The World Today Series®
Stryker-Post Publications, Harpers Ferry, WV • USA

SEP 1 7 2008

Western Europe

Wayne C. Thompson

2008

27th edition Next Edition: August 200

Graphic Materials Acknowledgments

For their generosity in providing certain visual material for use in this book, and in order of their appearance, special thanks to the following:

European Community Information Services
Delegation of the European Union in Washington
North Atlantic Treaty Organization
The Swiss National Tourist Office
The Government of Liechtenstein
The Government of Andorra
French Cultural Services, New York
The Royal Netherlands Embassy
The Embassy of Belgium

The Embassy of Ireland
The British Embassy
The Embassy of Italy
The Embassy of Malta
The Sovereign Military Order of Malta
The Government of Monaco
The Embassy of Spain
The Embassy of Portugal

First appearing as *Western Europe 1982,* this annually revised book is published by

Stryker–Post Publications
P.O. Drawer 1200
Harpers Ferry, WV 25425
Telephones: 1–800–995–1400 (U.S.A. or Canada)
    Other: 1–304–535–2593
    Fax: 1–304–535–6513
    www.strykerpost.com
    VISA–MASTERCARD–AMERICAN EXPRESS

The World Today Series has thousands of subscribers across the U.S. and Canada. A sample list of users who annually rely on this most up-to-date material includes:

Public library systems
Universities and colleges
High schools
Federal and state agencies
All branches of the armed forces & war colleges
National Geographic Society
National Democratic Institute
Agricultural Education Foundation
Exxon Corporation
Chevron Corporation
CNN

International Standard Book Number: 978–1–887985–98–7

International Standard Serial Number: 0084–2338

Library of Congress Catalog Card Number: 83–643780

Cover design by nvision graphic design

Cartographer: William L. Nelson

Typography by Barton Matheson Willse & Worthington
Baltimore, MD 21244

Printed in the United States of America by United Book Press, Inc.
Baltimore, MD 21207

Photographs used to illustrate *The World Today Series* come from many sources, a great number from friends who travel worldwide. If you have taken any which you believe would enhance the visual impact and attractiveness of our books, do let us hear from you.

DEDICATION

To the memory of my mother and father

ACKNOWLEDGMENTS

I am especially grateful to the Alexander von Humboldt Foundation, a farsighted German organization which, since 1869, has persistently nurtured the spirit of intellectual discovery and has sought to tighten the links between Europe and the rest of the world, for having granted me a two–year research fellowship at the University of Freiburg in Germany. Without its aid, I would have been unable to complete the first edition of this book.

No author could possibly write a book with the breadth of this one without the assistance of numerous persons and organizations. Mark H. Mullin, a Harvard graduate who earned an M.A. as a Marshall Scholar, Oxford University, wrote all but the political and economic sections of the chapters on the United Kingdom and the Republic of Ireland. I have updated them over the years. I thank my fellow author, Malcolm B. Russell, whose chapter on Cyprus we have moved to this volume after its accession to EU membership in 2004. We have also moved Greece to this book from our *Nordic, Central and Southeastern Europe* volume in order to group Mediterranean Europe together.

I wish also to thank my colleagues and acquaintances throughout Western Europe and the U.S. who took the time to read or to comment upon various chapters dealing with their own countries or specialties. They include: David M. Keithly, Richard Laurijssen, Jacky Paris, Philippe Vidal, and Maureen and Peter Ward. I am grateful to my students at the College of Europe who critiqued the chapters on their native countries. They are: Andres Arnaldos Montaner (Spain), Ritienne Bonavia (Malta), Nuno Borges (Portugal), Diego Calatayud (Spain), Núria Carrasco Comes (Spain), Isabelle Costa (Monaco), Laurence Deglain (France), Yannis Couniniotis (Greece), Francisco Bossa Dionisio (Portugal), Elena Donnari (Italy), Sylvain Dufeu (France), Javier Fernandez Gonzalez (Spain), Maaike Göbel (Netherlands), Gregory Gosp (France), James Hughes (UK), Vincent Imperiali (Belgium), Eelco Keij (Netherlands), José Maria Lanzarote (Spain), Koen Lenssen (Netherlands), Antoine Kopp, Jean Micallef Grimaud (Malta), Bérénice Orban de Xivry (Belgium), Nuno Queirós (Portugal), Laura Requejo (Spain), Alejandro Ribo Labastida (Spain), Emmanuel Lenaerts (Belgium), Panagiotis Papadopoulos (Greece), Chryso Ritsou (Greece), Hélène Stergiou (Netherlands), Sabine Tomordy (Liechtenstein), Tim Van Broeckhoven (Belgium), Edwin Van Os (Netherlands), Stijn Van Wesemael (Belgium), and Giuseppe Zaffuto (Italy). Renée Maeyaert and Anne Heber-Suffrin, librarians at the College of Europe, Bruges, consistently gave me important assistance in obtaining European newspapers and visuals for this book. Jean-Michel Cassiers and Monika Sapilak provided me in Brussels with information and materials on Belgium's language laws and practices. Michael Nix did a wonderful job in 2006 of reading every word of this book and making copious editorial changes based on his decades of experience as a Canadian government editor. I am deeply grateful for the generous gift of his time and talent. The late Catherine L. Lowe thoroughly read the entire manuscript in order to comb out style, spelling and typographical errors. My wife, Susan L. Thompson, took some of the photographs and carefully proofread some of the manuscript. My daughter, Juliet Bunch, also provided photos for this book.

I am grateful to Pro Helvetia, which arranged and financed a week-long study tour of Switzerland, as well as to numerous embassy and foreign ministry officials who provided information and arranged visits to Western European capitals to speak with representatives of parties, parliaments, universities, research institutes and news media about this book. A Fulbright Teaching Fellowship to Estonia in 1995–96 enabled me to become more familiar with Nordic Europe. A second Fulbright professorship in the spring semester of 2001 at the College of Europe in Bruges provided me with intellectual stimulation by top graduate students from all over Europe, in addition to an in-depth look at the BENELUX countries and EU and NATO institutions. My dear friend, the late Philip F. Stryker, was without doubt one of the most competent, encouraging and congenial publishers with whom an author could work. Finally I would like to thank my partner at Stryker-Post Publications, David T. Wilt, who supports my work in countless ways.

W.C.T.

Lexington, Virginia, July 2008

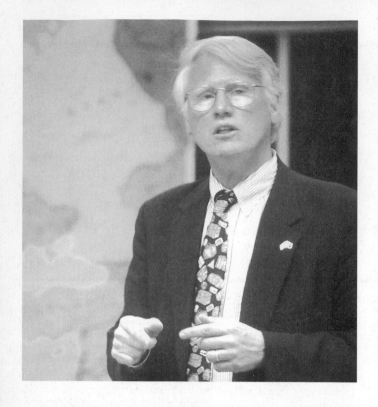

Wayne C. Thompson . . .

Professor Thompson teaches politics at Washington and Lee University, Lexington, Virginia. Professor Emeritus of Political Science, Virginia Military Institute, Lexington, Virginia. Ohio State University (B.A. in Government); Claremont Graduate University (M.A. and Ph.D., with distinction). He did further graduate study at the universities of Göttingen, Paris/Sorbonne and Freiburg im Breisgau, where he was subsequently a guest professor. He studied and researched many years in Germany as a Woodrow Wilson, Fulbright, Deutscher Akademischer Austauschdienst (DAAD), Earhart and Alexander von Humboldt Fellow. He served as scholar–in–residence at the Bundestag and as a Fulbright professor in Estonia. During the 1999–2000 academic year, he was a visiting professor at the Air War College in Montgomery, Alabama. In the spring semester of 2001 he had a second Fulbright professorship at the College of Europe in Bruges and continued for seven years to teach at the Bruges and Warsaw campuses of that graduate institution. In the fall semester of 2003 he was a visiting professor of politics at the American University of Bulgaria. He is the author of *In the Eye of the Storm: Kurt Riezler and the Crises of Modern Germany* (Iowa City, University of Iowa Press, 1980), *The Political Odyssey of Herbert Wehner* (Boulder, CO: Westview Press, 1993), *Historical Dictionary of Germany* (Metuchen, NJ: Scarecrow, 1994), and coauthor of *Redefining Transatlantic Security Relations: The Challenge of Change* (Manchester University Press, 2004). He has written two other books in The World Today Series: *Canada*, as well as *Nordic, Central, and Southeastern Europe*. He also co–edited *Perspectives on Strategic Defense and Space: National Programs and International Cooperation*, and *Margaret Thatcher: Prime Minister Indomitable* (Boulder, CO: Westview, 1987, 1989, 1994). He has written many articles on European politics, philosophy and history which have appeared in such periodicals as *The American Political Science Review, Western Political Quarterly, East European Quarterly, Journal of Politics, Central European History, The American Review of Canadian Studies, German Studies Review, Das Parlament, Current History, The Yearbook on International Communist Affairs, The History Teacher, Armed Forces and Society, Freedom at Issue, Communist and Post–Communist Studies, Contemporary French Civilization, Europe-Asia Studies*, and *Virginia Social Science Journal*. He is currently Editor-in-Chief of Stryker-Post Publications.

CONTENTS

September 27, 2001: Former European Commission President and subsequently Italian Prime Minister Romano Prodi, Former Belgian Prime Minister Guy Verhofstadt and President George W. Bush

Courtesy: Central Audiovisual Library, European Commision

Countries using the euro

»McDonald's? Ich? Immer!!!«

"McDonald's? Me? Always!!!"

In 1945 much of Europe lay in ruins, its peoples destitute and demoralized following a war on its own soil more destructive than any conflict in history. Two world wars in the 20th century (World War I from 1914 until 1918 and World War II from 1939 until 1945) had brought Europe's dominance over world affairs to an end and had led to a rise of the United States of America and the Soviet Union as the world's most powerful nations. These wars also ended Europe's colonial hold on much of the world, a hold which, despite some negative effects, had spread European civilization to the Western Hemisphere, Africa, the Middle East and the Far East.

Western Europe is a region rich in diversity, with a population of 262 million

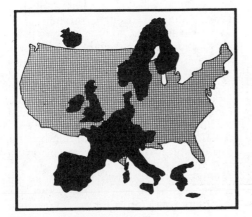

persons (382 if one adds Germany, Austria and the Nordic countries and 490 if one considers the entire European Union). This compares to 300 million in the U.S.

Geographically, western Europe is much smaller than the U.S. The entire region is scarcely more than twice the size of Alaska and would easily fit into the continental U.S. west of the Mississippi with much room to spare. Like the U.S., western Europe offers a very rich diversity of climates and landscapes, from the permafrost and midnight sun of northern Norway to the hot, dry, sunny Mediterranean; from the fog and rain of northern Germany to the warm blue skies of the Azores and to the snows and arctic winds of Iceland, from the Alpine peaks of Austria and Switzerland to the flat and sub–sea level terrain of the Netherlands.

With the collapse of communism in Europe, the unification of Germany, and the dissolution of the Soviet Union, Europeans are faced with the most significant alteration of their continent's political map since World War II. Because two hostile Europes no longer face each other, Europe has doubled its size from 382 to 700 million people. From Moscow to Lisbon and Dublin to Budapest democracies exist in which free elections provide the only legitimate claim to power and which are basically committed to freedom, individual rights, and some variant of capitalism.

Looking eastward, western Europeans see more than a dozen newly independent

nations and a few more emerging, all in difficult economic circumstances, some with ethnic scores to settle and millions of discontented and frightened citizens who may decide to seek a better future in the West. Most are clamoring for admission to the plentiful western European table and a place under the Atlantic Alliance's security umbrella. The December 1991 collapse of the former Soviet Union temporarily destroyed central authority and dispersed power among its various republics.

Western Europe still has many cultures and many lands and regions with characters and appearances of their own. However, there are many things which make much of modern western Europe and the U.S. look similar: large shopping centers, fast-food stores, freeways, modern cities with skyscrapers and much concrete, many automobiles and everywhere signs of prosperity.

Americans and western Europeans face many of the same problems and have many of the same concerns, though in differing degrees: the role and rights of women in modern society, illegal immigration, the integration of racial and religious minorities, a steady stream of political refugees, urban violence, the protection of the environment and the quality of life, the defense of their homeland and values in an age of terrorism and weapons of mass destruction, the provision of adequate supplies of energy and raw materials and the maintenance of prosperity and generous social security programs in an age of globalization.

The reader will confront numerous abbreviations and acronyms, and one must understand not only what the letters signify, but also what function the indicated institutions serve. Therefore, in the following pages, these acronyms will be presented in the context of a more general discussion of some of the more important European bodies and organizations.

Today, western Europe is a region that is, on the whole, highly prosperous, though it is relatively poor in natural resources. It

Western Europe Today

has a large industrial base, much capital and know–how and a highly educated and skilled work force. It is also secure militarily. Such prosperity and security are partly due to the countries' high degree of voluntary cooperation, formalized in numerous international organizations. All major western European countries are full members of the United Nations (UN), and all participate in the many organizations linked to the UN, such as the UN Educational, Scientific and Cultural Organization (UNESCO), the UN Conference on Trade and Development (UNCTAD), the World Court, which sits in the stately Peace Palace built with funds contributed by Andrew Carnegie in the Hague, Netherlands, the International Labor Organization (ILO), the UN Industrial Development Organization (UNIDO), the World Health Organization (WHO), the Food and Agriculture Organization (FAO) and a number of others.

Defense

Most western European countries would be unable to defend themselves alone. Therefore, the majority has chosen to join the North Atlantic Treaty Organization (NATO), also known as the Atlantic Alliance. Created in 1949, NATO links the power of the United States and Canada, and the geographic position of Iceland (which has no military) with the military resources of Belgium–Netherlands–Luxembourg (BENELUX), Great Britain, Norway, Denmark, the Federal Republic of Germany (FRG or Germany), Italy, Portugal, Turkey, Greece, France, Spain, and (since 1999) Poland, Hungary and the Czech Republic. At its November 2002 Prague summit, NATO invited seven more countries to join in April 2004: the three Baltic States (Estonia, Latvia, Lithuania), Slovakia, Slovenia, Romania, Bulgaria. At its April 2008 summit in Bucharest, NATO leaders invited Albania and Croatia to join. The alliance has 26 members. The only major western or Nordic European countries

NATO Headquarters, Commemorating 9–11 Victims

that remain neutral or nonaligned are Ireland, Switzerland, Austria, Sweden, and Finland.

When the question arose concerning the organization of a European military combination, France, Italy and West Germany initiated in 1952 a treaty creating a European Defense Community (EDC). It was intended to bring into being an integrated European army under a unified command structure, which would ultimately include troops from West Germany and the BENELUX countries. However, in 1954 the French National Assembly rejected this plan, fearing the possible loss of its sovereignty if it relinquished command over its army.

As a compromise, Great Britain proposed a Western European Union (WEU), composed of the BENELUX countries, France, Italy, Germany, Great Britain, Greece, Spain and Portugal, with headquarters in Brussels. Turkey, Norway and

Iceland became associate members. It conducted contingency planning, organized and controlled small all–European military operations (with the possibility of using NATO units and equipment), and attempted to coordinate the defense policies and armaments programs of its members.

At the 1991 EU summit meeting in Maastricht, it was agreed that the WEU would be Europe's own defense system, albeit "linked to" NATO. It largely ceased to exist the end of 2000, and most of its staff and activities were folded into the EU. At its Helsinki summit in 1999, the EU decided to create a 60,000-strong rapid reaction corps, officially operational in 2003, to act in crises when the U.S. and NATO choose not to get involved. It also began the creation of about a dozen "battle groups" of 1,500 soldiers for rapid deployment anywhere in the world. In July 2003 the French formed such a group, which included Swedish troops for the first time, to carry out a limited peacekeeping mission in the Democratic Republic of Congo. This was the EU's first solo military mission outside of Europe. In July 2006 the Germans commanded a similar battle group to the Congo to oversee elections, and in the spring of 2008 the French organized a battle group to deal with violence in Chad.

In December 2003 the EU adopted its first security doctrine, entitled "A Secure Europe in a Better World." It emphasizes that the Union is a global actor and that the alliance with the United States is indispensable. An informal organization within NATO known as the "Eurogroup," composed of all European members of NATO except France, Portugal and Iceland, serves as a forum for some European

A Changing Alliance: The Candidates Become Members, April 2004

Source: *The Washington Post*

Western Europe Today

states within NATO to discuss their special defense needs.

NATO itself has both political and military components. The highest political organ and decision-making body is the North Atlantic Council (NAC). It selects the secretary general of NATO, who chairs all meetings and seeks consensus among members. By tradition he is always a European. On January 1, 2004, George Robertson, former British defense minister, was replaced as NATO secretary general by former Dutch foreign minister, Jaap de Hoop Scheffer. Each member country sends a permanent ambassador to NATO Headquarters in Brussels, and these ambassadors meet once a week. Less frequently, the member countries' heads of government, foreign, defense or finance ministers meet to iron out higher-level political problems. All decisions are reached by consensus, not by majority vote. In other words, each member has an actual veto power although such vetoes are seldom cast.

The ambassadors or ministers of all but those nations that do not participate in the integrated defense system (France and Iceland) also take part in the Defense Planning Committee (DPC), which is assisted by a variety of committees and working groups. A staff of about 1,000, divided into divisions of Political Affairs, Defense Planning and Policy, Defense Support and Scientific Affairs are in Brussels to assist in the NATO effort.

The highest NATO military authority is the Military Committee, made up of the chiefs of defense from all states participating in the NATO military command plus France (since 1995). By tradition it is chaired by a European officer, but in 2006 a Canadian general, Ray Henault, occupied the post. Although the chiefs–of–

defense meet infrequently, their permanent representatives meet regularly in their absence. The Military Committee's primary role is to advise the DPC.

NATO has an integrated system of commands. The Supreme Allied Commander Europe (SACEUR), who by tradition is always an American, heads the Allied Command Europe (ACE). He also commands all U.S. forces in Europe, and his European Command encompasses Russia and all of Africa except the Horn. In 2002 Marine Corps General James L. Jones became SACEUR. Having grown up in Paris, Jones is the first SACEUR to speak fluent French and the first Marine to become SACEUR. He was chosen because he is an innovative thinker who, as a Marine, can help reshape NATO into a more mobile expeditionary military alliance. In 2006 he was replaced by Army General John Cradock. The position of Deputy SACEUR alternates between a British and German officer.

ACE is based outside Mons, Belgium, at the Supreme Headquarters Allied Powers Europe (SHAPE). In case of war, ACE is responsible for military operations in the entire European area and wherever in the world NATO forces are deployed. Since the 2002 Prague summit, this strategic command for operations, which remains in Belgium, was made leaner, more efficient, more effective and more deployable. A British or a German general alternate in commanding one of its two top regional subcommands in Europe, the Regional Command North, in Brunssum, Netherlands. The Regional Command South in Naples, Italy, is always entrusted to an American admiral. The French advocate turning this command over to a European officer. However, the United States, whose Sixth Fleet provides the most potent naval

forces in the Mediterranean area, rejects this suggestion.

Before the 2002 Prague summit, the other major NATO strategic command was the Allied Command Atlantic (ACLANT), commanded by an American admiral or general and headquartered in Norfolk, Virginia. Now a new strategic command is based in Norfolk, Virginia, with a presence in Europe. It is responsible for continuing transformation of military capabilities and interoperability of allied forces.

Only the U.S. engages in negotiations with Russia aimed at limiting nuclear forces in Europe. But western European members are consulted about any American negotiating positions which might affect European interests. Europeans have developed bodies, such as the NATO Nuclear Planning Group (NPG) and the less formal Special Consultative Group, which serve as channels to inform the U.S. of its allies' views and to keep the latter informed of U.S. objectives.

In 1989 the Conventional Forces in Europe (CFE) negotiations in Vienna replaced the moribund Mutual Balanced Force Reduction (MBFR) talks. This culminated in an agreement between NATO and the now defunct Warsaw Pact in 1990 to thin out their military equipment in the center of Europe. It did not apply to troops. Several years after the Warsaw Pact collapsed, the terms of the CFE Treaty began to be reexamined, at Russia's insistence, to take account of the fact that Moscow no longer has allies and has potentially serious internal instability.

In 1991 President George H.W. Bush announced unilateral nuclear cuts that went far beyond the Strategic Arms Reductions Talks (START) agreement reached in July. European allies and Soviet President Mikhail Gorbachev gave Bush's plan unanimous backing. The greatest impact was on Europe, where the only targets for NATO's tactical nuclear weapons were in areas that are no longer enemies, such as Poland and eastern Germany. Officially endorsed by NATO, the cuts did not make Europe nuclear–free: NATO still has some atomic bombs on dual–capacity aircraft to provide a measure of nuclear deterrence against unknown threats. Also, Britain and France retain some of their nuclear systems. But European defense has become almost entirely nonnuclear.

The sweeping American disarmament proposals, following the disappearance of a clearly identifiable foe, prompted Europeans to try to develop a distinct European Security and Defence Identity (ESDI); this was the NATO term for the EU's European Security and Defence Policy (ESDP) and was, in essence, the same thing. A consensus exists that such a Eu-

Western Europe Today

The European Council and European Commission, Brussels
Courtesy: Central Audiovisual Library, European Commision

ropean identity is necessary, while preserving NATO in one form or the other.

In 1999 the EU created a new post of "high representative" to breathe life into its Common Foreign and Security Policy (CFSP) and named Javier Solana Madariaga to occupy it. To give CFSP a military arm, the EU created ESDP with a rapid reaction force. This enabled the EU to take command of the small peacekeeping force in Macedonia in 2003 and in Bosnia December 2004. By 2008 the EU was running more than a dozen foreign operations, and there were nearly 200 admirals and generals based in EU institutions in Brussels. They are increasingly engaged in planning, an activity always dominated by NATO.

No European country wants the total withdrawal of American troops, which had already been drawn down from 320,000 to 100,000 (plus 14,000 in the Sixth Fleet) by the beginning of the century. That downward trend will continue to roughly 70,000. Americans have called on Europeans to bear a greater responsibility for their own defense, but not in competition with NATO, which remains the major pillar for American influence in Europe. One American diplomat said: "Sure, we want the Europeans to do more, but we're always going to be wary of anything that looks like it could push the U.S. out of Europe."

In order to facilitate greater European security independence, NATO in 1998 reduced the number of its command headquarters from 65 to 20, emphasized a multinational approach to the manning of these headquarters, and arranged them in a way that they can support both regular NATO tasks as well as Combined Joint Task Forces (CJTF), authorized in 1994. If certain members, such as the U.S., do not

wish to participate in a certain military operation, a coalition of those that do can use NATO units and assets under EU leadership. This is called "Berlin Plus." Non-NATO countries can also be included in such Combined Joint Task Forces.

International military groupings have proliferated in Europe since the end of the Cold War. Within NATO, a Dutch–German corps under alternate command has been formed; its troops use English. British, German, Dutch and Belgian troops constitute a multinational division with an airmobile brigade. It is part of the ACE Rapid Reaction force. The Dutch navy has merged its naval headquarters with those of Belgium. A corps has been created with headquarters in Szczecin, Poland, that comprises Polish, German and Danish troops and is commanded by a Polish officer. This unit was modeled on the French-German Eurocorps in Strasbourg, France, created in 1992. The Eurocorps now includes BENELUX and Spanish troops and uses English as its common language. In the summer of 2000 this Eurocorps took temporary charge of the NATO-led peacekeeping operation in Kosovo (KFOR); in 2003–4 it fielded peacekeeping forces in Afghanistan.

A U.S. combat division serves in a German-led corps, while a German division is part of a U.S.-led corps. Outside NATO, Italy, Austria and Slovenia created a joint land-based force, and the Spanish, French, Portuguese and Italians formed a rapid operational force called EUROFOR based in Florence. Many NATO troops served alongside other European and non-European soldiers in the Stabilization Force (SFOR) to guard the peace in Bosnia Herzegovina, as well as in KFOR.

In 1991 NATO was transformed into a more political organization seeking to

reach out to its former enemies. It created a North Atlantic Cooperation Council (NACC, renamed in 1997 the Euro-Atlantic Partnership Council—EAPC) comprising 44 countries at century's end to provide for regular consultations between NATO and the former Soviet republics and eastern European nations on subjects ranging from security issues, arms control, and the conversion of defense industries. In 1994 NATO initiated the Partnership for Peace (PFP), which links a dozen and a half nonmember countries, including Russia, in bilateral treaties with NATO. The purpose is to expand and intensify political and military cooperation and to strengthen stability and peace, primarily through training forces for peacekeeping operations. A special NATO– Ukraine Commission was established to deepen cooperation with that important country.

These nations are also linked in the 55–member Organization for Security and Cooperation in Europe (OSCE, known until 1994 as the CSCE), to which all European states, former Soviet republics, and the United States and Canada belong. It meets irregularly to consider how to defuse threats to peace through mediation, crisis management, and the dispatch of observers during elections.

Many countries regard PFP as a stepping–stone to full NATO membership. In principle, the alliance is prepared gradually to accept new members, on the condition that they have solid democratic credentials, including a firm civilian grip on the armed forces, and can make a genuine military contribution to the common defense. The door remains open to European democracies.

Russia once opposed such enlargement, especially insofar as former Soviet republics, such as the Baltics, are concerned. To assuage Moscow's fears, the Atlantic allies signed with Moscow in 1997 a NATO–Russia Founding Act. This is not a legally binding treaty, but it states that

EU Members

4

NATO has no need, intentions, or plans to create additional capabilities or permanently station troops or nuclear weapons in the new member states. Agreements in 2006 permit such stationing of small numbers of American forces in Romania and Bulgaria. NATO also created a Permanent Joint Council (PJC) at its headquarters in which Russian officials could discuss, though not veto, NATO policies and decisions. In the wake of close Russian-U.S. cooperation in the war against terrorism after the September 11 terrorist attacks in New York and Washington, the PJC was upgraded and renamed in 2002 the Russia-NATO Council.

NATO's outdated doctrine of containing Soviet power through "forward defense" and "flexible response" was replaced by one that gives NATO a reason to exist in the changed European environment. Smaller, highly mobile, conventional, and multilateral forces are being created which can be deployed on short notice anywhere in the world, and which can help manage unpredictable crises and instability in eastern Europe, the Balkans, the Mediterranean area and beyond. NATO chose at its 2002 Prague summit to create a multinational rapid deployment force of 21,000 troops for use against enemies far outside of Europe. NATO provides peacekeepers and combat soldiers to Afghanistan.

European Integration

No region in the world has been so successful in creating voluntary economic unions of sovereign states as western Europe. In 1922 the Belgium and Luxembourg Economic Union (BLEU) was created, which made the two countries a single unit for importing and exporting purposes and established a unified currency. In 1944 the Netherlands joined to form BENELUX, which was later extended to include even non–customs matters.

In order to help the devastated countries of Europe recover economically, the United States offered Marshall Plan aid in 1947, but insisted that all countries receiving such aid sit down together and decide as a group how the money should be spent. Thus, the U.S. provided an important initial impetus for a unified Europe. In response, the Europeans created, in 1948, the Organization for European Economic Cooperation (OEEC) for making the decisions and the European Payments Union (EPU) for administering U.S. funds.

In 1960, the U.S. and Canada joined the OEEC which was renamed the Organization for Economic Cooperation and Development (OECD), with headquarters in Paris. Later other western industrialized nations, and Japan, Australia and New Zealand, joined OECD, making a total of 30 members by 2007. It does economic analysis and forecasting for industrialized countries, including estimates of future growth, inflation, unemployment, and Gross Domestic Product (GDP, a measurement of an economy's total production of goods and services. A related and less used term, Gross National Product—GNP—adds to this value citizens' foreign earnings and subtracts foreigners' income within the country.) The OECD also attempts to coordinate members' economic and development aid, and it provided a forum for member states to hammer out an anti–bribery convention in international commerce. All western European countries belong. Wanting closer contact with the world's industrial leaders, the Czech Republic, Hungary, Poland and Slovakia joined, and Russia decided to enter. With only 16% of the world's popula-tion, its 30 members produce two–thirds of the world's economic output.

The Council of Europe was created in Strasbourg in 1949. Its 40 members include all western European countries and most newly independent countries in eastern Europe. Its assemblies of parliamentarians from the member states serve as a forum for discussing political, economic, social and cultural issues of interest to all European countries. Perhaps its main contribution has been its various conventions, especially its Convention for the Protection of Human Rights and Fundamental Freedoms (known as the European Convention on Human Rights—ECHR), adopted in 1950. Acceptance of all the Convention's principles is a precondition for EU membership. Since 1991 it has been particularly active in trying to strengthen democracy and human rights in eastern Europe. The United States requested and was granted observer status in 1996 in order to be able to promote democracy more effectively in eastern Europe.

The BENELUX countries, together with France, West Germany and Italy, made in 1951 the first significant move toward transferring a portion of their national sovereignty to a supranational organization by creating the European Coal and Steel Community (ECSC). Many persons could scarcely believe at the time that six countries that had been locked only six years earlier in a bloody struggle would be willing to transfer sovereignty over questions relating to these commodities, which are so crucial for heavy industry. Not only was it bold and farsighted to share these important goods rather than to fight wars over them, but the ECSC gave these nations the practice in economic cooperation needed to convince the six that a move to create a unified Europe could succeed.

The same six nations signed the Treaties of Rome in 1957 which created both the European Economic Community (EEC, frequently called the "Common Market") and EURATOM, which seeks to coordinate the six countries' atomic research and policy. Both came into existence the following year and merged with the ECSC under the same overall organization. This union provided for the elimination of tariffs and customs among themselves, common tariff and customs barriers toward nonmembers, the free movement of labor and capital within the union and equal agricultural price levels through the establishment of the Common Agricultural Program (CAP). To avoid giving the impression that the three communities were only *economic* in nature and to express the fact that they are managed by common institutions, they were referred to in the sin-

European Parliament building, Strasbourg, France

Courtesy: Central Audiovisual Library, European Commision

Western Europe Today

gular as the European Community (EC). On January 1, 2002, when its 50-year mandate came to an end, the ECSC was fully absorbed into the EU.

The 27 member states (with about 490 million citizens, almost two-thirds more than the U.S.) which now include the BENELUX countries, France, Germany, Italy, Great Britain, the Republic of Ireland, Denmark, Greece, Spain, Portugal. In 1995 Austria, Finland, and Sweden joined. In 2002, 10 more countries were invited: Estonia, Latvia, Lithuania, Poland, Hungary, the Czech Republic, Slovakia, Slovenia, Malta and Cyprus (the Greek section); they entered on May 1, 2004. Romania and Bulgaria followed on January 1, 2007. With their entry, the EU for the first time has more members than NATO, which has 26.

Because of its questionable human rights record, constitutional grant of political power to the military, continued Greek wariness, and fear by some western European countries that a flood of Turkish immigrants would arrive at their doorstep, Turkish consideration for entry was postponed until 2006. The Turkish part of Cyprus must also await unification of the island before becoming part of the EU. The irresistible logic of European unity has affected countries all over the continent. Norway was offered membership in 1972 and 1994, but its voters rejected it both times.

The issue of immigrants and refugees is a very sensitive one. Some western Europeans fear that they bring in crime and terrorism and overburden their generous welfare states at a difficult time when their economies are suffering under the challenges of the global economy.

Controlling the movement of outsiders who have entered the EU area has been made more difficult by the Schengen agreements of 1985 and 1990 that eliminate many of Europe's internal border controls. The idea is that one need only go through border formalities when entering one of the membership states; then one can pass freely into the others, submitting only to occasional spot checks. All of the earlier 15 EU members except the UK and Ireland have joined. Since the Nordic countries long since abolished internal border controls among themselves, Norway and Iceland are automatically included. In 2005 Swiss voters chose to take part starting 2007. On December 21, 2007, nine more countries joined the Schengen zone: Estonia, Latvia, Lithuania, Poland, the Czech Republic, Slovakia, Hungary, Slovenia and Malta.

On November 1, 1993, the Maastricht treaty came into force, bringing with it terminological confusion. It created a European Union (EU), which added common foreign and security policy and cooperation in justice and police matters to the EC. But unlike the EC, the EU has neither a single decision–making process or a legal persona; it cannot conclude international agreements. Although the EC and EU are technically not exactly the same entities, most scholars and journalists now employ the term EU instead of EC. The term EU will be used throughout this book.

It is this political element that had prevented some other European states such as Switzerland from joining the EU. But the EU has successfully dealt with this problem by granting associate membership (which generally excludes agricultural aspects only) to most non–full–member states in western Europe. Regular contacts are also maintained with 70 African, Caribbean and Pacific (ACP) countries linked to the EU through the Lomé Convention of 1975. Since 2002 the EU has a European Neighborhood Policy (ENP) to facilitate ties with former Soviet Republics in Europe and with Middle Eastern countries from Morocco to Turkey.

Most of the success the EU can claim has been in the economic field. The record is most impressive. With only 6% of the world's population, the EU countries accounts for about a fourth of the world's economic output and 47% of the development aid. Together, the U.S. and the EU states account for over half of the world's GDP and around 40% of global exports. Their annual commercial relationship, including investments, amounted in 2005 to $2.5 trillion, the equivalent of 20-25% of each side's GDP.

José Manuel Barroso
President of European Commission

In terms of foreign direct investment (FDI), they are each other's favorite targets. Two-thirds of America's FDI flow to Europe, while three-fourths of Europe's are directed to the United States, with Texas as the favorite state. America's preferred investment site is the UK, where total U.S. investment is roughly equivalent to that in Asia, Latin America, Africa and the Middle East combined. It invests ten times more in the Netherlands (and two and a half times more in Ireland) than in China. No wonder many observers claim that economics is the stabilizer of the European-American relationship.

Having cornered a fourth of global trade, it is the world's largest trading power. Politically, western Europe is and will probably remain a region of sovereign states, which ultimately make their own decisions about the vital matters that affect them. This is especially true since May and June 2005, when French and Dutch voters decisively rejected an EU constitution that would have strengthened Europe's political union. About 90% of lengthy document's contents were salvaged two and a half years later in the EU treaty signed in Lisbon.

European Union

The EU has a well–developed institutional apparatus. It has a dual executive: the European Council is the major decision–making body and is composed of the heads of state or government; it is called the Council of Ministers when member state ministers with responsibilities for finance, agriculture, etc., depending upon the specific matter which is pending, meet.

Italian election poster for the European Parliament: "Your vote for your Europe"

The second part of the executive that directs the day–to–day business of the EU is the European Commission which meets in Brussels. The Commission is composed of 27 members, one from each member state. The 2000 Nice Treaty stipulates that there be fewer by 2009. If the Lisbon Treaty is ratified by June 2009, which is unlikely, each member would lose the right to send a commissioner. The total number instead would be capped at a rotating two-thirds of the number of member states. In the meantime, up to three members are proposed by the government of his or her country for five– year renewable terms. The EC president selects one and assigns that commissioner a specific portfolio. After joining the College of Commissioners, each commissioner is expected to make decisions based not upon the interests of his or her home country, but upon the interests of the EU as a whole. The commissioners decide issues by a simple majority vote; none has the power of veto.

After 2009, the Lisbon Treaty (rejected by Irish voters) fixes the problem of the rotating six-month presidency of the all-powerful European Council (which is composed of the chiefs of government) by creating a standing president elected by the Council for a two-and-a-half-year term, renewable once. The Council would have a simplified voting system relying more on majority voting as long as 55% of the states containing 65% of the total EU population say yes to a measure. Members try to make as many decisions as possible by consensus. A high representative would be foreign minister in all but name, combining the posts of commissioner for external affairs and foreign policy spokesman for the Council, and assisted by an external action service (a diplomatic corps).

A total of 34,000 persons work in the EU institutions. Two-thirds of them are at the Commission and most are in Brussels, with a minority working in Luxembourg and Strasbourg. This amounts to fewer civil servants (dubbed "Eurocrats") than work in medium-sized city governments in Europe. The highest EU official is the European Commission president, selected by member countries for a five–year renewable term. In 2004 President José Manuel Barroso, former Portuguese prime minister, replaced Romano Prodi, returned to his native Italy to become prime minister in 2006.

The 785–seat European Parliament, which might be lowered to a maximum of 750 after 2009, is the world's only directly elected international legislature. The formula for seats is based roughly on the population size of the member states, but larger states are under-represented and smaller ones overrepresented. It meets seven to eight times a year for one–week sessions. Formerly, the Parliament met in both Strasbourg and Luxembourg. However, in 1981 the Parliament voted to hold all its sessions in Strasbourg, leaving only the administrative headquarters in Luxembourg. Parliamentary committees meet in Brussels. Since most of the real bargaining and revising takes place in the committees and since "additional" plenaries can be held in Brussels, most Members of the European Parliament (MEPs) do all of their work in Brussels.

Since 1979 its members have been elected directly in their home countries according to each country's own preferred method of election. Its members do not sit in national delegations, but in party groupings, such as the Communists and Allies, Socialist European People's Party (Christian Democratic), European Progressive Democratic and Liberal and Democratic Groups. There are a few unaffiliated members.

The European Parliament is officially entitled to oversee the work of the European Commission and to approve or reject the EU's budget. Since the SEA was introduced in 1987, the Parliament's power and influence have grown. Some legislation, most importantly that covering measures to bring into effect a unified European market, can be altered or amended by the Parliament. It must approve the budget. It can veto the accession of new member states to the EU, as well as new trade agreements with non–EU countries. It can launch investigations. Finally, it oversees the Commission, a power that was dramatically demonstrated in 1999 and 2004.

For years it had been asking questions about waste and mismanagement, but the Commission responded with arrogance and indifference. In January 1999 the Parliament threatened a vote of censure; a two–thirds majority could have removed all the commissioners. This threat was averted when a panel of five independent experts was appointed to investigate financial impropriety. In March the panel published a devastating report accusing the well–paid commissioners ($200,000 salary and expenses in 1999) of tolerating widespread fraud, corruption, nepotism, favoritism and mismanagement. All commissioners felt compelled to resign.

The consequence of this scandal was not only more democratic accountability, but a dramatic alteration of the political balance of power in favor of the elected European Parliament. It showed its muscle again in 2004, when it questioned the competence of five of the commissioners proposed. This forced EC President Barrosa to reshuffle his lineup of commissioners in order to win parliamentary approval. This was the first time this had ever happened.

Finally, there is a European Court of Justice with its seat in Luxembourg and composed of 27 justices, each chosen by member states for six–year renewable

Old currencies go ...

Western Europe Today

THE EURO BANKNOTE DESIGNS
LES MAQUETTES DES BILLETS EN EURO
DIE ENTWÜRFE DER EURO-BANKNOTEN

EUROPEAN MONETARY INSTITUTE

ECHELLE · SCALE · MABSTAB · 1,5:1

... and a new one arrives

Courtesy: Central Audiovisual Library, European Commision

terms; they are assisted by eight advocates general. The Court judges violations of three major documents, the ECSC, EU and Euratom Treaties, as well as all subsequent EU treaties that are collectively called the Treaty of the European Union (TEU). This includes the Nice Treaty of 2000. It redistributed national votes, restricted vetoes, revamped certain institutions, limited the number of commission-

ers and granted the European Parliament more power and seats. The court rules on whether national laws are in accordance with European laws in those fields within the EU's competence (jurisdiction).

The court would have been the final arbiter of that constitution drafted in a constitutional convention, chaired by former French President Giscard d'Estaing and attended by 66 representatives from mem-

ber states and 39 non-voting delegates from applicant states that joined in May 2004. It was intended to be ratified and adopted by the time the 10 new members joined, but the members failed to reach agreement on all aspects of the document at their December 2003 summit in Rome. Proponents had hoped that the new constitution would democratize the EU, make its internal structures more comprehensible and efficient, and put teeth in the CFSP. The Lisbon Treaty of 2007 would give the Charter of Fundamental Rights legal force, and the court would probably be the ultimate arbiter after 2009.

The Single European Act (SEA) amends the European treaties by spelling out certain EU objectives: completion of the European internal market, creation of a great area without frontiers, technological development, progress toward economic and monetary union, improvement of the environment and working conditions, creation of more effective and democratic institutions, and institutionalization of cooperation among member states in the field of foreign policy. The target year 1992 was chosen for its symbolic importance: 500 years after the discovery of the New World.

From 1979 the European Monetary System (EMS) attempted, not always successfully, to coordinate the monetary affairs of certain western European countries by attempting to link their currencies. At their 1991 Maastricht summit, EU leaders agreed to create a single European currency (called the "Euro") and a European Central Bank (ECB) located in Frankfurt.

The criteria for joining this Economic and Monetary Union (EMU)—a budget deficit of not more than 3% of GDP and a total national debt not in excess of 60% of GDP—placed enormous political strains on member governments. The inevitable austerity policies were resented by many of their voters. Many Europeans thought that the price to be paid for the euro was not worth it.

In 1998 the governments of 11 members (known unofficially as the "euro zone") decided to adopt the euro as of January 1, 1999, with Britain, Sweden, Denmark, and Greece waiting until later to join. Danish voters rejected the euro again in a September 2000 referendum. Greece enthusiastically entered on January 1, 2001. Despite the fervent support by their government, Swedish voters rejected the new currency in 2003. Slovenia joined on January 1, 2007, and Malta and Cyprus joined a year later, making 15 EU member states in the euro zone.

The participating countries phased in the euro until it became the exclusive currency of members between January and March 2002. In order not to hurt national feelings, the new euro bills bear generic European designs: Gothic arches, bridges, windows, and a map of Europe. No scene from a particular country is recognizable. The only national concession for paper money was made to Greece, which does not use Roman letters. The word for the currency appears both as "EURO" and "EYPO." Bulgaria became the first EU member to use the Cyrillic alphabet, and that may be added as well. The coins are uniform on one side, but each participating country made its own design for the reverse side. Thus 12 different coins circulate but are legal tender throughout the eurozone. The new EU members are expected to join the euro zone within four to five years after entering the EU in 2004 and 2007. The euro is an undeniable success: by 2007 there were more of them in circulation around the globe than U.S. dollars although the dollar remained the favorite reserve currency for central banks.

A few countries that are not full members of the EU belong to the European Free Trade Association (EFTA), which was created in 1959 and whose headquarters are located in Geneva. Whereas the EU has a huge bureaucracy and budget, EFTA is a shoestring operation, with about 60 full-time staff. English is the working language, even though no member nation uses it as its mother tongue. EFTA has no political objectives, and its members have not relinquished a shred of sovereignty.

EFTA eliminated tariffs and customs on all industrial products bought or sold from all member nations, but it does not include agricultural or fishing products.

All EFTA members have separate free-trade agreements with the EU. EFTA's economic importance declined after Great Britain, Ireland and Denmark left to join the EU in 1972 and Finland, Sweden and Austria in 1995. To restore EFTA's significance, its members—Switzerland, Liechtenstein, Norway, and Iceland—concluded cooperation agreements with Egypt, Morocco and Tunisia.

In 1991 the EU and EFTA countries agreed to form a European Economic Area (EEA), which creates a market of 500 million customers extending from the Mediterranean to the Arctic and accounting for over 40% of world trade. Within the EEA, EFTA members enjoy the EU's "four freedoms": of goods, services, capital, and people, but EEA does not include agriculture, fish, energy, coal and steel. EFTA members live under many EU rules although they have no voice in their writing; this lack of representation gives them added incentive to join the EU as full members.

All Scandinavian countries are in the Nordic Council, which meets regularly to discuss nonmilitary problems that they have in common. Eleven nations belong to the European Space Agency (ESA) which, with American assistance, launched the first European Spacelab into orbit at the end of 1983. On board this Spacelab was the first European astronaut to travel into space with Americans—Dr. Ulf Merbold, a German physicist. In 1988 ESA also joined with the U.S. and Japan to begin construction of the Space Station Freedom.

Western European countries are active in such international economic treaties or organizations as the General Agreement on Trade and Tariffs (GATT), the World Trade Organization (WTO), which since 1995 attempts to resolve disputes relating to the GATT Treaty, the International Monetary Fund (IMF), which provides funds for countries with balance–of–payments problems, the International Bank for Reconstruction and Development (World Bank), and the European Bank for Reconstruction and Development (EBRD). Headquartered in London, the EBRD was created after the collapse of communism to help Central and eastern European countries make successful transitions to free–market economies.

The International Energy Agency (IEA) exists to insure that all industrialized nations have minimally sufficient energy supplies in times of crisis. No European country belongs to the Organization of Petroleum Exporting Countries (OPEC), whose headquarters is in Vienna. Nevertheless, those western European countries which export large quantities of oil, such as Great Britain and Norway (from the North Sea), note what is charged by the OPEC countries before setting their own prices.

Interpol, headquartered in Paris, provides some coordination in fighting international crime. Europol, based in The Hague, shares information among national police forces and cooperates in a limited way with the U.S. SitCen exists for intelligence sharing among EU countries. Eurojust coordinates the EU countries' prosecuting authorities. Following the September 11 attacks in the U.S., EU governments rapidly accepted a single European arrest warrant to facilitate the struggle against terrorism.

This high degree of cooperation and organization explains in great measure the tremendous growth of the economy of western Europe. In a sense it may be likened to the United States, which, after discarding the Articles of Confederation and creating the present Constitution two centuries ago, abolished tariffs on goods shipped between the states and laid the groundwork for ever–closer cooperation among formerly sovereign entities.

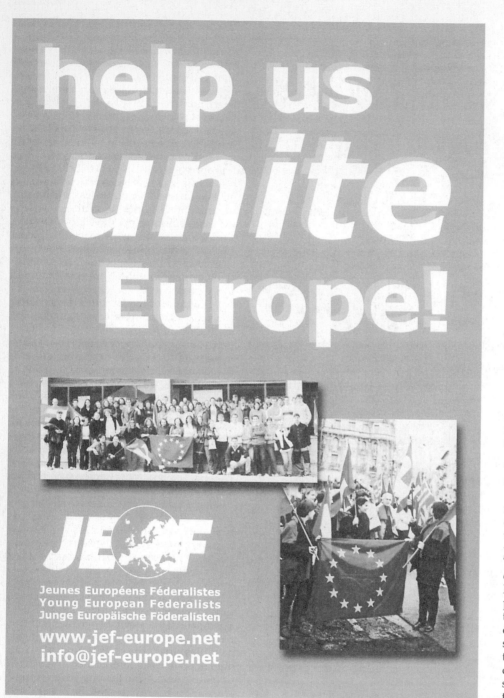

help us *unite* Europe!

JE F

Jeunes Européens Féderalistes
Young European Federalists
Junge Europäische Föderalisten

www.jef-europe.net
info@jef-europe.net

ropeans and Canadians. They responded with emotion and resolve. Within 36 hours of the attack, NATO offered to invoke the mutual defense clause, Article 5, for the first time in its half-century history.

Former EC President Romano Prodi called an emergency session the next morning. After a moment of silence for the victims of the attacks, he decided to send "the strongest possible signal of European solidarity with the American people" and to "call for a common European approach to all aspects of this tragedy." In moving language he announced, "this barbaric attack was directed against the free world and our common values. It is a watershed event, and life will never be quite the same again. . . . In the darkest hours of European history, the Americans stood by us. We stand by them now."

In a poll taken a week after the attack, Europeans showed a strong willingness to support a U.S. military assault: 80% in Denmark, 79% in Britain, 73% in France, 58% in Norway and Spain, and half in Germany. The EU called for a three-minute silence on September 14, and from Finland to Italy and Berlin to Paris, businesses and stock exchanges, buses and shoppers stopped to honor the dead and reflect upon their world that had changed so suddenly.

The Complexity of U.S.-European Cooperation

The transatlantic relationship is intense, multilayered, exceedingly complex, increasingly interdependent, and fraught with fluctuations and frictions. It takes place within several interrelated channels. The United States and all European states conduct bilateral relations with each other. In times of crisis, Washington tends to prefer these bilateral contacts because they bring action and cooperation more quickly than does a complicated evolving structure like the EU. The same applies to European governments. The German daily, *Die Welt*, called the antiterrorist crisis "the moment of the nation-states, the time in which individual European governments turn to the American partner after consulting among themselves."

The allies interact closely within NATO. The highest political leader within the alliance, the secretary general, is always a European. But American military leadership is institutionalized through the permanent appointment of an American general as the SACEUR. Decisions are reached on the basis of consensus. However, not all European countries belong to this organization, and not all members participate in the integrated command structure, such as France and Iceland although they have a part in NATO's political structure. The partners collaborate in a

Through the many organizations they have formed and joined, western European nations are better equipped and prepared to face the complicated problems of today.

September 11, 2001

For the United States, the world changed dramatically on September 11, 2001, when fanatical Islamic al-Qaeda terrorists, trained and financed by Osama Bin Laden and sheltered in Taliban-ruled Afghanistan, hijacked four American commercial airliners and crashed three of them into the twin towers of the World

Trade Center in New York and the Pentagon in Washington, killing more than 3,000 persons from 81 different countries. More British and French citizens perished that day than in any previous terrorist attack.

Americans' feeling of invulnerability from outside threats went up with the noxious smoke from the buildings' rubble. Any temptations to pursue an isolationist, North America-focused policy disappeared, at least temporarily. A shaken America looked for help from its friends, and the most steadfast of them were Eu-wide variety of international fora, such as the OSCE, the G-8 (which includes Japan, Canada and Russia), and most importantly the United Nations. Finally and of ever increasing importance, the U.S. has had to adapt to and work intensively with an evolving EU. This was symbolized in February 2005 by the first visit by an American president to the EU institutions in Brussels.

The transatlantic partnership involves the meshing of many different systems of government—the U.S. central government and individual American states, the EU, its member states and, in some federations such as Germany, states or "*Länder.*" Thus political authority is dispersed, and there are many points where one or more of the numerous players can veto policies. On both sides of the Atlantic, domestic politics is of vital importance. Negotiators often need to make domestic tradeoffs that adversely affect the foreign policies they are trying to pursue. Since all the states involved in this thick network of links are democracies, electoral cycles strongly affect the effort to reach agreements. On the American side, it is often pointed out that presidents and Congress find it especially harrowing to make bold, potentially unpopular moves within a year of reelection. It is no different in the EU.

The American political system divides power both geographically (between the central government and the states) and within the governing institutions inside Washington and the 50 state capitals. This can create diplomatic nightmares for both American and European leaders. For instance, American states have become more and more assertive in global politics and conduct their own foreign policies, particularly in economic and trade matters. Ignoring Washington, the Massachusetts legislature passed a "Burma Law" in 1996 forbidding the state and its agencies from buying anything from companies or individuals that invest in or trade with Myanmar (Burma), which is under military rule. The same can happen in Europe. Germany's *Länder* have supremacy over certain aspects of immigration policy. Thus they can impede both the policy of the German central government in Berlin and that of the EU itself.

Europeans must deal with America's large, highly decentralized institutions, which wield power of their own and often seem to be hostile to each other. Separation of powers is particularly troublesome for foreign policy: it is often impossible for a president to produce what he promises to foreign leaders. An American president occupies a central position in the making of effective foreign policy. If he is not personally involved or committed to achieving important foreign policy goals, little gets done. The political system enables persons who are largely unknown in Europe to rise to the highest national political office through a painfully long and complicated electoral system. The unique American selection procedure permits a person to arrive in the White House who had pursued a nonpolitical career as a soldier (Eisenhower), farmer (Carter), actor (Reagan), or governor of a state (Carter, Reagan, Clinton, George W. Bush). It almost always brings to the White House a neophyte in foreign policy; Eisenhower and the first George Bush were the exceptions. Most presidents learn diplomacy as on-the-job training, learning by doing.

When that president seems to overlook the multilateral dimension of America's dealings with the outside world and the need to engage former adversaries, Europeans react negatively. Although many of the red-letter issues—such as the Comprehensive Test Ban Treaty, the Kyoto Protocol, and the International Criminal Court—had gained prominence during the Clinton administration, Bush's predecessor was able to give the appearance in public that he supported these issues and to put the blame on the Republican Congress for not ratifying them.

President George W. Bush took more straightforward opposition to policies he thought would damage American interests, and he suffered for it in European public opinion. Most Europeans were convinced that he knew less about Europe than did his predecessor even though Clinton's opinions did not substantially differ from Bush's on many key issues. The sole Bush policy favored by Europeans was his decision not to withdraw American troops from Bosnia and Kosovo. Bush's gestures to patch up the transatlantic relationship after his reelection in 2004 were unprecedented.

A newly elected president may have little or no experience in foreign affairs and yet have the power to select a multitude of foreign policy advisers, secretaries and agency chiefs, many with little or no foreign or defense policy background themselves. Such a presidential "team" appears often to operate in an uncoordinated way, frequently sending off widely differing signals. This inevitably creates and fuels doubts about American leadership capabilities and the continuity of U.S. foreign policy. The complicated and extensive interagency bargaining in Washington confuses many people, European and American alike.

The powerful U.S. Congress can also be frustrating. In the last two decades of the 20th century Congress underwent significant changes: the seniority system in committees had weakened, and the number of committees and subcommittees proliferated. Also, the workload became so demanding that congressmen and senators are retiring earlier. Therefore, an increasingly high percentage of the legislators are new in Congress. For example, by the mid-1990s half the members of the House of Representatives had entered the chamber after the fall of the Berlin Wall. What these changes did was to take much of the

Western Europe Today

power that used to be concentrated in a few key figures and dispersed it within Congress. In this more decentralized (or, more positively, "democratized") Congress, legislative work has become much more complicated. For instance, more than 40 congressional committees and subcommittees deal with the defense budget alone.

In the absence of the kind of strong party discipline that exists in most European parliaments, American congressmen and senators are more protective of their constituents' interests and can safely vote against their party leaders or the president if an issue of great interest in their districts or states is at stake. Thus there is no stable coalition on foreign policy matters. Nevertheless, the Congress is not as obstructionist and isolationist as it might sometimes seem from across the Atlantic. For example, in the 1990s and the first half-decade of the 21st century, it supported the United States' entry into the North America Free Trade Association (NAFTA), the World Trade Organization (WTO) and two enlargements of NATO. Its unflagging and vigorous support of President Bush's antiterrorist measures after September 11 revealed yet again that presidential-congressional unity is the norm in times of crisis.

Complexity on the European side of the Atlantic

One exasperated American official during the Nixon administration described the European Community to be "as mystifying as the Tibetan theocracy." William Wallace was more subdued, calling the EU institutional structure "complex and opaque." Desmond Dinan attributes this to the "incremental, often untidy nature of European integration." The European Union is in the process of steady evolution; it is a polity in the making. The American ambassador to the EU, Richard Morningstar, put it this way: "If we look 20 years into the future, we will know what the U.S. will look like. But Europe? It is hard to predict what the relationship will be when we do not know what one part will be."

Those who deal with Europe must constantly adapt to its changing institutions. It is therefore not simple for Europeans and Americans alike to know precisely who has the authority to make decisions on what, what exactly is the division of labor among many bodies of the community, or where is the line between EU competence and that of the member states. This is one reason why the United States still prefers to utilize its bilateral ties with European allies in times of emergency.

European countries all have variations of parliamentary systems, which simplify the conduct of foreign policy. Responsibility is clearer than one finds either in the EU or the U.S., and once policy is established by the central government, there are fewer obstacles to its implementation. Given party discipline and the fact that a prime minister or chancellor is in office precisely because his party or coalition has a parliamentary majority, it is not easy for its foreign policy to be thwarted by legislative action. Nor does a European government need to worry as much about ratification after having negotiated a treaty as does an American president.

There are, of course, some exceptions. In order for ex-Chancellor Gerhard Schröder to carry out his historic decision to send German military forces to South Asia to support the American and British military action in Afghanistan in 2001, he had to win a majority vote in the *Bundestag*. Not wishing to see his Social Democratic-Green coalition weakened by having to rely on opposition votes, he combined this vote with a vote of confidence and narrowly carried the day with a two-vote margin.

One of the difficulties of EU foreign policy is created by the presidency of the European Council, which, until the Lisbon Treaty becomes operative after 2009, revolves every six months. The member states alternate, and each brings its own perspectives and priorities to its presidency. For instance, the Spanish presidency brought a redirection of attention to Latin America, something in which Finland would have only mild interest. But the Finnish presidency heralded the

Jaap de Hoop Scheffer, Secretary General of NATO

"Northern Dimension", with which Spain would not share a strong affinity.

The member states have differing opinions on how the community's relations with the US should be, and this can affect the transatlantic relationship. A country can assume the presidency with a firm agenda, but find it high jacked by international events. The presidency is so important for setting the EU agenda that the US and other nonmembers cannot ignore it. But such a short presidency inevitably creates discontinuity and can disrupt or complicate ongoing negotiations.

In determining who really makes decisions in EU external policy, the outsider must decide now among a variety of powerful figures: the EC president, the EC commissioner for external relations, the European Council's High Representative for CFSP, the trade commissioner or the prime minister or foreign minister of the current presidency. A prestigious German daily wrote what many people already know: "Neither the European public nor Europe's partners understand the distribution of competencies (if there is one) among the foreign policy representative, Mr. Solana, the commissioner responsible for external relations, Chris Patten, and the council president. . . . who all travel around the world speaking 'in the name of Europe'." It continues: "The same applies to operative politics. The EU has countless commissioners and representatives for special regions or issues, but outside the EU apparatus, nobody knows what powers they have and in whose name they speak."

Despite the many-headed EU leadership that still exists, this stable of influential EU leaders represents considerable progress toward enhancing the community's ability to conduct foreign policy. Referring to the gibe Kissinger once made about not having a phone number when he wanted to call Europe, former Senior Director for European Affairs on the U.S. National Security Council, Antony J. Blinken, argues that there is now a number to call at the EU, depending on the problem. "It is true, however, that while each has the receiver in one ear, he also has 15 [now 27] European ministers whispering in the other. As a result, Brussels' executive decision-making authority is circumscribed." In an interview with the German weekly, *Die Zeit*, ex-Commissioner for External Affairs Chris Patten admitted: "I don't claim for a minute that there will be one single telephone number in the near future, which a Secretary of State Kissinger could dial. Incidentally it's a rare silly question, which Henry Kissinger asked at the time. Which number do you dial if you want to phone the United States?"

The United Kingdom of Great Britain and Northern Ireland

with Mark H. Mullin

Political power's most coveted address: 10 Downing Street, residence of the Prime Minister

Area: 89,038 sq. mi. (230,609 sq. km., slightly smaller than Oregon).

Population: 59.7 million (estimated).

Capital City: London (Pop. 7 million, estimated, including the city's sprawling suburbs).

Climate: Mild and temperate, rarely above 86° F (30° C) or below 14° F (210° C).

Neighboring Countries: Ireland (a short distance across the Irish Sea to the west); France, Belgium and the Netherlands (a short distance across the English Channel or North Sea to the east).

Official Language: English.

Other Principal Tongues: About a fourth of the population of Wales speaks Welsh, and about 60,000 Scottish speak a form of Gaelic. Both are Celtic dialects.

Ethnic Background: Angle, Saxon, Celtic and Nordic.

Principal Religions: Christian 90%. In England, Church of England (Anglican) 49%; Roman Catholic 7%; in Scotland, Church of Scotland (Presbyterian) 19%; in Wales, Church of Wales; Muslim 3%; Sikh and Hindu 2%; Jewish 1%; other 4%.

Main Exports: Finished and semi-finished manufactured products, oil and gas, foodstuffs, chemicals, motor vehicles.

Main Imports: Manufactured goods, foodstuffs, fuels.

Main Customers: EU25 (56.8% of exports and 55.8% of imports), U.S. (14.6% of exports and 7.9% of imports), Germany (10.9% of exports and 13.8% of imports), France (9.4% of exports and 7.9% of imports), Ireland (7.8% of exports), Netherlands (6% of exports and 7.3% of imports), Belgium-Luxembourg (5.4% of imports).

Currency: Pound sterling.

National Day: Celebration of the birthday of the Queen is in June, although she was actually born on April 21.

Head of State: Her Majesty Queen Elizabeth II, b. 1926. Married Lieut. Philip Mountbatten (Prince of Greece and Denmark) on November 20, 1947; he had been created Duke of Edinburgh on the preceding day and (in 1957) Prince of Great Britain. Queen Elizabeth II succeeded to the throne on the death of her father, George VI on February 6, 1952; her coronation took place on June 2, 1953.

Heir Apparent: His Royal Highness Prince Charles (b. Nov. 14, 1948), Prince of Wales. His son, Prince William of Wales (b. June 21, 1982) is second in succession to the throne.

Head of Government: Gordon Brown, Prime Minister (since June 2007).

National Flag: The Union Flag—a dark blue charged with the white cross of St. Andrew (for Scotland), the red cross of St. Patrick (for Ireland), surmounted by the red cross of St. George (for England) bordered in white. Sometimes called the Union Jack.

No country in the world has closer ties with the United States in language, history, shared assumptions and emotion than does the United Kingdom. In the capital of each country there stands a prominent statue of one of the greatest leaders of the other. Abraham Lincoln gazes at the Houses of Parliament in London, and in a prominent section of Washington, Winston Churchill (himself half

13

The United Kingdom

American) stands giving his famous "V" for victory salute. Although the British influence on the United States is not surprising, what is remarkable is the influence that the United Kingdom has had on the rest of the world. It is striking that a moderate–sized island off the coast of Europe should achieve first a pivotal role in European affairs and then domination of much of the entire globe.

Britain is blessed with a moderate climate, despite its northerly location, due to the warmth of the Gulf Stream, which after originating in the Caribbean Sea crosses the Atlantic. Its waters provide a warmer, albeit moister, climate than would otherwise be the case. Rain is frequent, but not overabundant. The sun shines in most parts for one out of four to eight daylight hours during the winter. The mountains of the west modify this pattern, condensing the clouds into rainfall, which is more abundant there.

The climate is not suited to plant life needing heat, but it is ideal for water–seeking crops, particularly grasses. With a population density of about 640 persons per square mile, much of Britain is urbanized. In spite of the fertile soil, it is an importer of foodstuffs. The industrial revolution, for which Britain is renowned, resulted in a particularly dense type of city building construction. Wales is a mixture of industry, agriculture and herding. Virtually all sheep and cattle are consumed within the country; the sheep support production of fine woolens, few of which are exported. Scotland, about one quarter the size of England and Wales, consists of a small area of lowlands and the larger highlands, which actually reach a maximum height of only 4,400 feet. The cities of Glasgow on the Clyde River and

Edinburgh on the Firth (Bay) of Forth are seats of heavy industry and highly urbanized. The mountains are widely interspersed with valleys where intensive sheep–raising supports the production of world–famous Scotch tweeds and plaids, treasured by tailors throughout the world.

While Roman remains can be found in various parts of England today, the most important architectural work is virtually invisible. London, located at the spot closest to the sea where the Thames could most easily be bridged, was walled and became a Roman center, even though the Celtic name was retained. It became the hub from which spokes of roads headed out to other parts of the island. This pattern still shapes the roads and rails of Britain. The city today extends far beyond the boundaries of the original wall.

Natural resources that were important in the early Industrial Revolution in the late 18th and 19th centuries have been a second blessing. Its island location has protected it from invasion for more than 900 years and encouraged it to use the sea for commercial and political gain. But its greatest blessing has been a relatively stable history that developed quite early in a tradition of freedom and representative government. Americans are sometimes confused by the various names applied to Britain. Its official name is The United Kingdom of Great Britain and Northern Ireland. Four areas combine to make up the country: England, Wales, Scotland and Northern Ireland. The word "Britain" encompasses the first three. The last is composed of the six northern Irish counties. Because England is the site of the capital and over the centuries came to control the other areas, the term "England" or "the English" is sometimes (but

inaccurately) used to describe the whole country. Residents of Wales, Scotland and Northern Ireland prefer to use the term "Great Britain" or "British."

The growth toward world leadership and representative democracy in Britain has not been smooth or steady, but the history of Britain has been a stage on which royal pageantry has combined with remarkable commercial, industrial and political success of more humble citizens.

HISTORY

The Early Period

It must have been quite a shock for the Roman legionnaires who left the brilliant sunshine of Italy, marched across Gaul, and then made the short but perilous crossing of the English Channel. They arrived in a land of soft greens, frequent rains and fearsome warriors who painted themselves blue and drove chariots armed with sharp blades at the axles. These Celts had come to the island during the Iron Age, spoke a dialect known as Brythonic, and thus their land was known as Britain.

Julius Caesar led two expeditions to Britain in 55 and 54 B.C., but it was not until 43 A.D. that the Roman Emperor Claudius began to establish settlements. The campaign to stamp out Celtic Druid beliefs, with all of their mysticism, that have faded into the mists of time, produced the first of the great British queens, Boadicea, who managed to kill several thousand Romanizing Britons before finally being captured and committing suicide. While the popular image has always seen the British as chauvinists in their men's clubs, the fact that in the 1980s both the throne and the office of prime minis-

The prehistoric ruins of Stonehenge on the Salisbury Plain which scholars date from 1800 to 1400 B.C.

The United Kingdom

ter were occupied by women is less surprising when one remembers that the first resistance leader and the monarchs with two of the greatest reigns in English history, Elizabeth I (1558–1603) and Victoria (1837–1901) were women, however different they were. The first was an astute monarch, who is reported to have utilized amorous affairs to advance the affairs of state. The latter was conservative, conventional, prudish and astute, devoted only to her husband Albert. Indeed, rightfully or wrongfully, an entire age is known by the name of each in the English–speaking world.

Celtic tribalism continued in the mountains of Wales and Scotland. Hadrian's Wall ran for miles to seal off the northern borders of the Roman area since the people in the mountains there were beyond conquest. No attempt was made to invade Ireland.

The Early Christian Era

Roman soldiers and merchants brought Christianity with them to the island. Their persecution by Emperor Diocletian produced the first Christian martyr of the island, St. Alban. But after Emperor Constantine legalized Christianity in the empire, the Church began to flourish in Britain.

The Romans occupied England for about 400 years, but as the empire collapsed inward, barbarian pressure on England increased. Angles, Saxons and Jutes, Teutonic tribes from what is now northern Germany and Denmark, filled the vacuum left by the Romans. Now it was the Celts leading their tribal lives in Wales, Scotland, Ireland and Cornwall, who kept alive the light of Western civilization and Christian culture.

King Arthur may be more legendary than historical, but his story represents the urge to restore Christian order during the dark period that lasted for two centuries. In 597 the monk Augustine (named for the more famous St. Augustine of Hippo) was sent from Rome to convert the English. He established Canterbury as his see and became its first archbishop. As Roman Christianity spread, it came into contact and then into conflict with Celtic Christianity. The synod of Whitby, meeting in 664, decided that Roman Christianity would prevail. This proved to be a most significant decision, for England was thus brought once more under the influence of Rome; its culture, its politics and religion would be shaped by events on the Continent. Nearly 900 years later, when England turned away from Roman Christianity, the effects would be even more important. During the 8th century, English culture flourished. The first English historian, Venerable (later Saint) Bede,

A castle in Wales

wrote his *Ecclesiastical History of the English People*; the great Anglo–Saxon epic *Beowulf* was written; and the Saxon monk Alcuin of York was a leading intellectual of Charlemagne's court.

Viking Invasion and Expulsion

By the 9th century, Vikings (Norsemen, Northmen, Normans) from Norway and Denmark attacked and then conquered much of the British isle. In response, the only English king to be known as "the Great," Alfred of Wessex, whose capital was at Winchester, organized an army, developed a navy, founded schools and stopped the growth of Norse–Danish power. It is ironic that the Norsemen then invaded France, where their region became known as Normandy. Almost two centuries later, one of their leaders would head the last successful conquest of England. Although Alfred died in 899, his son, Edward the Elder, conquered the remaining Danish–controlled areas and thus became the first king of a united England.

For the next 100 years, Anglo–Saxons and Norsemen merged during a golden age of relative peace. As the English historian Trevelyan said, "Had it not been for the Scandinavian blood infused into our race by the catastrophes of the 9th century, less would have been heard in days to come of British maritime and commercial

enterprise." Again ironically, at about the same time, the Scandinavians were invited to Russia to establish order among the belligerent, disorganized Slav warlords.

By the start of the 11th century, a weak king, Ethelred the Unready, allowed his kingdom to fall into confusion. The Danish king, Canute, invaded the island in 1016 and England became part of an empire that included Denmark and Norway. Canute was followed by his two sons, each of whom died shortly after ascending the throne. Ethelred's son, Edward the Confessor, who was half Norman and had lived in Normandy during the reign of Canute and his sons, was placed on the throne. He made two decisions with far–reaching consequences. He founded Westminster Abbey outside of London, starting the separation of the government from the city. Because he was childless, he promised his cousin, William Duke of Normandy, that the throne would one day be his.

The Final Conquest and the First Plantagenets

The year 1066 is to the English school children what 1492 is to Americans. In that year, Edward the Confessor died. The Witan (national council) elected his brother–in–law, Harold, as his successor. A Norwegian invasion in Yorkshire called Harold to the north. Seizing the opportunity, William landed a Norman force in the south of England. Harold raced south to meet his death—at the Battle of Hastings he was killed by a sword blow, and William established himself and his Norman lords as rulers of England.

William chose to rule by a rigorous system of feudalism. He established Normans loyal to himself as lords of all the great manors. But they were tenants on the land; ownership was the king's right. The most important lords made up the Great Council, the forerunner of parliament. William also placed Normans in the most important positions in the church hierarchy and ruled that clergy would be tried in ecclesiastical, rather than secular courts.

All over England, Norman buildings characterized by massive rectangular towers, showed that the conquerors had come to stay. The most notable were the Tower of London and Westminster Hall. Scores of parish churches, castles and monasteries dotted the landscape. William dispatched Norman legal scholars to go among the people and inquire by what laws (including customs which were virtually laws) they lived. These were organized into the Common Law—the law of the people, which were to be used in secular courts. This greatly pacified the conquered people, since they corresponded with what had prevailed before the Norman conquest. Writs were established which were an intriguing combination of Latin, Anglo–Saxon and French—*Assumpsit*, *Trespass Quare Clausum Fregit*, *Indebitatus*, etc.

William's great–grandson, Henry II (the first of the Plantagenets), came to the throne in 1154. He asserted the power of the king at the expense of the barons by tearing down unlicensed castles, creating a militia instead of depending upon the nobility for armed troops, and created traveling judges. The decisions of these judges were based on the Common Law, which operated by establishing written precedents rather than a codified law. Henry II also invaded Ireland, and, with the permission of the Pope, established himself as king of England's western neighbor. No one could possibly foresee what enormous consequences this would have for England in the years to come— consequences that affect Britain to this day.

Henry might have foreseen the consequences for which he is most remembered. He got into a dispute with his Archbishop, Thomas Becket, over the issue of whether the clergy should be tried in Church courts or civil courts. Whether Henry ordered that Becket be killed, or merely hinted that it would please him, will never be known. But Becket's murder turned him into a martyr and Canterbury

Mark H. and Mrs. Mullin chat with Prince Charles

into a shrine. Henry's two sons, Richard and John, were low points in the history of the English monarchy. Richard (who came to be known as the Lion–Hearted) spent most of his reign out of the country as a crusader, trying to wrest Jerusalem and Israel from the Arabs. His absence did England little good, but it did provide that great scene in stories and movies where, when he returns to England, he reveals himself to Robin Hood.

John was not only ineffective but also very unpopular. He lost English possessions on the Continent, including Normandy, and ran up such a debt that the barons were able to force him to sign the *Magna Carta* in 1215. This document was not the forward–looking cornerstone of freedom that it is sometimes portrayed to be, but rather it guaranteed the rights that the nobility and the Church expected. At the same time, it established the principle that there are limits on the powers of the monarch, and thus it was a first step toward the largely unwritten constitutional monarchy of today.

The 13th century was a time of intellectual growth. Groups of scholars gathered at Oxford, and a splinter group later moved to Cambridge. Roger Bacon was a leading teacher stressing scientific experimentation. The King's Council was expanded to include representatives of shires and boroughs; thus the way was prepared for a representative House of Commons. At the end of the century, Edward I epitomized the medieval monarch. Physically imposing, he aided the growing spirit of nationalism by checking the power of the barons and the Church, and by increasing English power in Wales and Ireland. However, unsuccessful attempts to invade Scotland led Edward into financial difficulties, and in 1297 he was forced to sign a confirmation of the Magna Carta.

He agreed that the king could not impose taxes without the consent of the newborn parliament.

Edward's grandson, Edward III, attempted to reassert English power on the continent. In 1337 the Hundred Years War began. At first, success came to the English and the war strengthened the nation. However, in 1348 the Black Death (Bubonic Plague) swept the country and nearly half the population died. The country sank into economic depression, and by the time the king died in 1377, all the lands he had conquered in France had been lost except for a small area around Calais.

The period produced the first great work of literature in primitive English, Chaucer's *Canterbury Tales*. For centuries, Latin had been spoken by the Church and French by the nobility, but now the nation was uniting with the use of the English language.

The War of the Roses and the House of Tudor

Among Edward's sons were John of Gaunt, Duke of Lancaster, and Edmund, Duke of York. During the first half of the 15th century, the Lancaster branch held the throne, but in 1455 the Wars of the Roses, symbolized by the red rose of Lancaster and the white rose of York, subjected the country to a brutal civil war. Shakespeare puts the words "Uneasy lies the head that wears a crown" in the mouth of Henry IV, the first of the Lancastrian kings. The instability of a monarch's life continued throughout the 15th century. Perhaps the best example was Richard III of the House of York, who gained the crown by allegedly having two of his nephews, young princes, murdered in the Tower of London, and lost his own life in a battle against Henry Tudor of the House of Lancaster. Despite the battles for the throne, the 15th century was one of growing prosperity for England, especially in wool and foreign trade. To this day, the Lord Chancellor's seat in the House of Lords is a woolsack.

With the arrival of the Tudors, the medieval world drew to a close. During the first Tudor reign (Henry VII), Columbus sailed for the New World. The wealth that Spain acquired there provided constant problems for the Tudors, and it was not until their successors, the Stuarts, that English colonies were firmly established. Soon the winds of the Reformation would bring even greater changes to England. Henry arranged for his eldest son, Arthur, to marry Catherine of Aragon, daughter of the king of Spain. This was a particularly important match for diplomatic reasons, because Spain controlled the Netherlands through which much of English trade entered the continent.

The United Kingdom

King Henry VIII

Anne Boleyn

Arthur died in 1502 before his father. Despite both scriptural and canon law injunctions against marrying one's brother's widow, the Pope granted a dispensation allowing Arthur's brother, Henry, to marry the young widow. Henry's sister, Margaret, married the king of Scotland, thus providing England with marital allies on several sides. When Henry VIII assumed the throne after his father's death, he realized the importance of a male heir. But his union with Catherine only produced a daughter, Mary. It is important to note that Henry was initially loyal to Roman Catholicism, and because of a work he authored attacking the doctrines of Martin Luther, the Pope granted him the title "Defender of the Faith." It is ironic that his non–Roman Catholic descendants still carry that title.

Because Henry realized that Catherine would not produce a son, and because he was lusting after the attractive, dark–haired Anne Boleyn, he asked the Pope to grant him an annulment of his marriage to Catherine, claiming that it was illegal in the first place. Unfortunately for Henry, Catherine's uncle, Charles V of the Holy Roman Empire, had his troops in Rome at the time. When the Pope refused to grant Henry's request, in an unprecedented move, Henry had himself declared Head of the Church in England. His marriage to Anne Boleyn, however, produced only a daughter, Elizabeth, and Henry then proceeded through four more wives, making six in all, only one of whom produced a son, Edward.

Pupils learn to keep track of Henry's wives by the saying "Divorced, beheaded, died, divorced, beheaded, survived."

Edward VI followed his father to the throne in 1547 at 11 years of age. His guardians moved the country rapidly in the direction of Protestantism. But the sickness–prone boy died six years later (he was possibly murdered), and the first of Henry's daughters, Mary Tudor, assumed the throne. Had Mary wanted to move England back to the religious position of her father, she probably would have lasted. But she felt a calling to return the nation to full Roman Catholicism and further alienated her subjects by taking Philip of Spain as her husband.

Although the number of resisting Protestants who were burned at the stake was actually quite small, there were enough prominent bishops ignited to earn the Queen the historical title of "Bloody Mary." The words of one of these bishops—"Be of good cheer, Master Ridley, we shall today light such a candle as will by God's grace never be extinguished in England" proved to be prophetic. At Mary's death after only five years on the throne, her half–sister, Elizabeth I became queen, and with her, one of the great ages in English history began.

The Elizabethan Period

Since the Catholic Church considered Elizabeth illegitimate, she moved the country back toward Protestantism. It was a moderate protestant position, with the old forms of worship retained in English and no vigorous attempt to be overly scrupulous in matters of doctrine. As Elizabeth put it, "We shall make no window into any man's soul." Elizabeth's cousin, Mary Stuart, abdicated the throne of Scotland in favor of her son, James, and fled to England. For years, Roman Catholic attempts to oust Elizabeth flurried around Mary, who was Catholic. Despite "that divinity that doth hedge a king," (or queen), Elizabeth finally yielded to the advice of her court and had Mary beheaded in 1587.

That same year, Sir Francis Drake, having already stolen Spanish gold from the New World, raided the port of Cadiz. In reprisal, the next year Spain sent a Great Armada to invade and conquer England. But a "Protestant wind" and English naval tactics carried the day; less than half of the Armada managed to limp back to Spain. England had established itself as a ruler of the seas, a position it would continue to enjoy for almost 400 years.

The Elizabethan Age was a flowering of English culture and the brightest blooms were uses of the language that still affect our thought and speech. Although William Shakespeare was the most magnificent of the blossoms, others, such as Spenser, Drayton, Donne and Marlowe bloomed in the sunshine.

Thomas Cranmer produced a Book of Common Prayer in 1549 whose magnificent collects shaped the way the English–speaking world addressed God and whose words start the most important ceremony in most people's lives: "Dearly beloved, we are gathered here together in the sight of God and in the face of this company to join together this man and this woman in holy matrimony: which is an honorable estate instituted of God, signifying unto us the mystical union that is betwixt Christ and His church." The musical liturgy of the book was done with assistance from Lutherans, who had retained Catholic plain song chant traditions in German; they were adapted to English. Further, harmonized Anglican chant was first produced. All of this is preserved with little change in many churches to this day.

In the last part of Elizabeth's reign, William Shakespeare began to write his plays. Their plots shape our view of history, or romance, and of humor, and his phrases fill our speaking and our reading, even when we do not know the source of the words. Finally, shortly after Elizabeth's death, the language of the Book of Common Prayer and the language of Shakespeare came together in the most influential of all English books, the King James Bible. Until recently, it was read by more people than any other book in the English language, and for many Americans on the frontier, it was their only book in the English language. It has been only in the past five decades that serious attention was paid to any of the "modern" English translations.

The Tudor monarchs were able to dominate England by their political skill and by the force of their personality. All except Edward and Mary enjoyed considerable popularity, and if those who followed them had enjoyed similar success, the parliament might have melted out of British life. But the Stuarts, of whom it could be said, "They learned nothing and forgot nothing," tried to push the doctrine of the Divine Right of Kings farther than the English wished to have it carried. When Elizabeth died unmarried in 1603, James Stuart, king of Scotland, became James I of England and the whole island was united under one monarch.

The Stuarts Brief Tenure

The second of the Stuarts, Charles I, came to the throne in 1625. He soon began to have trouble with parliament over taxation, and his inflexibility and demands for royal absolutism only angered the democratic movement within the country. Moreover, Charles was a "high" churchman, with Roman Catholic leanings, and most members of parliament were Puritan protestant in inclination (i.e. a full, chanted Eucharistic service with all ceremonial acts, including incense, holy water, etc. versus three hymns, a psalm, lessons and sermon). For 11 years Charles managed to rule without parliament and his persecution of Puritans led to the founding of the colonies in New England. In order to raise revenues, Charles reconvened parliament in 1640 and soon civil war broke out in England. Catholics, high churchmen, the nobility and the rural people of the north and west supported the king; Puritans, people of trade and commerce and most important, Londoners, supported parliament.

Religious and Civil Turmoil

Unlike the Wars of the Roses, the Civil War of the 17th century was not simply a fight over who should occupy the throne, but an ideological struggle to determine the very nature of English society. Oliver Cromwell emerged as leader of the parliamentary forces after Charles had been captured. Cromwell purged parliament of all but his loyal supporters, abolished the House of Lords, and in 1649, had Charles beheaded. He was the only English monarch to die for religious reasons, and the last to be killed for political reasons. Whether Charles was a martyr for the causes of royal stability and the Anglican Church or whether he justly died for opposing the representatives of the people depends on one's viewpoint—and perhaps both views are true.

The Commonwealth Period and Return of Monarchy

Cromwell had hoped to rule in a liberal and democratic way, but continued factionalism and the threatening anarchy in English society caused him to assume absolute power as Lord Protector. This period was known as the Commonwealth. When Cromwell died in 1658 and the monarchy was restored in 1660, Charles II, the son of the dead king, returned from the continent to which he had escaped and was greeted by a joyful people.

Queen Mary I

Queen Elizabeth I

The United Kingdom

During Charles' reign, English culture extricated itself from the heavy burden of Puritanism and flourished again; Bunyan, Milton and Pepys were the most famous writers. The great fire of 1666 destroyed much of London, but allowed such master architects as Christopher Wren to rebuild a new and even more glorious city. On another continent, the Dutch were driven out of North America and New Amsterdam became New York.

James II followed his brother to the throne, but did not renounce his faith in Roman Catholicism. The English then turned to William of Orange, a grandson of Charles I, who came to England and later defeated James in the July 1690 Battle of the Boyne in Ireland. From then on, the fact that England was Anglican (not Roman Catholic or Puritan) was settled. But both William of Orange and his wife were childless. The most logical successor was Queen Anne, daughter of James II, but she died childless in 1714. What was the answer for a people accustomed to a monarchy?

The House of Hanover (later Windsor) and Parliament Power

Britain turned to George of Hanover (a great–grandson of James I, and a Protestant) to become king. The fact that he could speak no English (only German) was of immense importance. It meant that the king had to leave many of his powers in the hands of the chairmanship of his council, and that person was the leader of the Whig Party, with a majority in the House of Commons. Thus, England developed the tradition of having a prime minister preside over a cabinet that grew out of parliament.

During the middle part of the 18th century, the first British Empire took shape. English forces defeated the French for control of much of India and the defeat of the French forces at Quebec in 1759 meant that Canada and the area west of the thirteen colonies were brought under British rule. In 1760, George III succeeded to the throne. Since he believed a king should rule the country, he suspended the cabinet government, intending that the king and the "king's friends" would rule.

As the British Empire expanded with Captain Cook's discovery of Australia, relations with the 13 American colonies deteriorated. By 1782 they had been victorious in their revolution and the period of the First British Empire was largely over. With the disaster in North America came the return of the cabinet system to England as William Pitt the Younger became the new prime minister. For the next 50 years the Tories would lead the country and maintain a steady and conservative posture while the French Revolution and then the armies of Napoleon forced Britain once again to demonstrate its mastery of the seas.

Nineteenth Century Change

At the turn of the century, the Act of Union dissolved the Irish Parliament and incorporated Catholic Ireland into the United Kingdom. Tragically, religious persecution of the Catholics kept the Irish from full integration into British society and thus, the Union was doomed from the start.

But change was occurring in England. The Industrial Revolution, gradual at first, gathered momentum. Early machines made of wood were replaced by stronger and more efficient ones of iron. James Watt's inventions harnessed the power of steam. Reforms in agriculture improved food production, but caused many farmers to leave the land. Thus, as industry and commerce were growing, along with the wealth and power of those who controlled them, so, too, there was a growing urban class kept in degrading poverty. As populations shifted, parliament became less representative.

In so–called "rotten" boroughs, a few voters could control who was elected to parliament. In one district in Cornwall a single voter could elect two members! It is coincidental, but symbolic that in 1830, the Reforming Whigs Party obtained a majority in parliament and the first railroad line on which the Rocket whizzed along at 35 miles an hour was opened.

The Whigs were able to get their Reform Bill through parliament in 1832. This most important piece of legislation abolished many "rotten" boroughs, gave representation to the new towns and significantly lowered the property qualifications necessary to be a voter. Many observers think that this Reform Bill saved the country from revolution, which had become so popular in the rest of Europe. Certainly, it gave new power to the middle classes, and was an important step toward mass democracy.

Victoria

In 1837 the 18–year–old Victoria began the longest reign in British history. As the

George III (1738–1820)

John Constable's *Hay Wain* **(1821)**

National Gallery, London

democratic form of government. Nations under the constant threat of attack often could not afford the luxury of a relatively inefficient and cumbersome governmental order that involved parliamentary meetings, long debates, votes, press coverage and criticism. As a nation equally invulnerable, the Americans shared this advantage with their English forebears.

Also, Britain did not need to maintain a large standing army. As the history of many countries indicates, ambitious soldiers, led by prestigious officers close to the political heart of the country sometimes cannot resist meddling in the political affairs of a nation. The British never had difficulty in maintaining control over their military; a military putsch is unthinkable in the British context. Fortunately, the tradition of civilian supremacy over the military was passed on to many (though not all) of its former colonies, including in the United States.

Political Power Struggles and Social Change

A watershed year in the growth of power of the House of Commons was 1911. The Liberal Party government had proposed a land tax, and although tradition had it that only Commons controlled finances, the House of Lords rejected the bill. The parliament bill of 1911 deprived the Lords of any control of finance and limited their power over other bills to a two–year delay. In a move to make the Commons more responsive to the popular will, the maximum life of a parliament was reduced from seven to five years. When it appeared that the Lords would veto this bill, George V threatened to increase the number of Lords and pack the Upper House with those favorable to the bill. The Lords yielded to the threat and thereafter the House of Commons gained virtual total control of legislation. In the same year, members of the House of Commons began to receive pay, and thus, those without independent incomes could be in Parliament.

World War I not only devastated a generation of Englishmen—it helped to produce changes in society. As recognition for their part in the war effort, women received the vote in 1918. Because they involved so much of the population, both world wars did much to further popular democracy and reduce the differences between social classes. Shortly after World War I, the southern part of Ireland left the United Kingdom and achieved dominion status as the Irish Free State. Protestants living in the north clung tenaciously to their membership in the United Kingdom and their loyalty to the crown, but their conflict with Catholics living alongside them has not been solved to this day.

last half of the 17th century had belonged to Elizabeth, so the 19th century belonged to Victoria. During Victoria's reign, reform acts gradually increased the number of people enfranchised and gave protection to the lower classes. The repeal of the "Corn Laws" and free trade not only stimulated industry, but also reduced the cost of living for the poor. Thus, under the leadership of such greats as Palmerston, Gladstone and Disraeli, Parliament found a course that kept England moving toward democracy without being caught up in the excesses that racked so much of the continent. By 1846 Canada had been made self–governing, and within a few years, Australia and New Zealand were given internal self–rule. Thus, the concept of the Empire of free countries bound to the mother country by loyalty to the Queen was born.

Two great events marked the reign of Victoria. The great Exhibition of 1851 demonstrated British industrial might and middle class prosperity, whereas the

Golden Jubilee of the Queen in 1887 marked the high point of the Empire. The claim that the sun never set on the British Empire was indeed true. Its members included Canada in North America, British Guiana in South America; the United Kingdom in Europe; South Africa, Kenya, Somaliland in Africa; India and Ceylon in Asia; and Australia and New Zealand in the Pacific. The greatest problem, however, was closest to home, and various attempts to solve the Irish problem through Home Rule were unsuccessful.

Until 1900 the roar of the British lion could be heard throughout the entire world. Britain controlled over one–fifth of the earth's land surface and ruled a quarter of the world's population. Its flag flew on every continent and the largest and most powerful navy in the world protected its magnificent empire. At the same time, Britain was invulnerable to foreign invasion. This meant that, unlike many other nations with frontiers instead of shorelines, it could leisurely develop a

The United Kingdom

THE
BRITISH NAVY
guards the freedom of us all

Following World War I, trade unions grew in power and were able to call a general strike in 1926. But the great depression of the 1930s significantly reduced the power of the Labour government, and the Conservatives led the country in the years before World War II. The last crisis to affect the monarchy occurred in 1936. Edward VIII ascended the throne, but within months he abdicated so that he could marry the divorced Wallis Simpson, an American.

The Hitler Threat and World War II
As Hitler began to threaten more and more of Europe, Prime Minister Neville Chamberlain practiced a policy of appeasement. This only whetted the German appetite; after an attack on Poland in September 1939, Britain joined France as allies in World War II. In May of the next year, Winston Churchill became prime minister. His courage and his words epitomized the best of the British spirit and inspired the nation to withstand withering aerial attacks from bombers and rockets. With tremendous but belated assistance from the U.S., Britain and its allies were victorious, but prostrated and devastated by the end of the conflict in 1945.

The Postwar 1940s and 1950s
Two world wars in the 20th century brought enormous changes. These included revolutions in many European countries, the rise of the United States and the Soviet Union as the most powerful countries in the world and the relative decline of the traditional global powers, including the United Kingdom, in terms of political and military significance. As a victorious ally, Britain gained a veto right in the United Nations Security Council,

but it had to liquidate most of its foreign investments to finance its own recovery; these foreign investments had once paid for a third of British imports. The merchant marine was depleted and factories and equipment were either destroyed or obsolete.

The negative economic consequences of the wars reduced Britain's ability to be a global power and stimulated in many British colonies the desire for independence. By proclaiming the Truman Doctrine, the U.S. assumed from Britain the burden of economic and military aid to Greece and Turkey and relieved the U.K. of its responsibility for supporting the struggle against communist forces in the Greek civil war. The British also found themselves in the crossfire between Jews and Arabs in Palestine and Hindus and Moslems in India and were forced in 1947 to abandon both important regions. In 1952 it lost control of Egypt. When Egypt seized the Suez Canal in 1956, Britain, supported by France and Israel, attempted to reconquer that important waterway. However, stiff joint United Nations, U.S. and Soviet opposition to this move, which seemed like the last gasp of colonialism, forced the British, French and Israelis to back down.

In 1959 Britain still ruled over 53 countries with a population of 81 million, and 86,000 British troops were deployed around the world outside of Europe. But the floodgates opened, and by the 1960s a tidal wave of separations swept through Africa, the Middle East and Asia. Having lost most of its Asian empire in the late–1940s, the British recognized the inevitability of African independence. Fortunately, Britain had trained many Africans as capable administrators and had established there a relatively efficient system of local administration. Therefore, when they gradually relinquished their hold, well–trained Africans were usually able to take their places. An exception was Rhodesia, whose tiny white minority took power in 1965 and held it for years before finally handing the reins of power to the new black–ruled state of Zimbabwe.

Britain spearheaded the international UN boycott of Rhodesia. But the UK was in the throes of such economic distress that it was not only unable to steer events in Africa, but it was also forced in 1971 to terminate most of its military and political responsibilities "East of Suez." This withdrawal was unfortunate for the U.S., which was trapped at the time in the quagmire of Vietnam. The U.S. felt compelled to assume Britain's prior responsibility for maintaining "stability" in the Middle East. It thereby became embroiled in one of the world's least stable regions. This untimely responsibility prompted

American administrations in the 1970s to help build up the Shah's power. The hope was that a modernized and well–armed Iran could maintain order in the oil–rich Persian Gulf region and keep the Soviet Union's power and influence out of the area. The Americans paid heavily in the 1980s for this gamble.

Elizabeth II succeeded her father, George VI, on the British throne in 1952. Thirty generations separated her from her ancestor, William the Conqueror, and she began her reign in a nation struggling to find a new role in the modern world. The Empire became a Commonwealth of independent nations, bound together by language, democratic principles and a residue of loyalty to the person (but not the power) of the British monarch. Decolonization had a serious negative economic impact on Britain by depriving it of many protected markets, sources of raw materials at low prices and cheap food. The resulting economic difficulties harassed the United Kingdom for a quarter of a century following the Second World War.

Domestic Politics before Thatcher
On July 5, 1945, voters delivered a dramatic blow to the Tories by electing the first Labour prime minister with a clear majority of 145 seats in the House of Commons, Clement Attlee. Although the British deeply admired Churchill as a great wartime leader, they associated his Conservative Party with the soup lines and unemployment of the prewar depression. Labour had ably guided the home ministries in the national government during the war. It had impressed the British as being the best team for creating full employment, housing and better social security and health care for a people that had just sacrificed so much in the war effort.

Although ideologically divided, as always, between more pragmatic and radical wings, the Labour Party moved boldly to make many sweeping economic changes, including the nationalization of the Bank of England, hospitals, railways, aviation, public transport and the gas, electrical, coal and steel industries. Unlike France and Italy, though, the newly nationalized industries were placed under the direction of autonomous corporations (subsidized from the state treasury), rather than government agencies and ministries. In 1946 the National Insurance Act and National Health Service Act were the prime examples of popular social welfare legislation which strengthened or created old–age pensions, unemployment compensation, education, social insurance and free health service. No sooner were these innovations in place, though, than the Labour government began losing pop-

Horse Guardsmen leaving their barracks for duty at Buckingham Palace

ularity. It was badly divided, British influence abroad was noticeably eroding, the pound was losing its value, and economic recovery was painfully slow.

At age 77 Winston Churchill was returned to power in 1951, and his Tories ruled until 1964, the longest period of continuous party government in modern British history until Margaret Thatcher and John Major ruled 18 years from 1979 to 1997. His government returned the iron and steel industries and road transport to private ownership, although Labour renationalized iron and steel in 1967. However, accurately sensing the sentiments of the British nation, the Tories did not make a radical U–turn. It accepted the national welfare and health services, as well as the commitment to full employment.

Following a stroke, Churchill was finally persuaded to step down in 1955. His successor was his longtime foreign minister Anthony Eden. After only a year Eden had to resign in the aftermath of the Suez crisis of 1956. He was followed by Harold Macmillan, who like Churchill had an American mother. He optimistically predicted a turnaround in Britain's economic fortunes (for which reason he was dubbed "Supermac"). There was a short–lived economic boom in the late– 1950s, and the living standards of some British rose. But inequalities of wealth remained which the

government could not alleviate because of a rising imbalance of payments and a serious sterling crisis. Britain was obviously not keeping up with its international trade competitors, and management and trade unions were not inclined to introduce more efficient and modern methods of

production. In an attempt to protect the value of the pound, the government had to introduce an unpopular wage freeze and raise the bank rate. Macmillan sought to halt the growing economic malaise and increase British industry's competitiveness by leading Britain into the EU, but

Winston S. Churchill, surrounded by the royal family

The United Kingdom

French President Charles de Gaulle vetoed its entry in 1963.

Following this humiliation came the *coup de grace* for the Macmillan government: a lurid sex scandal involving Secretary of War John Profumo. He was alleged to be involved with a call girl who had been asked by the Soviet naval attaché to gather information from him on the UK's nuclear weapons. No government could possibly benefit from such a spicy and embarrassing affair. But what forced Macmillan to demand Profumo's resignation was not so much the illicit activity itself as the fact that he had insulted parliament by lying to it about his involvement. He thereby dragged both himself and the prime minister down.

The colorless Sir Alec Douglas–Home replaced Macmillan in the fall of 1963. Home (pronounced Hume) was a rare example of a prime minister being drawn from the House of Lords, even though he scrambled to win a by–election seat to the Commons. Home could not quiet the growing desire for a change, and with only a razor–thin majority he could not prevent Harold Wilson's Labour Party from winning power in October 1964.

A former Oxford University economics don (lecturer), Wilson was from the more conservative, reformist wing of the Labour Party. Faced with daunting economic problems, he not only pared down the UK's military commitments abroad, but he applied the traditional conservative policies of increasing taxes and reducing government spending. These unpopular economic policies widened ideological divisions within his own party, sparked industrial unrest and strikes and brought Wilson into a head–on collision with the trade unions. Widening trade imbalances, another devaluation of the pound, and a renewal of strife between Catholics and Protestants in Northern Ireland, all spelled disaster for Wilson in the June 1970 elections, when the Tories, led by Edward Heath, returned to power.

Heath's government knew little happiness, aside from Britain's entry into the EU in 1973. His bitter confrontations with the assertive coal miners brought serious economic disruptions and forced the prime minister to declare states of emergency five times. The crippling coal strike in the winter of 1973–4 destroyed what credibility remained for the cabinet. Voters brought Wilson's Labour party back to power in February 1974 on the assumption that they would have better relations with the powerful unions.

Wilson had only a miniscule majority which he widened in a snap election in October 1974. He expended precious energy and patience fending off an ambi-tious radical left wing within his own party which sniped at him constantly and openly advocated such unpopular policies as a "socialist transformation" of British society, massive nationalizations of large companies, the abolition of elite institutions such as the House of Lords and private schools, withdrawal from NATO and the EU, and unilateral disarmament. These leftist antics ultimately drove some moderates out of the party and led to the formation in 1981 of the now defunct Social Democratic Party (SDP).

It is hardly surprising that Wilson was unable to improve the economic situation. The skyrocketing price of oil resulting from the 1973 OPEC embargo hit the struggling British economy hard, despite the discovery of oil in Britain's own sectors of the North Sea. Inflation rose to a dizzying level, and for the first time since the war unemployment reared its ugly head. These problems made hopes for harmonious labor relations a pipe dream, as the spate of disruptive strikes indicated. In 1976 an exasperated and tired Harold Wilson turned the keys to Number 10 Downing Street over to his foreign minister, James Callaghan. The new prime minister was no more successful than Wilson had been in controlling the unions, improving the overall economy, and coping with rising violence in Northern Ireland and growing separatist movements in Scotland and Wales.

It has been said that the world stands aside for a man who knows where he is going. By the spring of 1979, the British voters were prepared to do just that, with one historical twist: they brought to power the first woman prime minister in British politics, Margaret Thatcher. She acted with such determination and decisiveness that by January 3, 1988, she had become the longest continuously serving British prime minister in the 20th century. Ruling over a country with the highest economic growth of any major economy, low inflation, declining unemployment, a rising pound, and tamed unions, she had every reason to believe that she would remain at the helm into the 21st century and perhaps even overtake the record of Sir Robert Walpole, whose 21 consecutive years of service as prime minister began in 1721.

Attitude and Political Change

Terrorism related to the unsolved problem of Northern Ireland, along with rising crime in Britain, helped shift British voters' view of the world in an important way. It helped many of them shape a tough–minded attitude and become more receptive to political appeals based on "law and order," replacing the compromise politics of the 1960s.

The parliamentary elections of 1979 and 1983 took many foreign observers by surprise because they revealed that the political landscape in Britain had dramatically changed. Upon closer scrutiny, it can be seen that these changes are the consequence of important changes in Britain's economy and society in the course of the decade of the 1970s. Those changes broke down much of the class structure of Britain, which traditionally had shaped British politics to such a large extent.

Public opinion polls and election analyses continually confirm that fewer and fewer British spontaneously identify with a particular class, and that class–consciousness has and is declining markedly. Class itself has become only one of many factors shaping individual attitudes and preferences. It has become harder to classify Britons by class, which has increasingly become more a matter of taste and culture, rather than of income and occupation. With less than a quarter of workers in manufacturing jobs, fewer than two workers in five belong to a labor union. Two–thirds of all British own or are buying their homes; even one of three unskilled manual laborers is a home–owner. Also, leisure is no longer the privilege of a few; instead, almost all full–time workers receive four weeks of leave. In short, more workers have become middle–class. Young people from all economic strata mingle more easily and are more likely to intermarry than they used to. Since Britons have become more individualistic, their social attitudes and political behavior have become less predictable. These changes are bound to have a negative effect on political parties whose appeals have traditionally been heavily class–based, especially the Labour Party.

Since 1979, Britain's population has barely grown, but the size of the electorate increased from 39.3 in 1970 to 42.2 million in 1983. The voting age was dropped to 18 in 1970, but the number of pensioners has grown, so the average voter today is actually older than in 1970. He or she is also more highly educated, more likely to be divorced and live alone or in small households, own his own home, and, despite high unemployment, have a higher standard of living than in the 1970s. Disenchantment with unions and changes in social patterns (see Culture) that were occurring in the 1970s set the stage for dramatic political shifts in Britain. After 1979 these effectively altered much of the conventional wisdom about British politics and realigned the structure.

Although the diminishing numbers of unionized workers in the mines and factories retained their traditional loyalty to the Labour Party and the managers remained steadfast to the Conservative Party, their diminishing numbers hoisted the flag of change on the pole in the 1970s. Soaring inflation and rising unemployment, accompanied by increasingly strident union demands alienated the people. Their revulsion at the excessive "unelected power" which union bosses wielded boiled to the surface in "the winter of discontent," 1978–79, when coal and transportation strikes threatened to paralyze the entire nation.

These changes led to conditions whereby a party leader would advocate a policy based on the notions that the best help was self help, that initiative deserved rewards, that an economic pie must be baked before it is divided, that welfare could not produce prosperity, that private business is better than nationalized industries, that the problem of inflation is more important than the problem of unemployment, and, finally, that the government cannot control the economy. In other words, traditional Keynesian economics was no cure for British problems, but was part of the disease. That leader was Margaret Thatcher, leader of the Conservative Party (Tory) since 1975, who was elected prime minister in 1979. Leading a changed party, she captured the mood of an altered society and spoke for the new social realities.

Return to the Conservative Party

When she moved into the prime minister's office, she promised "three years of unparalleled austerity," and for three years the pain of Thatcherism was far more evident than the benefits. Unemployment rose and economic conditions worsened. She was unable to cut government spending significantly because of greater numbers on welfare and pay raises for government workers to bring them into equity with the private sector. Nevertheless, the "iron lady," as she began to be called, held firm to her monetarist policies (restricting the money supply) and vowed, "I will not stagger from expedient to expedient." By 1982 her party was well behind the Labour Party in the polls and she seemed to be heading for sure defeat in the next elections when the unexpected occurred.

The Falklands War

Argentine troops invaded and captured a small group of offshore islands that had long been settled and ruled by the British. Mrs. Thatcher galvanized the nation with her firmness and resolution in organizing the recapture of the Falklands Islands. The British basked again briefly in imperial glory, and an overwhelming majority of them applauded their leader for her ability to deal with a crisis, winning back control of the islands, albeit at a tremendous financial cost. The Falklands War boosted her party's popularity, and the economy fortuitously began to revive at the same time, with inflation shrinking to the lowest level in 15 years. The electorate became convinced that her economic medicine had been a harsh necessity and that she was a true leader. Sensing the political winds blowing briskly at her back, she took advantage of the prime minister's privilege to set an election whenever it suits his or her party. It was called for June 1983 and demonstrated beyond doubt that the party landscape had greatly changed and that a new Conservative Party had become the dominant force in British politics by the mid–1980s.

Her astonishing electoral triumph in June 1983, which made her the first Conservative prime minister in the 20th century to be reelected to a second term, revealed both her leadership image, established in the Falklands War, and the extent to which most social and economic groups in Britain accepted her diagnosis of the nation's problems. Most voters did not even blame her for the country's most pressing problem: continuing unemployment, which shot up from 5.4% to 13.3% during her four years of rule. They clearly patted her on the back for bringing inflation down.

"The Iron Lady"

She was a fundamentally cautious politician, whose bark was often more powerful than her bite. She did take modest steps to return some of the nationalized industries to private hands, but she did not precipitously withdraw the public from the economy; in 1988 government spending amounted to 42% of GNP, about the same as in 1979. Nor did she dramatically reduce public employment, welfare assistance or taxes; she disliked spending what she did not have. Therefore, most voters did not see in her a fanatic ideologue who wished to turn the clock backward.

She never enjoyed "popularity," as her many nicknames reveal: "Leaderene," "Attila the Hen," "Rhoda the Rhino" and "Nanny," to mention only a few of the "kinder" ones. Many saw her as uncaring, cold and obsessed. But she had authority and respect because of what she accomplished and what she represents. She strode firmly forward to remake her country in her own self–image: brisk, hard–working, frugal and self–sufficient. She combined some of the best 19th century values with 20th century energy. She was a strong leader who entered office with a sense of mission: to make Britain great again. Of course, she benefited from an opposition that was in disarray.

Part of Thatcher's appeal was that she represented a new kind of Conservative Party that had emerged. The image of the party as the preserve of the landed gentry, bankers or high–level civil servants, which could display charity when needed toward the lower classes, and which assembled in prayer in the Church of England, has changed.

The attitude of most citizens, an overwhelming majority of whom are baptized protestant, is now indifference toward religion—its traditional role in politics has all but vanished. Tory leaders cannot count on the support of the Church of England, containing many clergy bitterly opposed to its policies.

Thatcher was an example of the "new" kind of Tory, who worked her way up in the world. The daughter of a dressmaker and grocer from Grantham, Lincolnshire, she lived with her family in an apartment above the shop and worked all her childhood in her father's store. She studied chemistry at Oxford, where she led the Conservative student organization and held off–campus jobs. She later acquired a law degree after marrying a successful

Mr. Denis Thatcher and former Prime Minister Thatcher

The United Kingdom

Her Majesty Queen Elizabeth II opens Parliament in the House of Lords

businessman, Denis Thatcher, who served as the nation's "First Gentleman," staying a discreet half pace behind the prime minister. She was never an insider in "the establishment," and, like Ronald Reagan, she harbored a bias against the party elite. She served only four years in the early 1970s as Education Secretary before gaining the party leadership in 1975.

Having emerged from the middle class herself, she was well able to forge an alliance between skilled workers and the middle class, in a society which is becoming more and more middle class. She capitalized on the dream of owning one's home by giving residents of government–built houses the opportunity to buy them at bargain prices. About a half million gratefully did so. This was the greatest transfer of wealth to the British working class in history. By the time her Tory party was voted out of power in 1997, 68% of all housing units were owner–occupied, a higher percentage than in the United States or elsewhere in Europe.

She benefited from a transformation within the party, which extends from the grass roots all the way up to parliament. Its seats are no longer occupied primarily by traditional local notables, but increasingly by insurance agents, housewives, teachers, salesmen and self–made middle management types. Perhaps as good an example of the new kind of Tory as Thatcher herself was a speaker of the House, Bruce Bernard Weatherill, a former tailor who always carried in his pocket a thimble to remind himself of his humble background. It is said that when he entered parliament, one aristocratic Conservative MP was overheard saying to another: "I don't know what this place is coming to, Tom: they've got my tailor in here now!" The point is that the tailor to whom they were referring was a Tory.

GOVERNMENT

Simplicity and Flexibility

Speaking of his country, the great Victorian Prime Minister Benjamin Disraeli stated: "In a progressive country, change is constant, and the great question is, not whether you should resist change which is inevitable, but whether that change should be carried out in deference to the manners, the customs, the laws and the traditions of the people." Americans often imagine the British as a conservative nation. In fact, Britain has skillfully adjusted to change for centuries, and today it confronts fundamental shifts in its society, economy, political system and place in the world. The British genius is to combine astonishing continuity with necessary change; they excel in pouring "new wine into old bottles."

Great Britain remains a monarchy with a noble class that still enjoys certain privileges. However, Britain is the birthplace for the most durable democratic model of government in the world. Unlike the complicated American democratic system, which has almost never been successfully adapted to other societies, the "Westminster model" not only fits the British people and circumstances, but it can quite easily be made to fit other nations as well. Its secret lies in its simplicity and its flexibility. It can be modified and tailored to other peoples' needs and circumstances without losing its essentially democratic character.

British politics operates according to an unwritten constitution that prescribes the "rules of the game" and places limits on the rulers. In the UK voters elect 646 members of the House of Commons, the lower house of parliament. The leader of the party that wins a majority of the seats (or has more seats than any other party) becomes the prime minister, the most powerful political figure in the land. The monarch is the head of state, but her role is largely symbolic; she makes no important political decisions. The prime minister selects other ministers, who are also experienced parliamentary leaders in the party, to sit in the cabinet.

Together the prime minister and cabinet are called "the government" which rules "collectively." This means that all members of the government must publicly support its policies or resign from office, in great contrast to the United States. Further, the entire team assumes responsibility for the overall policy. The government normally rules as long as it maintains a majority in the House of Commons. It rules until it loses a "vote of confidence" it has called on an important bill. There have occasionally been minority governments, when the ruling party does not have a majority in the House of Commons. The prime minister must call a new election at least five years after the preceding election, but she or he can call one earlier if that would be to the party's advantage.

Contrasts with the U.S.

Unlike the United States, where both houses of Congress are equally powerful, the British upper house, the House of Lords, has far less power than the House of Commons. Also, unlike in the United States, there is neither "separation of power" among the executive, legislative or judicial branches, nor a distribution of political powers among the national government and many state governments. Executive and legislative powers are fused, and the prime minister is both the chief executive and the chief legislator of the land. Through party discipline the prime minister controls the House of Commons. Further, political power is concentrated in the central government. Britain is a *unitary*, not a *federal* state, so he/she does not have to contend with separate states that wield constitutionally granted powers of their own. No court in the country can judge a law unconstitutional. Parliamentary supremacy is the fundamental principle of British government.

This setup is the basic model for most democracies in the world. Even the founders of the American government, whose political views had been shaped by British political ideas but who had consciously sought to depart from that model, adopted more from the British system than many Americans care to remember. After all, what the founders had deemed to be so unjust and tyrannical was the fact that Americans had been "denied their rights as Englishmen." Even the arguments and wording of the Declaration of Independence bore striking resemblance to the work by the 17th century English philosopher, John Locke, entitled *The Second Treatise of Government*, an important blueprint and philosophical foundation for British government.

The American founding fathers were certainly aware of their debt to Westminster when they included in the American constitution such provisions as the necessity of senatorial confirmation of cabinet ministers, congressional election of the president in the event that no candidate wins a majority in the electoral college, and the possibility for the national legislature to impeach and remove a president. It is indeed fitting that the statue on the top of the Capitol faces toward London, symbolic of the extent to which the American government, the political habits, and the thinking of its people have been shaped by Great Britain.

The Unwritten Constitution

As the British political system is more closely examined, perhaps the first striking aspect is the fact that the country's constitution is *unwritten*; that is, there is no single document, as in the United States. One must refer to one or all of five sources to know what is constitutional: first are particularly important documents, such as the Magna Charta (1215), the Habeas Corpus Act (1679), The Bill of Rights (1689) which, unlike the American Bill of Rights, defines rights of parliament, not rights of individual citizens, the Parliament Act of 1911, and the Statute of Westminster (1931). Then there are interpretations of courts of law and principles of common law (which has itself been in a constant state of change). For example, basic individual liberties, such as the freedom of assembly, speech, and religion are all derived from common law. There is the Law and Custom of Parliament, which deals with the special privileges which parliament and each Member of Parliament (known as MP) enjoy.

Finally there are wholly unwritten elements, known as conventions. These include such practices as: parliament must meet at least once a year, the government must resign if it loses a vote of confidence, the monarch cannot attend cabinet meetings or enter parliament without permission. However, the monarch always opens parliament with a speech from the throne in the House of Lords. She is there in all her finery, displaying the majesty and royal tradition that stretch back continuously over so many centuries. Yet, she is surrounded by members of parliament, freely elected by the people and operating within the context of an effective multiparty system. Her speech does not contain her own ideas, but puts forward the program of the prime minister and the government which holds a majority in the lower house of parliament. Members of the opposition party, often called the "Loyal Opposition," listen to it. Because the monarch delivers the speech, tradition requires that even critics refer to it as "the gracious speech." For example, opposition leader John Major responded to Prime Minister Tony Blair's text read by the Queen in May 1997 as follows: "The road to hell is paved with good intentions, and this gracious speech is very full of good intentions."

Perhaps no other idea has been a more important gift of the British to the growth of free government than the concept of the "Loyal Opposition." That someone may be opposed to the present government in its policies and yet still be loyal to the country and not subject to political punishment is incomprehensible in totalitarian or one-party states.

The United Kingdom

The Order of Succession to the Throne

Her Majesty Queen Elizabeth II with her successors Charles (left) and William (right)

The Heir Apparent, eldest son of the queen:

1. His Royal Highness The **Prince CHARLES Philip Arthur George,** Prince of Wales and Earl of Chester, Duke of Cornwall and Rothesay, Earl of Carrick, Baron of Renfrew, Lord of the Isles and Great Steward of Scotland, b. November 14, 1948. Married Lady Diana Frances Spencer (3rd daughter of the 8th Earl Spencer) July 29, 1981.

> The Prince and Princess of Wales separated in 1992 and were divorced in 1996. Diana, Princess of Wales, died from injuries received in a car crash in Paris on August 31, 1997. On April 9, 2005, Charles married Camilla Parker-Bowles, who became Her Royal Highness the Duchess of Cornwall. Unless Parliament passes legislation to the contrary, she will receive the title of Queen when Charles becomes King.

The sons of the first union:

2. His Royal Highness **Prince WILLIAM Arthur Philip Louis of Wales,** b. June 21, 1982.
3. His Royal Highness **Prince HENRY Charles Albert David of Wales,** b. September 15, 1984.

The second son of the queen:

4. His Royal Highness The **Prince ANDREW Albert Christian Edward,** Duke of York. b. February 19, 1960. Married Miss Sarah Margaret Ferguson July 23, 1986. They separated in 1992 and were divorced in 1996.

The daughters of that union:

5. Her Royal Highness **Princess BEATRICE Elizabeth Mary of York,** b. August 8, 1988.

6. Her Royal Highness **Princess EUGENIE Victoria Helena of York,** b. March 23, 1990.

The third son of the queen:

7. His Royal Highness The **Prince EDWARD Antony Richard Louis,** b. March 10, 1964. Married Miss Sophie Rhys-Jones June 19, 1999.
8. *The daughter of that union:* **Lady Louise Windsor,** b. 2003.

The daughter of the queen:

9. Her Royal Highness The **Princess ANNE Elizabeth Alice Louise,** Princess Royal, b. August 15, 1950. Married (1) Captain Mark Anthony Peter Phillips, November 14, 1973. The marriage was dissolved April 23, 1992. Married (2) Commander Timothy James Hamilton Laurence, RN, December 12, 1992.

The son and daughter of her first union:

10. **PETER Mark Andrew Phillips,** b. November 15, 1977.
11. **ZARA Anne Elizabeth Phillips,** b. May 15, 1981.

The sister of the queen:

12. **DAVID Albert Charles,** Viscount Linley, b. November 3, 1961. Married Hon. Serena Alleyne Stanhope (only daughter of Viscount Petersham, son and heir of the 11th Earl of Harrington) October 8, 1993.
13. The Hon. **Charles Patrick Inigo Armstrong-Jones** (1999).
14. The Hon. **Margarita Elizabeth Rose Alleyne Armstrong-Jones** (2002).
15. Lady **SARAH Frances Elizabeth Chatto,** b. May 1, 1964. Married Daniel Chatto July 14, 1994.

The son of that union:

16. **SAMUEL David Benedict Chatto,** b. July 28, 1996.

The first cousin of the queen:

17. Master **Arthur Robert Nathaniel Chatto** (1999) [son of Lady Sarah].

Buckingham Palace

18. His Royal Highness **Prince RICHARD Alexander Walter George,** Duke of Gloucester, b. August 26, 1944. Married Miss Birgitte Eva Van Deurs (of Denmark) July 8, 1972.
The son and daughters of that union:
19. **ALEXANDER Patrick Gregers Richard,** Earl of Ulster, b. October 24, 1974.
20. **Lady DAVINA Elizabeth Alice Benedikte Windsor,** b. November 19, 1977.
21. **Lady ROSE Victoria Birgitte Louise Windsor,** b. March 1, 1980.
The first cousin of the queen:
22. His Royal Highness **Prince EDWARD George Nicholas Paul Patrick,** Duke of Kent, b. October 9, 1935. Married Miss Katharine Lucy Mary Worsley, June 8, 1961.
The first son of that union:
GEORGE Philip Nicholas, Earl of St. Andrews, b. June 26, 1962, is no longer in line of succession having married a Roman Catholic, Miss Sylvana Palma Tomaselli, January 9, 1988.
The son and daughters of that union:
EDWARD Edmund Maximilian George, Baron Downpatrick, b. December 2, 1988. (became R.C. excluding himself)
23. **Lady MARINA-CHARLOTTE Alexandra Katharine Helen Windsor,** b. September 30, 1992.
24. **Lady AMELIA Sophia Theodora Mary Margaret Windsor,** b. August 24, 1995.
The second son of the Duke of Kent:
Lord NICHOLAS Charles Edward Jonathan Windsor, b. July 25, 1970. (Lady Helen skipped her brother)
The daughter of the Duke of Kent:
25. **Lady HELEN Marina Lucy Taylor,** b. April 28, 1964. Married Timothy Verner Taylor, July 18, 1992.
The sons of that union:
26. **COLUMBUS George Donald Taylor,** b. August 6, 1994.

27. **CASSIUS Edward Taylor,** b. December 26, 1996.
28. Eloise (2003) (daughter of Lady Helen Taylor)
29. Estella (2004) (daughter of Lady Helen Taylor)
His Royal Highness **Prince MICHAEL George Charles Franklin of Kent,** b. July 4, 1942, brother of the Duke of Kent married a Roman Catholic, Baroness Marie Christine von Reibnitz, June 30, 1978, and under the terms of the Act of Settlement of 1701, he is no longer in line of succession to the Throne. *The son and daughter of that union, however, remain in the line of succession:*
30. **Lord FREDERICK Michael George David Louis Windsor,** b. April 6, 1979.
31. **Lady GABRIELLA Marina Alexandra Ophelia Windsor,** (known as Lady Ella) b. April 21, 1981.
The sister of the Duke of Kent:
32. Her Royal Highness **Princess ALEXANDRA Helen Elizabeth Olga Christabel of Kent,** born December 25, 1936. Married the Honourable Sir Angus James Bruce Ogilvy (second son of the 12th Earl of Airlie), April 24, 1963.
The son of that union:
33. **JAMES Robert Bruce Ogilvy,** b. February 29, 1964. Married Miss Julia Caroline Rawlinson, July 30, 1988.
The son and daughter of that union:
34. **ALEXANDER Charles Ogilvy,** b. November 12, 1996.
35. **FLORA Alexandra Ogilvy,** b. December 15, 1994.
The daughter of the union of number 32:
36. **MARINA Victoria Alexandra Mowatt,** b. July 31, 1966. Married Paul Julian Mowatt, February 2, 1990. They were divorced 1997.
The son and daughter of that union:
37. **CHRISTIAN Alexander Mowatt,** b. June 6, 1993.
38. **ZENOUSKA May Mowatt,** b. May 26, 1990.

The United Kingdom

Hyde Park Corner, London

No politician could violate these conventions without touching off a serious political crisis. The well–informed and respected *Economist* described Britain's constitution as a "contraption, stuck together from old laws, bits of precedent, scraps of custom and practice and blind faith in the steering ability of its driver, the prime minister of the day. The machine is notoriously short on brakes: the checks and balances which are a feature of written constitutions."

Why does a nation of almost 60 million persons have no written constitution? One reason is that Britain is one of the few democracies in the world to enter the democratic age without a revolution. After successful revolutions, winners are far more inclined to put in writing the kind of guarantees and rights that had been denied them by the former rulers. The outlines of the British regime were established before the industrial revolution in the 19th century. Therefore, the economic and social conflicts which that revolution sparked could ultimately be reconciled within the system. Also, the British aristocracy had the foresight to make concessions to the middle and working classes, prompting the latter to realize that they could achieve change and satisfaction through reform, rather than rebellion. This is one reason why Marxism was never as potent a political force in Britain as it was on the European continent. Further, Britain is not a federal state, so there is no need for a careful delineation of jurisdictions between various governments, as in the U.S.

Most important, however, is the kind of political culture one finds in Britain. There is widespread agreement on basic political values, and the population broadly supports the leading institutions. This consensus has meant that disagreements over policies have (except under Cromwell) never led to fundamental challenges to the regime and constitution. The British have changed their political system only gradually. Important changes usually only occur after much dialogue and after the major parties have reached general agreement on them. The British also are a law–abiding people, a fact that makes it especially shocking to read about bombings or racial riots in that country. They tend to be moderate and pragmatic and are remarkable for their unwillingness to mount the barricades over abstract or idealistic principles.

They are inclined to boil political disputes down to conflicting interests rather than to conflicting morals or ideas, and this makes compromise much easier. Finally, there is a widespread acceptance of democracy and pluralism. Any foreigner who needs a reminder of the fact that there are many different groups or viewpoints which have a right to exist and be heard in Britain can go to Hyde Park on any Sunday morning to hear the soap–box speeches of dozens of advocates.

The Monarchy

Britain is a monarchy, and in theory the queen or king has sweeping powers. She theoretically appoints the prime minister, assembles or dissolves parliament, approves of all laws, makes foreign policy, commands the "Armed Forces of the Crown," and appoints officers who hold their rank by "Royal Commission." The trappings of political power would seem to confirm this. The "Queen's government" contains "Ministers of the Crown," who propose laws which always begin with the following words: "Be it enacted by the Queen's Most Excellent Majesty, by and with the consent of the Lords Spiritual and Temporal and Commons in this present Parliament assembled . . ." She is the temporal head of the Church of England, the country's official religion, and she appoints the leading priests. Also, in theory, sovereignty resides not in the people, but in the "Crown," which is not the person of the monarch, but rather the symbol of supreme executive power.

Actually, she no longer exercises any of the above powers. She "reigns but does not rule." The "Glorious Revolution" in 1688 established parliamentary supremacy and spelled the end of any monarchical pretense to rule absolutely. The last exercise of royal veto power was in 1707. Walter Bagehot wrote in 1867, "the greatest wisdom of a constitutional king would show itself in well-considered inaction," and Queen Elizabeth II has obeyed this dictum. By the 21st century, the real reason why "the Queen can do no wrong" is that the government never permits her to make any important decisions. In the case of Elizabeth, she does not even express her opinions publicly. This does not mean that the monarch does not perform any important functions whatsoever. She retains the right "to be informed, to advise and to warn." This right confers no power, but it does provide influence. As constitutional expert Ivor Jennings notes, "she can be as helpful or as obstreperous as she pleases: and she is the only member of the Cabinet who cannot be informed that her resignation would assist the speedy dispatch of business."

In unusual circumstances or in times of crisis, the monarch could actually exercise considerable influence. If a prime minister dies or resigns and a successor has to be appointed from the same party, or if an election yields no majority, the queen could wield authority, so long as she would not act according to personal preference. For instance, in 1963 Queen Elizabeth named a member of the House of Lords, Sir Alex Douglas Home, as prime minister, an exercise of her theoretical powers about which many Britons were unhappy. Home survived in office for one year when his party was defeated in elections. The monarch holds other significant "prerogative powers," such as dissolving parliament or rejecting requests for dissolution. The ultimate guarantee that the monarch will not overstep her bounds is the British people, who are sovereign in reality, if not in theory. Prince Charles, who turned 60 in November 2007, admitted this fact frankly, saying, "something as curious as the monarchy won't survive unless you take account of people's attitudes. I think it can be a kind of elective

Charles, Prince of Wales, and Camilla, Duchess of Cornwall

institution. After all, if people don't want it, they won't have it."

Much more importantly, she symbolizes the unity of the nation and the continuous thread through a millennium of English history. She is thus the focus of national pride. Politics touches not only the mind, but also the heart, and she helps to provide her subjects with an emotional attachment to their country. She is therefore an important cornerstone for the kind of low–keyed, but deep–rooted, patriotism most Englishmen share. Finally, because of her dual position as head of state and defender of the faith, she helps to link governmental with religious authority in the minds of many Englishmen.

In his brilliant book published in 1867, *The English Constitution*, Walter Bagehot distinguished between the "dignified" and "efficient" parts of government. The "dignified" parts, especially the glittering monarch and nobility, were useful in securing authority and loyalty for the state from the citizenry, while the "efficient" parts actually used the power and resources of the state to rule. In his book, *The Body Politic*, Sir Ian Gilmour argued that "legitimacy, the acceptance by the governed of the political system, is far better aided by an ancient monarchy set above the political battle than by a transient president, who has gained his position through that battle. . . . Modern societies still need myth and ritual. A monarch and his family supply it; there is no magic about a mud–stained politician."

Bagehot had written, "we must not let daylight in upon magic." But in an age of non–deferential journalists and citizens in Britain, royal indiscretions have completely exposed that "magic." In the wake

of lurid reports in the tabloid press about marital breakdowns and infidelity within the royal family, which over the years have included Elizabeth and especially Philip themselves, the succession to the throne and the very future of the monarchy in Britain are being questioned. The concept of a family monarchy, a Victorian–era notion that granted a symbolic and public role to royal offspring and consorts as well as to the king or queen, has been severely shaken.

Three of Queen Elizabeth II's four children have been unable to sustain a stable first marriage. The year 1992 saw the formal separation of Prince Charles from Diana, a superstar princess who overshadowed the estranged crown prince until her tragic death in Paris in 1997. In 1999 he began appearing in public with his long–time love, Camilla Parker Bowles. On April 9, 2005, he became the first heir to the throne to marry a divorcé. They were betrothed in a civil ceremony that the queen and her husband, Prince Philip, refused to attend. However, his parents were present at the church service that followed.

Polls indicated that most Britons either approved of or were indifferent to the wedding. However, a sizable majority does not want to see Camilla become queen. To assuage that sentiment, Charles emphasized that Camilla wants only to be called "princess consort" and will have the lower title of "Duchess of Cornwall," not "Princess of Wales," as Diana was called. Nevertheless, the Department for Constitutional Affairs confirmed that the marriage would not be "morganatic," meaning one in which the spouse of inferior status has no claim to the status of the

other. Unless parliament passes a law barring Camilla from becoming queen, she will assume that title the moment Charles becomes king.

Prince Andrew is divorced from Sarah Ferguson. In 1992 Princess Anne, who divorced her first husband, Mark Phillips, became the first top–ranking British royal since King Henry VIII to divorce and remarry. She wed a divorced naval commander, Timothy Laurence. The ceremony had to be held in Scotland because the Church of England does not condone second marriages. In November 2002 she suffered the indignity of becoming the first member of the royal family to be convicted of a criminal offense since Charles I was beheaded for treason in 1649. Her loose English bull terrier, Dotty, bit two children in Windsor Great Park. Although she drove the kids to the hospital and apologized for her dog's behavior, a judge fined her $620 for violating the Dangerous Dogs Act. Edward announced his engagement to Sophie Rhys–Jones in 1999. They married and had their first child in 2003.

Personal revelations about the royals are dangerously corrosive because an unelected institution in a democracy depends on the popular will for its legitimacy. Despite the bad publicity, a MORI poll in 1996 confirmed that the royals still enjoy considerable trust: when voters were offered a choice among 13 candidates for an elected president, the clear favorite was Princess Anne. A 1997 poll taken September 7, the day after Diana's moving funeral and an outpouring of grief that saw 60 million bouquets placed around the royal palaces, revealed that the mood toward the monarchy had changed: 73% of respondents (82% if Diana's eldest son William were to be the next monarch) favored its retention (down from 85–90% a decade earlier); fewer than half thought it would survive the next 50 years; and 39% thought less of the royal family.

Prince William

The United Kingdom

A hostile mood was shown in the reaction to a fire that caused $90 million worth of damage to Windsor Castle in 1992. The royal family had invented its name Windsor after this favorite castle in 1917 in order to shed its German name (Saxe–Coburg-Gotha) during the war against Germany. Popular outrage greeted the government's decision to pay the costs of the repair, which were completed beautifully in 1998.

The flames reignited the debate over whether the monarch should pay taxes and whether the state should provide annual incomes to the members and staffs of a very wealthy royal family. To quiet the fury, Queen Elizabeth announced that she would pay income taxes amounting to about $4 million annually and about $1.9 million to most members of her family out of her own fortune. She noted in 1997 that the cost of operating the monarchy had fallen by 39% since the beginning of the decade and that the royal yacht, "Britannia," had been decommissioned for financial reasons. It is understandable that on the fortieth anniversary of her coronation she publicly described 1992 as an *annus horribilis*.

Princess Diana's death in 1997 was one of the few times the Queen was ever personally criticized by the media; she felt obliged to share her grief publicly and to lower the flag at Buckingham Palace to half-mast. She made a rare gesture of humility by bowing her head when the princess's casket passed Buckingham Palace on the way to the funeral. Her predicament and the role played by the newly elected Prime Minister Tony Blair in helping point Elizabeth in the right direction were portrayed with insight and sympathy in the British film, *The Queen*. Helen Mirren, herself an opponent of the monarchy until she immersed herself in the role of Elizabeth II, won an Oscar as best actress.

After Diana died the royals made a real effort to be more accessible and open. They hired pollsters to help them come closer to the people and to read the public's message. Elizabeth II admitted: "Read it we must." It appears to be working. In 1996 only 41% of Britons thought that Charles would make a good king; by 1998 that had risen to more than 60%.

The year 2002 was the Jubilee to celebrate Queen Elizabeth II's half-century on the throne. But it was also a year of death. On February 10 Princess Margaret died, and she was followed on March 30 by the most popular royal, the 101-year-old Queen Mother. The splendor of her burial showed that the British public still likes monarchical dignity and theater. But the funeral could not stifle the noisy national debate about the role of an inherited monarchy in a nation that champions democracy and meritocracy. One caller to the BBC said: "The Queen Mum had 40 people waiting on her, and we taxpayers had to cough up 600,000 quid [over one million dollars] to support it. What did she do to deserve it, except marry the right bloke 80 years ago?"

On April 21, 2006, Elizabeth II celebrated her 80th birthday as a remarkably popular monarch after 54 years on the throne. By the end of 2007 she had both become the first reigning British monarch to celebrate a diamond (60 years) wedding anniversary and the oldest-ever monarch 243 days after her 81st birthday. In 2015 she will surpass Queen Victoria's length of reign. She now elicits almost no criticism from politicians or press. Polls show a steady rise in Britons who think the monarchy will exist ten years into the future even though only 10% of those between the ages of 16 and 24 think the monarchy is important to their lives.

Parliamentary Government

The seat of power was once the House of Commons, which elected and controlled the prime minister and the cabinet. It debated the great issues of the day and shaped the laws of the land. It was supreme, and no political institution in the entire kingdom can block its will. A century later this was no longer true. The rise of powerful catch-all parties firmly controlled by party leaders had largely converted the majority in the House of Commons into the tail wagged by the dog in Number 10 Downing Street, the residence of the prime minister. Observers gradually stopped speaking about parliamentary government and began talking first of cabinet government, then prime ministerial government.

The prime minister is not all–powerful. He must face a powerful civil service (collectively called Whitehall), sometimes count his votes carefully in the Commons, and deal with a multitude of quasi–governmental and interest groups. In theory, the British political process is simple; in practice, it is surprisingly haphazard. British governments do at least as much "muddling through" as they command. The need to persuade, coax, beg, threaten or compromise with so many groups and institutions, all with independent standing of some sort, changes the traditional picture of British government, which is centered on the prime minister and cabinet, who can do anything they want. In truth, British government has never been exactly as it appears to be on the surface. While clothed in basically the same institutional garb, the reality of British politics is always changing.

The House of Commons

Since 2005 the House of Commons has 646 Members of Parliament (MPs, 639 in 2007) elected at either general elections, which must be held at least every five years, or at by–elections, held when a seat falls vacant because of the death or resignation of a member. From the Great Reform Bill of 1832 until the electoral reform of 1970, the suffrage was gradually ex-

House of Commons. View of the Chamber showing the Speaker's Chair, seating for Clerk of the House and assistants.

panded until all men and women 18 years and older can vote. Also, all citizens of the Republic of Ireland who reside in the United Kingdom are allowed to vote. Compared with American elections, British campaigns are very short.

Usually only about four weeks elapse between the time the prime minister sets the date for new elections and the polling day. Many voters complained that the six–week campaign in 1997, the longest in 70 years, was much too long. The threat of sending MPs out on the hustings with very little notice is a powerful tool of persuasion in the hands of the prime minister. The MP does have certain advantages over the U.S. Congressman at election time: the parties pay the bulk of the campaign expenses. Also, since the MP's constituency has only one–seventh as many inhabitants as an American congressional district, he or she is able to canvass the voters at their doorstep and get the full blast of public opinion face to face.

MPs are elected by a system that is very simple and controversial: the single–member simple plurality. The candidate with the most votes in each of the 646 constituencies is elected, even if he or she won fewer than 50% of the votes. This electoral system has the advantage of preventing many parties from gaining seats in parliament. By bolstering the two–party system, proponents say it enhances political stability. Since one or the other of the large parties usually has a majority in the House of Commons, there has never been the need for a formal coalition to rule.

Opponents say that it is undemocratic and unfair because it favors the larger parties by enabling them to win a far higher proportion of parliamentary seats than the percentage of votes they won nationally. For example, in the 2005 elections, the Labour Party was returned to power with only 35.2% of the total vote, the lowest share for a government since the Reform Act of 1832. Nevertheless, it received 355 seats, or 55% of the total. By winning 32.3% of the vote, the Conservative Party captured 197 seats or 30.5% of the total. The Liberal Democrats, with 22% of the total vote won only 62 seats or a mere 9.6% of the total. It is increasingly common for MPs to be elected with the support of fewer than half the voters; in the House of Commons elected in 1997, 312 of 659 were in this situation. A Liberal Democrat, Sir Russell Johnston, won his Inverness constituency in 1992 with only 26% of the votes.

It is no surprise that the Liberal Democrats are strongly in favor of a proportional representation (PR) system, which would award seats in proportion to the total votes won. A 1997 MORI poll revealed

The funeral cortege of Diana, Princess of Wales, proceeds through Hyde Park toward Westminster Abbey.

Photo: Edward Jones

that two–thirds of voters agree. The question is: exactly how could this be done?

Virtually every other European democracy has some form of PR. Tony Blair confessed before his party won a huge majority in 1997, "I personally remain unpersuaded that proportional representation would be beneficial for the Commons." Aside from the obvious fact that his party benefited from the old system, he points out that a fair electoral method must not only reflect opinion, but "it must also aggregate opinion without giving disproportionate influence to splinter groups." This is "particularly important for a parliament whose job is to create and sustain a single, mainstream government." The political system needs an electoral method that offers voters a clear choice between the governing party, whose performance can be judged, and an opposition party, whose promises can be weighed and considered. The clear distinction between the two sides necessarily discourages third parties and splinter groups from developing.

In 1998 then Prime Minister Blair appointed a commission under Lord Jenkins to examine the electoral system but with two stipulations: that the need for "stable government" should be kept in mind and that the link between MPs and their constituencies should be preserved. The conclusion was that a "lack of democracy" would have to be accepted at the national level in the interest of retaining stable, one–party government, while proportional representation could be practiced at the regional and local level. That is exactly what was done in regional elections in Scotland, Wales and Northern Ireland, as well as in elections to the European Parliament.

The very organization and physical structure of the House of Commons depends upon a government and an opposition, without a wide spectrum of opinion. The House of Commons is arranged in rows of benches facing each other rather than in seats facing the podium. This arrangement encourages debate and questions because members of the opposing parties sit facing each other across an aisle. By ancient custom, and for good reason, the aisle is two sword lengths wide so a man may not reach across it with a sword and skewer his opponent during debate. The government sits on the front row to the right of the speaker's throne, and the leaders of the opposition (known also as the "shadow cabinet") sit on the first row to the speaker's left. Because of the massive Labour majority after May 1997, some of its members had to stand when the House was full. MPs on the lower end of the pecking order in their respective parties sit higher up on the back rows and are therefore called "backbenchers."

The speaker, who since 2000 is Michael Martin, a former sheet metal worker, directs the debate. By tradition the speakership alternates between the two main parties, and the new speaker resigns from his party. But like his predecessor, Betty Boothroyd, Martin is a Labour MP. A former shop steward and son of a stoker, he grew up in poverty in Glasgow. He observed the tradition of feigning reluctance to assume the post and having to be tugged to the speaker's chair, a throwback to the days when speakers were occasionally beheaded because of their uncomfortable position between the Commons and the monarch. When he strides into the

The United Kingdom

chamber, his aides call for the long–standing ritual of respect: "Hats off, strangers!" The speaker has little control of the Commons' business. The Leader of the House, who belongs to the cabinet, organizes this. However, a skillful speaker can protect the prerogatives of the House against the government.

Unlike in the United States, the opposition party in Britain has an alternative cabinet that is pre–selected and ready to assume office at a moment's notice. Indeed, a major strength of British parliamentary democracy is that talented leaders in a government which loses an election still retain their front–row seats in parliament and are therefore kept in reserve until a later date when the electorate's moods change and their services are again desired. This shadow government leads what is known in Britain as "Her Majesty's loyal opposition," a concept grounded in the notion that two persons of good will can disagree agreeably on an important issue. In contrast to the U.S., though, the "loyal opposition" has no means of delaying governmental action through filibuster in parliament.

In theory, parliament checks and controls the executive (the prime minister and the cabinet). In practice, it is normally the other way around. Parliament lacks the facilities to watch over the government competently, and MPs are underpaid, understaffed and under–informed. Despite some recent pay increases, MPs still earn far less than their American counterparts. In 2006 they raised their salary to £60,277 ($120,500), plus more than $72,000 for secretarial and research assistance. MPs do receive expenses for travel, phoning, postage and housing allowances (if they must maintain two homes). After the 2001 elections the salary for a cabinet minister was raised to the equivalent of about $155,000 and that of the prime minister in 2006 to £186,362 or the equivalent of $372,000.

Two–thirds continue working at their normal jobs. For centuries until 2002 the hours of the parliamentary sessions had been set from 2:30 p.m. to 10:30 p.m. in order to accommodate that need. Now parliamentary business starts at 11:30 and must normally be concluded no later than 7:30 p.m. in order for MPs to have a more "family-friendly" schedule. Exceptions are sometimes approved. One–third even work for private lobbying firms and other businesses with interest in legislation, something forbidden for U.S. congressmen. They have inadequate office space and receive only a modest sum for secretarial and research assistance while the average American congressman has 16 aides and the average senator 36. With such minuscule staffs, ordinary MPs have great

difficulty acquiring sufficient information to challenge the government, which has the entire civil service to provide it with facts.

Unlike the U.S. Congress, the House of Commons does not have a well–developed committee system to do the detailed work which cannot be done on the floor of the House. The ad hoc "standing committees" have too little expertise and are too large to be truly effective. The smaller "select committees" have a relatively permanent membership, are often chaired by an opposition MP, and do play a more important role. In 1980, new committees were set up to oversee the work of specific ministries and to deal specifically with Scottish and Welsh affairs. There is considerable discussion of reforms to improve the committee structure in the House, but in the absence of successful reforms, it is likely to remain more a forum to debate the important issues of the day than a powerful lawmaking body. In 1988 the Commons voted to allow television to record its often rowdy deliberations.

It remains the government's job to determine what will be the law of the land. All important legislation, including the budget, is drafted by the government and Whitehall. Since the government determines the order of parliamentary business, its proposals always take priority over those of private members or the opposition. Parliament can make amendments and must give its approval, but the government has numerous ways to insure that its policies will be accepted. First, all MPs are almost always party members (after 2001 there were three independents, one of whom had been elected as such), and they can jeopardize their careers if they defy their party leaders. Renegades

are seldom reelected. Second, as many as 110 MPs are actually members of the government, and all are expected to vote with the government.

Finally, since the very survival of the government depends upon maintaining a majority, MPs are under far greater pressure from the cabinet to support the government than is the case in the U.S. Rigid party discipline on most bills has always been essential in order to make the political system work. MPs are permitted to "vote their conscience" on moral issues, such as abortion and gun control (Britain has a near total ban on handguns.). In 2005-6 it applied to votes to outlaw smoking in public places by summer 2007, to permit pubs to remain open after 11 p.m., and to allow same-sex partnerships. The latter grants the same property and inheritance rights as married heterosexual couples and gives partners the same pension, immigration and tax benefits. Among the first takers was pop singer Sir Elton John, who formalized his relationship with David Furnish.

Control by the government is much less effective than it once was. From 1945 to 1970 no government lost a vote of the full House of Commons. The 1970s brought a significant change. The Conservative government of Edward Heath suffered defeat in parliament six times. Before 1970 it would have been unthinkable for a government so defeated to remain in office, but he returned to the 19th century practice of resigning only upon losing a declared vote of no confidence. The Labour government that ruled from 1974 until 1979 suffered 23 such defeats, and Thatcher was defeated twice. MPs can now often vote against the government without bringing it down. This encour-

Queen Elizabeth II and six former prime ministers celebrate the 250th anniversary of 10 Downing Street as the official residence of the Prime Minister.

34

ages backbenchers to revolt without severely endangering their careers. The days are over when the backbenchers automatically vote as their leaders order.

The Blair government changed the raucous "prime minister's question time" in the House of Commons by converting it into a more serious, once–a–week half–hour session every Wednesday in which more questions from opposition backbenchers are allowed. The leadership confrontations with the opposition leader remain the most entertaining and sometimes most embarrassing interchanges for the prime minister. In order to be able to prepare better for these weekly duals, Blair switched the day for his weekly half–hour audience with the Queen in 2004 from Tuesdays to Wednesdays after question hour.

Such audiences date back to 1739 and are a valuable opportunity for the head of government to tap the vast reservoir of knowledge Queen Elizabeth has accumulated in her more than half a century on the throne. Gordon Brown is her eleventh prime minister since Churchill, and George W. Bush was the tenth president with whom she has dealt. By tradition, the opinions expressed at such audiences are strictly confidential. Even the prime minister's closest aides are kept in the dark.

Harold Wilson (1964–70) regarded the queen as the only person with whom he could confide without thinking a knife was being sharpened behind his back. John Major (1992–97) said no notes were taken, and the sanctity of the event was preserved by the "total block" on the discussions. He remembered that he could talk to the monarch in a way he did to no one else. Tony Blair (1997–2007) initially viewed the meetings as "ancient etiquette." But he soon found them to be a great opportunity to talk to a very wise person in the knowledge that it would go no further. Only Margaret Thatcher (1979–1990) is reported to have had an uncomfortable relationship with Elizabeth.

The House of Lords

Great Britain is a monarchy, and it should therefore not be surprising that its aristocracy continues to enjoy certain political privileges. These are institutionalized in the upper house of parliament, the House of Lords. Before 1999, of the 1,164 members (known as the "peers") 650 had hereditary titles. This meant that all the offspring of these peers who inherited the titles would automatically be entitled to a seat in the House of Lords. These titles range, in order of precedence, from Duke, Marquess, Earl, Viscount and Baron, all except Dukes being commonly addressed as "Lord." Some peerages have ancient origins, such as the Marquis of Salisbury

or the Duke of Norfolk, but half the hereditary peerages were created in the 20th century "for services to the nation." No new hereditary peerages were created after 1964 until Prime Minister Thatcher ennobled senior minister William Whitelaw and retiring Speaker of the Commons George Thomas.

A law of 1958 creating "life peers" set an irreversible trend. Such peers are appointed for their learning or their distinguished public service. However, after they die, their heirs cannot claim their seats. Among the life peers named in 1997 was composer (now Baron) Andrew Lloyd Webber. Sir Paul McCartney (now a knight) and "Dynasty" star Joan Collins (now an Officer of the Order of the British Empire) were not awarded peerages.

Only 746 peers remain in the reformed House of Lords, of which 92 are hereditary peers, whose tenure remains uncertain. There are about a dozen law lords (who form the highest appellate court in the land) and 26 Church of England Bishops. The rest are life peers, half of whom entered the House of Lords since Labour came to power in 1997. Approximately 67 are peeresses, such as Margaret Thatcher. By 2006 the largest party was Labour (206 seats), followed by Tories (205) and Liberal Democrats (74). In this new House of Lords, most peers attend regularly and are less inclined than earlier to do what the governments tells them. A 2006 poll revealed that 68% of respondents think it is all right for the Lords to vote against government bills.

As the democratic wave caused a steady expansion of the franchise in the 19th and 20th centuries, the powers of the House of Lords came under increasing attack. In the Parliament Acts of 1911 and 1949, its veto right was taken away; now the only kind of bill it can veto is one to prolong the life of parliament beyond five years. Also, its power to delay legislation was reduced; it can now hold up bills for 13 months at the most (only 30 days for a financial bill). Until the Thatcher era, it seldom exercised its power out of fear that if it fully used its powers, it would ultimately lose them.

The Labour Party has long sought "to abolish the undemocratic House of Lords as quickly as possible." One of Labour's most influential leftists even renounced his title of Viscount Stansgate, giving up his right to sit in the House of Lords. He also shortened his name from Anthony Wedgewood Benn III to the more proletarian Tony Benn. One cannot say, however, that he "put his money where his mouth is" because he did not renounce his considerable fortune. His son, Hilary Benn, shares his father's appearance and mannerisms. A state secretary for international

development in Tony Blair's government, he emphasizes that he is "a Benn, not a Bennite."

In normal times, opposition to the prime minister's policies is exercised in the House of Commons. But Thatcher so dominated that body until 1990 that another institution performed that function: the House of Lords. One Labour Lord said in 1988: "It hurts to admit it, but on many issues we are the government's only real opposition." A Liberal baroness added: "As an unelected body, it would obviously be quite improper for us to try to kill a bill outright. But there is nothing to stop us from being an utter nuisance to the government. We call it playing Ping–Pong—holding up a bill for so long that the government is compelled to accept our amendments just to get the thing passed." In fact, by 1988 Thatcher had suffered 107 defeats in the House of Lords, compared with only two in the House of Commons. Between 1999 and 2007, the Lords defeated more than 350 government bills.

Why is such a privileged house, to which no one is elected, retained in a democratic country? In fact, debates in the House of Lords are at least as well informed and much less partisan than in the lower house. In order to demonstrate this fact, debates in the upper house began to be televised in 1985. The lords' main job is to examine and to revise bills that have proceeded too hastily through the House of Commons. With such experienced peers, the most active of whom had already distinguished themselves in all walks of life outside parliament, the lords perform an important function in improving legislation. Also, the fact that the most active lords are persons of great prestige and influence in British society means that no government systematically ignores the House of Lords.

Supported two–to–one in a 1997 MORI poll, Tony Blair's Labour government moved swiftly to enact its campaign promise to remove "the absurdity of the hereditary element." He appointed a royal commission that produced a white paper in 1999. It recommended that the hereditary peers' right to sit and vote be removed, that the nomination of life peers be accomplished through an independent appointments committee (not the prime minister), that some be indirectly elected by bodies such as the new regional assemblies, and that longer–term reform be considered.

To move this reform through the legislative process, Blair agreed to a temporary compromise with the Tory leader in the House of Lords: 92 hereditary peers were permitted to stay until a final second–stage reform of the house could be

The United Kingdom

undertaken; over 600 life peers retained their seats.

After facing further opposition in the upper house, the Blair government proposed additional constitutional reforms. It abolished the ancient and powerful position of Lord Chancellor, who was speaker of the Lords, a cabinet minister, head of the country's judiciary and titular member of the highest court, the Law Lords. Since 2005 a Speaker of the House of Lords presides over the upper house. In 2006 a Labour Party Baroness, Helene Hayman, became the first elected lord speaker. The Lord Chancellor's other roles were assumed by a Department for Constitutional Affairs. The reform also will replace the 12 Law Lords with a Supreme Court, which would be the highest court in England and Wales.

The House of Lords had been doing a good job scrutinizing laws, producing quality reports, and challenging Commons; that is why the pressure to reshape the Lords comes from politicians, not the voters. In March 2007 a majority in the House of Commons voted in favor of an all-elected House of Lords. This was a non-binding vote, but it will guide the government's future choices. It is unclear what will ultimately happen to the Lords.

Prime Ministerial Government

The nerve center of British politics is "the government," a collective term to describe the prime minister, the 16 to 23 cabinet ministers and the parliamentary secretaries or junior ministers, a team which may total from 70 to 110 members.

In theory, the prime minister is the 'first among equals' within the governing team. But as a senior Whitehall official noted at the end of the 20th century: "The idea that the prime minister is primus inter pares is wrong. The prime minister is not pares. He's way above that. Like Caesar he bestrides the world like a colossus." The prime minister is the leader of the party that has a majority (or at least a plurality) in the House of Commons. Thus, the holder of this highest office is an MP who has worked his or her way upward through the legislative system. The average prime minister has served a quarter of a century in the House of Commons. It is virtually inconceivable that a stranger to the national capital, such as Jimmy Carter, Ronald Reagan, Bill Clinton, or George W. Bush, could become prime minister. In actuality, the powers of the post are so great that the description 'first among equals' is misleading.

The prime minister's powers, which are almost nowhere clearly spelled out in statute, strike the American as sweeping. As the nation's chief executive, chief legislator and chief administrator he is the primary focus of political attention. After the election, he is rather free to appoint and dismiss cabinet members, thereby largely determining the broad political direction the government will take. The convention of 'collective responsibility' prevents his ministers from criticizing him in public, and the tradition of secrecy shields many of his decisions and actions from the public eye. He decides on the agenda for cabinet meetings and appoints the cabinet committees, which prepare government policies or deal with crises and carry out most ministerial business. For example, in 1982 Thatcher formed a 'war cabinet' to manage the Falklands crisis; she also had influential committees for economic, foreign and defense, domestic, and legislative policy. Such grand committees have subcommittees. There are no votes taken in cabinet meetings, and the prime minister interprets the sense of the cabinet. Cabinet minutes are sparse in detail and taken in long hand to keep them that way.

Given the tradition of cabinet secrecy, the Brown government was shocked in February 2008 when Britain's information commissioner, citing the "gravity and controversial nature" of the decision to go to war in Iraq in 2003, ordered the government to release the minutes of two cabinet meetings discussing the legality of the invasion. The government appealed the order, arguing that it set a "dangerous precedent" for releasing cabinet papers, which cannot normally be published for thirty years.

Regardless of how the debate in the secret cabinet meetings might have gone, he can always announce the meaning in a way which conforms to his own views. As ex–Labour cabinet member Richard Crossman revealed, any prime minister who is subordinate to the cabinet is "consciously refusing to make use of the powers which now constitutionally belong to the office." In practice, most issues are decided either in Whitehall or in cabinet committees and are not even discussed in full cabinet meetings, which are normally held twice a week, including each Thursday morning. The modern cabinet is increasingly a reporting and reviewing body and less and less an executive one. Crossman was correct. Collective decision-making has been replaced by a system in which ministers have been reduced to agents of their leader, forced to deal with him bilaterally rather than as part of a collectively responsible group.

The prime minister directs the nation's sizable civil service. He determines the country's foreign and defense policies and can commit Britain to a policy that the cabinet and Commons can do little to alter. He can even enter treaties with foreign nations that need not be approved by parliament; foreign policy was a 'royal prerogative' which was never passed to parliament although a prime minister does customarily discuss with it treaties and declarations of war. The 2003 war in Iraq demonstrated that even a strong and activist prime minister like Tony Blair must be very attentive to both British law and popular and parliamentary sentiment when using the prime minister's war powers. Finally, as leader and chief strategist for the national party, he alone can decide the date of the general election and thus determine when the entire government and Commons must face the voters. He is burdened neither by separation of powers nor by a federal structure. No American president wields such power.

Limitations on the Prime Minister

A closer look at the contemporary British political system reveals that the prime minister's power is far more restricted that initially meets the eye. Although he appoints and dismisses the cabinet members, he can hardly lord over them. Unlike most American cabinet members, the British ones are experienced and influential parliament members with whom the prime minister has usually worked for many years. He cannot scout the country for talented individuals whose main responsibility is to carry out the chief executive's policy; he can only choose from his close colleagues in parliament who have powerful political bases of their own in the party and in the nation. He thus does not deal with minions, but with powerful political office–holders, who would be far less afraid to stand up to him in private.

He must retain the confidence of the most important factions within the parliamentary majority party. He must inevitably take into the cabinet some persons who disagree with him on some fundamental issues. This has tended to weaken the convention of cabinet solidarity. Thatcher had to cope with scarcely concealed criticism from those within her own cabinet whom she dubbed "wets." John Major lost the 1997 elections in part because he never succeeded in silencing Tory colleagues who opposed his policy toward Europe. Finally, since 1999 the prime minister must deal with regionally–elected parliaments in Scotland, Wales, Northern Ireland, and since 2000 a Greater London Assembly.

It is often argued that the prime minister enjoys the advantage of not having to direct huge ministries, as cabinet members do. Therefore, he is freer to deal with larger political questions. To some extent, this is true, but the other side of the coin is that he lacks manageable administrative backing. He has no department to provide him with independent analyses and advice. His "private office" at his residence, Number 10 Downing Street, is too small. More valuable to him is the "cabinet office," headed by a top civil servant, which organizes the agenda for cabinet discussions. Thatcher established a "policy unit" at Number 10 composed of some expert advisers. Yet these specialists were no match for the massed expertise available to departmental ministers. Thus, the quality of the prime minister's information is not generally better than that of his cabinet members.

He must deal with a complicated network of ministries and departments with diverse views and a good deal of autonomy in their own areas of responsibility. By American standards, there is virtually no "spoils system" in British politics. The prime minister is able to send to each ministry only one minister and one to three parliamentary secretaries. But when they arrive, often with little or no detailed experience in the particular areas of responsibilities and with no staffs of their own, they are faced with a permanent secretary, the senior civil servant of his department with several decades of experience. He and his subordinate civil servants have the facts at their fingertips and brief the minister.

Although it is his job merely to give technical advice and let the minister set the political direction, it is but a short step from persuasively "giving the facts" to actually determining departmental policy. Usually continuity, not change, wins out. New policies must be negotiated with these bodies, not simply imposed upon them. Nevertheless, if the minister comes to clear, firm decisions, then his officials will almost always carry them out.

Bureaucracy and the Civil Service

As in all advanced countries, much of the work which used to be done by leading politicians has now been delegated to the civil service, which numbers about 640,000 bureaucrats. Most do not actually work in Whitehall, that small area in London where the chief administrative buildings are located. Britain is fortunate to have civil servants who generally work efficiently, who are almost entirely uncorrupted and whose decisions usually arise not from personal or political reasons, but from good administrative ones.

Personnel are frequently criticized because they, the top people, come from too narrow a social background and because they operate under a blanket of secrecy. It remains essentially true that the top 3,500 administrators are drawn heavily from the "Oxbridge" (Oxford and Cambridge) universities after having received a gener-

View of London across the Thames, with "Big Ben" (right)

alist's education, despite the fact that the three–class hierarchy was replaced in 1971 by a single, open structure. The recruitment system remains largely unchanged.

Not only the cabinet, but the top 3,500 or so civil servants must take oaths of secrecy. Among cabinet ministers, this convention is breaking down somewhat, as they leak information to the press or write revealing memoirs. The civil servants' oath makes it a crime to disclose any official information, whether it is classified or not; he is bound to remain silent for life.

A vigorous campaign was launched by a variety of groups to punch some holes in this screen of secrecy by adopting a law similar to the U.S. Freedom of Information Act. One hole appeared in 1991 when for the first time the newly appointed chief of the MI5 Security Service (counterespionage), Stella Rimington (the first woman ever to occupy the post), was identified by name. This agency, as well as Secret Intelligence Service (SIS, still widely referred to as MI6), which deals with foreign intelligence, has long inspired the imagination of thriller writers. When a disgruntled former MI6 agent, Richard Tomlinson, put the names of more than a hundred British secret agents on the World Wide Web in 1999, British security officials conceded that the Internet is so far–flung that no government can control the flow of information on it.

Despite the Official Secrets Act and tradition, the British news media have always been an important check on governmental power. Britain has more newspapers per capita than any other country. Nevertheless, Prime Minister Blair's government introduced in 2005 a Freedom of Information Act, a reform with the backing of three–fourths of the population.

Unlike its equivalent in the U.S., where Americans have to take their government to court to force it to share its secrets, a British information commissioner does this job for Britons.

Acts of parliament usually merely establish the basic principles of law, and the civil service fills in the details. Bureaucratic regulations now vastly outnumber actual laws, as is the case in the United States. Traditionally, the Treasury, led by the Chancellor of the Exchequer (Treasury minister), has been the main coordinator of the many departments and ministries. Since it was responsible for the budgets of the various departments, it gained the right to comment on any policy proposal from any department. There is some skepticism about the Treasury's ability to oversee and review all policy effectively. But if anybody is master of Whitehall, it is the Treasury and not the cabinet as a whole.

In addition to the huge bureaucracy, the prime minister must deal with a maze of so–called "quasi–autonomous nongovernmental organizations," mercifully shortened to "quangos." Depending on how wide the net is thrown, these organizations number up to 5,521 and include such bodies as the Arts Council, the University Grants Committee, the Commission for Racial Equality, the BBC, Trustees of National Museums and the nationalized industries. Many are purely advisory, but some dispense large sums of money. All consider themselves to be more or less autonomous, but most are financed, and most members are named, by the central government, usually by a department of Whitehall. The government can sometimes force these "quangos" to comply with overall policies by giving or withholding grants, but it frequently faces stiff

The United Kingdom

opposition and must often modify its policies in order to win compliance. They have taken over many services formerly performed by local authorities.

Alongside the "quangos" are especially important interest groups that have semi–official status with the government or with various ministries. They include the Church of England, the universities and the umbrella organizations for the unions and industry—the Trade Union Congress (TUC) and the Confederation of British Industry (CBI). The latter is the largest employers' association in the world, with a highly professional bureaucracy. Sometimes the government is driven to very close negotiations with one of these. From 1974 to 1978 the Labour government agreed to a "social contract" with the unions, swapping legal concessions and price restraints for limits on wage increases. More often, the government tries to conduct "tripartite" negotiations with both the TUC and the CBI to maintain economic stability. The fatal flaw in this effort is that the CBI and the TUC (whose constituent unions are autonomous and therefore negotiate their own wage agreements and decide when to strike) cannot bind their members to whatever agreements are reached under the auspices of the government.

The Judiciary

Another limitation on the government's power, which has long been one of the chief cornerstones of British liberty, has been an independent judiciary. Political leaders are forbidden to obstruct the judicial process, even though judges make decisions that significantly influence politics. As with most other aspects of the British public life, the legal structure is fragmented and complicated. There are different court systems: one for England and Wales, one for Northern Ireland and one for Scotland, which has always retained its own separate, Roman–based legal system. There are different layers of courts. At the pinnacle are the 10 to 12 Lords of Appeal (known as the "Law Lords"), who sit in the House of Lords and who, constituted as the Judicial Committee of the Privy Council, can even hear appeals from some parts of the British Commonwealth.

Usually the Law Lords' hearings are dry and poorly attended; they involve less pomp and ritual than does the U.S. Supreme Court. But the eyes of the world were on them in 1998–9, when former Chilean leader, General Augusto Pinochet, went to Britain for medical treatment. While there, Spain and other European countries demanded his extradition because of his alleged international human rights violations. He claimed immunity as a former head of state and current member of the Chilean senate, so the Law Lords were asked for a ruling. Normally these jurists do not have reputations for their political leanings, as do American Supreme Court justices, but their politics became an issue in the long legal battle. In the end, they rendered seven judgments that revealed differing interpretations on points of law. Nevertheless, they ruled that Pinochet could be extradited to Spain to face charges of torture, but only for those acts committed after December 1988 when Britain implemented the 1984 Torture Convention.

They made another landmark decision in December 2004 when, sitting for only the second time since the Second World War in a panel of nine justices instead of the usual five, they struck down the government's practice of detaining terrorist suspects indefinitely without trial. They ruled in December 2005 that evidence obtained through torture in other countries could not be used in British courts. Four months later they struck down a key provision in the government's anti-terrorism law allowing house arrest for suspects. In 2005 the House of Lords voted down the Blair government's antiterrorist package four times until the prime minister offered an acceptable concession: to allow parliament to review it within a year.

Much of criminal law and most civil law in Britain do not come from acts of parliament, but instead from "common law." Unlike "civil law," which most European democracies have, "common law" is based on tradition, a slow development of rules based on previous cases ("precedents") which are reported in writing, indexed and published in an elaborate system for reference. It is law made by judge and jury. In order to make legal language more comprehensible for litigants, civil courts eliminated Latin legal terms from proceedings in 1999, replacing them with plain English.

Britain's tradition of parliamentary supremacy excludes the possibility of "judicial review," such as exists in the United States. This would permit the courts to overturn acts of parliament on the ground that they were unconstitutional. This was theoretically impossible since no body could be superior to parliament. That ended in 2000. A kind of individual bill of rights went into effect by incorporating into British law the European Convention for the Protection of Human Rights and Fundamental Freedoms (often referred to as "the European Human Rights Charter" or EHRC). This convention includes such protections as rights for criminal defendants and freedom of speech, religion and assembly. These are rights that have been recognized for centuries under common law. To these freedoms is now added a defendable right of privacy.

A half century earlier, British jurists had played a leading part in drafting the charter, and it has applied to British citizens since the UK entered the EU in 1973. But it was not enforceable in British courts. That has changed. Parliament should not make laws that violate the EHRC. Judges still do not have the right of judicial review, that is, the right to strike down legislation. However, they can now make a "declaration of incompatibility" when British laws conflict with the EHRC. Parliament or the government must determine whether the "incompatible" statute can remain. The government can bypass parliament by amending the law by statutory instrument. Although the legislative and executive branches have the last say, political pressure is very strong to bring any law in line with the European charter.

Only a small part of the governing of Britain is carried out by parliamentary acts. Ministers, civil servants, local government authorities and "quangos" must use discretion in applying general laws to concrete situations, and it is precisely this

Feeding the pigeons, Trafalgar Square, London

discretion that can be checked by the courts. In the 1970s a group of parents took the minister responsible for education to court on the charge that the way in which he had applied the school reform was illegal, and the court ruled in their favor. In order to deal with concrete cases, judges must decide what the laws mean. It is in such interpretation that judges have most of their power; the whole thrust of a law can be changed or bent by judges. When judges have this kind of power, one might ask who needs judicial review.

As in the United States, there is much controversy over the question of whether the courts have too much power and whether they are, in fact, political. There can be no question that judges' ability to assess the propriety of ministerial actions opens up another course of action to persons who oppose the government's policy. Of course, if parliament does not like what the courts are doing, it could make new laws that are clearer and more specific, but parliament has taken that step only once since 1945. It is far too busy to monitor the judges' use of their discretionary power. Whether one likes it or not, the impact of judicial interpretations will remain political and will continue to place limits on governmental power. However, judicial restraint still prevails in Britain to a greater degree than in the United States.

Local Government

Largely because of historical circumstances, the United Kingdom is a unitary, not a federal state. That is, it is not a collection of "united states." Unlike the United States of America, the UK was not consciously created by sovereign states that carefully retained important powers. The English conquered Wales militarily in the 12th century; it was politically integrated with England in 1536. The thrones of England and Scotland were united in 1603, and the process of union was completed in 1707. The question of succession to the throne led to Anglo–Scottish conflict in 1715 and 1745, which culminated in the occupation of Scotland by English armies. Ireland was simply taken by force, and the six northern counties remained in the United Kingdom in 1922, when the southern 26 counties became independent.

Therefore, the British government is, in theory, freed from the problems of getting its policies accepted by powerful states or provinces. This centralization would seem to fit well with the land and its people—it is a small country, no bigger than the state of Oregon, with a population of almost 60 million. It is highly urbanized, with 40% of the population living in only seven urban centers that account for less than 4% of the total land area.

London, with a population of seven million (over 15% of the United Kingdom's total), is seven times larger than the second largest city, Birmingham. Only four other cities have more than half a million inhabitants: Liverpool, Manchester, Sheffield and Leeds. Unlike Washington, New York, Ottawa or many national capitals, London is simultaneously the center of government, finance, the mass media and the arts. Nearly three–quarters of the people who earned a place in Who's Who live within a 65–mile radius of London. Half the MPs never resided in their constituencies before their election, and many of them are from London. Further, most ambitious civil servants climb the career ladder in London.

Nevertheless, unitary government does not mean that orders from Number 10 Downing Street, Westminster, or Whitehall are automatically carried out in all corners of the UK. There are many institutions that give much scope for local resistance to central authority. Let us look first at local government.

It is not a surprise that, like most other British political and legal institutions, the structure of local government is diverse and highly complicated. In 1974 a reorganized structure of local government came into effect in an attempt to produce a fairly uniform pattern throughout the entire kingdom. This reform scarcely made the structure of local government easier for the foreigner to understand. To begin with, local government still differs in England, Wales, Scotland and Northern Ireland. In the first three, there are two tiers of administration, each with elected councils, taxing authority and its own powers. The top tier (composed generally in England of metropolitan or county councils, and in Scotland of nine regional councils) and the lower tier (composed of borough, or district councils) together provide schools, local roads, government–owned housing (known as "council housing"), and an array of services, such as buses, garbage pickup, libraries, swimming pools and (except in London) police protection.

These two tiers often clash with each other, especially in metropolitan areas. To muddle things even more, there is usually even a third tier composed of parish or community councils with powers of their own. In all, there are more than 14,000 local governments in Britain. These local units account for a quarter of all government spending. Most is handed out by the central government rather than raised locally, but they do provide for close to half of their own expenses through local property taxes (known as "rates") and fees for services. They employ almost three million people (over 12% of the total work force), far more than the central government.

Former Prime Minister Thatcher locked horns with local authorities. In 1988 she sought to abolish the existing system of local taxes, based on the size and value of personal property, and to replace it with a flat–rate levy, or community charge, which would spread the tax burden to residents of all incomes. Opponents said this was regressive and unfair, while she said that by spreading taxes evenly, the new tax would bring pressure to bear on local councils, many of which are dominated by Labour politicians, to reduce their budgets. Thus, a motive to modernize the tax system was mingled with one to reduce the opposition's power even further. So unpopular was this flat–rate levy that it helped lead to her downfall in 1990.

She also moved to abolish the metropolitan councils, at least in part because some of them had become centers of leftist power. These included the Greater London Council (GLC) and what was sometimes derisively referred to in Tory circles as the "Socialist Republic of Yorkshire." While eliminating the GLC in her 1986 reform, the elected councils in London's 32 administrative areas, such as Kensington and Chelsea, Westminster, and Lambeth and Hackney, continued to exist. Within days of assuming office in May 1997 Prime Minister Blair proposed a referendum for Londoners to create an elected government and mayor.

In 1998, 72% voted in favor of a directly-elected mayor, and in May 2000 self-proclaimed socialist Ken Livingstone, running as an independent, was elected London's mayor. He is known as "Red Ken" because of his outspoken opposition to Thatcher and his earlier policies as GLC head of declaring the capital a nuclear-free zone, making common cause with IRA supporters, and backing gay rights. He vowed to rid Trafalgar Square of pigeons, which he described as "rats with feathers."

In 2003 he launched a revolutionary program to diminish central London's traffic congestion, among the world's worst. Every private automobile and truck driving into an eight-square-mile area in the heart of the city on weekdays between 7 a.m. and 6:30 p.m. must pay the equivalent of $14 per day for the privilege. The proceeds are spent on public transport projects. When in 2006 the U.S. embassy and other foreign embassies called this a tax (from which they should be exempt) and refused to pay it, Livingstone called the U.S. ambassador "a chiseling little crook" and a "car salesman." The forthright mayor was also suspended from office for four weeks in 2006 for saying a Jewish reporter was "just like a concentration camp guard."

Even Blair had called him and his colleagues a "ragbag of Trotskyists" and

The United Kingdom

threw him out of the Labour Party a couple of months before the election. The Labour and Conservative parties each won nine seats in the new 25-seat Greater London Assembly.

Sometimes strong–armed measures toward local governments do work, depending largely on the skill and determination of the prime minister. Nevertheless, it would be more accurate to describe the overall relationship in terms of bargaining between interdependent levels of government.

Island Governments

The United Kingdom includes certain island groups, such as the Outer Hebrides, Orkney and Shetland, which have more local authority than county, district or metropolitan county councils on the mainland. For instance, Shetland controls oil developments in its own territory and has launched a strong movement toward total internal autonomy. The Isle of Man in the Irish Sea and the partly French–speaking bailiwicks of Guernsey and Jersey off the French coast already have autonomous legal status, Norman–based legal systems, their own parliaments and governments which control domestic, fiscal and economic policy. They are quaint anomalies in that they are not part of the UK, but are Crown dependencies. They are also not in the European Union, so their citizens do not enjoy the freedom to move and work in its member states.

The Channel Islands had been occupied by 30,000 Germans during World War II. In 1993 embarrassing evidence was released that islanders had collaborated with, profited from, or slept with the German masters. In one notorious incident in 1942, local authorities helped the Germans identify 2,100 Jews and English–born residents to be deported to camps in Germany. These revelations reopened old wounds and prompted Britons to think about how they might have reacted if Hitler's forces had overrun the entire country.

Wales, Scotland and Northern Ireland

The three large regions on the outer fringe of the United Kingdom comprise less than a fifth of the UK's total population: Wales (2.9 million), Scotland (5.1 million) and Northern Ireland (1.6 million). These populations compare with 48.7 million in England. By 2004, however, the usual migration had been reversed, and Scotland and northern England were gaining people. Until 1999 all were, in varying degrees, Celtic in background and relatively poor economically. All three were ruled by departments of the central government: the Wales Office, the Scottish Office and the Northern Ireland Office, each with a mini–Whitehall at its disposal. The prime minister appointed a secretary of state for each, and these politicians, who never come from the areas they control, sat in the cabinet.

Although these regions' relations with London have rarely been smooth, regionalism was seldom a major factor in British politics. The differences were masked by a common language, the facade of unitary government and economic prosperity. This changed dramatically in the 1970s. Strapped with a disproportionate number of dying industries and unhappy with the remoteness of central government, nationalist parties in Wales and Scotland grew. At the end of the century Westminster transferred important powers to these regions. "Devolution," which resulted in all three having their own elected parliaments in 1999, represents a historic shift in the way Britain is governed.

Wales

Wales is technically a principality whose titular ruler is the Prince of Wales, who is always the heir apparent to the English throne. It lost all traces of political identity through the Act of Union with England in 1535. However, its social integration with England proceeded much more slowly. English was the language of the government after 1535, but until the 19th century the Welsh language, which is a Celtic dialect related to Irish, Scottish and Breton, was spoken by a majority of the people. Now only one–fifth of the Welsh population speaks it, mainly in rural areas and small towns in North Wales, but one–third claims to have "some understanding" of the language. Welsh speakers form a majority in outlying areas in the West inhabited by only 10% of the population.

Unlike Scotland, it was the preservation of the language, more than independence from England, which fired the Welsh nationalist movement in the 1970s. Lacking its own aristocracy, the Welsh always tended to be somewhat more egalitarian in their outlook. The coal mining and basic industry, especially in the more populous South Wales have always made it a Labour Party stronghold. In 1978 London offered both Wales and Scotland regional assemblies whose powers would have fallen short of American state legislatures. But in a 1979 referendum, Welshmen rejected such an assembly by a margin of four–to–one, largely because of the revulsion English–speaking Welshmen felt toward the pretensions of the Welsh–speaking minority.

To help satisfy Welsh nationalist urges, Welsh–language schools were established. By 2006 they numbered 448 primary and 54 secondary schools that teach mostly or entirely in Welsh. Since they tend to be good schools, parents want their children to attend them. The result is not only that a new generation of articulate nationalists is graduating from Welsh-language schools. But for the first time since reliable statistics have been taken, the proportion who claim to speak Welsh is rising: between 1991 and 2001 the proportion grew from 19% to 21% (and from 5.8% two decades ago to 10.9% in the capital, Cardiff). Teenagers are more likely to speak than their parents. Since 1993, public agencies are obliged to provide service in both languages, and court cases can be heard in Welsh if the plaintiff or defendant wishes. Welsh speakers are favored in the job market and earn 6-8% more than English-only rivals.

Second, a separate Welsh–language television channel was established (Sianel Ped-

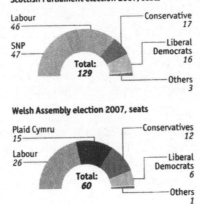

Less for Labour

Scottish Parliament election 2007, seats

Labour 46
SNP 47
Conservative 17
Liberal Democrats 16
Others 3
Total: 129

Welsh Assembly election 2007, seats

Plaid Cymru 15
Labour 26
Conservatives 12
Liberal Democrats 6
Others 1
Total: 60

Sources: Scottish Executive; Welsh Assembly

Source: *The Economist*

war Cymru—channel four—S4C), which, due to the small viewing audience, is one of the most expensive television channels in the world. Finally, the Welsh Language Act of 1993, which declared that Welsh and English were to be considered "on a basis of equality," enabled Welsh speakers to be more insistent that Welsh be spoken more. Language disputes are mild compared with Belgium or Quebec.

A colony of a few thousand Welsh-speakers was found in Patagonia. Having emigrated to Argentina in the 19th century, they are being actively recruited to return to Wales to help keep the language alive, despite their noticeable Spanish accents. In 2004 one such Patagonian lady became the first person to take her naturalization oath in the Welsh language.

Welsh nationalism is alive though not robust. A nationalist party, *Plaid Cymru* (pronounced "Plide Cumry"), founded in the 1920s amid anti–English feeling, no longer talks much about an independent Wales with a seat in the United Nations since most citizens do not want that. A pressure group, the Independent Wales Movement, was organized in 2000 outside Plaid's ranks. It is more exuberantly nationalist, forcing Plaid leader, Ieuan Wyn Jones, to speak of "full national status" for Wales. He explains that this means the same standing as Ireland has within the EU.

It settled for the referendum leading to an elected Welsh Assembly. In 1997 a razor–thin majority in Wales, with only half the eligible voters participating, voted in favor of its first elected parliament in nearly 600 years. Its powers are more limited than those of the new Scottish Parliament. It can amend certain acts of Westminster, but it cannot pass its own laws or raise taxes. It can decide how to spend the budget formerly administered by the

Welsh Office, including for health and education, and scrutinize and alter the administration of Wales.

In May 1999 the first elections were won by Labour. A new electoral system modeled on that of Germany was used: each voter has two votes, the first for his preferred representative (called Member of the Welsh Parliament—MWP) in the 40 constituencies and one for the party of his choice. Thus it is a combination of Britain's "first–past–the–post" system and proportional representation. Secretary of State for Welsh Affairs Alun Michael of the Labour Party handed over his powers to himself in his new capacity as first secretary of the Welsh Assembly. In 2000 Labour's popular Rhodri Morgan was elected as first minister.

In the May 2003 Welsh elections, the first since devolution, voters decided that Labour still best represented their interests, giving it 36.6% of their votes in a low turnout of 38.2%. *Plaid Cymru* slid downward by 10.8%, winning only 19.7% and 12 seats. The Conservatives almost overtook the Welsh nationalists, winning 19.2%, and the Liberal Democrats garnered 11.7%. The weakened *Plaid Cymru* shelved the question of ultimate independence.

A 2007 survey revealed that a majority of Welsh believe devolution has improved the way Wales is governed and favor more powers to their own assembly, which will come. Though not as desirous of independence as are Scots, three-fifths of them prefer to call themselves "Welsh" rather than "British." In the May 2007 elections Labour remained the largest party, but it lost seven percentage points mainly to *Plaid Cymru*.

Scotland

Scotland, which is still a kingdom in its own right, joined England by agreement in 1707. Although the Scottish parliament voted itself out of existence at that time, other institutions remained intact, such as the legal system, based on Roman law, a distinctive educational system and a Presbyterian Church of Scotland. By long–standing custom, the Queen worships as a Presbyterian in Scotland and as an Episcopalian in England. One should therefore not wonder at the fact that the Scots have a secure sense of separate national identity that has survived union with England.

Scottish nationalist feeling has simmered for two and a half centuries, but the intensity and strength surged furiously in the 1970s when oil was discovered in the North Sea off Scotland's coasts. The Scottish Nationalist Party (SNP), founded in 1928, argued that "It's Scotland's Oil!" and that it would make this relatively poor region in the UK wealthy and capable of independence. In the 1974 parlia-

The United Kingdom

mentary elections, its vote surged to 30%. In the face of such rising nationalism in their traditional party stronghold, the ruling Labour government offered to create a popularly elected Scottish assembly if such a move were approved by a majority in a referendum.

Such an instrument of "direct democracy" means that between parliamentary elections, the people, not parliament, decide. Because of the tradition of parliamentary supremacy, there were no referendums in Britain until the 1970s. Parliament did stipulate that at least 40% of the eligible Scottish voters had to approve the transfer of powers to the region (a process known as "devolution"). The referendum was held in March 1979, and 51.6% of the voters approved of the assembly; however, only 33% of the eligible voters participated, so parliament repealed the devolution act for Scotland. The Labour Party, which had always won most of the Scottish seats, reasserted itself in Scottish affairs and picked up the torch of devolution.

The 1990s witnessed a resurgence of Scottish nationalism and the SNP. Polls in 1992 indicated that 80% of Scots wanted either a Scottish parliament or outright independence. One native son, actor Sean Connery, compared Scotland to the independent Baltic states. This was quite a role reversal for "James Bond," who on screen risked everything to serve the British crown. He said he would permanently move from his adopted home in the Bahamas back to Scotland if it were ever to win its independence. The hit movie "Braveheart" in the mid–1990s also

boosted the movement for greater Scottish independence. Even more Scotsmen began saying: "We're not free. We need a William Wallace." This feeling helped fuel an upsurge of interest in learning Scotland's Gaelic language, which had declined to only 80,000 speakers, or about 3%-4% of Scotsmen, who may use it in the assembly if they choose. Still there is no language motive to Scottish nationalism, as in Wales. Nor are there religious ones, as in Northern Ireland, or ethnic motives, as in eastern Europe. Former SNP leader Alex Salmond remarked, "we are a mongrel nation."

In the 1997 elections the SNP, which captured six seats, for the first time in Scotland's history drove the Tories out completely. Scottish MPs in Westminster enjoy the privilege, known as the "West Lothian question, that they can vote on all matters that concern the entire UK, whereas English, Welsh and Northern Irish MPs cannot vote on matters devolved to Scotland. This quirk helps stimulate "English nationalism." Some polls have shown that two-thirds of the English support an English-only parliament, and the proportion who define themselves as "English, not British" had by 2005 risen to 40%.

With Labour dominating Westminster again, devolution of powers to Scotland and Wales came back on the agenda. A referendum in Scotland in September 1997 paved the way to a democratically elected assembly in 1999. Voters overwhelmingly approved a 129–seat parliament, Scotland's first in 300 years, with wide powers over such local matters as health, education, municipal government, economic

**Scottish First Minister
Alex Salmond**

development, housing, criminal and civil law, fisheries and forestry. They also voted for the right to raise or lower income taxes by up to 3% and to levy charges, such as road tolls. Each Scot continues to receive about 1,000 pounds ($2,000) in subsidies from London.

The polling set the stage for the most important constitutional change in British government in modern times. It also signaled the peaceful rebirth of a nation in an extraordinary way: no guerrilla army, separatist terrorists, civil disobedience, or even mass demonstrations. Edinburgh has become Britain's second diplomatic capital, with 16 foreign missions established there by 2005. A couple of dozen Scotsmen work in "external relations," a term carefully selected so as not to irritate British diplomats in the "foreign office." Half of those diplomats work in Brussels, Washington and Beijing.

On May 6, 1999, voters elected their first Members of the Scottish Parliament (MSP). Using the same mixed single–member constituency/PR electoral system as the Welsh, they favored Labour. This was a setback for the SNP's independence cause. In 2000, Labour's leader, Donald Dewar, slipped on his front porch and quickly died of a brain hemorrhage. This was a blow to those who advocated autonomy rather than separation from Britain.

The SNP, under John Swinney, had clearly failed to persuade voters in May 2003 that it would be a plausible government and that full independence would be a good thing. The party was divided between those who wanted to return to being a protest party and those who believed that a gradual accumulation of power by the Scottish parliament is the best route to go.

SNP Leader Alex Salmond, a former economist with the Royal Bank of Scot-

Holyrood, Scottish Parliament

land, concluded that an election victory in Scotland would no longer be a sufficient mandate for independence. It would need to be followed by a referendum before an SNP government could enter negotiations to remove Scotland from Britain. Scots appear to want to see how devolution works before leaping into independence. Indeed it seems that devolution, not independence, is still the preferred direction, even among some SNP voters. Although three-quarters of Scots prefer to be called "Scottish" than "British," only about a third favor independence, according to polls. But "independence" can mean different things to different people. When they went to the polls in May 2007—the 300th anniversary year of the Treaty of Union with England—to elect a Scottish parliament, two-thirds voted for parties that favor union with Britain.

Although there was no mandate for independence in 2007, the results were still a sensation: for the first time since 1959 Labour came out in second place, winning only 46 to the SNP's 47 seats in the 129-seat assembly. The Tories got 17 and the Liberal Democrats 16. This ended a half of a century of Labour dominance of Scottish politics. It presents a real problem for Labour and its leader Gordon Brown (also a Scotsman): they cannot win Britain without winning Scotland. An elated Salmond, who still has a seat in Westminster, declared that "never again will the Labour Party think it has a divine right to govern." He became first minister in a minority government. No other party would enter a coalition with his party even though there are other small parties that favor independence—the Greens, Solidarity and Scottish Socialist Party. With the SNP in power, the English can no longer be blamed for everything that goes wrong in Scotland even though Salmond never misses an opportunity to stand up to the prime minister. His rapid pace as first minister has provided a mighty boost to the SNP's approval ratings, and Salmon talks confidently of a referendum in 2010 or after. By the standards of separatist movements around the world, Scottish nationalism has been a peaceful success story.

In October 2004 the Queen officially opened the new ultra-modern Scottish Parliament building, Holyrood, right across the street from her official Scottish residence. Housing 129 lawmakers, it was three years late and at £431 million ($862 million) ten times over budget. Sitting in its beautiful interior, MSP can look out over the rugged hills that symbolize their land.

Northern Ireland

The UK's most serious regional problem by far was Northern Ireland. The Irish island can be said to be England's oldest colony, having been invaded by the English in the 12th century and ruled as a colony until 1800, when it received its own parliament. Ireland remained legally a part of the United Kingdom until 1922, when the 26 predominantly Catholic southern counties formed what is now the Republic of Ireland. The Protestant majority in the six northern counties rejected "home rule" (independence from Britain). The British at the time pledged that no change in the link between Northern Ireland and the United Kingdom would occur without the consent of the majority of the people. Every subsequent British government held firmly to this commitment.

The largely Presbyterian and Church of Ireland Protestants are descendants of Scottish immigrants who began arriving in the 17th century. Their loyalty to the English crown is based upon the monarch's historical status set forth in the 1689 Bill of Rights, as "the glorious instrument of delivering this kingdome from Popery and arbitrary power." It is not surprising that this historical attitude, along with the Protestants' rejecting unification of the two parts of Ireland, has always antagonized the Catholic minority in Northern Ireland (who comprise 42% of the population of 1.6 million). Although Northern Ireland is officially a secular (i.e. non–religious) state, in actual practice the friction between Catholics and Protestants dominates politics there.

Northern Ireland was in turmoil since 1968, when a Catholic civil rights movement organized internationally publicized street demonstrations to object to Protestant discrimination in housing, jobs and electoral representation. British governmental pressure on the Northern Irish parliament (which has existed since 1921 and is known as "Stormont" because it met in Stormont Castle) to meet many of the Catholic demands created a Protestant backlash. Peaceful street demonstrations in 1969 gave way to open violence, and British troops were sent to reestablish order.

The Irish Republican Army (IRA) sprang to life again and launched a modern terrorist campaign to remove the British from the territory and to reunify the entire island. It received money and arms from overseas sources ranging from Gadhafi in Libya to the Irish Northern Aid Committee—NORAID—in the United States. Due to bad publicity, IRA fund-raising in the U.S. became more difficult. It found a lucrative substitute: extortion and racketeering in Northern Ireland itself. Because it also seeks the overthrow of the Dublin government, it has been banned in the South since 1936.

In retaliation, some Protestants in the North organized illegal forces. The best-known illegal Protestant paramilitary group, known for its violence, is the Ulster Volunteer Force (UVF). This illegal unit should not be confused with the Ulster Defence Regiment (UDR—the British army in Northern Ireland), the Royal Ulster Constabulary (RUC—the mainly Protestant police force) or the Ulster Defence Association (UDA—a moderate and legal Protestant paramilitary group). In 1993 Protestant gunmen murdered more people than did the IRA.

The British disbanded Stormont in 1972 and resorted to the unpleasant task of ruling the region directly, through a Secretary of State for Northern Ireland. Successive British governments sought earnestly for ways to devolve governmental power to the Northern Irish themselves. The problem was always how to protect the Catholic minority's interests against a perpetual Protestant majority. This difficulty revealed a major weakness of the English model of parliamentary democracy, which presents great power to any political group that commands an electoral majority: the model does not work well in societies which are divided religiously, ethnically or racially, because minorities can be voted down so easily.

Realizing this, the British government had to reject in 1975 a proposal by the leaders of the Protestants that a constitution be drawn up for Northern Ireland that would copy British parliamentary practice. Instead, British governments sought some form of "power–sharing" arrangement that would guarantee the minority Catholic parties a place in any Northern Irish executive. This idea infuriated the two Protestant political parties, the Ulster Unionists and the Democratic Unionists.

The IRA, which became a dedicated and ruthless band of 400 to 500 paramilitaries operating in small cells called "active service units," was divided into two groups: the "official" IRA was formerly Marxist, but now it seeks power through elections; the "provisional" IRA (Provos) was strictly nationalist, but it shifted to armed struggle to convert Ireland into a Marxist state. This shift was one reason why Irish–Americans became less generous toward the IRA. Both these wings face some competition from the smaller, but more radical Irish National Liberation Army (INLA, the paramilitary wing of the Marxist Irish Republican Worker's Party).

From 1976 to 1982 the IRA campaigned for special treatment as "political prisoners." After the failure of such tactics as refusing to wear prison garb and smearing the walls of the cells with their own excrement, they resorted to hunger strikes. The deaths of ten IRA hunger strikers in Maze

The United Kingdom

Prison in 1981 sparked renewed militant Catholic nationalism. Shortly before his death, one of the hunger strikers, Bobby Sands, even managed to win a seat in the House of Commons, while he was still in prison.

In response, the British government tried again to restore a measure of devolved government by means of the 1982 Northern Ireland Act. Elections for a 78–seat Northern Ireland Assembly and an executive branch were held in 1982. This new body was to have the power to make proposals to the British government on how to return to self–government. It failed. Neither the mainly Catholic, moderate and law–abiding Social Democratic and Labour Party, nor the militant *Sinn Fein* (the political arm of the IRA, pronounced "Shin Fane," receiving only 10% of the total votes), took their seats in it. The Ulster Unionist Party also walked out and vowed that it would not return until security had been restored in Northern Ireland.

That is exactly what the British tried to do. In 1975 it ended the detention of both Catholic and Protestant terrorist suspects without trial, and it refused to declare martial law in the violence–torn area. Because of the risk of intimidation against jurors, non–jury courts (known as "Diplock Courts") were created for those accused of terrorist–related offenses. The British have always contended that the fundamental principles of British justice— a fair trial, the onus on the prosecution to prove guilt, the right to be represented by a lawyer, the right of appeal if convicted— are maintained for all.

The most effective antiterrorist measure undertaken by the government in 1983 was the granting of pardon or lenience to onetime terrorists if they would tip off the police (in Northern Irish slang, 'to grass') on the whereabouts of active terrorists. The testimony of such 'supergrasses' led to a dramatic number of arrests in both the IRA and Protestant Ulster Volunteer Force. These organizations were so paralyzed that terrorist deaths in Northern Ireland dropped by half in one year, from 97 in 1982 to about 50 in 1983. IRA terrorists did give British Christmas shoppers a grisly indication they were alive in 1983, however, when they exploded a bomb outside of the bustling Harrods Department Store in London, claiming still more innocent lives (including an American teenager, a fact that hurt IRA fund–raising in the U.S.) in their ruthless struggle.

The Brighton bombing of 1984 was another grim reminder of the IRA's intent to wreak as much havoc as possible, this time by assailing the highest levels of British government itself. Having organized into "cells," the IRA became more

difficult for police to combat. The violence prompted the Irish Republic to ratify the European convention on terrorism, which requires the extradition of terrorists.

By 2003 the toll stood at over 3,600 since 1969. In doing its bloody work the IRA had the tactical advantage over the 30,000 security forces, which were kept on the defensive by the IRA's meticulous planning and constant shifting of tactics. To minimize its own losses, it increasingly struck at "soft targets," such as bands, military hospitals, off–duty RUC officers, and civilian firms that supply goods and services to the security forces. It also acquires state–of–the–art equipment; for example, it has surface–to–air missiles to use against army helicopters.

Democracy still existed at the local level in Northern Ireland, and voters send 27 MPs to the House of Commons in London. Protestants win a majority of these seats. Catholics would take more if the competing SDLP and *Sinn Fein* would unify in constituencies with predominantly Catholic populations. In the 1997 elections the two Catholic parties captured an unprecedented 40.2% of the votes.

The Protestant Unionist parties also have trouble working together, with Ian Paisley's hard-line Democratic Unionists taking five seats and David Trimble's larger Ulster Unionist Party winning six. *Sinn Fein* traditionally refused to take any seat in the British parliament, whose authority it does not recognize and which would require them to swear allegiance to the Queen. In 2002 Adams and three other party members took a historic step by going to the House of Commons and signing up to use all of the facilities except actually occupying a seat. Adams emphasized: "There will never ever be *Sinn Fein* MPs sitting in the British houses of parliament." In 2005 the party's parliamentary expenses of £400,000 ($800,000) were withheld to punish the party for IRA crimes.

In 1997 *Sinn Fein* won an all–time high of 16% of the votes in Northern Ireland. Two of its candidates, Gerry Adams and Martin McGuinness (an IRA leader who has served jail sentences), won seats, which remained vacant. *Sinn Fein* does occupy seats in local councils on both sides of the Irish border and in the Northern Ireland Assembly. In 2002 it decided to run for seats in the Irish Republic's elections and it won five; there was general relief when it lost one of those seats in May 2007. In June 2002 *Sinn Fein* won control of Belfast, and Alec Maskey became lord mayor.

There was progress in addressing the problem of social and economic discrimination. For members of the growing Cath-

Mr. Gerry Adams
President, *Sinn Fein*

olic middle class, life has never been better. They are upwardly mobile and increasingly move into middle-class Protestant neighborhoods, where they are tolerated. Catholics now outnumber Protestants at universities by four to three. The unemployment gap is shrinking. Three out of ten persons are employed in the public sector, and hiring policies are scrupulously equal and fair. They have begun to intermarry; one tenth of marriages are mixed. Tourists are returning to the province, which has the lowest rate of violent crime in the UK. Investment is entering from the Irish Republic, which has become Europe's third-richest country. Businesses on both sides of the border are working together. There would be even more cooperation if corporate taxes (30% in Northern Ireland and 12.5% in the Republic) were more equal. However, there is still mistrust. A quarter of respondents said in a 2004 poll that a close relative had died in the Troubles. That figure is probably higher in working-class areas.

In 1985 former Irish *Taoiseach* (prime minister) Garrett FitzGerald and British Prime Minister Thatcher signed an Anglo–Irish agreement on Northern Ireland. This marked the first time the British government formally permitted the Irish Republic involvement in Northern Ireland's affairs, a concession many Northern Irish Protestants could not accept. It is regrettable, but perhaps not surprising, that all groups in Northern Ireland condemned this landmark act, despite the fact that its first article stated that no change in the province's status would come about without the consent of a majority of its people.

Peace Talks in Northern Ireland
In 1993 optimism was ignited by a joint declaration by the British and Irish prime

First Minister Ian Paisley and Deputy First Minister Martin McGuinness enjoy their historical moment

ministers offering *Sinn Fein* a seat at the bargaining table to discuss Northern Ireland's future if the IRA renounced violence. Former Prime Minister John Major, who admitted that his government had conducted secret contacts with the IRA, promised that Britain would not stand in the way of a united Ireland if a majority of Northern Ireland residents supported such a step. His Irish counterpart pledged that there would be no change in the six counties' status without majority consent.

The following year President Bill Clinton, betting that the IRA wants peace in Northern Ireland, made a risky decision to grant a visa to *Sinn Fein* leader Gerry Adams to come to the U.S. Although the British government criticized him for this, it triggered a series of historic events. On August 31, 1994, the IRA declared a cease–fire, which prompted the Irish government to begin meeting with *Sinn Fein* leaders. Six weeks later Protestant loyalists also declared a truce. While paramilitaries on both sides continued to terrorize their own communities, inter–sectarian violence and IRA attacks on British forces stopped. As a result, the British government relaxed its security measures in Northern Ireland and began drawing down its 18,000 troops. In December London opened direct talks with *Sinn Fein* and, later, with the Protestant paramilitaries. In February 1995 the British and Irish governments issued a "Framework for Agreement," outlining their proposals for Northern Ireland's future.

The U.S. government did its part to keep the momentum going by permitting *Sinn Fein* to open an office near Dupont Circle in Washington in 1995 and to raise money legally in the U.S. Much to London's displeasure, Clinton invited Gerry Adams to a St. Patrick's Day party in the White House honoring Ireland's *Taoiseach*. In May the U.S. also organized a Northern Ireland Investment Conference in Washington that brought together more people from more different Northern Irish parties under one roof than ever before. It was also attended by top government officials from the UK and Ireland and was the venue for the first meeting between Gerry Adams and Britain's ex–Secretary of State for Northern Ireland Patrick Mayhew. This was the highest–level meeting between British and IRA leaders in 75 years and a giant step toward Adams' goal of receiving the same recognition and treatment accorded to Northern Ireland's other political leaders.

Clinton gave another powerful boost to the peace process in November 1995 by paying the first visit to Belfast ever made by an American president. It was a triumph. The very approach of his historic visit helped dissolve a stalemate in the talks and revitalized cooperation. Hours before his arrival the Irish and British prime ministers met and agreed to a breakthrough: preliminary all–party talks, led by former U.S. Senator George Mitchell, would be held while an international "decommissioning commission," led by former Canadian chief–of–staff and ambassador to Washington, General John De Chastelain, sought a way around the weapons impasse.

John Major admitted that Clinton's coming helped "concentrate the mind." Greeted everywhere in Belfast by cheering crowds waving American flags, Clinton addressed over 100,000 people, the largest throng in memory to gather in the square of Belfast City Hall. He appealed to everyone to put aside "old habits and hard grudges" and to seek peace. One witness said: "I've never seen anything like this before. Everybody's come together." His American optimism reportedly made a deep impression. He met with all major leaders in the conflict and invited them to a reception at Queen's University; most came, which would have been unthinkable earlier. It was a very different Belfast that he saw: gone are the soldiers on the hunt, the countless roadblocks and the barbed wire. Although the ugly wall topped with razor wire separating Protestants and Catholics, inaptly called the "peace line," still stands, most of the blockaded streets have been reopened in Belfast.

There is little support in Northern Ireland or elsewhere for immediate reunification of Ireland. But not since 1969 had there been so many grounds for optimism that "the troubles" can end and that the Northern Irish can discuss their future peacefully. As a symbol of returning normalcy with Britain in 1995, Prince Charles became the first member of the royal family to make an official visit to the Irish Republic since 1922. Also in 1995, David Trimble, leader of the Ulster Unionist Party, the main Protestant group, traveled to Dublin and met with the Irish *Taoiseach*. This was the first time since 1922 a Unionist leader was received in Dublin. In 1996 the IRA ended an 18–month cease–fire and launched a bombing campaign in Britain and Northern Ireland. Negotiations resumed in June 1997.

Since the Labour government is not dependent upon Unionist MPs from Northern Ireland to win important votes in parliament, as John Major was, it had more political flexibility on Northern Irish issues. A couple of weeks after becoming prime minister, Blair lifted the ban on official contacts with *Sinn Fein* in order to explain London's position and to assess whether the IRA was really prepared to renounce violence. Gerry Adams accepted the offer. Blair dropped London's insis-

45

The United Kingdom

tence that terrorists disarm before joining peace talks. He visited Northern Ireland on May 16, 1997, in order to demonstrate that he is willing to take risks for peace in the six counties.

To continue the negotiation process, he invited Gerry Adams to a meeting in Downing Street in December. This was the first visit by an Irish Republican leader to the prime minister's private residence in 76 years. It was a richly symbolic encounter, with the meeting over tea held in the cabinet room, the target of an IRA mortar attack only six years earlier. A month later, in January 1998, Adams returned to Downing Street to hear from the prime minister that the peace process is an "absolute priority" and that "the status quo is not an option." To balance his gesture to *Sinn Fein*, Blair told Protestants that "none of us . . . , even the youngest, is likely to see Northern Ireland as anything but a part of the United Kingdom."

Talks, involving eight Northern Ireland parties and the British and Irish governments continued, despite the outbreak of renewed violence following the assassination of a Protestant terrorist, Billy Wright, in Maze prison just after Christmas. American George Mitchell emphasized the importance of the negotiations: "We're talking about, literally, people's lives, the possibility of the resumption of the terrible conflict that enveloped this society with fear and anxiety. So, frustrating and tedious as it seems—and it is—you have to be patient and recognize how tough it is for them to move."

Good Friday Agreement

In the early morning hours of Good Friday, 1998, after a series of marathon sessions, all parties at the table reached an historic agreement: a new 108–member Northern Ireland Assembly would be elected using the Irish Republic's system of proportional representation with the transferable vote. To protect Catholics from being permanently outvoted on sensitive "cross–community" issues and to necessitate consensus, a majority of both Catholic and Protestant blocs or an overall "weighted majority" of 60% would be required for decisions. The cabinet would consist of 10 seats distributed proportionally to the four largest parties.

The assembly would share power with a new North–South Ministerial Council, composed of ministers from the Republic and Northern Ireland. This gives the Irish Republic its first formal role in Northern Ireland's affairs. In return, Ireland's leaders agreed to give up the Republic's claim to the North. All parties pledged to use their influence to persuade armed groups to turn in their weapons within two years, and imprisoned members of those armed

groups would be released within two years as well.

On May 22, 1998, referenda were held on both sides of the border, and 71% of Northern Irish and 94.4% in the Republic approved of the Good Friday settlement. The following month, the first elections to the new assembly were held, and David Trimble's UUP came out on top with 28 seats. John Hume's SDLP (later led by Seamus Mallon) was second, with 24 seats. For their indispensable role in the entire peace process, Trimble and Hume shared the 1998 Nobel Prize for Peace. Hume had declared that "we finally decided that agreement for the whole community is more important than victory for one side." Other seats went to the DUP (20), *Sinn Fein* (18), the Alliance (6), the UKUP (5), Independent Unionists (3), and the Women's Coalition and PUP two each. The great number of parties winning seats demonstrated the effect of the proportional representation electoral system. Trimble became first minister, and the body met for the first time in the traditional Stormont building on July 4.

This being Ireland, an island with so much history and so many memories, things were not destined to go smoothly. In August a fringe Catholic organization calling itself the "Real IRA" exploded a car bomb in the Northern Irish city of Omagh, killing 29 people. The public was so repelled by this grisly act that the "Real IRA" apologized and announced a permanent cease–fire on September 12. This was soon broken, and the IRA was forbidden from raising money in the United States.

After the BBC named four men it said were involved in the attack, three were arrested in 2000. In 2002 the first was convicted and sentenced to 14 years in jail. Colm Murphy, a wealthy pub owner and building contractor, was found guilty by a three-judge panel in a special criminal court in Dublin. To the chagrin of the victims' families, Murphy's conviction was overturned by a Dublin appeals court. He faced retrial. Another suspect, Sean Gerard Hoey, was charged in 2005 for participating in the bombing. But all convictions were subsequently overturned, including that of Hoey in December 2007. Nevertheless, the tragedy ultimately strengthened support for the peace process.

The "Real IRA" were also the prime suspects in the September 2000 rocket attack against the London headquarters of MI6, Britain's foreign intelligence service. To maintain his credibility in the Protestant community, Trimble called for a beginning of "decommissioning" (turning in) of weapons even before the creation of a Northern Ireland cabinet. Noting that this precondition had not been in the

agreement, *Sinn Fein* balked at completing the peace process.

Endless haggling over paramilitary groups laying down their arms threatened the peace deal. However, both sides began taking cautious steps to implement the agreement. On December 1, 1999, a new coalition government in Ulster was formed that shared power devolved from Westminster in London. It included both the party of hard-line Protestant, Rev. Ian Paisley, and former IRA commander, Martin McGuinness, as minister of education. However, this government was suspended in February 2000 after the IRA failed to meet the Unionists' deadline for starting turning in its arms.

Power-sharing was reestablished in May 2000 when the Unionists accepted an IRA pledge to put its arsenal "beyond use" and to allow limited inspections by international observers to verify that that the promise is being kept. Such visits were conducted in June and October 2000, and the arms dumps were reported to have a substantial amount of military material that was safely stored. For a year and a half the IRA dragged its heels. As a result David Trimble, leader of Northern Ireland's power-sharing government, quit in 2001, and things came to a standstill.

In November 2001 the IRA finally began destroying some of its weapons under international supervision. In quick response to this breakthrough, Britain began demolishing military installations, including army watchtowers overlooking regions with high IRA support. Trimble led his Ulster Unionist Party back into the assembly and was narrowly reelected first minister with the help of the Alliance Party, which had steered a middle road between unionists and republicans. Peace was back on track.

Genuine struggles remain on such emotional symbolic issues as flying flags over official buildings and reforming and renaming the Royal Ulster Constabulary (RUC), which is 93% Protestant. A top American law enforcement official, Tom Constantine, former head of the Drug Enforcement Administration (DEA), was appointed as "oversight commissioner" to scrutinize changes in the RUC. But progress is undeniable. The bloodletting has subsided although armed dissidents abound. Maze prison, just outside of Belfast, was emptied and closed in September 2000. Ex-prisoners had played a role in the peace process; they were crucial in the maintenance of their various organizations' cease-fires. The British closed six bases along the Irish border and looked forward to reducing the number of bases from 64 to no more than 20 and of troops from 13,500 to 10,500 in 2005 and ultimately to only 5,000.

In July 2002 the IRA stunned everybody with an expression of "sincere apologies and condolences" for all the persons it had killed in the Northern Irish sectarian violence. The "troubles" appeared to be close to an end when a spy scandal at the heart of the Northern Irish government broke in October 2002. After raiding *Sinn Fein* homes and offices at the Northern Ireland Assembly, British authorities charged three members of gathering intelligence from Britain's Northern Ireland Office that could be used for terrorist operations. Police found sensitive political material, including minutes of conversations between Blair and his Northern Ireland secretary of state, and names, home addresses and license plate numbers of many provincial police officers and British security personnel. It was feared that some of the information could be used for assassinations.

Sinn Fein leaders denied the allegations and claimed the police had orchestrated a frame-up. The British suspended the assembly, and Protestant leaders vowed that they would not resume participation unless the IRA renounces violence unmistakably. The IRA then broke off all contact with the independent panel established to oversee disarmament, which had already supervised the destruction of two caches of IRA weapons. One *Sinn Fein* leader, Martin McGuinness, announced that he had abandoned his fight with Britain and was committing himself to preventing the deaths of any more people. "My war is over." Nevertheless, the peace process had suffered its most serious blow since the Good Friday Agreement five years earlier.

In April 2003 President George W. Bush visited Blair and Irish Prime Minister Bertie Ahern in Belfast to lend his endorsement to the peace plan. The president had aroused the ire of the British government when Gerry Adams was invited to a White House St. Patrick's Day party in March, this when IRA operatives had been arrested while traveling undercover in the U.S. Although Blair sensed that breaking the stalemate was "frustratingly close," all his efforts to get the IRA to make a crystal-clear statement that it had given up paramilitary activities like gathering intelligence, threatening and attacking adversaries and acquiring weapons failed. Adams' statement that there would be "no activities which will undermine in any way the peace process or the Good Friday Agreement" was not enough.

The atmosphere became even more strained when the head of London's Metropolitan Police released evidence in April that agents working for the British army had worked with death squads in Northern Ireland. This included the 1989 murder of Belfast lawyer, Patrick Finuncane,

who had represented IRA terrorists. Two gunmen from the outlawed Ulster Defence Association broke into his home and shot him 14 times at point-blank range before the very eyes of his wife and three children. One of the gunmen left prison in May 2006 under the terms of the 1998 peace accord.

Despite unprecedented direct talks in the fall of 2003 between David Trimble and Gerry Adams, the results of those elections, which were finally held in November 2003, brought a cruel surprise: the confrontational parties outpolled the conciliatory ones, which were the architects and supporters of the peace process. Ian Paisley's Democratic Unionists (DUP) won 30 seats in a 108-seat assembly that does not function, and David Trimble's Ulster Unionist Party (UUP) captured only 27. On the nationalist side, *Sinn Fein* got 24 seats, while the more moderate Social Democratic and Labour Party (SDLP) fell from 24 to 18. The nonsectarian Alliance Party held on to its six seats, and independents got three.

The same thing happened in the May 2005 British parliamentary elections, which delivered convincing victories to the hard-line parties and moved Northern Ireland closer toward a two-party system. David Trimble resigned his leadership of the Ulster Unionist party after losing the seat he had held for 15 years. This capped a decade of steadily declining influence for the party. In June 2006 he was granted a life peerage in the House of Lords. Ian Paisley's Democratic Unionists captured half of the 18 seats allotted to Northern Ireland. *Sinn Fein* took five, and Gerry Adams won easy reelection. The SDLP held on to its three seats. Blair noted in 2003 that "it is more than a little frustrating." Paisley's DUP must be included in any talks to restore devolved government. But Paisley's position as of May 2005 was that the Good Friday Agreement is "finished completely" and "only paper."

A hoped-for settlement ended in December 2004 when the IRA refused to permit photographic verification of its disarmament. Then the IRA was accused of masterminding a spectacular £26.5 million ($50 million) bank robbery in Belfast. A month later, a Catholic father of two, Robert McCartney, was beaten and stabbed to death by a dozen IRA thugs outside a Belfast pub. Seventy-two witnesses in the pub were intimidated in the usual IRA way from testifying. But the man's wife and five sisters decided to depart from the traditional code of silence and bring the matter to international attention.

With increasing publicity on both sides of the Atlantic, *Sinn Fein* found itself in the limelight as the incident galvanized pub-

lic opinion against the IRA. It made one of its most extraordinary blunders ever: it offered to shoot all the IRA members involved in the killing, an offer McCartney's family rejected out of hand. Four of the sisters were invited to *Sinn Fein*'s annual conference in March 2005 and were seated in the front row to hear Gerry Adams call on the killers to turn themselves in and to confess. However, since *Sinn Fein*/IRA rejects police authority, it advised witnesses to offer statements to lawyers, a policy widely criticized in Northern Ireland.

An even greater invitation was extended to the six women from the American president, who met with them on St. Patrick's Day, while refusing to receive Adams, the first time in 10 years this had happened. Adams was also denied the kind of visa that would have permitted him to raise funds in the U.S. More and more families of persons murdered by Catholic and Protestant paramilitaries are coming forward with their stories and standing up to the terrorists they once feared. Adams appealed to the IRA, which British and Irish intelligence officials no longer believe is a separate entity from *Sinn Fein*, to use words, not guns to end British rule in Northern Ireland. But he faces a stark choice: remain linked to an increasingly discredited IRA, or break with it and lead his followers into modern democratic politics without the backing of a murderous paramilitary force.

In July 2005 the IRA formally declared an end to its armed struggle against British rule and pledged to pursue its aims of uniting Ireland through "exclusively peaceful means." In September General John de Chastelain certified that the IRA weapons dumps had been destroyed. Some Protestants, especially Ian Paisley, claim that the IRA had not, in fact, disarmed. A half year later a report by the Independent Monitoring Commission (IMC) stated that the IRA is moving in the right direction, but that some IRA members are still armed and involved in robbery, gasoline smuggling, and financial crime, perhaps without the knowledge of the leadership. The IRA admits that.

British intelligence reports also contend that the IRA kept some weapons, but Chastelain disagreed. Other reports say that the IRA's intelligence service, a formidable group, is still active spying on public officials and providing information to organized crime networks. None of the reports contend that the IRA is still engaged in terrorist operations. However, there were suspicions of that in April 2006, when a senior official in *Sinn Fein*, Denis Donaldson, admitted to having been a British agent for 20 years and was soon thereafter shot dead after being tortured. The IRA denied responsibility. That

The United Kingdom

Northern Ireland is more peaceful is beyond dispute. In 1972, 500 persons were killed; in 2005, the number was only five.

A glimmer of hope was produced in May 2006, when the Stormont assembly met for a ceremonial hour. *Sinn Fein* proposed that the leader of the largest party, Ian Paisley, lead a power-sharing executive to revive the stalled peace effort. This was perhaps a ruse to portray itself as cooperative and Paisley as intransigent. In any case, Paisley, whose DUP had never accepted the 1998 peace agreement, declined, remarking that *Sinn Fein* had not done enough to disarm and distance itself from violence: "I am not saying I will never sit in Stormont with the IRA. I am saying I will not sit in Stormont until the IRA gives up its weapons. It's a conditional no, not a 'No, I'll never do it.'"

In the meantime, an impatient British government, which had funded the assembly and the members' $60,000 annual salaries for the previous three years, joined with the Irish government in setting a deadline of November 24, 2006, for the formation of a Northern Irish government that would take over from London such responsibilities as education, health care and transport.

That got people's attention. The Royal Ulster Constabulary (RUC), which had once been 97% Protestant, was transformed into the Police Service of Northern Ireland, with one-fifth of the officers Catholic. In January 2007 Sinn Fein recognized that force. In March the voters went to the polls and confirmed that Paisley's DUP (with 30% of the votes) and Adams' Sinn Fein (with 26%) are the dominant groups. This enabled them both to claim a mandate to strike a deal, which they did. Both announced their willingness to share power.

On May 8, Paisley was sworn in as first minister, with Sinn Fein's Martin McGuinness as deputy first minister. The formerly recalcitrant Paisley said: "I believe Northern Ireland has come to a time of peace, when hate will no longer rule." After more than 3,700 deaths, this was a very welcome message. Bertie Ahern hailed Tony Blair as the driving force behind the peace effort and declared that "we can, and are, shaping our future in a new and better way." A few days later Ahern became the first Irish leader to address a joint session of the British parliament, and he got a standing ovation. Blair noted at the power-sharing ceremony that "these islands have at last escaped the heavy chains of history." The settlement may well be his most illustrious legacy after a decade in power.

In the end, Blair had high praise for Paisley, whose "contribution to peace, after all the years of division and difference,

was decisive and determinative." Both prime ministers convinced him that only a man of his stature could bring peace. Paisley succeeded in bringing most of his community on board, but the diehards in his unionist movement felt betrayed and could not forgive him. Their loathing was only increased by the jovial photos in the press of him and McGuinness enjoying each other's company. This ultimately forced him to shed his leadership positions. Rather than risking ouster as head of the Free Presbyterian Church of Ulster, which he had founded 56 years earlier, he stepped down in January 2008. In May he quit as first minister and as leader of the Democratic Unionists, which he had created 37 years earlier. His replacement for both is long-standing number two in the party, Peter Robinson. Paisley remains only as an MP in London and member of the Stormont assembly. Power-sharing continues.

Resistance to the agreement was softened by a generous hand extended by then Chancellor of the Exchequer, now Prime Minister Gordon Brown. He offered a financial package of £50 billion ($100 billion) over 10 years to an area where one in three jobs and two-thirds of economic output comes from public sector. The central government spends over £2,000 more per capita than it does in Britain as a whole, and income will continue for some years to be only about 80% of the British average. But this is important because getting the economy moving will not be easy in a corner of Ireland where violence has discouraged both investors and local entrepreneurs. By 2008 more than $6 billion in foreign investments had poured into the North. One sign of the economic renaissance is the glittering new Victoria Square in Belfast, a $800 million shopping center with a huge glass dome hovering over the downtown skyline.

Securing the peace is the highest priority. Within days after the agreement, the oldest loyalist paramilitary group, the Ulster Volunteer Force (UVP), announced that it was going out of existence although its weapons were merely put out of reach, not destroyed. Britain created a new Catholic-Protestant panel to oversee the police force, and for the first time it includes Sinn Fein officials. However, policing remains a problem even though crime by 2008 had gone down six consecutive years, and overt sectarian violence is increasingly rare. The British army officially ended "Operation Banner," its longest continuous operation ever, in effect since 1969. But it left a garrison of 5,000 soldiers to offer support to the police. Few people are ready to remove the 50 "peace walls" that separate Catholic and Protestant housing, and a few more have been con-

David Cameron, leader of Conservative Party

structed. More time is needed to build trust and complete the healing. (See Ireland)

Today's Political Parties

Like any modern democracy, the British system could not function without parties. They recruit and select candidates, define issues which are important, educate voters about them, finance and fight electoral campaigns, put up governments which rule at all political levels, and provide well–organized opposition which continually remind the electorate of the government's shortcomings. For the government, the party is an essential tool for maintaining a parliamentary majority, and for the individual politician, it is the ladder to power. For the political activist it is an important means for putting his ideas into practice. For the voter, it is an indispensable label for a set of politicians, policies, sympathies or interests.

British parties bear some similarities to those of America, but there is a striking difference which stems from a fundamental difference in the two political systems: the real power in American parties is at the bottom of the hierarchy; a national party in America is nothing more than a loose coalition of state and local parties. By contrast, in Britain the real power within the party is at the top.

Basically, all British parties have a similar organization. At the lowest level are party units in the wards, which are grouped together into 646 constituency parties, each of which struggles for a seat in the House of Commons. These ward or constituency parties raise funds (part of which must be passed up to the national party), recruit members, campaign at election time and select candidates.

National parties rarely try to overrule constituent parties' choice of candidates, although the national parties clearly influence the selection. The most obvious evidence is that about a half of all MPs do not reside in their constituencies before their election to parliament. Unlike the U.S., there is no legal requirement for this. The national party leaders search all over Britain for "safe seats" for important MPs. Constituency party leaders often decide that national party interests override their own local desires. All constituency parties are grouped into regional organizations, which, except Wales and Scotland, have little importance.

At the national level, each party organizes an annual conference to which each constituency sends representatives. This large conference debates and adopts the party's overall policy (which is never binding on the party if it is in power) and, in the case of Labour, elects the party's leadership. At the national level, two other party organizations also exist. The central bureaucracy assists the party at all levels. The parliamentary party consists of the MPs and members of the House of Lords belonging to it.

All British parties are coalitions of differing interests and ideologies. It is often assumed that British parties are class parties. While this, to some extent, is true of the Labour Party, the Conservative Party has always had an appeal which cuts across class lines. In terms of policy, the major parties have normally been far closer together than is often assumed. From 1945 until the early 1970s, there was a large measure of consensus among the major parties. All were agreed on a welfare state, the mixed public–private economy which permitted much state intervention in the economy and employer–union–government collaboration (sometimes referred to as "corporatism").

Some observers even spoke of the "end of ideology" in Britain. That broad consensus collapsed in the 1970s, and both the Conservative and Labour parties became more ideologically oriented. By the 1983 elections the major parties had become more polarized than they had been in a half-century. Margaret Thatcher's embrace of market–oriented economics and rejection of state intervention, of "welfarism," and of "corporatism" was matched by revived class–warfare rhetoric in the Labour Party. Its moderate wing found itself placed on the defensive by the left–wing, which demanded radical changes in Britain's social, economic and political power structures. Sir Winston Churchill's observation was no longer correct that "four–fifths of the two major British parties agree about four–fifths of the things that need to be done." But four defeats in a row from 1979 to 1992 prompted Labour to move toward the political center. The payoff exceeded its wildest expectations.

The Conservative Party

The Conservative Party is conscious of its heritage, which it traces back to the 17th century. Its pragmatic approach has always enabled it to appeal to British from all classes, even though its strongest appeal could be found among those who were well–off economically. At the heart of the Tory Party, as it was formerly known, is the unity of the whole nation. It has always preferred voluntary effort to public assistance, and this stems from its insistence on free enterprise in industry, advocacy of the profit motive and of indirect (sales) taxes rather than direct (income) taxes.

It has never argued that the state has no role in the economy, and it even nationalized industries under certain circumstances, such as the Central Electricity Board in 1926 and Rolls–Royce in 1971.

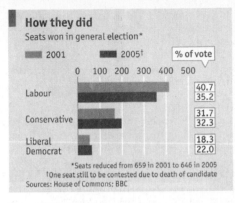

Source: *The Economist*

Nor has it ever rejected the notion that the state should provide social welfare services sensibly. In her 1987 campaign Margaret Thatcher said that all decent people want to help the ill, the unemployed and the aged, but that a healthy economy is needed to provide the level of services which the British want.

There has, of course, always been division within Tory ranks between proponents of more state intervention and those who favor less regulation and a much freer market economy. Some of the differences in political orientation within the party are reflected in well–established pressure groups: they include the Bow Group, which presses for policies which benefit all classes, the Monday Club (the old right), the Tory Reform Group (progressives) and the Charter Movement, who want to democratize the party.

It was publicly known in 1975 when Thatcher defeated Edward Heath for the party leadership that the new leader represented a different Toryism than Heath. After she became prime minister in 1979, those persons in her cabinet who loyally supported her views were dubbed "dries." Those who had doubts about her medicine, especially about how it would affect millions of citizens and their families, were dubbed "wets." In a cabinet reshuffle after the 1983 and 1987 elections, she dismissed the "wets" in her cabinet.

Thatcher's stunning victory in the 1987 elections revealed that although she was an unpopular and unloved leader, British voters respected her no–nonsense competence and will. They grudgingly accepted her bitter economic medicine of sound money, hard work, and standing on one's own two feet. She was the first prime minister to win a third consecutive term in modern British history and surpassed Winston Churchill and H.H. Asquith as Britain's longest serving prime minister in the 20th century. Why did she win?

The first reason is that her opposition was severely divided. Second, the prime minister had won considerable stature

View of London from St. Paul's Cathedral

The United Kingdom

and influence in the international arena. She could boast with justification that "we have put the Great back into Britain." The main reason for her victory was the undeniable economic success her government had achieved.

Thatcher's Fall

The willingness of France and Germany to relinquish more sovereignty to Europe widened the chasm between the UK and its continental partners. Thatcher's cabinet had been rocked by high–level resignations stemming from disagreements over Europe. In 1986 Michael Heseltine stormed out because he wanted a European consortium, not one from the U.S., to purchase a British helicopter company. In 1989 Nigel Lawson left because he wanted to include the pound in the European Monetary System (EMS). The fatal resignation—and the catalyst for her downfall—was that of Sir Goeffrey Howe, the last surviving member of her original 1979 cabinet and an architect of "Thatcherism." He charged in parliament that her obstruction in Europe carried "serious risks for our nation."

The devastating speech led to a successful challenge to her leadership in November 1990. After a historic 11–year rule, the longest prime ministership since the Victorian era and the longest consecutive one since the Napoleonic age, Thatcher resigned. The events leading to her fall related to Europe, but the reason why 45% of her parliamentary party colleagues voted against her was that she was guiding her party toward defeat in the next elections. For 18 months her party had trailed in the polls a Labour Party that had become more moderate, had overthrown its suicidal commitment to nuclear disarmament, and had embraced the EU. Her country was experiencing high inflation, a growing trade deficit, a slowdown in economic growth, and intense domestic opposition to her poll tax for local governments.

With her leaving, the UK entered a period under John Major, Britain's youngest prime minister in the last century, until Labour leader Tony Blair evicted him from Number 10 Downing Street. Major was a self–made man from a very humble background and with no university education. His father had been a circus performer and minor league baseball player in the U.S. Major was the Iron Lady's protégé and hand–picked successor. Nevertheless, he backed away from strident Thatcherism, abolishing the hated poll tax in 1991. He buried the grudge Thatcher had borne against both the EU and Germany and became a more cooperative European. Like Thatcher, he benefited from an unexpected war, this time in the Gulf

in 1991, which went very well for Britain and its allies.

He entered the 1992 elections with the highest popularity rating of any British prime minister in three decades, but nobody expected his stunning victory in the midst of Britain's worst recession in a half century. He led his party to a 21–seat majority, based on 42% of the votes and 336 seats (down from 376).

The Tory party was deeply divided, especially over Britain's role in the EU. Major's government was sometimes held hostage by several dozen vocal "Euroskeptics" in his own party, including Thatcher herself, who were determined to sabotage all moves to closer European union. The government appeared to be at war with itself and was dogged by a succession of scandals and sleaze. Voters were tired of Tory rule after 18 years. Even the party's most significant achievement—a booming economy and unemployment half as high as when Major took office in 1992—played in the opposition's favor since voters seemed to think they could afford the risk of voting Labour.

The 2001 elections brought the second devastating defeat in a row for the Conservative party. It won only one constituency in Scotland and none in Wales. It has become a regional party confined to the southeastern English countryside. It failed to win a single seat in any major city outside London, where it captured only 13 out of 74. It was demoralized after its two worst election defeats since 1906. Party leader William Hague resigned immediately. His replacement, Iain Duncan Smith, was selected by a new kind of primary election: first the parliamentary party voted on the contenders. The top two candidates then were submitted to a vote by all 250,000 registered party members in the UK (average age over 65).

The Tories were jolted in 2002 by stories of another sensational sex scandal, this time involving John Major. Miffed that he had not mentioned her in his autobiography and had not given her a cabinet post during his prime ministership, former Education Minister Edwina Currie and later talk-show host revealed in her published diaries that she and Major had had a four-year affair from 1984–8. She had indirectly alluded to this in her 1997 novel, *A Parliamentary Affair*. This lapse of judgment blemished both Major's reputation for honesty and the wisdom of his 1993 campaign, "back to the basics," calling for strict moral values.

Most Tories supported Prime Minister Blair's decision to participate in the war against Iraq in 2003, but this did not help the party in the polls. It remained internally divided, and Duncan Smith was a poor manager of people, a bad communi-

cator and debater, and an uninspired strategist. In October 2003 he was deposed, becoming the first Tory leader to be dismissed without having the opportunity to fight an election. He confided to his colleagues that "only a lunatic would want to lead the Conservative Party."

He was replaced by Michael Howard, who was unopposed. The son of a Romanian-born father and Russian-born mother, Howard is the first professing Jew to lead a major British party. (Benjamin Disraeli was baptized as a child into the Church of England.) He led his party to defeat in the May 2005 parliamentary elections. Although the Tories gained 33 seats for a total of 197, it advanced less than 1% in the popular vote, climbing from 31.7% in 2001 to only 32.3% in 2005. It has won only about a third of the votes for three elections in a row. It gained some ground in the southeast and in prosperous London suburbs. But its continued division over Britain's place in Europe and campaign focus on the problem of immigration, demanding annual limits, turned many voters off.

Part of its problem is that Tony Blair's Labour Party adopted Margaret Thatcher's market reforms and notions of economic efficiency. By doing that, New Labour not only made itself electable, but it also made it very difficult for the Conservatives to define how they are different from Labour. In 1998 *The Economist* called Blair "the strangest Tory ever sold."

Howard announced immediately that he would step down. His replacement was his young (39) protégé, David Cameron, a down-to-earth politician who quickly managed to make the Tories look human and approachable again. He lured William Hague back into the front bench as shadow foreign minister. In January 2006 he gave the Conservatives their first opinion poll lead over Labour in more than a decade: 37% to 35%, with the Liberal Democrats 20%. By October 2007 that 2% lead had not widened, even after the Tories came out on top in the May 2007 local elections, when they took back some of Labour's footholds in the South. But Prime Minister Gordon Brown made a serious mistake. Thinking he could win a snap election on November 1, he mused out loud about it. But he got cold feet when his advisers told him that his 66-seat majority would drop by as many as 46 seats, and he called the election off. This deflated Labour and transferred the momentum to Cameron's Tories, who entered 2008 with 40% support, about a seven-point lead over Labour. However, that is not enough for a majority.

Knowing how damaging the Europhobic image had been to the Tory Party, he hesitantly fulfilled a promise made in the

50

Campaign brochure for Charlotte Atkins

'New Labour has the vision – and the energy – to build a strong dynamic economy breathing new life into Britain'

leadership struggle to draw his party's Members of the European Parliament (MEPs) out of the European People Party (EPP) group. That move reaped more criticism than Cameron had anticipated even though a July 2006 poll had revealed that only 31% of Britons trust the EU. The Conservative Party remains bitterly divided over Europe, but its relations with America are cordial for the most part, despite Cameron's statement that "we should be solid but not slavish in our friendship with America." "I and my party are instinctive friends of America and passionate supporters of the Atlantic alliance."

A couple of months after the election, former Tory Prime Minister Edward Heath (1970–74) died. He had led his country into the EU in 1973 and was ousted from party leadership in 1975 by a then little-known Euroskeptic named Margaret Thatcher. Asked in 1990 if it were possible that she had done a few good things as prime minister, he roared: "Name one!" To his dying day he considered the Tories' increasingly anti-European stance to be responsible for their string of three election losses.

The Labour Party

Although its roots extend far back into the 19th century, the Labour Party was officially founded in 1900. Under the influence of the small but well-connected Fabian Society, which sought to reform British society gradually from above rather than through violent revolution or labor union agitation from below, the party adopted in 1918 a new constitution which transformed it officially into a socialist party. It proclaimed that the goal of the party is to "secure for the producers by hand or by brain the full fruits of their industry and the most equitable distribution thereof that may be possible upon the basis of common ownership of the means

of production and the best obtainable system of popular administration and control of each industry and service."

That purely Marxist objective helped prevent the Labour Party from sharing the fate of many socialist parties in Europe that split apart in the aftermath of the Russian Revolution. However, it became the source of continuous intra–party friction ever since. During most of its history the party was in reality more moderate than its constitution might indicate. It sought to "democratize" the economy by nationalizing key industries and regulating others, to distribute wealth more equally, to expand social welfare services and to eliminate class differences.

During the Thatcher government Labour took a leftward lurch and embarked upon an almost suicidal political course. Grossly underestimating Britain's first woman prime minister and the public support for her economic austerity policies, the Labour Party committed itself to radical promises: unilateral nuclear disarmament, withdrawal from the EU, massive nationalization of industries and huge increases in public spending.

This led to an electoral disaster, and in the 1983 elections, it suffered its worst defeat in 60 years. Its 27.6% was Labour's lowest popular vote since 1918 and was 20 percentage points lower than in 1966. Almost a quarter of those voters who had identified themselves consistently with the Labour Party abandoned it.

It failed to win a majority of the votes among the working class or among labor union members. This was a severe setback for a party created by and organizationally linked to the unions; it seriously hollowed out the party's claim to be the party of the worker. Only the traditional working class remained more loyal: that segment which worked in nationalized or "smokestack" industries or which lived in

council housing, Scotland, Wales or the North of England. This represented the most significant basic shift in the social basis of British politics since World War II.

Within hours after the polls had closed, the move to replace the ineffective Labour leader, Michael Foot, began. The choice was Neil Kinnock. He began immediately to mend the gaping, intra–party split between the left and right which had led to electoral disaster and the massive drop in party membership between 1979 and 1983 to a level comparable to that of 1945. He moderated his party's views on the EU, defense and the status of capitalism. With a sharp eye on the social changes which have occurred in Britain, Kinnock announced that Labour must appeal to the "newly well–off" and should be a party which appeals to the haves, as well as the have–nots.

Going into the 1987 elections, the party shied away from extremism. Its platform purged the earlier pledges to abolish the House of Lords (which has been critical of some of Thatcher's policies), to nationalize much more industry and to control the country's banking system. It accepted the principle of selling public–owned houses, and it no longer opposed the UK's membership in the EU. An enormous electoral liability was Kinnock's decision to stand by his party's unilateral nuclear disarmament position. The electoral effect was suicide. The party suffered its second worst defeat in more than a half-century, capturing only 32% of the votes and 229 seats.

British students celebrate the special relationship

The United Kingdom

In the 1992 elections it faced important social changes which worked against it: its traditional support base—trade–union members, manual laborers and tenants of state–owned housing—is shrinking. Party leaders conducted a thorough rethinking of its positions. In order to be able to present a credible challenge to the Conservatives, Labour had to develop a moderate, non–socialist program. It unveiled its new policy, which scrapped unilateral nuclear disarmament, as well as vote–losing calls for withdrawal from NATO, removal of U.S. military bases in Britain, scuttling the Trident nuclear submarine program, and state ownership of industry. It reconciled itself to the market system.

The year 1992 seemed ideal for a Labour victory, but voters handed Labour its fourth consecutive defeat, even though it climbed to 35% of the votes and 271 seats. Voters continued to associate it with crippling strikes, chaos, and economic decline. Kinnock had begun to introduce the kinds of changes that would ultimately lead his party to victory in 1997, but he had failed at the time to persuade his countrymen that Labour's transformation and pragmatism were genuine and lasting.

In 1994 another leader who could bring the party victory was chosen: Tony Blair. The son of a life–long Conservative, Blair was educated at a private boys' school and studied law at Oxford. He took no interest in student politics and spent his spare time singing in a rock band called "Ugly Rumours." He entered parliament in 1983 representing a traditional Labour constituency in the North. He bore no scars of Labour's dismal rule in the 1970s, and he was its first leader with no roots in the labor movement and with no grounding in traditional socialism.

This made it easier for him to complete the process of modernizing his party. He lessened its dependency upon and identification with unpopular unions. In the 1960s, union money made up 80% of the party's budget; by 1995 that figure was 50% and then 30% by 1998. That began rising again to 57% in 2005, 78% in 2006 and nearly 90% in 2007. He remained silent during a 13–week railway strike in 1994, breaking a long tradition of unfailing party support for the unions' actions. He curbed the voting power of union leaders, who had controlled large blocks within the party. Their power was diluted by changes in the complicated rules governing party voting and policy making.

He persuaded the powerful NEC to accept his revision of Clause IV of the party constitution, setting aside the party's 1918 commitment to public ownership of key industries. This had been a major obstacle to its return to power. Blair confessed later that scrapping Clause IV had "shown me

what I intuitively thought but wasn't sure of: that the party was actually behind change." Since it was a democratic process every step of the way, he was sure that most of the party's rank and file had changed and were behind the reform.

Through his patience, charm, and power of persuasion, he reversed the radicalism within the party and opened it up to fresh ideas. He led Labour toward the political center. He ceased regarding Labour as a tribal party focusing on the working class. By enhancing its appeal among the middle class in the heavily populated south of Britain, he aimed directly at the bedrock of the Tories' support. He was highly confident, disciplined, focused, energetic, and quick to master a brief. He was also sometimes accused of being brutally autocratic when it came to bringing his party in line with his reforms, a quality Margaret Thatcher is said to have admired in him. Unlike Thatcher, though, who relished battering her opponents into submission, Blair preferred logical argument and persuasion.

In the 1997 elections he demonstrated what a skillful campaigner he was. He could orchestrate a tightly organized campaign, present himself convincing in two television debates with his opponent (an innovation in British campaigns), "work a crowd" very effectively, and inspire voters without promising too much. His main challenge was to convince voters that his party had indeed shed the heavy baggage of the past. He stuck to a single message: that his party was now "New Labour." "The old ideologies are dead. New Labour is offering a new and different form of politics. . . . There has been a revolution inside the Labour Party. We have rejected the worst of our past and rediscovered the best. . . . We have made ourselves fit to face the future."

He distanced his party from the "outdated ideology" of high taxes financing expensive government programs, from powerful unions, and from unilateral nuclear disarmament. He established friendly relations with business leaders. He vowed neither to renationalize industries nor raise income taxes. Instead, he pledged to keep inflation low, to spend no more than the Tories had already budgeted, but nevertheless to improve the struggling National Health Service and the school system, to introduce a minimum wage, to combat crime, and to reform the constitution.

Seeing too little difference between his program and that of the Tories, some observers dubbed him "Tony Blur." He responded by arguing, "I do not think everything that has happened in the last 18 years has been bad. My attitude is: keep what is working and change what is

not." Clearly Britain's economy was already working well. This fact persuaded even more voters that there was little danger in voting for a Labour Party that promised not to tamper with one of Europe's most robust economies. Blair assured his countrymen within hours after his victory: "We ran as New Labour and will govern as New Labour."

The electoral payoff for Labour was historic: it won 418 of 659 seats on the basis of 43.1% of the votes. Its majority of 179 seats was its best performance ever. It wiped the Tories out of Scotland and Wales altogether and made deep inroads into Tory strongholds in southern England and London, capturing even Thatcher's north London Finchley constituency. In a stunning turnaround women flocked to Labour, which won 53% of their votes (compared with 30% who voted Tory). The number of women with seats in the House of Commons shot up from 63 to 120, and 101 of them were from Labour. Most of the nine ethnic minorities, including a wealthy Muslim, elected to parliament ran on the Labour ticket. Blair's cabinet also contained many firsts: five women, an openly gay man (Chris Smith, secretary of state for culture, media and sport, who later admitted that he is HIV positive), and a blind man, David Blunkett, education and employment secretary. Plunkett resigned in 2004 because of his affair with a married woman and his attempts to speed up the visa process for her nanny.

In the June 2001 elections, which saw a startling 12% drop in turnout to 59%, the lowest since 1918, Labour slipped to 42% and lost six seats. Nevertheless, with 413 seats it still commanded two-thirds of the seats in the House of Commons. This was the first time in its century of existence that it had succeeded in being reelected to a second full term. A few weeks before the 2005 elections former Labour Prime Minister James Callaghan (1976-79) died. A decent man and a skilful politician, his failure as leader of his party and country stood in stark contrast to the success of Tony Blair.

Turnout rose slightly to 61% in the May 2005 elections. Labour's share of the votes fell by 4.5% to 35.2% of the total votes, the lowest percentage ever recorded by a winning party since 1832. Hurt by the growing unpopularity of the Iraq war, new tuition charges at universities, foundation hospitals and damaged credibility from a wide range of other domestic policies (more than half the voters surveyed a few days before the elections said he could not be trusted), Labour also suffered a loss of over half its majority in the House of Commons, falling to a nevertheless comfortable 67. As in the two earlier elections, it benefited from the division of the opposition.

Blair became the first Labour prime minister in British history to win a third straight term, which is an admirable accomplishment. Turning 52 the day after the elections, he said that this would be his last election as prime minister. This was an unprecedented declaration for such a relatively young leader to make.

On June 27, 2007, he passed on the leadership to his Chancellor of the Exchequer Gordon Brown, the intellectual son of a Presbyterian minister, an admirer of the United States, and excellent manager of the economy. He had entered Edinburgh University at the age of 16 and was elected its rector at 21. Hard-working and extremely smart, he holds strong views about poverty and injustice. Blair went out of his way to call him "the best chancellor in 100 years" and said what "an excellent prime minister" he would make.

The Liberal Democrats

In reaction to the Labour Party's earlier swing to the left, a group from the party bolted and in 1981 formed the Social Democratic Party (SDP). This new grouping sought to occupy the center ground of the British political spectrum, which had opened up because of the polarization between the two larger parties. Its strategy was to align with the older Liberal Party of the center.

The Liberals had been one of the two major parties during the 19th century, but it had not been in power since the Labour Party eclipsed it just after World War I. Their heaviest emphasis has been on individual freedom, and it speaks for decentralization of state power, for a greater focus of local political issues and for workers' (not union) councils sharing control with management. Both the Liberals and the SDP strongly support European integration and reform of the electoral system in favor of proportional representation.

Just how important such a change would be for the SDP–Liberal Alliance was demonstrated in the 1983 elections. It won 25.4% of the vote, the best performance of center parties for 60 years. Its remarkably even support across the entire class spectrum proved that it was not merely a fashionable "wine and cheese" grouping, as critics had charged. But it won only 23 seats in the House of Commons. The SDP was reduced to a tiny rump within parliament. The Alliance did even worse in 1987, falling to 22% of the votes and only 22 seats.

Many analysts had believed that the Alliance could supplant the Labour Party and that the new Social Democrats and the traditionally independent, undisciplined Liberals could forge a partnership

that could "break the mold of British politics." But the Alliance had failed to establish itself as an electable non-socialist alternative. Therefore, in 1988 the SDP dismembered itself. It merged with the larger Liberal Party to form a new party, the Social and Liberal Democrats ("Lib Dems"), led for 11 years by Paddy Ashdown.

He stepped down as leader in 1999, having rescued the party from the splits and name changes of the 1980s and having moved it close to the center of power. Former journalist Charles Kennedy, a good-humored Scotsman, replaced him and led the party in the June 2001 elections, in which they captured an impressive 18.8% of the votes and 52 seats. The party's opposition to the 2003 war in Iraq paid political dividends as enthusiasm for the war wore off.

The party did quite well in the May 2005 elections, climbing from 18.3% to 22% of the votes. However, the electoral system had its usual negative effect on the Lib Dems, garnering for them only 62 seats (11 more than in 2001), under 10% of the total. Because of the party's opposition to the Iraq war and raised university tu-

ition, they won a few of their added seats from Labour. It remains in the opposition.

In 2006 Kennedy stepped down as leader after being forced to admit that he had sought medical treatment for a drinking problem. He was replaced by former Olympic sprinter Sir Menzies Campbell, who in December 2007 handed the leadership over to Nick Clegg after the party had been the big loser in the May local elections. Clegg, a 40-year-old former Member of the European Parliament, hopes to prevent either larger party from winning a parliamentary majority in the next elections. This would make his party the king-makers. But there is no consensus among the Lib Dems which of the two parties they would prefer as partners or even whether they would want to be the junior partners in a coalition government.

RECENT FOREIGN AND POSTCOLONIAL POLICY

Today the sun technically does not set on the British Empire. Ten dots on the map are still ruled by Britain: Pitcairn in

The United Kingdom

the south Pacific Ocean; Bermuda, British Virgin Islands, Caymans, Leeward Islands, Turks and Caicos in the Caribbean area; the Falkland Islands, St. Helena in the south Atlantic Ocean; Gibraltar in the Mediterranean; and Diego Garcia (where the U.S. leases a military base) in the Indian Ocean. Yet it must still deal with many problems that stem from its colonialist legacy. They have included both foreign policy problems and domestic political difficulties, such as how to control and treat millions of immigrants from the former colonies (see Culture).

The Commonwealth of Nations is a loose, voluntary association of the former ruler and the ruled, and the head is the British monarch, even though some of its members are republics. In 1995 it opened its doors to such states as ex-Portuguese Mozambique, formerly French Cameroon, and ex-Belgian Rwanda. It holds its members to the Commonwealth's declared values. Zimbabwe was suspended and then it quit in 2003. In 2005 Fiji was suspended. Member states, which numbered 53 in 2008 encompassing two billion people (half of them Indians), regularly confer at Commonwealth gatherings, and sometimes Britain must assume additional, unwanted responsibilities under the aegis of the Commonwealth, such as in helping to arrange a transition to democracy in the tiny Caribbean island of Grenada after four years of totalitarian rule and an invasion by the United States and six other Caribbean island states.

Britain also faces terribly complicated problems with the smaller enclaves it rules because local inhabitants there fear their larger neighbors and look to Britain for protection. It has declared that the principle of self–determination must not be violated and that a neighboring land can absorb subject peoples only by their consent. The principle is an admirable one, but it has a high cost. The 2,900 inhabitants of the Falklands, located 300 miles (480 km) off Argentina's southern tip, called upon Britain to defend them when Argentina occupied what it calls the "Malvinas" islands for 73 days in April 1982. These islands had first been discovered by an Englishman in 1690. After the French and Spaniards had claimed them, the British established a naval garrison there in 1833. Sovereignty has been disputed ever since. It has never been tested in an international court. In 1984 a House of Commons committee decided it was "unable to reach a categorical conclusion" on the validity of the UK's claim.

Britain's military victory in 1982, costing 258 British and 649 Argentine lives, did not convince Argentina to renounce its claims to the islands. No doubt Buenos Aires also has its eye on the Falklands' potential offshore oil reserves of perhaps 500,000 barrels a day. As a deterrent, London stations 2,000 troops on the islands.

Although Britain still refuses to discuss its sovereignty over the islands unless the 3,000 largely British inhabitants request it, it established friendly relations with Argentina. The two countries set up a "sovereignty umbrella," under which they cooperate on practical issues while maintaining their separate claims to ownership. They established commercial flights between the Falklands and Argentina and collaborate on fishing licenses worth $40 million each year. A memorial to the 649 dead Argentine war dead was constructed on the islands. President Carlos Menem received a warm welcome in London in 1998, where he laid a wreath to the Britons who died in the war. Prince Charles visited Argentina the following year.

Nevertheless, Argentine politicians, including presidents, still cannot resist whipping up support at election time by verbally attacking "illegal" British rule over the "Malvinas." In 2007, on the 25th anniversary of the war, Argentine President Néstor Kirchner called again for an end to the "illegitimate" occupation, cancelled charter flights to the islands, pulled out of a 1995 agreement on oil and gas exploration, and banned energy companies that did business with the Falklands. In part because of these economic ties, Falklanders have a per capita GDP of $50,000, one of the world's highest.

The 32,000 inhabitants of Gibraltar cling to their rock and are largely self–ruling. But they rely on the protection of 5,000 British troops stationed there because they are afraid of becoming a part of Spain. In 1985 the border between Gibraltar and Spain was reopened, and discussions over its sovereignty and eventual disposition continue. [See Spain]

Painstaking negotiations with the People's Republic of China (PRC) over Hong Kong resulted in an agreement that gave the PRC sovereignty over the colony in July 1997. But it committed China to guarantee Hong Kong's capitalist economy and lifestyle for 50 years.

Special Relationship with United States

Britain's foreign policy involves close cooperation with the United States and a primary focus on Europe. As separate sovereign states with their own interests, the Americans and British sometimes have different views on issues, ranging from the British–French invasion of Suez in 1956 to the American invasion of Grenada in 1983. But many people on both sides of the Atlantic still talk of a "special relationship" between the two countries stemming from their common language and heritage, as well as from their alliance during two world wars. They cooperate closely on defense, intelligence gathering and nuclear technology.

This relationship does not exclude disagreement. Ex–Foreign Minister Geoffrey Howe spoke in 1983 of the "special intimacy and a special mutual confidence that we're able to talk with each other with the candor which one would normally expect only between one's own advisers." But some Europeans suspect that Britain is a sort of Trojan Horse for American objectives on the continent. This, among other things, influenced former French President Charles de Gaulle to reject Britain's first attempt to join the European Community.

No country's leader seized the moment more decisively after the September 11, 2001, terrorist attacks against the U.S. than did Tony Blair. They claimed 100 British lives and thereby became the worst terrorist strike against British citizens in history. He flew to America immediately after the disaster, visited "ground zero" where the World Trade Center once stood, listened to President Bush's speech to the nation from the gallery of the House of Representatives, and offered stirring words to the Americans and his own people: the terrorists "have no moral inhibition on the slaughter of the innocent. If they could have murdered not 7,000 but 70,000, does anyone doubt they would have done so and rejoiced in it? There is no compromise possible with such people, no meeting of minds, no point of understanding with such terror. Just a choice: Defeat it or be defeated by it. And defeat it we must. To the Americans, we were with you at the first. We will stay with you to the last." The queen awarded former New York Mayor Rudolph Giuliani an honorary knighthood for his leadership in the aftermath of the crisis.

Blair put his country's money where its mouth was. Within two months Britain had sent 4,200 troops to the war zone in and around Afghanistan. In the opening salvos against the Taliban regime, British submarines fired cruise missiles at key targets and put special operations forces and Royal Marines on the ground to assist the opposition's push to rout Taliban forces. In 2002 its commandos joined the Americans and other allies on search-and-destroy operations aimed at remnants of al Qaeda and Taliban forces. For a half-year it commanded the international peacekeeping forces in Kabul trying to stabilize the traumatized country. The UK took command of NATO peacekeeping forces in Afghanistan in May 2006, under Lt.-Gen. Sir David Richards. In July it announced an increase in its troop strength from 3,600 to 4,500 amidst debates at home over whether the mission has been under-resourced, misrepresented or misconceived. By 2008 it had 7,800 troops in Afghanistan, mainly in the dangerous South, to deal with fierce Taliban raids and tribal complexities though challenging counter-insurgency tactics; 87 of its soldiers had died. Between them, the U.S. and UK contribute more troops to NATO's effort in Afghanistan than all other allies put together.

The American president and people benefited greatly from Blair's support, and the two leaders developed a close personal relationship. The prime minister was mocked in left-leaning British media as the "president's poodle." He was criticized at home for getting too little in return. However, his position was always that it is difficult or impossible to do much good in the world without a powerful and engaged American partner.

The March–April 2003 war in Iraq offered a further opportunity for Britain to act as a transatlantic bridge; it provided 45,000 well-trained troops, 15% of the total. With a sensitivity to growing European concerns about the U.S. role in the world, Blair stood up for a disliked and distrusted American president and repeatedly condemned anti-Americanism, reminded his countrymen of past American contributions to their security, and warned that opposing the U.S. would merely reinforce American tendencies toward unilateralism. He did this at considerable temporary damage to his popularity at home, and even 139 of his own Labour MPs voted against the war, one of the largest rebellions in parliamentary history. He tirelessly argued the case for military action against Saddam Hussein's dictatorship and withstood merciless heckling and a strange British form of disagreement toward speakers—slow hand clapping.

His eloquence and persuasiveness paid off; at the beginning of 2003 only 13% of Britons thought their country should go to war against Iraq; by the time war began, 56% were in favor. He was able to demonstrate that America did not stand alone in the world and that the transatlantic divide ran down the middle of Europe rather than through the Atlantic. The result was a strengthening of the "special relationship" and an elevation of British influence in the world. One senior Bush official put it this way: "The special relationship had become a cliché which was being constantly trotted out, but all of a sudden it is very real. It is very deep and very operational." He continued: "This kind of partnership makes the United Kingdom a world player."

For his part, Blair reminded his party comrades at Labour's 2002 conference: "For all the resentment of America, re-

Britain's most famous lieutenants: Princes William and Harry

member one thing. The basic values of America are our values too. . . . My vision of Britain is not as the 51st state of anywhere, but I believe in this alliance, and I will fight long and hard to maintain it because alliance with America is in the interests of this country." Nevertheless, Blair was weakened politically by having led Britain into a war against Iraq that many British consider to have been unnecessary and for having gotten so little from the American president in return for his loyalty. "Bush's poodle" was a tag that hurt the prime minister.

The government was bruised by several inquiries into the political conduct of the Iraq War. In July 2004 the "Butler report" argued that the government had oversold the case for war and that there had been intelligence failures. But it refrained from questioning Blair's "good faith," criticizing the prime minister individually, or saying that he or his government had distorted the evidence to build a case for war. "There was no deliberate attempt . . . to mislead."

Just days before the May 2005 elections, confidential documents from the attorney general's office at the time of the war seemed to indicate concerns about the legality of the war, even though the attorney general stated publicly that the war was legal, in his judgment. The documents did show some diplomatic discord between London and Washington. Both agreed that Saddam had weapons of mass destruction and had to be removed. But Blair wanted to work harder to "construct a coalition" and to "exhaust" efforts to deal with the problems within the UN. The British were also somewhat more concerned about what could go wrong once war began. In 2007 Britain reduced its troops strength in Iraq from 7,000 to 5,500. About 150 British soldiers had been killed there by mid-2007. Prince Harry, who had completed his officer's training, threatened to resign if he was prohibited from deploying to Iraq with his regiment. Military leaders decided against sending him

on the grounds that his presence would make his unit an irresistible target for insurgents. However, in March 2008 he returned home from ten weeks of combat duty in Afghanistan. His tour had to be cut short after American and other foreign news media reported his deployment, which British outlets had vowed to keep secret.

The government and public were stunned by photos in newspapers of British troops in Iraq seeming to abuse Iraqi prisoners in 2003. Blair described them as "shocking and appalling." In February 2005 four soldiers were convicted of abusing prisoners, and in July 2005 eleven more were charged for mistreating prisoners in Basra, the headquarters of the British troops in Iraq. These trials strike at the heart of the government's portrayal of their soldiers as less aggressive and more adept as peacekeepers than their American allies.

Nothing tarnished the last stage of Blair's prime ministership more than the bloody aftermath of the Iraq war. Gordon Brown's tricky task is to distance himself from Blair's Iraq commitment without being tagged as soft on defense. In December 2007 the British handed over Basra province in southern Iraq to Iraqi control and began a slow withdrawal from the country possibly to be completed by the end of 2008. Only special forces and aircraft supporting U.S. soldiers will remain. Winston Churchill's words in 1926 echoed in some British ears: "I hate Iraq. I wish we had never gone to the place." Staying there, he continued, was like "living on an ungrateful volcano."

Defense

For centuries Britain was a global power, whose interest in Europe was merely to prevent any one power or combination of powers from upsetting the military balance there and dominating the entire continent. After the Second World War it shifted its primary focus to Europe. This is best seen in defense. It was a founding member of NATO, and until 1990 it organized its defense on the assumption that the chief threat was the Soviet Union. It therefore channeled the bulk of its resources into strengthening NATO rather than defending British outposts elsewhere. In 1971 it abandoned its defense commitments east of Suez.

The "NATO–first" policy necessitated fundamental changes in defense structure. Britain converted the once–mighty Royal Navy into a specialized force whose purpose was primarily to assist the American navy and to defend against submarines. In the 1970s it phased out its attack aircraft carriers. The Falkland Islands war in 1982 revealed how this change in force

The United Kingdom

structure could affect Britain's commitments outside of Europe. It had to lease luxury liners and merchant vessels just to transport its troops and equipment to those faraway islands. The conflict prompted Britain to bolster its capabilities to project military power in the world by canceling the scheduled deactivation of an aircraft carrier and the Royal Navy's last two amphibious assault ships.

The heart of the British defense effort today is the army. It has thousands of soldiers on station in Northern Ireland. It deploys a diminishing number of troops on the European continent, mainly in Germany. The costs for this force are great, especially since Britain has a volunteer army. With the disappearance of the Soviet threat to Europe, NATO faces fundamental restructuring that affects the British military. In 1991 the allies decided to establish a sizable rapid reaction force to confront unforeseen threats anywhere in Europe. This new force is stationed mainly in Germany and is commanded by a British officer.

Within Britain itself, the most controversial aspect of British defense was its nuclear arsenal. Aside from France, the UK is the only European country to possess atomic weapons. The Thatcher government decided to replace the aging Polaris vessels (each carrying 16 missiles) with more modern submarines, capable of firing ultramodern American–made Trident missiles, each of which could attack eight separate targets. As part of its nuclear modernization program, the UK also equipped Tornado jets with the capability of delivering nuclear bombs. The new Labour Party, which took power in May 1997, dropped its long–standing opposition to Britain's nuclear force. But in post–cold war Europe, nuclear weapons have become largely irrelevant. The UK decided in 1998 to halve the number of its nuclear weapons at sea to about 200 on four Trident submarines. This is its total number of warheads.

The government debated what do about its four Vanguard-class Trident submarines that will reach the end of their lives in 2024. The Blair government decided in 2007 to devote £20 billion ($40 billion) to build a new generation of nuclear submarines to carry a reduced number (ca. 160) of American-supplied Trident missiles. This makes Britain's nuclear arsenal the smallest among the five permanent UN Security Council members and the only one of them whose warheads are based on a single platform. Since it relies on American Trident missiles, it keeps the cost of its nuclear arsenal at half the level of France's. Nevertheless, the government faced the biggest revolt in parliament since the onset of the Iraq war, with 95

Labour backbenchers voting no. But approval was won because of solid support from the Tory opposition.

Although nuclear targeting is coordinated with the United States, only the British prime minister can order the use of Britain's nuclear weapons. The willingness of the British government since the 1950s to permit the deployment of American nuclear weapons on British soil, which are not under the direct command of the British prime minister, reflects NATO's importance in British defense planning. "Dual–key" safeguards were considered unnecessary because the UK had a firm agreement with the U.S. (which has never been published) that no American nuclear weapons could ever be launched from Britain without the approval of the British government.

In 1991 Britain's participation in the war to drive Iraq out of Kuwait was solidly supported at home. The UK sent a powerful contingent of land, air and naval forces serving under the overall command of American General Norman Schwarzkopf, whom the Queen knighted after the successful campaign. In 1998 it dispatched an aircraft carrier back to the Persian Gulf to show its solidarity with the American and UN efforts to force Saddam Hussein to open his weapons facilities to international inspectors.

No sooner were the warriors home than the government began a steady reduction. In the decade and a half to 2004, it cut the army from 156,000 to 116,670 and then further to 102,000 in 2007, the navy and marines from 63,000 to 42,370, and the RAF from 89,000 to 53,620. Infantry battalions sank from 55 to 40 and front-line tanks from 699 to 304. The British Army of the Rhine was halved to 22,000. How-

ever, Britain built up its special operations forces to 2,000–3,000.

The Royal Navy has responsibilities in the south Atlantic, off west Africa, in the Caribbean and around the Middle East. It operates in Iraqi waters protecting oil terminals. In March 2007, fifteen of its sailors were temporarily abducted by Iran. Its Harrier pilots support ground operations in Iraq and Afghanistan, and its marines fight in Afghanistan. To perform these functions, it retains its three small (a fourth the size of America's larger ones) but expensive aircraft carriers and four ballistic-missile submarines (Tridents). But its fleet of 28 attack-submarines was cut to 11, and its 49 frigates and destroyers to 25. The RAF lost nine of its 30 front-line combat squadrons; its total front-line fighters and bombers sank from 630 to 500, some of which are flown by women. Its ships must often put to sea without their full crew or equipment. The air force has taken control of the navy's Harrier jump-jets, and in 2007 its carriers sailed without planes four-fifths of the time. To keep up the crews' training, the navy allowed allied aircraft to land and fly off its ships. The Brown government hinted in 2007 that two new aircraft carriers may be ordered that would carry Joint Strike Fighters, co-produced with the U.S. Any acquisitions are bound to strain an annual military budget of £30 billion ($60 billion), constituting 2.3% of GDP, compared with America's 4%.

Britain sent 35 combat aircraft, eight ships and 6,600 troops to participate in the air war over Yugoslavia in 1999. The UK has increasingly assumed peacekeeping responsibilities. In 2004 it had 1,400 deployed to Bosnia, 1,400 to Kosovo (900 in 2007), and 431 to Cyprus.

Navy to cut its fleet by half

■ Six destroyers and frigates to be mothballed ■ Retired First Sea Lord attacks 'outrageous' plans

The ruling Labour party produced a long overdue Strategic Defence Review published in 1998. It emphasized mobility, flexibility, sustainability, interoperability, and rapid reaction. It called for a nimble British military capable of going quickly "to the crisis, rather than have the crisis come to us." It followed up with a major restructuring of its military, announced in December 2003, calling for increased spending to enhance interoperability with U.S. forces. It is assumed that Britain could fight a large war only alongside the U.S. and that its soldiers should be better prepared for multiple, smaller sized expeditionary operations in remote places, capable of taking on terrorist groups. They should therefore be lighter, quicker and more technologically capable.

In July 2004 further cuts were announced, ultimately bringing down total strength of the armed forces to 179,000. With 22,000 British soldiers operating abroad and in Northern Ireland at the time, this would be a strain. The air force lost some training planes and an air base, and the navy shed three aged destroyers and three new frigates. In exchange the military received more special forces and high-tech weaponry. Defense spending was cut by over a fifth from 1990 to 2007, to 2.5% of GDP, the lowest since 1930. Despite the reductions, defense spending is still one of the highest percentages in Europe.

The government shows an increased interest in a European defense capability that could, when necessary, operate without the U.S. The prime minister met with French President Jacques Chirac at St. Malo in December 1998 to give his blessing to the European Security and Defence Policy (ESDP), which decided a year later to build a European rapid-reaction force that can act when NATO chooses not to do so. Britain's cooperation with France and Germany has tightened.

As viewed from London, the latter two countries' attempt at the time of the 2003 Iraq war to assume joint political and economic leadership over Europe was unsuccessful. In order to lead in Europe, they need Britain's support, especially in the fields of foreign and defense policy. Blair saw that the UK had become the indispensable link between the "old" and "new" Europe. This was confirmed by France's Dominique de Villepin, who said in London that "there can be no Europe without defense and no European defense without Britain."

Blair made clear that his country would support neither a separate EU military headquarters (the Franco-German plans for which were scrapped in the fall of 2003) nor participate in any "autonomous" operations unless NATO declined

to be involved. He began meeting separately with the French and German leaders to discuss the direction Europe should go and particularly to spearhead European defense efforts. Before leaving office, Blair stressed that Britain must preserve and fund a military able not only to keep the peace, but also to fight wars. His successor continued the quiet talks with France's new president, Nicolas Sarkozy, to work out a new accord on European defense. France discovered in the Iraq crisis that it could not unify Europe against the Americans and British, and it is open to closer cooperation with both.

ECONOMY

Britain for almost two centuries has been a highly industrialized and developed nation. It led the Industrial Revolution in the 18th and 19th centuries, but after World War II it enjoyed less efficiency than some of its newer rivals. Only 23.4% of the present gross domestic product now comes from industry and manufacturing (employing 22%), while service industries provide 75.4% of GDP and 77% of jobs and agriculture 1% of GDP and 1% of employment. British farmers produce more than half of the country's food requirements. Two–thirds of Britain's agricultural land is used for grazing; the main field crops are wheat, barley, oats, potatoes and sugar beets.

Because of the extraction of oil and natural gas from the North Sea, Britain became self–sufficient in these sources of energy in the 1980s. It remains one of the dozen or so largest oil producers in the world. But the North Sea supplies are gradually running out, and British drivers pay the highest gasoline prices in the world ($6.65 per gallon in 2008). It already gets a third of its electricity from gas and does not want a greater reliance on this one source. The UK is no longer the biggest coal producer in western Europe, but its coal supplies could last for another 300 years if needed. EU environmental rules and halts in government subsidies caused many coal plants to shut down. Along with Sweden and Germany, Britain is the only country in Europe that is meeting its Kyoto greenhouse gas emissions target, so it does not resist such closures. Unlike Germany, which gets 28% of its electricity from renewable sources, Britain gets only 3%.

Having calculated that world energy demand will increase by 50% in 2030, especially given the increased needs of China and India, and worried about climate change, the Brown government declared in 2008 that investment into a new generation of nuclear reactors is needed. In 1996 the government had privatized its

nuclear-power arm, British Energy, but the upfront capital costs of atomic plants make long delays inevitable. However, nuclear energy produces little carbon dioxide, the technology is well developed, and uranium can be bought from stable countries like Australia and Canada.

No reactors have been built since the 1980s, and its two oldest commercial nuclear stations were closed in January 2007. Nuclear power provides about a fifth of Britain's electricity, but its 10 plants are aging, with only one to be left running in 2023. This sudden turn-about is controversial, but voters and the Tory party are generally receptive to the idea that nuclear power should continue to make up a part of the nuclear mix. Polls show that more British now favor it than oppose it. Waste is stored temporarily at the Sellafield site, and plans call for a long-term underground facility to be built.

Temporary Decline in Economic Performance

Economic and social shifts in Britain helped to bring important changes in some fundamental assumptions. From 1945 to 1970, it had generally been assumed (and was broadly the case) that despite temporary ups and downs, the economy would always continue to improve, that inflation was unimportant, that full employment was normal and that if the economy got a little out of kilter, it could be put back on course by reducing or raising demand through taxes and public spending (classic economic methods of the late British economist, John Maynard Keynes). It was therefore widely accepted that governments should regulate the economy in order to maintain employment while expanding the welfare state out of ever–increasing national prosperity. By 1975, state spending amounted to more than 60% of national income.

The Keynsian assumptions, which more or less enjoyed an acceptance by both major parties, were torn asunder in the 1970s. At the beginning of the decade inflation began to rise, reaching the stratospheric level of 25% annually in the mid–1970s and 22% in 1980. Unemployment began to rise steadily, and the old cure did not seem to work any more.

As economic growth slowed to a standstill, governments were faced with an unpleasant dilemma: demand for welfare services continued to grow while the national income to pay for them did not. British economic discussions began to be preoccupied with "managing decline." The nationalized industries (most of which had passed to public control in the immediate postwar years) were performing poorly and were becoming an increasing drain on the nation's productivity,

The United Kingdom

thereby discrediting the very idea of public ownership. Everywhere people began talking about the "English disease."

The Thatcher Revolution

Margaret Thatcher brought dramatic economic changes during her prime ministership from 1979 to 1990. Neither the Tory government of John Major nor Tony Blair's Labour government, which took office in 1997, moved to undo her reforms in any fundamental way. She denationalized more than a third of Britain's nationalized industries, including Rolls–Royce, British Airways and the British Gas Corporation. The sale of these brought more than $40 billion into the state treasury, eliminated the need for taxpayers to subsidize them, and reaped handsome annual tax revenues. In 1987 the government began selling shares of British Petroleum. In 1988 plans were announced to privatize the electric industry in England and Wales. British Telecom was sold, and in 1996 its merger with the American MCI was made public. Thatcher's large–scale privatization program included two-dozen major companies. Nevertheless, state spending still accounts for 39% of GDP (compared with 30% in the U.S.), roughly the same percentage as when she took office.

Thatcher had argued that the state was overspending, and the shortfalls were being covered by public borrowing and expanding the money supply, rather than by taxes. These expedients stimulated inflation and absorbed the capital that was desperately needed to finance industrial innovation. The cure, she argued, was to restrict the money supply and cut public expenditures, which would both reduce inflation and free investment capital. To create economic incentives, income taxes should be cut. Finally, trade union power had to be curbed.

Her pride and her optimism were borne out by the facts: Since the country began pulling out of recession in 1981, productivity increased at an annual rate of 3.5%. The economy grew at an annual rate of 3%. Inflation was down from a high of 24.2% to 3.3% in 1995. Taxes had been reduced slightly, and the average voter's real pre–tax income had increased by 25% since 1979. From 1971 to 1994 real disposable income grew by almost 50%, and spending on social benefits increased by 168%. Britons live more prosperous lives. Nevertheless, the UK is the only EU country in which working hours have increased, to 43.4 hours.

Unemployment was higher when she left than the 4.3% when she took office. Nevertheless, a million new jobs had been created under her rule, in part because of incentives to small enterprises. Also, the jobs of those who were employed seemed far less threatened than in the early 1980s. Interest rates were falling, and the pound was much stronger. Its stock market was booming, and the UK had again become a leading creditor nation. Public borrowing had fallen to 1% of national income. Most important, she had restored morale and seemed to have ended decades of relative economic decline.

After her 1987 victory, London's *Sunday Times* pronounced that Thatcher has brought about Britain's "biggest transformation since the Industrial Revolution." Indeed, her economic performance profoundly changed her country. She created what she calls a "property–owning democracy," in which "every earner shall be an owner." Two–thirds of Britons now own their homes, compared to 50% in 1979, and car ownership has risen from 54% to 66%. In 1979 four times as many Britons belonged to trade unions as owned shares in the stock market. But by 1989 the number of stock–holders had tripled from 7% to 21%. As a result of a fall in union membership by one–fourth to nine million, the number of union members and stock–holders are now equal.

Thatcher enormously reduced the power of the once–mighty labor unions, which had been able to topple the governments of her two predecessors. She introduced laws that limit unions' legal immunities. They restrict picketing rights, ban secondary picketing and political strikes, make national unions financially responsible for the actions of their members, and require unions to have a secret balloting of members before declaring a strike. She rooted out one of the main causes of the "English disease" by taking on the bosses of the most powerful unions and crushing them: the steel workers in 1980, the coal miners in 1985 and the teachers in 1986. By 1987 strikes were at a 50–year low; workdays lost to union disputes declined from 29.5 million in 1979 to 1.9 million in 1986.

The reduction in the number and length of strikes was, in part, due to workers' and employees' fear of losing their jobs and to their realization that real earnings for those with work has risen almost 35% between 1980 and 1987. There has also been a change of attitudes: many workers associate unions with strikes and therefore have increasingly turned their backs on the unions, whose membership has continued to decline. An important result for the overall economy is that the unions are no longer able to block the introduction of state–of–the–art technology in order to protect jobs. Thus, while from 1974–80 output per worker in British manufacturing did not increase at all, from 1981–7 it grew by 40%. So powerful had the unions been that many people wondered: "Who governs?" After she was finished, no one would suspect that it was the union bosses.

More and more workers became homeowners (43% by 1983 and one–third of even unskilled laborers by 1988) thanks in part to Margaret Thatcher's policy of selling many state–owned council houses to their occupants. By the time her party finally left power in 1997, 68% of all households owned their own homes. It is not surprising that the percentage of Britons who consider themselves to belong to the middle class increased from 30% of the population in 1979 to roughly 50% in 1987. Their lifestyles became more and more like those of the middle class; this was given added impetus by the education changes in the 1970s that largely did away with the several schooling tracks and brought most British schoolchildren together in one school. The massive occupational shifts and breakdown in elite structure in the educational system fostered increasing social mobility. It is no wonder that persons who lived in several classes in their own lifetime ceased to use class as a major political reference point. It is quite simply no longer accurate to speak of "two Britains," one a deprived working class and the other a traditional upper class.

Thatcher created a more prosperous and productive Britain that is still the basis for the country's exemplary economic performance. But her chief economic legacy was one of the mind. The pursuit of comfort and wealth had become marks of bad form. But she made prosperity an acceptable goal and free–market capitalism morally defensible. Tony Blair's Labour Party not only embraces both, but he won the 1997 elections by promising that his government could manage Thatcher's economy even more competently. By the 1990s anybody working in Britain's offices and factories could see that they are much better and more productively run than was the case two decades earlier. Industrial relations have improved dramatically.

Labor Unions

Public sympathy and enthusiasm for labor unions gradually eroded in the 1970s and early 1980s. In order to gain wage restraint from the powerful unions, Labour governments made so many concessions to them that many persons began to blame the unions for high prices and many of the economic problems. Their revulsion at the excessive "unelected power" which union bosses wielded boiled to the surface in the 1978–9 "winter of discontent," when coal and transportation strikes threatened to paralyze the entire nation.

Both the economic recession and the Conservatives' broadside attacks against the Labour Party in general and the unions in particular greatly weakened the latter. Between 1979 and 2007 their membership dropped from 12 million to 7.5 million. In 1979 more than half the workforce was unionized; 38% was in 1990 and 29% in 2002. In 2007, 16.6% of private sector employees and 58.8% of public-sector employees were unionized. Union-negotiated settlements cover more than 70% of those public-sector workers. By election time in 1983, almost three–fourths of all Britons favored stricter laws to regulate unions; an astonishing three–fifths of all trade unionists also favored legal curbs on union power. Union popularity declined further as the result of a protracted coal miners' strike in 1984–5. Union leader Arthur Scargill fanned the flames of anti-unionism with public pledges to bring down Thatcher's government. He failed, and her ability to break trade union power is her most lasting legacy.

In the 1990s strikes were at their lowest level in more than a half-century. In 1979, 29.5 man–days were lost to strikes; in 1995 that figure had fallen to 4.15. In the 21st century the figures are even more dramatic: only 158,000 working days were lost to strikes in 2005, compared with 12.9 million in the 1970s and 7.2 million in the 1980s. This is fewer than in the U.S. and Canada, and about half the rate for the EU and OECD countries. Perhaps because of affluence and higher home ownership, strikes also tend to be much shorter. One expert noted: "It's much more risky to strike now. If you don't do it right according to the law, you end up in court."

Unions affiliated with the TUC lost a third of their members after the Tories came to power in 1979. Even within the Labour Party the unions' influence has been reduced, though not eliminated. The support of the trade unions for the party can still be helpful in a crunch. They provide more than half of its money.

The gap between the working and middle classes has also been narrowed by the changing composition of the labor unions. The increase in the number of civil service employees, the growth of the service sector within the economy, and the rise of computer–related and other high–technology industries in the south of England and especially around London and Cambridge prompted the growth of so–called "white collar unionism." That is, union members were no longer exclusively manual workers in factories and mines, but they could be teachers, engineers in a nationalized industry, secretaries in Whitehall, etc.

With rising inflation and talk of "paring down the public sector," these white–collar unions even became quite militant in pressing their demands. Thus, Britain began to experience a different breed of striker, from nurses and hospital personnel to civil servants. This militancy among the white-collar employees has helped even more to bridge the social gap between workers and employees and to break down class divisions.

There are still workers concentrated in large manufacturing or mining industries living in rented council housing in working class sections and remaining in a largely isolated social environment. They confront employers and managers whose political attitudes are also traditional and are diametrically opposed to those of their workers. These groups are far more likely to retain a strong loyalty either to the Labour Party or the Conservative Party and a strong class–consciousness. However, these kinds of workers and managers are becoming a diminishing minority in Britain's more service–oriented economy. Union members in the service sectors work in an environment that brings them into contact with all other classes, a factor that reduces, rather than sharpens class-consciousness. As a consequence, their voting behavior is far less class–bound. They can be attracted to parties that portray a new, non–class image and seem capable of overcoming the old social divides.

Britain and Europe

In 1973 the UK entered the EU, a move that has had a dramatic impact on its economy. The EU25 now buys 56.8% of British exports, compared to 31% in 1972. It provides 55.8% of its imports. Still, many British remain critical of their country's entry into the EU. A 2006 poll indicated that only 31% of Britons trusted the EU.

In practice, British governments have tended to put British interests ahead of European interests. They have been cool on a common EU energy policy, a directly elected European Parliament and European Monetary Union (EMU). Britain traditionally showed little interest in deepening European integration, and it tends to be opposed to political and supranational integration. But it supports enlargement, perhaps to water down the union, as some critics contend.

Margaret Thatcher tried hard to reduce the British contribution to the EU budget. Declaring that "I want my money back," she insisted on a "British rebate" of two-thirds the difference between what Britain paid into the EU and what it got back out. The Blair government declared in 2005 that it will not give this up until significant changes are made in the Union's Common Agriculture Policy (CAP), which gobbles up 40% of all EU spending; about a quarter of CAP spending goes to France. By 2005 Britain had become the fourth-largest net contributor as a percentage of national income and the second largest in total cash contribution, two and one-half times more than France pays in.

Thatcher signed the Single European Act in 1986 because it was an economic, not political, step toward integration. In 1989–90 she remained suspicious of "deepening" EU unity on the grounds that it would undermine national sovereignty and that it is no time to create new bureaucracies and weaken national parliaments just when Eastern European nations are digging themselves out from underneath their bureaucracies and breathing new life into their legislatures. Not all British, not even all Tories, agreed with her foot–dragging, and this contributed to her fall.

At the historic 1991 summit in Maastricht, Britain agreed to greater economic and political union on the condition that the UK could "opt out" of an eventual single European currency, which it chose to do when the euro was introduced in 12 EU countries. It also rejected moves to make an EU "social policy" mandatory for all members, and the Euroskeptic Tories threaten to stop observing it. There was much resistance in all parties, especially the Conservative party, to the Maastricht Treaty. However, parliament finally accepted it in 1993.

The Labour governments are more supportive of British membership in a more united Europe although Prime Ministers Blair and Brown promised to put British interests first. The UK would have to worry about meeting the criteria for EMU. Its budget in 2008 had a deficit of 3.2% of GDP, and overall public debt stood at 33% of GDP.

One of New Labour's first acts was to transfer the power to set interest rates from the then Chancellor of Exchequer Gordon Brown to an unelected panel of the Bank of England. Greater independence for central banks is one of the EU's prerequisites for participation in the common currency. The euro remains unpopular in the UK. The Blair government decided that the UK would not join the first wave of monetary union, and the prime minister found it publicly expedient to announce in 2000 that "people don't want Europe interfering in every aspect of people's national lives." But he continued to steer a course toward Europe and the euro.

In April 2004 he stunned Europe with an announcement that he would call for a referendum over whether to adopt the EU's new constitutional treaty that the leaders of the 25 member states agreed on. This would have been the first time a Eu-

The United Kingdom

ropean treaty had ever been put to a vote in the UK. All agreed that he had taken a very risky step. London bookmakers immediately gave such a referendum 1-to-6 odds of succeeding in a country where, according to a 2004 poll, only 28% of Britons thought EU membership was "a good thing."

The Blair government was saved from certain defeat by the French and Dutch voters' rejection of the treaty on May 29 and June 1, 2005. This was a blessing for Britain, which has always had two chief aims in Europe: slow down the drive for political union and prevent Franco-German domination of European politics. The death of the EU constitution accomplished both, and it is primarily France, not Britain, that bore the blame for it. French ex-President Jacques Chirac had foreseen this and warned in his final TV address before the vote that defeat would be a victory for those (read Britain) who had always wanted Europe to be little more than a "free-trade zone."

In the campaign the French government had heaped criticism on what it saw as the "Anglo-Saxon" economic model. In supposed contrast to France's and Germany's shorter work week, higher welfare benefits and restrictions on the influx of low-wage workers from central Europe, Britain

is an economic free-for-all that lacks all these amenities. This is a caricature. Since New Labour assumed power in 1997, unemployment has fallen to 5.2% in 2008 (compared with France's 7.9% and Germany's 8.1%). Blair asked a valid question: "What type of social model is it that has 20 million unemployed in Europe?"

The failed EU constitutional treaty was doctored up by getting rid of the most unpopular provisions (about 10% of the original text). The revised version, which was not labeled a "constitution," was adopted by the member states in Lisbon in December 2007. The Lisbon Treaty is deeply unpopular in Britain, and the Tories regard it as only cosmetically different from its ill-fated predecessor. Prime Minister Brown, never known as an EU enthusiast, showed his displeasure by turning up three hours late for the official signing in Lisbon. This infuriated his fellow chiefs of government, who were already seething because Blair had negotiated various opt-outs for Britain. However, Brown reversed Blair's earlier promise of a plebiscite and announced that the new treaty would be ratified by parliament. To mend fences with the EU, he made a charm offensive to Brussels seven months after taking office and declared that "Britain must be at the centre of Europe."

Current Economic Situation

Spending for social welfare and health care has been greatly increased. Child and pensioner poverty rates have declined to near average EU levels. All this is paid for by tax levels on a par with most continental countries; government spending is 42% of GDP.

The Blair government introduced new market and financial discipline to the National Health Service (NHS). A 2006 study concluded that middle-aged English are "much healthier" than their American counterparts even though the health-care system costs half as much ($5,635 versus $2,231) per capita than in the U.S. Smoking and drinking rates are slightly higher in England while there is greater obesity in the U.S. Life expectancy at birth is 77.2 years in America and 78.5 in Britain (77.2 for men and 82.7 for women). The NHS universally covers all citizens, while 16% of Americans under age 65 are without health insurance. The NHS therefore provides important psychological reassurance.

The British and French finally agreed to construct a twin–bore, 32–mile channel tunnel (dubbed "Chunnel") through which an auto–rail link between the two countries passes. Road vehicles are loaded on trains at terminals on both sides of the Channel and whisked at a speed of 100 miles per hour from one side to the other. The Channel became what Napoleon had described as "a ditch that will be leaped whenever one has the boldness to try." The two nations' leaders shared a bold vision of the future. In 1990 the burrowing French and British crews linked up under the Channel, and the Chunnel opened in 1994.

It is mired in serious financial difficulties, having cost twice as much to build as projected. Repayment of the $11.2 billion debt had to be suspended while its finances were restructured, which was done in 2006 and 2007. The problem is that too few passengers are using this undersea link even to pay the interest on the construction costs. It was assumed that 10 million passengers would use the Chunnel each year, but in 2003 only 6.3 million did so. Also only 1.7 million tons of freight was shipped through in 2003, far short of the 5 million ton estimate each year. The result was a severe cash crunch although the tunnel operator, Groupe Eurotunnel, reported its first annual net profit in 2007.

In November 2007 Britain completed its $12 billion 109-kilometer (68-mile) high-speed railway linking the Channel Tunnel to the newly renovated terminal, St. Pancras station. Its imposing ironwork trainshed had once been the world's largest enclosed space. The train journey to Paris now takes two and one-quarter hours going 186 mph, and passengers can also travel to Brussels.

The 600–foot long boring machine which led others in clawing through 7.5 million cubic meters of chalk–marl one mile beneath the sea which divides Britain and France.

The United Kingdom has been heavily involved in overseas trade for many centuries, and the importance of that trade continues to grow. In the last 50 years, the export of goods and services has moved from being one–fifth of the gross domestic product to one–third. Of these exports, 15% go to the United States.

After the U.S., Britain is the world's largest investor abroad. After the U.S., it was also the favorite destination of foreign direct investment (FDI). Many well–known "American" brands are now British: Brooks Brothers belongs to Marks and Spencer, and Diageo owns Burger King and Pillsbury. Foreigners own everything from London's water supply to its airports. Its steel industry has almost been entirely purchased. In 1995 it surpassed Japan to become the largest source of foreign direct investment in the U.S. By 1999 the UK was directing 30% of its direct investment to America, while the U.S. sends a fifth of its foreign direct investment to Britain. By 2003 the U.S. had invested almost as much in the UK as it had in all of Asia, Latin America, Middle East and Africa. After the turn of the century only the U.S. and China attract more money from foreigners than does Britain. In part, this is due to the fact that Britain's labor costs are lower than in some major industrialized countries.

The City of London (a small area within greater metropolitan London) is of immense significance in international finance. It has the world's largest insurance market, the lengthiest listing of overseas securities, the highest proportion of the Eurodollar market, the biggest foreign exchange market and the largest secondary market for Islamic bonds. It generates a fifth of all corporate-tax revenues in the UK. In 1986 a "big bang" occurred in the London financial world: the financial markets were largely deregulated, and foreign companies were permitted to trade in British financial markets for the first time. The overall effect has been to make London the world's most important financial center. Each day, 600,000 people go to work in 580 banks; that is more than the total population of Frankfurt. Big American banks have their continental headquarters there, and London's traders have grown to control 30% of global foreign exchange trading. Britain's financial institutions are fully competent in dealing with the euro, even though its political leaders are not yet ready for it. All this financial activity has helped make London the world's second-most expensive city in the world for expatriate employers, after Moscow; New York was not even among the top 10.

Brown inherited an economy that no one would call "diseased" any more. Its growth rate was 2.7% per year from 1998 to 2006, and 2.9% in 2008. This steady expansion pushed up per capita GDP above that of Germany and France. At 5.2% in 2008, unemployment is one of the lowest of any major country in Europe. Inflation is 2.2%. The budget deficit was 3.2% of GDP in 2008. Roughly a quarter of all foreign direct investment flowing into the EU15 nations goes to the UK.

Britain was hurt in 2007 by the credit crisis in the U.S. The two countries' business cycles have historically moved together. Northern Rock became the first British bank since the Victorian era to experience a run, and in February 2008 the Labour government did the unthinkable: it nationalized it, the first such action since 1984. This hurt the image of "New" Labour, which under Blair's leadership had discarded the commitment to "common ownership of the means of production."

Living standards are below those in the United States. Productivity lags behind that of the U.S., Germany and France. It is higher in foreign multinational firms, which employ two million Britons, primarily because they invest more. The Blair government introduced the country's first minimum wage law. But the current economic success is also due to less cumbersome business regulations, cost effectiveness, and a flexible labor market. Privatization is well advanced.

In 2002, 400,000 rural Britons marched in London to dramatize what they called a "crisis in the countryside." It suffers from a depression in agriculture, made worse by the disastrous handling of the foot-and-mouth disease. Since the mid-1990s farm incomes have halved, and weekenders and 100,000 Britons resettling in rural Britain each year have driven house prices so high (overall they trebled in the decade to 2007) that many locals can no longer afford to live where they grew up. The positive side of this real estate inflation is that the value of farmers' assets has risen by about 40% since 1992. Thus the average farmer possesses an average net worth of 700,000 pounds ($1.4 million). In 2004 fox hunting that involves a pack of dogs sniffing out foxes and killing them was prohibited. Riding with hounds is still permitted, as is the shooting of foxes forced out of cover by a maximum of two dogs. Some judges have found the Hunting Act confusing and poorly written, and only a handful of hunters have been convicted of violating it.

Britain is the fifth most popular tourist destination in the world, attracting 25 million foreign visitors annually; it is Americans' most popular destination. The 125,000 mostly small tourist businesses employ 1.75 million people, more than agriculture, food production, coal mining, steel, car and aircraft manufacturing, and textiles combined. In the 1990s it was responsible for creating a sixth of the new jobs.

CULTURE

The impact and pervasiveness of British culture on the rest of the world has been out of all proportion to the size and population of the United Kingdom. While those who participated in the Beatlemania of the 1960s might disagree, two British

Globe Theatre

The United Kingdom

gifts to world culture stand out as most important. First, the achievement of English writers in producing a magnificent body of literature has influenced the way people think around the world. Within English literature, certainly Shakespeare and the King James Bible have been most important. One-third of the world's most translated authors come from the UK.

Second, the development of constitutional, parliamentary democracy set an example to all the world of how men and women may live in freedom and guide their own destinies. It also shows how compromise and civility rather than coercion are the best ways to pull together the social fabric. In a world in which the majority of human beings do not enjoy political or individual freedoms, and other countries that attempt democracy are unable to achieve stability, the United Kingdom stands a worthy example of a free society living under laws.

The widespread knowledge of English as a first or second language throughout the world speaks for itself, be it the Americanized or British version. It has become the language of scientific expression almost worldwide. English is not spoken throughout England, Wales, Scotland and Ireland in an identical fashion. Local expressions and local pronunciations vary widely. The urbanized lower classes of London traditionally speak "Cockney" English, which the average American can seldom understand. Language has traditionally been a key to identifying the social class of a British person. The reason lies partly in the educational system.

Education and Class in Britain

The traditional school system had been tracked in such a way that a child's educational program was more or less fixed at age eleven. After the crucial "eleven-plus exam," some children went into trade or commercial schools. Others went into the more elite, state–supported grammar schools or the independent, privately endowed "public schools" (the most prestigious being Eton, Harrow and Winchester). "Public Schools" were especially geared to preparing pupils for the few seats in universities, especially at Oxford and Cambridge (known collectively as "Oxbridge"), which held the keys to success in politics, industry and scholarship. A 2007 study concluded that the top ten universities in the world were either American or British: Cambridge and Oxford placed second and third, Imperial College London fifth, and University College London ninth.

In a 1992 study of the top 100 persons in Britain's elite, *The Economist* found that two–thirds had attended public schools, and more than half had studied at Oxford

Eton boys

and Cambridge. Only a decade later, in 2002, those percentages had fallen noticeably to 46 public school and 35 Oxbridge graduates. The number of women had climbed from four to a mere five. The loosening hold of public school and Oxbridge alumni reflects the growth of competition, especially in business, which has resulted from deregulation and globalization. Life in Britain's larger and more multinational companies is no longer as cozy as it used to be. Ambitious products of the country's expanded university system have claimed top positions once reserved for the well-born and those from famous schools.

Critics had long charged that the traditional educational system actually hardened and perpetuated class lines in British society. That is a major reason why the old grammar and secondary modern schools were fused into "comprehensive" secondary schools, in which all pupils learn under one roof. State-sponsored schools can no longer select for ability, and state scholarships to the coveted private schools were eliminated. About a tenth of all pupils attend the fee–paying "public schools." Some say that these reforms actually lowered educational standards, and the gap between rich and poor people's education has in fact widened. However, to make the testing easier, less intimidating, and fairer, the old A-levels taken in the pupil's final year of secondary school, which were crucial for university admission, were changed. They now take "Advanced Supplementary," or AS-level, exams in their second-to-last year in school, and they are permitted to retake some of those tests to improve their grades. They then take the more difficult A2 exams at the end of their last year. Their final grades are based on the results of the two years combined.

In 1993 the government introduced an Education Bill to parliament that took school reform another step forward. After haphazard and underfunded reforms un-

der Thatcher and Major, British schools still reflect the social stratification of the country. A majority of pupils leave full–time education or training at age 16. As a result, less than half the work force is classified as skilled, compared with 85% in Germany and 75% in France. Tony Blair's campaign appeals in 1997 for higher academic standards and lower class sizes fell on sympathetic ears. The feeling is widespread that British schools are not fully prepared for the challenges of the 21st century. About 7% of pupils attend independent fee-paying schools that provide a good education for £7,000 ($14,000) per year.

Two-fifths of university–age Britons (up from 5% in 1960 and one–eighth in 1980) study in one of the 87 universities or polytechnic schools. The Labour government wants to raise this to 50%. This dramatic increase in enrollment broke the budget and required that students contribute to the cost of their education.

Many of these students were distressed by the Labour government's decision to end tuition–free higher education and to levy in 2006 a flat-rate £3,000 ($6,000) yearly tuition charge. Adding the £5,000 ($10,000) the taxpayer provides, this falls well short of the $18,700 *The Economist* estimates it costs each year to educate a student at Oxford or Imperial College. This is on top of the more than $3,000 room and board costs, much of it borrowed or obtained through grants, including from local governments. Although Britons with a university education earn 17% more over a lifetime, there is resentment over such tuition and any talk of raising it to a level needed to cover the annual cost of a student.

Some enterprising British universities attract large numbers of non-EU foreign students and charge them American–level tuition of £5,000 ($10,000) per year (almost two times higher). Britain attracts more than 15% of the world's international students. For instance, one half of all undergraduate students at the London School of Economics (LSE) are non-EU foreigners. In 2005, some 9% of university students came from outside the EU; that is one fourth more than in the preceding year. To improve its bottom line and be more able to compete with top American universities, Oxford plans to raise its number of non-EU students from 8% to 15% over a decade, deemphasize undergraduate teaching, get away from its hallmark tiny tutorial groups and have graduate students teach undergraduates.

Despite the emotional resistance to higher tuition, the Blair government succeeded in winning a House of Commons vote in 2004 by a whisker-thin five-vote majority authorizing a rise in tuition in English universities (Wales and Scotland are different) up to £3,000 ($6,000) from 2006.

Only the most affluent pay the full amount. Those from lower–income families paid less, and the lowest 30% paid nothing. Students will borrow the money through a state-managed loan system and begin paying it back after graduation and when their income reaches $25,000 per year. Although low by American standards, this rise reflects an important shift in thinking that is very controversial in Britain.

The educational system remains a target of criticism. Critics argue that spending for it was cut by 10% in real terms under Thatcher. Even her minister for information technology, Geoffrey Pattie, had complained, "schools are turning out dangerously high quotas of illiterate, delinquent unemployables." According to an *Economist* survey in 2007, more than a third of adults left school with no formal qualifications. A sixth were judged functionally illiterate and a fifth innumerate. In 2002, spending on higher education was a mere 1.1% of GDP, compared to 2.3% in the U.S. A passionate controversy also rages in England over allowing schools to select their pupils according to academic ability.

While there is considerable dissatisfaction with the educational system, there is little doubt that Britain's establishment and class system have changed dramatically in the last decades. Intelligent and ambitious individuals have always been able to succeed in Britain, whose society has long been less rigid than in many other countries. But in the UK today, status is largely earned, not inherited. BBC producer Nick Guthrie speaks of a revolution in the class system and argues, "it's not so much your family that matters; it's what you've achieved, and of course how much money you've got." Prime Minister Gordon Brown agrees, noting that on corporate boards, "titles are out, for the most part. Today it's not who you are, but what you have done. . . . The old class system is not dead. But it is much weaker than ever before."

An example of the new kind of establishment, based on money, athletic prowess or celebrity, is the knighthood conferred in 2002 on Sir Michael Jagger. The musical superstar asked meekly, "does this mean I'm part of the establishment?" Considering his global reputation, massive wealth and elegant country estate, the answer is yes.

Religion

Polls in 1990 revealed that 71% of Britons believed in God (77% in 1965), 44% in life after death, and 30% in the devil. The Anglican Church of England (in Scotland the Presbyterian Church of Scotland) is the official state religion. The queen is its head, and parliament approves its prayer book. Only in 2007 did the prime minister relinquish the right to select its bishops, 25 of whom have seats in the House of Lords. The Archbishop of Canterbury is the spiritual leader of the world's 80 million Anglicans. It claims up to 30 million members on paper, but only a fifth of religiously active Britons belong. Church attendance has fallen dramatically in the Church of England. In 1960, 2.1 million attended on Easter Sunday, a figure that had fallen to 1.3 million by 1994. It is estimated that it lost about 1,000 church–goers every week during the 1990s. By 2008, only 1.7 million persons attend its services regularly.

In 2005 only three in ten Britons even belonged to a religion and attended services, down from nearly three-quarters in 1964. one study in 2007 showed that more people visit bingo clubs each week than go to church. The joke is that the C and E in the Church of England's abbreviation stand for "Christmas" and "Easter." Polls in 2002 indicated that barely one in 50 British families say grace regularly before meals, compared with close to half in the U.S.

Most worshipers are drawn to religions that are better able to satisfy the thirst for spirituality: immigrant religions (mainly Islam, Sikhism and Hinduism), cults, Pentecostal or charismatic Christian churches, or new age, non–mainstream faiths. In an attempt to lure worshipers back to the Church of England, its General Synod voted in 1992 to ordain women, a decision which had to be approved by parliament and the queen in 1993. In protest, traditionalist Anglicans threaten to split away from the Church, and some may migrate to Catholicism. The Anglican establishment is holding firm against ordaining gays to the priesthood, as is practiced in some American dioceses. But this issue has the potential of creating a schism in the Church.

In 2008 Archbishop Rowan Williams found himself in a furious tempest when he suggested that some aspects of the Muslim Sharia law, such as those regulating marriage, property and inheritance, be recognized and formalized. He failed to anticipate the explosive effect of the very word "Sharia" in a public that has deep concerns about Islam in Britain. He was condemned by all political parties and even some Muslim leaders, and the prime minister himself phoned him to request that he calm the storm. The besieged archbishop publicly apologized explained that he was not advocating that Islamic law be granted equal status with British law.

Thanks to the influx of as many as 500,000 central Europeans since the 2004 EU enlargement, about two-thirds of them Poles, many Catholic churches are experiencing a boom. One London church had fallen to 20 members when it introduced masses in Portuguese. Suddenly its attendance soared to about 1,400 each Sunday.

The Media

Britain has 11 country-wide newspapers, and London boasts both high–

A Truly European Newspaper

The United Kingdom

quality titles, such as *The Guardian*, *The Times* and the *Financial Times*, as well as the more popular *News of the World*, *Daily Mirror* and *Sun*. Two–thirds of the papers sold are conservative; in order of circulation, they are the: *Sun*, (which nevertheless endorsed Labour's Tony Blair in 1997), *Daily Mail*, *Daily Express*, *Daily Telegraph*, *Daily Star*, and *Times*. Fewer than 10% are non–aligned: today, *The Independent*, and *Financial Times*. In 2005, the latter was judged the world's best newspaper by the Swiss-based consultant Internationale Medienhilfe. Only a fourth

are left–leaning, chiefly *The Guardian* and the *Daily Mirror*.

The latter, with a circulation of about two million, was dealt a severe blow in May 2004 when its editor was forced to resign after publishing shocking photos showing alleged British mistreatment of Iraqi prisoners that were proven to be fakes. The following year similar photos appeared in the press, which were regrettably not fakes. With one of the world's most competitive and irreverent presses, Britain sells 14 million newspapers a day. However, most newspapers face financial

problems, and they are losing readers. Since 1990 overall national readership has fallen by a fifth. Most troubling is that young people are not buying newspapers as their parents did and have not developed the habit of reading a daily at the breakfast table. Instead they are getting their news from TV, radio or online.

The news wire service, with particularly good international coverage, Reuters, is renowned for its meticulous accuracy and avoidance of editorializing. In spite of the fact that ownership of these London dailies is concentrated in a few hands, they keep a sharp eye on Downing Street, Westminster and Whitehall. Bringing the important political news to all corners of the country, they do not stifle the lively regional press. They are also reinforced by widely read weekly news magazines, such as *The Economist* and *The Observer*.

The written media is supplemented by radio and television, which are controlled by two public bodies, the British Broadcasting Corporation (BBC), whose directors are nominated by the government, and the Independent Broadcasting Authority (IBA), which permits private advertising. Both receive revenues (in the case of BBC over £2.5 billion annually) from licenses which everyone who owns a TV must pay. Both are expected to remain politically impartial, and both vigorously resist being used by the government in power.

In 2004 the world-famous BBC (popularly dubbed "Auntie Beebs") found itself implicated in the worst crisis in its 82-year history. It had carried a story from a government weapons expert, who later committed suicide, that the Blair government had "sexed up" a dossier on weapons of mass destruction (WMD) in order to strengthen the case for war against Iraq. The government was furious. An independent judicial inquiry in February 2004 issued the Hutton Report that cleared the prime minister and his aides of charges, reported without scrutiny by the BBC, that they had exaggerated or falsified intelligence reports to bolster the case for war against Iraq. It argued that the BBC had broadcast "unfounded" allegations against the prime minister and his aides and had failed to investigate its source's charges and the government's complaints properly.

BBC's two most senior officials resigned. But a majority of Britons did not believe the report's findings. Soon afterward, the government felt obligated to launch a formal inquiry into the reasons why Britain's (and America's) intelligence services apparently failed in their prewar assessments of Saddam's weaponry. His government was again found innocent of wrongdoing, despite some exaggeration of the threat. Nagging questions about his use of intelligence information to justify going to war weakened Blair and cost his party some seats in the past election.

Although a 2004 poll revealed that the BBC was still trusted by three times as many Britons as was the Blair government, it had to deal with the damage and with the erosion of its viewership over the years to only 33% of the total TV audience in 2007, barely more than for all digital channels. It is more popular among the wealthy and elderly than it is among the poor and young. Since multi-channel TV came to Britain in 1990, a flood of American shows began to appear on screens.

The BBC finds itself torn between its responsibility as a neutral public service news broadcaster and its desire to compete for its viewership by taking a more aggressive and controversial approach to the stories it covers. It got into trouble in 2007 when it manipulated bits of footage in its documentary, "A Year with the Queen," to make it look like she had stormed out of a photo-shoot when she had not. In addition to "Crowngate," the BBC had to admit that it had faked the winners of phone-in competitions on several programs. These scandals left the BBC's reputation with the public tarnished. It launched a 24-hour news service, News 24, to compete against Sky News and CNN. It continues to produce high-quality films, which Americans like to watch on public television. In 2005 BBC secured its future with another decade of generous public funding. It remains popular even though its audience share is dropping.

The British film industry is far too small to compete with Hollywood. But those who go to the cinema found 2007 a very good year, with the British films, *The Last King of Scotland* and *The Queen*, winning Oscars. In 2008 *Atonement* was nominated as best picture. In 2007 Britain created a tax credit of 16% of the cost of big productions and 20% of smaller ones for films that express British culture and national identity. Among the main beneficiaries of this tax subsidy, however, are big American studios, which figure that the tax break makes films 23% cheaper to make in the UK than in the U.S.

Ethnic Changes in Britain

A basic change in British society is ethnic—it had for 900 years experienced almost no immigration, except from Ireland. Now it is no longer a racially homogeneous society. As a consequence of decolonization, Asians and blacks poured into Britain from India, Pakistan, Africa and the Caribbean. The population is 8.1% non-white (half of them Asians of Indian, Pakistani, and Bangladeshi descent), a percentage that is likely to grow because of the declining birth rate of white Britons.

In 2006 the Muslim population constituted an estimated 1.8% of the total. Of these, 45% were of Pakistani origin, 19% from India, and 13%–16% from Bangladesh. Muslims have the youngest profile of any religious group in Britain. About a third is under age 16. Their unemployment rate is more than double the national average; among those between the ages of 16 and 24, joblessness was 27.6% in 2006.

Britain is faced with the difficult problem of integrating large groups of non–white minorities, who tend to be concentrated in the decaying inner cities (half are in London), even though there is less residential segregation by race in Britain than in the U.S. Such concentration gives the impression that the minority presence in the UK is far greater than it actually is. A fifth to a third of London's population belongs to an ethnic minority. They often speak little or no English, worship religions that are quite unfamiliar to most British, and groom themselves or dress in very different fashion from the rest of the population. Critics disparage the city as "Londonistan."

Foreigners continue to pour into London at a faster rate than at any time in its history, while Britons are moving out. Other cities' populations are declining. For example, Manchester's population shrank by 10%, Liverpool's by 8%, Newcastle's by 6% and Birmingham's by 3% in the 1990s, while London's grew by 4.8% over that period. The mix has also changed: in the 1970s newcomers came mostly from India, Pakistan and Bangladesh.

Today two-thirds of new immigrants come from high-income countries. Among

Statue of Martin Luther King

the wealthiest are Russians, whose numbers in London are over 200,000 and climbing. Faced with the prospect of a flood of immigrants from the eight former communist countries (as many as 600,000 came) that entered the EU in May 2004, Britain declared that they would be permitted to seek work in Britain, but those without jobs are not permitted to claim most welfare benefits for two years after arrival.

This central European influx has been good for the economy, and they pay more in taxes than they take out in benefits. Nevertheless, some Britons feel overwhelmed. Many feel that they push up house prices, pour into schools without knowing English and keep down wages. In response, Britain announced temporary restrictions on migrants from the two newest EU members, Romania and Bulgaria. But thanks to immigration, the UK is one of the few developed countries that have a growing population. Foreign-born women are helping to stabilize the birth rate at 1.84 children. If this continues, Britain's population would rise to roughly 71 million by 2032 and 77 million by 2050.

Ethnic minorities suffer the most from any economic downturn, especially unemployment. British blacks have not penetrated the top levels of business, the professions, judiciary, or the cabinet, as the American black elite has. Only 1% of soldiers are minorities (compared with 27% black in the U.S.), 2% of the police (3.3% in London) and 5% of civil servants. This may change as a result of an increase in non–white enrollment at British universities; 12% of students are from ethnic minorities, double their representation in the overall population. In London 29% of nurses, 31% of doctors, and more than 20% of civil servants are already from ethnic minorities.

In an effort to improve their public image, the London Metropolitan Police and other police forces in the country have recruited more black policemen. This is the kind of policy enacted to prevent black-white racial conflict that has proved successful. Ethnic minorities no longer have to deal with the earlier combined hostility of the police, the local government and public opinion. Only seldom are there clashes with whites or the police; more common today are clashes between ethnic minorities themselves.

In some ways Britain is a more integrated society than is the U.S., at least if one observes only the Afro-Caribbean population. There is more dating and intermarriage between white and black men and women. According to a 2007 survey, almost half of Afro–Caribbean men have a white partner; the figure for women was about a third. This is lower among British–

The United Kingdom

'HEY, DID I JUST GET SCREWED BY THE 40-YEAR-OLD VIRGIN?'

Canada's 106-year-old soldier tells all

WHO IS CANADA'S FATTEST BANKER?

CANADA'S MAGAZINE OF THE YEAR

MACLEAN'S

www.macleans.ca

JUN. 11th 2007

ENGLAND'S SHOCKING DECLINE

The Queen's once-proud subjects now lead Europe in illiteracy, unemployment, teen pregnancy, divorce, drug use, obesity, alcoholism, crime and STDs. Bloody hell. P.24

Display until June 29, 2007
$4.95

born Indians, but the figures still show change: 20% for men and 10% for women. In the U.S. only 4% of black men and 2% of black women have a white spouse.

Since 1999, more immigrants are coming from outside the Commonwealth and the EU than both of those sources combined. This means that there are more black Africans with large families. They intermarry far less. Tolerance for inter–racial marriage is strong: 74% of respondents said in a 1997 poll that they would not object to one of their close relatives marrying a black, and 70% said the same about Asians. Bangladeshis, Pakistanis and Indians remain more to themselves, though; fewer than 5% live with whites.

A glowing example of integration is Trinidad-born V.S. Naipaul, who won the 2001 Nobel Prize for Literature. He graduated from University College at Oxford in 1953 and remained in England. An eternal outsider, he is a prickly critic of religious extremism. The panel praised him for transforming "rage into precision" in such books as *Among the Believers*. Another foreign-born British novelist, 88-year-old Doris Lessing, won the Nobel Prize for literature in 2007. Born in Iran, she moved with her parents at age six to Southern Rhodesia (now Zimbabwe), where she grew up. Her writing draws heavily from her experiences in Africa. A school drop-out at age 14, she moved to Britain in 1949, where she joined the Com-

munist party and became a fierce critic of the South African regime. She explored the divide between whites and blacks in her autobiographical *The Grass Is Singing* and in her series of novels entitled *Children of Violence*.

A combination of tough anti–immigration policies, unusually detailed laws against racial discrimination, and the fact that legal immigrants have always been treated not as migrant workers but as permanent settlers, with automatic rights to vote, to run for office, and to claim social security benefits, had prevented the spread of the kind of anti–immigrant sentiment and support for racist parties seen on the continent. But this has changed, as more than half a million immigrants pour into the country each year. There are fewer asylum seekers than before; the bulk are workers and people entering as spouses or relatives of Britons. The government unveiled plans in 2005 to apply an Australian-style point system, ranking applicant workers according to their skills and occupations. Those with little or nothing to contribute to the British economy or who risk becoming a burden to the welfare system would be weeded out.

Anti-immigrant feelings are rising: 68% of respondents indicated in a 2007 poll that there were too many immigrants, and 72% thought their government did not have the influx under control. Polls in 2007 showed that race and immigration have become main concern in the UK. In a 2005 poll, 54% had agreed that "parts of the country don't feel like Britain any more because of immigration." At the same time, 62% of the general public (and 87% of Muslims) had favorable views of multiculturalism, and 48% believed that "immigration is generally good for Britain." Only a quarter of Britons worry about racial balance in their country. They tend to regard ethnic minorities and immigrants as one and the same whereas in America they have always been viewed as two different things. The fact that immigration has less to do with race in Britain makes it easier to criticize immigrants.

That gave hope to those whites who want to exploit the rising tensions at election time, such as the neo–Nazi British National Party (BNP), which favors repatriation of nonwhites, and the UK Independence Party (UKIP), which promises "freedom from overcrowding" and an end to economic migration. As usual, these parties fell flat on their faces in the May 2005 parliamentary elections. But even the Tory party made immigration one of its major campaign issues, something that was a turnoff for many voters.

Labour, which has always presented itself as the party of the underdog, receives the overwhelming majority of nonwhite votes. In the 1987 election, 27 nonwhites ran for office, and for the first time since 1922, nonwhites took seats in the House of Commons. In 2007, there were 15 Members of Parliament from ethnic minorities, and there were even more in the House of Lords. Most blacks in the UK are either British citizens or Commonwealth citizens who can vote in Britain. That is changing, though, as black Africans arrive in greater numbers.

It has been difficult to integrate blacks and Asians into the political process, except in direct defense of their own interests. But there has been progress. Nonwhites in the UK have visible positive role models in sports, the arts, business and the professions. There are grounds for optimism that the lauded English tolerance and gradualism will lead more British to accept the immigrants and their children as nonwhite Britons. It is symbolic that in 1998 a statue of Martin Luther King was placed in the last remaining niche above the Great West Door of Westminster Abbey. In 2007 a nine-foot bronze statue of Nelson Mandela was unveiled outside Parliament to honor his campaign to end apartheid in South Africa. It joins statues of Abraham Lincoln and Winston Churchill in Parliament Square.

British Muslims and Terrorism

Just as the celebrations over winning the 2012 Olympic Games were dying down, during the morning rush hour of the July 7, 2005, death struck 52 commuters in the heart of London. Four young British Muslims, three of Pakistani origin and one convert from Jamaica, killed themselves and as many as they could take with them in three Tube (subway) stations and one double-decker bus in al-Qaeda-linked attacks. Not surprisingly for a multicultural city like London, half the victims were foreign-born, and one was an American. They included victims from all major religions. Two weeks later similar attacks were botched without fatalities.

The bloody attacks on the 7th seemed to have been planned to coincide with the G8 summit meeting in Scotland, hosted by Tony Blair. He rushed back to London, vowing that "our determination to defend our values and our way of life is greater than their determination to cause death and destruction to innocent people in a desire to impose extremism on the world." In their usual way, British citizens and parties rallied around their leader in such a time of crisis and sorrow to show that they will not be intimidated. Then opposition leader Michael Howard extolled "the calm resolute and statesmanlike way in which the government has responded." London Mayor Ken Livingstone assured

the terrorists: "Even after your cowardly attacks, you will see people from around the world coming to London to achieve their dreams." He continued to go to work every day by subway.

Such attacks had been long feared and expected. London's antiterrorism precautions are among the most elaborate and well-practiced in the world. Intelligence services in London said that many such attacks had been thwarted in recent years. After much experience with aerial and terrorist bombing, Londoners are very resilient people. The very next day they returned to their daily routines.

But life was not the same for Britain's 1.8 million Muslims. A generously defined tradition of free speech had allowed extreme clerics to preach hatred and violence, to the frustration of the majority Muslim moderates. It is not clear what motivates homegrown terrorists. Most are not poor, and they are no more likely to live in heavily Muslim neighborhoods than in mixed or white ones. Three of the bombers had been born and raised in Britain; all four were British citizens. But a 2006 Pew Global Attitudes poll of Muslims found that 81% of British Muslims considered themselves Muslims first and Britons second. That is stunningly high when compared to France, where only 42% considered themselves Muslim before French.

Britons are looking for answers to the question of why young men who had grown up in Britain and seemed to be at least partly assimilated could become so alienated that they would commit such treacherous acts against ordinary citizens in their adopted country. Three had spent some time in Pakistan, receiving some schooling and training. Al-Qaeda's leadership, based in Pakistan, has easy access to thousands of Britons of Pakistani origin who visit their ancestral country easily and frequently.

But it is a disturbing thought that Britain now has homegrown suicide bombers who are difficult to catch. Police and intelligence agencies must contend with diffuse and overlapping *jihadi* groups, who are willing to die in an effort to kill as many people as possible. A *Times* poll showed that 86% of British respondents supported giving the police new powers to arrest people suspected of planning terrorist attacks. Yet the surge in recruits and supporters of radical Islamic networks continues.

The UK is faced with the task of persuading moderate, law-abiding Muslims, who constitute the large majority, to rally around the Muslim Council of Britain (MCB) to try to root out extremism on the fringes of mosque life. The government would like to draw Muslims into the

policing of their own communities. The Sunni Council in the Birmingham area responded by issuing an edict condemning "all forms of terrorism, be it state terrorism or otherwise." A 2005 poll indicated that 86% of British Muslims believed the use of violence for political ends is unacceptable, even though four out of five considered the "war on terrorism" to be a war against Islam. In 2007, 79% answered that suicide bombings are rarely or never justified, while 15% thought they were often or sometimes justified.

Polls a couple of weeks after the 2005 bombings indicated that two-thirds of Britons believed their country's involvement in the Iraq war had something to do with their being targeted. Britain's prominence as America's ally both in Iraq and Afghanistan no doubt feeds some persons' rage. In February 2008 a Muslim man in Birmingham was sentenced to life in prison for plotting to kidnap and behead a British Muslim soldier and to record it all on video "to cause panic and fear within the British armed forces and wider public." In secret recordings played in court, the man was heard instructing his 5-year-old son on how to behead a person.

Blair took another position, arguing that such people as the bombers can always find an excuse to persuade themselves to take other people's blood. But one thing is incontrovertible, he said: nothing justifies such slaughter of innocent people. The attacks reinforced his case for achieving the long-term task: help establish stable democracy in Iraq, promote peace between Israel and Palestine, and support democratic reform elsewhere in the Middle East.

Terrorism is a threat whose prominence in the public's mind was greatly enhanced by the grisly killings in July 2005. But the government's response reflected Blair's extraordinary gift for articulating the public mood at moments of crisis. This was one of his greatest strengths as a political leader. Many European governments have been extending their surveillance and prosecution powers. But he had to accept the judgment of the House of Commons. On November 9, 2005, his proposal to allow terrorism suspects to be held for as many as 90 days without charge was defeated by 322 to 291; 49 members of his own party deserted him, a record number in a Commons vote. Later in the day Commons approved a compromise of 28 days and legislation to toughen penalties for terrorist-related activities and to broaden government powers to ban organizations thought to support terrorism. In February 2006, however, Commons again defeated a government bill to ban religious hatred. In January 2008 Prime Minister Brown un-

The United Kingdom

veiled a plan to hold terrorist suspects up to 42 days without charges.

The relevance of these laws was highlighted on August 10, 2006, when police thwarted a huge terrorist plot to blow up in midair ten American planes departing from Heathrow Airport causing what was described as "mass murder on an unimaginable scale." Authorities arrested two dozen young Muslims, most of them British citizens of Pakistani origin; accomplices were also detained in Pakistan. Fueled by disenchantment at home, poor educational achievement, high unemployment, discrimination, and rage about fighting in Iraq, Afghanistan and Lebanon that they see as part of a western "war against Islam," the ranks of violent Islamic extremists are growing in Britain. Many Britons are wondering whether their country has struck the right balance between encouraging cultural diversity and insisting on a shared national identity.

FUTURE

Britain now has a higher per capita GDP than France, Germany and Italy although it has embarrassingly been overtaken by Ireland. Oxford Economic Forecasting predicted that the British economy will by 2030 be the largest in Europe, beating out even the more populist Germany.

Nevertheless, the country has some serious social issues it will have to face in the future: UNICEF ranks it, along with the U.S., at the bottom of the scale among industrial nations in terms of the well-being of children. Child poverty doubled between 1979 and 1998. It has Europe's highest teen-age pregnancy rate, which is five times that of the Netherlands. Sexual activity begins young, and condoms are used infrequently. The proportion of children born outside marriage has risen to 42%, and it leads Europe in single-mother households. It has Europe's highest obe-

sity rate. It leads the continent in cocaine abuse and has one of the highest alcohol abuse rates. Along with Ireland and the Netherlands, it has the highest crime rate in Europe. London has more violent crime than New York. There is a worrisome alienation of large segments of Britain's young people, especially Muslims. The UN Human Development Index ranked the country 18th in the world, behind the Nordic countries, Canada and the U.S.

In July 2005 London received the sweet news that it would host the 2012 Olympic Games. It beat out the likes of Paris, Madrid, Moscow and New York to become only the third city in history to host the Games three times. Then Prime Minister Blair had spent three intensive days in Singapore lobbying successfully for the London site. Now the UK faces the usual problems of rising cost estimations and an outcry against the pink logo adopted as the Games' symbol. Some called it a bro-

International edition
Friday 18.05.07
guardian.co.uk

theguardian

Britain's two prime ministers

- I will lead a new government with new priorities
- A different type of politics, a more open dialogue
- My passion is education. My priority is the NHS

- I do not regret close relationship with Bush
- I would take the same position again
- There is still work to do for the common good

ken swastika, and others winced at the £400,000 ($800,000) price tag for its design.

With at least 30 habitual Labour rebels in parliament and many others ready to join them to embarrass Blair, it became increasingly difficult for him to find a parliamentary majority. His party performed poorly in the May 2007 local and regional elections. Scandals involving questionable party donations, sexual misbehavior and ministerial failure, along with the unpopularity of the Iraq war, beset Labour. These prompted irresistible calls for Tony Blair to make way for his successor. An increasingly popular Tory Party with a dynamic new bike-riding green leader, David Cameron, was able to exploit this. On June 27, 2007, Blair handed the keys to the prime minister's office to Gordon Brown, his chancellor of the exchequer for a decade. What many analysts will discuss for years in the future is the legacy that this extraordinary politician and statesman will leave behind.

Leading his party to three straight electoral victories (something no Labour leader had ever done), Blair was Britain's most successful Labour prime minister ever. He moved his leftist party to the center, where elections can be won, and he eliminated Labour's reputation for incompetence in government. He made British politics competitive by making Labour electable again. He removed hereditary peers from the House of Lords and reformed that upper chamber irreversibly. He extended self-government to Scotland and Wales. He was also the driving force in achieving a power-sharing agreement in Northern Ireland, perhaps his greatest success.

He left Britain a better country. The average citizen is more prosperous, and Britain's openness to large numbers of immigrants boosted the economy without producing a serious backlash. The war in Iraq cost him his popularity. He persuaded a majority to allow universities to charge higher tuition fees, thereby beginning to solve higher education's chronic underfunding. Now 40% go to universities.

In his decade as prime minister, the challenges facing his country shifted from domestic to foreign policy, as he was forced to face terrorism, energy shortages and climate change. He was Britain's most pro-EU leader ever. At the same time, he attempted to guard his country's traditionally close ties with the United States. More than any other leader, he built the coalition that ended genocide in Kosovo and terminated the murderous career of Serbian President Slobodan Milosevic. He was a key player in the successful war to end Taliban rule in Afghanistan. He brought peace to Sierra Leone, after murderous rebels kidnapped 500 UN peacekeepers and threatened to renew warfare.

Blair is still young and vigorous, and he remains an international star. The UN tapped his expertise on the Middle East by appointing him special Middle East envoy for the Quartet (UN, EU, U.S., Russia) the day he left Number 10. He was appointed a senior adviser at JP Morgan Chase and a consultant on international politics for Zurich Financial Services, Switzerland's largest insurer. He lectures for astronomical honoraria and signed a lucrative deal for his memoirs. He agreed to teach a course at Yale University during the 2008-9 academic year on faith and globalization and to work with the divinity and management faculties as a Howland Distinguished Fellow. Both his successor and French President Nicolas Sarkozy are recommending him to be the first full-time president of the EU's European Council some time after 2009. He speaks respectable French, which would be essential, has the ear of the Americans, and is the most pro-European leader Britain ever had. However, he would have to overcome the rancor over the Iraq War and the UK's semi-detached attitude toward Brussels.

Few British political leaders veer far from Blair's legacy, certainly not Gordon Brown. He was an important part of Labour's transformation and will not retreat from it. He is unloved and enigmatic. Often referred to as the "dour Scot," he is sometimes accused of being a brooding and cold "control freak," who is stiff and formal with the electorate.

Brown changed the political tone somewhat, but he did not pursue a substantially different foreign policy. He ordered a gradual withdrawal from Iraq leaving special forces and fighter aircraft after 2008. He shows a bit more independence

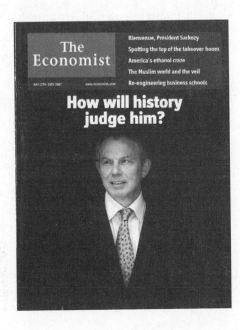

from the U.S. government although he remains instinctively Atlanticist. He never challenged the conventional wisdom of the foreign policy establishment that the alliance with the U.S. is the UK's pivotal security relationship. He declared that America is Britain's "most important bilateral relationship" and vowed not to "allow people to separate us from the United States of America in dealing with the common challenges that we face around the world."

Nor has he ever as much as hinted that that Europe might be an alternative pillar of his country's security. He has held the EU at arm's length and stuck to the "red lines" restrictions his predecessor negotiated at the EU summit on the amended constitutional treaty a few days before ceding power. He showed his disdain for the EU by showing up three hours late for the official signing of the Lisbon Treaty in December 2007. He decided that there is no longer a need to submit the treaty to a referendum, as the opposition Tories insist and as most of the public favors. Parliament will probably ratify the treaty after a bruising debate. He argues the Lisbon Treaty (rejected in Ireland) halts the tide of European integration. His belated trip to Brussels in February 2008 did not dispel the suspicion some Europeans have toward his commitment to the EU.

Since he was in control of the government's economic policy for a decade and is highly respected in international financial circles, that has not changed. He has until May 2010 at the latest to convince his countrymen that he is the right person at the helm. His hints that he might call an early election backfired, and his subsequent change of mind took the momentum out of the "Brown bounce." This non-election destroyed the sense that he would bring change.

Other events were not kind to him in his first year in office. Britain experienced the first run on a British bank (Northern Rock) since the Victorian era, and the government ultimately decided to nationalize it. This was a violation of New Labour's policy to privatize the economy. A junior civil servant lost a disc containing the personal data of 25 million child benefit claimants. Revelations that a Labour cabinet member, Peter Hain, had accepted unlawful party donations given by a shady businessman under various names and accounts destroyed Brown's hope to cast his government as squeaky clean compared with that of his predecessor. Worse still are reports of his style of leadership. Insiders say that he is intellectually curious but cripplingly indecisive. He has difficulty making decisions. It is not surprising that the Tories have a 7% lead over Labour in the polls.

The Republic of Ireland

with Mark H. Mullin

Area: 27,136 sq. mi. (70,262 sq. km., slightly larger than West Virginia).

Population: 4.1 million.

Capital City: Dublin (Pop. one million, estimated); a third live in or around Dublin.

Climate: Cool and damp (rarely above 65° or below 40° Fahrenheit).

Neighboring Countries: Great Britain lies a short distance eastward across the Irish Sea.

Official Languages: English, which is the first language of 98% of the population. Irish (Gaelic) is spoken as a native language by only 2% (ca. 70,000).

Ethnic Background: Celtic (some Norman and Norsemen).

Principal Religions: Roman Catholic 88.4%, Church of Ireland (Protestant) 5%, Presbyterian .4%, Muslims 19,000 and growing.

Main Exports and Imports: Machinery and transport equipment, chemicals, foodstuffs and tobacco, high–tech equipment, petroleum and other fuels.

Main Trading Partners: EU25 (63.3% of exports and 57.4% of imports), United Kingdom (17.4% of exports and 31.2% of imports), United States (18.7% of ex-

ports and 14.1% of imports), Belgium (15.1% of exports), Germany (7.5% of exports and 14.1% of imports), France (6.4% of exports), China (6.6% of imports), Netherlands (4% of imports).

Currency: Euro.

Former Colonial Status: "Given" to England in 1155 by the Pope, turbulent English control until 1922; its own parliament, diminishing control until independence.

Independence Dates: December 6, 1921 (Dominion status); April 18, 1949 (independent republic).

Chief of State: Mary McAleese, President (since October 1997).

Head of Government: Brian Cowen, *Taoiseach*, pronounced "Tea–such," or Prime Minister (since May 2008).

National Flag: Three vertical stripes of green, white and orange.

Green fields, white–washed thatched cottages, leprechauns and men sitting in front of a peat fire spinning tales that are part fact and part fiction are images of Ireland that the first–time tourist seeks. This scene is also found in St. Patrick's Day cards, framed in green. While the tourist

may miss much of what is new in Ireland, both the green fields and the confusion of fact and fantasy are still there for him to find. And both are largely the result of Ireland's location—it lies at the spot where the warm air and water of the Gulf Stream confront their cold rivals of the northern latitudes. This produces a climate in which temperature variations are rare; it is an unusual day when the temperature is more than slightly warm or cold.

The confrontation of warm and cold produces air that is frequently moist—thus the lushness of the green, and skies that are always changing—gray and sad one minute, brilliant and joyful the next. If the sky is not constant, why should reality be constant? And, perhaps it is the soft, moist air that blurs fact and fantasy. George Bernard Shaw wrote of Ireland to an English friend, "You've no such colors in the sky, no such lines in the distance, no such sadness in the evenings. Oh the dreaming! The dreaming!"

If one may generalize about the people of a nation, the Irish people reflect their climate. There is a gentleness about the Irish, an essential sadness punctuated by flashes of sparkling wit. And there is a willingness to let the line between reality and dream be as indistinct as that between the distant mountains and the evening sky.

If its location has shaped the green beauty of Ireland and the character of its people, its location has been more responsible for shaping its history. Ireland is not merely an island; it is an island off the coast of another island. While its contact with the continent has usually been indirect, its subjugation to England has been of paramount influence. Being one step removed from the mainland has kept continental armies, and the cultural influences that they brought, out of Ireland. Roman legions never tramped across its fields. Although Norsemen settled on the east coast and raided many other areas, Irish culture achieved a flowering of learning and artistic brilliance while the rest of Europe slipped into the Dark Ages.

As nation–states developed on the continent, Ireland was involved in European dynastic wars only when England had a stake in the contest. The last continental troops to be in Ireland made an unsuccessful attempt to export the French Revolution. Ireland even managed to be one of the few European countries to be neutral during World War II. As the English, century after century, negotiated and fought rivals on the continent, they did not want to have to worry about the island on their other side. The English always felt a domination of Ireland was essential to their security. The Irish Sea, after all, varies in width from 120 miles to only 11 miles, thus the fates of England and Ireland have been intertwined for the past 800 years.

Ireland is like a small bowl floating in the Atlantic. Its mountains ring the coastal region; they seldom reach more than 3,000 feet (914 km.) into the sky. But the steepness with which they meet the sea gives them the appearance of considerable height. The center of the island is relatively flat, with the Shannon River flowing from north to south like a fine crack in the bottom of the bowl. West of the Shannon, peat bogs provide much of Ireland's fuel. East of the Shannon, the plains are rich grasslands, superb for cattle or horses. In fact, the Curragh, the finest stable and racetrack in the land, has 5,000 acres of grass uninterrupted by either a tree or a fence. But even in the center of Ireland, one is never far removed from the sea, for the whole island is only 150 miles wide and 275 miles long.

Ireland is a beautiful and gentle land. Tragically, its history has not always been so.

HISTORY

The Early Period

The earliest remains of humans in Ireland date from about 7000 B.C. These hunters and food gatherers lived along the coasts and near the rivers. By 3000 B.C. Neolithic settlers had introduced agriculture and pottery. Their most spectacular accomplishments, elaborate Megalithic burial chambers, can still be seen today. At Newgrange one may enter the massive chamber by crawling through a tunnel 62 feet long. It is so constructed that only at the summer solstice does sunlight come down the tunnel and illuminate the interior chamber.

About 300 B.C. the Gaelic Celts used their knowledge of iron weapons to gain control of the island. Celtic Ireland was divided into some 150 local kingdoms under the loose control of the Kings of the Five Provinces. Meath later became part of Leinster, but the four provinces of Ulster in the north, Leinster in the southeast, Munster in the southwest and Connacht in the west have retained fairly similar boundaries to this day.

Saint Patrick

One of the High Kings who ruled at the Hill of Tara from 380 to 405 A.D. was Niall, an ancestor of the O'Neills, an important family in Ulster until the 17th century. Niall's troops attacked both Britain and Normandy. On one raid, a young Briton named Patrick was brought back as a slave. After several years in Ireland, Patrick escaped to the continent where he entered a monastery. In 432, after being consecrated as a Bishop, Patrick returned to Ireland. He spent Lent in prayer at the top of Croagh Patrick, a mountain overlooking the Atlantic in County Mayo. Bound by age–long tradition, even now, more than 50,000 people a year make the strenuous 2,700-foot climb to the top. And it is typical that some do it as an adventurous outing and some do it as a religious penance. In fact, thousands climb over the rough stones with bare, and therefore bleeding, feet. The story is told that two young men were climbing and one of them saw some attractive girls up ahead. He said, "Let's hurry and catch up with those girls." The other one replied, "Oh, I wouldn't dare. It's for too much foolin' with the girls that I'm havin' to make the climb."

Certainly Patrick was one of the most successful missionaries of all time. Within a few years after his death, the whole island was Christian. Celtic Christianity developed in unusual patterns. Instead of the bishop and his diocese being the chief authority, the abbot and the monastery were the center of ecclesiastical life. The emphasis on monastic life had three major effects on cultural developments.

First, monks often practiced extremes of asceticism. To this day, Irish Christianity has maintained an emphasis on self—

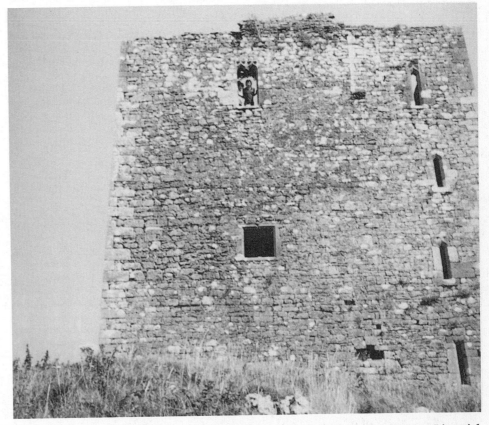

The ruins of Rocktown Castle, County Limerick

Ireland

denial and penance that affects the Irish character. Second, while the rest of Europe descended into darkness, Irish monasteries kept the light of western culture burning. Piety, painting and learning were combined into one art form: the illuminated manuscript of the scriptures. Flights of imagination turned the letters of holy books into fantastic geometric shapes and celestial beings. The most famous illuminated manuscript, the Book of Kells, may be seen today in the Library of Trinity College, Dublin.

Third, because monastic orders thought beyond the geographic boundaries of the Diocese, Irish missionaries carried Celtic Christianity to Britain and the continent. The Irish St. Colombo established a famous monastery at Iona off the coast of Scotland. But perhaps the most interesting missionary was St. Brendan—medieval manuscripts describe how he and a group of monks sailed in a leather boat from the coast of Kerry. They visited a land of sheep, then an island occupied by giant blacksmiths working at their forges, and later an area of great fog. Finally, they reached a new land of beauty and richness that was divided by a large river. Brendan returned to Ireland just before he died. The story has usually been dismissed as a fanciful legend. In 1977, however, a group of men built a leather boat and sailed from Brendon's creek in Kerry. They were blown to the outer Hebrides (where there are many sheep), wintered in Iceland (where volcanoes might be confused with giants' forges), were becalmed in the fog off the Grand Banks, and finally, in 1978, washed ashore in Canada. Perhaps Brendan, not Leif Ericson nor Christopher Columbus, was the first European to reach the New World.

Viking Raids and Norse Settlements

Unfortunately, the very success and more particularly the wealth of the monasteries brought trouble. Beginning in the 9th century, Viking raiders began to attack monastic and other settlements, plundering them for gold and valuables. Inevitably, the monks sought refuge in remote places. The most spectacular of these is Skellig Michael, a tiny island off the coast of Kerry. Today, those who brave the four miles of rough seas in an open boat can climb the steps cut into the stone face by monks over a thousand years ago and visit the remains of the beehive huts perched 550 feet above the water.

By the 10th century, the Norsemen began to plan settlements. The Vikings established the first cities in Ireland near the mouth of important rivers. Dublin, Waterford, Cork and Limerick all began that way.

At times the Celtic Irishmen intermarried with the Norse and at times they tried

Skellig Michael

to drive them into the sea. Brian Baru, after defeating the Norsemen in Munster, established himself as High King of all Ireland in 1002. Brian married the beautiful Gormflath whose six feet of height was crowned with flaming red hair. Unfortunately, as so often happened in Irish history, treason destroyed a chance for national unity. Gormflath's half–Danish son by an earlier marriage plotted with his mother, his uncle and other Danish chieftains to attack Brian. At the Battle of Clontarf in 1014 in which 20,000 men took part, Brian's forces were victorious and broke the Viking domination of Ireland. Tragically, at the end of the battle, a Danish soldier broke free and killed Brian in his own tent. It is even more tragic that neither Brian's brief unification of Ireland nor his freeing it of foreign domination proved lasting. No clear successor to him was able to establish control, and strife between local warlords continued as an Irish tradition. Because of these rivalries, new invaders arrived within 150 years.

The name Dermot MacMurrough has been a black one in Irish history for eight hundred years. It was he who invited British troops into Ireland. But it is easier to see the tragic consequences of his act in retrospect than it would have been in the 12th century. In fact, it was Adrian IV, the only Englishman ever to be pope, who set the stage. Wishing to bring the practices of Celtic Christianity into conformity with the rest of Roman Christianity, Adrian issued the papal bull *Laudabilitier* in 1155 that granted Henry II of England permission to control Ireland. For 20 years, Henry did not make a move across the Irish Sea. However, when Dermot Mac-Murrough lost control of the Kingdom of

Leinster, he asked for help from the Normans who had then been ruling England and Wales for a hundred years.

Norman–Anglo Saxon Invasion and Control

Strongbow, Earl of Pembroke, led a group of Normans into Ireland in 1170. He married MacMurrough's daughter and for a while it appeared that an independent Norman kingdom might be established. A year later, however, Henry II himself brought a large force of British Normans into Ireland. With the murder of Thomas Becket less than 12 months behind him (see The United Kingdom), Henry may have thought it was a good time for some foreign travel. He not only established Normans loyal to himself as local rulers, but did away with the Celtic form of worship and brought Irish Christianity under the control of the Roman Church.

Two legacies of the Normans are still plentifully evident in Ireland. Many of the great names of Ireland came with the Normans: Joyce, Fitzgerald, Barry and Burke. These names can still be seen on many store and pub fronts. A person driving through Ireland also still sees the remains of castles, the prototypes of which were built by the Normans. These are usually rectangular stone towers three or four stories high. Most are in ruins, but a few such as Bunratty, Blarney, Dungory, Cahair and Knappogue have been restored and are open for visitors or popular medieval banquets. Over 300 castles still stand in Ireland.

As the Anglo–Normans became settled in Ireland, they adopted more and more of the Irish ways. The old saying is that

"They became more Irish than the Irish themselves." Eventually, of course, such assimilation began to threaten the rule of the British crown. The attitude of the English was shown in the statutes of Kilkenny in 1366. These provided a punishment of the loss of lands for any Englishman who spoke Irish, married Irish people or adopted Irish customs.

English authority was strongest in the area around Dublin, known as "The Pale." Outside this region, local rulers paid only nominal homage to the British Crown and British ways. Thus the expression "Beyond the Pale" as a term of derision expresses things from the English point of view. While they had only small loyalty to Britain, the Irish rulers could hardly be described as ardent nationalists. Ireland was so fragmented politically that the idea of allegiance to Ireland itself was not an effective alternative. Rather, each local lord simply looked after his own interests.

Religious Intolerance after the Reformation

It is interesting, but futile, to speculate what would have happened to relationships between Britain and Ireland if the Reformation had not come to England. Perhaps Ireland would have gone the way of Scotland and Wales and become part of the United Kingdom. But the Reformation drove an irreconcilable wedge of hatred and mistrust between the English and the Irish.

England vacillated between Roman Catholicism and Protestantism through several monarchs, but with the crowning of Elizabeth I, the English were ready to try to export the Reformation. For the next 400 years, religion and nationalism would be intertwined in Ireland. In 1579, armed rebellion arose in the southwest of the island. As a reprisal against the rebels and as a reward to her soldiers, Elizabeth confiscated vast areas of land from the Irish and gave them to Englishmen. On one such parcel of land, Walter Raleigh planted the first Irish potato. It was a crop well suited for growing by the Irish and they soon became dependent on it, much to their regret during the potato famine 275 years later, one of the greatest tragedies in Irish history.

By 1588 Elizabeth's rule was strong enough that as the ships of the Spanish Armada wrecked against the rocky shores of Ireland, the Irish obeyed her orders and slaughtered the would-be invaders. Only in Ulster in the north were the Spaniards spared. This was ironic; because Ulster held out against English rule, a sequence of events began that led in the 20th century to the north being the one area of Ireland loyal to the British crown.

At the end of the 16th century, Hugh O'Neill led a rebellion in Ulster. He embarrassed Elizabeth's current favorite Essex, but finally in 1601 was defeated at Kinsale by Mountjoy. In 1607 he and other Ulster chiefs fled to the continent in "the flight of the Earls." James I filled the vacuum by sending Scots Presbyterians to settle in Northern Ireland. These are the antecedents of today's Protestants in Northern Ireland loyal to the British. It is significant that the only Protestants in Ireland were imported.

Upheavals in the British monarchy brought violence to Ireland in the 17th century. Oliver Cromwell beheaded Charles I and in 1649 landed in Ireland. His purpose was to establish his brand of Puritanism in Ireland and end the possibility of rebellion. Tens of thousands of Irish were killed or driven into exile. Irish landlords in the fertile east were given the choice of death or migration to the rocky areas of the west. "Hell or Connacht" are still remembered as the only options open to them. By 1660, only one quarter of the country was owned by Irish Catholics.

When James II, a Catholic, came to the throne of England, there was a chance of reconciliation. But there was an immediate rebellion of Protestants against James, who chose William of Orange, a Netherlands Protestant as King of England; the decisive battle was fought in Ireland in 1690. Protestants in Ulster still celebrate the anniversary of the Battle of Boyne, fought on Irish territory, where William defeated the forces of James. This greatly irritates their Catholic neighbors.

As retribution for support of James, the English confiscated more areas of Irish land and imposed the Penal Laws. These forbade Catholics to vote, to hold office, to send their children to anything but a Protestant school or to have wealth above a set limit.

The Georgian Era

Much of Dublin and many beautiful country homes were built by the Protestant aristocracy during the Georgian era of the 18th century. The vast majority of the population, Catholic peasants, subsisted on potatoes grown on tiny plots of land. The success of the American and French revolutions inspired hopes among the downtrodden people. The ideals of equality and fraternity were imported from the continent. Theobald Wolfe Tone founded the United Irishmen, a group that sought to include those of different religions in the establishing of a republic. In 1798 a French force with Tone in attendance landed in Mayo on the west coast. The British commander, Cornwallis, was more successful than he had been at Yorktown, and the French–Irish forces were soon defeated.

The English now tried to have Ireland conform to the pattern that Scotland and Wales had followed years earlier. The Act of Union, passed in 1800, abolished the Irish parliament and gave the Irish representation in the British parliament at Westminster. Robert Emmet tried an unsuccessful revolution in 1803; his statue stands today in Washington, D.C., but his words were engraved on the heart of

The ancient mansion of Sir Walter Raleigh, Youghal

Ireland

every Irish revolutionary who came after him: "When my country takes her place among the nations of the earth, then and not till then let my epitaph be written."

Further Attempts at Freedom and the Potato Famine

Two names dominate Irish attempts for freedom in the 19th century: Daniel O'Connell and Charles Stewart Parnell. But their periods of influence were separated by the most terrible tragedy Ireland ever knew. In the first half of the century, Daniel O'Connell worked to improve the position of Catholics. He won election to the House of Commons in 1828 even though, as a Catholic, he could not take his seat. A year later, the Penal Laws that accomplished this were replaced. In the 1840s O'Connell developed a large following that demanded the repeal of the Act of Union. However, when he obeyed an order by the British government to cancel a mass meeting in Clontarf, his political support soon failed.

By the 1840s more than half the people of Ireland were dependent on potatoes as their principal source of food. In the wet summer of 1845, blight attacked the crop, and it appeared again in 1846 and 1847. Famine and death spread across the stricken land. The relief efforts of the British government were too little and too late. In a population of 8.5 million, one million starved and another million fled their country. English–speaking countries around the world, particularly the United States, received a transfusion of Celtic, Catholic blood that would, in turn, help shape their destinies. Even as the famine subsided, immigration continued and for the next 40 years, 1% of the population left each year. Many found their way to America, where in the 2000 census, 10.8% identified themselves as of Irish descent, more than five times as many as inhabit the whole island of Ireland. One hundred years after the great famine, the population was only one–half what it had been before the blight struck.

As Irish immigrants prospered abroad, many did not forget the cause of Irish independence. Money and occasionally arms or leaders flowed back into Ireland and supported various movements. The Fenians, a secret society favoring armed revolution and also known as the Irish Republican Brotherhood, was founded in 1856 in Ireland and the United States. In 1879, the Land League was founded by Michael Davitt and was supported by American money. It worked through parliament to achieve land reform. Charles Stewart Parnell became the leader of the Irish Parliamentary Party. He controlled enough seats in the British parliament to tip the balance of power at various times.

His Home Rule Bill passed the House of Commons, but was defeated in the House of Lords. His next try for home rule might have been successful, but in 1890 a scandal broke when Parnell was the cause of a divorce between Kitty O'Shea and her husband. Although Parnell married Kitty, neither Victorian England nor Catholic Ireland would forgive him. How ironic it was that one man's illicit love of a woman

delayed the possibility of home rule until it was too late to be effective.

In 1912, after severely limiting the power of the House of Lords, the House of Commons finally passed a Home Rule Bill, but by that time the Protestants in Ulster were afraid of being controlled by a Catholic majority. Sir Edward Casson organized the Ulster Volunteers, a military group armed with German guns to op-

The potato famine struck a severe blow to Ireland

pose the move. The next year the Irish Republican Brotherhood and the *Sinn Fein* (pronounced "Shin Fane," meaning "Ourselves Alone") formed the Irish Volunteers to oppose the Ulster Volunteers.

But the outbreak of World War I caused Britain to postpone home rule for the duration of the war. With British attention focused on the continent, the Irish Volunteers and the Irish Citizens Army staged an armed rebellion. On Easter Monday, 1916, rebels captured the center of Dublin. At the General Post Office, they proclaimed the Irish Republic: "We declare the right of the people of Ireland to the ownership of Ireland and to the unfettered control of Irish destinies to be sovereign and indefeasible. The long usurpation of that right by a foreign people and government has not extinguished the right nor can it ever be extinguished except by the destruction of the Irish people. In every generation for centuries the Irish people had and have asserted their right to national freedom and sovereignty. Six times in the past 300 years they have asserted it in arms. Standing on that fundamental right and again asserting it in arms in the face of the world, we hereby proclaim the Irish Republic as a sovereign, independent state, and we pledge our lives and the lives of our comrades in arms to the cause of its freedom, of its welfare, and of its exultation among the nations."

Within a week the rebellion was crushed; because the British were at war, they reacted to the rebellion as treason, and with great severity, executing most of the leaders. Eamon deValera was spared because he had been born in the United States. Those executed instantly became heroes and martyrs to the Irish people, and hatred toward England became even deeper.

When World War I ended, the *Sinn Fein* again proclaimed an Irish Republic. DeValera was President and Michael Collins led frequent terrorist raids on British installations. The British fought back with the Auxiliary Cadets (former officers) and the Black and Tans (former enlisted men). Both sides practiced atrocities, murders, burnings and lootings. The Irish desire for freedom received world–wide publicity when Terrence McSwiney died in a British prison after a 74–day hunger strike. This strategy would later be used in the fight by India for its freedom from Britain and again in Ulster in the 1980s and 1990s.

Strife and Freedom

The three years of fighting are still known by the Irish as "The Troubles," though many years in Irish history could qualify for that title. Parliament passed the Government of Ireland Act in 1920 that allowed for two types of Home Rule, one for the six counties in the north and

The Counties of Ireland

another for the rest of Ireland. In early 1922 the republican government led by Arthur Griffith and Michael Collins accepted a treaty that made 26 counties a free state within the British Commonwealth, and left the six northern counties a province of the United Kingdom. DeValera refused to accept the treaty, and for a year and a half led a civil war against his former friends. Collins was killed in a battle and Griffith died, but deValera was forced to give up his fight. William Cosgrave became head of the Irish Free State; the boundary between the Free State and Northern Ireland was accepted in 1925.

Eamon deValera returned to power in 1932 as head of the *Fianna Fail* ("Warriors of Destiny") Party that held a majority for 16 years. In 1937 a new constitution declared Ireland to be "a sovereign, independent, democratic state." Only formal ties with Britain remained. Ireland was officially neutral during World War II, but many Irishmen served in the British armed forces. Further, it was an important refueling stop for transatlantic military aircraft during the strife.

In 1949, a coalition government led by John Costello took Ireland out of the Commonwealth and made it an independent republic. DeValera served as *Taoiseach*, (pronounced "tea–such"), a prime minister, several times, but in 1959 he gave up leadership of the *Fianna Fail* and was elected president of the republic. During the 1950s, Ireland began a major push toward industrialization. Foreign capital was invited into the country and given tax incentives. By the mid–1960s, industrial output was growing at over 5% a year. Ire-

Ireland

By the sea in County Cork

land joined the EC (now EU) in 1973, which gave a great boost to both its agricultural and industrial production. The improved economic situation brought about a rising standard of living. Automobiles and televisions became commonplace.

POLITICAL SYSTEM

A Written Constitution Derived from an Unwritten One

The Republic of Ireland (Eire) is Europe's newest independent state, having been founded in 1921 and having separated itself completely from Britain in 1949. It devotes much attention to strengthening a sense of Irish national identity, and the resentment resulting from recent British occupation is still very strong. Because of its long domination by Great Britain, it is hardly surprising that the Irish political system so closely resembles that of its former conqueror. Before Ireland gained its independence, many Irishmen had served in the British House of Commons. Therefore, they had not only gained their parliamentary experience in Britain, but had also contributed to the very development of the British political system.

In some important ways, however, Irish democracy differs from the "Westminster model" of Great Britain. The Republic of Ireland has a written constitution that it

adopted in 1937. Article 2 of that document mandated the eventual reunification of Ireland: "The national territory consists of the whole island of Ireland, its islands and the territorial seas." This article was removed in 1998 as a contribution to a daring Northern Ireland settlement.

The Catholic Church

The constitution also pledges to support the teachings of the Roman Catholic Church. Except for the Vatican itself, Ireland has traditionally been the least secular state in all of Europe. The Catholic Church maintains considerable influence in social affairs. It controls all but 462 of the 3,940 primary and secondary schools. Senator Donal Lydon once noted, "the Church has contacts at every level of society, in every corner. Its influence is everywhere. Any politician who ignores the views of the Church would need to be crazy."

In recent years, the church's political influence has declined significantly, as a younger generation is more reluctant to accept Catholic teachings. In the 21st century six in ten Catholics regularly attend Sunday mass, down from 87% in 1984 and 91% in 1974. Only 38% of Irish Catholics regularly take communion. Contraceptive devices are now legal, but that does not prevent almost a third of all children from being born out of wedlock. The birth rate is falling dramatically, largely because

more and more Irish women have entered the workforce.

Following referenda in 1992 and 1995, Irish women are permitted to have abortions abroad; this was confirmed by a 2007 court ruling. Abortions may be performed in Ireland if the life of the mother is threatened. The constitutional ban does not disallow these exceptions. In March 2002 voters rejected a government effort to reverse a Supreme Court ruling that permits a pregnancy to be terminated when there is a risk that the mother may commit suicide. By 2006 more than 6,000 women were going to Britain to have an abortion, up from 578 in 1971. This would be as if 500,000 American women had to go to Toronto each year to obtain an abortion. By 2002 the abortion rate was over 10%. In a March 2002 referendum Irish voters rejected by the narrowest margin (50.4% vs. 49.6%) a proposal to tighten abortion laws.

As a result of a close vote in 1995 (50.2%, with urban support outweighing rural opposition), couples are allowed to divorce after a four–year separation. The 60% yes vote in Dublin swung the result. All the parties and most of the media supported it. The campaign was bitterly fought: opponents' posters read "Hello Divorce, Goodbye Daddy!," while proponents, irreverently referring to the spate of revelations about child–molesting and sexual transgressions by priests, waved signs reading "Let the bishops look after their own families!" These scandals involving clergy have shaken respect for ecclesiastical authority. The divorce rate is creeping up.

The government became involved in 2002 by ordering the police to set up a special team of detectives to investigate every case of sexual abuse involving priests ever reported. It also reached an agreement with 18 religious orders indemnifying them against abuse claims at state-financed schools they operated.

Critics charged that the government was slow to acknowledge the extent of the abuse and quick to exonerate the Church. Taoiseach Bertie Ahern therefore ordered a retired judge to launch a new investigation. The report published in November 2005 revealed one of the worst pedophile scandals ever in the southeastern diocese of Ferns. It identified 100 children who had complained of being sexually abused by priests. Some involved repeated rapes. It charged that the church and state had collaborated in covering up the abuse, and incriminated priests were transferred rather than punished. Compensation to victims could run into hundreds of millions of euros. There are signs that some parishioners are forgiving of priestly foibles. When a 73-year-old priest admitted in 2006 that he had fathered a child

Only recently did it become possible to receive a School Leaving certificate without passing an examination on the Irish language. Parliamentary documents are translated into it, and parliamentarians sometimes begin their speeches in the language. After a few sentences, though, they usually switch to English with the words "As I was saying ..." Some persons wonder what good a sign does which reads *Roinn na Plandeolaiochta. Aonad an Leicteron Mhiocrascóip'*, when the following words must be written underneath it to make it comprehensible: "Department of Plant Science. Electron Microscopy Unit."

Although Irish is still declining in the Gaeltacht areas, there is a trend among urban middle class families to send their children to Irish-language schools. The state devotes 500 million euros ($625 million) to Irish instruction every year. When protesters confronted a government minister demanding that Irish be made an official EU language, he discovered when talking to them that they did not even speak the language. Nevertheless, in 2007 the EU gave Irish the official status as the 23d official language so that it could be spoken in the European Parliament. When it joined the EU in 1973 it had chosen English as its working language.

In 2005 a law came into force forbidding the use of English names in road signs, government documents or survey maps. Another law mandates that outside the Gaeltacht signs bear the Irish version of the place names along with the English. A further change in road signs was made in 2005: speed limits are now posted in kilometers per hour, not miles per hour.

The Supreme Court

As in most countries, a written constitution also calls for the supreme court to uphold that fundamental document. The republic has one consisting of a chief justice and five others. It is empowered to decide on the constitutionality of laws if the president of the republic asks for an opinion. This provision, known in the United States as "judicial review," is not present in Great Britain because there is no writ-

with a local school teacher a year earlier, they closed ranks in his defense and agreed to let it go.

The 2002 referendum manifested an open revolt against the Church's dominance. Former President Mary Robinson spoke of the country's "new pluralism," which "means the movement of a predominantly Catholic country, where the Catholic moral code and doctrines had a very significant place, to a society still influenced by the role of the Church but having other voices and having a sense of space between legislators and the Catholic Church." In the spirit of the times, the 30-year censorship ban on *Playboy* magazine was lifted in 1996.

Whereas Protestants in Northern Ireland outnumber Catholics by about 58% to 42%, in the republic they constitute only about 5% of the population. Since Independence their numbers have declined by two-thirds. Many younger Protestants left; of the 115,000 who remain, most are elderly. Nevertheless, they have played and continue to play a role out of proportion to their size. They were important in creating modern Irish nationalism, from Wolfe Tone and his United Irishmen at the end of the 18th century to Charles Stewart Parnell and the home rule movement in the 19th. The republic's first president, Douglas Hyde, was one, as were great Irish writers like W.B. Yeats, Samuel Beckett and Oscar Wilde. They were products of the Dublin Protestant middle class. Ireland's premier university, Trinity in Dublin, was opened to Catholics only in recent years. Protestants created even such recognizable Irish products as Jameson whiskey and Guinness stout.

Two Languages

The constitution recognizes two official languages: English and Irish, the latter of which is a Celtic language, closely related to Scottish, Gaelic and more distantly, to Welsh. It was spoken by a majority of Irishmen until the first half of the 19th century when it rapidly lost ground to English. Irish is now "used frequently" by only about 5% of the people and is spoken as a native language by only about 2% (about 70,000 people) in seven small pockets along the western seaboard, an area known as The Gaeltacht. There are three dialects, and the speaker of one will not necessarily understand everything said in the other two.

Ireland is experiencing a resurgence of the Irish language. In 1996 polls, more than a million claimed "some proficiency" in it, and a half million said they were "fluent" or intended to become so. Those numbers justified the creation of an Irish-language television station, called *Teilifís na Gaeilge* (literally "Irish TV"), which broadcasts home-grown soap operas and news and sports programs aimed primarily at educated and urbanized Irishmen. They also prompted the education ministry to create a dozen new all-Irish primary schools.

With state policy to promote the use of Irish, it is a required subject in the schools.

Ireland

President Mary McAleese

ten constitution. However, English legal concepts and common law did replace the ancient Irish law (known as the Brehon law) by the 17th century. Thus Irish justice does bear an unmistakable British stamp. One British usage that was done away with in 2006 was that supreme court and high court judges are now addressed as "judge," not "my lord." The supreme court demonstrated its power in 1993 by declaring hundreds of EU directives unconstitutional because they had bypassed the Irish Senate.

The President

The most notable divergence from the "Westminster model" is that the Republic of Ireland does not have a monarch and all links with the British crown were severed in 1949. Instead of a monarch, the republic has a president, elected by the whole people for a seven–year term. This term can be renewed only once. The office is chiefly ceremonial, but unlike the British king or queen, Irish presidents have been leading political figures who continue to exercise considerable influence within the system, even if their powers are restricted.

The first woman president in Irish history, Mary Robinson, was elected in 1990. For years she had opposed Catholic positions on contraception, divorce, and homosexuality. Her election signaled an important change from traditional social attitudes. She became one of the most popular presidents in Irish history, enjoying a 93% approval rating in 1996. Not inclined to shy away from controversy, she unofficially met *Sinn Fein* leader Gerry Adams in 1993 and shook his hand in public in 1996, a political act that won her countrymen's praise. She became the first Irish chief of state to meet a British monarch. The fact that she is married to a Protestant manifests tolerance on this religiously torn island. In 1997 she became UN High Commissioner for Human Rights.

Robinson's election as president in 1990 forced Ireland's leaders to take a fresh look at Irish society, which has proved to be more receptive to change than most had realized. She became Ireland's most respected politician and helped pave the way for many women to win seats in parliament.

Her successor is Mary McAleese, a Belfast lawyer and vice–chancellor of Queen's University, who was the candidate of *Fianna Fail*. A resident of Northern Ireland, she is the first British subject to be elected president of Ireland. Under the Irish constitution, residents of the six "partitioned" counties of the North are considered citizens of the republic. She is a conservative Catholic who opposes the legalization of abortion and divorce, but she favors the ordination of women. She admits that she is an unabashed nationalist. She was not helped by the fact that Gerry Adams said during the campaign that she would make a fine president and by the fact that she has a cousin serving a life prison term for an IRA murder. She disavowed any links with Adams or *Sinn Fein* and pledged to stand above politics, to "seek to heal the hurt of divided Ireland," and to "build bridges." In October 2004 she was reelected without opposition.

The Parliament

Despite the differences described, the Irish political system developed by using Britain as a model. Irish government is parliamentary. This means that there are no checks and balances among three equal branches of government as in the United States. The lower house of parliament is supreme because unless the government can find a majority in it to carry forth its policies, that government must resign. Parliamentary government in the Republic of Ireland has usually been stable and durable. Conflict in the republic now takes place almost entirely within the parliamentary traditions and standards of conduct left by the British.

The Irish parliament (called the *Oireachtas*—pronounced "or–rock–tas") is bicameral. The upper house is the Senate (*Seanad*) composed of 60 members, 11 of whom are named by the prime minister and six by the universities. The remaining 43 are selected from five panels of nominees representing the national language and culture, agriculture and fisheries, organized and unorganized labor, industry and commerce, public administration and social services. The Senate has the power to delay legislation for up to 90 days in order to try to amend bills. However, the lower house can always outvote it.

One might ask why such a weak body should even exist. Upper houses usually have the greatest importance in federal

states where regional interests must be represented within the national government. However, the four traditional Irish provinces (Ulster in the north, Connacht in the west, Munster in the south and Leinster in the east) are not political units. Further, the 115 local authorities are supervised by the National Department of Environment. Local budgets are financed partly by grants from the national government, since local property taxes (known as "rates") cannot possibly provide enough revenue. In other words, the Republic of Ireland is a unitary state, and political authority rests largely with the central government. This centralized system exists even though local concerns are very important to Irish politicians. Thus, the Senate's purpose was never to represent provincial interests, but instead to give some political power to certain groups which could not win it in free elections before the whole people.

Political power is centered in the lower house of parliament known as the *Dáil* (pronounced "Doyle"). This house is composed of 166 members known as *Teachtái Dála*, or TD for short), elected from 41 constituencies. Elections must be held at least every five years. The prime minister (called the *Taoiseach*—pronounced "tea-such") may choose to hold earlier elections if he desires to reestablish or widen his party's majority in the *Dáil*. The *Taoiseach* is by far the most important political figure in the republic. With his cabinet, which is composed of from 7 to 15 members, he establishes the country's policies and dominates his party in the *Dáil* in order to get his government's bills through parliament. He is also the best paid head of government in the world. His salary is 310,000 euros ($446,000) per year, compared with the U.S. president ($400,000) and the British prime minister ($387,700).

Electoral System: Proportional Representation

In any democratic system, parties usually play a key role, presenting candidates and policy issues as alternatives from which to choose. They educate the voters, wage election campaigns and, above all, rule or prepare to rule. Political parties are especially important in the Irish Republic because interest groups are far less tightly organized than in most other European countries. Thus, Irish parties are particularly important channels for interest groups expressing their concerns and wants at high policy levels.

Parties seek seats in the *Dáil* by means of a particularly complex electoral system—a form of proportional representation system involving what is known as a single transferable vote in multimember constituencies. The voter marks his ballot by placing the numeral 1 opposite the name of the candidate of his first choice and may then place the numeral 2 opposite the name of his second choice, continuing on until he has numbered all the candidates. Thus the voter is able to say in effect, "I wish to vote for A, but if he does not need my vote or if he has no chance of being elected, transfer my vote to B. If B in turn does not need my vote, or he has no chance of election, transfer my vote to C," and so forth.

Thus, the system reflects more completely the voters' preferences for the three to five seats filled by each constituency. This makes it easier for smaller parties and independents to win parliamentary representation. At the same time, it is designed to prevent fringe politicians and a high number of small parties from winning seats in the *Dáil* and thereby adversely affecting the stability of the parliamentary system. It is therefore one of the better proportional representation systems in Europe. However, this complicated system enormously slows down the tabulation of the votes, and it often takes several days to determine the final results of an Irish election.

The republic's electoral system affects Irish politics in several important ways. By permitting voters to discriminate among candidates of the same party (as does the American primary system), it pits members of the same party against each other. Thus, the individual candidate's appeal must veer from the policy of the national party and be far more closely tailored to local concerns. Politicians compete with each other to perform a variety of services for local constituents, and this strengthens an important characteristic of Irish politics: personality and personal ties become far more significant than national policy issues.

Moreover, the local political clubs, not the national parties (which have very small staffs), recruit candidates and wage campaigns. Although it is not required by law, *Dáil* members almost always come from the constituency in which they are elected. Also, most TDs continue to hold local political office at the same time. All of these factors represent a strong decentralized tendency in Irish politics: politicians show strong loyalties to their local constituencies, but at the same time the national party leadership needs to maintain strong party discipline as it seeks a majority in the *Dáil*. Without such discipline, no government could possibly survive.

Political Parties

Irish political parties are noticeably different from British parties whose bases were traditionally rooted in different social classes. The Republic of Ireland is a more homogeneous country, and it has historically been economically underdeveloped. It has no major national, regional, religious or racial differences that could become the basis for different parties. There are, of course, social cleavages, but these do not have the overriding significance that they do in many other European countries. It is more likely that the dividing line between the two major parties is determined by the position one's father or grandfather took on the signing of the Anglo–Irish treaty in 1921, which divided the island and created the Irish Free State. In 1932, after a bloody civil war followed by intense domestic political rivalry, the party that had accepted the treaty (now the *Fine Gael*, pronounced Finna Gwail, meaning "Family of Irish") suffered an election defeat and relinquished power to the *Fianna Fail* (pronounced Fee–anna Foil), which had originally opposed the treaty. The 1932 elections firmly established democratic government, which stands or falls on the parties' willingness to alternate power peacefully, in response to the wishes of the voters.

The "pro" or "anti" distinction between the two major parties does not mean very much today. But the importance of family ties in Irish politics inclines Irishmen to vote as their fathers and grandfathers did, and it encourages political activists to become leaders in those same parties. It is hardly surprising that parties that are not formed along class or religious lines are not very ideological in their orientation.

North Americans who observe the two major Irish parties have the same difficulties distinguishing between them that Europeans express about American parties. Perhaps the 1960s saying of George Wallace about the American mainline parties applies to their Irish counterparts: "There's not a dime's worth of difference between them." Both parties in the republic are catch–all parties that attract voters from all social groups. Both are rather conservative, anti–secular, nationalistic and predominantly male. Both are what one would call Christian Democratic parties elsewhere in Europe.

The Irish party system has developed into two more or less stable blocs. In the past three decades, the government has alternated between the *Fianna Fail* and a coalition combining *Fine Gael* and the Labour Party. Traditionally *Fianna Fail* did not enter coalitions, but it must often rely on support from small parties, making its governments more fragile. *Fine Gael*–Labour coalitions were made easier by the fact that there is very little ideological distance between them.

Hon. Bertie Ahern
former *Taoiseach* of Ireland

Fianna Fail has governed most of the time since 1932. It is moderate to conservative on economic matters; it still has a slightly anti–British attitude although it has eliminated many of the more militant elements in the aftermath of a party split in 1970 over the question of Irish unification. It attracts considerable support from businessmen and professional people as well as parts of the urban working class. However, its greatest strength remains in the rural western regions. The native Irish–speakers solidly support it because it has stamped itself as a party seeking restoration of the Irish language (at least nominally). It often sees itself as a grass roots party and demonstrates populist tendencies.

Fianna Fail was able to stay in power after 1989 only by forming a historic coalition with its most bitter political enemies, the Progressive Democrats. This was the first time ever that *Fianna Fail* has shared power while ruling. In 1992 Charles Haughey (who was given a state funeral in June 2006) was finally forced out after it had been revealed that he had been aware of police bugging of two journalists' phones. He was replaced as *Taoiseach* by Albert Reynolds, a self–made pet–food tycoon.

After calling his own *Fine Gael* coalition partner "reckless, irresponsible, and dishonest," Reynolds lost a vote of no-confidence in 1992 which prompted a snap election. *Fianna Fail* suffered its worst electoral setback in 50 years. Reynolds emerged from the polling badly wounded and had to enter *Fianna Fail*'s first coalition with Labour in order to stay in office. With 100 seats, the coalition had the biggest *Dáil* majority in Irish political history until a crisis broke it apart in 1994 and forced *Fianna Fail* out of the government. Bertie Ahern became party leader.

Ireland

Hon. Brian Cowen
Taoiseach of Ireland

Ahern led the party to victory in the 1997 elections. As usual, it took weeks of haggling and deal making before the new prime minister could go to the elegant Phoenix Park residence of the president and ask for permission to form a government. A populist Dubliner from a lower class background who is separated from his wife and lived openly with his girlfriend, Ahern vowed to "cut taxes, cut crime and work for peace in Northern Ireland." Although reputed to be "green" or pro–Catholic on the volatile subject of Northern Ireland, he pushed hard for progress in the peace talks.

The cloud of financial scandal was looming over the party when a judge found former *Taoiseach* Charles Haughey guilty of accepting gifts of almost $11 million from business interests while in office and then stashing it away in offshore bank accounts, presumably in order to hide it from the tax collectors. A 2006 official report raised that figure to $15 million. He paid $1.4 million in back taxes in 2000, and in 2003 he was required to pay another $5.3 million to tax authorities. Ahern had been a close colleague of both men for many years, and their sins greatly embarrassed him and his government.

Riding on a tide of popular contentment with the economy in 2002, Ahern's *Fianna Fail* became the first government in more than 30 years to be reelected. He did it again in May 2007, when his party captured 78 seats, making him the first *Taoiseach* since Eamon deValera to win three elections in a row. With 11 years in office, he became the longest-serving Taoiseach in modern Irish history.

Until only a few weeks before the 2007 election it had appeared that he would lose. He had to make a public apology for accepting financial gifts and loans as finance minister in the early 1990s. The issue came up again in September 2007 when he had to call a vote of no-confidence over it, which he won 81 to 76. His reputation as the "Teflon Taoiseach"

failed him in April 2008. He decided to resign on May 6 before being pushed out of office because of the financial investigation against him. Half the electorate indicated in a poll that it no longer trusted him to run the country. He had become an electoral liability that could threaten passage of the EU Lisbon Treaty in the June referendum.

He had gained stature as a statesman in May 2007 when he helped facilitate a dramatic Northern Ireland agreement and became the first Irish leader to address both houses of the British parliament. His last hurrah was a speech before a joint session of the U.S. Congress just a week before leaving office on May 6, 2008. Bill Clinton and Tony Blair gave him glowing testimonials for his effectiveness in the Northern Irish negotiations. He also had presided over Ireland's most successful economic boom, which reversed the traditional emigration.

Ahern was replaced as Taoiseach by Brian Cowen, who had been in politics since age 24 when he succeeded to his father's parliamentary seat. He is known to be highly intelligent and articulate, as well as pugnacious when he has to be. In his long career, he has occupied most top cabinet posts, including the foreign and finance ministries, and shown in competence in each.

Fine Gael is a traditional establishment party that draws a disproportionate share of its votes from the upper and middle classes and from farmers with large holdings. Its leaders also tend to be drawn from somewhat higher social strata. Although it tends to be moderate to conservative on economic matters, the party has moved slightly to the left to accommodate the Labour Party. *Fine Gael* is the most centralized and hierarchically organized in the republic. Led by John Bruton, a wealthy rancher with long governmental experience, *Fine Gael* slipped in 1992 to less than 25% of the votes and 45 seats. Nevertheless, Bruton was able to form a center–left governing coalition with the Labour and Democratic Left parties in 1994 and become *Taoiseach*.

In 1997 Irish voters continued a tradition maintained from 1969 to 2002: never reelect a government no matter how good its record. Despite the fact that the *Fine Gael* government presided over the strongest economy in the 75–year history of independent Ireland, with the fastest growth rate in the EU that won it the nickname, "Celtic Tiger," and living standards that were near the EU average, it was thrown out of power. Its partner, the Labour Party, collapsed in the voting booths. The two parties were rudely reminded of an old saying in Irish politics: No good turn ever goes unpunished.

In 2002, *Fine Gael* nearly experienced collapse. It fell from 54 to only 31 seats and only 22.5% of the votes. Its humiliation signaled a realignment of Irish politics, as the votes of the two traditional rival parties dropped from 84% in 1982 to only 64% in 2002. The Irish party divide may now develop along left–right lines, as is typical in the rest of Europe. In 2007 it made a comeback, winning 51 seats. But it is in the opposition.

Unlike in Britain, the Labour Party in Ireland has never articulated socialist or Marxist ideologies. In fact, by western standards, it is hardly a party of the left although it does have a left–wing minority. It had been virtually excluded from urban politics in the eastern part of the country, and most of the working class voted for one of the two major parties, especially the *Fianna Fail*. But its former leader, Dick Spring, an astute rugby–playing lawyer with a wife from Virginia, brought Labour more into the public eye. Labour's main electoral support is found among rural, agrarian workers. Its importance in Irish politics was greatly enhanced by the fact that until 1997 it had been an essential part of any ruling coalition led by either *Fine Gael* or *Fianna Fail*. Labour experienced disaster in 2002. But with a new leader, Pat Rabbitte, it held on to 20 seats in 2007 and is in the opposition.

Minor Parties

Despite the proportional representation electoral system, which usually permits many parties to enter parliament, small parties had almost entirely disappeared from Irish parliamentary politics. Twelve representatives of minor parties and five independents did win seats in the 2007, elections. The environmentalist Greens grew in 2002 to 3.8% and six seats and held on to all its seats in 2007. This was enough to enter a governing coalition with Ahern's Fianna Fail in 2007; this is the first time it has been in government. Their price was a proposed carbon tax and measures to deal with climate change. They might create problems for Ireland's relations with the EU since they have opposed membership and every new EU treaty, including Nice, since Ireland joined in 1973.

The Progressive Democrats (PD) broke away from *Fianna Fail* in 1985 in protest against its hard–line Northern Ireland policy. It temporarily displaced Labour as third largest party, a position that Labour had occupied since 1922. The PD appeared to break the mold of Irish party politics; it supplanted Labour as *Fine Gael*'s favorite coalition partner although *Fine Gael* and PD compete for the same kinds of voters. In 2007 it captured only two seats and moved closer to political irrelevance.

The Marxist–oriented Communist Party of Ireland seeks to unify the entire island under an orthodox communist regime. It plays no significant role whatsoever in Irish politics. The Trotskyite Socialists captured one seat in 1997. The Workers' Party took that name in 1976 following a split six years earlier among the ranks of the small *Sinn Fein* Party, which was the political arm of the Irish Republican Army (IRA). The split resulted in two distinct groups: the first is an "official" IRA, whose political arm—the Workers Party—has for years competed in parliamentary elections in the republic and has accepted the few seats which it has won.

The second group is the "provisional" IRA (Provos), which became Marxist and fervently nationalist. Until 1987 it refused to recognize the Dublin parliament as a legitimate Irish parliament, and it therefore refused to participate in elections, except for town councils in which it occupies a few seats in both parts of Ireland. Its suspicions that it would win precious few votes were confirmed in the 1997 elections, when *Sinn Fein* won a paltry 2.5% of the votes. Caoimhghin O Caolain became the first member of *Sinn Fein* ever to win a seat in the Irish parliament since independence in 1922. The result underscores two facts: although polls indicate that two–thirds of Eire's population believes ideally that Ireland should one day be a unified nation, the overwhelming majority abhors the violent attempt to unify Ireland by bullets and bombs.

It is precisely to try to overcome its isolation that leader Gerard (Gerry) Adams ended the party's boycott of the Irish (though not of the British) parliament. As he stated: "We've lost touch with the people for the simple reason that we have not been able to represent them in the only political forum they know. To break out into the broad stream of people's consciousness, we have to approach them at their own level." To many traditionalists, this approach smacked of betrayal. As one die–hard remarked, "when you lie down with the dogs, you get up with the fleas."

Nevertheless, *Sinn Fein* made dramatic gains in 2002, capturing 6.5% of the votes and five seats, nearly winning three more. It is the only party with parliamentary seats in both parts of Ireland (and in London although it refused to occupy its Westminster seats). Analysts concluded that *Sinn Fein*'s success was not primarily due to a rise of nationalist sentiment in the republic. Instead its young candidates exuded dynamism and concern in poorer areas on the island. It appeals mainly to the urban poor. All other parties were worried about its electoral success and gave a sigh of relief when it lost a seat in 2007, winning only four.

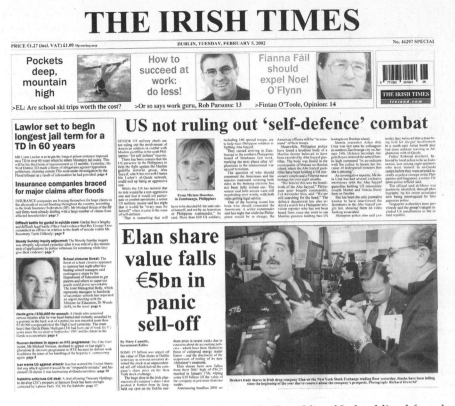

Foreign and Defense Policies

A central reality in the republic of Ireland's foreign and defense policy is that the Irish live on a politically divided island and are a politically and religiously divided people. Few foreign policy issues can be treated entirely separately from these facts. Most Irish citizens and politicians in the republic want to see these divisions overcome, and no Irish republican government has ever recognized the division of the island as permanent. Most people in the republic do not use the term "Republic of Ireland." which implies permanent division, but instead refer to their state almost exclusively as "Ireland." But the unification issue is no longer as important in Irish politics as it once was.

Younger leaders with no direct memories of the bloody struggle and with far greater interest in Ireland's economic development replaced the old revolutionary elite who fought for independence against Britain. A 2004 British Council poll of young Irish professionals revealed a dramatic transformation of Irish attitudes toward Britain: three-fourths have a broadly favorable view of Britain, and 81% described the relationship between the two countries as good to excellent. Irish unity remains important, but it is no longer as pressing as it once was. In fact, personal links with Britain are stronger than with Northern Ireland: only half the respondents had ever visited the six northern counties, whereas 84% had been to London.

The Republic of Ireland lived for a long time in the shadow of Great Britain although it has become a much more confidant nation and is no longer obsessed by its ancient hatred of the British. Because of Britain's part in Irish history and the continued presence of the British in Northern Ireland, the republic is inclined to remain neutral in conflicts where Britain is involved. It remained neutral in World War II—in fact it even refused to observe blackouts in its cities at night. Thus German bombers were able to orient themselves by regrouping in the skies over Dublin and then flying in a direct line toward such British cities as Liverpool. In 1982, the republic also refused to go along with EU sanctions against Argentina when Britain, a fellow member, was engaged in an armed struggle for control of the Falkland Islands.

Ireland's policy of neutrality does not mean that the republic is ideologically neutral or politically indifferent. It shares the basic democratic, political and economic values of other countries in Europe and North America. However, it is only one of four EU countries that have not joined NATO. This fact does cause disputes sometimes. For instance, when the *Dáil* debated the ratification of the EU's Single European Act (SEA), which calls for majority votes in the EU Council of Ministers and a completely free market, some members questioned how the republic could remain neutral and still take part in the security and foreign policy coopera-

Ireland

tion for which the act called. The Supreme Court found that the SEA's political cooperation section was unconstitutional and therefore ruled that a referendum on amending the constitution was necessary. In the 1987 voting, 70% voted in favor of it and 30% against. This perennial question arose again in 2008 when Irish debated whether the EU's Lisbon Treaty (a revision of the failed EU constitution) violated their treasured neutrality.

Ireland's long–established policy of military neutrality is increasingly irrelevant since the country cooperates on European security matters, and Irish and British troops coordinate the fight against the IRA. In 1999 it decided to establish formal links with NATO through the Partnership for Peace (PfP). Following the September 11, 2001, terrorist attacks against the United States, Ireland offered its airspace and airfields to American military planes. In 2003 about 30,000 American soldiers passed through Shannon Airport during the military buildup around Iraq. However, *Taoiseach* Ahern declared, "Ireland cannot engage in support of military action because we work under the UN resolution." It had served a two-year term on the UN Security council from 2001–2.

The republic is so enveloped by the military forces of the Atlantic Alliance that it is able to keep its own defense forces very small. Internal security rests almost entirely with the unarmed police, the 10,000-strong *Garda Siochana* ("guardians of the peace"). External defense is the responsibility of the permanent defense forces that number 10,460, about 8,500 of whom are land forces. The Navy has 1,100 personnel and seven coastal and patrol vessels. The Air Force has 860 troops and is composed of fewer than 40 aircraft, including helicopters. Military service is voluntary, and there is also a reserve defense force of 14,800 that could be mobilized in time of crisis. Ireland has contributed troops to UN peacekeeping units throughout the world, including in southern Lebanon, Bosnia, Kosovo, Croatia, Cyprus, Western Sahara, Ethiopia/Eritrea, and East Timor. In 1991 the Irish government supported UN policy toward Iraq. Although Ireland played no direct role in the war, it did permit U.S. military planes to refuel at Shannon Airport, thereby prompting many domestic critics to cry that its neutrality had been breached.

Out of sheer economic necessity, Ireland joined the EU in 1973, at the same time that Britain entered. Ireland stood to benefit from EU regional aid and the Common Agricultural Program (CAP), which in 2002 accounted for 4% of its GDP or $1.5 billion and in no year exceeded 5% of its GDP. In three decades, such assistance has totaled over $32 billion. EU aid helps modernize Ireland's infrastructure. For a few years CAP funds were a boon to Irish farmers, but their benefits were not lasting. Adjusting to CAP, western Ireland has been forced to change from its traditional dairy and beef farming economy to tourism and forestry. In 25 years its forestry industry is expected to be as important to the economy as its food industry is now. Its trade volume with Britain (to which a fifth of its exports still go) remains very high.

EU membership has served to shift Irish foreign trade and political attention away from Britain to a broader view of the rest of Europe. Former President Robinson argued, "it lifts the burden of the relationship with our close neighbor. We are now partners with them in Europe. The history is still there, but it is less a tight connection and burden between us." For centuries Ireland had defined itself in relation to Britain, as a victim. That is far less prominent now. Today it is more inclined to define itself in relation to Europe and the EU, in which it is recognized as an equal. It distinguishes itself from Britain and benefits from being the most pro–European anglophone country in the EU. This foreign policy reorientation has not altered the fact that hundreds of thousands of Irish still live and work in Britain, where they enjoy the same political, legal and social welfare rights as British citizens.

Some Irish worry that increasing integration with Europe may have negative effects on Irish culture. Arts Minister Sile de Valera, granddaughter of Eamon de Valera, said during a visit to Boston that EU regulations and directives "often seriously impinge on our identity, culture and traditions." Ahern's deputy prime minister, Mary Harney, also warned against a more centralized and bureaucratic Europe. She claimed that spiritually Ireland is "probably a lot closer to Boston than to Berlin."

In a June 8, 2001, referendum marked by massive abstention and indifference, a majority of Irish slapped the EU in the face by rejecting the Nice Treaty, which had laid out the process for enlarging the community. Many Irish were smarting from an earlier EU rebuke of the country's economic policy, were fearful of losing EU funding if a dozen poorer countries were admitted, and were uneasy that its neutrality was being threatened by Europe's acquisition of its own defense and security role.

A second referendum was held in October 2002, and this time the government spent ten times more on the referendum campaign than it had the first time. Voters overwhelmingly endorsed the Treaty of Nice 54% to 46%, with a turnout of 48.5%, giving the green light to EU institutional reform and enlargement and causing a sigh of relief throughout the community. Ireland is the only EU country whose constitution required that the new constitutional Lisbon Treaty be submitted to a referendum in June 2008. Voters rejected it.

In 2002 Ireland gained more visibility in the EU when Pat Cox was elected president of the European Parliament. Thanks to his admirable performance, he was placed on the short list for the exalted post of European Commission President to succeed Romano Prodi.

In the first half of 2004 Ireland assumed the EU presidency, oversaw the entry of ten new members and guided the discussions to salvage the new constitutional treaty on which the members could not agree the end of 2003. In 2004 former Taoiseach John Bruton was selected to be the EU's ambassador in Washington. Inspired as a youth by John F. Kennedy, he entered politics right after graduation from the University of Dublin, becoming a member of parliament at age 22 before studying law. A key part of his job is to help repair transatlantic relations. "I always enjoy a good argument. In America people are much more willing to be forthright and to debate with no hard feelings."

Leaders of the accession states were welcomed in a glittering ceremony in front of the presidential palace in Dublin on May 1, 2004. They looked to Ireland more than any other country as their model. Charles Grant of the Center for European Reform noted: "Ireland is a poor country dominated by a big neighbor, and all of the new countries except Poland are small countries dominated by big neighbors."

But all know that it is poor no more. When it joined the EU in 1973 its per-capita income was a mere 62% of the EU average; by 2003 it had reached 136%. It slashed its top corporate tax rate from over 40% to 12.5% and the state's share of GDP from 54% in the 1980s to only 33% in 2004. Foreign investment poured in. Unemployment fell from 17% in 1987 to 4.3% in 2006. Cox stated the obvious: Membership "turned us from a stagnant, backward, failed part of the British regional economy into a modern and prosperous European country." This tiny land has become the third richest country in the EU. That is exactly what fascinates the new eastern partners and what they want for themselves. But this wealth has a significant consequence: Ireland has become a net contributor to Brussels' coffers and therefore helps finance the assistance for the poorer new members.

Reunification

The vast majority of the citizens of the Irish Republic and virtually all of its political leaders share the goal of reunifying

Ireland

all 32 Irish counties. But they eventually wish to see this accomplished peacefully and with the consent of the Northern Irish. In Northern Ireland, about a million Irish Protestants outnumber the half million Catholics, so Irish unity must take a form palatable to the Protestants. Violence spilled over from Northern Ireland to the South. The Irish government outlawed the provisional IRA; government raids and arrests provide frequent reminders that the IRA can expect no tolerance within the republic. In 1982 a Dublin court convicted an Irishman for possessing explosives, even though the crime was committed in Britain. This was the first application of a 1976 law that was part of an ongoing Irish–British cooperation against terrorism in both countries.

In 1981 a U.S. court convicted the Irish Northern Aid (NORAID) committee for failing to list the IRA as its principal foreign agent. The Irish government ordered its diplomatic representatives in the United States to boycott the 1983 annual St. Patrick's Day parade in New York City because the organizers of the parade had chosen an IRA supporter as Grand Marshal. In explaining its decision, the Irish government noted that the IRA's actions, which include collecting money from unsuspecting Irish–Americans to finance violent operations in Northern Ireland, "have deepened the wounds of our troubled history and continue to postpone the day of Irish unity and reconciliation." Dublin frequently appealed to Americans not to support violence in Ireland. Funds from NORAID declined, and the IRA sought to fill its coffers by means of extortion and racketeering in Northern Ireland.

The Irish government realizes that unification can be accomplished only in cooperation with Britain and Northern Ireland. This has brought the Irish and British prime ministers together for periodic high-level meetings to discuss the developments in the area. This was dangerous as was shown by the attempt on Prime Minister Thatcher's life in the grisly 1984 IRA bombing of the hotel in Brighton where she was staying. She narrowly escaped death, and several Tory leaders were killed or wounded. The bombing inflamed anti–Irish sentiments to a height unequaled since the IRA murdered Lord Mountbatten in 1979, and it set back progress towards peace.

Nevertheless, consultation between representatives of Eire and the UK continues within the rubric of the 1985 Anglo–Irish accord. For the first time, this permitted Dublin some say in Northern Ireland's affairs. The agreement enjoys majority support in the republic. In 1990 the Pope appointed Bishop Cahal B. Daly, a fierce critic of IRA terrorism, as Ireland's primate. In 1993 optimism was ignited by a joint declaration by the British and Irish prime ministers offering *Sinn Fein* a seat at the bargaining table to discuss Northern Ireland's future if the IRA renounced violence. Prime Minister John Major promised that Britain would not stand in the way of a united Ireland if a majority of Northern Ireland residents supported such a step. *Taoiseach* Albert Reynolds pledged that there would be no change in the six counties' status without majority consent.

As a symbol of returning normalcy with Britain in 1995, Prince Charles became the first member of the royal family to make an official visit to the Irish Republic since 1922. Also in 1995, David Trimble, then leader of the Ulster Unionist Party, the main Protestant group, traveled to Dublin and met with *Taoiseach* Bruton. This was the first time since 1922 a Unionist leader was received in Dublin. On November 26, 1998, Tony Blair became the first British prime minister since Ireland's independence to speak to the Irish parliament.

Talks involving eight Northern Ireland parties and the British and Irish governments continued despite sporadic outbreaks of violence. In 1998 a majority in Eire backed the deletion from their constitution of the mandate to unify the island. As a result of the 1998 Good Friday Peace Agreement, followed by dramatic "yes" referenda votes for the accord in both the republic (94.4%) and Northern Ireland (71.1%), Ireland reached the doorstep of peace. Trimble and his Catholic counterpart, John Hume, received the 1998 Nobel Peace Prize for their role in reaching a historic peace agreement in Northern Ireland that year. Despite continuing setbacks, there is optimism that "the troubles" will end.

In February 2005 the Dublin government named *Sinn Fein* leaders Gerry Adams, Martin McGuinness and Martin Ferris as members of the IRA's ruling

**Mr. David Trimble
Former Leader, Ulster Unionist Party**

army council. Joined by the British government, it dropped the polite fiction that the leaders and organizations of *Sinn Fein* and IRA are separate. Ahern declared an end to "creative ambiguity." They are both to be regarded as one and the same. Justice Minister Michael McDowell called the IRA a "colossal criminal operation" and launched a major campaign against IRA racketeering. For decades the IRA has operated a range of criminal enterprises to finance IRA operations, including robbing banks and armored cars, counterfeiting currency and goods, smuggling fuel and cigarettes, and trafficking in drugs.

In February 2005 the Irish government ordered the police to move in on IRA money-laundering operations, believed to center on hotels and pubs. £3 million in cash were seized at the home of a businessman. Five young men were convicted in a Dublin court after their vehicles were found filled with fake police uniforms, stun guns, balaclavas, lump hammers and lots of *Sinn Fein* election posters. The Irish and British governments agreed to share cross-border policing duties.

At Easter 2006 the Dublin government revived the tradition of commemorating the failed 1916 rebellion against the British by marching 2,500 soldiers and veterans down the main boulevard, O'Connell Street, where most of the fighting had taken place. To showcase the current friendly relationship, the British ambassador joined the leaders of the six main political parties in attendance. The republic is divided over whether the 1916 rebels were heroic patriots or trouble makers, and there was lively debate over whether the parade was an appropriate way to remember the event.

In an attempt a month earlier to demonstrate fairness and tolerance of a unionist alternative tradition, the government had permitted a march down O'Connell Street, past the Post Office, by 300 loyalists, most of them relatives of IRA victims. However, they were blocked by republican dissidents. The result was the largest riot Dublin had seen for a quarter of a century. Gangs of young and drunken thugs wrecked cars and looted stores. The damages were set at 10 million euros ($15 million). *Tanaiste* (Deputy Prime Minister) Mary Harney admitted that the riots had brought "shame on the city, shame on the country."

On May 8, 2007, a power-sharing agreement in Northern Ireland was celebrated after three decades of violence and five years of rule from London. (See United Kingdom)

ECONOMY

In the last half century, Ireland has undergone an economic revolution. The in-

Ireland

flux of foreign investment as a result of generous incentives and the increase in trade have added significantly to the prosperity of Ireland. More than 1,100 foreign firms employ half of all Irish workers involved in manufacturing. Foreign companies are also responsible for 80% of the country's non–food exports. It has also acquired an impressive high-tech industry. By 1986 it had already achieved the highest ratio of high technology to total exports of any EU country.

What made Ireland so rich so quickly? There is a combination of factors: It cut spending, taxes and borrowing, and it adopted the euro. It established a social partnership between trade unions and management that keeps wages down and respects the opinions of the unions. Labor markets were liberalized making businesses relatively free to fire and hire. Also employer social security payments are lower. The EU poured in transfers equivalent to almost 5% of Ireland's GDP. The European single market was a boon to trade. Personal taxes are kept low, and generous corporate taxes of 12.5% attract lots of foreign direct investment (FDI).

Roughly a fourth of all American investments in Europe go to Ireland; this is more than America invests in China. Educational standards, including in business administration, engineering and the sciences, are kept high, and English is spoken.

Although Ireland's birth rate is now falling, it still has a relatively young population. Finally, more people are working. More women are in the work force, and labor-force participation for both sexes has risen from 60% in the 1980s to 70% today.

Outmigration has ended, and immigrants are pouring into the country, one-third to one-half of whom have Irish roots. By one estimate, a quarter of a million people immigrated between 1995 and 2000. The Irish government estimated that 14,000 Irish returned from the U.S since 2001, more than half of them from New York. The U.S. Census Bureau reported that by 2005 the Irish population in the U.S. had shrunk by 28,500 to 128,000; the number of illegal Irish had dwindled to 25,000 to 50,000.

Like the UK, Ireland opened its doors to citizens of new EU member states after May 2004. There has been an influx of 300,000 from those countries, mainly from Poland, who have registered for work. This includes many students looking for temporary jobs while polishing up their English. Dublin's main afternoon newspaper, *The Evening Herald*, includes a Polish-language supplement, and there are other locally published newspapers and magazines available in Polish. Some Irish sus-

Irish village life

pect uneasily that there are now more Polish speakers in the country than Gaelic speakers.

These newcomers are a key factor in the continued strong economic growth rate and for the construction boom. There is no evidence that they have displaced Irish workers, and they are still paid less than Irish although the gap is narrowing. But their presence has sparked a debate over whether they are driving down wages. Trade unions pointed to Irish Ferries, which wanted to employ cheaper Latvian crews. An *Irish Times* poll in 2006 revealed that three-fourths of respondents favored the reintroduction of a permit system for new EU arrivals.

Growth and prosperity in Ireland have been dramatic. Less than 30% of all households are rented. The Irish entered the 1990s with a 50% gap between their living standards and those of the EU average. By 1998 income in Ireland had caught up with the European mean and surpassed Britain in per capita GDP for the first time in history. Also a variety of social welfare indicators in Ireland are as good or better than in Britain. Life expectancy is about the same for women (81.4 years) and men (76.5 vs. 76.7 years). Ireland spends a higher percentage of its GDP on public education. Per capita consumption rose 10.5% from 1990 to 1996, twice the average rate of increase in the rest of Europe. Sustained economic growth (down to ca. 5% in 2007), low inflation, a hard currency (the euro), a healthy trade surplus, and low unemployment cohabit with a growing income gap between rich and poor.

It is an extremely productive, capital–intensive and modern economy, only partly owned by foreigners, including companies like IBM, Intel, Fujitsu, and Motorola, as well as banks and financial institutions, like Citibank, Merrill Lynch, and Daiwa. Nine of the world's ten top

drug companies are there; one third of all personal computers sold in Europe are manufactured in Ireland; it is the world's largest software exporter (ahead of the U.S.). Dell's computer plant in Limerick is one of the company's most productive; HP Compaq is Galway's largest employer. The country is trying to invest more in research and development so that its own companies can grow to such status.

Agriculture has declined in importance in the last four decades—the percentage of the working force employed in farming dropped from 43% to 6% in 2008; they produce only 3.3% of GDP. Industry's share in employment is 28%, producing 38.8% of GDP. Services account for 66% of employment and 57.9% of GDP. The agricultural life of Ireland benefited from EU membership, although income from the CAP helped fuel the rapid growth of welfare spending and thus contributed to the country's debt problem. Income in the farm sector has doubled in the past three decades, and today one–half of the value of agricultural production is exported. However, family farming remains relatively unsophisticated, and food processing has not developed as far as in some EU countries.

Two other sources of revenue are important to Ireland: tourists and pubs. By 2000 Ireland was the fastest growing tourist destination in Europe, growing by 12% during the 1990s. Each year 5.5 million tourists (that is more than the number of Irishmen there are to receive them) visit the nation despite the fact that Ireland is the only EU nation not directly linked to the continent since the opening of the English Channel "Chunnel" in 1993. Americans account for 14% of the total, although they tend to spend more money than other visitors.

They drink in over 11,000 pubs; the ratio of one pub for every 300 people is even more striking when one knows that half the population is under age 25, and thus the ratio of pubs to those old enough to drink is even higher. Annual alcoholic consumption per Irish adult jumped from 10.6 quarts of pure alcohol in 1985 to nearly 15.8 quarts in 2000, compared with the EU average of 9.5 quarts, despite high taxes on wine and spirits. This is the highest increase in the EU and has brought with it more social problems, such as higher absenteeism on the job, auto accidents and medical care costs.

With alcohol consumption up 17% in the decade before 2008, both parts of Ireland moved to lower the legal driving blood alcohol content from .08% to .05%. This raised concern from an unexpected quarter—the Catholic Church. Since the number of priests is rapidly decreasing, more and more of them have to drive from church to church to say two or three masses per day. After each service, the priest must consume any communion wine left over since it is considered to be Christ's blood in the Eucharist; throwing it out would be blasphemous. The clergy must therefore sometimes drive impaired from parish to parish.

Pubs have been healthier since 2004 when smoking was banned throughout the republic in all pubs, restaurants, and work places (including company cars and trucks). Only prisons, police cells, psychiatric hospitals and hotel rooms were exempted.

The Irish economy is dependent on events outside of the country because of the important roles that trade and foreign sources of energy play in the life of the island. It is a land that must import many essential raw materials. It does have a large quantity of zinc ore, as well as copper, sulphur, baryte, gypsum and dolomite. Its only valuable energy source is peat, or turf bogs, which cover parts of the Central Plain and large areas along the south, west and northwest coasts. It lacks sizable coal deposits, but it extracts natural gas near Kinsale Head.

Although recent discoveries on the ocean shelf may produce oil for Ireland, at this time the country has very little. Yet 70% of its energy needs are supplied by oil. Thus, the Irish economy was drastically affected by changes in oil prices, while remaining dependent upon unstable world trade for its strength. It generates no nuclear power.

Almost 90% of Ireland's GDP is generated by trade. Manufactured goods account for well over half the value of exports. Since almost a third of these go to the United Kingdom (and the percentage is steadily declining) and another third to the continental EU members (a percentage which has steadily risen since 1973), Ireland is vulnerable to economic ups and downs in those industrialized countries. In an attempt to reduce that vulnerability somewhat, the Irish severed the link between the British and Irish pound in 1979 and tied its currency later to the European Monetary System. In 2002 it joined 10 other EU nations in adopting the euro. Ireland presents an image of financial stability that foreign investors like.

In 2005, total public debt stood at 33% of GDP (down from 131% in 1987), and its 2004 budget deficit was only .4% of GDP, well below the 3% limit required to meet the EU's convergence criterion for the European currency. Taxes are kept low for foreign firms in order to attract them to invest in Ireland, making it the EU's biggest tax haven. New investors receive tax breaks, and overall corporate tax rates are 12.5%, far below the EU average of more than 30%. Personal taxes also began to be reduced sharply. Ireland still has Europe's highest VAT at 21%.

The economic growth that Ireland has enjoyed since the mid-1950s is impressive. After averaging 6% from 1993–8, it slowed down. It stood at around 4.5% from 2004 to 2007, but by 2008 it was the lowest in two decades. Inflation at 3.9% in 2006 is a worry. The economy has speeded ahead so rapidly that Ireland has not had time to revamp its infrastructure. Roads are often clogged, hospitals are overcrowded, and housing is tight and expensive.

Average Dublin real estate prices quadrupled in the decade 1994-2004. Average Irish homes in 2006 cost $450,000 ($600,000 in Dublin), nearly ten times the average level of industrial wages. This affects a lot of people since almost a third of the Irish population generating close to 40% of GDP live in or around Dublin. Elsewhere, housing prices rose by 14% in 2003 alone. However, the housing bubble began bursting in 2007, falling almost 4% in that year alone. This hurt the economy since a quarter of it was dependant on the property market, and construction accounted for 13% of economic output.

Ireland has some of the highest prices in Europe. One study found that it is just behind Finland as the most expensive country in the eurozone. Denmark is more expensive, but it does not use the euro. Wages do keep up with prices. From 1998 to 2003, they rose 37.1% before taxes, or 12.1% in real terms after accounting for inflation. Gross average pay in 2004 was 38,140 euros in Ireland, 35,750 euros in Britain, and 40,470 euros in the United States.

Inflation might be even higher were it not for a "social partnership" created by government, labor and business to slow wage-rate increases and secure labor peace. Its 4.3% unemployment in 2006 is far lower than the 20% posted at the low point of the 1980s and about half the EU average. This is partly due to the annual investment by offshore companies, creating directly or indirectly more than 300,000 jobs.

As the country with the EU's highest sustained growth in population (more than 8% in four years to 2006, by far the EU's fastest) and labor force, the republic must provide jobs for those Irishmen who continue to move back to Ireland and from the agricultural into the manufacturing and service sectors. But it must continue to provide work for the growing number of young persons and women who are entering the labor market. The economic boom is also attracting other nationalities, including British. Immigration to this once-poor island exceeds emigration. Net immigration by 2005 was running about 30,000 per year. The government's strategy to create jobs for the EU's youngest labor force has been through rapid industrial development.

In the past high unemployment set in motion a disappointing wave of emigration. Almost a fourth of Ireland's adults have lived abroad at some point in their lives. The impressive economic growth reversed the population flight, and skilled workers are returning to Ireland. Labor became scarce in such sectors as electron-

Aerial view of Dublin

Ireland

U2   Credit: Anton Corbijn

ics, computers, information technology, and building. American firms advertise in American newspapers to fill vacancies in their Irish businesses. The state training agency (FAS) conducts worldwide recruitment, known as Jobs Ireland, to fill vacancies.

The republic's population had soared to over four million in 2006, the highest since 1871 and up a million in only a generation. Its population is growing by 2.5% annually and is projected to reach five million by 2019. This is true despite the fact that its fertility rate has plummeted and is below the level usually required for a stable population. The country remains underpopulated when one considers that the Irish island had more than eight million inhabitants in 1841. Both parts of Ireland have only six million today.

Immigrants from all over the world are pouring into Ireland, particularly to Dublin, where more and more Irish are also moving. The republic's immigrants and asylum seekers each year are per capita four times the rate in the United States. An immigration expert noted that "Ireland is changing so fast that it's hard for the country to catch its breath." The overall Catholic population has fallen from 91.6% in 1991 to 88.4% in 2004, and the number of Muslims has quadrupled to 19,000 in the same period and is still growing.

The Irish know that they need workers, given their declining birth rate. For example, in 2003 Ireland had to offer 47,000 work permits to foreigners in order to meet its labor supply requirements. But Irish have conflicted feelings about the climate of fear and uncertainty that the resulting diversity has created. Their country has become multicultural, with 11% of the population foreign-born, nearly as high a percentage as in the U.S. Such diversity has not provoked the kind of conflict found elsewhere in Europe. But there

are undercurrents of racial unease, and regrettable racist incidents occur. This is made worse by an economic downturn. The government responded by denying automatic citizenship to immigrant children born in Ireland. This was overwhelmingly approved by almost 80% in a June 2004 referendum.

Ireland grants to citizens of the eight former communist countries that entered the EU in May 2004 the right to enter the country to seek work. But like the UK, it sets a two-year waiting period for them to qualify for social benefits although the attorney general indicated that such a waiting period might be illegal in the EU. No such limits apply to job seekers from Malta and Cyprus.

The tradition of spirited trade union activity has remained in Ireland. This is reflected in the 94 member unions of the Irish Congress of Trade Unions (ICTU), which have affiliates in Northern Ireland. About 60% of working Irishmen are members of unions, which were one among the strongest and most militant in the world. This is no longer true.

CULTURE

Ireland's culture, like its history, reflects the problem of a native people being dominated by a more powerful neighbor. For centuries the natives spoke Gaelic (usually called Irish); the Norman invaders spoke French; but as the English Anglicized them, they came to speak that language as it had evolved in the 14th century. As so many of the Irish–speaking people died or immigrated after the Potato Famine in the mid–19th century, English came to be the predominant language. Despite efforts to require school children to learn Gaelic, only 2% of the population (located primarily in the rural areas of the west) speaks Irish as a first language. The fact that road signs and of-

ficial government publications are still in Gaelic is quaint, but hardly necessary. In fact, it is so difficult to find someone who speaks it that fluent speakers can wear a lapel pin called a *fainne* to invite others to address them in Irish.

Because of the poverty in which they lived for many centuries, the Irish developed worldwide recognition in only one art form; it required no capital investment—the use of words. The Irish have always prided themselves in their ability to talk and write. Celtic history is rich in legend and folklore, and more recently, a number of authors, poets and dramatists have achieved international prominence. Whenever one thinks of masters of the English language, the names of Irishmen come to mind. Jonathan Swift, Thomas More, James Joyce, Oliver Goldsmith, John Millington Synge, Sean O'Casey and Brendan Beehan are influential in all of literature. And four Irishmen, William Butler Yeats, George Bernard Shaw, Samuel Becket, and in 1995 Seamus Heaney, have won the Nobel Prize for Literature. Born in Belfast the son of a potato farmer, Heaney's poetry is stamped by the simplicity and nature images of his boyhood farm. With his characteristic modesty, he said that he is a mere "foothill of a mountain range" compared to Yeats and Becket. Writers like Colm Toibin, Dermot Bolger, Mary O'Donnell, Evelyn Conlon, and Nuala Ni Dhomhnaill are widely read.

The Irish are indeed a musical people, but their music has most often taken the form of widespread participation rather than special expertise of outstanding composers or professional performers. The

A new generation of Irish youth, Kinsale

Celtic harp, along with the shamrock, is one of the most frequently used symbols of Ireland. Harp playing is heard wherever there are groups of expatriate Irish. Many American pioneer songs, bluegrass and country music (but not western) have Irish roots. In rural Ireland, amateur nights where performers display a variety of talent are still popular. Even today, a visitor to a rural cottage may be told, "Now you mustn't leave until we have a little sing–song." Then all those present will sing together, usually unaccompanied by any musical instrument. The Cork jazz, Wexford opera, and Waterford light opera festivals attract thousands of visitors.

Among the most famous Irish musicians was U2, a successful rock group and winner of two Grammy awards in 1988. Although three out of four are Protestant, their unmistakable Irishness is revealed by the political content of some of their texts, which deal with fighting and dying on their island. The repertoire of the popular Irish–American rock band, Black 47, is also overtly political, as the title of its debut album, Fire of Freedom, indicates. Other musicians, such as Moving Hearts, Fleagh Cowboys, and Mary Coughlan, mix musical styles like rock and traditional and demonstrate that Ireland is still fertile ground for creative music. Ireland is also producing world–class films. A Dublin native, Glen Hansard, and his Czech partner, Marketa Irglova, won the 2008 Academy Award for best song, "Falling Slowly." It was the theme song for the Irish independent movie, "Once," filmed in Dublin and funded by the Irish Film Board.

Celtic dancing (rhythmical patterns formed by four or eight dancers using rapid foot movements, with the arms usually held down at the sides) has spread around the world. Irish step dancing has burst out of the local parish hall and onto a world stage. The dance show–musicals, Riverdance by Bill Whelan and Lord of the Dance starring Chicagoan Michael Flatley and Jean Butler, are performing before packed audiences everywhere and are receiving global acclaim. After one performance, an observer claimed, "the speed and coordination took my breath away!" Another noted that Irish vernacular is being married to "American razzmatazz." These dance sensations were part of a larger cultural phenomenon in the 1990s. The Irish are becoming more urban, secular, experimental, self–confident, and less attached to nationalist certainties. Their once rural–based arts are being transplanted to Dublin, where they find a new cosmopolitan expression and no longer serve a nationalist agenda.

Irish art in both Celtic and medieval times displayed a wild imagination with brightly colored swirls and fantastic figures best represented in the illustrated manuscripts. Until recently, Irish art has tended to copy work being done in England or on the continent. But in the last quarter-century, there has been a revival of crafts that have used the old Gaelic and medieval symbols to create the beginnings of an indigenous modern art.

Until the 20th century, Ireland had only one university, Trinity College in Dublin, which was founded in 1591 by Queen Elizabeth I. Only recently was it opened to Catholics. In 1908 the National University of Ireland was founded. It has branches in Dublin, Cork, Galway and Limerick. Education is free and compulsory for children through the age of fifteen. The system pays its teachers more in relation to average earnings than any other land in the OECD. It produces a well–educated work force, especially at the upper end. This and the use of the English language are very appealing to foreign investors.

Both the postal and telephone services are operated by the government, which claims that 90% of all letters mailed reach their destination within one day. There are seven daily newspapers, five in Dublin and two in Cork. An autonomous public corporation operates radio and television broadcasting; licensing fees are charged and advertisements also produce revenue.

Dublin, whose graceful Georgian buildings are now falling into the shadow of taller concrete and glass structures, continues to dominate the life of Ireland. A fifth of Eire's population lives within the city's boundaries, and over a quarter lives in greater Dublin. This reflects the fact that Ireland has become much more urban than it once was. It also means that some of Eire's poverty, which was largely confined to rural areas, is now more visible in the congested capital city. Dublin is the center of the nation's cultural, financial and political life.

FUTURE

The Irish can be proud that Robert Emmet's vision has come true—his country has taken its place among the nations of the earth. They still aspire to unify with Ulster. But election battles are now fought on economic grounds and not over Northern Ireland. Ireland has acquired the nickname, "Celtic Tiger." It has undeniable economic strengths. Its growing standard of living during the past 50 years reached that of the EU, and for the first time in history it overtook that of Britain. This wealth and success have significantly increased the expectations of the Irish people and their demands on the government for continued prosperity.

The failure of any party to gain a majority in parliament and the frequent elections point to the difficulty any government will have in satisfying these aspirations. With typical Irish wit, FitzGerald said before the 1982 election, "Whoever wins the election should have first choice on going into opposition."

By electing two female presidents in a row, including British subject from Northern Ireland Mary McAleese, voters signaled receptivity to reforms which enabled the country to enter the 21st century as a modern European nation. In 1994 a bill was passed "without a ripple of controversy" legalizing homosexuality. Abortion and divorce are also legal now in certain circumstances. The traditional bastions of power and paternalism—state, church, and family business patriarchs—are under assault as never before.

The Ahern government, reelected in 2007 with a majority coalition with the Greens, had watched its popularity decline, and his *Fianna Fail* party had fallen to its lowest level in two decades. It had lost public trust by failing to deliver promised public-service reforms. It promised "world-class health service," but citizens still have to wait to get a hospital bed. It was unexpectedly reelected, but the Greens' price was a proposed carbon tax

Saucy Irish youth

Ireland

and measures to deal with climate change. A growing burden to his party, Ahern decided to resign before being forced from office. On May 6, 2008, he was replaced as Taoiseach by Brian Cowen, who is known for his intelligence and experience.

Economic performance might not stand out quite so much in the future because it has caught up with the rest of Europe. It no longer has the low-cost advantage over its rivals it once had. The country is facing a slowdown and has been shaken by a burst in the housing bubble and by America's financial problems. Nevertheless, Ireland is justified in being optimistic about its own future. It no longer suffers from a lack of confidence, and it is no longer as sensitive about its relations with Britain.

At least one village watched the 2008 U.S. presidential elections closely. Moneygall has unearthed records indicating that Barack Obama's great-great-great-grandfather, Fulmuth Kerney, grew up there before leaving for America at age 19. His line eventually produced Obama's mother, Ann Durham. A bemused Obama had to admit that "I've got pieces of everybody in me."

Ireland's culture is attracting attention far beyond its borders. When leaving for Paris in 1939, Irish dramatist Samuel Becket claimed that he preferred France at war to Ireland at peace. His country has changed dramatically. Frank McCourt, whose best-selling *Angela's Ashes* describes his youth in a poor and hide–bound Ireland before and during the Second World War, said about Ireland in the late 1990s: "When I go back I see it in a way the kids walk. The confidence. It's almost saucy. We have entered the age of Irish sauciness. God help us all."

There was nervousness throughout Europe over how unpredictable Irish voters would decide in their June 2008 referendum over the EU's constitutional revision, known as the Lisbon Treaty. Ireland is the only member state whose constitution required such a plebiscite.

On voting day, the Irish shocked the rest of Europe, just as they had done in June 2001 when they rejected the Nice Treaty. This time, in a convincing vote of 53.4% against and only 46.6% in favor, voters said NO to the reform that is intended to enable the enlarging EU to make quicker and more coherent decisions in vital areas. The results dramatized the inability of EU leaders to persuade citizens that they can benefit from reforms described in a long, dense, complex 277-page legal document.

At a time when economic growth is slowing and the real estate market is collapsing, it was easy for opponents of the treaty to exploit the fears of anxious Irishmen. Many worry about immigration and the possibility that Brussels could usurp their power to levy their own taxes, determine their own family law, and decide when and how to use their own armed forces.

Prime Minister Brian Cowen acknowledged that there was "no obvious solution before us." Nobody knows if a compromise can be found to salvage the Lisbon Treaty, which had already been ratified by the parliaments of 18 member states. It would be difficult for the government to ask Irish citizens to vote again. EU officials hope to deal with the problem by offering the Irish government more treaty protocols that would guarantee the Irish the right to determine policy in sensitive areas, such as family law, military affairs, and taxation. In the meantime, Ireland finds itself somewhat politically isolated from the rest of Europe.

The French Republic

Vichy France (1940–42)

Wine Regions

Area: 211,208 sq. mi. (547,026 km.). This is the largest country in Western Europe, four fifths the size of Texas and four times the size of New York State.

Population: 61.4 million.

Capital City: Paris, population 2.4 million within city limits, 9.1 million within Metropolitan Paris.

Climate: Pleasant, rather temperate, except in the south, where the weather resembles that of Florida.

Neighboring Countries: Belgium, Luxembourg, Germany (North and Northeast); Switzerland (East); Italy and Monaco (Southeast) Spain and Andorra (Southwest).

Official Language: French.

Ethnic Background: Indo–European, of diverse origin.

Principal Religions: Roman Catholic (85%), Muslim (8.3%), Protestant (2%), Jewish (1%).

Chief Commercial Exports and Imports: Capital equipment, consumer goods, automobiles and transport equipment, agricultural products, including wine and spirits, energy.

Major Customers: EU25 (65% of exports and 61.3% of imports), Germany (14.5% of exports and 17.2% of imports), UK (8.8% of exports and 5.9% of imports), Spain (10.2% of exports and 7.1% of im-

ports), Italy (9.2% of exports and 8.6% of imports), U.S. (8.1% of exports and 8% of imports), Belgium-Luxembourg (8% of exports and 8.5% of imports).

Currency: Euro.

National Holiday: July 14, anniversary of the storming of the Bastille Prison in Paris in 1789, the spark that brought the French revolution to an explosion.

Chief of State: Nicolas Sarkozy, President (since May 2007).

Head of Government: François Fillon, Prime Minister (since May 2007). Unlike many nations where the presidency is merely ceremonial, France has a Chief Executive with broad powers. The

France

Prime Minister concerns himself primarily with the daily workings of the government, and he also can wield great power if he is from a different party than that of the president.

National Flag: The tricolor—three broad vertical stripes, blue, white, red.

France is a land of visible contrasts. In many ways it appears divided. Within the past two centuries, during which time the United States has had one continuous political system, France has experienced three monarchies, two empires, a half dozen republics and more than a dozen constitutions; its history is strewn with revolutions, counterrevolutions and *coups d'état*, and its political party system is extremely fragmented. General de Gaulle, the founder of the present French Republic, once asked in exasperation how one could ever rule a land that has more than 300 different cheeses! Yet there is an underlying stability in contemporary France and a strong consensus concerning the importance of respecting individual rights and of maintaining a republican, democratic form of government. Indeed, France is one of a minority of stable democracies in the world and is therefore a haven for political refugees.

France also is highly centralized politically, economically and culturally. The predominance of Paris is undeniable. No successful revolution ever began outside of Paris. King Henry IV's famous statement in 1593 justifying his conversion to Catholicism, that "Paris is worth a mass," was an early reminder that control over France must emanate from Paris and not from the provinces. The French capital often seems to be the place where French history is made and then merely presented to the provinces as the finished product. With a population as great as the entire continent of Australia (roughly one out of five Frenchmen lives in Paris or its suburbs), it is the residence of a fourth of France's civil servants and doctors, a third of its students and half of its university professors, two-thirds of its artisans and authors, a fifth of its factory workers and factories employing more than 25 persons and two–thirds of its company and bank headquarters. Efforts since 1955 to decentralize the French economy have met with little success.

At the same time, France is a land of great diversity in terms of religion, landscape, language, customs and styles of living. Such ethnic minorities as the Basques, the Alsatians, the Bretons, the West Indians and the Corsicans preserve their own languages and cultures. Only in Corsica is there a serious movement for autonomy that enjoys any appreciable popular backing. There are other small and largely irrelevant movements in Brittany, the Basque region and elsewhere. In general, ethnic diversity does not threaten the present French state to the degree that it does other European countries such as Ireland, Belgium and Spain.

France, it has often been said, is "weighed down by history." Frenchmen have a long memory for their own past although they do not always agree about its high and low points. Yet, far from being a country exclusively living in the past, contemporary France is a highly dynamic and forward–looking nation. It is among the wealthiest, most technologically advanced and influential countries in the world. Clearly, France has a future, but Frenchmen would say that they have a *destiny*. From the time of the Crusades, the first of which was practically an entirely French affair, to the present day, Frenchmen have felt a sense of mission to civilize the world. In the 21st century they still believe in "French exceptionalism," even as they grope for a clear French identity in the face of massive Arab and African immigration and de facto multiculturalism.

Perhaps no one expressed this mission better than the great realist de Gaulle, who opened his war memoirs with the following words: "All my life I have had a certain idea of France. This is inspired by sentiment as much as by reason. The emotional side of me tends to imagine France, like the princess in the fairy stories or the Madonna in the frescoes, as dedicated to an exalted and exceptional destiny. Instinctively I have the feeling that Providence has created her either for complete successes or for exemplary misfortunes. . . . But the positive side of my mind also assures me that France is not really herself unless in the front rank; that only vast enterprises are capable of counterbalancing the ferments of dispersal which are inherent in her people; that our country, as it is, surrounded by the others, as they are, must aim high and hold itself straight, on pain of mortal danger. In short, to my mind, France cannot be France without greatness."

The general, who once admitted that he preferred France to Frenchmen, disdained the petty squabbling of everyday politics. He denied that the essential France was to be found in the yawning provincial bureaucrat, the scandalous French president (Felix Faure) who died in the presidential palace while making love to his mistress, or the impetuous Parisian pamphleteer who plots to bring down the regime. He believed that one must inhale the heady air of the mountain peaks in order to see the true France: "Viewed from the heights, France is beautiful."

France is at the same time an Atlantic, Continental and Mediterranean country, and it is territorially the largest country in Europe west of Russia. The country is somewhat hexagonal in shape with rather regular contours. It stretches roughly 600 miles (960 km.) from north to south and west to east. Through it flow five great rivers, the Seine, Loire, Garonne, Rhône and Rhine, which originate in the central land mass (Massif Central) or in the mountains of the Alps and the Pyrenees. It faces three seas (the North Sea, the Atlantic Ocean and the Mediterranean), and has a coastline of more than 1,200 miles (1,930 km.).

In the North, there are no natural barriers to separate France from northern Europe. Elsewhere, the Rhine River sepa-

From atop Notre Dame Cathedral, a stone gargoyle stares vacantly over the Seine River and the rooftops of Paris to the distant Eiffel Tower.
Courtesy: Jon Markham Morrow

rates France from Germany, the Alps from Switzerland and Italy, and the Pyrenees from Spain. The geographical relief of France begins from the coastline to the valleys, and then rises to plateaus, highlands and finally to mountains, the highest being Mont Blanc in the Alps (15,777 feet, 4,807 meters) and Mont Vignemale in the Pyrenees (10,804 feet; 3,293 meters).

Although France is large, it has the lowest population density in the European Union (EU). Its total population and economic riches are very unevenly distributed geographically. If one were to draw a line on the map of France from the northern port of Le Havre to Grenoble and then on to Marseilles (which school children learn as the *"diagonale du vide"*—diagonal of emptiness), one could see two halves of a country as different from one another as northern Italy is from southern Italy. The western half of France contains 56% of the territory, but only 37% of its people, and is steadily losing population. It tends to be less industrialized, and its agriculture is based on small farms and is therefore less efficient. East of the line are 80% of France's industrial production and three-fourths of the industrial employees. Economic development is particularly rapid in the northeast of France, and recently in Rhône–Alps and Marseilles regions. Farming tends to be more intensive and efficient, and a far smaller percentage of inhabitants live agriculturally.

Geographic and demographic statistics can hardly convey the beauty that for centuries has been called *la belle France*. The visitor invariably finds himself charmed by the smell of rich vines heavy with grapes, by the rolling green countryside studded with more castles than one finds in any other country, by the towering cathedrals whose bells resound throughout the countryside, by the warm beaches along the Riviera and by the majestic, snow–capped peaks. As one begins to realize how this beauty blends with the Frenchman's proverbial *joie de vivre* ("joy of living"), one sees why the Germans have always described the good life as "living like God in France."

HISTORY

The Early Period
Although France has played a prominent role in European history for at least 1,500 years, it did not become a national entity or even approximately achieve its present shape until the 16th century A.D. The legend of French unity goes back to Vercingetorix, the chief of a Gallic tribe called the Arverni, who led a coalition in an uprising against the Roman occupiers in 52 B.C. Although he placed his foot soldiers in a hopeless strategic position and

squandered his cavalry before the critical phase of the battle had begun, resulting in his troops' and his own capture, he is seen as the first patriot and resistance hero of French history.

The French profess a close kinship to the Gauls. But the latter were a people who left no literature, no language, no laws, who worshipped many gods and practiced human sacrifice, and who, according to the Roman arch at Orange, fought naked, their hair buttered and in a long looped knot, with drooping mustaches and long narrow shields. It is doubtful that such a race had a profound impact on the French people and their civilization. Frenchmen today are amused by the caricature of the early Gaulois in the popular *Asterix* comic books.

They no doubt owe far more to the Romans, who occupied for centuries much of what is now France. The Romans built towns, roads, aqueducts and theaters. They provided examples of centralization, efficient bureaucracy, written law and a periodic census. They brought education and culture to France and gave the French an appreciation of abstractions. They also left a tradition of grandeur, spotting France with statues and monuments. Finally, their language—vulgarized by common usage—later developed into French.

Even before the fall of the Roman Empire in the 5th century, France had become an invasion ground for tribes from all over the known world: Visigoths, Burgundians, Alemans, and Franks (Germans who eventually gave the country its name). In the 8th and 9th centuries, Charlemagne, the warrior king who established himself as "Emperor of the West," absorbed what is now France into a huge political unit encompassing much of present Europe, from Saxony to the island of Elba, including Bavaria and most of Lombardy in Italy. This great empire, however, did not survive his death in 814 A.D., and France again became fragmented.

The Capets Claim Paris
Not until a century and a half later did conditions begin to develop which were favorable to unity. In 987 the Capet family, which owned large tracts of land around the region now called the *Île de France*, raised a claim of dynastic leadership over France. The Capetians chose as their capital a small town nearby, which had been established in 100 B.C. on a five–acre island in the middle of the river Seine by a curly headed Celtic tribe of fishermen and navigators called *Parisii*. The Romans had named this city Lutetia and had built it up to a town of from 6,000 to 10,000 inhabitants. The city had also served as capital for the Frankish King

Clovis, who had defeated the last remnants of the retreating Romans in 486.

The Capetians adopted *Francien*, a Latin–based dialect spoken around Paris, as their official language. Hugues Capet, born in 938, was the first Frankish king who could speak no German, and as a result of the Capetian example, German and Latin soon disappeared from the early French court. French became the language of the elite, both at the court and abroad (for example, Marco Polo wrote about his travels to China in French!), and the political and military successes of the French dynasty gradually led to the language's adoption by all the people. This language became a powerful agent in the formation and expansion of the French nation and civilization. For that reason, few peoples in the world try so hard to preserve and spread their language as do the French.

Crusades
The first Crusade in the 11th century, sponsored by the French Pope Urban II, and organized by the French cleric Peter the Hermit, was conducted almost exclusively by the French knights. While building castles in Lebanon and establishing a Kingdom of Jerusalem (which endured at least in name until the 15th century), they showed a zealous sense of mission in extending French civilization, which they tended to see as embodying Christian values. This became a major rationale for most French military and colonial enterprises in the centuries to follow.

A crucially important by–product of the Crusades was the weakening of the feudal bonds which tied serfs to their lords. French noblemen were often left penniless by the military expenses they bore, and many times they obtained needed money by freeing serfs and selling charters to cities. By the 13th century, serfdom had almost disappeared in France, and cities had sprung up everywhere, partly because of the trade the Crusades had created. Spices and textiles from the Orient were highly desired by the Europeans, and cities became the crossroads for such trade. France prospered.

Another indirect example of French expansionism occurred when William (the Conqueror) invaded England in 1066, conquering the Anglo–Saxons by 1070. Although French largely displaced Anglo–Saxon initially, at least at the court, the latter soon revived, and the two languages were combined, enriching each other. Court decisions and proceedings by the 12th century were written in a curious combination of English, French and Latin. But William retained his holdings in Normandy, Maine, Touraine and Anjou within what is now France; this later became a source of friction between the French and

France

Crusaders and Saracens in Battle
(From a 12th century stained-glass window)

the English. William's great–grandson, the incompetent King John of England, lost many of the French territories in the early 13th century.

By the end of the 12th century, France, especially Paris (which by that time was the most populous city in Europe), was considered to be the world center of science and culture, having replaced Athens and Rome. In the 14th century one–half of the people in the Christian world lived in what is now France.

Disorganization and Weak Monarchs

Despite the establishment of a unique language and a French dynasty, French history, until the 16th century, continued to be characterized most of the time by weak kings struggling against foreign rulers and by powerful, rebellious French noblemen, who often did not hesitate to ally with foreign powers against their king. Such division exposed France to the danger of absorption into a large kingdom dominated by England because of its control over much of France. But in the 13th and 14th centuries, three powerful French kings, Philippe Augustus, Louis IX (canonized in 1297 as Saint Louis) and Philippe IV (the Fair), succeeded in wresting control of some of the English domains in France.

They began the slow process of patching France together, sometimes by legitimate feudal claims, often by intermarriage, and very often by war. However, England maintained its huge foothold in Aquitaine, acquired in 1154 and encompassing most of southwestern France below the Loire River; England was also allied with the Burgundians north of the Loire. In the 14th and 15th centuries, the French kings waged a "Hundred Years War" to finally drive the English out of France.

Joan of Arc

In the midst of this struggle, a female savior emerged from the small village of Domremy in Lorraine. At the age of 16, Joan of Arc, the daughter of a French shepherd, claimed to have heard the voices of the Saints Michel and Catherine commanding her to free the besieged city of Orléans and to have the French king crowned in Reims. Having persuaded a French captain to give her a horse and an armed guard, and flying a white flag, she set off to find the king. She told a distrustful Charles VII that she would drive the English out of France and be "the lieutenant of the king of heaven who is king of France."

Dressed in a man's armor, and displaying remarkable skill in improving offen-sive military operations, she liberated Orléans, defeated the enemy forces at Patay and Troyes, and amidst enthusiastic crowds, proceeded to Reims to have the 26–year–old Charles VII crowned on July 17, 1429, in the way traditionally prescribed for French kings. Whenever she addressed the crowds as "Frenchmen," the response indicated that a new nationalism mingled with a divine mission was emerging.

Short–lived was the fortune of this girl. Dressed in men's clothing and violating the feudal law barring women from combat, she was distrusted by the clergy, the nobility and even the newly crowned king. Mounted on a beautiful horse, she led her forces in a vain attempt to storm Paris and Compiègne, and though wounded by an arrow, she tried unsuccessfully to rally her troops. She was captured in May 1430 and delivered to the Duke of Burgundy, who was allied with the English and who sold her to them for a high fee. She was tried in Rouen by a French ecclesiastical court and, despite her own eloquent defense, was pronounced guilty of heresy. On May 30 she was burned at the stake in Rouen's marketplace, without the ungrateful king having made the slightest effort to save her.

Centuries later there is still no consensus in France concerning the legacy she had left. A monarchical France before 1789 had little use for saviors from the masses, and her mystical, religious aura made her out of place in an enlightened, revolutionary France. Nevertheless, Napoleon had a beautiful statue of her erected in Orléans in 1803, and the process to have her made a saint was initiated in 1869. Not until the humiliating defeat of France at the hands of the Prussians in 1870 was she embraced as a symbol of vengeance toward an outside power that had taken her native Lorraine. She was finally canonized in 1920.

Joan of Arc is to many Frenchmen the ideal symbol of patriotism: a pure lady warrior with a sense of mission who placed God solidly on the side of the French. She is undoubtedly the Madonna in de Gaulle's memoirs who incorporated France, since the great French leader also adopted the cross of Lorraine as his own symbol. His stubborn, righteous defense of France's destiny moved an exasperated Englishman, Sir Winston Churchill, to remark that "of all the crosses I have had to bear, the heaviest was the Cross of Lorraine."

Further Union Followed by Religious Wars

By 1453 the English had been driven from France, except for a tiny foothold in the northern port city of Calais. The "Hundred Years War" had nevertheless been a cruel disaster for the French people. Within a century, the war and the plagues that had struck at roughly the same time had reduced the population by almost one-half. In the closing years of that century Brittany, which had been independent, was integrated into France. Anne of Brittany, who in 1491 married the French King Charles VIII, sealed the union. She took her native Brittany as a dowry. Upon his death she married the next French King, Louis XII, in 1499 in order to preserve this union. Though France had made impressive strides toward territorial unity in the 15th century, the century to follow was not to be one of peace and unity.

In 1519 a minor German priest named Martin Luther courageously raised a challenge of faith to the powerful Catholic Church and began the Reformation that spread throughout the Christian world. A Frenchman, John Calvin, also developed a religious doctrine hostile to the Church and was forced to flee to the Swiss city of Geneva, which he soon shaped into a Protestant "capital." He left behind a France seriously divided into two sects: the Huguenots (Protestant) and the Catholics. From 1559 until 1598, the Wars of Religion raged in France; this was a chaotic period dotted by eight distinct wars, assassinations and massacres. These unfortunate events were related to the issue of the king's and other nobility's respective powers, as much as to theological matters.

The situation became particularly grave in 1572 when 4,000 Protestants gathered in Paris for the wedding of the 19-year-old King Henry of Navarre to Charles IX's sister. Henry, whose life was under threat, had announced his conversion to Catholicism, ostensibly to heal fanatical religious divisions in France. The Protestants were massacred on orders of the French king, and they promptly responded to this "St. Bartholomew's Day Massacre" by announcing that such a treacherous king was no longer to be obeyed. Henry quickly reassumed the Protestant faith and the wars raged on. All involved finally realized in 1598 that the strife was without any redeeming value. Upon becoming king, Henry issued the Edict of Nantes, which promised Frenchmen religious freedom. Nevertheless, the religious issue continued to gnaw away at the unity of France for more than three centuries.

The French Century

The 17th century became "the French century" in all of continental Europe. This was a period when forceful French kings and brilliant royal advisers succeeded in reducing much of the French nobility's powers and in establishing the present

Joan of Arc triumphantly enters Reims

borders of France. The glitter of the royal court soon dazzled Europe.

When in 1624 Louis XIII chose an ambitious cardinal to be his chief adviser, he gained at his side a tireless servant of the French crown and the French state. Cardinal Richelieu was not a man given to courtly debauchery, theological hairsplitting or listening for voices from God. "Reason must be the standard for everything," he said, and "the public interest ought to be the sole objective of the prince and his counselors." *Raison d'état* ("reason of state"), the interests of the community, became for him the overriding concerns.

Since Richelieu was convinced that only absolute monarchical authority could elevate his country to the highest rank in the world, he proceeded to neutralize any powers that could challenge the central authority of the king. He had torn down all castles not belonging to the king that could be used to resist royal authority. In a swashbuckling era presented so vividly in Alexander Dumas' *The Three Musketeers*, Richelieu dared to ban dueling, a favorite pastime of the nobility, on the

grounds that weapons should be drawn only against enemies of the state. While not attacking religious principles, he whittled away at the privileges granted in 1598 to Protestants, believing that a free, powerful Protestant party in France could easily undermine the centralized power of France.

At the same time he sent money and troops to support the Protestants in the Thirty Years War that ravaged Germany from 1618 to 1648. His reasons were simple: although Austria and Spain were fighting in the name of Catholicism, their victory in the struggle would have strengthened these great powers and thus presented a greater threat to France. Further, by sending French troops southward, eastward and northward, France acquired territory along the way. France's borders thus moved outward. Clearly, the Cardinal did not think religiously; he thought *French*. When he died in 1642 (followed in death a few months later by Louis XIII), he left behind an almost unchallenged central authority, a powerful French army, a small but effective fleet and a highly or-

France

ganized professional diplomatic service. He also established French as the new diplomatic language for the world, a position it enjoyed for more than 250 years. Above all, he left a tradition of total dedication to the power and glory of France.

Louis XIV, Cardinal Mazarin and Anarchy

Louis XIV became king in 1643 at the age of five This renowned monarch was able to build on the great works of Cardinal Richelieu and on the works of another Cardinal who, though extremely unpopular, held France together against an angry and dangerous storm until the young king was ready to assume the reins of government. Cardinal Mazarin was a wealthy Italian, whose love of money did not prevent him from energetically serving the young king's mother and regent, Queen Anne, with whom he reportedly had more than just cordial relations.

Picking up where Richelieu had left off, Mazarin led France to victories over Austria. The Treaty of Westphalia in 1648 and subsequent victories over Spain left France the foremost power in Europe. Austria was seriously weakened, and Germany was fragmented, depopulated and exhausted. French strength and German "weakness" through division remained a cornerstone of French politics until 1990. Indeed, many Frenchmen would have echoed the words spoken by the 1952 Nobel Prize for Literature laureate and Gaullist political commentator François Mauriac after the Second World War: "I like Germany so much that I am glad there are two of them."

Having achieved a position of power in Europe, France became seriously weakened internally. From 1648 to 1653 it was rocked by a complicated series of civil disturbances which threatened the young king's hold on the throne, and which in some ways anticipated the French Revolution that came a century and a half later. The parliament, the bourgeoisie (a class of persons who had risen socially above the level of peasants and manual laborers, but who had no titles of nobility), and the Parisian mobs, all for their own reasons, created such an anarchical situation in Paris that the king and his mother were forced to flee to the palace of St. Germain, where they lived at Mazarin's personal expense.

Some French nobles invited the Spanish troops to reenter France, and Parisian mobs erected barricades and took law into their own hands. In the prolonged confusion, battles raged in the countryside and the streets of Paris, and finally Mazarin was forced to flee to Germany. However, after all order had disappeared, the key figures of this uprising, known as the *fronde* (named after the French word for slingshot, used by rioters to smash windows in Paris) surprisingly lost their nerve, and this revolt against the centralized monarchy and the unpopular Mazarin gradually collapsed.

The 14–year–old Louis led his loyal troops in 1652 into a tired and shamed Paris. Louis never forgave the rebellious city and wasted little time in removing himself from the clutches of this beautiful, but tempestuous and unfaithful mistress. The rupture between the king and Paris would later have disastrous consequences for the monarchy.

Louis Comes of Age

Immediately after Mazarin's death, the young king called a meeting of all the court's advisers and announced: "Now it is time that I rule!" No one questioned this. By then, the 23–year–old monarch's imposing physical dignity and his polished manners, combined with an unhesitating decisiveness, rapidly brought him respect within France, which sometimes bordered on worship. France was weary of chaos and was ready to kiss the hand that ruled with firm authority. His prodigious lovemaking at the court, which has certainly lost nothing in the telling, greatly irritated his mother. But it did not prevent him from being a hard–working and effective king. Almost no state affairs escaped his attention; in 1661 he commanded his ministers not to sign or seal any order without his permission.

The entire kingdom increasingly felt the impact of the royal government. When the affairs of state became too great for one man to handle, he developed a bureaucracy and efficient procedures to enable his government to absorb the workload. All aspects of French foreign affairs, defense, finance, commerce, religion and the royal household were channeled through the king's court. He appointed officials to secure royal control over all activities in the various regions in France. He supervised all major appointments in his bureaucracy and the army. Although there is no evidence that he ever really said "I am the state," there was no question that he would have readily agreed with such an assertion. He actually worked very hard to live up to his rather arrogant motto: *Nec pluribus impar* ("None his equal").

As a symbol of his magnificence, the "Sun King" ordered that a royal palace be built in Versailles, which would not only be at a safe distance from Paris, but would be unsurpassed in all of Europe for its beauty and dignity. For 20 years he had this gigantic structure, with its surrounding gardens, fountains and smaller palaces, built and rebuilt. His finance minister, Colbert, was exasperated by the project, which almost emptied the royal treasury and which could only be financed by selling many of the state's treasures. However, once finished, this palace became the assembly point for much of France's ambitious nobility. There Louis could keep an eye on them and busy them with ritual duties, such as buttoning his coat or escorting the servants who brought his food to the royal table. Louis' preeminence was such that nobles competed for the honor of performing even the most menial functions at his court. For instance, the Princess of Ursins, who later became the queen of Spain, was considered one of the luckiest persons at the Court of Versailles because she performed the task of handing the king his dagger and night pot each evening as he retired to his private bedroom.

Paris in the 17th century

France

Under the conscientious guidance of Louis XIV, France achieved an incomparable political, military and cultural ascendancy. The arts bloomed, and France was the richest and most populous country in Europe. It also acquired the most powerful army on the continent, and Louis was more than willing to use it. He conducted almost continuously destructive wars. He thereby was able to establish France's present borders, but he ultimately converted almost every country in Europe into an enemy of France. He ordered that the Palatinate in the western part of Germany be burned, resulting in the destruction of Heidelberg, Mannheim, Speyer, Worms and hundreds of smaller towns. His soldiers ripped the bones of earlier Holy Roman emperors out of their graves in Speyer, a sacrilege that was not soon forgotten in Germany. The Treaty of Utrecht finally established an uneasy peace in 1713, two years before the king's death.

Even if France gradually exhausted itself financially and physically through almost continuous warfare, it was certainly well administered. Louis' powers were broad, and he used them with great energy. However, he could by no means be called a dictator in the modern sense. He had to deal with a limited national treasury, an absence of a national police force, ineffective and slow means of communication and regions that still jealously guarded their remaining powers. All in all, he gave Frenchmen an era which they still proudly call "the grand century."

Stirrings of Discontent

The "Sun King" long outlived all of his children, and upon his death his five-year-old great-grandchild was crowned Louis XV. The new King ruled until 1774, when Louis XVI, a good man who never wanted to be king, succeeded to the throne. Both were rather weak and increasingly unpopular kings who were unable to guide their country's adjustment to the changes that occurred in French society during the 18th century. This was a formula for revolution. Greatly contributing to and benefiting from France's prosperity, the bourgeoisie resented its exclusion from political responsibility, which was almost entirely in the hands of the aristocracy. The rural peasantry, which comprised 80% of the population and owned 40% of the land, resented the aristocracy's rights to hunt on their land, its local police power and its near monopoly over rural mills, bakeshops and wine presses. The manorial lords appeared to live well without performing an obviously useful function.

The dissatisfaction with the aristocracy was fed by the enlightened ideas of the time. In the course of the 18th century,

Louis XIV, the "Sun King." Probably painted at about age 55+, it indicates he had lost his teeth, was overweight, had bunions from wearing high heels, and a double chin.

thinkers such as Montesquieu, Voltaire and Diderot had brilliantly chipped away at the foundations of aristocratic society. An irreverent Frenchman named Jean–Jacques Rousseau had written in his bombshell book, *The Social Contract*, that "man was born free, but everywhere he is in chains," and he had proposed provocative ways of breaking these chains and creating a society of free and equal human beings. Rousseau was driven from France because of these ideas. He died in 1778.

Events in America that same year caused revolutionary ideas to pour in that brought the soup to a boil. A young revolutionary named Thomas Jefferson from Virginia had written, "all men are created equal and are endowed with unalienable rights." In rapid succession, the 13 colonies began to produce democratic constitutions, which were translated almost immediately into French and avidly read by intelligent persons grown weary of social hierarchy and inherited privilege.

The Mature Benjamin Franklin, 1777
Courtesy of Special Collections,
University of Virginia Library

France

Benjamin Franklin, who was sent to France to persuade the government to help the American colonies in the struggle against the English, was lionized by France's high society. His rustic, egalitarian wisdom was the talk of Paris. Most importantly, he persuaded France's leaders, who had lost their colonies in North America to the English in the Seven Years' War (1756–1763), to enter the struggle against the British. French assistance to the rebellious colonies was a very important contributing factor in the American victory; without the French army and navy, perhaps the ill–equipped and militarily untrained colonists would never have prevailed against their masters.

While the French government slapped its traditional enemy in the face, it had unknowingly allowed the bacillus of freedom to enter France through the back door. Some officers and many noncommissioned officers returned to France deeply moved by the events in America of which they had been a part, and they were very sympathetic and supportive of revolutionary movements in their own country. The world now had a concrete model of a large country ruling itself in a republican way.

Financial Woes Lead To Revolution

Another unforeseen consequence of France's aid to the Americans was that it brought France to the brink of bankruptcy; it doubled the national debt and consumed more than one–half of the crown's income. It was not an extravagant court that caused France's desperate financial situation; only 5% of the public expenditures were devoted to the entire royal establishment. The French Revolution did not spring from a naive, spendthrift Queen Marie Antoinette (called by the people "Madame Deficit") who was reported (incorrectly) to have asked why the peasants did not eat cake if they had no bread.

One–fourth of France's budget was devoted to war costs, and a whopping one–half was needed to service France's debts. Other countries, such as England, had similar expenditures, but France's financial crisis could not be solved because of its archaic and unequal tax system. The aristocracy and the wealthy bourgeoisie either evaded or won exemptions from taxation. The Church also refused to pay taxes, so the tax collectors could turn only to the poorest French citizens. Thus, although the country was generally prosperous, the public treasury was empty.

Louis XVI, who like his predecessor had often opposed the aristocracy and sought strength from the bourgeoisie, well understood the problem, but he was so weak and unpopular that he could do nothing about it. In desperation, he convened an Estates General in May 1789, the first such meeting in a century and a half. However, the class antagonism in France was such that the three classes assembled (clergy, aristocracy and bourgeoisie) simply could not work out reform in cooperation.

On June 17, 1789, the bourgeois element (the "Third Estate") decided to declare itself the "National Assembly." When the king panicked and closed the hall in which the Third Estate met, the latter moved to a nearby indoor tennis court and proclaimed in the "Oath of the Tennis Court" that it was the true representative of the people and that it would not disband until it had produced a constitution for France. This was a revolutionary step, unleashing explosive events that an irresolute king could not control. It was the first act in the French Revolution, which went through many stages and lasted ten years. Whether or not these events represented "the end of history," as the Prussian philosopher Friedrich Hegel maintained, neither France nor the world would thereafter be the same.

Revolution

The events at the Versailles meetings stirred up crowds in Paris, which began to look for weapons in arsenals and public buildings. On July 14, 1789, a crowd went to the Bastille, which, like the Tower of London, was a stronghold built during the Middle Ages to overawe the city and to provide a place of detention for influential prisoners. When the official in charge of the stronghold refused to distribute any weapons, the crowd successfully stormed the fortress. The mob, infuriated that almost a hundred persons had been killed, slaughtered the guards who had surrendered. They then beheaded the commanding official with knives and paraded around Paris with the heads of their victims on spikes. This bloody skirmish and macabre display was a harbinger of ferocious acts to come. Nevertheless, Frenchmen celebrate July 14 today as their major holiday.

The unrest and violence spread to the countryside as manorial lords saw their properties sacked and burned by bitter peasants. The more fortunate escaped with their lives, but royal power vanished quickly. The Marquis de Lafayette, a revolutionary–minded aristocrat who had been a favorite on George Washington's staff during the American War of Independence, was given command over the guard in Paris. He designed a flag for the new France to replace the blue and white *fleurdelis* ("lily flower"). He combined the colors of the city of Paris, red and blue, with the white of the House of Bourbon. Thus, the tricolor, which is France's flag

Lafayette and Washington in Harlem, New York

today, represented a fusion of the new and old regimes.

The sudden acts of violence had frightened the ruling group into granting important concessions. On August 4, 1789, the nobles relinquished their feudal rights, and on August 27 the National Assembly promptly proclaimed the Declaration of the Rights of Man. The U.S. ambassador to France and author of the American Declaration of Independence, Thomas Jefferson, was asked to read and improve this French equivalent before its publication. He was also requested to sit in the Na-

Thomas Jefferson
Courtesy of Special Collections,
University of Virginia Library

96

Count de Mirabeau
Courtesy of Special Collections,
University of Virginia Library

LA MARSEILLAISE.

tional Assembly during the writing of the French constitution. He declined both requests for diplomatic reasons although he was a passionate supporter in the young U.S. of the French Revolution. This French declaration was one of history's most eloquent assertions of equality before the law, of the opening of public service to all classes, and of freedom as an unalienable individual right, limited only by the freedom of others. An enlightened constitutional monarchy was established. The king was forced to return to the Tuileries palace in Paris. There he would be under the watchful eye of France's new, moderate regime, guided by Count de Mirabeau, who, like many aristocrats, had concluded that the future lay with the Third Estate.

Revolution Out of Control

It is always a great misfortune when moderate and democratic revolutionaries cannot control the beast of revolution once it has been uncaged. As in Russia a century and a quarter later, a more radical "second revolution" often overtakes the first one, wiping away many of the democratic gains in the process. This misfortune befell the French Revolution.

The first signal for such a change came on the night of June 21, 1791, when the king and his family attempted to escape to Germany. Caught at Varennes, close to the border, two days later, they were brought back to the Tuileries without glory and locked up in their palace. After this clumsy move, the king's commitment to the new order was no longer credible, and the people's loyalty to the king, which had already been eroded, disappeared entirely.

This new situation greatly angered the other monarchies of Europe, especially those of Prussia and Austria. The moderate "Girondists," members of a revolutionary club whose name derived from

the department (state) of Gironde and who had gained a majority in the National Assembly in 1792, responded to what they saw as a clear external threat to the Revolution. They declared war on Austria. It went badly for France, but it quickly added a new element to the Revolution. Seeing the "fatherland in danger," the citizens took up arms, and patriotism rose to fever pitch. Nationalism and revolution joined hands as the French national anthem, the Marseillaise, indicates.

The newly unleashed popular tide became extremely difficult to control. The Tuileries palace was stormed by a mob and forced a humiliated king to wear a red hat of the Revolution and to drink with them from a common bottle. The constitutional monarchy was overthrown, and in September 1792 suspected royalists were hunted down and massacred in prisons, monasteries and elsewhere. In December the king was tried and convicted of conspiring with the enemy (a charge which was no doubt true), and he was beheaded one month later. Scarcely had the king's head fallen into the basket of the guillotine before France found itself at war with all the major monarchies of Europe.

Faced with a frenzied, imperiled nation, the moderates were pushed aside by the radical Jacobins, a revolutionary club

which had met regularly since 1789 in the Jacobin Convent in the Rue Saint-Honoré and which was led by the fanatical Robespierre. A Committee of Public Safety was formed to cope with enemies abroad and at home. On October 10, 1793, the new revolutionary leadership declared that the government of France must remain "revolutionary until the peace." In clear text, this meant a "reign of terror," and political "trials" were begun at once.

On October 16 Queen Marie Antoinette was guillotined, followed by all the Girondists who could be arrested. For the next nine months the guillotine would never cease from doing its grisly work. Until Robespierre and his followers' own execution in July 1794, France was subjected to a dictatorship in the hands of fanatically self–righteous people who asserted, "terror is nothing else than swift, severe, indomitable justice; it then flows from virtue."

Enlightened democrats make no claims to know absolute truth and therefore tolerate other men's views and weaknesses. By contrast, the ideologues who controlled France in those bloody days had such an abstract conception of liberty that they lost sight of man. Out of love for humanity and the truth, they would have eradicated the human race.

France

The noted French author, George Sand, wrote that "during the terror, the men who spilled the most blood were those who had the strongest desire to lead their fellow men to the dreamed–of golden age, and who had the greatest sympathy for human misery ... the greater their thirst for universal happiness, the more relentless they became." Charles Dickens was no doubt correct when, in the opening sentence of his *A Tale of Two Cities*, he referred to the French Revolution: "It was the best of times, it was the worst of times, it was the age of reason, it was the age of foolishness . . ." Perhaps at no other time could one see so clearly the worst and best in man.

Although Frenchmen today tend to remember mostly the noblest aspects of the Revolution, the terror made it difficult then and now for persons outside of France to have a unified opinion of this first great European revolution. No doubt, many of the 17,000 victims of the terror were in fact enemies of the new republic. Only 15% of the executions took place in Paris, and more than half took place in western France, where the resistance to the new order was the greatest. Only 15% of the victims were aristocrats or clergy-men. To some extent, then, the terror was a defensive measure. However, the number of innocent persons who were caught in the grinder was so great that the new republic disgusted highly respected friends abroad. Also, although France's foreign enemies were ultimately defeated, the French Revolution was knocked off its democratic path, and it was almost a century before France was able to return to relatively stable, republican government.

The French Revolution in Retrospect

The year 1989 marked the 200th anniversary of the French Revolution, and 5,000 events around the country commemorated this great convulsion. It created the opportunity for Frenchmen to look both back into their past and forward into their future. Not all Frenchmen cherish the spirit of 1789, as was shown by Catholic counter–demonstrations to remember martyrs in the Place de la Concorde on August 15, 1989, the production of a movie called "Vent de Galerne" that depicts the savage repression of peasant rebels in the Vendée, the tracing of descendants of the 3,000 persons executed in Lyons by the Jacobins, and the widespread apathy in many parts of the country.

There has been a fundamental rethinking of the causes and meaning of the revolution, and many simplistic explanations have been replaced by a much more complex picture. Some myths were corrected: only seven prisoners were freed at the Bastille; execution by guillotine often took several "chops," and only 10% of those beheaded were nobles; most of the revolution's victims were shot, burned or drowned, rather than beheaded; the statement attributed to Marie Antoinette, "Let them eat cake!", appeared in Rousseau's Confessions at least two years before Marie arrived in France in 1770.

Frenchmen have even become more ambiguous about their heroes and villains. Polls indicated that the era's most revered character is the Marquis de Lafayette, who broke with the Jacobins and fled France. He became a favorite on the staff of General George Washington at age 19 living in his house and riding at his side in parades and into battle. Biographer Douglas Southall Freeman wrote: "Never during the Revolution was there so speedy and complete a conquest of the heart of Washington." A televised reenactment of Louis XVI's trial with the ending left open so that viewers could decide his guilt or innocence also produced astounding conclusions: only 27% of viewers favored beheading him, versus 55% who voted to acquit him.

It is therefore not surprising that the government decided to focus as little as possible on the bloody elements of the past and almost exclusively on the idealistic achievements of the revolution that have undeniable relevance for France's future, such as the Declaration of the Rights of Man and the Citizen. This focus on human rights and the question of what it means to be a citizen in a free and modern republic relates directly to France's future as a multiracial, multicultural society. Some citizens are also beginning to ask whether France needs to have such a brutal national anthem, which calls on them to "drench our fields" with the enemy's "tainted blood." According to a July 14, 1992, poll, 40% of the French find the lyrics too bloodthirsty, but 75% are staunchly opposed to altering the hallowed verses.

Napoleon

Robespierre was overthrown and beheaded on July 27, 1794. That date fell within the month of Thermador in the revolutionary calendar, which had been introduced on August 18, 1792, the date the constitutional monarchy began. The notables who assumed power moved rapidly to restrict suffrage and eliminate the masses from political influence in a tired, internally paralyzed France. In 1795

The Palace at Versailles

Napoleon returns from Elba (Karl Stenben)

they created a Directory, led by five directors, but this new form of government could not create order in France.

In the midst of such instability, a brilliant young general saw his great opportunity. Born into an Italian family from Corsica in 1769, Napoleon Bonaparte had been educated in French military schools and had gained notoriety by suppressing an uprising against the Directory shortly after its founding. An ingenious innovator of lightning military tactics combined with effective use of field artillery, he understood how to win the unswerving devotion of his soldiers. He achieved great victories in Italy, and in 1799, while his troops were conducting a major campaign in Egypt, he returned to Paris and seized power at bayonet point.

For the next 15 years, France followed this man, who though slight of stature

(barely five feet tall), was a great leader in many ways. He clearly preferred order to liberty, and he quickly moved to establish order in France. Despite his authoritarian style of rule, he was an immensely popular leader who quickly showed that he was, at least to some extent, a child of the revolution. He introduced financial reforms and tightened the centralized administration of France. He promulgated a new constitution and a civil code which reflected the major accomplishments of the revolution: popular sovereignty, underscored by Napoleon's practice of submitting every constitutional change to a plebiscite; trial by jury and equality before the law; a citizens' army; office holding based on competence; abolition of feudal privileges; freedom of religion; and freedom of speech and press (at least in theory). Though they had often been ignored in practice during the ten years since 1789, liberty and equality had within a decade become so embraced in principle that they have remained permanent elements of French public life.

Napoleon may appear today as a greater friend of monarchy than of the revolution. He signed a Concordat with the Catholic Church in 1801, reintroduced slavery in French colonies in 1802 and allowed émigrés to return to France and reclaim their unsold properties. In 1804 he crowned himself "Emperor of the French," and during his reign he divorced his wife Josephine in order to marry an Austrian princess. He also placed his brothers, son and marshals upon thrones throughout Europe as he proceeded from conquest to conquest. Nevertheless, in his own day, the other peoples of Europe saw

him as a very embodiment of the revolution who carried its ideals to every part of Europe. These principles were always among his most effective weapons.

Napoleon remained a great military leader who sought both to secure France's "natural borders" and to pacify Europe under French leadership. This was essentially accomplished by 1802. However, his ambition was to be more than a peacemaker, and his lack of moderation not only sapped his own country's vigor, it ultimately doomed him to defeat. In May 1803 he began an endless series of wars aiming far beyond the mere protection of France's frontiers. Due to stunning victories, French domination by 1806 extended from Holland and the German North Sea coast to the Illyrian Provinces along the east coast of the Adriatic Sea. Italy was completely under French control, and some territories (including Rome itself) were annexed to France. But his very successes helped to bring about his downfall.

His invasions stimulated nationalism outside France, and the other governments of Europe felt compelled to imitate France by making popular reforms and raising citizens' armies. Soon Napoleon discovered that he faced opposition, not just from hostile governments and ruling groups, but from entire nations in Europe. He fought an unsuccessful guerrilla war in Spain, and in 1812 his Grand Army suffered a disastrous wintertime defeat in frigid Russia. The following year he was defeated at the "Battle of the Nations" in Leipzig that pitted France and its allies, chiefly the Rhineland Germans, against Prussia, Austria, Russia, Sweden and England. His enemies pursued his disintegrating army into the heart of France, capturing Paris itself on March 31, 1814.

Napoleon was forced to flee to the island of Elba, where the victors erected a small kingdom for him, but in less than a year he returned to France in order to regain his empire. Though exhausted from

Napoleon's tomb in Les Invalides

France

At the Court of Napoleon I

long sustained warfare, the French succumbed once more to Napoleon's magic. In a hundred days he prepared a new army, but his dreams were crushed by a united Europe on the Belgian battlefield of Waterloo on June 18, 1815. His wars had claimed the lives of almost two million soldiers. This time he was held as prisoner on the small British island of Saint–Helena in the South Atlantic while the victorious European powers gathered at the Congress of Vienna to reconstitute Europe.

Napoleon died in lonely exile in 1821, but the "little corporal," as he was often called, still casts a giant shadow in the memories of Frenchmen. He brought France pride, and he rests in magnificent glory in the Invalides, a military hospital in Paris, where the mutilated from his Grand Army were cared for. To this day, the elite professional officers of the French army descend at midnight to their knees at the foot of Napoleon's giant illuminated statue to receive their commissions at St. Cyr, the military academy he had created.

The Monarchy Returns

In 1815, with 150,000 occupation troops on French soil, the Bourbons were again placed on the throne. Although one spoke of a restoration and although 70,000 returned from exile abroad, few believed that the clock was to be turned back before 1789. The royal family was compelled to live in Paris under the eyes of a population that had never made the kings' lives comfortable. The new king, Louis XVIII,

the brother of the ill–fated Louis XVI, wanted no part of the revolutionary flag, the tricolor. He did accept a constitutional order which left things more or less as they were before 1815; feudal customs and special privileges of the nobility were not reintroduced, and France's law code, formalized under Napoleon, the tax system, personal freedoms, centralized administration and the principle of equality before the law remained.

Louis' other brother, who was crowned Charles X in 1824, showed that he had learned little about France since 1789. He believed in the divine right of kings to rule, and he tried to restore the earlier authority of the Catholic Church. His men sought revenge against former Jacobins and Bonapartists, and the ultraroyalists demanded restitution of their properties. In 1830 he made his final mistake by suspending liberty of the press, dissolving the French legislature and so restricting the electorate that practically only noblemen could vote. While the oblivious king was hunting in Rambouillet, dissidents publicly waved the tricolor and erected barricades in the streets of Paris, some of which reached a height of up to 80 feet. One nobleman, sensing danger, noted to his friend: "Things look bad. They are singing La Marseillaise!"

Three days of bitter street fighting (known as the *trois glorieuses*) convinced Charles that he could not master the situation, so he set sail immediately for Scotland. No Bourbon ever ruled France again; their last King had failed to notice that although the French population had

grown tired of revolution and war, it nevertheless continued to take equality and liberty seriously. However, unlike the Americans, the French did not experience one successful 18th–century revolution which established a new democratic political order once and for all. The French Revolution had to be refought at intervals, and each revolution left France divided. It remained a country with a seed of civil war.

Another monarchy was established in 1830. The new king was the 57–year–old Duke of Orléans, Louis–Philippe, the son of the renowned Philippe *Egalité* ("equality"), who had voted for the beheading of Louis XVI and who soon thereafter was also beheaded in the name of the Revolution. Louis–Philippe had fought for the revolution at Valmy and Jemmapes and then had gone into exile, visiting the United States at one time. Despite his romantic past, the new king was an uninspiring man. He was intelligent enough to disavow the divine right of kings and to proclaim himself the "citizen's king." He restored the revolutionary tricolor as the nation's flag, lifted censorship and doubled the suffrage (although only about 200,000 in a nation of 32 million had the right to vote).

He was a moderate, business–oriented king who brought France more prosperity at home and peace abroad. But the fact that he was the target of more than 80 assassination attempts indicated that his rule was not universally acceptable to Frenchmen. He did not pursue glory, a fact the poet Lamartine lamented: "France is a bored nation." Although an admirer of the king, even Victor Hugo wrote in that great work of fiction about post–Napoleonic France, *Les Misérables*, that "his great fault was that he was modest in the name of France . . . His monarchy displayed excessive timidity which is offensive to a nation that has July 14 in its civil traditions and Austerlitz in its military annals."

An economic crisis in 1846 made the voteless urban workers in Paris nervous, and the middle classes wanted an end to the narrow elite composed of a few thousand noblemen and upper bourgeoisie. The influence of the extremely unpopular premier, François Guizot, who was reputed (incorrectly) to have advised those in power to "enrich yourselves," helped fan the republican and democratic revival which was gaining momentum. On January 27, 1848, Alexis de Tocqueville, who had gained a great reputation for his perceptive study Democracy in America, told the French Parliament, "I believe that at this moment we are sleeping on a volcano." The volcano erupted in Paris only a few days later. Wanting no bloodbath on his conscience, Louis–Philippe abdicated and departed for England.

The Second Republic, More Anarchy and another Napoleon

The Second Republic was declared immediately, and a highly idealistic government under Lamartine's leadership proceeded to introduce universal male suffrage, to abolish slavery in the colonies again and to guarantee every citizen a job by establishing national workshops at the state's expense. To the new leaders' surprise, their government suffered a crushing defeat in the first parliamentary elections in the spring of 1848. A new legislative majority eliminated the costly socialist experiments, most notably the national workshops. This action provoked desperate workers and idealists again to erect barricades in the streets of Paris and to resist the reaction that always follows each radically democratic experiment in France. In four bloody "June Days" of street fighting in Paris, General Cavaignac crushed the rebels, killing 1,500 and arresting 12,000 in the process; 3,000 persons were hunted down and executed later.

The frightful events in Paris set off rebellions in capitals all over Europe. French workers were left bitter and smoldering. Class hatred was hardened, feelings which remained a part of French life for the rest of the century and which, to a limited extent, continue to exist in France today.

After the June convulsion there was a widespread desire for a return to order. A new constitution was written, calling for presidential elections by universal male suffrage. In elections held late in 1848 the winner by a landslide was a man who in the past had not displayed any political talent. He was not a dashing figure. He was short and rather paunchy, and his appearance was once described as that of a "depressed parrot." However, he enjoyed two immense advantages: his name was Louis Napoleon Bonaparte and he was the nephew of the former emperor.

He had been raised in Germany and always spoke French with a slight German accent. He had served as a captain in the Swiss army and had participated in revolutionary events in Italy. In 1836 and 1840 he had made two almost comic attempts to overthrow the dull regime of Louis–Philippe. In his trial in 1840 he had cried: "I represent before you a principle, a cause, a defeat. The principle is the sovereignty of the people; the cause is that of the Empire; the defeat is Waterloo!" Though he did not persuade the court, he managed to associate his name in the minds of many Frenchmen with the Napoleonic legend, which had been experiencing a rise in popularity at the time.

Streets in Paris had been named after Napoleonic victories, the Arch of Triumph that Napoleon I had ordered had been finally completed, and the "little corporal's" remains had been brought back to France and solemnly transported through the city before the wet eyes of thousands of nostalgic Frenchmen.

For his revolutionary activities in France, Louis Napoleon had been imprisoned for life in the fortress of Ham, where he spent his time in luxurious confinement, writing tracts on such topics as "The Extinction of Poverty." One morning early in 1846, Louis Napoleon slipped into workman's clothes and with a pipe in his mouth and a board over his shoulder walked out the front gate of the fortress. He was in England the next day, where he awaited his opportunity. In May 1848 his chance came, and he returned to France; by the end of the year he had been elected France's president.

Louis Napoleon invoked the revolutionary principle of popular sovereignty, but he left little doubt that his would be an authoritarian regime. He once remarked: "I do not mind being baptized in the water of universal suffrage, but I do not intend to live with my feet in it." With his four–year term of office approaching its end, and with a hostile parliament that refused to change the constitution so he could succeed himself, he sent his troops to occupy Paris the night of December 1–2, 1851, and to arrest most of his opponents. When Parisians awoke the next morning, they learned that a *coup d'état* had just effectively put an end to the Second Republic.

In characteristic post–1789 style, Louis Napoleon asserted the sovereignty of the people as the first law of the land and promised a referendum on all constitutional changes. Also, in characteristic fashion, the Parisian population refused to accept this change without a fight. The barricades went up again; at one across the Boulevard de Montmartre near the Saint–Denis Gate, a military column panicked under the insults of the mob and opened indiscriminate fire on the fleeing citizens. Two hundred persons lay dead as a result of this unfortunate carnage. Although a terrified Parisian populace did not rise up again for 20 years in 1871, Louis Napoleon's hope for a bloodless takeover was dashed; the December massacre was never forgotten or forgiven. Years later his wife Eugénie confided to a friend: "A *coup d'état* is like a convict's ball and chain. You drag it along and eventually it paralyzes your leg."

Observing the usual practice, Louis Napoleon proceeded rapidly to rewrite the constitution. He created a weak legislature and a strong president who could ap-

peal directly to the people by means of plebiscites. After a year, he could no longer resist one last temptation: on the first anniversary of his *coup d'état*, he submitted a referendum to the people asking whether they favored "restoration of imperial dignity." Almost eight million votes indicated yes against only a quarter of a million who said no. On December 2, 1852 he was proclaimed Napoleon III, Emperor of the French.

For all his talk of restoring France's glory, Napoleon III desired above all to establish order and to make it a prosperous, industrially advanced country. He expanded credit and stimulated new investment. Everywhere new industry and railroads sprang up. He liberalized trade, which boosted French commerce. Overall, French industrial production doubled under his rule; signs of dynamism were everywhere.

Perhaps the most lasting of his public works can be seen in the large cities such as Marsailles and Paris. Napoleon III appointed Baron Haussmann to administer the department of the Seine in which Paris is located. Haussmann completely transformed the city. He built the Paris Opera. He destroyed the narrow, medieval streets and laid wide boulevards and broad squares (such as the Place Étoile) with radiating avenues. It was noticed immediately that such wide boulevards would make barricade building, a periodic Parisian pastime, almost impossible and would facilitate military mobility inside the city. Nevertheless, these changes were badly needed to accommodate the capital's rapid growth and to make it a more modern, livable and beautiful city. During the Second Empire Paris was a prosperous, carefree and culturally active city that attracted admirers from all over the world.

In the first decade of his rule, Napoleon III restricted political parties and freedom of the press. He was a very popular ruler in France, however, and seeing that he had nothing to fear he introduced greater political freedoms in the 1860s. He even took what at the time seemed to be a very radical step: he legalized trade unions and granted workers the right to strike. His regime certainly did not come to an end due to domestic resistance. Instead, he shared the fate of his uncle, falling victim to foreign policy entanglements. He conducted a very active colonial policy in Africa, the Near East, China and Indochina, bringing the latter under French control in the 1860s.

In 1861 he decided to take advantage of the United States' preoccupation with its own Civil War by trying to establish a monarchy in Mexico dominated by France and ruled by Archduke Maximilian of Austria. In 1863 French troops entered

France

1900 Paris World Fair: Petit Palais

Mexico City and placed the Archduke on the newly created throne. But he never developed popular backing and as soon as the American strife ended in 1865, the U.S. invoked the Monroe Doctrine and demanded that France get out of Mexico. Napoleon III complied, and when by 1867 no French troops were left in Mexico, the naive Maximilian, who had decided to remain with "his people," was executed by a firing squad. The Mexican adventure was a blunder that greatly diminished Napoleon III's prestige at home.

The fatal blow to the Second Empire was delivered in 1870 when the emperor tried to enforce France's long–standing policy of keeping Germany permanently divided. Provoked by the Prussian Chancellor Otto von Bismarck, who sought to create a unified Germany under Prussian domination, the French government declared war against Prussia. Napoleon calculated that the southern German–speaking states would not support Bismarck and might even side with France, but he had made a grave miscalculation; southern Germans were swept up in the new tide of German nationalism.

War and Defeat

France entered the war extremely unprepared. Prussia had a far superior general staff, supply system and strategy. Also, because of their faster mobilization, the German soldiers outnumbered the French two to one. Smashing through Lorraine, the Prussian Army cut Paris off from the two main French armies and delivered a devastating blow to the French at Sedan on the Belgian border. Napoleon

III and more than 100,000 French soldiers were captured there, and the Empire came crashing down. In Paris, a republic was declared and the Parisians prepared for a long siege. The new government's 32–year–old leader, Léon Gambetta, escaped from the surrounded city of Paris by balloon and tried to raise a new army in the Loire area. However, the capture of the last trained French army in Metz in October 1870 demoralized the remaining untrained troops in France. In early 1871, after every last scrap of food in the capital had been consumed, including the rats in the sewers and the animals in the zoo, and after the trees in the Bois de Boulogne and the Champs Elysées had been chopped down for fuel, Paris and the troops in the provinces surrendered.

A humiliated France looked on as the German Empire was proclaimed in the Hall of Mirrors at the Versailles Palace. Germany then proceeded to set a very bad precedent by imposing a harsh peace on a prostrate France: Alsace and most of Lorraine, with their rich iron deposits and industry, were annexed by Germany. Further, France was required to pay the victor a very large reparations sum and to allow German occupation troops to remain in France until the sum was paid. For the next half century, French policy would revolve around undoing these terrible losses. Referring to the lost provinces, Gambetta told his countrymen: "Never talk about them, always think about them."

France Drifts

While a new government under Adolphe Thiers saw no alternative to ac-

cepting this bitter peace, hundreds of thousands of Parisians saw the matter differently. They had suffered the most during the war and had been humiliated both by the Prussians' triumphant entry into Paris and by the transfer of the French capital to Versailles. Further, this traditional hotbed of republicanism resented the monarchist sentiment that dominated both the provinces and the newly elected National Assembly. Finally, Parisians greatly resented the new government's termination of the wartime moratorium on rents and debts and of all payments to the National Guardsmen, who had defended Paris, and who, because of France's financial collapse, were now out of work and without subsistence. Again, Paris became a powder keg.

On March 18, 1871, the government sent cavalry troops commanded by two French generals to remove the guns from the promontory of Montmartre that overlooks the city. An angry mob attacked the cavalry and lynched the generals. Violence spread throughout the city, prompting the government's troops to withdraw hastily. Recalling the radical days of 1793, a new Commune of Paris, composed of radical republicans, socialists and National Guardsmen was formed. However, this strange mixture of idealists and rowdies spent more time debating socialist and political experiments than in preparing for their own defense. The government immediately besieged the city and, reinforced by French prisoners of war whom the Germans had released for just that purpose, prepared to storm the city.

The troops struck on May 21, and for one bloody week the street battle raged. In the closing days of the struggle, the Communards, as the dissidents were called, shot their hostages, including the Archbishop of Paris, and set fire to many public buildings, including the Tuileries palace and the Palais Royal. Finally the remaining Communards were trapped in Père–Lachaise Cemetery, where they were executed against the Mur des Fédéré (now highly revered shrines for socialists and communists all over the world).

The government's vengeance was severe: any person caught wearing a National Guard uniform or army boots was shot immediately without trial. In all, about 20,000 Communards were killed in battle or executed without trial. Thousands more were imprisoned or driven into exile. Both sides, fired by hatred, had fought like animals. Reflecting on the events, the French novelist Flaubert wrote: "What an immoral beast the mob is, and how discouraging it is to be a human being." Karl Marx, in his widely read pamphlet *The Civil War in France*, made a legend of the Commune, and these violent events widened the gap created in 1848 between the workers and the political left, on the one hand, and the rest of France on the other. A constant reminder of this gulf is the beautiful white Sacre Coeur (Sacred Heart) church that overlooks Paris from the top of Montmartre. Built to commemorate the suppression of the Commune, it remains for the French left a prominent and hated symbol of a reactionary France.

For a while a monarchist majority in the National Assembly pressed for the restoration of the monarchy, and Bourbon, Orléanist and Bonapartist pretenders waited for the call. There were very good prospects for the aging Bourbon pretender, the Count de Chambord, who would rule as Henry V. But the Count quickly showed how little he had learned about his own country. He insisted that the king have absolute authority, unrestrained by any constitution. He also insisted that the old *fleur–de–lis* flag of the former monarchy replace the revolutionary tricolor. Even the most die–hard royalists could see the folly of such demands.

Meanwhile the French people, who in the past 100 years had experienced about every conceivable regime and who were growing tired of provisional governments, pressed for a decision. In 1875 important constitutional laws were adopted calling for the establishment of a two–house parliament and a weak president. The wheel that always alternates in France between a strong parliament and a strong executive had again come full circle. The Third Republic lasted until 1940, longer than any French scheme of government since the revolution.

The capital was moved back to Paris from Versailles in 1880; July 14 was established as the national holiday and *La Marseillaise* was made the national anthem. Paris began to bustle with artistic creativity. By the time the Eiffel Tower was unveiled at the World Exposition in 1889, Paris had assumed the place, in many foreigners' minds, as the intellectual and artistic capital of the world, of which it was often said: every person in the world has two capitals—his own and Paris. Gertrude Stein put it this way: "America is my country, but Paris is my home." One can scarcely imagine contemporary culture without the creative contributions of artists, writers and scholars in Third Republic France: impressionism in music and art (e.g. Renoir, Monet, Degas, Debussy) and the reaction to it (e.g. Bracque, Picasso, cubism or fauvism); the positivism of Auguste Comte, the *"élan vital"* of Henri Bergson, and the discoveries of Louis Pasteur in medicine or Pierre and Marie Curie in physics.

Stung by its territorial losses in 1870, France, with Bismarck's encouragement,

Renoir's *The Luncheon of the Boating Party* (1881)

sought to reestablish a world empire such as the one it had lost a century earlier. It created French Equatorial Africa and protectorates in Tunisia and Indochina (presently Vietnam, Cambodia and Laos). Thus, by 1914 the tricolor flew in most of North, West and Equatorial Africa, in Madagascar, in several West Indian and South Pacific islands and in small holdings elsewhere. Such a policy was not universally popular in France, but a colonial empire offered France the opportunity to resume expansion of its culture overseas. It also offered some economic benefits to France, which was experiencing a slower rate of population growth and economic progress than Germany and Britain.

Many French industries remained small, family–owned and cautious, a situation which persisted in France until after World War II. At the same time, there was considerable worker unrest and violent strikes during the Third Republic. Legalized trade unions tended to remain dedicated to direct, sometimes violent action, rather than to pursue gains through the parliamentary political process. Such "syndicalist" tendencies (to which French trade unions are still attracted) reveal that the deep wounds of the Paris Commune never healed entirely.

At the beginning of the Third Republic, more than half of the population lived in rural areas, and that number had declined to only about one–third by 1940. While the visitor to France has always been struck by the amount of acreage that is cultivated, many farms remained small and relatively inefficient. In the 1870s plant lice threatened the wine industry with extinction. Only by importing American plant grafts was this precious jewel saved. Thus, in a certain sense, French wine is actually American wine.

Third Republic Politics

The Third Republic was seriously rocked by religious disputes, parliamentary instability, scandals, a world war and economic depression. The new republic moved in traditional French revolutionary fashion to reduce the influence of the Catholic Church. Its anticlerical policies included the permission to divorce and the loosening of the Church's grip on the school system. The result was a total separation of church and state in most of France by 1905.

The absence of party discipline and the distrust of any president who tried to play a guiding role in French politics (Third Republic presidents were said to be merely "old men who wore evening clothes in the afternoon!") produced a constant rotation of weak parliamentary coalitions. The resulting "parliamentary game" inclined French citizens to view politics with increasing cynicism and decreasing trust. Representatives rarely hesitated to vote themselves frequent and large salary increases. At the occasion of one such increase in 1905, a socialist member of parliament was heard to say "my indignation is matched only by my satisfaction."

Scandals further shook the confidence in France's political institutions. In the 1880s a dashing general named Boulanger was reputed to have wanted to put an end

France

to the republic after gaining power legally. When he was summoned to the Senate in 1889 to answer to charges of conspiracy against the state, he lost his nerve and fled to Belgium, where he committed suicide two years later. Scarcely a year after his death, another scandal came to light. Since the 1870s a private French company had been attempting to build a canal across the Isthmus of Panama. Unwise engineering and yellow fever bankrupted the company in 1889, but its directors bribed politicians and press in order to secure public subsidies for the project. The revelation of such bribery in 1892 helped convince many Frenchmen that all politicians were corrupt, an attitude which has by no means disappeared from France today. The French still tend to be far less shocked by political scandals than is the case in the United States.

A further scandal convinced many Frenchmen that it was not only politicians who could not be trusted, but military leaders as well. In 1894 Captain Alfred Dreyfus, the first Jewish officer to be assigned to the French general staff, was convicted of selling military secrets to the Germans and was sent to the infamous Devil's Island off the northern coast of South America. Later, probing journalists, aided by a skeptical army officer, discovered that the documents presented by the military had been forged and that Dreyfus had been framed. The army, seeing its honor at stake, refused to reopen the case, and many French conservatives and clergymen openly supported the army.

Dreyfus was later pardoned, promoted to lieutenant–colonel, and awarded the Legion of Honor. But for more than a generation this sordid affair, with its implications for anti–Semitism, the army, the Church and democracy in France, weakened the republic. Not until 101 years later, in 1995, did the French military formally and publicly acknowledge that the army had been wrong. On January 13, 1998, the 100th anniversary of Émile Zola's sensational headline article, "J'accuse" (I Accuse) in *L'Aurore* newspaper, Prime Minister Lionel Jospin laid a wreath on Zola's tomb in the Pantheon and called the Dreyfus affair "one of the founding events in the history of our country." In 2006 the French president and prime minister publicly honored Dreyfus on the 100th anniversary of his rehabilitation.

Until the 1890s Germany's Chancellor, Bismarck managed to keep France diplomatically isolated in Europe. However, after the Chancellor's fall from power in 1890, France was able to improve its relations with Italy and in 1894 to forge a military alliance with Russia. France's intense colonial activity led it into frequent conflicts with the greatest colonial power of

The Café concert by Edward Manet

the time, Britain. Nevertheless, after the turn of the century France gradually settled its differences with England, and military and political cooperation between the two countries became much closer. Thus emerged the outlines of the Triple Entente alliance against Germany and Austria–Hungary before and during the First World War. Eventually, crises in Morocco and then in the Balkans brought about the devastating explosion which Bismarck had predicted shortly before his death in 1897: "One day the great European war will come out of some damned foolish thing in the Balkans." It did.

World War I

The outbreak of World War I in August 1914 unleashed an outburst of patriotic sentiment in all major countries of Europe. Even workers rallied to the French cause, and trainloads of enthusiastic troops left their hometowns in railroad cars with words "*à Berlin*" written on the sides. Although not openly avowed, many French undoubtedly viewed the affair as an opportunity for revenge of the dismal defeat of 1870 and recovery of the "lost provinces." Never since that time did France experience such unity of purpose.

The British and French armies were able to stop the German advance within heavy artillery range of Paris. Thereafter, the armies faced each other during four weary and bloody years of trench warfare. This unimaginative method of fighting made it exceptionally difficult for either side to win. The enthusiasm faded quickly as 300,000 French soldiers lost their lives in the first five months. Colonel de Grandmaison's axiom that "there is no such thing as an excessive offensive" produced untold carnage on battlefields such as Verdun, where a half million soldiers were

slaughtered in the spring of 1916. A young second lieutenant named Charles de Gaulle, who was wounded and sent to a German prisoner of war camp for two years, noted: "It appeared in the wink of an eye that all the virtue in the world could not prevail against superior firepower."

The defeatism and demoralization which such mindless frontal assaults produced led to large–scale mutinies on the French front from April to October 1917. Miraculously, the Germans never heard about them at the time. They also produced a frame of mind which the novelist Jules Romains described in his book, *Verdun*, which first appeared at an unfortunate time—1938: "Men in the mass are seen to be like a school of fish or cloud of locusts swarming to destruction. The individual man is less than nothing—certainly not worth worrying about . . . My most haunting horror is not that I see men now willing to suffer and act as they do, but that having so seen them, I shall never again be able to believe in their good intentions."

Ultimately a million fresh American troops in France tipped the balance, and on November 11, 1918, the exhausted and starving Germans saw no alternative to capitulation. France had technically been victorious, but it was left breathless and demoralized; 1.3 million Frenchmen had been killed and more than a million crippled. Northeastern France, the country's most prosperous industrial and agricultural sector, was largely devastated. France's enormous human and material losses inclined French leaders to demand a heavy price from Germany in the Treaty of Versailles.

Germany and its allies were branded as solely responsible for the war, and Germany was therefore required to pay exorbitant reparations. France regained Alsace and Lorraine, established temporary control over the German Saar, stationed its troops in Germany west of the Rhine and obtained mandates in the former German colonies of Togo and Cameroons, and in Syria and Lebanon as well. While France's demands were somewhat understandable, they played into the hands of a future German rabble–rouser named Adolf Hitler, who promised to undo the hated treaty. The settlement is a glaring example of the fact that policies that may be righteous are not always wise.

The Post–World War I Era

The French expected to rebuild their land with the reparations from Germany, but when it became apparent that an impoverished Germany could never pay the sums demanded, the French set about to do the work themselves. Displaying re-

France

German troops enter Paris, 1940

markable resilience, the French had, by the mid–1920s, cleared away the rubble, rebuilt homes, factories and railroads, and achieved a measure of prosperity which exceeded even that of Britain. Unfortunately, many of the economic gains were wiped away by the great depression that spread to France by 1932. The last European country to be affected by "Black Friday" on Wall Street, France was so jolted that when democracies all over Europe toppled, France tottered also.

The Nazi seizure of power in Germany in 1933 further destabilized France by pumping new life into right–wing and, in some cases, openly fascist groups in France. The best–known was the *Action Française*, which had emerged from the Dreyfus controversy, and whose leader, Charles Maurras, powerfully and eloquently railed against Jews, Protestants, foreigners and the French Republic generally. Offshoots and competitors of *Action Française* such as the *Camelots du Roi* or the *Francistes*, bullied people in the streets, dressed like Hitler's storm troopers, and ceaselessly pointed to the difference between the vigor and effectiveness of the dictatorships in Italy and Germany and the tired, ineffective parliamentary system in France. Royalist and fascist groups, supported by thousands of students and some communists gathered on February 6, 1934, at the Place de la Concorde and stormed the National Assembly, located just across the Pont de la Concorde. The police stopped the assault, but 21 persons lay dead and more than 1,600 were injured in this violent action against the feeble republic.

Storm Clouds and Paralysis

As storm clouds gathered over Europe, France had only short–lived, stop–gap governments that could not begin to cope with the mounting crises. In desperate economic straits, no French government could propose military increases to counter the dictators. Also, the memories of the First World War were so horrifying in the minds of many Frenchmen that they could not tolerate the thought of participating in another war, for whatever cause. *Surtout pas la guerre* ("Above all, no war!") was the slogan of *Action Française*. It was uttered with all the energy of "Hell no, I won't go!" in the America of the 1960s and 1970s.

Pacifism was widespread and was manifest in the writings of many of France's literary figures. In a letter to a friend, novelist Roger Martin du Gard wrote: "I am hard as steel for neutrality. My principle: anything, rather than war! Anything, anything! Even fascism in Spain . . . even fascism in France! . . . Anything: Hitler rather than war!" The highly respected writer, Jean Giono, dared to write: "I prefer to be a live German than a dead Frenchman!" Even the Minister of Public Works, Anatole de Monzie said publicly, "I prefer to receive a kick in the behind than a bullet in the head." French patriotism after World War I had become tinged with the fear that the costs of war were simply too great.

A state of mind jelled that prepared France for defeat in the next war. As noble as it may seem sometimes, pacifism usually plays into the hands of the world's bullies, as France was soon to see.

With the fascist leagues active in the streets of France, the parties of the left began to speak of unified action for the first time. In 1935 the Socialists and Radicals formed a Popular Front that won a great victory in 1936 parliamentary elections. Under Léon Blum, the first Jew and first Socialist to serve as prime minister of France, the Popular Front, with the parlia-

mentary support of the communists, proposed a 40–hour work week, paid vacations, collective bargaining and the partial nationalization of the Bank of France. However, Blum was unable to find a solution to the problem of lagging production, and in 1938 the government fell.

France was the helpless observer of an aggressive German government which in the mid and late 1930s reoccupied the Rhineland, sent troops and squadrons to Spain to fight for Franco in its civil war, absorbed Austria and occupied part of Czechoslovakia. After World War I, France had not only constructed the Maginot Line, it sought to protect itself by surrounding Germany with enemy powers. It forged military alliances with Belgium, Poland, Czechoslovakia, Romania and Yugoslavia. Hitler merely pointed to this encirclement to justify his own aggressive policies.

In 1930, before Hitler came to power, just 12 years after the end of World War I, the French Parliament voted funds to build an allegedly impregnable defensive line against invasion from Germany. The Maginot Line consisted of an elaborate system of underground bunkers, fortifications and antitank devices and extended all the way along France's border with Germany. It was based on a conclusion drawn from the previous war that all advantages lie with the defense. Colonel Charles de Gaulle disagreed. He warned at the time in his controversial book, *France and Its Army*, that modern warfare requires great mobility with tanks and aircraft. Regrettably the book was read only by the German commanders, who reportedly carried it with them when they invaded France in 1940. Unfortunately the designers of the line neglected one of the basic principles of fortress–building: protect all sides. It was thought that the line could stop at the Belgian border since that state was supposed to remain neutral.

Gen. Charles de Gaulle, London

France

This shield mentality naturally meshed with the pacifist feelings in the French population and political circles. Léon Blum, who apparently believed in the power of a strong world conscience that hated war, opposed the extension of military service from one to two years and continued to speak of the need for France to take unilateral steps toward disarmament, as if such a French policy could incline Hitler to be more peaceful. As his government fell, France was frozen with fear. Political parties and alliances were such that the country was ungovernable. Complicating the scene was journalism at its lowest. Most political parties and groups printed their own newspapers that propagated untruths daily about opposing parties, groups and people. There were 39 regularly published in Paris alone.

World War II

Thus, when Germany invaded Poland on September 1, 1939, and when France reluctantly and finally felt compelled to declare war three days later, it entered a disastrous conflict militarily and emotionally unprepared and half–consciously aspiring more to an armistice than to a victory. Germany and the Soviet Union quickly partitioned Poland, but Hitler delayed military action against France for three–quarters of a year. In France, one spoke of a "phony war" or a *Sitzkrieg*, and precious little was done to prepare for a future onslaught. The German tank commander, Heinz Guderian, later wrote, "the relatively passive attitude of the French during the winter of 1939–40 incited us to conclude that the adversary had little inclination for war."

On May 10, 1940, Hitler unleashed his armies against France. Invading the Netherlands and Belgium (both neutral countries, thereby avoiding the face of the Maginot Line which was unprotected from the rear), German forces used lightning warfare (*Blitzkrieg*) tactics against a French army that was poorly and lethargically led and in some respects technologically outdated. French leaders refused to withdraw troops from the Maginot Line to confront actual German advances to the north, and their administrative confusion prevented badly needed French aircraft and artillery from being transferred to the actual front. This produced such disastrous reversals that the French government was forced to abandon Paris within one month. British Prime Minister Winston S. Churchill testified that French soldiers fought valiantly, but their political and military leaders were so quickly seized by defeatism that the French cabinet could not muster the tenacity or eagerness to persist after the shock of initial defeats.

French resistance leader Jean Moulin

Britain pleaded urgently that France both honor its earlier agreement not to seek a separate peace and even consider a political union of the two countries. The latter proposal was understandably unwelcome to a country that had spent centuries ridding itself of English domination and influence. A demoralized French cabinet, under the influence of the First World

Allied invasion of Normandy, June 6, 1944

General de Gaulle inspecting Free French troops, London
Courtesy of Special Programs, University of Virginia Library

War hero, aging Marshal Pétain, chose instead to surrender on June 22, 1940, barely 40 days after the German attack.

The terms were very harsh. The northern half of France, including Paris, and the whole of the Atlantic coast to the Spanish border, were to be occupied by German troops at French expense. Alsace and the Moselle Department were annexed by Germany. The rest of France was to be ruled by a French government friendly to Germany. This government was to supply its conquerors with food and raw materials needed for the German war effort. The French army was to be disbanded and its navy placed in ports under the control of the Germans and the Italians.

The fate of the French navy especially distressed the British. They were unaware that the French naval commander–in–chief, Admiral Darlan, had secretly ordered his fleet commanders to scuttle his ships if the Germans or Italians tried to seize them by force. When the British tried to take control of the French squadron in Mers–el–Kebir in Algeria, the French commander resisted. The British destroyed the squadron, an action that caused a wave of anti–British feeling in France. This sentiment played into the hands of the cunning Premier Pierre Laval and the 80–year–old Pétain, who had long opposed the Third Republic as a decadent, inefficient regime.

They quickly abolished the Third Republic and established a repressive Vichy Republic (named after the spa in France where the new government established its seat of power). Without prompting by the Germans, they denied Jews and Freemasons the protection of the law. In the July 1942 "Vélodrome d'hiver" roundup, 8,000 Jews were arrested over two days and detained at a Paris sports stadium. A former police barracks outside Paris, called Drancy, served as a transit camp.

In all, 76,000 of the 330,000 Jews in France at the beginning of the war were, with the help of the French police, deported during Vichy. Only 2,500 returned. In June 2006 a French court ruled that hundreds of Jewish families or their relatives are entitled to compensation paid by French railway (SNCF) for its role in deporting them.

Foreigners who had come to France to escape Hitler's persecution were penned up in French concentration camps and, unless they were able to escape, were later returned to Germany where an uncertain, usually fatal, future awaited them. In fact, most Jews deported to Germany had been new arrivals in France who had fled Nazi persecution elsewhere. By the time Paris was liberated in 1944, about 60,000 Jews were left in the city, half of whom in hiding.

Many Frenchmen were relieved to have achieved a peace at any price; nevertheless, they felt a numbing feeling of humiliation and an awareness that this was a tragic debacle which had befallen the French nation. What followed was as much a French civil war as a war against the Germans. For the next four years there were two Frances, one fighting against the Germans and one trying to ignore the conflict and to minimize damage to the French population. Any single Frenchman could find sound patriotic reasons for supporting either, and it was up to the individual to decide which France was his.

France still has not fully recovered psychologically from the terrible tension of the Vichy years. A poll in 1992 showed that 82% of Frenchmen considered the Vichy government to be guilty of "crimes against humanity," and 90% thought that their country should admit it. In a July 2004 ceremony to commemorate the "Vélodrome d'hiver" roundup, France's top public figures acknowledged the evils of anti-Semitism during the Vichy regime. Until Jacques Chirac assumed the presidency in 1995, the opinion of every president was that the Vichy state was not France.

In 1994 the trial of Paul Touvier captivated France. Convicted of murdering Jewish hostages in 1944, he became the first Frenchman charged and convicted of a crime against humanity. This was also the first time a French court blamed Vichy for its role in the Nazis' Final Solution. In 1995 Jacques Chirac became the first president to accept the responsibility of the

Gen. Leclerc and his troops preparing to capture Paris

France

French state for the arrest and deportation of Jews during Vichy. In 1997 the Bishop of St. Denis admitted for the first time the French Catholic Church's guilt in "acquiescing by its silence" in the persecution of the Jews: "We beg God's pardon and we ask the Jewish people to hear our words of repentance."

Maurice Papon was a police supervisor in Bordeaux from 1942–4, who, according to documents first revealed by the satirical *Le Canard Enchaîné*, was instrumental in the arrest and deportation of 1,690 Jews; very few returned. Still defiantly maintaining that he only done what the Germans had made him do and that he had been a loyal member of the resistance, he became de Gaulle's post–war police chief in Paris, member of the National Assembly, Gaullist party treasurer, and budget minister under President Giscard d'Estaing. He was found guilty in 1998 and sentenced to ten years in prison, becoming the highest-ranking Frenchman ever convicted of complicity in crimes against humanity.

His trial had been the longest and most expensive in modern French history, and it forced the country to confront a part of its past that many still try to forget. After executing the Vichy leaders for treason, the policy was to keep France united, to avoid recriminations and to draw a veil over the past. Vowing that he would "go into exile" rather than spend his last years behind bars, Papon fled to Switzerland. He was quickly apprehended. In 2000 President Chirac rejected his plea for release. Nevertheless, in September 2002, less than three years into his sentence, Papon was discharged under a law allowing early release for the ill and aging. He sparked anger when he walked unassisted from jail after the doctors had determined he was lacking in mobility. Controversy still surrounded him after his death in February 2007 at the age of 96. Many were shocked to learn that he had asked to be buried wearing his Legion of Honor medal he had received from de Gaulle's very hand.

France has a respectable record in returning assets seized from Jews. A study in 2000 found that about the equivalent of $1.3 billion had been taken: 80,000 frozen bank accounts, 6,000 safe deposit boxes, 38,000 confiscated apartments, 50,000 "aryanization" cases to seize businesses and homes, 100,000 works of art. About 90% of these were compensated in some form within a decade of war's end. Some were never reclaimed. France still has about $3 billion in unclaimed funds, earmarked for a "National Foundation for Memory" to keep alive the awareness of the Holocaust. In 2003 the government-appointed Commission for the Compensation of Victims of Spoliation recommended that the government and French banks pay Jews an additional $84 million.

While working together with the Germans, the Vichy government introduced what it called a "National Revolution." Although this was, in some cases, fascist in inspiration, it sought among other things to strengthen the role of France's regions, to introduce economic planning at the highest political level, to concentrate small agricultural holdings into larger, more efficient farms and to stimulate population growth through family allowances for children. Postwar France actually built on some of these Vichy innovations.

The Vichy government's powers were drastically reduced at the end of 1942 when the Germans, in response to Anglo–American military landings in North Africa, occupied all of France. Vichy's prestige declined rapidly and when Frenchmen were sent to Germany involuntarily in order to work in German war industries, the ranks of the resistance began to grow.

By 1943 command over the entire French resistance movement had been gathered into the hands of General de Gaulle, who had fled to Britain in 1940 and who had organized there the Free French Movement. He reminded his countrymen by radio, "France has lost a battle, but not the war." His claims to be the le-

De Gaulle leaves Notre Dame Cathedral after the liberation of Paris   Courtesy: Central Audiovisual Library, European Commission gal French government in exile and the sole spokesman for France greatly irritated Churchill and Roosevelt, who, for a time, found it politically wise to maintain diplomatic recognition of the Vichy government. Further, when Admiral Darlan was assassinated three weeks after he scuttled the French navy, Britain and the United States recognized another French general as "chief of state" in French North Africa. Roosevelt greeted him warmly in Washington, which infuriated de Gaulle. His wartime experiences with the British and Americans did not leave him with a strong admiration for the two countries, and his resentment was to disturb these two nations' relations with France even after 1958 when he became France's leader.

The French resistance fighters helped protect unfortunate Allied pilots and often provided useful military intelligence and other support to the Allies. There is no doubt that resistance against the Germans was very dangerous business. De Gaulle later estimated that 20,000 French resistance fighters had been executed and more than 50,000 deported from France before the Allied landings in Normandy. But German documents reveal that this movement had not constituted an effective military threat to the Germans, as had the resistance movements in the Soviet Union and Yugoslavia. Still, when the Allies landed on the Normandy beaches (which today are sobering and moving sites for visiting and reflecting), the French resistance played an important part in destroying bridges, assembling paratroops for action and providing Allied units with useful information. Also, French military units that had been organized in London under de Gaulle's overall command fought side by side with the Americans, British and Canadians.

Local resistance forces and delegates from de Gaulle's headquarters in London assumed political control in liberated France, arresting or executing Vichy officials. On August 19, 1944, resistance fighters rose up in Paris against the German occupiers. Six days later, Free French units commanded by General Philippe Leclerc took control of the city, which a disobedient German commander had saved from senseless destruction by refusing to burn and destroy as ordered by Hitler. De Gaulle arrived with the French troops, and the following day he led a triumphant march down the broad Champs–Elysées.

The Vichy government fled to Germany, and for the next year and a half, de Gaulle's provisional government exercised unchallenged authority in liberated France. The resistance movement had brought together persons from all backgrounds and political convictions, and de Gaulle hoped that this predominantly

One of hundreds of plaques honoring the Battle for Paris

young, patriotic, idealistic, but at the same time practical core of Frenchmen would provide the spark for national revival and change. He announced during the war, "while the French people are uniting for victory they are assembling for a revolution."

His movement also encompassed French communists although he was always suspicious that his desired revolution was not the same as theirs. French communists displayed undeniable courage and commitment after Germany had attacked the Soviet Union in 1941, "but never, as an army of revolution, losing sight of the objective, which was to establish their dictatorship by making use of the tragic situation of France ... I was quite as decided not to let them ever gain the upper hand or bypass me, or take the lead." He successfully blocked their efforts to gain a ministry controlling foreign affairs, defense or the police. French Socialists and other groups also learned then and later what a mixed blessing cooperation with communists can be.

The End of Conflict and the Beginning of Bickering

De Gaulle engaged in feverish diplomacy in order to reestablish France's position in world affairs: he traveled to Moscow in November 1944, helped create the United Nations, fought successfully for a permanent French seat on the Security Council and secured a French occupation zone in Germany as a victorious power. He also initiated a program of nationalizing the nation's coalmines, electrical production, natural gas, some banks and other basic industries, such as the Renault

auto company. Since many French business leaders had collaborated with the enemy during the Vichy years and since a national effort to rebuild the French economy was so obviously necessary, few people opposed such a policy.

Frenchmen shared an almost universal desire for the creation of a Fourth Republic, but they split on the perennial French dispute concerning the kind of republic that was appropriate for France. De Gaulle stood aloof from these controversies, although it was widely known that he preferred a strong executive and a weak parliament. "Deliberation is the work of many men. Action, of one alone!" Sensing that the old bickering party and parliamentary activity was about to reemerge, that his coalition was collapsing and that his views on the future republic were not gaining support, he announced in January 1946 his resignation as temporary president. He apparently expected a wave of popular support to swell in his favor, allowing him to strengthen his hand in shaping the new republic, but such a movement failed to materialize. For seven years he tried to return to power, but in 1953 he withdrew completely from direct involvement and lived for the next five years in the political desert, awaiting a crisis that would direct his countrymen's eyes again on de Gaulle, the savior.

In 1946 that kind of political regime was created which de Gaulle had most feared: a parliamentary system with a weak president—practically a restoration of the Third Republic which, in his eyes, had so thoroughly discredited itself and France in 1940. In the plebiscite of late 1946, a

France

bare majority voted in favor of the new constitution, an ominous sign for the new Fourth Republic. There was no clear majority, either in the parliament or the nation, so subsequent political instability was hardly surprising. There were ten governments in the first five years, and by 1958 Frenchmen had witnessed no fewer than 25 governments. A coherent policy was very difficult to achieve, and the "parliamentary game" appeared more and more to be divorced from the pressing needs of the public.

The governments of the Fourth Republic were faced with many crises in economic, foreign and colonial policy, some of which they mastered and most of which weakened or destroyed them. Nevertheless, it is a great mistake to view France from 1946 until de Gaulle's return to power in 1958 as a hopelessly paralyzed country. France had a resilient population, a rather competent and dedicated bureaucracy and a few leaders with sound judgment.

Economic Growth and European Cooperation

France set about very quickly to repair the destruction from the long war and to reestablish economic strength. The results, with massive assistance of the United States' Marshall Plan, were impressive. Between 1949 and 1957 its GNP increased by 40%, and from 1952 forward, its growth rate was more than 10% a year, consistently among the highest in Europe. Frenchmen poured into the urban areas from the countryside, thereby dramatically changing the face of French society. Fortunately, French industry was able to absorb them. At the same time, agricultural production increased by 24% from 1949–1957. Government financial subsi-

dies for families with children, coupled with the people's increasingly optimistic view of the future, helped bring about one of Europe's highest birth rates, a welcome development for a country which for more than a century had experienced relatively low population growth.

France's rapid economic growth was greatly aided by economic planning, which, in contrast to planning in communist countries, is entirely non–compulsory. These periodic plans set targets and suggest investments to French industry, with a view to making the economy as efficient and modern as possible. Perhaps most important, such planning has helped Frenchmen believe strongly in the possibility of progress. The Marshall Plan assistance which the United States gave to France and other Western European countries encouraged such planning. It even had a further long–term benefit for Europe: a condition for aid was that European countries discuss and agree among themselves how such help should be used. These discussions opened possibilities of European cooperation that laid the foundations for the creation of NATO and the EU.

The fruits of this were not long in coming. In 1950, France's brilliant foreign minister, Robert Schuman, proposed an imaginative European Coal and Steel Community, which within two years provided a common market for these two critical commodities among West Germany, France, the BENELUX countries and Italy, a step unthinkable five years earlier. Seven years later, Schuman and his countryman, Jean Monnet, de Gaulle's wartime representative for economic negotiations with Washington and London, and from 1946 to 1952 chief of France's General Planning Commission, were key figures in the creation of the EU by the

Jean Monnet   Courtesy: Central Audio-visual Library, European Commission

same six powers. The French were not inclined to transfer any French sovereignty to the EU; indeed, de Gaulle later reiterated that this was to be a "Europe of Fatherlands," i.e., of entirely sovereign nation–states. Yet they have clearly recognized that French interests are best served in a cooperative, democratic Europe and they have strongly supported such a Europe.

At one time France sought to extend European cooperation into the military sphere as well. When the Korean War began in 1950, there was fear in Europe that the Soviet Union might be considering an aggressive assault against Western Europe. When the United States suggested that West Germany be permitted to rearm, the French became uneasy. Therefore, the government proposed a European Defense Community (EDC) that would integrate German soldiers into an overall European command. There would be no German general staff. However, Britain refused to join and French public opinion also gradually turned against it. In 1954 the parliament, not wanting French troops to be under supranational control, rejected the proposal. After the vote the Gaullist and communist deputies stood up and sang the *Marseillaise*. France, however, remained a member of NATO, which had been formed in 1949 and which West Germany also joined in 1955.

The Empire Crumbles

While France's economic recovery and contribution to a unified Europe, which included former enemy powers, were glittering successes of the French Fourth Republic, the government was brought to its knees by the painfully traumatic disinte-

Captain (later General) C. E. Vidal shaking hands with his French troops, in Koblenz, Germany, 1945.
Courtesy: The late General C. E. Vidal

gration of the colonial empire. The two world wars had stimulated a desire in colonies all over the world for independence, but many Frenchmen believed it was impossible to restore French power, prestige and prosperity without aid from the colonies.

The first disaster occurred in Indochina, which the Japanese had occupied during the war. When the French attempted to reestablish control after liberation, a powerful native communist resistance movement called the Viet Minh and led by Ho Chi Minh opposed them. Fighting broke out in December 1946 and all French political parties, including the communists, initially supported the war effort. However, eight inglorious years of fighting without victory created powerful domestic opposition to continuation of the conflict. The United States refused in principle to help the French in a colonial war although it did provide about $1 billion in financial assistance. When in 1954 France sought relief for its embattled stronghold Dien Bien Phu and a quick solution to the war by asking that the U.S. use atomic bombs against the Viet Minh, the request was turned down. After the Viet Minh captured that garrison in the same year, the French agreed to a temporary division of Vietnam and to a permanent withdrawal after free elections. For complicated reasons, such elections were never held.

Having had no time to recover from the shock of loss of Indochina, the French had to turn their attention immediately to a rebellion in Algeria that erupted in November 1954. Algeria was a much more complicated problem. Legally it was not a colony, but an integral part of France, as Hawaii is part of the U.S. Located directly south of France, it (unlike Indochina) had an immediate strategic importance for the country. Further, there were more than a million French settlers living there, some of whose families had been in Algeria for more than three generations. Many were farmers, producing semitropical foodstuffs for France.

The Algerian rebellion shook France to the core. It unleashed conspiracies against the government, assassinations and ill-fated military *coups d'état*. A half million troops were sent to Algeria to suppress it. It was a struggle that prompted the French military, which was left more or less to its own devices, to conduct unconventional warfare and atrocities against an enemy that often used terrorist methods and melted into the general population.

In response, French methods were sometimes unsavory. In 2001 a former French general in the secret service, Paul Aussaresses, wrote a book, entitled *Special Services in Algeria 1955–1957*, in which he described in a matter-of-fact way how he and other French military routinely tortured and executed suspects, noting that as many as 3,000 suspects had simply "disappeared." He admitted having executed 24 suspected guerrillas himself and claimed to have only "followed orders." The book was a sensation in that he showed no remorse, and it reflected a "cold tone, lacking any hindsight and any humanity," in the words of the judge who fined him for "complicity in justifying war crimes." France has never officially apologized for its conduct during the war, which claimed the lives of 30,000 French men and women and at least a half million Algerians.

The process by which Morocco and Tunisia gained their independence went much more smoothly. One of the most important and influential politicians to steer France through its crises in the 1950s was Pierre Mendes-France. Serving as premier from 1954-55, he extricated France from Indochina, helped facilitate Tunisian independence in 1956, and began talks with Moroccan nationalists that would lead to France's withdrawal from the country. An ardent opponent of colonialism, he also favored concessions to Algerian nationalists.

The war brought an aging man out of retirement from the eastern village of Colombey–les–deux–églises: Charles de Gaulle. When the French military seized power in Algeria's capital city, Algiers, in May 1958, and soon thereafter on the island of Corsica, Napoleon's birthplace, many, especially French generals, believed that only de Gaulle could save Algeria or protect the country from civil war.

De Gaulle haughtily said that he would respond to the call of his fellow citizens only on his own terms: that he be granted unrestricted authority to cope with the crisis. In mid–1958, he was appointed prime minister, and he quickly went to Algeria and gave an enthusiastic French throng the highly ambiguous assurance "I have understood you!" He undoubtedly knew the situation was hopeless. In late 1958 an electoral college of notables elected him president of the republic. Parliament also approved his new constitution. This spelled the death knell of the Fourth Republic and the birth of the present Fifth Republic.

The de Gaulle Years in Power

Always a realist under his mantle of magnificence, de Gaulle was convinced that Algeria could no longer be held by force, but he proceeded very cautiously in seeking a settlement of the crisis. He did not want to provoke a military *coup d'état* in France itself. He shrewdly allowed all groups to think that he shared all of their own objectives. Sensing that the right time had come, he announced a referendum for early 1961 to decide whether Algeria should be granted self–determination. Fifteen million said yes; only 5 million said no. He thus had received a free hand to pursue negotiations with the Algerian National Liberation Front (FLN), and he directed Prime Minister Georges Pompidou to lead the negotiations.

This was an extremely unstable time in both France and Algeria, and de Gaulle felt compelled to assume sweeping emergency powers to master the situation. The cloud of a military takeover loomed over

France

the country. Indeed, some French officers regarded the president's policy as "treachery" and formed the Secret Army Organization (OAS) with the aim of keeping Algeria French by any means possible, including terror, bombings and assassinations. De Gaulle himself barely escaped three assassination attempts in 1962.

A breakthrough occurred in March 1962: France granted Algeria full sovereignty in return for the Algerian promise to respect the French settlers' lives and property, as well as French oil interests in the Sahara and military interests in a port city. Ninety percent of the people approved this settlement in a referendum. Three–quarters of a million French settlers from Algeria (known in France as *pieds noirs*—"black feet"), as well as a few Algerians who had fought for France (known as *harkis*) left for mainland France. The promise regarding oil interests was not fully kept by the Algerians.

De Gaulle had already offered all the other French colonies the option of becoming independent while retaining cultural ties with France. By 1960 all had accepted this option, with the exception of Guinea, which rejected all ties with the French Community that was to be established. Thus by 1962 the French empire had practically ceased to exist.

It now possesses four overseas departments (Guadeloupe and Martinique in the Caribbean, French Guiana in South America, and Réunion in the Indian Ocean), five overseas territories (New Caledonia, French Polynesia, Wallis and Futuna in the South Pacific, and French Southern and Antarctic Territories, a smattering of islands in the southern part of the earth), and two special status territories (Mayotte in the Indian Ocean and Saint–Pierre and Miquelon in the Atlantic near Newfoundland). The inhabitants are French citizens with a right to vote and economic subsidies that enable them to enjoy a standard of living comparable to that of metropolitan France. Far from weakening France, the shedding of the colonial burden freed its hand for a more assertive foreign policy in Europe, the Middle East, and elsewhere and it eliminated the searing domestic division that stemmed from unpopular colonial wars. In the years that followed, de Gaulle was able to show his countrymen that it was possible to have a measure of grandeur without a colonial empire.

Prosperity and Social Benefits

While de Gaulle provided France with a constitution that could maintain a greater measure of political stability, he also sought to eliminate the bases of social conflict by introducing needed social reforms. The often enigmatic, but always

pragmatic general was a point of intersection between two seemingly contradictory forces. He was an agent of French modernization and also the guardian of the idea of French mission and grandeur. His task was to change France without discarding her glorious tradition. Among his followers were traditionalists, technocrats, social reformers, French nationalists, dreamers and realists.

He continued work begun before 1958 to expand education opportunities, thus facilitating greater mobility, especially for workers and other formerly underprivileged groups. He stabilized France's currency and helped bring about a rise in real wages. He expanded the social security net that protects Frenchmen against ill health, unemployment and old age. He also proposed that large firms distribute a portion of their shares to employees and include workers in the firms' decision–making practices, which some companies such as Renault actually adopted.

In general, he furthered efforts to provide his countrymen with prosperity and higher common consumption standards shared by all. He could write with pride, "once upon a time there was an old country hemmed in by habits and circumspection . . . Now this country, France, is back on her feet again."

Foreign Affairs—Estrangement from U.S. Hegemony

With social peace and economic prosperity at home, de Gaulle could turn full attention to that which was undoubtedly his major interest: foreign affairs. He had been greatly displeased with France's position in the world when he came to power. Colonial wars had sapped almost all of France's attention and military strength. What was worse, the fate of Europe had been determined by the Soviet Union, the U.S. and Britain, and after the advent of the Cold War in 1946–7, French security had fallen almost exclusively into the hands of NATO, with an American general in command. That is, France's security was basically in the hands of the U.S., a friendly, but foreign country, which in his words, "brings to great affairs elementary feelings and a complicated policy."

De Gaulle and all his successors knew that the Soviet Union posed a threat to Western Europe, which ultimately needed American protection. He also knew that the United States' tolerance level toward its European allies was high. He therefore decided that France needed and could achieve foreign policy independence. He unquestionably also had bitter memories of what he considered a personal snub by

"... the whole room might tilt everyone into the garden."

112

Churchill and Roosevelt during the struggles of World War II.

His first step was to develop French atomic weapons. When he was informed in 1960 of the successful French explosion in the Sahara, he exclaimed: "Hurray for France!" This nuclear capability, known in France as the *force de frappe* has come to be supported by most of the French political parties, including the Communist Party.

Seeking to strengthen the center of Western Europe, he signed a treaty with West Germany in 1963. It basically called for regular consultation and semiannual state visits between the leaders of these two European powerhouses. A disappointed de Gaulle later referred to this treaty as a "faded rose" because it had failed to persuade the West Germans to loosen their own ties with the U.S., as he had hoped. Nevertheless, it was an extremely important and imaginative policy observed by all his successors. For example, the first meeting President Mitterrand had with a foreign political leader after his election was with the West German Chancellor. Further, Helmut Kohl's first foreign visit after becoming German Chancellor in 1982 was to Paris. De Gaulle had provided an enormous boost for a development which few Europeans would have considered possible in 1945: for the first time in European history, the idea of a war between France and Germany had become unthinkable.

In 1967 he announced an "opening to the East" which amounted to direct French contact with the Soviet Union and actual participation in the era of détente. In 1967 when war broke out between Israel and its Arab neighbors, de Gaulle, unfettered by a colonial policy in North Africa, chose to adopt an openly pro–Arab position. Although many Frenchmen were displeased by his anti–Israel (and occasionally unconcealed anti–Jewish) remarks, this policy was not reversed by his next two successors, who were only too well aware of France's dependence upon Arab oil. Mitterrand promised a more evenhanded policy toward Israel and the Arabs.

The U.S. reluctantly honored de Gaulle's demand that American troops (whom he called "good–natured but bad mannered") be withdrawn from French soil, a move that greatly increased NATO's logistical problems. This was a logical step to follow his announcement a year earlier that France would withdraw from NATO's integrated command (although not from NATO itself). He did not oppose the presence of American troops elsewhere in Europe because he did not want to remove France from the NATO shield. It was always assumed that France would support NATO in the event of a

Subway entrance, Paris. The Louvre is on the left.   Photo by Susan L. Thompson

Warsaw Pact attack against Western Europe. This assumption was underscored by the fact that France continued to maintain 70,000 troops in West Germany and participates in many joint military exercises. De Gaulle was convinced that in case of a ground war in Europe, Frenchmen would be more willing to make sacrifices to defend Europe because they would see this as primarily a French defense effort, not an American one. Thus, in his opinion, the Western alliance would be strengthened, not weakened.

American leaders in 1967, bogged down in a hopeless Vietnam War, had little understanding for such logic. Many Americans remembered the many American soldiers buried in France as a result of World War II. However, after 1968, the White House had far more admiration for de Gaulle's character and policy. Kissinger noted in his memoirs that de Gaulle's policies "so contrary to American postwar preconceptions, were those of an ancient country grown skeptical through many enthusiasms shattered and conscious that to be meaningful to others, France had first of all to mean something to herself."

The changes were by no means universally supported in France at the time, but by the early 1970s they had been embraced by all political parties, including the communists. The basic Gaullist goal to

create an independent Europe under French leadership, and thereby to diminish U.S. influence in Europe, has not been accomplished. Nevertheless, his design to create an independent French foreign policy has been followed by his presidential successors, despite some changes in emphasis and style.

He gave France a role of which it could be proud, and he ultimately won the world's respect for his country. Kissinger recalled that the general "exuded authority" and told of de Gaulle's attendance at a reception given by former President Nixon on the occasion of General Eisenhower's funeral in Washington: "His presence . . . was so overwhelming that he was the center of attention wherever he stood. Other heads of government and many senators who usually proclaimed their antipathy to authoritarian generals crowded around him and treated him like some strange species. One had the sense that if he moved to a window, the center of gravity might shift and the whole room might tilt everyone into the garden."

The "Events of May" and de Gaulle's Exit

Under de Gaulle, France had not become a land of complete satisfaction and harmony. Many Frenchmen grew weary of his paternalism. His preoccupation

France

with foreign affairs gradually slowed down the reformist impulse. While most Frenchmen shared in the increasing prosperity, income differences had actually widened during the Fifth Republic. Further, despite the educational reforms, only 1% of the children from the working class families entered the universities. Class stratification was not breaking down as much as some would have liked. At the same time, some Frenchmen, especially the young and the educated, were becoming afraid that the new consumption–oriented society was not good for France; it became apparent that France's traditional schizophrenia about change and modernism had not been entirely erased.

Before departing for a state visit to Romania in May 1968, de Gaulle announced that France was an "island of calm" in a very troubled world. Scarcely had he arrived in Budapest when a furious storm erupted in France that brought the Fifth Republic to the brink of extinction. Student unrest at the new University of Nanterre, a slogan–besmeared concrete complex located at the edge of Paris, spilled over to the Sorbonne and to other universities in the country. Many small groups of anarchists, Trotskyite and Maoist students believed that the university was the ideal place to launch a revolution against the capitalist society. Trying to reestablish order, the police violated an old taboo by entering the university grounds. This tradition stemmed from the time when the universities actually exercised the privilege of ruling themselves, a privilege long since revoked by a highly centralized French regime.

With vivid pictures of the Paris Commune in their heads, students erected barricades in Paris, and night after night they battled police with bricks from the cobblestone streets for control of the Latin Quarter. For this reason, Parisian authorities later paved over all of the city's cobblestone streets, thereby eliminating this arsenal of projectiles. Miraculously, the chaos claimed only two dead.

De Gaulle's number-two man, Prime Minister Georges Pompidou, was very conciliatory toward the students, but before he could restore order, French workers were on strike and the French economy practically came to a standstill. The Paris Stock Exchange was burned and the threat of civil war was in the air.

De Gaulle developed a bold plan of action. He quietly flew by helicopter to Baden Baden, the headquarters of the French Forces in Germany, in order to assure himself that the French military no longer bore grudges against him and would help him in the crisis. Returning to Paris, he announced new parliamentary

elections in a radio speech that reversed the entire situation.

The campaign that followed was one of the shortest (19 days) and crudest in France since 1945. De Gaulle presented the basic issue as a choice between himself or anarchy. He successfully raised the specter of a communist danger to France. He also freed the remaining OAS prisoners in order to placate the army and right–wing elements. Opposition collapsed when the communists decided that it was not yet time for a revolution in France and advocated a return to order. The elections held in June 1968 were a virtual landslide for the Gaullists. The left lost half its seats and found itself in utter shambles.

The "events of May" had so shaken de Gaulle's grip on power he decided that he needed to restore his authority. He announced a referendum for April 1969, and, as usual, warned that if his recommendations were not accepted, he would resign. He combined a rather unpopular reform (a change in the election of senators), with a more popular measure designed to strengthen the French regions. It was clear, however, that the chief issue was de Gaulle's popularity and his continued presidency, and on election day 53% voted against him. The general was thus handed the first referendum defeat in French history—a stinging rebuke.

Never tempted by dictatorship over his country, he resigned immediately and returned for the last time to his estate in Colombey–les–deux–églises in eastern France. Many Frenchmen asked whether this would be the end of the Fifth Republic, but they soon saw that he had not left a political void. He had left a sturdy constitution, in many ways well tailored to French needs. He had left a successor who easily won the presidential elections and whose greatest contribution to France was that he showed how the Fifth Republic could survive its creator.

In a 2005 television poll, de Gaulle was elected as the greatest Frenchman of all time. This was not merely a matter of popularity. The general remains as a kind of moral guarantor of today's French state, as well as of the Gaullist party. He provides comfort and inspiration in the midst of uncertainty, decline, political stagnation and a renewed search for French identity.

Georges Pompidou and Valery Giscard d'Estaing

The new president, Georges Pompidou, had been educated at one of France's elite *Grandes Ecoles* and had quietly taught French literature in a Paris *lycée* during World War II. He was characteristic of many successful French political leaders, including Mitterrand: highly literate and

intelligent, with a humanistic education and a sharp, practical sense for the realities of modern and political economic life.

In foreign policy, Pompidou was only slightly less Gaullist than de Gaulle himself, although he was always more modest and less abrasive than the general had been. He did break with his predecessor's policy by allowing Britain to enter the EU. He stressed continued industrial growth and the protection of French economic interests in the world. He also sought to modernize Paris by constructing urban freeways and skyscrapers in the city. However, Frenchmen, who are always sensitive to any alterations of their capital, widely condemned this "Manhattanization" of Paris, and his successor therefore abandoned this face–lifting operation.

Pompidou died in 1974 and was succeeded by Valéry Giscard d'Estaing, who won a razor–thin victory over Socialist leader François Mitterrand. A product of the super–elite *Ecole Nationale d'Administration* (ENA) and a former finance minister, Giscard, who possessed distinguished aristocratic looks and a logical and photographic mind, had emerged as leader of a cluster of parties in the center and moderate right of the French political spectrum which came to be known as the Union for French Democracy (UDF).

Giscard entered the presidency determined to establish a more relaxed style in the Elysées Palace. Calling himself a "conservative who loves change," he wore a business suit instead of formal wear to his inauguration and after the ceremony walked instead of motored down the Champs–Elysées. He allowed himself to be photographed in a V–neck sweater and took a ride on the Paris Metro. For a while, he even ate monthly dinners in the homes of ordinary Frenchmen, and once he invited a group of Parisian garbage men to breakfast in the presidential palace. But he, like U.S. President Jimmy Carter, discovered that his people did not necessarily respect folksiness in their highest leaders. Soon he withdrew to the dignity of his office and eventually assumed such an aloof and aristocratic air that his political opponents were always able to score points with voters by attacking his "monarchical" style.

The only president to be elected under age 50, Giscard was a reform-minded leader. He brought question time to the National Assembly and gave the opposition the chance to challenge legislation in the constitutional court. He also introduced some social changes. During his term the minimum voting age was lowered from 21 to 18, divorce laws were liberalized, abortion was legalized, a minimum wage was made available to

Hon. Valery Giscard d'Estaing

Hon. Jacques Chirac
Ex-President of the French Republic

agricultural workers, and most of the emigrants housed in embarrassing shanty towns, known as Bidonvilles," on the periphery of France's metropolitan areas, were resettled in newly–built public housing. He also made the decision to permit immigrant families to rejoin their relatives in France, a policy that later became highly controversial.

In foreign affairs he observed the basic Gaullist principles of French independence and active presence on the international scene. He modernized the *force de frappe*, sent warships to the Persian Gulf to underscore French interests in the area and took an active hand in Zaïre (Congo) and the former French West Africa. About 6,000 French troops, including Foreign Legionnaires, are stationed in Africa, where about 300,000 mainland French still live. The largest units are in Djibouti, Senegal, Ivory Coast and Gabon.

He sent French troops in 1977–8 to Shaba (formerly Katanga) Province in Zaïre to halt an invasion of Angolan and rebel forces. While France continued to sell arms to Libya, Giscard approved French military operations against Libyan moves in Mauritania (1977 and 1979) and Tunisia (1980). He joined anti–Libyan efforts in Chad. He also approved the use of French soldiers in 1979 to help depose the butcherous leader of the Central African Republic, Jean Bédel–Bokassa, a man who figured in one of Giscard's most embarrassing and damaging scandals: while finance minister under Pompidou, he had accepted gifts of diamonds from Bokassa.

Giscard prided himself on his support of European cooperation. He increased France's role in NATO planning and exercises although he never hinted at any willingness to lead France back into full participation. Sometimes, though, he chose to act alone, reaping condemnation not only from France's western allies, but from many French as well.

Giscard's main objectives were to reorder in a systematic and long–term way French industrial priorities. Industries such as textiles or steel that could no longer compete in international markets were denied government subsidies and were therefore often forced to cut back on their operations. Future–oriented sectors, such as telecommunications, microelectronics, nuclear and aerospace technology and seabed research, which could compete successfully, were granted support. To reduce French energy dependence on oil from over one–half of energy needs to less than a third, Giscard supported an atomic energy policy that made France Europe's largest producer of nuclear power.

On the whole, France was more prosperous and economically prepared for the future than when Giscard entered office. But his effort to strengthen the economy by making firms more competitive put many Frenchmen out of work. Combined with growing revulsion for Giscard's aloof and aristocratic manner and a scandal involving his acceptance of diamonds from an African dictator, this convinced a majority of the French voters in 1981 that it was time for change. Power passed to the Socialists under the leadership of François Mitterrand.

GOVERNMENT IN THE FIFTH REPUBLIC

In his famous Bayeux Manifesto of 1946, de Gaulle had repeated the rhetorical question posed by the ancient Greek thinker Solon: "What is the best constitution?" He answered: "Tell me first for what people and during which period." De Gaulle suggested to his countrymen "Let us take ourselves as we are." He asserted that French political parties, as indeed most individual Frenchmen, traditionally obscured the highest interests of the country and thereby created confusion in the state. He admitted that a parliament is necessary, but it could not be entrusted with the destiny of the French nation. Due to its very nature, France requires a powerful, popularly elected president who stands above the parties, focuses on the "national purpose," and wields the supreme power of the state.

The constitution of the Fifth Republic, adopted in 1958 and still in force, reflects these convictions. It contains a workable compromise between the need for national unity and the legitimate expression of many political ideas, social classes and interests; between the need for a strong executive and a representative parliament; between lofty politics and common, day–to–day politics. It also incorporated the Napoleonic practice of involving the citizens directly in the political process. Beginning in 1962, they directly elected the president for a seven–year renewable term, lowered to five years in 2000. Through referenda, they are called upon occasionally to give opinions on major national policy issues.

The Presidency
The French president's constitutional powers are immense, and the character of the presidents since 1958 expanded these powers far beyond the letter of the constitution. Unless his party lacks a parliamentary majority (a situation called "cohabitation" that did not exist before 1986), he appoints the prime minister and cabinet, chairs all cabinet meetings and actively directs the work of the cabinet ministers. Within any one-year period, he may dismiss the National Assembly (lower house of the parliament) for whatever reason he chooses and call new elections. He may question the constitutionality of any law and require parliament to reexamine any piece of legislation. He may submit any issue to a referendum, including constitutional amendments.

These infrequently held referendums almost always demonstrated confidence in the president and therefore invariably strengthened him with respect to the parliament. He is commander–in–chief of the nation's military forces, and he negotiates and ratifies all treaties. He may not issue

France

decrees. But if, in his opinion, the Republic is in danger, he can assume emergency powers that enable him to wield full executive, legislative and military authority. He is formally obliged to seek the advice of the Constitutional Council and is not permitted to dismiss parliament during this time. There is no provision for terminating such emergency powers. In effect, the French president determines domestic and foreign policy and has veto power over every imaginable aspect of policy, including constitutional amendments. Unlike his American counterpart, though, he cannot veto an act of parliament. He can be removed from office if he is convicted in a special tribunal (not by the parliament) of high treason. In February 2007 parliament approved a constitutional amendment creating an American-style impeachment procedure to check the president's powers.

De Gaulle in 1964 described the presidency which he had created in breathtaking terms: "It must of course be understood that the indivisible authority of the State is confided in its entirety to the President by the people who have elected him, that no other authority exists, neither ministerial nor civil nor military nor judicial, which is not conferred and maintained by him . . ."

Clearly this is hardly a presidency of the American type. The U.S. president must deal with 50 powerful states and what has become the most powerful and assertive legislature in the world. One foreign minister complained that in matters involving the United States he had to deal with 535 secretaries of state. The French president traditionally appoints the prefects (governors) in the 96 departments (states) and until 1986 faced neither serious regional resistance nor a powerful legislature. In the 21st century the power of prefects has been diminished by the requirement that they share responsibility with the departmental presidents and the 22 elected regional councils. Whereas the American president must deal with such nonconstitutional checks as an influential, independent and often fiercely investigative press and electronic news media, the French president faced a meeker press for a long time. Until 1984, radio and television networks were controlled by the government and were hesitant to attack the president openly.

In contrast, the American president must operate in an environment in which the Freedom of Information Act and various "sunshine" laws have made more visible the working of government. The French traditional cult of secrecy and more impenetrable bureaucracy are a haven for the chief executive. The public appears to be more used to viewing the state as something that is walled off.

Some prefer to describe French presidentialism as monarchy, in which the incumbent's whims and favors are crucially important. The French satirical magazine *Le Canard Enchaîné* ("The Chained Duck") once put it: "There's the President, and under him there's a vast void. And afterwards there is a nothing. And below that, nothing. But finally one stumbles over the government." Edouard Balladur asked with a degree of exaggeration: "In which other democracy is the president in charge of the executive and the legislature and the judiciary; in charge of the order of business in parliament, where by intimidation, force or a reverential majority he gets the votes he wants; in charge of the promotion of magistrates and of the public prosecution that sends them cases; in charge of a government that moves only at his whim?"

The powers of the presidency grew so much that President Mitterrand pledged to reduce them and to pass back to parliament some of the powers it had lost. He had always been a vocal critic of the Fifth Republic's constitution, as the title of his 1964 book indicated: *The Permanent Coup d'Etat*. In office, he did nothing to diminish presidential powers. Like all presidents, he succumbed to what political writer Denis Tillinac called the "Versailles syndrome."

Changes in the imperial presidency are underway. Growing public cynicism toward the political establishment emboldened journalists to break hallowed taboos against reporting on politicians' private lives. In 1994 the weekly *Paris Match* published a cover photo of Mitterrand in public with his daughter born from an extramarital affair two decades earlier. Mistress and daughter had been housed in government guesthouses and had traveled at taxpayers' expense. Although the magazine was sold out within hours, there was an outcry among public figures that it had crossed the line. Unlike in the U.S., this harmed neither Mitterrand, who made no attempt to conceal his daughter's paternity, nor his party. At his funeral in January 1996 his wife, Danielle, stood for the first time with his daughter out of wedlock, Mazarine Pingeot, and her mother, Anne Pingeot.

Mitterrand died of prostate cancer. He had been informed of this condition several months after his election in 1981, but he ordered that it be kept secret. In 2005 a feature film on Mitterrand, "Le Promeneur du Champ de Mars" (The Stroller in the Champ de Mars, by Robert Guediguian) portrayed a cancer-weakened president in his final months in office with all his human frailties and missteps outside the view of the public.

In order to reduce the risk of seeing the same person occupy the presidency for 14 years, 73.5% of the voters in a 2000 referendum opted to reduce the term of office to five years with no limit on the number

Cafe life in Sarlat.

Photo by Bill Remington

LE FIGARO

« Sans la liberté de blâmer, il n'est point d'éloge flatteur » Beaumarchais

Cannes
« Les Chansons d'amour », une comédie musicale de Christophe Honoré
Page 28

Sarkozy charge Fillon d'une « politique nouvelle »

Le nouveau premier ministre a été nommé hier.
La composition du gouvernement doit être annoncée ce matin.

Prime Minister François Fillon and President Nicolas Sarkozy

of times to be reelected. All the major parties supported this reform. Even though only about one out of three eligible voters bothered to go to the polls to record their opinion, this change could dramatically alter the balance of power in the political system. Referring to such a significant shift by means of a referendum, political analyst Dominique Moïsi said this "ends Gaullism in a very Gaullist way."

The unusually long tenure of seven years had been designed to create a powerful chief of state who could provide France with the kind of stability that had been lacking in earlier republics. By the end of the century France had achieved that stability, so an imperial presidency is no longer needed. The special aura of the magisterial presidential office declined. The reform reduced the periods of power sharing with parliament, known as "cohabitation." By making presidential and parliamentary elections coincide more frequently, France gains more coherent governments. However, critics argue that parliamentary elections only six weeks after presidential ones mean that the National Assembly has only a weak democratic mandate of its own since it is filled with members who rode the president's coattails. The president still has the power to dissolve parliament once within a year's time.

The Prime Minister and Cabinet

The prime minister and the cabinet ministers (the "government") have usu-

ally been drawn from all the parties in the president's majority coalition, although some have belonged to no political party. They are forbidden from having seats in the National Assembly. Ministers, including prime ministers, must give up their seats to substitutes, and if they later leave the government, they can reclaim their seats only by persuading the substitutes to stand down and by winning a by-election. If the prime minister and president are from the same party, the former is responsible for explaining and gaining support for the president's policies and for insuring that the president's overall directives are carried out in practice. The prime minister executes the laws. He supervises the drafting of the budget, which is submitted to the parliament for overall approval, but which parliament rarely alters. Finally, he determines the agenda of parliament; government legislation always takes priority. He is the president's lightening rod and is dependent on him; from 1958 to 1991 only one prime minister resigned voluntarily. None survived a full five-year legislative term until Socialist Lionel Jospin managed to do that from 1997 to 2002.

If the president's party does not have a parliamentary majority, then the president must select a prime minister whose party or coalition can get a majority of votes in the National Assembly. In this case, the prime minister is a very powerful political figure who establishes the main lines of French domestic and economic policy

and shares with the president responsibility for foreign and defense policy. He appoints and instructs the top officials in the foreign ministry.

Parliament

The parliament has two houses: the Senate and the 577–seat National Assembly. Deputies to the National Assembly are elected for five years by universal suffrage. The president can call new elections before the end of the five-year term. The Senate has 260 members elected since 2003 for nine–year terms. One-third of them are renewed every three years, by members of the National Assembly and elected officials at all levels down to municipal counselors.

Both houses of parliament have essentially the same powers with two exceptions: the National Assembly has the privilege of examining the government's budget first. Further, only the National Assembly can force the government to resign by assembling a majority against an important piece of government legislation. However, the Fifth Republic's constitution places severe limits on this latter practice, which in past republics had been abused and which therefore brought a merry–go–round of governments with extremely short life spans. Such a vote may be submitted only once during any legislative session, and all abstentions or blank ballots count automatically for the government. Also, if such a vote succeeds, the National Assembly is dissolved immediately and new elections are called. This latter provision takes the fun out of the former "parliamentary game" of shooting down the government for the most trivial reasons and makes such a vote of censure a much more serious step for the parties and the individual deputies.

An additional limitation of the parliament's powers is that much of what is considered "legislation" in other democratic countries is defined in the French constitution as "rule–making." The president signs decrees issued by the prime minister, thereby circumventing the parliament altogether for a limited period of time (ca. 18 months). There is a debate whether the president can refuse to sign a decree. Decrees authorized by parliament are called ordinances; an example was privatizations while Jacques Chirac was prime minister from 1986–88.

Approaching the 50th anniversary of the Fifth Republic in 2008, which has provided a degree of political stability unknown in France's past, President Nicolas Sarkozy commissioned his former mentor, ex-Prime Minister Edouard Balladur, to review the constitution. The latter submitted 77 reform proposals, some of them strengthening the presidency, such as al-

France

lowing the president to address parliament (now forbidden). Some would strengthen parliament's role: it would share the right to determine the daily agenda, which is now the government's prerogative; the government's right to pass laws by decree would be limited; parliament would get new powers over presidential nominations. Any changes in the constitution would have to be approved by a congress of both houses. One reform that must have pleased the president has already been enacted: his salary jumped from 101,000 euros to 240,000 ($360,000). This compares with the American president's salary of 343,000 euros (over $500,000).

The number of parliamentary committees (which enable a parliament to develop the expertise to challenge the executive) is limited to six, and even these few committees are not permitted to amend a government bill before it comes to the floor. Such an increasingly weak parliament has been called "a device to provide majorities." There is little public interest in its debates, and people turn to their mayors rather than to their local deputies to pursue causes and grievances.

A final striking innovation in the constitution is the Constitutional Council, composed of nine members appointed by the president of the Republic and of the presidents of the two houses of parliament for nine–year terms. Its purpose is to guard the constitution. De Gaulle did not originally design this body to protect individual rights, but rather to protect executive power against parliament. It is ironic that today it emphasizes the protection of parliamentary and individual rights. In 1971 the Declaration of the Rights of Man became a reference used by the Constitutional Council.

Upon request of the three above mentioned presidents or the prime minister or, since 1992, 60 members of either house of parliament, it can review the constitutionality of laws, treaties, elections and referendums. The Council cannot be compared to the far more prestigious United States Supreme Court, which possesses the power of unlimited judicial review. But in France a piece of legislation can be challenged in the Constitutional Council before it goes into effect; in the U.S., this can happen only after the law is in effect.

From 1986 to 1988, when for the first time since 1958 the prime minister came from a different party than the president, the Constitutional Council was called upon to determine which powers and responsibilities belong to each office. It became the ultimate referee in the political system. A Council of State also exists to deal with administrative and public law. It provides re-

course to individual citizens who have claims against the administration.

Political Parties

It has always been difficult to rule France from the center, long referred to as the "swamp." Since the founding of the Fifth Republic there has been a steady reduction in the number of parties with any hope for electoral success. The major parties on the right are the UMP, the UDF and the National Front. On the left are the Socialists and the Communists.

Union for a Popular Movement (UMP)

After numerous name changes, including the Rally for the Republic (RPR) until 2002, the Gaullist party renamed itself the Union for a Popular Movement (UMP). It is a federation of parties that grew out of Jacques Chirac's successful electoral alliance in 2002, then called the Union for the Presidential Majority, with the same acronym. It merged several conservative and centrist groups, including the Liberal

Democrats (DL), the free–market quasi–Thatcherite party of ex-Prime Minister Jean-Pierre Raffarin. For the first time in the Fifth Republic, the French right can reasonably claim to be united in a single party.

Founded in 1976, the RPR and its successor seek to preserve the fundamental Gaullist values: foreign policy independence, caution toward a more united Europe, maintaining the institutions of the Fifth Republic and economic and social expansion and progress. Even a third of a century after his death, de Gaulle basks in widespread approval. His predictions seem to have come true in the 1990s: the collapse of communism and the USSR, upheaval in Eastern Europe, the unification of Germany, which Frenchmen accepted with only a little uneasiness, the emergence of a Europe more independent of the superpowers. "Europe from the Atlantic to the Urals" was his concept before Mikhail Gorbachev picked up on it. In 1990, to celebrate his famous call for resis-

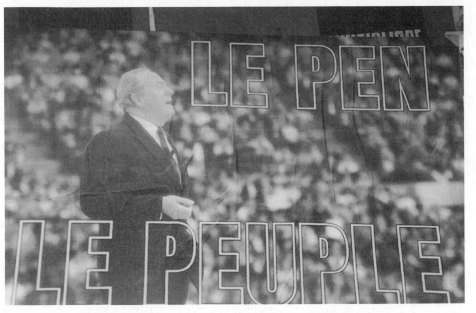

Le Pen: The People. National Front campaign poster

tance on June 18, 1940, the obelisk at the Place de la Concorde was draped with a 35–meter high radio model blaring popular songs of the time and coded messages from London to the Free French.

In May 1995 Jacques Chirac was elected president. But he was reduced almost to the status of a figurehead after the 1997 parliamentary elections, when the RPR crashed from being France's largest party with 258 seats to a minority with only 134 seats. In 2000 the party picked the first female leader of a major French party, Michele Alliot-Marie, a law lecturer and later defense and interior minister. The RPR struggled to unify itself and to find a new identity more compatible with the rise of a global economy and the EU and the reduced French role in the world.

Chirac and his party faced the 2002 presidential elections in serious trouble. Former interior minister, Charles Pasqua, broke away and created the Rally for France (RPF). They were also mired in scandals that came perilously close to Chirac himself. During the 18 years Chirac was mayor of Paris (1977–1995), fictitious jobs were created at the taxpayers' expense, and grateful public-works contractors made contributions to parties, especially the RPR. In 2000 a videotape surfaced in which a deceased property developer described illicit RPR fund raising, including a $660,000 cash payment in Chirac's presence.

The president called such allegations "abracadabra," but three-fourths of the public thought he should tell what he knows. François Bayrou, then leader of the UDF, spoke menacingly of "a moral

and political crisis without precedent." To protect himself, he appointed three cronies to key positions before leaving office: one became the public prosecutor in the Nanterre tribunal, where a trial would likely be held. Another was made public prosecutor for Paris. A third, Jean-Louis Debré, was appointed president of the powerful Constitutional Council.

Chirac's immunity from prosecution was lifted when he left the presidency in May 2007. Two months later he was called for questioning concerning the Clearstream scandal, an alleged conspiracy to smear Sarkozy a year earlier. However Chirac refused to appear, citing the constitution, which states that "the president of the republic shall incur no liability by reason of acts carried out in this official capacity." But he could not escape charges stemming from his time as Paris mayor. He was interviewed in July 2007 by an investigating judge and was charged in November with embezzlement of public funds relating to the fake jobs. After further inquiries, his case could either be dropped, or he will stand trial. This would be without precedent in modern French history.

Chirac and his party did well in the 2002 elections. He won a massive reelection as president thanks to voters' revulsion for his chief opponent, Jean Marie Le Pen. He then organized a conservative grouping broader than his RPR to win the June 2002 parliamentary elections—the UMP. It decimated the left, winning 355 seats, up from the RPR's 1997 showing of only 134. He greeted an end to cohabitation with the Socialists as well as massive defections from the RPF and the UDF.

The UMP's leader and most ambitious politician in France is President Nicolas Sarkozy. In November 2004 he won the party presidency with 85% of the votes at an American-style party convention complete with French flags, music and a giant video screen. A first-generation immigrant son of a Hungarian nobleman (real name: Sarkozy de Nagy-Bocsa) and of a French mother with Jewish roots, he had made it known to his school classmates that he would be president one day. Unlike most of the elite, however, he studied law instead of attending the National School of Administration (ENA).

He entered politics at age 20 and became a mayor at age 28. Chirac heard him speak at a rally and told him: "You are made for politics." Sarkozy is still France's most gifted orator. He was catapulted into national fame in 1993 when, as mayor of Neuilly-sur-Seine, he personally negotiated with a hostage-taker, who had stormed a local kindergarten, while the police sneaked into the school and shot the man dead.

He became a Chirac protégé and was very close to him until he decided to back Chirac's rival, Edouard Balladur, for the presidency in 1995. It took the fiercely ambitious Sarkozy five years to make his comeback. He made a name for himself as a law and order minister. He was determined to show the country that he is responding to a widespread feeling that France is engulfed by a wave of crime, especially violent crimes against innocent victims.

France needed a new generation of leaders, and Sarkozy most represents that new France. He brings to the presidency fresh ideas that are changing the terms of public debate and are stirring a debate on how the future France may look. He does not shy away from controversial subjects, such as the need to change the country's economic model. He speaks of the erosion of the work culture and the importance of self-reliance, achievement and social mobility.

He speaks effectively to multiple constituencies. He takes on the complex question of how to integrate millions of North African immigrants. He recommends some kind of affirmative action and suggests that the strict separation of church and state should be modified so that the government can fund mosques instead of leaving that task to foreign fundamentalists. This is heresy to many Frenchmen. As interior minister, he pursued a law-and-order policy to crack crime and drug rings in immigrant neighborhoods.

He showed energy in dealing with the three weeks of urban violence in November 2005, claiming that it illustrated the "exhaustion" of the French political sys-

France

tem. He vowed to deport any foreigners involved in the riots. It turned out that only 8% of them were not French citizens. Some French disliked his choice of words: he called rebellious youths "scum" and said they should be cleaned out with an "industrial power hose." His detractors suggested that he used such language intentionally in order to attract far-right voters in the 2007 presidential election. If so, it worked: he won 63% of Le Pen's second round votes, to Ségolène Royal's 12%. This was his most controversial maneuver and a break from the party's old guard. In any case, 56% of the public supported his handling of the crisis.

He opposes Turkey's entry into the EU. He believes that the Franco-German duo can no longer steer the EU and that the time has passed when France can shape the entire European debate. He has an uncomplicated approach to America and advocates closer relations. He revels in comparisons with California Governor Arnold Schwarzenegger; both are self-made men from foreign backgrounds with names that are difficult to pronounce.

Sarkozy came to the presidency without the usual French anti-Americanism. He offers a fresh start for Franco-American relations. He urges French youngsters to embrace as a role model Martin Luther King, Jr., and he says his favorite author is Ernest Hemingway. During a highly publicized (and in France criticized) visit to the U.S. in September 2006, he argued that "friendship is respect, understanding, affection, but not submission….I ask our American friends to let us be free, free to be their friends."

In the first paragraph of the English translation of his best-selling campaign book, *Testimony: France in the Twenty-First Century*," he calls America "the greatest democracy in the world." Later in the book, he wrote that "I don't see why my country doesn't take inspiration from its great ally" and that "I love the value Americans place on work and the desire for excellence that you find everywhere." On election night he assured America that France would "always be at its side when it needs her." However, the realities of French politics require that he be cautious to leave some light between his foreign policy views and those of Washington. He acquired the tag of "*Sarko l'Americain*," and one of his Socialist opponents in the election called him "an American neocon with a French passport."

Sarkozy is a convinced Atlanticist, and in his first summer in office "I came to visit the United States on holiday, like 900,000 French do every year. It's a great country." He paid an informal visit with both Presidents Bush at Kennebunkport, Maine, and was served his choice of ham-

burgers or hot dogs. He was granted the privilege in November 2007 of speaking to a joint session of Congress and was received with warmth and enthusiasm. Undersecretary of State Nicholas Burns spoke for many Americans when he said, "we admire the way he has opened up to our country." His willingness to reintegrate with NATO's command structure (on the condition that European defense capability is improved) is appreciated. His foreign minister, Bernard Kouchner, made clear that France cannot pursue its interests through "permanent anti-Americanism." Both Frenchmen also have the hardheaded calculation that if France's ties with the U.S. are not strong, its weight in the world is diminished.

Dominique Moïsi noted: "He has so much energy and is so quick, sometimes it's almost frightening." He is also resilient, bouncing back from many setbacks on his three-decade steeple chase to the presidency. Chirac's own chances for re-election in 2007 were demolished by the failed referendum to ratify the EU constitution on May 29, 2005, and by the serious rioting and strikes in the year that followed. His approval ratings fell to 21%, the lowest of any president in the Fifth Republic.

Sarkozy persuaded the party over which he presides to select its presidential candidate by means of primary elections involving all party members. He reached the presidency in May 2007, becoming the first French president born after World War II, the first Gaullist president never to have served under de Gaulle himself, the first Gaullist president since Georges Pompidou not to have graduated from ENA, and the first president whose father was not French. In the June parliamentary elections, his UMP became the first ruling party to be reelected since 1978.

The Union for French Democracy (UDF)

Former President Giscard d'Estaing had founded his own Independent Republican Party in 1966, renamed the Republican Party (PR) and then Liberal Democracy (DL), which joined the UMP in 2002. In order to enlarge his electoral and parliamentary base, he forged in 1978 a larger, loosely–knit group of parties called the Union for French Democracy (UDF), which is more pro–Europe and free–market oriented than the UMP. The UDF has several thousand direct members who strive to unify all disparate groups within the umbrella organization.

In addition to diverse centrist political groups, the UDF includes The Democratic Force (FD), formerly the Center of Social Democrats (CDS). Now centrist, devolutionist and strongly pro–European, this is the last remnant of the postwar reformist

Popular Republican Movement (MRP), which had played such an important political role in the Fourth Republic. It also includes the Radical Party, a pro–Europe social democratic product of 19th century liberal tradition and one of France's oldest parties. During the Third Republic it almost dominated French politics and led a particularly determined campaign against the power of the Catholic Church in politics and society. This always undisciplined party shrank in importance after World War II, and in 1971 its more leftist–oriented members broke away and formed the Leftist Radical Movement (MRG), a tiny party which closely cooperated with Mitterrand's Socialist Party. A final party in the UDF is the pro–European Popular Party for French Democracy (PPDF).

The UDF was never a sufficiently powerful political base for Giscard, although it was constructed around him. Conservatives were always plagued by divisions and bickering. In 1996 the former president retired from politics. François Bayrou assumed the leadership in 1998. He is a gentleman farmer from the South, who had taught classics history and served once as education minister. To make it look fresher, the party's name was officially changed in 2000 to "*Nouvelle UDF*" (New UDF). But it is a difficult task to make this loose collection of disparate parties into a credible political force. Finding itself in disarray, it formed an Alliance of various conservative groupings in 1998 to present a unified image for the 1999 European elections and beyond. But this experiment did not succeed.

Bayrou carried his party's banner well in the 2007 presidential election campaign, almost catching the two leading candidates, Sarkozy and Royal, at one point by claiming the center ground. He finished third with 18.6% of the votes in the first round, up substantially from his 6.8% in 2002. He refused to support either Sarkozy or Royal in the second round, and these top two each attracted 40% of his first-round voters. Entering the parliamentary elections a month later, he broke away from his own party to create a new one, the Democratic Movement (MoDem). Few of his comrades followed him, and MoDem failed miserably, winning only 7.6% of the votes in the first round and .56% in the second. It won a mere four seats; his own was secured by a decision of President Sarkozy to withdraw the UMP candidate in Bayrou's district and let him win.

The National Front

The phenomenal rise of the extreme right–wing National Front (FN), led by the former paratrooper, Jean Marie Le

Pen, was the 1986 election's biggest surprise. Foaming against France's 4.2 million immigrants, whom he accused of being responsible for high unemployment and crime, Le Pen's party won 9.7% of the votes. It did particularly well along the Mediterranean coast, where there is much hostility to North African immigrants.

The timely abolition of proportional representation in 1988 practically eliminated the party from parliament. But its 14% showing in the 1988 presidential balloting and 15% in 1995 indicated that racist fears and resentments on which the party feeds are strong in French society. Its high vote (*e.g.* 28% in Marseilles) in regions, towns and suburbs with large concentrations of immigrants, unemployed, and crime, as well as in some rural areas, is a warning to the government to eliminate the seeds of discontent that keep the National Front alive.

Although Le Pen insists he is not a racist, a court ordered him to pay a fine of $180,000 to nine French deportee organizations for his reference to Nazi gas chambers as a mere "detail of history." Because of this remark the European Parliament, in which he had won a seat in 1994, lifted his immunity. He did it again in 2005 when he told a rightist weekly that the Nazi occupation of France was not "particularly inhumane," that "excesses" were inevitable and that France had to be delivered from "lies about its history." He also found himself convicted in court for assaulting a Socialist politician at a 1997 rally; he was banned from voting or holding office for most of 1999. He complains repeatedly about Jews having excessive power in the French media, a view that, according to a poll, was shared by 88% of the delegates at the party's 1990 congress.

The other conservative parties have refused to deal with this overtly racist, xenophobic party, which opposes greater European unity. A populist, he presents himself as a supporter of the "little guy" against a corrupt establishment. Le Pen's supporters are predominantly young, urban, poor and unemployed. Le Pen captured 15% of the votes in the first round of the 1995 presidential elections. In 1997 the party also won 15% of the votes in the first round, but because of the electoral system it received only one seat in parliament, which it lost in a by-election in 1998.

In 1999 Le Pen's number two, Bruno Mégret, a well–educated man who graduated from the Ecole Polytechnique and received a master's degree from Berkeley, launched an intra-party putsch against him. Mégret sought to turn the party into an acceptable mainstream party although his political views differed little from those of Le Pen, who expelled him and 19 other leading party officials from the party. The party was left in tatters, and Mégret formed a new party, the National Republican Movement (MNR).

Le Pen's youngest daughter, Marine, is maneuvering to become his political heir. A young working mother with her father's gravelly voice and combative spirit, she was appointed vice president of the party in 2003. Toning down her father's notoriously aggressive rhetoric, she is trying to improve the party's image and broaden its electoral base.

The party faced a potential danger in the Chirac government's 2003 change of the electoral system for regional councils and the European Parliament. By raising the thresholds for winning any seats to 10% in the first round of regional elections and 5% in eight regional areas for the European Parliament, the National Front and a host of small parties were in danger of being locked out. The result, Chirac claimed, would be "stable majorities" of the UMP or the Socialists. In the regional elections in March 2004 the National Front did not win control of any region, but it remained very much alive, capturing 16% of the votes overall and as many as 40% in Orange. It has no members in the National Assembly.

Le Pen enjoyed a surge of popular support after crippling immigrant rioting in November 2005 and a steady stream of political crises that had, in his words, turned France into a "banana republic." Le Pen called on the increasingly fragmented far right to unite behind him in the 2007 presidential elections. However, his support was undercut by Sarkozy, who also talked about law-and-order, restrictions on immigration, and the need to address the underlying issues which had fueled Le Pen's strength in the past: uncertainty and insecurity, unease over immigration and crime, disillusionment with the political class and a faltering economy. The 78-year-old Le Pen suffered a crushing blow, his worst since 1974, by placing only fourth in the presidential race, with about 10% of the votes; 63% of those went to Sarkozy and 12% to Royal in the second round. The National Front did even worse in the parliamentary elections, winning only 4.3% in the first round, .08% in the second and no seats. Some thought that France had seen the last of Le Pen, but in November 2007 he was reconfirmed as party chairman, running as the only candidate and gathering 97% of the votes.

The Communists

The main reason why the left had difficulty assuming power in France is that it has always been fragmented, with two parties particularly prominent: the French Communist Party (PCF) and the Socialist Party (PS). The PCF was founded in 1920 when delegates to the Socialist Party congress walked out to join the Comintern, the external arm of the Soviet's party. It converted the Socialist newspaper, *L'Humanité*, into an organ through which the new party consistently advocated a hard–line, class–conscious revolutionary policy, closely attuned to the aims of the Soviets. In 1936 the PCF refused to join the Popular Front because Socialists dominated the coalition, and it loyally supported Stalin's nonaggression pact with

The more just, the stronger
France will be

Together, everything
becomes possible

France

Street musicians in Southern France.

Photo by Bill Remington

Hitler, which was the prelude to the devastating German attack on France in 1940. Once the Soviet Union was invaded by Germany, though, the PCF joined the resistance to Hitler's Germany and fought valiantly, thereby winning the admiration of such diverse persons as de Gaulle and Mitterrand.

When the Cold War poisoned relations between the West and the Soviet Union, the PCF did not hesitate to orient itself toward the latter. The Soviet suppression of uprisings in Eastern Europe in 1953, 1956 and 1968 all ultimately won the PCF's approval. In the 1970s a thaw in the party began to occur. It officially disavowed the Marxist–Leninist concept of "dictatorship of the proletariat" and accepted in 1972 Mitterrand's offer of a common program of the left, including both socialists and communists. The course was an entirely new concept for Western European socialists, who had seen clearly what happened in Eastern Europe after socialist and communist parties had agreed to cooperate.

The PCF showed itself to be a difficult partner. Mitterrand's PS could count on only about 5% of the vote in 1972, whereas the PCF consistently received over a fifth of the vote in any election (and a third of all workers' votes). Therefore the PCF be-

lieved that it would soon be able to control its "junior" member. It was badly mistaken. The PS grew very rapidly in voter appeal and eventually overtook the PCF. Not wishing to be the smaller member of a parliamentary majority, the PCF torpedoed the chances for a leftist victory in the 1978 parliamentary elections.

The PCF had second thoughts about its Eurocommunist course. It openly supported the Soviet invasion of Afghanistan and was returning to its pro–Soviet position. This was disastrous. To halt its stunning erosion, the PCF saw no alternative in 1981 to joining forces with the Socialist Party, but this alliance collapsed within three years. The PCF has suffered a steady decline in votes and membership, especially among the young and intellectuals. The Socialists overtook the Communists in the traditional "red bastions" in the north. The PCF declined to where it stood a half century ago.

The PCF shed such dogmas as the pledges to "abolish capitalism" and "nationalize the means of production." It entered the Socialist Party's governing coalition in 1997 and had four ministerial posts. It was staunchly opposed to the European constitution and helped defeat it in the May 29, 2005, referendum. One of

its leaflets opened with the words: "For years, one has been constructing Europe on the backs of the workers and against them."

The party is struggling to avoid disappearing completely and is trying to reinvent itself. If it modernizes its policies to adjust to a market-oriented new world not understood by Marx and participates in governments, it loses many of its core voters. If it does not do this, it becomes irrelevant and seals itself off from new voters. The results of its dilemma are obvious. Robert Hue lost his seat in 2002 after an election he called "catastrophic." He turned the leadership over to Marie-George Buffet in April 2003. The PCF's steady downward slide continued in 2007. Buffet won only 1.9% of the votes in the presidential race, and it captured a record low of 4.3% of the first-round votes in the parliamentary elections. It ended up with 18 seats, down from 86 in 1978.

It lost many of its votes to other leftist groupings, which together captured 11% of the votes in the 2002 presidential elections and far fewer in 2007 (3.4% in the first round of the legislative elections). They include such parties as the Workers' Struggle (Trotskyite), the Revolutionary Communist Party, the Workers' Party (Trotskyite), and the Radical Party of the Left, led by Christiane Taubira, Guiana-born Member of the European Parliament, the only candidate who is both black and female. Although they are electorally insignificant, these far-left groups are still a strong political and social force in contemporary France.

The Greens

The French public now focuses greater attention on environmental protection because of such highly–publicized problems as the Chernobyl nuclear accident in the Ukraine, chemical factory accidents which polluted the Rhine and Loire rivers, depletion of the ozone layer, global warming and deforestation. They are also untainted by scandals, which have shaken other parties. French Greens (*Les Verts*) are on the left of the political spectrum, although they advocate protecting the high material standard of living, rather than radically changing the structure of French society. They call for restraints on foreign capital in France and the preservation of small neighborhood stores, which are increasingly threatened by supermarkets. Led by Dominique Voynet, who was environmental minister, the Greens captured seven seats in 1997. A Citizens' Movement also won seven seats in 1997.

Because of France's electoral system and because it lacks a tradition of pacifism, nuclear protest or respect for the environment, the Greens do not have the political

Hon. François Mitterrand

clout that their German counterparts do, even though both are in their respective national governments. Desiring to overtake the Communists as the second-largest party on the left, they chose as their standard bearer in upcoming elections a German citizen, Daniel Cohn–Bendit. Known earlier as "Dany le rouge" (Dany the Red), he had been expelled from France for playing a leading role in the 1968 student rebellion. Known for his pugnacity, charisma and rhetorical skills, he is an outspoken Europhile who already represented the German Greens in the European Parliament. He is the first foreigner to head an electoral campaign in France. He could not rescue the party in 2002, when it won only three seats; the most prominent victim was Voynet. It did no better in 2007, winning only 3.3% of the first round votes for parliament and four seats.

The Socialists

The chief opposition party is the Socialist Party (PS). After it lost its parliamentary majority in 1993 and the presidency in 1995, Lionel Jospin took the reins of the party and breathed new life into it by imposing his authority on this fractious party. The PS, entered a new period of cohabitation after the 1997 parliamentary elections, when it won a resounding victory, electing 253 members (including 12 Radical Socialists) to the National Assembly, up from only 63 four years earlier. The new parliament doubled its female membership to 11% thanks to the PS's policy of fielding women for nearly a third of the seats. Of Jospin's 27 ministers, 30% were women.

Disaster befell the Socialists in the 2002 presidential and parliamentary elections. Penalized by the voters' perception that they had failed to address the twin problems of crime and growing insecurity, they fell precipitously from 241 to only 140 seats. Many prominent heads rolled. Jospin relinquished the party leadership to François Hollande.

The party became terribly divided over whether to support the EU constitution in the May 29, 2005, referendum. Although 59% of its members had voted to back it, deputy party leader and former Prime Minister Laurent Fabius defied the party line and opposed it. In June he and a dozen of his supporters who sided with the left and campaigned against it were ousted from their party positions.

The party entered the 2007 presidential elections with many ambitious contenders, but one clear front-runner: Ségolène Royal. She is the daughter of an army colonel and graduate of the prestigious ENA, where she met her ex-common-law partner and father of her four children, Socialist chairman François Hollande. She is fresh, attractive, intelligent and extremely media-savvy, with political experience as former minister the environment and for family and education. She argued for a crack down on teenage criminals by dispatching first-time offenders to community service boot camps run by the military (a notion that 69% of French and 81% of National Front supporters like). Parents of delinquents should be sent to schools for instruction on how to be better parents, an idea that 55% favor.

She experimented with a new style of participatory politics by engaging voters on her interactive website and posting her positions on a blog site. Her entries were gathered into a book since by tradition it is essential that serious French presidential candidates publish a book during their campaign. Because she lacked deep roots in the PS, she attempting successfully to shape public opinion before the 219,000 registered party members had a chance to elect the party's candidate in an open primary November 2006. She won a landslide 60%, with 80% of party members participating. By summer 2006 she enjoyed a 10% lead over Nicolas Sarkozy, but that evaporated over time.

Party leaders, including her partner, expressed outrage over her outspoken ideas, her populist methods and her candidature in general. Former Prime Minister Laurent Fabius sneered, "Who will look after the children?" This remark would be a guaranteed vote-loser in many other democracies, also in France. At the end of a hard-fought election, she garnered a respectable 46.94% of the votes, and she led her party to a better-than-expected result in the parliamentary elections a month later, winning 205 seats, up from 140.

She has her eye on her party's leadership. That means that her former partner, François Hollande, who had expected to be the party's candidate, has to step aside in more that one respect. In her book published six weeks after the presidential election, *Behind the Scenes of a Defeat*, she admits that she had asked Hollande to leave her home for cheating on her. This is very unusual for French politicians to be so open about their private lives. But the French press has become more intrusive, and she preferred that "things be clarified for everyone." There will be a bitter struggle for control of a divided Socialist Party.

Socialist Past

The PS was created in 1971 from the staunchly anticommunist French Section of the Workers' International (SFIO,)

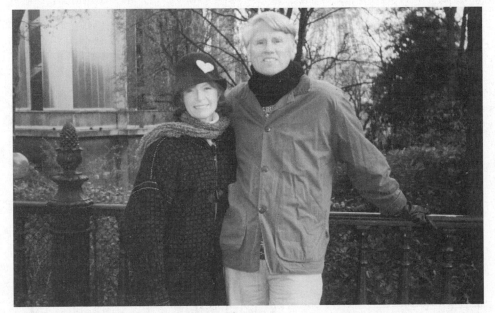

Autumn in Paris ... Susan and Wayne Thompson

France

François Mitterrand's own Convention of Republican Institutions and various other socialist elements. Its rapid growth was partly due to the decline in some social groups which traditionally supported parties of the right: farmers, small shopkeepers, wealthy bourgeois families and nonworking women. But the Socialist Party's success can be attributed mainly to the work of a man who was both farsighted and persistent, but who, like de Gaulle, was also mysterious, elusive and unknowable: François Mitterrand.

He was born into a piously Catholic bourgeois family in the Cognac region of France in 1916. His father was a railway stationmaster who inherited a thriving vinegar business. Brought up on Balzac's panoramic novels, Lamartine's romantic poetry and Barrès's patriotic fiction, he acquired a love for literature; which remained his primary passion. He authored ten books himself and certainly ranks with Léon Blum and de Gaulle as one of the most literary figures in French politics. His career did not always follow a consistently left–wing course. At age 18 he joined the youth group of the far–right *Croix–de–Feu* (Cross of Fire) and wrote for right–wing journals.

He studied law and political science at the Sorbonne in Paris. A sergeant in the army, he was wounded in the chest at Verdun in 1940 and was sent to a POW camp after his capture. After two unsuccessful attempts to flee, he finally succeeded. Asked many years later why he thought he could win the presidency after two unsuccessful attempts in 1965 and 1974, he noted that in 1941 he had succeeded in returning to France only on his third try. He became a civil servant and admirer of Marshal Pétain. He was awarded the highest honor given by the Vichy state, the *Francisque* in 1943, and from 1986 to 1992 he laid a wreath on Pétain's tomb every Armistice Day. He also maintained personal contact with a number of collaborators, such as René Bousquet, who had overseen the deportation of French Jews. Mitterrand joined the resistance movement under the cover names of "Morland" and "Monier" in mid-1943. He changed his address at least weekly and narrowly escaped arrest and almost certain execution by the Gestapo a few days before being flown to England on November 16. There he was interrogated by British intelligence and transported to de Gaulle's Free French headquarters in Algiers before returning to France in early 1944. During this time he gained respect for French Communists and a strong distaste for de Gaulle, who had demanded that he subordinate his activity to the general's leadership.

Mitterrand was hardly a new face in Fifth Republic politics, having occupied many ministerial seats during the Fourth Republic under diverse governments. His political views continued to be very changeable, leading to charges that he was a political opportunist. In the Fifth Republic, though, he was a consistent and ferocious opponent of Gaullism, in part because he wanted power himself. He was a man determined to unify the left in order to take control of France's destiny.

His first task was to establish a program acceptable to his own heterogeneous party. He set a clear leftist course for the 1981 elections. However, he never mentioned the word "Marxist" in the campaign, even though the party's program did contain some Marxist references and principles. In the campaign, Mitterrand hammered away at the many inequalities in French society and Giscard's unpopular style. He presented himself as the "tranquil force" which France needed. His countrymen listened.

Mitterrand's 1981 Election

Mitterrand's triumph was the first time that an entire generation of Frenchmen had experienced a transfer of presidential power from right to left. One of his first acts in office was to dissolve the National Assembly and to call new elections. This reveals a fundamental characteristic of the French political system. Despite the powerful office of the presidency, no incumbent had been able to rule long in the face of a determined, reasonably cohesive opposing majority in the National Assembly because of its budgetary and legislative approval powers. For the first time in the history of the Fifth Republic, a president faced a hostile parliamentary majority. The elections in June produced a landslide victory for the PS, which won an absolute majority with 288 out of 491 seats in the assembly.

The new government wasted little time in seeking legislation for the most far-reaching of its proposed reforms: the nationalization of certain industries and the decentralization of the French political system. Although Mitterrand's plan to extend state control over more of the French economy appeared at first glance to be a radical move, three things had to be borne in mind: first, France has a long tradition of extensive state intervention in the economy, at least since the time of Louis XIV. Laissez–faire economics (believing that the government should intervene as little as possible) never really took hold in France, and for a long time the government has heavily subsidized industries for one reason or another. Second, 12% of the French economy had already been nationalized before Mitterrand was elected. The state–owned sector was already France's largest employer and responsible for 30% of all industrial output.

Third, the French state has supervised economic planning since the end of World War II. Managers, union representatives and government officials have always drawn up "Le Plan," and parliament debates and approves it. It usually extends for a five–year period and sets economic targets, investment priorities, statistical analyses of past, present and future economic performance and needs. The aim is to sustain balanced economic growth. Traditionally, there have been no coercive measures associated with the plan, but the state has always offered industries many incentives to participate: it provides useful statistics and analyses, grants tax relief and tariff concessions, awards government contracts or provides loans for investment funds.

Decentralization

The second fundamental reform was the decentralization of the political system. Since at least the 17th century, French national leaders consistently strengthened the powers of the central government at the expense of the regions and communes. In 1792 France was divided into 96 departments, each headed by a prefect, a powerful and uniformed official appointed by and answerable to the national government. The prefect oversaw the work of locally elected mayors and councils in the 37,500 municipalities. For economic and administrative purposes, 22 regions, whose borders roughly approximate those of France's ancient provinces, each headed by a regional prefect, were created. The essential fact is that all important initiatives had either to originate or be approved in Paris. For example, the designs for school cafeterias, soccer fields, swimming pools and other public facilities had to clear numerous bureaucratic and political hurdles in Paris.

This not only required personal connections and caused serious delays, but many Frenchmen feared that it was creating excessive visual uniformity in a land admired for its rich diversity. Many observers also believed that centralization stifled individual civic action and stimulated suspicion toward the French state. Mitterrand took seriously his pledge to reduce the power the central government and the prefects had over subnational political units and to allow popularly elected regional and local assemblies and executives to handle their own affairs.

Within two years, his government announced ten devolution laws and 50 decrees designed to decentralize France. Perhaps the most significant change was that the prefects, renamed "Commissioners of the Republic," were stripped of many of their administrative, financial, judicial and technical powers. They must share re-

French National Assembly elections: 577 Seats

The pendulum of French politics: left, right, left

1988 — Others, UDF (Giscard), Socialists, RPR (Chirac), Communists

1993 — Others, UDF (Giscard), Socialists, RPR (Chirac), Communists

1997 — Others, UDF (Léotard), Socialists, RPR (Chirac), Communists

sponsibility with the elected presidents of the departments and the 22 regional councils, which were strengthened. During the 1980s local governments were granted more autonomy in spending, taxation, and borrowing. The result was more local activity to build new airports, wider streets, pedestrian zones, museums, concert halls, and stadiums. However, the shift of power from civil servants to local politicians also brought a higher level of local indebtedness and corruption.

A political problem that devolution presented to the Mitterrand government was that his conservative opponents did very well in local and regional elections after 1982. Thus, he created a troublesome territorial set of checks and balances that provide departmental and regional restraints on the Paris government.

A Conservative Turn

The Socialists promised France in 1981 fundamental changes, but few persons expected to see France emerge as a more pragmatic, conservative country with a more robust brand of capitalism. After it was clear by 1983 that his socialist revolution had failed, the Mitterrand government pursued a more austere economic course and stressed modernization, rather than socialization of France.

As an intellectual force, Marxism became far less popular than it once had been. Partly because of Mitterrand's maneuverings, the Communist Party became practically impotent and became locked in a steady decline. The trade unions, a traditional pillar of the PCF, have never been weaker in modern France.

As Socialists began to talk about modernizing France and going "back to the basics" in schools, French society was beginning to manifest more conservative changes as well. Support for government–subsidized Catholic schools was so great that the Mitterrand government had to back down from efforts to restrict their independence. The government grip on

the airwaves was also loosened, as private radio and TV stations sprang into life.

Cohabitation—1986 to 1988

The 1986 electoral results created something entirely new since the beginning of the Fifth Republic in 1958: a president whose party was a minority in the Na-

tional Assembly. The traditional conservative parties won a whisker–thin majority. Therefore, Mitterrand was compelled to appoint a conservative prime minister, Jacques Chirac.

Chirac had studied international relations at Harvard, paying his way by working as a waiter at Howard Johnson's. Dur-

France

ing the Algerian War he served in the French Foreign Legion, after which he entered the prestigious *Ecole Nationale d'Administration*. His subsequent political rise was meteoric, working, as always, so energetically that Pompidou gave him the nickname "the Bulldozer." From 1974–76 he had served as prime minister under Giscard. However, believing that he was given too little leeway to pursue his own policies, he became the only prime minister in the Fifth Republic to quit due to disagreements with the president.

Observers coined the word "cohabitation" to describe the relationship between a strong president and an equally strong prime minister who is not willing merely to execute the will of the president. This relationship changed the basic rules of the French political game from 1986 to 1988. It also showed that the institutions of the Fifth Republic are more adaptable and resilient in democratic politics than even de Gaulle had ever imagined.

The president's actual powers diminished somewhat, but they nevertheless remained formidable. "Cohabitation" was not a return to the parliamentary politics and "games" of the Third and Fourth Republics because the powers the president lost fell to a powerful prime minister, not to parliament. Nevertheless, it was a difficult relationship with which the French had almost no experience. Both the president and the prime minister had an interest in making this power–sharing succeed. French politics has traditionally been characterized by polarization between the left and the right; the new experiment of cohabitation proved they could find common ground and cooperate with each other in the interest of the French nation. In fact, by election time in 1988 it had helped diminish the ideological gulf separating the major parties. Therefore, it actually strengthened French democracy. "Cohabitation" proved to be a workable alternative, and 70% of the French found it to be good.

As soon as Mitterrand appointed Chirac prime minister, the latter declared that he would play an active role in French foreign and defense policy, fields traditionally reserved for the president. Although Chirac and Mitterrand thought almost alike on these issues, their struggle was over constitutional power, not policy.

In domestic affairs, Chirac moved extremely quickly, hearing loudly and clearly the countdown to the 1988 elections. His government probably put through the largest number of reforms by any French government since 1958. Although Mitterrand initially balked at some of the conservative government's initiatives, he could not stop a single policy the prime minister wanted to pursue.

He was the first Fifth Republic president to have his wings clipped while still in office. He watched most of his power drain away from the Elysée to the Matignon palace. However, by knowing how and when to assert his residual authority, he succeeded in halting the trend. Having preserved his authority, his popularity soared. By standing above the political fray and focusing on the nation's interests, he let Chirac, who was in the trenches doing day–to–day combat, acquire some serious political bruises. Mitterrand thereby enhanced his own prospects of reelection in 1988 and diminished Chirac's chances to win the presidency.

1988 Elections

The strength of de Gaulle's constitution had been demonstrated by the two–year "cohabitation" experiment, which coupled a Socialist president with a conservative prime minister. The 1988 elections led the country into yet another untested experiment: a minority government.

In presidential elections Chirac garnered only 46% of the votes to Mitterrand's 54%. In the subsequent parliamentary elections in June, the PS fell 14 votes short of a majority. Mitterrand appointed a popular and capable rival within his party, Michel Rocard, as prime minister with a cabinet containing some nonsocialists.

The minority government had to work with other parties to make the system work. But this is nothing unusual in Europe, where most major democracies have coalition or minority governments. The constitution had been designed in 1958 to enable a country with a fractious parliament to enjoy stable rule. No new elections can be called for 12 months, and governments cannot be brought down unless a majority unites against it. In other words, it is the opposition, not the government, which needs a majority. Rocard went far in introducing non–socialist ideas on how an advanced economy should be run. He deserves much of the credit for transforming the PS from a party of doctrine to one of government.

In many ways Mitterrand had done more to transform French society and politics than de Gaulle. No one would have expected that he would be so able to convert the French to an acceptance of a market economy and the need for stable and rigorous economic management. In foreign policy he swept away some of the most important cornerstones of Gaullist foreign policy by nurturing a more trusting relationship with the United States and by championing greater European integration, including in the field of defense. In a 1992 referendum to accept the Maastricht Treaty, only a hair–thin 51% voted *Oui*. The narrowness of that margin in one

of the EU's founding nations was a stinging blow to France's political elite. It was in the context of greater European integration and closer Franco–German relations that Mitterrand sought to contain an enlarged, unified, and dynamic Germany within a Europe whose map is being redrawn.

He oversaw the most ambitious building program in Paris since Haussmann remade the capital more than a century earlier. I.M. Pei's glass pyramid in the court of the Louvre had shocked Parisians at first, but it gave new life to one of the world's finest museums. The Grand Arch at the heart of the suburb of La Défense, completed for the bicentennial in 1989, is a majestic, modern, 360–foot steel–and–glass version of Napoleon's Arc de Triomphe. The Bastille Opéra, opened in 1989, has been less successful in winning public admiration, but numerous other *Grands Travaux*, such as a new National Library, leave Mitterrand's stamp on Paris. In 2003 a street in central Paris was named after him: Quai François Mitterrand runs beside the Louvre along the Seine.

1993 Parliamentary Elections

Mitterrand's party, which had been in power too long and had run short on vision, ideas, and energy, was swept from power in the most devastating defeat in modern French electoral history. It was a hard verdict, but it was not an ideological one, since the Socialist Party had already shed most of its socialist ideology. Before stepping down in May 1995, Mitterrand admitted that with all the formal powers a French president has, he had "underestimated the ponderous nature of society, the slowness of its wheels, the weight of its traditions. You don't change society by an act of legislation." Mitterrand remains the only Socialist ever to win the presidency in the Fifth Republic.

The conservative victors captured 80% of the seats in the National Assembly, and for two years France again experienced rule by cohabitation. Prime minister of the conservative government was Edouard Balladur.

1995 Presidential Elections

Balladur's government was embarrassed by charges of American industrial espionage in France and subsequent expulsion of four U.S. diplomats. This was the first time France had publicly sought the removal of alleged American agents from its soil. It was also a setback for the two countries' intelligence cooperation, which had been instrumental in France's 1994 capture in the Sudan of the world's most wanted terrorist, known as "Carlos the Jackal." The government's handling of the spy affair widened a serious breach in the cabinet between Balladur's supporters and those of party leader Jacques Chirac. The latter had put Balladur into the prime ministerial hot seat to free himself to run for the presidency, which had eluded him twice before. Boosted by temporary popularity, Balladur's ambition grew, and he decided to make a bid for the presidency himself. Chirac felt double-crossed, and the stage was set for a tense race.

In the second round in May, Chirac and Socialist Lionel Jospin agreed not to bargain with Le Pen, who had received 15% in the first round, even though unemployment and immigration were the dominant issues on the minds of voters. Chirac campaigned energetically under the banner, "France for All," to try to show that he stood above party politics. He repeated in his standard stump speech that French society "is more divided and dangerous than ever." With a turnout of 80%, Chirac won 52.6% of the votes, doing best among farmers, business people, shop–keepers, artisans, and the professions, such as doctors and lawyers. For the first time, a conservative candidate won a majority of voters under age 35, as well as more than 40% of blue–collar workers and French describing themselves as under–privileged. Since a record 6% of blank ballots was cast, he actually won only 49.5% of the votes cast, making him the first president to be elected with fewer than half the total votes.

Chirac's victory left the right in control of the presidency, 80% of the seats in the National Assembly and two–thirds in the Senate, 20 of 22 regional councils, four–fifths of the departmental councils, and most of the big cities. Never in the history of the Fifth Republic has there been such a concentration of power.

Chirac promised a less monarchical presidency than that of his predecessor. He ordered that the fleet of military jets and helicopters at the disposal of the president and cabinet be disbanded and that ostentatious signs of power, such as motorcades with screaming sirens and motorcycles racing through the streets, be banned.

During his campaign, Chirac promised "profound change." As it became obvious that Chirac could not fulfill his campaign promises of lower taxes and bountiful jobs, his approval rating plummeted. Without preparing the public, he suddenly announced an abrupt reversal of his economic policy from creating jobs to cutting the deficit in order to ensure that France would be able to join Europe's monetary union in 1999.

The sense of betrayal over the unexpected U–turn from job creation to austerity ignited in 1995–97 the worst strikes since 1968, involving millions of citizens, from civil servants and truck drivers to students, actors and doctors. Unlike in 1968, though, there is no unified political idea behind the unrest. Demonstrators in 1968 had risen up against materialism and an allegedly soulless affluent society. Many French now revolted, not just because they refused to relinquish treasured welfare benefits and special privileges, but also because they had a feeling that life was getting worse and worse and that affluence and security might be slipping away from them. This is why strikers enjoy strong public support and why the government caves in to them so often.

1997 Parliamentary Elections

President Chirac dissolved parliament and called new elections. In the June 1997 final round of elections, control of the National Assembly changed hands for the fifth straight parliamentary election in 16 years. Tired of Chirac's broken promises made only two years earlier, voters turned back to the Socialists, led by Lionel Jospin, a former diplomat, economics professor, and education minister. They believed in Jospin's promises to create 700,000 jobs for the young—half of them in the public sector, to create more jobs by reducing the work week from 39 to 35 hours with no loss of pay, and defending the welfare state without raising taxes. Jospin pledged not to allow global market forces to condemn France to the "cruelties of 19th century capitalism," which many French identify with American–led economic reforms sweeping the industrialized world.

Running in both 1997 and 2002 under a loose umbrella called the "pluralist left" (*la gauche plurielle*), the Socialists captured 253 seats (including 12 Radical Socialists) in the 577–seat Assembly. Since that is short of an absolute majority, the government Jospin formed had to rule with the support of the Communist Party, which won 38 seats, and the Greens, which got seven. President Chirac, who had disastrously misread the mood of the French public, was obligated to accept cohabitation for the third time in 11 years. Jospin became the first prime minister in the Fifth Republic to serve a full five-year term.

2002 Elections

France was reeling after the 2002 presidential elections. With 16 candidates running in the first round and with an unprecedented 28% of the voters too disillusioned even to vote, Chirac won just under 20% of the votes, the lowest ever for an incumbent president. Socialist challenger, Prime Minister Lionel Jospin, fell to a disgraceful third place, with about 16% of the votes, behind Le Pen, who won almost 17%.

In the campaign Jospin had come unhinged, venting his frustration by questioning Chirac's age and stamina and thereby violating an unspoken rule against negative campaigning. Even though he had presided over a growing economy and falling unemployment, he failed to recognize early enough that the real issues for French voters were crime, which had risen to American levels in such categories as armed robberies and car theft, and fear of foreigners, whom many French blame for the ascending crime rate. He was also handicapped by an electoral system that allowed many other candidates to compete for the left, which together won a respectable 44% of the total votes. Even one of his former cabinet members, Jean-Pierre Chevènement, created a breakaway party, Citizens' Movement, which won 5% of the votes and thereby deprived Jospin of the crucial margin that would have put him into the second round and perhaps into the presidential office. All together the two largest parties, the RPR and the Socialists, gathered only 35% of the votes.

It was Le Pen and his National Front who benefited from the sense of insecurity that had gripped the country, especially in the aftermath of the September 11, 2001, terrorist strikes against the U.S.,

Typical World War I monument seen in every French village

France

which fueled fears of Arab terrorists moving within France's large immigrant minority. This feeling of insecurity was exacerbated by the physical attacks by Arab immigrants on French Jews and synagogues. He said, "I want to reestablish security throughout the territory." Despite the country's strict gun control laws, more and more crimes now involve firearms, including pistols, machine guns and grenade launchers. This was brought home again by a man who went berserk and burst with guns blazing into a meeting in a Paris suburb, killing eight city councilors before leaping out a window to his death.

Le Pen was thus a symptom of a wider political malaise, including the fear of globalization, ugly xenophobia, and gloomy feeling of decline. He spoke of France as a country "in regression": in its economy, its public safety, and its morality. The endless series of corruption scandals surrounding the political class, including Chirac, whom a nightly satirical television show routinely lampooned as "Super Liar," had sickened many French, especially the "little people" to whom Le Pen appealed.

The shock to the nation caused by Le Pen's success in the first round brought millions of Frenchmen of diverse political persuasions into the streets demanding a massive show of opposition to Le Pen in the second round two weeks later. These were anti-Le Pen rallies, not pro-Chirac ones. The most common slogan for the demonstrations was "Vote for the Crook, Not the Fascist." The usually neutral French media broke with tradition and endorsed Chirac. *Le Figero* carried a banner headline, "For France."

This worked. In the second round, Chirac captured an unprecedented 82% of the votes with a turnout of 80%. He faced the anomaly of having been elected by the largest margin in French history, outdoing even his hero Charles de Gaulle, but having very weak support from the public. A Harris poll revealed a day after the tally that only 13% of voters supported him because of his program; 75% gave as their main reason to shut out Le Pen.

Chirac's newly formed conservative Union for the Presidential Majority (UMP) dominated the parliamentary elections that followed on the heels of his presidential landslide. The right captured 399 of 577 seats, leaving only 140 for the humiliated Socialists. This victory not only left the right in control of the Senate and local government, but it ended cohabitation of a conservative president and a Socialist government. Voter abstention was a record 40%. Promising all things to all voters—tax cuts, subsidies to help women and the young to find employment, more

police on the streets—he appointed a diversified 39-minister cabinet that included 11 women, one of whom was of North African descent. Of the 577 parliamentary seats, 73 were won by women.

Chirac appointed Senator Jean-Pierre Raffarin as prime minister before the elections. He was from the provinces with a reputation as a popular speaker with a sensitive ear for what he terms "France down below." He served as the president's lightening rod until the end of May 2005, when Chirac replaced him with Dominique de Villepin. Seeing the writing on the wall, Raffarin had provided himself with a political parachute by winning a Senate seat.

2007 Elections and the Chirac Legacy

An era came to an end in 2007: Jacques Chirac, the only remaining politician who served every Fifth Republic president since de Gaulle, left power after 12 years as president. He departed as the most unpopular president in the history of the Fifth Republic. He came into office in 1995 promising to "mend the social fracture," get people back to work, ease tensions in the explosive suburbs, cut taxes, and insure prosperity. He accomplished none of these goals. Instead he left a France that was frightened by high unemployment, growing debt, and a strong feeling of political and economic stagnation.

During his tenure, joblessness averaged 10% (21.5% for those under age 25 and almost 50% in the housing projects of some suburbs), wealth per capita slid from 5th to 13th place in the world (surpassed by Ireland and Britain), and public debt (at 66% of GDP) grew faster than in any other EU country. The French social system, while performing well in certain sectors such as health care and public transportation, is in financial trouble. Yet he never stopped arguing that "our French model" must never be dismantled. His loss of the May 2005 referendum on the ill-fated EU constitutional treaty was a stinging personal rejection.

He consistently backed down from pushing through unpopular reforms. Although he billed himself as a politician of the right, he ruled more like one from the left. He went so far as to compare the dangers of free-market economics to those of communism.

Nevertheless, he occasionally took some courageous stands: he spoke out against racism and anti-Semitism, and he admitted France's official culpability in deporting Jews to their deaths in concentration camps during the Second World War. He took the unpopular stand of advocating Turkey's membership in the EU. Although subsequent research revealed that he and his government wavered

2007 Parliamentary Election
Source: *Financial Times*

about whether to join the war against Saddam Hussein's Iraq in 2003, his ultimate decision not to participate was appreciated by a large percentage of his people. He enjoyed brief popularity although France's diplomatic influence steadily declined after 2003.

He was a master of political opportunism. Respected Socialist politician, Dominique Strauss-Kahn, stated that "Chirac has more qualities to conquer power than to exercise it." A half a year before he left office, France 2 television aired a four-hour documentary on his presidency. This was the first time a sitting president has been assessed on prime time public TV. One after the other political leader told stories about his hunger for power, his opportunism, his betrayals and his nastiness. His tendency to change policies earned him the nickname, "The Weathervane."

It is no wonder that the three most promising candidates to succeed him—Nicolas Sarkozy (UMP), Ségolène Royal (Socialist) and François Bayrou (UDF)—all campaigned on anti-Chirac platforms in May 2007. In their varying ways, all ran against the current French system. This was especially remarkable for the winner, Sarkozy, who had occupied several posts in Chirac governments. Yet he and Royal were considered outsiders in their parties and were willing to challenge their conventional wisdom.

Twelve persons (down from 16 in 2002) competed for the presidency, but only the three of them had a realistic chance. Three of the others were Trotskyites, one was a Communist, and one was a alternative, anti-globalization, McDonald's-hating gad-fly (José Bové). The high turnout in the presidential voting (84%, the highest since 1974) was not only a testament to the vibrancy of French democracy, but also a signal of how important voters considered these elections to be for their future. They gave the three leaders three-fourths (76%) of their votes.

Sarkozy won 30.5% of the votes in the first round and 53.06% in the second round by sticking resolutely to his central message: France must change, the French must work more and be rewarded for their work, law and order must be restored, and immigration must be tightened. This was the highest result for a center-right candidate since 1974 and 10 points higher than Chirac ever got in the first round. Surprisingly since his chief opponent was an impressive woman, he captured 52% of the female vote as well as a majority of voters aged 25 to 44 and over 60.

Royal, the Socialist candidate, captured an impressive 25.5% in the first round and 46.94% in the second. She failed to transform her leftist party into a modern social democratic one in the center of the political spectrum. When she tried to do this in the second round and called for an electoral alliance with Bayrou, who had presented himself as a bridge-builder between left and right, she lost credibility. She won 11 of 20 Paris *arondissements*, many ethnically-mixed working-class suburbs, large parts of central and south-western France, and voters under age 24. In polls asking voters which characteristics most apply to the two top candidates, the only category in which she beat Sarkozy was "friendliness" (57% to 29%).

Bayrou won 18.6% in the first round, but he failed to get into the top two. A collective sigh of relief was heard when Jean-Marie Le Pen, leader of the extreme right-wing National Front, received only 11% of the votes and a humiliating fourth-place finish. In the second round, 63% of his voters turned to Sarkozy and only 12% to Royal. Sarkozy had succeeded in absorbing Le Pen's voters and, it is hoped, defanging them.

Entering the parliamentary elections a month later, in June 2007, Sarkozy became the first president in two decades to intervene in his UMP party's campaign. This marked a change in style from Chirac's aloof stance. But the new president had won a mandate to reform the country. He stated after his victory: "The French people have chosen change, and it is change that I will implement." For this he needed a strong parliamentary majority. The French gave him that, but without the margin that he had hoped. They seemed hesitant to place too much power in his hands and wanted a parliament that could slow him down when needed.

The UMP captured 39.5% of the votes in the first round and 47.79% in the second. This left them 324 of the 577 seats. To this must be added the 22 seats of its ally, the New Center. With 60% of the seats, Sarkozy had won a solid legislative base for his reforms. The Socialists did quite well, winning 28% in the first round and 45% in the second, securing an impressive 205 seats, up from 140 in 2002. Bayrou created a new Democratic Movement (MoDem) for these elections, but it captured

only 7.6% in the first round, winning a mere four seats including his own. The other big loser was Le Pen's National Front, which won only 4.3% of the votes and not a single seat. The Communists garnered 4.3% of the votes and 18 seats, while the Greens captured 3.3% of the votes and four seats.

Dubbed the "hyper-president" in the press, the frenetic Sarkozy wasted no time in assembling the most diverse and inclusive cabinet in French history. He concentrated as much power in his Elysée Palace as possible, signaling his intention to be

much more active in domestic politics than his predecessors. His prime minister is François Fillon, a lawyer and former education minister, who was a former enemy but later jogging buddy. A model of calm restraint, he is an amateur race driver, born in Le Mans. Like the remarried Sarkozy, he has a foreign wife, Penelope, who is Welsh. After one year in power, his popularity ratings were above those of the president, and this has increased the tension between the two. Not unexpectedly, he has been entirely overshadowed by his boss, who is sometimes called the "om-

Socialists, not Sarkozy, Down in the Dumps

France

nipresident." He resents the put-downs and snubs from Sarkozy, who has referred to him as a mere "collaborator" and "assistant."

Sarkozy appointed a sleek 16-person cabinet, half the size of previous ones. It contained Socialists and centrists. Only one member (Higher Education Minister Valérie Pécresse) had attended the elite ENA. It included seven women. Nine are lawyers, including Christine Lagarde, a former head of a large American law firm, who was tapped to be the country's and G-8's first female finance minister. Rachida Dati was named justice minister. She was one of 12 children. Her parents had emigrated from Morocco and Algeria, and her mother had worked as a cleaning lady to put her through law school. Sarkozy often includes her in his foreign trips. A militant Arab feminist, Fadela Amara, became deputy minister for urban affairs. Sarkozy reasons that only a government that looks like France can persuade his countrymen to accept profound change. However, such a heterogeneous grouping is bound to create internal tension.

Perhaps the most surprising appointment was Socialist Bernard Kouchner, who is consistently rated in the polls as France's most popular politician. His Socialist party called him a traitor and kicked him out for joining a conservative president's government. Co-founder of Doctors Without Borders and former UN head in Kosovo, he is one of very few French who supported the U.S. decision to go to war in Iraq although he later criticized its management. As foreign minister, he visited Baghdad for three days, the first such trip since 1988, in a gesture aimed at healing the wounds caused by the war.

He is a long-time critic of French anti-Americanism (once calling it "the motor of French foreign policy"). He joins the president in toning down the rhetoric in Franco-American relations. He also gives the new government a strong human rights stamp. To assist both of them is a new American-style national security adviser, Jean-David Levitte, an ex-ambassador to Washington. Together, they intend to conduct a foreign policy that is less "arrogant," more sympathetic to America, Britain and Israel, less friendly to Russia, and more transparent on Africa.

FOREIGN AND DEFENSE POLICIES

German unification in 1990 led many French to fear that their country would be overshadowed by Germany and would be driven to the margins of international politics. That has not happened. France plays an important role as a medium–sized

power willing to use its force abroad. It preserves its independence and has not rejoined NATO's integrated command structure, although it has intensified its contacts with the alliance. For example, in 1994 it began attending NATO defense minister meetings again. In 1995 it rejoined NATO's military committee, which brings the service chiefs together, and its officers began working more closely with SHAPE. It did not join the Defense Planning Committee, which in 2003 became the forum for a NATO decision to send support to Turkey in the face of fierce French opposition.

President Sarkozy is rethinking his country's relationship with NATO. He recognizes its permanence and importance in Europe and the world and said that France must play "a full role" in NATO. On a visit to Washington in November 2007, he indicated that he had already made his decision to rejoin the alliance's command structure on the condition that the U.S. put aside its objections to expanding the EU's capabilities. In giving European defense a push, he stresses that this effort would not be in competition with the U.S. and NATO, but would complement them both. Nor would it be Europe's intention to duplicate the capabilities that NATO already has.

Of its 10,000 soldiers deployed in missions abroad, one third serve under a NATO banner. In 2008 it had 1,600 soldiers in NATO's force in Afghanistan, and at NATO's April summit in Bucharest President Sarkozy offered to deploy 800 more in the dangerous southern part of the country. This was a risky move considering polls at home showing that 68% opposed sending extra troops and only 15% favored it. However, it was a clear

sign that his talk of renewed Atlanticism is not mere rhetoric. A French general commands the NATO stabilization force in Kosovo.

Chirac's meeting with British Prime Minister Tony Blair at St. Malo the end of 1998 agreed on a blueprint for such a new European defense. From the fall of 2003 on, British prime ministers met frequently with the French and German leaders to give impetus to a kind of European military force that would complement NATO. France's first female defense minister and Sarkozy's interior minister, Michèle Alliot-Marie, considers the EU to be a multiplier of French influence, and "defense is the area where Europe has progressed the most in the last three years" since 2002. Within the EU, France and the UK provide over two-thirds of military research funds and half the money for equipment. She assures that "Europe's progress in defense will not be in competition or contradiction with NATO. The EU is the only international actor with the complete range of civil, police and military tools to manage crises."

The creation of Combined Joint Task Forces (CJTF) allows some of NATO's European assets to be used in military operations where the U.S. has no interest in participating. The concept is meant to work within NATO and not against it. Also an agreement between the EU and NATO called "Berlin-Plus" makes available to the EU a variety of NATO planning capabilities and equipment for operations without NATO participation. After all, 21 of the 26 NATO members also belong to the EU. There is some disagreement on how Berlin-Plus should work. The French do not accept that the EU can act only when NATO chooses not to.

Le Monde

www.lemonde.fr

59e ANNÉE - N° 18078 - 1,20 € - FRANCE MÉTROPOLITAINE   DIMANCHE 9 - LUNDI 10 MARS 2003   FONDATEUR : HUBERT BEUVE-MÉRY - DIRECTEUR : JEAN-MARIE COLOMBANI

SUPPLÉMENT
La mode de l'été 2003,
énergique,
sophistiquée,
c'est de l'athlétisme
pure soie

CORSE
Polémique sur
la prison de Borgo   p. 8

SUPPLÉMENT
Le Monde ARGENT
Placement immobilier

La France dit non à l'ultimatum

LES ÉTATS-UNIS, le Royaume-Uni et l'Espagne ont déposé vendredi 7 mars à l'ONU une nouvelle version d'un projet de résolution qui constitue un ultimatum à l'Irak. Dans ce texte, Bagdad est en effet sommé de démontrer, d'ici au lundi 17 mars, « une coopération entière, sans condition, immédiate et active » sur son désarmement, sous peine d'une action militaire. L'ambassadeur américain auprès des Nations unies, John Negroponte, a déclaré que la date du vote serait déterminée lors des consultations entre les membres du Conseil, lundi. En fait, ce vote pourrait avoir lieu dès mardi.

Face à cette accélération des événements, le ministre français des affaires étrangères, Dominique de Villepin, a affirmé à l'ONU que Paris « ne laisserait pas passer une résolution qui autoriserait le recours à la guerre ». « La France, a-t-il ajouté, dit non à la logique de guerre (...). Nous ne pouvons pas accepter un ultimatum dès lors que les inspecteurs font état de progrès ». Le chef de la diplomatie française a proposé que les chefs

d'État et de gouvernement se réunissent la semaine prochaine au Conseil de sécurité, à New York, à l'occasion du vote sur la nouvelle résolution. Les États-Unis ont rejeté cette offre.

En matière de désarmement, le chef des inspecteurs de l'ONU, Hans Blix, a salué dans son rapport « une accélération des initiatives de l'Irak depuis la fin janvier ». « Vérifier le désarmement,

a-t-il conclu, même avec la coopération active de l'Irak, ne prendra pas des semaines ou des années, mais des mois. » Colin Powell a qualifié ce rapport de « catalogue de non-coopération ».

▸ Nouveau projet de résolution : l'ONU sommée de constater avant le 17 mars que Bagdad n'a pas désarmé

▸ Le texte est déposé par Washington, Londres et Madrid

▸ Les inspecteurs font état de progrès et contestent les « preuves » américaines

▸ Villepin : « non à la logique de guerre »

Lire pages 2 à 4

The wars in the Persian Gulf and the former Yugoslavia convinced France that it could not do much in military operations without NATO assets and American help. It put some of its ships and aircraft under American control in the Balkans. Its troops that enforced the Bosnian peace settlement served in a NATO force, which in December 2004 was converted into an EU-commanded force. France dispatched the largest foreign contingent—4,000 troops—to Bosnia to play the leading role in the UN Protection Force, led initially by a French general. Its combat pilots helped enforce the "no–fly zone" over war–torn Bosnia. When NATO created a rapid–reaction force in 1995 to protect UN peacekeepers in Bosnia, France contributed 1,500 elite troops and assumed overall command. France was a major participant in the Implementation Force (IFOR) in Bosnia, assuming responsibility for maintaining peace in the most complicated spot imaginable: Sarajevo. Its troops remained after IFOR ended.

In 2004 it offered several thousand troops and two generals in key command slots to NATO's new Rapid Reaction Force. French generals also commanded NATO forces in Kosovo and Afghanistan; France has 1,900 troops deployed in the latter country, roughly half in Kabul. In January 2007 it withdrew its 200 special forces troops working directly under U.S. command, but 50 remained to train Afghan commandos, and more are slated to return. France has also sent additional combat aircraft to Kandahar. For the first time since France left NATO's integrated command in 1967, it hosted a gathering of NATO defense ministers in Nice in 2005.

Many of the country's leading intellectuals embraced the cause of direct military intervention in the Balkans, fearing that "ethnic cleansing" could spread across Europe. This mood reflects a sharp break with the pacifist traditions of French intellectuals. That support continued in 1999 when France contributed 61 combat aircraft and five ships to conduct an air war against Yugoslavia in a NATO attempt to stop ethnic cleansing in Kosovo.

What replaced antipathy toward America is fear of the sole remaining superpower's domination of world affairs. Most French discount the idea that American policy abroad, including in the Balkans and Iraq, is motivated by ideals of human rights and democracy. Former President Chirac and the Socialists believe that there must be a counterbalance to American power: a "multipolar world" with multiple centers of power is "a fact." President Sarkozy and Foreign Minister Kouchner have a more Atlanticist view. The president has stated that it is "unthinkable for Europe to forge its identity in opposition to the United States." Now that the U.S. has seen its influence and prestige in the world reduced by its Iraq policy, it no longer appears as the "hyperpower" so many French feared or distrusted. This makes it easier for France to strengthen its ties with America.

France disagrees with the U.S. less than before. In 1996 Paris proposed reforms in the NATO command structure as a price for its further reintegration into the alliance. Specifically, it demanded that the Southern Command headquartered in Naples be led by a European officer, preferably by a Frenchman. The U.S., whose Sixth Fleet comprises the main military force in the Mediterranean, refuses. Paris believed that France's reintegration into NATO had to be contingent upon a European's receiving that southern command. is desirable. Now the main condition is that Washington accept a more capable EU defense organization that could complement NATO, and that the UK get fully behind this European effort.

Referendum on EU Constitution

The strong Gaullist antipathy toward a more centralized Europe is gone. Nevertheless, France was the most nervous of all the 15 earlier EU members about the enlargement that came in May 2004: 55% opposed it, compared to 36% in the EU as a whole. Only 21% of French had ever traveled to any of the 10 new member states. The government fears its loss of leverage and leadership in an expanded EU, especially given the strong American influence in former communist countries.

Enlargement is painful for the French, who fear their voice is becoming diluted, their language threatened, and their jobs at risk. Europe once represented reassurance and comfort for them; now it seems to be a threat to their identity and prosperity. It used to be a means of spreading French values and influence outside France. Now the EU is seen as a way of imposing outside values and influences on France itself. Europe has been an instrument for preserving and multiplying French power. Now some perceive it as weakening France. France thought it could once dominate and control Europe; that is no longer possible with 27 members.

The country found itself in an unprecedented debate over Europe. This was manifested in the referendum on May 29, 2005, whether to ratify the EU constitution, drafted under the guidance of former President Giscard d'Estaing. Those who saw the wrong kind of Europe taking shape banded together to vote it down, 55% to 45%, with a turnout of 69%. What went wrong?

The entire French political establishment, elderly voters, the more affluent and better educated, and two-thirds of voters in the 20 arrondissements of Paris supported the constitution. The unlikely coalition of opponents included renegade Socialists like former Prime Minister Laurent Fabius, the Communist Party, manual laborers (79% of whom voted no), Trotskyites, anti-globalization activists like José Bové, the anti-European right that advocates unfettered French sovereignty, the right-wing National Front, young voters and baby boomers between ages 35 and 65.

The motives for rejecting it were multiple, but they mainly boiled down to one overriding concern: the specter of a bigger more powerful Europe destroying the superior French social model and impos-

France

ing upon the continent the British economic model of reduced subsidies, longer working hours, more flexible labor markets and greater competition. The majority associated Brussels with free-market reforms that would endanger workers' protections and accelerate the "delocalization" (a favorite slogan in the campaign, meaning outsourcing) of their jobs to low-cost eastern Europe or China.

A deep anxiety over globalization came to the surface. This fear was embodied by a mythical "Polish plumber," whose kind would flood France undercutting its wages and stealing its jobs. "British liberalism," "competition" and "profit" were dirty words in the campaign. The French have an especially ambivalent attitude toward Britain, which has a lower unemployment rate (5.2% vs. 7.9% in 2008) and income per capita that overtook France's in 1995. Nicolas Sarkozy, who supported the constitution, asserted: "The best social model is the one that gives work to everybody. It is not, therefore, our own." Turkish entry into the EU symbolized borders that are too open. It unnerved voters even though the constitution said nothing about Turkey, and the government promised a later referendum on Turkish accession. In general, the NO vote was a protest against a Europe the French no longer recognized and a project they no longer dominated.

Perhaps the main source of opposition was a deep revolt against the political elite that does not seem to understand the concerns of normal citizens. It commits the people to ever closer European union without being able to explain to voters why this would be better for them. Related to this was a protest against an increasingly unpopular Chirac government. Indeed the 2007 presidential election was on the mind of every citizen who voted.

Chirac did what French presidents always do when they make mistakes and things go wrong: sack the prime minister and appoint another. This time it was his protégé Dominique de Villepin, even though he epitomized the very mandarin class against which the majority appeared to have rebelled. He demonstrated more denial than understanding the kind of new world in which France finds itself. "The French know it and tell it to us with force: globalization is not an ideal, it cannot be our destiny." He vowed to stay "deeply attached to the French model."

President Sarkozy recognized this unease. Although stating that he favors globalization and free markets, he used his first appearance at an EU summit meeting in June 2007 to eliminate the wording, "free and undistorted competition" from the EU's objectives. He returned to France hailing this change as opening the door to greater protectionism, an industrial strat-

French recruitment poster

egy and "European champions." "A country that abandons its factories is a country that has lost its identity."

Nevertheless, Sarkozy guided his country back into the EU's good graces. He strongly supported the new treaty that was adopted in Lisbon the end of 2007 to replace the more ambitious constitution his countrymen had rejected two and one-half years earlier. This time he decided to have the parliament, not the people, vote on the Lisbon Treaty. This succeeded in February 2008 after Foreign Minister Kouchner reminded the deputies: "All of Europe is waiting for this signal from France." Perhaps this caution was unnecessary. At the time the treaty was signed in Lisbon, polls indicated that fully 68% of French voters would have accepted it in a referendum. Sarkozy had already underscored the importance of the EU for France: "The construction of Europe will remain the absolute priority of our foreign policy. France is not strong without Europe, just as Europe is not strong without France."

Franco-German Cooperation

Another important departure is a dramatic increase in France's military cooperation with Germany. The two neighbors created an experimental joint brigade, whose command alternates between French and German officers. In 1991 they agreed to expand that unit to a corps size—35,000 troops. Actually most of the units are stationed in their home countries while Eurocorps headquarters in Strasbourg is only a staff. The French eased some of America's and NATO's fears by

conceding that this Eurocorps, which also includes troops from Spain, Belgium and Luxembourg, could operate under NATO for international peacekeeping and in time of war. In Afghanistan it commanded NATO's peacekeeping forces.

France has close links with the FRG. Bilateral ties, EU integration and NATO tether Germany securely to the West. German unity made Germany, not France, the leader of a strengthened Europe, and France seeks to act with Germany's support in the name of "European interests."

In January 2003 the two neighbors celebrated the fortieth anniversary of the Franco-German friendship treaty in grand style. Former President Chirac and ex-Chancellor Schröder met at the Elysée Palace, and 603 German parliamentarians joined 577 counterparts in the palace of Versailles. The next day, the two leaders met in Berlin. In their "Elysée Declaration," they agreed to increase the frequency of their special meetings to every six weeks, to appoint in each other's capital a "secretary-general for Franco-German cooperation" who would coordinate, prepare and follow up their common European policies, to dispatch the relevant minister to the other country's cabinet meetings when discussing a subject of interest to the other, and to propose common Franco-German legislation to each other's parliaments. In 2004 three Germans joined the French civil service. At one EU summit in 2003, Schröder even asked President Chirac to stand in for him so that he could return home for a day.

It is uncertain how durable this special Franco-German partnership is. From the beginning it was a reconciliation of opposites, and the two partners have always had world views that were not totally compatible. Although the two countries' interests converged in the early 21st century, including their publics' aversion to war in Iraq in 2003, they both continue to pursue their own national interests, which are not always the same.

A prevailing opinion in Berlin is that Franco-German agreement is a "necessary, but not a sufficient condition for moving the EU forward." Agreement between the two countries is still necessary for any serious EU initiative to get off the ground; if they can agree, a measure has a good chance of being accepted in Brussels. But they can longer dictate policy. The French hand in EU leadership is diminished and more controversial in an enlarged EU. France's worst fear is that a Europe of 27 will be an unworkable uncontrollable mess. In such an EU, the Franco-German partnership might end up dividing Europe more than unifying it.

They hope that such integration at the top, along with partner relationships between cities (numbering 2,500 in 2006) and combined military units, will help warm their citizens' hearts toward the other nation. A weakness in the relationship is that the two sides have to work so hard to maintain it. One French diplomat said: "It's the result of will and effort, not natural instinct." The reality is that French and Germans are not particularly at-

tracted to each other. One can see that in the choice of languages schoolchildren take. In 2006 only 800,583 French secondary-school pupils (15.7%) were learning German, and only 5% of German children were still learning French in their final year. But there is a reservoir of trust. A 2004 poll in *Liberation* revealed that 84% of French respondents said they trust the Germans, but only 51% trust the British. In 2006 educators in both countries completed a common history book to be used in their schools.

Both countries faced a change of leadership, with Angela Merkel the German chancellor after the September 18, 2005, elections and Nicolas Sarkozy French president after May 2007. Merkel and Sarkozy have not found a comfortable and trusting rapport with each other. She is not amused by Sarkozy's tendency to steal the limelight. For example, after months of delicate EU negotiations with Libya to liberate six Bulgarian medical staff who had absurdly been sentenced to death for allegedly infecting children with HIV, Sarkozy sent his ex-wife, Cécilia, to whisk them back to Bulgaria and claimed the credit for France. He also neglected to inform Germany of his agreement to sell weapons and a nuclear power plant to Libya. Finally, his idea of a "Mediterranean Union" linking states around that sea appears designed to exclude Germany. But both agree that the German-French "engine" remains important even though

it is now insufficient to drive the enlarged EU. Sarkozy noted that the Franco-German axis has sometimes "in the past been seen as a threat or a worry to our other partners."

The well-practiced institutional machinery will remain in place and work as usual. But the desire to cooperate so closely has cooled. There is a conviction in the Merkel government that the two nations are on different economic paths, with Germany far more positive toward globalization and the market economy. The French weekly newsmagazine, *L'Express*, wrote of a "Grand Disillusion."

Military Forces

The end of superpower confrontation meant that France had to reexamine the three pillars of its defense policy—its nuclear forces, its draft army, and its operational independence from permanent alliances. Without a Soviet threat it had problems defining a clear purpose for its atomic *force de frappe*. It became difficult to maintain its expensive triad of forces, which in 1991 consumed a fifth of total defense spending.

Its underground nuclear test series in 1995–96 unleashed a violent world outcry, especially in Asia and the Pacific, where they took place. Taken aback by the worldwide protest, Chirac swore that these tests were needed to perfect computer simulation programs that would make further testing unnecessary. They enabled France to sign an international treaty banning nuclear testing in 1996. In 1991 the French had finally signed the nuclear Non–Proliferation Treaty to emphasize the need to stop the spread of atomic weapons.

France continues to maintain the largest and most diversified military capability on the European continent outside of Russia, as well as a credible nuclear force. Despite the changed security environment in Europe following the end of the Cold War, a consensus remained to maintain as the ultimate security guarantee a minimal nuclear force posture for the purpose of "dissuasion," the French version of deterrence. There is little public debate over this. A significant change is that these nuclear weapons are to be linked to European security, not just the defense of French territory and interests. The French are aware that there is little current interest in Europe for such a link and that the establishment of a European defense identity would be a precondition.

French nuclear strategy also changed in 2001 with a move away from an "anticities" "all or nothing" strategy to a wider, more discriminate range of options. This is made possible by advances in the weapons' precision. In 2006 former Presi-

France

dent Chirac spoke openly of one new option for French nuclear weapons beyond the vague defense of France's "vital interests": retaliation against a terrorist strike against France backed by a sovereign state. He did not mention any specific countries, but he was probably thinking of Iran.

The consequence of France's decision to maintain only a minimal dissuasion policy is that major reductions in its nuclear force posture and infrastructure became possible. In the course of the 1990s, France reduced its nuclear spending by more than 50%. It started eliminating its 18 land–based nuclear missiles on Plateau d'Albion (completed by 2005), reduced to four its planned new ballistic missile submarines, and closed its plants at Pierrelatte and Marcoule that produce fissile material for atomic weapons. Of the five nuclear submarines in use the end of the century, four are always operational and two at sea. One sub has 16 M4 missiles, each carrying six warheads. Four new strategic subs carrying upgraded missiles entered the force: "Le Triomphant" in 1996, "Le Téméraire" in 1999, "Le Vigilant" in 2002, and finally "Le Terrible" in 2008. This submarine force represents four–fifths of the total French nuclear arsenal of 350 warheads. An airborne component remains: three squadrons of Mirage 2000 N planes are equipped with ASMP missiles; and two fleets of Super Etendards, equipped with ASMPs, are stationed on aircraft carriers.

The aircraft carrier "Clemenceau" was decommissioned in 1997, and the following year it was announced that the aged "Foch" would also be withdrawn from service. In 2000 after a four–year delay the "Charles de Gaulle" came on line. This is the first French carrier constructed to be interoperable with U.S. Nimitz–class carriers. It has compatible catapults, can receive U.S. aircraft, and carries U.S.–built Hawkeye planes flown by U.S.–trained pilots that control the airspace around the carrier and guide planes to their targets. Plagued by troubles, including the loss of a propeller during a shake-down cruise, the Charles de Gaulle must spend four months a year in port for maintenance. A second carrier has been ordered to accompany it. In the summer 2005 the Charles de Gaulle stole the show in a naval review of allied ships sponsored by the British to commemorate the Battle of Trafalger.

The 1991 Gulf War revealed that France's conventional forces were not equipped or structured to cope with far-away crises. Its draftees could not be sent out of France, and its equipment was found wanting. The war reinforced the case for a more professional army. Consequently, France began in 1996 to phase out

its 10–month conscription and to create an all–volunteer army. By 2004 France had a total force of 259,050 troops, including 22,790 women. It also has 100,000 reservists. Over a five–year period, it disbanded 38 of its 180 regiments, including 12 in Germany, where only 3,200 soldiers remain. Army manpower was reduced from around 400,000 to 137,000, which includes 14,700 "marine infantry and artillery" and 13,490 women.

It also includes 7,655 members of the Foreign Legion. In the past, most senior noncommissioned officers and a few officers were German. The majority of legionnaires killed in the Indochina War were Germans. But that has changed. Recruits for the five-year stints now come from 136 countries; 80% say they join for economic reasons, not for adventure. Each must give up his name and choose an assumed one. Only 18% are French-born, and they must give up their passports and be issued one from another French-speaking country. East Europeans make up 40% of its new recruits, and Asians and Latin Americans are among the fast-growing cadres. There are no women, and the command language is French.

They serve with regular French military forces wherever the latter are deployed, especially in Africa. Some served under General Norman Schwarzkopf in the 1991 Persian Gulf War, and they deployed with U.S. military forces in Somalia in 1992. They are part of peacekeeping forces in Kosovo, Rwanda and Cambodia. Recruits must demonstrate computer and technol-

ogy skills. They are now as likely to work side-by-side with French police and army fighting terrorism in metropolitan France. They also participate in humanitarian relief missions, such as in South Asia after the 2004 tsunami.

France has trained 2,700 special operations forces, and these elite troops have fought with the Americans and other allies in Afghanistan. The navy has 44,250 sailors, including 1,700 naval marines, 6,800 naval air, and 3,000 women. Its air force consists of 64,000 troops, including 6,300 women. There were cuts in the land–based nuclear deterrence force, military bases, schools and hospitals, and civilian defense contractors; 16 warships are being decommissioned. The professional officer corps remains at about 38,000.

France no longer spends more than most European countries on defense: 1.7% of GDP in 2007. The government embarked in 2002 on a costly defense modernization plan and shifted France's strategy toward creating a force that can be projected anywhere in the world. It ordered a second aircraft carrier, new spy satellites, reconnaissance drones, 50 new Airbus A400M heavy-lift transport planes, 34 helicopters, and 57 Rafale combat aircraft. By 2008 it was hoped that total armed forces, including the paramilitary gendarmerie, would rise to 446,000. The goal is to catch up with Britain's armed forces in terms of professionalism, equipment and global reach. It aims to improve France's interoperability with allies, but at the same time to protect

French troops in Kosovo

Photo by Gerald Camier

Le Monde

www.lemonde.fr

19ᵉ ANNÉE – Nº 18072 – 1,20 € – FRANCE MÉTROPOLITAINE – DIMANCHE 2 - LUNDI 3 MARS 2003 — FONDATEUR : HUBERT BEUVE-MÉRY – DIRECTEUR : JEAN-MARIE COLOMBANI

SUPPLÉMENT

Le Monde ARGENT
Charmes et dangers
de la « love money »
Marché de l'art

AUTRICHE
Schüssel reconduit
la coalition avec
l'extrême droite   p. 3

RÉPUBLIQUE TCHÈQUE
Vaclav Klaus,
nouveau président   p. 3

THAÏLANDE
Guerre contre la
drogue : plus de 1 000
morts en un mois   p. 6

VERTS
Affaiblis et toujours
divisés   p. 7

DÉCENTRALISATION
Raffarin a présenté
son projet   p. 8

PARFUMERIES
Bataille entre Sephora
et Marionnaud   p. 10

LUTTE ANTI-DOPAGE
Réunion à Copenhague
pour définir
un code mondial

France-Algérie, les retrouvailles

C'EST LA PREMIÈRE visite d'État d'un président de la République française depuis l'indépendance de l'Algérie. Du 2 au 4 mars, Jacques Chirac se rendra à Alger puis à Oran, et les autorités algériennes lui ont organisé un accueil exceptionnel. Pour Paris, il s'agit, après les dix années de guerre civile qui ont dévasté l'Algérie, de regarder désormais « vers l'avenir » et de « refonder » les relations entre les deux pays. Lundi, devant les parlementaires algériens, M. Chirac devrait souligner la destinée commune de la France et de l'Algérie, plaider pour la démocratie et la relance des réformes économiques aujourd'hui en panne. Histoire et mémoire seront également présentes lors de ce voyage. M. Chirac se rendra au Monument des martyrs algériens de la guerre d'indépendance et dans un ancien cimetière français. Cette visite devrait également relancer les relations économiques entre les deux pays, la France étant le premier partenaire commercial de l'Algérie.

▶ La première visite d'État d'un président français depuis 1962

▶ Une déclaration solennelle signée par Jacques Chirac et Abdelaziz Bouteflika

▶ Dans un discours devant le Parlement, M. Chirac devrait faire l'éloge de la démocratie

▶ ONG et familles de disparus s'inquiètent

Lire pages 2 et 3 et l'éditorial page 11

Le Monde DOSSIER

VIVRE À ALGER

Alger, la ville, le jour, la nuit

AVANT la visite de Jacques Chirac, une équipe de journalistes du Monde s'est promenée à Alger en toute liberté.

Lire notre dossier pages I à VIII

La guerre inéluctable de Washington

A L'ISSUE d'une réunion technique avec des experts des Nations unies, l'Irak a annoncé que la destruction des missiles prohibés Al-Samoud 2, réclamée par les inspecteurs, commencerait samedi 1ᵉʳ mars. Toutefois, le porte-parole de la Maison Blanche a présenté cette décision comme un élément du « jeu de tromperie » pratiqué par Saddam Hussein pour éviter un changement de régime à Bagdad. Pour l'administration américaine, les missiles en question ne sont que la « partie émergée de l'iceberg ». Pour sa part, le ministre français des affaires étrangères, Dominique de Villepin, a estimé que la décision de Bagdad « confirme que les inspections donnent des résultats ». C'est également l'avis...

▶ Bagdad annonce la destruction de ses missiles

▶ Une « tromperie » selon les Américains

PATRIMOINE

Bartabas installe son Académie équestre dans les écuries du roi

---

its ability to act alone "should it be necessary" and to "assume the role of lead nation" in any coalition.

Its independent stance had been challenged by the reality of emerging European defense identity, which the French government advocates. More than any western country, France was rocked by the breakup of the old world order. It can no longer pose as an independent force between two superpowers; such a state of affairs has ceased to exist. Under President Sarkozy, it no longer hopes to put itself in a position of leadership in Europe with the future possibility of heading a counterweight to American predominance in a more multipolar world. But it insists on its independence and the right to disagree with its allies.

Response to Terrorism and War in Iraq

When terrorists hijacked four commercial airliners and flew three of them into the World Trade Center and the Pentagon in 2001, killing 3,000 persons, including many French, France did not hesitate to help. It shed its usual hesitation toward collaboration with the U.S. President Chirac was the first foreign leader to visit Washington after the attacks. He told the American president that France stood in total solidarity" with the United States and "our forces will take part. We will assume our role in a spirit of solidarity and responsibility." Ex-Prime Minister Lionel Jospin also declared, "the struggle against terrorism calls for solidarity and cooperation. Our solidarity is first with America,

the ally to which we owe victory over Nazism, the friend with whom we jointly affirm the ideal of democracy."

French public opinion backed these stands. A charmed Chirac escaped an assassination attempt when an assailant fired at him while he was passing in the annual Bastille Day parade. The July 14, 2002, event was dedicated to Franco-American friendship and featured marching West Point cadets and 75 relatives of victims of the September 11 attacks on the World Trade Center.

As military action against Afghanistan began, it had a refueling ship and an Exocet-rocket launching frigate patrolling the waters close to the war zone with the American and British navies. It quickly put intelligence agents on the ground to work with the Afghan opposition and dispatched special forces who fought under U.S. command. It deployed 2,000 on three naval vessels, as well as combat and reconnaissance aircraft. It stationed some of its fighter-bombers in neighboring Tajikistan and ordered six of them back to the war in Afghanistan. It also sent some of its AWACS airborne control aircraft to the Balkans to relieve NATO AWACS planes for use in protecting the U.S. East Coast. French leaders regarded America's turning to its friends as inevitable. One advisor was correct when he said: "America's power in the world may be unrivalled in military, political and economic areas, but in the era of globalization even a superpower cannot disregard the need for allies."

According to a book published in France in October 2004, *Chirac Contra Bush: L'Autre Guerre* (Chirac vs. Bush: The Other War), written by two journalists for *Le Parisien*, Cantaloube and Henri Vernet, France was prepared in the fall of 2002 to provide from 10,000 to 15,000 troops for an invasion of Iraq. France agreed to Security Council Resolution 1441 putting Saddam Hussein on notice to disarm. Chirac sent General Jean Patrick Gaviard to the Pentagon in December 2002 to discuss a French contribution. Reportedly they were especially interested because they believed that sitting the war out would have left French forces unprepared for future conflicts.

Another French author, Pierre Péan, in a best-selling book, *L'Inconnu de L'Elysée* (The Unknown of the Elysée), wrote that France maneuvered for months while deliberating on whether to join an American-led invasion of Iraq. Research by former assistant secretary of state for public affairs under President Clinton, James Rubin, also showed France "scrambling to avoid a showdown with the United States." Robin reported that the French government even advised at one point "the Americans to bypass the Security Council altogether." French intelligence agreed in part with the analysis that Iraq wanted to acquire a nuclear weapon, but it could not prove it. After weapons inspectors seemed to be having success in Iraq and public opinion in France became so hostile, the French president changed his mind. Relations soured between the French and American governments. The Chirac government later refused to admit that there had been any hesitation on his part.

In the end, the French government opposed military action against Saddam's Iraq, with which France had long enjoyed lucrative commercial ties. Chirac and his ex-Foreign Minister (later Prime Minister) Dominique de Villepin argued that UN arms inspectors needed more time to complete their work and that such a conflict would breed even more terrorism and easily spill over into France itself, especially given its large Arab immigrant population, which solidly supported Chirac on this question.

Chirac, who enjoyed overwhelming backing within his own country and majority support in public opinion elsewhere on the continent, believed that the crisis offered him an ideal opportunity to enact his version of the earlier Gaullist doctrine: that Europe must act as a counterweight to a much too powerful United States and that France, with German backing, must be the directing force in Europe. Whereas British policy aimed to promote unity with Washington rather than trying to rein

France

it in, French policy sought the recreation of a multipolar world in which Europe, led by France, could stand up to the sole superpower. The UN Security Council would be the sole source of legitimacy for countries going to war. With its veto power, it could stop or limit the use of American military force whenever it chooses to do so. In the process, France's diplomatic weight and prestige would be greatly enhanced and its interests served.

This grand design ran into almost immediate difficulties. Chirac's tactless remarks at an EU summit meeting caused unexpected indignation throughout Europe that undermined any chances of placing France at the forefront of a united Europe. After 18 European governments, including most of those in central and eastern Europe, signed letters supporting U.S. policy toward Iraq, he hinted in frustration that France might veto the application by former communist countries to join the EU. Chirac said that they "have not been very well behaved and have been rather reckless of the danger of aligning themselves too rapidly with the American position." Referring to Romania and Bulgaria, who were still waiting for an invitation to join, he stated, "if they wanted to diminish their chances of joining the EU, they could not have chosen a better way." The new partners in the East were furious.

Chirac's policy also poisoned France's relations with many of its other allies, including the U.S. When he declared on March 10 that he would veto "in all circumstances" any new resolution to bring about Iraqi disarmament, he unwittingly had called an end to all chances for a diplomatic settlement of the crisis. The U.S. and Britain proceeded to defeat Saddam's regime in three weeks without France's support, even though the French government permitted coalition warplanes to use its airspace.

In France's own press and elsewhere, it began to sink in that France might have overreached its capacities. Chirac's condescending treatment of central European governments had split and weakened Europe, rather than uniting it. The EU's nascent Common Foreign and Security Policy (CFSP) was left in shambles, thereby destroying any hope for a European pole dominated by France. France's dogged resistance to war had paralyzed the UN Security Council, thereby possibly weakening the only body in which France has equal standing with the U.S. France was temporarily left on the sidelines in a new post-Saddam Middle East, and it faced a difficult task in repairing its relations with the United States and Britain. Sarkozy, who almost never uses words like "glory" and "grandeur" in his

speeches, had also opposed the war in Iraq, but he sees a need to restore good relations with the U.S. He finds a chastened America a more willing and cooperative partner.

In 2005 the U.S. joined hands with France in a successful effort to order Syria to pull its troops and security forces out of Lebanon. In August 2006 they co-sponsored a UN resolution that ended the fighting between Israeli and Hezbollah fighters. The U.S. and European allies asked France to take the lead in organizing a peacekeeping force in Lebanon after the military conflict between Hezbollah and Israel was over. At first Paris offered to contribute 200 soldiers, but it ultimately dispatched 2,000 troops despite its nervousness about getting involved in a country as lethal as Lebanon and doing anything that could cost it good-will with Arabs at home.

It also came to light in 2005 that the French and American intelligence services had created in 2002 a top-secret center in Paris, code-named Alliance Base, to analyze terrorist suspects' transnational movements and to develop operations to catch or spy on them. Funded largely by the CIA's Counter-terrorist Center, it is directed by a French general assigned to France's equivalent of the CIA—the General Directorate for External Security (DGSE). It also brings together case officers from Britain, Germany, Canada and Australia. To play down the American role, the working language is French.

Chirac phoned President Bush after the short war was over, expressing his pleasure that Saddam's government had been demolished and offering to be "pragmatic" about postwar reconstruction. France refrained from telling Washington, "I told you so," and it pledged to forgive some of Iraq's foreign debt. He ordered its navy to cooperate with the U.S. Navy in securing the sea lanes in the Indian Ocean, sent troops to Haiti under American command in 2004 to help create order after the Haiti's president was forced to flee, invited President Bush (as well as the German chancellor for the first time) to attend the 60th anniversary of the D-Day invasion in June 2004, when 100 Americans were awarded the *Légion d'Honneur*, publicly kissed the hand of Laura Bush when she visited Paris in 2003, and agreed to cancel several Air France flights to the U.S. when Washington requested that it do so due to terrorist concerns.

Although only 37% of the French admitted in 2004 to having a favorable impression of America, the French government seeks to reconcile its worst differences with the U.S. The United States remains France's largest trading partner outside the EU, with $50 billion in annual

France welcomes the euro

trade. Chirac dropped France's longstanding resistance to NATO's formal assumption of command over the international security force in Afghanistan. In 2005 France agreed to take part in NATO's effort to train 1,500 Iraqi security forces, albeit outside of Iraq.

After reelection in November 2004, President Bush made it one of his top priorities to restore good relations with Europe. His efforts were unprecedented. In February 2005 he became the first American president to visit the European Union headquarters in Brussels, and he sent Secretary of State Condoleezza Rice to Paris a couple weeks later. This was desperately overdue. A German Marshall Fund poll in France had revealed at the time that 88% of French disapproved of Bush's foreign policy. The newspapers wrote of a "charm offensive." A former Stanford University professor, she gave a lecture to the political elite at Sciences Po and talked of a "new chapter" in Franco-American relations and of the need "to turn away from the disagreements of the past." The French were receptive. Political analyst François Heisbourg concluded that it was not really rapprochement, but "we've both decided it's not in our interests to be at each other's throats."

Activism in Foreign Policy

France always tried to remain largely independent of other western industrialized nations in its dealing with the "third world." No other country of comparable size maintains as big a military presence abroad; it has soldiers stationed in some three dozen countries and territories. It maintains permanent military bases in three African ex–colonies (Djibouti, Gabon and Senegal) with about 5,000 soldiers; 2,800 troops are stationed in Djibouti on the East coast. It has about 4,000 troops in other African countries in order to protect French interests and citizens, who number about 130,000 in Sub–Saharan Africa. In 2008 there were 2,600 French soldiers on a peacekeeping mission in the Ivory Coast. When rebels tried to topple the government of Chad in February 2008, France had 1,500 troops on the ground to rescue 500 foreigners and the American and German ambassadors. Although French troops did not enter the fighting, they were ready to evacuate President Idriss Déby, who had studied at the Ecole Militaire in Paris, or prop up his corrupt government if necessary. Sarkozy declared "If France must do its duty, it will do so," despite earlier declarations that he intended to modernize France's Africa policy by refusing to defend dictators.

France also sends two–thirds of its foreign aid to Africa, making it, the UK and the U.S. the continent's major patrons. Since 1990 it encourages the trend toward democracy in Africa by linking its aid to democratic reforms.

Although it convenes a Franco–African summit each year, it decided to trim its costs on that continent. Its military interventions have become rarer although in 1992 it joined other allies to participate in the UN humanitarian relief operation in Somalia. It was the only European country to send troops to Rwanda in 1994. Its 2,500 soldiers managed to interrupt the first round of genocide and save thousands of lives.

In 1997 the Socialist government called for a complete rethinking of France's policy in Africa. It ordered a reduction in French troops permanently stationed in Africa from 8,400 to 5,000 although it has least 9,000 troops in the continent propping up weak governments in places like Chad and the Central African Republic. Two bases in the Central African Republic were closed, and military cooperation agreements with 23 countries were reviewed. Ex-President Chirac reiterated at a Franco–African summit in 1998: "The period of outside interference is over."

That declaration had to be put aside in 2002 when French forces were rushed to the Ivory Coast, a former French colony that was once a model of stability in West Africa. A bloody and confusing uprising got out of control, endangering 20,000 French nationals and prompting the rescue by French soldiers of 191 American school children trapped in the crossfire. Paris tried to mediate a peace pact. By November 2004 there were 4,600 French troops, including Foreign Legion and elite reconnaissance forces, trying to protect the government and enforce the oft-violated ceasefires. This was France's biggest foreign military commitment. France called on the UN to become more involved, and 6,000 UN peacekeepers, mainly from West African countries, were sent.

In November 2004 government forces broke a longtime cease-fire and bombed a French peacekeepers' camp, killing nine French troops and an American aid worker. France hit back immediately, destroying the entire Ivorian air force. Demonstrators then turned on Abidjan's sizeable French community, looting houses, burning businesses and schools, and forcing over a hundred French nationals to flee in terror each day. This festering crisis exposed the limits of France's new Africa policy of intervening less and resorting more to multilateral action.

In 2003 it attained EU and UN mandates to send its troops, accompanied by a small number of allied European soldiers including, for the first time, Swedes to northeastern Congo to secure the airport around Bunia. This mission, called "Artemis," was the first EU military deployment outside of Europe and was done with no coordination with NATO. President Sarkozy ordered more transparency in relations with Africa and downgraded a special presidential unit that once dealt with African heads of state.

France has long–standing interests in the Middle East. It sent a powerful 12,600–man air, naval and ground contingent in 1991 to help drive Iraq out of Kuwait. This was a bold move, considering the large Arab population in France and the fact that Iraq had been France's best Middle Eastern customer, and owed France $3 billion. In doing this it violated one of de Gaulle's most basic teachings: French troops should never be under U.S. command. Former President Mitterrand answered critics, saying "we are linked, we are allies, and we intend to do what we are committed to do."

France demonstrated that it is ready to move outside its traditional area of operations and to match its military presence to its strategic interests rather than to its colonial links. It announced in February 2008 the opening of its first permanent base in the Persian Gulf: in Abu Dhabi in the United Arab Emirates (UAE). Its 400-500 troops there will man a depot to support French maritime surveillance operations in the Gulf region. This is the first permanent French base outside of Africa and in a country where it has no colonial ties. In March 2008 French forces took part in large-scale war games in the Gulf. In a separate deal, France also agreed to help the UAE build two nuclear energy reactors.

Other countries look to France to take the lead in deciding how to respond if Algeria, to which France annually provides $1 billion in aid, becomes a fundamentalist Islamic republic. France is torn between the desire to prevent Muslim extremists from coming to power and fear of making irreconcilable enemies out of potential rulers of Algeria. It supports the military junta in power, reinforced by its election, even though it has outlawed the popular Islamic Salvation Front (FIS). This policy creates problems within France itself.

France's nervousness is understandable. The threat of violence on French soil had become real. Out of a total of about five million Muslims in France in 2005, about 30% or 1.5 million are of Algerian origin. Authorities believe that fundamentalists wield influence over a small but growing minority of them. This was demonstrated in 1994, when terrorists hijacked an airliner in Algiers, intending to blow it up in the skies over Paris. It was intercepted in Marseilles when police stormed it. After the September 11, 2001, terrorist strikes, French security services noted an especially strong Algerian influence within terrorist groups in Europe.

In March 2003 Chirac made the first ever state visit to Algeria since independence four decades earlier, and he was welcomed with enthusiasm. The government in Algiers treated this high-profile visit as a momentous event in its post-colonial history. Its purpose was to redefine the tortured relationship with Algeria, gripped by a deadly civil war that had claimed at least 120,000 deaths. It was time for reconciliation.

Chirac, who had served there as a second lieutenant during the Algerian war, said that that conflict had been "a painful moment in our common history that we must not and cannot ignore, but it is time now to move forward." He signed a "declaration of Algiers," forerunner to a formal treaty underscoring a "special partnership" between the two nations. Everywhere he went he was greeted with cries of "visa, visa!". He promised to improve visa procedures, while his interior minister at home vowed to crack down on the large increase in visas issued. France's pro–Arab foreign policy, driven in part by domestic considerations, put the country in conflict with the U.S.'s basically pro–Israel leaning. But that has diminished somewhat under Sarkozy's presidency.

Corsica

France also must deal with domestic terrorism from Corsica. Since the 1970s Corsicans have suffered an average of 400 explosions a year by various and divided nationalist groups, who finance their

France

operations by extorting "protection money" from local businesses. Supported by no more than one Corsican in ten, these groups do not agree among themselves about whether they are seeking independence or more autonomy. But in 1996 they took their struggle to the French mainland, bombing a courthouse in Aix–en–Provence and the Bordeaux office of the prime minister. The Corsican National Liberation Front (FNLC) claimed responsibility for the multiple explosions.

In 1998 the troubles escalated on "the impossible island." France's prefect, Claude Erignac, was murdered, and the assassins were never found. Bernard Bonnet replaced him and was given *carte blanche* to crack down on separatist terror, corruption, organized crime and clan vendettas. He succeeded in reducing bomb attacks to 96 in 1998, armed robbery fell by two–thirds, and scores of separatist extremists were arrested. Dozens of local politicians and dignitaries were placed under investigation in some 80 corruption scandals.

In 2000 the French government sought to end the violence by recognizing the island's unique identity and history and by offering Corsica a limited form of self-government. Responsibilities would be transferred in two stages. If peace prevailed and the terror stopped by 2004, the French constitution would be amended to grant some legislative powers. However, the parliament in Paris would have to approve of any laws recommended by the Corsican assembly. Islanders would have more authority over culture, education, economic development and the environment. The teaching of the Corsican language would be required in all nursery schools. In December 2000, a large majority in the island's legislature approved this plan for greater autonomy.

However, some Frenchmen regard the decentralization plan as nothing short of heresy. Spokesmen from the right reacted with fury, decrying this "tearing apart of the French republic." Former Socialist Interior Minister Jean Pierre Chevènement resigned in protest, saying: "There is a political current that wants to see decentralization and a move to a federal constitution. It's against the history of France!"

Unfortunately the reform proposals did not bring peace; in 2001 alone there were 28 killings in the murky world of separatists and gangsters. There was also scant interest in Corsica among the electorate. The Senate objected to the devolution of legislative powers. Finally the Constitutional Council ruled in 2002 that it was unconstitutional to give Corsica limited autonomy. It determined that other parts of the reform, such as teaching the Corsican language in local schools and giving

tax incentives for regional investment, were all right.

Greater autonomy for Corsica is on hold. The government announced in 2002 that Corsican devolution would be placed into an overall policy of greater decentralization in all of France. Its plan is to take some powers from the central government and give them to the regions, which would be authorized to bypass Paris on some aspects of tax collection and spending. The constitutional description of France as "an indivisible, lay, democratic and social republic" would be amended to add the words, "its organization is decentralized." Thus Corsica, which is to receive close to $2 billion in development aid over 15 years, would become a "precursor" for this reform. But 51% of Corsican voters rejected this plan in a July 2003 referendum. Nevertheless, the Corsican National Liberation Front announced an unconditional suspension of its military actions in October 2003.

ECONOMY

After World War II France experienced an economic miracle no less impressive than that of West Germany. The U.S. Marshall Plan, economic planning, membership in the EU and decolonization were important factors in this success. France possesses enough raw materials to supply about half of its overall needs, and it has a diversified and modern industrial base and a highly skilled labor force, 24% of which is employed in industry (producing 21.4% of GDP) and 74% in services (producing 76.4% of GDP). Most of the job creation in recent years has come from the dynamic services sector. Women constitute 43% of the work force, compared with 36% in 1968. With its cultural riches and geographic beauty, France employs many people in its tourist industry. With 78 million visitors every year, it is the world's most visited country, ahead of the U.S., Spain and Italy. It is Americans' second-favorite destination after Britain. A film-commission survey in 2005 concluded that 62% of tourists chose to visit France after seeing it in a film. But the French do not reciprocate. With more second homes than any other nation, 90% of them stay in France for their holidays. In 2008 it was the sixth-richest country in the world, despite the fact that it has only 1% of the world's population.

At 3.2% in 2008 its inflation was rising, and salaries have not been rising fast enough to match price increases. Unemployment declined to 7.9% in 2008 (21% among the young under 25 years, 22% and rising for unskilled workers, and up to half for Algerian and Moroccan immigrants in some suburbs). One major rea-

French bread for euros

son for the problem is the high cost of French labor. Employers must pay a high minimum wage, plus an added 50% in benefits. It is politically impossible to create new jobs by cutting the pay and benefits of those working.

Half the households in France pay no income tax. To strengthen incentives to invest and to produce, the government lowered the tax rates in 2000. The top personal rates dropped from 54% to 52.5% and corporate rates to 33.3%. Low-paid workers pay lower social security contributions, and the car license tax was abolished. Trumpeted by the government as the most dramatic tax cut in half a century, the changes still leave the French with a higher tax bill than most of their competitors: 45% of GDP. Government spending accounts for 54% of GDP, far above the OECD average of 38% and 30% in the U.S. In 2008 its budget deficit had declined to 2.8% of GDP, but its public debt, at 66% of GDP and rising fast, was five times higher than 1980 and exceeded EU guidelines for the euro.

The workweek was lowered to 35 hours for private companies and public workers. After fighting hard against the new law, employers discovered that by averaging the hours over 52 weeks they now had more flexibility to increase hours in busy periods and reduce them during slower times. They could respond better to seasonal demands. Thus workers found themselves doing shift work at awkward hours and six–day weeks. Also coffee breaks do not count in the 35 hours. Although wages were seldom cut, they were often being held down, and overtime was capped to the detriment of those wanting to earn more. The law neither created new jobs nor boosted productivity. It is more difficult to judge whether a further aim of the reform—to balance the work-life for the benefit of women—had succeeded.

The unintended results disappointed many employees, and some of them did what frustrated French workers always do: went on strike against the 35–hour week. More than 350,000 then took to the streets in 2005 to defend it. While many private-sector employees concluded that the 35-hour week should be scuttled, the middle class in the public sector loved this latest entitlement, which permits French to work about 15% or 300 fewer hours per year than Americans. A 2005 poll revealed that 77% of respondents liked their new lifestyles and did not want to work longer hours. However, it was blamed for 15,000 deaths in the 2003 summer heat wave, which depleted hospital and nursing home staffs.

In order to "increase the ability of workers to make their own choices," in the words of a government spokesman, legislation in March 2005 effectively scuttled the 35-hour workweek in all but name. It allows employees to swap time off for money and to work as long as the 48 hours per week allowed by EU law. The state-imposed ceiling on overtime was progressively raised from 130 to 220 hours a year. President Sarkozy made any time worked over 35 hours free of tax and social-insurance charges, and two-fifths of the companies employing more than ten persons have taken advantage of this rule.

The country has, in effect, a two-tier labor market: sheltered jobs for those lucky enough to have them and precariousness or joblessness for the rest, especially the young. It is a paradox, as the OECD confirmed in a 2005 study, that despite their layers of job protection, the French feel significantly less secure in their jobs than do Americans, Danes, Britons or Canadians. That was a major reason for the "no" victory in the May 2005 referendum on the EU constitution. Without a more flexible labor market, unemployment will remain high. The French labor code has 30 pages detailing the procedures for dismissing an employee, beginning with warning letters and meetings with the person. Even after dismissal, an estimated 25% of cases end up in court, with the employee winning three out of four times. This nightmare makes employers reluctant to hire in the first place.

Within days after the lost referendum in May 2005, France had a new prime minister, Dominique de Villepin, and a militant declaration of war against joblessness. "Unemployment," he declared, "is the true French disease." A biographer of Napoleon, he gave his government "100 days" to reduce it. In an attempt to encourage employers to hire, he rammed legislation through parliament by decree in the middle of the night, without adequate debate and discussion with effected groups, extending the probation period for new workers under age 26 from three months to two years.

This first job contract, known as CPE, tapped into deep-seeded fears of job insecurity and became a battle cry for millions demonstrators who filled the streets for almost two months in March and April 2006. These were the largest demonstrations in decades. The massive presence in the streets sometimes sparked violence, wounding about 500 policemen. Roads were blocked, airports and railway stations were invaded, and many of the country's 82 universities were shut down for over a month by strikes. Decrying "institutional insecurity" and grasping for the symbolism of protest in May 1968, the 17th century Sorbonne building was occupied. The special CRS police had to use teargas to evict the strikers. Ultimately the government caved in and scrapped the law. This buried any hopes that even bolder changes in the labor market could be made, and it ended de Villepin's presidential aspirations.

What united the trade unions, civil servants, students and the majority of the general public was a kind of conservatism: the wish to hang on to an idealized world of life-long jobs and an economy insulated from the constraints of globalization, which has strongly negative connotations in France. Even free-market capitalism, which has made France the sixth-richest country in the world, is in disrepute: only a third (36%) in 2006 found it the best available system, compared with 71% of Americans and two-thirds of British and Germans. Three-quarters of young French indicated in a 2006 poll that they would like to become civil servants, with iron-clad job protection. Only a fourth of all jobs are in the public sector. "Jobs for life" are so protected and hard to get rid of that fewer and fewer employers produce them any more. Two-thirds of young French who have a job a year after ending their schooling are on temporary contracts. By 2005, 70% of all new contracts are only temporary, and half of those (four-fifths for the young) last less than a month.

The government must avoid anything that smacks of what the French call "liberalism" (meaning a flexible labor market that responds to global challenges). Both unions and citizens fear the kind of global challenges that face all countries now, and they wish to build barriers against them. Pandering to these anxieties, de Villepin stated: "Globalization is not an ideal; it cannot be our destiny."

It is a glaring contradiction that France, which is the world's fifth-largest exporter, has an economy that is, in fact, more and more open and globalized. France fully exploits the open world economy and benefits enormously from it. It had steady trade surpluses until 2007. For example,

Jacques Rupnik, a specialist on eastern Europe, estimates that France lost 6,500 jobs to companies moving operations to eastern Europe. But these were dwarfed by the 150,000 jobs in France created by its trade surplus with these countries.

Its private sector boasts world-class producers of cars, cosmetics, and insurance. A French company (Sodexho) feeds the U.S. Army. Top managers, like Jean-Philippe Courtois who runs Microsoft International, make decisions for the largest companies on the globe. In June 2005 Cadarache in southern France was selected as the site for a 10 billion euro international nuclear-fusion reactor, the world's first. The government vows to defend national champions (huge companies with identifiable French names, like Danone, which PepsiCo decided in July 2005 not to attempt to buy) under siege from hostile bidders. Two-thirds of the public believed in 2006 that it is the government's job to intervene to stop foreign bids for French businesses.

At the same time, there is another French economy that coexists with the one that cowers before the threat of globalization. It is dynamic, highly trained, and comfortable in the private sector. French companies are brutally aggressive overseas. In the half-year to mid-2005, French companies bought $34 billion worth of foreign businesses, more than the $28 billion in all of 2004. French multinational corporations were the world's third-largest source of global cross-border takeovers. They are dynamically expansionist and are exploiting the globalized economy. Finance Minister Christine Lagarde, a former managing partner of a Chicago-based law firm, rightly disagrees with many of her countrymen, asserting in 2005: "France has a lot to win out of globalization. We have incredible talents. We have great know-how. We have got a lot to offer."

France has usually had relatively peaceful labor relations. In part, this is because France's social security programs have taken much of the heat out of the issue of unequal income distribution. Only 8% of the work force in the private sector belongs to labor unions (compared with 12% in the U.S. and nearly 30% in Britain), and membership continues to decline. However, in the public sector the share is about one-fourth (compared with 37% in America). This gives France the least unionized work force of any industrialized country.

Nevertheless, its unions are socially and politically strong in spite of their numerical weakness. The reason is that they have an ensconced place in positions of power. They conduct all national collective-bargaining agreements, which apply to all employees within an industry, they be-

France

long to the union or not. By law since 1945, every company with over 50 employees must have a works council (*comité d'entreprise*), financed by the companies. This body, dominated by unions, must be consulted on many major decisions that go far beyond working condition. The unions and employers are joint managers of the health, retirement and social security organizations. Unions belong to every labor tribunal. They also maintain a conflictual culture in industrial relations where dialogue with the government is often piped through a megaphone by striking workers. The timing for strikes can seriously harm the national interest. This happened in March 2005, when strikes in Paris were called on the very day the International Olympics Committee was in the city to evaluate it for the 2012 Games. Not surprisingly, it lost its bid to London.

Unions representing public sector workers are a mighty force, and they insist at a minimum on preserving what their members already have. Unions were once the vanguard of the leftists, but they are now the country's most conservative force. With their secure employment, public-sector employees are sheltered from the globalized competition that demands change and adaptation. The Communists dominate the largest union, the General Confederation of Labor (CGT). By 2006 the CGT had lost two-thirds of its members since the 1970s, with only 700,000 remaining. The French Democratic Confederation of Labor (CFDT) displays moderation, as does the leftist but anticommunist Workers Force (FO). The powerful National Education Federation (FEN) and the Confederation of Supervisory Grades (CGC) organize teachers and engineers and skilled technical personnel. Some nonunionized French, especially in the public sector, belong to so–called "coordinations," *ad hoc* bodies that serve as liaisons between competing unions or spring up in protest at the unions' inattention.

Although many signs of the old France remain, the economy is being modernized at an impressive rate. The Jospin Socialist government privatized far more of the country's industry than its center-right predecessors had done, leaving about 1,500 companies (compared with 3,500 in 1986) in which the state has a controlling share. It did all this without once using the world "privatize" in public. In 2003 the state also continued to hold large shares of some of France's key industries: 15% of Renault, 22% of Thomson Multimedia and 55% of France Télécom. France has accelerated asset sales to lower its budget deficit, selling shares in Renault and Thomson in 2003 and announcing

MARS 1990: 32ᵉ RECENSEMENT DE LA POPULATION POUR PRÉPARER L'AVENIR DE LA FRANCE.

Toi, moi, lui, tout le monde compte.

RECENSEMENT RÉALISÉ PAR VOTRE MAIRIE ET L'INSEE

Poster for the French census

plans to sell 20% shares in two toll-road operators.

One sign of the ascendancy of the "new economy" is the fact that half the graduates of the elite École polytechnique now go into private business, rather than into the civil service or large corporations. The result in the 21st century is an undeniable boom. Foreign investment plays a part in this. The U.S. is France's largest source of foreign investment, and American companies employ 500,000 in France. Pfizer in France produces 80% of the Viagra consumed in America. Most of the shares in listed French companies are also owned by foreign investors, mainly American and British.

The Socialist government also quietly legalized practices that once raised ideological red flags: stock options for young companies were legitimized in 1999, and private pension funds, heretofore illegal, are being discussed under the innocuous heading, "workers' savings plans." Nevertheless, fewer than 13% of French own shares, compared to 23% of Britons.

Health care, costing 10% of GDP, remains among the best in the world, and the poor receive free treatment. In 2003 the government tackled an old health problem: cigarette smoking by a fifth of the adult population (50% of those aged 15 to 24). Taxes account for 80% of the cost of cigarettes, and three steep tax increases on tobacco raised the price of a package of cigarettes by 50% to 5.40 euros ($7.70), making France one of the most expensive places in Europe to smoke. For the first time, tobacconists responded by calling a nation-wide strike, burning mountains of

cigarettes in town squares. Although 90% joined in, the strike failed.

In 2006 lawmakers banned the sale of cigarettes to youth under 16 and cracked down on public smoking. Supported by an overwhelming majority of its population, France joined a European-wide movement by banning smoking in all public places. In January 2008 this process was completed by including every commercial corner of "entertainment and conviviality," that is, bars, cafes and restaurants. Some expressed amazement that this could happen in the country that gave the "cigarette" its name, has a Museum of Smoking in Paris, and even named a Parisian street after Jean Nicot, the 16th-century diplomat who took American tobacco to Catherine de Medici to treat her migraines and gave "nicotine" its name.

A country where 80% of the women work, France is experiencing a rising birthrate of 2.0 children per woman, Europe's highest, even ahead of Ireland (1.99). This trend is encouraged by a number of government-funded programs, including free nursery schooling. The state offers a monthly allowance of about $400, which is raised at age 11. Families with three or more children are deemed *"familles nombreuses"* and are eligible for heavily subsidized rent and transportation, zero income tax and state-funded parental leaves that can be extended for years. Nevertheless, the French face a demographic time bomb: whereas there are two workers today supporting one pensioner, by 2040 there might only be one.

In accordance with its unsustainable traditional "pay-as-you-go" pension system, current workers are taxed to pay pen-

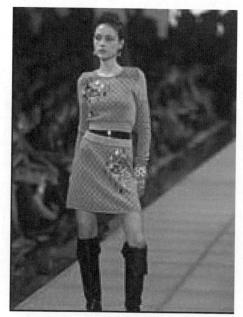

French model

sions of today's retired people. Public sector workers could retire after 37.5 years with a full pension, the private-sector after 40 years. This meant that many could retire at age 55 with a full pension. Railway, electricity and gas workers could retire as young as 50 with full pensions, since the rules for such "special regimes" had been made in days past when such work was dangerous. Only 16% of French citizens aged 60–65 are still working. Ex-Prime Minister Raffarin noted: "Conceived more than 50 years ago, our retirement system no longer corresponds to the current and future demographic reality."

The government confronted the unions over this issue in 2003 and won. The reform brought public sector workers in line with the private sector by 2008, requiring all persons to work 40 years (42 by 2020) in order to get a full pension. Government support for early retirement is being phased out, and tax incentives are being introduced to persuade workers to invest in company-based savings programs like those in the U.S. Finally, a pension bonus is offered to those who work beyond 40 years.

The massive street demonstrations and strike action that greeted this reform failed to stop it, as did the nine-day strike in November 2007 to prevent its enactment and, more generally, to try to stop President Sarkozy's reform plans in their tracks. Railway, bus and metro workers brought France to a standstill, and teachers, students, town-hall staff, post-office workers, magistrates and other civil servants also got into the act. However, unlike earlier strikes, this time the public supported the government, not the strikers. Also the president showed himself to be more conciliatory toward the unions than had his predecessors. He extended his charm to union leaders, took them to lunch in fancy restaurants and emphasized that his door was always open to them. In the end, he won: "I promised this reform, and I have kept my promise." From January 2008 on, railway and metro strikes will lose much of their potency because a new law requires a minimum service on public transport.

Agriculture

Two per cent of Frenchmen are now employed full-time in agriculture (compared with more than a third in 1945); they produce a mere 2.2% of GDP. De Gaulle had once said: "A country that cannot feed itself is not a great country." France is self–sufficient in all foodstuffs, and it gets tropical produce from the Antilles and la Réunion. It is the major agricultural country in the EU, producing 21% of the Community's total output (before enlargement to 25 members in 2004) and possessing about a third of all agricultural land within the EU. It is the world's fourth-largest producer of cereals and meat. Only the U.S. exports more food and drink products.

France remains one of the world's leading producers of wine although by 2002 its wine industry was unable to sell all it produces. The country's largest wine-producing region, Bordeaux, supplies two-thirds of the French market and has avoided the worst of the slump. But winegrowers in Beaujolais, Burgundy and elsewhere face ever stiffer competition from aggressive wine-exporting countries like Australia, New Zealand, South Africa and Chile. In 1996 it exported three times as much wine as these countries combined; a decade later it exported 15% less than they did. France's share of the American wine market fell from 26% to 16% in 2004 and from 37% to 23% in Britain.

The main reason for declining wine revenues comes from a dramatic reduction in wine consumption in France itself. Sipping wine throughout the day has gone out of fashion. The average Frenchman today drinks fewer than 60 liters of wine a year compared with 120 in the mid-1960s. By 2005 only 23% of French drink wine each day. Desperate winegrowers even resorted in 2002 to suing the government unsuccessfully over its campaign against drunk driving, claiming that it is illegal to discriminate between products, even those that make one intoxicated and those that do not. Speed cameras are everywhere now, and road accidents fell by 30% and traffic fatalities by 21% in the two years since 2002; during that same time wine consumption in restaurants declined by 20%. Regrettably more than twice as many people die in road accidents in France as in Britain.

As in other European countries, the farm lobby wields influence out of all proportion to its numbers. French farmers get around a fourth of the EU's farm subsidies through the Common Agricultural Policy (CAP). This cornucopia means that Britain, despite its EU "budget rebate" of about 5 billion euros each year, still pays two and a half times more into the EU budget than does France. EU subsidies account, on average, for 90% of a farmer's pre-tax income. Without it the average farmer would barely survive. But CAP funds are distributed very unevenly. A fifth of the largest and richest farmers, especially the grain growers, receive 80% of the funds. The largest 30 farmers, including Prince Albert of Monaco, annually get an average of over 390,000 euros ($580,000). Some, such as wine producers, were traditionally able to compete well on the world market and therefore had no need for the assistance.

The importance of agriculture, not only for the French economy but for the country's emotional rural roots in *la France profonde*, was demonstrated in the farmers' violent reaction to a compromise reached in 1992 between the EU and the U.S. regarding GATT limits on agricultural subsidies. They took their tractors and manure to the streets of France, targeting not only the National Assembly and the European Parliament, but also Coca–Cola plants and the 1,040 McDonald's restaurants, each of which serves 1,000 to 1,500 customers per day. All of them use only French farm products, and the head of McDonald's Europe, Denis Hennequin, is a Frenchman. However, the facts that Coke had cornered half of the soft drink market by the mid–1990s and McDonald's continued to grow steadily gave them symbolic value.

The emotion and fury of their clashes with the police underscored their intense concern about the effects a slash in subsidies would have on rural France. Ex-President Chirac was able to persuade the German government to postpone full-scale reform of CAP until 2013, and he refused even to consider an EU budget compromise that would reduce any of its free money from Brussels. By contrast, Sarkozy recognizes the need for CAP to be overhauled after 2013 and promises to initiate a fundamental debate about it. This is a dramatic change of approach, compared with his predecessor.

Farming is part of France's culture. Since they are rooted in the land, farmers cannot be transferred from one location to another like factories. The main issue is protection of France's farm interests, not of its consumers. Food constitutes only 16% of an EU family's budget compared with over 50% when CAP started in 1968.

Already barely surviving economically, many farmers would be forced off the land and into crowded cities, leaving depopulated regions behind them. From 1993 to 2004 the number of farms declined by a third to fewer than 700,000. Only half of these are run by full–time farmers; 40,000 farms go out of business each year. Without the CAP subsidies, an estimated third to two-thirds of the farms would go under, with as few as 150,000 remaining. Farms grew in size by 40% between 1995 and 2005, but they still are less than a fourth as big as the average American farm.

Energy

France is concerned about its future energy sources. Its energy consumption doubled during the 1970s. It is heavily dependent upon the importation of fossil fuels. It imports 96%. It obtains roughly half its needs from Persian Gulf countries,

141

France

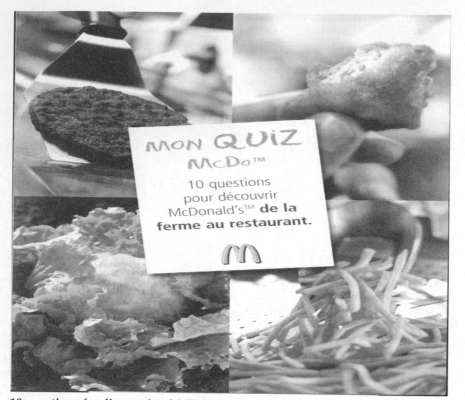

10 questions for discovering McDonald's from the farm to the restaurant

one–fourth from Mediterranean countries and one–eighth from Black Africa. It imports 90% of its natural gas. Some is produced in the southwestern region of Aquitaine, but these wells are rapidly being depleted.

By 2008 the high tax levied on fuel (75% of the price) helped drive gasoline prices to about $6.52 per gallon. In the past, such costs sparked severe demonstrations in strike-prone France. Truckers, joined by farmers, ambulance and taxi drivers, and Paris tour-boat operators, stopped work and blockaded oil refineries and fuel storage depots. Paris and other cities were partially brought to a standstill. The government stated that it would not give in, but then it reduced diesel fuel taxes after all. This capitulation helped spark similar outbursts elsewhere in Europe. The events underscored that while the "new economy" has contributed much to France's economic boom, the old economy remains very much alive.

Nevertheless, France produces about half the total energy it needs. The reason is that it launched a full–scale program to develop nuclear power, especially fast breeder reactors. Now Europe's largest producer of nuclear power, producing half the EU's nuclear energy, it is the world's fourth richest country in uranium, with 10% of all known reserves. Its Eurodif enrichment plant at Tricastin represents a third of the western world's

capacity and feeds a third of the world's nuclear reactors. By 2006, 78% of its electricity (compared with 19% in the U.S., 19% in Britain, 28% in Japan, and 33% in Europe as a whole) was generated by 59 nuclear reactors employing 100,000 people. This is the highest percentage in the world.

The last plant was completed in 1999. In 1994 it fired up the world's only working fast–breeder reactor, which creates plutonium while generating electricity. Nuclear power provides the country with the EU's cheapest electricity, except in Denmark. France even has an overcapacity in electrical generation that allows it to export about 13% of its production. Its nuclear industry has also given it an edge in developing nuclear technology. It is the world leader in reactor design and construction, supply of nuclear fuel and treatment of waste. This enabled it to win the contract to build in Finland the first of a new generation of pressurized water reactors and to land in 2005 the world's first international nuclear-fusion reactor, a 10 billion euro project in Cadarache in southern France. Since May 2007 President Sarkozy has signed nuclear cooperation agreements with Morocco, Algeria, Libya, the United Arab Emirates, and China. In 2004 it closed its last coal mine.

There are critics who argue that France has become overly dependent upon a single energy source and that such heavy use

is unsafe. But its reactors are among the safest in the world. Its decision to build a single standard reactor design not only reduces construction costs but enables technical personnel to be used interchangeably in all the sites, rather than being trained to work only in one site. Nuclear waste is stored on site at reprocessing plants. Because of violent local opposition, it has still not succeeded in finding a deep–storage site for nuclear waste. In the meantime, low–level waste is stored above ground, while high–level waste is stored in vitrified form in both steel canisters and concrete pits at La Hague and Marcoule.

CULTURE

The French have long fought what some critics see as a futile battle to preserve the purity of the French language, which is spoken as a native tongue by about 90 million persons throughout the world. This struggle is waged particularly against the powerful onslaught of the English language. One author even wrote a book with the provocative title *Parlezvous Franglais?*, "franglais" being a combination of the words meaning French and English. The number of pupils learning English in school quadrupled in the 1980s although a 2004 study found that French children speak English worse than all their neighbors. French scientists find it increasingly necessary to publish their works in English, and they often choose to deliver their lectures in English at international conferences held in France. English is the most frequently used language in the EU except at the European Court of Justice in Luxembourg. A 2007 survey of officials from the new EU member states revealed that 69% of them use English as their second language. To help them function in French, France offers them free crash courses at a castle near Avignon.

Jacques Chirac stormed out of an EU summit meeting in 2006, taking two ministers with him, when the French head of the EU's business organization, Ernest-Antoine Seillière, addressed the gathering in English. The president (who speaks English) claimed to have been "profoundly shocked" that a French industrialist would speak English in an international meeting. Seillière explained later that he was speaking "the language of business."

Indeed he was. In many French companies, such as Danone and the oil giant Total, it is English that is spoken in the boardroom, in part because of the increased foreign presence there. Air France-KLM holds its meetings of "le strategy management committee" in English. Renault requires all of its management recruits to be fluent in that language. One French businessman recalled a meeting at the engineering group Alstom, where English was spoken even though every person in attendance was French. Business schools require much of their instruction and most of their readings to be in English. Commercial French is filled with anglicisms, including "le spin-off," "les road-shows" and "le cash-flow." At the same time, foreign companies must be careful. GE was fined 580,000 euros ($870,000) in 2006 for failing to translate English documents into French.

Ordinary Frenchmen have adopted English words so quickly that in 1975 the parliament passed the Bas–Lauriol law requiring that trade names, advertising material, product instructions and receipts use only the French language. The text of the law even specified French replacements for such common expressions: "savoir–faire" (for "le know–how") "boutique franche" (for "le duty–free shop"), "mini–marge" (for "le discount"), "aéroglisseur" (for "le hovercraft"), "credit–bail" (for "le leasing"), "matériel" (for "le hardware"), "gros porteur" (for "le jumbo jet"), "astronef" (for "le spacecraft"), "boteur" (for "le bulldozer"), "retrospectif" (for "le flashback"), "spectacle solo" (for "le one–man show"), "palmarès" (for "le hit parade"), "baladeur" (for "le Walkman"), "mercatique" (for "le marketing"), and "zonage" (for "le zoning"). Some words escaped the sharp eyes of the language legislators: "le football," "le shopping," "le parking," "le living," and "le footing" (a word which is gradually being replaced in common usage by "le jogging").

Economic–Cultural Influences

Whether "le come–back" of pure French will succeed depends in part on "le mar-keting" of American investors in France. In 1983, the state's High Committee of the French Language stepped in to ban English words in the audio–visual field. Thus, "cameraman" and "close–up" became "cadreur" and "gros plan," and "drive–in theater" gave way to "ciné park." It also banned Anglo–Saxon terms in all government publications and speeches, legal contracts and schoolbooks. The counterattack has been generally successful in the computer field, such as "logiciel" (software), "la toile" (the web), "courriel" (email), "arrosage" (spam) and "bogue" (bug), despite the persistence of a few terms such as "un batch" of data or "un floppy disk."

In 1996 the High Committee sued the American sponsors of an English-only site on the World Wide Web because the material is not also available in French. It was thrown out of court in 1997 on a technicality. Former President Chirac argued, "the stakes are clear. If, in the new media, our language, our programs, our creations are not strongly present, the young generation of our country will be economically and culturally marginalized." In 2005 he advocated setting up a French rival for Google's search-engine, whose French-language version is used for 74% of internet searches in France. Google was invented by two Stanford graduate students. In typical French fashion, this French version would be created by the government.

The government has created a process to prevent English from dominating. Seven committees, including one in the economy ministry, suggest French replacements for English terms. These suggestions are sent to the Academie Française. If it and the economy ministry approve the changes, their use becomes mandatory for public bodies and law courts.

The French government wages a difficult battle. By 1995, 83% of high school pupils in EU countries were learning English (84% in France itself), compared with 32% learning French and 16% German. Only in Romania do more secondary-school pupils learn French than English. In an editorial, the *Washington Post* spoofed the apparent obsession with enforcing language purity by imagining a bureau in Washington sending a disk jockey a letter like this: "It has come to our attention that you have repeatedly used the word 'taco' to describe the comestible for which the officially sanctioned word is 'corn meal crispette.' Please be advised that ... a *Dictionary of Official Terms* contains 3,500 new French words for advertising, broadcasting, public notices, official documents and those dealing with goods, services and conditions of work. All international conferences held in France must allow participants to speak in French if they want and must provide French translations of foreign–language speeches and documents.

French is the mother tongue of about 90 million people in the world and the occasional language of another 60 million. As such, it ranks only ninth in the world, behind English, Spanish and Portuguese. The French insist that it remain one of the two official languages in most international bodies, but only a tenth of the documents produced by the UN Secretariat are in French. Already, about 85% of EU officials prefer to get information in English, which is their preferred second language. In an attempt to promote use of the language worldwide, France also foots the bulk of the bill for Francophonie, an assortment of 53 countries from Congo to Cambodia who enjoy "a shared use of the French language." Since French need not be the country's dominant or official language and since the membership includes such lands as Egypt and Moldova, it is doubtful that this organization is effective in achieving France's lingual goals.

Fifty percent of the films French cinema fans went to see in 2002 were American, almost double the proportion a decade ago, but below the EU average of 70%. Of the tickets fans purchased in 2004, 47% were for American films, 38% for French, 4.9% for British, .8% for German and a mere .2% for Italian. Four of the top five box-office films in 2004 were Hollywood blockbusters, as were two of the top three in 2006. The top film in 2005 was *Star Wars: Episode 3*, which did not quite reach the box-office champion of all time in France, *Titanic*. Steven Spielberg was invited to the presidential palace to receive the Legion of Honor award.

French cinema has made some impressive advances. In 2005, French films at-

Trompe l'oeil: false painted storefront in Lyon. Which are the real pedestrians?

France

tracted larger audiences abroad than in France, increasing by 50% in only one year. Its films are appealing more and more to foreign general audiences rather than to the traditional art-house patrons; an example is Louis Leterrier's *Danny the Dog*. Three of its films were nominated for Oscars in 2005: *March of the Penquins*, *Joyeux Noël* and *Darwin's Nightmare*. The first of these helped France have its best year ever in the U.S., where viewers tend not to like foreign-language films.

The French still make more films than do their European neighbors (200 features in 2005 compared with fewer than 40 in Britain). In the 21st century the lead has been taken by a new wave of creative directors who are products of French film schools and criticism: Olivier Assayas, Catherine Breillat, Claire Denis and Erick Zonca. The 2001 blockbusters, *Le Fabuleux Destin d'Amélie Poulain* (The Fabulous Destiny of Amelie Poulain) and *Le Pacte des Loups* (The Pact of the Wolves), were smash hits in France and drew large crowds abroad. French films are making a comeback.

In 2008 a French performer, Marion Cotillard, won the Best Actress Oscar for her lead in *La Vie en Rose*, a depressing story of the life of singer Edith Piaf. A delightful animated story of a rat with a genius for smells who rescues a posh Parisian restaurant's kitchen walked away with several Oscars in 2008. Though an American film, *Ratatouille* was a hit in France and won praise from French chefs and the high-brow *Le Monde*, which called it "one of the greatest gastronomic films in the history of cinema." Not bad for a cute little rat with a golden nose!

Television has been influenced even more strongly by America. The most popular soap opera in 1992 was called "Santa Barbara," and a French clone of the game show, "Wheel of Fortune," topped the popularity charts. "Who Wants to Be a Millionaire" and "The Weakest Link" became the new hits. Reality TV made its debut in 2001 with "Loft Story," which drew one of the largest TV audiences ever and divided France between millions of viewers who love such lowbrow entertainment and incensed critics who dismissed such trash television as the dumbing-down of French society. In 2004 the opening night of another reality-TV show, *"La Ferme des Célébrités"* ("Celebrities Farm") attracted 46% of the TV audience. Viewers were fascinated by the celebrities' incompetence in dealing with farm life, something that has always had a special grip on the French imagination.

Ratings for American programs are as high as for French ones. About 70% of foreign TV shows purchased are from the U.S. Nevertheless, by law, 60% of TV pro-

Market in Southern France

Photo by Bill Remington

gramming had to be European (of which two–thirds French); 40% of songs on FM radio must be French, instead of less than 20% before the law was passed. Many of the teeth were extracted from this law in 1995 when the Constitutional Council ruled that it conflicted with freedom of expression. Nevertheless, in 2004 French music accounted for 63% of sales, up from 51% in 2000.

Anti–Americanism still exists on both the political left and right. De Gaulle's humiliation during World War II is no longer relevant, and thanks in part to the writings of Alexander Solzhenitsyn the Soviet model fell from grace in French eyes. *Le Nouvel Observateur* even criticized anti-Americanism as "socialism for imbeciles." The dethroning of France as the world's cultural leader has hurt many Frenchmen. However, as ex-communist and singer Yves Montand remarked, "if America has succeeded in invading us culturally, it is because we like it."

In the 21st century what antipathy exists between the two countries, which have never fought a war against each other, has been fueled by the 85% disapproval rating in France of President George W. Bush's foreign policy. However, the French do not seem to generalize this dislike: in 2004, 72% had a favorable view of Americans, and 68% agreed that what unites the two nations was more important than what separates them. But as France's economic and military influence

has declined, its independence from the U.S. and its support from European allies seem to be ways to enhance French power. Some French identify America with things they fear: globalization, capitalism and the free market. The Socialist Party campaigned unsuccessfully for the new EU constitution under the banner: "Strong in the face of the United States." Anti-Americanism is strongest at times of French uncertainty.

One earlier sign of America's acceptability was the hard–won contract negotiated by a Socialist government to build a $4 billion Disneyland 20 miles east of downtown Paris. It opened in 1992 promising to create 12,000 new jobs. The only saving grace for hard–line Americanophobes is that Disney, himself, is of French lineage; the family's name was not Disney at all, but *D'Istng*.

In 1999–2000 the reaction against American popular culture was perhaps symbolized best by the antics of José Bové, a farmer who became something of a national hero for trashing one of McDonald's many new restaurants in the southern town of Millau. Using tractors, he literally brought down the roof. This act, along with protests at 40 other McDonald's establishments around France, was ostensibly in protest against the American decision to levy high tariffs on certain luxury foods imported from France, such as Roquefort cheese and *pâté foie gras*, in retaliation for the EU's and France's decision to ban American hormone-treated beef. By linking French culture with the protection of its food, Bové enormously widened his support within French society.

Chirac joined in by announcing that he "detests McDonald's food," and then ex-Prime Minister Jospin also went on record that "I am personally not very pro-McDo," as the chain is called in France. How shocking it must have been when French nutritionists determined in 2004 that a Big Mac has a higher protein-to-fat ratio and is actually healthier than the French classic, quiche lorraine. McDonald's cannot be blamed for the fact that 40% of French are now considered overweight, according to a 2005 report by the French Senate. The fact is that young French have always liked McDonald's since its first restaurant opened in the country in 1979. France is the chain's most profitable European country, and the European manager is French. KFC is expanding in its footsteps.

In order not to turn Bové into a martyr, McDonald's decided not to take civil action against him. Instead it launched a publicity campaign stressing that its more than 1,040 franchises in 750 French cities are owned by French, employ thousands of French workers, and use French products almost exclusively (80%). Nevertheless, Bové was tried in July 2000 for his destructive acts and sentenced to several months of prison. Over 40,000 of his fans came to Millau to cheer him as he went to court. In 2002 France's highest court upheld his conviction and six-week jail term; he exhausted all appeals. In 2003 the court ordered him to serve an additional 10 months in prison for damaging fields of genetically modified rice in 1998. He was released in August. In 2005 he was one of the leaders in the successful campaign to reject an EU constitution. The following year he was denied without explanation entry into the U.S. In 2007 he ran for president, winning 1.38% of the votes.

Bové's crusade taps into far deeper issues gnawing at the French. They include fear of globalization, a general annoyance with the vigor of the American and British economy, and nostalgia for a bygone way of life, including long lunches. French voters on both the left and right instinctively mistrust globalization, which erodes French sovereignty and smacks of unrestrained free markets and American hegemony. The conventional wisdom is not that globalization should be prevented, but that it should be regulated. A 2000 poll found 12% of respondents who admired the United States, 46% who were either critical of or worried by it, and 75% who favored less American influence on "economic and financial globalization."

Academie Française

Since 1635 the "Academie Française" has striven, in the words of its first patron, Cardinal Richelieu, to "preserve the purity of the French language." The body itself selects individually 40 distinguished literary figures known as "immortals." In 1932 they finally completed a French grammar book. They now meet every Thursday in order to compile and a dictionary that is to serve as a criterion for good usage rather than as a list of all the words in the French language. After 60 years of work, the immortals reached the letter R. Each word proposed for inclusion is first brought up before a special committee and then is voted on by the Academy as a whole. In 1986 the Academy added 912 new words; three-fourths of them were based on English or technical terms.

Such great French writers as Voltaire, Racine and Victor Hugo were members, but no female writer, such as Madame de Staël or George Sand (pseudonym for Aurore Dupin, later Baroness Dudevant), ever managed to break the Academy's all-male tradition. Finally, in 1980 it chose Belgian-born Marguerite Yourcenar, who at age 16 had begun to publish her string of poems, novels and historical works, culminating in her monumental *Memoirs of Hadrian*. When World War II broke out, she decided to join the faculty of Sarah Lawrence College in New York, and she became an American citizen in 1947. After teaching 10 years, she moved to a wood frame house on Mount Desert Island in Maine, where she could escape the literary circles and gossip of Paris and New York, which she detested.

In December 2003 former President Valéry Giscard d'Estaing was elected into the Academie with 19 out of 34 votes, despite vigorous criticism by some members, such as Maurice Druon, that "his works do not stand out in the history of French literature." His literary output consisted of four books on politics, two volumes of memoirs, and a steamy novel, *The Passage*, which *Le Monde* dismissed for its "total absence of originality." A year later he became the first former president to join.

All ambitious French politicians must write books. Excellent command of French is an essential prerequisite for the elite. Both top candidates for the presidency in 2007 came out with one or more during the campaign. Dominique de Villepin has eight to his credit, including two collections of poetry. François Mitterrand wrote over 20. Jacques Chirac seems to have been the least productive, with five to his name, including his student thesis, "The Development of the Port of New Orleans."

In 1989 the French Academy found itself in the midst of a storm over a proposal to simplify French spelling by, for exam-

Lycée students take a break in Paris.

France

ple, eliminating the circumflex accent in such words as *être*, replacing the "x" on the end of plurals such as *bureaux* with a simple "s," writing "f" instead of "ph" (thus *filosofes*), and doing away with unexpected double consonants in words like *traditionnel* when the noun is *tradition*. A government survey had revealed that about 20% of the adult population is functionally illiterate, twice the percentage in Britain. One poll of teachers revealed that 90% favor making French easier to write in order to combat both such illiteracy and to enable French to hold its own as a world language.

Proponents of simplification point out that French has in the past been changed by decree and that another change is long overdue since the last one came in 1832 when King Louis–Philippe ordered all public servants to conform strictly to the French Academy's dictionary. As expected, the opposition to change is strong and furious. One teacher warned his colleagues acidly to "keep your filthy hands off our language." Therefore, the Academy ruled in 1991 that changes should not be enforced, but should instead be subject to the "test of time." They have been blithely ignored.

The language watchdogs were stirred again in 1998 when the Academie Française, whose members wear green medieval costumes and carry swords when they meet, stoutly resisted female government ministers having themselves referred to as "Madame la Ministre" (the word being masculine). The "immortals" cringed when the education ministry declared that all women's job titles should be linguistically feminized: a female member of parliament should be a "député*e*," a lawyer an advocat*e*, an inspector an inspect*rice*. Just how much the French admire their wordsmiths was revealed again on November 23, 1996, when André Malraux, a wartime hero, adventurer, and writer was reinterred in the Panthéon. The ceremony was televised live on national TV, and his creative career was discussed exhaustively in the other media.

Although all citizens of France can speak French, there are many tongues spoken by ethnic minorities, primarily on the periphery of the country. These languages include Provençal, Breton, Corsican, Italian, Catalan, Basque and Alsacian. In 1993 the government faced protests because of its refusal to sign the European Charter on Minority Languages, adopted in 1988 by the European Parliament. In 1999 the Socialist government adopted only 39 of the Charter's 98 clauses and again set off a wave of nationalist passion. The youngest member of the Academie Française, Jean-Marie Rouart responded defensively: "At the very moment that our language is being bastardized by Anglo-Saxon expressions, it is to be undermined from within by having to compete with local dialects!"

Immigration and Ethnic Minorities

France's World Cup championship soccer team in 1998 demonstrated how multicultural France has become. Of 22 players, eight were nonwhite (most of them born and bred in France), another four of recent Armenian, Argentine, Kalmyk or Spanish descent, not including the Bretons and Basques on the team. The same applied to its 2006 team, which came close to winning the World Cup until the national emblem for minority accomplishment, Zinedine Zidane, intentionally head-butted an Italian player and was ejected from the game and from the sport in dishonor.

France has always been a magnet for foreigners, and today a third of all Frenchmen have at least one foreign grandparent. By 2007, 8% of residents were foreign–born. Six percent of the population had foreign passports in 1994. This was the same percentage as 25 years earlier, but then three–fourths were Europeans compared with only 40% now; 39% of foreigners come from North Africa and 6% from Sub–Saharan Africa. There is also a rapidly growing Chinese immigration.

Partly as a result of frightening unemployment, non–European immigrants face growing rejection and violence in communities where they live in large numbers. Except for music and sports, nonwhites are noticeably underrepresented in business, politics, media and the professions. In parliament some nonwhites represent the 22 overseas French territories, but none has a seat from metropolitan France. In 2002, a black presidential candidate, Christiane Taubira, an economist from French Guiana, won 2.3% of the votes. A black journalist from Martinique, Harry Roselmack, was finally chosen in 2006 to anchor TF1's popular news program during the summer. Of the 555 deputies representing districts in continental France, none is of North African descent. Only one out of 36,560 mayors and none of the regional parliamentary members is nonwhite. Yet they are visible in the streets. Blacks officially number about 1.5 million, but the unofficial number is higher. President Sarkozy asked after a trip to the U.S. in 2006: "Where is the French Condoleezza Rice or Colin Powell?"

Mosques spring up next to empty churches, and exotic North African commercial establishments are everywhere. Some Muslim girls wore scarves to school, igniting an emotional debate about whether such headgear should be permitted in secular schools. The French ideal envisions a secularized, uniform French identity as the most effective guarantee of national unity. Citizens in France are regarding as belonging to the whole republic, not to separate communities, and by tradition state schools are to be protected from all forms of religious proselytizing.

The issue came to a head in 2004 when a law, unlike any other in Europe, was enacted prohibiting ostentatious religious symbols like headscarves in public schools. The law was directed against Muslim fundamentalists; in Chirac's words, "fanaticism is gaining ground." Many French, 69% of whom favored the law, are uneasy about culturally assertive Islam, and this fear is easily exploited by the far-right National Front. French feminists consider the headscarf a symbol of female oppression. To appear fairer, the law also banned the wearing of Jewish yarmulkes, Sikh turbans and large Christian crosses.

Although 49% of North African immigrant women in France favored the ban (43% opposed it), thousands marched through the streets of Paris and other cities throughout the world to protest the action. Even the U.S. State Department publicly questioned whether "it is really necessary to be outlawing their manifestation of their own faith" when people are "peacefully practicing their faith." In an attempt to defuse the tension, the government appointed the first North African immigrant prefect, Aïssa Dermouche (in Jura), whose car was bombed within days of his assignment. The ban was widely accepted when schools opened in the fall of 2004. The education ministry reported in March 2005 that only 48 pupils had been sent home for wearing religious symbols, including three Sikh boys.

Violence has escalated in crowded schools and bleak housing blocks heavily occupied by North African immigrants. Eight in ten Frenchmen said in 1999 that urban violence has reached "unprecedented proportions," and many blamed foreigners and call on the government to act.

Called *Beurs*, (*Beurettes* for a females) a term that North Africans do not consider derogatory, French–born Arabs sometimes face resistance from their own families when they try to integrate into French society. The animosity toward them has helped far–right parties, such as the National Front, to make significant electoral gains in those areas. In their defense, an antidiscrimination lobby, SOS–Racisme has emerged.

France has the largest Muslim population in Europe: over five million or 8.3% of the total population. Their numbers are growing by 3.4% per year; 30% are from Algeria, 20% from Morocco and 10% from

Turkey. More than half the prison population is Muslim, and they are prime targets for proselytizing and terrorist recruitment. The percentage of population climbs in Marseilles to about 10% Arab and 17% Muslim. Half are French citizens. A third of French residents of North African descent live in about 750 suburban ghettos where unemployment is three times higher than the nationwide rate. Life is so desperate that in one Paris park, Buttes Chaumont, radicals opened a training camp for Muslim boys in 2004 to prepare them for holy war in Iraq. Some were in their teens, and some spoke no Arabic. The police, who pursue zero-tolerance policing, identified about 150 "no-go zones" in these dangerous suburbs (*banlieues*).

In November 2005 they exploded with an intensity that stunned the entire country. Two boys in Paris were electrocuted in a high-voltage transformer. Rumors immediately raced through the city that they had sought refuge there from overzealous pursuing police. It turned out that there had been no pursuit, and the two officers present were later charged for failing to assist people in danger. But a wave of nightly clashes ensued. It spread to other cities throughout France. This was France's worst social turmoil since 1968. Mainly young Arabs clashed with police during three frightening weeks. More than 10,000 cars were burned, 255 schools, 233 public buildings and 51 post offices were attacked or torched, 140 public-transport vehicles were stoned, and 4,770 people were arrested. One person died.

Using cell phone text messages, they coordinated their attacks and ambushed firefighters and police who arrived to restore order. The French government was shaken by its inability to contain the anger and violence. Finally it declared a controversial state-of-emergency based on a law not used since its enactment in 1955, during the Algerian War. This allowed local authorities to impose a curfew, restrict movement and launch raids on residences 24 hours a day. The only sense of relief came from the gradual realization that there was no apparent Islamic inspiration to these riots.

In November 2007 even more ferocious violence erupted in another suburb (Villiers-le-Bel) north of Paris. As two years earlier, this was sparked by an incident in which two teenagers without helmets, riding a mini-motorbike at 70 kilometers per hour, collided with a police car and were killed. For two bloody nights, scores of cars and buses were torched, and a police station, library, nursery school, local train station, car dealer, shops and a McDonald's were destroyed. Of 82 police injured, six were victims of serious gunshot wounds. The fact that rioters were prepared with shotguns signaled a worrisome escalation. It is not as if the government had done nothing since the last round of violence. There have been large injections of public money (six billion euros annually) to renovate housing projects, demolish tower blocks and improve lighting. But with youth unemployment doggedly remaining at 40% in the suburbs, the danger of explosion is always present.

The prolonged violence was a crushing blow to the country's self-image as a model of social equality and tolerance. Its roots lie in the economic and social alienation of the mainly North African population, who face bad housing, poor schools, social exclusion, discrimination and mass unemployment. A study in 2005 revealed that job applicants with French-sounding names were 50 times more likely to be granted a job interview than those with an African- or Arab-sounding name. Even President Chirac admitted that France confronts "an identity crisis."

The second- and third-generation immigrants do not feel part of French society even if they are French citizens. Because France's notion of supposedly color-blind equality does not acknowledge racial or religious minorities, there are no programs or concepts in place to help groups that face discrimination or social inequality. Minorities are forced to integrate with the strictly secular society, but they are victimized by discrimination. Like many other European countries, France is experiencing dangerous disenchantment.

France is vulnerable to a spillover of violence from the Middle East. This occurs when conditions of warfare and suicide bombings prevail in Israel and Palestine. There is often a direct correlation between events in the Middle East and the level of intercommunal tension. Whereas incidents against Jews in the 1990s were mostly carried out by white supporters of Le Pen, most attacks are now committed by young North African men. This is a major reason why ex-President Chirac was determined that France not become embroiled in the 2003 war in Iraq; French Arabs cheered the president for his decision to abstain.

France also has Europe's largest Jewish population (650,000, the fourth largest after the U.S., Israel and Russia), which becomes a soft target to Arab radicals in times of tension. Despite the prime minister's plea that "passions that flare up in the Middle East must not flare up here," an appalling desecration of Jewish graves occurred at Carpentras, a synagogue was gutted by fire in Marseille over Passover, and attacks on Jewish sites dramatically increased. In 2003 vandals torched a new two-story wing of an Orthodox Jewish school in Paris. The next year, a Jewish community center in the center of Paris was set on fire. On the walls of the ruins the words "Death to Jews" were written.

Violent hate crimes quadrupled in 2002 to the highest level in a decade, and in 2004 they doubled again, reaching the highest level since France began keeping statistics on them. The number of attacks against North Africans more than doubled in 2004. The majority was committed by supporters of the far right. However, two-thirds of attacks were aimed at Jews, mainly perpetrated by North Africans. A shocking example was the death in March 2006 of a young Jewish man. He had been kidnapped for ransom, brutally tortured for three weeks, splashed with acid and left out to die. The perpetrators were youths of immigrant and white French descent, some Islamic militants, all educated in France. A poll a month earlier had revealed that 57% of respondents thought anti-Semitism was on the rise, even though police records showed that the actual number of attacks had fallen by 50% since 2004.

Parisian rabbis advise Jewish boys to wear baseball caps over their yarmulkes and girls to hide their Stars of David under their clothing to prevent attacks. The number of pupils in Jewish schools in greater Paris has doubled to 30,000 in a decade, with thousands more on the waiting lists. The issue is the children's safety. More and more French Jews are also deciding to immigrate to Israel. The numbers climbed from 1,366 in 1999 to 2,083 in 2003; the numbers jumped by 40 percent in the first half of 2005.

Chirac declared that "an attack on a Jew is an attack against France," and the government ordered schools to show films like "Schindler's List," "Sophie's Choice," and "The Pianist" to combat the dramatic rise in racism. North African leaders in France condemn the violence but cannot stop it. Complicating the problem is that European public opinion is broadly critical of Israeli policy toward Palestinians. These attacks fed the existing fear of rising crime and a feeling of vulnerability to global terrorism since September 11, 2001.

With its large North African population and colonial history there, France is a kind of bellwether in Europe for dealing with a Muslim population. The center-right government elected in 2002 sought to create a model Muslim citizenry, which would be French-speaking and law-abiding, would honor the 1905 French law establishing separation between church and state, would incline females not to wear veils at work or school, and above all to consider themselves French first and Muslim second. The government adopted a two-

France

prong strategy to achieve this: give them a "place at the table" while at the same time regulating their activities through, for example, French intelligence monitoring of Friday sermons in mosques and prayer centers and deporting radical imams (clerics) who do not have citizenship.

To help integrate Muslims into French society, the government created in 2003 a French Council of the Muslim Faith (CFCM), with members elected by representatives of the country's mosques and prayer groups. It is a platform for discussions with local and national governments about such things as building more mosques and Muslim cemeteries and wearing veils in schools, an issue that seriously split the Council. Catholics, Protestants and Jews have had such councils for decades. Participation was high, with 992 of 1,200 (1,600 by 2007, only 50 of which are deemed "extreme") eligible mosques voting. The authorities were not entirely pleased with the outcome of the elections since fundamentalist Muslims in the Union of Islamic Organizations of France (UOIF) came in second and won a strong voice alongside moderate groups. This prompted the government to warn that it would deport immigrant Muslim leaders if they espoused violence or anti-Semitism. In new elections in June 2005 power was tilted away from the UOIF, the most radical grouping.

There is widespread uneasiness over the presence of millions of immigrants, the majority of whom Arabs and blacks. A 1998 poll revealed that almost 60% of respondents thought there were too many Arabs in France (down from 71% five years earlier); over a quarter believed there were too many blacks (down from almost a half), and 15% said there were too many Jews. Four out of ten admitted to being "racist" or "fairly racist," almost twice as many as in Germany, Britain or Italy. Other polls revealed that half no longer feel "at home" in France and want a "large number" of immigrants to leave. Half expressed a belief in the "inequality of the races." Although 10% of respondents in a 2004 poll admitted disliking Jews, 23% expressed prejudice against North Africans. Thus the latter face much deeper discrimination than do Jews.

Earlier immigrant groups are often among the opponents of the new arrivals. Portuguese– and Spanish–born workers in the Marseilles area are among Le Pen's most fervent supporters. But the polls show that racist feeling goes far beyond the 15% who vote for the National Front. About 28% of those who say they are "racist" or "fairly racist" vote for leftist parties. Le Pen's ranting against "invading Muslim hordes" who allegedly threaten Frenchmen with the same fate as

America's "Red Indians—annihilated by immigration," prove so seductive that the leaders of more respectable parties borrowed from his xenophobic vocabulary. Chirac once criticized their "odor" and "noise." Giscard d'Estaing warned of an "invasion" and called for nationality laws based on blood to replace the statutes that grant French citizenship automatically to anyone born on French soil. By 1996, almost half of respondents said they share some of Le Pen's ideas although two–thirds claimed to have been "shocked" by his comments that races are unequal and that the French national soccer team was not "representative" of the country since so many of the players are nonwhites.

There is positive news, though. A Pew poll in 2006 showed that only 46% of French Muslims considered themselves to be more Muslim than French, compared with 81% of British Muslims. A May 2007 survey showed that the French are the most immigrant-friendly population in Europe: 52% thought that the number of immigrants in their country was "about right," compared with 43% in the U.S., 32% in Germany and 20% in Britain. They were also more likely to invite a member of an ethnic minority into their home for dinner. Six in ten white Frenchmen said in 1998 that they would not try to stop their child or sibling from marrying a Muslim. In fact, half of boys and a quarter of girls of Algerian origin in France have their first steady relationship with a white. Fremainville, a tiny farming hamlet just outside Paris, even adopted a black Marianne, the potent bare–breasted symbol of French republican liberty springing from the French Revolution.

The government responded by declaring that France "can no longer be a land of immigration." It introduced policies to stop the influx of foreign workers, refugees, and their families, as well as to tighten citizenship rules, while speeding the integration of foreigners already there. In 2004 the number of asylum-seekers had again risen to 61,600, the highest in the world. The number of other foreign immigrants was cut by a third. However, once they arrive, most illegal immigrants are unlikely ever to leave. For instance, close to 44,000 foreigners were ordered to leave in 2000, but only 9,230 were expelled. From 400,000 to a million illegal aliens remain underground, despite a dramatic increase in forced deportations.

In an attempt to get the problem under control, the government announced a tougher immigration policy in May 2006. Under the prevailing system, three-fourths of legal entrants were family-related. The new law aims to raise the proportion of skilled immigrants, who are lured by three-year "talent" work permits. Newcomers are required to take lessons in civic education and the French language. To crack down on sham marriages, those bringing in a family must demonstrate the financial means to support them. The National Assembly passed a law in September 2007 authorizing the use of DNA testing to see if foreigners who apply for visas are really related to the family members they want to join in France. Finally the automatic right for illegals to remain after ten years in France was ended. As in the past, the effort to deport those without proper papers is fiercely resisted, especially if it involves school children.

France's law-and-order president, Nicolas Sarkozy, carefully explained: "France needs immigrants, but France cannot and should not welcome all immigrants." Determined to crack down on illegal migrants and people-smuggling networks, the center-right government that took power in 2002 made a decisive move. Under pressure by Britain, it closed an overcrowded and uncontrollable refugee camp at Sangatte on the north coast set up by the Red Cross three years earlier. Located near the entrance to the "Chunnel," it had attracted thousands of immigrants who were trying to enter Britain illegally and who were willing to risk their lives to hop the fast-moving trains or follow the tracks through the darkness to the other end. Sarkozy's new ministry of national identity and immigration proposed that proficiency in French and knowledge of the "values of the Republic" be required of those settling in France. New legislation would also permit authorities to gather census data on the racial and ethnic backgrounds of residents.

The French government is cracking down on immigrants in other ways. It has declared a zero tolerance policy toward radical Muslims who incite violence, deporting imams (Muslim clergymen) who do. It uses its two domestic intelligence services to keep an eye on what goes on in Mosques. Sarkozy wants France to train imams; of the 1,200 or so in France, three-fourths are not French, and only a third speak French. The minimum age for girls to marry was raised from 15 to 18 in a bid to clamp down on forced marriages. The judicial system pursues terrorists vigorously. For example, six Algerians were sentenced in March 2004 for attempting to blow up the American embassy in Paris in a suicide attack, and 10 were found guilty in December of the same year for plotting to blow up a Christmas market in Strasbourg in 2000.

Religion

Almost nine out of ten Frenchmen are baptized Roman Catholic, and two-thirds describe themselves as Catholic. Since 1905 churches in France have been separated from the state, except in Alsace, Lorraine and the Moselle Department, which then belonged to Germany. In these areas, church–state relations are governed by the Concordat which Napoleon I signed with the Vatican in 1801. Protestants constitute barely 2% of the population, but their influence far outweighs their numbers in business, the civil service and intelligencia. Three former prime ministers, including Lionel Jospin, Michel Rocard and Couve de Murville, are Protestants. In the French public mind, Protestantism is almost synonymous with austerity and moral rigor.

Only one in 20 French still goes to mass regularly, according to a 2003 survey. A 1997 poll by the Catholic newspaper, *La Croix*, indicated that two–thirds of the youth believe that the church has little influence on their lives. While 90% of Americans indicated in 2006 that they believe in God, only 50% of French respondents said that. Because of the principle of "secularity," whereby the state must be strictly separated from religion, the government's involvement in the pope's visit to France in 1996 sparked months of controversy and hostility. Also, many French resent any attempt by the Catholic Church to interfere in their private lives. Contraception is widely practiced, and abortion is common.

By 2007 the number of weddings had fallen by more than 30% in a generation. Only half of those weddings took place in church, compared with almost all of them only a quarter century earlier. France has the lowest marriage rate in Europe after Belgium and Slovenia; it was 40% below American figures. Marriage is in decline in most of northern Europe. In 1998, one in seven couples lived together outside marriage, a number seven times higher than a couple of decades earlier and double the proportion a decade ago; only 7% of French respondents considered such an arrangement "living in sin." French family structures have not disintegrated because society has accepted this.

The Socialist government decided in 1999 that it was time to offer some legal recognition to the new kinds of unions although it refused to call them "marriages." It introduced "civil solidarity pacts" (PACS) allowing couples, of the same sex or not, to enter into a union and be entitled to the same rights as married couples in such areas as income tax, inheritance, housing and social welfare, though it does not grant homosexuals the right to adopt children. Any two people sharing a home can sign a contract before a court clerk, and any partner can revoke it by giving the other person three-months advanced written notice. Charging that this law further undermines the family, the Catholic Church, half the country's mayors, and 200,000 irate marchers in the streets of Paris vigorously protested against it. A poll taken in 2000, one year after the PACs were introduced, revealed that 70% of respondents favor them. The opinion survey revealed other evidence of attitudinal evolution: As many French favor homosexual marriage as oppose it. Two years after the introduction of the PACs there was no discernible effect on the number of weddings since most of the 45,000 PACS were between gay couples.

With the average French woman bearing only 1.8 children in the mid–1990s, there was fear that the country faced the prospect of a declining native population. But by 2006, the fertility rate had risen to 1.94% (almost 2.0 by 2008), the highest in Europe after Ireland. More than 48% of all babies (59% of all first-born children) are now born out of wedlock, the highest rates in Europe outside the Nordic countries. This is mostly by choice, not by chance. Clearly illegitimacy no longer carries a stigma. Children born out of wedlock have the same inheritance rights as others, but unwed partners are not auto-

I.M. Pei's glass pyramid at the Louvre   Photo: Susan L. Thompson

France

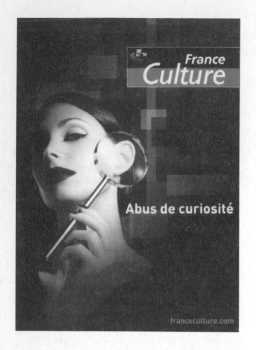

France Culture

Abus de curiosité

franceculture.com

matically entitled to inherit property after a companion's death. When then President Chirac proudly announced in 1996 the birth of his first grandchild, no one seemed to care that his daughter Claude was not married to the child's father, an ex–judo champion turned television presenter.

EDUCATION

Control over the school system is concentrated in Paris. Education is free and compulsory between the ages of six and 16, and approximately five out of six children attend public schools. Mitterrand stirred up much controversy by promising to do away with private schools, which receive state subsidies, and to create a unified, secular school system. A half million persons protested in the streets against this policy, the largest public demonstration in French history. Such widespread protests prompted him to withdraw the contentious private school bill in 1984.

From ages five to 11 children attend elementary school, and then they spend four years in an "intermediate school," called a "college." After this, they proceed to a high school, called a "lycée," which provides either vocational training or a baccalaureate degree leading to university study. In 1998, 75% were still in school pursuing the "bac," double the proportion only a decade earlier. In 2007, 83% passed it (compared with about 60% in the 1960s), a rate that diminishes its value, in the view of critics. As the number receiving the bac grows, youth without it become

sidelined in the job market. The examination for the baccalaureate is a traditional intellectual one. France is one of the few countries that still include philosophy as one of its obligatory high school subjects. In a 30-page "letter to teachers," President Sarkozy complained about too much "theory and abstraction." That could be one reason why 38% of pupils have to repeat a year by age 15.

Based on pupils' performance on the bac in 2005, all but one of the top 29 lycées in France are private. The exception is the famed Lycée Henri IV on Paris's left bank. This is why many parents choose private schools for their children: 14% of primary pupils and over 20% of lycée pupils go to private school, many of which are Catholic and some are Jewish. The state pays the teachers' salaries, and fees are normally under 3,000 euros ($4,500).

Any student with a bac is allowed to study at a university; universities are barred from rejecting students from entry. About 1.5 million students are enrolled in the 82 universities or special advanced schools, and about a third of these students are in the 17 universities in the Paris region. In 1968 a fourth of 18–year–olds and 4% of 20–year–olds were in a school or university; in 1990 the comparable figures stood at 55% and 22%. That latter percentage continues to grow. University fees are about 165 euros per year ($250). The rapid growth of enrollment has brought severe overcrowding, and almost half drop out before completing their undergraduate degree. Universities are underfinanced, disorganized and resistant to changes demanded by the outside world. Professor salaries are low by American standards. Graduates find that their degrees are now worth less and that there are too few jobs for them after graduation. Not a single French university was among the top 40 on Shanghai's Jiao Tong University's global ranking in 2007; the highest, Paris VI, placed 45th.

The unemployment line never threatens graduates of the elitist *grandes écoles*, who are selected by highly competitive nation–wide examinations (*concours*) following two further years of intensive preparation in the lycée after the "bac." Many students at the universities still suffer from a sort of second–class status, as they watch the best jobs being filled by graduates from the *grandes écoles*. Some of the best university students are admitted to these extremely selective institutions, which are prestigious and produce an elite in teaching, industry, government and the armed forces. They educate only 4% of French students but absorb 30% of the state's budget for higher education. They are well-organized, well-equipped, and overwhelmingly white and upper middle

class. Few children of working-class families find their way into these schools, and their numbers have steadily declined since the 1950s. Three-fourths of the Jospin Socialist government and half of the top 200 business bosses had attended a *grande école*.

Following the military debacle of 1870, the *Ecole des sciences politiques* (called "Sciences–Po"), which offers advanced training in political science and economics, was created to improve the quality of senior civil servants. It leads France in offering a three-year undergraduate degree, followed by "*un master*." In 2003–4 the education ministry advocated such degrees for all universities. All spend a year abroad, learn two foreign languages, and take a third of their classes in a language other than French. A third are foreigners, including many Americans.

In 2001 *Sciences-Po* caused a stir by introducing a kind of affirmative action plan, later ruled unlawful by a Paris court, to create a special admission track for secondary school students in seven poor neighborhoods whose population contains large concentrations of Arab and African immigrants. Such pupils would be exempt from the stiff competitive entrance exams other applicants must pass, but there is no fixed quota. In fact, three such students were admitted in 2007. No one disputes that the *grandes écoles* have always recruited almost exclusively from a limited sociological pool of white, well-connected and wealthy families. There is a growing minority of students from farm and working-class families.

The *École nationale d'administration* (ENA, whose graduates are called *Énarques*) accepts 120 students (a fourth to a third female) by examination from the other *grandes écoles* each year for the 27–month program. It was set up after the defeat in 1940 and the shame of Vichy to train elite administrators who would put the interests of the state above their own. It was in Paris until 1992 when ENA was moved to Strasbourg. Study at ENA is particularly important to those persons aspiring to top civil service positions.

Currently about two–thirds of such offices are held by *Énarques*, who form a highly useful informal network of contacts for each other. Only about 6,000 of its graduates are alive today. Among them were all the major contenders for the presidency in 1995—Jacques Chirac, Lionel Jospin, and Edouard Balladur—as well as former President Valery Giscard d'Estaing. In 2007, Nicolas Sarkozy was not an ENA graduate, but his rival, Ségolène Royal, was. It is perhaps not surprising that Sarkozy included only one *Énarque* in his cabinet, but nine lawyers. Prime Minister Dominique de Villepin and six out of his nine predecessors were *Énarques*. The mayor of Montpellier spoke bitterly of the influential *Énarques*: "France is still run by civil servants. There is no difference between a socialist *Énarque* and a neo–Gaullist *Énarque*. They are intelligent, incorrupt and absolutely convinced they are right. The country is run by thousands of little Robespierres." One conservative politician, Alain Madelin, even said in 1997: "Ireland has the IRA, Spain has ETA, Italy the mafia, but France has ENA." One contemporary reason for the disdain toward the highly selected *Énarques* is that ENA produces technocrats wholly imbued with a theoretical, state-oriented way of thinking that is not well adapted to a world of global capitalism.

The glory of ENA is fading somewhat. Between 1995 and 1999, applications for its notoriously difficult entrance exams declined by 30%. *Sciences–Po*, which supplies 90% of the external exam's successful candidates, has a special program to prepare students for the entrance test, but aspirants enrolling in that program have dwindled from 1,000 per year a decade ago to 200. A major reason is that in France's changed economic environment, it is the private sector, not the civil service, which beckons ambitious young people.

In addition, there are three *Écoles normales supérieures*, one in Paris—ENS Ulm (in the Rue d'Ulm), which concentrates on the sciences and humanities—and two in Lyon, one of which focuses on the sciences and the other on the humanities. Both institutions in Lyon want to merge and become identical to their counterpart in Paris. These elite schools train the top lycée and university professors, who must pass a rigorous final examination called the *agrégation*. Finally, there are the *Hautes Études Commerciales*, (HEC) and other business–oriented schools. They do well in international comparison: in 2006 the British *Financial Times* picked seven French business schools as among Europe's top ten. There are also the *École des mines*, and similarly specialized schools, such as the military academy at Saint–Cyr. In 1794 the military *École polytechnique* was established as a military school. Now it trains top public officials. Cadets begin with one year in the military to undergo officer training and then spend two years doing top-level engineering and scientific study.

In protest against under funding, overcrowding, decrepit buildings, insufficient security at inner–city schools, and bleak employment prospects, especially in nontechnical fields, thousands of lycée and university students again took to the streets in 1998 and engaged in pitched bloody battles with the police. One 15–year–old demonstrator was killed. The ed-

ucation minister admitted that the system of lycées and colleges is "archaic," but he pleaded for patience until reforms could be enacted. Teachers sympathize because half their classes have over 30 pupils, and some have over 40. One result is that one in four teachers requests a transfer or job change every year.

There were renewed strikes in 2003–4 by university students protesting American-style reform plans to make the universities more autonomous and to offer a three-year degree followed by a two-year master's degree. The education minister backed off in 2005 and agreed not to mod-

ify the *baccalauréat* exam. Scientists also took to the streets or resigned to demand more state support for research to stem the brain drain abroad and to protest plans to cut funding and 550 permanent scientific posts. The frightened government pledged to restore 120 of the jobs and invest 3 billion more euros in research by 2007.

The American film, *Dead Poets Society*, which portrayed a rebellion against a hidebound educational system, had a profound effect on debates in France concerning reform of the school system. The government proposed reforms to humanize

France

the grueling "bac." A major stumbling block for change has been the resistance of powerful teaching unions. In the meantime, many French ask why their once excellent educational system is soaking up more and more resources and producing students with less knowledge.

The Press

Financial difficulties have steadily reduced the number of daily newspapers to fewer than a hundred. The most widely read is *Ouest France* published in Rennes, a regional paper with a circulation of 762,450, twice as many copies as any of the national papers. The best-selling national newspaper is the lively daily tabloid *Le Parisien-Aujourd'hui*, with a circulation of about 400,000. The largest and most influential of the national papers is the moderately leftist and intellectual *Le Monde*, with a declining circulation of 399,000 and a readership of 2.1 million. The conservative *Le Figaro* (with receding circulation of 359,000) was purchased in 2004 by Serge Dassault of the airplane company of the same name. The left intellectual *Libération*, co-founded by Jean-Paul Sartre, also faces declining circulation with 142,000. All three—*Le Monde*, *Le Figaro*, and *Libération*—have seen a large industrialist or banker take control or a significant share (Edouard de Rothschild in the case of *Libération*). All are from Paris. One of the few dailies with climbing sales is *L'Equipe*, an all-sports newspaper.

In order to halt the growing concentration of the French press, the Socialist government approved in 1984 a law prohibiting publishers from owning both Parisian and regional newspapers, and from controlling more than 15% of either Parisian or regional circulation. Many educated French read certain political and economic weeklies, such as *L'Express*, *Le Nouvel Observateur*, *Le Point*, and *L'Evenement du Jeudi*, which offer in–depth analysis and criticism.

The stock and trade of *Le Canard Enchainé* is satire, a weekly that is thriving, with sales of 450,000 to 500,000. It was founded in 1915 by two left-wing journalists to circumvent army censorship during the First World War. It is owned by its staff of about 40 journalists and cartoonists and is so fiercely independent that it carries no advertising. Its investigative reporting can drive cabinet ministers out of office, but it has a strict ban on writing about the private lives of public figures.

As elsewhere in the world, many French have turned increasingly to television and radio for news. Fewer than 5% of French between the ages of 15 and 25 believe newspapers will be their first source of information in five years. The trends that face French newspapers are fa-

miliar in other nations: aging readers, plus competition from free newspapers, TV and the internet. Most face the prospect of being bought by investors to stay alive. Newspaper readership has dropped over three million since 1970. Even *Le Monde*, founded in 1944 at the instigation of General de Gaulle to provide journalism untainted by Vichy, is losing money and circulation. Until Arnaud Lagardère bought the largest share in 2005, it was owned and operated entirely by its employees. In the 1980s it temporarily improved its sales and financial condition by making its format more attractive and by selling and leasing back its headquarters building near the Opera. In 2008 it faced another crisis. With losses and debts mounting, there is a drastic need for refinancing. But the staff associations reject any solution that would remove their 60.4% controlling stake.

Renowned as rigorously intellectual and overwhelmingly serious, *Le Monde* received a black eye in 2003 when two journalists published a bestseller, *The Hidden Face of Le Monde*, accusing it of bias, conflicts of interest, hypocrisy, and business mismanagement. They argued that *Le Monde* twisted facts to cover up scandals, influenced French politics without declaring its interests, and hide the newspaper's financial weakness. The paper rejected the charges as an amalgam of "errors, lies, libels and calumnies." In 2003 it promptly fired Daniel Schneidermann, author of a follow-up book, *The Media Nightmare*, which attacks the French press generally and *Le Monde's* reaction to *The Hidden Face* in particular.

Until 1984 the state had a monopoly on television and radio. Radio programs are produced by Radio–France, and French government holding companies partially own three independent radio stations (Radio Luxembourg, Europe No. 1 and Radio Monte Carlo), which broadcast from outside of France. Radio–France and the state–owned television companies were financed by annual license fees paid by those persons owning sets.

Critics charge that these companies, although nominally independent and responsible for their own programming, have been manipulated from the Elysées Palace. Mitterrand proposed reducing government influence over them by placing control into the hands of an independent board of directors that would include government officials, media specialists and private citizens. In fact, little has changed in the management of the state–owned media.

The big changes in 1984 came with the legalization of private radio and television stations. So many private radio stations had cropped up that they could no longer

be controlled. By legalizing them, the state broadcasting monopoly had been so irreparably punctured that it was only a matter of time until private television was permitted. More than 800 private radio stations exist already, providing a voice for all kinds of minority interests. Many local TV stations exist around the country. In 1987 the government took another momentous step by selling the largest of the old state networks (TF1) to the private sector. This was the first sell–off by any government of a state–owned TV network. The state kept two of the six channels.

To strengthen Franco-German familiarity with each other, the two countries started a joint satellite TV channel called Arte. However, its total audience had by 2003 stagnated to about 13 million viewers, nine million of them in France. Many judge Arte as too high-brow and tend to associate it with Paris elites.

In 2006 France 24, the long-planned French rival to CNN and BBC World, went on the air with international news around the clock. It broadcasted in both French and English and was supposed to add an Arabic channel later. But the Sarkozy government produced a plan to strip it of its independence and to combine it with Radio France Internationale and TV5Monde to form France Monde. Broadcasting in English and Arabic was dropped.

The Arts

France continues to be a land rich and creative, and performing arts, although no longer occupying indisputably primary position in the world, are topnotch. Its artists have also declined from their pinnacle, but their past greatness is preserved for the world to admire in such great French museums as the Louvre, the Musée d'Orsay, the Beaubourg, and the Picasso Museum. Traditions date back hundreds of years in literature, art, music and the theatre. The writings of Voltaire and Rousseau are landmarks in rich French enlightenment. The music of father and son François Couperin were classic; that of Frederic Chopin, Jules Massenet, Camille Saint–Saens and Claude Debussy richly post-romantic. During the Third Republic before World War I, Paris was enriched by impressionism in art, e.g. Renoir, Monet, Degas, and the reaction to it (Bracque, Picasso, cubism or fauvism). During the same period there was the positivism of Auguste Comte, the *élan vital* of Henry Bergson, in medicine the discoveries of Louis Pasteur and in physics the discoveries of Pierre and Marie Curie. In 1988 Maurice Allais became the first Frenchman to win the Nobel Prize for economics, for his study of markets and efficient utilization of resources.

France

The job of French minister of culture is one of great influence and patronage. Today, the arts in France, as almost everything else, receive state subsidies and are highly concentrated in Paris. To try to spread French cultural activity into the provinces, de Gaulle's minister of culture, André Malraux (himself a leading French writer and art critic, who incurred the wrath of Parisian traditionalists by ordering that all public buildings in Paris be sandblasted to eliminate centuries of soot which had accumulated on them) created cultural centers in ten provincial cities, financed and operated jointly by the central government and the municipalities. These centers are designed to promote artistic creativity and to bring the performing arts into the provinces. They also serve as places for discussions on contemporary problems. Despite such attempts, many persons still speak with some justification of "Paris and the desert."

FUTURE

It is very difficult to change France. Jacques Chirac spoke in 1997 of the "extreme difficulty of changing anything at all in a profoundly conservative and fossilized country." By 2007 he had come to embody France's political incapacity to renew itself. Less than a year before the April 2007 presidential elections (with parliamentary elections following a month later), France's trust in its unpopular president and prime minister was gone. His and his imperious unelected Prime Minister Dominique de Villepin's approval ratings had sunk to around 25%.

The preceding year was one of the worst in recent French political history. Following the failed referendum on the EU constitution in May 2005, France lost the 2012 Olympics to Britain. It had not helped that French unions called Parisians out on strike the very day the IOC delegation arrived to study the feasibility of the city hosting the games. It suffered frightening urban riots by disenchanted unemployed young Arabs in November. They destroyed any lingering illusions that multiethnic France was indeed at ease with itself, and they brought into full focus the existence of two separate and unequal societies.

The government then witnessed widespread labor and student strikes and unrest in March-April 2006 that forced the government to back down from its timid labor market reform. Finally, it endured shameful abuse-of-power scandals. Such defeats and scandals rendered any meaningful reforms virtually impossible before the 2007 elections. Chirac left his country paralyzed and fearful of the future.

France faces the perennial challenge of corruption. In its 2002 report, Transparency International, a Berlin-based organization that campaigns against corruption, ranked it 25th in order of perceived lack of ethical cleanliness, equal with Portugal and behind all other EU countries except Italy and Greece.

Chirac was dogged by allegations of corruption from the time he was mayor of Paris, but the courts ruled that he had immunity from prosecution as long as he was in office (that is, until May 2007). The judge who led the earlier main investigations was removed from the case and resigned from the bench, saying that his investigation had been sabotaged at every turn: "I've had my eyes opened. People who make off with large sums of money escape justice or get insignificant sentences, while the thief who steals a handbag on the subway gets six years. We have a two-speed justice system."

With his immunity now stripped from him, he was called to court to testify on the charges stemming from his time as Paris mayor. He was interviewed in July 2007 by an investigating judge and was charged in November with embezzlement of public funds relating to the fake jobs. After further inquiries, his case could either be dropped, or he will stand trial. This would be without precedent in modern French history.

In 2006 the "Clearstream affair" helped paralyze the government, disgust the public, derail then Prime Minister de Villepin's hopes to become president in 2007, and damage France's image in the world. It involved a baffling web of judicial and intelligence inquiries into secret investigations initiated by de Villepin alleging that Nicolas Sarkozy and other politicians had received kickbacks and bribes laundered through the Luxembourg clearing house, Clearstream. French judges quickly determined that the accounts supposedly traced to Sarkozy were fabrications.

Even though de Villepin acknowledged that he had asked a fellow ENA graduate and secret service officer in 2004 to investigate Sarkozy for the possible money laundering, the public impression was that the prime minister was trying to smear his political rival. Shortly after leaving the prime minister's office, he was summoned in July 2007 to meet two investigating judges and was placed under formal investigation for his involvement in the affair. He denies any wrong doing. The scandal transcended the affair itself and revealed something about the power games played by the narrow political, industrial and administrative elites. Even ENA's old-boy connections seemed to be at work in this scandal intended to undermine Sarkozy, who did not attend the powerful school.

Some French intellectuals are gripped with a growing sense of France's decline, judging from a flood of bestsellers on the subject. Under titles like *New World, Old France* (Nicolas Baverez), *The French Arrogance* (Romain Gubert and Emmanuel Saint-Martin), *The French Disarray* (Alain Duhamel), and *West against the West* (André Glucksmann), they write that Europe no longer seeks French leadership, that French foreign policy is arrogant and ineffective, and that the country is adrift from its great past and unable to inspire allegiance or emulation. Baverez concludes that "the decline of France is accelerating at the same rhythm as the vast changes in the world." In a 2006 poll, 70% believed that future generations would live less well than they do today.

France is indeed undergoing introspection over its place in an enlarged Europe and a world seemingly dominated by American and Anglo-Saxon culture and economic practice. By 2008 it had slid from 6th to 21st place in the global ranking of GDP per capita. In a July 2006 poll, 85% of respondents thought France was heading in the wrong direction; only 9% thought it was on the right track. Three months before the May-June 2007 elections, 54% of French told pollsters their country was in decline; only 12% believed the opposite.

The incredible fact is that the Socialist Party, which had been out of power for five years, was unable to benefit from these problems, whereas the right, which had governed during this decline, was viewed at the party of hope. The Socialists seem to be paralyzed ideologically by the challenges of globalization; theirs has become the party of fear. They have not reshaped their party since its creation in 1971. They need new ideas and leaders.

The "Sarko-Ségo" contest between two such colorful and contrasting personalities captivated the attention of the public and the media. Sarkozy's and his UMP party's victories in the 2007 presidential and parliamentary elections offered promising reform to France. A majority of voters thought that he was best able to lift the "sick man of Europe" tag from the country and guide the necessary reforms through a difficult political environment. He has some accomplishments to his credit. He made peace with Washington and restored France as a serious player in the EU. Within France, he has shifted the argument from whether France should reform itself to one about how far and fast it might do so. But he suffered one of the most dramatic collapses in popularity in modern French history. Only 10 months

France

after taking office, his approval rating stood at only 38%.

The reasons for his problems are various. During his election campaign, he had pledged to boost stagnant incomes, promising to become the "president of purchasing power." However, the world economy has taken a turn for the worst, and he has not been able to keep that promise. Further, many French do not like his autocratic style, concentrating power in his own hands and overshadowing the ministers in his cabinet. Prime Minister Fillon has surpassed him in popularity. His inexhaustible energy strikes many observers as directionless activism. They ask what he is actually achieving.

Finally his personal life is not what French people expect from their presidents. His brash informality seemed refreshing at first, but it increasingly strikes people as undignified. The French are not accustomed to seeing their leader jogging in a t-shirt. Some even call him vulgar and self-centered. This applies especially to his private life, which has become very public.

In October 2007 he became the first French president to divorce while in office. He parted with his wife of 11 years, Cécilia. The next month he met a woman at a dinner party whom he courted in the most public way. On February 2, 2008, he became the first French president in over seven decades to marry while in office. During their 80-day whirlwind romance, their photos adorned the covers of scores of magazines, and their moves were reported non-stop in the media.

Carla Bruni is no ordinary lady. She is a beautiful Italian heiress to a tire fortune, who grew up in France, was a supermodel and then became a pop singer. She thereby is the first French "first lady" to work for a living although she said she would retire after her third album is finished. She is also no doubt the only first lady whose nude photo can be admired on the Internet. Cristie's auction house sold a decade-old nude shot of her while she was a top model. She had never been married and had been romantically linked to such celebrities as Mick Jagger, Eric Clapton, Kevin Costner and Donald Trump. A year

before her marriage to Sarkozy, she confessed in an interview with the magazine *Figaro Madame* that "I am faithful—to myself! I am bored to death by monogamy." In March 2008 Sarkozy's first wife, Cécilia, married her long-time lover Richard Attias, an event planner, in a New York ceremony.

The left-wing *Libération* newspaper dubbed Sarkozy "President Bling-bling" because he seemed to be ignoring France's business and having too much fun. He was widely criticized in his first year in office for his flashy habits, quick temper and frenetic style. A December 2007 poll revealed that almost half (45%) of respondents thought he displayed "too much of his personal life in public." A month later 93% said the news media were giving too much importance to the president's private life." Other polls were no kinder to him. In April 2008, two-thirds believed he had failed to make good on his electoral promises, and 72% were dissatisfied. Over half (53%) thought he represented France badly while 88% said the opposite about Charles de Gaulle.

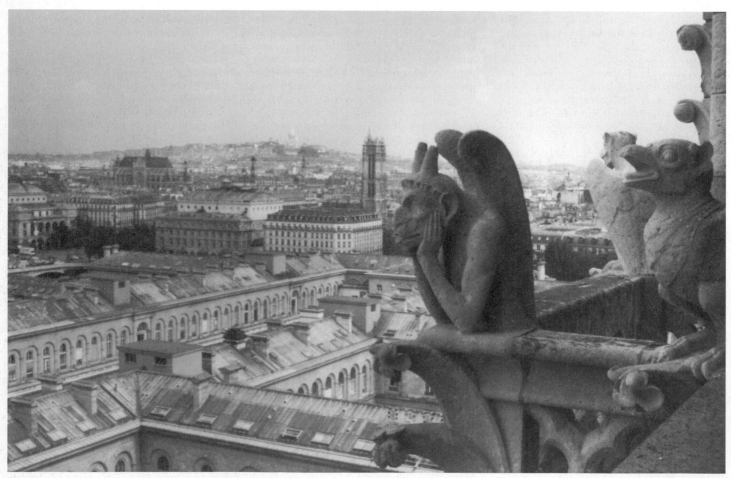

Finally, Notre Dame's gargoyles ... possibly pondering the mysteries of French politics

Courtesy: Jon Markham Morrow

The Principality of Monaco

Aerial view of Monaco showing the Port of Monaco

Area: .575 sq. mi. (1.95 sq. km.).
Population: 33,000 (estimated).
Capital City: Monaco–Ville.
Climate: Mild Mediterranean.
Neighboring Country: France.
Official Language: French.
Other Principal Tongues: Italian and Monégasque (a mixture of French and Italian) are also spoken.
Ethnic Background: French (50%), Italian (15%), native Monégasques (about 7,100), and diverse other European peoples.
Principal Religion: Roman Catholicism is the state religion.
Major Industries: Banking, tourism, postage stamps, gambling, small industries, such as cosmetics, chemicals, food processing, precision instrument manufacture, glassmaking and printing.
Main Customers: France, Italy.
Currency: Euro.
Year of Independence: 1338.
National Day: November 19.
Chief of State: His Serene Highness Prince Albert II Sovereign Prince of Monaco, Marquis of Baux (b. 1958), performed duties since July 13, 2005, enthroned November 19, 2005.
Heir Apparent: Princess Caroline.
Head of Government: Minister of State in Charge of Foreign Affairs.
National Flag: Red and white horizontal stripes.

The Principality of Monaco is one of the smallest sovereign countries in the world, smaller even than New York's Central Park. A densely populated, hilly city overlooking the Mediterranean Sea, Monaco is surrounded on three sides by the French Department of Alpes–Maritimes. The French city of Nice is nine miles (15 km.) to the west of Monaco and the Italian border is five miles (8 km.) to the east. Three picturesque settlements are now unified into one city. Its older section, situated on top of a steep rock, has maintained its medieval flavor despite some characterless high-rise blocks on the skyline.

Overlooking crowded Riviera beaches and some of the most luxurious tourist resorts in the world is the 13th century Genoese palace, which was remodeled in the 16th century in Renaissance style. Here resides the Prince of the House of Grimaldi, whose family has ruled Monaco, with periodic interruptions, since 1297. On January 8, 1997, the late Prince Rainier launched a year–long, $270 million celebration of his family's 700–year reign, the longest of any European dynasty.

Evidence of Stone Age settlements has been found within the present borders of Monaco. Founded much later by the Phoenicians, the city was known to the ancient Greeks and Carthaginians. Under the domination of the Romans (who called the city Herculis Moenaci Portus), Monaco was quite prosperous, and it was from Monaco that Julius Caesar set sail for his campaign against Pompeii. Its wealth was destroyed by the invading barbarians, who brought the once mighty Roman Empire to its knees. In the 7th century Monaco became a part of the Lombard Kingdom. Later it was absorbed into the Kingdom of Arles and was also subjected to a period of Mohammedan control. In 1191 the Genoese took control of Monaco, but they ceded domination in 1297 to the reining Grimaldi family.

As a minuscule land in a restless world, the independent principality of Monaco always needed the protection of a stronger power in order to survive. It allied itself first with France. In 1524 it accepted Spain's protection instead, but it returned to French safety in 1641. In 1793 the radicalized French National Convention dispossessed the wealthy and aristocratic Grimaldi rulers and annexed the entire Monacan domain to France. After Napoleon's fall from power, the Congress of Vienna awarded Monaco to the Kingdom of Sardinia as a protectorate in 1814. France repossessed the principality in 1848 and after greatly reducing its territory, granted independence to the present tiny remainder in 1861.

France today continues to assume responsibility for Monaco's defense, and a 1918 treaty stipulates that Monaco's policies must conform to French political, military, naval and economic interests. A further treaty of 1919 stipulates that Monaco would be incorporated into France if the reigning prince dies without an heir. This means that the city's self-rule depends entirely on the royal family. A former adviser to the prince explained: "The independence is given to the prince, not to the

The Principality of Monaco

His Serene Highness Prince Albert II and the late Prince Rainier III

people and not to the country, and this is why the prince is so important."

To prevent absorption by its huge neighbor, the palace made constitutional provisions in 2002 permitting the older of Prince Rainier's daughters, Princess Caroline, to assume the throne in the event that the bachelor ruler, Albert II, dies without a child born in wedlock. The next in line for the throne after Caroline would be her eldest son, Andrea Albert Pierre, who was 20 at the time his uncle, Albert II, became ruler in 2005.

Prince Rainier III died April 6, 2005, within days of the pope's death. He had been Europe's longest-reigning monarch. Rainier had been educated in Britain, Switzerland and France and had volunteered for service in the French army in 1944. He married the late American actress Grace Kelly in 1956. She epitomized American affluence and Hollywood glamour and attracted the world's attention to the ruling Grimaldi family. She met an untimely death in an automobile accident on the hilly roads of Monaco in 1982. Their offspring insure survival of the principality.

Since 1865, an economic union with France governs customs, postal services, telecommunications and banking. The principality even used the French franc until it adopted the euro when France did in 2002. Although it is not in the EU, it was permitted to mint its own euro coins with its own motif on the back. Monaco refuses to tax its own citizens, who number only about 20% of the principality's residents. Most of the rest are French. These 7,100 Monégasques also receive preferential employment and housing subsidies. The latter are needed since land, at 24,900 euros per meter (compared with 14,522 in Central London and 6,667 in Paris), is the most expensive in Europe. They are guar-

anteed government service jobs, and all companies must make their first job offers to them. There are 33,000 residents, but 43,000 work in the principality. Most Monégasques go to France for higher education, but thanks to the principality's healthy economy, they return.

More than half the residents are French, many of whom chose to reside and to locate their businesses in Monaco in order to avoid French taxation. French protests of this situation in 1962 unleashed a serious dispute. Nevertheless, a compromise was worked out in 1963; all French companies that do more than 25% of their business outside of the principality were brought under French financial control. French living in Monaco must pay French taxes. Other nationalities do not. In 2000 verbal warfare broke out again when France threatened to punish the principality unless it took effective measures against money laundering, tax evasion and drug barons. It demanded that Monaco impose a wealth tax on French residents and disclose details of bank accounts. Compliance would make the principality less attractive.

In 2008 trouble erupted again in the wake of a tax-haven scandal involving tiny Liechtenstein. Attention focused on the other two blacklisted ministates which the OECD has declared "uncooperative states" in terms of taxes: Monaco and Andorra. The principality faces the dilemma of how to maintain its banking secrecy while not being misused for tax evasion. The prince met with Germany's Chancellor Angela Merkel and approved the commencement of negotiations on a bilateral taxation agreement.

Prince Rainier was not pleased, calling the French attitude "incongruous" and demanding a renegotiation of its treaties

with France "to give Monaco back to the Monégasques." The principality likes to portray itself as a secure haven for the well-behaved rich. In response to EU pressure, Monaco agreed in 2003 to collect taxes on foreign accounts and to return 75% of the levy to the country of residence without revealing account holders' names.

Monaco has undergone a remarkable economic transformation in recent decades. At the end of the 19th century, gambling and the *belle époche* casino accounted for 95% of the state's revenues. When Prince Rainier took the throne in 1949, at age 26, his realm was seen, in the words of Somerset Maugham, as "a sunny place for shady people." It was a glitzy but sleazy gambling center. The prince sought to upgrade its image in order to attract wealthy, respectable visitors, depositors, and residents, and to provide long–term employment opportunities for native Monégasques.

His main achievement was to stimulate the local economy by creating thriving banking and tourist industries. Benefiting from tax advantages, banks have doubled in number since the early 1980s to nearly 40. It is estimated that there is one cashier for every 400 residents. Tough laws permitting the seizure of profits from drug operations were introduced in 1993 in an effort to keep the banks' money clean. The principality now attracts 4 million visitors a year, 3 million of whom are day-trippers from Italy and France. The annual Grand Prix auto race attracts 150,000 alone. Tourist spending accounts for 25% of GDP. Monaco also has experienced a blooming of commerce and light industry.

Monaco mourns the death of Prince Rainier III

The Principality of Monaco

In 1967 Prince Rainier won a long struggle with the Greek shipping magnate, Aristotle Onassis, over control of the famed casino of Monte–Carlo. Monaco's native citizens are not permitted to gamble in the casino, which is now owned by the Societé des Bains de Mer. Contrary to popular belief, less than 5% of the principality's revenues are now derived from its gambling royalties. Still, the social life of Monaco centers around the Place du Casino, with its lovely gardens. The Monte Carlo Philharmonic is one of the world's most recorded orchestras. The principality also boasts first–rate opera and ballet companies, as well as 55 galleries and 50 open–air sculptures.

The deceased prince also oversaw a major building program that changed both the look and the size of the city and won him the nickname, "the builder prince." Few capitalist countries have such close ties between government and business. Since the town is hemmed in by its land borders, it could only expand outward into the sea. That is what happened. By filling land, he was able to expand Monaco's size by 23% at the expense of the Mediterranean. To win more space, a tunnel was built for the railway that used to dissect the principality. The old harbor was extended by constructing a pier to accommodate the largest cruise ships. Prince Albert II founded an ecology foundation and aims to make the environment his highest priority when developing the city.

Monaco's present constitution, which was promulgated December 17, 1962, reduced the prince's powers somewhat and increased parliamentary powers. Executive power is vested in the hereditary prince, who rules through his appointed minister of state. The latter official must be a French citizen and must be selected from a slate of three candidates put to the principality by the French president. Three state counselors (one of whom must be French) and palace personnel who are appointed by the prince assist the minister of state. France supplies senior civil servants, judges, policemen and firemen. The French judicial system applies in Monaco, and two Parisian judges form the Court of Appeal. Prisoners must serve their sentences outside the principality, usually in France, since its only jail can accommodate suspects awaiting trial, but not convicted criminals.

Legislative power rests with an 18–member National Council elected by universal suffrage for five–year terms. The prince shares the legislative powers in that he retains the right to initiate legislation. Although four political parties are now active in Monaco, one party, the Na-

tional and Democratic Union (UND), dominated for four decades and controlled all 18 National Council seats. That ended with the 2003 elections, when the Union for Monaco coalition won an overwhelming majority.

The funeral of Prince Rainier III, attended by kings, queens and presidents, was held in the very cathedral where he had married Grace. On July 12, 2005, Prince Albert II, whose photo is displayed in every shop, assumed the duties of the throne to become the 31st descendant of Otto Canella, who had founded the house of Grimaldi. He was formally enthroned on November 19, 2005, with only one head of state (the Icelandic president) in attendance. He had graduated from Amherst College in Massachusetts. He began early preparing for the transition to rule. He attended government meetings and assumed his father's duties during his frequent illnesses in the last years of his life. Albert was a member of Monaco's bobsled team in the 2002 winter Olympics in Salt Lake City. He is also a passionate supporter of AS Monaco soccer team, which stunned Europe in 2004 by defeating Real Madrid in the semifinals of the Champions League. It also led the French league. The French cried foul, noting that non-French foreigners on the team do not have to pay income taxes. This enables the under-funded club to attract good players.

No sooner was his father laid to rest than a former Air France flight attendant from Togo announced that she had had an affair with Albert lasting several years and that her two-year-old son, Alexandre, had been fathered by him. She had been living

All Europe chatters about Albert's new girlfriend and children

in the prince's Paris apartment and had access to a villa on the French Riviera. After successfully suing the French weekly magazine, *Paris Match*, for 50,000 euros (about $62,500) for invading his privacy by publishing photos of him holding the child, Albert publicly recognized his paternity of the boy.

The prince admitted in June 2006 that he had also sired a daughter, Jazmin Grace, by a then-married California waitress on holiday along the Riviera, Tamara Jean Rotolo. Jazmin was born in 1992 and is a schoolgirl in Palm Desert, California. There could be even more. Given the fact that his sister Stephanie has three children out of wedlock, this news did not shock the principality as one might have expected. Each child whose paternity he recognizes will have a share of his inheritance estimated at close to $2 billion. This will have no effect on the principality's dynastic succession since only children born in wedlock are eligible. He announced in 2006 that he has a serious girlfriend, Charlene Wittstock, a 28-year-old South African swimming star. The 48-year-old monarch also made it known that he would like to marry, but does not want to be rushed into anything.

France controls Monaco's foreign relations, and the principality is included in the EU through its customs union with France. Since 1993 it is a full member of the United Nations, and it serves on several UN specialized agencies. It also maintains four embassies (in Paris, Brussels, Bern and Rome) and 110 consuls of its own, including ones in Washington and New York. In 1994 it signed a cultural convention under Council of Europe auspices. But because it is not considered to be either completely democratic or independent, it has never formally asked nor been invited to join the Council of Europe.

Monaco has no newspapers of its own, but there is a private radio station (Radio–Monte–Carlo) with programming in French, Italian and Arabic. Also, Trans–World Radio has a seat in Monte–Carlo and broadcasts in four languages. One private television station (Tele Monte–Carlo) transmits programs in French and Italian.

FUTURE

Before his death in 2005, Prince Rainier III could look back on half a century of successful rule in his ministate. With a new prince, Albert II, a clear succession to the throne, and an active program of home–based economic diversification, this minuscule 700–year–old principality can expect not only to exist, but to prosper in the coming years.

157

The BENELUX Nations

NORTH SEA

NETHERLANDS

GERMANY

BELGIUM

FRANCE

LUXEMBOURG

Belgium, the Netherlands and Luxembourg are located at the crossroads of Western Europe. Although they are collectively called "BENELUX," a word derived from the first letters of each country's name, these small countries have developed differing traditions, national characters and problems. Still, they have many things in common, and it is no accident that they cooperate with each other more closely than any other nations of the world. In fact, their example of international cooperation and their steady encouragement of tighter European integration have made them the core and motor for greater unity. The vast majority of the EU's institutions are located in Belgium and Luxembourg.

All three countries are very small and have no natural frontiers that could serve as barriers to unwanted intruders. They have therefore suffered recurrent invasions by all the great European powers. For a century and a half they tried to keep themselves out of the grips of the major powers by declaring a policy of neutral-

ity. But two disastrous world wars in the 20th century, which spared only the Netherlands from 1914 to 1918, left such a policy and the three countries in shambles. No one can easily forget the lines which the poet John McCrae wrote after visiting the Flemish battlefields: "In Flanders fields the poppies blow between the crosses, row by row . . . ."

Having paid a heavy price for their neutrality, all three countries became founding members of NATO in 1949. Its political headquarters are now located on the outskirts of Brussels, and its military headquarters, the Supreme Headquarters of the Allied Powers in Europe (SHAPE), are located outside of Mons, Belgium.

The Netherlands and Belgium have the highest population density of all Europe. All three have great numbers of foreign workers who bring both needed labor and social problems with them. These countries are not particularly rich in raw materials, but they have productive economies that have provided standards of living and social welfare systems for their popu-

lations that are almost unmatched in the world. Their central location and access to the sea made them prosperous trading nations, and the ports of Rotterdam and Antwerp are the largest and most active in Europe. With relatively small populations and high prosperity, these countries are heavily dependent upon trade, and, therefore, upon economic and political conditions beyond their borders. Roughly half of these countries' GDP results from foreign trade. This heavy volume is an economic blessing as well as a possible liability for the future.

To help secure their trade, they were pioneers in economic unions. In 1922 Belgium and Luxembourg formed the Belgium-Luxembourg Economic Union (BLEU), which made the two countries a unit for importing and exporting purposes. It also established a unified railway, customs area and currency for the two countries. Luxembourg coined and printed money below one hundred francs for local circulation, but Belgian currency remained dominant until the euro in 2002. The three countries' governments–in–exile in London in 1944 formed a customs union called BENELUX, which was later extended to include even non–customs matters. Because of the striking difference in postwar recovery, BENELUX did not come into effect until January 1948.

In 1952 they were founding members with France, West Germany and Italy of the European Coal and Steel Community (ECSC), with headquarters located in Luxembourg. Not only was it a farsighted idea to share these commodities, so crucial for heavy industry, rather than to risk fighting over them, but the ECSC gave these nations the practice in economic cooperation needed to convince the six that a bold move to create a united Europe could succeed. The six signed the Treaty of Rome in 1957 and in 1958 the European Economic Community (Common Market) came into existence. Later the Community grew, and its name was changed first to European Community (EC) and then in 1993 to European Union (EU) in order to emphasize that the union was someday to become a political one, as well as an economic one. None tried harder than the BENELUX countries to keep the idea of a united Europe alive in the 1960s, when the six were seriously split over the question of British entry.

All three countries are constitutional, parliamentary monarchies, whose monarchs are relatively popular, though not powerful. As modern constitutional monarchs, they "reign but do not rule." In contrast to the monarchy in Great Britain, which can be traced back more than a thousand years, the BENELUX monarchies are young. The oldest, in the Netherlands, dates back to 1813. Throughout the centuries these small countries have been tossed back and forth among the great powers of Europe and have sometimes been forced together and sometimes split apart. A quick glance at their history shows why they have so much in common and are nevertheless different from each other.

Early History

The early history of these three countries is so intertwined that it is best considered by grouping them together.

About a half-century before Christ, after a long and destructive campaign, the Roman legions conquered the tenacious Celtic tribes, including the Belgeai and Treveri. In his commentary *The Gallic Wars*, Julius Caeser used the name "Belgium" to refer to all the territory we now call the BENELUX countries. This area, especially what is today Belgium and Luxembourg, was dominated for more than 300 years by the Romans, who built roads and villas and introduced agriculture, especially vineyards and fruit orchards. They also brought Christianity to the area, but it did not begin to flourish until the 6th and 7th centuries.

When Attila the Hun invaded what is now Germany, Germanic tribes were thrown into the Low Countries (the Netherlands) in about 300. Two centuries later another Germanic tribe, the Franks, invaded the area and established a linguistic frontier that exists today in the middle of what is now Belgium. North of the line the Germanic tongues evolved into the Dutch language and into Flemish, a Dutch dialect spoken in northern Belgium. South of the line, vulgarized Latin, which developed into French, was spoken. Thus in Belgium the Latin and Germanic worlds met face to face and presented Belgium with a problem which many centuries later threatened to tear the country apart.

In the 8th and 9th centuries the entire territory that had been fragmented into many duchies, principalities and other political units, became a part of Charlemagne's empire. This was the time when the political center of gravity in Europe shifted from the Mediterranean to the northwestern regions. His great empire fell apart soon after his death, and for several centuries the BENELUX people saw their land converted into a constant battlefield between French and German contenders for control. During this time the crusades opened up trade with the Orient, and especially Belgium experienced a flowering of trade and urban development. The beautiful canal city of Bruges became a wealthy city of trade and the arts. In the 15th century, the Dukes of Burgundy, who were among the most powerful in Europe, began to acquire control over what is now Belgium and Luxembourg by means of conquest, marriage or land purchase.

Only the Netherlands was able to resist the Burgundian encroachment. As a country whose development had been retarded by its preoccupation with fighting back the sea, the Netherlands was not a very tempting target for Burgundian expansion anyway. At the end of the 15th century the last descendent, Mary of Burgundy, married Maximilian of Austria, and the Burgundian holdings in the area passed into the Hapsburg family. Their son, Philip the Handsome, married the Spanish princess, Juana of Castile; Spain and Spanish America also came under Hapsburg control.

A son born of this union in 1500 in the Flemish city of Ghent was destined to become one of Europe's greatest rulers. He became King of Spain in 1516 and the Holy Roman Emperor in 1519. He was Charles V, and by 1543 he had unified all of what is now the BENELUX area, except the county of Liège, which led a separate existence until the 18th century. Charles ruled his far–flung empire from Brussels, a city established in 979 on the islands of the Senne River, which was then called "Bruocsella." His reign was a time of great economic prosperity, artistic and intellec-

CAROLVS R○MA   N○R̄ IMPERAT○|
HISPANIARV̄   REX FOELICISS-
ATQ̄ CATHO|-

The Holy Roman Emperor, Charles V

159

The BENELUX Nations

tual bloom for the "Seventeen Provinces," as the Luxembourg area was then called. This was the time of the great humanist, Erasmus of Rotterdam, of Mercator, the most widely known cartographer in the world, of the painters van Eyck and Pieter Breugal.

The unity of the Seventeen Provinces might have survived if the Reformation which Martin Luther unleashed in 1519 had not divided Europe and with it the Low Countries. Charles V abdicated in 1555 in favor of his son, Philip II who had been raised in Spain; he decided to rule the empire from Madrid, leaving the administration of the Seventeen Provinces to governors. He was, however, determined to defend the Catholic faith, and he was cruel and inflexible in attempting to suppress the Protestant movement, which in its Calvinist form, was particularly strong in the Netherlands. William of Orange–Nassau led Protestant resistance in the northern provinces. Because Spain was so severely weakened by its continuous struggles against England and France during the second half of the 16th century, the Netherlands was able to secure its independence in 1581.

Until Napoleon's conquests in the 1790s the Dutch took control of their own destiny, while the Belgians and Luxembourgers continued to be dominated by other powers. In order to give the latter a sense of autonomy, Philip gave the southern provinces to his daughter, the Archduchess Isabella, and her husband, the Archduke Albert of Austria. It was a relatively happy time when the painter Peter Paul Rubens reached the height of his creativity. When Albert and Isabella died childless, the provinces reverted to Spain in 1621, and until 1713 the Hapsburgs fought over control of the area.

In one campaign in 1695, the French Marshal Villeroy, under orders of Louis XIV, bombarded the beautiful Grand Place in Brussels with its majestic town hall, built around 1400; it survived only with its tower and its thickest walls. This disaster merely stiffened the courage and determination of the Brussels population, which began the very next day restoring the structure. The best artistic and architectural talent in the city joined in recreating one of man's greatest architectural treasures. Jan Van Ruysbroeck, the city's master mason, rebuilt the town hall. Wishing to retain the foundation and porch of the old bell tower while extending the new walls as far as possible, he placed the main portal of the town hall off center with the central axis of the tower. Legend wrongly has it that he threw himself to his death when he discovered the error, but the "error" was in fact intentional. The Grand Place remains the vibrant heart of

the city and has always been a favorite subject for painters and poets. It is a place for open–air markets, public meetings, political assemblies, royal receptions and coronations. Earlier it was the favorite place for launching revolutions and for public executions. Each year on a summer evening the Grand Place is transformed into its medieval setting for a historical procession called the "Ommegang."

Both Luxembourg and Belgium passed into the hands of the Austrians, who renamed Belgium the "Austrian Netherlands" and who ruled over these provinces until 1794–95, when French troops snatched them away. The Austrians had exercised a benevolent dictatorship, but some Luxembourgers, Flemings and Walloons were infected by the fever of revolution emanating from France and welcomed the changes that came with the French republican troops. Belgium fell to the French in 1794 and the following year French revolutionary forces conquered Luxembourg and the Netherlands, which had been greatly weakened by its series of wars against England.

The French occupation brought fundamental changes to the Netherlands, which had been ruled by an enlightened oligarchy, with a high official called a *Stadhouder* (not a monarch) at the top. Although it was not a modern democracy in that leaders who were exercising power had been elected by universal suffrage, the Dutch republic had nevertheless been one of the most democratic countries in Europe with the possible exception of Switzerland. The old republic had been highly decentralized, with each province

stressing its independent powers. The new regime that the French created and called "The Batavian Republic," named after one of the tribes which had populated the country in the Roman period and which had revolted against Roman domination, was highly centralized in conformity with the French constitution.

The Napoleonic Code of laws and the selection of members of parliament on the basis of limited but free elections were also introduced. The Dutch grew restive under French control, especially after the Batavian Republic was abolished and Louis Napoleon, the brother of the French emperor, was made king of Holland in 1806. Quarrels with his brother forced Louis to abdicate in 1810, but only after he had tried unsuccessfully to have his son, who later became Napoleon III of France, crowned in his place. The Netherlands was annexed directly into the French Empire in 1810. Again, Napoleon's reversals gave the Dutch the chance to reassert their independence. In 1813, after Napoleon's defeat in the Battle of Leipzig, the son of the last Dutch *Stadhouder* who had fled to England, landed at Scheveningen, not far from The Hague, and was proclaimed William I of the House of Orange–Nassau, king of the Netherlands. For the first time the Netherlands became a monarchy with a Dutch monarch on the throne. Dutch troops took an active part in the final defeat of Napoleon.

In late 1794 French troops besieged the fortress of Luxembourg, which did not fall until mid–1795. It was annexed to France in the fall; French rule was very unpopular at first, but Napoleon was gradually

Gustav Wappers Episone of September Days 1830

160

able to smooth out many problems. When the French left the duchy in 1814 they left behind many positive and lasting gifts: the idea of equality, centralized and efficient administration and the Napoleonic Code.

The French were at first widely greeted in Belgium as liberators, and the introduction of the Napoleonic Code and an efficient, centralized administration was generally seen as an improvement over the old regime. Almost no one seemed to have realized at the time that decentralization would have helped Belgium's language groups to live together more harmoniously in a unified Belgian state. But the seemingly endless Napoleonic Wars soon sapped the Belgians' enthusiasm. After Napoleon began suffering disastrous reversals, especially in Russia in 1812, the Belgians joined the enemies of France. It was outside Brussels near a small town named Waterloo that the little dictator was defeated for the last time.

When the great powers of Europe met at the Congress of Vienna in 1814–15, they combined the Netherlands, Belgium and Luxembourg to form the "Kingdom of the United Netherlands," with the monarch William I as king. European leaders, who suspected that they had supported the French too enthusiastically, distrusted the Belgians. They believed that the Belgians, therefore, needed to be controlled by the Dutch king. Further, the East Belgian cantons of Eupen, Malmedy and Saint Vith were ceded to Prussia, whose borders had been moved as far west as possible in order to prevent any future eastward French expansion.

The union of the three countries did not last long. In 1830 the sparks of revolution flying from Paris landed in Brussels. The overwhelmingly Catholic Flemings and Walloons (Belgians who speak French) sensed religious discrimination by the predominantly Protestant Calvinist Dutch, despite the tradition of religious tolerance in the Netherlands.

Although it was the only thing that drew Flemings and Walloons together, Catholicism was enough to unify them against the Dutch. Such religious unity was later to prove the weakest of glue to hold the state of Belgium together. The use of Dutch in the South and in Brussels had been resented by the economically and culturally more influential French– speaking Walloons. The determination to elevate the French language above Dutch also was later to create extremely serious problems for this bilingual country. The eruption occurred in 1830 after an opera performance with a liberation theme. After a brief skirmish in Brussels, Dutch troops withdrew, and a provisional government proclaimed independence within three months. Seeing the utility of a buffer state on the European continent, the British announced that they would thenceforth guarantee Belgium's neutrality.

A liberal constitution, which is still in force, was proclaimed placing sovereignty in the people and providing for a constitutional monarchy. A German prince, Leopold I of Saxe–Coburg who happened also to be a British citizen, became king in 1831. Since sovereignty was placed in the hands of the people, there was no doubt that the parliament, as the representative of the Belgian people, would be superior to the monarch. French was also declared to be the new country's official language.

The Dutch reacted to these events by attempting to invade Belgium, but the French and British announced their determination not to allow the Dutch to reassert their control. At a London Conference of 1831, a border between the Netherlands and Belgium was drawn, but this settlement pleased neither the Belgians, who claimed about half of Luxembourg, nor the Dutch, whose king wanted no settlement at all which would reduce the size of his kingdom. Finally, the Treaty of Twenty–Four Articles, signed in London in 1839, granted the Dutch a slice of northern Belgium. Belgium, in turn, was compensated through a grant of about half of Luxembourg's territory. Further, the great European powers guaranteed the neutrality of Belgium and Luxembourg. This settlement finally satisfied all but the Luxembourgers, who saw their already tiny state reduced to about one–fourth of its pre–1815 size.

The Congress of Vienna had made Luxembourg an autonomous duchy with the Dutch king as the grand duke, but Luxembourg lost all its territory east of the Moselle, Sure and Our Rivers. The congress also made Luxembourg a member of the German Confederation and granted the Prussians the right to man the fortress in the capital city in order to be able to keep a closer eye on the recently defeated French. This arrangement meant that Luxembourg was wide open to Dutch royal ideas, Prussian military demands and Belgium's liberal cravings.

At first the Dutch king ruled in a rather authoritarian way, and when the Belgians rebelled against Dutch rule in 1830 most Luxembourgers outside the capital city also arose. Although they were unable to establish their independence, Luxembourgers were gradually able to create separate institutions and administrations. Political autonomy was granted in 1839 and in 1848 the country received a liberal constitution similar to that of Belgium. The Dutch became more benevolent rulers and cooperated in Luxembourg's movement toward democracy and independence. Finally, in 1867 the Treaty of London, drawn up in an attempt to reconcile differences between Bismarck of Germany and Napoleon III of France, proclaimed Luxembourg an independent and neutral country. Only a year later Luxembourg adopted a constitution that in revised form remains in force. Upon the insistence of Napoleon III, the Prussians withdrew from the duchy and the fortress was razed.

The only disappointment for the Luxembourgers was that the Dutch king remained the grand duke. However, when in 1890 there were no male heirs to the Dutch throne, Adolf of Nassau, whose family was related to the Dutch ruling family, became the grand duke of Luxembourg and chose to reside in Luxembourg City. Nevertheless, the close historical ties with the Netherlands continue to be symbolized by the fact that the two countries have almost exactly the same flag.

From 1890 on, all three BENELUX countries have been fully independent and sovereign states. Proximity, economic interests and political values continue to bind these three democracies very closely together.

The Monnaie Theater, Brussels, where the torch of liberation was lit

The Kingdom of the Netherlands

NORTH SEA

Land reclaimed from the sea since 1200

Delta dams

Earlier under consideration for reclamation (inpoldering), this area is now under approximately 15–20 feet (4½–6 meters of fresh water, the shallowest portion of this man made lake.

For clarity, several dozen cities with populations ranging from 50,000 to well over 100,000 are not shown on this map.

Groningen

Slochteren

BARRIER DAM

IJSSELMEER

Haarlem

AMSTERDAM

Enschede

Leiden

THE HAGUE

Utrecht

Delft

Arnhem

Rotterdam

Nÿmegen

Rhine

Breda

Tilburg

Eindhoven

Meuse

GERMANY

Scheldt

Maastricht

BELGIUM

N

The Netherlands

Area: 16,163 sq. mi. (41,863 sq. km., twice the size of New Jersey and one-half the size of Virginia).

Population: 16.4 million.

Capital City: Amsterdam (Pop. 1,000,000, estimated). The seat of government is The Hague (Pop. 530,000, estimated).

Climate: Temperate, with mild winters, cool summers.

Neighboring Countries: Germany (East); Belgium (South); England (West, 90 miles across the North Sea).

Official Languages: Dutch, Frisian in Friesland in the North.

Other Principal Tongues: English, German.

Ethnic Background: Frisian in the North, Saxon in the East and central part of the nation, Frankish south of the rivers.

Principal Religions: Roman Catholic (about one-third); Dutch Reformed-Lutheran (about one-fifth); Muslim (5.5%, growing by 3.9% per year); Hindu (about .5%); about 40% profess belief in no religion.

Main Exports: Machinery and transport equipment, chemicals and plastics, agricultural products, largely dairy, processed foods, fish and fish products, petroleum products and natural gas.

Main Imports: Machinery and transport equipment, chemicals, foodstuffs, fuels, clothing and cotton, base metals and ores, pulp, pulpwood, lumber, feed grains, edible oils.

Major Trading Customers: EU25 (75.8% of exports and 56.9% of imports), Germany (28.7% of exports and 19.6% of imports), Belgium (14% of exports and 10.8% of imports), UK (10.7% of exports and 6.5% of imports), France (10.7% of exports and 5.9% of imports), U.S. (9.1% of imports).

Currency: Euro.

National Day: April 30th, Official birthday of former Queen Juliana, mother of Queen Beatrix. Liberation day, May 5th, is celebrated every five years.

Chief of State: Her Majesty Queen Beatrix (b. 1938), married the late Claus George Willem Geert von Amsberg on March 10, 1966, a German diplomat who was proclaimed H.R.H. Prince of the Netherlands a few weeks before the wedding.

Heir Apparent: His Royal Highness Crown Prince Willem-Alexander (b. 1967).

Head of Government: Prime Minister Peter Jan Balkenende (since May 2002).

National Flag: Three horizontal stripes of red, white and blue, almost identical to the flag of Luxembourg, which has a pale blue stripe.

Benjamin Franklin once said: "In love of liberty and in the defense of it, Holland has been our example." Indeed, when the Dutch declared their independence from Spain in 1581, they justified their act in words which in some ways are very reminiscent of those which Thomas Jefferson wrote in the American Declaration of Independence almost 200 years later: "As it is apparent to all that a prince is constituted by God to be the ruler of the people . . . and whereas God did not create the people slaves to their prince, to obey his commands, whether right or wrong, but rather the prince for the sake of the subjects. . . . And when he does not behave thus, but on the contrary oppresses them . . . they may not only disallow his authority, but legally proceed to the choice of another prince for their defense. . ." Although their independence was not recognized internationally until 1648, the Dutch had already taken command of their own destiny and established a republic based on the ideas that government should be limited and directed exclusively toward the well-being of the people.

A thousand-year struggle against the sea helped to shape a people who are hard working, persistent, efficient and imaginative. It is a fact of history that nations have expanded their borders at the expense of other nations. The Netherlands, which even the Dutch call "Holland" though North and South Holland were traditionally merely the richest two provinces in the country, is one of the few nations whose expansion has been at the expense of the sea, not of other peoples. According to an old Dutch saying, "the Lord made heaven and earth, but the Dutch made Holland!" For centuries the Dutch built and strengthened dunes and dykes to hold back the sea. Since the 15th century they constructed windmills everywhere to convert the sea winds into energy to pump water back into the sea. Today, over one-fourth (27%) of the country is below sea level, and if the Dutch were not constantly vigilant, about one-half of the country would disappear under water or become unusable for any purpose. It is precisely in that half that more than 60% of the Dutch live and work and that most of Holland's industry is located. Amsterdam is built entirely on piles and has so much water that it has 1,281 bridges. The visitor flying into Holland can scarcely imagine that Schiphol Airport, near Amsterdam, where he would probably land, is 4.5 meters below sea level. It is the only airport in the world that was once (in 1573) the scene of a naval battle.

Despite the almost miraculous land reclamation the Dutch have achieved, there is still too little land. The Netherlands is the most densely populated country in Europe, with an average of almost a thousand people per square mile (480 per sq. km.). If the United States were as densely populated, it would have about

HOLDING BACK THE SEA: DUNES, DIKES, DAMS

163

The Netherlands

The Barrier Dam under construction

... and completed in 1932

three billion inhabitants. Of course, density is even greater in the horseshoe-shaped megalopolis surrounding a "green heart" of lakes and woods, called the *Randstad* (literally "rim-town"), which encompasses the capital city of Amsterdam (where merchants traditionally lived), The Hague (the seat of the government and the royal residence), Rotterdam (the trade center and the largest port in the world), as well as the cities of Delft, Leiden and Utrecht.

Its population density is twice that of Japan. Almost half the country's population lives in this area, which covers only about one-fifth of the total land area. Such concentration has made urban difficulties the most pressing of all Dutch problems although the *Randstad* provides a model for meeting the needs of its seven million inhabitants.

The Netherlands is located on the North Sea at the mouth of three large rivers—the Rhine, the Meuse and the Scheldt—and with the large port in Amsterdam as well, it truly deserves the name "Gateway to the heart of Europe." It has a predominantly low-lying, flat landscape; the highest elevation is only 323 meters. It is criss-crossed by lakes and waterways, which cover a total of 10% of the country's land area, about half of which consists of polders—land surrounded by dykes and drained artificially. There are many hundreds of such

polders because in earlier times the areas were pumped by windmills, which were not powerful enough to drain them. Now, with modern technology, much larger polders can be created. Dutch hydraulic engineers have been among the most ingenious in the world and have successfully tackled projects one can only call gigantic in scope. The Zuiderzee (renamed Ijsselmeer) and Delta projects have attracted particular attention.

The Zuiderzee Project was begun in 1920, with the expectation that it would be completed within 40 years. The idea was to seal off the Zuiderzee Bay in the northern part of the country from the North Sea by means of a 20-mile dam called the Barrier Dam. This created a large, freshwater lake, the Ijsselmeer, parts of which have been pumped dry and converted into farmland and recreation areas. If needed, residential areas for Amsterdam also could be created. The Barrier Dam was completed in 1932, and four out of five of the planned polders were created. Extremely high costs, environmental worries and disagreements concerning how the reclaimed land should best be used prevented the fifth from being completed.

In the 1950s a much larger project dramatically claimed a higher priority in the minds of the Dutch. On February 1, 1953, flood waters from the North Sea surged

into the Delta area in the southwestern corner of the country, covering many of the islands there and killing almost 2,000 persons. An audacious plan was promptly adopted to close off most of the waterways of the Rhine, Scheldt and Meuse rivers from the sea by a chain of dams and artificial islands. They would shorten the coastline by 440 miles, reverse the increasing salinity of the inland waterways and enable the Dutch to claim an additional 25,000 acres of land from the sea, if they ever choose to do so.

Only one dam across the Eastern Scheldt was left to be completed when a violent verbal storm erupted over the effect such a dam could have on the plant and animal life in the estuary. The environmentalists' influence was so great that parliament decided to build a costly storm-surge barrier instead of the planned solid dam. This change, which would better protect the ecological system, added more than a billion dollars to the costs, delayed completion until 1986, required entire new technology and could result in a barrier that might not last more than 50 years.

Queen Beatrix officially opened the Oosterscheldedam, assuring her subjects that "nature is under control but not disturbed." Indeed, this two-mile dam is "the ultimate insurance policy." This barrier, costing $5 billion, is the most expensive

The Netherlands

maritime project in the nine centuries since the Dutch have been building dykes to hold back the sea. It is a movable barrier, anchored by 65 concrete piers as large as grain elevators, which lowers 62 gigantic steel gates at the touch of a button to block off the rampaging North Sea whenever a serious storm threatens. Unless they are lowered, the tides continue to flow into the Rhine estuary as usual. This "compromise barrier" was a victory for the vocal Dutch environmental lobby. Large, man-made changes in the Netherlands' geography on the scale of the past are more difficult. But in 1997 the Dutch completed a storm surge barrier to protect Rotterdam.

Experts calculated that the gates will need to be closed only once every five years or so. When another storm like that in 1953 raged again in 1995, a quarter of a million Dutch were forced to evacuate their homes. Such a dam could mean the difference between survival and total disaster for the inhabitants of Zeeland.

In 1995 the Dutch were caught looking the wrong way. Having focused on the North Sea, they were struck this time by man-made perils along the Rhine and Meuse rivers. Marshes and floodplains once acted as sponges, soaking up surges of water. But in order to create residential and industrial property, people all the way along the river have dried out, asphalted and cemented, and buttressed with embankments the earlier waterlogged land. Changes in farming practices have also reduced the land's capacity to absorb rainwater. Worst of all, stretches of the Rhine have been straightened, reducing the meander to the sea and doubling the water's speed from Basel. This lessens the river system's ability to accommodate floodwaters. Holland's dykes held in 1995, but they were weakened by what many called "the flood of the century." Alarm bells were rung alerting the Dutch, more than a third of whom live below sea level, that they must again mobilize for a renewed campaign to salvage their lands.

The Netherlands is still a country where the old can be seen alongside the new. Windmills are plentiful, although only about a thousand serve their original purpose. For centuries the flowerbed of Europe, Holland in April almost seems like a gigantic bouquet of tulips, daffodils, narcissuses and hyacinths. In a few isolated villages one can find men in baggy pants and wooden shoes and women in floppy hats and bustling skirts. Yet the Netherlands is an extremely prosperous and heavily industrialized country, with a people whose dress is now more casual and modern. The Dutch stand out as among the tallest people in the world, with the average Dutchman five feet and eleven inches (1.85 meters) and women five feet six (1.71 meters), more than two inches taller than their American-born counterparts. It is a dynamic country whose modern look prevails over the traditional.

HISTORY

The Emergence of the Netherlands

Protestant leaders in the northernmost provinces of the Spanish empire signed, in 1579, the Declaration of Utrecht swearing to defend liberty and religious freedom. Predictably the Catholic Spanish King was unwilling to accept such freedom in the area he controlled, so in 1581 the northern provinces declared their complete independence of Spain. William, Prince of Orange-Nassau, also known as William the Silent, became the first head (stadholder or *Stadhouder* in Dutch) of the newly born Dutch Republic. He was assassinated by order of Spanish King Philip II, but the young Republic was able to resist Spanish efforts to reassert control. Aided initially by the English and by a fortuitous storm which decimated a mighty Spanish naval armada in 1588, the Dutch conducted a brilliant land campaign, led by Prince Maurice, son of William the Silent, and forced the Spanish to vacate the Netherlands in 1595. Although more wars with the Spanish followed, the Peace of Westphalia internationally recognized Dutch independence in 1648.

The 17th century was one in which the Dutch were involved in almost constant war, but it was for them also one of commercial success, naval supremacy and cultural bloom. It was the Netherlands' "Golden Age," and Dutch confidence and prosperity were vividly recorded in the paintings of the Dutch masters. It was the century in which Amsterdam quadrupled its population to 200,000 inhabitants and became a major point of departure for the entire world. It was also a city that even at that time was constantly *moving inland* as more and more land was reclaimed from the sea. In 1609 the Bank of Amsterdam was established, 85 years before the Bank of England, and Dutch financiers were among the most influential in the world. It was also a time of philosophical and scientific discovery.

Trade and Colonization

By the middle of the 17th century the Dutch had 16,289 seagoing vessels and 160,000 seamen. Their traders could be found in every corner of the globe, most often representing huge private companies such as the Dutch East and West India Companies, which had been chartered by parliament, called the States General. They traded virtually all over Europe, and their activities extended to Central Asia, where they had obtained the first tulip bulbs in the 16th century, India, Ceylon (now Sri Lanka), Japan, Formosa and Indonesia, where they established a

On top of the Zeeland storm surge barrier.

The Netherlands

Manhattan Island about 1627 . . . and today

colony which they controlled until 1949. In 1652 they established a colony at a good stopping-off place on the southern tip of Africa.

This Cape Colony was snatched by the British in 1806, but the Dutch descendants packed their belongings in 1836–8 and moved in a "Great Trek" into the interior of what is now the Republic of South Africa and established the Afrikaner colony of Transvaal in 1852 and the Orange Free State in 1854. Ultimately these Dutch (together with French Huguenot descendants), who speak a dialect of Dutch called Afrikaans, became the predominant white group in the Republic of South Africa that was created from a union of Dutch settled areas and British colonies. Until well into the 20th century the Dutch retained great sympathy for their Afrikaner relatives, who had created an economically prosperous state in an inhospitable land and who had successfully

resisted cultural assimilation by the British who previously had political control of the area as a colony. However, the Dutch gradually turned against the Afrikaners because of the latter's policy of racial segregation known as apartheid, an Afrikaans word meaning "separate." Until majority rule was introduced in 1994, the Dutch were among South Africa's most determined foes.

In 1609 a navigational failure brought the Dutch to North America. In that year Henry Hudson, an English sea captain in the service of the Dutch, sailed westward in search of a passage to the East Indies and China. He failed in his mission, but he bumped into what is now New York and sailed up a hitherto unknown river that now bears his name. It was the fate of America in its earliest days to be visited by seamen who actually wanted to get somewhere else. Hudson's contact with America resulted in the establishment of

the Dutch West India Company and in subsequent settlement of the New World.

Six years before the Pilgrim fathers landed, in 1614 the Dutch established Fort Nassau on an island just below the present-day city of Albany, New York, a city which the Dutch incorporated in 1652 as the town of Beverwych. In 1625 an even more important fort and town had been founded on Manhattan Island, and five family farms were established to supply the soldiers and merchants. The name of the town was Nieuw (New) Amsterdam, and it was soon to become the most important city in the Dutch North American Colony, called New Netherland. Only a year later the Dutch Governor made the famous deal with the local Indians, buying the whole of Manhattan Island for 30 guilders' worth of merchandise, which by today's exchange rates is worth only about $12, but which was worth considerably more in 1625. It was nevertheless an extraordinarily favorable exchange for the Dutch.

In the next two decades New Netherland continued to grow, but at a much slower rate than the British colonies in New England and Virginia, whose populations outnumbered the Dutch settlers by at least four to one. New Amsterdam had a population that did not exceed 700 by 1647. Its boundaries, if one looks at a present-day map of New York City, extended to Pearl Street and to the northern wall, called *de wal*, which gave the name to what is now perhaps the richest street in the world, Wall Street. Under the last Dutch governor, Pieter Stuyvesant, the city grew to 1,500 (1664) and boasted two windmills and one church. It was a very cosmopolitan city in which reportedly 18 languages were spoken. In strict accordance with Dutch West India policy, religious or other discrimination was forbidden. It was therefore much more tolerant than the Massachusetts Bay Colony to the north. It was also much more fun to live in New Netherland. There were many inns for drinking and dancing, and sports were a favorite activity. One such sport imported from Holland was called *kolf*, which developed into modern golf.

The Dutch continued to found cities in their colony. Among them were what are now the Bronx, Staten Island, Breukelen (Brooklyn), Haarlem (Harlem), Bergen (now Jersey City), Hackensack and Ridgewood. But the growth of New Netherland was halted abruptly by one of the three wars Holland fought against England in the 17th century. When British ships of war sailed into the harbor of New Am-

sterdam in 1664, Governor Stuyvesant saw no alternative to surrendering the colony to the English.

Although the Dutch won the colony back for a year in 1673-4, the Dutch foothold on North America was lost. They also lost their settlements in Brazil, although they managed to hold on to Dutch Guiana (since 1975 the independent nation of Suriname) on the northern coast of South America and to a handful of Caribbean islands known as the Netherlands Antilles, which still belong to the Dutch. But Dutch influence did not totally disappear from North America. Governor Stuyvesant returned to his beloved city, renamed New York, to live on his farm on Manhattan Island. His *bouwerij*, the Dutch word for farm, gave the name for a famous rundown area now undergoing gentrification in New York City known by its Americanized name—the Bowery.

Holland and the United States

In 1775 the Netherlands was the first foreign nation to fire a salute to the newly designed American flag, and in 1782 it was the second country formally to recognize the independence of the U.S. It was America's major source for loans, although it must be said that Dutch lenders at the same time provided loans to the British.

The Netherlands also left influences in the New World that became a part of American history and culture. Many famous Americans, including James Madison, Martin van Buren, Zackery Taylor, Ulysses S. Grant, Jefferson Davis and Theodore and Franklin D. Roosevelt de-

scended from Dutch settlers. Also, some words such as skate (from *schaats*), cookie (*koekje*), cole slaw (*kool sla*), cruller (*krullen*), halibut and pickle, as well as such seafaring expressions as skipper, marline, hoist and yacht entered English through the Dutch language. Perhaps the most famous, however, was the corruption of the popular Dutch name in the 17th century, Jan-Kees, which came to be applied to all persons from the United States: "yankees." The first serving American president to visit the Netherlands was George Bush, who in July 1989 paid tribute to the contributions made by the Dutch in America, especially their strong spirit of freedom.

Decline and Political Change

In the numerous wars during the 17th century, particularly against the English, the Dutch did not always fare badly. One time during the reign of Charles II of England, as Samuel Pepys described in his diary, the Dutch Admiral de Ruyter sailed up the Thames, burning British warships at Chatham right outside of London harbor and putting the city into a panic. This event was a high point in Dutch history and is still commemorated in Holland. The Dutch were also able to frustrate the plans of Louis XIV to conquer the Netherlands.

Nevertheless, Holland was exhausted by almost continuous war, and it became clear by the end of the 17th century that the Netherlands had assumed a position in the world that was out of proportion to its resources and size. It was propped up to some extent in the 18th century by a close tie with England. When James II of England decided to remain a Catholic, parliament offered the throne in 1688 to the Protestant Dutch stadholder, Prince William III of Orange-Nassau, who had fought the English only ten years earlier. William reigned with his wife, Mary, the daughter of the deposed James II. The childless couple ruled until 1702, and it was after them that the College of William and Mary in Williamsburg, Virginia, was named, as well as Nassau Hall at Princeton University. The 18th century was for Holland one of political and cultural decline. When the French came again in 1795 the Dutch were unable to offer serious resistance.

The Netherlands for the first time in 1813 created a monarchy of its own. In 1848 the revolutionary tide in France, Belgium and elsewhere in Europe reportedly converted King William I into a "liberal overnight." and he accepted a constitutional revision which made the government responsible to parliament rather than to the king. Thereafter, the Dutch monarch reigned but no longer ruled and became merely the first citizen of the king-

Golf and skating on ice, 17th century (van der Neer)

The Netherlands

dom. This was in effect the same position the Princes of Orange had earlier occupied as stadholders of the Dutch Republic and remains essentially true today.

After 1848 the Netherlands was confronted with tensions arising from industrialization. Though it came later than in Belgium or England, it nevertheless spawned a trade union and socialist movement. Holland also was confronted with struggles between the churches and the state, particularly over the creation of religiously affiliated schools that would be financed by the state. Not until 1920 was the present system of full state subsidies for parochial schools established. In all of these disputes, the Dutch displayed their characteristic willingness to abide by established rule of the democratic game and to find harmonious solutions to conflicts and differences.

The World Wars

During World War I, the Netherlands remained neutral and unoccupied. Sniffing the winds of change this mighty conflagration released, the Dutch did introduce universal suffrage for men in 1917 and for women in 1919. Because it had not joined Germany's enemies, the last German Kaiser fled to Holland after his abdication, living there until his death in 1941. The war radically disrupted the trade on which Holland has always been so dependent, and after the war its prewar prosperity did not return. The economic depression of the 1930s created greater unemployment, which stimulated radical movements on the left and right.

When the German army was hurled westward again in May 1940 the Dutch were unable to remove themselves from the melee. The Dutch army was facing east. The Germans flew around to the western part of Holland and attacked them from the rear. In the first large-scale aerial bombardment of a densely populated city, German dive-bombers destroyed 90% of Rotterdam's city center within 40 minutes. The German attempt to capture Queen Wilhelmina and the Dutch government by dropping crack paratroop units over The Hague failed, and the queen, Crown Princess Juliana and the cabinet managed to escape to London; they worked during the entire war to bring about a German defeat.

Holland fell within five days and a Nazi-appointed Dutch Reich Commissioner, an Austrian named Seyss-Inquart, ruled the country for the remainder of the war. This was an especially hard time for the Dutch, especially for Jews. The *Diary of Anne Frank*, whose setting is Amsterdam during the Nazi occupation, remains a moving testimony to the suffering inflicted upon the chief victims of Nazi racial theories and policies. More than 100,000 Dutch Jews—three-quarters of the community—were deported and perished in concentration camps. Unfortunately, some Dutch people were among the persecutors. As late as 1980, an art-collector, Pieter Menten, was imprisoned and fined for his role in the murder of 20 to 30 Jews in Poland in 1941. In 2000, compensation payments totaling $240 million were offered to about 35,000 Jews for damages

they or their relatives suffered in the Netherlands. In 2005, six decades after the war ended, the national rail company formally apologized for its role in deporting Jews.

Thousands of Dutch were active in the resistance movement against the occupation forces although many did collaborate with the German occupation forces. Despite the successful Allied landing in Normandy in June 1944, because of strong German resistance north of the Rhine and Allied policy to drive toward Berlin, that part of Holland north of the Rhine was not liberated until May 1945; the area south of the Rhine was freed in September 1944. When the horror was over, the Netherlands was left with 280,000 civilian dead, vast expanses of flooded areas, wrecked harbors and industries, and an economy close to total collapse. Dutch memories and emotions remain strong, which is one reason why a West German chancellor's trip to Holland in December 1987 was only the third official visit there in a quarter of a century.

Recovery

The very popular Queen Wilhelmina returned to Holland in 1945 amid enthusiastic cheers of her people, and the Dutch set about to mend their physically broken country, a task they were able to complete surprisingly quickly. In 1948, Wilhelmina abdicated in favor of her daughter, Juliana, and all would have gone well if the Netherlands had not been forced to face the same searing problem which was plaguing several other European powers at the time: decolonization.

The jewel of the colonial empire was Indonesia. In 1619 the Dutch East India Company had created a city it called Batavia (now Jakarta) on the island of Java. From this base the Dutch extended their control over most of the 3,000 or so islands of the Indonesian archipelago; for more than 300 years they retained firm control over the colony, but their policy of drawing a rather distinct line between themselves and the native population was a major factor which fanned the flames of an independence movement in the 20th century. The islands were an attractive target for Japanese expansion after 1940. The Dutch government, which was trying to maintain a policy of neutrality in the Pacific war, could not organize a credible defense. Indonesia was captured in February 1942.

Decolonization

When the Dutch returned at the end of the war in order to reclaim what they believed was theirs, they found that they were not wanted by a native population whose leaders had declared the islands'

Queen Beatrix with her children and grandchildren

independence in August 1945 immediately after the Japanese surrender. After four years of tension, military conflict and American pressure, a settlement was reached which recognized an independent Indonesia within a kind of union the Dutch equated with the British Commonwealth of Nations.

This agreement by no means settled all the difficulties. The Dutch had insisted on retaining full control of their economic investments, which at the time accounted for almost 15% of their national income. Indonesia's flamboyant and unpredictable President Sukarno solved the problem single-handedly by simply nationalizing all Dutch properties in 1957. Relations between the two countries also remained sour because of the Dutch retention of West Irian, part of the island of New Guinea, which the Indonesians claimed. Finally, in 1962, an American mediator proposed the face-saving procedure of turning West Irian over to the UN, which seven months later transferred sovereignty to Indonesia.

After a painfully drawn-out severance from Indonesia, the Netherlands was more than cooperative in aiding its other colonies to gain their own independence. In 1975, Suriname was freed in the midst of widespread fears among the Surinamese that such independence would lead to violent racial measures against the whites and East Indian Hindustani. More than a quarter of the population fled to Holland in the final days before independence. In order to help Suriname adjust to

its new status, the Netherlands promised it aid amounting to $100 million for each of the following ten years. This was certainly one of the most generous foreign aid programs on a per capita basis in history. However, because of the Surinamese government's flagrant human rights violations, the Netherlands suspended its assistance programs in 1983.

The Netherlands notified the six islands in the Netherlands Antilles that they must prepare for their independence. They organized themselves into four self-governing communities: Aruba, Bonaire, Curaçao and the Leeward Islands (southern portion of Sint Maarten, Sint Eustatius and Saba). The island of Aruba became an independent state in 1986 within the Kingdom of the Netherlands. It does not make its own foreign and security policy, and its highest court is still in the Netherlands.

In 2000 voters on the island of Sint Maarten opted to break away from the Dutch Antilles federation and become a separate country within the Kingdom of the Netherlands. Amsterdam feared that the islands would not be able to find a long-term alternative to economic dependence on Holland. Therefore, Dutch officials opposed Sint Maarten's independence, believing that it would be a bad precedent for the other islands.

On November 28, 2005, the Dutch government and the islands' other governments signed a new status agreement, effective July 2007. The Netherlands Antilles was dissolved. Curaçao and Sint Maarten are new associated states within

the Kingdom of the Netherlands. Bonaire, Saba and Sint Eustatius are directly part of the Netherlands as Kingdom Islands.

POLITICS AND GOVERNMENT

The Monarch

The Netherlands is a constitutional monarchy whose character is prominently visible during the investiture ceremony when a new king or queen begins to reign. The monarch takes an oath of allegiance to the constitution. Also, the royal crown is not placed on the head of the new ruler (for which reason the ceremony is called an investiture, not a coronation), but it and the other symbols of royal authority—the orb and the scepter—are arranged on a table around the constitution.

The royal family is the House of Orange-Nassau, whose descendants are inseparably tied to the Netherlands' entire history as an independent state. This is one reason why there is very little opposition to the monarchy in Holland and why most Dutch remain firmly attached to their monarchs. It was therefore a shock to many Dutch to witness the violent disturbances in Amsterdam, Rotterdam and Utrecht on April 30, 1980, when the popular 71-year-old Queen Juliana, who died March 20, 2004, abdicated after 31 years as queen in favor of her daughter Beatrix. While orange flags and streamers were displayed everywhere and while the mood around the royal palace in Amsterdam was royally festive, elsewhere several thousand protesters waged such vio-

The Netherlands

Princess of the Netherlands Maxima and Prince of Orange Willem-Alexander

lent battles with the police that more than 50 policemen and 100 demonstrators were injured. The slogan of the protesters was "No apartment, no coronation," which referred to the serious housing shortage in the capital city. No doubt some of the protesters wished also to show disapproval of the monarchy and of a family which is among the richest in the world and which draws over $5 million a year from the state treasury to maintain a royal household with 250 servants and other assistants. The area in which the ceremony was held had to be sealed off by the police.

Queen Beatrix was well prepared for her position, having studied law, politics and history at the University of Leiden. She has a pleasantly dimpled smile and is extremely knowledgeable and interested in politics. But she tends to be a strong-willed and impatient person whose manner is often stiff and aristocratic. For a while her manner appealed less to her people than did that of her unpretentious mother Juliana, who rode her bicycle in public, shopped in supermarkets, poured her own tea and abolished the curtsy. But the nation's respect for Beatrix has grown considerably since she became queen. It was her mother's enormous popularity that had enabled the family to overcome an extremely embarrassing scandal in the last decade of her reign. It was prompted by revelations that her German-born husband, Prince Bernhard, had accepted payoffs totaling $1.1 million from the Lockheed Aircraft Corporation for his assistance in helping the company to secure lucrative contracts from the Dutch air force. He was forced to resign from his post as inspector-

general of the armed forces. He died of lung cancer in 2004, age 93.

Beatrix's marriage in 1966 to a German diplomat, Claus, had created quite an uproar at the time, but the marriage became accepted, and Claus proved himself to be an effective promoter of good Dutch relations with developing countries. He acted as an adviser to the minister of development. Suffering from Parkinson's Disease, he died in October 2002 at age 76.

Crown Prince Willem-Alexander served as a lieutenant on a guided missile frigate, is trained as a pilot and holds the rank of lieutenant-colonel. However, he is not a career soldier. He studied history, but he is a specialist in water management and is on the International Olympic Committee. In 2002 he married Maxima Zorregui-eta from Argentina. Since her father had been a cabinet member during the time of Argentina's military dictatorship, he was not permitted to attend the wedding. On December 7, 2003, they had their first child, Catharina-Amalia Beatrix Carmen Victoria (called "Amalia" for short), who became third in line for the throne. On June 26, 2005, they had their second daughter, Alexia Juliana Marcela Lourentien.

The crown prince's younger brother, Johan Friso, studied engineering at Delft and at the University of California at Berkeley. He was dropped from the succession to the throne when he insisted on marrying Mabel Wisse Smit, who had once had a relationship with a violent drug kingpin, murdered in 1991, as well as with a former Bosnian foreign minister and UN ambassador charged with misappropriating millions of dollars in public

funds. Parliament must approve of all royal weddings. After extensive investigation by the Dutch intelligence services, an interview with the queen and three with the prime minister, Wisse Smit and Johan Friso were declared to have provided incomplete and incorrect information. According to a government spokesman, a prince "has to be as white as snow to be in a position so near to the throne." Denied the title of "princess," she and Johan Friso nevertheless married in April 2004, while the public remained sharply divided over the issue. A third brother, Constantijn, remains a part of the royal house and is in line for the throne.

Queen Beatrix is extremely hardworking and spends hours preparing for her speeches and meetings, and reading proposed legislation. She was very frank in her inaugural speech about the unromantic side of being queen: "It is a task no one would ever seek. The glitter is visible, but not the burden and perpetual self-denial." In most matters she is prevented from making any mistakes by the requirement that the appropriate cabinet member also sign all her acts and decrees. However, she is technically a part of the government, defined as the "queen and her ministers." She plays an important role in forming a government. Only the D66 party wants the monarch to be completely out of the government.

Entangled in a rare scandal in 2003, the queen was sued for $53 million by her niece, Princess Margarita, who accused her of abusing royal privilege and behaving like a "tyrant" by bugging her Amsterdam apartment, recording her telephone calls, intercepting her letters and spying on her commoner husband. Responding to evidence that the palace had indeed ordered a surveillance operation without the government's knowledge, Prime Minister Jan Peter Balkenende issued an apology. Claiming that these tactics had ruined her husband's business and amounted to "psychological terror," Margarita's lawyers took the unprecedented action of filing criminal charges against the state and considered calling the queen to appear in court. Because of a special immunity law of 1840, Beatrix cannot be prosecuted for any crime, but she can be summoned as a witness. The angry niece also took the opportunity to reveal that the queen's father, Bernhard, had had a secret love affair.

Although the case was dropped, polls in 2003 revealed that 54% of Dutch believed that the revelations had compromised Beatrix, and the percentage of subjects no longer happy with her role as head of state rose from 8% to 28%. Margarita subsequently divorced her husband, who is still in possession of the tapes and threatens to publish them. She is back in the family's good graces.

Forming a Parliamentary Government

She is certainly very capable of performing the one public act she is charged to accomplish independently: to coordinate the long coalition talks that are necessary to form a government after a parliamentary election. Because the Netherlands uses the proportional representation electoral system, many parties are able to win seats in the lower house, and no single party can even come close to winning a majority on its own.

The formation of a government out of almost a dozen parties that win parliamentary seats is therefore a very delicate task, requiring a firm but subtle lead on the part of the monarch. She consults numerous party, parliamentary and other political leaders in order to acquaint herself intimately with the political climate. Then, acting entirely independently, she names an *informateur*, who is usually a leading politician, whose task is to advise her of the most promising formula for constructing a government. She then appoints a *formateur*, a person who must seek to form a government in which he himself would probably be the prime minister. He is usually the leader of the party that has won the most seats in the election. His task includes the establishment of a program acceptable to several different parties. Such a broad program is necessarily moderate; no remotely radical program would be acceptable to several parties. The entire process takes a very long time, usually two to four months. Fortunately the work is done carefully and normally results in a government that can survive for at least three years.

In the carefully constructed cabinet, ministerial seats are usually distributed according to the proportion of seats the various governing parties have in the lower house, the most important positions being that of prime minister and minister of finance. Cabinet members, including prime ministers, need not be members of parliament, and some ministers are specialists who had never even run for elective office in their lives.

Compared with other parliamentary systems in which a prime minister is the most important political figure, the Dutch system is almost unique in that it calls for a separation between the executive (cabinet) and the parliament. All cabinet members must resign their seats in parliament, and the new government need not seek the formal approval of the lower house. Nor is there such a thing as a vote of confidence in which a majority in parliament can vote against the government, causing it to fall. The government is, however, always free voluntarily to pose a "question of confidence" to the lower house if it chooses. It is acutely interested in maintaining a majority without which it could not gain approval for important legislation, which is almost always written and submitted by the government, not by members of parliament.

The Parliament

The Dutch Parliament, called the States General, remains powerful in comparison to many other parliaments in Europe. One reason is that the lower house has permanent committees that correspond to each ministry. Therefore, parliament members can develop the necessary expertise to question and control the work of the ministries. Further, parties in parliament do not require absolute discipline from their members, who according to the constitution represent the entire nation, not a regional or party constituency. Therefore, the government can never be absolutely sure that its measures will pass in both houses. It must design its legislation in such a way that it would be acceptable to more than a slim majority, and it must work very hard to persuade parliaments to support its programs. Parliament is by no means dominated or overshadowed by the cabinet.

The States General was first established in 1464 by the Burgundian kings as an advisory body. After independence in 1581, it considered itself the keeper of Dutch sovereignty and granted an hereditary official, the stadholder, the right to exercise executive power. The States General is bicameral, and both the First and Second Chambers meet in the Binnenhof (Inner Court) in The Hague. The First Chamber, or upper house, is composed of 75 members elected by the 12 provincial parliaments for six-year terms, with one half of its membership being elected every three years. Since the provincial chambers are elected directly, the upper house usually has roughly the same party composition as the Second Chamber. This First Chamber cannot introduce or amend bills, but it is far more than a mere advisory or delaying chamber as is the British House of Lords. It has the right to approve or reject all legislation.

The Second Chamber is composed of 150 members elected at least every four years by all citizens 18 years or older. In contrast to most other European countries, elections are not held on Sundays. Nevertheless, voter turnout is high (78% in 2006) in contrast to U.S. presidential elections which are also held on Tuesdays and which now rarely attract more than 60% of the voters. One reason for the high participation is that Dutch law permits a family member or other designated individual to cast a person's ballot upon presenting a valid, signed voter card. The Second Chamber generally meets three days a week, Tuesday through Thursday, and its members are expected neither to reside in The Hague nor to give up their normal employment while they serve. About a third of its members are women.

Both chambers are regarded as the chief interpreters of the constitution, and together they are empowered to initiate the process to amend the constitution. If a majority in both houses finds a constitutional amendment necessary, then both houses are dissolved, new elections are held, and the amendment can then be accepted by a two-thirds vote in both chambers. No court in Holland has the right to declare a legislative act unconstitutional. The highest court of the land, the Court of Cassation, can only nullify a statute that is in variance with an international agreement. Its chief tasks are to insure the uniform administration of justice and to serve as the court of high appeal for decisions made in lower courts. Presiding over those lower courts are independent judges who apply Dutch law. There are no juries; the Dutch want a professional administration of justice by judges who serve for life and who are as free as possible from popular influences.

Dutch law has its origins in Roman law. However, the Dutch copied and codified the French civil code in the 18th century. After a significant recent reform of its Citizens' Law Book (*Burgerlijk Wetboek*), based on a major comparative study in 1992, the Dutch private legal system now functions as a guideline for democratizing countries, such as Estonia.

Assisting the queen and government as the highest advisory body is the Council of State, which is composed of a crown prince or princess over the age of 18 and no more than 24 persons appointed for life, although they normally step down at the age of 70. They are expected to have political, commercial, trade union, diplomatic or military experience. The queen officially presides over the council although it is actually guided by a vice president who is selected from among the members. The cabinet can seek expert advice from the council and is always responsive to any constructive advice it might give.

Political Parties

At all levels of government, Dutch political parties play a key role in informing voters about the most important political issues, conducting election campaigns, and then forming coalitions to rule. Dutch political parties have always tended to represent particular subcultures in society, such as Catholicism, various shades of

The Netherlands

Protestantism, socialism or liberalism. At the same time, they must adjust their aims to those of other parties in order to be able to participate in government. Therefore, compromise and mutual adjustment have been their basic rules. In a small country with such a highly homogeneous population, the range of political interests and opinions is somewhat narrower than in a large, multi-racial, multilingual and multinational country. Thus, a consensus regarding the political system and rules of the game has always been relatively easy to maintain in Holland, and this has made it less difficult for such a multiparty state to have such a high degree of parliamentary stability.

It has, however, become increasingly difficult to form coalition governments in Holland. This results partly from a change that is occurring in party politics. In the past, no Dutch government could ever be formed without the participation of confessional (religious) parties, particularly the Catholic party. Therefore, the secular parties always had to moderate their programs in order to be able to coalesce with them. But as the importance of religion declines in Dutch society, fewer and fewer Dutch vote for a party exclusively for religious reasons. Therefore, the strength of the confessional parties has declined in recent years. Seeing this, the major secular parties have sharpened their own programs and have moved more clearly to the right or left in order to draw the formerly religiously oriented voters away from the politically heterogeneous religious parties. In other words, the major secular parties often have intentionally tried to polarize Dutch politics in order to attract more votes. They have even publicly stated that they are not interested in entering into any coalition with each other.

A couple of dozen parties usually competed for seats. Some of them, such as the Party for the Liquidation of the Netherlands, the God is With Us, the Live or Die Together, the hard-line Communist Party of the Netherlands (CPN) and the Pedophile Party (which advocates lowering the age of consent and legalizing sex with animals, child pornography, bestiality and hard drugs), could not seriously hope to win seats. But profiting from proportional representation, which grants a parliamentary seat for roughly 55,000 votes, several parties manage to win seats.

The Green Left, which rallies radicals, socialists, pacifists, and communists, won 7 seats (from 8) in the November 2006 elections with 4.5% of the votes. Dutch voters are very sensitive to environmental issues. The crowded population, flatness, and the fact that half of it is below sea level make it a first victim to any rise in

Prime Minister Peter Jan Balkenende with the picture of Harry Potter

water levels due to the "greenhouse effect." In fact, in 1989 a Dutch government became the first in Europe to fall in a crisis over the environment.

The leftist Socialist Party, led by former Maoist Jan Marijnissen, promotes an anti-globalization, anti-European platform. It blends leftist populism with nationalism and isolationism. He was the most prominent face of the NO campaign in the 2005 EU constitutional campaign. In 2006, the party nearly tripled its seats from 9 to 26, and 16.6% of the votes. It received considerable support from the kinds of Dutch who had earlier voted for Pim Fortuyn.

The more conservative of the main secular parties is the People's Party for Freedom and Democracy (VVD). It is usually referred to as the Liberal Party because of its century-long struggle to reduce the influence of the churches in Dutch public life, especially in the schools. Individual freedom is its chief tenet, and it favors lower taxes, an even lower government deficit, a shrinking of the increasingly

Wouter Bos, Leader of Labor Party

costly welfare state, higher criminal sentences, a strengthening of the police in order to curb crime and severe restrictions on immigration. It supports a free market economy, but it also favors profit sharing with workers. It draws voters particularly from the upper and middle classes.

It was in Peter Jan Balkenende's governing coalition and entered the November 2006 elections under Mark Rutte, who defeated the ambitious Immigration Minister Rita Verdonk as party leader in June 2006. It got a rude shock, dropping 6 seats to a total of 22, based on 14.6% of the votes.

It was weakened by the defection in 2004 of Geert Wilders, a hard driving anti-Islam and immigration campaigner. His newly formed Party for Freedom (PvdV) came out of nowhere to capture 9 seats on 5.9% of the votes. Like the VVD, it finds itself in the opposition. But in December 2007 Wilders was picked as politician of the year in a poll run by the public broadcaster NOS; 13% would vote for him. He is a skilled parliamentarian, and his parliamentary outbursts have introduced an adversarial style to debates, in contrast to the consensus politics to which the Dutch have been accustomed.

Another major secular party is the Labor Party (PvdA). It is a moderate socialist reform party, which traditionally favors what it calls *Nivellering*, or the elimination of differences in citizens' power, knowledge and income. It supports an increased workers' share of profits and decision-making in the factories. Although the coalition governments Wim Kok had led for eight years had achieved "the Dutch miracle" of low unemployment and solid economic growth, it was rudely thrown out of power in the 2002 elections.

However, it bounced back vigorously in the 2003 elections, led by a dynamic, telegenic and charismatic young leader, Wouter Bos. A former Shell manager, Bos had entered parliament only five years earlier at age 34 and had become a junior finance minister in 2000. To shake its aloof image, the party selected its new leader in a rare primary election open to all members, thereby breaking from its former practice of having the party elite decide behind closed doors. Bos spent as much time criticizing his own party for past mistakes as he did his opponents.

Like Balkenende's Christian Democrats, the Labor Party avoided the explosive issues of immigration and Islam during the campaign. It was disappointed with its result in the 2006 election. It lost 10 seats and held on to only 32, with 21.2% of the votes. Although it was the biggest loser in the election, it joined the new government in February 2007. Bos occupies the post of finance minister.

The moderately left-wing party called Democrats 66, had been founded in that year in order to present voters with a clear alternative to the established parties, especially the PvdA, whose strong, paternalistic leadership was widely resented at the time. It opposes the ideological approach to politics and sees itself as a practical, problem party. It advocates reforms in the society and the constitution, such as the direct election of the prime minister. Once a trendy, intellectual party that appealed mainly to young voters from the upper and middle classes, it broadened its base temporarily. It had participated in the Balkenende government, but in June 2006 it pulled out, depriving the coalition of its majority. In the 2006 elections that followed a half-year later, it continued its steady downward slide, losing half its seats and ending up with only 3, and 2% of the votes. It faces extinction.

Fighting for its political life until 2002 between the secular parties of the left and right was the Christian Democratic Appeal (CDA). Faced with the gloomy prospect of watching their voters run to the increasingly polarized secular parties, the three major religious political parties, which had long since severed their direct ties with the churches, decided in 1973 to join forces for electoral purposes. In a nostalgic ceremony of prayers and hymn singing in 1980, they went a giant step further by disbanding themselves entirely and becoming full members of the larger CDA.

The merger in 1980 brought birds of many different colors together, which are difficult to control. They all agree basically that Christian principles must be applied in politics and that both a free enterprise economy and the present social welfare system should be defended. The fact that the CDA encompasses a broad political spectrum gives it the advantage that the party can easily form a coalition with almost every other party. Therefore, the CDA has survived the secularization and polarization of Dutch politics.

In the 2002 elections the CDA emerged as the strongest party. Its leader, Peter Jan Balkenende, became prime minister. He is nicknamed "Harry Potter" because of his resemblance to the boyish film character. He is not always flattered. In 2005 he won a court case over an advertising campaign that depicted him as a child. He also received an apology from Belgian Prime Minister Guy Verhofstadt after the Belgian foreign minister had referred to him in an interview as "Harry Potter, but without the charisma."

Balkenende is a former professor of Christianity and head of the Christian broadcasting network. He had entered parliament only four years before becoming prime minister. During the electoral campaign, he expressed concerns about his country's euthanasia policy and drug laws and called for more rigorous measures of integrating immigrants, such as required language and culture courses. His short-lived government in 2002 announced plans to put these campaign promises into practice. He thereby turned away from Holland's multicultural approach to immigration.

In the 2006 elections the CDA lost 3 seats, but hung on to 41 in the 150-seat assembly. Capturing 26.6% of the votes, Balkenende's party is the country's largest. His impressive comeback to win his third election in four years is in large part due to the end of economic stagnation: unemployment fell to 5.6%, growth of 3% was Europe's highest, and disposable incomes had risen.

After more than two months of tortured negotiations, he constructed a kind of grand coalition with Labor. To get the few extra seats needed to form a majority, the Christian Union (CU), led by André Rouvoet, was included in the government. It had doubled its seats to 6, with 4% of the votes. CU combines leftist economic policies with conservative social values. It is fiercely critical of anti-immigration policies and has forced the Balkenende gov-

Rembrandt's House in Amsterdam

The Netherlands

ernment to soften its approach to immigration. They rule over a parliament with a confusing array of 10 parties (out of 24 that competed for seats), including a Party for Animals (PvdD) and a Reformed Political Party (SGP), both with two seats.

The 2002 election campaign witnessed the emergence of one of the Netherlands' most colorful and controversial politicians, who was assassinated a week before the elections. Pim Fortuyn was the antithesis to Dutch consensus politics. An openly gay sociology professor and ex-Marxist, who became a prominent talk-show guest and columnist for the weekly magazine, *Elsevier*, Fortuyn was an effective antiestablishment populist. He dared to express in public his reservations about the effects of burgeoning immigration on Dutch culture and society, something that Dutch political correctness had hitherto forbidden. Even many who did not agree with his views found his directness a breath of fresh air in a stuffy political environment. Three months before the national elections he had been named leader of the Livable Netherlands Party, but he was soon thrown out for violating its nondiscrimination policy. He then formed his List Pim Fortuyn (LPF), which immediately captured a stunning 35% of the votes in Rotterdam's municipal elections. He expressed contempt for green politics.

On May 6, 2002, he was shot dead by an environmental activist, Volkert van der Graaf, who in April 2003 was given a shockingly lenient sentence of 18 years in prison, read amidst the boos, curses and sobs of Fortuyn supporters in the courtroom. This shocked his countrymen, who had never imagined that such violence could happen in their well-ordered country. He was the first Dutch politician killed since a mob lynched the De Witt brothers in 1672.

The party capitalized on this feeling in the May 2002 national elections, which saw an unusually large turnout: 79%. It won an astounding 26 seats, becoming the second largest party and partner in the ruling coalition. Not since 1945 had a new party won so many seats in its debut. Its success reflected the increasing worry that the political establishment was not in touch with the voters' concerns about a level of immigration that could no longer be absorbed. This eclectic "List" included a young West African entrepreneur, a former Miss Netherlands beauty queen, and a pig farmer. Almost all were political novices. Dutch politics was temporarily changed dramatically by the LPF.

The list failed miserably as a governing party in Prime Minister Balkenende's ruling coalition, with four novice politicians in ministerial posts. The party's continu-

Balance of seats in the Dutch parliament

Christian Democratic Alliance (CDA)
Labour party (PvdA)
Socialist party (SP)
People's party for freedom and democracy (VVD)
Party for freedom (PvdV) **9** (+9)
GreenLeft (GL) **7** (-1)
Christian union (CU) **6** (+3)
Democrats 66 (D66) **3** (-3)
Party for animals (PvdD) **2** (+2)
Reformed political party (SGP) **2** (−)

41 (-3) 32 (-10) 26 (+17) 22 (-6)

Total: **150** seats
Figures in brackets indicate gains/losses of seats

Vote share (%)

Voter turnout: **80.1%**

		% point change since 2003
CDA	26.6	-2.0
PvdA	21.2	-6.1
SP	16.6	+10.3
VVD	14.6	-3.3
PvdV	5.9	+5.9
GL	4.6	-0.5
CU	4.0	+1.9
D66	2.0	-2.1
PvdD	1.8	+1.3
SGP	1.6	−

Source: *Financial Times*

ous internal feuding and power struggles, culminating in the raucous resignation of two of its ministers, blew the three-party government apart after only 87 days in office. Returning to the voters again in 2003, the Pim Fortuyn List was issued a rude rebuke for their irresponsibility, losing all but eight of their seats. However, the party could take some consolation in the fact that all the established parties adopted much of the Fortuyn platform, calling for tighter immigration policies and the need for more integration.

The unruly List Pim Fortuyn quickly resumed its self-destruction. Facing a probe by public prosecutors into alleged fraud within the party's finances, its eight deputies unanimously agreed in August 2004 to sever their ties with the party's executive board saying that its "power struggle, chaos and unrest" hampered their work as parliamentarians. In 2006 Fortuyn's party imploded. It remains to be seen if the follow-on party, One Netherlands (EenNL), led by Marco Pastors, can pick up any of the pieces.

Unitary System, Regions, Municipalities

The Netherlands is a unitary, not a federal state. There are elected provincial and municipal governments which deal with matters of regional or local concern, but about 90% of their income is channeled to them by the central government. In each of the 12 provinces voters elect by means of proportional representation a Provincial Council. This assembly appoints from among its own members a Provincial Executive who is responsible for the day-to-day administration; retaining a French practice, the central government appoints a Queen's Commissioner, who presides over the Provincial Council and Executive and seeks to insure that nationwide interests will not be overlooked. The Provincial Councils elect the members of the First Chamber in The Hague, a provision that helps insure that provincial interests in turn will not be passed over by the central government.

Considerably more important in Dutch government are the Municipal Councils, which are also elected by proportional representation in the cities and towns. Each Municipal Council appoints Aldermen from their own members who serve as the executive. Presiding over both the executive and the Council is the *Burgemeester* (mayor), who is appointed by the central government for a six-year term. Although he usually does not come from the city in which he serves, he very often becomes the locality's most effective spokesman in The Hague. Increasingly, several municipalities are joining to form regional authorities to tackle such matters as the location of industry, housing, transport and environment. The need for action on a larger scale than the municipality has led to a proposal to increase the number of provinces and to allow the new provincial governments to perform such tasks.

Other very important local bodies in the Netherlands and among the oldest form of democratic administration in Europe are the Water Control Boards. Property owners within a board's jurisdiction elect a general council, which in turn elects an executive committee. The central government chooses the executive committee for the most important Water Control Boards. These are responsible for what might be considered the most important task in Holland: defending the land against water.

Housing Shortages

The Dutch government must grapple with some very difficult problems. One of the thorniest is the desperate housing shortage in the *Randstad*. People disagree on how such a shortage arose and how it should be eliminated. The shortage is due in part to changed demands for housing. As young people leave home earlier, as the divorce rate climbs and as an increasingly prosperous people demand larger and better quality housing, the demand for existing housing increases. Like other European countries, the Netherlands is experiencing a dramatic increase in homeless persons. In a controversial effort to help them, Rotterdam began in 1993 distributing tent-shaped waterproof cardboard boxes to the estimated 3,500 homeless in that city.

About half of the Dutch housing stock is owner-occupied. Rotterdam is an exception, where nearly all the land is owned by the city, and 80% of its housing is rented. Private investors are discouraged from building more new apartments because the government forbids the returns on housing investments to exceed the returns paid on state bonds. No government has been able to find a way out of this trap. With low rents, many landlords refuse to pay for the kinds of renewal which much housing needs. According to the Amsterdam municipal council, as much as 60% of the city's housing is in need of renewal. In some districts, three-fourths of the houses have no bathrooms. Thus, rather primitive accommodations are hidden behind many of the stately facades that foreign tourists admire in the capital city. On top of this, the Netherlands experienced an end to its housing boom from 2003 on.

Social Welfare Problems

The government was confronted with the problem of how to finance its generous social welfare system. Unlike many Western European countries, where welfare states were created after 1945 as a compromise between capitalism and socialism, and as an essential ingredient for social peace and political stability, Holland's welfare system (called the *verzorgingsstaat*) was built more on a Christian imperative, rather than on a political necessity. It reached the limits of the welfare state and must realistically revise downward its earlier version of a new society. Both the Christian Democrats and the Labor party cut back the welfare system.

It is understandable that the Dutch want to cling to the social welfare system. Parents receive special allowances for children, and widows and orphans receive special benefits although widows who can work must do so. Health insurance has been privatized, is universal, and includes dental care. It covers treatment and nursing in institutions for the physically and mentally handicapped, nursing homes, hospitals, sanitariums and similar establishments.

Workers who are declared to be fully or partially disabled are entitled to benefits in amounts up to 70% of their wages. Since 1968 when these disability benefits were expanded, the nation's health has seemingly declined rapidly. In that year 5.5% of the work force was considered to be at least partly disabled. In the 1990s this disability scheme (called WAO) was reformed slightly. The qualification criteria were tightened and benefit levels cut to 70% of previous salary. Nevertheless the number of claimants continued to rise, especially after psychological problems and stress were added. By 2002 nearly a million persons qualified for WAO out of a work force of seven million on the basis of complaints ranging from claustrophobia to chronic backache. Many had been added to the rolls because it was easier for employers to get unwanted employees on this list than to fire them. The government decided to do something about this outrage in 2003 when it tightened eligibility rules, reexamined all existing cases, limited levels of payments and required those on welfare who can work to seek work.

All in all, only one out of two adults worked by the 1990s (compared with 63% in the U.S.), which is one reason why economic growth lagged behind most industrialized countries for years. All Dutch who cannot support themselves, including artists, are entitled to state aid. Employers and employees contribute 50-50 to the unemployment and health insurance, but the employers and, in some cases, the state treasury pays for all the other benefits. Generous retirement benefits await all employees who contributed to special pension plans, but the Balkenende government introduced tough measures in 2003 to end the practice of early retirement at only 57 years.

The luxurious social welfare system grew out of the unpleasant memories of the depression of the 1930s and of the war. At first it was paid for by rising productivity and prosperity, and after large natural gas reserves were discovered in the late 1950s, budget deficits resulting from the social welfare bill were simply paid for by large government revenues derived from the export of natural gas. But the government, wishing to conserve the country's precious supply of natural gas, announced that all export contracts were to be terminated in the 1990s.

Public sector spending is half of GDP. How should the welfare system be financed? The Dutch government believes that the welfare state can be maintained only if it is operated more strictly and efficiently. Therefore, in 1994 it privatized sickness insurance and shifted responsibility for social security from the government to companies. It hopes to improve greatly the ratio of active to inactive persons in a land where almost half the population lives on benefits.

In 2003 the Balkenende government produced an ambitious reform package that sent the message that the days of cradle-to-grave government care are over and that the new society can expect more from its citizens in the way of individual responsibility. After four years the prime minister had cut spending, trimmed the welfare state by reducing benefits, scrapped incentives for early retirement and introduced more competition in health care.

European and Third World Relations

The Netherlands is a founding member of the EU and has long been one of the

Peace Palace in the Hague

175

The Netherlands

chief proponents of a more unified Europe. The Hague is the site of several supranational institutions, including especially the International Court of Justice, which is the supreme UN legal body in theory. This International Court meets in the stately Peace Palace built by money donated by the American steel magnate, Andrew Carnegie. The Hague has, in a way, become the center of a world system of justice. The Balkan war-crimes tribunal, which tried the now deceased ex-Serbian President Slobodan Milosevic for war crimes, is there, as is the new International Criminal Court. The world appears to trust the Dutch sense of justice and fair play.

Holland has especially distinguished itself in development aid. In 2008 it gave .82% of its GDP, tied for the world's third highest per capita donor after Norway and Sweden (.94%), with Luxembourg, and ahead of Denmark (.81%). It is the fourth-largest financial backer of the UN refugee agency, the UNHCR. One Dutch official commented, "development aid is a breed of sacred cow with us. We carry it out with the zeal formerly reserved for our country's Christian missionaries."

By 2002 the Netherlands had also become the second-biggest net contributor to the EU budget (after Germany); in per capita terms it pays more into the EU coffers than any other member. Prime Minister Balkenende admitted: "For me it is difficult to explain why an ordinary Dutchman is paying six times more than a Frenchman." It came out better in the 2006 EU budget, lowering its payment even though it remains a net contributor.

Dutch voters shocked Europe on June 1, 2005, when they rejected a new EU constitution by two-to-one (62% to 38% with a turnout of 63%) in their first ever national referendum. This was only three days after French voters did the same although only 4% of Dutch said their decision had been influenced by the French NO vote. When two founding members of the EU put their feet down on such an important issue, all of Europe pays attention.

An ever-larger Europe is in danger of losing its truest believers. It is all the more worrisome since they are two founding members on opposite sides of the ideological divide: France is in the "federalist" intervention camp, while the Netherlands is among the "Atlanticists," who favor a looser, less regulated Europe. All the main Dutch parties, representing 85% of the MPs, as well as the trade unions and almost all the main newspapers, supported the YES campaign. But by the time the YES campaign got going, the NO voters had already set the agenda and were fighting on a broad front.

Opponents' reasons were many. The main one was fear that the Netherlands would lose influence in a Europe dominated by big countries. Close behind were concerns that their leaders had failed to consult the people; it was a kind of confrontation between the political elite and the Dutch people. The unpopularity of the current government and its policies of austerity and immigration at a time of economic slowdown hurt. More than a fourth of the NO voters opposed Turkey's entry into the EU, and many also feared they could lose control of immigration policy. The latter is especially important in a country that was still reeling from a Muslim extremist's terrorist act half a year earlier. Almost a fourth feared a European superstate.

A third of NO voters cited opposition to the euro, which is widely blamed for inflation; in 2005 only 39% of Dutch thought the euro has been a success. After the Dutch government fought hard for a strict interpretation of the rules on budget deficits in the eurozone, France and Germany simply overruled it and did what they wanted. Liberal Dutch voters feared that a more conservative EU might interfere with policies on soft drugs, gay marriage and euthanasia. The vote was a slap in the face for the government, which vowed to slow the pace of European integration, reduce the relatively large Dutch contribution to the EU budget, and lay greater emphasis on the member states' sovereignty. In December 2007 the Dutch government voted in favor of the slimmed down Lisbon Treaty that replaced the failed constitution. After much passionate debate, the cabinet and the main parties decided not to hold a new referendum, but to allow parliament to decide whether to ratify the treaty or not. The Dutch remain committed to the EU: one year after the referendum, three-fourths (74%) said membership was a good thing.

Defense Policy

Its defense policy is based on its membership in NATO. Dutch troops are well-trained and equipped and are considered to be among the best-prepared forces in NATO. One unique feature of the Dutch military is that it officially recognizes almost a dozen official personnel associations that function very much like labor unions except that they have no right to strike.

Another unique feature is that the Dutch military was the first in the world to assign to combat units any woman who volunteers and who can satisfy the physical requirements. They also are permitted to serve on all naval vessels and to fly combat aircraft. The Dutch invested several million dollars on such things as developing backpack straps which do not irritate women's breasts, constructing separate quarters and conducting studies to determine how valid the Israeli experience is that military units are more quickly demoralized when women are wounded than when men are hit. In 2001 there were 1,920 women in the Dutch forces, 7.6% of the total. They serve in all branches.

Other armies, including that of the U.S., watched the Dutch experiment closely, as they did Holland's policy since 1974 to allow gays in the military. Gays have their own Foundation for Homosexuality in the Armed Forces (FHAF), which represents gay interests in the services. For example, when Dutch troops serving in the Balkans in 1993 were sent complimentary copies of *Playboy*, homosexual soldiers were sent issues of a corresponding gay publication. Self-declared homosexuals are officially welcome in the volunteer army although most experience difficulties.

The Dutch have abandoned conscription and created a flexible volunteer army designed to be used in rapid deployment actions and UN peacekeeping operations. The force has been cut 37% from 101,000 to 53,130: 23,150 in the army, 12,130 in the navy, and 11,050 in the air force. They are backed by 32,200 reservists. Stricter discipline and grooming standards have been introduced. Earrings and ponytails have been curtailed, and the use of cannabis has been banned. The non-saluting policy was not changed.

Some army bases were closed, and 2,300 of the army troops and 300 air force personnel are assigned to a joint German-Dutch corps headquartered across the border in Münster. The command for this joint corps rotates between a German and a Dutch general, and English is the unit's official language.

The air force, which since 1977 has used the American F-16 fighter, has the task of protecting Dutch air space and of contributing to the tactical air forces of the alliance. The navy plays a part in defending the Atlantic, the English Channel and the North Sea. Its most important assignment is to keep the Dutch coast clear of mines and to defend the Dutch ports, which are critical for NATO supply lines. To utilize their assets more rationally, the Dutch and Belgian navies and air forces coordinate some of their operations close to home. Several Dutch naval vessels were sent in 1991 to the Persian Gulf, and missile batteries were deployed to Turkey and Israel. The U.S. had reduced its troop level in the Netherlands from 2,200 to 780 by the turn of the century. In 2001 the Dutch entered a treaty with the U.S. allowing American aircraft to use Dutch bases on the Caribbean islands of Aruba and Curacao as staging areas to fight drug trafficking.

In the Balkans Dutch soldiers serve on the ground, in the air, and at sea. Their humanitarian image was badly tarnished by allegations in 1995 that they had stood aside after Srebrenica fell to Bosnian Serbs while 7,000 Moslem men and boys were butchered, and while the women and girls were raped and expelled. The troops had been sent into the area under an ill-defined UN mandate, with none of the weaponry necessary to withstand the onslaught of thousands of Serb troops. The Dutch commander on the ground had separately sought air strikes, but failed to get any support from allies, including the U.S. The Dutch government absolved them in 1995 of any wrongdoing in that complicated and tragic situation. However, it commissioned an inquiry, which issued its report in April 2002 that Dutch troops had been sent on an "ill-conceived and virtually impossible mission." Even though the fault lay with the UN and some allies, the incident haunted the Dutch conscience for seven years, and it prompted former Prime Minister Wim Kok to resign after the report was issued.

In 1999 it deployed one ship, 16 combat aircraft, and 738 troops in the NATO air war against Yugoslavia to stop ethnic cleansing in Kosovo. A tenth of its peacekeeping forces there is female. It has 1,070 soldiers in Bosnia. Its maintenance of peacekeepers in the Balkans, Cyprus and the Middle East underscores its changed emphasis from home defense to peacekeeping.

Following the September 11, 2001, terrorist attacks against the United States, the Netherlands sent troops to Afghanistan both to serve as peacekeepers and to fight alongside American and other allies to root out and destroy the remnants of Taliban and al-Qaeda fighting forces. In February 2003 it joined hands with Germany to command all peacekeeping forces in Afghanistan for half a year. After months of debate in parliament and pressure from the U.S. and NATO, the government decided in February 2006 to deploy 1,700 troops in Afghanistan as a part of a NATO-led reconstruction mission. Fearing that the troops would be drawn into combat with Taliban fighters, D66 opposed the mission, but Labor decided to support it. The force includes up to 1,400 troops dedicated to public works efforts, with the remainder flying and maintaining Apache helicopters and F-16 fighter jets.

Given the sacrifice their troops are making, which includes 14 combat deaths,

Hand painting Delft Porcelain

Dutch officials did not appreciate a remark by U.S. Secretary of Defense Robert Gates in early 2008 that most European forces "are not properly trained" in counterinsurgency. The Dutch defense minister demanded a clarification. A backtracking State Department spokesman explained that Gates "was not directing his comments at any one country in particular, but at the alliance as a whole, which includes us."

During the 2003 American-British war against the regime of Saddam Hussein in Iraq, which most Dutch opposed, the government permitted the American and British allies to move troops, tanks and other military supplies through the Netherlands to the Persian Gulf. This included airspace and airports, rail lines and Rotterdam harbor. Defense Minister Henk Kamp stated, "the Americans are our friends. They are here in Europe to help and protect us." The government also stood by NATO and shipped three of its four Patriot air-defense batteries and 370 soldiers to operate them to Turkey after France, Germany and Belgium had blocked Turkey's request for NATO protection against Iraq. Kamp justified this action by explaining, "we are an independent country. We have certain obligations in NATO and no one can prevent us from honoring them."

During the crisis over Iraq in the early months of 2003, the Dutch government supported the American position politically while not alienating its European allies. In order not to inflame contradictions

The Netherlands

A residential area in Amsterdam

among Europeans, it declined to sign the letter of eight European NATO countries criticizing French and German opposition to the war. But after the rapid victory in April 2003, it agreed to provide 1,500 troops to help police postwar Iraq and to enable an equal number of U.S. Marines to rotate home. Its peacekeepers applied their preferred soft touch: eschewing armored vehicles, helmets and mirror sunglasses, encouraging interaction with the people, and generally making their soldiers accessible and vulnerable to their surroundings. In May 2004 its troops suffered their first fatality in Iraq. In March 2005 it withdrew its remaining 1,400 troops.

The Netherlands was determined not to permit transatlantic ties to deteriorate any further. Referring to the countries that opposed the war, the then Foreign Minister Jaap de Hoop Scheffer explained, "Belgium and France will not guarantee our security. Germany will not guarantee the security of the Netherlands. I cannot imagine a world order built against the United States." Prime Minister Balkenende put it this way: "The Netherlands has become a builder of bridges, both within Europe and across the Atlantic." Having proven himself as a master compromiser, Hoop Scheffer became in January 2004 the third Dutchman to be named NATO secretary-general, strongly supported by the United States.

ECONOMY

The Dutch economy is the sixteenth largest in the world. It is almost entirely in private hands and the government restrains itself from subsidizing or assuming a direct or indirect ownership of Dutch companies. Nor does it engage in compulsory economic planning. The state nonetheless is active in the economy. For example, it is a major participant in the Netherlands Gas Company. The state employs 12% of the nation's work force, and including all social security programs, it spends half of the country's GDP.

The government is also closely tied in with the highly structured Dutch system for dealing with conflicts of economic interests. The labor unions (which have unionized about 40% of employees) send representatives to the Joint Industrial Labor Council, established in 1945; employers, primarily the Federation of Netherlands Industry and the Netherlands Federation of Christian Employers, send an equal number of representatives. The Council not only engages in collective bargaining, but serves as an official advisory body to the government.

Another important body is the Social and Economic Council (SER), which is composed of 45 representatives: 15 each from the labor unions and the employers' organizations, 13 academics, and the heads of the central bank and planning agency. The government is required to ask its opinion on all proposed economic and social legislation, and the council is free to give unsolicited advice. The cabinet is not required to follow the advice, but if the council's recommendations are supported by a large majority of its members it is very difficult for the government to disregard them.

The Netherlands has long since shed its traditional character as an agricultural country. Nevertheless, Dutch agriculture is important. It is very intensive, and farms in Holland, which are predominantly small family operations, are the most productive in all of Western Europe. The Netherlands is the world's third-largest agricultural exporter after the U.S. and France. The percentage of Dutch engaged in agriculture or fishing has dropped by two-thirds in the last three decades to only 3% of the total population, who produce 2.7% of GDP. Since three-quarters of them are unionized and their representatives sit in all economic advisory organs and political parties, they still can wield considerable political clout.

Two-thirds of the land is used for agricultural purposes, of which 62% is used for grassland, 32.5% for cultivation and 5.5% for horticulture. A consequence of so much farmland is that the bulk of the population is squeezed into the remaining third. The visitor notices much cultivation under glass. Of course, no one can overlook the most beautiful crop of all: flowers. The Dutch have grown and exported all over the world a wide variety of plants ever since the first tulip bulbs arrived from Central Asia in the 16th century. Their most splendid showpiece is Keukenhof and its environs, which in the months of April and May must surely be the largest and most colorful garden in the world.

The country is heavily industrialized. Its highly diversified industry employs 20% of the work force and accounts for 23.1% of GDP. For such a small country, it has an exceptionally large number of big-name international corporations. Some of the most prominent industrial names in the world are based in Holland: Phillips, Unilever and Royal Dutch Shell. In 1993 the giant music company, PolyGram NV, purchased the legendary symbol of African-American music, Motown Records. Services provide employment for 74% of the Dutch and produce 74% of GDP.

Almost 70% of the industrial turnover is in chemicals and petroleum, metals, biotechnology products, food, drink and tobacco. Chemical and petroleum industries, which include the processing of natural gas and the refining of oil, alone account for one-half of all exports. The Netherlands does have some lame industries, such as shipbuilding. It is, however, trying to gear up for future trade competition by exporting such sophisticated products as microcomputers and precision optical equipment. The government is strongly supporting the search for new Dutch markets abroad and does offer export subsidies to Dutch companies.

On the family tulip farm in Northern Holland

For centuries this has been a trading country, and today it is the world's eighth largest trading nation. Over half of its GDP is derived from the export not only of its goods, but also the services. It always has invested heavily abroad, ranking second behind the U.K. in total foreign investment in the U.S. It has always been a particularly important transit country because of its ports and inland waterways.

Of all goods loaded or unloaded in the EU destined for or arriving from overseas, 30% pass through Rotterdam, the world's largest port. The port moves almost half of all cargo entering or leaving ports between Le Havre in France and Hamburg in Germany. In 1996 the Dutch state and city of Rotterdam launched an investment program valued at $6.1 billion to boost the harbor's capacity. It includes building eight new state-of-the-art terminals capable of serving jumbo container ships. Because a deep channel was dug in the bed of the North Sea, the port can accommodate heavy tankers. Over half the cargo tonnage handled by the port now consists of crude or refined oils, and it is the world's chief oil port and "spot market" on which oil is bought and sold on a supply and demand basis. Pipelines have been constructed which can move petroleum to Germany and Belgium. Rotterdam alone provides more than 10% of the country's GDP.

Because of its inland waterways, which include Western Europe's most important rivers, the Dutch ports of Rotterdam and Amsterdam have the capacity to transport goods by water to markets that serve over 200 million persons. Dutch companies are responsible for 40% of the EU's inland waterway transport. About 70% of the transport between the ports and the European hinterlands moves on water, but Holland also has an excellent road and rail net that is connected with those of neighboring countries. Finally, the national airlines, KLM (now linked to Air France), ties Schiphol airport near Amsterdam to cities all over the world. Schiphol is Europe's second biggest airport for goods transport. In 2006 the government offered 49.9% of the shares to the public, but a year later the new Balkenende government scrapped the plans to privatize the airport.

Holland's chief customer by far is Germany, whose unity was a powerful stimulus for Dutch goods and which accounts for 28.7% of exports and 19.6% of imports. Belgium provides 10.8% of its imports and buys 14% of its exports. In all, the EU25 accounts for 75.8% of its exports and 56.9% of its imports. U.S. trade makes up 9.1% of the Netherlands' imports. But the U.S. is Holland's largest source of private foreign investment; a fifth of American (and a third of British) investment in the EU goes to the Netherlands. In fact, the U.S. invests ten times as much in the Netherlands as in China and twice as much as in Mexico. The amount of American dollars per capita invested in the Netherlands is larger than in any other European country. The U.S. has 1,100 companies there, including 42 of the top 50 American Fortune 500.

Energy

The Netherlands must, with a few exceptions, import almost all the raw materials its industries need. It has large salt deposits in the eastern part of the country, and it also is able to produce about 5% of the oil it needs. The principal exception is natural gas. Huge gas reserves were discovered in 1959 in Slochteren in Groningen Province. This became the largest producing gas field in the world and contained about half of all natural gas reserves in Western Europe. Its gas reserves were the world's fifth largest. The Slochteren fields produced 84% of the country's gas, and the remaining 16% came from Holland's continental shelf off shore. It exported about one-half of its gas, which was the country's most valuable source of foreign exchange. As its reserves dipped, it has had to be more sparing with this dwindling treasure.

The proceeds from these exports have not only kept its balance of payments in surplus since 1982, but the government, which claims a 90% share of all gas export income, also derived about 10% of its revenues from this source. In 1980 Holland renegotiated its ten-year gas sales agreements with its Western European customers in order to bring the price more into line with world energy prices.

When the Dutch first discovered their large gas reserves, they decided to exploit them very quickly because they saw that a rapid worldwide conversion to oil was in process. They foresaw the prospect of atomic plants supplying a high percentage of the industrialized world's needs in the future. Therefore, they rapidly converted 90% of Dutch homes and other buildings to gas heat. They also sought to sell their gas quickly while there was still a market for it. Almost all Dutch now regard this decision to have been a very serious mistake.

In the 21st century natural gas accounts for about half of the nation's energy supplies, while oil accounts for 37%, coal 12.6% and nuclear less than 1%; its one nuclear plant produces 4% of its electricity. In order to stretch out their gas supplies at least until the year 2000, the Dutch decided to terminate all gas export contracts in the early 1990s, to limit their own gas use to high-priority needs, such as home heating, and to mandate home insulation and the conversion of industry from gas to coal and oil. They also decided to begin buying gas from abroad, especially from Russia. The government negotiated contracts with Moscow whereby Dutch gas companies would provide assistance in helping it extract gas, which would then be sent to Western Europe.

Oil had to take up the energy slack, a fact which not only damaged Holland's balance of payments, but also made it far more vulnerable to an oil boycott such as the nation faced in 1973–4, when the Arab-

The Netherlands

dominated OPEC nations singled out Holland for its support of Israel. New discoveries in the North Sea enable the Netherlands to supply 20% of its own oil.

The future reliance on oil can be relieved also by increased use of coal and nuclear power. The Netherlands wanted to raise coal's share of electricity generation from the present 5% to 40% by the end of the century. This is made difficult by the fact that since Holland has already shut down its coalmines, most of the coal will have to be imported. Also, coal has a frightening effect on global warming, a pernicious development that threatens the Dutch almost more than any other nation. Holland has two nuclear power plants, but there is strong opposition to nuclear power generation; a 1990 poll showed 85% opposed building new reactors. The Labor Party even advocated the shutdown of the existing plants. With razor-thin majorities, and with the 1986 Chernobyl nuclear accident in the Ukraine still in people's minds, shaky coalitions can seldom afford to touch such hot potatoes. Holland's energy problems will not be alleviated by nuclear power.

Current Economic Situation

Dutch industry faces several problems. The workweek has fallen to 36 hours. Wage costs are very high, and, if one adds employer contributions to social security, wages are on a par with Belgium. Employers must also pay employees a holiday bonus of 8% of their annual pay. Normal wages are not indexed, but pensions and certain benefits are. The trade unions are still moderate, but they are often tempted to seek wage increases that could heat inflation (2% in 2008), and they resist reductions in social welfare benefits.

Despite high wage levels and the maintenance of extensive job protections and cooperation with the unions, unemployment was a remarkable 4.1% in 2008, the lowest in four years and well below the EU average. Part of the success has been the willingness to create incentives to work by lowering unemployment benefits and to make the labor market less rigid by reducing job security and increasing temporary employment. Of all jobs, 15% are temporary (compared with 13% in the U.S. and 30% in Spain).

By deregulating work hours and allowing previously unthinkable part-time work contracts, part-time employment now constitutes 40% of all jobs, the highest proportion in all Europe. Workers with such contracts continue to get benefits like vacation and health insurance, and after six months they begin to accumulate pension rights. Thus the Dutch labor market combines flexibility with protection: workers now accept more uncertainty in

return for the reassurance of welfare assistance if all goes wrong. It is women, 66% of whom work, who are most involved in this kind of work: 61% of working women in 2006 worked only part-time. This helps explain the pay gap between the sexes of 19% to 24%, one of the highest in the EU.

Unlike most European countries, the Netherlands actually created jobs in the late 1990s and early years of the 21st century, and this is a particular boon to younger Dutch. Success is due in part to the Dutch tradition of consultation and cooperation. It is also a small enough country that all the key political, labor and employer figures know each other and can work together. There is hidden unemployment, such as early retirement and disability payments.

At the onset of the 21st century the Netherlands showed some of the healthiest economic indicators in the EU. Half a decade later its economy is strong. In 2008 it was growing by 2% annually, and it achieved a budget surplus of .3% of GDP. Government spending and taxes are sinking. In order to attract foreign investment and improve competitiveness, the Balkanende government lowered corporate taxes from 34.5% to 30% by 2007, close to the EU average. Its national debt, at 51% of GDP in 2004, is stable. Its welfare program has become less generous, but unlike some of its EU partners, it faces no "welfare crisis." The Dutch have already tackled most of the economic problems that are now afflicting other EU states.

CULTURE

No longer a homogeneous country, the Netherlands has a growing nonwhite racial minority. However, except for about 400,000 in the province of Friesland northeast of Amsterdam who speak a German-Dutch language called Frisian and can use it to communicate with the government there, all whites speak Dutch as their mother tongue. Thus, the country avoids the terrible language problems found in neighboring Belgium. At the same time, the Dutch are very open to the world, and most school children learn English, German, and to a lesser extent French and Spanish. Visitors who seek information from or contact with the Dutch are relieved that most Dutch have learned these languages rather well: three-fourths speak at least one foreign language, 44% speak two and 12% three or more.

Holland is a very pluralistic country in which diversity is institutionalized in a way that the Dutch used to call *Verzuiling*, or "columnization." This means the coexistence in political and social life of separate religious organizations which operate

parallel to one another, but which aspire to the same goals. Such columnization is no longer relevant, but diversity still is found in education, the mass media, sports and social clubs. Dutch school children are free to attend either state or private (mainly religious) schools. All are financed by the government although religious schools receive some funding from religious communities.

Primary schooling lasts six years, and 70% of primary school children attend private schools. Secondary school pupils can choose either to go straight into vocational education, which would lead to careers in the trades, services or sales, or into a general secondary education, which paves the way to the university. Approximately 60% of the secondary school pupils attend private schools. Parents can choose their children's public school if they wish, and Dutch schools are permitted to select their pupils. There are 14 universities, four of which are private. Only 3% of Dutch students of university age attend them, compared with approximately 50% in the U.S. Over 70% of university students attend state institutions. Many Dutch attend religious schools from the beginning through the university. Aside from some supervision to ensure minimum standards, the government does not attempt to influence the private schools.

Religion

In the Netherlands religion has always been an important force shaping the national character. The Reformation took seed in Holland and it was the attempt of the Spanish king to re-Catholicize Holland that sparked the Dutch rebellion in the 16th century. It remains a tradition for the Dutch royal family to belong to the Protestant Dutch Reformed Church. When the queen's younger sister Irene left the Netherlands in 1963 to marry Prince Carlos Hugo de Borbon y Parma, a Catholic pretender to the throne of Spain, the very enemy her forefathers fought for almost 100 years, she threw her family and her country into a rage. But in fact, the Netherlands was never thoroughly converted to the Protestant sect of Calvinism. Even today a third of the population is Catholic, 21% Protestant, 5.5% Muslim (rising by almost 4% every year), .5% Hindu, and 40% who profess no belief in religion at all. Still, those observers are to some extent correct when they say that every Dutchman is somewhat a Calvinist.

The Dutch take a moral approach to most human affairs. One sees this in the tone and content of Dutch politics. Moral arguments are invariably made to support many political issues, including social welfare, human rights, nuclear disarmament, environmental protection and aid to

The Netherlands

developing countries. Some political parties are organized around religious principles. Although Dutch voters are less likely than they once were to vote primarily out of religious considerations, political parties often cannot resist the temptation to sprinkle their appeal with biblical messages, even if practical political considerations far outweigh religious ones. Most radio and television organizations and some newspapers have religious affiliations. Further, despite the fact that church and state are officially separated, the school system offers both religious and secular schools, with the state picking up the bill for both; 70% of these schools are privately owned, often nominally religion-based.

Despite their religious and moral approach to many human affairs and despite the religious strife that one still finds in the country, the Dutch have never practiced the kind of intolerance Calvinists practiced in, for example, the Massachusetts Bay Colony. Most of its people continue to practice some of the tolerance toward other ideas and ways of living for which the Dutch were once famous and without

which no democracy can function properly. Some Dutch are increasingly inclined to cast off their tolerance and to attack violently those views they do not accept. For instance, when the pope visited the Netherlands in 1985, he was greeted by bottles, cans, bombs and such obscene chants as "Kill, kill, kill the Pope!" A majority of Dutch Catholics opposes the Vatican's teachings on contraception, abortion, celibacy and the ordination of women, and John Paul had gone to Holland in the first place to heal these divisions.

While religion plays a role in many facets of public life, church attendance is actually falling. The importance of religion in everyday affairs is no longer as great as it once was. Polls in 1987 indicated that 27% of Dutch adults attend church regularly (vs. 14% in the U.K. and 12% in France). The fact that both religions draw believers from all occupations prevents them from being linked closely with any particular social class, as is the case in Northern Ireland.

The churches' influence at election time is also declining. In 1963, for instance, 83% of Catholics voted for the Catholic Peo-

ple's Party, but in 1972, only 38% did. Still, there are fewer interfaith marriages than in most European countries.

The Dutch remain a family-oriented people, who tend to treasure family life and prefer private to public amusement. There is little outright class discrimination. Nevertheless, there is still a large income gap among citizens, and people of different social classes tend not to mix as frequently and as easily as in the U.S.

Diminishing Tolerance for Minorities

Holland was always a land of refuge. It absorbed religious refugees from England, Belgium and France, and Jews from Spain and Portugal. In fact, because of the tolerant and relatively enlightened and prosperous conditions inside the Netherlands, the Dutch never poured out of their country and colonized foreign lands in great numbers. Presently almost 20% of the population is visibly different ethnically from the native Dutch. The percentage in Rotterdam is one-half, and in Amsterdam, The Hague and certain other large cities it is one-third.

When Indonesia won its independence from the Netherlands, many people of Indonesian ancestry came to Holland and assimilated rather well. Exceptions were the 15,000 South Moluccans, Christians who had fought with the Dutch army. They had been promised autonomy, but the new Indonesian ruler, Sukarno, forbade this. They could not get along with the new regime and were permitted to resettle in Holland. Their community has since more than doubled to 40,000.

When Suriname became independent in 1975, more than 140,000 Surinamese, who were Dutch citizens, left their newly freed country to go to Holland. The Dutch did almost nothing to stop or discourage them until the 1980s. Referring to these Surinamese, who now number 180,000, one Dutch clergyman spoke for many of his countrymen when he said, "they are here because we were there." The Netherlands continued to provide $1.5 billion of aid to Suriname annually. Surinamese and immigrants from the Netherlands Antilles continue to enter Holland.

In the 1960s when the labor-starved Dutch economy was in desperate need of more workers, thousands of guest workers poured in from the Mediterranean area, primarily from Turkey, Morocco, Spain and Italy. They concentrated in the cities of Rotterdam, Amsterdam and The Hague, and today Dutch talk openly about "black schools" and "black zones," referring to schools and neighborhoods where nonwhites are in the majority. The majority of the children under age 14 in the three largest cities are of "non-Western background," mostly Muslim. Half the prison

The Netherlands

population is comprised of ethnic minorities. These facts put wind in the sails of politicians like the late Pim Fortuyn, who helped break down the traditional political correctness about tolerance and the multiculturalism among all the mainstream parties except the Green-Left. Their insistence that newcomers integrate into Dutch society, learn the Dutch language, and realize that they cannot recreate their old lives at government expense in the midst of one of the world's richest nations has become official government policy.

Immigrant minorities are not on an economic or social par with the Dutch. The percentage of low-income households is three times higher among immigrants than native Dutch. Unemployment is also two to three times higher among these groups. In the 21st century the gulf between immigrants and native Dutch is widening. Nevertheless, immigrants have a higher economic standard of living in the Netherlands than in many other European countries. There is no immigrant underclass and no real ghettos, and some enter the middle class.

The Dutch government bends over backwards to serve them if they stay. More than 40% of immigrants receive some form of government assistance. This is a source of resentment among Dutch tax-payers. Mobile caravan schools have been organized for gypsy children, and all minorities are entitled to the same social welfare benefits as are the native Dutch. The Dutch Broadcasting Foundation beams television shows in five languages with subtitles. Since 1986 'outlanders' (as the resident foreigners are called) are permitted to vote or run for office in municipal elections. A 1998 survey on racism in Europe revealed that about a third of Dutch admit to being "racist" or "fairly racist." This regrettable statistic was nevertheless far below that in Belgium (55%) and France (48%).

The earlier Labor government claimed in 2002 that its tightening of the rules, especially on asylum, had cut the numbers of new arrivals by 25%. The center-right Balkenende government created a ministry of immigration and integration and tightened restrictions even further. They included admitting fewer immigrants and making it more difficult for ethnic minorities to bring a partner from their home country. Between 1997 and 2001 half the immigrants who entered the country had arranged for a spouse or family to follow. "Marriage migration" is a concern since 60% to 70% of second-generation Moroccans and Turks marry somebody from outside the Netherlands; this impedes integration.

Those seeking permanent residency have to pay in advance for a compulsory course on integration, and the sum is re-imbursed only upon completion of the course. Newcomers must take about 600 hours of "culture classes." To receive a passport immigrants must demonstrate competency in the Dutch language. Illegal immigrants' home countries were put on notice that they would not be eligible for Dutch development aid if they refuse to take back subjects whom the Netherlands had refused asylum. Those whose applications were rejected face criminal charges if they remain in the country.

Further steps were taken in 2006. An entrance examination tests whether applicants can speak some Dutch and are aware of the country's liberal values, even if they do not agree with all of them. Citizens of EU countries and of certain democratic states, such as the U.S., are not required to take it. The exam costs 350 euros and the preparation kit for it an additional 60 euros. The government produced a two-hour movie, "To the Netherlands," showing, among other things, women bathing nude and two men kissing. Its purpose is to cause applicants to ponder whether they really would fit into one of the world's most permissive countries. In response to fierce criticism, a blander film was released, with bare breasts and kissing deleted.

Many Dutch have never come to terms with the reality that the Netherlands has become an immigrant and multicultural country. A social worker in Utrecht admitted that "as much as we are called a multicultural city, we are living next to each other, and not with each other." Holland's 20% visible ethnic minorities are a higher percentage than in France or Britain. About half the nonwestern population was born in the Netherlands.

Approximately 5.5% (over one million and rising) of the total population is Muslim; the figure rises to 13.2% in Amsterdam and more than 10% in both Rotterdam and The Hague. It is estimated that by 2020 ethnic minorities will constitute the majority in the four largest cities: Amsterdam, The Hague, Rotterdam and Utrecht. Their birth rate is double that of native Dutch. Most come from the poorer parts of Turkey and Morocco, and the majority has citizenship. Two-thirds said in a 2005 poll that they would not want their daughters to marry a non-Muslim. Most take spouses from their home country, thereby delaying integration by a generation or more. Islam is a religion that now outnumbers Calvinism in the Netherlands. Polls in Amsterdam in 2007 revealed that more residents identify with Islam (12%) than with Catholicism or Protestantism combined. A minority of Muslim children attend 37 Islamic schools, financed by the state in the Dutch tradition.

The secret service recognizes that al-Qaeda is succeeding in recruiting young Muslims in mosques, cafes and prisons in the Netherlands for a "holy war" against the U.S. and its allies. In 2002 two men were accused in a Rotterdam trial of plotting to attack the American embassy in Paris. A year later Dutch authorities arrested an accomplice in a plot to send militants to Iraq for suicide attacks against U.S. forces. Nervous Dutch authorities requested the U.S. in 2003 to move its embassy from the middle of The Hague for security reasons.

In November 2004 the nation was given a horrible shock by a second political murder in only two years. Theo van Gogh, a provocative film director and distant relative of the famous 19th century Dutch painter, was murdered in Amsterdam in broad daylight while riding his bicycle to work. A 26-year-old Dutch Moroccan, Mohammed Bouyeri, emptied a magazine of bullets into Van Gogh's body, then slit his throat and left a note with verses from the Koran and threats to other Dutch stuck to his lifeless body with a knife. The murderer was wounded in the leg and apprehended after a shoot-out with the police. This crime has been called the "Dutch September 11."

In July 2005 Bouyeri was given a life sentence, the first person to be convicted of terrorism in the Netherlands since its anti-terror laws were toughened in August 2004. Claiming to be waging a holy war against the "enemies of Islam," he said he dreamed of replacing the Dutch government with an Islamic theocracy and that he was supported by a network of like-minded fanatics. He rejected the validity of the Dutch legal system, admitted guilt, showed no remorse, and swore he would do the same again if he were ever freed. The most frightening thing about Bouyeri was that he had not been a victim of social exclusion. He had been a good student, spoke good Dutch, and was active in community affairs before falling in with extremist elements.

This grisly act of intolerance by a religious fanatic who had Dutch citizenship has convinced many Dutch that building a multicultural society has failed. This comes on top of a longer-term Dutch backlash that had fueled the spectacular rise of Pim Fortuyn, who was also gunned down in the street. Nine other Islamic radicals were tried and convicted in March 2006.

Twelve more suspects from a radical Islamist cell, the Hofstad group, which had compiled a death list of Dutch politicians, were arrested a day after the van Gogh murder. Hundreds of police had conducted a 14-hour standoff. Two were jailed for 15 and 13 years for throwing a hand grenade at police officers, wounding five. The 30-man cell is mostly composed of second- or third-generation Dutch Muslims of Moroccan origin, but two were Dutch-American converts. Police uncovered plans for blowing up Schiphol airport, the Dutch parliament, the headquarters of the General Intelligence and Security Service and one of the country's nuclear reactors. A number of the arrested had trained in Pakistan to carry out armed attacks. In the days after the van Gogh murder, there were attacks on Muslim sites. An Islamic elementary school in Eindhoven was bombed and two mosques burned. Prime Minister Balkenende visited a Turkish mosque in a show of solidarity.

Van Gogh, an outspoken critic of Islam, especially its treatment of women, had directed a film, "Submission," for Dutch TV. It featured a Muslim woman in a see-through *burqa* (robe) telling a story of abuse within her marriage. Text from the Koran condoning family violence was written on her naked body.

The script for the film had been written by an outspoken Somali refugee, Ayaan Hirsi Ali. She was a member of parliament who had to live for a while within the protected confines of a naval base to avoid murder. When she could finally live in a normal apartment, a court ordered her to move out after neighbors complained that her presence brought them into danger. She said she had entered parliament in order to highlight the oppression of immigrant women and to make politicians aware that key aspects of Islamic doctrine, as practiced today, are incompatible with an open society. Among her parliamentary goals was to outlaw honor crimes. She became a symbol for resistance to Muslim fundamentalism.

In May 2006 her life in the Netherlands faced a crisis. A TV documentary about her highlighted some embarrassing facts that she had already long since admitted publicly, including when she was vetted for parliament. Coached by groups helping immigrants, she had lied in her 1992 asylum application about the route she had taken, her real name, and her true date of birth. She still insists that she had come under duress, to flee an arranged marriage to a cousin from Canada.

Her political ally, friend, and party colleague, Rita ("Iron Rita") Verdonk, the tough former immigration minister decided she had to be even-handed. She withdrew Ali's citizenship and ordered her to leave the country. Ali abruptly resigned from parliament and a day later announced that she would accept a position in Washington at the conservative think tank, American Enterprise Institute (AEI).

The expulsion order set off a political storm. Parliamentarians of all parties were enraged and held an all-night session to demand Verdonk to back off. After a further grilling from parliament, reprimands by cabinet members, and an order from the prime minister that her citizenship be restored, Verdonk relented. Ali's citizenship was returned to her, but the entire trauma caused the breakup of the governing coalition. The Hirsi Ali affair especially embarrassed the Dutch because it make them look both cowardly and anti-immigrant.

For more than a year, the Dutch government paid $4 million for her personal protection while in Washington. But when the U.S. granted her permanent residency, that assistance ended. The U.S. could not provide it, and the French government rejected her request for citizenship. But Paris promised to support her appeal to the EU for round-the-clock protection in America. She finds herself in an unenviable dilemma.

Another parliamentarian, Geert Wilders, had to go into hiding. He has six bodyguards and often sleeps in a protected prison cell with no windows. He noted: "The people who threaten us are walking around free and we are the captives." This kind of security is something entirely new for Dutch politicians. A soaring number of politicians, academics and public figures have been compelled to go into hiding or accept 24-hour protection after receiving assassination threats. Elsewhere in Europe, Muslim terrorists unsettle the societies through indiscriminate attacks. In the Netherlands they single out individuals for assassination.

In the opinion of Amsterdam's left-wing mayor Job Cohen, firebrands like Wilders are reaping what they have sown and are largely responsible for the situation that fear and suspicion among ethnic groups in the country are at a postwar peak. Wilders is an outspoken critic of radical Islam and immigrants, and radical Arab internet sites call for his beheading.

He made everybody nervous when he announced in 2007 that he was producing a film that compares the Koran to Hitler's book, *Mein Kampf*. He said the 15-minute film, entitled "Fitna" (meaning "civic strife" in Arabic), shows how the Koran inspires people "to do the worst things." The Dutch government tried but failed to persuade him not to broadcast it; warnings had come from all over the Muslim world. Since no television station would air the film, he temporarily put it on the internet until the servers bowed to threats and took it off. It portrays Islam as a ticking time bomb aimed at the West, and it shows beheadings, violence against women, anti-Semitic tirades by imams,

Rembrandt, self-portrait

and the aftermath of the New York and Madrid terrorist bombings, including charred remains of victims. The clips are alternated with images of Koranic verses purporting to saw where the inspiration for such acts come. It opens and closes with the same image of Mohammed with bombs in his turban published by a Danish cartoonist in 2005.

He has radical suggestions: stopping all Muslim immigration, banning the Koran and the construction of mosques, and giving the one-million Muslims in the Netherlands the choice of "going to their own countries" or renouncing their religion. He also proposed a general ban on wearing burqas, but the government decided that this would violate the freedom of religion guaranteed by the constitution. However, it did prohibit the wearing of burqas and full-face veils at schools and government work places. Wilders publicly questioned the loyalty of two cabinet members with dual citizenship (Turkish and Moroccan, in addition to Dutch).

The goal now is integration, meaning that the time has come for the growing Muslim minority (40% of whom come from Turkey and 34% from Morocco) to adjust to where they live and adopt Dutch values. The price for living in this open, law-governed society is to acknowledge the right of others to think differently. This conviction has entered the political mainstream.

More and more Dutch citizens feel threatened by the immigrant presence and the terrorist threat, and politicians have taken note of this. Laws were introduced permitting authorities to close mosques, confiscate Dutch passports from dual citizens, and deport radical imams (clergymen). Many demand that in the near future all imams be Dutch-educated. Uni-

The Netherlands

versities are given subsidies to create theology departments that train Muslim prayer leaders. The education ministry now requires that any school (meaning Muslim school) that is opened must prove that it intends to transmit the values of Dutch society.

This comes at a time when Dutch are worrying about a general weakening of their social cohesion, symbolized in many minds by the omnipresence of immigrants. How far should liberal societies tolerate the intolerant? It is perhaps not surprising that half of Dutch respondents in a 2006 poll had a dislike of Islam, and 43% thought Islam is not a peaceful religion. But some political figures are calling on Muslim groups to accept the liberal Dutch society they live in or be forced to do so.

Sexual Tolerance

The hallmark of modern Netherlands has become to acknowledge common practices and to decriminalize them. An example is prostitution, which has long been legalized. However, brothels were not. In 2000 parliament passed a law making the 2,000 brothels legal and subjecting them to government regulation and regular inspections. A job category for the 30,000 registered prostitutes was created: "freelance workers." They have employment rights and the right to establish a trade union, a process that began in 2001. Not all "sex workers" like their new legal status because they have to pay taxes.

In 2007 the Amsterdam city government strong-armed Charlie Geerts, the property magnate known as the "Emperor of Sex", to sell his third of the city's famed red-light district windows and to convert the buildings into public housing. The mayor explained that prostitution, which will remain legal, attracts money laundering and other criminal activity; he wants to gentrify the area. City councilwoman Karina Schaapman, herself a former prostitute, calls the popular tourist district "a cesspit. There's a lot of exploiting of women and a lot of social distress. That's nothing to be proud of."

Homosexuals in the Netherlands have wider civil rights than anywhere in Europe. Since 1999 they could register their partnerships in a civil ceremony and receive almost the same rights and obligations as heterosexual couples. In 2000 the Netherlands became the first country in the world to allow same-sex couples to marry on the same terms as heterosexuals. They can take each other's surname, inherit their property, receive alimony, enjoy the same tax status, and opt for prenuptial agreements. The restriction that a homosexual couple may adopt only a Dutch child, not one from abroad, was lifted in 2005. As many as 8% of all marriages are of the same sex. In 2006 the Dutch ambassador to Estonia was transferred to Montreal when he complained that his black Cuban male partner suffered racist and homophobic abuse on the streets of Tallinn.

The Netherlands is also the first country to experience gay divorces, which must be obtained in court and which sometimes result in alimony payments. Polls indicate that most Dutch support these reforms, and it has ceased being a contentious issue. In the words of one of the bill's sponsors, Boris Dittrich: "A person's sex is not important for marriage."

Euthanasia

Another case of legalizing what has been long-standing practice is euthanasia. Passive euthanasia (halting life support systems to allow natural death) was long permitted, and doctors in the 1990s were virtually never prosecuted for assisting in thousands of suicides of terminally ill patients. In 1995, for the first time, a physician was found guilty of murder for ending the life of a deformed newborn who was unable to ask explicitly that a doctor do so. But as a sign of how torn even judges were over this issue, the court ruled that the doctor's actions were justifiable under the Netherlands' tolerant euthanasia laws and refused to punish him.

The Netherlands moved toward permitting voluntary euthanasia ("mercy killing" through fatal injections to hopelessly ill patients); 80% involve cancer patients. Only 3.5% of deaths (ca. 5,000 per year) are mercy killings, a number that is stabilizing. Polls have long indicated that three out of four Dutch support this, although

Coffee shop, not to be confused with cafe (a bar) or coffee house (for coffee and tea).

Photo by Juliet Bunch

184

the practice remains ethically troubling and controversial. Dutch courts stopped prosecuting and jailing doctors who, according to a 1993 law (the first of its kind in an industrialized nation), followed a detailed 28-point checklist: the patient had to be terminally ill and in a clear state of mind, and he or she, not family or friends, had to have asked repeatedly to die. A second opinion had to be obtained. A 2005 study showed that of all the requests for euthanasia, nearly half are carried out, in a fourth the patient died before it could be done, 13% changed their mind, and physicians refused in 12% of the cases.

In 2000 euthanasia and assisted suicide were decriminalized under certain circumstances: A patient need not be actually dying. People over age 16 who suffer acute and unremitting pain may ask to die (parents may decide for sufferers under age 16). Doctors are not allowed to recommend suicide as an option and must inform the patient of all other alternatives known. They must get a second medical opinion and be sure that the patient's request is well considered and that he has acted voluntarily. In 2001, the Netherlands became the first country in the world to legalize mercy killing for terminally ill persons with "lasting and unbearable suffering" with no hope of improvement, as long as the volunteer's doctor and an independent consultant approve.

Drug Policies

In the early 1970s, the Dutch had another opportunity to show their toleration when Amsterdam became the favorite destination for longhaired, guitar-toting young people who were called at the time "hippies," as well as other younger people with different lifestyles. While these young people horrified the established citizens almost everywhere they went, the Dutch accepted them with good humor and tried hard to find them temporary shelter and areas where they could meet freely. They also tried to look the other way when the visitors chose to use "soft" drugs or violate the sexual standards of Dutch society.

By the mid-1980s, though, Dutch patience with hard drug trafficking and crime in Amsterdam had visibly begun to wear thin, and neighborhood vigilante groups were organized to protect against lawbreakers. On the whole, the crime rate remains low compared with the U.S. and many other European countries. But street crime has increased dramatically. Some politicians suggest that judges hand out sentences that are too lenient. In 1986, for instance, a punker who stabbed to death a young man outside a disco was sentenced to four years in prison, two of which were suspended. Dutch jails are

The Netherlands

known throughout Europe to be the hardest to enter and the easiest to leave. Even hardened criminals in prisons are permitted to vote and to have overnight visits with their families, girlfriends or homosexual partners in special rooms with complete privacy. Two-thirds of all prisoners are hard drug addicts, which points to a further problem.

Polls in 1996 showed that only 5% of the population uses cannabis regularly. It is still illegal to sell it without state supervision, but possession has been decriminalized. The state taxes the profits from the sale of cannabis, and police put the lowest priority on preventing its sale and use in small amounts. Marijuana is so tolerated that 782 coffee shops put it on their menus and serve it to customers. The number of such coffee shops has declined by a third since 1997 as a result of tougher enforcement of the rules. In 2003 the Netherlands became the first country to make cannabis available as a prescription drug if it is approved by doctors to alleviate acute pain after conventional treatments had been exhausted or if other drugs had negative side effects.

There are some legal problems. Dutch law prohibits substances that have been "processed." Does that include mushrooms merely if they have been dried? Authorities are well practiced at turning a blind eye. When ecstasy tablets became popular in the 1980s, they were declared illegal. But the police were told to ignore consumption and to try to curb manufacturing.

Uncomfortable with its reputation as being soft on drug users, Dutch authorities cracked down on the larger-scale commercialization of soft drugs. Neighboring countries put pressure on the Dutch government to enforce stricter laws on drugs. The German government once blamed it for the vast amount of drugs crossing the German border. The Netherlands was sensitive to those concerns. Cafe owners were put on notice not to call attention to their wares, deal in carryout quantities, sell more than a sixth of an ounce at a time, or sell cocaine and heroin under the counter. Coffee shops caught selling cannabis to children under age 18 are to be shut down. The Balkenende government pledged in 2002 to enforce the criteria governing the coffee shops more strictly and not to allow them to be located close to schools or the national borders. One earlier justice ministry spokeswoman had commented: "We want just enough to cater to our own citizens, not to the drug tourists." In 2006 a pilot program to regulate marijuana farming on the model of tobacco was introduced in Maastricht.

Police are cracking down on drug dealing at highway rest stops and parking ar-

eas. They have especially gone after the traffic in hard drugs, even though users are not arrested unless they commit other crimes. Such tolerance had been extended to ecstasy use. Although the country produces an estimated 80% of the world's supply, its trafficking and manufacturing are illegal. The government in 2002 pledged a crackdown on ecstasy, summarizing its tougher approach toward drugs: "The production of and trade in drugs in the Netherlands has reached unacceptable levels and must be tackled more firmly." Authorities believed that their tolerating soft drugs was responsible for the decline in the percentage of young people using hard drugs from 14% in the 1980s to only 1.6% in 1997, compared with 3% in Italy, 2.8% in France, and 1.5% in Germany.

Addicts are steered into treatment and are provided with clean new needles to prevent AIDS. In 2000 only 10% of AIDS victims in the Netherlands were intravenous drug users, compared with nearly 40% across Europe. The publicly visible use of drugs has caused some Dutch to wonder if their country has indeed become too permissive. Ed van Thijn, former mayor of Amsterdam, confessed that "in the past 15 years tolerance became synonymous with permissiveness and softness on law-and-order." In 1990, the Washington-based Drugs Policy Foundation awarded the Dutch government a prize for "its effective and humanitarian drug policies." Said one senior Amsterdam policeman: "We do not say that our way is right for them [Americans], but we are sure it is right for us." Nevertheless, in the 21st century more and more European countries are inclined to follow the Dutch lead in this matter and to turn away from America's more militant "war" on drugs.

The Dutch, as a people, are inclined to cling to tradition and to be conservative. At the same time, they are open to new ideas and are relatively tolerant toward all forms of individualism. This is why criticism and protest can be so firmly entrenched in the Dutch tradition, but why the Dutch are at the same time not inclined to be revolutionary. Compromise is a highly developed art in the Netherlands, and protest groups have often been smothered by tolerance. It saps one's strength to beat one's head against a richly padded, sympathetic wall.

Media and Arts

"Columnization" is also found in the press and electronic media. Newspapers and magazines reflect the opinions of many diverse groups in society, and the average reader expects to find his own opinions expressed in the news he reads. Financial problems have resulted in the

concentration of most newspapers in the hands of a few large companies, although 60% of the dailies still manage to take an independent editorial line. To help preserve their independence the government provides financial support to newspapers and magazines that are undergoing reorganization to become profitable again. The major dailies, in order of circulation, are *De Telegraaf* (conservative, now with a Sunday edition), *Algemeen Dagblad* (neutral), *De Volkskrant* (progressive), *Het Parool*, (center-left) and *Trouw* (Protestant). Top people tend to prefer the *NRC-Handelsblad* (liked by intellectuals) and the *Financieele Dagblad*. The number one magazines are *Elseviers Magazine*, *Elseviers Weekblad*, followed by *Vrij Nederland*. In a 2002 study by the professional group, Reporters Without Borders, the Netherlands ranked third in the world after Finland and Iceland in terms of press freedom. The U.S. placed 17th.

There are three public television channels, which have difficulties competing with commercial channels. There is a public educational and cultural channel (Nederland 3), and five public radio stations. Also on the air are 400 local radio stations, including a handful that broadcast legally from abroad, especially Luxembourg. Commercial TV channels have operated since 1992. Programming is in the hands of both the state and a variety of private broadcasting organizations that largely operate free of government control. Some of these organizations represent the basic pillars of society. For instance, KRO is Catholic, NCRV is Protestant, VPRO is liberal Protestant and VARA is socialist. Unlike many newspapers, however, the broadcasting companies attempt to broaden their appeals to include all social groups. They are, therefore, actually able to overcome some of the cleavages in Dutch society.

These four private organizations operate within the framework established by the government-related Netherlands Broadcasting Association (NOS). The NOS, a quasi-governmental broadcasting foundation, is charged with producing programs "in the general interest," such as news bulletins. The ministry of welfare, health and culture is the authority that oversees its operations. The postal service, privatized in 1989, no longer collects fees to finance broadcasting; it is paid out of taxes. The NOS also controls the amount of advertising that may be broadcast.

When one thinks of Dutch culture, perhaps the first words that come to mind are the names of painters: Hieronymus Bosch, with his powerful and sometimes terrifying scenes, brought to European art in the 16th century a form of symbolism which reflected the mind of a great vision-

The Netherlands

Johannes Vermeer, Girl with a Pearl Earring　　　**Mauritshuis, The Hague**

The Dutch consider art to be so important for the society that they maintain, at public expense, some 3,000 artists who are unable to make a living. Although they must demonstrate that they are full-time and professionally trained artists with talent, once they are selected they merely have to deliver a modest number of paintings each year to the state in return for their pay.

Most of the paintings go into storage and are never seen again. Some critics argue that this subsidy lowers the quality of painting and is merely an example of the welfare state run wild, and these funds have been heavily cut. The government also helps to finance experimental theater, orchestra, ballet and film companies. Over 4% of the central government's budget is devoted to supporting the arts. Even Dutch businesses are financing a variety of artistic groups from jazz to chamber music artists in order to improve their image with customers.

Historically, Holland is rich with philosophical and intellectual leaders. Hugo Grotius founded the study of international law. René Descartes, a Frenchman who was living in the Netherlands, developed a new starting point for philosophy when he asserted, "I think, therefore I am." Baruch Spinoza wrote treatises on the relationships between the human intellect, the state and religious belief. Anton van Leeuwenhoek invented the microscope that thereby revolutionized the study of biology. Christian Huygens invented the pendulum clock, and the Dutch have been a very punctual people ever since.

There are more than 22 million people inside and outside the Netherlands who speak native Dutch, and as many as 35 million can read Dutch literature in the original. The Foundation for Promoting the Translation of Dutch Literature seeks to introduce the nation's writings abroad. Before the 16th century, literature was primarily composed of plays, religious literature, folk tales and stories of chivalry. In the 17th century, Joost van den Vondel's writings were read all over Europe. The most noted author of the 19th century was Multatuli (pseudonym for Douwes Dekker), who worked in the colonies and observed the mistreatment of the native populations. His 1860 novel, *Max Havelaar*, attacked colonialism. The works of novelist Louis Couperus evoke the atmosphere of the turn of the century. After 1945, Holland rapidly lost its rural character. The postwar literature of such younger writers as Jan Wolkers, W.F. Hermans, Harry Mulisch and G.K. van't Reve often deals with the problems arising from life in a highly urban and industrial society.

ary. In the 17th century, Rembrandt, Franz Hals and Jan Vermeer established an artistic tradition through their vivid depiction of early Dutch life. In the 19th century J.B. Jongkind became a precursor of impressionism, and Vincent van Gogh, in a short but wild life, helped create the romantic picture that many people have of artists. He sketched the drab and dreary life of persons living in working-class and rural areas in the late 19th century, going later to Paris and southern France where he established his personal style of short brushstrokes in brilliant colors, which pointed the way to a new, expressive style. The Netherlands has almost 1,000 museums, with 42 in Amsterdam alone.

In the Dutch artistic tradition of accurately recording the landscape around them, Hendrick Willem Mesdag painted in 1880 the world's largest panoramic painting, portraying Scheveningen, a fishing village on the outskirts of The Hague. Displayed in a museum in The Hague, called the "Panorama Mesdag," the painting completely surrounds the viewer and gives him the most vivid possible impression of Holland in Mesdag's time. Piet Mondrian, the greatest and most consistent renovator of modern Dutch art of the 20th century, began with experimental nature paintings, but gradually he departed from nature and sought harmonious and universal images. His paintings of lines and colors are among the world's most treasured modern art works. Willem De Kooning and M.C. Escher also enjoy worldwide fame.

The Netherlands

FUTURE

The legendary Dutch tolerance and consensus orientation have become frayed. The "polder model," the popular name for the practice of policymaking by consensus between government, employers and trade unions, is no longer what it was. Political correctness has weakened. More and more Dutch are willing to support politicians who openly defy the old rules of the game and speak publicly of problems on many voters' minds, such as crime, immigration and terrorism.

Conservative Prime Minister Peter Jan Balkenende's coalition government collapsed after the country was cast into an emotional immigration debate after the renunciation in June 2006 of Hirsi Ali's citizenship, a former refugee who had a seat in parliament. That debate continues as she desperately seeks personal protection abroad. The prime minister could count on the contentment of the Dutch, which has prevented any prime minister from being voted out of office since 1973. He emerged from the November elections with a kind of grand coalition with

Labor and the fast-growing Christian Union.

The Dutch feel less comfortable about an enlarged EU, but parliament can be expected to approve the new Lisbon Treaty, which replaces the failed EU constitution that voters rejected in 2005. They are also less liberal toward any person who does not share their notion of liberalism. Nevertheless, they are optimistic about their future. With the economy buzzing, 95% told pollsters they were happy with their lives and more confident than most Europeans about their economic prospects.

NORTH SEA

NETHERLANDS

Ostende

Bruges

ANTWERP

Antwerp

Ghent

WEST-FLANDERS

EAST-FLANDERS

LIMBURG

GERMANY

FLEMISH BRABANT

Brussels

Leuven

Kortrijk

Tongeren

Ronse

Waterloo

Liège

WALLON BRABANT

Meuse R.

LIEGE

FRANCE

HAINAUT

Mons

Charleroi

Namur

Sambre R.

NAMUR

N

0   10   20 Miles

LUXEMBOURG

Bastogne

LUXEMBOURG

"The Language Line" — Dutch-language area in the north (Flanders), and French-language area to the south (Wallonia).

Ardennes Forest

German-speaking areas (in the province of Liège).

Area: 18,991 sq. mi. (30,562 sq. km., somewhat larger than Maryland and about 200 miles or 320 km. wide, taken from its northwest to southeast points).

Population: 10.54 million (6 million in Flanders, 3.4 million in Wallonia, .95 million in Brussels, 2007).

Capital City: Brussels (Pop. 950,000, estimated).

Climate: Temperate, with rather mild winters and comfortable summers.

Neighboring Countries: Germany (East); the Netherlands (North); France (South); Luxembourg (Southeast); England is about 54 miles (87 km.) away across the English Channel.

Official Languages: Dutch (59%), French (40%). Both languages are spoken by about 10%, principally those living in and around Brussels, 80% of whose citizens are native French speakers. German is the native tongue for 1%.

Principal Religion: Roman Catholic (95%).

Main Exports: Chemicals, transport equipment, machinery, food and animal products. Also 70% of the world's cobalt, 60% of the world's diamond dealing and 40% of cutting.

Main Imports: Chemicals, machinery, transport equipment, food and animals.

Major Trading Customers: EU25 (76.3% of exports and 73.4% of imports), Germany (17% of exports and 15.8% of imports), France (17.6% of exports and 12.8% of imports), Netherlands (12.4% of exports and 21.1% of imports), UK (8.1% of exports and 7.1% of imports).

Currency: Euro.

National Day: July 21st.

Chief of State: His Majesty King Albert II (b. 1934). Ascended the throne on August 9, 1993. Married Paola Ruffo di Calabria (Italy), 1959.

Heir Apparent: His Royal Highness Prince Philippe (b. 1960).

Head of Government: Prime Minister Yves Leterme (March 2008).

National Flag: Vertical stripes of red, yellow and black, with the black stripe at the pole.

In some ways Belgium is a very unnatural country. It has no natural frontiers, such as a mountain chain or wide river, to set it off from its neighbors. It has therefore always been very vulnerable to foreign invasion. Belgians have no common language and are extremely sensitive about being forced to speak the one not used in their half of the country. Their tradition as a unified country is only a century and three-quarters old and is too weak to give its citizens a strong common identity. Unlike the Swiss, many Belgians never really devel-

Belgium

Market Square in Bruges

oped the habit of thinking in terms of a single nation.

It sometimes seems that there are just six million Dutch–speaking Flemings and four million French–speaking Walloons, who must try very hard to live with each other. Unfortunately, the forces that once held them together—Roman Catholicism, economic and political opposition to the Dutch—are no longer strong. Belgium appears almost like a shotgun wedding—like a hopelessly broken marriage which held together only because the partners could find no other place to live. Walloons, who bitterly oppose a break-up of the country because their economy depends so heavily on government subsidies, feel like the wife who fears that her husband is about to run out on her.

Parties that preach language radicalism are still being defeated at the polls. Economic performance and stable government, as well as language issues, are important in Belgians' minds. This is baffling to political scientists. Belgium may be the only dysfunctional state in the world that is both stable and prosperous and in which government services are efficient. Belgians have many trumps in their hands as they face the future. They are rather cautious, conservative people, a fact that causes some critics to call Belgium a private, family–centered country.

It also means that while their conflicts are often verbally bitter and serious and sometimes erupt in street brawls between the rare hotheads, Belgians are very unlikely to resort to outright violence and terror to accomplish their goals. They have always shown a genius for compromise by very small steps. Thus, no one expects the community problems, as the language issue is called, to explode into a bloody and tragic Northern Ireland–style conflict. However, they can still cause a government to collapse and can prevent a new government from being formed ten whole months after elections are held, as was the case in 2007-8. The divide is beginning to sound permanent. Given this ongoing crisis, one can no longer be certain that Belgium will remain a unified country. The country's motto, "Strength Through Unity" sounds hollow these days. In a September 2007 poll, over 60% of all Flemings and 40% of Walloons said they thought Belgium would not exist in another decade; close to half of the Flemings already favor that outcome.

It still has many valuable economic resources. It has a very skilled work force with a proven willingness to work. Its economy remains highly productive; this has usually kept inflation low and has maintained for Belgians one of the highest standards of living in the world. Its central location in Europe remains a very significant trading advantage for the country. It is an important partner in a unified Europe and in the Atlantic Alliance, and its capital city, Brussels, is in many ways the "capital of Europe," housing the headquarters for both NATO and the EU.

One in three residents of Brussels is now non–Belgian. There are an estimated 30,000 foreign EU bureaucrats (dubbed "Eurocrats"), diplomats, journalists, lob-

Belgium in NATO

byists and their families in Brussels and perhaps another 15,000 Europeans whose jobs are linked to the EU. Such massive presence and the decision to hold all European summits in Brussels starting in 2002 have prompted the European Commission to consider declaring the city the "capital of Europe." Some countries, including the United States, even send three ambassadors to this city: one to the king of the Belgians (i.e. to the government), one to NATO and one to the EU.

Belgium is a picturesque country with scenery varying from Gothic medieval university cities to countless towns and villages located along winding rivers with steep bluffs. The country is mainly flat, but it rises toward the south, away from the North Sea coast and toward the Ardennes Forest. The country can be divided roughly into three geographic parts. In the North is the Flemish plain, which extends westward from a 41-mile (60 km.) North Sea coastline, with its sandy beaches and luxurious and expensive resorts. Flanders presents a pastoral landscape with small farms and most of Belgium's agricultural production. With 59% of the Belgian population, it is the most densely populated part of the country which itself is the second most densely populated land in all Europe, behind the Netherlands. Here are the Flemish cities of Bruges (with its many bridges which gave the city its name), Ghent and Antwerp, all three towns filled with cathedrals and other medieval structures. Most of Belgium's newer industries are located in Flanders, which is the country's most economically dynamic section, a fact that greatly riles the Walloons today.

At the center of Belgium are rolling fields of grain and many villages with houses grouped around the parish church. In the middle is Brussels, and below it are heavy industrial centers, clustered around the formerly rich Walloon coalfields, which are now largely exhausted and closed. This was the area of the country's industrial revolution in the 19th century, which occurred in Belgium earlier than almost anywhere else in Europe. It is where such industrial cities as Mons, Charleroi and the ancient and dignified city of Liège are located. South of the Sambre and Meuse rivers is the third area, with no large cities or industries. It is a region of fields and pastures with woods thickening as one travels southward into the Ardennes Forest.

Running west to east just south of Kortrijk, Ronse, Brussels, Leuven (Louvain) and Tongeren is an invisible line established 1,500 years ago and now of far greater significance for contemporary Belgium than the geographic areas mentioned above. This is the language line that separates the Flemings from the Walloons. Along the German border is also the German–speaking minority numbering about 64,500 people. Because most Belgians live on "their" side of the language line, they have fewer language problems, now that Flemish (a language which differs from Dutch about as much as American from British English), French or German is used exclusively in all affairs, including education, law, government and business, within each respective region.

The people in the various sections do not look or act very differently, although some observers claim to notice differences in the people's characters—the Flemings being severe and serious and the Walloons being more outgoing, volatile and fun–loving. In fact, the visitor would scarcely notice any difference at all if it were not for the fact that he hears different languages spoken on the streets and sees different languages on street signs and on billboards. The language separation is greatly complicated by the capital city of Brussels, which has 11% (1 million) of the country's population, 80% of whom speak French as a mother tongue. This city is situated uncomfortably north of the language line and is surrounded by Flemish speakers. It is over the hurdle of Brussels that all proponents of regional language reform have tripped. If Belgium ultimately holds together, it may very well be because of Brussels: with its 11% of the population and 20% of the country's GDP, it is simply too entangled to unravel.

One would not expect language difficulties to trouble this small, cosmopolitan country which is located at the very crossroads of Europe and which has been one of the most persistent and constructive proponents of European integration. But it is exactly this problem that has caused many people to wonder how many more birthdays this country will be able to celebrate.

HISTORY

Shaky Independence

Belgium proclaimed its independence from the Netherlands in 1830, and its new king took the name of Leopold I. Because the Dutch king refused to recognize Belgian independence until 1839, Leopold's most immediate goal was to win recognition for his new state, a goal that was greatly boosted by his marriage to the daughter of Louis–Philippe, king of France from 1830–1848. Having adopted a modern liberal constitution in 1830, Belgium was scarcely affected by the storm of revolution that blew across Europe in 1848 and could turn its attention to economic development.

Following Britain's example, Belgium adopted a policy of free trade and plunged headlong into industrialization, using its large and easily extracted coal resources. This effort was aided by an agreement with the Dutch in 1863 ending tolls for the use of the Scheldt River, which passes through Dutch territory before emptying into the North Sea. This agreement enabled the Belgians to develop fully the port of Antwerp that now plays such a key role in their trade.

The rapid industrial growth also gave birth to an urbanized working class and ultimately to socialism, which along with liberalism and Catholicism became one of the three main political "families" or social cleavages in Belgian society. Divisions still exist although groups are now less hostile to each other than they once were. The liberal and Catholic "families" squabbled throughout the 19th and early 20th centuries over the relations between church and state, especially insofar as the schools were concerned. Their struggle roughly ended in a draw, and state financial support continues to flow to secular, denominational and free schools.

King Leopold II actively engaged in colonial activity in order "to secure for ourselves a slice of this magnificent African cake." Henry Stanley, the famous Welshman who fought on both sides of the U.S. Civil War after emigrating to America, proceeded on an arduous journey to Africa in search of the Scottish missionary, Dr. Livingstone. He initially wanted Britain to take the Congo, but it already had too much on its plate and was not interested. Leopold summoned him to Belgium and engaged him to explore the Congo area of Africa (not on behalf of Belgium, but on behalf of the king). Stanley accepted, left for Africa and negotiated many favorable treaties with local chiefs that resulted in the establishment of the Congo Free State.

Conditions were harsh, since Leopold reportedly condoned labor and torture as instruments to produce wealth. Some say that about eight million Africans lost their lives during 23 years of Leopold's exploitation. Novelist Joseph Conrad, who was no anti-imperialist, described what he had seen in the Congo as "the vilest scramble for loot that ever disfigured the history of the human conscience." Bowing to strong international pressures after a commission reported that administration of the colony was scandalous, parliament passed an act in 1908 annexing the Congo state of Belgium. But Leopold had already enriched his treasury with the immense copper deposits in Katanga Province (now Shaba) and with rubber from the Congo during his years of possession. While

King Leopold II of Belgium

Belgium

The smallest street in Bruges

king, he did much to beautify and modernize Brussels.

Another problem began to bubble in the 19th century: the conflict between languages. French so dominated the over centralized bureaucracy, the court system, schools and businesses in the entire country that ambitious Flemings felt obligated to observe the rule "French in the parlor, Flemish in the kitchen." In the long run, such suppression of the Flemings' language, and with it their identity as a people, could not last. In 1898 Belgium officially became a bilingual state although it was not until 1932 that Dutch could be used in the national administration and not until the 1960s that Dutch became fully equal to French. Flemish is a dialect of Dutch, and it is the word "Dutch" that is used in the constitution and laws. An organization, Nederlanse Taalunie, exists to promote the correct usage of Dutch.

Failure of Neutrality and World War I

Since independence, Belgium tried to preserve its neutrality, which had been guaranteed by the great powers in Europe. However, when this was put to a test in 1914, the result was disastrous. Imperial Germany had set its gun sights toward France and demanded the right of free passage through Belgium for its troops. The Belgians refused, and the British announced that they would stand by the treaty of 1839 and support the Belgians to the end. Winston S. Churchill, the First Lord of the Admiralty, wrote later that the British cabinet had been "over-

whelmingly pacific" at the beginning of August 1914, but the direct appeal from the king of the Belgians for French and British aid raised an issue which united an overwhelming majority of ministers."

In a meeting with the British ambassador to Berlin, the German Chancellor, who thought he was speaking off the record, expressed amazement that the British would go to war over a mere "scrap of paper." Of course, the treaty rested on more than paper. It was anchored to the British national interest of preventing the North Sea coasts from being dominated by a hostile power and of preventing any European power from dominating the continent, as would have been the case if the Germans conquered France. The Germans conquered the Belgians in a few weeks, but their bravery against truly insurmountable odds was one of the most important factors in preventing a German victory in World War I.

The German violation of Belgian neutrality conformed with the German "Schliefen Plan," designed to meet the danger of a two–front war in the East and West through a strike at the heart of France on the well–fortified Franco–German frontier, which extended 150 miles (240 km.) from Switzerland to Verdun. German forces were to be concentrated on the right flank, which would sweep through Luxembourg and Belgium into northern France. Paris would be enveloped and the French troops would be pushed back toward the Moselle where they would be met by the German left flank.

By late August 1914 this plan appeared to have succeeded. German troops, which had bypassed Antwerp and the Belgian coast were dangerously close to Paris, with only a retreating French and British army before them. However, the German commanders grew increasingly nervous about the Belgian army, which was in a position to strike at the Germans' right flank and perhaps even to sever their lengthening lines of communication and supply in Belgium. Therefore, some German troops were detached from the main invasion force in order to contain the Belgian army in Antwerp. Seeing a chance to increase the Germans' nervousness, the British sent a brigade of marines (about 3,000 men) to Antwerp and leaked rumors of much more massive British landings and of totally fictitious British–aided Russian landings involving more than 80,000 troops.

This partly contrived danger to the German right flank, along with the Belgian army's refusal to surrender, influenced the German decision to avoid Paris and to slow down their advance. This interruption of momentum proved to be crucial during the four–day Battle of the Marne

in September and turned the tide of the war. The Belgian military effort was an example of how seemingly hopeless defensive operations, when seen in a larger strategic context, can be crucial for overall victory.

The Germans occupied most of Belgium for the remainder of the war although the king and the remains of the Belgian army held out in Ypres on a few square miles of unoccupied Belgian soil on the western tip of the country. This small salient was pulverized by four years of constant bombardment, and by the time the armistice was signed, it resembled a crater–filled lunar landscape. The three Ypres battles claimed an estimated 850,000 Allied and German casualties.

Initially the Germans found some favor among some Flemings, who saw the possibility of liberation from Walloon control. Such sympathy, which was again manifested in World War II, created great distrust in Wallonia toward the Flemings and has still not been entirely forgotten by Walloons. However, the Germans also found some support in Wallonia. The REX party, led by Léon de Grelle, was pro-German, and the Walloon Legion fought with the German military.

Further complicating the picture was a feeling on the part of some Walloons that the French had "defaulted" in both World War I and World War II, and that Belgians had to pay a high price in helping pull French irons out of the fire. This strengthened the realization that union with France was unthinkable. Thus, although "estranged," the couple (Walloons and Flemings) had no choice but to remain in the same house.

German plunder of Belgian industry led to high unemployment and the mass deportation of Belgian workers to Germany, creating downright hatred. Even the German military commander in Belgium had to protest the policies he was asked to enforce. He remarked sarcastically that "a squeezed–out lemon has no value and a slaughtered cow gives no milk!"

The Inter–War Period and World War II

After World War I, Belgium entered the League of Nations and was given the German–speaking area of Eupen, Malmedy and Saint Vith, as well as a League of Nations mandate over two former German colonies in Africa, now called Rwanda and Burundi. It also abandoned its earlier policy of neutrality and negotiated a military agreement with France and Great Britain. As the clouds of war became more ominous in the 1930s, however, Belgium again proclaimed a policy of neutrality on October 28, 1936. It was thus without allies when on May 10, 1940, German troops again invaded Belgium. After 18 days of

Belgian soldiers mounted on bicycles, 1940

bitter fighting the Belgian army was forced to capitulate. The government escaped to London, but the king of the Belgians became a prisoner of the Germans.

Although Belgium was liberated after the Normandy invasion in the summer of 1944, war returned when Hitler threw his last tanks into the Ardennes Forest in order to recapture Antwerp and break the Allied advance. The decisive action took place at the southern Belgian town of Bastogne, where the surrounded U.S. forces under General Anthony McAuliffe refused to surrender. When called upon to recognize the hopelessness of his situation and to give up, he reportedly answered defiantly, "nuts!" It has long been rumored that the general actually used a different expression, but decorous military historians chose to report it in the now famous way. Fortunately, foggy weather broke and enabled the necessary air support to preserve the general's position. After the war, Bastogne's main square was renamed "Place McAuliffe." The Bastogne Historical Center was opened to commemorate one of the most important battles of the war, and every December a "Nuts Festival" is held.

Postwar Reconstruction and "The Royal Question"

Belgium's postwar reconstruction was accomplished very rapidly. Partly because it had been liberated so quickly, the country had not been as heavily bombed and shelled as the Netherlands, and Antwerp was virtually undamaged. It adopted a financial policy to strengthen the Belgian franc, which soon became one of the most stable currencies in Europe. It also blocked all bank accounts and levied a high tax on fortunes acquired as a result of collaboration with the Germans.

From 1945 until 1950 Belgium was rocked by the so-called "royal question." Unlike his Dutch and Luxembourg counterparts, King Leopold III refused to leave Belgium when the government fled. He argued that as Commander-in-Chief of the armed forces he was compelled to stay where he could help his people more than by leaving. He did deal with the German occupiers, and some of his countrymen claimed he had actually *collaborated* with them. Shortly before liberation, the Germans moved him to Austria, where he remained until 1950.

During the war he had angered many Belgians by courting and marrying his second wife, Liliane Baels, a Flemish commoner and daughter of an activist in the Flemish national party. His first queen, Astrid of Sweden, had been beloved. In 1935 she had died in an auto accident in Switzerland with Leopold at the wheel.

Until his wartime role could be determined, his brother Charles served as regent. A parliamentary commission appointed in 1947 returned a favorable verdict as far as the king's wartime actions were concerned, but the socialists and communists continued to oppose his return. In an attempt to settle the question once and for all, a referendum was held in 1950 in which 57.7% of all voters approved of the king's return. Significantly, 58% of the Walloons and 52% in Brussels were opposed, while only 28% in Flanders were against his rule. When he reentered Belgium in 1950, the resulting disorders were so intense that Leopold III felt obligated to abdicate in favor of his eldest son, Prince Baudouin, on July 16, 1951.

Ever since the "royal question" divided the country, the Belgian king has never been able to exercise the considerable influence on Belgian affairs that he formerly had. None of his acts is effective unless the responsible ministers countersign his orders. The king is the commander-in-chief of the country's armed forces, but a royal military staff in the palace has to coordinate any action with the defense minister. The king can make no independent decisions on the deployment of troops. Baudouin was a popular monarch who restored dignity to the Belgian throne while stripping it of much of its earlier pomposity. The monarch is now expected to be a symbol of the nation, but to perform this role he often has to bend over backward to please the Walloons, whose hatred of father Leopold III still smolders. Of course, overt efforts to satisfy the Walloons inevitably stimulate Flemish criticism.

The king is not a member of the government, but he can play a role in facilitating the formation of cabinets. Since more than 30 have been formed since 1945, this is no small task. It is after parliament has been dissolved and a new cabinet is being sought that the king's influence is greatest. After elections he names an *"Informateur"* to advise him on who should form the next government. Then he names a *"Formateur"* to do it. This person is almost always the leader of the party that got the most votes.

Belgium

Their Majesties King Albert II and Queen Paola

In the event of deadlock, the king must keep negotiations going, and he can ultimately influence the solution. The limited nature of his other power was shown in 1981 when he called together 18 political, labor and business leaders in order to appeal to them to end the country's political instability. Some criticized this, accusing the king of going beyond his established powers. However, in 2007-8, when it took ten months to form a permanent government after elections, the king played an indispensible in keeping the parties talking to each other until a settlement was reached. This is the kind of practical political influence the monarch has. The fact that the king is a limited, if useful, monarch and knows what his boundaries are helps explain why there is no republican movement in Belgium. He is kept informed about political business through weekly meetings with the prime minister.

One of Belgium's most serious and prolonged postwar crises was the painful decolonization of the Belgian Congo, 76 times the size of Belgium with a vastly larger population. Over 100,000 Belgians had settled in the Congo, and Belgium had certainly developed economic interests there, although it sought to avoid mutual economic dependence between the colony and mother country. Belgium opened up the colony to foreign investment and trade. In the 1950s winds of African independence began to reach gale proportions, especially after the new French President, Charles de Gaulle, offered the French colonies in Africa their independence in 1958. A Congolese leader, Patrice Lumumba, emerged as a highly visible proponent of a free Africa. On January 4, 1959, riots broke out in the Congo; 42 persons died in events that deeply shocked the Belgians.

The Congolese had not been prepared for independence. Belgium quickly granted it on June 30, 1960. Unfortunately, a series of bloodbaths ensued, sparked by greed for power and wealth as well as by tribalism. It was not until seven years later that the Congo became orderly, in part because of vigorous efforts of the Belgians and of UN troops.

In 2002 a parliamentary commission concluded that Belgium shared moral responsibility for the assassination in Katanga province of Patrice Lumumba on 17 January 1961, seven months after being elected to lead Congo. It concluded that the Belgian government and king had known of plans for the police to kill him, but they did nothing to stop the assassination, which occurred in the presence of Belgian police and officials. Belgium's ex-Foreign Minister Louis Michel apologized to the Democratic Republic of the Congo on behalf of the government.

The copper, cobalt and uranium mines in the southern Shaba Province are still of great interest to Belgium. When this province was invaded from Angola in mid-1978, Belgium and France sent paratroopers to evacuate white families and to secure the area. In 1979 the Belgian government again sent paratroopers to join its soldiers in training exercises near Kinshasa, the capital city. Thus, Belgium retains a great interest in its former African colonies, and the great bulk of its relatively large development aid (.53% of its GDP in 2008) has gone to the Congo as well as to Rwanda and Burundi, which had been granted their independence in 1962. The Congo is not always a grateful recipient of such aid, and by the end of the 1980s Belgium's importance as a source of trade and aid had declined. In 1989 Belgium halted all development plans there in response to President Mobutu's suspension of payments on Belgian loans. In 1990 it used its diplomatic influence to try to sort out civil unrest in Rwanda, and in 1991 it sent 750 commandos to help evacuate Belgian citizens from the riot–torn country. Its troops were under a UN mandate, and ten Belgian soldiers were killed in 1994. The follow-up Rwanda Commission was Belgian, and Prime Minister Guy Verhofstadt offered a gracious apology for any shortcomings his country might have shown.

GOVERNMENT AND POLITICS

Overcoming the Language Barrier

Any discussion of Belgian politics always has to begin with the ever–present language problem. No major issue could be divorced from it, and it exhausted, paralyzed and fractured coalition governments to such an extent that the country was scarcely able to tackle the extremely important economic problems which it increasingly faced. Belgium was seriously distracted.

Flemings have fought hard and successfully for the complete equality of their language and culture. The principle of equality is essential for both sides. Now cabinet posts are distributed exactly equally between the French and Flemish speakers. This protects francophones, and the same principle applies in the Brussels regional government. The office of the prime minister technically remains outside of all language quotas or restrictions. However, given the permanent Flemish majority in the country, every prime minister since the 1970s has come from Flanders. Most francophone politicians do not master Dutch and therefore would not be representative of the entire country. All discussions in cabinet meetings are conducted through simultaneous interpreters. All major political parties are formally split along language lines, as are most military units and most labor unions.

Even the prestigious medieval Catholic University of Louvain, which had become a bilingual university, had to be split in 1968 because it was located in the Flemish area a few miles north of the language line. The French–speaking part was moved just below the language line and was renamed *Louvain–la–Neuve* ("The New Louvain"). When it came to deciding how to divide the holdings in the famous university library, one of the oldest in Europe, the only solution which was acceptable was that all books with an even file number would remain in Louvain (now called by its Flemish name of Leuven), and all books with an odd file number would be moved to the new campus.

The tension between Flemings and Walloons has been exacerbated by the economic disparities that have developed between them. In the words of ex–premier Leo Tindemans, whose government

The Flemish Separatist Temptation

foundered on the rocks of language regionalization in 1978, "the basic problem is not linguistic. It is the unequal economic development of two regions which speak different languages, have a different mentality and different dynamics, with the jealousy between them that often results and that can be easily exploited by politicians." Political scientist Marc Swyngodouw warns: "If the differential between Flanders and Wallonia continue to grow, it will become impossible to conceive of an economic policy for the country as a whole."

The economic inequality was becoming more apparent. Wallonia had once been one of the richest regions on the continent while Flanders was a poor, rural area. Some of the bourgeois elite in Flanders began to speak French at home, and to this day there is a sizable French-speaking minority of Flemings in Gent, Antwerp, Bruges and Leuven. Then the tables turned with a vengeance. Wallonia's coal industry disappeared, and its antiquated steel plants are in desperate need of streamlining and restructuring. Other traditional industries such as textiles lost out to competition from Third–World countries, where labor costs are very low. Thus, unemployment and labor unrest were higher in Wallonia. The EU declared Wallonia a "development area." Unfortunately, because of the psychological shock caused by crossing the linguistic border, unemployed Walloons are not inclined to

move to Flanders to find work. Thus, there is little labor mobility.

While Wallonia faced an uncertain economic future, Flanders experienced an economic boom, based on research and development, high-tech manufacturing and future–oriented industries such as chemicals. Output per capita is higher in Flanders than in Wallonia. Because of Antwerp and the other thriving ports of Zeebrugge and Ghent, foreign investments poured into the area. Earlier, most foreign investment went to Wallonia, but by 1979 it received only 10% of the total. Brussels received the same amount and Flanders a gigantic 80%. By 2004 almost 80% of Belgium's exports originated from Flanders. Distrust made both decisive governmental action and the establishment of some kind of national consensus, so strong in the Netherlands and Luxembourg, almost impossible in Belgium.

Since the mid–1980s Wallonia has experienced an economic turnaround although in 2006 it still accounted for only 23.5% of GDP (57.3% for Flanders) and had a growth rate of 1.6% (2.2% in Flanders). Investment, including high–technology, has flowed in, industrial output has risen, and the economy has shifted from one in which 53% of the gross regional product is derived from industry and 42% from services to one in which 36% comes from industry (including chemicals, food processing and light engineering) and 60% from services. Unfortunately services can-

not provide sufficient employment; in 2006 Wallonia's jobless rate was still higher than that of Flanders (18.5% compared with 8.5%).

There was general agreement in Belgium that Wallonia and Flanders had to be given more powers to control their own affairs, but there was much haggling on the details. As early as 1963 the two respective languages were given supremacy in the two main regions, and Brussels was declared to be a bilingual city. In 1971 the constitution was revised to permit the establishment of two cultural councils within parliament with authority over certain cultural and linguistic matters. The revision also established the necessity for special majorities (mostly two–thirds) for legislation touching these matters. Such special majorities were demanded by Walloons, whom the Flemish outnumber 60–40 and who have a lower birthrate as well. The amendment called for the establishment of a federal state composed of two lingual communities and three precisely defined regions, each empowered to legislate within carefully drawn limits.

Eight years and a string of cabinet crises later, two–thirds of both houses of parliament approved an autonomy plan establishing regional assemblies and executives with authority over cultural and family affairs, public health, roads, urban projects, energy, environment, hunting and fishing, water resources, land use, housing, employment and many other matters. In 2000 they gained control over agriculture and in 2002 over much of foreign trade. Each has its own foreign trade department, and to raise its international profile Flanders maintains "embassies" abroad called Flanders Houses. Brussels and Wallonia also has "delegations" normally located within embassies, but sometimes with separate facilities. The regions receive a total of 10% of the national budget to finance these tasks. However, the central government retains control over national finances, social security, foreign and defense policy, justice and police. Belgium thereby ceased being a unitary state and became more decentralized.

The new arrangement is messy. Borders differ for "regions," which deal with political, administrative and economic matters within territorial areas, and for "communities," whose competencies relate to language, culture, radio-TV and sports. These issues are linked to persons, not areas. Flemings choose to have one government for both, with its capital in Brussels, but Walloons and German-speakers keep them separate. Also, some of the ministries at the federal and regional levels share the same responsibilities. There are one central government and five regional and community governments and parlia-

Belgium

ments—one Flemish, one in Brussels, two in Wallonia (with its regional capital in Namur) and one in the German-speaking area. There are a total of 58 ministers and junior ministers. In a country with one of Europe's highest tax rates, this seems wasteful and inefficient.

This act of parliament was an important step, and the establishment in 1981 of regional and community institutions has sparked enthusiasm and energies to improve life in the language regions. Nevertheless, there are still many problems in the two larger regions that must be solved. There are small language enclaves on the wrong side of "the line." In 1987 the Belgian government collapsed over such an issue. Because of its location, the small, predominantly Walloon town of Fourons (or Voeren, depending on where one stands on this dispute) had been transferred in 1963 to the Flemish province of Limburg. Although most of the inhabitants of the town actually speak a dialect of German among themselves, two–thirds consider themselves French speakers.

They elected as mayor a militant French–language campaigner, José Happart, who refused to speak Flemish or take a Dutch–language test. The Belgian Supreme Court ruled that Happart's appointment was therefore illegal. This village incident mechanically set off reactions which would be possible only in Belgium: Flemish ministers in Prime Minister Martens' cabinet threatened to resign if Happart was not sacked, and their French–speaking colleagues said they would leave if he was. Evicted from the mayor's office, Happart won a seat in the European Parliament and remained one of Wallonia's most popular politicians. An exasperated Martens had to resign over the issue, which he and many others considered absurd. He was understandably furious that such a parochial dispute could prevent his government from solving the critical economic challenges facing the country. In 1992 power sharing was introduced to such mixed communities. But Belgians remain acutely aware of the underlying message of the dispute: never underestimate the importance of language factors in Belgian politics.

Belgium's high unemployment rate has created an interesting situation: in the past, the only Belgians who were bilingual were Flemings, since the francophones traditionally refused to learn Flemish. Brussels' bilingual status has placed a premium in the job market on the ability to speak both official languages, and that means that the Flemings there have a leg up on their Walloon competitors. This economic fact has bolstered a significant trend since the 1980s: many Walloon parents, especially those living close to the

Don't touch democracy! Bilingualism in Brussels

language border, are sending their children to Dutch–language schools in order to improve their employment prospects. In more and more schools in French-speaking communities, some or all subjects are taught in Flemish in order that pupils can become bilingual. This is occurring while fewer Flemish children are learning French.

The two regional governments, along with three additional separate governments of the country's francophone "communities" in both Wallonia and Brussels and of the tiny German-speaking "community" in the east, work alongside the traditional provincial and communal governments in Belgium. The country had always been divided for administrative purposes into nine provinces, each with a provincial council of 50 to 90 members and a governor chosen by the cabinet and officially appointed by the king. Four of the provinces are French-speaking—Hainaut, Namur, Liège and Luxembourg (a large chunk of the Grand Duchy of Luxembourg which was transferred to Belgium in the settlement of 1839). Four are Flemish-speaking—East and West Flanders, Limburg and Antwerp. In the 1990s Brabant, which had been bilingual, split into Flemish Brabant and Walloon Brabant, making 10 provinces today. Brussels is not a part of any province, but is a region in itself.

In 1989 parliament passed legislation to devolve further power to the regions, and

a special court was created to solve problems stemming from devolution. In 1992 an elected regional government for Brussels was approved, and the following year Belgium became even more federalized. The regional governments were granted all powers but those of the treasury, defense, and foreign policy. In 1995 their parliaments, as well as local parliamentary bodies, were directly elected for the first time. There are potential problems in foreign affairs because the three regions have the right to sign treaties with other nations. Flanders signed one on water with the Netherlands and set up a network of 70 economic representatives in five continents; it also has its own diplomats in Vienna, The Hague, Washington, Tokyo and Brussels. Such separate foreign ties could diminish the standing of the federal government.

Local governments in Belgium have a long tradition stemming from the Middle Ages and have had much autonomy. Each has an elected council of aldermen, who serve six–year terms. As a holdover of Napoleon's reforms, the mayor (called *Burgemeester*) is nominated by the city council, approved by the cabinet and officially appointed by the king. Direct elections were scheduled to be introduced in 2006. He presides over the city council and is expected to insure that national interests are considered. They very often become skilled defenders of local interests in opposition to the central government.

Prince Philippe and Crown Princess Mathilde with Princess Elisabeth

Since the early 1990s, Brussels is officially a bilingual Brussels Capital Region with enhanced competencies. The city is broken down into 19 bilingual and six Flemish communes. The latter are ruled by a separate Flemish regional council. There is sufficient language tension in the capital city and its suburbs that the Council of Europe formally rebuked Belgium in 2002 for violating minority rights. The facts that Dutch is an official language and that Brussels itself was once predominantly Flemish but is now about 85% francophone make Flemings all the more determined that only Dutch will be used in the suburbs regardless of the fact that 120,000 Walloons live there. All local council proceedings and all official mailings must be in Flemish. Anyone showing up at a council meeting who cannot speak Flemish must bring interpreters. Belgium signed the Council of Europe's convention on protecting minorities. However, all seven regional and national parliaments would have to ratify it, and few expect the Flemish parliament ever to agree.

It was the issue of the Brussels suburbs that was most bitterly fought over in the painstaking and seemingly endless ten-month negotiations to create a government after the June 2007 elections. More and more French speakers are moving into the tidy and prosperous Dutch-speaking suburbs on the Flemish side of the line. In some small towns and villages they already constitute a majority, and there are francophone mayors and parties.

In November 2007 politicians from the Flemish majority called a vote in a parliamentary committee abolishing the bilingual rights of some of the 150,000 French-speakers in the suburbs. An electoral district known as Brussels-Halle-Vilvoorde (BHV for short), which straddles the Brussels border is to be split up in a way that francophones in the "Halle-Vilvoorde" part of it would lose their right to vote for francophone politicians from Brussels. They would also lose the right to have court cases heard by French-speaking judges. Nine out of ten Flemings favor this move. However, the way this was done violated a long-standing taboo in the "Belgian pact." This forbade the two language groups from confronting each other directly by holding a straight sectarian vote. Walloon deputies stormed out as soon as the motion was proposed; this bodes ill for the future. This BHV matter is highly symbolic and explosive.

In general, government at the provincial and communal level works rather efficiently and has been able to keep an important part of the governmental machinery running smoothly at times when the central government has been paralyzed. Also, city officials have much influence on the central government; more than three-fourths of the members of the Belgian parliament are at the same time local government officials, and this fact strengthens the ties between the national and local governments.

The National Government

Belgium is a constitutional monarchy in which the king exercises largely ceremonial powers. The established tradition is that he signs all legislation passed by democratic methods. That is why there was dismay in 1990 when former King Baudouin announced that he could not sign a bill liberalizing abortion within the first 12 weeks of pregnancy. The childless, devoutly Catholic monarch asked: "Would it be normal that I be the only citizen in Belgium to be forced to act against his conscience? Is freedom of conscience a privilege for all except the king?" The pragmatic Belgians found a way out of this dilemma: invoking Article 79 of the constitution on April 3, the government declared the king "temporarily incapable of ruling," and it hurriedly promulgated the abortion law in his absence from the throne. Then on April 5 a joint session of parliament, invoking Article 82, offered him his job back. This bizarre episode prompted some Belgians to question again whether their country really needs a monarch after all.

After reigning for 42 years, King Baudouin died suddenly of a heart attack in Spain on July 31, 1993. Though his official powers were limited, he was popular among both Flemings and Walloons, and many credited him for helping preserve Belgian unity. Childless, he was succeeded by his brother Albert while Queen Fabiola kept her title. Thus Belgium has two queens because Albert's wife, Paola, also has the title of queen.

King Albert II never expected to become king and was a relative newcomer to the political world. However, he is familiar with the leaders of all three regions and is experienced in business. He had stated that he would step aside and allow his son Philippe to assume the throne. However, since the king's influence is considered essential to a smooth transition to greater

Canal in Ghent

Belgium

federalism, he was convinced to become king himself "in the interests of continuity." He has performed well, and his role in keeping the delicate and exhausting negotiations going over a ten-month period after the June 2007 elections was indispensable. His down-to-earth genuine nature and his lack of arrogance appeals to Belgians, who forgave him for siring a daughter out of wedlock. His popularity is confirmed by opinion polls: 70% of Belgians want to maintain the monarchy, with an equal percentage of Flemings and Walloons in favor of it. This remains true despite the expense. The king receives an annual allowance of almost 8 million euros ($12 million) plus the expenses for representation and the court. The crown prince receives 800,000 euros ($1.2 million) per year.

In December 1999 Philippe married a glamorous speech therapist, Mathilde d'Udekem d'Acoz, who is now in line to become the kingdom's first Belgian-born queen. In 2002 they had a daughter Elisabeth, and the next year a son named Gabriel was born; a third child followed. The royal family's main contribution to Belgium is to be one of the few remaining symbols of unity. Royals now learn Flemish and do a part of their schooling in Flanders. When officials at the Catholic University of Leuven decided in 2002 to award Crown Prince Philippe an honorary doctorate for his service to Belgian unity, 200 scholars signed a petition protesting the degree because of Philippe's earlier poor performance as an engineering student.

Real power is exercised by coalitions of parties that can maintain a majority in the Chamber of Representatives, the lower house of parliament. This is never easy because the proportional representation electoral system enables almost ten parties to win parliamentary seats. Therefore, until the mid-1990s Belgian governments tended to be very fragile and seldom lasted the entire four years for which a parliament is elected. Now governments are more stable.

It is striking that few cabinets are overturned by votes in parliament. Members of parliament are firmly bound to the party leaders through party discipline, so it is the powerful party leaders who make or unmake governments. Even when cabinets fall, the new governments are usually formed after minor reshuffling of cabinet posts. For example, after 1978 Wilfried Martens was prime minister in six governments, and they came to be known as Martens I through VI. Thus, there is usually more governmental stability in Belgium than meets the eye. This is particularly so because of the nature of Belgian political parties. Although they

Children during Carnival at Binche, Hainaut Province

are very different ideologically and linguistically, they are normally willing to compromise in order to form a government. This stems in part from the tradition of elite cooperation in Belgium that has always helped to bridge some of the differences in the heterogeneous Belgian society. Nevertheless, the delicate compromises necessary to form and preserve a government make it very difficult to attack the country's pressing problems head–on. The process of forming a coalition is so complex that it took the daily *Le Soir* 20 installments to explain it to readers in the lead up to the 2007 elections.

The Parliament

The Belgium parliament is bicameral, and both houses constitutionally have the same powers. However, tradition has made the lower house, the Chamber of Representatives, the more important. Its 150 members (reduced from 212 in 1995) are elected at least every four years by all citizens 18 years or older, who are required to vote; 34.7% of deputies are women. Nevertheless, in the 2003 federal elections 10% of voters abstained in cer-

tain areas. Since 2003, parties are required to win at least 5% of the total votes to get any seats at all; this is intended to reduce the number of parties in parliament and make governments more stable. The great majority of its members continue to perform their normal jobs and commute to Brussels for parliamentary sessions. Most legislation is discussed first with the major Belgian interest groups and is introduced into the Chamber before being passed on to the upper house.

The Senate accepts about 90% of the laws without change. The 181 senators are elected for four-year terms in three different ways. Fifty are elected by the provincial councils, 25 by the Senate itself and the rest directly by Belgian voters. The heir–apparent to the throne, presently Prince Philippe, is always a member, and the senate almost always has roughly the same party composition as the lower house.

Both houses are empowered to amend the constitution by simple majority in both houses. However, such changes must first be announced in parliament and then voted on only after the next elections. A two–thirds majority is now necessary for certain language and cultural legislation. The highest court in the land, the Court of Cassation, whose chief justice is chosen by the government and formally appointed by the king, cannot declare acts of parliament unconstitutional. In the Belgian legal system, which is modeled on the French, there is no provision for judicial review, but the Court of Cassation can rule administrative acts unconstitutional. A separate body, the Council of State, is permitted to give advisory opinions on the legal suitability and constitutionality of major legislation. An arbitration court was created in the 1980s to act like a constitutional court to deal with federal competencies.

Political parties in Belgium follow the cleavages of society. There are specific language parties whose main objective is to preserve or extend the language rights of their particular groups. The three "traditional" parties spring from the three great movements in Belgium during the 19th century: Catholicism, liberalism and socialism. Coalitions always require the participation of at least two of these, and one usually leads the opposition. None of the traditional parties is highly ideologically oriented, and all are rather flexible. These parties have been challenged by three language parties whose demands in behalf of Walloons, Flemings and residents of Brussels have been so appealing that these three language parties have increased their electoral strength enormously in the past two decades. This challenge was so great that all three traditional parties have split into separate French–speaking and Flemish–speaking parties that limit their appeal strictly to their own region. However, they are inclined to cooperate with their former party comrades when it comes to constructing a national governing coalition. There are no major national parties in Belgium today. One can scarcely imagine governing a nation with only regional parties. Energy is expended on the pettiest of issues.

The Christian Parties

Until 1999 the largest twin party was the Christian Democrats and Flemish (CD&V) party, as it is known in Flanders, or the Christian Democrat (CDH) party in Wallonia. Participation of the CD&V and CDH was crucial in all coalition governments from 1958 to 1999. Recent prime ministers, Leo Tindemans, Mark Eyskens (son of earlier Prime Minister Gaston Eyskens, who played a key role in the development of a satisfactory regionalization plan) and Wilfried Martens were all from the CD&V. Martens was a particularly important integration figure for the party. He started his political career as an

Hon. Yves Leterme
Prime Minister of Belgium

ultranationalist Flemish radical who painted over signs at the 1958 World's Fair because they were not written in both Flemish and French. He later became a convinced federalist and a model of adaptability. He was one of the few Belgian politicians trusted by both language groups.

Formerly a single Catholic party, it severed all its formal ties with the Catholic Church in 1945 in order to become the two mass parties they are today. Nevertheless, the two parties are still the only ones many Belgian Catholics find acceptable. Their program endorses a policy guided by Christian principles (liberally interpreted), and they have always been staunch proponents of state support for parochial schools. They favor a free market economy and the protection of private property. At the same time, they advocate equality of opportunity, an active state role in the economy and state assistance for those persons who cannot compete successfully in the capitalist economic order. These positions enable them to work sometimes with the Socialist parties. The CD&V is relatively stronger in Flanders than the CDH is in Wallonia, where the Christian Socialists have always taken a back seat to the Socialist parties. Both find the bulk of their voters among the middle class, farmers and Catholic labor movement, particularly within the Christian Trade Union Federation (CSC), Belgium's largest trade union. The CVP also attracts upper–class voters, such as prosperous merchants and high–ranking military officers.

In 1992 Jean-Luc Dehaene, who is from the trade union wing of the Flemish Christian Democrats, became prime minister. He was known as the "Bulldozer," "Carthorse," and "Plumber" because of his ability to fix problems. What awaited

the new government was a host of difficult decisions, such as direct election of regional and communal assemblies. Dehaene pushed hard to get parliament to accept constitutional reforms devolving additional power to the regions and trimming the large budget deficit to qualify for the euro.

The CD&V was confident as it entered the 2007 parliamentary elections after occupying the opposition benches for several years. The Flemish party, led by the premier of that Dutch-speaking region, Yves Leterme, captured 30 seats based on about 30% of the votes there. This made him the favorite to become the next prime minister at the end of Belgium's notoriously long post-election negotiations.

Leterme is the son of Dutch- and French-speaking parents, so he speaks both languages as a native. He was an accountant and Eurocrat in his early career before turning to politics and embracing Flemish nationalism more and more. He is anything but a unifying figure, and his ascendance has greatly heated up language tensions. In 2006 he had called the 176-year-old Belgian state an "accident of history" that was so worn down that it amounted to no more than a king, a national soccer team and well-known beer brands. He criticized King Albert II for not speaking Dutch well enough, and he once joked that Belgium's French speakers are too stupid to learn Dutch.

The Socialist Parties

The Socialist parties (Social Progressive and Alternative—Sp.a—in Flanders and PS in Wallonia) are a strong twin party nationwide. The Socialist party is one of the oldest parties in Europe. It was never an extreme left-wing party and always sought to work within the constitutional system. Winning elections always took priority over doctrine. The best-known Belgian Socialist, Paul-Henri Spaak, former prime minister, foreign minister, first president of the UN General Assembly and NATO general secretary, expressed the character of his party this way: "There are two kinds of Socialists—Socialists and real Socialists. Me? I am a Socialist."

Its program presents a parliamentary–reformist path to a socialist society. The party congress of 1974 defined the party's aim as democratic socialism, which gives each individual the possibility for full social, economic and cultural realization. They once found their voters chiefly among lower-level employees and workers, especially those without strong ties to the Catholic Church and those who belong to the second–largest trade union, the Federation of Belgian Labor (FGTB). Today they are parties less for workers and more for intellectuals.

Belgium

The Flemish party is generally less friendly to far–reaching reform than the Walloon party, which must stay left in order to compete in the more socialist Wallonia. The Socialists are considered to be especially useful coalition partners because of their ability to help control the powerful Belgian labor movement. Belgian Socialists are among the very few outside the United States who allow their parliamentary candidates to be chosen by means of party primaries, with all party members entitled to vote.

Led by Elio de Pupo, the Socialists were defeated badly in the 2007 parliamentary elections, in part because of local corruption scandals. *Le Soir* called the party's result "the Socialists' Waterloo."

The Liberals

The third traditional party group is the Party for Freedom and Progress, renamed in Flanders the Flemish Liberals and Democrats (VLD), and calling itself "Open-VLD" in 2007. It is called the *Mouvement Reformateurs* (Movement of Reformers—MR) in Wallonia and Brussels. Both parties are generally referred to as the Liberals. They pursue traditional European liberal policies, such as the limitation of the power of the state in society and the greatest possible freedom for private initiative. They generally want to prevent the socialization of the economy, to reduce taxes and to cut state expenditures. They do, however, accept gay marriage and legalized marijuana. Perhaps the only expressly conservative parties in Belgium, they appeal mainly to middle class voters, especially small businessmen and professionals.

Also divided by regions, the Liberals were the big winners in the 1999 elections and became the country's largest party after being in third place for more than 80 years. This electoral triumph represented the most dramatic turnover in Belgian political history. It repeated its victory in Flanders, narrowly beating out the Flemish Socialists in the 2003 federal elections and remaining the senior member of the governing coalition.

The Flemish Liberal leader is Guy Verhofstadt, who in 1981 at age 28 became the youngest major party leader in Belgian history. At age 32 he was already a vice-premier and budget minister. Over the years he changed his conservative views and moved closer to the political center, especially since he had to lead a center-left governing coalition with the Socialists from 1999. He cast his earlier heroine Margaret Thatcher overboard and embraced Tony Blair's "third way."

His center-left governing "rainbow" coalition capitalized on the economic achievements of the previous Duhaene government, which had sharply reduced the country's budget deficit. Bolstered for a while by a growing economy, Verhofstadt could make popular promises, such as across-the-board tax cuts and a more efficient public service. As prime minister in league with the Socialists, he changed his priorities by showing sympathy with the anti-globalization movement, legalizing marijuana and gay marriage (including the equal right to adoption), becoming the second country, along with the Netherlands, to end the ban on euthanasia, and joining with neighboring France, Germany and Luxembourg to oppose U.S. policy toward Iraq.

The Liberals lost badly in the 2007 parliamentary elections, tumbling from first to third place in Flanders. This cost Verhofstadt his job as prime minister. Voters had tired of him after eight years in power, and he was seen as not having backed Flemish interests strongly enough.

Smaller Parties

A relatively new party is the Greens, which are divided into Flemish and Walloon parties. They do meet together but make decisions separately. As in other European countries, they find voters among those who are concerned about environmental protection and nuclear dangers. They are convenient parties for expressing discontent and protest. They are the only partner parties whose French and Flemish factions cooperate easily in parliament.

The oldest of the Belgian autonomy parties is the Flemish People's Union (VU), established in 1954. The VU draws almost half its votes from workers and half from the middle and upper classes. It supports a free market economy and Flemish and Wallonian autonomy bound together loosely in a Belgian state. From 1987 to 1991 it was in the ruling coalition. It subsequently split into two parts: SPIRIT, which entered a coalition with the SP.A, and the Nieuwe Vlaamse Alliantie (NVA), which allied with the CD&V.

Vlaams Belang (Flemish Interest)

The hard-line anti-immigrant law-and-order Flemish Bloc (*Vlaams Blok*) changed its name at the end of 2004 to Flemish Interest (*Vlaams Belang*—VB) and reformed itself as a new party with a new flag and program. Belgium's appeals court had banned it in 2004 for racism, advocating the forcible repatriation of immigrants, and saying such things as Islam and democracy cannot go together. Marching under the banner, "Our People First!", it is the largest party in Antwerp, where it wins a third of the votes. Because of the scare of Islamic terror, many persons in Antwerp's sizable Jewish community support it. From 4,000 to 5,000 Flemish residents leave Antwerp every year while 5,000 to 6,000 non-European immigrants arrive annually. It also does well in Brussels, where half the newborns are from Arab parents.

In the May 2003 federal elections, held five months after serious race riots erupted in Antwerp, it gained 17.9% of the votes in Flanders and 18 seats for its best result in its 25-year history. It also did very

One Wallon, One Fleming = Two Belgians. Long Live Belgium!

Women in armed forces

well in the 2004 regional elections in Flanders, winning 24% of the votes. It continued its winning ways in June 2007 by overtaking the Liberals to become the second-largest party in Flanders. Nevertheless, the other parties continue to refuse to allow it into the governing coalition.

Its performance was helped by former beauty queen Anke Vandermeersch, who ran for a senate seat and helped soften the Bloc's edge. However, while beautifying the package somewhat, the message Vandermeersch delivered was the same: "We still are very much against the multicultural society. We need people who emigrate here to adapt. If they don't adapt to our systems, to our laws, to our values, they should go back to where they came from."

Filip Dewinter from Antwerp is one of the party leaders. The titles of his three books succinctly express his point of view: *Our People First, We Stand Alone,* and *Masters in Our House.* He opposes letting in more non-Europeans and insists that those already in Belgium "assimilate" or leave. Because of its views, no other Belgian party will team up with it, and this keeps it out of office, even in Antwerp. However, by closing ranks against the *Vlaams Belang,* forming what is known as the *cordon sanitaire,* the other parties have provided it with a monopoly on the protest vote.

Privately some mainstream politicians sense that this approach is backfiring because it strengthens the party's image as an antiestablishment party that responds to a widespread feeling of insecurity in Belgium. Thus the shunning of the party might actually enhance its popularity. The party also benefits from its ability to mix anti-immigration rhetoric with a call for Flemish autonomy or independence. Its insistence that taxes from Flanders should not be channeled toward poorer Wallonia

attracts votes from the richest Flemish neighborhoods. The party is further strengthened by the fact that it is less reliant on a single, charismatic leader than are other European right-wing parties although Dewinter is still its most visible leader.

It is changing its image from a radical to a conservative party without overt racial overtones. It does not mention immigration as much as earlier and states in public that its earlier program is no longer applicable. For example, when a Muslim woman felt compelled in 2005 to resign from her job following a series of death threats against her employer for allowing her to wear a head scarf at work, both Dewinter and the king condemned the threats. The party is moving toward the political center while trying to hold on to its traditional voters. This frightens the other parties.

The *Vlaams Belang's* steady rise has also generated another challenger to the country's respectable parties: an Arab pride movement called the Arab European League, which claims to be the voice for frustrated Muslims in Belgium. Its leader, Dyab Abou Jahjah, a Lebanese-born son of university teachers who speaks five languages, demands affirmative action in schools, the workplace and housing and the elevation of the Arabic language, spoken by the roughly 5% of Belgium's population that is of Middle Eastern descent, to the fourth official language. Calling assimilation "cultural rape," Dyab became the target not only of the *Vlaams Belang,* which demanded that his Belgian citizenship be revoked, but also of Prime Minister Verhofstadt. The latter had tried to avoid discussing the explosive issue of immigration. But after two days of rioting broke out in Antwerp in December 2002 in which a young Moroccan teacher was killed by a deranged elderly white man, the prime minister went on television and blasted the Arab European League as a "threat to our society that thrives on confrontation and provocation."

Although Dyab and his league had largely disappeared from public view by 2005, he forced Belgians to think more deeply about whether their traditionally tolerant country really welcomes immigrants and who precisely is a Belgian. He has also pointed to a political truth that the *Vlaams Belang* has more influence on mainstream Belgian political parties than many people realize: "*Vlaams Blok* talks about security, so they start talking about security. *Vlaams Blok* talks about assimilation, they speak about assimilation. That's the power of the *Vlaams Blok.*"

The Flemish Bloc's French equivalent is the National Front, which made some in-

Belgium

Politics in the Big Leagues. Louis Michel (2nd from right) with (left to right) Chris Patten, Javier Solana and Colin Powell. Source: Central Audiovisual Library, European Commission

roads in Wallonia in 2003. In Brussels the Democratic Front of French Speaking Brusselers (FDF), which advocated a redrawing of the boundaries separating Flemish from French speakers, was absorbed by the *Mouvement Reformateur* (MR).

In a 1998 survey on racism, 55% of Belgians admitted to being "racist" or "fairly racist." This was the highest percentage in Europe. Nowhere is this stronger than in Antwerp, a hotbed of the extreme right. A string of racially motivated crimes culminated in a particularly shocking act in May 2006. An 18-year-old secondary school expellee bought a hunting gun legally and walked through the city center shooting at nonwhite people. He shot and critically wounded a Turkish woman wearing a head scarf. Then he shot dead a Malian baby sitter and the white child for whom she was caring. During his interrogation he admitted that he sympathized with the extreme right, but *Vlaams Belang* denied any culpability for the gruesome acts. The boy, Hans Van Themsche, was sentenced to life in prison, the maximum sentence for murder.

In an attempt to reduce the number of illegal immigrants, the government in 2000 offered citizenship to 38,000 illegals in the country, while tightening controls at its borders to prevent such persons residing in other European countries from streaming into Belgium to gain a permanent right of residence.

The Communist Party (KPB in Flanders and PCB in Wallonia) is a small, politically insignificant party that appeals almost exclusively to workers and which is strongest in Wallonia, and Brussels. In 1971 it separated into regional organiza-

tions although it did not formally split. Its program is orthodox Marxist. It generally pursued a Moscow-oriented line. For instance, while most Western European communist parties denounced Soviet policy in Poland from 1980 on, the Belgian communists announced that Soviet pressure on Poland to limit or eliminate the free trade unions within the country was "perfectly understandable and exclusively defensive in nature." The party's offer to participate in a ruling coalition has never been accepted. One unique practice observed earlier by the party's

representatives in parliament was that each paid his parliamentary salary into the party coffers and accepted in return only a worker's wage from the party. This practice is irrelevant, though, since the communists have been shut out of parliament since 1985.

Foreign and Defense Policy

As a small country, Belgium's foreign policy is anchored in international organizations that seek to maintain peace and prosperity in the world, especially in Europe. The EU continues to give an important boost to this small trading nation, one–half of whose national income is derived from foreign trade.

Belgium is also a founding member of NATO, but in recent years it has been among the alliance's least enthusiastic members, due in great part to its severe financial difficulties and to its preoccupation with its internal problems. Some of its equipment is outdated. It has a total active force of 40,800, including 2,570 women; its reserves number 13,750. Its air force of 10,250 troops, including 800 women, modernized its force by purchasing American F–16 combat aircraft. In order to cut costs, Belgium is coordinating some of its air operations with the Dutch. The U.S. maintains approximately 1,400 military personnel in Belgium. In December 2007 police detained 14 Islamic extremists on suspicion of planning to free from prison an Al Qaeda supporter, former professional soccer player from Tunisia Nizar Trabelsi. In his trial he had been convicted of organizing an attack on

Bilingual Recruiting Poster

202

Belgium

a Belgian air base, Kleine Brogel, where about 100 American troops are stationed.

The navy, with bases in Ostend and Zeebrugge, has 2,450 personnel, including 270 women, and is mainly a coastal defense force, composed of three frigates and a dozen minesweepers. The Belgian and Dutch navies are combined in a joint operational command based in Den Helder, Netherlands. In 1987–8 it sent three of those mine sweepers to the Persian Gulf to help in the allied effort to keep that important waterway open to world shipping. In 1991 it again sent four warships, including two mine-sweepers, to the Gulf, and in 1992 its troops were dispatched to the Congo, where violence threatened the lives of Europeans, and Somalia. In Somalia its soldiers were regarded as tough, unforgiving, disciplined (despite several incidents of racism and violence toward the local population) and skilled, traits acquired in previous interventions in Africa.

Belgium has an army of 24,800 soldiers, including 1,500 female troops. Troops are separated as much as possible into separate language units and divided generally into two armies. Most soldiers are stationed in Belgium, but 2,100 serve in Germany until the end of 2005. In 2003 it had peacekeeping forces in Afghanistan and Kosovo.

Critics, including high military officers, fear that the drastic cuts deprive Belgium of the bare minimum needed to defend the country. In 1993 the government decided to participate in the Franco–German Eurocorps, the embryonic European army.

This decision provoked criticism in Flanders because Dutch would not be one of the languages used. The memory is still alive that Flemish troops sometimes died during the First World War because they could not understand the orders of their overwhelmingly francophone officers.

In the lead-up to the unpopular 2003 war in Iraq, the Belgian government took an aggressively critical stance, which boosted Prime Minister Verhofstadt's and Foreign Minister Louis Michel's popularity before the May 2003 elections. Teaming up with France, which Belgium usually supports unswervingly in NATO, it helped veto a request from Turkey for NATO protection, a decision that was popular with voters but was decried by many Belgian political veterans and business leaders. An editorial in *De Standaard* read: "Belgium is grandiosely overplaying its hand." A couple of weeks later, the government relented, and it supported the assistance to its NATO ally, Turkey.

Following the war, which Belgium vehemently opposed, it joined with France, Germany and Luxembourg to create on paper a joint rapid reaction unit built on the existing French-German brigade. Belgium offered to contribute commandos. In addition, the four said they would set up a multinational headquarters and a separate military center in the Brussels suburb of Tervuren to command and plan EU military operations when NATO is not involved. Belgium had even recommended that a "hard core" of EU countries form a defense organization entirely distinct

from NATO, but that went too far even for its French partners. The four invited other European nations to join their effort, but sensing that its real purpose was to weaken the transatlantic alliance, none did. Neither Belgium nor the other three pledged to raise their defense spending to cover the costs of these innovations, and the idea of a separate command in Tervuren was temporarily dropped.

Such a bold foreign policy places Belgium above its usual weight class in world politics. It did not shrink from publicly castigating the United States and such traditional partners as Britain. Perhaps the best example of a small country overstepping good sense and its own influence while seeking a special moral role in the world was a 1993 law granting Belgium "universal jurisdiction" to try the perpetrators of war crimes, crimes against humanity and genocide even if there was no Belgian connection with the alleged crimes, victims or perpetrators. Ten years later about 30 political leaders, including Palestinian leader Yasser Arafat, Israeli Prime Minister Ariel Sharon, and Cuban President Fidel Castro had been charged under the law.

The sweeping law became untenable in March 2003 when Iraqis charged former President George H.W. Bush, Vice President Richard Cheney, Secretary of State Colin Powell, and Generals Norman Schwarzkopf and Tommy Franks in Belgium for alleged war crimes in Iraq. Powell issued a stern warning that Belgium's status as an international hub could be jeopardized by such legislation. At the June 2003 NATO summit U.S. Defense Secretary Donald Rumsfeld questioned whether the alliance could continue to hold meetings in Brussels and whether the U.S. would withhold financing for the new NATO headquarters to be built across the street from the present building if the law remained in place. Under such pressure, Belgium all but scrapped the law especially after ex-Foreign Minister Louis Michel himself was charged for authorizing the sale of machine guns to Nepal. He responded indignantly, calling the suit "mad, pernicious, irrational and malign" that would make Belgium a "laughing stock."

Realizing that it had overstepped its capacity as a moral force in the world, the Belgian parliament and government amended the law in 2003 by deleting the phrase "universal jurisdiction," limiting applicability to complaints in which either the victim or defendant is a Belgian citizen or resident for at least three years, and granting automatic immunity to any official of a NATO or EU country or to citizens of a democratic country where they could be tried in their own courts.

The Grande Place, Brussels

Belgium

Belgian Cuisine: Mussels and "French" Fries

Photo: Juliet Bunch

ECONOMY

Belgium was one of the first countries in the world to become heavily industrialized; this was possible because of large deposits of coal and to a lesser extent of iron ore. The industrialized areas became heavily urbanized, and a well–trained and powerfully organized work force emerged. Today, two–thirds of Belgium's workers are unionized, the highest percentage in Western Europe. They are divided almost evenly among socialist, liberal and Christian unions.

As in every other Belgian institution, language separations weaken the unity of the unions. The country experienced its first general strike in 58 years in 1993; it was aimed at the austerity program of a shaky government, which beat a tactical retreat. The government can weather many such labor disturbances because the mainly French–speaking socialist unions and the dominant Christian unions in Flanders cannot pull together sufficiently to bring the government down.

Over the years, a highly elaborate system of formal discussions between labor unions, employers and the government has developed. These discussions facilitate the exchange of conflicting views and aim at establishing the framework for agreements in economic matters that would protect the well–being and future of the entire country.

Sometimes this cooperation breaks down, but as a rule, the unions take a constructive, pragmatic approach to economic matters. They have much to show for their high productivity and cooperative policies: wages which, though declining in real terms, remain among the world's highest, one of the world's shortest work weeks (less than 38 hours), pensions and social security benefits which until the 1980s were fully protected from inflation by means of indexing, which means that they were automatically raised to keep step with rises in retail prices. Such indexing took some of the heat out of labor relations, but it invariably contributed to inflation and to government spending deficits.

Like many European countries that were left in a condition of devastation and destitution at war's end in 1945, Belgium passed sweeping social welfare legislation within a few months which could give the people some economic hope for the future. Benefits were continually expanded. For instance, generous unemployment benefits take much of the sting out of losing one's job. The state medical insurance reimburses three–fourths of all medical and pharmaceutical expenses and pays persons with long–term illnesses—60% of their salaries for the first two years and 40% for the next two years. Belgium's social welfare net has attracted many admirers, but such a net became extremely expensive. Its nominal costs multiplied twelve–fold from 1960 to 1980, and the government exhausted domestic sources of credit to pay for them.

After 1978 the government had to borrow heavily abroad, not merely to finance foreign trade, but to meet the budgetary demands created by what many consider to be an overly generous social welfare program. With its high standard of living and small domestic market Belgium is extremely dependent upon foreign trade; about half of its production must be exported. In 2003 the World Trade Organization (WTO) ranked it as the 11th most important exporting nation in the world. Of course, it has many foreign trade advantages. Its central location in the middle of major European economic centers and its membership in the EU are very significant.

Belgium lies within a 300-mile radius of a market containing 350 million consumers. Almost three–fourths of its exports go to the EU15, and close to half flows to its three neighbors—Germany, France and the Netherlands. In 2000 the Brussels, Paris and Amsterdam stock exchanges merged to create Euronext, joined later by the Portuguese exchange and the London International Financial Futures and Options Exchange. Brussels is home to Euroclear, the world's largest clearance and settlement system for internationally traded securities, employing 1,800.

Also, it has the second largest port in Europe and one of the most modern, best equipped, efficiently operated and busiest in the world—Antwerp. This port, which is owned by the city, is located within 250 miles of Frankfurt, Düsseldorf, Lille, Paris, Amsterdam and London. Situated 45 miles (72 km.) inland along the Scheldt

School children parading before King. By Jan Verhas, 1878.

River, its access to the open sea was always a problem because the Scheldt passes through Dutch territory before emptying into the North Sea. For centuries the Dutch, wishing to minimize competition for their own port of Rotterdam, limited or prevented traffic heading to Antwerp from passing though their territory. Excellent relations with the Netherlands finally enabled the two countries to sign a treaty eliminating such hindrance, and Antwerp now thrives.

The port has the largest underwater warehouse facilities in the world, and is especially noted for its lightning–fast turnaround. More than 75,000 are employed by the port or by companies that in some way service the port. The port complex, which covers 27,000 acres, contains entire industrial plants, including factories owned by such multinational companies as General Motors and Bayer.

About half of the traffic entering and leaving the port is moved by Belgium's 930 mile (1,500 km.) canal system, which links it to all major Belgian cities and rivers, which are easily navigable because of their slow current. The inland waterways also connect the inland ports of Brussels, Ghent and Liège and plug into the Rhine River. Antwerp can call itself the gateway to Europe. The North Sea port at Zeebrugge is an important container terminal, and the one at Ostend is being restructured after losing much of its passenger trade following the opening of the Chunnel to the UK.

Backing up this inland waterway is a very well developed internal transport system. Zaventem, outside Brussels, is Eu-

rope's fifth most important airport. In 2002 the SN Brussels Airlines, formed from Delta Air Transport, a regional subsidiary of bankrupt SABENA, commenced operations. The first railway in Europe formally opened in Brussels in 1835. With its 2,536 miles (over 4,000 km.) the Belgian railway net is now the densest in the world. The Eurostar line speeds passengers from Brussels through the Chunnel to central London in a little over two hours, and Thalys trains race to Paris in an hour and a half and provide links to

the Netherlands and Germany. Its toll-free international motorways are plentiful and fully lighted at night.

Many of the factors that once made Belgium an economic powerhouse have now disappeared. Easily extractable coal, traditionally Belgium's only significant raw material, has been almost completely exhausted in the South, where most of the mines are closed. Belgium's steel industry, which grew up around the coalfields, had become inefficient and obsolete; EU policies to reduce European steel production have cost thousands of jobs in Belgium. Steel towns such as Liège, Charleroi and Mons are now economic and political trouble areas. The Belgian government felt compelled to subsidize many lame industries, particularly in the steel and textile sectors. This aid almost always flowed to Wallonia and enabled labor unions to achieve higher wages in some of the lame industries, especially steel, than those paid in the more productive mills in Flanders. Indeed, the strike record in Wallonia is three times the rate per capita than in Flanders. This only increases resentment toward Wallonia, which many Flemings believe is in essence being subsidized by Flanders.

The world economic turndowns since the oil shocks of 1973–4 struck a hard blow at Belgium's trading position. A half century ago, Belgium's own coal supplied 90% of the country's energy needs, but that figure has now sunk to about 20%. About 40% of its present energy needs are covered by oil; almost all of it must be imported and most comes from the Middle East. The oil company, Petrofina, now

Pieter Bruegel, the Bethlehem Census

Belgium

merged with Total, provides a small portion of the country's oil through its concession in the U.S., Canada, the Congo and the North Sea. Natural gas provides for 17% of its energy consumption. It hopes to be able to develop on–site gasification of coal, which could have the effect of reviving the lagging coal mining industry. More than a quarter of its energy is produced by seven nuclear power plants. In 2003 the parliament approved a law that would shut all of them down between 2015 and 2025, when each had reached the age of 40 years.

An unpleasant development for Belgium was the slowdown in foreign investment caused, in large part, by the country's high wage costs and drop in profitability of Belgian firms. The World Economic Forum ranked Belgium 31st in its 2006 Global Competitiveness Report, behind Portugal but one notch above France. American investors, who in the 1960s accounted for 65% of all foreign investment in Belgium, had reduced their share to less than a third by the 1980s, and some of the most visible U.S. firms such as RCA, General Electric and Holiday Inn, have withdrawn altogether. This is a serious problem because multinational companies control an estimated one–third of all manufacturing jobs and almost one–half of all industrial assets in Belgium. Thus, their confidence in the Belgian economy is crucial.

The government is trying to lure foreign investment by providing subsidies, reducing interest rates and giving capital bonuses and tax breaks, but the results are mixed. The French automaker, Renault,

found out in 1997 what can happen in Belgium when it decided to close its plant in Vilvoorde and lay off 3,100 Belgian workers. Ex-Prime Minister Dehaene proclaimed the action "brutal and unacceptable," and a hundred thousand people staged a protest march in Brussels.

Foreign workers were once concentrated primarily in the Wallonian industrial areas and Brussels, but now they are spread throughout the country. The capital city has a particularly visible foreign presence. The thousands of EU bureaucrats, international businessmen and especially foreign laborers now comprise almost 30% of the city's population. The most common name given to sons born in Brussels today is Mohammed.

Foreign workers are a convenient target for extreme right–wing groups, and they face discrimination in the larger society. The extent of the problem of integrating the predominantly African and Mediterranean workers was revealed by the passage of a law in 1981 directed against racism and hatred toward foreigners. It is now forbidden by law to put up signs such as "Foreigners unwanted" or "No entry for North Africans," as once one saw in Belgium. Public services may no longer be denied to foreigners.

Like many other rich Western European countries, Belgium has become a magnet for persons from the Third World seeking asylum. A fourth of Brussels' residents are immigrants, mainly Moroccans and Turks. With the situation worsening monthly, the government became a firm advocate of strict border controls. The government tightened controls on illegal refugees in

1993 and speeded up the application processing and deportation of such foreigners.

Belgian agriculture is still relatively efficient by European standards and provides 80% of the country's food needs. There are problems, however. Farm incomes have stagnated for years, but farmers have managed to stay afloat because of subsidies from the EU's Common Agriculture Program (CAP). Most Belgian farms are mixed, producing grains and raising livestock and, except for Italy, Belgium has the smallest farms in the EU. Therefore, there is a great need for amalgamation and modernization. But with a high unemployment rate in Belgium, the 2% of the population working in agriculture (producing 1.1% of GDP) must be kept on the land until some can be absorbed by industry, which employs 25% of the workforce and produces 24% of GDP, or services, which provide work for 73% and create 74.9% of GDP.

Despite some improvement, Belgium faces economic problems. Although its government deficit had disappeared by 2002, over a quarter of the budget is devoted to paying interest on the national debt. Its public debt, at 95% of GDP, is one of the highest in the industrialized world. The government's stiff austerity program since the 1980s was partly successful. The government's borrowing, spending and deficit have all been reduced. It had six budget surpluses in a row but showed a .6% deficit in 2008. Unemployment in 2008 was 10.8%, one of the highest rates in Europe, and inflation 3.5%. The economy shrank by .8% in 2002, but it was growing again in 2008 by 2.6% on an annual basis. Tax rates continue to be reduced. The corporate income tax rate for large corporations has fallen from 40.17% to 33.99% (ultimately to 30%) and from 28.24% to 24.98% for small and medium-sized businesses. One can no longer call the country "the sick man of Europe."

CULTURE

Belgium has more than one culture, and to understand the cultural dimension of the country, one must unravel the strands of Roman, Frankish, Spanish, French, Austrian, German and Dutch influences. With no common culture, there is very little feeling of Belgian national identity, especially among the Flemish. Unlike in Wallonia, there is a vocal separatist movement in Flanders. It is mainly when they are outside of Belgium that many Flemish and Walloons begin to feel like Belgians.

Today, Belgium is secularized, and few Belgians vote primarily along religious sect lines. Also, there is a trend away from doctrinaire religious positions on social and political matters, even among the Ro-

The Adoration of the Lamb. Jan and Hubert Van Eyck   **Sint-Baafskathedraal, Ghent**

206

man Catholics. Catholicism is still a significant social force, especially in Flanders. Catholics organize trade unions, youth movements, hospitals, sports clubs, political parties and schools, and these organizations are thriving. Perhaps this helps partly to explain the conservatism of the Belgians, who remain largely a rather private, family–oriented people.

The best example of the vitality of Catholicism is the separation of the school system into state schools, which accommodate approximately 43% of the pupils, and "free" (chiefly Catholic) schools, which are largely financed by the state and accommodate 57%. The long and emotional dispute over state support for Catholic schools was finally settled in 1958. The compromise that was reached probably put to rest the last religious dispute that would significantly affect Belgian politics. Such Catholic schools are open to all children and continue to be state financed. They are reputed to be slightly better academically than other schools. In 2003 same-sex marriages were legalized, followed the next year by legislation permitting homosexual couples the right to adopt children.

In Wallonia children are permitted to choose English as their first foreign language; 49.2% did that in 2007, in contrast to 42.3% who chose Flemish. In Flanders children start with French and begin English at about age 13. There has been an increasing tendency to use English as the common language between Flemings and Walloons, including in corporate boardrooms. Even José Happart admitted after a fierce TV debate, "after all, everybody will speak English in 20 years." There is, at the same time, an encouraging trend for ambitious francophones to buckle down and learn Flemish. Most educated Flemings continue to speak fluent French although the percentage that can do so is declining. There are many variants of Walloon French, which is closer to the old rather than to the modern Parisian form. There is diversity at the university level. There are many universities that include four Dutch–speaking ones and four French–speaking. Some are Catholic, such as Leuven and Louvain–la–Neuve, and some are not, such as the University of Brussels, Ghent and Liège.

The news media use both languages. The *Radio Television Belge de la Communauté Culturelle Française* (RTBF) and the *Vlaamse Radio en Televisie* (VRT) are separate public utilities with state financing but without direct state intervention in their management. Both are run by ten–member administrative councils, of which eight are representatives of political parties and are appointed by the parliament. Belgians were pioneers in radio broadcasting and

now have numerous German, French and Dutch channels. There are French- and Dutch–language television channels and many private channels.

There are newspapers in all three languages. The leading French papers are *La Libre Belgique* (Catholic) and *Le Soir* (independent). Flemish dailies include *Het Laatste Nieuws* (Liberal) and *De Standaard* (Catholic). One daily, *Grenz Echo*, appears in the German language. Most Belgian dailies have a political affiliation and are owned by one of four large chains, although each newspaper has a great measure of autonomy within each group.

Simply by driving through Belgium, one realizes that the country is filled with art treasures. One can see splendid medieval cities such as Bruges, Ghent, Antwerp, Liège, Brussels, Leuven (Louvain), Tongeren, Namur and Tournai, which are filled with castles, abbeys and venerable public buildings. But it is in art museums throughout the world that one can best see the impact of Belgian artists.

Painting was the medium in which artists came to be known best of all, and by the 16th century, Flemish painting with its bold personal expression and vitality marked the high point of the northern Renaissance. Jan Van Eyck was the first Flemish master to arouse the admiration of Italian painters, and his brother Hubert Van Eyck also produced masterpieces of lasting value. Pieter Bruegel the Elder combined religious, moral or satirical subjects with vivid descriptions of the Flemish rural environment. He broadened the art of landscape painting through a masterful, sweeping concept of nature.

Peter Paul Reubens became the most famous exponent of Baroque painting; he

also was a noted diplomat and worked for Marie de Medici, Philip IV of Spain and Charles I of England. His collaborator, Anthony Van Dyck, became the court painter of the English royal family. David Teniers was a master at painting highly realistic popular scenes. Flemish artists were pioneers in giving depth to painting, instead of rendering a flat appearance. They paid very close attention to detail and to common people. Thus, they gave us the most vivid picture imaginable of their surroundings and have kept their own time alive in the mind of the modern viewer.

Since ancient times, Belgian literature was bilingual. Until the 19th century its painters overshadowed its writers, but after Belgium gained its independence, literature began to bloom. Hendrik Conscience attracted attention to his homeland through his novel *The Lion of Flanders*. Reminiscent of Sir Walter Scott's romantic novels, Conscience rekindled Flemings' pride and interest in their past. He also wrote other delightful novels depicting life in the Flemish countryside and towns that sparked a literary revival. Another great 19th century Flemish figure was the poet, Guido Gezelle, whose poems presented religious sentiment with great eloquence. Karel van Woestijne was also a brilliant poet who wrote about the eternal conflict between body and soul. Perhaps the greatest 20th century authors are Hugo Claus and the late Baron Marnix Gijsen.

Walloon literature was revived under the leadership of Max Weller, whose literary review *La Jeune Belgique* encouraged experimentation and cosmopolitanism in the late 19th century. Charles de Coster wrote *Uilenspiegel* in 1867, a ribald tale so filled with the spirit of liberty that it became a symbol of Belgian resistance in both world wars. Perhaps the greatest French–speaking Belgian writers were Maurice Maeterlinck, who won a Nobel Prize in 1911, Emile Verhaeren and Michel de Ghelderode. Paradoxically, all three were Flemish. With such a composer as Cesar Franck and ballet artist as Maurice Béjart, Belgium has also gained world acclaim in music and dance.

In general, Walloon literature is strongly oriented toward France, while Flemish literature is concerned chiefly with maintaining and broadening Flemish cultural identity. The state has established "Houses of Culture" all over the country. These houses enrich the quality of life of the communities in which they are located, but it is doubtful that they contribute much to welding together two so distinct cultures. The Flemish community government and Dutch national government co-sponsor similar "Houses of Culture" abroad and offer common literature prizes.

Belgium

FUTURE

Despite serious economic difficulties and a dysfunctional central government, Belgium is still wealthy even by the high European standards. Its greatest problem in the future will be to manage the perpetual and exhausting strife sparked by the existence of differing language communities that find it difficult to coexist with each other.

It must also attempt to control migration into the country and to assimilate refugees and immigrants who are already living there. Like other European countries, it confronts a frightening terrorist presence. Authorities have unearthed sleeper cells for future acts and face the difficulty in sorting out suspicious behavior from imminent danger. One Belgian woman, who converted to Islam during her two marriages with Arab men, became the first Belgian woman to die in a suicide attack in Iraq. Parliament passed a controversial bill in December 2005 giving police additional powers to fight terrorism. Belgium is aggressive in arresting al-Qaeda suspects and in backing tough EU measures to combat terrorism in Europe.

The Flemish party, led by the former premier of the Dutch-speaking region, Yves Leterme, captured 30 seats and about 30% of the votes there in the June 2007 national elections. This made him the prime minister in March 2008 after an excruciating ten months of post-election negotiations. The compromise deal worked out by a "wise men's group" from the five main parties (both Christian Democrats, both Liberals and the French Socialists) promised even more self-rule for the regions and foresees the devolution of various powers over housing, agriculture and industrial policy. However, since the governing coalition represents a broad range of opinion and contains most of the large parties, it could last three years or more, even though two out of three respondents expressed doubts about this in a March 2008 poll. The result continues the three-decade tradition of having only Flemish-speaking prime ministers.

Leterme's ascendance will not have a significant influence on foreign policy. But it heated up language tensions that even seeped into the crowning ceremony of the Miss Belgium pageant the end of 2007 in Antwerp. When the shapely Alizee Poulicek, who is trilingual in Czech, English and French, was asked a question in Dutch and had to admit she could not understand, she was booed. In 2006 Leterme had called the 176-year-old Belgian state an "accident of history" that was so worn down that it amounted to no more than a

king, a national soccer team and well-known beer brands. An opinion poll in 2008 revealed that 54% of Flemings and 92% of Walloons did not trust him as prime minister. He has never served in a federal cabinet and has little experience negotiating with leaders from the other linguistic group.

These tensions are not new. But in the opinion of former prime minister Wilfried Martens, the current problems are made worse by the fact that politicians from the two regions do not share similar goals and lack the informal contacts they once had. "We are the center of the European Union. How could we give such a bad example to all the member states if we were to split?" The minister in charge of foreign affairs for the Flemish government, Geert Bourgeois, agrees: "We are two democracies with different parties and totally different needs. We speak different languages. We don't watch the same television. We don't read what is written in the south, and the Walloons don't read what our opinion-makers write." The country is close to the point where the central government would be irrelevant. Power has been either devolved to the regions or passed up to the EU. What is left?

Many Belgians cling to their country as was demonstrated in November 2007, when 35,000 from both regions demonstrated in Brussels to support unity and protest the lack of a government. It is re-

markable that, thanks to their efficient bureaucracy, Belgians' daily lives were barely disturbed by the prolonged crisis: social security benefits and salaries were paid regularly, and the trains ran on time. But the fragility of the Belgian state had been starkly displayed by the reaction to a fabricated TV "news" report on the French-language RTBF December 13, 2006, the day before an EU summit. With a straight face, a well-known francophone news presenter interrupted the normal programming and announced that Belgium had just split apart after Flanders declared its independence. He cut to familiar reporters "on the spot" and showed film clips of the royal family departing from the Melsbroek military airport and of the number 44 streetcar being stopped as it tried to cross from Brussels into the Flemish-speaking suburb of Tervuren.

The portrayal was so believable and realistic that diplomats called the foreign ministry to confirm whether it was true. Many Walloons panicked briefly. But all they would have had to do to verify that the report was a spoof was to flip on the Dutch-language channels. Few did this. The incident was a scare for some Belgians, a hilarity for others and a bad joke for the government. Coming at the end of a year of increasing talk about further decentralization, it demonstrated that the debate about Belgium's future was no longer restricted to political circles.

St.-Boniface Bridge in Bruges

The Grand Duchy of Luxembourg

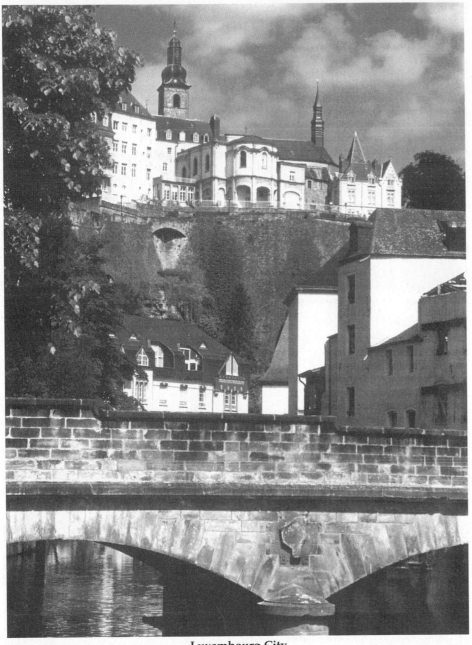
Luxembourg City

Chief of State: His Royal Highness the Grand Duke Henri, b. 1955. Married in 1981 to Grand Duchess Maria Teresa. He succeeded his father upon his abdication in 2000.

Head of Government: Jean–Claude Juncker, Prime Minister (since 1995).

National Flag: Three horizontal stripes of equal width, red, white, blue (The flag closely resembles that of the Netherlands).

Since the Roman legions came to what is now Luxembourg in 57 B.C., the Luxembourgers have tenaciously clung to their separate existence. Caesar wrote that the Treveri tribesmen who resisted his troops "never submitted to commands except under the compulsion of an army." In the two millenia that followed, the Franks, Burgundians, Dutch and Germans controlled this tiny land. But, unlike most small nations, the Luxembourgers never allowed themselves to be absorbed entirely by another power. They well deserve their national motto: *Mir wolle bleive wat mir sin!* ("We want to remain what we are!").

Luxembourg is the smallest independent state in the EU, encompassing only 999 square miles, less than the state of Rhode Island. It has a growing population of 450,000, fewer than one–third that of Brussels and one–twentieth that of Paris. Nevertheless, it is one of the most prosperous countries in the world, with an industrial productivity and international significance far out of proportion to its size.

The northern half of the country, called Oesling, is a rugged territory of low mountains and forests. It is a continuation of the Ardennes forest area of Belgium. The southern half is within the Lorraine Plain and is rolling, wooded countryside. Because of its lush pastureland and fertile soil, this area is called the Gutland or Bon Pays (Good Land). It also contains most of Luxembourg's industrial centers and its capital city.

With its many international organizations and multilingual citizens the capital is a very cosmopolitan city. Having only about 80,000 inhabitants, it is no metropolis, but it is a charming, almost fairytale city built in the late 16th century in Spanish Renaissance style and remodeled at the end of the 19th century. Two rivers, the Alzette and Petrusse, flow through the city, which is located on a plateau, and through the centuries they have cut deep, narrow valleys with very steep sides dropping 200 feet. The old section of the city is perched on the highest part of the plateau. Located on one of the many narrow, twisting streets of the old city is the Grand Ducal Palace, built in 1573, with

Area: 999 sq. mi. (2,586 sq. km., somewhat smaller that Rhode Island).

Population: 459,000, of which over a third are foreigners.

Capital City: Luxembourg (Pop. 80,000, estimated).

Climate: Temperate, with mild winters and summers.

Neighboring Countries: Luxembourg is wedged between Belgium (West); Germany (East) and France (South).

Official Languages: Luxembourgish (a Moselle Franconian–German dialect with numerous additions of French words), French and German.

Ethnic Background: Indo–European, Germanic.

Principal Religion: Roman Catholic (94%).

Main Exports: Iron and steel products, chemicals. International banking activities are extremely important.

Main Imports: Minerals, metals, foodstuffs, machinery.

Currency: Euro.

Major Trading Customers: EU (84.6% of exports and 90.1% of imports), Germany (25.4% of exports and 34.2% of imports), France (19.7% of exports and 26.5% of imports), Belgium (12.1% of exports and 15.3% of imports), U.S. (3.2% of exports and 4.3% of imports).

National Day: June 23rd.

Luxembourg

colorful guards always standing or marching in front of it.

HISTORY

The Early Period

Luxembourg's independence was established in 963 A.D. Siegfried, the Count of Ardennes, hewed powerful battlements in the cliffs where Luxembourg's capital city is now located. Until it was demolished by international agreement in 1867, this almost impregnable fortress was called the "Gibraltar of the North." In fact, the word Luxembourg meant "little fortress." The visitor can still climb on the ruins of this stronghold and wander in the maze of passages underneath it.

Independent Luxembourg was linked to the Holy Roman Empire, and in the beginning of the 14th century Luxembourg's Duke, Henry VII, was crowned Holy Roman Emperor. Luxembourg ultimately provided four Emperors during this heyday of the Duchy's power. Henry's son, John, a man very fond of travel, women, horses and dice, became the King of Bohemia. After losing one eye in battle and the other to disease, he became known as John the Blind. His bravery became legendary in the Battle of Crecy in 1346 against the English. Unable to see, John galloped to the head of his troops by having his steed tied to those of several loyal aides and then ordering them to advance. Not surprisingly, he did not survive the battle.

John's grandson, Charles IV, was also a Holy Roman Emperor and built the beautiful city of Prague, now the capital of the Czech Republic. The Luxembourgers' golden age of power gradually declined, and in 1443 the Duchy was conquered by the Duke of Burgundy; for more than four centuries, foreign powers gave the orders in Luxembourg.

Neutrality and War

Luxembourg evolved into a neutral country in the 19th century, but this lasted less than a half-century. It was violated by German troops in August 1914. The Grand Duchess Marie–Adelheid remained in the country during the entire four–year occupation, and in the opinion of many Luxembourgers she collaborated with the Germans. Whether this was true or not, she felt obliged to abdicate in early 1919, and her popular sister, Charlotte, ascended the throne. A referendum in 1919 confirmed the constitutional monarchy, but proclaimed the people to be sovereign and introduced universal suffrage for men and women. This referendum established a fully democratic parliamentary form of government in the Grand Duchy.

As small countries often do, Luxembourg felt the need to seek a union with a larger power, so in a referendum in 1921, Luxembourgers voted three to one to enter an economic union with France. The latter country, however, advised Luxembourg to enter a close economic relationship with Belgium; both smaller countries agreed to this in 1922.

In 1940 Luxembourg was given another reminder that a policy of neutrality alone cannot guarantee the security of a country. German troops again occupied the tiny state in 1940 and within a few weeks virtually annexed it. In August 1942 Luxembourg was officially incorporated into Hitler's Reich. When the population responded with a strike, about 30,000 Luxembourgers, or about 10% of the population and most of the country's young men, were deported. Many were forced to serve in the German army and until liberation the population continued to suffer greatly from a brutal occupation.

Having learned from her sister's mistake in 1914, Grand Duchess Charlotte fled in 1940 with her entire government, first to London and then to Montreal. She worked tirelessly to assure that Luxembourg would be recognized as an independent country at the war's end. Her son, Crown Prince Jean, served as an officer in the British army, and landed with his unit, the Irish Guards, on the beaches of Normandy on June 11, 1944, five days after the first Allied troops had landed. On September 3 his unit entered Brussels and on September 10 it crossed the Luxembourg border between Rodange and Pétange, exactly at the spot where his parents had left the country in 1940. The same afternoon he reached the capital city—his

Luxembourg

arrival was hailed by thousands of his countrymen. His father, Felix, had reached the city that morning with an American tank division.

Unfortunately, the war was not yet over for Luxembourg. Hitler's forces made a last offensive at the end of 1944 in order to stop the Allied advance toward Germany. During this Ardennes offensive, known as the Battle of the Bulge, the American commander, General Omar Bradley, made Luxembourg City his headquarters, but a large portion of the Duchy was nevertheless recaptured by German troops. In the fiercely fought Battle of the Bulge such destruction was visited upon the land that it took until 1952 to repair all the material damage. American losses were also very great, as one can see at the American military cemetery in Hamm, located about a mile from Luxembourg Airport. There rest 5,000 American soldiers, including General George Patton, who was killed in a jeep accident in December 1945. Most cities in Luxembourg have a street or square named after Patton, who is hailed as the country's liberator. Ettelbruck in the Ardennes unofficially calls itself Patton Town.

GOVERNMENT AND POLITICS

The Grand Duke

Luxembourg is a constitutional monarchy, whose constitution of 1868 was amended in 1919 to invest sovereignty in the people, rather than in the crown. Executive power is formally vested in the Grand Duke Henri, who assumed his father's legislative powers in 1998 and ascended to the throne in 2000 when his father, Jean, abdicated in his favor. The grand duke possesses no actual crown to wear. He is the sixth grand duke since 1890. Jean's decision to step down at age 79 followed a precedent set by his mother, Charlotte, who abdicated in 1964. Jean also ordered that Luxembourg's quota of euro coins, which went into circulation in 2002, bear Henri's head on them.

The grand duke, who underwent officer's training in Britain, is a popular monarch, and the Luxembourgers' enthusiastic response to his marriage in 1981 demonstrated this sentiment. Henri met a beautiful and intelligent Cuban exile, Maria Teresa Mestre, while both were studying in Geneva. Although she was not of noble birth, he chose to marry her, and their wedding in the Luxembourg Cathedral drew a large assemblage of European nobility.

The grand duke, who takes his duties seriously, has considerable influence in the political process. As all constitutional monarchs, he "reigns but does not rule." To be effective, one or several members of the

Former Royal Highnesses The Grand Duke Jean and Grand Duchess

government, who alone assume political responsibility, must countersign his orders. Nevertheless, he could be an especially important figure in times of national crisis when either the parties are unable to form a government, or the nation desperately needs a symbol of national unity. In normal times his actual powers are limited.

Executive Power

Executive power is actually exercised by the president of the government (the prime minister) and his Council of Government (cabinet). The latter body is composed of 11 or 12 persons, each usually holding several ministerial posts. During the five years between elections, the cabinets are occasionally reshuffled, but the resulting "new" governments are seldom significantly different from the ones they replace. In order to try to create some separation between the parliament and the executive, as mandated by the constitution, all cabinet members are required to resign their parliamentary seats when they assume a cabinet post.

The cabinet drafts and submits legislation, which is debated in parliament. The most important professional organizations, especially the six official groups representing agriculture, handcrafts, commerce, civil servants, private employees and labor, are consulted on legislation affecting their interests. The smallness of the country enables this process to work smoothly. Passage after two rounds of debate is usually a foregone conclusion, since the governing parties' approval had already been reached in advance. Particularly important legislation can be submitted directly to the voters in a referendum

if the cabinet and parliament approve, but such referendums very seldom occur.

Legislative Structure and Powers

The grand duke must formally sign all legislation and appointments. The president and Council of Government are not responsible to the monarch, but to the lower house of parliament, the Chamber of Deputies. Its 60 members (lowered from 64 in 1989 to reflect the declining population) are elected every five years by a system of proportional representation tailored to a small or medium–size country, in which voters live close to the candidates and may even know them personally. Almost a fourth of deputies are women. Luxembourg is divided into four electoral districts, and seats are distributed to each depending upon population. The largest receives 23 seats and the smallest seven. Each voter is permitted to cast as many votes as there are candidates to be elected and may even cast two votes for the same candidate if he wishes. The seats are then distributed to the candidates who receive the most votes.

Summaries of parliamentary debates and election information are sent to all citizens of voting age, who are required to vote. As in all parliamentary democracies, if the president and Council of Government lose their majority in the Chamber, then the grand duke can call new elections although such early elections are seldom necessary.

Political Parties

Since 1925 no political party has ever been able to win a majority of seats in the Chamber of Deputies, so all governments

Luxembourg

are coalitions of two or more parties. Luxembourg's three main parties have led Luxembourg for about 50 years and have helped create a democracy based on party cooperation. Although each major party represents a distinct political subculture, they all seek a solution to problems in a way agreeable to all three, no matter which is in government at the moment. All three are willing to form coalitions with each other. Neither ideologies nor historical resentments prevent them from sharing responsibility for their nation's future.

The largest is the Christian–Social People's Party (CSV), which represents the bourgeois values of a predominantly Catholic population. Its votes are drawn primarily from practicing Catholics, although the gradual disappearance of church–state issues has greatly reduced the religious component of its program. It does draw votes from the nation's farmers and workers. The party's program calls for support of a social market economy and special attention to the needs of citizens who earn below the national average. It is a middle–of–the–road party which supports the extension of the country's already generous social welfare system. With a loosening of religious bonds and a decrease of the number of farmers, the CSV gets fewer votes than it once did.

The CSV has for years been the key coalition party, and no ruling coalition since World War II has been formed without first trying to win its direct participation. In 1994 Jean–Claude Juncker replaced as prime minister Jacques Santer, who left office to be EU president from 1995 to 1999. One of seven children of a steelworker and trade union militant, Juncker went to school in Belgium and studied law in Strasbourg. He came from the left of the CSV and joined the cabinet in 1984 at age 29. He quickly gained a reputation as an intelligent, well–connected man in the EU with integrity, a broad mind, and a knack for grasping both practical detail and conceptual problems. A chain-smoker, he has an unruly air and a common touch. By 2005 he was the EU's longest serving leader with a reputation as a wily, multilingual political operator and negotiator, a blend of casualness and working energy.

In 2004 he was the French and Germans' choice to be president of the European Commission, but he turned it down in order to remain Luxembourg's prime minister and finance minister. He accepted the EU role as spokesman for the euro. In the June 2004 elections, Juncker's Christian Democrats increased their dominance with 36% of the votes and 24 seats, up from 19.

The second-largest party is the Luxembourg Socialist Workers Party (LSAP), known generally as the Socialists. It was founded at the turn of the century to protect workers from the seamy consequences of industrialization. Because it views itself as the party of the working class, it is strongest in the highly industrialized South. The LSAP got 23% and 14 seats in the 2004 elections, and it entered the governing coalition with the CSV.

The third-largest party is the Democratic Party (DP), usually referred to as the Liberals. Its support is found primarily in the middle class, professions and skilled working groups. It strongly supports a free market economy and opposes excessive government control over the economy. In 2004, it captured 16% and 10 seats and moved into the opposition.

Small parties capture some votes. The Action Committee for Democracy and Pension Justice (ADR) received 9.9% and five seats. It had begun as a one–issue party, calling itself the Five–Sixths Party because it advocated raising all pensions to five–sixths of a person's last salary, as government employees receive. It is now often referred to as the Nationalists. The Greens (*Déi Gréng*) won 11.6% and seven seats in 2004. It did even better in the European Parliament elections held the same day, winning 15%, the largest percentage increase of any European Green party. Profiting from the unpopularity of the Cattenom nuclear reactor three kilometers (two miles) across the French border, its slogan was: "You decide! Your vote blows nuclear power away."

The only party that never participates in governing coalitions is the Communist Party of Luxembourg (KPL). It finds its electoral support primarily in the industrialized South. Its electoral support has continuously declined. A major reason is that it never fully embraced the more moderate form of communism known as Eurocommunism, which seeks to respect the democratic process and pursue policies oriented toward the particular needs of their own countries. The KPL's ideological rigidity will probably keep it in the political cold, especially following the collapse of communism in Eastern Europe. Neither it, the New Left, nor the Populists won seats in 2004.

Although the parliament is technically a one–chamber assembly, the 21–member Council of State traditionally functions as an upper house. It is appointed by the grand duke, acting upon the advice of the cabinet, Chamber of Deputies and the Council of State itself. Mainly an advisory body, the Council of State must be consulted on all legislation and can actually postpone its enactment. Ultimately, however, the Chamber of Deputies can always override it. Eleven of the Council's members function as the nation's highest administrative court. On the whole, the Council plays an important role in the governing process.

Royal Highnesses The Grand Duke Henri and Grand Duchess Maria Teresa

Prime Minister Jean-Claude Juncker

Local Government

For administrative purposes, Luxembourg is divided into three districts: Luxembourg, Diekirch and Grevenmacher, which are further broken down into 12 cantons and 118 communes. Each commune has authority over local affairs and elects a Communal Council every six years. To maintain some measure of national control, the central government appoints a burgomaster (mayor) to every commune, who presides over the Communal Council. All appointments must, however, enjoy the confidence and support of a majority among the locally elected members of the Communal Councils; no mayor is ever imposed on a commune. In order to make the system of local government more efficient, the central government has proposed that all the present communes be fused into a total of 30, with none having a population under 3,000. Local resistance so far has prevented the realization of this plan.

Defense and Foreign Policy

Two world wars in the 20th century convinced Luxembourgers that neutrality offered their country no protection whatsoever. Their government–in–exile supported the Allied cause, and in 1949 the country joined NATO. With such a small population, it cannot contribute many troops to the alliance. In 1967, it abolished its conscript army, created in 1945, but it maintains a voluntary army of battalion size (900 light infantry troops), including a 60-man band. More importantly, it provides storage sites for NATO equipment. In 2006 the U.S. Army announced that it would close its facility in Bettembourg, where it stored equipment and material used to supply its troops on military deployments. Luxembourg pledged in 2002 that it would purchase an Airbus military transport plane to help provide lift to NATO or EU military units.

In the aftermath of the 2003 Iraq war, which Luxembourg opposed, it joined with France, Germany and Belgium to create a joint rapid reaction unit built on the existing French-German brigade. Luxembourg would contribute a reconnaissance team. In addition, the four said they would set up a multinational headquarters and a separate military center in Belgium to command and plan EU military operations when NATO is not involved. The four invited other European nations to join their effort, but sensing that the real purpose of this effort was to weaken the transatlantic alliance, none did. The plan was therefore dropped a few months later. Neither Luxembourg nor the other three pledged to raise their defense spending to cover the costs of these innovations.

Luxembourg was a founding member of the EU, a fact that has greatly enhanced its prestige. It amended its constitution in 1956 to permit the transfer of certain of its sovereign powers to the EU. At first, the EU's founding fathers suggested that tiny Luxembourg, which is the geographic center of the six nations, become a kind of Washington, D.C., for the new United States of Europe. This never happened. EU officials travel back and forth from Brussels, Strasbourg and Luxembourg, a necessity that many officials and observers find wasteful and irritating. It is now the home of many EU offices and institutions, a large part of which are located on the Kirchberg plateau in the Europa Center, a cluster of EU institutions containing several of Luxembourg's few skyscrapers. In 2005 it was a vast construction site as Luxembourg expands and improves the EU officials' working environment in the wake of the May 2004 enlargement to 25 members. In all, about 9,300 EU employees and even more foreign business executives live in Luxembourg.

Among the EU offices located in the grand duchy is the Secretariat for the European Parliament, which is the largest contingent, employing over 2,500 persons. There are also Euratom, the European Court of Justice, the European Audit Court, the European Investment Bank and the European Currency Union. In 1988 Luxembourg won an important victory in its bid to become the center of the EU's legal operations. A new Court of First Instance was created there to assume some of the growing workload of the European Court of Justice.

The European Parliament used to meet there sometimes, and a new European parliament building was constructed for these meetings. But in 1979 the parliament decided to hold all sessions in Strasbourg. This decision infuriated Luxembourg, which turned in vain to the European Court of Justice for help. A massive office complex was constructed in Brussels that includes an Assembly Chamber large enough for the European Parliament. Luxembourg tenaciously guards against Brussels its retention of the parliament's secretariat, a body of about 2,500 European officials who make the parliament work. Most of the parliament's committee work already takes place in Brussels, and all the major political groups within the parliament have established their headquarters there.

Entrance to the Grand Ducal Palace in Luxembourg

Luxembourg

It has been estimated unofficially that 10% of all retail spending in the city of Luxembourg comes from EU employees and their families. Thus, their disappearance could severely affect retail businesses and property values. Thanks to the presence of these European institutions, Luxembourg is not only the richest member of the EU, but also its biggest net recipient per head of EU funds. Luxembourgers converted their European Parliament building to other purposes, such as an international conference center.

Luxembourg's chief foreign policy goals are to be a significant partner in the building of a politically and economically integrated Europe, After French and Dutch voters turned down the ill-fated EU constitution in May and June 2005 referenda, Luxembourgers voted in favor of it (57% to 43%) on July 10, 2005. No one doubted that its parliament would approve the revived treaty signed in Lisbon in December 2007.

ECONOMY

Luxembourg is a highly industrialized and prosperous country. In 2003 it had the world's highest per capita GDP. Since 1945, it has known a high degree of political and social peace. Its economy has always been based so heavily on iron and steel that it is often said, "Luxembourg is as much a gift of iron as Egypt is a gift of the Nile." This has been especially true since 1877, when the Englishmen Sidney, Thomas and P. Carlyle Gilchrist discovered the Gilchrist-Thomas process for removing the phosphorus from Luxembourg's iron ore. Its largest steel company, Arcelor (formerly ARBED) was partly foreign–owned, but the Luxembourg state became its major stockholder. Only a fifth of its turnover was in Luxembourg; its operations were worldwide and it had major plants in France, Spain, Germany, Belgium, Holland and South Korea. ARBED, Usinor from France and Aceralia from Spain merged to form Arcelor, the world's biggest steel producer with roughly 5% of global output.

The competition among the world's steel producers had become so strong that production outstripped demand. In response, Luxembourg reduced its production. In 1970 the steel industry produced nearly a third of the country's GDP; by 2006 that figure was down to less than 3%. This forced the Luxembourg steel industry to restructure itself and ultimately to merge with two other foreign companies in 2002. This was also required by the EU, which now seeks to save the European steel industry by requiring it to modernize in member countries.

In June 2006 Arcelor agreed to a hostile merger with the Indian giant, Mittal Steel

The Château de Berg, Grand Ducal country residence

to form the world's largest steelmaker in terms of market value, revenue and output. The chief executive, backed by France, had vigorously resisted this move for over five months. But the selling price (25.6 billion euros or $38 billion) carried the day. Mittal contented itself with a 43.6% stake in the company and only three of the seven seats on the management board, but Lakshmi Mittal took over as chief executive.

There has been a gradual reduction of the steel industry's work force in Luxembourg from 25,000 in 1974 to 6,500 by 2006. These reductions resulted in a rise in productivity per employee. Arcelor remains the country's biggest employer after the state. In order not to disrupt social peace, they were accomplished by retirement of workers as early as age 57, rather than by massive layoffs. It is this kind of practice that has enabled Luxembourg to hold its unemployment rate to 2.2% in 2004, among the lowest in the world and best in the EU.

It has a labor shortage, and over 80% of new jobs are filled by cross border workers, called "*Frontaliers*"—approximately 90,000 enter daily to work in Luxembourg, chiefly in the financial services sector. Together with resident aliens, they constituted over 53% of the workforce in 2003; in the financial services sector that figure is two-thirds. Since Luxembourgers grew up speaking French and German, the foreign commuters face no language barriers.

The country's political and economic leaders saw the problem of excessive dependence upon steel and banking well in advance, and, since 1950, they have made a steady effort to diversify the economy. The Goodyear Tire and Rubber Company began building plants in the Grand Duchy in 1951 and is now its second largest employer. The program got a particular boost from the industrial diversification law of 1962; this has been renewed regularly and provides state financial assistance for industrial development that contributes to the construction, conversion and rationalization of industries, crafts and commercial operations. The program has greatly stimulated the service industries, which now employ about three-fourths of the work force, and has attracted over 60 new companies to Luxembourg, which have created employment for more than 11,000 persons. The most important newcomers have been American, such as DuPont.

The program has also helped to attract foreign banks to the country; the number of banks increased from 13 in 1955 to 230 in 1998 and then declined to 185 by 2002. Luxembourg has become one of the financial centers in Europe. When the Eurodollar market (in which Luxembourg had specialized) declined, and London deregulated the British financial industry, Luxembourg shifted deftly to other retail banking services and maintains its place in the world market. This has greatly benefited the country. Banks employ 24,000 and generate a quarter of the GDP and a third of government revenue in 2004. One can almost speak of an economic revolution in the grand duchy.

In the 1980s, one job in banking was being created for every job that was disappearing in the steel industry. By 1988 the number of Luxembourgers employed in banking overtook those working in the steel industry, and that gap has continued to widen greatly. In 2006 financial services, such as banking, investment funds, corporate finance and clearing houses, accounted for 30% of GDP. Sometimes its easy business environment creates problems. This was the case in 2006 when a clearing house, Clearstream, landed in the middle of a French political scandal for allegedly laundering dirty money for high-level politicians. Although the indicated accounts turned out to be fabrications, the affair raised questions about what kind of money flows through the grand duchy. In response, it promised to scrap a law that gives tax exemptions to certain holding companies.

To attract funds to Luxembourg banks, the country has doggedly pursued its right to guarantee bank secrecy, despite pressure from the EU and U.S. to cooperate more closely in cases involving crime, money laundering and tax fraud. Germany suffers most from the capital flight to Luxembourg. Along with other powerful neighbors, it pressured the duchy to harmonize its low tax regime (30.3% corporate tax) with its EU partners and abandon its zero withholding tax on foreigners. Because the financial services sector now accounts for more than a fifth of its GDP and employs one in ten persons in the work force, it remains the motor for the country's economic growth. Luxembourg resists these efforts as best it can. However, it pays attention to proposals to reform EU banking policies. In 2003 it agreed, along with Belgium, to levy withholding taxes of 15% (20% in 2008) on foreign accounts and pass them on to other EU governments while keeping the bank secrecy rules in place. It is preparing to expand beyond its traditional banking activities to offer financial services unavailable in other European countries.

Because of its low sales tax (VAT 15%), the country has become a center for e-commerce, including iTunes, Skype, eBay, AOL, Amazon.com and other large Internet companies. This is part of its effort to diversify its economy from an excessive reliance on banking. It therefore resists EU efforts to get rid of its tax advantages and to go after it as a "tax haven." Prime Minister Juncker admits: "We have not made ourselves extremely popular in Europe."

The financial services sector has emerged as the economy's largest taxpayer. To keep the economy growing, the government introduced in 1986 the most sweeping tax reform in the nation's history. Taxes were cut and loopholes were closed. Just over half the cuts are enjoyed by the business sector, prompting some critics of the reform to charge that it is a device primarily to improve the financial environment for bankers.

In 1991 further tax cuts went into effect. Luxembourg was the first EU country in 1997 to meet all the Maastricht treaty convergence criteria for economic and monetary union (EMU). The banks had mixed feelings about the new euro; they quailed at the cost of introducing it, estimated to be 4% of their total revenues. They also feared that the euro could bring with it an EU-wide harmonization of withholding tax, which could be a severe blow to Luxembourg's competitiveness as an offshore financial center. The country's government debt is a mere 6.7% of GDP, its budget showed a 2.5% surplus in 2003 but a 1.4% deficit a year later, its inflation was steady at 2.1% in 2004 despite wage indexing, and its economic growth, although down from 6% annually from 1996–2001, was healthy at 2.5% in 2004.

As a tiny but mighty economic dynamo and financial center in the heart of Europe, Luxembourg's influence over the regions it now borders has grown dramatically. It has adapted more successfully to new economic realities than have the German, French and Belgian areas along its borders. Germany's Saarland and Rhineland-Palatinate, France's Lorraine, and Belgium's Wallonia have experienced retarded economic development and have in some ways become economic satellites of Luxembourg. This has been facilitated by the EU's "single market," which promotes the free movement of capital and labor. Employment opportunities in the duchy help relieve the high rates of unemployment in those neighboring areas. In such a *Grande Région*, as it has been called, the economic, social and cultural ties will continue to deepen, and the borders between them will fade.

With a very small population and a high standard of living, Luxembourg is absolutely dependent upon foreign trade. Exports and imports account for 85% of its GDP, compared with 50% for Belgium, 20% for France and 10% for the U.S. Such dependence indicates why Luxembourg's membership in the EU has been a matter of economic life or death. It sends 85% of its exports to its EU partners and gets 88% of its imports from them. At 4% of its total, Luxembourg's trade with the U.S. remains relatively insignificant. Primary imports are iron ore, coke and all energy sources except hydroelectricity.

Its steel companies own some coalmines in Germany, but its dependence upon imported oil, gas and coal is a major problem. With the highest per capita number of automobiles in Europe, oil is a particularly sensitive import, but by 1991 oil accounted for only 10% of Luxembourg's imports, down from 17% in 1973. To increase its energy supplies, an atomic plant along the Moselle River was planned, which would have supplied most of the power needs until the year 2000. However, the nuclear accident at Harrisburg, Pennsylvania, created political problems that caused the plans for this plant to be dropped. Luxembourg also declined to join with France in developing a nuclear power plant at Cattenom, located only two miles (three kilometers) from the grand duchy. After the 1986 nuclear accident at Chernobyl in the Soviet Union, the Luxembourg government and, according to polls, 80% of the citizens began to worry more about the safety of the Cattenom plant. Winds blow west from Cattenom through Luxembourg. However, demonstrations and diplomatic protests have had no influence on the French in this matter.

An important factor in maintaining industrial production in such a small country has been the importation of foreign workers, especially from Portugal, Italy and Spain. Together with their families, they now account for over a third of the population (36.5% of the total population over age 15) and come from a hundred other countries. This is the highest percentage of foreign workers in the EU. If trends continue, the proportion will be one-half within the lifetimes of most living inhabitants. Over half of Luxembourg City's population is already foreign.

Nonnationals, especially immigrants from Portugal and Italy, hold about half of all jobs in the country. Foreigners provide 52% of the workers in all of Luxembourg's industries, although the percentages differ in the various economic sectors. They account for 85% of the construction workers, 66% of the craftsmen and 35% of the laborers in the iron and steel industry. Their visibility was manifested in a frightening incident in June 2000 when a 39-year-old Tunisian immigrant held dozens of school children cap-

Luxembourg

Museum Modern Art on Kirchberg, Luxembourg City

tive in the predominantly Portuguese-inhabited village of Wasserbillig, close to the German border. Because so many of the children were of Portuguese origin, the Lisbon government closely monitored the crisis. It ended after 28 hours when a sharpshooter posing as a cameraman shot and killed the hostage-taker with a gun concealed in a TV camera.

Foreign workers and their families are not permitted to participate in the national political life, although they can vote in European parliamentary elections. But even if there is little integration with the native population, they are generally well treated. Unlike in many European countries, there is no seriously destabilizing antiforeigner sentiment. This is partly explained by the fact that most immigrants share the same Catholic religion with 94% of the native Luxembourgers. In 2000 Luxembourg had the largest percentage of asylum-seekers per capita in the EU. There was a public protest when 40 of them were deported in 1999.

The dependence upon foreign workers seems irreversible, given Luxembourg's alarmingly low birth rate. Unlike the case in most European countries after 1945, there was no baby boom in Luxembourg, and since 1960 the birth rate has steadily declined to one of the lowest in the world—since 1968 the native population has declined by about 1,000 each year. This is not only a serious problem for the very survival of a small nation, but it creates an increasingly aging population that must be supported by fewer and fewer persons of working age. A fifth is already over 60 years of age, the largest percentage in the EU. Life expectance is rising: 74.9 years for men and 81.5 years for women. This will put increasing pressure on the country's generous pension system.

It is hoped that this unpleasant development can be rendered less serious by automating and modernizing industry. This would establish a productive industrial base that could create a high degree of wealth with fewer workers. The government provides a multitude of inducements to raise the birthrate: increasing family allowances, extending maternity leaves and helping single or divorced women raise children. Few people are optimistic that these measures will reverse the demographic downturn. One parliamentarian worried: "Our country is like an aging couple. We live well, but we don't know what tomorrow brings. We have no grandchildren."

Maintaining economic stability and prosperity will remain a major task for the future. This will require maintaining not only a high level of productivity, but also the labor peace that has prevailed since the end of World War II. There has been scarcely a strike since 1945. This enviable record is due to the well–organized process of consultation among employers, employees and the government, and to the great care taken not to allow the rate of unemployment to increase. In part, this has been successfully accomplished by introducing extensive public works and part–time work schedules with the state paying for the hours not worked.

This daring policy is one that most observers agree will become too costly in the long run. Labor peace was also preserved by indexing incomes and pensions to adjust automatically to inflation although such indexing fans the flames of inflation and damages trade competitiveness. In addition, this desire to maintain purchasing power clashes with the desire to increase social benefits, which already cover virtually the entire population.

Slightly more than half of Luxembourg's land is used for agriculture, of which 54% is used for grazing. A third of the country is planted with forests. Meat and dairy production dominate, accounting for more than 80% of the farm income. Wine production is also important.

Currently fewer than 6% of the population is engaged in agriculture, and this number is steadily declining. Yet even nonfarming Luxembourgers are not very far from the natural environment of their rural compatriots. A population density below the EU average, the absence of large cities, and the nearness of wooded areas, together with a relatively unspoiled countryside available for many kinds of relaxation, all contribute to making Luxembourg a pleasant place to live.

CULTURE

Tiny Luxembourg has always been heavily influenced by its neighbors, and nothing shows this quite so clearly as the polyglot of languages that every Luxembourger masters. The everyday language of the people is Luxembourgish, an old Moselle–Frankish dialect of German, which has taken on many altered French expressions, such as *d'fotell* (*le fauteuil*, armchair). The language has become the country's one real symbol of national identity. Even modern Germans have difficulty understanding it.

This native language is spoken at home, in parliament and sometimes in the courts, although documents and formal proceedings are in French. It also has a written form. Despite an official spelling, most Luxembourgers write it phonetically. There are no textbooks clarifying the grammatical rules. Some literature exists in the language, and local publishing houses are producing scores of books in it, spurred by such successful authors as Jhemp Hoscheit, who writes wildly popular children's books in Luxembourgish. Local radio thrives on it. There is a daily one–hour TV news broadcast in it since 1992. The 1990s witnessed a renaissance in interest in written Luxembourgish. A movement has risen to promote the language because many fear it will die in the face of massive migration to the duchy. The government declared it to be the official language and requires applicants for citizenship to study it. More and more foreign residents are learning to speak and write it as employees are increasingly required to use it on the workplace.

The German language is primarily used in most primary schools, criminal court proceedings, church, and the press, although it is not uncommon to see articles written in all three national languages on the same page of a newspaper—*Letzebuerger Journal*, *Luxemburger Wort*, *Tageblatt*. Finally, French is the language that is used most in administration, civil courts, parliament and secondary educa-

tion. Since most immigrants living in Luxembourg come from countries (particularly from Portugal, Italy, France and Belgium) where Romance languages or French are spoken, French is an easily learned unifying language that binds the newcomers with native Luxembourgers. Two German invasions in the 20th century caused the elite to align itself more toward France and francophone culture. Until 2006 the country lacked a university, but a new one opened its doors in 2006.

All Luxembourgers are completely trilingual, a fact that spares the country the terrible language conflicts that plague neighboring Belgium. In Luxembourg, culture, including theater, film and literature, is very dependent upon the surrounding French and German worlds, and citizens have realistically accepted this without resentment. Luxembourgers' national identity is so strong and seems so natural that no language issue seems capable of altering it.

Luxembourg introduced Europe's first commercial radio station in 1934. In 1988 it seized the lead in the satellite broadcasting of commercial television when an Ariane rocket placed its Astra satellite into orbit. Luxembourg now has Europe's largest satellite operator, Societé Europeenne des Satellites (SES). It has 16 channels that can beam to Britain, France, Germany and the BENELUX and Scandinavian countries.

Radio–Télé–Luxembourg (RTL) broadcasts to 500 million viewers across interna-

tional borders. It purchased a second satellite doubling capacity to 32 channels. It is the first European country to have an entire satellite system for TV. Some EU members, such as the UK and the Netherlands, oppose such open broadcasting, but Luxembourg is determined that the EU's principle of a "Single Market" should apply to TV viewing. This single market can also have other effects: Ufa, the TV and film subsidiary of the German media giant, Bertelsmann, merged in 1996 with the Compagnie Luxembourgeoise Radiodiffusion (CLR/now CLT), one of the pioneers of the European media industry. One of Luxembourg's largest businesses, RTL is now a majority-owned subsidiary of Bertelsmann and remains Europe's leading broadcasting company with interests in 24 TV channels and 17 radio stations. It boasts 26 channels in nine countries.

In 2006 the Grand-Duc Jean Museum of Modern Art opened on Kirchberg plateau, overlooking the capital. Dramatically designed with much glass by the Chinese-American architect Ieoh Ming Pei, it is the centerpiece of a vast cultural investment program aimed at transforming Luxembourg into a center for the arts. Lacking a world-class permanent collection, its first special exhibition featured the Luxembourg-born artist, Michael Majerus. The grand duchy also inaugurated a new philharmonic concert hall (Christian de Portzamparc's Philharmonie) next door and a national library within walking distance from the new museum. A new TGV fast-train line from France opened in 2007 to speed visitors to these sites.

THE FUTURE

Luxembourg's economic task will be to maintain the productivity, prosperity and social welfare net it has achieved. It is already Europe's richest country in per capita terms ($77,760 in 2008, compared with $41,640 in the U.S.). As an exporting nation, it worries about recession in the rest of Europe, especially Germany, and about its increasingly uncompetitive cost structure. It can be expected to maintain the political and social stability that has prevailed since 1945.

The duchy's goal of becoming Europe's capital will remain unfulfilled although its role in Europe is important. Prime Minister Juncker was honored in 2003 with Germany's first Quadriga Prize as "European of the Year," and in 2004 he was Germany's and France's candidate for the presidency of the European Commission to replace Romano Prodi. He turned it down to remain Europe's longest serving prime minister and to be "Mr. Euro."

The Swiss Confederation (Confoederatio Helvetica)

The nucleus of Swiss nationalism: Schwyz, Uri, and Unterwalden

Each of the cantons sends two members to the Council of States (Senate). However, the half-cantons listed send each one.

UNTERWALDEN
1. Nidwalden
2. Obwalden

APPENZELL
1. Inner Rhodes
2. Outer Rhodes

BASEL
Basel-Stadt (the city)
Basel-Land (countryside)

Area: 15,943 sq. mi. (41,292 sq. km.). Roughly the size of Vermont and New Hampshire together.

Population: 7.3 million. Average annual growth rate is .1%. One fifth of residents are foreigners.

Capital City: Bern (Pop. 122,560).

Climate: Owing to great variations in altitude, rapid changes in weather are typical.

Neighboring Countries: France (West); Germany (North); Austria and Liechtenstein (East); Italy (South).

Languages: Swiss nationals—German (64%); French (20%); Italian (6%) Romansch (.5%), Other (9.5%). Total population: German (64%); French (19%); Italian (8%); Romansch (.5%); other (8.5%).

Ethnic Background: Swiss nationals—German (74%); French (20%); Italian (4%); Romansch (1%); other (1%). Total population: German (69%); French (19%); Italian (10%); Romansch (1%); other (1%).

Principal Religion: Swiss Nationals—Protestant (55%); Roman Catholic (43%); Jewish (.2%); other (1.8%). Total population: Protestant (47.8%); Roman Catholic (49.4%); Jewish (.3%); other (2.5%).

Main Exports: Chemicals, machinery, watches and jewelry, metals and manufactures, precision instruments.

Main Imports: Chemicals, machinery, motor vehicles, textiles, precision instruments.

Major Trading Partners: EU25 (62.1% of exports and 82.8% of imports), Germany (20% of exports and 33.3% of imports), U.S. (10.7% of exports and 4.6% of imports), France (8.5% of exports and 9.4% of imports), Italy (8.1% of exports and 11.2% of imports), UK (5.1% of exports and 4% imports), Netherlands (5.2% of imports), Spain (4.3% of exports), Austria (4.6% of imports).

Currency: Swiss franc.

Independence: August 1291.

National Day: August 1.

Chief of State: A seven–person collegiate Federal Council; ceremonial functions are performed by the Federal President, a member of the Federal Council chosen by Parliament for a one–year term. In 2008 he is Pascal Couchepin, Interior Minister.

Head of Government: The Federal President's position is merely "first among equals" in the Federal Council.

National Flag: Square with a white cross on a red field. The flag of the International Red Cross is exactly the same, except that the colors are reversed.

Few visitors ever left Switzerland without feeling that he has been in one of the most extraordinary countries in the world.

218

With its stark Jura Mountains, jagged snow-capped Alps with tidy, rustic villages dotting their valleys, clean, mountain–fed lakes with cosmopolitan, manicured cities such as Geneva, Lausanne, Lucerne, Zurich and Basel on their shores, Switzerland seems to be the epitome of natural beauty, cleanliness, prosperity and stability. Its people speak a polyglot of languages, but such diversity does not threaten the country as it often does elsewhere.

In general, the Swiss are disciplined, thrifty, realistic, cautious, prudent about change and ingenious about using the resources they have at their disposal. They are not an exceptionally outgoing people, but they are renowned for their tolerance. Therefore, Switzerland is a dreamed-of refuge for political and economic disadvantaged and advantaged from all over the entire world.

A small, landlocked, mountainous country, Switzerland is located in the heart of western Europe. New Hampshire and Vermont could easily fit into the entire country, and 41 of 50 American states are larger than it. The Jura mountain chain covers approximately 10% of the country in the west and northwest and separates the city of Basel from the rest of the nation. Of the country's entire land area, 60% is located in the Alpine mountain chain, which runs roughly west to east through the southern part of the country. Often called "the mother of rivers, Swit-zerland, or more precisely, the Gotthard Massif, is the watershed for some of Western Europe's most important rivers: the Rhône flows through the canton of Valais, Lake Geneva and France to the Mediterranean Sea. The Rhine forms the border with Liechtenstein, Austria and Germany; it flows through Basel, where because of its large harbor, one has the impression of being closer to the sea than to the Alps. It forms part of the border between Germany and France, and after flowing through the Netherlands, it empties into the distant North Sea. The Ticino River flows into Italy and into the River Po, which ultimately empties into the Adriatic Sea. Finally, the Inn River, rising in the Swiss Engadine Valley flows through Austrian Tirol, the city of Innsbruck and empties into the Danube, which is destined for the Black Sea.

The remaining 30% of Switzerland's land area is composed of the rolling lowlands of the Central Plateau, extending from the northern shore of Lake Geneva (Lac Leman), northeast past Lake Lucerne and Lake Zurich to Lake Constance (Bodensee). This part of Switzerland is one of the most densely populated and heavily industrialized areas in Europe. Here are located three–quarters of the country's population, the bulk of its industry and agricultural crops, and most of its large cities, which by comparison with many other European cities, are relatively small. The largest is Zurich, with only about 720,000 inhabitants, including suburban residents.

Switzerland's central location has made the country a transportation hub for at least 2,000 years. Through it run important arteries connecting Paris with the Balkans, Munich with southeastern France, and northern Europe with Italy. This central location has, throughout the centuries, brought both prosperity and war to the fiercely independent Swiss people. It has presented them with their greatest opportunities and their greatest problems.

HISTORY

The Early Period

Since about 4000 B.C. Celtic tribes settled the fertile plain between the Jura and Alpine mountain ranges. One such tribe, which had moved from the banks of the Rhine, called themselves Helvetians. Scribes at that time described the Helvetians as "wealthy with gold" and as "outdoing all others in martial valor." They also knew how to write, applying the Greek script to their own spoken tongue. These ambitious warriors had been seriously bitten by the restless spirit of the migrations and set their eyes on the lands of the richest empire in the known world: Rome. When they tried to move into what is now southeastern France in 58 B.C., they clashed head on with the legions of

An Alpine village, Château d'Oex, in the canton of Vaud

Switzerland

Julius Caesar, which decimated the Helvetian army. For the next four and one–half centuries, Switzerland was a Roman outpost, an important buffer between the Germanic tribes in the North and the Roman Empire.

The Helvetians prospered under Roman domination. The new masters built cities in which trade, arts and crafts flourished. They secured the mountain passes and opened the Great Saint Bernard Pass for wagon trains in 47 A.D. Thus, military and trade routes between the two halves of Europe separated by the formidable Alpine mountains were created, which proved to be of lasting importance for the future development of Europe. The Roman legions also brought Christianity to Switzerland in the 4th century A.D.

As a Roman rampart and thoroughfare leading to the heart of the Roman Empire, the Helvetians were among the first to face the attacks by northern "barbarian" tribes who were bent on moving south against Rome. By the beginning of the 5th century, the Romans were compelled to withdraw, and the entire area lay open to invading Germanic tribes.

Two Germanic tribes moved to fill the rich vacuum left by the Romans. Christianized Burgundians settled in the western part of the country and gradually adopted Latin as their language. Ultimately their Latin idiom was the source of the French language. Shortly afterwards, the hardy and uncivilized Alemans from north of the Rhine River moved into the central plains and the Alpine area. They refused to give up their Germanic tongue and eventually displaced the Latin language and the Roman culture wherever they settled. Only the Rhaetians, who were firmly settled in the southeastern part of Switzerland (now the canton of Grisons), and the inhabitants of the valleys on the southern slopes of the Alps (now the canton of Ticino) escaped Burgundian or Aleman mastery. They were able to continue speaking Latin, which gradually became vulgarized into Romansch and Italian, respectively. By the 6th century the division of Switzerland into four separate language zones was established—three of Latin origin and the last, spoken by the majority, German.

From the 6th century on, another Germanic tribe, the Franks, established their control over large parts of Europe north of the Alps. During the reign of Charlemagne, who crowned himself Emperor in 800 A.D., the future Switzerland was absorbed into an Empire that scarcely survived his death. Switzerland was partitioned in the 9th and 10th centuries between the Kingdom of Upper Burgundy and the Dukedom of Swabia, both parts of the Holy Roman Empire. Switzerland's history from then on was closely linked to Germany, particularly to the House of Habsburg in Austria.

Although the new masters tried very hard to impose feudal ties on the Swiss, these attempts were never completely successful. The Helvetians and Alemans both had firm traditions of local autonomy and of personal freedom, traditions clearly visible in Switzerland today. By the 13th century, when Europe's feudal orders had been severely weakened by the crusades, important developments began to take place that ultimately resulted in an independent Switzerland.

In the year 1230 the St. Gotthard Pass was opened. Earlier, only two major, direct roads for crossing the Alps had been open, one in the West and one in the East of Switzerland. The opening of the Gotthard Pass now brought traffic to and from Italy through the heretofore relatively isolated central portion of the land. The great powers of Europe now eyed with much greater interest this valuable piece of territory astride a crucially important trade route.

At the foot of the northern slope of the Gotthard Massif, at opposite ends of Lake Lucerne, are located two small areas: Schwyz (from which Switzerland later got its name) and Uri. Far in advance of their time, these rugged mountain people met in assemblies to elect their leaders and to decide on the administration of common lands. In the 13th century they rebelled against the local dynasties and achieved a semi–independent status linked with the Holy Roman Empire. Schwyz had adopted its own banner, a white cross on a red field, the present Swiss flag.

The Beginning of Independence and Allegiance

The Habsburg ruler Rudolf I died in 1291, and two weeks later, representatives

The Oath of the Three Swiss (18th century)

of Schwyz and Uri, joined by those of a third Swiss area, Unterwalden, which is located on another arm of Lake Lucerne, met on the meadow of Rütli. There they signed a peace alliance in the beginning of August 1291, declaring their right to choose their own judges from among men of their own valleys and pledging reciprocal aid if one of them were wronged by an outside power. Indeed this alliance proved effective in 1315 when a thousand Swiss mountain men trapped and slaughtered two to three thousand knights sent to reestablish full Habsburg control. Although this alliance does not seem very revolutionary today, it was a momentous step at the time and established the cornerstone for modern Switzerland. These voluntary agreements formed the basis for the Swiss *"Willensnation"*—a nation created not by blood ties, but by the acts of diverse people's free will.

What it created was a loose confederation without central authority, army, police, court, or executive. Ultimate power remained with the individual states (called

Huge mural in Parliament—Lake Uri where Switzerland was founded

220

Switzerland

cantons after 1803). Decisions were made in regular meetings among the cantons' leaders and were made not by majority vote, but by consensus. In other words, solutions had to be found to which all parties could agree. These principles of reaching agreement for all decisions, known in Switzerland today as "amicable agreement," and of working out problems in a confederal, not centralized way, have become deeply rooted in Swiss democracy.

The legendary William Tell of Uri, immortalized in Friedrich Schiller's drama, remains a symbol for the liberty these three "forest cantons" on the shores of Lake Lucerne pledged to defend. Forced by the tyrannical bailiff Gessler to shoot an apple from the head of his own child, Tell took revenge by shooting a fatal arrow at Gessler himself.

Present–day Switzerland gradually took shape in the following centuries as other cantons or cities joined this original alliance. The major motive for the cantons' joining or remaining in the alliance was usually to defend themselves against the Habsburgs' repeated attempts to regain or tighten control over them. The cities and territories of Lucerne, Zurich, Bern, Glarus and Zug joined in the 14th century. At about the same time Uri conquered the Italian–speaking Levintina, a valley along the Ticino River on the southern slope of the Alps. This was the first time that a non–Germanic-speaking area became a part of the confederation. In 1477 Bern snatched stretches of land in the Vaud from the Duke of Savoy. Again, people who did not speak German were incorporated into the confederation. Later in joining were Fribourg and Solothurn in 1481, Basel and Schaffhausen in 1501 and Appenzell in 1513. The land between these cantons was gradually purchased or conquered, so that by the early 16th century, Switzerland was a more or less contiguous territory.

Initial Alliance Organization

The terms for each entry were often different, and most maintained their own alliances with outside powers. Thus, Switzerland was at this time a "system of alliances," a patchwork of independent countries with different political systems. What they agreed to do was to assist each other militarily, to consult one another and to hold conventions (Diets) at fixed times and places. Only unanimous decisions were binding. There were certainly powerful disagreements among the members, which sometimes led to wars among themselves. This system of alliances was the first in Europe to combine cities with rural states, and there were persistent disputes stemming from the different interests of town dwellers and peasants. Also,

some cantons wanted the confederation to expand in a westerly direction toward France, while others wanted it to expand in a southerly direction toward Italy.

The Swiss temptation to become a great power through territorial expansion was rapidly extinguished in 1515, when the French decisively defeated the Swiss forces at Marignano. The bravery of highland infantrymen was no match for modern cavalry and artillery in the plain. This disastrous battle, in which only about one–half the cantons chose to participate, made the Swiss realize two things. First, the headless Confederation, with its web of alliances and no overall executive, did not permit ambitious Swiss projects beyond their territory. It decided thenceforth to make key decisions by majority vote, but it was no longer a match for the surrounding monarchies. Second, having eliminated the last vestiges of Habsburg influence from Switzerland in 1499, the Swiss decided to pursue a policy of maximum independence from the alliances and political intrigues of all other European countries. A treaty signed in 1521 with France became the only alliance signed by all the cantons of the confederation with a foreign power.

Arms, Mercenaries and an Independent Tradition

In return for French protection and the right to trade freely with France, the Swiss obligated themselves to provide soldiers for the French king's infantry. At the same time, the Swiss were permitted to provide military units to other European states. This practice meant that on occasion, Swiss troops faced each other on the battlefield. It was, nevertheless, often economically important for Swiss communities which accepted contracts for the troops. The hiring of mercenaries did not end until 1859, with the one exception of the colorful Swiss guards who still staff the Vatican today.

Due to the outstanding reputation of Swiss troops throughout Europe, these soldiers were very much sought after. Louis XI of France paid Swiss troops premium wages for their services, and when word got around that the Swiss were being paid so well, men from all over the French– speaking world attempted to enlist under the guise of being Swiss. Thereupon, Louis decided that a Swiss was only a person coming from a German–speaking canton, and anyone else who claimed to be Swiss was hanged promptly for "fake advertising."

The excellent Swiss military reputation stemmed from several things. First, Swiss troops served their own cantons' interests, fought under their own cantons' banners, obeyed their own officers and were gov-

erned by their own codes. This made them far braver than other mercenaries, who were well known for the speed with which they left the battlefield at crucial times. Swiss troops, with their capacity to stick together and to offer themselves wholly to a collective, were prepared to fight to the last man.

The Swiss soldiers also had certain capabilities that were highly valued. They could march with great rapidity and they could operate very effectively in mountainous areas. Because they could scale cliffs so easily, they could capture fortresses better than any others. Therefore, before heavy artillery was perfected, the best weapon against a fortress was a unit of Swiss troops.

The Swiss infantry units also were the first to use a weapon that was terrifying to knights in armor—the halberd. This hand–wielded weapon, now frequently carried by the Swiss guards at the Vatican, basically stood in the same relationship to a knight's armor as a can–opener now stands to a can. Johannes von Winterthur recorded in his chronicle of a ghastly picture of row after row of dead knights lying on the battlefield, their helmets split wide open.

The Swiss were, and still are, a people in arms. This fact has been a key to Switzerland's survival as an independent country in the heart of Europe. It has also been a key to its establishment very early of an exceptionally high degree of personal freedom for more and more of its own people. Among the first things which European feudal lords did, in order to insure their mastery over serfs, was to disarm them. Thus, in the rest of Europe, fewer persons were armed than in Switzerland. This meant not only that their rulers treated peasants and other citizens of Swiss cantons with greater respect. It underscored the principle that gradually became accepted in Switzerland that the people were sovereign and that no ruler could rule legitimately without their consent.

Although many Swiss did not achieve equality until the 19th century, the ruling nobility in other European countries were well aware after 1291 that a different kind of society existed in some parts of Switzerland, especially in Schwyz, Uri and Unterwalden. They harbored fears that the Swiss example might destabilize the nobility and lead to the liberation of peasants all over Europe. For example the Burgundian king, Charles the Bold, once ordered that all captured Swiss soldiers be exchanged immediately so that they could not infect peasants from elsewhere in Europe with their independent ideas.

While noblemen throughout Europe regarded Swiss progress toward democracy

Switzerland

and respect for personal freedom as an ominous development, the Swiss themselves were never crusaders for their own ideas. They satisfied their yearning for freedom neither by trying to spread an abstract idea of justice throughout Europe, as the French did after their revolution, nor by trying to establish a *Pax Helvetia* in the entire known world as the Romans had done. Swiss democracy was always linked with moderation and the willingness to compromise. The Swiss almost always showed common sense by recognizing their own limitations.

The Reformation

Switzerland in the 16th and 17th centuries was shaken and divided by a development that changed the soul of Europe: the Reformation. From Swiss soil the great humanist Erasmus had long criticized the all–too–worldly popes and the many petty clerical abuses, and had advocated a return to the simplicity of the earlier Church. Only two years after Martin Luther had tacked his revolutionary 95 Theses on a cathedral door in Wittenberg, Germany in 1519, Ulrich Zwingli, a priest, army chaplain and humanist known as the "Reformer of Zurich," denounced on his own the abuses of the Catholic Church and began to preach sermons no less inflammatory than Luther's. Several Swiss cities followed his call, but the more rural cantons around Lake Lucerne resisted Zwingli by force. Ultimately he was killed in the violent atmosphere he helped to create. In the Peace of Kappel (1531) the cantons accepted a confessional division of the country into Protestant and Catholic cantons. Thereafter, all citizens in the same canton had to subscribe to the same form of Christianity. Where this was difficult, cantons split into half–cantons, as Appenzell did in 1597.

In another city linked by alliance to the Swiss Confederation, Geneva, a Frenchman named Jean Calvin successfully established in 1541 a strict, Protestant religious government. His pious religious ideas spread quickly to central Europe and across the Netherlands to England and Scotland. Geneva itself became a strict city, where frolicking and frills of all kinds were frowned upon. For example, it was forbidden to wear chains, bracelets, necklaces and gold objects. It became known as the "Protestant Rome." Interestingly, Calvinism as a faith had almost no impact on the rest of Switzerland; its theological radiation was felt chiefly outside the country. It did attract thousands upon thousands of skilled, ingenious, but brutally persecuted French Huguenots into Switzerland during the 17th century. These French Protestants were the first of many waves of immigrants seeking political or

Statue of Zwingli, Zurich

religious asylum in Switzerland. The Huguenots also brought skills in banking, trading and manufacturing (especially watch making) which were of enormous economic benefit to Switzerland.

To its great fortune, Switzerland was able to remain almost completely uninvolved in the confused, bloody conflict known as the Thirty Years War, which ravished parts of Europe from 1618 to 1648. The religious split a century earlier did slow the development of central institutions in the Confederation. Yet, Switzerland was always fortunate to have its internal divisions overlap one another. The many differences among language and religious groups, as well as between urban and rural areas, had and now have the effect of pulling the Swiss back together. For example, two residents of the city of Zurich may belong to different religions, but the fact that they are German–speaking city dwellers means that they have important things in common. A French–speaking and a German–speaking Swiss may both live in a rural environment and belong to the same religion. These overlapping divisions and the traditions of tolerance, moderation and readiness to compromise are important reasons why a multilingual, multinational, multireligious Swiss state is still able to manage the searing problems of division so well.

Industrialization

Swiss ingenuity and the economic shot in the arm the Huguenots provided were especially crucial in the 17th and 18th centuries because the discovery of America

gradually led to a shift in the center of world trade toward the Atlantic coast. One could almost say that Christopher Columbus had placed severe strains on the economic progress of Switzerland and of many other central European lands. In order to overcome the resultant economic stagnation, the Swiss had to raise capital to develop the country's manufacturing facilities, to expand Swiss banking operations and to build a global trading network. These efforts later put Switzerland in a position to be one of the first countries on the continent of Europe to undergo an industrial revolution, a fact which has enabled the country to achieve a level of prosperity which is still envied throughout the world.

Democratic Ideals

Switzerland in the 18th century became a cauldron bubbling with explosive democratic political ideas that were to have a dramatic impact all over Europe. One reason was that a trend had gathered momentum in Switzerland since the 17th century which saw a narrowing ruling class, rich and often highly cultured, gaining hold over almost all the coveted public offices, monopolies or privileges. Zurich became known as "the little Athens of the North," and after the 1760s Geneva became a magnet for brilliant minds such as Gibbon, Voltaire and Rousseau. Jean–Jacques Rousseau, a citizen of Geneva whose politics made him unwelcome in France, challenged the very legitimacy of all contemporary regimes and societies. His opening to the famous *Social Contract* became a starting point for many revolutionaries, including Karl Marx—"Man was born free, but everywhere he is in chains." In Geneva, which had become known as the "political laboratory of Europe," such ideas helped ignite an unsuccessful revolution in 1782. This was the first in Europe since the American Revolution and seven years before the outbreak of the French Revolution.

As Germany's greatest poet, Goethe, said at that time, "With Rousseau a new world begins. "The momentous events in France after 1789 unleashed aftershocks that ultimately tottered the fragile confederal structure of Switzerland. In 1792 Geneva exploded, and the revolutionary fever spread throughout the confederation. Republican France intervened openly in Swiss affairs, and in 1798 French troops invaded Switzerland, partly in order to secure the Alpine passes. This was the first time since the Thirty–Years War (1618–48) that the Confederation had been occupied by foreign troops. Further, in 1799 Austrian and Russian troops also entered Swiss territory, but the French drove them out. The ease with which the well–commanded armies conquered Switzerland was another reminder of its inherent weakness. Such an excessively decentralized Switzerland was completely unable to withstand a determined attack. By the end of 1799 war had ravaged large parts of Switzerland, and the French held the cantons firmly under their control.

The conquerors created a "Helvetic Republic," which was a highly centralized state modeled after France. This new republic was almost the complete opposite of the traditional Swiss Confederation and therefore sparked severe disorders within the country. It was replaced in 1803 by a new constitution drafted by Napoleon and called the Act of Mediation. This document permitted more decentralization, and it drew considerable inspiration from the newly developed U.S. Constitution in that it combined federalism, separation of powers, popular sovereignty, individual rights and the central government's authority over foreign and military policy. It reestablished the cantons, and to the older ones it added six new ones: French–speaking Vaud, Italian–speaking Ticino, partly Romansch–speaking Grisons and the three German–speaking, St. Gallen, Aargau and Thurgau. Thus, under French influence, Switzerland, which had hitherto been a predominantly German–speaking country, was converted into a truly multilingual state.

For the next ten years Switzerland remained a scarcely disguised French protectorate. Much to the disgust of many Swiss, it was compelled to supply a contingent of 16,000 men to the French army. In 1812 Napoleon's dominance of Europe received its fatal blow in the snows of Russia, and in 1813 Napoleon's enemies marched through Switzerland on their way to conquer France. When Napoleon escaped from Elba the following year and attempted to pick up his tattered imperial flag, Switzerland joined France's enemies in burying the Napoleonic Empire once and for all.

It received its reward at the Congress of Vienna, which put Europe back together in 1815. The European powers added three cantons: two French–speaking ones (Neuchâtel and Geneva), and the bilingual Valais, thereby completing the boundaries of present–day Switzerland. The Congress also proclaimed the neutrality and inviolability of Switzerland. From that date on, Swiss neutrality has been an established principle of international law.

Although the French Revolution had been crushed, its ideals retained their force and popularity in many countries, including Switzerland. Pressure mounted in the cantons to achieve more democracy. Such efforts received a powerful boost at the time of the Paris uprisings in 1830, which prompted some cantons to regenerate themselves by establishing fully elective governments. They were also furthered by the industrial revolution, which created a confident middle class and a growing urban working group. Both demanded greater influence in the political affairs of their cantons. The democratic movement rapidly gained steam, and between 1830 and 1848 conservatives throughout Europe viewed Switzerland as a carrier of dangerous democratic germs that could infect the rest of Europe.

By 1847 proponents of an even more democratic national constitution had won the majority in more than a dozen cantons. As in the U.S., a civil war had to be fought between those insisting upon states' rights and those advocating a stronger federal government. The conflict lasted little more than a month and claimed only about a hundred lives. But the federal victory was necessary for the pact among cantons to be converted into a truly federal constitution with institutions under which Switzerland still lives. A Swiss federal state with a democratic constitution inspired by the American Constitution and the 1803 Act of Mediation was created. This actually occurred before many revolutions had erupted throughout Europe in 1848, all of which ultimately failed. The only consequence of these outbreaks as far as Switzerland was concerned was that the European powers were far too busy with their own domestic problems to interfere in Swiss affairs at this crucial time. From 1848 on, Switzerland has been a democracy in the modern sense of the word. The industrial revolution, with a Swiss emphasis on watchmaking and fine machine tools and equipment, continued steadily during the balance of the century and the 20th century. Brilliant engineering enabled construction of a comprehensive rail system through the rugged terrain.

Rumblings and Difficulties during World War I

During World War I, tension between the German and French–speaking populations erupted over a scandal involving a high–ranking Swiss military officer who had passed intelligence information to the Germans. Also, thousands of refugees poured into the country; many continued political activity involving other countries from Swiss soil, a practice that threatened the country's neutrality. Perhaps the best known of these was Vladimir Ilyich Lenin. He was living in Zurich in 1917 when the Russian Revolution erupted, and he reportedly screamed in exasperation that he would gladly sell his soul to the devil for the chance to return to his country to take control of the upheaval. German leaders, desperately wishing to eliminate Russia as a battlefield foe, decided to support the Russian revolutionaries, who promised

The church in Meiringen (Bern canton) has frescoes from the 11th and 12th centuries

Switzerland

Scenic valleys in the canton of Bern

peace to their war–weary countrymen. Of course, the Swiss authorities were delighted to be rid of him and many other Russian radicals. The Germans provided him passage in a train closed to German officials of all kinds. As Winston Churchill later wrote, Lenin was sent "like a plague bacillus from Switzerland to Russia."

European wars always threaten the markets and raw materials that trade–dependent Switzerland needs in order to survive. Price controls and rationing had to be introduced during World War I, and the Swiss economy suffered greatly. In November 1918 the social discontent created by such setbacks exploded into a general strike with Marxist revolutionary overtones. Timely concessions, such as the introduction of a proportional representation electoral system, enabled the government to end the strike quickly, and thereby to avert the danger of further domestic tensions.

Switzerland made three significant foreign policy decisions in 1920–21. It turned down a request by the Austrians living in the Alpine area of Vorarlberg to become a part of Switzerland. It agreed to form a customs union with its small eastern neighbor, Liechtenstein. Third, it decided to become a member of the League of Nations, whose headquarters had been established in Geneva. Thus, it decided that

membership in international organizations did not violate Swiss neutrality so long as (1) the organization publicly recognized Swiss neutrality, (2) Switzerland be permitted to abstain from sanctions against other countries and (3) Switzerland be permitted to maintain its universal economic relations with all countries of the world, a principle which it considers essential for its prosperity.

The Depression and World War II

The great depression of the 1930s inevitably affected Switzerland because of its dependence upon foreign trade. The social unrest the economic shocks helped to create spawned some radical political movements such as the youthful Front groups that demanded a fascist order. Nevertheless, Switzerland managed to preserve its democratic order at a time when most of the democracies in Europe collapsed.

It also managed to remain neutral during World War II, which followed on the heels of the depression. Such neutrality was not entirely a gift of the neighboring fascist dictators. Switzerland mobilized 430,000 soldiers and threatened to destroy all major tunnels and bridges. It declared its determination to fight to the last man if it were invaded, although it was revealed after the war that only the heart-

land, including the St. Gotthard Pass and the Simplon tunnels, were to be defended to the end. This threat, backed by the Swiss military reputation and determination, helped to dissuade Hitler and Mussolini from attacking the country, which the former scornfully called "the anus of Europe."

But Switzerland did not remain free as a result of military deterrence alone. Faced with the prospect that it could share the fate of other occupied countries, it made compromises with Nazi Germany in the name of "neutrality" that now make it seem to many Swiss and non–Swiss that the country may have bought its freedom at a very high moral price. It continued to trade with Germany and Italy, and some of the products it sold were obviously used for armaments. Further, thousands of Jews and political refugees were denied entry into Switzerland and therefore ended up in prisons or extermination camps. An agreement with Germany in 1938 required Jews to obtain visas and have a special stamp in their passports. Elie Wiesel argues that the idea of stamping German passports with a "J" for "Jewish" came from the Swiss. Police officials who allowed Jews to enter the country illegally were punished.

Recently declassified Allied intelligence documents reveal the extent to which the Swiss also reaped handsome profits by serving as bankers both for the Nazis and their Jewish victims. Prominent Nazis were steady customers of Swiss banks: Hitler reportedly deposited royalties from *Mein Kampf*, and Hermann Goering made regular trips to Zurich to deposit art masterpieces stolen from museums in occupied countries. The banks purchased from the Nazis hundreds of millions of dollars of looted gold, and other looted funds were invested in Swiss enterprises. Bank secrecy was introduced in 1934 to accommodate Jews who wanted to deposit their assets quietly outside of Germany, and then those same secrecy laws were used to prevent the heirs from claiming those assets after the war. Jewish groups estimated in 1996 that the banks hold about $7 billion including interest that belonged to Jews who perished in the Holocaust, in addition to gold and other valuables looted from Jews. After years of denial, the government admitted that the Swiss secretly used some of these funds to compensate their own citizens for property confiscated by the Communists in Poland, Hungary and the former Czechoslovakia.

The Swiss refusal to discuss or deal with these problems cracked in 1996 under intense pressure from Jewish organizations, the American Senate Banking Committee, and other foreign governments. Attempting to contain this gigan-

Switzerland

tic public relations disaster, it formed one commission, chaired by former U.S. Federal Reserve Chairman Paul A. Volcker, to oversee the search for dormant accounts left by Jews. A second international historical panel was appointed to investigate the extent and fate of Jewish wealth and Nazi loot sent to neutral Switzerland during the war.

A further panel was set up under foreign pressure in 1996, composed of nine international historians with economists, legal experts and researchers to assist them in examining the country's culpability. In 2002 it issued its massive final report that concluded that Switzerland's politicians and businessmen had failed the country on three counts: They contributed to the Holocaust by turning back 20,000 refugees, at times discriminating against Jews, even though they knew what fate awaited them in Germany. They helped the Nazi war machine by going further than necessary in trade and financial support. After the war, banks and art galleries were negligent about restoring property. The end of 2002 the Swiss government supported a proposal to overturn the wartime convictions of people who broke the law by sheltering Jews and others fleeing Nazi Germany. The first pardon came in 2004, when a 79-year-old Jewish lady, who had served 15 days in jail for guiding other Jews across the border from France, was cleared. No compensation is allowed.

In 1997 Switzerland agreed for the first time to use the funds in Holocaust victims' unclaimed bank accounts to help survivors. It also set up a separate fund of about $200 million contributed by private banks to distribute to individuals who survived the Holocaust. In 1998 the two largest Swiss banks reached a $1.25 billion settlement of a lawsuit by Holocaust survivors and their descendants; $800 million is to go to bank depositors or their heirs and the rest to settle other claims, such as the looting of private property. Two major European insurers also reached an accord on life insurance claims for victims. In return, U.S. cities and states canceled an economic boycott against all Swiss banks, institutions and companies, and a $20 billion class-action suit brought against the banks was dropped. Ursula Koch, president of the Socialist party, said, "we have to come to grips with our history." Nevertheless, a judge in Brooklyn claimed in 2004 that Swiss banks were still denying wrongdoing and were stonewalling the settlement of some cases. That seemed to have ended in January 2005 when a list of 3,100 newly released names of Nazi-era depositors was published.

While few Swiss are proud today of such past policies, Swiss national survival

seemed to require them at the time. On the positive side, Switzerland was a base during the war for allied spies, such as Allen Dulles, as well as for international Jewish agencies operating in Europe. It also offered protection to 300,000 refugees who would otherwise have joined the many victims of fascism. Switzerland did not entirely escape the destruction meted out in other parts of Europe. In April 1944 U.S. squadrons mistakenly bombed the Swiss city of Schaffhausen, the only major Swiss city located entirely north of the Rhine River. Allied bombers also attacked other localities, such as Basel and Geneva.

In 1999 the Swiss government disbanded a special crisis task force looking into the country's role in the war. But it will take much longer for the bruised feelings to heal. The myth of wartime Swiss neutrality was exposed. Yet nothing in recent years unified this highly decentralized country as thoroughly as the world's condemnation of its actions during the war. The crisis opened Swiss eyes to their contemporary isolation. Many Swiss believe that their European neighbors and the U.S. had abandoned them by bearing down on them so forcefully over Nazi gold.

POLITICAL SYSTEM

In many countries of the world today, ethnic, lingual and regional diversity often create almost insolvable problems of political and social instability. This has not been the case in Switzerland. Thanks to its tradition of tolerance and compromise, its economic prosperity and its decentralized democratic order tailored to its particular needs, Switzerland enjoys a level of political stability envied in much of the world. But it is an undeniably complicated land. Napoleon Bonaparte confessed to a Swiss

delegation in 1802: "The more I think about your country, the more convinced I become that the disparity between its constituent parts makes it impossible to impose a common pattern on to: everything points to federalism."

The constitution, adopted in 1848, was considerably revised in 1874 to establish national responsibility for defense, trade and many legal matters. On the whole, it has served Switzerland well. Some Swiss now consider the much-amended constitution to be unwieldy and outdated, and since the 1960s the government studied the possibility of rewriting the document. In April 1999 voters, backed by all the major parties, approved a new constitution that abolished the gold standard for the franc and enshrined new rights in law, including the right to strike and the principle of equal opportunities for the handicapped.

The central elements of Swiss democracy remain unchanged: a federal form of government composed of powerful and confident cantons, jealously protective of their own powers; the participation of all major parties in the national, cantonal and communal governments; a collegial executive elected by, but not responsible to the parliament, rather than a one-man executive elected directly or responsible to the parliament; a method of decision-making known as "amicable agreement" involving consensus and respect for minority opinions, rather than the majoritarian approach and, finally, a system of semi-direct democracy at the national, cantonal and communal levels.

Canton Customs and Government

A Swiss person tends to consider himself a citizen of his commune or canton, and secondly of Switzerland. Only the 2,800 communes can grant citizenship, but

The government procession at Nidwalden

225

Switzerland

communal approval is normally a mere formality when the person meets all federal requirements. A quarter of the country's residents are foreign-born, and about 12,000 foreigners become naturalized citizens each year. Federalism, reinforced by strong regional pride, is very much alive in Switzerland, and as a result the 26 Swiss cantons have been considerably more successful in resisting the trend toward government centralization than most other countries, including the U.S. As is nominally true in the U.S., Swiss cantons in reality exercise all powers not explicitly granted to the federal government. In general, they have their own taxing authority, and the Swiss pay most of their income taxes to their cantons. The mix of spending among the federal, cantonal and communal governments is approximately 30:40:30. The cantons have the right to manage their own affairs and the responsibility to enforce the law within their own boundaries.

A proposal in 1978 to create a federal police force was rejected in a national referendum. In 1982, 74% of the voters rejected the creation of a federal anti–terrorist unit. Cantons also have the authority to decide who has the right to vote in their elections.

Because 60% of all voters in a 1981 referendum agreed to amend the constitution in order to give women and men equal rights, it was inevitable that women would ultimately get to vote at every level. In 1990 the Federal Tribunal ruled that Article 4 granting equal rights overrides Article 74 giving cantons the power to decide their own voting rules. Thus, in 1991 the last holdout, Appenzell–Inner Rhodes, counted women's votes in its open–air assembly. The trend toward full equality for women was continued in a 1985 referendum that granted them equal marriage rights. The husband was no

longer the legal head of the household who could decide where to live, to what schools the children should go or whether the wife could open a bank account or take a job. Since 1971 all women have been allowed to vote in national elections. Cantons also have the right to decide what kind of governments they will have, so long as they are democratic and conform to the federal constitution. All have chosen to have a collegial executive with a unicameral legislature.

On the last Sunday in April and the first Sunday of May the citizens of the five mostly rural Swiss cantons of Obwalden, Nidwalden, Glarus and the two Appenzell half cantons of Inner Rhodes and Outer Rhodes gather in annual open-air assemblies to elect their leaders and judges, vote on important laws, approve the budget and change their constitutions. In the early days attendance at such assemblies, which date back to 1231, was required for all male citizens old enough to fight, which was usually 14 years. Participants came to the assemblies armed. Male citizens in Appenzell must still appear with side arms in order to vote; women were granted an exception to this rule. A large, ornate sword, which is the symbol of cantonal authority, is carried into the assembly area (called the "ring") with great pomp. In Glarus, the presiding official (called the *Landammann*) even wraps his arm around the sword during the entire session. In the past, the people dismissed the *Landammann* by the simple act of taking the sword away from him.

The assemblies begin, proceed and end with ceremony and colorful folklore. They give vivid glimpses into Switzerland's past. Honored participants and guests are led into the ring by full–bearded attendants in long robes, baggy striped pants, fur or pointed hats, or plumed helmets. They carry the cantonal insignias, seals,

banners, keys and other relics with them. The leaders stand on a wooden stage surrounded by attendants, while the citizens stand or sit on long wooden benches. In Nidwalden, the assembly is opened by the blowing of a large curled horn, a word from a priest, the introduction of honored guests and an oath of the leaders to respect the constitution.

The visitor is usually so fascinated by the ceremonial aspects of the assembly that he forgets that the citizens have gathered in order to make policy, not to view a parade. There is a serious air, and participants in modern business suits and dresses far outnumber those wearing ornate traditional jackets and bonnets. All voters receive detailed information in advance on the issues that are to be discussed. Except in Appenzell, where there is no discussion at the assembly, each citizen has a right to speak. Speeches are well–prepared and short, and normal voting is done by raising hands, with officials in red robes judging the results from an elevated platform.

A 1982 vote showed how uncertain the outcomes can be. In Obwalden the president of the federal senate, Jost Dillier, one of Switzerland's leading national politicians, was voted out of office, even though he had no opposing candidate. Newspapers the next day wrote of "an absolute sensation," a "bomb which exploded." The Swiss emphasize continuity and stability so strongly that elected officials have no formal limits on the time they may serve. However, most retire when their terms expire. Dillier had violated two fundamental rules of Swiss politics. He had assumed too many offices in politics and business and thus had too much power in his own hands. Also, he paid more attention to politics in Bern than in his canton. Many said that he personified the "arrogance of power," and in Switzerland there is almost nothing which is more distrusted than obvious political ambition or heavy–handedness.

At the end of the four- to six-hour assemblies, ceremony again glosses over the differences that arose in the debates. The attendants lead the procession out of the ring and to the church or city hall, where the newly elected leaders are greeted before attending a banquet. The other citizens spend the rest of the day in a holiday manner.

In order to accomplish anything in such annual meetings, the canton must be rather small in size. It must also have a small and homogeneous population. Granting women the right to take part has created a particular problem by doubling the number of participants. Serious divisions between Catholics and Protestants or city and country dwellers have

The vote is taken in Glarus

wrecked such annual assemblies. There are many tales of brawls at meetings, even though such disturbances of the peace traditionally carried a higher sentence than at other times. To reduce the likelihood of these outbreaks, the consumption of alcoholic beverages at such meetings has long been strictly forbidden. Success requires concentrating on a few important issues, as well as discipline on the part of the individual citizens. Long–winded speeches would seriously try the patience of the participants, and filibusters would be a catastrophe.

One can call this form of direct democracy antiquated or mere ballast tradition. Yet every form of democracy has its advantages and disadvantages. This kind of colorful, but serious, gathering brings together several thousand citizens for public debate on political issues immediately affecting their lives. There have been practical reasons why some such assemblies have had to be abolished. But none has ever been cancelled because of lack of public spirit or citizen interest.

Trends toward Centralization

There is an undeniable trend toward greater governmental centralization because of the many knotty problems of modern life. Such issues as environmental protection, nuclear energy and especially economic matters including unemployment, inflation, foreign trade, currency controls and planning are increasingly seen to be problems with which single cantons cannot easily cope effectively. A rule of thumb is that whenever the Swiss economy is in a slump, there is a stronger demand for shifting more powers to the central government. When the economic picture is rosier, then the resistance to such transfer stiffens.

Over the years the principle has developed that "federal law is superior to cantonal law." The cantons are, nevertheless, far from helpless in the face of this powerful pull toward the federal capital city of Bern. Any constitutional change requires a "double majority" in a national referendum—a majority of all Swiss voters and a majority in more than half the cantons. For instance, in 1973 a majority of Swiss voters supported a proposal to give the national government authority to unify the country's schools, traditionally a cantonal power. However, a majority of the cantons rejected the proposal, so each still maintains its own preferred school system.

The Bicameral Legislature

Both houses of the national parliament, including the Council of States, must approve all national legislation. This upper house, modeled after the U.S. Senate, is

The Swiss Parliament, Bern

composed of two representatives from each canton regardless of size—and the cantons vary in population from 15,000 in rural Appenzell Inner-Rhoden to 1.2 million in Zurich. The cantons are free to decide how representatives are chosen; in fact, the 46 members are elected directly by the people in all but four. This Council of States tends to be far more conservative than the lower house of the national parliament, especially insofar as cantonal prerogatives are concerned. As is true of other Swiss political offices, the title of parliamentarian carries neither great influence nor prestige. Parliament meets for approximately 16 weeks a year divided into four sessions. Deputies are given only a part–time wage for their service and are even freed two days per week during the sessions to perform their regular jobs.

As the United States' leaders saw in the 1780s and as Belgium's leaders realized in the 1970s, federalism is a very important means of enabling a heterogeneous population to live together in harmony; it certainly has been a key ingredient in Switzerland's success as a multinational, multilingual state. Switzerland has had the flexibility to adjust its federal order when a serious problem developed, such as that which emerged in the bilingual canton of Bern. The French–speaking inhabitants in the Jura Mountains that border France sensed discrimination by the canton's German–speaking majority and desired to live in an autonomous canton of Jura. Mass demonstrations were organized, and a few extremists even planted bombs in prominent public places to underscore this separatist demand. In a national referendum held in 1978, 82% of all voting Swiss and a majority in virtually all cantons approved the creation of a new Jura canton, the first new canton to be cre-

Switzerland

ated in 130 years. Thus, instead of suffering a festering problem with a separatist minority, Switzerland now has an additional canton exercising all the powers enjoyed by all the other cantons. Again, federalism was able to act as a tranquilizer.

Below the cantons are some 2,800 communes of greatly differing size. They choose their own system of local government (with approval of the cantons). Some elect their own parliament, but most have a traditional community assembly that normally meets indoors where all citizens over 18 can show up and express their opinions. They elect their own officials and assume general responsibility for granting citizenship, administering public lands, such as the forests, and supplying citizens with water, gas, electricity, bridges, city administrative offices, schools, swimming pools, sanitation facilities, fire services and police protection. They have to submit to some supervision by cantonal governments, but their right to self–rule is guaranteed by the federal constitution, and they can appeal to the Federal Supreme Court if their autonomy is excessively infringed upon.

Political Parties

At all levels of government in Switzerland, political parties play a key role. In contrast to most other European parties, Swiss parties did not grow out of parliamentary groupings or honorary societies, but were mass parties from the very beginning. This was because Switzerland had introduced universal manhood suffrage as early as 1830. As in the U.S., Swiss parties were, and still are, organized primarily at the communal and cantonal level, and the national parties are little more than umbrella organizations for local parties, some of which even have different names than the larger national parties. As decentralized bodies, the national parties are all able to perform an important integrative function by cutting across most subgroups in Switzerland. The major Swiss parties encompass all language, regional, religious and occupational groups. Decentralization also permits maximum flexibility for local and regional solutions to problems.

Swiss parties have a few other important characteristics. First, organized interest groups are represented formally in the parties to an extent unknown in most other countries. Second, the parties demand almost no "party discipline." Members are left more or less free to vote as they please, and it is therefore often difficult to pin a particular policy to a particular party. Third, conflicts within the parties are settled by the principle of "amicable agreement." The majority tries to find solutions acceptable to the minor-

ity rather than merely voting it down. This is widely accepted as the best means of finding a common denominator for all the diverging language, religious and economic interests. At the same time, it makes parties and governments very cautious and deliberate and therefore helps give Swiss government and all major parties their rather conservative hue.

The principal parties' voting strength has remained stable since the end of World War I. In 1919 the four major parties received 88% of the vote; in 2007 they received just under 80%. All four support the existing political order, and until December 2007 none presented itself explicitly as an opposition party. For this reason, no major party and no government traditionally had a firm party or governmental program against which one could easily evaluate its performance. That began to change in 2003. Because of the proportional representation electoral system, votes for the 200–seat National Council (lower house) seldom produce dramatic shifts in political power. Until 2007 elections normally renewed the governing coalition.

The most traditional and oldest party is the Free Democrats/Radical Democratic Party (FDP/PRD), which after the October 2007 federal elections slid from 36 to 31 seats, based on 15.6% of the votes, its worst results ever. Founded in the 19th century as a radical (which in the traditional European sense means anticlerical) and liberal (meaning traditionally that it favored an expansion of individual rights and a reduction of governmental power) party, it now defends the economic and social status quo and is friendly to business. It has very close connections with private economic groups and influential molders of opinion in the mass media, schools and universities. It is no longer the most influential party.

The Christian Democratic People's Party (CVP/PDC) gained ground climbing from 28 to 31 seats in 2007, winning 14.6% of the votes. It received only one seat on the Federal Council. The bulk of its voters are practicing Catholics. It does recruit members and voters from all language and occupational groups; but although it has attempted to leap beyond the confessional barrier by attracting Protestants, it has not been very successful in doing so. The party sees itself as a "dynamic center" party.

From 1935 to 2003 the Social Democratic Party (SPS/PSS) received more votes than any other party, but now it has slipped into second place, falling to 19.5% of the votes and 43 seats (down from 55) in 2007. Founded in 1904, it was originally a working-class party dedicated to the class struggle. But the fascist threat and the eco-

Christoph Blocher

nomic crises in the 1930s convinced Social Democrats that support of reform policies in the existing Swiss state was its best course. It officially changed its program in 1959 and is now a moderate party that wants to reform the capitalist economic system by expanding the social security net, reforming the tax structure and evening out incomes. Its voters were once found only in the working class, but many intellectuals now support it. It helps to form every government in Switzerland, but it always tried to project an image of the "opposition within the government," a role it must now share.

Finally, the Swiss People's Party (SVP) skyrocketed in 2007 to 29% of the votes and 62 seats in 2007, up from 55. These gains made it the largest party since 1919. Its increased votes came mainly from the smaller rightist parties and increasingly from the FDP. The SVP traditionally tried to represent the interests of farmers, small businessmen and craftsmen, and it gets most of its votes in small towns and rural areas. It is more conservative than the FDP in the sense that it has been openly skeptical of any sign of a welfare state and European integration. The SVP is not an extreme right-wing party. It is deeply conservative, nationalist and populist. It exploits extremist ideas and plays on deep-seated fears of cultural dilution and being overwhelmed by larger neighbors. But it is committed to democracy and the constitution, and it vigorously defends popular rights and direct democracy. It does not advocate sending all immigrants home, only those who have committed a crime. It is a modern party that is well-funded, dynamic and professionally organized. It normally did well only in the rural German-speaking east, but it now wins seats in French-speaking areas. Its phenomenal electoral success not only upset governing traditions, but it threw the entire political landscape into chaos.

Led by outspoken and charismatic billionaire industrialist Christoph Blocher, one of the world's richest 300 people, the party appealed to voters worried about high taxes, closer ties with Europe, Swiss participation in peacekeeping operations and NATO's Partnership for Peace, a flood of illegal immigrants and asylum seekers, whom he blames for a rise in crime, and easier citizenship laws. He touches a nerve by implying that the EU would swallow their nation and jeopardize its direct democracy by accumulating powers in Brussels.

Some of his party's campaign posters were so racist that the UN High Commissioner for Refugees sternly rejected them. One showed a black face and the slogan: "The Swiss are becoming Negroes." It was withdrawn after an outcry of protests, but others displayed mug shots of criminals and the text: "Our Dear Foreigners." In the defeated referendum in September 2004 to ease citizenship rules for second- and third-generation foreigners, Osama bin Laden was portrayed on a Swiss ID card, and black and brown hands were depicted taking Swiss passports out of a box.

A 2007 poster depicted three white sheep kicking a lone black sheep off the Swiss flag; it bore the caption: "For Greater Security." Such provocations ignited a clash in Bern during the campaign when hundreds of leftist demonstrators tried to disrupt a march of about 5,000 SVP supporters. The demonstrators threw bottles and rocks, and the police responded with tear gas. Such violence at election time was unknown in such a placid land. It is significant that in the 2007 elections a black, Ricardo Lumengo, was elected to parliament for the first time.

The SVP success also reflects a continuing reaction to limits on bank secrecy and embarrassing disclosures about the country's role as the Nazis' banker during the Second World War. Blocher proclaimed: "As far as Switzerland is concerned, the threat to boycott Swiss banks in America is pure extortion." Many Swiss voters agree. Blocher's electoral fortunes have risen as some of the country's defining myths have weakened. The bankruptcy of Swissair, rising unemployment (hitherto unknown), increasing numbers of visible minorities, the international assault on bank secrecy, and the discovery of al-Qaeda terrorist cells have shaken Swiss pride in their unique land and stimulated a mood of self-doubt. Blocher offers a vision of Switzerland's return to its old values of prosperity and robust independence.

He made his mark in a September 2006 referendum when 68% of voters endorsed

Mass Immigration? No!

a tightening of asylum and immigration laws. Asylum-seekers face faster expatriation or loss of welfare benefits if they cannot present a valid identity document within 48 hours; three-fourths cannot. Voters also approved a law requiring foreigners to integrate into Swiss society. A triumphant Blocher then turned his attention to Muslims, fighting such things as minarets or veils. He demands a referendum over construction of mosques with minarets in Swiss cities.

The electoral outcome called into question the "magic formula" for distributing seats among the four main parties. As the smallest of the four parties, the SVP always had to be content with only one seat in the Federal Council, the Swiss governing body, while the other three each got two. As the largest party now, the SVP demanded and received two. Blocher became justice minister. The SVP's leading role in the government after 2003 represented the first political alignment to the right in more than four decades. It signaled a more confrontational style of government, which strains the consensual system. Blocher told the *Neue Zürcher Zeitung*: "Our success is a clear sign that people want another type of politics." Traditionally ministers are expected to come to unanimous decisions behind closed doors, whereby the outside world hardly ever learns how individual members argued. One of the least popular ministers in the Federal Council, according to polls, he often publicly alluded to disagreements with his fellow cabinet colleagues, a practice that is discouraged.

Blocher showed little respect for the traditional team spirit of collective responsibility. He combined a place in the government with an outsider's role, disapproving of legislation at odds with his party's policies. The consequence was almost constant tension and an end to the tradition that ministers drop their party loyalties to serve the state. Consensual politics came to an end after a half century. He paid the price in December 2007 when parliament, in a surprising vote, rejected Blocher and elected two other SVP members (Samuel Schmid and Eveline Widmer-Schlumpf) to the cabinet. As he had warned, he disowned the two who had accepted the cabinet positions, yanked his party out of the government and announced that the SVP would be an opposition party. He rudely gave Widmer-Schlumpf a 100-day ultimatum to resign from office and the SVP, but she resolutely refused. She was publicly insulted and even received anonymous death threats. Many viewed such warnings as a serious challenge to democracy in a country where ministers ride the streetcar and move around without bodyguards. These are uncharted waters for Switzerland. Since it is the largest party since 1919, the SVP can paralyze the government and threaten to call for a referendum for any legislation it does not like.

A few other parties receive a smattering of seats. The ecologically–oriented Green Party of Switzerland (GP/PES) continued to gain, winning 9.6% of the votes and 20 seats, up from 13 in 2003; it also won its first Senate seat. The GP, which is outside the government, can play a crucial role in assuring a majority for important legislation. A start-up center-right Liberal Green party won three seats. The Greens' success was a reflection of the salience of environmental protection in a country of so many glaciers and mountains. The party also enjoys a good reputation for efficiency in the cities and regions where it rules. Other parties won a half dozen seats.

Foreign Workers

The Swiss Democrats, formerly called the National Action for People and Homeland (NA), aims its arrows toward what it sees as a threatening perversion of the Swiss character caused by foreign workers, rapid urbanization and growing concentration of power in Switzerland. This openly patriotic and nationalist party reached its zenith in 1970 when a majority of Swiss voters was almost persuaded in a referendum to limit the numbers of foreign workers. In the 1990s the less democratic, neo–Nazi Patriotic Front, entered the anti–immigrant scene.

In their opposition to foreign workers the REP and NA unquestionably touch a

Switzerland

very sensitive nerve in Switzerland. The country has traditionally been very hospitable to political exiles; for example, it took in 16,000 Hungarians after 1956 and 14,000 Czechoslovaks after 1968. Swiss industry learned very early that high levels of production could be achieved only by attracting foreign workers. No one doubts that the hotel and restaurant industries would never be able to survive without foreign workers. About half of these workers are Italians, followed by Germans and Spaniards.

In 2008 foreign workers accounted for a quarter of the labor force. About 60% come from EU countries and another fourth from former Yugoslavia. All western European citizens are now free to work in Switzerland. An additional 150,000 people cross the Swiss border every day to go to work. In all, there are about 850,000 "guest workers" in Switzerland.

As classrooms in Swiss schools sometimes swell with foreign children and as run–down areas with predominantly foreign residents begin to appear in some cities, cultural clashes are inevitable. In fact, this same problem is seriously testing the tolerance of many European countries. In a 1994 referendum, a majority of voters accepted a government ban on all forms of racism, including a belittling of the Holocaust, and in 2002 a tiny majority rejected a proposal to make it more difficult for asylum seekers to enter the country. By 2004 the number of asylum seekers had fallen by over half because of the end of major fighting in the Balkans.

In five referenda since 1970, Swiss voters, not wishing to tarnish Switzerland's image as a land of refuge or to harm its economy, rejected proposed laws to limit the percentage of foreigners. A proposal in 2000 to limit it to 18% was defeated by 64% of voters in a referendum. For a while, the Swiss government responded to the discontentment by quietly reducing the percentage of foreigners in Switzerland to 17% of the total population. It could do this because, although foreign workers enjoy many rights and social benefits while in the country, many must renew their work permits every year. However, the country's dependence upon such labor is so great that by 2004 the percentage of foreign residents had grown to 20% and continues to rise. In 2002 voters rejected by the closest referendum margin since 1891 (50.1%) another proposal to curb the number of asylum seekers; none of the French- or Italian-speaking cantons approved of the proposition. In the previous year only 12% of asylum applications had been accepted.

Those with permanent work permits and the same employment rights as Swiss nationals slightly outnumber those with

Former President (1982) Fritz Honegger with the author's two daughters, Katie and Juliet Thompson, April 1982.

limited rights. Foreign workers must live in the country four years before they are permitted to bring their families. In one French-speaking canton, Neuchâtel, long-term foreign residents are permitted to vote in local elections.

In 1997, the Swiss Statistical Office calculated that, with declining birth rates, the working population would be reduced by almost a third by 2050 if the level of immigration were kept stable. This means that the foreign population would have to expand to a total of 23% by 2017 for the country's workforce to be kept stable. It is not easy for some Swiss to face this fact.

The Federal Government

The federal government, with its seat in Bern, is composed of a bicameral parliament similar, in some ways, to the U.S. Congress, and of a powerful seven–man executive elected by parliament. The National Council, elected every four years by male and since 1971 female voters over 18 years of age, represents the interests of all Swiss. Because elections almost never produce significant changes in the parties' strength in parliament, Swiss elections are never the heated, highly publicized affairs they are in the U.S. and many other European countries.

Both houses have equal powers. Although all bills are now drafted by the government and presented to parliament, both houses must examine them. Once both have passed a piece of legislation, the executive may not veto it, and the Supreme Court may not declare it unconstitutional. In drafting legislation, the government, by tradition, consults all interested groups inside and outside parliament. This is a clumsy, time–consuming process, but it helps to ensure better results: potential objections to the legisla-

tion are ironed out in advance. It also reduces the possible danger of a law being overturned in a referendum.

Both houses meet to elect the seven Federal Councilors (*Bundesräte*), who have steadily become more powerful in the Swiss political system. The parties carefully select on the basis of party membership and political experience at the federal or cantonal level. Highly charismatic figures are very seldom chosen because of the traditional Swiss aversion to a personality cult of any kind. The recommended candidates are almost always elected. Their terms are four years, during which time they cannot be removed by parliament for any reason. They are traditionally re-elected until they voluntarily choose to retire. Thus, strictly speaking, Switzerland does not have a parliamentary system as in most European democracies.

Since 1959 they have been selected according to a so–called "magic formula": two councilors are chosen from each of the three largest parties in the National Council and one from the fourth largest. At least two councilors must be from the French- or Italian–speaking sections, and it is usual that one comes from each of the country's three largest cantons—Zurich, Bern and Vaud. Finally, no two councilors may come from the same canton. One can imagine the compromises necessary to satisfy such a "magic formula."

Each directs one of seven ministries, called departments. Together the seven form the government, and they play the predominant role in drafting legislation, executing laws and dealing with the outside world. Until 2007 they made decisions collectively according to the principle of "amicable agreement." They are nominated by the major parties, but they are expected to cease being "party men"

Young woman gathers signatures opposing centralization of power

once they are in office. Therefore, they have no coherent government program. There was no formal opposition either within the government or the parliament before the SVP stormed out of the government in December 2007. This did not mean that a party could not oppose a particular issue; what it meant was that none of the major parties consistently opposed the government with a view to replacing it. In other countries such an "all-parties government," also known as "grand coalitions," are formed only in times of national emergency. Switzerland always had them. Due to Christoph Blocher's decision to take the country's largest party, the SVP, into opposition, a more adversarial system has replaced the earlier consensual practice. It is uncertain whether this change is permanent.

The year 1984 had seen a break in the tradition of parliament's more or less automatic acceptance of the parties' nominations to the Federal Council. Polls indicated that 64% of citizens thought it was time to have a woman federal councilor, so the Social Democrats nominated Lilian Uchtenhagen, a respected economist. Reportedly grumbling that she was "too emotional," "too elegant," "not enough of a mother figure" and "unable to stand the strain of high office," a majority in the Federal Assembly in a joint meeting of the two chambers rejected her.

The widespread bad feelings caused by Uchtenhagen's rejection no doubt helped Elisabeth Kopp, a lawyer and leading member of the Radical Democratic Party, to win a seat on the Federal Council in 1984. Unfortunately Kopp became implicated in Switzerland's biggest scandal in

years. In 1989 she resigned because of accusations that, as justice minister, she had used her influence to protect her lawyer husband against charges of complicity in a major drug money–laundering operation by leaking confidential information to him about the inquiry. She was later acquitted of violating the official secrecy laws.

In 1993 it was time for another woman to be named to the Federal Council. She had to be a Social Democrat from a French–speaking canton, and parliamentarian Christiane Brunner fit that bill. However, an overwhelmingly male parliament rejected her, some say for sexist reasons: she was a thrice–married blonde who liked flashy clothes, opposed the military, and was said to have had an illegal abortion and posed in the nude. She denied the latter charge. Switzerland had never experienced what followed: thousands of women gathered in front of parliament, spattering paint and eggs, and chanting: "We have lost the first battle, but only the first!" They were right. Ex–trade unionist Ruth Dreifuss of the SPS was promptly elected as interior minister. A close friend of Brunner, she concluded, "I reassure people because I look a little plain." In 1999 she became the country's first female and first Jewish president.

Every year the Parliament elects from among the seven a president and a vice president for one–year terms. They are not permitted to succeed themselves immediately, and by tradition, the vice president is elected President the next year. The president of the confederation is only a "first among equals," representing the government in ceremonial functions. In times of emergencies he may assume

greater powers than the other councilors. Under no circumstances can he be recalled or impeached.

Swiss presidents are so inconspicuous in comparison to French or American counterparts that most Swiss, when asked, are unable to name their own president in any given year. In a country in which the most glamorous figure is the head of the central bank, the president needs neither bodyguards nor staff cars, and he lives in his own house during his term of office. He goes unguarded to movies or restaurants and probably carries out his own garbage. When Kurt Furgler (1981) traveled to work or around the country, he either drove his own car or went by rail. Only when his schedule was particularly tight was he transported by helicopter. Once, when he was being flown to an appointment, his helicopter developed engine trouble and was forced to make an emergency landing. Undaunted, he merely walked to the nearest road and hitch–hiked the rest of the way.

The Courts

Since the Federal Supreme Court has no power to judge on the constitutionality of federal laws, it does not have the same prestige or importance as does the U.S. Supreme Court. It is chiefly the highest court of appeals for civil and criminal cases. Its judges are selected by both houses of parliament meeting together for six-year terms and must be chosen from all language and regional groups in order that the entire population be represented. Its seat is not in Bern, but in Lausanne. The administration of justice remains primarily a cantonal affair, but the supreme civil and criminal laws of the land are the federal code of civil law, in force since 1912, and the federal code of penal law, enacted in 1942.

Direct Democracy

Many European democracies permit citizens to vote directly on some particularly important political issues, rather than to leave virtually all such decisions to the parliament. This is called "direct democracy" because the will of the people is not filtered exclusively through parliament. In most countries this instrument is used very sparingly, particularly because it has often been a favorite tool for dictators to legitimize their power over a frightened people. The Swiss have never needed to fear such abuse in modern times, and direct democracy is a very important part of the political process at all levels of government.

If at least 100,000 voters sign a petition demanding a constitutional change, then such an "initiative" must be submitted to a direct vote of all Swiss. Initiatives have

Switzerland

a one-in-two chance of succeeding if they are put forward by parliament, whereas the success rate is only one in ten if voters launch them. If at least 50,000 demand in a petition that an act of parliament or an international treaty be approved by all the voters, then a "facultative referendum" is held. Parliament can declare an act to be too urgent to allow time for a referendum, but one is mandatory if parliament adopts any constitutional changes or approves of an international treaty of supranational or security character which affects the country's sovereignty.

Most Swiss now cast their votes for initiatives and referendums by mail. They are held on an extremely wide range of subjects: abortion, conscientious objection to military service, modernizing the armed services, restructuring civil defense, mandatory wearing of safety belts, increasing federal powers to tax and to control unemployment and inflation, mandatory retirement ages, gun control, bans on automobile driving and on leaded gasoline, daylight savings time, nuclear power, rent controls, euthanasia, worker participation in management, and many more topics. In 2004 voters backed proposals for some of Europe's harshest laws on violent criminals and pedophiles. "Extremely violent and dangerous criminals" can be incarcerated for life unless "scientific findings" show they are cured or no longer dangerous. In June 2005 Switzerland held Europe's first referendum granting more rights to same-sex couples. If registered, they have from 2007 the same tax and pension status as married couples except that they can neither adopt children nor undergo fertility treatment.

By threatening to organize an initiative or referendum, interest groups in Switzer-land can almost always secure a serious hearing for their concerns within the government or parliament. This insures that they will not be overlooked in the decision–making process and that the government will try to establish a consensus for all its acts. Still, the problems associated with direct democracy have increasingly become the subject of discussion. The first problem is that the number of referenda and initiatives at all levels has sharply increased. Between 1914 and 1934 there was an average of 8.5 referenda per year. At present, the average has climbed to more than 30, and this includes neither the many referenda at the communal and cantonal level, nor the up to four national initiatives per year. Constitutional changes since 1871 have been made an average of once every 13 months, and the frequency has risen in recent years. Further, the issues on which the people are asked to decide have become more and more complex, and fewer and fewer citizens are able to form a firm opinion about them. From 1971 to 1997 only five of 68 national initiatives passed.

The cost of gathering signatures by convincing enough people of an issue's importance has become very expensive, and the Swiss government must now spend more than four million Swiss francs (about $3 million) to conduct a referendum. The increasing dissatisfaction with this form of democracy is demonstrated by the rapidly decreasing voter participation. Few referenda, initiatives or national parliamentary elections attract more than 50% of the voters, and no one is surprised if only one–third of the eligible voters choose to vote on an issue; the average was 40% by 2004. In fact, Switzerland is the only democracy in the world where voter partici-pation (45% in federal elections) in major elections is lower than in the U.S. Nevertheless, Switzerland, with only 4.7 million voters, accounts for an estimated half of referendum ballots worldwide.

The people also express their will on emotional social issues through referenda. The Swiss try hard to find acceptable compromises with the youth because they fear that failure could damage or destroy a very delicate but essential ingredient of Swiss democracy: the inclination and ability to solve serious problems by means of consensus. Without its traditional "rules of the game," which include tolerance and compromise, Swiss democracy would lose much of its uniqueness.

For example, hard drug use is illegal, but the police almost never arrest anyone for mere possession. In 1997 voters overwhelmingly endorsed their government's liberal drug policies, including state distribution of heroin under doctors' care to longtime addicts. However, in 1998 nearly 74% rejected the legalization of heroin, cocaine and marijuana. Surveys found that a fourth of all Swiss had tried marijuana, and of the 90,000 daily users, a third were teenagers. In 2001 the government decided to remove penalties for consumption of marijuana and hashish. This drew the wrath of both neighboring countries and some UN agencies, which had already been critical of the earlier program of providing needles and heroin to some addicts. Swiss officials defended themselves by pointing out that the old approach had not worked.

Foreign Policy

Swiss foreign policy is based on five main pillars: (1) armed neutrality, (2) universality of diplomatic and economic relations with all countries of the world regardless of regime or foreign policy, (3) the readiness to provide its "good offices" to other countries (for instance, Switzerland represented the U.S. in Cuba and still in Iran, where no U.S. diplomats are allowed; it also represents Cuba in the U.S., Iran in Egypt, and Israel in Ghana), (4) providing its own territory for international organizations and conferences and (5) solidarity with other peoples of the world, especially when it comes to humanitarian actions.

There are many international organizations with headquarters in Geneva, including many UN specialized agencies such as WHO, ILO, ITU, and WTO. Numerous nongovernmental organizations have their headquarters in Geneva, such as the World Council of Churches, the International Committee of the Red Cross (for war emergencies) and the International Federation of Red Cross Societies (for natural disasters and peacetime emer-

Montag, 4. März 2002 · Nr. 52

Der Zürcher Zeitung 223. Jahrgang

Neue Zürcher Zeitung

INTERNATIONALE AUSGABE

Blutiges Wochenende im Nahen Osten
Über 20 Tote in Israel – Rund 30 palästinensische Opfer

Ja zum Uno-Beitritt der Schweiz
Knappes Ständemehr – deutlicheres Ja des Volkes

gencies). The latter organization was founded in 1864 by the Swiss businessman Henri Dunant, who had been shocked by the carnage he had witnessed on Italian battlefields during the campaigns of Napoleon III. Switzerland's close links to the Red Cross are still symbolized by the latter's use of the Swiss flag with reversed colors. The Red Cross is an important vehicle for international humanitarian actions involving prisoners and refugees.

Switzerland is often criticized for its mediocre record for foreign aid. In 2008 it devoted .44% of its GDP to helping developing countries, compared with .94% for Norway and Sweden, 82% for the Netherlands and 81% for Denmark. The U.S. spent only .22%. Yet, the quality of its assistance is very high, and there is scarcely a nation in the world that is more generous in time of crisis.

Switzerland is not a member of NATO, and its and Austria's neutrality separates NATO's northern and southern halves. However, it joined the "Partnership for

Peace" within NATO in order to strengthen its cooperation with that alliance. Its citizens also voted in 2001 to allow their soldiers to train with NATO forces. Earlier, its political leaders never publicly commented on foreign political events, such as elections or *coups d'état* or on foreign military actions such as the Soviet Union's invasions of Czechoslovakia in 1968 and of Afghanistan in 1979. This changed in August 1990, when for the first time Switzerland applied the UN sanctions against Iraq, which had invaded Kuwait. However, it staunchly opposed the military action taken by the U.S. and Britain against Iraq in 2003 and closed its airspace to military planes on their way to the front.

Until 2002 the Swiss conception of neutrality had prevented the country from joining the UN. It joined many of the specialized UN organizations, and it pays more than half a billion Swiss francs ($500 million, more than 72 Swiss francs per inhabitant). Geneva is the seat of the UN's European headquarters. It has held that the UN's provision for sanctions against member states is incompatible with Swiss neutrality. The Swiss Federal Council and parliament gradually reached the conclusion that Switzerland could no longer remain outside the UN, which they believed would officially take note of Swiss neutrality. They were supported by most university educated Swiss and by the country's most prestigious newspapers.

The Swiss government has steadily nudged the country in the direction of greater international involvement. In a 2002 referendum, a majority (54%) of Swiss finally voted to join the United Nations. They concluded that their country,

which sits in the middle of Europe, could no longer remain on the sidelines in an era of global politics and interwoven economics. Support for the move came from the government, most political parties, business and trade unions. Foreign Minister Joseph Deiss noted: "Switzerland needs the world and the world needs our country." The September 11, 2001, terrorist attacks against the U.S. boosted the vote because it shattered the Swiss sense that their country could remain outside of and immune from world events. In September 2002 it became the 190th member of the United Nations. President Kaspar Villiger said: "The people realized that they are no longer an island. We can be neutral—and be a good member of the UN."

Switzerland participates in international peacekeeping missions and helps finance UN peacekeeping operations. In 1989 it took the bold step of actually sending unarmed but uniformed medical personnel, administrators and observers to Namibia, and later to Western Sahara. Since the Swiss constitution forbade sending troops abroad, this was not an ordinary military unit: all were volunteers; a third were women, only a few of whom are members of the country's tiny women's military services (known best for their former work with carrier pigeons that has been abandoned with "Army 95"). Nevertheless, this marked the first deployment of Swiss troops abroad since the Battle of Marignano in 1515. Switzerland also sends officers and aircraft to assist the UN in the Middle East.

Following an unusually bitter campaign preceding a 2001 referendum, a narrow majority (51%) approved of arming Swiss soldiers participating in peacekeeping missions. Heretofore, they had been unarmed in accordance with the policy of neutrality. The government wanted to avoid situations such as in Kosovo, where its peacekeepers had to rely on German and Austrian troops for protection. Opponents had displayed posters showing the battered corpse of an American soldier in Somalia, with the words, "Die for foreign powers?" The country's neutrality continues to prevent its soldiers from performing peace-enforcing operations, as opposed to peacekeeping ones. In 2005 it had 220 soldiers deployed in Kosovo and a smaller contingent with three helicopters under EU command in Bosnia. It participates in UN missions on the Golan Heights, in Afghanistan and since 1953 along the DMZ between the two Koreas.

In 1996 it broke with its tradition by allowing NATO troops to pass through its territory and skies on their way to implement the peace in Bosnia. By giving sanctuary to 400,000 refugees from former Yugoslavia, it also turned its back on its

Swiss soldiers

Switzerland

refugee policy before and during the Second World War. The growing internationalism is strongest in the French– and Italian–speaking parts of the country.

Military Service

The Swiss have traditionally been armed to the teeth in order to demonstrate their determination to defend their neutrality and in order to dissuade any belligerent in a European war from viewing Swiss territory as a military vacuum and thereby inviting invasion. There is no general staff in peacetime, and parliament creates the rank of general only in wartime. There is only a skeleton standing army—about 1,500 career officers and NCOs. Defense spending has fallen to 9% of the confederation's budget and less than 2% of the nation's GDP.

The Swiss buy some of the most sophisticated military hardware available, including U.S. fighter aircraft. They also produce a wide range of military equipment that they sell—subject to certain restrictions—to countries as diverse as Australia, Turkey, Egypt, Saudi Arabia, Burma, Guatemala and Angola. Switzerland has built a network of bomb shelters that would protect 90% of the population in the event of nuclear attack.

Every Swiss male must serve in the national militia from age 20 to age 42 (age 52 for officers and 62 at the latest for generals). It has been aptly noted that Switzerland "has been in a state of war every weekend since 1945" and that "Switzerland does not have an army, it is an army!" Although there is a civilian service for those citizens who are morally or religiously opposed to all forms of military service, this service lasts 1.5 times longer than the minimum requirement for ordinary military duty. Avoiding the draft has become easier than before. Many young Swiss succeed in claiming to be mentally or physically unfit. Those who for any legitimate reason cannot perform military service must pay a fee to the Swiss state. If they want to do so, women can also serve in the armed forces, except in combat missions. After 15 weeks of basic training, soldiers are assigned to militia units and are required to perform three weeks of duty every other year. Special units such as militia pilots and tank formations, serve two weeks each year. Thus, the country could mobilize 351,000 soldiers within 48 hours.

The Swiss soldier is permitted to take his equipment, including his assault rifle and five sealed magazines of live ammunition, home with him, and many keep it all after leaving the military. He is required to practice his sharpshooting regularly in rifle associations. Former reservists are permitted to buy a weapon for private use. This policy of having so many weapons in the society came under close scrutiny after a grisly massacre that occurred in 2001. Using a semiautomatic weapon a man burst into the cantonal parliament in Zug and shot dead 14 people and wounded as many more before killing himself. This was the first time in more than 100 years that any Swiss politician had been murdered and was the biggest mass murder in the country in living memory. The man had never been in the military and had probably purchased the gun in a shop that sells semiautomatic weapons legally or from another person, also legally.

Although gun laws vary depending upon the canton, any citizen without a criminal record can buy one after an identity check and official approval. One may keep it locked up at home. There are an estimated 2-3 million guns in circulation. The total number of gun deaths, including accidents, was 6.2 per 100,000, second to the U.S. rate of 9.42 and more than double the rate elsewhere in Europe.

This practice of keeping guns at home is being widely criticized. A 2007 poll found that two-thirds (65%) were opposed to storing military guns at home, and three-fourths (76%) said it was not "necessary for the army's mission." But such traditions die hard, especially since the "porcupine" military doctrine has existed for generations: all the guns in closets or basements throughout the small but mountainous country are believed to act as millions of quills to deter invaders.

The Swiss ability to shoot straight is widely respected. As the Swiss often remind listeners: "William Tell was a man of courage and integrity—and he was a good shot!" The last German Kaiser, Wilhelm II, was also given a friendly reminder of this. Once, after inspecting a Swiss army unit, he turned to one of the Swiss soldiers and asked what his comrades would do if the German army were to invade Switzerland with twice as many soldiers. The answer: "In that case, each of us would have to fire twice!"

In 1989 the government decided to add some American firepower by acquiring several thousand shoulder–fired Stinger anti–aircraft missiles and 34 F/A–18 fighter airplanes. In 2005 parliament made the unusual move of rejecting Defense Minister Samuel Schmid's defense budget because it contained funds to purchase two Spanish military transport aircraft. He wanted them in order to make Switzerland less dependent on others to move its troops. The military has only helicopters to move soldiers, or it must charter planes.

In 1989 the revered armed forces, which in a country with so many ethnic divisions is one of the few truly national institutions, was seriously buffeted by the winds of détente. The end of the cold war greatly diminished the likelihood that Switzerland would ever face a serious external threat. Swiss feel less need to be as well armed as before, and they are reexamining their policy of armed neutrality. In a referendum, in which 68.6% of the eligible voters participated (the largest turnout in 15 years), 35.6% voted to abolish the military. Although the President at this time, Jean–Pascal Delamuraz, had called the initiative "an idiocy as big as the Matterhorn," (one of the highest and best known mountains in Switzerland), the results severely shook the armed forces. A coalition called Switzerland without an Army was able to resubmit the question of disbanding the armed forces to the voters in 2001. It was again overwhelmingly rejected; only 21.9% voted in favor of the initiative. Even though it had survived twice, the votes pointed to resentment against the army's influence in society, which has in any case diminished. The networking advantages have declined.

The army embarked on reform and rehabilitation. Former General Heinz Häsler admitted that "everything must be done to restore the people's confidence that military defense is needed." In 1994 voters were asked to decide on the questions: "Does Switzerland really need an army?" and "Does Switzerland need 34 new fighter airplanes?" Both votes passed by a small majority. By 2007 the Armed Forces had been reduced from 600,000 to 240,000 soldiers, in part by shortening the service time and declaring many draftees as unfit. It converted from a "static force" to a "dynamic force." The professional support comprises about 1,500 instructors, pilots and professional soldiers (to protect the underground installations). As a result of the most extensive armed forces reform since 1907, called "Army 95," the minimum total service time (after basic training) is 295 days for soldiers, 900 days for officers up to the rank of captain, and 1,200 days for colonels.

In May 2003, three-fourths of the voters agreed in a referendum to plans for reducing and professionalizing the military, ignoring arguments that such a reform could undermine the country's traditional neutrality. Quaint remnants of the past, such as bicycle units, were disbanded, going the way of carrier pigeons, whose use had ended only in 1994. The number of men in active and reserve service was drastically reduced. With the reforms completed, the army had shrunk to about half its size, and the remaining soldiers are more mobile, more flexible, better trained and better equipped. Military service was shortened. For most soldiers it will be over by the

Switzerland

time they are 26. At the same time, civil defenses were refocused from war to national catastrophes and terrorist attacks, and it will be possible for recruits to opt for civil defense duty instead of the armed forces. The Cold War requirement that all residences and businesses have their own nuclear fallout shelters was also relaxed. The government claims that Switzerland already has sufficient bunker places for almost the entire population.

Switzerland is home to about 350,000 Muslims, or 5% of the population. For years the Swiss assumed that their country would be one of the last for Islamic terrorists to attack or to use for planning attacks. That has changed. In 2006 police arrested a dozen suspects who allegedly conspired to shoot down an Israeli airliner flying out of Geneva. A North African man was also seized and charged with preparing to blow up the Spanish supreme court. An intelligence report in May concluded that the country has become "a jihadi field of operation" and predicted a rise in terrorist actions. The chairman of the parliamentary intelligence oversight committee noted realistically: "Switzerland is no longer able to exclude itself from the rest of the world in the face of a globalized threat."

ECONOMY

The overall Swiss economy is one of the most efficient and prosperous on Earth. In 2006 the World Economic Forum named it the world's most competitive. But there are at least two economies, not one. There is the efficient export sector dominated by large world-class companies such as Nestlé, Novartis and Roche, Swatch, and banks such as UBS and Credit Suisse. Then there is the inefficient domestic sector that only survives by being protected. Its per capita GDP and income were at one time among the highest in the industrialized world. Now Luxembourg, Norway and the U.S. are richer as measured by GDP per head at purchasing-power parity. Even tiny, neighboring Liechtenstein with its postage stamps and tremendous number of banks does better. In 1950 income per head was 80% above the European average; now it is only 14% above. The Swiss work longer than any nationality in the OECD (44.5 hours average per week). In 2002 they turned down a referendum proposal to mandate a 36-hour work week. The economy is firmly based on the principle of free enterprise.

The public sector accounts for a lower percentage of GDP than in most other European countries, and some public companies, such as telecommunications, are being privatized. There has traditionally been little protection for their industries, so

Swiss companies have always been stimulated by international competition to adapt in order to survive. However, as in all modern states, the Swiss state intervenes more and more in the economy. It offers export risk guarantees to exporters who doubt the viability of their customers. But it scorns central planning and other attempts to limit the flexibility of private firms.

The Swiss economy is influenced heavily by several basic factors. First, Switzerland is a very small country with almost no exploitable raw materials. This includes, most importantly, oil. Switzerland meets more than three-fourths of its energy needs with oil, and almost every drop must be imported from as many diverse sources as possible. It must also import natural gas—which constitutes about 4% of its energy consumption—and nuclear fuel for its four nuclear plants, which produce almost 40% of its electricity. In 2003 voters rejected proposals to impose a 10-year moratorium on new atomic plants, to require existing ones to be closed after 40 years of service, or to close nuclear power plants after 30 years. One of its few natural resources is mountainous terrain for waterpower, which provides the country with about 60% of its electricity. In 2008 this fact helped put Switzerland in first place among 149 countries in an international ranking of environmental performance. The U.S. was in 39th place. The only other natural resource is wood, available because forests cover one-fourth of the country.

Second, Switzerland has insufficient farmable land to feed its population. Since it has pasturelands, much of which is in or at the foot of mountains, it has a productive dairy industry. Milk has always been plentiful, and long ago the Swiss discovered that by converting it to cheese, it could export its milk to the world. This discovery made it famous for cheese. Its sunny hillsides also enable every single canton to produce excellent, mostly light dry white wine, which supplies well over one-half the Swiss market. Unfortunately, there is very little left over for export. Only 6.3% of Switzerland is suitable for grain crops, and this is the chief reason for its excessive dependency upon food imports. In 2005 voters approved a five-year ban on growing genetically-modified organisms (GMOs). In terms of calorie intake, Swiss agriculture produces only 60% of the national requirements, or 45% if one takes into consideration the imported feed component of milk and meat production. Switzerland is willing to pay a high price to keep farms operating in remote areas of the country in order to reduce the wartime vulnerability of its food supplies and to look after the countryside. Farmers comprise 4% of the labor force, compared

to 22% prior to World War II. They produce only 1% of the GDP, but they earn an average of 50% more than other European farmers. This has been due largely to the fact that Switzerland subsidizes agriculture and forestry more generously than does the EU's CAP. However, Swiss subsidies have been reduced in the 21st century. Tariffs on agricultural imports average 50%. This makes farming the least market-oriented sector of the Swiss economy. It also raises food prices, which are 40% higher than the OECD average, compared with 10% for France and Germany. In addition, heavy mechanization and the government-sponsored effort to combine more than half the arable land into larger farms more suited to efficient agriculture help keep farming alive.

Third, the lack of raw materials and sufficient home-grown food has forced the Swiss to make the most of their human resources. This means that they have had to industrialize and, above all, to become a trading nation. Almost no European country with such a high standard of living has reached such a high degree of dependence on the world economy. Almost two-thirds of its GDP is derived from foreign trade in goods and services. Exports account for a third of GDP, and about 60% go to Europe. This high volume of foreign trade is also made necessary both by Switzerland's small domestic market stemming from a small population and by its high level of prosperity.

Germany is its most important trading partner. The lion's share of trade is with European countries, particularly with the members of the EU: 62.1% of its exports and 82.8% of its imports. Of course, it benefits from being strategically located at the junction of Europe's main trade routes and from having an excellent road and rail network that plugs into the transportation nets of its neighbors. However, it has faced severe problems with terrible fires in key tunnels that are essential to through-traffic. After a fire in 1999, in which 39 people were killed in an inferno, Mont Blanc Tunnel was not reopened with new safety features until 2002. Another fire in the St. Gotthard Tunnel closed it for three months until the end of 2001.

Switzerland has an almost unique problem for a European trading nation: it is landlocked. It does have one important port on the Rhine–Basel. It maintains 29 merchant ships on the high seas and is in 50th place among 111 nations that maintain a merchant fleet. However, its lines to its overseas trading partners are very vulnerable.

This was one reason why it maintained its important air link through Swissair, a semipublic corporation that went bankrupt on October 1, 2001, a day the presti-

235

Switzerland

Cheese–making

gious *Neue Zürcher Zeitung* called "the blackest day in Switzerland's economic history." It was the first collapse of a European flag-carrier, and its demise was a huge blow to Switzerland's image as a solid business and financial center. Already terribly indebted before the September 11 terrorist attacks, it could not secure the funds to continue. It also caused the collapse of Belgium's Sabena, which was partly owned by Swissair. In 2002 the defunct Swissair was combined with Crossair, which flew routes within Europe, to form Swiss International Air Lines, known as "Swiss." It added international flights and used two-thirds of Swissair's planes. Despite the fact that it was Europe's fourth-largest fleet in 2003, its passengers were dwindling, and the company had to lay off workers, ground some planes and cut some routes to stay competitive. It was bought by Germany's Lufthansa in 2005. In 2007, 19 former executives faced criminal charges of mismanagement and fraud in a high-profile trial lasting two months. The airports at Zurich and Geneva remain among the busiest in the world.

Industrial Sector

Swiss industry, which was fortunate to survive World War II almost unscathed, produces a wide variety of quality, precision goods. It has some heavy–weight

multinational corporations, 12 of which are on the Fortune 500 List, led by Nestlé (which ranked number 12). Four out of Europe's 10 top multinationals in terms of market capitalization are Swiss: Novartis, Nestlé, Roche and UBS. Thanks to its lowered corporate tax of only 8.5% plus cantonal taxes as well as its central location, good transport links, well-trained multilingual work force and high quality of life, it has become the European headquarters of choice for many foreign multinationals, such as Colgate-Palmolive, DuPont, Catepillar, General Motors, Proctor & Gamble, Polo Ralph Lauren, Estée Lauder, Hewlett-Packard, Phillip Morris and Oracle. American and French companies prefer Geneva, while German multinationals like the German-speaking cantons. However, most of its factories are by world standards relatively small and widely dispersed throughout the country. About a fourth (23%) of all employed persons work in industry and 73% in services. Over a fourth (26.3%) of the GDP is derived from industry, compared with almost three-fourths (72.7%) from the growing service sector.

Approximately one–sixth of all employees work in the machine and equipment sector. It provides one–third of Switzerland's exports. It specializes particularly in equipment that does not lend itself to mass production, such as generators and turbines. It produces over 15% of the

world's textile machines and roughly 13% of the precision instruments. The country provides about 1% of the world's arms exports. In 1997 three–fourths of voters approved continuing arms sales despite reports that Switzerland had delivered about a fifth of the equipment for Iraq's atomic program. It is also a leading chemical exporter. Three Basel firms alone produce roughly 10% of the world's need for medicines, and Swiss chemical plants provide 13% of the world's production of paint materials.

The chemical industries in the Basel area created great concern and international consternation in November 1986. Accidents at the chemical plants of Sandoz and Ciba–Geigy spilled masses of toxic waste into the Rhine, undoing much of the hard work in the preceding 15 years to revive a river that had been declared ecologically dead. Countries all along the Rhine protested the Swiss handling of the disasters and the fact that information about them was withheld for many hours by Swiss authorities. These incidents were also a rude awakening for the Swiss, who had comfortably contended that nothing like that could happen in their country because their technology was too good and they were so careful.

Two of Switzerland's traditionally most important industries, watch making and textiles, have faced serious challenges. The textile industry is a victim of high labor costs and the rising value of the Swiss franc, which has priced many textile products out of the market; they cannot compete with cheaper Asian products.

In 1970, Swiss watchmakers had a third of the world's sales. By 1984 that share had fallen to 10%. Benefiting from the technological spin–offs of space exploration, the U.S. watch industry moved rapidly into the field of digital, electronic and quartz watches regulated by computer chips, and Japan was close behind. Swiss watchmakers responded by restructuring and investing effectively, diversifying into such products as heart pacemakers and by shifting some of the production facilities to foreign countries with low labor costs. To the horror of traditionalists, many "Swiss" watches bear the stamp "Made in Hong Kong under Swiss supervision." Two Swiss firms, (SSIH and Asuag) have also merged to form the world's second largest watch producer—Industrie Horlogère Suisse—and have met the challenge of the electronics revolution by introducing robots to produce such big, mid–price sellers as the "Swatch."

As a result, the restructured watchmaking industry has recovered steadily since 1982. It now employs 40,000 compared with 90,000 in 1970. It is also making advances in microchips for watches. Switzerland now has a 60% share of the world market, and watches account for 8% of exports. Top quality timepieces, such as Rolex, are among the most coveted in the world.

The undisputed leader is Swatch, the world's largest watch producer. It is best known for its low-cost but stylish plastic time pieces. They make a lifestyle statement and get much of the credit for making Swiss watch making healthy again. But Swatch also owns upmarket brands, such as Omega, Longines and Breguet. As the country's dominant supplier of mechanical watch movements, it sent tremors through the entire Swiss industry in 2005 when it announced that it would no longer supply them to other watchmakers. That means that the latter must either make their own movements or no longer advertise their watches as "Swiss-made" since the law requires that the movements, not just the assembled watch, be produced in the country.

Strikes in key sectors of the economy were almost unknown since 1937, despite the fact that nominal wage increases are traditionally the lowest of all industrialized countries. This fact is crucial for Switzerland's ability to maintain its international competitiveness. Consensus and conservative continuity are the foundation of the country's stability and steady economic progress. Wage negotiations are conducted at the local level, and the government stays out of them. Nevertheless, 2002 saw the first nationwide strike in Switzerland in 55 years. Construction workers protested their employers' refusal to sign a contract to allow early retirement at age 60.

A chronic problem had been a shortage of labor. That helped insure that Switzerland did not have the unemployment other European nations face. It was 4% (2.8% on a narrower national measure) in 2008. The labor shortage compelled Switzerland to attract foreign workers, who comprise a fourth of the labor force and are essential to Swiss prosperity. In earlier years the country could cope with the threat of unemployment by simply sending some guest workers home. However, criticism of this policy shamed the government into granting more permanent visas.

Tourism

An essential aspect of the economy is tourism, which accounts for about 8% of the overall national income. Swiss tourists re-spend about one-half of that income outside Switzerland. This industry is threatened by the high value of the franc. Nevertheless, it was ranked in 2007 as having the most competitive travel industry in the developed world. No one who

has seen pictures of Switzerland's majestic mountains, its sparkling spring-fed lakes and streams, or its beautiful meadows and valleys should have any difficulty understanding why the tourist industry is so successful.

It has also been the salvation for rural areas that would have become almost completely depopulated due to the economic and cultural attractions of the cities. Since the tourist trade is concentrated largely in otherwise economically disadvantaged areas, rural Switzerland has been kept alive and prosperous. Of course, some veteran travelers miss much of the color and folklore of the earlier rustic Switzerland, but they sometimes forget that such folklore often masked great poverty.

Banking

Since the 16th century Switzerland has been among the world's major banking nations. Geneva became an extremely successful banking city, which aroused admiration and exasperation throughout Europe. Voltaire once advised that if one sees a Genevese banker jump out the window, one should jump after him because there is bound to be gold on the pavement! The French novelist, Stendhal, called them "the foremost money men of the continent. In this *metier*, they have the foremost of virtues, that of eating less each day than they earn!" The U.S. also profited from this talent when the scion of a wealthy Geneva family, Albert Gallatin, was appointed Secretary of the Treasury in 1801. Later, as the U.S. Ambassador to France and Britain, Gallatin adroitly negotiated commercial relations between the U.S. and Europe.

Switzerland has more banks than it has dentists—one per 1,400 residents. The number of banks has declined from 495 in 1990 to 356 in 2002. Half of all banking business comes from outside the country. The traditional strength is in private banking, which is personalized service for the rich. They have a reputation for secrecy, security and efficiency. Financial services by banks account for more than 12% of GDP, twice that in Zurich and Geneva. If one includes insurance and pension funds, the figure rises to 16%, ahead of commerce and tourism at 15% and engineering at 9%. However, they have begun to lose ground to the three big world banking centers of New York, Tokyo and London. A third of its smaller banks have merged or closed. Even two of its largest banks, Union Bank and Swiss Bank, announced a merger, and the three largest banks reported financial losses in 1997. The banks' dealings with the Nazis have also tarnished their reputation. In 1997 California, New York City and other

U.S. cities even started boycotting their services.

Swiss banks have profited from Switzerland's political stability and hard currency, which is the most highly treasured in the world. By attracting funds to Switzerland the "Gnomes of Zurich," as the Swiss bankers have been called, in turn help to drive up the value of the franc. Combined with the Swiss National Bank's successful policy of restricting the domestic money supply, the high value of the franc has kept Switzerland's inflation rate (2.4% in 2008) under control. This is because with its valuable franc, it can buy raw materials abroad more cheaply than it could if its currency were worth less. Of course, the rise in the franc's value can increase the price of Switzerland's exports, thereby hurting Swiss industry. However, the extremely low inflation rate helps keep down the price of Swiss exports and thereby keeps the export industries competitive.

A very important ace which Swiss bankers hold in their hands is the country's bank secrecy laws, which sometimes make their banking system look like the Ali Baba caves. Their banks holds an estimated one third of the world's total offshore assets. These laws were introduced initially in 1934 to protect Jewish victims of Nazi persecution. They differed from bank secrecy laws in other countries in that bank information was also withheld from revenue authorities, and any breach of banking secrecy was a criminal offense. Yet since 1991 absolute secrecy is no longer possible. Swiss courts can order banks to divulge information or to freeze accounts, as they did when the U.S. Congress began investigating insider trading.

A 1973 treaty with the U.S. permits the divulging of bank information in cases where U.S. authorities can prove that a criminal offense is under investigation. This does not include U.S. tax evasion, which does not violate Swiss laws. After 1983 Swiss authorities were willing to extend legal assistance to other foreign governments seeking evidence to convict persons accused of tax fraud or other penal cases. The code was tightened in 1989 when the laundering of money obtained through illegal activities was made a criminal offense. This law was in part a result of American pressure, as was a 1985 measure dealing with insider stock trading.

The Swiss froze assets of deposed dictators Nicolae Ceausescu (Romania) and Manuel Noriega (Panama) and of the Medellin drug cartel, and they divulged information on accounts needed in the trial of Elizabeth Kopp. They agreed to cooperate with investigations on unclaimed Jewish assets from the Second World War. In 1997, they for the first time took action

Switzerland

LANGUAGE AREAS

against a ruler still in office, Zairian President Mobutu, who by the time of his death was said to hold $4 billion in Swiss bank accounts. In 1998, Switzerland's highest court ordered $500 million in assets belonging to the late Philippine ruler Ferdinand Marcos to be returned to the Philippine central bank. In 2001 Switzerland cooperated with the United States' anti-terrorist campaign by freezing 24 bank accounts linked with al-Qaeda. A year later it returned to Nigeria more than $1 billion the late dictator Sani Abacha and his family had embezzled and placed into Swiss accounts. A half billion dollars more were returned in 2005 when the court determined that the remaining funds from Abacha "were clearly of criminal origin."

In 2004 the accounts of Russia's formerly richest man, Mikhail Khodorkovsky, and 20 other Russian citizens were frozen. The sum linked to the Yukos oil group alone amounted to $5 billion. In August 2007, while Khodorkovsky sat in a Russian prison, the Swiss supreme court ordered authorities not to turn over bank documents that Russia was seeking on the grounds that the Russian investigation of Yukos was politically motivated. This was the first time the court rejected an international request for this reason.

The Trade Union Federation and the Swiss Socialist Party have long demanded that banking operations be opened even more to public scrutiny, and American law gave strength to these demands. Many other Swiss grew uncomfortable with the notion that their prosperity

might partly be based on the huge deposits of dictators and drug kings, especially as drug consumption is a growing problem in Switzerland itself. Finally, in 1991, Switzerland abolished its "Form B" accounts, which allowed clients to conduct bank transactions through intermediaries without revealing their own identities. Banks must now know who is behind each account.

Desiring to ward off dirty money in the first place, Swiss authorities tightened their "know your customer" rules in 1997 and introduced one of the world's strictest money-laundering laws. Bankers must report suspicious deposits or transfers to a special police office, and they must relinquish account details requested in criminal investigations. Legal procedures were streamlined to make it easier for foreign police or prosecutors to get assistance. In 1999–2000, authorities froze more than $1 billion in bank accounts. However, they need cooperation from foreign governments, which must be willing to prosecute. In 2000, the third Russian prosecutor was fired in Moscow after trying to build a criminal case with the Swiss.

In 2003 Switzerland grudgingly agreed with the European Union that it would discourage citizens from EU countries from using Swiss accounts. The EU is aggressively cracking down on tax evaders, and the trail all too often leads to the Alpine banking center. The drain on Swiss banking assets seems relentless, a very serious problem for a country whose banks manage about a third of the world's private savings (ca. $3 trillion). It reached an

agreement with the EU to collect withholding taxes for bank account interest (15% in 2005 rising to 35% in 2011) and return 75% of it to the country of residence without providing account holders' names.

By 2005 the flood of foreign money pouring into Switzerland had become a trickle for several reasons. It is no longer so attractive because of its new savings tax and laws on money laundering. Declining tax rates elsewhere in Europe have reduced the fiscal incentives. Finally, some countries have offered amnesties to entice wealthy foreigners to repatriate their funds.

The European Union

Switzerland is a member of several economic international organizations. In addition to the OECD, IEA and the WTO, it has belonged since 1960 to EFTA, which is now largely irrelevant. Although Switzerland signed an agreement with the EU that removed all tariffs on industrial products in 1972, it could not become a full member for three reasons: first, it would have had to relinquish a portion of its sovereignty to the EU; second, its neutrality could be affected; third are economic reasons. For example, it gives much higher subsidies to its farmers than the EU allows.

The EU's push toward greater unity stimulated fears of isolation in Switzerland. In 1992 the Federal Council formally applied for membership. In that year the Swiss voted to join the IMF and the World Bank. But in December they rejected by a whisker-thin 50.3% their country's entry into the European Economic Area (EEA), a link between the EU and EFTA. German speakers in the large cities said yes, but they were outvoted by rural and small town German speakers, whose traditional fear of being absorbed by a larger Germany was revived by the EU. By contrast, French–speaking Swiss, who have no fear of France, said yes. In a step to align their fiscal policies to the EU, voters in a 1993 referendum approved the introduction of a Value Added Tax (VAT).

The rejection of the EEA put the application to the EU, for which there is no parliamentary or popular majority, temporarily on ice. In a 2001 referendum, 77% of the voters in an unusually large turnout again rejected a proposal to enter negotiations to join the EU. French-speaking cantons were most inclined to favor entry. This blocked the government's hopes that talks with the EU could get underway during the 2003–7 legislative session. Thus EU membership is unlikely before 2015 or later, especially after the SVP's electoral success in 2003. Its laws have already been made "Euro–compatible" in

Jean Tinguely's *Chaos I* in Columbus, Indiana

Photo by Claude and Victor Thompson

most sectors. It has negotiated a series of sector-by-sector bilateral deals with the EU that give it access to most EU markets without loss of sovereignty. It can opt out of whatever EU legislation it or its citizens dislike. By 2005 its citizens were free to live and work anywhere in the EU.

In a June 2005 referendum 55% of voters chose to join the 13 EU countries in the Schengen passport-free travel zone. It would retain customs checks on shoppers and trade. The government reacted angrily when the EU Commissioner for External Affairs Benita Ferrero-Waldner said immediately after the vote that Switzerland would not be allowed to join Schengen unless its voters also voted yes on a more controversial question in a September 2005 referendum. The Swiss government denied that there was a legal link. Fortunately, backed by business groups and opposed by nationalists, a solid 56% of voters voted in that referendum to endorse the plan to open up the country's job market to workers from the EU's 10 new member states and to pay them an equal wage.

Swiss voters share many of the same fears that motivated French and Dutch voters to vote down the ill-fated EU constitution in May and June 2005: that eastern Europeans will swamp them and take their jobs from them. The country had already been criticized by the UN in March 2005 for introducing some of the toughest asylum and immigration controls in Europe. They would require refugees to pro-

duce a passport or identity papers to apply for asylum. Welfare payments would be cut off if those ordered to leave the country tried to remain.

Therefore, Switzerland has not suffered economically by not joining. However, this bilateral approach is both cumbersome and complicated as the EU constantly evolves. The Swiss worry about the fact that if it were ever to enter, their country would be the second–biggest financial contributor after Germany. But its small population means that it would be one of the smaller and therefore less influential members. Most of all Swiss fear the effect EU membership would have on their unique political system.

In May 2004 the government and the EU accepted a series of treaties to clear the way for a new savings tax regime, for the country's entry into the EU's Schengen passport-free area in 2006–2007, and for enhanced cooperation in areas like fraud. Whether and when they would be ratified remained an open question. It feels its close ties with the EU. Swiss voters approved a law in 2006 to give the 10 newest EU members $800 million in economic aid. It also had to accept EU criticism that its tax rate in some cantons, where profits foreign companies make in EU countries are not taxed, are a form of state subsidies.

The chances that Switzerland would soon join the EU are slim. If it did, its manner of governance would create a constant dilemma. How would the EU deal with a member that could call a referendum on

every major EU decision? Even the most pro-European Swiss treasure their country's unique system of democracy.

Refusal to join the EU hurts some industries, such as chocolate. To retain their market shares in other European countries, chocolate makers are shifting their production outside of Switzerland, thereby dulling the magic ring of "Swiss chocolate." At least they retain a huge market at home: the average Swiss consumes more than 22 pounds of chocolate per year, more than do Americans (10 pounds) or any nationality.

CULTURE

Switzerland is a multilingual country. The most widely used official language is German, spoken by 64% of the citizens. Actually, most German–speaking Swiss speak one of many different dialects of Aleman German, which differs from valley to valley and which is spoken very differently from that which is heard in Berlin. The other official languages are French, spoken in pure form by 18% of the Swiss, and Italian, spoken by about 8%.

A fourth "national language" is Romansch, a collection of five not always mutually intelligible Latin–based dialects spoken mostly in the more isolated valleys of Grisons. Some linguists argue that it is the closest living language to the late Roman Empire vernacular. It is spoken by about 40,000 (.6%) of the Swiss. That number has been declining as tourism has

Switzerland

helped encourage slightly more than half the residents in Grisons to speak Swiss German. To fight against this trend, linguists are busy standardizing the idioms and spelling and translating many texts, including income tax forms, into Romansch. TV and radio air–time is also being increased and broadened to include comedians and local pop groups. In 1996 the Swiss voted in a referendum to elevate Romansch to the status of a "semiofficial" language, meaning that speakers may use it in dealings with the federal government.

Although only a minority of Swiss is fully multilingual, as are Luxembourgers, the fact that the language groups are separated and largely concentrated in single–language, autonomous cantons prevents the language diversity from being a major problem as in Belgium. It is true, though, that French- and Italian–speaking Swiss somewhat resent the dominance of German in the federal institutions in Bern.

In 1998 a new language problem emerged: the most populous canton, Zurich, decided that English, not French, should begin at an early age, perhaps in the first grade. Its officials argued that in

the contemporary world pupils need more than the one or two years of English they used to get before age 16, when they can leave school. Education officials in 11 of 19 other German-speaking cantons want to follow Zurich's lead. This produced an uproar, especially in the French–speaking cantons. Many fear such a change could erode Swiss identity. But with no national ministry of education, it is difficult to establish and maintain one common policy in the cultural field. Federal Interior Minister Ruth Dreifuss argued in 2000 that English "should not be like a steamroller" crushing the country's languages. But she recommended that all Swiss children have a fair command of three languages, including two of Switzerland's official ones. Zurich also took the lead in reintroducing High German in the classroom after the promotion of dialect had been successful in the 1970s. A 2005 study showed that teaching in the local dialect may hold pupils back both academically and in terms of employment.

Switzerland is also multireligious. While Protestants outnumbered Catholics by nearly three to two in 1900, Catholics,

who now comprise 49.4% of the population, presently outnumber the Protestants, who comprise 47.8%. Each canton is free to decide whether or not to have complete separation between church and state, as in Geneva. The federal government does exercise some control over the churches by reserving the right to approve bishoprics and by banning members of the clergy from the National Council. Not until the 1970s did the government permit the Jesuits to resume activities in the country. However, one cannot say that serious tensions exist among religions or between the churches and the state. Religion also plays an insignificant role in Swiss politics today except when such issues as abortion are the subjects of referenda. Nevertheless, 58% of Swiss voted in 2005 to grant more rights to same-sex couples.

The cantons organize their own school systems, and this enables the schools to reflect their religious, lingual and cultural uniqueness. All children enter primary school at age six or seven. After four or five years of primary school, the children enter one of three different kinds of "upper school": an extended primary school makes the lowest academic demands; a second type, called a *Realschule*, prepares pupils for a commercial or technical career and a Gymnasium prepares pupils for the universities. After the mandatory eight or nine years of schooling, pupils can enter an apprenticeship, and roughly 80% do this; or they can continue their general education, aiming toward specialized training or the university. There are seven cantonal universities, one business and social science university in St. Gallen and two federally operated technical universities in Zurich and Lausanne.

Radio and TV operate under government license and are administered by a mixed state and privately owned body, the Swiss Broadcasting and Television Corporation (SRG). The SRG broadcasts in four languages from six radio studios and in German, French and Italian from three television stations. Of course, broadcasts from neighboring countries are also received in most parts of Switzerland. In 1983, the cabinet approved the establishment of Switzerland's first local radio and TV stations, which would supplement the existing national broadcasting network. These new stations will be nonprofit, and advertising will be limited.

With about 231 newspapers, the country also has the greatest number per capita in Europe although it has declined by 40% since 1939. Zurich has one of the most highly respected newspapers in Europe, the *Neue Zürcher Zeitung*, which celebrated its 225th birthday in 2005. Known affectionately as "Die alte Tante," (the old aunt), it has changed very little since the

Seite 27: Afghanistan, Qatar und der Irak: Ein Bericht des Filmers Christian Frei

Basler Zeitung

AZ 4002 Basel

Basler Zeitung – Aeschenplatz 7, 4002 Basel, Telefon 061 639 11 11, Fax 061 631 15 82, E-Mail: redaktion@baz.ch – *Abonnements- und Zustelldienst*: Tel. 061 639 13 13, Fax 061 639 12 82, abo@baz.ch, www.baz.ch/abo/ *Inserate*: Publicitas AG, Tel. 061 275 41 41, Fax 061 275 42 42

BaZ online: www.baz.ch

Montag, 17. März 2003   Nr. 64

161. Jahrgang

Fr. 2.50 (inkl. MWSt), Elsass/Deutschland: € 1.70, übriges Frankreich/ Eurogebiet (A, F, GR, I) € 2.–, Türkei TL 4 250 000, Zypern CYP 1.20

Teil I		Teil II		Teil III		Teil IV		Teil IV	
Zweite, Tagesthema	2, 3	Wirtschaft	9, 10	Region Basel, Aktuell	19, 21	Feuilleton	27	Sport	
Ausland, Inland	4, 5	Forum	12	Basel	22, 23				
Wetter, Fernsehen/Radio	6, 7	Bestattungen	16, 17	Baselland, Region	24, 25				
Letzte	8			Kultur aktuell	26				

Kein Triumphzug. Proteste gegen die Rückkehr Vittorio Emanueles. **8**

Luftfahrt-Pionier tot. Der Franzose Jean-Luc Lagardère ist gestorben. **9**

«Zürich-Häuser». Ein Gutachten lässt doch mehr Spielraum. **23**

Georges Simenon. Würe in diesem Jahre 100 Jahre alt geworden. **27**

Fünfmal bezwungen. Der sel verlor in Visp 0:5.

Fürstlicher Sieg

Vaduz. BaZ. Triumph für den liechtensteinischen Fürsten: Fast zwei Drittel der Stimmbürger stellten sich gestern hinter die Verfassung von Hans-Adam II. – bei einer Stimmbeteiligung von 88 Prozent. Die neue Verfassung räumt dem Monarchen das Recht ein, die Regierung zu entlassen, wenn diese sein Vertrauen verliert. Die Verlierer der Abstimmung kündeten bereits eine Beschwerde beim liechtensteinischen Staatsgerichtshof an.   **Inland, 5**

Wasser-Forum

Kyoto. BaZ. Rund 1,2 Milliarden Menschen weltweit leben ohne gesicherten Zugang zu sauberem Trinkwasser – und mit zunehmendem Wohlstand wird Wasser auch in Industriestaaten immer knapper. Am dritten Welt-Wasser-Forum, das am Sonntag in der japanischen Stadt Kyoto eröffnet wurde, beraten in dieser Woche rund 10000 Politiker und Fachleute aus aller Welt darüber, wie die Versorgung mit Wasser sichergestellt werden kann.   **Tagesthema, 3**

Weiter abwärts

Basel. F.E. Trotz den kräftigen Avancen Ende letzter Woche dürften die Aktien an den Börsen weiter fallen, sagt Novartis-Finanzchef Raymund Breu im Interview mit der BaZ: «Wir sind der Ansicht, dass die Bewertungskorrektur selbst auf dem heutigen Niveau nicht vorbei ist.» Für das Pharma- und Generikageschäft von Novartis rechnet Breu

Der «Moment der Wahrheit»

Der heutige Montag werde zum «Moment der Wahrheit», hat US-Präsident Bush gestern Abend erklärt. Die USA suchen im UNO-Sicherheitsrat das letzte diplomatische Gefecht, um anschliessend in den Krieg zu ziehen. Verloren haben sie schon jetzt ihre moralische Au

Auftritt der Kriegstroika auf den Azoren. Tony Blair, José María Aznar und US-Präsident George W. Bush bekräftigten ihre Entschlossenheit zum Krieg. Das kleines Eiland mitten im Atlantik war am Sonntag der einzige Ort, an dem sie vor Massenprotesten sicher sein konnten.   Fot

240

1930s. It is invariably high-brow and studiously avoids gossip. Perhaps that is why the average age of its readers has climbed to 50 and its circulation has fallen to 160,000.

Switzerland has a wealth of folk art and music and a rich cultural tradition of its own. The Swiss foundation, Pro Helvetia, seeks both to preserve and stimulate Swiss cultural activities. Yet the cultural and intellectual life of Switzerland has always been enriched by foreigners who were drawn to it or who sought refuge there. Such towering figures as Hans Holbein the Younger, Germaine de Staël, Franz Liszt, Richard Wagner, Friedrich Nietzsche, Thomas Mann, Jules Verne, Albert Einstein, Karl Barth, Karl Jaspers and Hermann Hesse chose to live and work part of their lives in Switzerland.

The proximity of great cultures that surround the country both stimulates Swiss writers and thinkers and draws their minds away. Any Swiss writer who does not feel himself a German, French or Italian, or who does not share in the intellectual life of the neighboring country where his native language is spoken, risks becoming narrow and provincial. But if he takes a much wider view, his work risks losing its Swiss character. Indeed, many Swiss writers have been frustrated and bored with the narrow confines of the small bourgeois and neutral Switzerland. The Swiss psychoanalyst, C.G. Jung, once described Switzerland as a country "beneath the battle," and two of the 20th century's greatest playwrights, Max Frisch and Friedrich Dürrenmatt, both Swiss, have expressed in their works gruesomeness and disillusionment and have generally debunked the lives of those around them.

Still, many Swiss artists have found great international recognition. Paul Klee, who was brought up in Bern and who later fled Nazi Germany, brought Swiss painting to the world stage. His modern art is represented in the great galleries around the world. The art theoretician and one of the greatest architects in history, Charles–Edouard Jeanneret (better known as Le Corbusier) designed buildings throughout the world, although he built very little in his native Switzerland. The modernist sculptor, Jean Tinguely, with his "free and joyous machines," ranks as one of the world's most inventive contrivers. An ingenious example of his work can be found in Columbus, Indiana. Using pieces he had found in the Columbus junkyard, he created his indescribable "Chaos" with such intriguing moving parts that the viewer can neither wholly understand nor forget it.

In February 2008 Switzerland was stunned by two spectacular art thefts. The first took place in the town of Pfäffikon, where thieves stole two Picassos worth an estimated $4.4 million. A week later in nearby Zurich, three men wearing ski masks walked into a low-security private museum in broad daylight and stole the first four paintings they saw, valued at $163 million. A van Gogh and a Monet were found a week later in an unlocked car in the parking lot of a mental hospital a few hundred yards away in perfect condition. But the most valuable painting, Cézanne's "Boy in a Red Vest," valued at $91 million, and a Degas remained missing.

Without a doubt, one of the most important influences on the Swiss culture has been and always will be nature. Perhaps the incomparable Swiss landscape is the focus of the greatest pages in its literature and of its greatest art. They evoke those magic moments when a person surrenders himself completely to the beauty of the world around him, when a person feels himself included for a moment in a great harmony.

Foreign writers could scarcely escape this magic effect of the Alps. Friedrich Nietzsche conceived his *Zarathustra*, which expressed his bold, heroic, over–proportional philosophy in the Alpine Engadine, and Thomas Mann set his *Magic Mountain*, one of the 20th century's greatest novels, in the crisp, sanitary Alpine air above Davos. Perhaps Hermann Hesse, who had been drawn permanently to Switzerland, expressed it best: "Everything merges into one, distance vanishes and time is done away with."

FUTURE

The Swiss are ruminating about their role in the modern world. Such problems as an aging population, political scandals, laundering of dirty money, and rising drug use have prompted the country, in the words of a Swiss official, "to redefine Switzerland by examining our internal problems and by looking at our future role in Europe and in the 21st century."

It will continue to enjoy a relatively high degree of domestic stability. The economy successfully reinvented itself in the face of globalization and is running well. The rising value of the franc is a worry for such an powerful exporting nation. In 2006 the World Economic Forum ranked Switzerland as the most competitive country on Earth. It will remain a prosperous country. As a member of the UN since 2002, its foreign policy has a much more international orientation, and its policy of neutrality continues to undergo change. The aftermath of the 2007 elections, with Christoph Blocher's People's Party becoming the largest party since 1919, continues to transform the basic rules of Swiss government. Consensus politics and amicable agreement appear weaker, and adversarial politics of a determined opposition nipping at the government's heels seems to be the rule for the next few years.

Distance vanishes and time is done away with.

The Principality of Liechtenstein

Area: 62 sq. mi. (160.475 sq. km.)

Population: 35,000, estimated.

Capital City: Vaduz (Pop. 5,000, estimated).

Climate: Alpine, with cool summers and cold winters.

Neighboring Countries: Switzerland (Northwest and South); Austria (Northeast).

Official Language: German (Aleman dialect).

Ethnic Background: Alemannic German. More than one–third of the residents are foreigners, chiefly Swiss, German, Austrian and Italian.

Official Religion: Roman Catholic (80%).

National Day: August 15 (birthday of Prince Franz Josef II, father of current reigning Prince Hans Adam II).

Main Industries: High technology, metal industry, especially production of small machines, textiles, ceramics, chemicals and pharmaceuticals, timber, hydroelectric power, building equipment, processed foods, tourism postage stamps.

Main Customers: EU (45%), EFTA (19%), Switzerland (27.3%).

Currency: Swiss Franc.

Date of Independence: January 23, 1719.

Government: Hereditary constitutional monarchy.

Head of State: His Serene Highness Prince Hans Adam II (b. 1945). Since August 2004 Crown Prince Alois conducts the day-to-day affairs.

Head of Government: Otmar Hasler (since 2001).

National Flag: Two horizontal bands, blue over red, with a gold crown in the blue field. (The colors of the House of Liechtenstein are gold and red.)

Liechtenstein is an almost unknown Alpine country with a territorial size slightly smaller than the District of Columbia and one–twentieth of that of Rhode Island with a population of only about 35,000. In fact, about the only thing big about this pint–sized state was the name of its late ruler, who died in 1989: Prince Franz Josef II Maria Aloys Alfred Karl Johannes Heinrich Michael Georg Ignatius Benediktus Gerhardus Majella von und zu Liechtenstein, Duke of Troppau and Jägerndorf, Count of Rietberg. It is the last existing intact remnant of the Holy Roman Empire and is the world's only remaining German–speaking monarchy. Its people, who have a strong feeling of independence and tradition, maintain their country's sovereignty without soldiers.

Separated from Switzerland by the Rhine River, a torrent rushing straight down from the mountains which at times threatens the country's fertile valley, Liechtenstein is squeezed between the Swiss cantons of Grisons and St. Gallen to the west and the Austrian province of Vorarlberg to the east. One third of the country, which is approximately 15 miles (25 kilometers) long and an average of four miles (six kilometers) wide, is a rolling, green and fertile area located in the Rhine valley. Most of the country's population, industry and agriculture is located in this area. The remaining two–thirds is composed of the rugged foothills of the Raetian Massif, with peaks ranging from 5,900 feet (1,735 meters) to 8,600 feet (2,599 meters), that form part of the central Alpine chain which runs east and west through the southern half of Switzerland. Surveyors re-charted and re-measured the borders in 2006 and concluded that they were one mile (or 2%) longer than previously assumed. Thus the tiny principality grew by a half of a square kilometer, or roughly 50 football fields. This forward–looking relic of the past is a land of almost unsurpassed natural beauty, colorful tradition and economic prosperity.

Liechtenstein

The Early Period

Situated on one of the oldest north–south transit routes in Europe, Liechtenstein was a logical area for continuous settlement since the Stone Age. In 15 B.C. the Romans under Caesar Augustus conquered the Celtic inhabitants and established an important highway through the area. This road helped open the land that is now Germany to Roman conquest, trade and administration. Later, it provided good access for German tribes or troops seeking wealth and power in Italy. Liechtenstein also lies astride the Basel–Vienna route, a thoroughfare that also brought soldiers and traders to the area. The remains of Roman villas and the castle in Schaan testify to the former Roman presence. Parts of the Alemannic (Germanic) tribe moved into the region in 264 A.D. Like many other tribes of northern and eastern Europe at the time, the Alemans had pulled up stakes and sought richer territories in western and southern Europe. They drove the Romans out of the area very quickly and have remained ever since. Today's citizens are descendants of these ancient Alemans and still speak their melodic dialect of German, which is also spoken in sections of eastern Switzerland and southern Germany.

The land was subsequently ruled by a variety of noble houses until Prince Hans Adam von Liechtenstein, an Austrian nobleman with a family residence near Vienna, purchased the Lordships of Shellenberg in 1699 and Vaduz in 1712. The calculation of the prince, who had tried for years to buy territory anywhere between Italy and the Elbe River, was that by purchasing these two independent lordships which were fiefs of the Holy Roman Empire, he could persuade Austria's Kaiser Karl VI to upgrade the united lordships to the status of the Imperial Principality of Liechtenstein. Karl did just this on January 23, 1719, and the House of Liechtenstein, which gave its name to the new principality, thereby gained a coveted seat in the Imperial Diet of the Holy Roman Empire. Karl's declaration made Liechtenstein the 343rd state in the empire and gave the principality its present form. The new ruling family remained in Vienna, caring very little for the small land that had brought it privilege and honor. For 187 years, Liechtenstein was ruled from a distance by an absolute monarch.

Napoleon

In 1806 Napoleon drove out the Austrian troops that had occupied the principality since 1794 and made the country a member of the Confederation of the

Prince Hans–Adam and Princess Marie

Rhine. Its ties with the Holy Roman Empire ended with the demise of that long paralyzed conglomerate of states, which, as was often said, was neither holy, Roman, nor an empire. Liechtenstein officially became a free and sovereign state. Napoleon respected Liechtenstein's independence, which was confirmed later by the Congress of Vienna in 1815. It is, in fact, the only part of the Napoleonic territorial system that survived unchanged to this day.

It is almost inconceivable that a country as small as Liechtenstein could exist without some form of economic union with a greater power. It joined the German Confederation after the fall of Napoleon and in 1852 it joined a customs union with the Austro–Hungarian Empire. From 1876 until 1918, the principality was a part of an even tighter customs and tax arrangement with the Austrian province of Vorarlberg. Its close ties with Austria made it unavoidable that it lent its support in Austria's feud with Prussia over the future shape of a unified Germany. Nevertheless, Liechtenstein maintained a rather free hand. It resisted all efforts to draw it into the First World War as an ally of Germany–Austria.

After World War I

The links between Liechtenstein and its eastern neighbor were severed in 1918 with the collapse of Austria–Hungary. World War I brought about the collapse of centuries–old dynasties all over Europe in the face of revolution, famine, misery and the widespread evaporation of former ideals. Liechtenstein's partner, Austria– Hungary, had been whittled down to its German core, a mere splinter of the earlier multinational empire. Such a ruined and chaotic country could no longer offer a promising future to Liechtenstein. In fact, Austria's collapse and dizzying postwar inflation

wiped out Liechtenstein's entire savings. Therefore it saw the need for far–reaching changes. It both proclaimed the present democratic constitution on October 5, 1921, and reoriented itself toward its other, more fortunate neighbor: Switzerland. A customs treaty was signed with that nation in 1923, and this relationship, updated and deepened by subsequent agreements, is now firmly established.

Depression and World War II

In the 1930s Liechtenstein was severely shaken by the economic depression and narrowly escaped being swallowed up by Hitler's Third Reich. Austria was absorbed by Germany in 1938 and the shadow of the swastika was cast over Liechtenstein's border. The 85–year–old monarch, Franz I, was without heirs, and he feared that his death would be the signal for a Nazi takeover of the principality. He therefore appointed as regent one of his grandnephews, the present monarch's father, Franz Josef II. On July 26, 1938, Franz Josef II ascended the throne. A small minority of Liechtensteiners had actually been attracted to Nazism, and in March 1939 local Nazis attempted unsuccessfully to overthrow the government. This determined minority remained undaunted and continued to publish a semiweekly Nazi newspaper. A few of them even joined the armed sections of the Nazi SS.

Not included in the Swiss defense system during World War II, Liechtenstein miraculously managed to maintain its neutrality throughout the conflict. German troops could have captured the country within half an hour, especially since the fifty–man auxiliary police corps was under orders to offer no actual or symbolic resistance whatsoever. This corps occupied itself chiefly with trying to control the great number of foreign deserters,

Liechtenstein

conscientious objectors and refugees who streamed into the country.

After Germany's collapse, the border posts were strengthened and a barbed–wire barricade was strung along the entire border with Austria. However, in the night of May 2, 1945, the barricade was trampled and crossed by armed soldiers of the First Russian Army of Liberation, who were fleeing from Red Army units that had been ordered to send them back to the Soviet Union. They were disarmed and interned with thousands of other refugees in camps near Ruggell and Schaan. Despite attempts by a Soviet investigating team that came to Vaduz to demand possession of all Russians, these refugees remained until 1948, when they were permitted to emigrate to Argentina.

POLITICAL SYSTEM

Liechtenstein is a constitutional monarchy in which sovereignty is theoretically shared by the hereditary monarch from the House of Liechtenstein and the people. The prince's constitutional powers were dramatically increased as a result of a referendum in March 2003, in which 64.3% of voters supported his proposals to strengthen his political prerogatives. Only 35.7% opposed them, with a voter turnout of 87.7%. The reforms made the ruling prince the most powerful monarch in Europe within his realm. It can no longer be said that this royal "reigns but does not rule." His acquisition of sweeping powers caused concern in the Council of Europe. It set up a commission that concluded that the constitutional revisions are "a serious step backward" and could "lead to the isolation of Liechtenstein within the European community of states." Former Prime Minister Mario Frick agreed: "We have made ourselves an international laughing stock." However, both the prince and two-thirds of Liechtensteiners waved off these worries. In the prince's words, "the princely house and the people of Liechtenstein can walk hand in hand into the future."

The country has a 25–member unicameral parliament elected by proportional representation for four–year terms. The voter turnout at elections is quite high, ranging from 76% to 95%, and citizens 18 years of age or older are permitted to vote. Not until 1984 were women granted the right to vote and to hold public office. Earlier, an antiquated law stripping all locally born women of their citizenship if they married foreigners was repealed. Liechtenstein has ceased being politically a "man's world."

As in Switzerland, the highest executive authority is a collegial board. All five members of the cabinet serve four–year terms. The majority in parliament selects the leading member (called the head of government). The deputy chief is chosen in the same manner, and by tradition is from an opposition party. Parliament also chooses the remaining members (called Government Councilors). The prince formally appoints all of them. Since 2003 he can unilaterally dismiss the government, which is responsible to both parliament and to the prince.

The prince must formally approve all legislation although he has not vetoed a law since the 1960s when he disapproved of the legislature's proposed change in hunting rights. Since 2003 he can kill legislation passed by parliament by not acting on it for six months. He has the right to introduce legislative proposals in the parliament. In time of emergency, he can, with the permission of the head of government, decree laws without seeking approval from parliament.

In 1993 he flexed his constitutional muscles by dissolving parliament and calling new elections after the ruling party revolted against its leader, Markus Büchel, whom it accused of incompetence. Such a rejection of a parliamentary no–confidence vote is inconceivable in any other European monarchy. The prince noted: "There is no majority for a figurehead," and the 2003 referendum confirmed this.

In the past the prince made no attempt to dominate the political process. However, in 1997 he demanded and later received the right to approve the appointment of judges. He had said he would pack up his family and move to Vienna if this power were denied him. Even one of his critics in parliament, Peter Wolff, admitted that losing the prince would be a terrible setback: "The monarchy gives us our national identity." The speaker of parliament agreed, asserting: "Without the prince, we are nothing." The referendum gave him the power to approve all judges and to be removed from the jurisdiction of the constitutional court.

The prince found solid support among the political parties and the people. Citizens were divided on his proposed constitutional changes, which some saw as an excessive strengthening of the monarchist element. Some local politicians resent his semi-feudal powers although they want to retain a constitutional monarchy. The constitutional struggle culminated in the 2003 reform, which for the first time grants citizens the right to call a referendum to express any displeasure in the prince's performance. If that were to happen, various males in his extended family could decide whether to replace him. According to custom, the prince receives no pay from his subjects although he accepts a token expense allowance of 250,000 Swiss francs. His popularity helps give stability to the country's politics.

The prince is married to Prague–born Countess Marie Aglae Kinsky, and they have four children. When Crown Prince Alois, who graduated from Britain's famed Sandhurst military academy and Salzburg University law school, was married to Duchess Sophie of Bavaria in 1993,

The Prince and Princess of Liechtenstein with their children—(on the stairs) H.S.H. Princess Tatjana and H.S.H. Prince Maximilian, and (left and right) H.S.H. Prince Constantin, H.S.H. Hereditary Prince Alois.

The Castle at Vaduz, residence of the Reigning Prince of Liechtenstein

the entire Liechtenstein population was invited to join the festivities in a garden party. Having won the referendum after a decade of bickering and criticism, Prince Hans Adam II, who remains head of state, handed over day-to-day responsibility to Alois on August 15, 2004.

Liechtensteiners generally know how to reconcile their love for the royal dynasty with their right to self–rule. Thus, their traditionally firm attachment to the monarchy was rather surprising to the outsider, considering the facts that the first time their ruler even visited the tiny country was in 1842 and that the rulers declined to live permanently in the land until 1938. Until then, princes always preferred the splendid family palace, Burg Mödling, near Vienna. But when he ascended the throne in 1938, the quiet and unassuming Prince Franz Josef II, who had been born in 1906 and educated in agriculture and forestry in Vienna, chose to reside in the 100–room medieval castle perched on a high cliff crowning Vaduz. The prince of Liechtenstein's family possesses an art collection whose estimated value is from $150 million to $500 million.

In 1989 Franz Josef II died, less than one month after the death of his wife, Princess Gina; he collapsed at his wife's bedside and never recovered. His successor, Hans–Adam, is an economist who has long administered the family's wealth, estimated at four billion euros ($6 billion). This includes a bank (LGT) with subsidiaries in London and New York, electronics and "software" investments in the U.S., and land holdings in Austria twice the size of Liechtenstein. It also owns jointly with the International Paper Company a 75,000–acre farming operation in Texas.

In one of Europe's most complicated and high-profile cases, the prince is demanding that the Czech Republic return lands confiscated after World War I 10–times the size of the principality. It began in 1991 when he discovered a painting in a museum in Cologne and on loan from Czechoslovakia that had been stolen from his family collection. A decade later he took Germany to court to recoup over a billion euros worth of property that it claims Germany had illegally expropriated to pay its postwar debts to Czechoslovakia. Prague keeps the properties on the grounds that Liechtenstein's royals are German-speaking and therefore German in nationality; that gave Prague the right to confiscate the property. The prince reminds the players that postwar Allied-sponsored legislation exempted neutral Liechtenstein, which was the only country to refuse to recognize the infamous 1938 Munich Agreement that ceded the Sudetenland to Germany, from paying Germany's reparations. Prague refuses even to recognize Liechtenstein officially, let alone discuss the case.

Political Parties

The two main political parties have programs that are difficult to distinguish from each other. They appeal to electors who, not surprisingly in such a small country, are often inclined to vote for the man rather than the party. In the 2005 elections to the 25–seat parliament, the conservative Progressive Citizens' Party (FBP) and the centrist Fatherland Union (VU) won the most seats. They formed a coalition government headed again by Otmar Hasler with the FBP occupying three cabinet posts and the VU two. A left–wing environmentalist group, the Free List (FL),

had entered parliament with one seat in 2001.

Liechtenstein has an independent judiciary and a legal system based on Swiss, Austrian and its own law. For administrative purposes, the country is divided into 11 communes, which are governed by mayors and city councils elected locally every three years. A civil service staff of approximately 600 officials administers the government's political decisions.

This is a sovereign state that, because of its extremely small size, has chosen to align itself politically and economically very closely to Switzerland. This places severe limits on its powers, but as a sovereign state, Liechtenstein is free to take back its full powers at any time. It does differ with Switzerland on some diplomatic issues. In 1980 Liechtenstein broke with the Swiss policy and supported the U.S.–led boycott of the Moscow Olympics to protest Soviet intervention in Afghanistan.

He also announced Liechtenstein's entry into the UN, rather than to wait for the Swiss to make up their minds. In 1992 it announced that it would not enter the EU, even if Switzerland decided to do so. The voters accepted the referendum on the European Economic Area (EEA) treaty in 1992 under the condition that the customs union with Switzerland be maintained. Unlike Switzerland, it joined the EEA in 1995. In 2007 it joined the EU's greenhouse gas trading system.

EEA membership gives it most of the advantages of EU membership and few of the burdens. Prince Hans–Adam called it "the best of all possible worlds for Liechtenstein. We have our cake and eat it too." The greatest beneficiary is its manufacturing sector, which accounts for almost half of the country's 20,000 jobs and which is almost totally dependent upon exporting.

Liechtenstein belongs to several special organizations associated with the UN, such as the International Court of Justice, the International Atomic Energy Agency and the UN Conference on Trade and Development. It belongs to EFTA (to which a substantial amount of its exports go), the OSCE, and the Council of Europe in Strasbourg at which it has taken its turn as chair.

At one time, Liechtenstein maintained embassies only in Bern, Switzerland, (which in turn represents its tiny partner throughout the world) and in Vienna, Austria. It now has eight foreign missions, including in such international centers as Brussels, Berlin, New York and Washington. It has agreed not to conclude trade or customs treaties with other states, but is bound by most treaties into which Switzerland enters. In general, it avoids any international dealings that would dis-

Liechtenstein

please Switzerland. It has renounced its right to coin its own money, with the exception of gold coins that have no legal value as currency; Swiss currency has been used since 1921. Swiss officials have full responsibility for all customs questions arising out of the 1924 customs union.

Beautiful postage stamps are printed in Liechtenstein, which it sells profitably throughout the world. In fact, such sales provide 10% of the government's revenues. Switzerland once shared responsibility for the postal, telephone and telegraph systems, although Liechtenstein owned the equipment. In 2000 the principality assumed full control of its postal and telecommunications systems.

Swiss border guards also control Liechtenstein's boundaries. Officially, all able–bodied males to age 60 are required to be ready for military service. However, there has in fact been no army since 1868. It maintains merely a 55–man police force.

Liechtenstein was most recently invaded on March 1, 2007, a dark and rainy night, when 170 confused Swiss infantry soldiers mistakenly crossed the unmarked border into Liechtenstein during a routine training exercise. After two kilometers of marching, they realized they had made a mistake, so they turned around and sneaked back home undetected. After a few hours sleep, they called the Liechtenstein authorities and apologized for the embarrassing border violation.

ECONOMY

The visitor to Liechtenstein most often remembers the romantic side of this Alpine retreat, which seems to have slumbered almost unnoticed into the modern age. What he often overlooks is the fact that this principality is the second richest, second most industrially productive country in the world when measured in per capita income terms. Only Brunei, with its tremendous oil deposits, earns more per person each year. This economic prosperity tends to change the traditional, overall picture of this nation. Though traditional in so many ways, it has shown itself to be extremely open to progress in research, technology and production. Before World War II more than a third of the population worked on the land, and there were only four factories.

Now only 1.7% of the population is engaged in agriculture, and there are 45 factories. This leap into the modern industrial age is a result not only of extraordinarily stable political conditions, but also of minimum investment requirements, a very liberal tax policy and strict bank secrecy. The tax laws encouraged from 20,000 to 30,000 foreign businesses,

often called "letter box companies," to maintain nominal headquarters in Liechtenstein. It also allows the establishment of anonymous foundations, of which there are about 50,000, more than there are inhabitants. About 30% of GDP and a third of Liechtenstein's total fiscal revenues are derived from such companies and foundations. The government prefers to call this "wealth management," and it traditionally refused to assist foreign tax evasion investigations. It is untrue that no individual or company pays taxes there. Income taxes range from 8% to 10% for individuals and 6% to 18% for companies. Property is also taxed.

It grew tired of its reputation as a country that caters to persons and groups who want to hide "dirty" money. French and German reports had linked it to Russian and American organized crime and South American drug dealing. Such criticism prompted Prince Hans Adam, whose family owns Liechtenstein's largest bank (LGT, managed by second son Prince Max), and the elected government to appoint a financial investigator from Austria to look into corruption.

A police raid in May 2000 led to the arrest of a handful of leading citizens, including the brothers of the economics minister and the chief judge. The embarrassed principality amended its laws to facilitate the search for dirty money, dubious depositors, and other shady individuals who maintain mailbox corporations. It reached an agreement with the EU in 2003 to collect taxes for bank account interest and return 75% of it to the country of residence without providing account holders' names. In 2005 it returned to Germany about 2.6 million Swiss francs, which East German embezzlers had deposited in the closing days of their sinking state.

In February 2008 disaster struck when Germany revealed that it had a disc purchased from an anonymous former LGT employee for nearly five million euros

containing the names of thousands of investors who were hiding money in the principality. British tax authorities also paid the same informant. After Germany announced that it would share the information on accounts with any government that wanted it, Liechtenstein was faced with its greatest financial crisis ever. Berlin accused it of "encouraging lawbreaking" and threatened to oppose its entry into the EU's Schengen area to end border controls. The usually quiet and reflective Crown Prince Alois shot back against this "attack" on his country and accused Germany of "trafficking in stolen goods." He canceled an exhibition of the royal family's paintings in Munich.

Although his spirited defense won him adulation at home, he faced charges from many European countries, which had long pressured Liechtenstein to adopt OECD rules on secret accounts and to loosen its bank secrecy laws. They demand the same kind of transparency standards as the United States negotiated with Vaduz committing the principality to provide financial information on U.S. citizens living abroad who invest there.

Determined to change its shady image in order to attract tourists and legitimate investments, the principality set up the Image Liechtenstein Foundation in 2002 and hired a global branding specialist, Wolff Olins, to polish up its image. When day-to-day power was transferred to the crown prince on August 15, 2004, a new national logo was unveiled. Called a "democratic crown," it is red and blue, the royal colors, on an aubergine-colored background. It is used on official documents and on materials in the private sector.

Liechtenstein's industry is very diverse. High technology and the metal industry, which specializes in small machines, are the leading ones, followed by the ceramic, chemical and pharmaceutical industries. The country produces a wide range of goods, including ultrahigh vacuum technology, miniature calculators, boilers, tex-

Liechtenstein princely moments   **Logo: democratic crown**

Liechtenstein

tiles, furniture, varnishes, fountains, canned foods, prefabricated houses and protective coatings for spaceship windows and artificial teeth, for which it is one of the world's biggest producers. One of its companies even produced a component for a solar wind experiment that went to the moon with the Apollo astronauts.

Because it has practically no natural resources, Liechtenstein has no heavy industry. The relatively small size of factories and the fact that the firms have been consciously dispersed throughout the country away from urban areas has had the favorable effect of both preventing large industrial plants from dominating the landscape and of preserving the country's environment from the kind of damage that has often accompanied rapid industrialization in other countries. This fortunate situation greatly benefits not only the inhabitants, but also the country's tourist industry, which is the nation's fourth most important source of income. With tourism down in 2003, an innovative "rent-a-state" program was introduced. It offers the whole principality except the Vaduz Castle as a destination for conventions and corporate retreats. For a daily fee of about $320 to $530 per person for groups up to 1,200 people, an organization could reserve entire hotels, restaurants, meeting places and sports facilities and even temporarily put their own logos on buildings.

The thriving economy has enabled the residents to enjoy a high standard of living and a generous social welfare system. It has also brought certain economic and social problems to the country. First, since there is almost no domestic market for its high technology products, Liechtenstein is overwhelmingly dependent upon exporting. It is extremely vulnerable to international developments that might adversely affect world trade. Second, with only 1.7% of its population working in agriculture, it must import 70% of the food needed to nourish its well-fed population. Third, the small size of the domestic work force has necessitated the importation of foreign workers. Approximately 12,000 such workers, who come chiefly from Switzerland, Austria, Germany and Italy, and who are often accompanied by their families, now constitute a third of the country's population. Adding 6,500 commuters who come daily to work, about 60% of the workforce is foreign.

This large percentage of foreigners has placed strains on the tolerant and hospitable Liechtensteiners. They can seldom be absorbed into the political life of the country; an ancient practice permits foreigners to become citizens only if the popular assemblies in one of the 11 communes approve them individually. Few of the foreigners ever gain the right to vote. In 2000 a new law was passed to make it easier for foreigners who have been living in the principality for 30 years to become citizens.

Many native Liechtensteiners became concerned about the possibly negative social effects that the presence of so many foreigners might have on the country. Therefore, since 1962 the government has placed severe limits on the influx of foreign workers. This policy has produced undeniable economic difficulties. Without an available pool of labor, Liechtenstein's domestic industry cannot grow. Because of this limitation, almost all of the country's major industries, which need to expand because of the high volume of orders, have begun to transfer substantial portions of their production activities to foreign countries.

Liechtenstein has a good network of roads, but has no airport and no rail service to the capital city. The railway facilities in the north of the country linking Switzerland and Austria are owned and operated by the Austrian Federal Railways.

CULTURE

As a small country with very few citizens, Liechtenstein is heavily dependent culturally on its German-speaking neighbors. Two German language newspapers appear in the capital city of Vaduz: the *Liechtensteiner Vaterland* published six times weekly by the Fatherland Union, and the *Liechtensteiner Volksblatt*, published six times weekly by the Progressive Citizens Party. Except for a Liechtenstein station called Radio L, all radio and television programming comes from Switzerland, and the Liechtenstein postal ministry pays fees for this service.

Cultural efforts receive generous subsidies from the government. Permanent art collections are maintained in two museums. In the second half of the 1980s a new art museum was supposed to be built in Vaduz to display the bulk of the Prince's collection of paintings, sculptures, old weapons and furniture. However, bickering and red tape held up the construction. Most of these treasures are stored in the royal castle in a five-story depot as large as a medium-sized department store. A few can be seen in a new museum that replaced the old Engländerbau in 2000. An impatient Prince Hans–Adam reportedly thought about establishing his own art museum by blasting a huge cavern into the cliff under his castle in Vaduz. The high cost of constructing the new museum was such a political hot potato that it prompted new parliamentary elections in 1989 to try to sort it out. Theater am Kirchplatz in the town of Schaan attracts leading performers from throughout the world.

Liechtenstein's people are 80% Roman Catholic, and in 1999 it finally got its first archbishop. His limited political influence was displayed in 2005 when an initiative he had supported to prevent abortion, birth control, assisted suicide and living wills was favored by fewer than one in five voters. Nearly 80% ratified a government counterproposal that brought the principality's birth control and abortion laws in line with European standards.

The school system offers kindergarten, elementary and secondary educations, and is modeled largely after the Swiss school system. There is one elite *Gymnasium* (high school) in Vaduz for those pupils who wish to pursue university studies. Students must enter universities outside the country, since none exists locally. The literacy rate among the country's citizens is 100%.

Future

Liechtenstein's close association with Switzerland and its highly advanced and diversified economy will continue to be crucial for its existence as a sovereign microstate in the modern world. It can be expected to remain politically stable, despite the fact that over one–third of its residents are foreigners. After constitutional reform in 2003, the principality now has Europe's most powerful monarchy with everyday powers being wielded by Crown Prince Alois. Liechtenstein will remain somewhat vulnerable economically because of its dependence upon exports, a static domestic labor pool and dubious financial services. It suffered its greatest economic crisis in 2008 when the names of thousands of tax evaders fell into the hands of European tax authorities. This will likely lead to a loosening of its bank secrecy and greater transparency in its financial service sector, which accounts for 30% of the principality's GDP.

The Hellenic Republic (Greece)

Area: 50,961 sq. mi. (131,900 sq. km., somewhat larger than Louisiana).

Population: 11.2 million (2001 census).

Capital City: Athens. (Population 3.3 million). The number in the Greater Athens area, including Athens, Piraeus (its port) and surrounding municipalities is estimated to be 5 million.

Climate: Generally mild, with the summer hot and dry, tempered in the vicinity of the coast where sea breezes blow in every afternoon.

Neighboring Countries: Turkey (East, across the Aegean Sea, with many scattered Greek islands lying close to the Turkish coast, bordered on the northeast by *European* Turkey); Albania, Bulgaria, Macedonia (North).

Official Language: Greek.

Other Principal Tongues: There is a small Turkish–speaking minority (about 1.5% of the population) in Thrace.

Principal Religion: Greek Orthodox (over 95%).

Main Exports: Machinery, food and beverages, transport equipment, petroleum products, chemicals, non-ferrous metals, textiles.

Main Imports: Machinery, chemicals and plastics, foodstuffs, automobiles, petroleum and fuels, iron and steel.

Major Trading Customers: EU25 (53% of exports and 55.7% of imports), Germany (12.4% of exports and 12.7% of imports), Italy (10.4% of exports and 12.4% of imports), UK (6.7% of exports), United

States (5.3% of exports), France (5.2% of imports), Russia (7.8% of imports).
Currency: Euro.
National Holiday: March 25 (Independence Day).
Chief of State: Karolos Papoulias, President (since 2005).
Head of Government: Costas Karamanlis, Prime Minister (since March 2004).
National Flag: Four white and five blue alternating stripes, with a white cross on the upper left hand corner.

Greece is a land with many islands that, at times in the past, has been the geographic, military, economic, cultural or philosophical heart of the Western world. Its mainland portion is for the most part mountainous and hilly. Its geographical position at the intersection between East and West and between the Balkans and the Mediterranean has made it a springboard to the Orient and a thoroughfare for invasion by Moslem peoples heading west. For ancient Romans, Christian crusaders and European merchants, Greece was the doorway to the East. For Arabs, Turks, Serbians and Bulgarians, it was an important gateway to Western culture. Throughout the centuries, Greece's position at the bridgehead of three continents inevitably drew it into most conflicts between the peoples of Europe, the Near East and North Africa.

This central position of Greece remains largely unchanged in the 21st century. Even today Greece retains its key geostrategic position. With its many islands, it is the heart of the Aegean Sea and the eastern Mediterranean. But contemporary Greece is much more than that. It is a society that is experiencing a shift from traditional values and economic ways to those more compatible with Greece's new role as a full partner with the prosperous and advanced states of western Europe. It is a land that is open to the major influences of the modern world. All changes in Greece are always viewed from outside the country with a mixture of hope and anxiety.

HISTORY

Greece is both a very old and a very new country. Not until 1829 were Greeks able to end four centuries of Turkish domination and to create an independent nation–state. However, the Greek state which was proclaimed in that year and the country's contemporary society and culture bear little resemblance to the ancient Greece which so many people have admired throughout the centuries. The large body of Greek classical literature and the many magnificent ruins reflect the grandeur of the ancient past. But the modern Greek's approach to life and his understanding of himself have been shaped far more significantly by the Byzantine past (324 A.D. to 1453), the Orthodox Church and four centuries of Turkish domination than by the Greece of antiquity. At the very most, the modern Greek shares with his ancient forefathers an ardent passion for political discussion, a talent for daring economic activity and a proverbial hospitality.

The Early Periods

Nevertheless, a presentation of Greece without the classical period would be unthinkable, for ancient Greece was the cradle of Western culture and civilization. Most Western philosophical, political, scholarly and artistic achievements have their roots in Greek antiquity. Ancient Greece has served in many respects as a model worthy of imitation or, at the very least, as an almost inexhaustible, examinable reservoir of human experience and thought. It is rightly referred to as the founder of Western thought and culture. That torch still to a degree burns today.

It is often the case in history that the new and the extraordinary emerge at the point of contact between various cultures and peoples. From roughly 1600 to 1200 B.C. Greece attracted a flood of Indo–Germanic tribes from the north, who came into contact with older cultures from Crete, Egypt and other areas of the Middle East. These highly intelligent and agile newcomers borrowed the Phoenician letters and numbers and developed a written Greek language; they took the religiously oriented astronomy of the Middle East and developed it into mathematics. They also freed the ancient Egyptians' great, but static, art of sculpture from its immobility and produced an art capable of portraying the idealized likeness of man.

When the first Greek immigrants arrived on the coast of the Aegean Sea, they came upon a highly developed culture, whose mysterious ruins on the island of Crete provide evidence of the Minoan cul-

The Parthenon in Athens (temple of Athena, goddess of wisdom) dominates the Acropolis, that flat–topped natural stronghold of early times which was the heart of the city.
Photo by Susan L. Thompson

Greece

ture, named after the legendary king of the island, Minos. It began to rise around 3000 B.C. and had developed brilliantly by about 2000 B.C. The unearthed palaces, ceramics and frescoes give exciting glimpses into a highly developed and cultivated civilization. The Minoans apparently maintained a very powerful fleet because excavations provide no evidence of fortifications. The origins of this culture, its social structure and its decline remain a mystery to the present day.

The Greeks began to burn and sack the Minoan strongholds around 1400 B.C. and a new culture emerged—the Mycenaean, named after the town of Mycenae in the Peloponnesus—the peninsula forming part of the mainland of Greece. The remains of this culture can be seen around the Peloponnesian coasts and up the eastern seaboard of Greece all the way to Thessaly (Thessaloniki), as well as in the southern islands of the Aegean Sea, the islands of Rhodes and Cyprus, and the west coast of Asia Minor. Through the decoding of many clay reliefs from this period (roughly 1600 to 1150 B.C.) we know that the civilization was organized in small, Greek–speaking governmental structures. Even the names of Greek myths appear as historical realities in these carvings, so this society unquestionably provided material for these myths and system of religion.

It was around 1200 B.C. that the legendary siege and destruction of Troy (a city whose ruins can be seen on the northwestern coast of Turkey) is said to have taken place. This exciting tale, which may even contain a tiny bit of truth, sprang from the alleged kidnapping of Helen, the beautiful wife of the Spartan King, Menelaüs, by Paris, a prince of Troy. King Agamemnon of Mycenae, Menelaüs' brother, led a ten-year Greek expedition

to Troy to recapture the queen. Finally the Greeks pretended to give up the fight, leaving behind a large wooden horse as a supposed gift of congratulations to the "victors." During the same night that the gullible Trojans broke a hole in their walls to bring the fatal trophy into the city, Greek soldiers sprang out of the "Trojan horse" and captured the city from within.

A System of Religion

Sometime between 900 and 700 B.C., the Greek poet Homer described the siege in the Iliad and the Odyssey and the Greek warriors' adventures on their way home. The same author may not have written these long poems. Nevertheless, they are the beginning, and, in some experts' view, the best of Greek literature. They quickly became the standard texts that were memorized by Greek pupils and influenced Western literature as have few other works. They also reflected, and may even have influenced, the Greeks' view of the gods who, they thought, took a direct part in their daily lives. Homer poetically presented a host of particular gods, with well–defined characteristics, names and places of residence.

Zeus, ruler of the heavens was of primary importance. Hera, his wife and sister, was queen of the heavens. Poseidon ruled the sea and unleashed earthquakes, and Hades lorded over the underworld. Athena was the goddess of wisdom and skills, including those of the household, Aphrodite of love and beauty, Eros, her son, god of love (thus the word "erotic"), and Apollo of youthful manly beauty, of light, healing, young men's arts, such as archery, music, prophecy and poetic inspiration. Artemis, sister of Apollo, was goddess of the moon, wild animals and hunting, Demeter of grain, Hephaestus, god of

fire and metalworking, Hermes, messenger of the gods and god of the roads, Ares of war, and Dionysus of wine (and thus, drunkenness).

All Greeks ascribed to the gods at least some influence over their lives and cities, but it would be a mistake to think that Greek life was dominated by fear of the deities, as was the case in some primitive societies. Religious dogma, clergy or temples never profoundly shaped Greek political, economic and intellectual life. They sought human achievement and pleasures, and their endeavors were, on the whole, secular rather than religious. In this respect, the Greeks distinguished themselves from most other ancient civilizations. Nevertheless, the authority of the gods continued to be invoked in order to bolster political authority within the cities. Therefore, as the philosopher Socrates experienced in the year 399 B.C., a person could lose his life for defaming the gods in public, especially within earshot of impressionable young people.

City–States

The onset of a second migratory wave into Greece from 1200 to 900 B.C. led many Greeks to flee across the Aegean Sea to the Near East, on whose coasts they founded cities such as Ephesus and Miletus. Athens was located on the peninsula of Attica, an inverted triangle about 20 miles (30 km.) wide at the base and 35 miles (56 km.) from top to bottom. Attica, which had allegedly been united by the legendary King Theseus, was able to remain an undisturbed enclave during this second migration.

As was often the case, geographic factors left their stamp on Greek history. The mountainous terrain, with small river valleys and almost no large plains except in the North, favored from the beginning the formation of a kind of small political organization known as Polis (from this the words "politics" and metropolis" are derived). The *Polis* was a city–state, which in some cases included a number of small towns. Its limited size later made possible the unprecedented development of democracy in some Greek cities, especially Athens, and it helped stimulate the development of political awareness and interest among the citizens of the cities.

The Greeks' passion for politics was one reason why the philosopher Aristotle defined humans as "political beings." However, the intense interest in politics and the small scale of Greek political units were also factors which helped perpetuate the never–ending and exhausting conflicts among the various city–states. These conflicts helped prevent the integration of the Greek settlements into a larger political order, such as a nation state, as we know

Detail from a piece of Minoan pottery

it today. Citizens in the city–states viewed the world strictly on the basis of their narrow local patriotism and never developed a sense of Greek national identity. For the Greeks, including the Athenians, there was hardly a period of more than two years that was free of conflict with other cities. In general, the history of ancient Greece is one of almost constant war.

Had it not been for the temporary predominance during the 8th to the 6th centuries B.C. of the cities' aristocracies (often called "oligarchies") who gradually dislodged the cities' kings from power, and who maintained some close ties among the various city–states, Greece would probably have suffocated very early in the stifling spirit of provincial narrow–mindedness. It is because of this aristocratic class that the poetry of Homer, with its portrayal of the Olympian world of the gods, became standard references for all Greeks. The aristocracy was also responsible for developing the Greek education of man in the arts as well as in athletic competition.

The periodic gathering of Greeks for the Olympic Games, first organized in 776 B.C. at the city of Olympia in the western Peloponnesus, and thereafter held every four years, reflected the spirit of competition which became a precedent for the knightly tournaments in the European Middle Ages. Those with Olympic prowess and the virtues espoused by the noble class greatly overshadowed those persons who merely showed the simpler virtues, such as trading skills and industriousness, and sometimes they even overshadowed sculptors and architects who adorned the cities in which the Greeks lived. There can be no doubt that the Olympic Games brought Greeks together and showed them some common ideals. But these games never succeeded in creating peace or political unity in the Hellenic world, any more than have the modern Olympic Games eliminated wars or divisions among the peoples of the world today.

The governing cliques of aristocrats did begin to establish the political principles that the privilege of ruling should be passed around periodically and that rulers should not be above an established body of rules of law. Such laws were independent of the will of the temporary ruler and could be invoked if the rulers appeared to be abusing their powers. Thus, a notion of "limited government" by consent of the governed existed in most Greek cites from the 8th century on. This was a principle that was scarcely known in any other civilization of the era.

Politically, the aristocracy's domination over the masses was already being challenged from the 8th century. Rapid population growth, increasing tensions among

Greek legend tells of Hero, a priestess of Aphrodite, whose lover, Leander, swam to her each night across the strait between Europe and Asia. On one stormy night he drowned, his lifeless body washing to the shore. In grief, she cast herself into the raging waters.

the social classes and changes in warfare (which made citizen armies militarily superior to ones based primarily on noblemen) became important factors in further Greek developments. Increasing conflicts between the aristocracies and the common citizens created the right kind of conditions by about 600 B.C. for dictators to seize power in most of the cities. The threatened or dispossessed noblemen called them *tyrannis*, or "tyrants," a word which had formerly been applied to absolute rulers and one which still retains its negative connotation.

It is true that most tyrants disregarded many previously established laws and conventions. But most came to power by promising to break the power of the aris-

tocracy, and the common citizens usually favored them. They frequently launched conspicuous building programs to create public works which would both provide people with jobs and improve the economic base, living conditions, beauty and therefore, the prestige of the city. They also proclaimed laws that would benefit small tradesmen, artisans and farmers, and sometimes they gave subsidies to these groups. To pay for these policies, they often expropriated the property of the noblemen (and of their own opponents). Such property could thus be dispersed to some persons who had possessed none. They often abused the power they wielded, but because they did tend to have an ear attuned to the wishes of the

Greece

lower classes of citizens they, too, made a contribution toward the development of democracy in Greece.

Those Greek cities that had only small agricultural hinterlands close by could relieve the pressures created by rapidly growing populations only by founding colonies overseas to which their excess people could emigrate. Between 750 and 550 B.C. such Greek colonies were created along the coasts and on the islands of the entire Mediterranean and Black Sea, including one at Byzantium (later Constantinople, now Istanbul, Turkey). Greek colonies sprang up from the eastern coast of Spain to the mouth of the Dnieper River in what is now the Soviet Union and from what is presently the French Riviera and Sicily (where Syracuse was built) to the toe of Italy, which, along with Sicily, became known as "Greater Greece."

By means of these colonies, the Greek language, culture and influence were extended over much of the known world. Almost all of these colonies quickly broke the umbilical cords that tied them to their mother cities and became politically independent. There was no all–powerful overlord to subordinate the cities through taxes or military means as was the case in the Middle and Near Eastern empires. They continued to share similar viewpoints on ruling, culture and religion, and they almost always maintained sentimental ties. They also traded with the older Greek cities, and such trade was the foundation for an enormous growth of wealth in the entire Greek world. This wealth provided some Greeks with leisure, which was essential for their being able to produce beautiful poetry, usually about various forms of love. Leisure was also the starting point for rational, systematic speculation about nature. Thus, the Greeks began to free philosophy from mythology, which had characterized speculation in other ancient cultures.

The philosopher Plato coined the expression that the Greeks sat around the Mediterranean like frogs around a pond. In a short period of time, the Greeks showed themselves to be daring seafarers, traveling as far as Britain. It was the Greeks who gave meaning to the saying that "oceans are bridges," and they established the foundations of a Greek maritime predominance that indirectly continues to exist today.

Athens and Sparta

As could be expected, these cities often became bitter rivals. In the motherland political developments came to be dominated by the rivalry between the land power, Sparta, and the sea power, Athens. By the late 8th century B.C., Sparta had acquired the entire southern part of Peloponnesus.

Frieze of a Greek athlete

Its expansion had always been of a military rather than of an economic nature, and it did very little colonizing. The political organization of Sparta consisted of the exclusive domination by a warrior caste over the subjugated masses, who practically were kept in a condition of slavery and who were responsible for the economic maintenance of their masters.

According to law, all members of the warrior caste were equal and were not allowed to possess private property. The elite, whose reputation of being unconquerable, lasted until the 5th century B.C., was shaped from early youth by strict breeding and upbringing in a collective (thus the expression "Spartan discipline"). They performed permanent military service until age 60 and had a very restricted private life. The Spartans' thoughts centered almost exclusively around the triangular fortress, the mess hall and the battlefield. Most standard forms of pleasure and luxury were abolished in order to make military life more attractive. This kind of life would appeal to few people today, but a form of it was presented as an ideal state in one of the greatest books ever written, *The Republic* by Plato.

The Spartan political system blended elements of monarchy, aristocracy and democracy. Two kings had limited power and had supreme authority only in time of war. A Council of Elders, whose members were elected by an assembly of soldiers, made the really important political decisions. The brand of Spartan perfection, whose purpose was permanent military preparedness, tolerated no change and therefore soon became frozen in conservative rigidity.

Athens, a late bloomer among the Greek city–states, assumed a unique position from its onset because it encompassed the entire Attican Peninsula and became master of the sea. Perhaps most important, it developed a new kind of political order. As we have seen, the domestic political conflicts between the nobility and other classes of citizens had gradually led to the rise of tyrants in most cities. In the course of the 6th century B.C., a few of these cities experienced the emergence of a more democratic political order, in which the principles of equality before the law and the right to vote were extended to that part of the inhabitants who were citizens. Foremost among these was Athens.

Athenian law was codified and made public by 621 B.C. This enabled anyone who could read or who was informed to compare the behavior of the city's rulers with the established laws. In 593 the highly respected public figure, Solon, introduced a complete legal reform that provided the lower classes with financial relief, legal protection and a powerful voice in the city's government. The reform abolished property requirements for participation in the Assembly, which elected the city's leaders and which served as the final court of law for important cases, including those for public officials accused of abusing their power. For such cases, the judges were selected by lot from the entire citizen body.

The reform also transferred from the upper class to the other classes the right to determine the Assembly's agenda. Thus, the lower classes gained an important influence, perhaps even control, over the election of the city's officials, over legislation and over the Athenian judiciary. These reforms cannot be said to have secured democracy in Athens, but they laid the foundation for the Athenian democratic tradition. It was not until the reform of the statesman Cleisthenes in the years 508–507 B.C. that the power of the aristocracy was completely broken and all the important political decisions began to be made by democratic institutions.

The most important organ in the Athenian political system, and that which wielded legislative authority, was the Assembly, in which all citizens could attend and vote. This form of parliament did have some important drawbacks. One was that citizenship in Athens, as well as other Greek cities, was denied to women, foreign residents and slaves. Slave–ownership was widespread. Small farmers and shopkeepers usually had two or three and the rich could own thousands. In general, slaves were at least as numerous as were citizens. In any case, never did anything close to a majority of adult residents have the right to vote in the Assembly, so Athenian democracy, as advanced as it was for its time, was still ruled by a minority.

A second drawback stemmed from the fact that the Assembly met on a regular basis every nine or ten days. Since such meetings were too frequent even for most of the passionately political Athenians, few citizens attended most sessions, and the wealthier ones, who had more leisure to pursue their political interests, were often able to dominate the proceedings. Not until the 5th century B.C. were citizens paid to attend the sessions so that they could receive financial compensation for being away from their work.

The government's supreme executive functions were performed by the Council, composed of 500 representatives drawn by lot from the ten districts of the city. For the sake of convenience, the Council was divided into ten committees, each of which served a tenth of a year, during which time the chairmanship changed daily. The Council and the committees always remained subordinate to the Assembly, though. The sovereignty of the people was, in principle, exercised through the Assembly, but those who really had the decisive influence were the ones who

could have their point of view accepted by the often fickle and easily changeable majority in the Assembly. This fact put a high premium on the ability to speak eloquently and persuasively in public. Thus, these skills formed the basis of Athenian education. It also gave rise to a whole new profession: sophistry, so named because the sophists claimed to make men wise (*sophos*). Sophists made good money by teaching people how to win arguments in the Assembly and courts of law.

The volatility and changeability of the majority within the Assembly meant that policy could switch suddenly, and yesterday's powerful and honored leaders could be disgraced and dismissed the very next day. This led to great political instability and to a form of permanently latent revolution in Athenian political life. It is not surprising that many a leader was sent into exile, not because he had disregarded Athenian law or interests, but because his political opponents had successfully seized the chance to get rid of him. It is clear that such a political order was an ideal setting for golden–tongued demagogues and intriguers. This is one reason why such profound political thinkers as Socrates, Plato and Aristotle condemned democracy as an inferior type of political organization.

Only the most competent politicians, who could persuade the masses at any moment, could conduct a coherent and consistent policy under these circumstances. These leadership qualities were best reflected by Athens' greatest political figure, Pericles, who from 461 to 428 B.C. was able to guide the city to the summit of its power, glory, prosperity and architectural achievements. Of course, there were courts of law in which all citizens' rights were to be protected. But Plato's description in the Apology of Socrates' trial in 399 B.C. indicates that court proceedings could be uproarious and outrageous affairs, in which political or personal interests often weighed heavier than the evidence, to say nothing of justice.

With all its shortcomings, though, Athens extended wealth, luxury, leisure and political power more broadly among its citizens than did any other city. Also, democracy was an essential step in the direction of placing ultimate political power in the hands of the ruled, instead of those of arbitrary rulers. In Athens, the citizens exercised final control over all aspects of government. This first great example of democracy in action influenced western political thought from then on and helped to inspire the democratic revolutions of

Simplified map of Sparta and Athens with certain major cities of the area

Greece

the 18th, 19th and 20th centuries A.D. in America, western Europe and modern Greece itself.

Athens existed under conditions of almost permanent mobilization and imperialism, maintained by sea power and the exploitation of allies. It was able to survive a grave external threat to itself and to the rest of Greece in the first decades of the 5th century B.C., namely that of the mighty Persian empire to the east. The power of this great empire already extended into India and, by the middle of the 6th century, to the Greek cities along what is today the western coast of Turkey. When these cities, especially Miletus, revolted in 500 B.C., they were brutally crushed by the Persians within a few years.

The easterners, under the Great King Darius, decided to eliminate the sources of support for the Greek cities under their control, and especially to punish Athens for its aid to the rebels. Darius threw his military forces against the Greek mainland in 492 B.C. and conquered Macedonia and Thrace. However, during a violent storm his navy was wrecked off Mount Athos. But he resumed the operation two years later, landing an expeditionary force of 20,000 troops on the Attican coast; a far smaller force of Athenian citizen soldiers on the Plain of Marathon easily defeated these troops. A messenger ran as fast as he could for 26 miles (42 km.) in order to bring the news of victory to Athens, where he reportedly died upon arrival. The mod-

ern Marathon runs, in which both Olympians and many thousands of avid joggers now participate, commemorate the feats of both the Athenian soldiers and their prodigious messenger. Athens' victory secured for it enormous importance and prestige in all of Greece, and it ushered in the "Golden Age" of Athens, the 5th century B.C., when its power and cultural achievements were at their peak.

After Darius' death his crown prince, Xerxes, laid careful plans for a final blow to Greece. It certainly is wrong to assume that the Greeks displayed solidarity and fraternity with each other in the face of the Persian threat. Such concepts, as well as nationalism, were still unknown in the ancient world, as many Greeks showed in this great struggle. Xerxes was able to persuade the Greek trading power in the western Mediterranean, Carthage (located near the present–day city of Tunis in Tunisia), to tie down the western Greek forces by means of an attack against Sicily. All of northern Greece offered Persia indispensable support. Greek architects and engineers built the pontoon bridge over the Dardanelles and dug a canal in order to spare the Persian fleet from having to sail around the perilous Mount Athos. Most of the sailors in the Persian fleet were Greeks, and Athenians who had been driven out of their city served the Persians as highly paid military advisers. Basically, only a large part of those cities in central Greece and the Peloponnesus, including Corinth, Thebes and a couple of dozen smaller city–states fought under the leadership of Sparta and Athens.

In the summer of 480 B.C. the numerically vastly superior Persian units, with an estimated 100,000 foot soldiers and 1,000 ships, descended upon central Greece. They confronted the Greeks' first line of defense at Thermopoly, where in a legendary effort, a Greek force of 7,000 courageous soldiers, under the command of Spartan King Leonidas, held back the entire Persian army for a week before withdrawing. The enemy was then able to march almost unopposed into Attica and to occupy and completely destroy Athens, which had been evacuated just in the nick of time.

The Athenians were by no means defeated. In the narrow straits between the Attican coast and the island of Salamis, the Athenian admiral, Themistocles, lured the Persian fleet into a trap and destroyed it. Also, the land battle at Plateaea in 479 B.C. demonstrated the superiority of well–trained and motivated citizen soldiers over a huge immobile army, which was largely composed of a colorful mixture of diverse peoples who had been involuntarily drafted into service and who had been left on the Greek mainland without logis-

tical support. At the very same time, the news arrived that the Sicilian Greeks had stopped the Carthaginian invasion and that the remainder of the Persian fleet in Asia Minor had been cornered and destroyed at Mount Mycale, located immediately north of Miletus. After these sobering dual victories, the Persian threat was ended, and many of the Greek cities on the Aegean coasts rebelled anew against Persian domination. For the next 280 years the Greek world was spared from any serious external threat until the Roman Empire absorbed all of it in 190 B.C.

The Delian "League" and the "Golden Age"

Athens, which had carried the main burden of the Persian War, took quick advantage of its undisputed mastery at sea in order to construct a widely–spun web of alliances, which extended throughout the entire Aegean area and which Athens dominated. After Sparta had relinquished its leadership in the Greek alliance against Persia, Athens organized in 478–477 B.C. the Delian League, which maintained a common treasury on the island of Delos, where the League's representatives occasionally met. As the largest contributor, Athens was assured political and military predominance within the League. Soon, its allies discovered that they were veritable subjects of Athens, especially after 454 B.C., when the treasury was transferred to Athens and when meetings of the council were terminated.

Athens experienced an almost unbelievable economic upswing and it had a democratic order that inspired both loyalty on the part of its own citizens, as well as some admiration and support on the part of the lower classes in the other Greek cities (to the chagrin of their non–democratic leaders). Conditions were favorable to a cultural flowering that still testifies to Athens' "Golden Age." Out of the rubble of Athens emerged the classical Athens, with its grandiose structures on the Acropolis (literally "high city" which in most Greek cities was first a place of refuge from enemies and, later, the place for temples). Under the leadership of Pericles the living conditions of the poor were improved. After a few unfortunate military adventures, Pericles again launched Athens' deliberate, major policy of colonization, sending settlers to Thrace, Euboea and Naxos in 447 and then on to other Aegean islands, Macedonia, southern Italy and the Black Sea. These settlements provided land for Athens' allies and poorer citizens, as well as markets for its trade.

Art, science and philosophy flourished. Sculpture achieved its eternal classical form under artists such as Phidias and Ply-

An Athenian lady

254

An artist's concept of ancient Athens at its height

clet. The dramatists, Aeschylus (525–456), Sophocles (496–406) and Euripides (485–408) produced timeless tragedies. It is characteristically Greek that the victory over the Persians did not produce feelings of superiority among the Greeks. In his famous tragedies, Aeschylus portrayed the Persians with sympathy and sorrow. In bitingly critical comedies, Aristophanes took hilarious, but deadly, shots at the politics of the day. He is the only 5th century author of comedies whose complete works survived. On the southern slope of the Acropolis these dramatists presented plays in festivals, at which winners were chosen. A special tax on the rich enabled those from all classes to enjoy the performances.

In the writing of history, Thucydides approached his subjects far more systematically and analytically than had Herodotus in his narrations. Thucydides presented a concept of history as a structure of interlocking effects, which themselves become causes in human affairs. He sought to delve into the motives and interests of conflicting parties in historical events, and his historical method is still important today. In medicine, Hippocrates demanded that the body be studied as a whole. Hippodamus of Miletus redesigned Piraeus (which was and is, in effect, the port of Athens) and introduced gridiron planning for cities, instead of building towns with wildly winding streets.

A Second Round with Sparta

The enormous growth of Athens' power and its imperialist foreign policy again led almost unavoidably to a collision with Sparta, the second greatest power in Greece. When Athens turned on its major trade competitors, Corinth and Megara, which had been joined by Thebes, Corinth appealed to Sparta for help. The tension boiled over in the Peloponnesian War, which lasted almost three decades from 431 to 404 and which ended in Athens' defeat and ruin. This war was conducted with a brutality that had been almost unknown up to that time. Because of the alliance systems which Sparta and Athens had built up, almost every city in Greece was ultimately drawn into the conflict.

Based on what he witnessed in this war, Thucydides, the former Athenian general who had been exiled from Athens during the first part of the war for failing to save Amphipolis from the Spartans, developed his pessimistic view that man's insatiable striving for power was the sole motor of history. In his fascinating classic book, History of the Peloponnesian War, he described very impressively the restless and unlimited political passion that was a basic characteristic of the Greeks, along with the yearning for perfection and order in art and philosophy. On the one hand, Greeks were politically volatile and unreliable; on the other, they left timeless works.

As a sobering example, Thucydides described the political mistreatment of a small state by a more powerful one. When the island of Melos refused to join the Athenian naval league, the Athenians stormed the capital city, killed all the men and sold the women and children into slavery. And that was done by a democratic Athens. Thucydides' observations on foreign relations remain largely valid today. Military power and the willingness to use it are significant factors in international politics. Modern countries, large and small, must still adjust to this reality or suffer the consequences. The challenge to men remains to create a system of international law and widely respected codes of international conduct that would greatly diminish the significance of military force in human affairs.

At the onset of the war, Sparta marched into Attica and drove much of the rural population into the city of Athens, where close quarters and insufficient sanitary conditions created ideal conditions for a deadly plague, which broke out in 430 and which reduced the population by a third. It so frightened the rest of the people that, as Thucydides described so vividly, all respect for morality, social ties and law broke down for a time, since all individuals expected to be dead by the next day. The great leader Pericles died in 429. Fortunately for Athens, the Spartans were unable to launch any decisive attacks, so an armistice was arranged in 423 and a peace treaty in 421.

This first phase of the war accomplished nothing. Athens was interested only in having a temporary breather, and in 415 it sent an expedition under the leadership of the wealthy, brilliant and handsome young general, Alcibiades, to Syracuse (a former colony of Corinth) on the island of Sicily. As happened so often in Athens, he no sooner left the city with his large army and navy than his political enemies at home turned on him and demanded that he return home to stand trial.

Greece

The Lions of Delos, guardians of Apollo's sacred island

Courtesy: Dorothy L. Lewis

Knowing that he would be returning to sure death, Alcibiades fled instead to the Spartans, whom he persuaded to recommence hostilities against Athens in 414. The next year, the Syracusans proceeded to decimate the Athenian force.

By 412 both Syracuse and Persia had entered the war on Sparta's side, and Athens' allies along the Ionian coast had revolted. These setbacks so discredited the democratic order that an oligarchy was temporarily established, but the people in Athens could not accept this for long. Therefore Alcibiades was called back to Athens as the city's supreme commander, and democracy was restored. However, Athens was so ridden by party squabbles and demagoguery that it could not possibly conduct a successful war against its enemies. After a stinging naval defeat, Alcibiades was again driven into exile, and the Persians ultimately executed him. Demagogues in Athens persuaded the volatile majority to execute most of the successful commanders, and after its last fleet was destroyed in 405, the Athenians were exhausted. In 404 they surrendered to the Spartans, and Athenian greatness came to an end. In fact, none of the Greek cities ever fully recovered from the wounds they suffered in this terrible war.

The Athenian empire had existed for a shorter period of time than had any of the famous empires of antiquity; it had risen and fallen in three–quarters of a century. It was also the smallest of the great empires, comprising only a corner of Greece, most of the Aegean islands and colonies along the western coast of Greece, in Asia Minor around the Black Sea and in southern Italy. It probably never had a citizen population of more than about 60,000 and the population of Attica was certainly never more than a half million; in all likelihood it was a lot less.

The Postwar Period; Socrates, Plato and Aristotle

The Peloponnesian War accelerated the breakdown of morality, restraint and harmony among citizens in Athens and elsewhere in Greece. Greek politics was in a state of chaos. The probing, analytical minds of Greek thinkers had revealed that the gods in which Greeks had believed did not really sanction the moral order or back up the laws of the various cities as the people had thought. These insights created problems for the rulers, who now had greater difficulty persuading their people to obey them. If the gods did not determine what was just and what was not, then who did? What was justice? That was the fundamental question that a stone carver and former private in the Athenian infantry liked to discuss at the Athenian marketplace (agora) with anyone who wanted to talk about it.

His name was Socrates, and he particularly attracted a following of young, rich and ambitious Athenians, who were itching to become rulers themselves. He impressed and entertained them by skillfully cross–examining influential and supposedly wise men in public on subjects dealing with justice and morality. In reality, he was teaching by questioning. He was invariably able to reveal that they did not really know much about these subjects. He claimed not to know anything about these difficult concepts, but because of his skepticism and willingness to examine any question at its very roots, the oracle of Delphi (a pronouncement by a religious group with political clout) declared him to be the wisest of all men.

The rulers of Athens did not agree. Aristophanes revealed in his hilarious play, *The Clouds*, that most of the people regarded him as a mere gadfly, who taught young people how to lie, to avoid paying their debts and to turn against their parents with a good conscience. He was perceived to be undermining the already corroded authority of the city, and he was therefore put on trial in 399 B.C. for allegedly defaming the gods and corrupting the youth. He was condemned to death. But this questioning stone carver, who never wrote a word (he was described by others, such as Plato or Xenophon), influenced western civilization as almost no other human being.

After the fall of Athens in 404, the greatest power in Greece was Sparta, which established oligarchies in most cities. Even Athens experienced a "reign of terror," under the "thirty tyrants," led by a former pupil of Socrates and cousin of Plato—Critias—whose bloody deeds did much to assure his teacher's execution. The heavy Spartan hand provoked revolutions everywhere, and Greece experienced a long period of power struggles with Persia, Sparta, Athens and Thebes as the main contenders. By about 370 B.C. Spartan predominance in Greece ended once and for all.

Greece entered the 4th century B.C. in pitiful condition. The constant war had devastated much of the countryside, impoverished or destroyed many of the cities and disrupted the patterns of travel and trade. It was a time of growing piracy and of economic depression. However, it was also a time of continued intellectual achievement. The most influential sculptor of antiquity, Praxiteles, was creating individual statues which could stand alone in their perfection, rather than having to blend into an architectural setting.

The philosopher Plato, a rich Athenian from a very influential family, focused on the legacy of one man who, in his opinion, stood out in the madness of Athens: Socrates. His poetic and literary style, filled with brilliant argumentation, common sense and moral concern, as well as with beautiful myths and metaphors, greatly enhanced his prestige in his own day and his scholarly reputation right up to the present time. He founded a school in the Athenian suburb of Academia (from which the words "academy" and "academic" are derived), which survived until the Christian emperor Justinian closed it in 529 A.D.

Out of this school came his most famous pupil, Aristotle, who classified the various branches of knowledge, created much scientific terminology, advocated close scientific examination and experimentation and established standards of definition and proof. He too created a school, called the Lyceum (after which the French high school *"lycée"* is named). In 1997 this school was accidentally unearthed on a construction site for a Museum of Modern Art, 600 meters from Athens' central Constitution Square. The large ancient complex that was rediscovered includes a central courtyard and palaestra (wrestling area). Although he had very little impact on his own contemporaries, his writings, which were preserved by Arab scholars and rediscovered in medieval Europe, became the basis of scholarship and university teaching in Europe and the U.S. until the 19th century.

Philip of Macedon and his Son, Alexander

The mainland of Greece had fallen into such political chaos that it was left to the mercy of Philip II of Macedon, a kingdom of a Greek–speaking population in the North (now the independent state calling itself Macedonia). Macedon was culturally attracted to Greece, and Philip brought to his court outstanding Greek artists, writers and scholars, including Aristotle, who tutored the monarch's son, Alexander. Macedon was a different kind of political entity than the city–states of Greece. It was a large kingdom, not a city.

Philip was able to extend his rule into Byzantium in what is now Turkey. He could take advantage of the web of rivalries among the Greek cities to the south so that he brought one city after the other under his influence. The warnings of one of antiquity's most famous speakers, Demosthenes, fell on deaf ears in Athens, and by the time he could organize a coalition of the most important Greek cities against the Macedonian king, it was too late. Philip's victory in 338 B.C. followed up by finishing operations in the Peloponnesus signaled the end of the cities' freedom. The king proclaimed a general peace and organized the Greek cities in a league under his control.

Philip had already begun preparations for war against Persia when he was assassinated in 336. His son, Alexander, later known as "The Great" (356–323), who had just turned 20 when he became king, turned a new page in the book of world history. In a breathtaking campaign, the young commander in only nine years conquered the Persian Empire that had reached its greatest expanse, and he also won parts of south Asia as far as the Indus Valley. By the time he arrived in Susa with his army, which had completed a 12,000 mile (20,000 km.) march, Alexander ruled over an empire which stretched from Greece over Asia Minor, the Phoenician coast, Egypt, Mesopotamia, Babylon, Persia and beyond.

It is true that the Persian Empire had been weakened by palace intrigues and rebellions, but nothing fell into his lap without his having to earn it. On the contrary, bitter struggles demanded the entire strategic genius of the young commander, and his army had to engage in constant and exhausting individual combat with wild mountain men, to face inconceivable perils in the extensive deserts and dry highlands, and to master difficult technical challenges, such as the siege of the sea fortress at Tyre in Palestine.

He also had the political sense to assume the right titles in order to win the loyalty of his newly conquered subjects. He became the Great King in Persia and the Divine Pharaoh and Son of the God Amon in Egypt. The Greek cities bent to his demand that he be proclaimed no less than a Greek god. Genius, energy, ambition and charismatic leadership so united in the person of Alexander the Great that he could inspire thousands to perform the most incredible feats, and he was honored as a demigod during his own lifetime.

The fascination for this great and unfathomable personality remains alive today, especially since his campaigns of conquest were not like the marauding of Mongols, who left nothing but devastation and terror in their wake. He placed the stamp of Greek civilization on the entire Near and Middle East, not by simply forcing the Greek culture on conquered peoples, but by attempting to foster an ingenious synthesis of the Greek and Oriental cultures. The most visible expression of this attempt was the mass marriage in Susa (today in western Iran) of 10,000 Greek Macedonians with Persian women in the year 324 B.C.

A by–product of Alexander's success was the release of the Jewish people from Babylonian captivity. They gradually returned to Palestine, but many, referred to in the Bible as Samaritans, adopted some

Frieze of a water bearer

Greece

Alexander

Greek customs, much to the consternation of those who had struggled to preserve their faith intact.

When Alexander died on June 13, 323 B.C., at the age of only 33, the gigantic empire which he had created fell into three large parts, which had been divided among his three main generals and which ultimately developed into a relatively consolidated system of states: the kingdoms of Egypt, Macedonia and Seleucid (the latter encompassing the bulk of the former Persian Empire). There were also minor states that developed, such as Pergamum, Rhodes and Syracuse. The thread of Hellenistic culture ran through all of these states. The century following Alexander's death witnessed constant border wars caused by the conflicting interests of the three major kingdoms. Also, a new rising power in the west, Rome, conquered all the Greek cities in Italy by 270 B.C. These conquests not only increased Rome's power, but enhanced the influence of Greek culture on Rome itself. Much of the Roman Empire retained Greek culture and usages, including the grisly custom of execution by crucifixion.

The creative genius of the old Greece had not entirely dried up after the death of Alexander. This was a time when the Greek heritage was preserved in great libraries in Alexandria (a Greek city and the capital of Egypt) and Pergamum (now in Turkey), where scholars carefully collected, classified, evaluated and edited classical texts and theories. Thinkers such as Euclid (in mathematics) Archimedes (in physics) and Theophrastus (in botany) absorbed what had previously been done in their fields. Their works later became the point of departure for the Renaissance in the 15th and 16th centuries A.D. Eratosthenes calculated rather accurately the circumference of the earth in 295 B.C. The astronomer, Aristarchus, even proposed the revolutionary theory that the earth revolves around the sun. Another thinker, Hipparchus, refuted his theory incorrectly in the 2nd century B.C. Ptolemy's explanation of the astronomical constellation was accepted for many centuries before it was disproved by the discoveries of Kepler and Galileo.

The classical Greek language gradually gave way to dialects and became a learned language of scholarship. The more simplified Greek that emerged facilitated communication among many different peoples. Greek remained the international language of administration, diplomacy, business, teaching and theology. It is no surprise that simplified Greek was the language of the first written New Testament known to exist. Greek knowledge, customs and administrative talents migrated to Rome as Greeks were taken as slaves by the Romans, who used them according to their knowledge and talent, often as civil servants.

The Roman and Byzantine Era

The road from classical to modern Greece passed through the gates of the Roman and Byzantine Empires. Byzantium, along with later Turkish domination, shaped modern Greece far more than did the Greece of Homer, Pericles and Socrates. Rome had conquered the entire Greek world by 190 B.C., and in 394–395 A.D. the Roman Empire was divided into a western and an eastern half. The latter, initially Rome, but later ruled from Byzantium (later Constantinople and now Istanbul), was the offspring of the union of classical Greece and Christianity. With Christian faith, Roman administration and Greek thought and language, Byzantium remained the preserver of classical philosophy and culture. This remains the Empire's greatest legacy to the west, providing the foundation for the later Renaissance (see Italy).

In a swift tide of events, the Romans expelled the Jews from Palestine (Israel) in 70 A.D.; they had already widely become dispersed throughout the Mediterranean area prior to that date, but became more so after the Diaspora (dispersal). Many settled on Greek islands and a substantial number, together with Jews in Rome itself, were converted to Christianity in the first centuries A.D. in spite of oppression.

Until the 11th century A.D. the Byzantine Empire, of which Greece was only a small part, was the leading country of its time in terms of military power, area and population, differentiated administrative organization, education level of its people and splendid mosaics and buildings, the most impressive example of which is the Hagia Sofia Church (now a mosque) in Istanbul, Turkey. From Byzantium the Slavic Balkans and Russians were Christianized, not by means of fire and sword, but by means of an alphabet. The monks Cyril and Methodius developed the Cyrillic script, which was molded to display graphically the Slavic languages and which Russians and other Slavic peoples, such as the Bulgarians and Serbs, now use. At its peak, the Empire under Emperor Justinian (527–565) extended to all of Italy, parts of Spain, North Africa and the Middle East, including Syria and Palestine.

This colorful mixture of peoples was ruled by a theocratic (religiously oriented) monarchy. The state and Orthodox Church were united in the person of the emperor, whose rule was absolute. Tsarist Russia later adopted this term, and the word "Tsar" was derived from the Latin word "Caesar" (emperor). For a long time, Byzantium served as a rampart against the onslaught of Islam. However, rivalry with the Roman Catholic West, whose fourth Crusade resulted in the plundering of Constantinople by Catholic knights in the year 1204 brought about a change. For a while, Frankish knights and Italian merchants dominated Greece, and Slavs who were moving southward threatened the empire. The constant battle against the Moslem pirates and later against the Turks weakened the empire and reduced it in size to Greece and the capital city. In 1453 the remainder of the empire fell into the hands of the Turkish Sultan Mohammed II, without the Christian west lifting a finger to help.

Islamic Rule: Church Preservation of Greek Culture

Greece lived under the sign of the Islamic half–moon for almost 400 years until it won its independence in 1829. But it was Byzantine tradition, embodied and preserved by the Orthodox (which literally means "worshipping correctly") Church, which provided the strength of survival and the sense of cultural independence. The Church kept Greek identity alive, operated underground schools, guarded Greek literature and culture, fought any attempt to diminish the use of the Greek language, and, with the approval of the Turkish masters, took full responsibility for such acts as baptism, marriage and burial, which until the early 1980s remained the exclusive privilege of the Church.

The Turks also granted the Orthodox Church tax exemption and the right to conduct court cases in civil matters. Thus,

the Church not only was responsible for religious matters, but also for most legal and civil administration over Orthodox Christians. This was because of the Turkish masters' desire largely to avoid contact with "infidels." In contrast to some other Islamic peoples, the Turks placed no importance on the religious conversion of their subjects. Such intense Orthodox political involvement in, and even control over, political, social and religious affairs created in Greece a kind of close union between Church and nation that was almost unique in the world. This union only now is breaking down, as the Greeks are becoming increasingly secular, and as the Church's political and social influence is being strongly challenged. Nevertheless, much of the prestige which the Church still enjoys today stems from the Greeks' awareness that in the past the Orthodox Church kept the Hellenic flame burning during four centuries of Turkish domination and that, as the chief patron for Greek nationalism, the Church was at the forefront of the struggle for Greek independence in the 1920s.

The Turks left their traces in Greece, even though the war of independence almost totally removed any visible traces of Turkish rule. Remains of medieval cities or of mosques can hardly be found in the country today. One does notice elements in the Greeks' everyday life, though: the warm hospitality and generosity, the food and the manner in which coffee is prepared and drunk, the men's habit of sit-

ting around cafés in midday, while the women are at home working, the music, the distinctly Balkan folklore, the peasant dress and the reels of red tape and almost impenetrable bureaucracy all reflect heavy Middle Eastern influences.

On the other hand, the unpleasant memory of long Turkish subjugation, the bloody and emotional struggle with the Turks to regain Greek independence in the 1820s and the effort, which continues to this day, to extend Greece's borders to include all Greek–speaking peoples, have combined to create a deep–seated hatred which always plays a prominent role in Greek politics.

Revolt

Exasperated by Turkish maladministration and inspired by the ideals of liberty ignited in Europe by the French Revolution, the Greeks revolted against the Turks in 1821. This struggle immediately stimulated sympathy in all of Western Europe, where the love for Greek antiquity was great and where only a few years earlier the young British poet, Lord Byron, had written of Greece lamentingly in Childe Harold's Pilgrimage: "Trembling beneath the scourge of Turkish hand, From birth to death enslaved; in work, in deed, unmann'd." Byron even went to Greece to fight for its independence, and his death as a result of fever at Missolonghi on April 19, 1824, lent the struggle an almost divine consecration in the eyes of many Western Europeans.

Alexander the Great's empire at its height

Greece

Greek history kept alive under Turkish occupation

As so often in 19th and 20th century Greek history, foreigners' admiration for Greek antiquity helped focus attention on modern Greece's problems. The Russian poet Pushkin found this fact disgusting. He wrote acidly: "This enthusiasm of all cultured nations for Greece is unforgivable childishness. The Jesuits have told us all that twaddle about Themistocles and Pericles, and so we imagine that the shabby nation of robbers and traders are their legitimate successors." Pushkin was certainly too hard on the Greeks, but it is true that foreign observers were all too apt to show disgust at Turkish atrocities in this brutal struggle and to overlook such behavior when the Greeks committed them. For instance, there was hardly a reaction to the Greeks' hanging, impaling and roasting alive 12,000 Turkish prisoners who had surrendered at Tripolitsa, but the outcry was deafening when the Turkish governor later systematically executed 30,000 Greek survivors at Chios and sold another 46,000 into slavery. The atrocities both sides were committing did not hinder the French, British and Russians from joining the struggle against the Turks in 1827 and by 1829 Turkey had to sue for peace.

A Wobbly Monarchy

In an ambassadorial conference in London, the major powers and Greece finally defined the boundaries of the new Greek state which was much smaller than present–day Greece. The first border extended only as far north as the line extending from the Gulf of Volos on the east to the Gulf of Arta on the west. This excluded such islands as Crete and Corfu. At the same conference, Prince Otto of Bavaria was named king of Greece and was placed on a royal throne that wobbled and shook almost continuously until it was finally abolished once and for all in 1974. The new king made one mistake after another. This foreigner refused to convert from Roman Catholicism to Orthodox Christianity in a land where the Orthodox Church was inextricably linked with the very idea of the Greek nation. Then he tried to impose tightly centralized government upon a people that had just fought for their independence. The first governor established himself on the island of Aegina in 1828. For idealistic reasons, Athens, a dusty village of 5,000 inhabitants at the time, was declared capital with the constitution of 1834.

It is not surprising that the Greeks could never settle down under such rule and that the two unfortunate elements in subsequent Greek politics developed like malignant cysts in the very heart of Greek politics. First, an unbridgeable gap between monarchists and republicans was created. Second, the Greek military began meddling in Greek politics. Such activity was partly the consequence of, and partly the cause of, the political instability that afflicted the country for the next century and a half.

This chronic instability and absence of even a minimal consensus ultimately left the Greek political landscape littered with the wreckage of two dynasties. Absence of political stability ultimately resulted in five removals of kings from power (1862, 1917, 1922, 1941 and 1967), seven changes of constitution, three republics, seven military dictatorships, 15 revolutions and coups (of which ten succeeded), 155 governments (43 since 1945), 12 wars and a bitter five–year civil war. Thus, in certain ways, modern Greek politics until 1973 was like a pendulum swinging constantly between the extreme democracy of Athens and the iron military sentiments of Sparta.

About the only thing the Greeks could agree on was that their borders had to be extended until all Greeks were citizens of the Greek state (a goal referred to as the "Great Idea"). Thus, where domestic politics divided them, intense nationalism, which can bubble to the surface of any Greek almost instantly, united them. The settlement of 1832 had not created a natural and mutually acceptable frontier between Greece and Turkey, and every Greek government pursued an ingathering policy of some kind to rectify this. This meant constant friction and occasional

Greece

war with Turkey, which greatly nourished the hatred Greeks seem almost always to bear toward their neighbor to the east.

It took time, but the Greeks have, with the notable exception of Cyprus and small pockets of Greeks in southern Albania, accomplished their "Great Idea." In 1864 the British turned over to them the Ionian Islands, including especially Corfu. In 1881 Greece received a third of Epirus and the bulk of Thessaly, but when it conducted naval actions against the Turks in Crete and the rest of Thessaly a few years later, the Turks declared war on Greece in 1897. They routed the Greek army and even threatened to take Athens—a humiliating defeat for Greece.

The emergence before World War I of one of Greece's greatest 20th century political leaders, Eleutherios Venizelos, brought Greece many benefits. He introduced important reforms to establish a modern state. An admirer of Western European democracy, he created the foundations of a state of law in Greece, expanded the school system, initiated a land reform program, legalized trade unions and created agricultural cooperatives. He was also able to utilize his international prestige and diplomatic skill to win for his country a handsome chunk of the spoils of distribution to the Balkan nations resulting from the Balkan Wars against Turkey in 1912 and 1913. Greece received a part of Macedonia, the island of Crete and the Aegean Islands. These additions enlarged the Greek land area by 75% and its population by 70%.

World War I and another Greek–Turkish Round

When World War I broke out, King Constantine I tried to remain neutral, but British and French pressure, which included the landing of French troops on Greek soil, caused the king to abdicate. Prime Minister Venizelos was able to have his country declare war on Germany and its allies. Its reward from its new allies was western Thrace, which it received in 1918 and a British promise of a part of Turkey around Smyrna (now Izmir).

On May 15, 1919, British ships transported Greek troops to Smyrna in order to collect its booty, but this adventure ended in a catastrophe. American President Woodrow Wilson opposed any carving up of Turkey in spite of its support of Germany in the war. Further, the greatest political leader in Turkish history, General Kemal Atatürk, who created the modern Turkish state, revived his exhausted and humiliated countrymen, who had been decimated during the war, and organized a heroic defense of Smyrna.

After the British stopped supporting the Greek expeditionary force, the Turks de-

livered a devastating and fatal blow to the Greeks. In bloody revenge, the Turkish sword swung freely, and practically the entire Greek population was either killed or driven out of the area around the coast of Asia Minor where Greeks had lived for 3,000 years. The French and British declared themselves to be neutral in the face of this massacre and refused to take Greek refugees on board their ships although it had been the British who had made promises to the Greeks that had unleashed this tragic adventure in the first place. In the end, 600,000 Greeks perished, and almost a million and a half were forced out of Turkey. In return, Turkey agreed to the repatriation of about 400,000 Moslems living in Greece.

Continued Political Conflict

The one positive thing this unfortunate conflict did produce was clearly defined borders between Greeks and Turks (except in Cyprus), with only negligible minorities on the wrong side of the lines. But the disaster sent Greek politics into a tailspin again. Venizelos and the King were forced into exile. The first Greek Republic was established in 1923, followed by military coups in 1925, 1926, 1933 and 1935, and a restoration of the monarchy in 1935, but one in which real power was held by General Joannes Metaxas. The latter suppressed most political groups and led a right–wing dictatorship until he was subsequently removed from power by the German conquerors in 1941.

World War II

Greece entered World War II on the side of Britain and France. On October 28, 1940, the Greek government said *ochi* ("no") to a host of unacceptable demands made by the impetuous Italian dictator, Benito Mussolini, who boasted of a "promenade to Athens." Italian troops entered Greece from Albania. Although the British hurriedly sent a limited number of troops to Greece from North Africa, the Greeks themselves were able to drive Mussolini's poor–quality forces back into Albania, where they could have destroyed the entire Italian army if Metaxas had not feared German retaliation.

Since Hitler had already decided that Greece, the "Achilles heel of Europe" should not be allowed to fall into enemy hands it mattered little what the Greek general feared. Hitler sent his storm troopers into Greece; their numerical superiority broke the Greek resistance on April 6, 1941. The last British bastion in Greece was taken within two months, the island of Crete, after the attackers launched the largest airborne operation against the island that the world had ever seen. The Germans then divided Greece into occupation

zones, awarding the lion's share to the defeated Italy, which perhaps could at least tend to a conquered country.

The suffering and humiliation of occupation created a resistance movement in Greece. Metaxas had destroyed all political parties and thereby had created a political vacuum. Therefore, the Greek communists, who had built up an underground apparatus, were able to form an effective resistance organization, the Greek Liberation Front (EAM), which had a fighting force, the Greek People's Liberation Army (ELAS). Not until 1943 was an anticommunist competitor created, the Greek Republic Liberation League (EDES).

The British supported both partisan groups in order to disrupt the Germans' supply links with their troops in North Africa. When the Italian fascist regime collapsed in 1943, its occupation forces left Greece after selling a large part of their weapons to the Greek partisans. The Germans responded to the resistance activity in Greece by shooting hostages and devastating entire villages. These measures merely drove countless young peasants into the arms of the communists.

Civil War

Even during its struggle against the Germans, ELAS began preparing a civil war against its Greek opponents. At first, the Soviet leader, Stalin, honored the agreement he made with British Prime Minister Churchill at the Tehran conference from November 28 to December 1, 1943, to divide the Balkans into spheres of influence with Greece falling at a ratio of 90% into the British sphere and 10% into the Soviet. Romania would be the reverse, while British and Soviet interests in Yugoslavia would be 50–50.

However, from March 1944 on, the Soviets began supporting their Greek comrades. Therefore, when the Germans pulled out of Greece in October, the communists were in a very good position. They controlled about 90% of the country when the exile government arrived at Athens from Egypt accompanied by about 15,000 British troops. Fearing defeat in a democratic election, ELAS resisted by force, and it took a full month of bitter house–to–house combat for the British and the Greek government troops to drive the communists out of Athens. Fighting again broke out in December 1944, but the communists suffered such losses they decided to lay down their arms temporarily.

The first elections, which were held on March 31, 1946, under the supervision of 1,200 American, British and French troops, produced a resounding victory for the conservative royalists. Also, in a referendum held on September 1, 1946 to determine the future form of government, 68%

Greece

of those voting supported the restoration of the monarchy. Along with the stern anticommunist measures of the right–wing extremist, Colonel George Grivas, this referendum made reconciliation with the communists impossible. They also made it difficult for noncommunist liberals and republicans to give the new regime their enthusiastic support.

With the aid of the Soviet Union, Yugoslavia and Bulgaria, the Greek communists resumed their armed struggle, which lasted three more years. Key factors in the ultimate noncommunist victory were American economic and military assistance to Greece (as a consequence of the "Truman Doctrine," which promised aid against communist threats to Greece and Turkey) and Yugoslavia's break with the Soviet Union in 1948. After the latter event, the Yugoslav leader, Marshal Tito, closed the Yugoslav–Greek border, thereby preventing needed supplies from being shipped to the Greek communist rebels.

In 1949 the communists finally gave up the struggle, which had cost them about 80,000 casualties and the government forces about 50,000. This tragic conflict polarized Greek politics for years, sapped Greece's economic resources and caused considerable destruction in the country. The civil war complicated the problem of reconstruction, despite generous infusions of Marshall Plan assistance from the U.S. Thus, while World War I lasted in reality ten—not four—years in Greece, World War II had also, in effect, lasted a decade in the battered country. The only tangible benefit from the settlement after the second conflict was that Greece was awarded the Dodecanese Islands in 1947.

Restoration and Recovery; the Status of Cyprus

The government turned to the task of restoring and improving the country's economy. It led Greece into NATO in February 1952 and into a Balkan Pact in August 1954, which was supposed to forge a military link among Greece, Turkey and Yugoslavia. This pact has, for all practical purposes, remained a dead letter because of Greece's chronic tensions with Turkey. Such tensions were again rekindled in 1954 as a result of events on the island of Cyprus, which had been a British base since 1878 and a Crown Colony since 1925, and more than 80% of whose residents are Greek. Cyprus had long aroused the emotions of Greek nationalists and the goal (called Enosis) of bringing the island's residents under Greek authority had long existed. Enosis was supported on the island by the Orthodox Church and by a large number of educated Greeks.

When some of them launched an indiscriminate terrorist campaign in 1954 in or-

REGIONS OF MAINLAND GREECE

THRACE
MACEDONIA
EPIRUS
THESSALY
CENTRAL GREECE EUBOEA
PELOPONNESOS

der to try to stimulate international sympathy for their cause, the Turkish minority on the island fought back. Although Cyprus was ultimately granted independence, the problems of how the two groups should administer the island and of what kind of relations Cyprus should maintain with Greece and Turkey has been and is a continuing, chronic irritant in the relations between the two NATO allies.

POSTWAR POLITICS

During the postwar period, Greece was a parliamentary democracy. King Paul succeeded his brother, King George II, in 1947. But there also was a strong military involvement in politics. Present party alignments emerged. There was almost continuous political instability after the communists were defeated, and cabinets sometimes lasted only a few months.

From 1954 to 1963 the key figure in Greek politics was Constantine Karamanlis, who later became president and who tried to steer Greece more closely toward Western Europe by establishing economic links with the EC. Almost two decades later, as prime minister and president, he finished his work by overseeing Greece's entry into the EC as a full member in 1981. He and many of his countrymen hoped that entry into the EC would help secure democracy in Greece.

The years from 1963 to 1965 were characterized by the sweeping social reform

efforts of Georgios Papandreou and by a situation in which neither the supporters of the monarch nor of parliamentary democracy could prevail. The political temperature in Athens rose extremely quickly in 1965. Young King Constantine II, who had ascended to the throne at the age of 23 when King Paul died in 1964, almost immediately locked horns with Papandreou over a number of constitutional issues, especially that involving control of the army. The king accused the prime minister of trying to infiltrate the military by means of a left–wing organization called Aspida, headed by Papandreou's son, Andreas (who became prime minister in 1981 and again in 1993). Papandreou saw the matter differently—he wanted to fire his defense minister because the latter balked at dismissing right–wing plotters within the army. In any case, King Constantine dismissed Papandreou in mid–1965, an act which set off two more confusing years of stopgap governments, trials, riots, strikes and political polarization, which cleared the way for the military to act.

On the eve of May 1967 parliamentary elections, in which Papandreou's Center Union Party was favored to win, perhaps with the electoral help of communist groups, a group of military officers seized power, pointing to the alleged communist danger and claiming to have the support of the king. It turned out that he had not even been informed about the plan. When they began arresting and exiling parliamentary leaders, including both Papandreou. King Constantine attempted a clumsy coup of his own, which failed miserably and which forced him to flee the country. Not until 1993 did a stable and democratic Greek republic inform Constantine, who had just announced his hopes of reclaiming the throne some day, that he could leave his London exile and return to Greece as a private citizen any time he wanted.

Some Greeks are convinced that the U.S., through its CIA, had a hand in this military coup, even though it is admitted that there is no absolute proof, and even though President Lyndon Johnson publicly denounced the coup. Reference is made to a so-called "Prometheus Plan" worked out by the King and the army, for a military coup in the event that the elections produced a government with communist participation. It is alleged that NATO approved this plan. Further, Andreas Papandreou frequently reminded his listeners that during the Nixon administration, Vice President Spiro Agnew, himself of Greek descent, traveled to Greece, thereby allegedly giving the dictatorship "full support."

It is, of course, true that the U.S. maintained its military presence in Greece and made arms sales to the new military rulers. Whether the rumors of U.S. complicity or foreknowledge of the coup are true or not, these allegations did help to create in Greece a strong anti-American feeling that remains strong. President Bill Clinton's state visit to Greece in November 1999 unleashed pent-up rage. Leftist groups organized advanced daily protests, mobilizing more than 10,000 before the American embassy. They forced the Greek government to close off the Athens city center and Clinton to pare down the visit to only 24 hours. Every November 17, the anniversary of a 1973 student uprising that helped topple the country's military rulers, demonstrators march on the American embassy in Athens because of alleged U.S. backing for the junta that seized power in 1967.

The bombing in Kosovo, which 90% of Greeks opposed, ignited the renewed anti-American fervor. But Clinton addressed the deeper cause, offering a near apology for the American stance during the seven years of repressive military dictatorship: "When the junta took over in 1967 here, the United States allowed its interests in prosecuting the Cold War to prevail over its interests—I should say its obligation—to support democracy, which was, after all, the cause for which we fought the Cold War. It is important that we acknowledge that." The audience erupted in applause.

Military Dictatorship

The seven–year military dictatorship, first under the leadership of Georgios Papadoupoulos and, after November 1973, under the chief of the secret service, Colonel Demetrios Ioannides, is remembered as a long and brutal period. The "colonels" converted Greece into a military camp in which political opponents were persecuted by all the means of state terror.

The regime put itself on the wrack when in 1974 Ioannides decided to overthrow the government of Cyprus' mercurial Archbishop Makarios and to try to install a government on the island subject to command from Athens. This heavy–handed action merely provoked the Turks to invade Cyprus and ultimately to partition the island. Since the Turks used American weapons in this invasion (referred to as Attila), many Greeks place partial responsibility on the Americans' shoulders. This is a deliberate distortion, however, since the Turks were using weapons received as a member of NATO, and there was no authorization by the U.S. to use them for an invasion of Cyprus. The use of such weaponry violated American law, and even when the U.S. thereafter cut off all arms sales to Turkey for several years, this event, which was clearly out of American control, created even more resentment in Greece against the U.S. In effect, the Americans were criticized both because they allegedly supported the "colonels" and because they allegedly did not.

Fortunately the crisis created a situation the "colonels" could not handle. Greece had been brought to the brink of war with Turkey, so important senior officers withdrew their support from the discredited Ioannides and called for Constantine Karamanlis to return from his Paris exile and to reassume the reins of power as the leader of a government of national unity. Thus, as in Portugal the same year, a foreign policy crisis cleared the way for the establishment of a democratic political order.

After years of intense political instability and harsh military rule, Greeks adjusted very well to democracy after 1974. When Andreas Papandreou called for *allaghi* ("change") in the 1981 parliamentary

October 1944: Prime Minister Georgios Papandreou on the Acropolis as Greek women carry the national flag to be raised over liberated Athens

Greece

election, a near majority of his countrymen responded. Greeks knew well that for the first time in decades that change meant a transfer of power from one democratic party to another, not a change of regime involving the destruction of democratic rule.

Despite many political and economic problems, Greece is experiencing unprecedented stability. The traditional Greek cycle of volatile democracy–military dictatorship, often punctuated by coups, has come to an end. Now the two largest parties, which received 85.9% of the votes in 2004, firmly accept the parliamentary system. Also, the soldiers have returned to their barracks once and for all, and Greek politicians no longer have to calculate the military's possible response to any decision. Despite the invariably inflated election rhetoric, the Greek body politic is no longer divided into hostile, enemy camps.

In some European countries, monarchs symbolize national unity, but in Greece they almost always tended to divide, not to unite the nation. Therefore, 69% of those who went to the polls voted in a referendum held on December 8, 1974, to abolish the monarchy and to establish a republic.

In 1981 the Greek leadership nervously allowed Constantine II to return briefly to Athens to attend the funeral of his mother, ex–Queen Frederika, at the Tatoi Palace on the outskirts of Athens. They feared that his presence in Greece, after 14 years of absence (first in Rome, now in London, where he is in the sales and public relations business) might destabilize the new regime. They permitted him to land at a military airbase near the palace and remain in Greece a few hours to attend. The leaders' risk paid off because only two thousand chanting admirers appeared to greet the king.

It became clear that what little support the monarchy had enjoyed earlier had largely evaporated. This realization bolstered the confidence and long–term stability of the republic. When the king and his family unexpectedly returned for a two–week holiday in August 1993, scuffles broke out between royalists and leftist protesters, prompting the government publicly to disapprove of the visit. An irritated President Karamanlis noted, "such affairs do not threaten democracy or our system of government but hold the country up to ridicule." In 1994 parliament stripped the king of his citizenship and remaining property in Greece.

At the European Court of Human rights in Strasbourg in late 2002, Constantine received an award of about 20 million euros as a settlement of the royal claims, a sum lower than that accepted by the Greek government. In February 2003 he also got

two palaces in Athens and Corfu, some compensation, but no pay. Since he refuses to adopt a surname, allow his name to be entered into the record of citizens, and carry an identification card, he cannot get a Greek passport.

PRESENT GOVERNMENT STRUCTURE

The Presidency

On June 7, 1974, a new constitution went into effect that described Greece as a "presidential parliamentary republic." Considering the Greeks' experiences during seven years of military dictatorship, it is not surprising that the new constitution contains extensive guarantees of individual rights and civil liberties. The head of state is a president without executive powers, who is elected for a five–year term by the parliament, which meets for this purpose as an electoral college. The constitution requires consensus in electing the president. A successful candidate must win a two-thirds majority on one of the first two ballots, or 60% on a third one. If the third ballot fails, parliament is dissolved, new elections are held, and a simple majority of deputies in the new house elects the president. This form of indirect election means that no president can claim to have a direct mandate from the people and thereby challenge the political direction taken by the majority in parliament. The presidential powers are largely ceremonial, and a responsible minister, that is, the government, must countersign most of his acts.

The parliament voted in 1986 to reduce the president's powers even further. He can no longer appoint the prime minister. He can dissolve parliament only if two governments fall in rapid succession. He can no longer call a referendum on what he regards as a major issue, address the people directly when his opinions differ from those of the government, or proclaim a state of siege.

The president's powers and actual influence in Greek politics depend upon the respect he enjoys in the eyes of the citizens or of the leading politicians. The president until 1985 was Constantine Karamanlis, one of the most highly respected leaders in Greece and widely regarded as one of the major architects and protectors of the democratic regime. No prime minister could overlook his views on important issues. He was succeeded by Christos Sartzetakis, a respected supreme court justice who became famous for cracking the notorious Lambrakis murder case in 1963 and who was immortalized as the incorruptible judge in the movie "Z", which portrayed Greek politics during the last years of the monarchy. In 1990 Karamanlis was again elected to a five–year term.

He was followed in 1995 by lawyer Constantinos Stephanopoulos, who had sought exile in Paris during the military dictatorship and who had never been implicated in a scandal. In 2005 the New Democracy government nominated an ex-foreign minister and a founding member of PASOK, Karolos Papoulias, for the presidency. He won by a record majority in parliament, receiving 279 of the 296 votes cast. The choice of Papoulias was supported by 80% of the population.

Parliament and Prime Minister

The most powerful political office in Greece is that of the prime minister, who must be able to find a majority for his policies in the 300–seat unicameral parliament (*Vouli*). All Greek citizens 18 years or older can vote. Voting is mandatory although not all eligible voters go to the polls. For example, in 2004, the turnout was 76.5%. Greek media are prohibited from publishing opinion polls in the final two weeks of an election campaign.

The members of parliament are elected by a modified form of proportional representation that favors the larger parties. This system is designed to increase the chances that one party will have a parliamentary majority even when none wins a majority of the votes cast. For instance, in the 2004 elections, the New Democracy party received 45.36% of the votes, but it won an absolute majority of the seats. In the 17 general elections following 1951, the government has changed the electoral system nine times within six months of the polling in order to maximize its seats.

In 1989 the system was brought closer to a strict proportional representation system, which improves the chances of small parties and thereby makes it more difficult to form a majority. This was further tweaked in 2007 to help little parties. Nevertheless, a party must win at least 3% of the total votes in an election to qualify for any parliamentary seats. This eliminates minuscule parties. For example, in 2007 only five parties cleared this threshold.

Because instability had long been a curse in Greek politics, it is logical that the framers of the present constitution would seek ways to insure stability within a democratic framework. Parliament is elected for four years, but the prime minister can arrange for early elections for any reason, especially in the event he cannot maintain a parliamentary majority.

Since 2003 a deputy is prohibited from holding other jobs. His influence depends largely on whether his particular party permits him to disregard the party's recommendations or policy when votes are taken. For instance, under Andreas Papandreou PASOK forbade its deputies to vote against the party leadership and would refuse a maverick deputy the chance to seek reelection under the PA-SOK label. A traditional source of influence for the deputy was *rousfeti* ("influence peddling"), by which he used the bureaucracy to get special favors, including jobs, for his constituents. This was a way for him to win and to maintain votes, but the massive migration from rural areas into the cities reduced its effectiveness. In the cities people are no longer so inclined to turn to their local political bosses and deputies for help or favors.

The traditional need for some practice like *rousfeti* reflected the difficulty Greek citizens have in attracting the attention of an overgrown and often lethargic, indifferent or corrupt bureaucracy in order to find solutions for individual or collective problems. At the same time, *rousfeti* helped to bloat or paralyze the bureaucracy because jobs were often filled or created for friends or constituents of influential politicians. Appointments and subsequent promotions were too often based more upon friendship and connections that upon merit. Mitsotakis vowed to end *rousfeti*, a move that was resented by many New Democrats, who wanted to place their supporters into positions after eight years in opposition.

In Greek political ideology, it is better to have a friend or relative hired or advanced rather than having a merit system. Added to the problem are job security for even the most incompetent workers, exaggerated respect for tradition which leaves little room for new ideas, lack of management skills and excessive fear of being blamed for mistakes: if you don't do *anything*, you can't be blamed for doing *something*. Even simple transactions required as many as a dozen signatures. A bureaucrat's typical response is understandably *avrio, avrio* ("tomorrow, tomorrow").

The government tried during the 1980s to do something about these problems within the bureaucracy. Papandreou pledged to end "partisanship and corruption in public administration," and he launched a program of decentralization to transfer some power from bureaucrats in Athens to local councils. His administration began by firing about 300 senior civil servants merely because they had been appointed during earlier administrations. This was too much shock treatment too early, and also many competent officials were sacked in this indiscriminate purge. He appointed hundreds of his own party people. Many of them were conscientious and well–educated, but inexperienced. By distributing so many jobs to PASOK supporters, he merely played the old game of *rousfeti* again.

Upon assuming office in 1996 ex-Prime Minister Simitis vowed to restrict patron-age and to reduce the public–sector payroll by hiring only one qualified civil servant for every three who retire. He faced stiff resistance from the 40% of PASOK members who are public–sector employees and who are used to securing jobs for their family and friends. Greece's high unemployment rate in the 21st century is in part due to the collapse of public-sector patronage as a way to win the voters' favor. Politicians do not have the opportunities they once had to divvy out jobs to their friends. There are also more jobs in the private sector than there used to be. However, patronage is still deeply entrenched, and party heavyweights still control most public-sector appointments, from hospital directors to university professors and local government officials. Corruption is still rife in state enterprises.

PASOK tried to make good its promise to decentralize power in a highly centralized country. The central government traditionally sent 55 *nomarchs* (governors) into the provinces to exercise nearly total power over local decisions. Local government received all their revenues from Athens and did not even have the right to levy taxes. The Papandreou government doubled the financial grants to local governments and set up committees, composed of city councilmen, farmers, workers and employers, to advise the *nomarchs*, whose control over the city councils was reduced.

Evzone (a Greek regiment) presidential guard in the traditional white foustanela
Courtesy: Jon Markham Morrow

POLITICS AND PARTIES

One of the most encouraging developments in Greek politics since 1974 is that the military no longer threatens to intervene in politics as it once did. Although soldiers were apparently still hatching plots in 1975, they concentrate now on purely military duties. Nevertheless, no Greek politician, especially no leftist prime minister, would dare overlook the possibility that the officers might return to their earlier self–appointed political role of "straightening up the mess" of democratic politics.

In order to help pacify the military, Papandreou increased their housing allowances and pay sharply. Also, his stridently nationalistic rhetoric was well received in the mess halls. As irritating and exaggerated as his nationalism may have been to foreigners, it did serve an important domestic political purpose of reconciling, if not totally integrating, ultra–conservative and military circles with the democratic regime.

Greece's two main parties are, in traditional Greek style, personalized in that they are built around, and largely dominated by, respected figures. They are run from the top. Central headquarters selects electoral candidates and controls patronage. In Greece, politics always revolves more around persons than policies. This characteristic of both major parties, which were created in 1974, produces both weaknesses and strengths. The most obvious disadvantage is that any party that is so dependent on one person could decline or disappear quickly if the leader were no longer there. One bullet could immediately change the party landscape. The advantage is that because of the personalities and political skill of Papandreou and Karamanlis, both were able to consolidate modern Greek democracy. They created parties of the right and left which are committed to the democratic regime.

PASOK
PASOK sprang from the Panhellenic Liberation Movement (PaK), an underground guerrilla group established to fight against the colonels' junta from 1967 to 1974. It grew extremely rapidly since its founding as a political party in 1974. It climbed from 14% of the vote in 1974 to 25% in 1977 and to 48% in 1981, to become the first non-conservative government since 1974. PASOK's rise to power would have been unthinkable without the inspiration and leadership of one man, Andreas Papandreou.

Young Andreas got a PhD in economics from Harvard University and became an American citizen in 1944. After serving in the U.S. Navy, he taught economics at

Greece

President Karolos Papoulias

such American universities as Minnesota (where he met and married his first wife, Margarete), Northwestern and Berkeley.

When in 1963 his father asked him and all other Greeks living abroad who could contribute to the nation's development to return to Greece, Andreas agreed. When the "colonels" seized power in 1967, he and his father were imprisoned. Andreas was kept in solitary confinement for eight months before he was released, thanks in large part to the efforts of his American wife and the U.S. Embassy. He again went into exile, first to Sweden and then to Canada, before returning in 1974.

Papandreou was a brilliant speaker with a knack for accurately reading the pulse of his audience. However, his eloquence often lapsed into demagoguery. He is very intolerant of criticism or diverging views. He ran PASOK and the Greek government with an iron hand.

PASOK's voter appeal was not limited to one class or group. Young voters were especially attracted to PASOK. It established a network of local organizations all over Greece, had a populist strain and it was very nationalistic, directing its venom toward the U.S., Turkey, NATO and the EU. Nationalist appeals always brought in the votes in Greek elections and they combined with the populist appeals to help PASOK win votes from a wide spectrum of groups, including farmers, workers, employees and mid-level civil servants.

At first PASOK presented itself as a somewhat Marxist movement for national and social liberation, and even shortly before the 1981 election Papandreou announced, "we plan to change the system, not to embellish it." Experience indicates that too much Marxism is bad politics in most democratic countries. The party quickly backed away from it and now merely advocates using certain aspects of Marxist thought "in a creative way."

It saw itself as a left wing party, as European socialist and social democratic parties go. For years it refused to join the Socialist International because Papandreou claimed that it was dominated by the social democratic parties in northern Europe, especially the German SPD, which he had branded as the European representative of "monopoly capitalism." Nevertheless, PASOK is extremely flexible (some say "opportunist") and can present itself in almost any democratic way, depending on the political climate and realities of the time.

As a governing party, it faced the typical problems of a radical party that finds itself in power and responsible for confronting concrete problems. The party was aware that the change for which many Greeks voted in 1981 was not socialism, but something less, and the party acted accordingly. This caused tension within the party.

Before the 1989 elections, Papandreou's popularity plummeted because of a serious financial scandal and his public love affair with Dimitra Liani, a divorced airline stewardess half his age. She accompanied him to London to be by his side during his open-heart surgery. She began serving as his official consort. Some feared that she influenced his political decisions. Pictures of her in the nude published in Greek newspapers shocked many Greeks.

To minimize electoral damage in socially conservative Greece, Papandreou divorced his wife a few days before the election, although for legal technical reasons he was unable to marry Liani before June 18. But he had already sacrificed the respect of many citizens. Many Greeks cringed in 1993 when he named Liani as his chief of staff, a powerful post managing his work schedule as prime minister and controlling access to him.

PASOK regained a majority in the 1993 elections, and the frail Papandreou again became prime minister. He suffered from heart, lung and kidney problems and was able to work only a few hours a day. He tried to demonstrate that he was firmly in charge by refusing to appoint a deputy prime minister and pushing potential rivals aside. By January 1996, after he had spent 44 days in the hospital on life-support machines, PASOK had to act. Polls in the fall had shown that 82.3% of Greek respondents were dissatisfied with the ailing Papandreou, and 87.7% wanted him to retire from politics.

The situation was particularly urgent because many thought that he was determined to make his unpopular wife Dimitra ("Mimi") his successor. They were irritated by the way she interfered in government, screened access to the prime minister, and summoned ministers for

meetings. She deepened the divisions within the party and strengthened fears that it would be punished severely at the next elections. Her efforts to change her image by having breast–reduction surgery, wearing more dignified clothing, and appearing to be the pious Orthodox wife by visiting churches were foiled by the front–page publication in 1995 of yet another photo of her bathing topless. She did not see a problem: "Should I not enter politics because I once bathed naked?" Her husband's death spelled the end of any serious political ambitions on her part. In 1999 she was charged with fraud and embezzlement of public funds, having evaded taxes on the purchase of land where she and her husband had built a multimillion dollar house.

In 1996 Papandreou was replaced as prime minister by Costas Simitis, a mild-mannered, statistics-quoting technocrat and reformer. He had been challenging Papandreou for months. He studied law

**Former Prime Minister
Andreas Papandreou**

in Germany and economics in Britain. A leftist in his earlier years, he was forced to escape to Italy on a forged passport for opposing the "colonels" when they seized power in 1967. Lacking his predecessor's charisma, he is nevertheless one of Greece's most popular politicians.

Within days of Papandreou's death in June 1996 Simitis quickly consolidated his power, with the crucial backing of Andreas's son, George Papandreou, by narrowly winning the leadership of the party and of the 200-member central committee, PASOK's main decision-making body. In 1996 he called an early general election and guided his party to victory. Most of Andreas Papandreou's staunch supporters lost their seats, leaving Simitis's economic reform faction in charge. He narrowly won the 2000 elections. This was the first time in Greece's post-war history

George Papandreau

that the Socialists won three electoral victories in a row.

Simitis, whom Papandreou had fired as finance minister in the mid-1980s, remade PASOK by introducing economic austerity measures, beginning to privatize state industries, and limiting patronage. All were designed to enhance the competitiveness of the Greek economy, reduce inflation and the massive public debt, and prepare the country's entry into the European single currency in 2001. He broke with PASOK's populist tradition of pandering to interest groups, including the powerful farmers, who make up a fifth of Greece's workers.

He changed PASOK by cleaning it up to make it more "European." He dismissed PASOK's old-fashioned populist secretary-general, Costas Laliotis, whose diehard anti-Americanism had become an embarrassment. During the Iraq war in 2003 Laliotis had encouraged the teachers' union to stay off work and organize elementary school children to participate in demonstrations and shout "American murderers."

Rapport with America was enhanced by the appointment in 1999 of the soft-edged George Papandreou as foreign minister. Born in the U.S. of an American mother and speaking perfect American English (and Swedish), he grew up in the U.S., Canada and Sweden and studied at Amherst, Harvard and the London School of Economics. He greatly benefits from his family's name and connections. But whereas his father was confrontational, the son is more inclined to build bridges and emphasize the positive. He is highly sensitive to the political realities of the outside world and worked hard to improve Greece's relationship with Turkey. Few Greek foreign ministers have been as

respected by their NATO and EU opposite numbers.

Seeing that it was heading for defeat in the 2004 elections, PASOK chose Papandreou, the country's most popular politician, to succeed Simitis as party leader. In his eight years as prime minister, Simitis had achieved much by making Greece a normal European country with a broad consensus for a market economy and good relations with its neighbors, especially Turkey. But he had largely failed to reform the state and to rid the country of much of its corruption. Greeks were tired of PASAK in power; after all, they had ruled in all but three of the preceding 22 years. They liked Papandreou's style, his soft-spoken talk of social inclusiveness, his folksy internet diary on the web, and his willingness to use his personal authority to break foreign policy molds. He is respected in part because of his name recognition. After all, politics in Greece is a family affair, as the two contenders—Papandreou and Karamanlis—demonstrated. In 2006 he was elected president of the Socialist International.

At the top of the ticket, Papandreou had too little time to make his mark. PASOK garnered 40.55% of the votes and 117 seats in 2004. In opposition he did not succeed in renewing his party by making it more like a western European social democratic party. He even lapsed into his father's populist rhetoric during the 2007 elections. But it fell to 38.12% of the votes and 102 seats.

Communists

One of PASOK's firmest political principles (dictated in part by political pragmatism) was to refuse to establish any direct links with Greek Communists. They are divided into two main parties. The

Former Prime Minister Costas Simitis

Greek Communist Party (KKE) is a rigid Marxist–Leninist party. It greeted the August 1991 coup against democracy in the USSR as a "welcome return to order." It is the only party in Greece today that had existed before 1974. The KKE has a well–organized and highly disciplined cadre and base. It controls much real estate around Athens, including a shipping company. Its domestic and foreign policy is predictable: state control over the economy and withdrawal from NATO and the EU.

In the 1989 elections, the KKE forged an "Alliance of the Left and Progress" with the Greek Communist Party of the Interior (KKES) and other small groups. KKES is so named because its leaders had remained in Greece after the civil war instead of fleeing to Eastern Europe. It advocates a softer, Euro–communist line, more in tune with the Greek democratic political order. Together they won 13% of the votes and 29 seats. Most of them went to the KKE. Another moderate Communist party is Sinaspismos.

Since neither PASOK nor New Democracy won a parliamentary majority, the Communists suddenly found themselves in a situation where they were courted by both large parties and could determine the composition of the Greek government. As the key to power, they attained a measure of influence they had not had since the civil war had ended in 1949 and since they had been legalized in 1974.

The Communists' electoral success brought mixed blessings. On the one hand, disagreements over cooperating with the bourgeois parties fractured the unity and prompted a wave of expulsions and resignations. Their new role in government eroded their popularity. In 1990 their 10.3% of the votes and 21 seats no longer enabled them to play the role of power brokers.

The Communists' success gave them political legitimacy and helped all Greeks to bury the hatchet that had been bloodied during the civil war. The term "civil war" officially replaced the previous term for the struggle: "bandits' war." The 40th anniversary of the last battle in the mountains of Epirus was redesignated a celebration of "national reconciliation." Some 16 million files the security police had kept on politically suspicious persons were burned, and full pension rights and social benefits were extended to anybody who had fought on the losing side.

Communist unity did not last. In the 2007 elections, the KKE got 8.13% of the votes (up from 5.89% in 2004) and 22 seats (up from 12). The populist Radical Left Coalition (Syriza or SYN) garnered 5% of the votes (up from 3.26%), which enabled it to win 14 seats (up from six).

Greece

The New Democracy Party

New Democracy, sprang up quickly around Constantine Karamanlis. He later became a cabinet member before the colonels overthrew the government in 1967. He was jailed briefly and later escaped to exile abroad. Returning to Greece in 1974 he served as minister of economic coordination and foreign affairs until 1981.

It is clearly the more conservative of the two major parties, but it is a party of the center and the reformed right, which is committed to democracy and social reform. It defines itself as a modern, pluralistic party. It is liberal in the European sense in that it favors a limitation of the state's role in the society and economy. It advocates a free–market economy, but one that does not overlook the economic needs of any groups, including those citizens with low incomes. New Democracy's foreign policy is strongly oriented toward the West, and it was Karamanlis who guided Greece into the EU and back into the NATO command structure.

New Democracy ruled Greece from 1974 to 1981 and again from 1990–93. Although it introduced many needed changes, it became tinged with accusations of corruption and favoritism, whose roots are deeply embedded in Greek politics and society.

New Democracy had come close to election victory in 1996. In 1997 it picked a new leader, Costas Karamanlis, nephew of the party's founder and the youngest man ever to lead a big Greek party. Born in 1956, he studied law in his native Athens, then earned an MA and PhD at the Fletcher School of Law and Diplomacy in the United States (1980–1984). Under his leadership it came within 1% of unseating the ruling PASOK party in the 2000 elections.

The party got a boost from the first woman to be elected mayor of Athens, Dora Bakoyanni. This was a major accomplishment in a country with so few women in elective office. For example, after the 2004 parliamentary elections, there were two women in the cabinet and 40 women in parliament, including the first-ever female speaker, Anna Psarouda-Benaki. Like Karamanlis himself, Bakoyanni is the product of a famous political family, being the daughter of former Prime Minister Mitsotakis. This is very important in Greece, where voters feel loyalty for familiar family names. She inherited her family's huge network of personal connections on Crete. Her first husband had been killed by November 17 terrorists in 1989, and she appeared as a witness at their trial. In 2006 she became the country's first female foreign minister.

The year 2004 was a charm for the New Democrats. In the March parliamentary

Prime Minister Costas Karamanlis

elections, they won 45.36% of the votes and an absolute majority of 165 seats. At 47, Karamanlis became the country's youngest prime minister ever and the first to be born after the divisive Greek Civil War from 1946–1949. Since the party had been out of power for 19 of the preceding 22 years, he and most of his 46-member government had never held a cabinet post before. Because of the urgent need to complete preparations for the Olympics in August 2004, he himself took over as minister of culture, in charge of overseeing and coordinating the Games.

Karamanlis steered his party toward the center on domestic policy and toward his predecessor's sensible policy of conciliation toward Turkey and healing the division of Cyprus. While still in opposition he had built a personal relationship with Turkish leader Recep Tayyip Erdogan, who invited him to address his party's congress in 2003. Ex-Foreign Minister Petros Molyviatis remembered the occasion: "Watching 7,000 Turks giving a standing ovation to a Greek leader was unprecedented." In January 2008 he made the first prime ministerial visit to Turkey since his uncle, Constantine Karamanlis, had done so 49 years earlier.

Arguing that he needed a new mandate to deal with the riotous public opposition to pension and university reform, he called new elections for September 16, 2007, six months early. He hoped that Greece's buoyant economy would win him reelection. The campaign was under a thick cloud of smoke as Greece experienced its worst forest fires in more than a century. Homes in more than 100 villages were gutted, and over 60 persons were killed. Firefighters succeeded in rescuing the marble temples and stadiums of the ancient Olympic site. But the fires dented support for his government, and he had to halt all campaigning to deal with the emergency. Nevertheless, New Democ-

racy emerged bruised but victorious with 41.86% of the votes and 152 seats, a mere two-seat majority. It can get some help from the Popular Orthodox Rally (Laos), a populist right-wing party led by George Karatzaferis, which entered parliament for the first time after winning 3.8% of the votes and 10 seats.

FOREIGN RELATIONS AND DEFENSE POLICY

Any government in Athens formulating Greece's foreign policy finds a complicated web of problems that confound most people who examine it. The ingredients include an American military base in Crete, Greek membership in NATO along with Turkey, the traditional enemy to the east that is competing for Cyprus, air-traffic lanes, offshore oil, mineral rights, and the delineation of international and territorial waters and the continental shelf. None of these problems can be sorted out and dealt with separately, and each problem with Turkey is overladen with heated emotion, the roots of which run more deeply than anyone can imagine.

Greece occupies a very important strategic location in the Mediterranean, which is a major lifeline for Europe. Much of Europe's oil moves through the Mediterranean, and this southern flank of NATO is a vital staging area for any possible European or American military operation in the Middle East. In order to bolster NATO muscle in this region, the U.S. has naval air facility in Suda Bay, Crete, with an airfield nearby. The U.S. Sixth Fleet is trained and equipped to operate without bases in Greece in case their use would be denied.

Greece still buys most of its weapons from the U.S., as well as from Germany, France and Britain. The Greek and Turkish air and naval forces are roughly equal in numbers. However, with 542,000 troops, the Turkish army outnumbers and outguns the Greek forces. The term of service for conscripts is 14 months, 16 months for navy and air force, depending on the branch. In 2004 the Karamanlis government expressed its intention to reduce military service gradually to six months and to use border-area residents as reserve forces. A professional army is still far off. Of 177,600 total troops (114,000 army, 19,000 navy, and 33,000 air force) 5,520 are female volunteers. There were 98,321 conscripts in 2004 (down from 105,820 a year earlier).

Among NATO countries, Greece spends the highest percentage of its GDP for defense: almost 5% in 2003, roughly twice the percentage spent by other EU nations. In 1997 Greece launched a $16 billion weapons modernization program, due for completion in 2007. It includes purchase of an AWACS early warning aircraft, 60 new warplanes and other aircraft, including training and transport planes and helicopters. In 2005 Greece decided to purchase from the U.S. 40 F-16 (block 52) fighter airplanes to be delivered by 2009. This was a bitter disappointment for the European allies that produce the Eurofighter. There will also be new tanks, antiaircraft systems, and new warships, including submarines and nine surface ships. It upgraded its antiaircraft capability by procuring six long–range American–made Patriot missile systems, 21 short–range Russian–made Tor missiles for the army, and 11 French–built Crotale missiles for the air force and navy.

It is unlikely that Greece will again leave the NATO command structure after having reentered it in 1980. It had left that command structure in protest against the Turkish invasion of Cyprus. However, when Greece sought reentry, it ran up against a Turkish wall. Any NATO member can veto entry into the alliance or its command structure, and Turkey wanted to use its veto to force Greece to make concessions in the Aegean and in Cyprus. On its part, Greece became so anxious to rejoin that it even wanted to make its reentry a precondition for the renewal of the U.S. base agreements, thereby giving the Americans a powerful motive to help it. It was primarily American diplomatic efforts that smoothed Greece's path back into NATO.

The basic traditional problem remains, but in significantly diminished form: that Greek eyes are cast eastward toward Turkey. Confrontation with Turkey is no longer a permanent operating factor in Greek foreign and defense policy. Greece contributed to its allies' war effort against Iraq in 1991 by sending one frigate. But Turkey's participation was much more visible.

In the 1990s both acquired huge quantities of modern offensive weaponry free of charge, as the U.S. and Germany transferred to them hundreds of helicopters, tanks, and artillery under the terms of the 1990 CFE treaty. The purpose of this conventional forces agreement was to diminish the threat of surprise attack in Central Europe. But it was an arms bonanza for Turkey and Greece and, in the opinion of some observers, created less, not more, stability in the Balkans. In 1998 the U.S. stopped all military aid, in the form of credits for purchasing American weaponry, to both Greece and Turkey.

Like its predecessor, the Karamanlis government supports reconciliation with Turkey, its accession to the EU and a unified Cyprus in the EU. It favors "a really European Turkey," and publicly supported the Annan Plan for creating an all-Cyprus federation, which failed in April 2004 after Greek Cypriots voted against it. [See separate chapter on Cyprus in this volume.]

The Balkans

While Turkey remains Greece's top concern, the dramatic changes in the Balkans and the breakup of the former Yugoslavia are very worrisome to Greeks. They fear that Macedonia to the north could make irredentist claims on their province with the same name. This prompted Athens in 1992 to oppose Macedonia's right to use that ancient Hellenic name when it declared its independence from Yugoslavia. In 1993 a compromise was reached to allow Macedonia to enter the UN under the clumsy temporary name of "Former Yugoslav Republic of Macedonia (FYROM)." Greeks call the country either FYROM or the capital's name, Skopje; they refer to the people as "Skopjans." No flag was hoisted because of Greece's objection to its 16–point star.

When the U.S. and Greece's EU partners formally recognized Macedonia in 1994, the Greek government imposed a trade blockade on FYROM. This deprived the struggling country, in which 500 American soldiers were performing peacekeeping duties, of access to the port of Salonika, through which three–fourths of its exports and imports and most of its oil passed. This move was devastating to Macedonia and incomprehensible to Greece's allies, who did not understand why it would want to destabilize a multi-ethnic country that could shield it from the turmoil in the former Yugoslavia. Greece was at odds with all its neighbors.

Through American mediation in 1995, Greece and Macedonia agreed to take steps to end their quarrel. Greece agreed to (1) recognize Macedonia as a sovereign and independent state, (2) lift its trade blockade imposed against Macedonia, which was hurting both countries financially, (3) stop vetoing EU aid to Macedonia, and (4) endorse its membership in the OSCE.

In return, Macedonia agreed to redesign its flag and change two articles in its constitution eliminating any hint of a claim on the Greek province of Macedonia. Li-

Zeus, from Artemision, ca. 450 BC

Greece

aison offices were established in each other's capital, and both countries enjoy mutual "unimpeded movement of people and goods." Trade is thriving, and in 1997 they participated in a joint military exercise. In 1999 the Greeks flew supplies to Macedonia to help that country cope with the flood of refugees from Kosovo. The policy of friendly support continues as a part of Athens' policy to promote stability in the Balkans. In 2001 Greece deployed 411 troops to Macedonia as part of a NATO force to disarm Albanian rebels, and it is Macedonia's largest investor.

Their relations with each other have been greatly improved as commerce has gained precedence over historical arguments. Greece supports Macedonia's application for EU membership although it insists that everything be done using the name FYROM. They opened a pipeline from Thessaloniki to Skopje to transport crude oil to a refinery in the capital purchased in 1999 by the Greek state oil company, Hellenic Petroleum. The refined oil is shipped north to Kosovo in a second pipeline. They own Macedonia's biggest bank, a leading supermarket chain and a mobile-phone operation. Both countries are worried about armed Albanian militants, which often maintain close ties with organized crime. However, Greece's policy in the Balkans is to maintain cordial relations and discreet communication with all groups, including Muslim ones.

Greece and Macedonia have not solved their name dispute, but in its first foreign policy act after reelection in November 2004, the U.S. administration said it would now recognize the country as "Republic of Macedonia." Washington gave an assurance that it would recognize any name that is eventually agreed on between the two countries. The change was angrily received in Athens, but its ire was restrained compared with 12 years earlier when the Macedonian republic was proclaimed. At that time a million Greeks joined in the country's biggest-ever nationalist rally. However, Greeks objected to Macedonia's decision to name its main airport after Alexander the Great.

In April 2008 the Greeks delayed Macedonia's admission to NATO, even though Macedonia had accepted "Republic of Macedonia (Skopje)." They pointed out that they would accept the name Macedonia with an "Upper" or "New" before it. But Foreign Minister Dora Bakoyannis explained: "When Marshal Tito of Yugoslavia changed the name of his country's southern province in 1944 from Vardar Banovina to the Socialist Republic of Macedonia, he did it to stir up disorder in northern Greece in order to communize the area and to gain an outlet to the Aegean Sea for his country."

Greeks made a great effort to establish good relations with the new regimes in Bulgaria and Romania. Since entering the EU in 2007, Bulgaria forms Greece's first border with the EU. This is good for trade. Greeks are already among the three largest investors in Bulgaria, Romania and Serbia, and overall Greek investment in the Balkans is increasing. By 2003, an estimated 3,500 Greek enterprises were active in the broad Balkan area with investments amounting to 4 billion euros. Greece is now the top foreign investor in Bulgaria, Albania and Macedonia. Its banking sector represents 16% of banking activities in the region, and Greek banks open a new branch in a Balkan country almost weekly.

Even in Istanbul there are 50 to 60 Greek companies, up from 3 or 4 only a decade ago. Companies in Greece are increasingly transferring manufacturing operations to the lower-wage Balkan countries. Average per capita income in the Balkans is less than one-fifth the level in Greece. The Greek vision is an integrated and open Balkan market of 65 million people with its own economy in the lead. Its trade with southeastern European countries more than doubled between 1996 and 2005. In short, it is the region's business center.

Greece is strengthening its relations with the Black Sea countries and Russia. In 2007 it signed a long-delayed agreement with Russia and Bulgaria to construct an oil pipeline by 2011 to convey Russian crude oil from Burgas on Bulgaria's Black Sea coast 175 miles (280 kilometers) to Alexandroupolis in northern Greece. Russia holds 51% of the shares, with Greece and Bulgaria each holding 24.5%. Since this "south stream" deal excluded Turkey, Ankara was not pleased. In July 2005 the Greek and Turkish prime ministers had launched a landmark cooperative project to build a natural gas pipeline connecting the two countries. Inaugurated in November 2007, it carries natural gas from Azerbaijan 170 miles (295 kilometers) through Anatolia in Turkey to Thrace in Greece beneath the Marmara Sea and eventually underneath the Adriatic Sea to Italy. This project highlights the American role in encouraging Greece and Turkey to reduce dependence on Russia energy supplies by tapping Caspian Sea resources. Their electric grids were linked by 2007. Construction of the continuing undersea gas pipeline between Greece and Italy began in 2008.

Athens utilized its traditionally close ties with Serbia to try to mediate a settlement to the bloody war in Bosnia. This effort led to friction with Turkey, against which Greece and Serbia share a historical antipathy. Greece forbade Turkish planes from flying over its airspace on their way to helping NATO enforce a

no–fly zone over Bosnia. It refused in 1994 to endorse NATO ultimatums against Bosnian Serbs or to participate in any military action in Bosnia. In 1995 Turkey used its veto to prevent the establishment of a NATO rapid deployment headquarters in Thessaloniki and a land and air headquarters in Larissa.

Greece welcomed the Bosnian peace agreement in 1995 and the lifting of UN trade sanctions against Serbia and Montenegro, which had hurt the Greek economy. It agreed to send a contingent of 1,000 troops to join NATO's multinational peacekeeping force in Bosnia, and it donated $7 million in reconstruction funds. In 1997 it put pressure on the Serb president to recognize opposition victories in local elections.

Albania presents a special problem. In 1987 Greece had officially ended the state of war with Albania and had sent the first cabinet–level delegation since 1940. In 1991 Mitsotakis became the first Greek prime minister to visit Tirana. Since 1994 Greece has been the largest investor in Albania. The partial opening of its borders resulted in thousands of ethnic Greeks from a part of Albania called North Epirus and other parts of Albania fleeing to Greece. After decrying their plight for decades, Greece could hardly shut them out.

In 1993, after some 300,000 Albanians had poured into Greece, the breaking point was reached. With illegal immigrants being blamed for rising crime and a lowering of wage rates, anti–Albanian sentiment prompted the government to try to detain and expel the estimated half million Albanians who entered Greece illegally in the three previous years. Deportations of Albanians began in 1993, and there was some frighteningly loose talk in Greece about autonomy for the Greek minority in Northern Epirus. Albania retaliated by cutting the number of Greek–language schools. Rarely had Greece's relations with Albania been worse.

A tentative rapprochement was reached in 1995, when Greek police arrested members of the Greek terrorist North Epirus Liberation Front, and the foreign minister visited Tirana. But when Albania later rejected Greece's request for the establishment of three Greek schools in southern Albania, Athens suspended the planned signing of an agreement on employment opportunities for the estimated 150,000 illegal Albanians residing in Greece. In 1997 Greece sent a sizable peacekeeping contingent to Albania as a part of a multinational force to restore public order. To demonstrate impartiality, its troops were not deployed in the south, where the Greek ethnic minority is concentrated. Athens also opened new border crossings

Greece

and increased its economic assistance to the small, destabilized neighbor.

Today 10% of Greece's population are immigrants, most of them legal. About 130,000 immigrant children are enrolled in Greek schools. Greece announced in 2006 that it would open its doors to workers from all the new EU member states.

In 2001 Greece conducted a vast drive to register hundreds of thousands of illegal immigrants, nearly all from Albania, so that they could acquire the proper papers and live and work without fear of deportation. There are about 1.5 million immigrant workers in Greece, over half of them (58%) Albanian. The approximately 800,000 Albanian immigrants mostly work on farms, construction sites and in services. They send an estimated one billion euros back home in the form of remittances. They find it difficult to gain acceptance. The hardships they face were described in a best-selling book written by an Albanian immigrant and journalist, Gazmend Kapllani, *A Small Diary of Borders*. He regrets that only a handful of Albanians, those considered to be of Greek origin, are granted Greek citizenship. The children of immigrants born in Greece are not entitled to citizenship.

Other immigrant waves came from Bulgaria, Romania, Ukraine, Georgia, Pakistan, Russia, Moldova, Turkish Kurdistan and Poland. Russia is home to about a half million Pontians, who are of Greek origin, having once lived along the southern coast of the Black Sea, which the ancient Greeks called "Pontos." Few of them speak modern Greek. By 1991 about 25,000 of them had found their way to Greece. They are a resourceful people who had already become masters of survival in the Soviet Union. Nevertheless, there were some protests against their being resettled in Thrace, one of Greece's poorest areas.

In 1999 Greece found itself in a difficult situation when NATO launched an air war against Serbia in an effort to stop ethnic cleansing in predominantly Muslim Kosovo. Greek leaders had been friendly to Serb strongman Slobodan Milosevic in the past. Most Greeks are fiercely pro–Serb, as are most of the country's newspapers and TV stations. Both nations are Orthodox Christian, and Greek churchmen are not shy about stirring up emotions against Muslims although the church as a whole is not anti-Muslim. But the Simitis government decided that Greece's wider interests—closer ties with western Europe and joining the euro—required that it support NATO.

As the alliance's sole Balkan country (except Slovenia), Athens said it could not join an attack against a neighbor. However, its airbases provided logistical help for AWACS surveillance flights over Yugoslavia, and it permitted supplies to pass through its port of Thessaloniki. Also its good relations with Belgrade enabled Greece to be the only NATO country that could actively support such non– governmental organizations as the Red Cross inside Kosovo. Simitis distanced his country from Serbia's leaders while improving relations with the rest of the Balkan countries. Greece sent 1,000 peacekeeping troops to Kosovo.

Following Milosevic's fall from power in October 2000, Foreign Minister Papandreou was the first EU minister to meet Yugoslavia's new president, Vojislav Kostunica, and stressed that Europe must seize the opportunity to transform the Balkans from a crisis region to one of stability and democracy. To put its money where its mouth is, Greece pledged $455 million over five years for Balkan recon-

Mount Lycabettus, Athens

Courtesy: Richard F. Strader

271

Greece

In traditional costumes of their region, young men from Crete perform a line dance

struction. Speaking in the European Parliament, Kostunica asserted that Greece was Yugoslavia's "window to the outside world." Greece now views the Balkans more from a commercial standpoint than from a strategic one. Their hope is that the oil flows and shopping trips and cross-border business deals will help prevent a renewal of armed conflict.

Greek-Turkish Hostility in the Aegean

Greece insists that its airspace extends 10 miles around each island rather than six miles, which Turkey recognized. Also, now that there are proven oil reserves in the Aegean, Greece is determined to maximize its economic rights on the continental shelf. Each country claims that the Aegean is a part of its continental shelf, and Turkey questions Greece's possession of the eastern Aegean Sea. Actually, both have shown noteworthy restraint in the past, accepting a six-mile offshore limit in the Aegean, compared with the internationally accepted 12 miles.

When Turkey occupied northern Cyprus in 1974, many Greeks asked: "What good is NATO to us if it cannot prevent the Turks from invading Cyprus or from threatening Greek interests in the Aegean?" Cyprus remains an issue although both Turkey and Greece supported a UN effort in 2004 to overcome the island's division. Pending a future settlement that satisfies a majority of both Turkish- and Greek-Cypriots can be reached, 40,000 Turkish troops will still occupy 37% of the island although the Turkish minority comprises only 18% of the population.

In August 2005 Greece supported France's objection to the opening of accession talks between Turkey and the EU un-

til Turkey formally recognizes Greek Cyprus and opens its ports to Cypriot-flagged shipping, something that Ankara resists. Prime Minister Karamanlis increased the pressure by postponing his planned visit to Turkey in August 2005. It would have been the first such visit by a Greek prime minister in more than 46 years. Accession talks began anyway. While continuing their demands on Turkey, most Greeks desire to see it pursuing peace and respectability through the EU. Ever since Turkey became a candidate for the EU, both Greece and Cyprus have sharply reduced their defense spending.

Greece focused on extracting NATO guarantees against possible Turkish incursions in the area. This was a guarantee that NATO was understandably unprepared to make against a fellow member. Greece also turned to the Americans to secure a more precise formulation of a vaguely worded guarantee that former Secretary of State Henry Kissinger had given in 1976 that the U.S. would not stand idly by if either Greece or Turkey attempted to resolve their disputes by force. This was a delicate request for the U.S. The Americans hinted that they might be prepared to give Greece a firmer guarantee if it would first try to mend its fences with Turkey.

At NATO's 1997 summit meeting the American secretary of state got the Greek prime minister and Turkish president to endorse a broad declaration of good neighborly relations in a nonaggression pact. But they rejected Washington's requests to cancel military maneuvers in sensitive areas. Instead they engaged in dogfight challenges over the Aegean, vio-

lated a moratorium on military over flights of Cyprus, and steered so closely to each other that two naval vessels nearly collided close to the Turkish coast. Nevertheless, in 1997 Mesut Yilmaz became the first Turkish prime minister to visit Greek territory since 1988. The occasion was the first summit of Balkan leaders since the breakup of Yugoslavia. The meeting was hosted by the Greeks on the island of Crete and ended with a pledge to work together to ease tensions. The Greek and Turkish prime ministers took the opportunity to hold private talks.

In the months before the dawning of the 21st century an almost miraculous change in popular attitudes occurred in both Greece and Turkey. After the Turkish prime minister asked Greece to endorse a bilateral agreement on combating terrorism, the PASOK government decided to drop long-standing objections to engaging in direct negotiations with Ankara.

Then a mutual disaster occurred. An earthquake struck Turkey on August 17, 1999, killing at least 15,000 people. Greek nongovernmental organizations rushed blankets, clothing and medical supplies to the stricken region, while Greek families on Greek islands off the Turkish coast offered to host children made homeless by the quake. Three weeks later a terrible earthquake struck Athens, killing 140. The Turks instantly sent rescue teams. The television images of Turks searching for Greeks trapped in the rubble stirred deep emotions that laid the foundation for undreamed-of rapprochement and optimism that the two nations could cooperate with each other.

The fruits were quick to come. In December Greece supported Turkey's candidacy for the EU, and Ankara subsequently announced that it backed Greece's efforts to recover the Elgin Marbles from Britain. George Papandreou became the first Greek foreign minister to visit Turkey in almost four decades, and in 2000 Prime Minister Simitis accepted an invitation to become the first Greek head of government to visit Turkey since the late-1950s. The two countries tackled numerous "soft issues," reaching agreements on such matters as tourism, commerce, the environment, combating organized crime and terrorism, and preventing illegal immigration. They set up a joint Greek-Turkish team to handle disaster relief. After their newly acquired habits of cooperation had been strengthened, they confronted the truly divisive problem of Cyprus in 2004, and they are doing so also in the Aegean.

A positive signal had been given in 2000 when for the first time in more than 20 years Turkish marines were permitted to land in Greece during NATO exercises in the Aegean. Defense ministers from both countries met in Greece for the first time to discuss how to cut military spending. At the beginning of a 17-day NATO exercise in October 2000 designed to showcase the new era of friendship between Greece and Turkey, Greek military planes landed in Turkey for the first time in 28 years. Greek frigates also called on a Turkish port. By 2006 both sides were busy implementing confidence-building measures, including a telephone hotline between both countries' military forces, avoidance of military exercises in the Aegean during the tourist season, and cooperating on air-sea rescue training.

But then an old controversy broke out that seriously set back the two nations' year-long attempt to improve their relations. Turkey objected to Greek flights over the Greek islands of Lemnos and Ikaria in the Aegean. Turkey considers the islands to be demilitarized zones, whereas Greece denies that there are any such international agreements. Greece maintains a large military presence on Lemnos, and Turkey has always claimed that Greece has no right to do so. Greece immediately withdrew from the maneuvers. To make matters worse, Russian-made antiaircraft missiles locked on to Turkish planes that flew close to the Greek-controlled part of Cyprus. Although Greeks did see in the crisis a danger of war, NATO's former supreme commander, Gen. Joseph W. Ralston, was called in to help broker a truce, and the other allies were relieved that the dispute had not led to war.

The rapprochement at the highest level continues, pushed especially by two ex-foreign ministers, George Papandreou and Ismail Cem. In 2001 they strolled together down the streets of Kusadasi, Turkey, and planted an olive tree near the ruins of an ancient temple; they agreed to clear land mines from their common borders; they decided to bid jointly to host the European soccer championships in 2008. Papandreou made an unprecedented overture during a visit to Ankara in 2001 to discuss with Turkish leaders the possibility of mutually agreed defense cuts. In 2002 they traveled together to Israel and the West Bank to offer their joint help in the search for peace and to show that traditional foes can choose a "different path."

They signed an agreement to build a pipeline to transport Central Asian and Iranian natural gas through Turkey to a Greek port and then on to western Europe. Christo Doulakis became the first Greek finance minister to visit Turkey, and Greece no longer blocks Turkey's EU application. This consensus among Greeks and their government in supporting the warming of ties with Turkey and a just and lasting settlement of the Cyprus prob-

lem prompted ex-Foreign Minister Molyviatis in 2005 to call the present "the golden age of Greek diplomacy." In January 2008 Costas Karamanlis became the first Greek prime minister in 49 years to make an official visit to Turkey.

The improvement of the diplomatic climate is not irreversible. There are many festering disputes, including Cyprus, seabed exploration rights, territorial waters, and airspace rights. In May 2006 two of their F-16 fighters collided in mid-air as they shadowed each other in disputed Aegean airspace near the island of Karpathos. The Greek pilot was killed. Trade and investment have remained limited even though cross-border trade doubled from 2002 to 2006, and an increasing number of foreign tourists pass from the Greek islands to the Turkish coast. But the policy of reconciliation continues under Prime Minister Karamanlis, and there are good grounds for confidence that these differences will be settled peacefully.

Terrorism

The November 17 Movement, Greece's deadliest terrorist group, claimed responsibility for a spate of attacks against U.S. targets, including the murder of four American officials, an antitank rocket blast at a Citibank branch in 1998 and bombings of tourist sites in 1999 in protest against the NATO bombing of Yugoslavia. Since 1975 it killed 23 persons, starting with CIA Athens station chief Richard Welch and continuing in 2000 with the daylight murder of the British defense attaché at a spot along a busy Athens street where U.S. Navy Captain George Tsantes and his driver had been murdered in 1983. Most of its victims are Greeks, usually political conservatives.

American intelligence and law enforcement experts widely suspected that the Socialist government tolerated November 17 because the group's overtly leftist and nationalist standpoints and strident anti-Americanism resonate with many Greeks. Its ideology had evolved from hard-core Marxism to nationalism and anti-globalization. Until 2002 not a single November 17 member had ever been arrested. When suspects were picked up, they were treated leniently. In 1999, for example, a woman was caught attempting to firebomb the U.S. consulate in Thessaloniki. After a few days' detention and a small fine, she was released.

In July 2002 Greek police made a rapid-fire series of raids arresting leading members of the November 17 terrorist group, named after the date in 1973 when soldiers and tanks crushed student-led protests in Athens. Known for its fanatical secrecy and ruthless precision, the organization had completely outwitted authorities during a

27-year spate of murders, robberies and bombings. The break came after a botched bombing attempt on June 29, 2002, left an injured terrorist on the scene who revealed information to the police that led to the sudden raids throughout Greece.

The captured operatives included an unassuming shopkeeper (Nikos Papanastasiou), a hospital telephone operator (Pavlos Serifis), who was accused of being the group's second in command, and a translator of French texts, Alexandros Giotopoulos, whom Serifs fingered as the gunman who killed the CIAs Athens station chief, Richard Welch, in 1975. That was the assassination that initially attracted attention to the terrorist organization. Also arrested were a bus driver, a religious icon painter and an elementary school teacher. Since the Welch murder, the group claimed responsibility for 22 more victims (including three Americans), the latest being the British defense attaché, Brigadier Stephen Saunders, in June 2000.

In September 2002 Greece's most wanted man, Dimitris Koufodinas, walked into an Athens police station and announced that November 17 was "finished." A series of revelations led to weapons stashes in Athens apartments. In March 2003 what the Greek press called the "trial of trials" began in a specially protected maximum security courtroom in the country's largest prison, where the leaders of the 1967–74 junta had been tried. The court rejected the suspects' charges that their crimes were political, not criminal, and it forbade TV coverage of the lengthy trial.

Even for prisoners condemned to multiple life sentences, Greek law permits a maximum sentence for murder of only 25 years with the right to apply for conditional release after only 20. In the trial that lasted until November 2003, the suspects faced 2,000 charges. Guilty verdicts were rendered against 15 of the 19 members of the "November 17" terrorist group. Four were acquitted for lack of evidence. The leader, Alexandros Yiotopoulos, got 21 life terms, the heaviest penalty in Greek legal history, and Dimitris Koufodinas 13 life terms. The remaining 13 received sentences ranging from eight years to life. Many were disappointed that the trials did not shed more light on the group itself and why it was able to act with impunity for 27 years.

The U.S. must spend more on diplomatic security in Greece than anywhere else in the world. The State Department's annual report in 2000, *Patterns of Global Terrorism*, placed Greece second only to Colombia in the number of terrorist attacks. In 2007 the far-left Revolutionary Struggle fired an anti-tank grenade into the heavily fortified American embassy. When claiming responsibility, the group

Greece

blamed U.S. policy in Iraq and the Middle East. There were no injuries and little damage, but the attack underscored continued anti-American sentiment and the potential for more homegrown terror.

There were serious concerns about terrorist violence during the 2004 summer Olympics in Athens. They embarrassed the government of former Prime Minister Simitis, which strove to convince the other EU countries that Greece is a well-run, law-abiding country. He agreed to a reorganization of the anti-terrorism police and to new antiterrorist cooperation with the U.S., UK and EU. The government also hoped that the trial would reassure the world that it could deal effectively with any kinds of terrorists who might threaten the 2004 summer Olympic Games, in which a record 202 nations participated. They were the first to take place since the September 11 terrorist attacks in the U.S. and a particular worry following the March 11, 2004, Islamic militant attack in Madrid that killed 192 persons.

The government allotted $1.2 billion for security during the Games, more than three times the amount spent four years earlier in Sydney, Australia. Security was coordinated by Greek authorities and by a seven-member intelligence Advisory Group that included the U.S., UK, France and Israel. The FBI and CIA were directly involved in the planning, and the U.S. Department of Energy supplied millions of dollars worth of radiation detectors to deal with "dirty bombs."

Greece asked NATO for help and received pledges of 24-hour air surveillance by AWACS aircraft. U.S. battleships patrolled offshore. The Czechs kept a biological warfare detection battalion on standby for the Games. No NATO forces served on Greek soil. For that the Greeks themselves assigned more than 50,000 police, army and other security personnel. To get ready, 1,500 Greek police officers and soldiers, joined by 400 American special-forces troops and soldiers from other allied nations, held a two-week exercise in March 2004 to train for "catastrophic scenarios." A June 2006 bomb attack on Greece's culture minister by the left-wing "Revolutionary Struggle" demonstrated that foreigners are not the only targets. No one was hurt.

When terrorists killed 3,000 persons in New York and Washington on September 11, 2001, the Greek government did not waver in its support of America's response to this mortal terrorist threat. It put sympathy ads into six major U.S. newspapers, reading: "Greece, the birthplace of democracy, mourns with America at this difficult hour. We have joined with the United States in the fight against terror-

ism. Our common values of freedom, democracy and humanism will prevail. Together we stand."

Greece provided to the U.S. and its other allies the use of its airspace, air bases and naval facilities on Crete. It shared intelligence and investigated suspect bank accounts. It offered to replace American peacekeepers in Bosnia and Kosovo (where Greece already had peacekeeping troops) if the U.S. soldiers would have to be withdrawn for service in Afghanistan or elsewhere. It dispatched a naval frigate to patrol the Arabian Sea. Its aircrews were among those of the NATO allies who manned five AWACS reconnaissance aircraft dispatched to the U.S. to help patrol the East Coast; this was the first time since the Revolutionary War that the U.S. needed foreign troops to protect its own territory.

Finally, Greece sent two C-130 transport planes and 128 soldiers (mostly engineers and medical personnel) to Afghanistan to support the war against the Taliban and al Qaeda. In 2005 it deployed a 45-man mobile medical unit, and at the end of the year it dispatched 44 air force officers to assume the administration of the Kabul airport for four months. Nevertheless, Greeks are the only Western Europeans who are not granted visa-free travel to the United States.

Entry into the EU

Under former Prime Minister Constantine Karamanlis Greece joined the EU in a hurry, primarily in order to strengthen democracy in Greece but also to benefit Greece's economy. During the 1980s Papandreou had often described the EU as a "rich man's club" which discriminated against the weaker economies (although all poor countries in western Europe entered). He had promised to pull Greece out of the EU if he were to be elected.

As on many other issues, he changed his tune after he found himself in the prime minister's chair. The EU, in contrast to NATO, is popular in Greece, and it is quite lucrative as well. Greece receives handsome annual subsidies from the EU coffers, for a while more than any other EU member. In the 21st century EU structural aid amounted to more than 1.5% of GDP annually. Greece still lacks the necessary administrative capacity to administer all these funds. In 2005 it had to repay almost 500 million euros ($750,000) in aid it had misspent; this was the first such instance in EU history.

In 2006 Greece succeeded in securing over 20 billion euros ($30 billion) through 2013. But these EU funds will decrease thereafter because needier new member states have a more urgent claim on them. Greece also receives stern economic warn-

ings and advice from Brussels. This is bitter but needed medicine; aid does not flow to Greece unconditionally.

Greece did not make the most of its first decade in the EU. In 1981 its per capita GDP was 58% of the EU average, but by 2006 it had risen to 77.3% of the EU average. Its citizens were asked to make sacrifices in order to get ready for the European single currency. With a government deficit at 5.2% of GDP (2.7% and declining in 2008) and a total national debt at 106.9% of GDP in 1997 (104% in 2007, the second-highest in the EU after Italy), it did not qualify for the first round. But it appeared to meet the convergence criteria by 2000, and it was invited to join the eurozone in 2001. A pleased Prime Minister Simitis commented at the time, "there were many doubts among people who said we did not have the discipline to meet the criteria for the euro. But we proved that when it comes to taking a historic step, we are able to make the necessary sacrifices."

It turns out that the Greek government had provided false budget deficit figures between 1997 and 2003 that disguised Greece's repeated breaches of the EU budget ceiling. When the European Commission discovered this in 2004, it ordered Eurostat, its statistical service, to begin supervising Greece's finances very closely. It admonished the country for widening the budget deficits, recognizing that at least half the overruns in 2004 were due to unexpected cost overruns to finance the Olympic Games. Brussels showed renewed skepticism in 2006 when Greece changed its method of measuring its economy by including parts of its large black economy, such as prostitution and money laundering. This increased the GDP figure by about 25% and both lowered the budget deficit and the public debt figure (to 85% of GDP). In any case, possessing the euro gives Greece a stronger sense of security and confidence.

During the first half of 2003 Greece occupied the EU presidency and reaped the praise of Secretary of State Colin Powell for its "great skill" in dealing with a difficult time of sharply divided opinions within Europe and between Europe and the United States over the war in Iraq. It was also a crucial time in Europe's history because of the writing of a new EU constitution, which the Greek parliament ratified in April 2005 by an overwhelming margin of 268 to 17, and because of the admission of the most new members ever—ten, including the Greek part of the divided island of Cyprus.

About 90% of Greeks opposed the U.S.-British war effort in Iraq, but Greece's role as EU president muted the government's criticism of the war. It did permit allied military aircraft to fly over Greek airspace on their way to bomb Baghdad. In 2005 it contributed 300,000 euros ($375,000) for training Iraqi security forces and military doctors in Greek hospitals. In the aftermath of the August 2006 Lebanese war, it helped more than 13,000 Americans who had to flee the country, and it contributed two naval ships and a Navy Seals unit to the international peacekeeping efforts.

Greece was in the spotlight on April 16, 2003, when the EU's leaders met with those of the ten prospective new members in the Greek resort of Porto Carras on the northern Aegean coast for the accession treaty signing ceremony. It was a glittering occasion that highlighted Greece as the cradle of democracy. It was held in a classical-era building, the Stoa of Attalos, restored to its earlier glory by American archaeologists and philanthropists.

ECONOMY

Herodotus wrote almost 2,500 years ago, "Greece always has poverty for a mate." After Portugal it is the poorest country in Western Europe; more than 15% of Greeks live below the poverty level defined by the EU. It is always tempting to use Western European standards when analyzing the Greek economy. In one sense, this is appropriate because many Greeks do, in fact, want to share western life and values. But it must be remembered that Greece is geographically isolated from the rest of western Europe and is Mediterranean and Balkan in character, as well as western European.

Greece has undeniably changed greatly since the 1940s, when foreign occupation and a destructive civil war stood in the way of economic improvement. In the 1950s it began to experience an economic boom, and in the years 1964 to 1975 it had an annual growth rate of over 10%. Between 2000 and 2006 that rate was over 4%, fueled by Olympic construction projects; by 2008 it was declining to 2.4%. Personal consumption rose almost as spectacularly, and improvements in living standards were visible. Half of the Greek families living in the cities own their own homes, and the figure is even higher in the countryside.

This is one of those countries in which real earnings and the actual standard of living are higher than official statistics would indicate. The secret lies partly in the flexibility and resilience of the Greeks and in the tightly-knit family, which is marked by hard work, saving for the future and the drive to get ahead.

It also lies partly in the extensive "underground" economy. It has almost become the norm for Greeks to hold down second and even third jobs, for which persons are paid in a way that goes unnoticed by the tax collectors and statisticians. It has been estimated that the underground economy may be equivalent to 15% to 20% of Greece's GDP. This thriving underground economy is one reason why more and more foreign refugees and mostly illegal migrant workers are immigrating to Greece, especially from Poland, and the Philippines.

Shipping

Ever since Jason and the Argonauts sailed away to find the Golden Fleece, Greece has been the world's leader in shipping. Today it has the largest merchant fleet in the world owned by one group of nationals—16.5% of the world's merchant fleet is Greek–owned. About three-fourths of the ships fly the Liberian, Cypriot, Maltese, or Panamanian flags for reasons of legal convenience. Most owners are based in Athens, and they are investing so much in new ships that 612 of a total of 3,700 Greek ships were new in 2007. For the first time, the average age of its ships fell below the world average of 14.4 years. Greeks own two-thirds of the EU's total merchant fleet and half of its tonnage. Greece was therefore given the chairmanship of the EU shipping committee.

Shipping is a vital part of the economy, providing about 114,000 jobs. It is estimated that one family out of 11 is directly or indirectly dependent upon shipping for its livelihood. After tourism, it is the country's top foreign exchange earner and has helped to alleviate Greece's chronic balance of payments deficits. Names like Onassis, Niarchos, Goulandris and John Spiros Latsis are inextricably identified with this entire industry.

Greek shipping is reaping handsome profits from delivering China's growing raw material imports. Greek ferries transport more than 10 million passengers a year. Recruiting can be a problem. Greek law requires that all captains be Greek nationals, and most personnel must be Greek or EU citizens. The rise in living standards on the mainland and islands have made the seaman's life of loneliness, long absences from families (the average time away is seven months) and the danger from storms less attractive. Greece's 10 training academies produce too few officers to man the ships. Therefore, ship owners are compelled both to pay extremely high wages and benefits, at EU levels. But they may hire more than 25% of their crews from outside of Greece, especially from Asia, and pay them less.

Tourism, Immigration and Industry

Its ancient ruins, beautiful beaches and almost perpetual sunshine, combined with the people's well–deserved reputation for hospitality and friendliness, have long made Greece a favorite tourist land. It welcomes 13.5 million tourists annually, more than the total Greek population. Crete is the most popular destination with more than 2.2 million visitors each year. It ranks among the 15 top tourism destinations in the world. Tourists leave large amounts of their currencies behind by the time they depart, 18% of GDP. Tourism is Greece's largest source of foreign currency and its biggest industry, employing 800,000 or a tenth of the population; it produces more than 10% of overall employment growth.

Altar boys in Serres

Greece

But there are problems with tourism. It is seasonal, so many facilities are not used in the off–season. Further, it tends to be concentrated in Athens and the islands, which become terribly overcrowded in the high season. Efforts to encourage tourists to visit less–frequented places, particularly the northern part, have not been successful. Since the arrival of the euro, Greece has lost its price-competitiveness compared with its Mediterranean rivals. Turkey, with beautiful beaches, friendly people, low prices, and almost as many ancient Greek ruins as Greece itself, is luring precisely the kinds of middle–class tourists as is Greece. Only 2% of tourists are Americans. Finally, Greece lies close to the Arab world. This has scared some tourists away. As the 1991 Gulf War showed, Greece is very sensitive to travel advisories issued by the U.S. government. Not until 2006 did the government decide to allow foreign investors to build large new resorts with world-class accommodations and golf and other sports facilities.

An increasingly prosperous Greece has a growing number of immigrants, who now number about 1.5 million working in the country. Including their families, at least one million residents in Greece were born elsewhere. Most live around Athens, and many of them perform many jobs Greeks no longer want to do, such as hard farm labor. Thus the economy could hardly function without them. That is why changes in the law resulted by 2006 in more than 400,000 immigrants acquiring work and residence permits and joining the social security system. Their presence in such large numbers is a considerable challenge to what is called "Greekness," everything that has to do with Greek culture, language and history. The number of immigrant children in Greek schools had risen by 2006 to over 130,000. In 2006 Greece opened its doors to workers from all the new EU member states. However, citizenship remains severely restricted. Law requires that illegal migrants arrested by the police be released within three months. Those denied asylum are released with a deportation order, and most of those go underground or move elsewhere in the EU.

Traditionally Greece has been relatively tolerant of foreigners. But in the early 1990s the country lost control of its borders, and hundreds of thousands of people poured over its frontiers. Some of them brought with them unwelcome problems, such as organized crime and illegal trafficking in women and children for the sex industry. The same applies to Cyprus, which is located less than 40 miles from the shores of Turkey, Syria and Lebanon. The furious debate ignited by proposals to build a mosque in Athens in

time for the 2004 Olympic Games showed just how sensitive the issue of accommodating outsiders is. There are at least 100,000 Muslims in or around Athens. Their presence taps into lingering resentments against Turks, with whom many associate Islam. Parliament had authorized a mosque for Athens in 2001, but not until 2006 were actual plans for constructing such a place of worship announced.

As measured by its employment structure, the Greek economy has become more modern: 65% of its workforce is engaged in the services sector, producing 78.7% of GDP, and 22% is employed in industry, creating 17.2% of GDP. Manufacturing is concentrated primarily in small, artisan industries. The average number of workers is 45, but about 95% have fewer than ten workers and about 80% fewer than four. Only companies producing basic metals, tobacco, paper, textiles, chemicals and petro–chemicals are in the medium to large–scale category. The hundred largest Greek companies combined do not approach the size of General Motors.

By EU standards Greek production methods are often antiquated and the management style is more appropriate to small artisan family businesses than to modern, aggressive ones. These are all too often one–man shows in which the family head runs almost everything and is very hesitant to delegate authority. One result is lower productivity than elsewhere in the EU. For example, manufacturing exports per capita are only about 4% that of the EU average.

Another problem with Greek industry is that it tends to be heavily concentrated in the Athens–Piraeus and Thessaloniki areas. About 30% of the Greek population, 40% of all enterprises and 50% of the total labor force producing half of the country's GDP are located in and around Athens, a sprawling megalopolis of 3.76 million. The capital is growing by 100,000 each year, despite the problems of smog (primarily from a million motor vehicles), high rents, poor sanitation and traffic chaos. There was a consensus that the best way of solving the city's traffic and pollution problems was to expand the subway system. Prodded by the Olympic deadline of 2004, much was done to accomplish this. By extending the metro, improving the suburban rail line, and creating a streetcar from the center of Athens to the beaches, traffic has been reduced and so has pollution.

Although Greece is not highly developed as a whole, it has pollution problems similar to those of many highly industrialized countries, thanks to the fact that its industry is greatly concentrated. For several years the government has tried to do something about this problem. Athens is

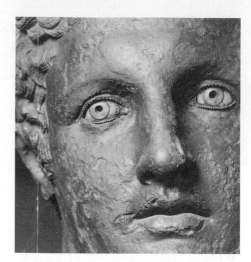

formally closed to new industry, and permits for modernization or expansion of existing plants are issued only under the condition that there be no further pollution. Also, large investments have been steered to northern Greece, and this area is now the fastest growing region, in terms of population.

The two main trade unions are the General Confederation of Greek Workers (GSEE) and the Civil Servants' Union. Together they represent more than 2.5 million workers and had traditionally been under the thumb of the government, which gave unions their money and usually managed to get their men installed in union leadership. Therefore Greek union leaders were almost always conservative. Andreas Papandreou allowed the unions to finance themselves through members' dues, and thereby gave them more independence from the state. Also, strikes became easier by eliminating such restrictions as cooling off periods and by making it more difficult for employers to use the "lockout" response to a strike. The result is that Greece loses the most work days to strikes among the OECD rich countries: 580 per 1,000 employees per year, compared with 197 for Spain, 113 for Italy, 16 for France, 5.3 for Germany and 2.4 for Austria.

Both their ability to disrupt daily life and the limits to their influence on the government were shown in early 2008 when they created labor unrest for a month to protest the government's plans to reform the fragmented pay-as-you-go pension system. It is one of the most generous in the EU and also so underfunded in a country with the EU's fastest aging population that it would go bankrupt in 15 years if unreformed. In March parliament approved measures to fuse about 170 pension funds into eight, to raise the retirement age of working mothers from 50 to 55 years, and to provide incentives for employees to work beyond the current retirement age of 65.

Agriculture

Greek agriculture has always been limited by the facts that the land is 80% mountainous, the soil is rocky and the climate is dry. Only 28% of the land is arable. Greece has the lowest proportion of forest cover of any EU country. That is diminishing rapidly because of fire destruction, which by the beginning of the 1990s had already claimed 1.5 million acres (or 4.8% of Greece's total surface area). Despite the massive exodus to the cities during the past three and a half decades, the farm population is still 13% of the total.

Living standards of Greek farmers have risen. Their frame of mind has also changed considerably in the last quarter of a century. They are now outspoken and ready to underscore their protests by blocking roads with their tractors. They are also far better organized. The former conservative government devoted an increasing share of its budget to modernizing agriculture, but Greek farms are still too small and fragmented to be competitive. The European Court of Justice gave cheese farmers a boost in 2005 by declaring that only Greece could call the salty, crumbly white cheese sold all over the world "feta." That is a major reason why agriculture produces only 4.1% of GDP. A further source of foreign exchange has been the remittances sent back to Greece by the close to one million Greeks living elsewhere in Europe. The country's fishing industry lands over half of the Mediterranean's total fish catch and employs 10,000 persons in places where there are few alternative job opportunities.

Resources

Greece is not rich in raw materials, but it does mine nickel, bauxite, chrome, zinc, asbestos and lignite (brown coal). It also has deposits of uranium, gold and silver. Heretofore it has had very little domestic oil and rapidly became very dependent upon import sources. Fortunately, the Greeks' energy consumption is the lowest per capita in western Europe, mainly because there is little need for heating in the warm climate.

The dry climate prevents a dramatic expansion of hydroelectric power, and the hundreds of scattered islands complicate energy delivery to the far reaches of the country. Greece is nevertheless determined to increase its domestic energy production. With so much sun and coastline, solar and tidal power is a possibility in the distant future. Greeks have been nervous about pressing ahead with plans to construct a nuclear plant that could supply a fifth of the nation's power. The major reason for their hesitation is that the country is very prone to earthquakes, which could dangerously damage a power plant. With its sizable lignite deposits, it still uses this brown coal for 60% of its electricity generation despite the negative environmental consequences. Renewable energy (primarily hydroelectricity) accounts for only 12% of its power. It can import harder and cleaner burning coals to replace the lignite. The goal is to reduce the oil component of electricity from 40% to only 2%.

The greatest hope is that offshore oil extraction can increase. In 1981 Greece began extracting its first barrels of low quality Aegean crude oil from Prinos, near the holiday resort island of Thasos in northern Greece. Its production is expected to supply from 8% to 10% of oil needs. Promising oil deposits have also been found off the Ionian Islands between Paxoi and Zakinthos, facing Italy. However, the extent to which Greece can use Aegean oil depends upon its ability to settle its differences with Turkey, which also raises conflicting claims in this disputed area. Dependency on imported oil will continue.

Most of Greece's trade is with the EU, the Middle East and North Africa. While Lebanon was in flames, Athens grew fast as a regional trade center for the Middle East, with many international businesses maintaining regional offices in Athens. However, Greece has not been a Mecca for foreign direct investments. The 2006 World Competitiveness Report ranked Greece 42d (up from 50th) out of the 60 countries it surveyed. It pointed to several obstacles for investors, including an inefficient bureaucracy, high income and corporate tax rates (cut to 25% in 2007), ill-defined land use, and popular resistance to the idea of foreigners benefiting from the development of Greek assets. The processing of investment applications is slow and the issuance of licenses and permits even slower. Many investors lack the patience to wait two years to complete the paperwork.

The Current State of the Economy

The budget deficit was brought down to 2.2% in 2007, below the 3% eurozone limit for the first time. Public–sector debt stood at 104% of GDP in 2007 (85% if different accounting methods are used). This is the second highest in the EU and almost double the EU average of 64.2%. Inflation stood at 4.4% in 2008 while unemployment fell to 9% in 2007 and 8.9% in 2008. This is low for heads of households, but is a frightful 24% for youth under age 24.

The economy is in need of further restructuring, and Greece still has a long way to go to catch up with the rest of its western European partners. Per capita income is 77.3% of the EU average, and it has failed to close the gap with its Mediterranean neighbors, Italy and Spain. The "new economy" has yet to arrive completely. Greeks own fewer computers per capita than any other nation in the EU. Nevertheless, its economic growth rate at over 4% from 2000 to 2006 and 4.3% in 2007 (dropping to 2.4% in 2008) was not

A Greek newspaper reports on the London bombing of the Queen's Horse Guards

Greece

only one of the highest in the EU15, but also in the OECD.

Much of the stimulus was provided by the push to be ready for the 2004 Olympics. A new metro line and airport in Athens were completed. A new highway around greater Athens was begun, as was a major project to link the Peloponnese to mainland Greece by a bridge. A new highway from the Adriatic to the Turkish border will speed up east-west travel and help tie the two cautious neighbors more closely together. All these projects contributed to the highly successful Olympic Games in 2004. Now Greeks face the difficult decisions of what to do with all their new specialized sports facilities.

CULTURE

Before the Byzantine Empire fell under the Turkish onslaught, the Greek culture had largely fallen into a state of religiously–induced rigidity. Under Turkish domination, cultural life oriented itself more around the simple roots of peasant and shepherd life. That is the reason for the fact that modern Greek culture, with its exotic charm, is strongly shaped by and fused with folklore.

Literature and Arts

In modern Greek literature one finds a strong orientation toward folk themes and styles. In the works of its most famous novelist, Nikos Kazantzakis (1883–1957), who was nominated for the Nobel Prize several times, one gains a deep insight into the suffering and the liberation of the Greek people. His novel, *Alexis Zorbas*, which was filmed in the 1960s became an enormous success. Greek music long kept its distance from the Western cultural tradition, and this film, as well as *Never on Sunday*, helped introduce to Western ears the oriental sound of the bouzouki, through the artistry of composers Mikis Theodorakis and Manos Hadjidakis. Greece has produced some leading classical musicians, such as singer Maria Callas and composer Dimitri Mitropoulos. Classical music is rapidly gaining in popularity, and Athens has a new concert hall, the Megaro Mousikis, for presentations of all musical styles.

The lyricist, Georgios Seferis (1900–1971) received the Nobel Prize in 1963 for his attempt to synthesize Greek folklore with the western cultural tradition. Odysseus Elytis was also awarded the Nobel Prize for his surrealist poetry. The hope and the suffering of the Greek left during the turmoil and civil wars of the 1930s and 1940s are chronicled by the astoundingly prolific Yannis Ritsos, one of Greece's most popular poets, especially among those who are young and on the political left. A staunch supporter of the Greek communists, he has published 86 books of his works in 48 languages, and he reportedly has 40 more ready for publication. Like many contemporary Greek artists, he has had much experience with arrests and exile because of his political activities and writings.

This also applied to Mikis Theodorakis, who was an active communist, and to Melina Mercouri, who became the PASOK minister of culture and science. The granddaughter of a former mayor of Athens and daughter of a former leftist politician, she played a prostitute in her most famous film, "Never on Sunday," which was shot in the lower–class section of Piraeus, which she represented in the parliament. Forced into exile in Paris and the U.S. when the "colonels" seized power in 1967, she publicly urged tourists to boycott Greece. After 1967 she devoted most of her attention to politics and held high political office until 1994. She created quite a stir in the male–dominated parliament by insisting on wearing trousers to its sessions. In 1990 she was defeated in her bid to become mayor of Athens. When PASOK returned to power in 1993, she again became culture minister for a few months until her death of lung cancer in a New York hospital in 1994. After lying in state at the Athens Cathedral, she effectively shut down the city of Athens by attracting 300,000 admirers to line her funeral procession.

Language

Modern Greeks cannot understand the classical Greek language although the modern dialects do retain some features of that earlier, far more complicated, language. Despite the changes over time, the Greeks are the world's only people (except the Chinese) who can look at a 2,500–year–old inscription and recognize it in their own language. A proposal by the education minister in 1987 to restore classical Greek to the higher–education curriculum revived a century–old dispute. Opponents say that teaching two Greek languages would slow down educational reforms, and communists and leftists branded the proposal as reactionary. But classicists responded that even Marx, Engels and Lenin learned ancient Greek. In 1992, after a 16–year hiatus, ancient Greek was reintroduced in junior high schools.

At present there is one modern Greek language since *Katharevousa* is no longer in use. The latter was devised in the 19th century to purify the language as much as feasible and return it to a form at least approximating classical Greek. It was used in the Church and for a long time in the administration, courts, elevated literature and the universities. The less formal and simpler *Demotiki* ("people's language") is exclusively used by 90% of the people. Those who only read it felt like quasi–illiterates whenever they entered those circles where *Katharevousa* was used. Since the restoration of democracy in 1974, the formal version has lost its privileged position. It was eliminated from the schools as part of a series of educational reforms introduced in 1976. The language used in Church liturgy is a mixture of some modern Greek and even more ancient Greek as reformed during the Hellenistic age. It is the language in which the Old and New Testaments were written.

Educational System

The school and university systems need improvement. Reform has focused on unblocking the bottleneck leading to the Greek universities. The government traditionally limits the number of openings to anticipated numbers of jobs for graduates. The country must face the problem of ill–equipped schools and universities staffed by poorly paid teachers. There are pockets of excellence within the university system, but state universities tend to be chaotic, highly politicized, ill-adapted to the requirements of the 21st century, and often unprofessional in hiring staff. Surveys show that only 30% of students at the 23 universities attend courses regularly, while graduation rates are among the EU's lowest. One result is that about 5,000 Greek scientists and professors have gone abroad, mainly to America, to work. Greece also sends more students per capita to foreign universities (about 10%)

Greek student in Warsaw

278

Greece

than most other countries despite free tuition. Britain is the favorite choice, followed by America and Germany.

Some private universities have sprung up to fill gaps. But a government effort in 2007 to change the constitution to end the state monopoly on higher education by encouraging private not-for-profit universities failed. The very idea, along with tightening state funding, making academic standards stricter and imposing a time limit on completing degrees, sparked prolonged strikes and disturbing street violence in Athens in 2007. Only the deadline for students became law. Polls showed that 99% of respondents objected to the aggressiveness and vandalism of these riots. Students and teachers seem always to favor the status quo. But since both Prime Minister Karamanlis and opposition leader George Papandreou both studied at elite American universities, they will not likely give up on education reform.

No doubt drawing on his experience in the U.S., Papandreou proposed that a system of junior colleges be established for those applicants not accepted to the universities. Such reforms inevitably run into opposition by educational bureaucrats and the highly–revered professors. Nevertheless, a 1982 Higher Education Law replaced the earlier university system built around a few almighty professors with broader American–style departments. It also created about 2,000 new teaching positions and permits undergraduate representatives to participate in university decision making.

In 1987 two new institutions, the University of the Aegean and Ionian University, opened their doors to all Greek students on many Aegean and Ionian islands. These branch campuses strive both to provide practical education and to revive Greek literary and artistic traditions. The professors are encouraged to live at the university sites. This avoids the problems at mainland provincial universities, where professors often appear only briefly during the week before returning to Athens. Greek student life remains highly politicized, and lecture halls and laboratories are still overcrowded in the metropolitan universities.

Cultural Heritage

Many Greeks are aware that the country's rapid economic growth and modernization have sometimes done violence to Greece's cultural inheritance. This is very much the case with Athens. When it was declared to be the capital of the newly independent Greek nation in 1833, it was "nothing but a pile of filthy ruins," in the words of an Austrian historian, von Prokesch–Osten, who visited the village at that time. When the German archaeologist Ludwig Ross saw the settlement, which had only 5,000 largely poor inhabitants, he was astonished. "One has difficulty believing that one is in Athens!" The new king, Otto I of Bavaria, brought in noted German architects, such as Leo von Klentze, Ernst Ziller and Friedrich von Schinkel, who designed and built glittering neoclassical buildings for the city.

Unfortunately most of these buildings fell victim to the construction boom after World War II, a period when there was little interest in conserving the monuments of the past. "Growth" was the consuming reality, and no major city in Europe grew as fast as Athens. At the turn of the last century, it had 120,000 inhabitants. In 1920 it had already 300,000 and by 1950 it had reached a million. At the beginning of the 1960s the number had passed the two million mark, and by now greater Athens has almost five million inhabitants.

Almost miraculously, there are no slums in Athens, and the crime rate is lower than in any other major European city. But one must live amidst countless blocks of unembellished apartment build-ings, traffic jams and noxious clouds of smog, called *nefos* by the Greeks; it is a mixture of smoke, dust, sulphur dioxide, carbon monoxide and nitrogen oxides produced by industrial discharges and car exhaust gases. Surrounded by mountains, Athens is as vulnerable to air pollution as is Los Angeles and Denver. When it rains, the sulphur dioxide in the air turns into sulphuric acid that dissolves stone, especially the marble of the city's few remaining monuments.

The previous government tried to make a start at controlling this by limiting the use of high–sulphur oil, but this measure had little effect. It also halted the movement of new industries into the area. Cars with alternating license numbers were banned from the center city, but public transportation has been greatly improved in preparation for the 2004 Olympic Games. More trees were planted in order to beautify the dusty cityscape. The pollution problem has been somewhat alleviated since the Olympics. The Parthenon, which dominates Athens' horizon, is linked with the city's other antiquities in

Gazing down from the Acropolis . . . and looking back on the glory of ancient Greece

279

Greece

Priests and soldier commemorate patron saint of Serres

a new four-kilometer-long archaeological park to display the capital's magic during the 2004 spectacle.

The remaining classical structures in Athens can almost be counted on the fingers of both hands. The previous and present governments have mounted an all–out effort to save the most precious jewel of classical Greece: the Acropolis in Athens. This monument to man's sense of beauty and proportion has led a tortured existence. It has been battered by wars, earthquakes and plunder from such varied groups as barbarian invaders and British diplomats. During the Turkish occupation, the temples were converted into mosques, and at one point were even used to house the harem of the Turkish commander.

Many of the marble statues and friezes can be seen in the British Museum in London, and the Greek government has formally demanded their return. In 2004 former British Foreign Minister Robin Cook, supported by 50 MPs, launched "Marbles Reunited," an initiative of British citizens who believe that the Parthenon Marbles should be returned to Athens. British opinion polls in 2003-4 showed that up to 80% of respondents are in favor of restitution. The Greeks hoped in vain to have them back in time for the 2004 Olympics. On a much smaller scale, the Getty Museum in Los Angeles agreed to return a few ancient Greek artifacts taken illegally out of Greece.

The four major buildings remaining atop the 512–foot (158 meter) hill now face their most serious challenge: tourists and air pollution. Three million tourists visit the Acropolis each year. They not only marvel and walk upon the stones, but in a few cases scratch, pound or etch their names in the stones. The acid rain is an even more formidable enemy, eating away

at the marble. Earlier suggestions to cover the entire Acropolis with a plastic dome were rejected as unfeasible. But many original statues are being placed into museums and are replaced on the site by copies. Also, next to the Parthenon, the huge Doric temple that once housed the gigantic statues of the goddess Passas Athena was closed to tourists. Work is now being done on all the temples to strengthen them. By the time the restoration is completed, the 230 restorers will have worked twice as long as the original builders and sculptors in the 5th century B.C. One stonemason on the project marveled at his ancient counterparts: "The attention to detail, the huge amount they knew about working marble—it makes you feel you're a beginner."

At one time one could wander and climb unimpeded within this magnificent structure, but now one may view it only from the outside. In anticipation of the eventual return of the Parthenon Marbles, a new museum opened in 2008 at the foot of the Acropolis that houses all the sculptures from the temples. It includes a huge empty space exactly the size of the Parthenon so that the 54 meters of frieze remaining in Athens can be reunited with the other 75 meters in London. This would allow the original sculptures to be seen in relation to each other as they once were. Other sculptures are displayed on the top floor surrounded by glass walls and roof so that the visitor can look back and forth at the Parthenon while admiring the art works.

Another segment of its heritage it fought hard to bring back to Greece is the Olympic Games, although no one contemplated trying to hold them in the ancient location. The first modern Olympics had been held in Athens in 1896. Greece's hopes to stage the centennial games in 1996 were dashed when Atlanta was picked over Athens. A stunned Melina Mercouri exclaimed: "Coca–Cola has prevailed over the Parthenon!" But jubilant Athenians won their bid to host the 2004 games.

Preparations for the 2004 games were long plagued by slow progress, infighting, sobering cost overruns, and worries about security. One special problem Greeks faced in rushing to finish all the needed construction projects was that builders had to be on the lookout for delicate remnants of the ancient past. When workmen turned up artifacts, work stopped immediately until archaeologists could be dispatched to the site, the artifacts were unearthed, photographed and documented,

Greek students at College of Europe, Bruges

A monastery on the Mount Athos peninsula

the information was passed on to the Hellenic Ministry of Culture, the Central Archaeological Council determined how to handle the findings, and archaeological excavation was completed. The costs for any such delays were borne by the builders. The Greeks hoped the games would provide an economic and development stimulus. They calculated an annual .5% boost in GDP until 2004, 30,000 to 40,000 new jobs per year, 14 new hospitals, 38 major new road works, and athletic and tourist facilities.

Foreign interest in the treasures of classical Greece remains strong. It is in part maintained by such institutions as the American School of Classical Studies located in Athens. This is an academy for rigorous classical scholarship and archaeological excavation founded a hundred years ago by a group of scholars from Harvard, Yale, Brown, Johns Hopkins and Cornell universities. It now has about 100 students and faculty from the U.S. and Canada and an endowment of $8 million. At the same time, Greeks maintain strong ties abroad, primarily with the U.S. There have been two waves of immigration to the U.S. in the 20th century, and now over three million people of Greek and Greek descent live permanently in the U.S. The third biggest Greek city in the world is Chicago, and Greeks in America have, on the whole, been very successful. They include not only such well-known entertainers as Maria Callas and Telly Savalas (Kojak), but former presidential candidate Michael Dukakis and ex-Vice President Spiro Agnew.

Greek-Americans form a potent lobby in the U.S. Congress. Sometimes they can even put pressure on Greece. For instance, in 1963 they erected a statue of President Harry Truman honoring his providing Greece with arms and money to defeat the communists in the Greek civil war. However, some Greeks saw this as a symbol of American tutelage. In 1986 left–wing extremists blew it off its pedestal. The former Socialist–Communist majority in the Athens city council voted to get rid of it altogether. At first Papandreou refused to intervene, but Greek–American delegations persuaded him to reconsider.

As elsewhere in the past, the Greek Orthodox Church holds the Greek communities in the U.S. and Canada together by organizing schools, cultural events and activities, social welfare and even camping holidays. As delighted audiences all over the world saw in the film, "My Big Fat Greek Wedding," this event is a rite and celebration that is unforgettable. Marriage remains strong in the homeland. Greeks marry more and divorce less than other EU citizens, and they have fewer children out of wedlock: 4% of births compared with Sweden's 55%.

Some progress has been made in the field of social reform, especially in matters involving women's rights. The 1974 constitution includes a provision that all laws that foster inequality between the sexes had to be wiped off the books. Such things are easier written than done in a country with such a powerful state church and in one which the man, as head of the household, always had the right to decide all family matters literally by decree.

The PASOK government was able to break the church's monopoly on marriage and to permit civil marriages. By the 1990s only three out of 20 couples in the cities married outside the church. But atheists can now marry in Greece. Further, there are no more criminal prosecutions for adultery. The government also prepared legislation to permit abortion on demand, although it in fact was already widely available. In the 21st century it has an exceptionally high incidence of abortion. Along with rising prosperity, this contributes to a dramatic plunge in the fertility rate. Combined with prodigious longevity, especially among women, this is having a frightening demographic effect. By 2015 the number of Greeks aged between 15 and 24 will have fallen by almost a quarter, and the number of octogenarians will have increased by 70%.

Parliament enacted in 1983 a series of important laws to protect women; it permitted divorce on mutually declared grounds of incompatibility and made it possible to name a child without baptism and to register the name with the civil authorities rather than with the church. It made it legal for a Greek woman to keep her own name after marriage, to have custody of small children, and to choose which schools they attend. It guaranteed to Greek women equal pay for equal work and forbade employers both to discriminate in hiring and to fire women for being pregnant. Greece has one of Europe's lowest percentages of women in the workforce. The government also proposed family planning centers and social benefits to unmarried mothers.

Orthodox Church

The Greek Orthodox Church remains influential in Greece although many Greeks no longer care about religion. Ex-

**His All Holiness
Ecumenical Patriarch Bartholomew**

Greece

cept for the Turkish–speaking minority concentrated in Thrace and constituting only about 1.5% of the total Greek population, 90% of Greek citizens are baptized and belong to the established church, whose position and powers are fixed in the constitution. At least five million adherents live abroad. Greece is the only country in the world today in which Orthodox Christianity is the official religion. Although only 4% of Greeks say they attend church regularly, religion remains a part of their daily lives.

The Ecumenical Patriarch of the Orthodox Church (currently Bartholomew) is the spiritual head of world Orthodoxy, but he has no jurisdiction over the Church of Greece. Since the great split with the Roman Catholic Church, he has always resided in Istanbul (formerly Byzantium), Turkey. Life in Islamic Turkey has not been easy for the patriarch, who must be a Turkish citizen and travel with a Turkish passport. His flock within Turkey has shrunk to only 3,000. During crises between Turkey and Greece, he must worry about being expelled from Istanbul, thereby surrendering his primacy over the other Orthodox patriarchs, especially the Russian Orthodox leader, as heir to the Byzantine tradition.

His place as head of world Orthodoxy is tenuous. Relations with the resurgent Russian Orthodox Church are not good. By tradition he is considered the first among equals over 135 million adherents of Orthodox Christianity, including 1.5 million in the U.S. He was permitted to restore the shabby buildings of his patriarchate, in part because of an appeal made to Turkey by former President Carter.

The church has, in the past, been able to use its influence to delay social reforms. In causing these delays it sacrificed much of its prestige in a society that is increasingly secular. The government had widespread approval for its plans to cut off state financial aid to the church and to amend the constitution in order to make all religions equal in the eyes of the law.

It also continued the efforts begun by New Democracy aimed at expropriating the landed wealth of the church, which, after the state, is Greece's largest property and enterprise owner. It owned forest and agricultural land, office and apartment buildings, bank shares, islands and businesses, in addition to churches and monasteries filled with treasures. Much of its land had been abandoned by Turkish landowners, and the state has often challenged the church's claim to it. Much of

the land is not used at all, in part because it is too hilly or mountainous.

In 1987 parliament approved a bill expropriating the Church's huge, 350,000 acres of landholdings and distributing them to farm cooperatives. The bill also called for putting laymen in charge of church administration. In an expropriating mood, the government also announced plans to take over most of former King Constantine's property in Greece, estimated to be worth about $40 million. Not surprisingly, the church announced at first that it would not comply with the new law. An amicable face–saving compromise was found, though. In his first journey to Greece in a quarter of a century, the patriarch agreed to a church–state committee to administer monastic lands and to leave the rest of the property under the control of the Holy Synod.

The leader of the Orthodox Church inside Greece from 1998 until his death in 2008 was His Beatitude Archbishop Christodoulos of Athens and all Greece. Although he succeeded the late Seraphim, who had been put in power by the rightwing colonels who ruled Greece from 1967 to 1974, he found himself at loggerheads with the government. He was a tireless meddler in politics. His message was stridently nationalist, and he expounded the tired conspiracy theory that "the world's big powers are working against the interests of Hellenism." He railed especially against the "eastern barbarians" (the Turks) and called upon Greeks to "liberate Constantinople." Since Orthodoxy is the country's established religion, such populist pronouncements were especially embarrassing to Greece's diplomats. His popularity rating of 75% was far higher than any politician, and he was able to raise church attendance. He worked to heal the centuries-old grievances with the Roman Catholic Church, and in 2006 he met the Pope in Rome. But he avoided the sensitive subject of dogma.

Elected by a conclave of 74 bishops in the main cathedral in Athens to take his place was Metropolitan Ieronymos of Thebes, a 70-year-old bishop, who has not courted conflict. The process lasted only four hours, when bells pealed and the light of an ancient lantern outside flashed on to signal his election. Minutes later, dressed in traditional black robes, he appeared on a balcony to acknowledge the cheers of thousands of faithful. He was enthroned February 16, 2008.

In general the church's influence is declining, although it will remain for a long time a political, social and economic force to be reckoned with. In the rural, mountainous areas, attendance at the breathtaking, ritualistic services is very high. A curious custom exists in some of these areas—a shortage of land means a shortage of cemetery land. A person is buried for a certain number of years; the women of the parish then dig up the bones, clean them and place them in the cellar reliquary of the church together with those of thousands already there. A new burial plot is thus created.

One place where the religious flame also burns brightly is Mount Athos, or the Holy Mountain, as many Greeks call it. It dates back to the 7th century when a group of hermits fled there and founded their "Garden of God," and it is one of the world's oldest Christian communities. Covering 225 square miles in an isolated forested and mountainous peninsula in northern Greece, and overlooking treacherous waters in which many a seaman drowned, Mount Athos contained 180 monasteries sheltering more than 10,000 monks in the 11th century. Now it has shriveled to about 20 monasteries and only 1,400 monks (up from 1,146 in 1972).

Mount Athos is beset with numerous problems. One is that female tourists, who sail within sight of the monasteries and sometimes even land illegally, have challenged its longstanding total ban on women (and even on female animals). It can no longer maintain the 20 monasteries and 1,700 auxiliary buildings, the 300,000 feet of frescoes, the 20,000 icons, 13,500 Greek manuscripts and a vast collection of relics and treasures which are irresistible objects for thieves.

The Greek state gives Mount Athos about $300,000 annually, but neither this nor the income it derives from subsistence farming, rent from outside properties and timber trading enable the monks to make ends meet. The entire area is an autonomous republic within the Greek state, and it rules itself entirely through an annually elected governing body of 20 abbots. All the monks categorically refuse to unite or reconcile their differences with the western churches, which they regard as heretical and corrupt. They all criticize the Greek state's decision to open diplomatic relations with the Vatican, as well as the Orthodox Church's ecumenical steps toward the Catholic Church in Rome.

One group of 117 Esfigmenou monks, which regards the dialogue with the Vatican as betrayal, was branded by the patriarch as "schismatic" and was ordered off the sacred ground in 2003. They refused to budge and stocked enough food to last for a two-year siege. Their dispute was taken up by Greece's highest administrative court. One young member of the group drove a tractor accidentally off a cliff while trying to dodge the police during a standoff.

In all, a minority of about 300 zealots within the compound accuses the other monks of religious impurity. This fanatic minority struggles with them over control of the monasteries. On several occasions, the Greek police have been called in to deal with violent skirmishes between zealots and moderates. Still, all the monks agree that Mount Athos is a gateway to higher spiritual levels and ultimately to heaven. One abbot explained with confidence that "for the rest of the world, we are a lighthouse, battered by the waves, but still lighting the way, as we have done for centuries."

Media

Since 1974 Greece has been a country that enjoys freedom of speech, and Greek newspapers make full use of this liberty. Although the newspaper readership is low by western European standards (about 80 per 1,000), about 85 papers appear daily. Athens alone has 14 morning dailies. Few could survive without the tax–free newsprint and guaranteed loans provided by the state. Greece's large public banks also give aid. Although only two papers are official party organs, *Rizospastis* (Communist) and *Avgi* (radical right), most other papers have a clearly recognizable political line.

Most foreign observers remark that the journalistic standards of the Greek press are rather low, with sensationalism and extreme politicization taking priority over

Hermes (or Youth) 4th Century B.C. Athens National Museum

283

Greece

objective reporting. News columns tend to be as politicized as the editorial pages, but this seems to be what most Greek readers expect of their favorite newspapers. Only such Athens morning papers as the independent *Kathimerini* and the pro–socialist *To Vima* even make a stab at objective news reporting. In 1991 the editors of seven newspapers went to jail rather than comply with a new law which, precipitated by the 1989 assassination of Mitsotakis' son–in–law by the November 17 group, prohibited them from publishing statements from terrorists. This measure reminded too many Greeks of the censorship practices during the military dictatorship from 1967 to 1974.

There are three state–owned television channels: two in Athens (ET1 and NET) and one in Thessaloniki (ERT3). They are financed by the state and by advertising fees. Since 1989 there are also many private channels, which are financed by advertising fees: 10 major ones in Athens and 13 smaller ones in other large cities. Countless local community channels broadcast throughout Greece. The programming consists of American films (70%), Greek films (20–22%), other European programs, and the normal fare of news, sports, documentaries, interviews and entertainment. There is also a mix of state–owned and private radio stations.

After exhaustive consultation among political parties and other interests, a bill for regulating privately–owned press and media was introduced in parliament. The aim is to restrict the excessive concentration of media ownership and the development of communications monopolies. It would prohibit companies that accept contracts with the state to have ownership in a mass media company. Also, no individual would be permitted to own more than a 25% stake in a television station. Finally, it would prohibit simultaneous participation in more than two media categories, such as television and publishing.

FUTURE

The sight of a snow-covered Acropolis in Athens at the onset of 2002 demonstrated in purity what a changed nation Greece is. It is a country that is trying to absorb four decades of rapid economic and social change. A predominantly rural way of life and a traditional system of values have been largely swept away. Greek democracy has become sufficiently robust to absorb a good deal of passionate debate and unrest. Though chronic economic problems are difficult to solve, there is noticeable improvement.

New Democracy rules, led by American-educated Costas Karamanlis, who pledged to root out corruption, which is deeply entrenched in Greek society. He has not succeeded in keeping his own government beyond suspicion of corruption. Governments traditionally appoint party loyalists, not professionals, as pension-fund managers, a practice that does not render the best returns. His poll ratings tarnished by this embarrassment and by crippling nation-wide strikes protesting pension reform, Karamanlis called early parliamentary elections for September 2007. His New Democracy won a two-seat majority a whisker ahead of the opposition Socialists.

His government's most immediate concern upon assuming office was that the 2004 Olympic Games in August go well. Greece made a mad dash to finish the preparations and the sites. Pessimists were grumbling everywhere. Security concerns, cost overruns, and missed construction deadlines plagued the birthplace of the games right down to the last minute. But Greeks rose to the challenge. By any standards, this was one of the most successful games ever. There were no major security incidents. The country kept its promise to link its ancient and 21st-century games, and its credibility as a modern state, capable of organizing a world class event, soared.

Relations with Turkey improved, and the Karamanlis government continues to seek better ties with this former enemy. Differences over the long-standing division of the island of Cyprus will continue to make this difficult. Cooperation with Balkan neighbors, including Macedonia, will also remain good.

Relations with the U.S. are more harmonious than in decades, despite the Greek government's and people's staunch opposition to the war in Iraq. Political commentator Jim Hoagland noted in May 2005: "Resentments about Turkey or the United States, while hardly erased, are not the festering wound they once were in Greece." It remains to be seen if and when the U.S. will include Greece in its visa-waiver program, offered to all other Western European countries.

Greece's support of the U.S. antiterrorism campaign has been firm and unwavering, and that is likely to remain so. Within days of the September 11, 2001, terrorist attacks, Greece put sympathy ads into six major U.S. newspapers, reading: "Greece, the birthplace of democracy, mourns with America at this difficult hour. We have joined with the United States in the fight against terrorism. Our common values of freedom, democracy and humanism will prevail. Together we stand."

Greek letters on Euro notes

Goodbye to world's oldest currency!

The Republic of Cyprus

Marketwoman in Nicosia: "Try these luscious grapes!"

Area: 3,572 square miles (9,251 sq. km.), the third largest island in the Mediterranean.

Population: 766,400 Greeks Cypriots; 87,900 Turkish Cypriots, an estimated 80,000 Turkish settlers and about 30,000 Turkish troops in the North.

Capital City: Lefkosia (Nicosia) (Pop. 303,000).

Climate: Rainfall is usually moderate, but periodic droughts may be severe. Summers are usually hot, humid on the coasts, dry inland; winters are mild, except in the mountains.

Neighboring Countries: The island lies 40 miles from the southern coast of Turkey and 65 miles west of the Syrian coast.

Official Languages: Greek and Turkish. English is widely used.

Ethnic Background: The people are divided by language and tradition into Greeks (about 78%); Turks (about 18%); Armenian, Maronites and Latins (about 1%), foreigners (3%).

Principal Religions: Most Greek Cypriots profess Greek Orthodox Christianity; most Turkish Cypriots profess *Sunni* Islam, but tiny religious minorities also are found.

Chief Commercial Products: Grapes, citrus fruits, potatoes, and grain. Light manufactures include textiles, food products, and pharmaceuticals.

Major Trading Partners of Republic of Cyprus: U.K. (17% of exports and 8.6% of imports), Greece (8% of exports and 17% of imports), Italy (11% of imports), Germany (5.4% of exports and 8.9% of imports), France (3% of exports), Lebanon (3.4% of exports).

Currency: Euro in the South since 2008. Turkish Lira in the North.

Former Dependent Status: British Colony (1925–1960).

Independence Date: August 16, 1960.

National Day: October 1; November 15 (Turkish Republic)

Chiefs of State: Demetris Christofias, president of the Republic of Cyprus since March 2008. Mehmet Ali Talat, president of the Turkish Republic of Northern Cyprus since April 2005.

National Flag: White field with outline map of the island in rich gold above two sprigs of green leaves. The Turkish Cypriot flag has two horizontal red bars, and between them a red crescent, on a white field.

GDP per capita: $25,820 (2007). Half this figure for Turkish Cypriots.

Cyprus is a pleasant, often dry, island in the northeast part of the Mediterranean Sea, located 65 kilometers (40 miles) off Turkey's coast. Along the entire scenic sweep of the northern coast are the Kyrenia Mountains, often snow–capped in the winter. The higher Troödos range in the west central region, covered with forests and vineyards, is crowned by a peak reaching 6,401 feet above sea level. This lofty mountain is called Chionistra by Greek-speaking Cypriots, but in English it is often known as Mt. Olympus in imitation of the more famous mountain in northern Greece. Between the two mountain ranges lies the central plain of Mesaoria, a rich agricultural region surrounding the capital, Lefkosia (renamed in English from Nicosia in 1995). Thanks to the normally adequate rainfall that favors it, more than half the island's total area is cultivated.

History

As early as 6000 B.C. this island was inhabited by people who built curious round houses, herded sheep and goats,

285

Cyprus

raised a few crops and wove textiles. The first mention of the island in written records occurred in the Nile Valley, whose ancient inhabitants traded with it, as did the Phoenicians and Greeks at a later time. Christianity began to spread on the island in the first century A.D., when it was part of the Roman Empire. By the fifth century, a Cypriot Church with its own Archbishop was recognized.

Cyprus remained part of the Byzantine Empire until 1191, when Richard the Lion Hearted of England conquered the island on his way to the Holy Land as part of the Crusades. The following year King Richard sold Cyprus to Guy de Lusignan, a former Crusader king of Jerusalem. From the Lusignan period, which lasted until 1489, come numerous examples of Gothic architecture in the form of castles and fortifications.

The merchant states of Genoa and Venice in turn sought control of Cyprus as a link in their trade with the Orient. Genoa held the port of Famagusta from 1373 to 1464, but it was Venice which finally wrested control from the Lusignan rulers. Fearing competitors and the growing Ottoman Turkish Empire, the Venetians built massive fortifications at the main ports. They taxed the Cypriots heavily, required free labor from them and attempted to impose Latin Christianity on them, as the Lusignan rulers before them had also done.

Because of the unpopularity of the European rulers, the Cypriots were not unhappy to see the Ottomans drive them out in 1570-71. As Ottoman subjects, the Cypriots were permitted civil autonomy within their religious community. The reestablished office of Archbishop for the Cypriot Orthodox Church became their link with the Ottoman government. The important role of the religious community and its head has persisted up to the present in varying forms. Poor administration and heavy taxation later in the Ottoman period led to much dissatisfaction.

The Ottoman government agreed in 1878 to let Britain take over the administration of Cyprus, but not sovereignty. The Ottomans were to receive part of the revenues and, in case of need, British aid in warding off Russian encroachment on Turkey's northern borders. Following Turkey's entry into World War I on the side of Germany, Britain annexed Cyprus in 1914 and in 1925 gave it the status of a Crown Colony. Britain continued to regard it mainly as a military base to defend the Suez Canal. It therefore did not pay much attention to the internal affairs until they became difficult after World War II.

The grievances of the Greek Cypriots, aggravated by an economic depression after World War II, found political form in the idea of *enosis* (union) with Greece. Some Greek Cypriots had long felt themselves part of the Greek nationalist movement. *Enosis* basically rejected Cypriot independence in favor of becoming part of Greece. As the idea gained support among Greek Cypriots, opposition to it grew among the Turkish Cypriot minority.

When the determined and energetic Makarios was elected archbishop and ethnarch of the Cypriot Orthodox Church in 1950, the *enosis* movement gained more political impact. British concessions came too late, and rioting came to characterize life on Cyprus. Murder and intimidation accompanied the breaches of the peace after the formation in 1955 of the EOKA, an underground military force.

Pressed by worsening conditions, negotiators from Britain, Greece, and Turkey met with representatives of both Cypriot communities and finally reached agreement in Zurich in 1959. The Zurich Agreement rejected both union with Greece and partition of the island. Instead, it granted Cyprus independence under a constitution containing collective safeguards for the Turkish minority. Britain, Turkey and Greece received the right to intervene, either jointly or singly, to uphold the constitution. Britain also retained sovereignty over about 99 square miles of territory for two military bases.

Archbishop Makarios

As specified in the constitution, Cyprus became independent with a Greek Cypriot president, Archbishop Makarios, and a Turkish Cypriot vice president, Dr. Fazil Küchük. However, independence did not dispel the old attitudes and suspicions. Turkish leaders used their constitutional veto to block laws and development programs allegedly favorable to the Greeks. Soon major government functions came to a halt, and in 1963 fighting broke out between the two communities. The constitution had failed to solve the conflict between the Greek Cypriot goal of majority rule throughout the island and the Turkish Cypriot goal of its partition.

To halt the violence, the United Nations voted to send peacekeepers (UNFICYP), who arranged cease-fire agreements between the two sides. They patrolled areas of possible renewed fighting. Established in 1964 for six months, this international force became the longest-serving group of UN peacekeepers.

For the next decade, general peace prevailed, but there was little cooperation between the two communities. The House of Representatives met with only the 35 Greek members present; the 15 Turkish members met separately and denounced the measures taken by the Greeks. Though representatives of the two factions met occasionally, they found no formula to resolve the constitutional issues. The Greek majority could not impose its will by force because of the constant threat of invasion by Turkey on behalf of the minority's interests.

The year 1974 proved critical. In January EOKA's leader died, and sentiment for *enosis* began to fade more rapidly. In sharp contrast to the multiparty democracy enjoyed by Greek Cypriots, Greece suffered a military dictatorship linked to NATO. Determined supporters of *enosis* saw the chances for union with Greece slipping away, and in a desperate effort engineered a coup by the National Guard. Archbishop Makarios himself barely escaped into exile.

The Turkish government seized the coup and the following disorders as an opportunity to invade Cyprus. Its forces attacked in July, rapidly seizing Greek-inhabited villages and towns in the north as well as Turkish ones. Successful in military terms, and arguably legal by the

Zurich agreement, the assault captured 37% of the island, ostensibly to protect the rights of 18% of the population.

The invasion displaced from 150,000 to 200,000 Greeks from their homes, farms, and businesses; an estimated 40,000 Turkish Cypriots fled in the opposite direction. The resort towns of Famagusta and Kyrenia lost practically their entire populations, and some small villages fell vacant. Other serious human rights violations included the disappearance and apparent execution of prisoners. Unique works of art and other antiquities were stolen from churches in the Turkish–occupied zone, a crime rendered easier by alleged neglect or even the connivance of officials and the military.

The invasion had an enormous political and economic effect on the Greek Cypriot community. It discredited the coup leaders, and Glafcos Clerides, speaker of the house, became acting president until Makarios returned. An expanded UNFICYP monitored an uneasy peace between the Turkish army and the Greek Cypriots along the "Attila Line" dividing the two zones.

When Makarios died in 1977, Spyros Kyprianou succeeded him, then won his own term. A hardliner, he demanded that the territorial division should be proportionate to the population of the two zones. In addition, he demanded a strong (and inevitably Greek) federal government. Equally uncompromising, the Turkish Cypriots continued to demand most of the territory north of the Attila Line (keeping

37% of the island for their 18% of the population) and virtual independence for their Turkish region. The two communities periodically bowed to international pressure and held talks on a settlement, but neither proved willing to compromise.

In 1981 Turkish Cypriot leaders finally approved an investigation of over 1,600 Greeks who had disappeared during the invasion, to little avail. In 1996, besides noting that hundreds of Turks were missing as well, Denktash finally publicly admitted the obvious: prisoners turned over to the Turkish–Cypriot militia had been executed.

In some technical cases the communities worked together. Water from the Turkish–held town of Morphou, purified by a Greek processing plant, was restored. The Greek sector supplies electric generating capacity for Turkish Lefkosa, while the sewage passes from the Greek to the Turkish side for treatment. Nevertheless, the Lefkosia (Nicosia) airport was closed, and the Varosha resort near Famagusta shuttered.

POLITICAL SYSTEMS

Political System in the South

The Republic of Cyprus has a presidential form of government. Under the 1960 constitution, the president is elected by universal suffrage to a five-year renewable term of office. If a candidate in a multiparty election does not succeed in winning an absolute majority in the first round of voting, there must be a runoff election between the two top vote-getters. The one who gets a simple majority wins.

The president is vested with executive power. He appoints and chairs the cabinet, called the Council of Ministers, which has 11 ministries. They are responsible for initiating legislation, coordinating and supervising the public services and finances and processing bills and the budget before they are presented to parliament. Members may be chosen from outside parliament, but they may not sit in the House of Representatives after joining the Council of Ministers.

The unicameral parliament—House of Representatives—was enlarged in 1985 to 56 seats, each elected by direct universal suffrage for five-year terms. The proportional representation electoral method is used, and parliamentary and presidential elections are not scheduled at the same times. Three seats elected in a separate vote are reserved for special representatives of the Maronite and Armenian minorities. Voting is compulsory, and heavy fines are levied for non-voting.

Parties range across the political spectrum. Those winning seats in the May 2006 parliamentary elections were: the

Turkish soldier guards Greek–Cypriot prisoners, July 1974

Cyprus

ΙΔΡΥΤΗΣ: ΝΙΚΟΣ ΧΡ. ΠΑΤΤΙΧΗΣ

ΓΡΑΦΕΙΑ: ΛΕΩΦ. ΒΥΡΩΝΟΣ αρ.36, 3ος ΟΡΟΦΟΣ και 34Β — 34° ΙΣΟΓΕΙΟ, ΜΕΓΑΡΟ «ΝΙΚΟΣΙΑ ΤΑΟΥΕΡ ΣΕΝΤΕΡ». ΤΗΛΕΦ. 463922 (12 ΓΡΑΜΜΕΣ) Τ.Κ. 1094. ΤΕΛΕΞ: 4999 PHILNEWS. ΤΗΛΕΦΑΞ: ΣΥΝΤΑΞΗ 366121, ΛΟΓΙΣΤΗΡΙΟ 366122. ΤΙΜΗ 25 ΣΕΝΤ

Ὁ ΦΙΛΕΛΕΥΘΕΡΟΣ

ΗΜΕΡΗΣΙΑ ΕΦΗΜΕΡΙΣ ΕΙΣ ΤΗΝ ΥΠΗΡΕΣΙΑΝ ΤΟΥ ΚΥΠΡΙΑΚΟΥ ΛΑΟΥ

20 ΣΕΛΙΔΕΣ
ΤΡΙΤΗ
3 Απριλίου 1990
ΛΕΥΚΩΣΙΑ, ΚΥΠΡΟΣ ΕΤΟΣ 35° ΑΡ. 1
ΤΗΛΕΓΡΑΦΗΜΑΤΑ: PHILELEFTHE
ΤΥΠΟΙΣ: Ὁ ΦΙΛΕΛΕΥΘΕΡΟΣ Α

ΛΕΥΚΩΣΙΑ ΕΝΩ ΕΤΟΙΜΑΖΟΝΤΑΙ ΟΙ ΕΝΑΛΛΑΚΤΙΚΕΣ ΕΙΣΗΓΗΣΕΙΣ

ΠΡΟΣ ΠΑΓΚΟΜΜΑΤΙΚΗ ΤΩΡΑ ΣΤΗΝ ΑΘΗΝΑ

Αμέσως μετά τις εκλογές

ΔΙΑΦΩΝΕΙ Ο Γ.Γ. ΤΟΥ ΑΚΕΛ

Γράφει: Α. Λυκαύγης

Η ΣΥΓΚΡΟΤΗΣΗ ευρείας σύσκεψης στην Αθήνα, με συμμετοχή των Κυπριακών κομμάτων και της νέας Κυβέρνησης που θα προέλθει από τις κάλπες της ερχόμενης Κυριακής, διαλαμβάνεται στα υπό μελέτη παραπέρα ενέργειες της Λευκωσίας σε σχέση με το Κυπριακό με στόχο, όπως γίνεται

Λένε ότι ο Νικολάου πλήρωσε το «πρόστιμο» στο Λονδίνο

Το ψευδοκράτος Ντενκτάς ισχυρίστηκε χθες ότι ο σπουδαστής Νίκος Νικολάου στον οποίο είχε επιβληθεί από ψευδοδικαστήριο πρόστιμο για δήθεν ζημιές που προκάλεσε σε αυτοκίνητο Τουρκοκυπρίου «το πλήρωσε (604 δολλάρια) στον αντιπρόσωπο της ΤΔΒΚ

ΛΕΜΕΣΟΣ

Τάφηκαν χωρίς νεκρώσιμη ακολουθία τα τέσσερα «θύματα μαγείας»

ΧΩΡΙΣ τη νενομισμένη νεκρώσιμη ακολουθία και χωρίς παρουσία οποιωνδήποτε στενών ή μακρυνών συγγενών τους, τάφηκαν χθες στη Λεμεσό οι τέσσερες αυτόχειρες της πρωτοφανούς «σφαγής» στο διαμέρισμα του θανάτου στη Λεμεσό. Κι' αυτό, αφού προηγήθηκε νεκροψία στα σε αποσύνθεση πτώματα τους, ενώ η Αστυνομία επεκτείνει τις έρευνες και προσπαθεί ν' αξιολογήσει κάποια στοιχεία και τεκμήρια,

ΛΕΜΕΣΟΣ ΣΤΙΣ 14 ΑΠΡΙΛΙΟ

Θάτσερ και Μπους συζητού το Κυπριακό κα αντιδρ έντονα η Αγκυρ

Τ Ο Κυπριακό έχει τοποθετηθεί στην ημερή διάταξη, των συνομιλιών ανωτάτου επιπέ που θα έχουν στις Βερμούδες, ο Αμερικανός π εδρος Τζωρτζ Μπους και η Βρεττανίδα πρω πουργός Μ. Θάτσερ στις 14 Απριλίου. Και όπ γράφει η Τουρκική εφημερίδα «Χουρριέτ»:

• Η ΑΓΚΥΡΑ αντέδρασε ήδη έντονα, χαρακτηρίζοντας την εξέλιξη αυτή, ως «αντίθετη προς τις καλές υπηρεσίες του Πέρεζ ντε Κουεγιάρ».
Παρόλο, προσθέτει η εφημερίδα ότι «ήταν αμοιβαία δεν

Μπήκε στα κατεχόμενα συνελήφθη

Lefkosia's *O Phileleftheros* headlines the Third Interparliamentary Union Congress held in Cyprus in April 1990

communist Progressive Party of the Working People (Akel), which won 31.1%, the moderate nationalist Democratic Party (Diko), which grew to 17.9%, the Movement for Social Democracy (Edek), which captured 8.9%, the right-of-center Democratic Rally (Disy), which received 30.3%, and the new right-wing European Party, which got 5.8%.

In the February 2008 presidential elections, former President Tassos Papadopoulos was surprisingly eliminated in the first round of voting. Emerging as victor was Demetris Christofias of the communist Akel party. With 53.5% of the votes in the second round, he defeated Yiannakis Kassoulides of the Democratic Rally party, who won 46.4%. Christofias was backed in the final round by the Democratic Party.

Aged 59 at the time of his election, Christofias is a populist politician who had studied political science in Moscow and still speaks fluent Russian. He is the first Communist to run for the presidency and is the first Communist ever to rule in an EU country. Despite the facts that Akel has not formally renounced Marxism-Leninism and that his supporters waved as many red banners as Cypriot flags at his victory celebration in a soccer stadium, he is no red firebrand. He owes his victory to the nationalist Democratic Party, whose support he needs. He has abandoned Akel's former euroskeptic position, and his party is friendly toward business. In fact, it controls a wide range of businesses, including an investment company. He as-

serted: "We shall become Eurofighters struggling on behalf of the poor."

The independent judiciary is modeled on the British system. A Supreme Court stands above lower Assize and District Courts. Most statutes and regulations relevant to business are in English.

Political System in the North

The 1985 constitution for the "Turkish Republic of Northern Cyprus" provides for a strong president, a prime minister, and an elected legislature of 50 seats. Although the constitution allows for an independent judiciary, individual freedoms are more limited than in the South. Military forces from mainland Turkey control the local police, and journalists questioning such links have been arrested on dubious charges.

In December 2003 a landmark parliamentary election ended in a draw. The Republican Turkish Party, which supported the Annan Plan for reunifying the island, won more votes than Rauf Denktash's National Unity Party, which opposed it. But both received 25 seats apiece. In effect, the election was a referendum on Denktash's rejection of the UN plan. The two parties had no alternative to forming a coalition government in January 2004.

New parliamentary and presidential elections were held in 2005. In February voters in the north sent a strong message to the EU to end their political and economic isolation. They returned then Prime Minister Mehmet Ali Talat and his Republican Turkish Party to parliament with 24

of 50 seats. Talat said he wanted "to extend the hand of friendship to the Greek Cypriot government."

As in the south, the political system is characterized by a strong presidency elected for a renewable five-year term. In April 2005 Talat easily won the presidential election with 56% of the votes on a platform of reuniting the divided island and joining the EU. He appealed to the EU and UN to put fresh impetus into reunification efforts.

After the 1974 invasion, the Turkish community organized itself north of the Attila Line (Green Line) across the island that the Turkish troops had established. In the absence of an agreement, the Turkish–Cypriot Legislative Assembly proclaimed the independent "Turkish Republic of

President Demetris Christofias of Cyprus

Northern Cyprus" in 1983. Only Turkey recognized this new state, while the Security Council of the UN asked that the independence move be withdrawn. Rauf Denktash, the former vice president of the entire island, became president.

Despite surviving for a generation, the Turkish sector technically remains an international illegality. It is recognized only by Turkey although the EU offered in 2004 to provide it with financial and trade benefits. Travelers can fly to northern Cyprus only from Turkey, greatly hindering business and tourism. Its products lack convenient access to foreign markets. International copyright laws are often not honored, thus permitting local bargains in counterfeit sports clothing and videos.

Per capita incomes now average only about one-half the Greek level. Even this meager existence depends on subsidies from mainland Turkey, which funds most major public works and is the main employer. However, this requires use of the Turkish Lira, one of the least valued currencies anywhere. It thus condemns the island's Turks to inflation sometimes reaching 100%.

The Turkish Cypriot state is starved of capital, faces a trade boycott, attracts few foreign investors, and lures less than a tenth of the tourists that are vacationing in the south. Despite the economic crisis, Rauf Denktash, nicknamed "Mr. No" for his intransigence, repeatedly won reelection as president. However, in early 2003 and again in April 2004, massive demonstrations against his uncompromising rejection of a compromise with the Greek Cypriots showed that he no longer held much public confidence. He was forced to step down.

THE SEARCH FOR CYPRIOT UNITY

Initial attempts to bring peace to the island during the 1970s and 1980s failed even in the humanitarian task of discovering the fate of the 1,600 Greeks and 800 Turks listed as missing persons. Greece suffered a shocking setback in 1983 when Turkish Cypriots declared an independent "Republic of Northern Cyprus," thereby undercutting UN efforts to find a solution to that conflict. Currently 1,200 UN peacekeepers patrol the line that divides the two communities, and the capital city of Lefkosia (Nicosia) is the world's last divided capital.

The Greeks long suspected that the Turks might try to seize other Greek islands lying close to the Turkish coast. Although such fears may seem farfetched, the Turks maintain a 125,000–man Army of the Aegean equipped with 110 landing craft on their southwestern coast. Turkish politicians have sometimes refused to rec-

Rauf Denktash
Ex-Leader of the Turkish–Cypriots

ognize that the Aegean islands are Greek, and they actually demonstrated in Cyprus that they were willing to use military means to back up their aspirations in the area. In 1996 U.S. diplomatic intervention was required to defuse a crisis over Turkish occupation of an uninhabited Greek island, Imia. Greeks conveniently forget that the Greek majority in Cyprus, particularly under Archbishop Makarios, had sometimes abused the Turkish minority Cypriots.

In 1992, the UN Secretary General proposed a "bi–zonal and bi–communal" settlement that required concessions from each side. "Bi-zonal" implied that the Greeks would have to abandon demands for one strong government for the whole island. Instead, a weak central administration would have been limited mostly to customs, the post office, the central bank, and the diplomatic corps. The two ethnic

zones would have remained and administered themselves with great autonomy. This would have required the Turkish community to accept the withdrawal of most Turkish military forces and a reduction in the size of the zone from 37% to 28%. This would have allowed one–third of the 1974 refugees to return to their homes while the other Greek and Turkish refugees would receive compensation. This proposal was unacceptable to both sides.

Greece's long-standing position until 2004 was that the Greek Cypriot side is the only legitimate government and the Turkish part was a breakaway entity that must rejoin the national government. Further, Turkish troops and settlers had to be withdrawn, and effective guarantees had to be given to a Cypriot Republic. The Turkish position until 2004 was that all talks must presuppose equal legitimacy of the two sides and that any solution must be based on a federation of two separate Cypriot states.

Former Greek Cypriot President Glafcos Clerides spurned earlier UN talks on Cyprus. To strengthen his hand, he won Russian agreement to sell 300 sophisticated surface–to–air missiles. The Turks said they would destroy them the moment they arrive. Also, a 1993 defense pact with Greece permitted construction of a military air base at Paphos that could accommodate Greek F–16s deployed there in time of crisis. One American official noted that "these are acid concerns for Turkey-Greek jets and Russian missiles on Cyprus." To prevent military conflict, an American diplomatic mission in 1997 got Clerides to postpone receipt of Greek F–16s. He also announced that the Russian missiles would not be deployed on Cyprus. Instead they were removed in 1999 to the Greek island of Crete, placing

A Greek Orthodox priest at his easel

Cyprus

ANGUISH: Clutching large photographs of missing loved ones, mothers and wives plead for information about men who have not been heard from since the Turkish invasion of July 1974, a full generation ago.   Courtesy: Embassy of Cyprus

One clear impetus behind the negotiations was "accession", the planned expansion in 2004 of the European Union to include Cyprus and nine other nations. Partly because it met the economic criteria for membership, and partly because Greece had threatened to veto all other new members if Cyprus was not admitted, the EU governments pledged to admit Greek Cyprus even without a settlement over the Turkish zone.

Despite months of negotiations with Clerides and even urgings by the Turkish prime minister, in early 2003 Denktash rejected a new UN plan accepted by the EU. Ironically, his rejection diminished the pressure for a Greek acceptance of the UN plan. It featured strongly in the presidential elections of early 2003, when President Clerides promised that if elected, he would serve only until Cyprus joined the Union. However, Tassos Papadopoulos, his leading rival and strong critic of the UN plan, managed to unite both right-wing and left-wing against Clerides. He defeated him, ending Clerides' 40 years at the helm of the island's politics. As the Greek Cypriot leader during the final negotiations, Papadopoulos demanded better terms for Greek refugees from areas that would remain Turkish.

Things moved very quickly in 2003 in the wake of the EU's "big bang" enlargement. Voters went to the polls in the north and strongly backed pro-settlement politicians in local elections. In February a third of the population in the north gathered in a huge demonstration and marched through the streets shouting anti-Denktash slogans and carrying signs reading, "Yes to peace, Yes to the EU." On February 28 UN Secretary General Kofi Annan met in The Hague with the leaders

Turkey well outside of the missiles' 90–mile range.

In 1997 the EU decided to consider Cyprus' application for membership, but it rejected Turkey's three–decade–old application. Greece refused to allow a linkage between Greek Cypriot EU entry and a final settlement of the island's division. It threatened to veto further EU expansion if such a linkage were made. The EU ultimately accepted Greece's position in 1999. Turkey objected in vain to an arrangement whereby a Greek Cypriot government would be admitted to the EU, while Turkish Cyprus and Turkey itself were left out. That could end Turkey's chances of ever joining because accession decisions are made by unanimous consent.

To the north of the dividing line, resentment among Turkish-Cypriots grew toward the presence and role of the 30,000 Turkish troops, in addition to the approximately 80,000 Turkish settlers who came since 1974. Turkish-Cypriots, who number about 100,000, find themselves in a minority *vis-à-vis* these settlers and soldiers. They were almost completely dependent on Turkish government handouts. For these reasons, public opinion in the north swung heavily in favor of a settlement that would have permitted the entire island to join the EU in 2004.

After two decades of discussing the bizonal, bi-community proposal, Denktash broke off negotiations in 2000. He demanded a new framework: a confederation of two independent states. While the practical difference may be nil between a

federation of autonomous regions and a confederation of independent states, Greek Cypriots feared that the Turkish terms amounted to creeping recognition for the northern republic.

Hopes rose on both sides of the buffer zone after the Cypriot President, Glafcos Clerides, met with Denktash several times in late 2001 and early 2002, even crossing into the Turkish zone. Taking a humanitarian approach to the missing persons, they sought to find mass graves and identify the dead, rather than concentrate on details of their capture.

Ancient theater at Curium (Limassol)

of both parts of the island to ask them if they accepted his compromise plan to have a referendum on unification a month later. The Greek Cypriot president said yes, but Denktash said no, thereby having to bear the stigma of sabotaging the UN plan. In April the south turned down his offer of a six-point confidence-building plan just two weeks before Greek Cypriot leaders signed the EU accession document at the Union's summit meeting in Greece on April 16. In July parliament approved entry unanimously.

In an attempt to prevent isolation and to keep the pot from boiling over, Denktash stunned everybody the end of April 2003 by throwing open the three-decade-old dividing line between the two parts and allowing citizens from both areas to cross into the other side for one-day stays. Within a week, 160,000 Cypriots had flooded both ways over the border to visit their old homes, to observe how the other people live, and to see for themselves just how much each community had grown apart from each other. Most found the mingling experience exhilarating. Cyprus' most famous refugee is Titina Loizidou. In December 2003 the European Court of Human Rights ordered Turkey to pay her 1.2 million euros ($1.7 million) for denying her the "peaceful enjoyment of her property" in Kyrenia. Similar cases are likely to follow.

Other long-awaited steps quickly followed, including reopening telephone lines, clearing minefields, removing trade barriers on Turkish goods, granting work permits and health benefits to Turkish Cypriots, and making it possible for Orthodox Christian Greek Cypriots to marry Muslim Turkish Cypriots. By the end of 2003, there had been 2.2 million border crossings; around 6,000 Turkish Cypriots cross into the more prosperous south each day in order to work or seek medical care. The government in the south was ambivalent and tried to put moral pressure on its citizens not to go north and spend money, particularly in hotels which it described as "stolen property." Nevertheless, the mutual fear that sustained the Cyprus problem for so long has largely disappeared. Some southerners visit the 20 casinos in the North since the Orthodox Church opposes such establishments in the South.

Denktash rejected an EU offer of eased trade restrictions and a $14 million aid package in June 2003, arguing that it was an attempt to force his republic to submit to the internationally recognized Greek Cypriot government. The northern leader found himself in a difficult position.

The Annan Plan, 2004

In 2004 a UN plan devised and personally negotiated by General Secretary Kofi Annan, and strongly supported by the EU and the United States, brought the two sides as close to accepting an agreement as they had ever been. The formation in January of a new Turkish Cypriot coalition government that included the Republican Turkish Party, which supports a settlement to end the division, set the stage for a new round of unification talks.

On February 13 the leaders of Greece and Turkey accepted the UN road map for reunification before Cyprus joined the European Union on May 1. Turkish Prime Minister Recep Tayyip Erdogan decided to put his weight behind an agreement because he knew that a settlement of the Cypriot issue is a precondition for Turkey's opening of negotiations to join the EU. It has been an official candidate for membership since 1999. He persuaded the Turkish generals that his way, not the obstructionist tactics of Turkish Cypriot President Denktash, was best for Turkey's future. Erdogan acted courageously in reversing decades of Turkish policy.

For several years the leaders of the Greek and Turkish governments had worked to lower the tensions between the two former arch enemies. In October 2003 they had decided to cancel their annual naval exercises in the eastern Mediterranean and not to participate in planned naval war games with their rival communities on Cyprus.

Six weeks of intensive UN-sponsored talks followed in New York, Cyprus and Switzerland. In the end, the two Cypriot presidents were unable to agree. But under the February 13 accord, they were obligated to help the UN organize separate referenda on Annan's plan, scheduled for April 24, 2004.

The UN plan called for a federation of two politically equal states under a weak central government. A "United Cyprus Republic" would handle relations with the EU. It would be governed by a nine-member presidential council of six Greek Cypriots and three Turkish Cypriots. Three members would have no voting rights, thereby insuring that the Greek majority could not simply outvote the Turkish minority. The presidency would be by rotation.

The area under Turkish control would have been reduced from 37% to 29% of the land area, allowing 120,000 Greek Cypriots to return to their homes and live under Greek Cypriot administration. The port city of Famagusta would be returned to the Greek Cypriots. Approximately 50,000 Turkish Cypriots would have been uprooted. There would be limitations on the settlement of one ethnic group in the area controlled by the other for 19 years, or until Turkey had entered the EU, whichever came first. Finally, Turkey and Greece would gradually reduce their military presence on the island from the present 35,000 Turkish and 6,000 Greek soldiers to no more than a total of 1,600 by 2018.

In the lead-up to the referendum on both sides of the line, the presidents of both parts of Cyprus opposed the plan. Most Greek Cypriots largely objected to limits on the right of *all* Greek Cypriot refugees to return to the homes they had fled in 1974, while permitting tens of thousands of Turkish settlers who arrived after the 1974 invasion to stay. In other words, not all Greeks could reclaim their lost property. Most Turkish Cypriots favored the plan because it was their ticket to greater prosperity and membership in the EU. The Greek Cypriots were aware that they would enter the EU on May 1 no matter what the outcome of the referendum in their part of the island. They would then have a veto over the future EU entry of both Turkish Cyprus and Turkey itself. Turkish Cypriots knew that they would enter the EU only if voters in *both* parts of Cyprus accepted the plan.

The outcome of the referenda on April 24, which was the first time Cypriots had ever had a chance to vote on any peace plan since 1974, was disappointing but not surprising. With a turnout of 88% in the south and 87% in the north, the results were predictable: 76% of Greek Cypriots rejected the plan, while 65% of Turkish Cypriots voted in favor of it. Opinion polls showed that three-quarters of Greek Cypriots opposed the UN blueprint because they distrusted Turkey. They believed that the Annan Plan offered too little restitution for the more than 160,000 people who were forced to flee to the south during the 1974 invasion. It would have left too many Turkish soldiers on the island (6,000) pending a withdrawal plan whose execution was not guaranteed. Turkish Cypriots sensed that they were on the brink of a historic change, and many supporters demonstrated outside the home of Rauf Denktash urging him to resign.

Denktash remained rejectionist to the end, promising to step down if the plan had been accepted. In practice, however, he had seen his power diminished as a growing number of moderate Turkish Cypriots showed that they want to coexist with like-minded Greeks. They won a moral victory by casting off their previous image as the main obstacle to a unified federal republic, which both sides claim to want. Cyprus became the only European country with UN peacekeeping forces (1,200) patrolling its interior.

Current Situation

On May 1, 2004, the Greek Cypriot republic entered the EU under a cloud of re-

Cyprus

sentiment for having turned down a compromise that many outside observers considered fair. The EU moved immediately to share the benefits of EU membership with both parts of the island and to send a positive signal to those in the north who had voted "yes." It agreed to end the economic isolation of northern Cyprus by allowing Cypriot goods to pass freely over the partition line without the need to prove that they are of purely local origin. These goods would enter the EU tariff-free. This would be a long step toward ending the international trade embargo against the north imposed in 1974.

To reward the north further, the EU decided to redirect to its use 259 million euros ($390 million) originally earmarked to back a political settlement. It made another offer of 139 million euros ($210 million) in 2006. Through maneuvering in Brussels, the Greek Cypriot government prevented all these steps from being taken. The north also added its own complication, refusing to accept the aid until its ports and airports are opened to EU traffic.

In the face of withering international criticism, former Greek Cypriot President Tassos Papadopoulos insisted that UN efforts to reunite the island would continue despite his own energetic opposition to them. He also pledged not to use his island's EU membership to block Turkey's effort to join. Few believed that. He added a proviso: Turkey must behave "like a European country" and adhere to European law and principles. Papadopoulos's true stance was intransigence rather than to work with the Talat government in the north. The UN-backed plan to reunify Cyprus as a bi-zonal federal state was on extended hold. Polls showed that three-quarters of Greek Cypriots continued to oppose the UN plan, and 48% in 2006 favored living separately from Turkish-Cypriots, while only 42% wanted to co-exist.

The South has a hammer hold on Turkey whose start of accession talks in October 2005 complicates matters. Ankara

**President Mehmet Ali Talat
of Turkish Cyprus**

agreed to sign a protocol to its customs union with the EU in 2005. But it emphasized that this did not mean it recognized the Greek Cypriot administration. Nor would it open its ports and airports to all EU members until the embargo against Northern Cyprus and its ports is lifted. It was unacceptable to some EU countries for a country to want to join an organization without recognizing one of its members. Progress stalled.

Cypriots on both sides of the line are entitled to European citizenship, and Turkish Cypriots have the right to request Cypriot passports. Many apply for a Greek-Cyprus passport so that they can work within the EU. "We're fed up with being isolated," said one businessman. "We want to join Europe." About 40,000 Turkish-Cypriots had received Greek-Cypriot passports by 2006, and others were in line to get them. These enable them to work outside their northern enclave and to vote or run for office in Greek-Cypriot elections. More than 30,000 immigrant workers are employed in the south, and 6,000 Turkish Cypriots cross the Green Line every day to work in the south, mainly in the booming construction industry.

In January 2007 Turkish Cypriot authorities sent a positive signal by ordering the demolition of a foot bridge that had been an obstacle to opening up Ledra Street, the main thoroughfare that runs through the heart of the city's tourist area. The South responded two months later by tearing down a heavy wall that had separated the two parts of the capital for four decades and replacing it with less daunting sheets of aluminum. However, it made clear that civilians could not cross it freely until Turkey removed its troops stationed in the area. This particularly ugly part of the "green line" had stretched along Ledra Street.

The February 2008 presidential victory of Demetris Christofias, who had been a rejectionist in the previous election but now pledged to "build bridges," showed that Cypriots on both sides want an end to division. Both the candidate he defeated, Yiannakis Kassoulides, and Northern Turkish President Mehmet Ali Talat, who stems from the same leftist camp as Christofias, promised to support his efforts. This signaled an end to a four-year stalemate in bringing the two parts of Cyprus together.

The two presidents met and decided to restart formal peace talks. They promptly ordered that the Ledra Street crossing be opened. Although the Turkish Cypriots had opened five other checkpoints in the preceding years, this one is especially symbolic because it is in the heart of Nicosia. Mines had to be removed, and

Turkish soldiers stationed there had to be moved out of sight. This dramatic step will help revitalize the center of the divided capital, parts of which had practically become a ghost town. Another successful confidence-building measure is the launching of investigations, funded by the EU and bilateral donors, to locate the sites of mass graves of victims of the 1974 war, exhume the remains and identify as many as possible for the families.

The EU was relieved to see former President Tassos Papadopoulos defeated. He had irritated them no end by exploiting the South's EU membership to force Turkey to accept concessions over Cyprus and to stymie EU-funded projects in the North. But northern President Talat is also burdened by having to follow Turkey's guidance on major issues. However, with pro-settlement leaders on both sides, the chances of a successful outcome are much greater.

CULTURE

Cypriots, whether Greek or Turkish, Christian or Muslim, share a number of basic cultural traits. In both groups the rural population is generally poorer than the city dwellers. Women of both groups traditionally led rather restricted lives and with very few exceptions did not participate in public life nor enter the professions. That is slowly changing. Greek Cypriot women increasingly enter the professions and exercise rights similar to those in the rest of Europe. The two communities were already socially separate before the geographical separation of 1974. This social avoidance resulted from reciprocal suspicions and hostility rooted more in tradition and emotion than in culture.

It has not been the similarities, but the differences that have been emphasized by the two communities. This is reflected by the remark: "There are no Cypriots living on Cyprus, only Greeks and Turks." In the cities, members of the two communities often cannot be distinguished by appearance, but in the countryside the style of clothing worn is frequently distinctive. They celebrate different holidays. The Greeks celebrate Easter in the spring, while the Turks celebrate their Islamic *Bairam* (at the time of pilgrimage to Mecca) at different times in each year according to a lunar calendar. Then the national holidays of Greece are observed by one community, while those of Turkey by the other.

Greek Cypriots traditionally dominated trade and industry, and this gave Turks the feeling that they were economically oppressed although relative to their numbers Turks traditionally owned more farmland. Education in the respective communities has tended to follow the systems used in Greece and Turkey and was largely separate even before 1974. Those countries are also the sources of most of the books and periodicals read by the two communities.

For decades, Cypriot students wishing to study most disciplines at the university level were forced to go abroad, and a high proportion did so. However, the University of Cyprus opened in 1992, incorporating the existing teacher–training institute. There are now 10 universities on the island after three colleges in the South were upgraded to university status in 2007. The six Turkish universities in the North have 32,500 students, most from mainland Turkey. The four southern universities educate 5,500 students. Three of them are private: European University Cyprus, Frederick's University and Nicosia University.

The Greek Cypriot government refuses to recognize any institution of higher learning in the North. This means that degrees from Turkish Cypriot universities are not recognized in Western Europe. Nevertheless, fewer than 100 Turkish Cypriot students cross the border to study in the South. Scholars in the South are prohibited from collaborating with their counterparts in the North. They are even discouraged from traveling there, especially with students. A Nicosia University dean lamented: "Students from both communities show a marked lack of curiosity about their compatriots."

Greek-Cypriot student at the College of Europe, Bruges

ECONOMY

The agricultural contribution to the economy varies, owing to occasional severe droughts. Water from the small rivers is used for irrigation, but this is insufficient during an extended period of below-average rainfall. So great has been the shortage of water that running water was not always available in homes. However, several desalination plants in Greek areas now ensure sufficient water there for households, industry and some irrigation. Tankers can transport water from Turkey to the northern zone.

The largest share of arable land is sown in cereal crops, but there is not enough grain produced to meet domestic needs. Production of olives, an important part of the diet, likewise falls short of domestic requirements. The agricultural exports are mainly citrus fruits, potatoes, raisins, carob beans and wine. The Orthodox Church is the largest landowner, a fact that lends it secular influence in the countryside.

Although copper was previously the chief Cypriot export—indeed, the island's name comes from the mineral—mining currently plays only a minor role in the economy. Light industry expanded substantially in recent years, and the British bases provide both jobs and foreign exchange. Nevertheless, the island still imports a far greater value of goods than it exports. The island's only globalized industry is shipping. By 2005 the Cypriot-flagged fleet totaled 1,084 vessels, down from 1,475 in 2000. This makes it the world's eighth largest fleet, down from fourth a few years earlier.

The 1974 Turkish invasion necessitated a drastic reorganization of the economy. For instance, all of the tobacco farms and more than half of the citrus groves and grain lands fell under Turkish occupation although they were mostly owned by Greek Cypriots exiled to the south. Though not as experienced in this work, Turkish Cypriots took over these agricultural resources. Citrus fruit now comprises half of the exports from the Turkish zone.

Although more than half of the tourist facilities are in the 37% of the island occupied by Turkey, few tourists go there aside from a half million Turks each year. All tourists to the north must fly over Turkey since there are no direct flights into northern Cyprus from elsewhere. The opening of the border for Cypriots does not apply to foreign visitors. The south bans tourist visits from the north.

By contrast, Greek Cypriots who were cut off from the hotels and restaurants they owned at Famagusta, Kyrenia and elsewhere, have built new tourist centers in the south, mainly along the southern coast. So well managed is their tourist business that the number of visitors both from Europe and Arab countries has grown by leaps and bounds. Britain alone accounts for 55% of the tourists. With more than two million tourists each year, the number of tourists entering the country triples the size of the south's population. Their need for hotels and apartments boosts the construction industry. Tourism is the main industry in the Cypriot economy, accounting for 12% of GDP in 2007 (down from more than 20% in 2002) and about 45% of foreign earnings. A problem is that it is rated a more expensive destination than its rivals Greece and Turkey.

Both sides are experiencing a property boom, especially in second-home sales, triggered by entry into the EU in 2004. This opened up the property market to non-Cypriot citizens. In the three years following membership, more than 120,000 such homes were purchased by foreigners. In the north, construction on land formerly belonging to Greek Cypriots is a source of division and tension. The Turkish Cypriot government had transferred deeds to Turkish Cypriots from the south, settlers from the Turkish mainland and the Turkish military. In the south most families own their own homes, and many have villas or apartments by the sea. President Talat argues that the property issue cannot be settled through individual claims in court, but only as part of an overall political settlement.

Violence and difficulties elsewhere in the Middle East presented Cyprus with the opportunity to become a center for banking, insurance, and shipping activities. In 2007, financial services accounted for about 7% of GDP, and the number of foreign companies registered increases by 20% annually. Simple regulations and a skilled population encourage companies to locate regional headquarters on the island.

The Greek Cypriot republic's bank secrecy attracts funds in need of laundering and avoidance of taxation. It has become a tax haven. Foreign currency deposits held by non-residents constitute about half of total bank deposits. The largest expatriate community is Russian, with an estimated 35,000 residents around the port of Limassol. An investigation by the UN War Crimes Tribunal in The Hague revealed that the Serbian government of Slobodan Milosevic had transferred several billion dollars to the Laiki Bank to purchase weapons, fuel and equipment for his wars. However, in 2000 Cyprus agreed to cooperate with international efforts to curb abusive and criminal tax-avoidance schemes. It received U.S. approval in its efforts to fight money–laundering and the drug trade. The U.S.

Cyprus

State Department lists the island as having Europe's worst record for trafficking of women.

Services now employ twice the labor force as agriculture in the Greek sector. The fact that three-fourths of the south's GDP comes from the services sector indicates that its economy is similar to those of the EU-15. Its GDP per capita is 80% of that in the EU-15 and the highest among the ten new states that entered the EU on May 1, 2004. Its infrastructure is very good, its educational system is sound, and the British-based legal system is transparent.

The Greek Cypriot economy is booming, with GDP growing by just under 4% in from 2004 to 2007 and 3.4% in 2008. In 2008, inflation stood at 3.9% and unemployment was only 4%. To attract foreign investment, the government reduced corporate taxes to 10%, the lowest in the EU. The South achieved its first budget surplus in 2007 and qualified to adopt the euro in 2008. Its total foreign debt was 67.4% of GDP in 2006, close to the 60% desired by the EU. It has initiated deep spending cuts, including in defense. The retirement age was lifted from age 60 to 63. Because of the small size of its economy, a determined effort to impose fiscal discipline can produce dramatic results within a relatively short period of time.

FUTURE

A mood of optimism has descended upon the island of Cyprus, and the prospects for a breakthrough have improved. The election in 2008 of a new president in the South, Demetris Christofias, who promised to "build bridges" with the North, is the best news in years. The key is for Cypriots on both sides of the Green Line to be persuaded that a deal is not a zero-sum game and that both sides will benefit. Such a prospect is now in sight, and final reconciliation appears to be closer. The North will still have to do without a significant boost from the EU, which was stymied in its efforts to extend benefits to Turkish Cypriots in consolation for the Greek Cypriot's disappointing rejection of unity in 2004. However, Cyprus might turn out to be a UN success story after all. Turkish Cypriot President Talat expressed hope: "I believe that it won't be a surprise if we solve the problem by the end of 2008."

The Annan Plan, 2004

Source: *The Economist*

The Italian Republic (Italy)

Italy

A rainy morning in Rome

Area: 187,176 sq. mi. (301,225 sq. km., about twice the size of California; about 750 miles—1,200 km.—from north to south and from 95 to 155 miles—152 to 248 km. wide).

Population: 58.4 million.

Capital City: Rome (Roma in Italian; Pop. 2.5 million, estimated).

Climate: From late spring to early winter the days are generally sunny and warm. Midsummer is quite hot in all but the North, where in the winter (the rainy season throughout the country) temperatures can sink to below freezing; the South is consistently warm.

Neighboring Countries: France (West); Switzerland and Austria (North); Slovenia (Northeast), with Croatia, Bosnia–Herzegovina, Montenegro and Albania paralleling its eastern coastline across the Adriatic Sea 50 to 100 miles (80 to 160 km.) away.

Official Language: Italian.

Principal Minorities: Predominantly German–speaking people with Austrian culture in South Tirol (Alto Adige); Albanian–speaking people in Calabria and Sicily; Greek–speaking people in Grecia–Salentin (Puglia) and some places in Calabria; French–speaking minority in Aosta–Valley; Slovene-speaking minority in the Trieste–Gorizia area;

Catalan-speaking minority in northeast Sardinia (Alghero).

Principal Religion: Roman Catholic.

Main Exports: Engineering products, textiles and footwear, transport equipment, chemicals, foodstuffs.

Main Imports: Engineering products, transport equipment, chemicals, energy, foodstuffs, textiles and clothing.

Major Trading Customers: EU25 (58.6% of exports and 57.2% of imports), Germany (13.6% of exports and 18% of imports), France (12.4% of exports and 11% of imports), U.S. (7.9% of exports and 4.3% of imports), Spain (7.3% of exports), UK (7.1% of exports and 4.3% of imports), Netherlands (5.9% of imports).

Currency: Euro.

National Day: June 2, (1946), Anniversary of the Republic.

Chief of State: Giorgio Napolitano, President (since May 2006).

Head of Government: Silvio Berlusconi, Prime Minister (since May 2008).

National Flag: From the pole, three equal vertical stripes of green, white and red.

Italy is easily recognized on every map by its boot shape. This narrow peninsula with the Apennine mountain range as its backbone extends from the Alps almost to the North African coast. It is flanked by the largest islands of the Mediterranean: Sicily (15,500 sq. mi.–25,000 sq. km.) and Sardinia (14,300 sq. mi.–23,000 sq. km.) in the western basin of the Mediterranean. With its own coastline extending almost 5,000 miles (8,000 km.) and its mild climate, Italy has lured people for thousands of years. However, most of its settlers did not come as polite guests, but rather as plunderers or conquerors who used force to overrun the land.

In the long course of Italian history, almost all the peoples of Europe have at one time or another either occupied or settled the country. From the ancient Greeks to the Spaniards, from the ancient Germanic tribes and Arab Saracens to the Holy Roman and Austrian emperors, peoples of the world have left their traces in Italy. This almost uninterrupted chain of foreign domination dating back to the classical period has decisively affected the traditions, behavior and mentality of the Italian. At the same time it has provided a basic impulse for Europe. Roman rule, which extended from the Mediterranean area through present-day Germany and France as well as all the way to Hadrian's Wall in Britain, and the Renaissance (meaning "rebirth") in the 14th and 15th centuries, decisively shaped western civilization.

In northern Italy the visitor witnesses a modern industrial and urban life. But in the South one finds the many typical characteristics of a developing nation with illiteracy, high unemployment and unproductive agriculture. Whoever takes the so–called "sunny freeway" to a village in the region of Abruzzi in central Italy finds himself in two different worlds: on the one hand, modern construction and, on the other hand, a medieval mountain village that has had electricity for little over a half a century. Old women clothed in black sit in front of their houses and look distrustfully at the stranger.

Even by Western European standards, Italy is a prosperous nation. At the same time, one is astonished by the social differences between the rich and poor. It has the sobering task of defending a 5,000-mile coastline. Given the strong centrifugal forces of highly diverse regions and countless competing political groups, it is no wonder that Guilio Andreotti wrote in his memoirs that Italy is almost ungovernable.

HISTORY

One of the major contradictions of Italian history is that the heroic epoch that was invoked and emulated by Mussolini, Italy's fascist dictator from 1922 to 1943, is actually not Italian history, but rather the history of a single city, Rome. This city rose to become the ruler of the entire Mediterranean world and, much more, of Europe. At one time, a person could truly say, "all roads lead to Rome." Italians themselves interpret differently the significance of Rome's earlier power and influence. If one were to ask inhabitants of southern Italy, particularly someone from Calabria or Sicily, whether they consider themselves descendants of the Romans, one would immediately receive a vigorously negative response. Even in the North the people, with their Celtic roots, do not consider themselves as descendants of the Romans. Southern Italians view Roman history as the beginning of perpetual foreign or outside control. The present form of this control is the economic predominance of the North over the South.

In a strict sense, Roman history cannot be called Italian national history because the concept of "the nation" was completely unknown in the ancient world. Yet, one cannot understand modern Italy without first viewing some of the principal features of Rome's development. This still vibrant past has had tremendous impact not only upon Italy itself, but also upon western Europe as a whole. The most evident examples of Roman heritage are found in the Romance languages, which include modern Italian, Spanish, Portuguese, Romanian and French. Without its Latin components, English would never have developed as it did and certainly would be incomprehensible to people today. The grammatical structure and vocabulary of all modern Germanic languages was strongly influenced by Latin (including the old rule that the verb comes last which gives non–Germans so much trouble). In law, civil administration, literature, art and engineering, ancient Roman civilization established the standards for many centuries.

The Early Period

The history of ancient Rome is long and exceedingly complicated, and is punctuated with magnificent victories and achievements, as well as ignoble failures, corruption and civil war. That history can be divided roughly into three periods: it was ruled by kings from roughly 753 B.C. (according to Roman legend) until 509 B.C., when a revolt led to the establishment of a republic, governed by elected consuls. The Roman Republic lasted until 45 B.C. when Julius Caesar established an empire subsequently ruled by emperors. In 185 A.D. this mighty empire began to fragment. It was divided under Emperor Theodosis in 395 A.D. into a Western empire, led from Rome, Milan and Trier in present–day Germany, and an Eastern empire, ruled from Constantinople (now Istanbul) in Turkey. The former empire finally collapsed in 476 A.D., whereas the Eastern one continued to exist for another thousand years.

According to their own legend, the Romans were descendants of a group of Greeks who had accompanied Aeneas, one of the sons of the Trojan King Priam. Aeneas, who many historians would say was not Greek, had escaped from the burning city of Troy and had sailed across the Mediterranean Sea before being blown ashore at the mouth of the Tiber River. There he allegedly founded a city called Lavinium. In fact, Italy was settled around 1200 B.C. by Indo–European tribes which moved into the area from the West, and since the Trojans were Indo–Europeans themselves, there might have been some truth in the Roman belief that they were descended from the Greeks.

The settlers in the Italian peninsula broke up into various warlike tribes: the Etruscans settled around the present city of Viterbo, located about 66 miles (110 kilometers) north of Rome. The Umbrians also settled north of Rome around the present city of Perugia. The Samnites built up their civilization south of Rome, while the Latins were based around the Tiber River. At the bottom of the peninsula and on the island of Sicily, the Greeks and Phoenicians established colonies, which thrived on trade and shipping.

Roman legends tell us that the city of Rome was founded in 753 B.C. by a Latin chief named Romulus, one of the infants allegedly reared by a she–wolf. The new city was situated on a hilly site about 20 miles (32 km.) inland from the former city of Lavinium in order to be out of reach of Phoenician and Greek raiders. Romans believed that Romulus made himself king of Rome and ruled until 716 B.C. He was succeeded by Numa Pomilius, who came from the Sabine tribe and who is said to have introduced Rome's first religious in-

Florence: Medieval parade

An Etruscan soldier

stitutions, which were largely copied from those of the Etruscans and Greeks. Many Greek gods were worshipped although the Romans gave them different names. For instance, Zeus became Jupiter, Hera became Juno, Hermes became Mercury and Athena became Minerva.

Under the rule of the Roman kings, the city's influence and control began to expand beyond the original seven hills, named the Palatine, the Capitoline, the Esquiline, the Aventine, the Caelian, the Quirinal and the Viminal. The most powerful foes were the Etruscans, a fierce, but civilized people, who had perfected the use of iron. The Etruscan leader, Tarquin, reportedly defeated the Romans and became king. Although it still became the leading city of the Latin League, a loose association of cities bound together for purposes of defense, Rome's subsequent kings were of Etruscan descent and were known as "the Tarquins;" they were elected by a small group of noblemen.

Under the Tarquin kings, Rome's class system became more firmly shaped. On top was the patrician class, consisting of free Romans who had the right to attend the assembly of aristocrats who advised the king. Eventually this assembly became open to all Romans who owned property. The plebeian class was composed of freed slaves who had immigrated to the city. The third class was composed of slaves, who had some rights, but who were not citizens. Only patricians and plebeians were allowed to serve in the army. Soldiers were at first required to provide their own uniforms, weapons and supplies, and they were paid by being able to share in the booty gained in victorious campaigns.

The last king was also named Tarquin, but his people called him Superbus because of his arrogance. He ruled very badly, involving Rome in expensive wars, arresting and murdering Roman citizens without trial and generally subjecting the city to a reign of terror. Finally in 509 B.C. two patricians staged a successful revolt and drove out the last of the kings, although it was not until 496 B.C. that the final attempt by the Etruscans and Sabines to restore the monarchy in Rome was suppressed.

The Republic

Because the kings had made themselves so hated, the Roman Republic was declared, which was ruled by two consuls elected by the People's Assembly each year for a one–year term. The first two consuls were the leaders of the revolt, Brutus and Collatinus, who were the most important founders of the Republic. Later, officials below the level of consuls were elected in pairs, and the normal career path to the post of consul was through a series of lower offices.

The republican constitution was not wholly democratic in the modern sense because it granted considerably more power to the patricians than to the plebeians and because most slaves were entirely excluded from politics. Only the election of the civil servants, consuls and judges by the People's Assembly can be regarded as democratic. There can be no doubt that a few influential Roman families wielded a disproportionate amount of power and authority. In general, the nobility and large landowners insured that all political functions were carried out honorably. Yet it was possible for common people with talent to acquire great political prominence and to influence Roman politics. For example, the well–known politician Cicero, who did not come from one of the few influential families in Rome, was the most famous orator of his time. Despite his great influence and fame, he suffered his entire life from an inferiority complex about his humble background.

The Roman constitution succeeded in solving many social crises and enabled Rome to establish and maintain a citizen's army. Realizing that victories were their own, these citizen soldiers were eminently more motivated than the disorderly mercenary armies of oriental dynasties. For the ancient world, the Roman civic virtues such as discipline, obedience and bravery were of great importance. They made their control over other peoples legitimate. Three essential pillars for the Roman state's strength were the exclusively Roman understanding of the commonwealth as *res publica* ("affairs of the people") from which the word "republic" is derived, the right of political participation, which was the highest goal of every distinguished Roman, and the disdain for all purely private matters.

In the Roman Republic important steps toward limited government were made: the very existence of a constitution, as long as it is observed, places limits on rulers' power. The Roman republican constitution, which was unwritten, especially embodied many principles essential for the development of modern democracy and did limit the state's control over citizens in several important ways. It was based on the separation of power between the executive and the legislature. Two consuls, who were elected by the People's Assembly composed of all citizens, provided the executive leadership. However, the electoral system gave more votes to those citizens who paid more taxes. Therefore, upper classes always had a majority of votes. The highest executive authority alternated each day from one consul to the other, although the consul not having the highest authority could veto decisions made by the other except in times of war. The yearly election and the mutual control over each other prevented the concentration of power in one person's hands.

The fact that the civilian rulers had command over the military, even in times of crisis, prevented the development of a "state within a state" and the use of war as an end in itself instead of as a political means. The daily alternation of supreme command over the military, however, caused many defeats, the most famous occurring in Cannae in 216 B.C. But these changes helped to prevent a military dictatorship. In time of extreme emergency, the People's Assembly could appoint a dictator to exercise full political powers until the grave dangers to the city had passed. The only exception to such a dictatorship limited in time was Julius Caesar, who at the end of the Roman Republic was appointed dictator for life.

The Senate wielded limited legislative power and had authority over foreign policy, including the declaration of war and ratification of treaties. In domestic policy it had only advisory power. In contrast to the consuls and other civil servants, Senators, who numbered up to 300 at any one time, were not elected; rather they consisted of retired high government officials, including all former consuls.

To protect themselves in courts of law, the plebeians forced the establishment of Tribunes for the People, elected by the People's Assembly and to whom any plebeian could turn for help whenever he believed that he was being treated unjustly. These People's Tribunes could even veto decisions made by the Senate and they could eventually veto any law. It was considered to be a very serious crime to attack the Tribunes during their term of office. Plebeians won the right for themselves (and for slaves) to stand for election to all city offices and thereby ultimately to gain seats in the Senate. Plebeians also won the right to marry patricians, thus making class lines less rigid.

Very significantly, the plebeians were able to have a written legal code adopted in 454 B.C. These laws were published on 12 bronze tablets, known as the Twelve Tablets of Law, and were kept in the heart of the city, known as the Forum. Every Roman schoolchild was expected to know them by heart, and they ultimately became the foundation of Roman law and of the legal systems of many modern European nations. Roman laws embodied all the important rules pertaining to contracts, the protection of private property, marriage and divorce and inheritance. Because private property was at the core of Roman legal thought, offenses were most frequently punished by requiring payment of property. The victims of petty theft and robbery and the families of murder victims were compensated by means of fines and confiscated property. The Romans had no clear-cut criminal law with the exception of a political penal code for corruption, abuse of public office and high treason.

Two important preconditions for the rise of Rome were the still unexplained decline of Etruscan rule over northern and central Italy in the 5th and 4th centuries B.C., as well as the Roman domination of the various tribes in Italy and the Greek cities in the South. Rome had been constantly threatened by various tribes within Italy and by Gauls who poured into the peninsula from the north. Once it was even captured and burned. The city was saved several times by such heroes as Cincinnatus and Camillus.

One Greek city in southern Italy, Tarentum, even sent for the help of Pyrrhus, king of Epirus in northern Greece, who arrived in 280 B.C. with a huge fleet carrying a herd of elephants and 25,000 troops. This army clashed with the Romans outside of Heraclea in 280 B.C.; the Romans fought extremely well, but when Pyrrhus sent his elephants roaring and screaming against the enemy troops, who had never seen such beasts before, the soldiers panicked and retreated. Though he won the battle, Pyrrhus had lost far more soldiers than the Romans had, and his weakened troops therefore were eventually beaten at Benventum. Today, the words "Pyrrhic victory" refer to any success achieved at too high a price.

Punic Wars

The victory over Pyrrhus, along with other swift and successful campaigns, established Roman domination over the Italian Peninsula in the first part of the 3rd century and permitted them to cast their sights farther for the first time. It is no surprise that Italy hurled a serious challenge against the major naval power in the western Mediterranean at the time: the Phoenician metropolis of Carthage (located a few miles outside the present city of Tunis in North Africa). Carthage had numerous colonies extending all along the coasts of North Africa and Spain, and it dominated Sardinia and the western part of Sicily.

In the first Carthaginian (Punic) War (264 to 241 B.C.) between the land power Rome and the sea power Carthage, Rome demonstrated its unusual adaptability by

Built by the first Tarquin king, the *Circus Maximus*, seating 300,000 Romans, saw the first chariot races

Italy

The Roman Senate

skillfully utilizing its allies in order to acquire sea power itself and by gaining the three large islands, Sicily, Sardinia and Corsica. From 218 to 202, after the Romans had finally expelled the Gauls from the mainland peninsula, Carthage, which had been provoked by Roman meddling in Spain, sought revenge in a second round of battles known as the Second Punic War.

The Carthaginians, led by a brilliant young general named Hannibal, threatened the very heart of Rome's Italian domain. In 218 B.C. he moved an army of 100,000 foot soldiers, 1,300 cavalry and 40 elephants from Spain over the Pyrenees and Alps right into Italy. But the climate was too cold in the mountains, and he lost all his elephants and many of his troops during this journey. Nevertheless, he was able to assemble an army on its soil in 218 B.C. Although the Romans tried to avoid open battle, except at Cannae, Hannibal's forces succeeded in destroying several Roman armies through skillful maneuvering, but they were never able to take Rome; he remained until 203 B.C. when he received word of an end run that the Romans were planning on Carthage itself. He departed hastily to his city's rescue, but to no avail. In the third Punic War, Roman troops captured the city and destroyed it, salting the soil in the hope that nothing would ever

grow again. From this harshness came the expression "a Carthaginian peace." At last, Rome was unchallenged master of the western Mediterranean. A treaty between Rome and Carthage, now outside Tunis, ending the Punic wars was finally signed in 1987 A.D.

Roman Imperialism

Rome could now direct its sights eastward toward Greece. Between 198 and 190 B.C., Rome won victories in Greece, which not only again opened the Roman door wide to Greek cultural influence, but it also gave the Romans a firm foothold in Asia Minor. This was the beginning of Roman imperialism. Hitherto, diplomatic balancing and management of conquered peoples were the primary factors in Roman foreign policy; in the new phase it adopted different methods of power politics. Punitive expeditions against disloyal allies and the destruction of cities like Carthage and Corinth in 115 B.C. revealed the foreign political pattern for the conquest of the eastern Mediterranean area. By 63 B.C. nearly all the countries in the Mediterranean region were paying tribute to Rome.

The burden of constant war and of administering the enormous empire overextended the resources of a small state that

had started on the banks of the Tiber River at the foot of the Palatine Hill. It had transformed itself into a large and powerful metropolis.

The Romans' encounter with Greece during the conquest of the eastern Mediterranean area influenced Roman life and thought in such a way that the Roman poet Horace could write that the "conquered Greeks conquered their victors." Greek slaves taught the children of the wealthy in the Roman Empire. The Greek language assumed a role during the Republic that in some ways corresponded to that of the French language in the 17th and 18th centuries. On the other hand, the Romans clung to their traditional political and cultural norms and deeply mistrusted foreign influences. They were willing to adopt those technical and institutional achievements of other peoples that the Romans considered worthy of copying. For instance, many weapons systems were patterned after those of the conquered peoples. The critical examination and adoption of whatever was considered better, combined with the steadfastness of a self–reliant identity, gave Roman policies their dynamism and flexibility.

After many years the republican constitution became increasingly incapable of solving the many social problems of such

CARTHAGINIAN EMPIRE
c. 300 B.C.

a large realm. The defense of the vast empire, with its many administrative requirements, called for an effective central bureaucracy, but the old republic did not have such an institution and was therefore unable to perform many essential functions. Numerous military campaigns claimed thousands of casualties and therefore left large tracts of land either to fall fallow or into the hands of the large landowners. Further, following the campaigns, many unemployed soldiers drifted into Rome, thereby adding to the city's mounting problems.

In earlier times no one was permitted to enter the city of Rome with weapons. Standing armies with nothing to do and former peasants who had lost their land to large landowners broke down the old customs that had integrated the army with the society and the state. At this point, the earlier observation of the Greek philosopher, Aristotle, applied to Rome: masters of weapons are also masters of the state.

The political order in the Roman Republic began slowly to disintegrate, and widespread dissatisfaction, lawlessness and corruption ran riot throughout the realm. The citizens' rights were gradually whittled away; the parties particularly established themselves in the social circles of the later republic from 133 to 45 B.C. The Senate Party represented the interests of the nobility and the large landowners, while the Popular Party was supported by the masses.

The Republic Falls; the Empire Arises

Early in the 1st century B.C. civil war between these two groups broke out which lasted on and off for most of the remainder of the century. The leading figure in this struggle was Gaius Julius Caesar, the best-known leader within the Popular Party. Born into a patrician's family, but always possessing strong plebeian sentiments, his extraordinary bravery and endurance endeared him with his troops. He was a talented general, politician, orator, poet, historian, mathematician and architect. William Shakespeare called this unique man "the noblest man that ever lived in the tide of times." In 60 B.C. he

was elected consul and set about to accomplish his two chief objectives of establishing order in Rome and the empire, and reconciling the conflicting classes. He spent nine years in Gaul (presently France) and Britain. This not only enabled him to win victories for Rome, but to write an eight-volume history entitled the *Gallic War*. This remains one of the most important books of ancient history.

When he wanted to return to Rome in 49 B.C., the Senate informed him that he was to disband his army and to return to Rome alone. Sensing that he was about to be arrested, he decided to cross the Rubicon River and to march his army against Rome itself. For four years he confronted his enemies, including his former friend and son–in–law, Pompey, in battles in Greece, Egypt, North Africa and Spain, before returning in 45 B.C. as master of the entire Roman world.

Julius was acclaimed dictator in 45 B.C. He proceeded to try to restore order and to introduce such measures as founding colonies inside and outside of Italy to provide new lives for Rome's unemployed, providing grain for the hungry, enabling non–Romans to become members of the Senate and making all residents of Italy Roman citizens. He also made no secret of his conviction that Rome could survive only if it had one ruler with absolute power that included the right to name his successor.

Fearing the restoration of kings, a group of senators let by Brutus and Cassius murdered Caesar in 44 B.C. in the theater of Pompeius, which was being used temporarily as the Senate. This act, vividly dramatized by Shakespeare, again thrust Rome into a civil war that touched every part of the realm. Not until Octavian, Caesar's grandnephew, established order in 31 B.C. did the bloody civil war come to an end. He became the first emperor of Rome, under the name of Augustus (meaning "the revered") and his successors bore the title of "Caesar" in honor of Julius. The Roman Republic was dead, and the Roman Empire had commenced. The Caesars served for life and were selected in many different ways. Most of them were not from the city of Rome. Some even came from Spain, (Trajan), Africa (Lucius Septimius Severus) or from what is now Yugoslavia (Diocletian).

Peace and Prosperity

Augustus restored order and revived trade, and his people again experienced the rare combination of peace and prosperity. He launched a building program in the empire and its capital that enabled him to say toward the end of his life in 14 B.C., "I found Rome a city of brick and am leaving it a city of marble." Despite a

string of less capable emperors, his life's work lasted almost two centuries.

There are many preconceived ideas about Roman emperors. They are often portrayed as degenerate beasts which practiced tyranny with Caesarian insanity, only to fall victims to palace revolts or poisonous death. This is only an anecdotal and superficial understanding. It is true that they sometimes directed political cruelty against other members of the noble class who might have presented a threat to them, but the Roman Empire and its citizens drew many benefits from the emperors' efforts.

It was precisely the centralized bureaucracy, which the emperors created, which made the Roman Empire the blooming civilization as we know it today. Some were wise and learned men, such as Marcus Aurelius, whose published volume, Meditations, is still a highly valued philosophical work. Impressive ruins bear eloquent witness to prosperous Roman cities from Germany to the desert sands of the Sahara. The empire reached its greatest expansion under Emperor Trajan from 98 to 117 A.D. From Iraq to Scotland, from Cologne to Libya, one spoke Latin and lived according to Roman law and customs.

A dark shadow over the cultural splendor of the Roman classical period was the fact that much of the economic prosperity was achieved by means of slave labor. Modern estimations are that at any one time between 300,000 and 500,000 slaves provided a luxurious life for many citizens of Rome, which by the 2nd century A.D. had grown to a city of over a million inhabitants, including slaves. Our present view of humanity inclines us to judge harshly the treatment of the ancient slaves, who without rights or status could be sold or even killed by their masters. Under Roman law they were considered to be nothing more than "animated tools." However, slaves were actually valuable property, especially an educated Greek.

The degree of suppression endured by a slave depended upon his type of work. Naturally, those slaves who served in public office, including the highest administrative positions, or who as scholars instructed the children of wealthy Romans were much better off than those who worked on the large plantations. The exploitation of the latter led to two slave revolts. In 136 B.C. the slaves in Sicily rose up under their leader, Syrer Eunus, and established a short–lived slave republic in the city of Enna. From 73 to 71 Rome trembled before the legendary slave leader, Spartacus, who led 90,000 rebellious slaves in southern Italy.

Very early the conscience of many persons was stirred by the injustice of slav-

Italy

Statue of the Emperor Trajan in Rome

ery. In Plautus' comedies the slaves always played the intelligent and superior roles. Stoic philosophy rejected such servitude entirely. In making a judgment against human bondage in the Roman world, one must remember that slavery existed in modern times as well. In addition, the history of human suppression and exploitation is a very long one. To say that a worker during the period of early capitalism in Manchester or a mercenary Hessian soldier bought by the English to fight against Washington's army during the American Revolution was better off than an ancient slave would be deceptive.

The Decline and Fall of the Empire

The emperors considered their main task to be the security of the Empire's extensive borders. However, as the threat of invasion became greater and greater, the ancient Roman world was unable to withstand after the beginning of the 3rd century A.D. the mounted attacks of Germans, Slavs, Huns, Persians, Turks, Mongolians, Berbers and later, of Arabs.

In 284 A.D. Diocletian, the son of a freed slave from Illyria (along the eastern Adriatic coast) became emperor. He realized that the Roman Empire had grown too large to be governed by one man, so in 285 A.D. he divided it into an eastern and a western part. He assumed rule over the eastern portion, with its seat in Nicomedia in Asia Minor. The subsequent western emperors held court at Milan and Trier. Emperor Constantine, who became sole emperor of Rome in 324 A.D., continued the reorganization of the empire initiated by Diocletian. He built a new city on the site of the former Byzantium, a strategically important crossroads between Asia and Europe, and named it after himself: Constantinople. From then on, the Roman Empire was administered from that city and Rome lost much of its significance. There, Roman civilization mingled with that of Greece and of Asia.

Disciples of and converts to Christianity had been circulating amid most parts of the empire since the 1st century A.D., converting many who held the ancient Greek and Roman beliefs in the classical gods to their belief in a single, almighty God. These beliefs and moral teachings were those of a mortal who claimed to be his son. A gradual Christian penetration of the Roman society and the emergence of Christianity to that of a state religion were not as commonly supposed. They were only persecuted when they directly challenged the traditional classical understanding of a state religion as a form of political loyalty. It would not have been possible for Christian beliefs to spread unless there had otherwise been an attitude of relative religious tolerance. In spite of some use of torture and martyrdom, this faith continued inexorably to grow, eventually becoming the most powerful and dominating concept of the Western and Middle Eastern worlds. It was supplanted by Islam to a large degree in the Middle East after the life of the prophet Mohammed.

Constantine decided to accept Christianity and to make it the empire's official religion. After his death in 337 A.D. there was less and less cooperation and coordination between the eastern and western parts of the empire. While Constantinople was a safe distance from the marauding tribes of Europe, the western part became the object of sustained attacks by Goths, Visigoths and Vandals. Rome was temporarily captured and sacked in 410 A.D. and in 476 the East Gothic chief, Odoacer, marched his troops into the city and deposed the last western Roman Emperor, Romulus Augustulus. Thereafter, sheep grazed on the overgrown ruins of the Forum, once the scene of the power behind the heart of the Empire.

Rome Destroyed

The destruction of Rome was without precedent. But many aspects of this great empire have been salvaged for posterity, including its literature, which was protected in the Christian cloisters, and its law. Further testimonies to the splendor of the Roman past are the unique accomplishments in architecture, such as domes, columns and basilicas, and in engineering, such as bridges, aqueducts and highways. Most of the important European roads today follow the same routes established by the Romans. Therefore, Italy's past is significant not only to Italians, but to all persons touched by Western civilization.

The "Middle Ages"

During and after the Middle Ages, Italy was so fragmented into feuding and ever-shifting states, papal holdings, kingdoms and foreign dominions that even well-educated Italians have difficulty comprehending their own history during that time. In the Middle Ages as well as in modern times, Italy was characterized by foreign domination, inner strife and parochialism of the Catholic Church. Over a span of a thousand years Byzantines, Germanic tribes, Arabs, Germans, Normans (Scandinavians), Frenchmen, Spaniards and Austrians marched across the land and levied taxes or subjugated the dependent minor princes in the peninsula to servitude.

Ideals such as freedom, unity and independence first became political realities in 1861 with the "Resurgence," or unification movement. With Italy's past in mind, it should be no surprise that Italians' identification with their state developed very slowly. The political culture was stamped with a combined feeling of powerlessness and distrust toward the state.

After the fall of the Roman Empire, centuries of gloom and of alternating domination, particularly by the Germans and Lombards, afflicted the peninsula until the Frankish King Pippin, father of Charlemagne, introduced in the 8th century A.D. a territorial order in Italy. It was divided into a Lombard-Frankish area in the North and a Byzantine area in the South, ruled ultimately from Constantinople. The results of this fateful division continue to be evident in the economic and cultural contrasts between the North and the South right up to the present day.

Along with the division of Italy, the so-called "Pippin Deed" had another extremely far-reaching consequence for the political development of Italy. The Deed assured the Pope an ecclesiastical state in the middle of Italy. Centuries later this was the last political entity in the nation that resisted unification with the national Italian state.

Meanwhile during the later Middle Ages, as the North was involved in and profiting from the constant conflict between the German Emperors and the Popes, the South was undergoing an entirely different development. The Byzantines, who were also occupying Sicily, could no longer fend off the attacks of the Moslem Saracens from North Africa.

The Roman Empire at its height

The Byzantines, who had become Eastern Orthodox Christians, could not count on the Roman Catholic Church for assistance in upholding their occupation. Around 900 Sicily blossomed into a rich and fertile garden under the new Moslem rule. The Saracens, reputed to be blood-thirsty pirates along the coast of Italy, exercised a clever and tolerant reign in which an enormous cultural flowering unfolded. They introduced lemons, oranges, cotton and pistachio nuts, the last being the island's most important agricultural export today. Only an entirely new actor who entered the world scene could put an end to such a rule.

The Power of the Holy "Roman" Empire

In 1080, through a shrewd marriage policy, southern Italy under the Normans (Vikings) became joined with the Holy Roman (actually German) Empire under Friedrich II of the Staufen dynasty. Known to his contemporaries as "the wonder of the world," Friedrich was an enlightened emperor who was as at home in the world of politics as in the world of scholarship. His reign was the last golden age in Italy before a long period of conservative-clerical foreign domination.

Despite their different life-styles, Friedrich succeeded in uniting the original inhabitants of southern Italy, the Byzantine Greeks and the Moslem Saracens, in a life of harmonious coexistence. Under his rule a cultural and economic highpoint was achieved which was unparalleled in Europe at the time.

The new spirit of tolerance as well as the encirclement of the ecclesiastical state by Friedrich's territories did not please the pope. The long-standing dispute between the German emperors and the pope reached a climax with the appeal for a crusade against Friedrich. Many had hoped that divided Italy would develop into a model state under the reign of the House of Staufen. These dreams were shattered, however, when the Frenchman, Charles of Anjou, protégé of the pope, overthrew Staufen rule in Italy. Southern Italy suffered terribly under the domination of the Anjou family until 1282, when the mounting hate against the uninhibited French arrogance erupted. The absolute monarchy of the French in southern Italy was consumed with uninterrupted wars, and could not withstand the attacks by the Aragonians from Spain, who, through intrigues, were able to undermine every French military unit.

Disunification

As a result of the disputes between the pope and the German emperor, the small and fragmented states and cities in northern Italy were able to achieve a certain degree of political independence. Loyalty to one side or the other varied, depending upon the political advantage at the time of a given battle.

The cities knew well how to exploit to their own economic advantage the disputes of the popes and the German emperors and the Crusades, which began at the end of the 11th century. The latter were medieval efforts directed at reclaiming Jerusalem from the Arabs. Of all cities, Venice profited most of all from these efforts. The Venetians did not in any way share the religious fervor or self-sacrifice of the German, French and English knights. The knights and pilgrims enroute to the Crusades and Jerusalem poured into rival Venice and Genoa in droves.

One of the most notable Crusades was the Fourth, which took place from 1198–1204. The aged, composed and politically gifted Doge (leader) Dandolo of Venice was able to redirect the course toward Constantinople and agreed to transport the crusaders to their destination on the condition that they stop along the way

Italy

Ideal of virility: Tiziano Vecellio, Portrait of a Man ("The Englishman")

Ideal of feminine beauty: Tiziano Vecellio, Portrait of a Young Woman ("La Bella")

and plunder Constantinople for Venice. Thus, instead of becoming conquerors of holy cities held by Moslems, the crusaders attacked and plundered a Christian capital city. The Quadriga, a large statue of four horses from the Hippodrome in Constantinople and now above St. Mark's Cathedral in Venice, bears witness to this strange event. In this way, a troublesome trade rival was seriously weakened. Venice was so powerful that it was not even perturbed by the resulting excommunication of the Venetian leaders by the pope.

Despite the continuing conflict, no other country in Europe achieved at this time the degree of economic development that took place in Italy. One of the most well–known and powerful families of bankers, the Medici, had gained far–reaching political influence in their home city of Florence, as well as in France, where marriage joined Catherine de Medici with King Henry II. In the economically developed cities of northern and central Italy, the transition had been made from a less productive barter economy to a money economy. The bases of this affluence were the development of industry and trade, especially with the Middle and Far East.

The Reawakening (Renaissance)

In 1492 the Italian, Christopher Columbus, discovered the "new world." Some would say that this ended the strategic importance of the Mediterranean Sea and the Italian peninsula. But in the 14th and 15th centuries northern Italy was the cradle of an intellectual and cultural rebirth known as the Renaissance. This reawakening was indirectly stimulated by Venice's refusal to support Constantinople when that city was subjected to a determined Turkish attack. When that last remnant of the Roman Empire finally fell in 1453, many highly cultured Greeks emigrated to Italy from Constantinople and gave the Renaissance movement a significant boost. They helped to reawaken Italian interest in the Greek classical authors. Had it not been for the efforts of the Italian scholars, who laboriously collected and preserved many ancient Greek works, the originals we possess today would have been lost forever.

In the depths of the foaming cauldron of bickering city–states a fundamentally new approach to life was born. Man was no longer the *viator mundi* (pilgrim seeking heavenly salvation) of the Middle Ages, concerned with the universal principle of salvation. He became the *faber mundi* (the creator and master of the world), who shaped his own destiny. Self–assured individualism and rational thought were reflected in the Renaissance conception of the state. Autonomous states were directed by paid public officials according to the guidelines of "reason of state," and carefully calculated business considerations determined politics and administration. Wars were conducted by mercenary enterprises (known as *condittieri*) that dared to do battle in the same way as one dares to make capital investment, that is, only if a profit is certain. The Florentine, Niccolò Machiavelli, developed the theory of politics that in no way was based upon religious principles.

Correspondingly, scholars who had until that time been considered as *ancillas theologiae* ("slaves of theology") divested themselves of that status and began working independently of theology. Above all, rediscovery of the classical authors advanced this secular conception to that of a rational principle. Spurred on by their Latin predecessors, Dante, Petrarca and Boccaccio, they created new literature in Italian (sometimes intermingled with Latin) but later a total variant of the historic language of Rome.

The universal man with his comprehensive wealth of knowledge represented the new ideal of the Renaissance man. The universal genius, Leonardo da Vinci, was a painter, artist, engineer, doctor, architect and politician and is a particularly prominent example of vast numbers of creative persons who contributed enormously to his culturally rich times. Inspired by the classical model of rounded arches that tied together the central construction, architects developed a totally new concept of space through emphasis on the vertical, with clear, well–formed proportions. Donatello and Michelangelo surpassed their classical predecessors in expression and monumentality. In painting, the central perspective was developed which strove for ideal anatomical proportion that were at the same time more realistic. Masaccio, Botticelli, Raphael and da Vinci, the best–known painters of their time, were the leading lights of an art movement that influenced the entire field of European painting.

Secular–Religious Relations

The popes themselves were responsible for directing the focus of the Renaissance from the religious realm to the secular princes and scholars. For instance, Pope Julius was Michelangelo's patron. As learned patrons of the arts, the popes accelerated the inner disintegration of the Church—the reconstruction of St. Peter's Cathedral, sponsored by a member of the Medici family, Pope Leo X, could only be financed by his system of indulgences (paying for forgiveness of sin). This way of raising revenue unleashed the Reformation in the early 16th century. When the popes became staunch supporters of the Counter–Reformation, Italy ceased being the center of the Renaissance, which thereafter found a more congenial setting in France.

Da Vinci Design and Backward Handwriting

In the conflict between the Habsburgs and the French, which was the central problem for the Western European states until the 18th century, the autonomous Italian city–states lost much of their independence. The plunder and devastation caused by the rival French and Habsburg armies, as well as pillaging and destruction by pirates from North African Barbary states, came to dominate life in Italy. The South gradually faded under Spanish domination and became unhinged from developments in the rest of Europe. The war of the Spanish Succession (1701–1713), which endangered the European balance of power between the Habsburgs and France, brought northern Italy under the domination of the Austrians and southern Italy under the control of the Spanish Bourbons. The popes retained their political hold over much of central Italy. Due to uncontrolled cuttings, the rich forests of Puglia, where Friedrich II had so happily hunted, were reduced to withering grasslands.

It is hardly surprising that the shock waves of the French Revolution of 1789 soon were felt in Italy, where feudal institutions and conditions were still present. French republican forces invaded Savoy and Nice in the fall of 1792 and in March 1796 a concentrated French campaign began in Italy. This resulted not only in temporary French domination of most of northern and central Italy, but also in brilliant victories for a young French general who soon became the leader of France, Napoleon Bonaparte.

In early 1798 French forces invaded the Papal States. The pope fled and a Roman Republic was established. Although the French were temporarily driven out of Italy in the latter part of 1799, Napoleon, who had seized power in late 1799, renewed his Italian conquests and soon secured much of Italy under his control. When Napoleon made himself emperor of France he also placed an Italian crown on his head, thereby becoming king of Italy, with all of northern and central Italy un-

Dante in Florence

der his authority. In the spring of 1806 French forces occupied the rest of Italy and on March 30, 1806, Napoleon's brother, Joseph, was proclaimed the king of the Two Sicilies. When Joseph became king of Spain in 1808, a French general, Joachim Murat, was crowned king of Naples.

Exit Napoleon

Although Napoleon's hold on Italy was finally broken in 1815, his legacy remained. He had decreed important reforms in the country. These included the Napoleonic Code, which together with Roman law, remains the foundation of Italian law today. He confiscated much of the Catholic Church's property, ended feudal privileges and immunities and improved roads and education. He thereby gave Italians a crucially important impetus for political, social, legal and economic reform.

The restoration of the old regime after the Congress of Vienna reestablished Austrian domination in northern and central Italy. The pope was granted the Vatican's pre–Napoleonic holdings again and the Bourbon king, Ferdinand I of the Two Sicilies, again became ruler of southern Italy. But the spark of the enlightenment, Italian nationalism and the right of Italians to establish a democratic state continued to ferment within a few secret societies of bourgeois intellectuals.

Fragmented Italy

Prince Metternich of Austria stated correctly in 1815 that Italy was not a nation, but rather a "geographic concept." The only state within Italy that played an active role in Europe was Piedmont–Savoy, where the unification movement originated. The remainder of Italy was either under foreign control or ruled by small splinter states. The parochialism that had its roots in Italian history also resisted the liberal ideas of the French Revolution and those of the few "middle and upper–class romantics" who dreamed of Italian national unification. Numerous uprisings, usually started by the secret societies against the established rulers from 1820 to 1831 were all crushed.

The revolutionary movement was not strong enough to overcome Austrian domination without outside help. The major European powers had concluded that the balance of power in Europe was more important than Italian unity. Further, the most important secret resistance movement, the *Carboneria* (literally "Charcoal Burners") had been so loosely organized, so heterogeneous and so unable to define its aims clearly that it was incapable of uniting in crucial moments.

It was these kinds of problems that certain subsequent Italian nationalists tried to avoid. The traveler to Italy notices that in every town, streets and plazas bear the names of Mazzini, Cavour and Garibaldi. They made up the triple constellation of the "Resurgence," the name they gave to Italian political unification in 1861.

Gradual Unification

In 1831 a young Genoan political thinker, Giuseppe Mazzini, founded the "Young Italy" movement. He had remained the intellectual head and prophet of the unification drive for a free, independent and republican Italy although he was unable to lead that movement to success. He died in 1872 bitterly disappointed about the kind of Italian state that had been created.

In 1848 uprisings again occurred throughout Italy, and the pope was even temporarily driven out of Rome. But with the aid of French troops, the rebellion was quelled. With its failure, nationalists' eyes turned increasingly toward the kingdom of Piedmont–Sardinia, whose capital was Turin and which was ruled by one of the oldest ruling families in Europe, the house of Savoy. It had been the only regime in Italy that had fought hard for freedom from Austria.

The new Piedmont king, Victor Emmanuel, who was to become the first king of a united Italy, was a man of rough manners and visible virility. He became a popular focus of attention for those who wanted change. But that he was also a politically shrewd man was revealed by his appointment as Piedmontese prime minister of a man whom he personally de-

Italy

Scene typical of the Renaissance—Dante in Florence

tested: Count Camillo di Cavour. He was not brilliant, but he was a pragmatic man who was well aware that Italy could never become independent as a result of spontaneous mass uprisings of idealists. The political hold of Austria had to be broken and he knew that Italians would need the help of a foreign power to do this. Therefore, he turned to the new French emperor, Napoleon III.

The French leader agreed to support Piedmont in any war against Austria under the condition that in the event of victory, France be rewarded with Nice and Savoy. The deal was sealed by the marriage of Victor Emmanuel's 15–year–old daughter, Clotilde, with Napoleon's lecherous cousin, Jerome. With such a commitment tucked away in his breast pocket, Cavour sought a way to bring about war with Austria. Two blunders by the latter country played directly into Cavour's hands. One was Austria's decision to impose military conscription on its dominions of Lombardy and Venetia, a move which drove many draft–dodgers into Piedmont. The tension which arose as a result of Piedmont's refusal to turn these young men over to the Austrian authorities gave Cavour the excuse he needed to begin military preparations.

The second blunder was committed just when the French emperor was beginning to have second thoughts about the prom-

ises he had made earlier to Piedmont. In the spring of 1859 Austria issued an ultimatum to Piedmont, demanding that it either disarm itself or go to war. Cavour, of course, chose the latter, and with Napoleon's assistance faced the powerful but indecisive Austrian Army and defeated it at Magenta on June 4 and at Solferino on June 24 and conquered all Lombardy and Milan.

After these important victories, Napoleon grew weary of the war and concluded an armistice with the Austrians at Villafranca on July 11. Cavour was understandably furious at the French, but the movement toward Italian unity had gained such momentum that it could no longer be stopped. Revolutionary assemblies in Tuscany, Modena, Parma and Romagna voted in August 1859 to unite with Piedmont; France and Britain spoke out against any foreign (i.e. Austrian) intervention to foil these popular decisions. In March 1860, plebiscites in the four areas confirmed the steps taken by the assemblies. True to his earlier promise, Cavour delivered Savoy and Nice to the French.

Southern Unification

With most of northern and central Italy now unified, the cauldron of unification began to bubble in the South. In the spring of 1860 revolts broke out in Sicily that gave a chance to reenter the center stage

in Italy to a highly talented military adventurer, Giuseppe Garibaldi. A former member of Mazzini's "Young Italy" movement, he had spent 13 years as a soldier of fortune in Latin America, where he became a master in the leadership of irregular forces and guerrilla warfare. He had raced back to Italy in 1848 when he heard of the revolutionary activity there.

He formed military forces first in Lombardy, then in Venice and finally in Rome, where he served under Mazzini to defend the Roman Republic which had just been created. From April to the end of June 1849, Garibaldi's legion, clad in red shirts and Calabrian hats, had defended the "Eternal City" valiantly against French troops that protected the pope. Prolonged resistance had proved to be impossible, so Garibaldi fled with his troops to the tiny independent republic of San Marino, where he disbanded his army and went into exile.

Revolts in Sicily in 1860 again drew him into southern Italy and in May he packed his 1,000 irregulars, mostly students, poets and soldiers of fortune, into rickety steamers and set a course directly to Sicily. When he arrived at Marsala, he declared himself dictator of Sicily and proceeded to defeat piecemeal the confused and divided Neapolitan troops that were supposed to defend the island. By mid–July he poised for his strike against the Bour-

A FOREIGN DOMINATED, POLITICALLY FRAGMENTED PENINSULA

1 DUCHY OF SAVOY
2 DUCHY OF MILAN
3 DUCHY OF MANTUA
4 DUCHY OF FERRARA

THE REPUBLIC OF GENOA
SAN MARINO
REPUBLIC OF VENICE
CORSICA (GENOA)
STATES OF THE CHURCH
ROME
THE KINGDOM OF SARDINIA (ARAGON)
THE KINGDOMS OF NAPLES AND SICILY (ARAGON)

5 DUCHY OF MODENA
6 REPUBLIC OF LUCCA
7 REPUBLIC OF FLORENCE
8 REPUBLIC OF SIENA

About 1450

SAVOY
MILAN
PIEDMONT
SAN MARINO
REPUBLIC OF GENOA
GRAND DUCHY OF TUSCANY
STATES OF THE CHURCH
REPUBLIC OF VENICE
CORSICA (GENOA)
ROME
KINGDOM OF SARDINIA
KINGDOM OF NAPLES (AUSTRIA)
KINGDOM OF SICILY (AUSTRIA)

1 MANTUA
2 PARMA AND MODENA

About 1722

NAPOLEON'S "KINGDOM OF ITALY" (1804–13)
FRANCE
SAN MARINO
OCCUPIED BY FRANCE
CORSICA (FRANCE)
ROME
KINGDOM OF SARDINIA
KINGDOM OF NAPLES (France, 1806–13)
KINGDOM OF SICILY

Under Napoleon, 1804–13

LOMBARDY (FROM AUSTRIA)
VENETIA
PIEDMONT
SAN MARINO
GRAND DUCHY OF TUSCANY
STATES OF THE CHURCH
CORSICA (FRANCE)
ROME
NAPLES
KINGDOM OF SARDINIA
KINGDOM OF THE TWO SICILIES (RULED BY SPANISH BOURBONS)
SICILY

1 PARMA
2 MODENA
3 LUCCA

The Unification of Italy, 1849–70

Italy

bon kingdom of the Two Sicilies with its capital in Naples.

Riding a tide of popular enthusiasm, Garibaldi's army, which had swollen to 10,000 men, crossed the Strait of Messina in mid–1860, and his units produced panic among the Neapolitan troops whenever they appeared. On September 7, a jubilant Garibaldi entered the city of Naples far in advance of his troops. In less than five months he had conquered the Kingdom of the Two Sicilies, a country of 11 million inhabitants.

He immediately set his sights again on Rome, which was still defended by French troops. Not wishing to lose entirely the initiative for unifying Italy, Cavour ordered his own troops to march southward into the Papal States. On September 18 they crushed the Pope's forces at Castelfidardo and then defeated a remaining Neapolitan army at Capua. These successes prompted the Piedmontese parliament to annex southern Italy. In October plebiscites in Naples, Sicily, the Marches and Umbria revealed overwhelming popular support for union with Piedmont.

On October 26, 1860, Garibaldi met Victor Emmanuel II at Teano. The warrior greeted Victor as king of Italy and shook his hand. When the monarch asked him not to start a war against the Vatican, Garibaldi reportedly replied: "*obbedisco!*" (I obey!) and resigned his command the next day. He retired on the rocky island of Caprera, refusing to accept any reward for his services. He was subsequently called the "hero of the two worlds" as a tribute to his military adventures in South America and Europe.

In February 1861 Victor Emmanuel II was proclaimed king of Italy. A new Italian parliament representing the entire peninsula except Rome and the province of Venetia assembled. Shortly thereafter Florence became Italy's new capital until 1870.

Differences within the Union

The historical differences between northern and southern Italy were not overcome through the unification and establishment of a monarchy. Despite the initial enthusiasm in southern Italy for joining the newly unified state, the northern rulers considered the southern half of the autonomous Italian national state more as a conquered province of the North. They displayed little respect for traditional practices in the South, regarding the people as backward and rural, and merely included it in a highly centralized governmental administration that was imposed on all of Italy. Therefore, the Italian king's popularity in the South disappeared almost overnight, and southerners again began to look northward with dis-

Engraved by W. Holl, from a Photograph.

Giuseppe Garibaldi

Courtesy of Special Collections, University of Virginia Library

trust and resentment that has yet to disappear.

The new national leaders next turned to the province of Venetia, which was still in the clutches of the Austrian Empire. When the latter entered a war in 1866 against Prussia, however, Italy immediately sided with the victorious Prussians, who granted their allies the prize Italians had wanted. Only Rome remained outside the new Italy.

The End of the Church State

The ecclesiastical state, under the Pope, remained a drop of melancholy in the wine of the unification. The Vatican resented the reduction of its secular power in the unification of Italy. As the new Italian state was officially declared in 1861, it was taboo even to speak of Piedmont and that part of Italy ruled by it. But when France became locked in war against

Prussia in 1870, French troops could no longer defend Rome against the rest of Italy. Hence, in September royal Italian troops marched into Rome unchallenged, and the national capital was transferred to the city without delay.

The ecclesiastical state came to an end, and the popes withdrew in bitterness behind the Vatican walls with utter contempt for the Italian kingdom. This papal rejection of the Italian state nipped in the bud all attempts to integrate Catholic elements in politics, and the Catholic prohibition against political participation gained strength especially in the more independent–minded South. It hardened many Italians' distrust toward their state, a problem that remains today. Leading liberals asserted their strong anticlerical position despite the Church's opposition. Only in the second decade of the 20th century did the Church support an Italian

Italy

Monument in Rome commemorating the unification of Italy

Popular Party (the *Popolari*), founded in 1919 and a forerunner of the now defunct Christian Democratic (DC) Party. Those historians are certainly correct who argue that an earlier integration of moderate Catholic forces would have helped stabilize Italy's political system and would have helped to prevent the later rise of fascism.

Continued Instability

The first years of unification were overshadowed by political instability, social opposition and an ever–growing gap between North and South. The inhabitants of the South continued to be looked down upon as backward, illiterate semi–North Africans. The people were also disadvantaged by the new liberal leaders' dropping of trade barriers, which clearly favored the industrially powerful North.

The one–crop agrarian society of the South bore the full economic weight of foreign grain imports. Malnutrition, health problems and child labor abuse set in motion an enormous emigration wave from the South. From 1886 to 1890 over 200,000 people left their homeland every year, most of whom sought refuge in the United States. Today, 25 million Americans are of Italian and/or Sicilian descent. The fact that most of their ancestors came from southern Italy helps explain why Americans often have a one–sided view of Italy, namely that of the impoverished South rather than the more opulent North.

Parliamentary proceedings degenerated quickly as deputies became so concerned about clinging to their seats that they avoided taking clear-cut stands on the pressing issues of the day. By means of a method which came to be known as

Trasformismo ("Transformism"), prime ministers and cabinets disregarded party affiliation and made delicate bargains with any interested deputies from the left, right or center in order to patch together a short–lived parliamentary majority. In the process, all political groups became highly fractured, and cabinets changed so constantly that no coherent and consistent governmental policy was possible. Major questions were avoided or postponed, and when domestic pressure for change became too great, governments tended to divert attention from them by taking refuge in such emotional campaigns as anticlericalism or colonialism.

Colonial Ambitions

In order to cope with the problem of a surplus of workers and to divert attention from the domestic political paralysis and tensions, Italy embarked on a colonial policy which was not only unprofitable, but which robbed it of its strength. After a casualty–ridden expedition into the East African coast of Eritrea (formerly in Ethiopia), Italy temporarily conquered this area in 1889–90. A subsequent campaign in Ethiopia ended in catastrophe soon thereafter, costing the lives of 15,000 poorly–equipped soldiers when the Ethiopians drove them out. Italy took Libya and the southeastern Greek islands (Dodecanese) from Turkey, which was in the process of disintegration.

All of these foreign adventures could not distract from the domestic social tensions and conflicts. Rebellions, violent protests, assassinations and bloody reactions against the forces of order became so commonplace by the turn of the 20th century that many observers believed that the young kingdom could not survive.

The most outstanding politician in the early 20th century was Giovanni Giolitti, who tried to fuse the liberal bourgeoisie and socialists who supported the state from 1903 to 1915. He was able to guide some progressive legislation through a highly undisciplined parliament. Factory laws were passed, insurance companies and railways were nationalized, trade unions were legalized, agricultural cooperatives were subsidized and collective bargaining was encouraged. However, he could not overcome the widespread impression among the people that Italy was not only standing still, but was decaying.

Sick and tired of these internal conflicts, a movement of bourgeois intellectuals under the leadership of the poet Gabriele D'Annunzio, and the political thinkers Gaetano Mosca and Vilfredo Pareto gained respect, and practically declared war on the parliamentary system. D'Annunzio called on young Italians to seek fulfillment in violent action that would put an end to parliamentary maneuvering, general mediocrity and dullness that characterized public life. Mosca and Pareto called for a new political elite that understood how to use power and to put an end to materialist values.

A jingoist National Party was created in 1910 under the leadership of Enrico Corradini, who never tired of painting an attractive picture of martial heroism, of total sacrifice of individualism and equality to one's nation, of the need for reestablishing discipline and obedience, of the grandeur and power of ancient Rome and of the personal gratification which comes with living dangerously. Many Italians needed only the travails of a long and disappointing war to make a dangerous leap toward fascism. They heard its extremist appeals with enthusiasm.

World War I

Although Italy had allied itself with Germany and Austria–Hungary in 1882, it declared its neutrality at the outbreak of World War I in 1914 on the grounds that its allies were waging an aggressive war. For more than 10 years it had pursued, under Giolitti's leadership, a policy of peaceful reconciliation in Europe. Italy did, in fact, enter World War I against Austria and Germany in 1915. In Hemingway's *A Farewell to Arms*, one sees that the Italian war against Austria was neither easily won nor advantageous for Italy. It lost 600,000 men in battle, and the Italian economy was wrecked by the war. The public debt swelled, inflation ran out of control and many of the demobilized soldiers left one kind of army for another: that of the unemployed.

To make things worse, the aftermath of the Paris peace settlement following the

309

Italy

war never fulfilled Italy's high expectations. Trentino and the city of Trieste became part of the country, as did the Istrian Peninsula and the German–speaking part of South Tirol, which even today remains a bone of contention between Austria and Italy.

Postwar Chaos

Italy had entered the post-World War I era as a society badly off balance. Without relief, lawlessness in the countryside and towns, strikes in the cities as well as sharp and often violent domestic differences of opinion, polarized the political scene. The war had brought revolution in Russia, and with that revolution a breaking away in Italy and elsewhere of radically revolutionary communists from the more moderate socialist parties. The establishment of the Communist Party of Italy (PCI) scared many anti–Marxist Italians, who became sympathetic to the idea of a strong leader who could protect Italy from the communist revolution. This included many wealthy landowners and industrialists.

The war had also frustrated the dreams of many Italian nationalists, who had believed that Italy should become a major Mediterranean and Balkan power. Millions of returning veterans were bitter about the fact that their country seemed to show no appreciation for the suffering and sacrifice they had endured. Even appearing on the streets in uniform was bound to evoke abuse. Finally, the traditional Italian parties and elites were almost wholly incapable of coping with the domestic political situation. Therefore, a vacuum and a constituency were created for a charismatic opportunist with extremely flexible principles and an emotionally appealing, but intellectually fraudulent political theory: Benito Mussolini.

Mussolini and the Fascists

Born the son of a blacksmith and a schoolteacher in 1883, Mussolini had been educated in a seminary, but had been expelled because he reportedly stabbed another student. After teaching school for a few years, he fled to Switzerland in order to avoid military service. He grew tired of exile after a couple of years and returned to Italy to serve in the army, rising like Hitler to the rank of corporal. He then became a prolific journalist, an activity he performed quite effectively and which helped launch a meteoric career in Socialist politics. He left behind 44 volumes of his collected writings. In 1911 he was jailed briefly for his inflammatory articles against Italy's colonial policy in North Africa, and in 1912 he was named editor–in–chief of the major Socialist Party newspaper, *Avanti*! ("Forward") of Milan. His writings and speeches sometimes

took excursions into anarchism, and they were always radical. At the Socialist Party congress at Reggio in mid–1912, he was among those party members who vehemently rejected a moderate course for the party and insisted that socialism must destroy the "bourgeois experiment" of democracy.

He never veered from his bitter opposition to liberal democracy, but after the outbreak of World War I, he revealed how fluid his political convictions really were. Unlike his former socialist comrades, he strongly supported Italy's involvement in the war. He maintained that it was one of the country's finest hours and that the conniving, greedy politicians at home had betrayed the young heroes. He had coined the slogan "war or revolution," which clearly presented the only alternatives as he saw them. The moving and persuasive eloquence with which he used the Italian language, his undeniable charisma and showmanship and his appearance of raw manliness (although he was in reality often a timid man in times of crisis when daring moves needed to be taken) greatly appealed to the lost, the frightened and the bored.

They flocked to the many loosely–knit *Fasci* (groups) that sprang into existence in imitation of the *Fascio di combattimento* (fighting group), which Mussolini had founded in Milan in 1919. Mussolini wanted to weld a coalition with the non–communist left, but he found little support for such a union. It took a couple of years for him to gain full control of the fascist movement, named after the Latin word *fasces*, which meant a bundle of sticks around an ax, an ancient Roman symbol of state authority. Not until 1921

Benito Mussolini

was the Fascist Party formally created. Mussolini quickly saw that the government's inability or unwillingness to step in and bring the rural and industrial violence under control offered a welcome opportunity for the Fascists to present themselves as the protectors of life, property, law and order.

His *Squadristi* (black–shirted bully squads) roamed the streets unimpeded and intimidated voters and opponents. When the Socialists proclaimed a general strike in August 1922, the Italian public became exasperated with this newest in a series of crippling strikes. It did nothing as the Fascists sacked or smashed trade union or Socialist party headquarters and presses all over Italy, including those of *Avanti*!, the paper which Mussolini once edited. They also seized control of the city

Benito Mussolini—*Il Duce*

Mussolini and his "Black Shirts"

councils in Cremona, Ferrara, Livorno, Parma and Ravenna. These brazen, but unopposed acts were merely the prelude to a Fascist *coup d'état* that had been long–planned.

After delicate negotiations with royalist and Church circles to assure their acquiescence, Mussolini mobilized his Black Shirts for a "March on Rome" on October 22, 1922. Mussolini demonstrated that he was not entirely confident such a seizure of power would succeed by remaining close to the Swiss border in order to be able to escape into exile just in case the march failed. The prime minister tried to persuade King Victor Emmanuel III to sign a declaration of martial law in order to deal with the crisis, but the latter refused. Informed that there would be no resistance whatsoever, Mussolini took a night train to Rome, where the King appointed him prime minister. After so much violence and lawlessness, Rome fell to the Fascists without a shot being fired. This outrageous act of political adventurers would have been foiled if the forces of order had only shown the smallest bit of courage.

Step by step, Mussolini (who named himself *Il Duce*—"The Leader") transformed Italy into the first European dictatorship outside of Russia. He combined workers, employers and other groups into organizations called corporations. This corporate structure was intended to convey the mistaken impression that class and other social conflicts had been or were being eliminated. It therefore was used to justify the abolition of trade unions and strikes, which were allegedly no longer necessary to protect workers.

His power was insured through the introduction of censorship, a strict administration, a youth movement led by the state, a sham one–party electoral system, the incarceration of all political opponents and the creation of a feared secret police (OVRA). The slogan *"credere, obbedire, combattere"* ("believe, obey, fight") reflected the new ideal. Although the king remained on the throne and the bicameral parliament was permitted to go through the motions as if it were functioning, all power by 1925 rested with Mussolini and his Fascist Party, whose organization reached from 10,000 *Fasci* (local) party groups all the way up to a Fascist Grand Council of about 20 men. All other parties were outlawed.

Fascist "Theory" and Administration

In the Fascist ideology Mussolini had helped to concoct, freedom had allegedly been created through authoritarianism, and nobility and heroism had been established through discipline and sacrifice. The state was glorified, and liberalism, democracy and socialism were condemned. On top of that allegedly well–ordered state stood the leader, Mussolini, a man with a knack for sensationalism, self–dramatization, effective oratory and heavy–handedness toward those who were weaker than he. The subsequent persecution of all opposition forces was restrained in comparison to the terror in Nazi Germany.

The dead–end policies to establish an autarkical (internationally independent) economy corrupted the initial economic successes resulting from protective tariffs and grandiose state-sponsored projects. The antiquated relationships of the property owners toward the peasants in the agrarian South remained unaffected, and the power of the Mafia was temporarily broken. Of far–reaching importance, however, were the Lateran Treaties (Feb. 11, 1929) with the Vatican. Mussolini settled the long–standing dispute with the Church over its role in Italian politics by granting it extensive opportunities to influence political and social affairs within Italy (see Vatican City State).

World War II

Italy was ill prepared for the wars it fought, at first on a small scale against Ethiopia in 1935, and then later against

Italy

Germany's enemies in World War II. After Mussolini's attempts to conquer Albania and Greece in 1941 had failed, Italy and the Duce became more dependent upon Hitler than the Italians had intended. Their initial enthusiasm about the adventure of war soon turned to resignation and disappointment. Although Italy was supposedly a "partner" in the Axis, Hitler and the Germans in some ways considered it as much a problem as an asset insofar as the war effort was concerned. Although Mussolini was arrogant and boastful in public, he was rather timid in reality.

Things got worse when the Americans, British and Canadians began to launch successful attacks against the Italian homeland. In mid–1943 British and Canadian forces landed on the east coast of Sicily and took Syracuse, while General George S. Patton's troops landed in the south of the island and took Marsala and Palermo. They then joined the British forces to expel the Germans who were in control of Sicily. The allies next turned toward the Italian mainland and began bombing Rome on July 19.

The sober reality of war right in the city of Rome brought the downfall of Mussolini. The Fascist Grand Council, formerly a malleable tool in Mussolini's hands, which had not met since 1939, demanded his resignation, which the king ordered the next day. The former *Duce* was arrested as he left the royal palace, but German paratroopers rescued him later in a daring, precision operation. Totally at the mercy of Germans, Mussolini eked out a temporary existence as head of a puppet fascist state in German–occupied northern Italy until April 28, 1945, when communist partisans murdered him and publicly hanged him and his mistress upside down. A few days later, his protector, Hitler, shot himself and had his body burned in Berlin to escape such ignoble public treatment.

Unfortunately, long, drawn–out negotiations in the summer of 1943 between the Anglo–American allies and the new Italian government under Marshal Pietro Badoglio enabled the Germans to improve their defenses in Italy. Therefore, when an armistice could finally be signed and an amphibious assault could be launched the very same day against the mainland on September 3, 1943, the Germans were well–prepared. The British Eighth Army under General Montgomery landed with little difficulty on the coast of Calabria. By contrast, the American landing at Salerno thereafter was resisted fiercely and almost ended in disaster.

The rugged and hilly Italian terrain, combined with the dogged German resistance under Marshal Kesselring, rendered

Uniformed police—*carabinieri*

Courtesy: Jon Markham Morrow

every mile of northward advance in the peninsula painful and costly. The Germans had dug in their heels along the so–called Gustav Line, in the center of which was located the almost impregnable 1,700 foot (510 meter) tall Monte Cassino, which guarded the road through the Liri Valley toward Rome. In order to try to circumvent these formidable defenses, the Americans made another amphibious landing at Anzio, located only 33 miles (53 km.) south of Rome. But the American troops were pinned to the slopes overlooking the beach under murderous fire for four months until they could finally break free. In April 1944 Monte Cassino finally fell at the cost of thousands of American lives and after the allies had made the much–criticized decision to bomb the Benedictine abbey there, which the Germans were effectively using for observation purposes.

In June 1944 allied troops entered Rome. When seven allied divisions were withdrawn shortly thereafter in order to take part in an amphibious landing in southern France, the possibility of driving the German armies entirely out of Italy quickly disappeared. Italy therefore remained partially occupied by the Germans until the end of the war. On the plus side, the Italian invasion diverted German troops which otherwise would have been available elsewhere. The expertise gained— in complex amphibious operations at beaches like Anzio and Salerno, in fighting as a large, multinational coalition, in occupying a big fractious defeated country, and in reorganizing civil society and infrastructure from the ground up—were very useful in the subsequent invasions of

France and Germany. Tactically, it was a costly mistake, since Italy presented no threat, and the terrain made it a defender's battlefield, not an invader's. This is reflected in the tremendous number of allied casualties. Three quarters of a million American GIs served in Italy, and 23,501 of them were killed in action.

The Italian resistance to the Axis powers was militarily significant in the course of the war. After the war the resistance became a symbol of solidarity, and it should have helped the Italians to put aside some of their many regional, political and social differences. Unfortunately, the adhesive effect of the resistance proved to be weaker and more transitory than many had hoped.

After the war, Italy found itself again in the strange position of being both the conqueror and the conquered. Regular troops and partisan units had fought against the Germans ever since the fall of Mussolini in mid–1943. However, the fact that this same Italy had been an ally of Nazi Germany and had led attacks against Albania, Yugoslavia and Greece, had not been forgotten. Historian R.J.B. Bosworth calculates that through his wars, Mussolini was responsible for the deaths of one million people. In contrast to Germany, Italy was able to preserve its national unity, but this was due chiefly to the crucial assistance of the influential Italians living in the United States.

The peace treaty that took effect September 15, 1947, required Italy to renounce all claims on Ethiopia and Greece and to cede the Dodecanese Islands back to Greece and five small Alpine areas to France. In addition, the Istrian Peninsula (including Fiume and Pola) was awarded to Yugoslavia. Trieste was made a free city until 1954, when it and a 90–square–mile (135 sq. km.) zone were transferred to Italy. The remainder went to Yugoslavia. In addition, Italy was required to pay reparations to the Soviet Union and Albania.

GOVERNMENT

A majority of Italian voters in a national referendum held in June 1946 chose to abolish the monarchy and to establish a democratic republic. Not until 56 years later, in 2002, did parliament agree that the ban against Italy's male royalty from entering the country would be lifted. Victor Emmanual, who left Italy at age nine, pledged allegiance to the Italian republic. He and his son Emmanuel Filiberto, live in Switzerland, where Victor was jailed in 2006 on charges of racketeering, gambling and prostitution.

With the unpleasant memories of a dictator and a rigid one–party state fresh in their minds, the framers of the postwar constitution made two important decisions which have made it difficult for the country's political institutions to cope with some of Italy's festering economic and social problems. First, they greatly curtailed the powers of the head of government in order to make the reemergence of a dictator almost impossible. Second, they adopted the proportional representation system of voting that gave parliamentary seats to as many parties as possible.

Italy is a centralized, unitary state. As in France, the prefect in each of the 106 provinces is appointed by and accountable to the central government. The 20 regions each elect regional parliaments and wield limited political power, but they still are chiefly administrative units for the central government. Five of these regions have had special statutes for a long time: Sicily, Sardinia, Valle d'Aosta, Friuli–Venezia Giulia, and Trentino–Alto Adige. Within the latter, known in Austria as South Tyrol, are two partly German-speaking special provinces, Trento and Bolzano, which enjoy autonomy. They benefit from a separate German-language school system and legally mandated bilingualism. When 113 of the 116 municipalities in Alto Adige signed a petition in 2006 asking Austrian authorities to help protect their language rights, they touched a raw nerve in Italy. The other 15 regions were created in 1970. This broadening of regional government led an actual decentralization of political power in Italy.

In 2001 a further devolution of power in the regions was approved in a referendum. The reform made the 20 regions responsible for everything, including raising taxes, not constitutionally granted to the central government in Rome. In September 2004 parliament accepted measures to grant the regions new powers over health, education and law and order.

In a June 2006 referendum voters rejected by a wide margin of 61% to 39% a proposal to change more than 50 of 139 articles in the constitution. Turnout was 52%; a 50% is required for any referendum to pass. Originally conceived by the Northern League, the reform would have transformed Italy into a quasi-federal state by devolving more powers to the regions. It would also have reduced the size of the legislature and strengthened the power of the prime minister by allowing him to disband parliament (which only the president can do) and appoint and fire cabinet members (of which the president must now approve).

The constitutional court judges the constitutionality of laws, decisions made by state or regional councils, and accusations against the president. It is made up of 15 judges, five of whom are nominated by the president, five by parliament in joint session, and five by the magistrates' supreme council. In 1985 the Italian government revised the 55–year–old concordat with the Vatican ending the status of Roman Catholicism as the state religion; Italy became a secular state. The Church accepted the civil court's right to decide on marital annulments, previously the exclusive right of the Church, and it agreed that religious instruction in public schools would be optional.

Post-Cold War Renovation

A political earthquake occurred in Italy that has brought about profound changes in the country's parliamentary system and party politics. Italians have always known that there was corruption in high places, but what they have now learned is taking their breaths away. It began in 1991 with the arrest of a Socialist Party official in Milan (Mario Chiesa) who was caught taking bribes on a cleaning contract in a home for the elderly. But it developed into an explosion that affected the nation's entire political order.

Investigations (called "Operation Clean Hands") into embezzlement, illicit bribes, and kickbacks to political parties and politicians in return for public–works contracts have produced the greatest public corruption scandal in modern European history. The estimated $11 billion in annual rip-offs was equivalent to the government's annual deficit. The investigations uncovered evidence that the Mafia and top government leaders might have cooperated for years. None of the traditional parties escaped unharmed; all were discredited.

Until the collapse of communism in Europe, Italians had grudgingly tolerated misgovernment by leaders mainly preoccupied with party intrigue and devious fund–raising because it seemed like the alternative would have been rule by the Communist Party of Italy, which had discomforting links with the Soviet Union. With that danger gone, most Italians saw no reason not to confront head on the rot in the political establishment. By mid–1993, more than 2,600 persons in the political and business elite, including top corporate executives, party chairmen, and three former prime ministers, had either been arrested or were under investigation. Entire regional and local governments had been jailed or forced to resign.

Voters' disgust came to a head in a historic referendum in April 1993. Voting on eight separate questions, over 90% voted to abolish state financing of political parties, and 83% chose to scrap the system of proportional representation in the Senate. Designed in the post–fascist era to prevent another single party, such as Mussolini's, from gaining power, this system created government by weak coalitions of quarrelsome partners and by an oligarchy of often corrupt party leaders.

The 1993 referendum was a stunning rebuke to politicians and their machinery of power. Operation Clean Hands officially came to an end in 2003. However, in the preceding decade all of the institutions and parties discussed below were changed or influenced by the rage and determination that had been expressed.

The pressure was kept on by a best-selling book published in 2007 by two journalists—Sergio Rizzo and Gian Antonio Stella—entitled *La Casta* (The Caste). They describe the many privileges and perks of the deeply entrenched political class. They estimate that from 600,000 to 700,000 live off the political machine. There will always be plenty of Italians clamoring to win parliamentary seats. Few benefit from high-paying jobs more than members of parliament (MPs). They have the highest salaries for parliamentarians in all of Europe: 16,000 euros ($24,000) a month, including funds for staff members whether they have any or not. After only 30 months they are eligible for a lifelong pension beginning as early as age 60. With such frequent elections, there are three times more retired parliamentarians than active ones. The turnover continued in the 2008 elections, when 40% of the elected MPs were new. It is little wonder that the annual cost of Italy's parliament is the highest in Europe.

The number of sitting MPs "in trouble with the law" remains high although the number had fallen from 91 to 70 after the April 2008 elections. On of them was the

Italy

newly elected Prime Minister Silvio Berlusconi, who still faced two court cases after more charges were dropped either because his earlier government had changed laws or because of the statute of limitations.

Parliament

Italy is a parliamentary democracy with a bicameral legislature. The Chamber of Deputies is composed of 630 members elected until 1994 and then again from 2006 by proportional representation in 32 electoral districts at least every five years. The 2005 electoral reform aimed to add more stability to governments by reducing the number of parties in the Chamber and giving a reward to the electoral coalition that wins the most votes. A party linked to a coalition needs to win at least 2% of the votes to win a seat. A party running independently must get at least 4%, and a coalition of parties needs to capture at least 10%.

The winning coalition is guaranteed a minimum of 340 seats, however narrow the margin of its victory. The intent is to increase the chances of a stable governing coalition composed of as few parties as possible. For example, in 2008 the center-right coalition led by Silvio Berlusconi's People of Freedom party got 344 lower house seats based on 46.81% of the votes. The center-left coalition under Walter Veltroni's Democratic Party got only 246 seats although it won 37.54% of the votes. The 9% advantage gave Berlusconi a 98-seat majority, more than enough to move into the prime minister's magnificent residence in central Rome, the Palazzo Chigi. This huge majority, combined with the fact that only six parties (plus three minuscule parties that took only 4 seats) won seats (compared with 23 parties in the previous parliament), promises a stable government that can serve out its full five-

year term. The 2008 elections produced the first Italian parliament with more than 20% women; the 170 places Italy above the European average. There is also one Muslim, Souad Sbai, a Moroccan women's activist.

The Senate is composed of 315 elected members. Every five years members representing the 20 regions (the exceptions being the valley of Aosta, which sends a senator and the province of Molise, which sends two) are elected. Beginning in 2006, members are elected by proportional representation. As in the lower house, the new system aims to reduce the number of parties with seats. A party linked to an electoral coalition needs at least 3% to win a seat. One running alone must get 8%. A coalition of parties must win at least 20%. Seats are distributed on a regional basis. The winner in each region receives at least 55% of the region's seats. It is possible for an electoral coalition to win the most votes but receive fewer seats. For example, in 2006, Berlusconi's center-right won 50.2% of the votes, but got only 156 seats. Prodi's center-left garnered 48.9% of the votes, but received 158 seats. That was not the case in 2008. Berlusconi's coalition captured 47.32% of the votes and 174 seats, while Veltroni's coalition won 38% and only 132 seats.

In contrast to the Chamber of Deputies, the Senate contains some non–elected members. Every ex–president of the republic is a senator for life, and the president appoints five other senators for life, based on their outstanding achievements in social, scientific, or artistic and literary fields. The oldest senator elected was 99-year-old Nobel Prize winner, Rita Levi Montalcini. The 3.4 million Italians living abroad elect 12 deputies and six senators to represent them; these are added to the 630 and 315 members. The constituencies for these seats are huge: Europe (including Russia and Turkey), South America, North and Central America, and Africa-Asia-Oceania-Antarctica. The speaker of the Senate is a powerful political figure and is the equivalent to the vice president of the republic. He takes over if the president is unable to perform his duties.

Both houses have identical powers. Both function and make decisions independently, and both must pass a bill before it is forwarded to the president of the republic for signature. The government must have the confidence of both chambers. The legislative system is slow and cumbersome, making passage of laws difficult. Because of the electoral system, almost the same constellation of parties is represented in both chambers with the same proportion of parties in the standing committees. The Senate has 11 such committees and the Chamber of Deputies 14.

In both houses party politics determines all aspects of the legislative process.

Since 1988 party discipline is easier to maintain because of the elimination of secret voting, which had permitted dissidents to vote anonymously against their own parties and bring down their own governments; the result was perennially weak government. Secret balloting had been one stumbling block to efficient rule under a constitution that had been designed four decades ago primarily to prevent another Mussolini from coming to power. Until 2006 no Italian legislature had lived its full five–year life.

Presidency

The president is elected by the members of both houses of parliament and by three delegates from each regional council for a seven–year term. Any citizen over the age of 50 is eligible. In order to maximize the possibility that the president be a national unifying figure and impartial, a two-thirds majority is required. But if such a special majority cannot be reached after two ballots, then a simple majority is enough. This was the case in May 2006, when three days were needed to select the winner.

The president is an influential player in the political system. He can veto a law, but a simple majority in both houses can override his veto. All acts of the president require the countersignature of the appropriate cabinet minister, who assumes political responsibility for these acts. He formally declares a state of war, calls elections, appoints the prime minister and dissolves parliament.

The presidency is gaining in influence. In 1991 Francesco Cossiga grew tired of his figurehead role and proclaimed his intention "to shake a few pebbles out of my shoes." He startled the nation by becoming more involved in everyday politics. His moves caused a storm of controversy. In 1992 he decided to give "a shock to the

President Giorgio Napolitano

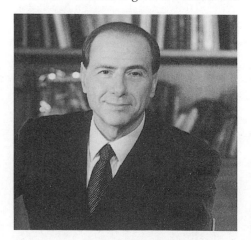

Former Prime Minister Silvio Berlusconi

The Senate and The Italian Chamber of Deputies (630 members), 2008

Source: *The Financial Times*

political classes" by resigning two months before his term ended. He charged that Italy's traditional politicians had ignored the electorate's reform message in the parliamentary elections.

His successor, Oscar Luigi Scalfaro, broke long–standing practices in 1993 by not consulting the ruling parties before selecting the first prime minister not to belong to a political party: Carlo Azeglio Ciampi, a respected civil servant and head of the independent Bank of Italy. Scalfaro charged him with enacting sweeping political reform, trimming the budget, and then bowing out after early elections. In the past, party leaders dictated the political direction to president. But in 1993 it was President Scalfaro who delivered the marching orders to the party chiefs.

In May 1999 Ciampi became president. He demonstrated that the president is no mere figurehead. In 2003 he refused to sign into law a controversial reform of the media sector that Berlusconi's government had pushed through parliament. A year later he blocked changes to the judicial system that seemed to curb the independence of judges and prosecutors.

On May 10, 2006, Giorgio Napolitano was elected. A former moderate communist leader until 1989 and president of the lower house, he represents the integration of former communists into the current political system. At 80 he was the oldest man ever to be elected to the office. Some noted that a gerontocracy had taken over the country, with the average age of the top four political leaders in 2006 being 71. No less a luminary than Cicero would approve. He once said: "Old age, especially an honored old age, has such great authority that it is of more value than all the pleasures of youth."

Normally the most delicate political act in which the president is fully involved is the formation of a cabinet. A prospective candidate for the prime ministerial post is charged by the president to form a government. The prospective candidate suggests the composition of the new government after extensive consultations with the possible coalition partners. Whether the prime minister can win and maintain a majority for his cabinet in both chambers is always the decisive question.

Political Parties and Alliances

In May 2008 Italy installed its 62d government since World War II. Until 2001 the average duration of each had been seven months. All governments are coalitions, with disagreement on a single point sometimes bringing down a prime minister. To understand why Italian governments are often so unstable, one must examine the past and current basic party structure.

The multiparty system has traditionally been highly fragmented. However, beginning with the 1996 elections many of the numerous parties grouped themselves into two loose alliances. The *Washington Post* aptly described them at the time as "not coalitions but collages, fragments of political movements thrown together without a cogent denominator other than the aim of power. As such they are prone to instability."

On the center-right in 2008 are the parties that formed Silvio Berlusconi's People of Freedom (formerly House of Liberties), which captured 46.8% and 344 Chamber of Deputies seats (47.3% and 174 Senate seats). They include his own People of Freedom (formerly Forza Italia—"Go, Italy!"), which won 37.4% of the votes and 276 seats (38.2% and 147 Senate seats). The National Alliance (formerly the neofascist Italian Social Movement—MSI), led by Gianfranco Fini (appointed speaker of the Chamber of Deputies and often mentioned as Berlusconi's likely successor) was absorbed by People of Freedom before the election. Coalition allies are the Northern League, led by Umberto Bossi, which doubled its votes from 4.58% and 26 seats to 8.3% and 60 seats (8% and 25 Senate seats), and its southern Italian equivalent, the Movement for Autonomy, which captured 1.13% of the votes and eight seats (1.1% and 2 seats in the Senate).

In the vanishing center was the Union of Center and Christian Democrats (UDC, led by Pier Ferdinando Casini), a breakaway minority from the former ruling Christian Democrats (DC), which got 5.6% and 36 seats (5.7% and a mere 3 Senate seats). His dream of holding the balance between left and right remains just that—a dream.

On the center-left is the Democratic Party (PD), which in 2008 won 33.2% of the votes and 217 seats (33.7% and 118 seats in the Senate). Its sole coalition partner, Italy of Values, climbed from 2.3% and 16 seats to 4.4% and 29 seats in 2008 (4.3% and 14 seats in the Senate). PD consciously excluded far-left parties from its coalition. As a result, the Communists were routed in the elections and for the first time in the history of the republic were not represented in parliament; they lost all 84 of their seats. The Greens were also kept out of parliament.

The PD leader is Walter Veltroni, popular former mayor of Rome, who had begun his career at age 21 as a Communist on the Rome city council. He later edited the Communist daily newspaper, *L'Unita*, for five years. In October 2007 he won a huge primary majority to lead the new party, which he promised would be "a

Italy

new force" with a "new language." He professed admiration for America's big-tent Democratic Party, especially John Kennedy, and he openly modeled himself and his new party on presidential candidate Barack Obama. An author of over a dozen books, including a novel, he wrote the preface for the Italian edition of Obama's book, *The Audacity of Hope,* and wrote: Obama is innovative, unifying and post-ideological." He included Obama's image in his election videos and even adopted as its slogan, "*Si puo fare!*" (It can be done!) While Berlusconi flew every-where during his campaign, Veltroni traveled throughout Italy on a green campaign bus called "Pullman." Almost 20 years younger than the 71-year-old Berlusconi, he called for a generational change in Italian politics. Desiring to make his PD party the sole party on the left, Veltroni announced in advance that he would make no alliance in either house of parliament.

PD had replaced "The Union," a broad nine-party coalition led by outgoing Prime Minister Romano Prodi. The old "Union" had included the "Olive Tree" coalition, a patchwork of ex-Communists, liberals, greens, some former Christian Democrats, and a few independents. Created in 1996, they had together made history by becoming Italy's first leftist government, under Prodi. They broke a long-standing taboo by including nine former communists in the ruling coalition, more than from any other single party.

In 2006 Olive Tree coalition took power for 20 months by combining the moderate ex-communist Democrats of the Left (DS, formerly the Communist Party of Italy—PCI) and *Margherita* (Daisy)-Democracy is Freedom. Prodi stepped in to organize the disparate groups for the April 2006 elections and moved the left closer to a unified party. He suggested an American-style primary election to select the left's leader (himself), who would thereby enjoy an unparalleled degree of legitimacy. That was done in October 2005, with the members of all the parties in the coalition having a vote; Prodi won 75%. To prevent the incessant warring on the left, he proposed a broad-based Democratic Party like its American namesake. The hard-line Refounded Communists, which broke off from DS in 1998, ran its own candidates. Groups on the left have their own daily newspapers wherein they passionately debate issues in which the average voters have little or no interest.

The shift to such a unified right and left had begun in 1993, when the entire political landscape began to change. Before that the political fronts in Italy were polarized and rigid. The problem was that parties cornering roughly a third of the vote—the PCI and the MSI—were unacceptable as coalition partners, leaving only two–thirds within which to find a majority. Neither of the two largest parties was capable of winning a majority. No governing coalition could be formed without the participation of the defunct Christian Democrats and the Socialists. Together with the Social Democrats, the Liberals and sometimes the Republicans, these two parties could paste together a wobbly temporary majority in parliament composed of five parties (called the *Penta-partito*), which were generally more interested in their own survival and in delivering maximum benefits to their own special constituencies than in providing stable government capable of dealing with Italy's pressing problems.

The DC and the Socialists were never natural partners for reasons of ideology and strategy. Any coalition between them was by nature unstable because the partners were fierce competitors. The DC could not win a majority by itself, and most Italians did not accept the Communists as ready for a place in the government. Thus, about a dozen small parties held the balance. This insured incoherence and produced a string of short–lived governments with narrow attention spans.

Even elections could not always produce a government; they could create only the raw materials for one. They seldom settled questions; they merely deferred them. Following elections, an acceptable coalition, composed almost invariably of the same parties which were in the last one, was hammered together only after a drawn–out process of bargaining. It could take weeks or months until the many demands of powerful party and factional leaders had been satisfied and balanced. While there was a certain stability inherent in this process, the damage to the political system was clear. Widespread corruption and cynicism toward rulers flourished in a fragmented political scene in which politicians were well entrenched with little possibility of being displaced. Nobody expected major changes. One voter remarked before the 1992 polling, "we all know that when the vote is counted we will be right back where we started."

That may be changing as Italy is moving toward a two-party system (or at least two opposing blocks) with fewer and fewer parties in parliament. In 2006, 39 parties won seats in parliament; in 2008 only six succeeded, all moderate. Even though the two main parties are still young and somewhat undefined, Berlusconi's People of Freedom victory in 2008 offers the reasonable hope that Italy's 62d postwar government will be stable and durable, lasting five full years. After all,

The National Alliance's Gianfranco Fini

he is the only postwar prime minister to have survived a full term, from 2001 to 2005. The left-leaning *La Repubblica* wrote of "an electoral tsunami that redraws Italy's political landscape." Becoming prime minister for the third time in a clear and convincing win, Berlusconi announced confidently: "Now we'll govern like major western democracies, with one major party in power and one major party in opposition."

THE RIGHT

People of Freedom (ex-Forza Italia)

At the head of this party is one of Italy's richest men (the world's 51st richest, according to Forbes in 2008), Silvio Berlusconi, an entrepreneurial superstar whose business empire, Fininvest, includes three TV networks dominating commercial television, Italy's largest department store chain, the top–selling newsmagazine, and an array of other investments, including the AC Milan soccer club. His opponents charge that he misused his three TV networks, which control 45% of the Italian audience, to propagandize voters. They also claim that a politician with such vast and varied investments cannot escape from conflicts of interest. He is a man with telegenic good looks, enormous energy and determination, an excellent business brain, and a shrewd understanding of the nature of power.

He claimed to have been forced into politics "to keep my country from falling into the hands of the communists." Centrist reformers had failed to organize an effective bloc against the communists' momentum. Its deputies tend to be young, ambitious professionals and business people who helped change the character of the parliament by lowering the average age (40% under age 50 and 25% under 40), raising the percentage of university graduates to 75, and increasing the number of women representatives from 51 to 170 (of whom 70 are from the conservative ruling parties). People of Freedom must coalesce with the autonomy–seeking Northern League, with its roots in the rich and industrialized Lombardy region around Milan (Berlusconi's home town), and its southern equivalent—the Movement for Autonomy. People of Freedom absorbed the National Alliance before the 2008 elections; its voters are concentrated in the impoverished South, and it advocates a strong central government.

In its first attempt at governing, Berlusconi's heterogeneous coalition could not give Italy what has eluded it for more than four decades: stable government. In December 1994 it collapsed after only eight months when the Northern League walked out. Berlusconi had refused to separate himself from his business empire. When he was formally placed under investigation for his business dealings, including tax fraud and corruption, he could no longer survive as prime minister.

Berlusconi was convicted in 1997 for false accounting (though his 16–month sentence was commuted). In 1998 he was sentenced to two years and nine months in prison for bribery although his parliamentary immunity and the appeals process kept him out of jail. In 2003 he became the first sitting Italian prime minister to be called to give testimony as a criminal defendant in his own bribery trial. Although he has never been definitely convicted of anything, his close friends, have.

Berlusconi used his majority in parliament to pass laws that make prosecuting corruption cases more difficult. They included a retroactive measure to restrict the use of evidence gathered abroad, especially secret bank account records, the decriminalizing of false bookkeeping convictions, amnesty for illegal transfer of funds outside Italy, change of venue for trials away from judges who are "legitimately suspected" of bias, and immunity for the country's top five posts from facing trial while they hold office.

When Berlusconi attempted in December 2003 to protect one of his family's TV networks, President Ciampi refused to sign the bill and sent it back to parliament. A month later the Constitutional Court struck down the law granting immunity from trial to the state's five highest officials, including the prime minister, on the grounds that it violated the principle that all citizens are equal before the law. This decision prepared the way for Berlusconi's suspended trial to reopen. He never enacted a law to deal with his conflicts of interest, and his family did not divest itself of the nation's three largest private TV channels. In any other democratic country he would probably have been forced to step down, but not in Italy. Not only had his popularity not suffered, but a poll published in *Corriere delle Sera*, revealed that only a third of Italians trust the judicial system.

Less than two months after losing his second prime minister's position in May 2006, Berlusconi was ordered to face trial on charges of fraudulent accounting and money laundering. He was back in court in March 2007 on bribery charges. But he

escaped conviction because Italy's statue of limitations and interminable judicial delays make it almost impossible to convict someone of a white-collar crime. Some Italians suspect that he remains in politics primarily to protect himself from the justice system.

In the April 2006 national elections Berlusconi tried for an unprecedented three victories in a row. Already his ruling coalition had been Italy's longest-serving government since the return of democracy in 1945 and the only government to serve out a full five-year parliamentary term. It provided unaccustomed continuity. He began his third run as prime minister in May 2008.

National Alliance

Until 1994 the neo–fascist Italian Social Movement–National Right (MSI–DN) could be found at the outer right fringe of the party spectrum. It understood how to capitalize on the disadvantaged population of southern Italy. But protests against the establishment and disappointment over the center–left governments never took it over 7% of the votes. In terms of a political program, the MSI maintained entirely the tradition of Italian fascism.

But then came a new and intelligent young leader, Gianfranco Fini, who steered the party away from the corporatism and exaggerated nationalism of old fascism and gave it a new program (which he calls "post–fascism") and a more respectable name: National Alliance. The MSI was dissolved in 1995. The fascist hardliners who could not accept this change broke away and created their own *Fiamma Tricolore*, which languished in irrelevance.

Fini studiously avoided contacts with extreme–rightist groups elsewhere in Europe and condemned anti–Semitism, attacks against foreigners, and skinhead violence. Emphasizing clean government, law and order (including reintroduction of the death penalty), stricter immigration controls, family values, and the preservation of Italian unity, he transformed the party into a broad–based mainstream conservative political force, modeled on the French Gaullists, and a major player in Italian politics.

Having been excluded from government for a half century, it could not be blamed for corruption and poor performance, as could Italy's traditional parties. Fini declared during the campaign: "Italy no longer divides itself between fascists and anti–fascists, but between thieves and those with clean hands!"

The reward came in the 1994 elections when it more than doubled its previous electoral score. Capitalizing on the dramatic decline of the former Christian De-

Former Secretary of State Madeleine Albright with ex-Prime Minister Prodi

Italy

**Former Prime Minister Romano Prodi
Ex-President, European Commission**

mocrats, who had long dominated the South, the National Alliance became the strongest political force in the southern half of Italy, including Rome. Fini later became a respected foreign minister.

Not everyone is persuaded that the party's transformation is genuine. Fini himself reinforced the skeptics by once describing Mussolini as "the greatest statesman of the century." Some party members demanded that Italian claims on parts of Istria and Dalmatia in the present Slovenia and Croatia be resurrected, but Fini assured the public that his party would not press this issue. Berlusconi asserted, "fascists do not exist in my government." Citing polls showing that less than 1% of Italians identify themselves as "fascists," he asked, "so how can this be considered dangerous?"

Fini moved resolutely to disavow the party's fascist roots. He referred to the fascist past as "shameful pages of history" and denounced the racism of Mussolini's regime. He visited Israel and advocated that legal immigrants be permitted to vote in local elections. This was too much for Alessandra Mussolini, granddaughter of the fascist dictator and niece of actress Sophia Loren. She temporarily left the party but held on to her parliamentary seat as an independent. A strident feminist, she became a member of the European Parliament. She briefly created her own far-right Social Alternative party, but she joined Berlusconi's People of Freedom in 2008. Some other National Alliance members are critical of Fini's turnaround.

Fini, who became the leader of the Chamber of Deputies in 2008, is arguably the most popular politician on the center-

right and is the man to watch. By joining forces with Berlusconi in the 2008 elections and agreeing to merge his party with the People of Freedom afterwards, he is positioning himself to be Berlusconi's successor, even though the latter is said to dislike him. Many observers suspect that Berlusconi will step down before the end of his entire five-year term.

That the party is on a roll was demonstrated two weeks after the 2008 parliamentary elections when Gianni Alemanno of the National Alliance won 54% of the votes and defeated former Rome mayor and national culture minister, Francesco Rutelli, to become Rome's mayor. It is the first time since Mussolini's time that a conservative has been elected to that prominent post. Alemanno was a former MSI youth leader, who served 14 years in parliament and then as agriculture minister in Berlusconi's previous government. His election created some unease, especially after youthful supporters greeted him following his victory with straight-armed "Roman" salutes, chanted "Duce! Duce!" and screamed abuse against communists and foreign immigrants.

Northern League

In the 1990s all of Italy's established parties anxiously witnessed the rise of leagues seeking regional autonomy in the North. The most successful was the *Lega Nord* (Northern League), led by Umberto Bossi.

The League stands for federalism and devolution of power to the regions. It capitalizes on local dissatisfaction against what is seen as misrule by Rome, which does not seem to act vigorously enough to stem the wave of immigrants and to re-

verse Northern Italy's subsidizing of the South. It charges, with considerable justification, that too much of those funds end up in the pockets of Mafia contractors. A clean–government party, the Northern League benefited from the country's massive corruption scandals. Its spokesman, Roberto Maroni, announced, "our purpose of breaking up Italy is not linked to ethnic or religious identities, but to economic issues." Nevertheless, there is a whiff of racism in its appeals.

Emboldened by its strong election showing in 1996, the League proclaimed northern Italy an "independent and sovereign" republic called "Padania" (for the River Po) and called on the United Nations to recognize its right of self–determination. Unlike the Basque country in Spain and France, Padania has never existed before. Nevertheless, its supporters are playing government. They moved their 15 "ministers" into a Renaissance building in Venice and swore in a self–nominated "parliament" in their "capital city" of Mantua. In 1997 they held unofficial parliamentary elections and charged the assembly with writing a new constitution that would make Padania either independent or loosely confederated with Italy. Advocates waved their own flag, wore green shirts and called themselves "citizens of the North." They called on northerners to refuse to pay their taxes to Rome.

By 2008 Bossi abandoned those calls for Padania secession. Despite such colorful trappings, opinion polls suggested that most northerners opposed secession although many agreed with some of the League's criticisms. Bossi had not helped his cause in 1997 by referring to the Pope

Demonstration by largest union, the CGIL

318

Former Prime Minister Massimo D'Alema, *DS*

as a "foreigner" and saying that the Italian flag belongs in the toilet. This remark brought a million Italians into the streets in Milan and Venice to demonstrate for national unity. In 2005 the League began a campaign to scrap the euro and reintroduce the lira.

In 2004 Bossi, a heavy smoker and hyperactive politician, suffered a serious heart attack, fell into a coma and was hospitalized for weeks. Gravely ill with his overall recovery uncertain, the League had reason to worry about its political future. He returned to politics in June 2005, but he is physically much diminished, and his speech is impaired. He never found it necessary to designate a successor. The up-and-coming star of the party is Roberto Calderoli, whose practical approach has advanced the League's core political projects.

The party was temporarily in disarray after the failed June 2006 referendum to decentralize Italy. But it roared back in the 2008 parliamentary elections, doubling its vote and seats and making itself the indispensable coalition partner for Berlusconi's ruling People of Freedom. Its dramatic revival stems from its strident anti-immigration, anti-crime and anti-globalization rhetoric. Newcomers to Italy are branded as a social and cultural threat.

THE VANISHED CENTER

Union of Center and Christian Democrats

In the center only the Union of Center and Christian Democrats (UDC), led by Pier Ferdinando Casini, retains a parliamentary presence. It is a breakaway minority from the former ruling Christian Democrats (DC). With only 36 seats in the lower house and a mere 3 in the Senate,

its hopes of holding the balance between left and right remains an empty dream.

What happened to the political center? Until 1994 the Christian Democrats (DC) had been the dominant party since 1945, and as such was hit the hardest by the political storm raging in Italy. It had placed in office all prime ministers until the Republican, Giovanni Spadolini, held the office from 1981 to 1982. The DC formed coalitions with all parties except the PDS (Communists) and MSI (neo-fascists). By 1983, 64% of all mayors, 57% of city councilors, 90% of the managers of state–operated businesses, 94% of all savings and loan presidents and 58% of all bank presidents were members of the DC. In addition to the broad spectrum of closely related organizations in all sectors of the society in which the DC party exercises influence, the party received special support from the Catholic Church. Two–thirds of the DC's 1,200 sections had been founded in 1946 at the insistence and under the influence of local clerics.

Ideologically, the DC built upon the two larger middle-class parties of the pre-fascist period. The Catholicism of the old Popular Party and the economic liberalism of the old Liberal Party were the pillars for the DC's political conception. In accordance with the Manifesto of Milan of 1943, the DC defined itself as a "Catholic People's Party" encompassing all classes. It had no binding party program. Instead, it was the classical example of the "catch–all party."

The DC's adaptability and its openness to coalitions toward both the right and the left were reasons why for so long it sur-

vived political and economic crises without suffering large electoral losses. However, it refused to agree to a "historical compromise" (*Compromesso storico*) with the Communists. Its heterogeneity helped it to stabilize Italian society and guarantee the proper functioning of the parliamentary system. But it was shaken by scandals that left few of its talented leaders untainted.

Staring electoral disaster in the face, DC renamed itself the Italian Popular Party (PPI) in order to try to improve its image and appeal. The new name was designed to signal a return to the Catholic values of Luigi Sturzo, the priest who had founded the Popular Party in 1919.

A minority refused to stay in the Popular Party, forming instead the Christian Democratic Center Party, which was largely irrelevant. To gain some name recognition, it recruited actress Gina Lollobrigida to be a candidate for the 1999 European Parliament elections. Also losing their political significance were the Italian Republican Party (PRI—the Republicans), the Social Democrats (PSDI), the Italian Liberal Party (PLI) and Italian Renewal. The only center party left standing in 2008 was the Union of Center and Christian Democrats. It rebuffed Berlusconi's request for support and is in the opposition.

THE LEFT

Since the 2008 elections, the left is dominated by the new center-left Democratic Party (PD—formerly the Olive Tree Coalition), modeled in many ways after its

Former President Scalfaro addresses the Chamber of Deputies

Italy

American namesake. It captured 33.2% of the votes and 217 seats (33.7% and 118 seats in the Senate). It absorbed the former Radicals and formed an electoral and parliamentary agreement with the much smaller Italy of Values party, led by Antonio Di Pietro, which garnered 4.4% of the votes and 29 seats (4.3% and 14 seats in the Senate). No other leftist party survived. For the first time since the Second World War, the Communists—represented by The Left-The Rainbow (which included Greens)—were routed and are absent in Parliament. However, the PD is young and fragile, and it is uncertain if and how long it and its leader, Walter Veltroni, will survive politically after its dual losses in the April 2008 parliamentary and Rome mayoralty elections.

Gone is The Union (*L'Unione*), created for the 2006 elections. The most important part was the Olive Tree, which embraced the Democrats of the Left, Daisy-Democracy is Freedom and the European Republican Movement. One of Italy's oldest parties, the Socialist Party, founded in 1892 and one-time political home to Mussolini, has all but disappeared; it won fewer than 1% of the votes for both chambers in 2008. Former communists had been key players in The Union, but they too have been wiped out.

The Communists

The various communist parties grew out of the now defunct Communist Party of Italy (PCI), which had emerged in 1921 and disbanded in 1991. It split into the Party of Democratic Socialism (PDS) and the Refounded Communists (*Rifondazione Comunista*). In 1998 PDS joined several smaller parties and became the Democrats of the Left (DS), which became the largest party on the left with 1.5 million members. In the same year, the Italian Communist Party broke off from the Refounded Communists. The old PCI overcame its political and social isolation of the 1950s and 1960s because it was able to reach beyond its traditional base in the industrial working class and to gain new voters from the middle class. A traditionally atheistic party, it could exist in a country closely associated with the Catholic Church because it quietly dropped atheism as a part of its platform. It also ceased being a Marxist–Leninist cadre party and instead became simply a leftist worker's party. It rejected the concept of its first postwar leader, Palmiro Togliatti, who had wanted to introduce socialism into Italy through revolution. History had proven that efforts to change Italian society through revolution simply helped to drive an uncertain middle class into the arms of the fascists.

In the 1960s the PCI was the first western European communist party publicly to reject the Leninist doctrine of a revolutionary seizure of power followed by a dictatorship of the proletariat. That is, it turned down the model of the Soviet Union and sought its own path to socialism.

This enabled the PCI to accept Italian membership in NATO and the EU. As western Europe's largest communist party, it could become the leader of so-called "Eurocommunism," a movement that discarded Marxist–Leninist orthodoxy as the basis of its ideology. The movement recognized parliamentary democracy as a prerequisite for socialism, which, it believed, could be achieved through a wide consensus of reform–oriented forces. It also rejected the planned economies found in eastern Europe, although this rejection did not imply total acceptance of a free market economy. It is no surprise that these policies led to tensions with the Soviet Union. The DS criticized Moscow over the Soviet occupation of Afghanistan in 1979 and the introduction of martial law in Poland in 1981. Other Italian parties cautiously welcomed such criticism.

In contrast to that of its voters, the social structure of the party members has not basically changed. The reservoir of the party is still industrial workers, who make up approximately three–fourths of its membership. An important lever for accomplishing party goals is the largest union in Italy, the CGIL, with 4.32 million members. One thing that weakened the party is that the number of industrial workers has declined in Italy's modernizing economy. Also, the growth of the service and white-collar sectors reduced the power of trade unions, and that has adversely affected the DS. The new groups in which the party was able to attract voters and members, such as the intellectual and technical elites as well as the civil service workers, remain under–represented in the overall party membership. However, just the opposite can be seen in the party's leadership organs. In the 36–member party directorate, a majority has full university credentials.

To hold on to the votes of young and well–educated people, the DS loosened the leaders' grip on the rank and file by making public criticism of the party no longer grounds for expulsion and by permitting elections to the party's central committee to be held in public. The formerly closed way of making party decisions was replaced by free and open votes in all party committees, from the national to the local level. It formally embraced the market economy and did not oppose the privatization of nationalized industries. It accepted NATO and American bases in Italy, and it rejected unilateral nuclear disarmament.

In 1991, the DS cast off both its name and hammer and sickle symbol and sought membership in the Socialist International. The events in eastern Europe had left the party with no choice. One member admitted, "in terms of Italian politics, this is our Berlin Wall that has come crashing down." The new insignia was a spreading tree, with the hammer and sickle practically hidden in the roots. With the total collapse of Moscow–led communism in Europe, the other parties lost their rationale for excluding the DS from government. It is now willing to enter a governing coalition with any major party. It was the main pillar of the Olive Tree coalition.

In October 1998, DS leader Massimo D'Alema became the first ex–communist to form an Italian government. A pensive former editor of Italy's largest leftist newspaper, *L'Unità*, which after a makeover still sells 50,000 copies a day (down from 300,000 in its heyday), and author of many books, one of which is aptly entitled *La Grande Occasione* (The Big Chance), D'Alema admires Tony Blair's style of reform and attacked irresponsible trade unionists. He broke a record by bringing nine parties into his government, sarcastically dubbed "the first center–left government of the center–right open to the radical left." It included Communists, ex-Communists, various Greens and centrists. This government fell in April 2000.

In 2006 D'Alema became foreign minister. Another former prime minister from DS, Giuliano Amato, became interior minister. In April 2007 D'Alema proposed that DS merge with Democracy and Freedom (Margherita), a suggestion that appalled some of his fellow former Communist comrades. D'Alema called for primaries to choose the first leader for the newly united Democratic Party.

Hard-liners broke from the DS and formed a separate party, Refounded Communist Party, led by Fausto Bertinotti. It advocated Italy's withdrawal from NATO and opposition to further European integration. The party refused to join the Olive Tree coalition, which, in Bertinotti's opinion, was too "heavily weighted on the side of centrists and moderates." But it joined the Prodi government in 2006. Bertinotti was elected president (speaker) of the Chamber of Deputies. However, in 2008 he resigned his party leadership after his electoral coalition, The Left-The Rainbow, which included Greens, was decimated at the polls, winning only slightly more than 3% of the votes.

SOCIETY

Civil Society and Terrorism

Italian society has often been characterized as an "uncivic culture." According to studies made by Almond and Verba in the late 1950s, two–thirds of the Italians refused to have anything to do with politics or to discuss the subject with anyone. Only 3% were proud of their state institutions, and only 10% approved of political participation.

An updated version of this study in 1980 revealed that Italians have become much more inclined to engage in direct political action, especially in the form of demonstrations, strikes, blocking of railroads or highways or even political violence. Many Italians cling to the view that laws have been made to be evaded, that taxes are hostile acts of the state against the individual, and that one who does not successfully embezzle the government when one has the opportunity is considered a fool. Public institutions were long regarded with an unparalleled carefree air. The citizen's contempt and irritation toward his state was almost nihilistic, as is manifested in the widely used expression *piove, governo ladro* ("It's raining on this corrupt state"). The political revolution in the 1990s showed that toleration of corruption and indifference toward elected representatives have dramatically changed.

The bad state of government affairs is not simply a result of the continuous public scandals that have brought down many governments and have helped paralyze the bureaucracy. For instance, in 1981 the Cossiga government fell because of an affair centered around an ultrasecret Masonic Lodge named P2 in which many of the country's leading politicians, industrialists and tax officials were closely linked in a scandal. This is rather the result of a historically developed behavioral pattern. For centuries the state meant nothing more to Italians than suppression by foreigners of subordination to the Doge princes, who themselves were dependent upon others. It has been difficult for Italians to believe that the state is working for their interests. One Italian expressed this in 1993: "We expect little of our politicians, and that's what we get."

The permanent crisis of the modern democratic state in Italy is scarcely suitable for developing a stronger sense of public spirit among its citizens. The work of many heterogeneous factions organized into many groups has made the establishment of a political consensus difficult. In Rome alone, over 25,000 politically active organizations have been counted. Some of these groups refuse to observe the democratic rules of the game and have become parts of the powerful terrorist movements that seek to achieve their political goals through violence. Terrorists on the extreme right have tried to upset the political system by means of countless indiscriminate bomb attacks. They have not been brought entirely under control.

The extreme leftists, the Red Brigades, posed a great problem for Italian domestic security through their precisely planned and executed attacks and kidnappings of high–ranking personalities. Their objective was to undermine the state and then to provoke a fascist reaction, which, they hope, would be the prelude to a "proletarian" revolution although the working class in Italy shows almost no sympathy for such aims. U.S. Brigadier General James L. Dozier, the highest ranking American general stationed in Italy, was kidnapped from his Verona apartment in 1981 and freed by a highly trained Italian antiterrorist unit in a daring and brilliant raid in 1982 after he had been held prisoner for over 40 days.

This spectacular kidnapping was intended to be the opening act for a carefully planned spree of further kidnappings, commando–style raids on jails to free arrested terrorists, and as a final bloody crescendo, the massacre of the entire Christian Democratic leadership at a DC gathering in Rome. Yet this campaign was foiled by the determination of the Italian government to put an end to left–wing terrorism. The government was greatly aided by the crack antiterrorist units, which had been created in order to achieve the same level of expertise as that of the astonishingly well-informed, well-armed and well–trained terrorists.

In 1982 almost a thousand suspected terrorists were arrested, including many of their known leaders. Bases, conspiratorial apartments and arms dumps were raided. The police and courts also made effective use of a temporary law permitting more lenient sentences for terrorists who tell on their former comrades. The state thus made a significant strike at left–wing terrorism. Very importantly, it did this without abandoning democracy or an observance of civil rights. But the causes of such violence remain: an immobile political system, a corruption–ridden bureaucracy, and the bleak economic outlook for many young Italians.

In 1999 there was a frightening reminder of Red Brigade terrorism when one of the government's top advisers, Massimo D'Antona, was gunned down as he walked to work. Prime Minister D'Alema vowed: "We are faced with a terrorist band that the state intends to find and to hit." In July 2005 three of the murderers received life sentences for this crime, and one got nine years.

In March 2002 Marco Biagi, a top economic adviser who was helping the government draft controversial changes to the labor laws making it easier to lay off workers, was murdered in Bologna. Au-

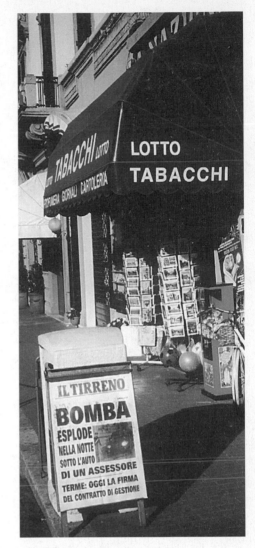

Report of car-bombing

thorities had ignored Biagi's pleas for protection. Forensic tests indicated that the assassination was the work of the Red Brigades. A Red Brigade member arrested a year later admitted that the assassination had been part of the group's strategy to derail the government's plans to reform Italy's labor laws. One of the murderers, a turncoat, was sentenced in 2005 to 16 years in prison. In October 2003 six further suspects were apprehended in raids throughout the country.

In March 2004 a breakthrough occurred in the battle against the Red Brigades. A gunfight broke out on a train from Rome to Florence when police asked two Red Brigade suspects to show their identity cards. A police officer and one suspect were killed, but police found notebooks filled with information about the gang. The clues gained from them led to a series of raids and arrests across the country. One of the apprehended, Cinzia Banelli, became the first Red Brigade suspect to

Italy

turn informant since the group returned to action, disclosing hiding places, secret codes, accomplices and crimes committed. In February 2007 police arrested 15 people accused of belonging to the Politico-military Communist Party (PCPM), a descendent of the Red Brigades.

Italians' worries about violence in their midst were fueled again in 2001 by the radical Islamic terrorist strikes in New York and Washington on September 11. Police authorities determined that al-Qaeda cells were operating in Italy and were planning violent attacks against such targets as the U.S. embassy. Police made many arrests of suspected terrorists. For example, in September 2002 they followed a tip from U.S. naval intelligence and seized a ship carrying 15 suspected terrorists. They also raided a farmhouse near Venice in January 2003 and arrested five Moroccans in possession of explosives and chemicals, plus maps of NATO bases in Italy and the London underground. Police have shut down money-transfer operations suspected of financing terrorist groups and concluded that Italy was being used by international terrorist groups as a transit and logistics center.

Cooperation with the Americans has been close, perhaps too close to suit some Italians. In July 2005 an Italian judge ordered the arrest of 13 CIA operatives (and 13 more in July 2006) on charges of kidnapping for carrying out an operation of "extraordinary rendition" on Italian soil. It occurred in February 2003 when a Muslim cleric, Abu Omar, who was suspected of belonging to a militant Islamic organization, was bundled into a van and transported back to his native Egypt, where he was jailed, tortured and released. The CIA claims that its Rome station chief had informed his Italian counterpart at the time and had received implicit approval for the operation.

Evidence emerged in July 2006 that Italy's military intelligence service, SISMI, had indeed been notified of the plans and had perhaps aided the CIA; in a letter the SISMI chief had notified political leaders at the time of the CIA's operation. In February 2007 an Italian judge indicted 25 CIA operatives for the kidnapping. The warrants will never lead to any arrests. The CIA agents had used false papers and were no longer in Italy. A State Department legal adviser confirmed that if Italy were to request the extraditions, the U.S. would not comply. In May 2008 the long-delayed trial of the CIA operatives in absentia and former Italian intelligence officials began.

Italians' fears were heightened after the July 2005 bombings in the London underground stations and the flight of one of the suspects to Italy, where he was tracked down and arrested by Italian police. A poll in *Corriere della Sera* found that 82% saw a serious risk that they will face similar deadly attacks. Sensing the popular mood, the government gained approval for many new security measures. They include strengthening border checks, the right to hold terrorist suspects for 24 hours (up from 12) without turning them over to a magistrate, broader access to the records of internet service providers (including internet cafes) and telephone and cellular companies, permission to take DNA samples from suspects, jailing suspects who provide explosives training, placing limits on pilots' licenses, quick expulsions for foreigners considered to be a danger to national security or who assist in terrorist activities, criminalizing the recruitment and training of people for terrorist activities, sequestering assets of firms suspected of financing terror, and checking on mosques and Islamic centers.

The Mafia

Organized crime is the country's number one plague. The most famous is the Sicilian Cosa Nostra, whose power extends from Sicily to Rome and the industrialized area farther north. Its regional competitors include the Sacra Corona Unita in Puglia, Camorra, an umbrella term for dozens of Neapolitan Mafia clans, and *Ndrangheta* from Calabria, the "toe" of Italy. Camorra smuggles uninspected Chinese goods into Europe, imports arms from Eastern Europe and transfers them to Basque terrorists, launders money, and reportedly has its hand in the highly lucrative business of collecting and disposing trash. It is widely believed that it dumps forbidden toxic wastes gathered from Camorra-affiliated companies all over Europe into public landfills around Naples.

Ndrangheta had been responsible for the kidnapping of the young American heir, John Paul Getty, Jr. Of all these groups, *Ndrangheta* is the most ruthless and prosperous today, having cornered the market for cocaine smuggled into Europe. Its annual narcotics income was estimated in 2008 to be as much as 40 billion euros ($64 million). It has eclipsed Cosa Nostra and the other mobs in power, wealth and international reach. It enjoys the advantage that there is little public protest in Calabria against it, while there is a growing outcry in Sicily against the outrages of Cosa Nostra.

The Mafia accumulated enormous wealth from lucrative bogus public works contracts, "protection," and international drug traffic, of which Sicily became the European center following the severance of the "French Connection" in the 1970s. The Mafia has lost ground in the global drug trade, supplying only an estimated 5% of the American market in 1993. As a result of its being progressively pushed out of international drug-smuggling, it has become more dependent on its traditional extortion business. A 1996 survey revealed that 23% of businesses paid racketeers an average of 10.7% of their annual sales. A decade later Sicilian entrepreneurs pay an estimated 8 billion euros ($12 billion) in "pizzo" (protection payment) to the Cosa Nostra each year. However, a small but growing number of mainly young businessmen defies the mob in Sicily by refusing to pay protection. The 2008 national budget contained tax breaks for those courageous entrepreneurs. Also this illicit means of collecting money actually makes Cosa Nostra members more vulnerable to the combined pressure of the government and business people who refuse to pay.

Italian mobsters also face competition from ruthless imitators from Russia, Colombia, and other countries. Italy is not merely a transit point for drugs, which increasingly flow into the veins of Italians themselves. It gives the country the shameful distinction of having the largest number of addicts in Europe.

With its wealth the Mafia has shifted its emphasis to becoming an entrepreneur. The Mafia bought into countless businesses and penetrated a portion of the Italian banking system, which it needs to "launder" its "hot" money. Whereas the Mafia's main profits were once from the drug trade, they are now from government contracts and extortion. In 1996 the Italian trade association, *Confcommercio*, estimated that a fifth of all trade and construction enterprises in Italy were controlled by organized crime and that the authorities discover no more than 8% of illegal businesses.

The competition among Mafia and Camorra families for larger shares of the drug trade unleashed ruthless gang wars that left the streets and countryside strewn with hundreds of bloody corpses. In 2005 a turf war over the drug trade erupted in Naples, claiming at least 135 lives. It also led the Mafia to aim its ugly pistol against the political process itself. In 1979 it began liquidating top Italian political officials in Sicily who stood in its way. The government responded to this deadly challenge by making membership in a Mafia clan a crime, by legalizing the confiscation of suspects' estates if they cannot demonstrate that their income was legally acquired, and by sending the new leader of the secret services to Sicily as that island's regional prefect. In 1987 courageous judges and prosecutors in Palermo, relying heavily on testimony from 14 Mafia members who broke the

The Northern League's Umberto Bossi and family

code of silence, convicted 338 Mafiosi of crimes ranging from murder to drug trafficking in the biggest Mafia trial in Italian history. For the first time, the leading mobster bosses received the stiffest sentences.

In the 1980s and 1990s the Mafiosi maintained a steady wave of killings, not only among themselves, but against the Italian state. In 1988 they murdered an active judge for the first time. The government cooperated with U.S. officials to crack a powerful transatlantic drug ring. Despite the scores of bosses arrested, all agree that only the tip of the iceberg had been shattered. Authorities are able to prosecute criminals more quickly because of a 1989 judicial reform aimed at streamlining the system. One headline read: "Perry Mason has finally entered Italy's old and decrepit courtrooms."

The criminal families not only expanded their operations into northern Italian cities, but began influencing municipal and regional elections by murdering or intimidating candidates. In 1991 five persons, including a member of a city council, were shot; one victim was even beheaded; his head was used for target practice. This horrified the Italian public and prompted the government to assume the authority to dissolve any city council or local authority infiltrated by the Mafia and to send judges, even against their will, to man understaffed courts in the three regions most plagued by gangs: Calabria, Sicily, and Campania. The government created in 1991 a special post, dubbed the Italian "FBI," within the Attorney General's office to coordinate the fight against organized crime.

Like some Latin American countries, Italy is fighting to prevent itself from falling under the control of unelected international criminals. At stake is the freedom of Italians to be ruled by leaders they elect, rather than by those who reap undreamed of profits from feeding human vices. After the Mafia murdered two top anti-Mafia officials (Giovanni Falcone and Paolo Borsellino) in 1992, the government deployed 7,000 soldiers to Sicily in July to crack down on the mob. This was the most drastic step taken since 1945 against a domestic disorder and the first time troops were used in a large-scale crackdown on the Sicilian mobsters. Also in 1992 law-enforcement officials joined Spanish, British, and American police to arrest Italians working with the Cali (Colombia) cocaine cartel. The biggest organized crime sweep in almost 10 years put scores of Mafia suspects in jail, including several mayors and three members of parliament.

Armed with strengthened antiracketeering laws permitting wider use of phone taps, property searches, confiscation of property of convicted or suspected Mafia people, state reimbursement to businesses that suffer for defying the racketeers, and guarantees of protection for state witnesses, police maintained this momentum in 1993. A startling development occurred when the late Pope John Paul broke the Church's long tradition of silence on Mafia matters and lashed out against organized crime. The Mafia's two top leaders, Salvatore ("Nitto") Riina and Benedetto Santapaola, as well as the only woman known to have headed an Italian crime syndicate (the Camorra around Naples), Rosario Cutolo, were captured. In 1996 one of the most powerful and ruthless bosses in the history of the Corleone clan, Giovanni Brusca (nicknamed "the Pig"), who had masterminded the murder of Falcone and Borsellino, was captured by 200 black-hooded special police troops.

The key has been a crumbling of the long-standing code of silence. By 1997 more than 1,200 arrested Mafiosi were collaborating with investigators. The growing number of *pentiti* ("penitents") has prompted Mafia organizations to retaliate brutally, departing from the older code of honor not to attack women, children, judges, government officials, and innocent bystanders. It has also been expensive for the taxpayer to take care of more than 6,000 people, including families, who need escorts, protection, money and shelter, special schools and churches. But organized crime really does seem to be on the run.

The resulting confessions of these *pentiti* led not only to the dramatic arrests of Mafia leaders. They opened perhaps the most explosive chapter in Italy's mega-corruption scandal: that top Christian Democratic leaders, especially seven-time prime minister, Giulio Andreotti, may have cooperated with and protected the Mafia. No Italian politician had as many revealing nicknames as he: "Machiavelli," "Mephistopheles," and "the Fox." Prosecutors claim that the Mafia had guaranteed his party votes and political control in Sicily in return for government contracts for Mafia-controlled companies and protection from police crackdowns. Andreotti denied the charges but agreed to have his senatorial immunity lifted in order to clear his name in court.

Commencing in 1995, this trial was a humiliating ordeal for Andreotti; two-thirds of respondents in a 1995 poll think he did indeed have a "relationship" with Mafia. The press called it "the trial of the century." In 1999 he was acquitted on charges that he had associated with the Mafia and had ordered it to kill an investigative journalist (Mauro De Navro) in 1979. The court decisions did not dispel all doubts about his activities, and in November 2002 this verdict was overturned in a court of appeals, and Andreotti was sentenced to 24 years in jail. He quickly appealed this reversal, as the country was aghast at this never-ending ordeal based on the testimony of a Mafia turncoat. A year later Italy's highest court overturned the conviction, and he was formally acquitted. In May 2003 he was absolved from another charge of having connections to the Mafia, and finally in October 2004 the highest criminal court acquitted him of all charges that he had colluded with the Mafia. In 2006 he was an unsuccessful candidate for speaker of the Senate.

Andreotti's seemingly interminable legal entanglement ignited attacks on the

Italy

controversial use of over 1,100 *pentiti*, on whose testimony all his cases had been based. This questioning became a furious public debate in May 2003 when a mobster convicted of a grisly murder was released from prison after only seven years behind bars. Enzo Brusca had kidnapped an 11-year-old boy and held him captive before strangling him and dissolving his body in acid. In 2001 parliament had already toughened the *pentiti* law by limiting the window for providing information and requiring them to serve at least 10 years of a life sentence.

Many Italians now believe that organized crime can finally be defeated. No longer able to act with impunity inside Italy, the Mafia and other organized crime groups are increasingly expanding their operations into other European countries. In 1998 one of the new generation's top bosses in Sicily, Vito Vitale, was arrested. Then in April 2006 the "boss of bosses," Bernardo Provenzano ("Binnu the Tractor"), was captured at a lonely run-down farmhouse in Sicily. Sentenced in absentia to life in prison in 1963, he had been on the run 43 years, sleeping in caves, stables and secluded cottages. He had been supported by a vast invisible web of protection that included businessmen and possibly prominent politicians. He is said to have steered the Mafia away from murder and into such rackets as drug dealing.

The arrests continued. In November 2007 Salvatore Lo Piccolo (nicknamed "the Baron"), the most senior Mafia "boss of bosses" still at large, was captured with his son and two other mobsters in a house near Palermo. He had been on the run for 24 years. An ecstatic chief anti-Mafia prosecutor declared that the mob had been "decapitated." Another gang leader, Pasquale Condello, was snatched in February 2008 after 20 years on the run. At the same time, Italian and American police arrested over 100 Mafia suspects in New York and Sicily, striking a fatal blow to the second largest crime group in the U.S., the Bambino family.

Italians remain fascinated by the Mafia. In January 2008 they were treated to a six-part TV miniseries called "Il Capo dei Capi" (The Boss of Bosses) about imprisoned chief Salvatore (Toto) Riina, who reportedly watched it faithfully from his cell. Seven million viewers (28% of the total TV audience) were glued to the series. Ironically, the American gangster series, "The Sopranos," was a flop in Italy.

Despite the fact that many bosses and their underlings are behind bars, the Mafia is far from destroyed. No part of Sicily is free of its influence, and extortion and protection rackets remain commonplace. In 2008 a magistrate in Calabria worried about the deeply rooted mob: "There is a virus, but no anti-virus."

The Italian Family

Despite the complicated historical development and the division into numerous interest groups, the Italian family has traditionally been responsible for Italy's national identity and strength. It is the most important institution and focal point of Italian life. Its strength permits society to function when government fails. Its significance has changed due to the modernization that accompanies industrial life. Italy reached zero population growth in 1987. By 2006 the average mother was producing only 1.34 children (up from 1.25 a couple years earlier), compared with 2.7 in 1964. The figure is especially low in the North. Italy now has one of the world's oldest populations. This is a ticking bomb for the nation. Current projections foresee Italians over age 65 accounting for a third of the population in 2050, up from 15.3% in 1991. The entire population could decline to 47 million in 2050.

Italians live long lives (83.5 years for women and 77.5 for men). After becoming, in January 2005, Europe's third nation (after Norway and Ireland) to ban smoking totally in public places, they may live even longer. The ban includes offices, bars, restaurants, and discotheques unless they have separate smoking areas with ventilation. In most years now, deaths outnumber births, and only immigration somewhat stabilizes the population.

The influence of the Catholic Church is growing again, and it takes an active and overt role in politics. A reminder was given in June 2005, when a referendum took place to decide whether to abrogate parts of a 2004 fertility law that banned research using stem cells from embryos. The law also imposed stringent requirements on test-tube pregnancies. In order to pass, a majority had to turn out to vote, and a majority had to vote yes. The new Pope, Benedict XVI, and the country's bishops and priests told the faithful to boycott the referendum. As a result, only 26% showed up to vote, and 90% of those voted yes. Italians once again showed the power of their church. This action convinced some students and academics that the Pope was hostile to science; he had once argued in 1990 that the Church's verdict against Galileo had been "rational and just." In 2008 he had to cancel a speech at the prestigious Sapienza University in Rome because of protests by professors and students.

To cool down a dispute with the Vatican in May 2006 then Prime Minister Prodi publicly reprimanded his health minister for supporting trials of the RU-486 abortion pill even though polls show that Italians strongly favor the 1978 law legalizing abortion in the first trimester. He also criticized his family min-

ister for defending proposed legislation to grant legal recognition to same-sex unions. However, in 2007 his government supported the Roman municipal council decree officially designating two blocks of bars and restaurants leading up to the Colosseum as a recreation ground for homosexuals.

Young Italians must postpone marriage for economic reasons. They do not finish university until about age 27. Due to low salaries, youth unemployment three times the national average (up to 40% in the South), and the employment trap of one after the other short-term contract, they cannot afford to leave home until they are around 30, to say nothing of having children. In 2005, 60% of Italians aged 18 to 34 and 40% aged 30 to 34 still lived with their parents. A "baby bounty" of 1,000 euros ($1,500) to couples for every child after their first has little effect on procreation. In contrast to most northern European nations, only 9.6% of Italian babies are born out of wedlock (EU average: 28%, and 55% in Sweden). Same-sex marriage is not allowed, but the government approved a bill in 2007 granting rights in areas like inheritance and health insurance to any two persons who choose to live together.

The worsening age distribution presents a ticking bomb for the pension system. In 2001 pensions claimed 60% of welfare spending, compared to an EU average of 45%. By 2007 the annual pension bill was 14% of GDP and rising to 17% by 2035 if future entitlements are not adjusted to rising life expectancy. It is estimated that by 2030 about 42% of Italians will be pensioners, the highest proportion in Europe.

The government introduced a pension reform in 2003 that brought hundreds of thousands of protesters into the streets. It had to water down the reform to get it passed in 2004. Only 30% of Italians aged 55 to 64 have jobs. The average Italian retires at age 59 (57 if he or she had worked 35 years). But starting in 2008 it was raised to 60, in 2010 to 61. In 2007, during Prodi's brief second government, the retirement age of 57 was retained only for those in "arduous" jobs. Others must wait until age 58 (down from 60) for the minimum retirement age, and by 2013 those who have contributed at least 36 years can stop working at 61. This can barely be called "reform." The country cannot afford such a pension system.

The Bureaucracy

Many political decisions are made within the various interest groups rather than in the official political channels. Italians therefore have a good understanding for the term "under government" (*sottogoverno*). Italian bureaucracy, with 1.7 million civil servants, has been reproached for its general inefficiency, inflexibility and corruption. Government employees have alarming absenteeism, and far too many who report for work either do nothing or use their time to do outside work in order to have a second income.

Government officials are, for the most part, recruited from the South, where an administrative position is for many the only opportunity for a job. The emphasis on authority, exaggerated bureaucracy and official government patronage and nepotism which characterizes public offices can be traced back historically to the behavioral patterns of the pre–capitalistic feudal states of the South. It is a curious phenomenon that in this land of contradictions the North conquered the South during the "Resurgence" partly through its economic predominance; however, the South conquered the North through the Italian bureaucracy.

The South

The main domestic problem remains the structurally underdeveloped South (*Mezzogiorno*). It comprises 40% of Italy's land area and 35% of its population, but only 24% of its GDP. When describing the Italian social and economic situation, one can speak of an industrialized state that has some characteristics of an underdeveloped country. Four–fifths of the industry is concentrated in the Turin–Milan–Genoa triangle. Although roughly one–third of the population is concentrated in the

South, two–fifths of Italy's unemployed live there. In 2006 the jobless rate in the South was three to four times higher than in the North.

The problem is bound to get worse because illiteracy is higher in the South. The average income per capita in the South is 70% of the Italian average, and it is widening. The per capita productivity in the South is 40% to 60% under that of the North. In the 21st century most of the gaps in the labor market in the dynamic

North of Italy are being filled by workers from central and eastern Europe, no longer by immigrants from the South of Italy. There are, of course, significant differences between regions within the South. For instance, Calabria and Campania are very depressed, while such areas as Abruzzi and Molise are catching up with the North. Clearly prosperity is not being shared equally throughout Italy. The South faces even more intensely a problem that threatens manufacturers in

Italy

all of Italy: too many of its industries—textiles, shoes, machine tools—are vulnerable to global competition, especially to low-cost China.

The traveler coming from the modern, industrialized North to Calabria or the Basilicata in the South has the feeling that he has left a highly developed country and has landed in an underdeveloped one. In order to compensate for this historical disadvantage, a governmental agency called the *Cassa per il Mezzogiorno* was established in 1950 to channel resources to the South and stimulate improvements. It accounted for a few worthwhile projects, including a turnpike from Milan to Palermo, which opened up the South to tourism. However, overall results were disappointing. Profit–seekers in the North benefited excessively, and the Mafia and the Ndrangheta used fraud to amass fortunes from the money it provided. It was therefore abolished in 1992.

The culmination point for misery in the South is Naples, the "capital of poverty," as the Turin newspaper *La Stampa* described it. The city, with its 1.3 million inhabitants, among which over 100,000 are unemployed, is practically incomprehensible. Speculation on construction projects has been boundless. Also, the absence of a sewage system has transformed the once renowned gulf into a cesspool that is five times more polluted than Italy's other coastal waters. Neapolitan newspapers read many days like a hair–raising chronicle of crime and catastrophe. The number of stolen vehicles is estimated at 40,000 annually. There are not enough orphans' homes to accommodate the deserted children of desperate parents living in a city known traditionally to be family–conscious. It is surprising that Naples has not collapsed under the pressure of such massive problems.

In 2007-8 the extent to which the public sector fails its citizens was demonstrated by the fact that Naples went months without trash collection. This was merely the latest rubbish emergency the city had faced in the preceding decade and a half. Garbage collectors stopped their rounds

on December 21 because the dumps in and around the city were full. A controversial modern incinerator was never built. The local organized-crime organization, Camorra, was also involved since it reaps large profits from disposing often toxic wastes from all over Europe in illegal dumps. Then Prime Minister Prodi tried desperately to deal with the stinking problem, even sending in the army to clear the city's trash. The inability to solve this putrid problem was an important reason why his center-left government was voted out in April 2008. The problem was so bad that in May 2008 the EU's European Commission filed suit against Italy in the European Court of Justice in Luxembourg charging that the state had failed to meet its obligations to its people.

Foreign Relations and Defense

Italy joined the UN in 1955, but the two main pillars of its foreign policy are membership in the EU, of which it was a founding member, and NATO. It has 200,000 men under arms including 20,100 conscripts doing basic 10-month military service. Plans have been made to abolish conscription. In 2000 the first female volunteers entered the military.

Italy's forces are supplemented by more than 7,565 U.S. ground and air force troops, mainly in northern Italy, and 4,400 U.S. naval personnel in the 6th fleet based in Naples. A spat over American plans to expand the size of its army base at Vicenza in northwestern Italy in order to unify all three elements of the 173d Airborne Brigade, a rapid reaction force of 4,500 soldiers, helped bring the Prodi government down temporarily in 2007. He favored the enlargement, but almost two-thirds of the city's residents and the most leftist groups in his 9-party coalition opposed it. He was quickly restored to power, and the construction plans proceeded.

Although it occupies a strategically important position on NATO's southern flank, its defense spending accounts for less than 2% of its GDP. This has dire consequences for the Italian navy, which must leave the defense of Italy's extensive coastline to the army and the air force, which are concentrated in the North. The navy is capable of defending only merchant vessels in the Mediterranean.

NATO membership for a country that had the largest communist party in western Europe caused some tensions. However, as the PCI moved steadily away from Moscow and renamed itself the PDS (then DS), it increasingly accepted national defense within NATO. The dilemma still gives Italian foreign policy one of its major characteristics: it is normally conducted quietly and with the utmost of discretion in order not to allow

Prosperous shoppers in Florence

foreign policy to become part of the always heated domestic cauldron.

Italy has long sought to play a more assertive role in the world, especially in Mediterranean affairs. It became the first European NATO ally to accept, without condition, U.S. medium–range cruise missiles, which began to be deployed at Comiso, Sicily, in 1983. Italian willingness to contribute to strengthening NATO was again shown in 1988 when its government termed the eviction of American F16 fighter aircraft from Spain as "disastrous" and agreed to their being based in Southern Italy. The end of the Cold War made that relocation unnecessary.

In 1991 it sent 10 Tornado aircraft and five naval vessels to the Persian Gulf to support its allies' war effort against Iraq. In 1993 Italy was one of the first countries to send troops on the UN humanitarian mission to Somalia, part of which had been ruled by Italy until 1960. Links with Somalia remained strong. Most educated Somalis still speak Italian, and many studied in Italy.

When NATO launched an air war against Serbia in 1999 to try to stop ethnic cleansing in Kosovo, Italy stuck with the alliance. Although its own aircraft were not involved, it sent 2,000 troops to Albania to administer humanitarian aid, and it permitted NATO pilots to use 14 bases in

Italy, including especially Aviano in the Northeast. Although some parties, such as the Northern League and the United Communists opposed the air strikes, then Prime Minister D'Alema, a former Communist, declared, "we'll be loyal to the end."

American flights from Aviano had become an emotional public issue in 1998–9 when a low–flying Marine Corps EA–6B Prowler aircraft passing through Aviano clipped the cable of a gondola killing 20 skiers. Anti–American and anti–NATO feelings were inflamed when an American military court acquitted the pilot on charges of negligence. However, he was found guilty of obstruction of justice for destroying a videotaped record, and the Americans agreed to tighten restrictions and accountability for training flights in Italy.

The Italian government responded without hesitation when radical Middle Eastern terrorists attacked the World Trade Center in New York and the Pentagon in Washington on September 11, 2001. It offered the aircraft carrier Garibaldi, two frigates, Harrier jump jets and Tornado aircraft, a supply ship, and 2,700 troops including 150 paratroopers. It also organized a rally in Rome called "USA day" on November 10. On the same day leftists organized a peace rally. This reflected the ambivalence and division within Italian society over the issue of going to war in Afghanistan. Opinion polls revealed only a slight majority favoring such participation.

When the U.S. and Britain went to war in Iraq to unseat dictator Saddam Hussein in March 2003, most Italians opposed the

Italian students celebrating end of course at the College of Europe.

conflict. But the Berlusconi government backed the American and British allies by offering Italian airspace, ports, highways and bases, provided that they were not used for actually launching attacks against the enemy. After the three-week conflict was over, Italy joined several other European allies in agreeing to send 3,000 soldiers to help humanitarian efforts in Baghdad, while maintaining 650 troops in Afghanistan. They have suffered casualties. In December 2003 suicide bombers blew up their military headquarters in Nasiriyah, killing 13 *carabinieri* paramilitary police, four soldiers and two Italian civilians. Italy also endorsed the call to cancel some of the $1.73 billion debt Iraq owes it.

Relations with the Americans were strained in March 2005 when an American soldier shot and killed an Italian intelligence agent, Nicola Calipari, who had just liberated a kidnapped Italian journalist in Baghdad. A U.S. investigation found that the soldier had acted properly, while admitting that it was a tragic accident. The Italian government accepted that it was an accident, but it held that the Americans had acted improperly. Calipari was given a hero's funeral with the prime minister in attendance. In June 2006 an Italian prosecutor asked for the American solider responsible to be tried in Italy, something the American ally cannot grant. Berlusconi had already announced the withdrawal of Italy's 2,600 troops from Iraq by the end of 2006. Subsequent Prime Minister Prodi, who called the war in Iraq a "grave error," accomplished this.

Italy under Berlusconi tried to help heal the wide transatlantic rift that had developed over the Iraq crisis. It had asserted itself in world affairs more than its predecessors, and it was less deferential to France and Germany within the EU. "Italy will make the Euro-Atlantic relationship a priority." The Prodi government is taking another look at the country's foreign and defense policy. It is attempting to steer a middle course between the desire to distance the country from the Bush foreign policy and to make a positive commitment to NATO and the long-standing alliance with the United States. The prime minister and Foreign Minister D'Alema want to show that Italy is independent but not instinctively anti-American. They want to realign Italian foreign policy more toward France and Germany.

Parliament had an emotional debate over funding combat operations in Afghanistan, which some communist partners oppose but which a large percentage of the Italian population supports. In February 2007 the government briefly fell over the issue of funding Italy's 2,500 troops in Afghanistan. A bipartisan vote of 524-3 quickly restored the government to power.

Immigration and Balkans

One of Italy's thorniest future foreign policy problems is immigration. By 2008 immigrants living there legally constituted 5% of the total population; adding those who are illegal, the number is over 3.7 million or 6% of the total population. More than 700,000 new immigrants arrive every year. Of the illegals who have slipped in, 10% come by sea, 15% over land, and 75% overstay their visas. Many Italians fear that some of these illegals are involved in prostitution and drug rings in the major cities. Other European countries fear that Italy could be a gateway into the

Chatting at the market

Italy

EU since Italy is a member of the EU's Schengen group, which lifts border controls for those persons already inside an EU country. But it is increasingly a place where immigrants want to remain.

Especially unsettling are the large number of Romanians (especially Roma—gypsies) who poured into Italy after their country entered the EU in January 2007. By the end of the year it was estimated that 556,000 had arrived. Many sleep in illegal camps or shanty-towns on the outskirts of major cities. Over a third of all crimes are committed by foreigners, with Romanians topping the list. Sensational incidents in Rome have spread terror. A Romanian women was caught on closed-circuit security cameras killing a subway passenger by stabbing her in the eye with an umbrella (for which the assailant was sentenced to 16 years in prison). After another woman was raped and brutally murdered by a Romanian immigrant, the government issued a decree permitting local authorities to expel from the country any EU nationals considered to be a threat to public safety. Earlier loopholes in the law had made it difficult to deport immigrants. The dramatic electoral success of the anti-immigrant Northern League in 2008 and the subsequent election of the first right-wing mayor (Gianni Alemanno) of Rome since Mussolini's time underscored the rising concern over crime in Italians' minds. Alemanno pledged in his campaign to demolish 85 unlicensed Roma encampments, expel 20,000 allegedly criminal foreigners, and generally to crack down on lawbreaking.

Until recently Italy was a land of emigration, but its long coastline facing North Africa has made it a natural bridge between the burgeoning populations of Africa and the rich nations of Europe. Not wishing to damage its good relations with its Arab neighbors on the other side of the Mediterranean and Adriatic Seas, Italy has not wanted to impose quotas. Its Muslim population has risen steeply to about 1.5 million, and the vast majority of them are immigrants who have little chance of ever getting citizenship. Only an estimated 4% regularly attend a mosque. Because of the discovery of numerous Muslim terrorist cells, Italians have mixed feelings about these new arrivals. There are attempts to reach out to them. The chairman of Rome's city council, Giuseppe Mannino, said: "Rome is a city that is open to everybody." To encourage its growing number of illegal residents to register with the authorities, it offered its generous welfare benefits to non–EU citizens, but this merely stimulated even greater immigration.

In a country that thought it was above racism, daily headlines now report racial strife. Nowhere was that more visible than

The frenzy of last–minute Christmas shopping in a Rome food market

in Florence, where the presence of hundreds of North African street vendors sparked protest marches to decry the influx. Gangs of white rowdies set upon the newcomers with baseball bats and iron bars.

To the East, the collapsed communist regimes in Albania and Yugoslavia have enhanced the specter of an immigration flood. Waves of Albanians, traveling across the Adriatic Sea in overcrowded boats, were washed ashore in 1991, only to be penned in coal docks and inside a local soccer stadium, which they proceeded to wreck out of anger toward their reception. One Caritas relief worker complained, "the police threw food at them like in a zoo."

In 1997, for the first time since the Second World War, Italy led a multinational force, including 6,000 of its own soldiers, to restore order in Albania, a country with which it has close historical and cultural ties. Violence and anarchy had broken out when thousands of people lost their savings in shady financial pyramid schemes. By the end of the year, order had been restored, and thousands of the Albanian refugees began to be deported. In 2004 it still had 1,100 troops in Albania, 3,700 in Kosovo and 1,500 in Bosnia. The Balkans are simply too close and too unstable not to warrant Italy's full attention. In the words of Lucio Caracciolo, editor of *Limes*

magazine, they "have become our top foreign policy priority."

Stung by the criticism, the government adopted a new policy to prevent the exodus of impoverished Albanians. Italian naval vessels help Albania patrol its shores. It also established a large emergency aid program within Albania itself. Italian soldiers distribute food and advice on improving the infrastructure, as a forerunner to a longer–term program to help stabilize the Balkan country's ailing economy.

By 2003 the main immigration route into Italy had changed. Instead of coming from the east into the southeastern region of Apulia, more immigrants now come north from Africa and land on the southern and southwestern shores. Italy also adopted a tougher law in 2002 making it harder for new immigrants to obtain residency permits. That made it easier for law enforcement authorities to expel those who do not have the right papers or consistent employment, to levy higher fines and criminal sentences, and to mete out stiffer penalties for employers and immigrants who violate the regulations. Non-EU immigrants must now be fingerprinted upon arrival in Italy.

ECONOMY

The motor that keeps the country operating despite all of the crises, scandals,

Italy

Coming home from school past the *Piazza San Marco*, Venice   Photo by Vincent Campi

strikes, poverty and natural catastrophes, is the Italians' ability to improvise and adapt to existing conditions. Such extraordinary resilience and resourcefulness have taken shape through centuries of foreign domination and of continuous threats along the coastline from pirates and conquerors. The everyday problems merely stimulate these qualities and enable one to understand why so many informed commentators on the state of Italian affairs are inclined to say with confidence that "the situation is desperate, but not hopeless."

Italy has a private enterprise economy, although the government has a controlling interest in some large commercial and industrial firms. Electricity, transportation, telephone and telegraph are largely owned by the state. Three TV channels are dominated by the state RAI network, although voters in a 1995 referendum chose to allow private shareholders to buy a stake in them. Silvio Berlusconi's Fininvest owns three other channels, with 65% of the advertising market, and voters in 1995 decided that he should not be forced to give up control of two of them.

The changes in wage indexation stabilized inflation (2.6% in 2008), despite a VAT of 19%. Italy suffers from chronically low productivity growth, the worst being the public sector, one of Europe's most expensive and inefficient. This is partly explained by the abysmally poor educational scores in international comparisons and the low level of computer literacy at the work place. A poll in 2005 revealed that 56% of respondents had never used a computer, and 72% had never been on the internet. Even though inflation is low, criticism against the euro is audible because it has allegedly increased the cost of living. After the Northern League called for a return of the lira, Berlusconi also blamed the nation's economic problems on the way his nemesis, Romano Prodi, while

prime minister, had steered Italy into monetary union. "Prodi's euro conned us all."

In the first five years of the 21st century, its economic growth averaged only .7% per year, the slowest of all the G8 and large OECD countries. It rose to 1.5% in 2006 and 2.3% in 2007, but it dropped to only .3% in 2008. In 2006 its per capita GDP fell below that of Spain. In 2008 it dropped below the EU average for the first time, and in 2009 it was predicted to be overtaken by Greece. Productivity growth is static, and competitiveness has declined. In 2005 the World Economic –Forum ranked Italy 47th in the world in competitiveness, just one notch above Botswana. Tourism dropped by a quarter after the September 11 terrorist attacks and the discovery of al-Qaeda cells in Italy. In 1970 Italy was the world's top tourist destination; today it is in fifth place after France, Spain, the U.S. and China. But Italy does have a modern economy: 65% of the work force is employed in services, who produce 68.8% of the GDP, while 31% is employed in industry, who produce 31% of GDP.

Italian firms have invested heavily in the latest technology and have some of the most productive factories in Europe. Italian companies are also actively investing outside the country. Northern Italy shows particular dynamism. Of Italy's 20 regions, the three northern ones—Lombardy, Veneto and Piedmont—produce almost 40% of the GDP. Lombardy alone generates 30% of the country's exports. The country has a high level of entrepreneurship: a third of all Europe's small- and medium-size enterprises are based in Italy.

Prodded by its desire to join the EU's single currency (euro), Italy has made some economic progress since 1992. By 2008 the budget deficit had fallen to 2.8% of GDP, below the required 3%; that is the major success of the Prodi government

that was voted out of office in 2008. Its total national debt is equal to 104% of its GDP, the world's third largest in absolute terms. It is the eurozone's most highly indebted country. Servicing that debt consumes a tenth of its GDP and a fifth of government spending. This leaves very few funds for needed investment in productivity improvement and research and innovation. At 1.1% of GDP, Italy's R&D is below the EU's average of almost 2%. Italy needs to be more internationally competitive. Fortunately, 90% of its debt is funded domestically, thanks largely to Italians' disposition for saving: they save 15% of their earnings, the highest rate in the EU. Much of it is in government securities. Thus, most of the interest payments are recycled into the economy.

Partly because of the shaky ruling coalitions that require expensive concessions to keep all partners satisfied, it has not been easy for any government to make big cuts in government spending and borrowing. The country's financial system both in banking and the stock market must be further modernized. Obstacles to business exist, such as rigid hiring and firing laws, high employers' social security contributions, and widespread price controls. These fuel unemployment, which stood at 6% in 2008, the lowest rate since 1993. This is below the EU average and is a success for the Berlusconi government, which reformed the labor market by making it easier for companies to hire temporary staff. Half the jobless have been out of work for more than a year, and a third of adults under 25 have no job. Joblessness is higher in the South (20%, and about 60% for youths) than in the North (7%). It is also higher for women, whose emancipation Italians say they want. Italy has the smallest proportion of participation in the workforce (57%) in Western Europe. Living standards are stagnant or declining.

Some argue that the South will get an economic boost from the construction of a bridge over the strait of Messina linking Sicily with the mainland originally scheduled for completion in 2012. The world's largest suspension bridge, it will stretch 2 miles (3.3 km), three times longer than the Golden Gate bridge, and have 12 lanes for cars, trucks and trains. Its towers will soar 1,230 feet above sea level. The megaproject could create 10,000 jobs. The failure to build this long-discussed bridge had become a symbol of the country's inability to modernize its road and rail infrastructure. But others argue that it will only benefit a few construction companies, the Mafia, and organized criminals who will be able to travel more quickly to the mainland. It would be in private hands and would charge more than boats now do. The project was scrapped by Prodi in 2006

Italy

Lucca

because the benefits could not justify the high costs, but it was resurrected by the victorious Berlusconi government in 2008.

A further problem is Italy's lag in innovation. A 2003 survey revealed that it holds a mere 1.8% of the world's high-tech patents, compared with Germany's 15% and France's 7.3%. Its citizens' scientific knowledge, internet use, and vocational training are low compared with many other European countries, and the resources it allots to research and higher education are inadequate. As many as 5% of its university graduates leave the country to work elsewhere. That is why the education ministry announced plans in 2003 to improve schools, to have pupils begin school at an earlier age, to study computers and English from the start, and to stay in school for a minimum of 12 years, two years more than before. There is a demonstrated need for improvement. Italian children did badly on the OECD's PISA cross-national comparisons, and none of its universities are in the world's top 90.

Nevertheless, Italy remains a visibly prosperous country. A reflection of such prosperity is the fact that almost two–thirds of Italians were homeowners by the end of the 1980s, and one Italian family in four has a second home. One explanation of such economic well–being, which defies the gloomy statistics, is the celebrated "submerged economy," a parallel unofficial economy, mainly behind the backs of government statisticians and tax collectors. In 2008 the black labor market was estimated to constitute one-sixth GDP, about 60% above the OECD average. Tax revenues equal about 41% of GDP (which is below the EU average), and it is conser-

Composer Puccini in his hometown, Lucca

vatively estimated that tax evasion amounts to around 15% of GDP. This kind of economic activity is done at home, in the streets or on the job, while the boss is looking the other way.

Under- and non-invoicing to avoid the VAT are common practices, and declarations of income are often much too low. For example, in 2008 most dentists and lawyers declared less than 50,000 euros ($75,000), restaurant owners 20,000 euros ($30,000), and taxi drivers only 11,500 euros ($15,750). In an effort to improve public finances, the Prodi government made some progress in tax collection. Days before leaving office in May 2008, it posted on the internet all 40 million tax returns so that journalists could report on the pitiful underpayment of taxes.

If the production of goods and services from such a submerged economy were able to be included in the official economic figures, an estimated 10% to 30% would have to be added to the national wealth. This "black economy" makes the country's high unemployment figure less serious politically than in many other western European nations. Also, whereas unemployment prevails in large parts of the South and in some cities in the industrial North, there are other regions where the demand for jobs must be filled with guest workers such as Tunisians in Sicily and Yugoslavs in Trieste.

Italy's dependence upon oil and raw material imports is excessive. It has almost no domestic energy sources except small amounts of natural gas (chiefly in the Po Valley) and very few other raw materials. Domestic oil production meets only 3.6% of needs. Government plans to expand nuclear power production were dealt a severe blow in an emotional 1987 referendum vote which stopped the build-

The Spanish Steps, Rome

ing of atomic power stations even though the country possessed an advanced nuclear industry. Italy has no functioning nuclear plants. It imports 80% of its energy needs, twice the Western European average. It imports about 16% of its electricity. Its vulnerability to disruptions is demonstrated by periodic outages; in 2003 the entire country except Sardinia was affected.

Such extreme dependence on energy imports explains the heavy Italian investment in a trans–Mediterranean gas pipeline, which began in 1982 to bring Algerian gas to the economically depressed southern Italy. Its large state-owned ENI jointly owns with Russia's Gazprom the giant South Stream pipeline that will deliver natural gas from Siberia via the Black Sea and the Balkans. Romano Prodi declined a proposal by the Russian president to head that project after leaving office in 2008. In a further effort to ensure its energy supply, Italy will increase its reliance on coal from 14% to 33% by 2013.

The country's periodic trade deficit results mainly from the import of consumer goods and even agricultural products that Italy itself produces. It is only 80% self-sufficient in food. It does have impressive trade successes, though, in clothing, shoes and mechanical goods; 90% of its total exports are manufactures. Almost two-thirds of its trade is with its EU partners.

Agriculture

The percentage employed in agriculture has dropped over the years from 38% in 1951 to 4% in 2008. Italy's agricultural population generates only 2.1% of GDP. The rather unproductive Italian agriculture suffers from the small size of farms and the advanced age of farmers. Also, about a fourth of the farmland is underutilized and about a tenth is not used at all.

A major agricultural obstacle is, of course, the problem of hill farming. More than 40% of Italy is classified as hilly, and such terrain merely intensifies the country's other agricultural problems of fragmentation and low productivity. Only about 23% of the land is classified as plain, most of it in the fertile Po Valley in the North, the Pontine Valley south of Rome and parts of Puglia in the South, although the latter is strapped by severe irrigation problems. The Po Valley is Italy's breadbasket, producing cereals, dairy products and sugar beets. In the South, Mediterranean produce predominates, such as citrus fruits, olive oil, wine and tomatoes. But Italy is faced with a particular dilemma as far as this kind of farming is concerned. On the one hand, it is inefficient. Yet, if farming in the South were reorganized, many agricultural workers would lose jobs.

One vintage Italian product, wine, has fallen on hard times. Domestic wine consumption has halved, especially in the south, where thirst increasingly demands beer and whisky. Production is still relatively impressive, supplying 30% of Europe's wine (second only to France) and 18% of the world total. The EU buys 52% of its exports and the U.S. 32%. With regard to the cheese to go with that wine, the European Court of Justice ruled in 2008 that the word "Parmesan" can apply only to the product made near the Italian city of Parma, not the fake varieties produced elsewhere, such as Germany.

Government–Owned Enterprises

Italy's enormous budget deficits in the past can be partly explained by the huge losses by some of the businesses that are wholly or partially owned by the state, the almost uncontrollable system of social expenditures, and the hostile attitude of the citizens toward taxes. The state's hand in the economy is large. In contrast to many other European countries, where left-wing governments once nationalized many companies, such work was done in Italy by Mussolini. The three large state-owned industrial groups—IRI, ENI and EFIM—account for about 10% of GDP. Some of the firms controlled by these huge holding companies are not profitable. These debt–ridden enterprises are an economic burden in a country in which most private concerns report a profit.

Therefore, the government decided to reduce the state's ownership in the economy. It is in no great hurry to privatize, and it has made no commitment to divest itself totally. The reason is political. Few of the country's leaders were convinced that privatization was a good way to improve the economy. During the 1990s the proportion of the banking system in state hands declined from 70% to 20%. The nation's flag air carrier, Alitalia, limps along on the brink of bankruptcy. Its union, as well as incoming Prime Minister Berlusconi, rejected a bid by Air France-KLM to

Italy

buy it in 2008. However, its future prospects are dim to hopeless. Italy is less able than most other European countries to reform its economy.

Unions

In the view of many analysts, it is an encouraging sign that the Italian trade unions, which in 2002 organized 35.4% of Italy's work force (down from 39.2% in 1990), have lost a considerable portion of their power and influence. In the past the unions had made the Italian worker one of the most protected in Europe, and they had gained a practical veto power over the country's economic and social policies.

The reversal in trade unionists' fortunes has come since the Communists have lost votes in successive parliamentary elections, and since a massive strike against the Fiat automotive company collapsed in the fall of 1980. Fiat had to keep its overseas prices competitive with those of other countries. Now only 30% of Fiat's work force is unionized. Italy enjoys better industrial relations as a result: from 2002 to 2004, it annually lost 113.2 working days per 1,000 employees to strikes, compared with 580 for Greece, 197.4 for Spain, 34.7 for the UK and 16 for France. Enhanced competitiveness enabled production and export of subway cars for the Washington D.C. metro.

The heavy political involvement of the unions has caused them to lose touch with the rank–and–file members, who are more interested in bread–and–butter economic issues. In the midst of a recession, more and more Italians have also come to the conclusion that private enterprise and market–oriented management are necessary if the country's prosperity is to be maintained. Further, the unions were forced to budge on wage indexation, which had kept the motor of inflation well lubricated. The result is a generally favorable economic outlook. At the same time, despite the fact that things Italian miraculously turn out to be less serious than they are usually predicted, the country continues to face some serious economic challenges.

Italy also has powerful professional guilds (*ordini*), which do not always get their way. For example, a state body, the Corte dei Conti, ruled in 2005 that all graduates of the recently revamped university system have the right to use the title "*dottore*" (doctor), even though it takes only three years to graduate. With two additional years they can be called "*dottore magistrale*," while the title "*dottore di recerca*" adorns those who complete advanced research degrees equivalent to an American PhD. The guilds argued that this cheapens the title. But they fought a losing battle in a society that loves inflated titles. Graduates of professional schools are addressed by their occupation (e.g. Architect Verdi or Engineer Rossi). Even post-elementary school teachers are called "*professore*" (professor).

CULTURE

No other country has both profited and been stifled by the wealth of its historical inheritance as has Italy. This inheritance has attracted educated tourists for over 200 years. Annually, 26 million tourists exchange their currencies in Italy in order to see its incomparable art treasures and to enjoy the usually mild climate. In addition, approximately 80 million individual pieces of art await restoration. The most dramatic reappearance in 1999 was Leonardo Da Vinci's "Last Supper," which had undergone a meticulous 21–year restoration in Milan.

Italy possesses 30,000 churches, 20,000 castles, 3,000 archaeological sites that are of value to art historians and shelters in its 712 museums countless important works of art. According to one UNESCO estimate, Italy possesses more than two-thirds of western civilization. With 39 (two more than Spain), it has more sites on the UN's coveted World Heritage List than any other country on earth. Its most recent additions were the Etruscan Necropolises of Cerveteri and Tarquinia, as well as the picturesque hills and villages of Tuscany's Val d'Orcia.

Only one who understands the ambivalent attitude of the Italian toward his history and state can excuse the fact that the money used by the state to maintain the irreplaceable wealth of arts corresponds to the amount needed to construct 18 miles of freeway. Since 1909 the immeasurable cultural inheritance has been administered by a small group of 284 highly placed civil servants. However, Italy alone cannot be expected to bear the burden history has placed upon it; the entire civilized world is also, to some extent, responsible for the vast historical wealth.

UNESCO provided a considerable contribution in order to save Venice, which was threatened by uninhibited industrial exploitation of the hinterlands. In 2003 one of the largest public works projects in a long time was launched to save Venice, which is threatened by rising sea levels and the sinking of the city itself, which had been built on a soggy foundation. It is flooded nine months a year. A series of 79 sea gates were being constructed to rise from the ocean floor if high tides in the Adriatic threaten to swell the lagoon in which Venice is located. This grand project was shelved by the Prodi government as too expensive, but the new Berlusconi government in 2008 was expected to resurrect it.

Many European and American organizations provided aid to cover damages caused by the catastrophic flood in Florence in 1966. It continues to face flooding, with the low–lying parts of the city inundated about every three years. Florence was again shaken in 1993, when terrorists exploded a car bomb in front of the 16th century Uffizi Gallery, which houses the world's most important collection of classic Italian art, including priceless paintings by Leonardo da Vinci, Michelangelo, Raphael, and Titian, and which is visited by more than a million persons each year. Six people died, three paintings and many medieval manuscripts in the library were destroyed, and 21 canvases and three statues were damaged.

The Uffizi's cash flow problem was dramatized in 2002 when the state electric company threatened to cut off its power if it did not pay its long overdue quarter of a million euro bill. This was symptomatic of a larger problem: the state spends much too little on maintaining the country's cultural treasures: only .18% of GDP. Since there are no tax deductions for private donations, the private sector lacks an incentive to step in and help.

The earlier Berlusconi government introduced an experiment to see if some of Italy's treasure trove could be privatized. A new state agency, Patrimonio dello Stato, was created to evaluate Italy's cultural patrimony and decide what could be sold or leased in order to generate income.

Garibaldi

Italy

The government promised not to sell off any treasures that are part of the country's national identity, such as the Colosseum, the leaning tower of Pisa, or the Uffizi. Nor would private owners ever possess a majority stake or hold leases longer than five years. The government also announced in 2002 that it would return to Ethiopia the prized Obelisk of Axum, dating from the 3d century A.D. and looted by Mussolini's soldiers in 1937. It is believed to be a grave marker for a king from the Axumite empire. It was erected near Rome's Circus Maximus. Italy's past reluctance over its repatriation stemmed from a worry shared by many European countries: once such repatriation of antiquities begins, where does it stop? The first part of the 160-ton monument was shipped in April 2005.

According to Italian law, any classical artifacts found on Italian soil belong to the state, even if they originated in Greece. The ministry of culture negotiated tenaciously with the Getty Museum in Los Angeles concerning the return of 46 antiquities from the American collection taken out of Italy under questionable circumstances or purchased from dishonest dealers. The Getty Museum offered 26 in 2006, which Italy's culture minister denounced as not meeting its demand for a comprehensive agreement, which was reached the following year. New York's Metropolitan Museum of Art agreed to return 21 disputed antiquities to Italy, and three other American museums also handed over artifacts. In all cases, such transfer was in exchange for long-term loans from Italy of artifacts of "equal beauty and historical and cultural significance." Such a quid-pro-quo was not possible for New York philanthropist Shelby White, who was persuaded to give up 10 classical antiquities. She became the first private collector to return art to Italy.

The unique Byzantine churches of Ravenna are threatened, the cathedral in Milan is unstable and there is danger that the Palatine Hill in Rome will collapse. Unfortunately, the international contribution has never been used in full because of competition and disputes among the different bureaucracies. The burden of history has not only left its imprint on the political culture and on the problem of southern Italy (*Mezzogiorno*) but also literally threatens to slip out of the Italian state's control.

Italy's extraordinary significance for the development of western civilization from antiquity through the Middle Ages and the Renaissance in the areas of science, the arts, architecture and finance is well known. The Italians have also accomplished much in more recent times. The recognition of Italian as the language of

music indicates the influence it had on the developing years. During the Baroque period (17th-18th centuries), composers such as Domenico Scarlatti, Antonio Vivaldi and Luigi Boccherini, just to name the most important figures, were prominent; (Bach was a great admirer of Vivaldi's works). The 19th century also produced world-renowned composers, such as Gioacchino Rossini, Giuseppe Verdi, Gaetano Donizetti and Giacomo Puccini. Even today, Italian composers such as Luigi Dallapiccola, Bruno Maderna and Luigi Mono are conspicuous. No singer of opera is a star until he performs at the incomparable La Scala in Milan. In December 2004 it was reopened after a three-year overhaul, staging the same obscure opera by Salieri with which it first opened in 1778.

Without even taking into account the countless artists of the 15th, 16th and 17th centuries, Italian artists include modern painters such as Amadeo Modigliani and Giorgio de Chirico and sculptor Marino Marini, who have maintained Italy's reputation in the international art world. In 1906 and 1936 respectively Giosuè Carducci and Grazia Deledda received Nobel prizes for literature. Significant writers such as the novelist Giovanni Verga and the romantic poet, Gabriele D'Annunzio, lead a long list of splendid literary figures. In lyric poetry, Giuseppe Ungaretti, Eugenio Montale and Salvatore Quasimodo (who won a Nobel prize in 1959) have made important contributions. Dramatist Luigi Pirandello and novelists Curzio Malaparte, Cesare Pavese, Tomasi di Lampedusa, Ignazio Silone and Alberto Moravia dominated the Italian literary scene until after World War II. The critical realist, Italo Calvino, enjoys postwar popularity.

International film, opera and theater festivals, as well as modern art exhibits reflect the ever–vibrant cultural life of Italy. In terms of cinema, Rome is to Italy what Hollywood means to the U.S.A. Italian directors have been and still are the leading film figures in Europe. Names such as Vittorio de Sica, Federico Fellini, Luchino Visconti and Pier Paolo Pasolini have decisively affected European films. With his commercial Italian Western (often referred to jokingly as "spaghetti Western") director Sergio Leone captivated masses of movie– goers all over the world. Italian cinema's stellar position was shown in 1999 by Roberto Benigni's "Life is Beautiful," which won two Oscars, including the best foreign–language film, and the Grand Jury Prize at the Cannes Film Festival. Italians continue to see many American feature films, and in 1999 two–thirds of its foreign TV programs were purchased from the United States.

In the natural sciences, the Italians have also distinguished themselves—Galileo

Galilei, Luigi Galvani and Alessandro Volta played a prominent role in the research of electricity. Guglielmo Marconi won a Nobel prize in 1909 for his discovery of the wireless telegraph. One cannot overlook another Nobel prize winner, Enrico Fermi, who investigated the peaceful use of the atom.

For the first time since Italy's creation, the press is no longer controlled by political power and parties, but by the normal business groups in the Italian economy. Major dailies include Rome's *La Repubblica* and *Il Messaggero*, Milan's *Corriere della Sera*, *Il Giornale*, and *Il Sole 24 Ore* (important financial newspaper) and Turin's *La Stampa*. *Il Foglio* is a clever four–page daily. The Communist *L'Unita*, founded by Antonio Gramsci in 1924, is no longer widely read, but it still sells 50,000 copies a day (down from 300,000 in its heyday). Italians buy no more dailies than they did in the 1930s—six million, compared with 22 million in the UK. The major newsweeklies include *L'Espresso* and *Panorama*.

As in France, the guardians of the language worry that English is encroaching on the Italian language. They deride the resulting mixture as "Italiese." The Academia della Crusca was founded in 1570 to promote the primacy of Florentine Italian, and the government maintains 89 Italian Cultural Institutes throughout the world to serve as disseminators of the Italian language. In 2005 the government jumped into action when the European Commission decided to drop Italian and Spanish and use only English, French and German in some news conferences. The EC backed off. This reaction underscored the fact that while many Europeans are willing to merge their currencies and cede some sovereignty to Brussels, they are not ready to give up their languages.

Despite its problems, Italy remains a prosperous, democratic country, in which civil rights are protected far better than in most countries of the world. It sometimes looks maddeningly chaotic. Even the hottest film in Italy in 2008 was entitled *Caos Calmo* (Quiet Chaos). But the Italian brand of chaos has a certain refreshing sweetness to it which is precisely why millions of non–Italians are fervent admirers, even lovers of this country and its friendly people. Perhaps a touch of chaos is essential to the renowned Italian *dolce vita* ("sweet life").

FUTURE

That Italy will survive its multifaceted ordeals is due largely to the fact that the Italians have an unshakable ability to adapt to existing circumstances with imagination and practicality. Some ten-

Italy

dencies toward integrating the otherwise centrifugal political forces are evident in the widespread rejection and struggle against corruption, terrorism and organized crime. Pressure for reform of the political system continues. However, in 2006 Transparency International ranked Italy 45th among 163 nations in terms of corruption, behind Greece. Pressure on the Mafia and the other organized crime families is being maintained.

Parliamentary elections in April 2008 took place against a backdrop of weak economic growth, increasing prices, a slipping standard of living, fear of immigration and growing crime (especially by foreigners), and a deep sense of national crisis and despondency. Italians are experiencing a more profound concern that their country is in serious decline relative to their European partners. This malaise put a severe dent in the popularity of Romano Prodi's government and ultimately brought it down in April 2008 after only 20 months in office.

The April 2008 elections were a clear victory for Silvio Berlusconi and his center-right coalition. Prodi faced problems not only of unifying the left, which is always a daunting task. But he had to rule with a shaky nine-party coalition government that relied on a wide spectrum of political forces, from moderate Catholics to communists and radical leftists, for a parliamentary majority. The government was at the mercy of the Refounded Communists, who had brought down Prodi's first government in October 1998. This was not a situation conducive to fundamental reform, and it is somewhat surprising that he booked a couple of successes: bringing more competition to the professions and retail trade and decreasing the budget deficit below 3% of GDP by raising tax revenues.

In an effort to tighten unity on the center-left for the 2008 elections, the Democrats of the Left announced its merger with the Margherita to form a new Democratic Party, supported by Prodi and led by former Rome Mayor Walter Veltroni. This created the novelty of a basically two-party political system. The daily *La Repubblica* wrote that "this is an electoral tsunami that redraws Italy's political landscape." One cannot say that this will last, though, because both large parties are still young and poorly defined.

The renamed party of Silvio Berlusconi—People of Freedom—proved formidable. Italian voters wanted strong leadership and returned to Berlusconi for the third time because they were tired of the bickering in Prodi's nine-party center-left government, did not like their higher taxes, were disgusted by the mounting piles of uncollected trash in Naples that

symbolized a failure of public services, and recognized that the broad reforms Prodi had promised had not been enacted. Berlusconi's party's victory was sweetened by the results of the Rome municipal elections two weeks after the parliamentary voting: for the first time since the fall of Mussolini in 1943 the capital had a rightwing mayor: Gianni Alemanno. Thus Berlusconi entered office with clear majorities in both houses of parliament and in Rome and Milan, his home town. This gave him mastery of the national political scene unparalleled in modern Italy.

His 21-member cabinet contains some familiar faces, including Franco Frattini as foreign minister and Giulio Tremonti as economics minister. The Northern League's Umberto Bossi became minister of reforms, and two of his party comrades also received seats at the table. The cabinet contained four women, including most controversially a 32-year-old former beauty queen and nude model, Mara Carfagna, as equal opportunities minister. Until two years earlier, Carfagna had been a presenter on one of Berlusconi's TV channels and had been in the middle of a public spat between Mr. and Mrs. Berlusconi when he told her at an awards ceremony that he would marry her if he were not already wed. The new government vowed to join the U.S., Britain, France and Germany in taking a tough line toward Iran's nuclear ambitions. It also moved quickly to fulfill a campaign promise to

crack down on immigration and to "empty illegal camps and get rid of nomads who have no residence and no means of subsistence." Within days of its taking office, 400 persons were arrested and 100 expelled.

One should not expect too much from his rule. Repeated massive demonstrations to protest his earlier government's changes to the pension and labor laws revealed how difficult and politically dangerous reform in Italy is. Elderly Italians, whose percentage of the total population is ever growing, wield impressive political clout. Economic growth has stalled, and the deep-seated structural flaws in the economy have not been corrected: too few big companies, too much regulation, poor competitiveness, low productivity, not enough investment in new technology, low investment in research and development (1.1% of GDP compared with EU average of almost 2%) and discouragingly high levels of youth unemployment. It is unlikely that the renewed Berlusconi government will make significant inroads in solving these problems.

But there is always room for some optimism in Italy. Public opinion polls showed in 2008 that three-fourths (74%) of Italians were worried about their economy. A majority (52%) thought their country was "moving in the wrong direction." Nevertheless, 71% said they were satisfied with their own lives as far as family, work and their personal future are concerned.

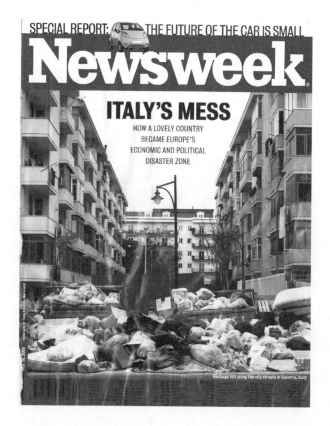

SPECIAL REPORT: THE FUTURE OF THE CAR IS SMALL

Newsweek

ITALY'S MESS

HOW A LOVELY COUNTRY BECAME EUROPE'S ECONOMIC AND POLITICAL DISASTER ZONE

Garbage left along the city streets in Caserta, Italy

The Republic of San Marino

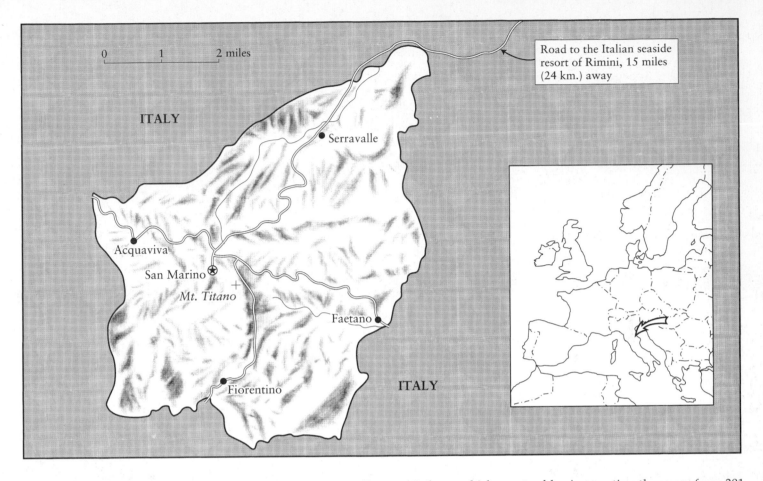

Area: 23.6 sq. mi. (61 sq. km.)

Population: 31,000 (UN 2007).

Capital City: San Marino (Pop. 4,500, estimated).

Climate: Mild and temperate.

Official Language: Italian.

Ethnic Background: Italian.

Principal Religion: Roman Catholic.

Main Industries: Tourism, postage stamps, cotton textiles, brick, tile, cement, furniture, craft goods.

Main Customer: Italy.

Currency: Euro.

Independence: Fourth Century A.D.

Government: Republic.

Chiefs of State: Two Captains Regent, selected every six months.

Heads of Government: Secretary of State for Foreign and Political Affairs (Fabio Berardi) and Secretary of State for Budget, Financial and Internal Affairs (Pierre Marino Mularoni).

National Flag: Two horizontal stripes, one white on the top and one blue on the bottom.

National Holidays: April 1, October 1.

Known today chiefly to collectors, who prize this tiny country's beautiful postage stamps, the most serene Republic of San Marino is a landlocked historical curiosity situated on the slopes of Monte Titano in the eastern part of central Italy, to which it is linked by a customs union and a treaty of friendship. The last remaining relic of the self-governing Italian city-states, San Marino is the smallest republic in the world (except Nauru), and it always has wanted to stay that way. Its residents once refused Napoleon's offer of more territory on the grounds that the country's small size and poverty were the greatest guarantors of its independence. It has an irregular rectangular form with a maximum length of eight miles (13 km.) The country's setting is dominated by the 2,424-foot-high (739 meters) Monte Titano, whose three summits are crowned by ancient fortifications. The medieval-looking capital city with its red-roofed stone houses is located directly below one of these fortifications and is surrounded by triple walls. Of its 31,000 residents, roughly 3,000 are non-citizens, mainly Italians. An additional 20,000 of the people (known as San Marinese) reside abroad, principally in Italy.

San Marino traces its origin to 301 A.D. when St. Marinus (from whom the country derives its name) and a small group of Christians fled to Monte Titano to escape religious persecution. In memory of their founder, the San Marinese do not date years according to Christ's life, but in-stead begin counting the years from 301 A.D. For instance, the year 2009 in San Marino is 1708. By the 12th century this tiny territory had become self-ruling. It has always managed to maintain its independence chiefly thanks to its geographic isolation, its mountain fortresses and its skill in playing rival noble families against one another. By the 15th century, it was a republic ruled by a Grand Council composed of 60 men from San Marino's leading families.

During the Italian unification struggles in the 19th century, San Marino offered asylum to revolutionaries, including the hero Giuseppe Garibaldi. This assistance enabled it to gain a guarantee of independence from the kingdom of Italy in 1862. San Marino remained neutral in World War II until September 1943, and in November of that year it was temporarily occupied by German troops. In June 1944 it was damaged by British bomber pilots who were attempting to dislodge the occupiers.

The Statutes of 1600, enlarged in 1926 and revised in 1939, serve as a constitution. They established a parliament, the Great and General Council, with 60 members elected every five years by universal suffrage since 1960. This Council in turn elects two Captains Regent, largely cere-

335

The Republic of San Marino

monial figures who formally exercise executive power for a period of six months. During their semiannual investitures on April 1 and October 1, the Noble Guard and Great and General Councilors all dress in brightly colored uniforms and parade through the capital's streets. The Captains Regent cannot be elected for a second term until three years have elapsed. In 1981, for the first time in the country's history, a woman, Maria Lea Pedini Angelini, was chosen. The Council also elects from among its members ten persons who serve as secretaries of state in the Council of State, the principal organ of executive power. These secretaries of state each head a government administrative department.

The Secretary of State for Foreign and Political Affairs and the Secretary of State for Budget, Financial and Internal Affairs are in fact the highest and most powerful government executives of San Marino. Finally, the Great and General Council elects a supreme appellate judicial body, the Council of Twelve, which hears appeals from the decisions of San Marino's two full–time judges, who need not be citizens. These judges decide on the basis of San Marino's own civil and criminal legal system, which has understandably been influenced greatly by Italian law.

The country has many political parties, which are heavily influenced by their much larger counterpart parties in Italy. They include the Christian Democratic Party (DCS), the Party of Socialists and Democrats (PSD), the Popular Alliance, the United Party and the New Socialist Party. Like their Italian counterparts, these parties are not rigidly bound to doctrine. In the June 2006 elections the Christian Democrats continued their dominance, winning 32.9% of the votes and 21 seats, compared with 31.8% and 20 seats for the Party of Socialists and Democrats.

A unique election feature is that the state pays 75% of the return fare for any

Monte Titano dominates San Marino

San Marinese living abroad to come home and vote in general elections. Over 5,400 did just that in 1988, returning from as far as Detroit, where many live.

This tiny mouse roars against the United States if it gets an urge to do so. In 1982 its parliament voted to "deplore" American policy in El Salvador and authorized a symbolic $4,500 contribution to the rebel forces there.

All parties in San Marino favor a broad social security system that, among other things, provides health care from state funds. Children up to the age of 12 receive a guaranteed summer holiday on the seaside, and up to the age of 14 a free public education. Those wishing to study further are eligible for state scholarships to Italian high schools and universities. Finally, the state of San Marino finds work for all citizens who cannot obtain employment privately. If no work at all can be found, then the state provides unemployment benefits amounting to 60% of the person's normal salary. Citizens inform themselves by the state-run radio and TV—San Marino RTV—and two daily newspapers: *La Tribuna Sammarinese* and *San Marino Oggi*.

This country has no army because Italy provides for its defense. It does have a military corps that performs parade duty during national celebrations. It has a gendarmerie that maintains public order. In 1988 San Marino entered the Council of Europe, and in 1992 it joined the United Nations. It sends athletes to the winter Olympics since 1976.

There are utterly no natural resources, so earnings must be made from farming (chiefly wheat and grapes), livestock raising, light manufacturing (chiefly cotton textiles, brick and tile, cement and pottery), the sale of postage stamps and tourism. Diplomatic relations between the EU and San Marino were opened in 1983. Its goods have free access to the EU. It not only adopted the euro in 2002, but it was permitted to mint its own euro coins with its own motif on the back.

It began to attract capital by being a tax haven. However, in 2000 it agreed to cooperate with international efforts to curb abusive and criminal tax-avoidance schemes. It reached an agreement with the EU in 2003 to collect taxes for bank account interest and return 75% of it to the country of residence without providing account holders' names. It aspires to be a financial center like Luxembourg, with light regulation and banking secrecy. It set up a central bank in 2005 and established eight banks since 2000, with insurance companies arriving thereafter.

Tourism accounts for over 50% of GDP. During the summer months, from 20,000 to 30,000 foreign tourists visit San Marino

each day. Unfortunately, the San Marinese welcome these tourists with solid rows of souvenir shops on both sides of the principal streets. Without doubt, it has more tourist stands and shops per capita than does any other country in the world. This creates an excessively commercialized air in this naturally beautiful mountain–top republic. Several handsome hotels and restaurants relieve this monotony. There are no railroad or airport facilities.

FUTURE

Although legally independent, San Marino has always been very vulnerable to pressure from the Italian government, political parties and trade unions. This situation will certainly continue. Its beautiful setting and the curiosity this tiny republic stimulates will help assure that tourism will continue to be a lucrative source of income. However, a shortage of energy will continue to exist, and San Marino will have great difficulty finding the necessary funds to finance badly needed expanded water and electric power systems.

The Vatican City State

St. Peter's Square

Area: .15 sq. mi. (.40 sq. km.)
Population: 1,000 (estimated).
Climate: Temperate.
Neighboring Countries: Italy.
Official Language: Latin. Italian is the working language at the Vatican.
Religion: Roman Catholic.
Currency: Vatican lira, interchangeable with euro.
National Day: June 30.
Chief of State: His Holiness Pope Benedict XVI (formerly Cardinal Joseph Ratzinger), elected pope April 19, 2005.
Suffrage: Limited to cardinals less than 80 years of age, who elect a Pope for life.
National Flag: Yellow and white stripes parallel to the staff, with the papal insignia on a white field.

Vatican City is the world's second smallest state. One can stroll leisurely around the full length of its borders in less than one hour. Located in the heart of Rome, near the west bank of the Tiber River, and surrounded by medieval walls and the Church of St. Peter, this tiny dot on the Rome city map is often said to wield more influence in the world than the entire nation of Italy. The reason is that this is the headquarters of the Roman Catholic Church, the largest body of

Christians in the world. Building began in the 8th century to create a residence for the popes. By the Middle Ages the Vatican had come to control a large part of Italy and was one of the most important and influential powers in European politics. In 1870 the government of the newly founded Italian state annexed the extensive Papal States throughout Italy. The pontiffs rejected all offers of financial compensation, choosing instead to withdraw behind the Vatican's walls in defiance.

In 1929 the pope chose to sign the Lateran Treaty with the then fascist government of Italy. This treaty established the independence and sovereignty of the State of Vatican City, fixed the relationship between the Italian government and the Catholic Church and set a cash payment for the earlier seizure of papal property. A revision of this treaty in 1984 ended the status of Roman Catholicism as Italy's state religion. Despite the loss of much of its property, the Vatican has very extensive investments throughout the world, especially in Italy.

The Church's wealth is widely assumed to be massive. Financial operations are handled by the Institute for Religious Agencies, better known as the "Vatican Bank," whose depositors are Catholic reli-

gious orders, Vatican employees and clergymen. For 2,000 years until 1987 the Vatican kept its financial operations strictly secret. However, an inspection of the books of the bankrupt Milan–based Banco Ambrosiano and the murder by the Mafia of that bank's president, Roberto Calvi, in 1982 revealed deep Vatican entanglement in questionable financial dealings. The Church hierarchy was so seriously embarrassed by this scandal that the pope ordered an end to the Holy See's dependence upon investment and speculation for its funds. It would rely instead on "the spontaneous contributions of the faithful and of other men of good will." The bank scandal made it more difficult to raise money. Five persons were ordered to stand trial for Calvi's death, but the Rome court cleared all of them in 2007.

In 1987 an Italian court issued an arrest warrant against the head of the "Vatican Bank," American Archbishop Paul Marcinkus, as "accessory to fraudulent bankruptcy." Because the archbishop, who the Vatican insisted was innocent, had moved inside the Vatican walls, Italian authorities could not arrest him; Italy has no extradition treaty with the Vatican.

There were no precedents for such a complex legal standoff between the two

Vatican City

sovereign states. According to Article 22 of the Lateran Treaty, the Vatican is obligated to surrender to Italian custody anyone who enters its grounds in order to escape from Italian law. However, Article 11 states, "central bodies of the Catholic Church are free from every interference on the part of the Italian state." During the Second World War, even the Mussolini government did not try to get possession of Jews and political refugees who had hidden within the Vatican's walls. Italy's highest court annulled the arrest warrant, and Marcinkus retired from papal service in 1991 and returned to Chicago as a parish priest. Supervision of the bank passed to an international board of five Catholic lay directors.

The Lateran Treaty established extraterritorial status, but technically not papal sovereignty, for 13 areas outside Vatican City. These are chiefly the major Catholic churches in Rome and the Pope's summer residence of Castel Gandolfo. In an agreement of 1951, the Vatican's radio station (*Stazione Radio Città del Vaticano*) also was placed under Vatican jurisdiction. This created tensions in 2001 when citizens charged that the electromagnetic emissions from the Vatican Radio's large towers on the outskirts of Rome cause cancer.

Insofar as the purely political functions of the Vatican are concerned, all executive, legislative and judicial authority is vested in the Pope. He appoints a governor and organs to administer the Vatican. The College of Cardinals serves as the chief papal advisers, and the Roman Curia carries on the central administration of the Roman Catholic Church's religious affairs.

Order within the small state is provided by a colorfully dressed regular army of Swiss guards. Recruitment is held in the

Author (l) with papal nuncio to the United Nations

cantons of Freiburg, St. Gallen and Lucerne; the men must be between 20 and 30 years old. They carry old–fashioned halberds, but they always have machine guns hidden close by. Perhaps former Soviet Foreign Minister Andrei Gromyko was wrong in calling them "the world's least frightening army."

Plainclothes Swiss guards and agents from the papal gendarmes always accompany the pope everywhere when he confronts audiences and crowds within the Vatican, just as Secret Service men accompany the president of the United States. One difference is that the agents never turn completely away from the Pope in order to scan for potential troublemakers. Paul VI ruled that it was disrespectful for the guards to turn their backs on the Pontiff. In 1998 a disgruntled guard fatally shot his commander and wife and then killed himself. This was the first time in 150 years that this had occurred, and it prompted the Vatican to review its recruiting procedures and administer psychological exams for new guards. In 2006 the head of the pope's bodyguards, Camillo Civin, retired after 58 years.

Within the Vatican live fewer than 1,000 persons, all of whom have Vatican documents, rather than other passports. They are chiefly permanent Vatican employees, the largest number being priests and nuns. Cardinals are considered to be Vatican residents whenever they are in Rome. When a citizen of the Vatican leaves the city limits of Rome, he automatically becomes a citizen of his original nationality (or of Italy if the original nationality does not permit dual citizenship).

Vatican City has within its borders its own telephone system, a post office (which uses the Vatican's own stamps), a radio station, a pharmacy, several stores, and a banking system with its own coins and the only cash machines in the world with instructions in Latin. It was also granted permission to mint its own euro coins with Pope John Paul's profile on the back.

In addition to the Church of St. Peter and the Vatican Apostolic Palace (which was expanded in the 15th and 16th centuries to become the largest palace in the world) with all its museums and library, the Vatican contains a score of administrative and ecclesiastical buildings, a "village" of apartments and the beautiful Vatican gardens. There is a small railroad station at the perimeter of the Vatican that is connected by 300 meters of track to the Italian state railway station.

Almost 300 permanent diplomatic representatives (known as *nuncios*) in 176 capitals throughout the world conduct the Vatican's external dealings; 78 countries maintain missions in Rome, including the United States since 1984. By tradition, papal nuncios are granted the first rank at any diplomatic ceremonies they attend. The Vatican also has permanent observer status at the United Nations (some of whose human-rights conventions it has signed) and at 15 other intergovernmental bodies, including the African Union and the Organization of American States.

Nuncios (all priests) are trained at the Pontifical Ecclesiastical Academy in Rome and are known to be very knowledgeable, highly cultured and facile in languages.

His Holiness the late Pope John Paul II

Fresco in the Sistine Chapel

They have a policy to be only lightly protected and never to pull out of dangerous situations. There are seldom more than two people in each mission, and their time is devoted chiefly to the life of the church, including the appointment of bishops. Their "headquarters" is the "Section for Relations with States" in Rome, which has only 18 diplomats and 29 other staff. A Pontifical Council for Justice and Peace serves as a kind of overseas-aid mission, while an independent Rome-based body, the Sant'Egidio Community, specializes in mediation work in crisis areas.

The Vatican possesses priceless cultural treasures, including the Vatican Museums, the frescoes by Michelangelo in the Sistine Chapel, frescoes by Pinturicchio in the Borgia Apartment, Raphael's Stanze and the Church of St. Peter, where such art treasures as Michelangelo's "La Pietà" are displayed. In 1983 more than 200 of these irreplaceable art works toured the United States, where they were viewed by millions of Americans in New York, Chicago and San Francisco. The Vatican Library contains a valuable collection of manuscripts from the pre–Christian era to the present. It also publishes an influential daily newspaper, *L'Osservatore Romano*.

The Vatican owns a press that publishes books and pamphlets in all languages of the world. In 2003 it published the latest edition of a two-volume Latin dictionary containing 15,000 modernized Latin words. The Vatican's Latin Foundation, set up in the 1970s to keep Latin alive in the Church after it had been decreed that

mass could be celebrated in local languages, is behind the project. Although Italian is the working language of the Vatican, Latin remains the Church's official language, and an up-to-date dictionary is needed for encyclicals and other scientific documents. It is not easy to keep Latin alive after more than two millennia, and many of the dictionary's new words are compounds of existing Latin words. For example, "dishwasher" is *"escariorum lavator"* and "disco" is *"orbium phonographicorum theca."*

The Papacy of John Paul II (1978–2005)

Sensitive to allegations that the Vatican had done little to condemn the holocaust or help Jews during the Second World War, the Vatican intervened to support the relocation of a cloister located on the edge of the Auschwitz death camp in Poland. The Holy See's relations with Jews had been strained for 2,000 years. But in 1965 the Vatican repudiated the doctrine of collective Jewish guilt for the death of Jesus. This was documented in "Nostra Aetate" ("In Our Time") published in 2002. The Vatican official in charge of Jewish relations, Cardinal Walter Kasper, stated in that year that Catholics and Jews may still disagree on some things, but they do so as brothers. In 1993 it signed an accord with Israel leading to full diplomatic relations the following year, and in 1994 it published a document acknowledging its past mistakes that had contributed to anti–Semitism.

In 1997 the pope condemned the actions of many Christians before and during the

Holocaust, saying that they contributed to the rise of anti–Semitism and then failed to help as Jews were being eradicated. Jewish groups criticized the fact that this strong statement fell short of an apology, which they have been demanding. In 1998 the Church, while defending the actions of Pope Pius XII as having been a quieter form of resistance against the Nazis, officially apologized for failing to take a more active role in stopping Nazi persecution of Jews. It also declared Edith Stein, an Orthodox Jew who had converted to Christianity and died at Auschwitz in 1942, to be a saint. One year after becoming pope, Benedict XVI was welcomed in Poland by two million faithful. He visited Auschwitz to signal reconciliation and called the Nazis "a ring of criminals."

Until 1975 the foreign diplomatic representatives to the Vatican had to be men. When the West Germans sent a woman counselor to its mission, they were reminded of the Vatican's "tradition that forbids Vatican officials from having business contacts with ladies." Finally the former African dictator of Uganda, Idi Amin, forced the Vatican to accept a female mission chief. The Church's ban on women priests is under increasing attack by Catholics. In 1987 it was revealed that a priest who had served in southern Italy for 25 years had undergone a sex change and become a woman. Church practice holds that an ordained priest remains one whatever his transgressions might be. Therefore, the Church granted her early retirement with the usual pension. The Church often acts slowly: in 1992 it for-

Vatican City

mally rehabilitated Galileo Galilei, whom the Inquisition had condemned in 1633 for daring to prove that the Earth orbited the sun, rather than the other way around. The Vatican announced in 2008 that a statue to Galileo would be erected and also that Martin Luther would be rehabilitated.

Italy assumes responsibility for defending the Vatican and for patrolling St. Peter's Square. When the Turkish gunman who shot the pope in May 1981 was captured, he was taken initially to the Commissariato Borgo, the Vatican police headquarters. He was then bundled very quickly into an armored car and driven to central police headquarters in downtown Rome. Not until March 2006 was there evidence "beyond any reasonable doubt," in the words of an Italian parliamentary commission, that the Soviet Union's military intelligence (not the KGB) was behind the assassination attempt. The motive was Moscow's fear of the pope's support of Solidarity in Poland. The pope

requested clemency for Agca, and the Italian president pardoned him in 2000. He was extradited to Turkey to serve a sentence for a prior crime, and he was released in 2006.

By the end of the decade, though, Mikhail Gorbachev's *Glasnost* had led to better relations between the Holy See and Eastern Europe, and the pope launched a campaign for a "Europe without spiritual frontiers." The reconciliation between communism and Christianity was crowned by Gorbachev's historic audience with the pope (whom he addressed as "Your Holiness") in 1989. A Vatican diplomat said: "Catholicism and communism are ideologies that cannot be reconciled. But there is space for common endeavor in the social, cultural and humanitarian fields." Gorbachev expressed interest in the pope's call for a third road between capitalism and socialism, a new social order that would combine social justice with economic efficiency and political pluralism. The USSR wanted to be a full partner in a common European

civilization, and the pope holds one of the keys to that community. In 1991 he named spiritual leaders for Soviet Catholics, published a social doctrine for societies returning to capitalism, and convened an unprecedented synod of bishops from the two halves of Europe to meet in Rome.

In 1996 Pope John Paul II received one of the world's last Communist leaders, Fidel Castro. In return, the Cuban dictator renewed his country's invitation of the pontiff; Cuba was the only Latin American nation the pope had not yet visited. The pope arrived in Cuba in 1998 to large and enthusiastic crowds. One million Cubans assembled to hear him read mass at Revolutionary Square. The political importance and influence of the pope were visible in the easing by Castro (who for the first time as president wore civilian clothes in his own country) of religious intolerance before the pontiff arrived and his public composure while the pope admonished the Cuban church to fight for "the recognition of human rights and social justice" and to take "courageous and prophetic stands in the face of the corruption of political and economic power." The pope also won the release of 299 prisoners. However, in 2003 he decried the harsh sentences against dissidents meted out by the Castro regime, as well as the execution of three men who had seized a ferry in an ill-fated attempt to escape to the United States.

The Vatican looked forward to a grandiose diversion to celebrate the dawning of the third Christian millennium in 2000. More than 30 million visitors journeyed to Rome for the event. Fearing that this celebration would be marred, the Vatican suggested that it would have been a "matter of common sense" for Italian officials to ban a World Gay Pride parade in Rome in July. Many persons were offended by posters highlighting God's hand touching Adam's private parts in Michelangelo's masterpiece in the Vatican's Sistine Chapel. However, the Holy See took no formal steps to stop the parade, especially since the most recent concordat between the Vatican and the Italian state, signed in 1984, deprives Rome of the "holy status" Mussolini had granted it in 1929. The event drew 70,000 participants, according to the police (200,000 according to organizers). The pope bitterly denounced it as an insult and an offense to Christian values, saying that homosexual acts are "contrary to natural law."

A Vatican glossary of sexual terms that appeared in 2003 asserts that homosexuals are not normal and that the increasingly large number of countries that allow gay marriages are inhabited by people with "profoundly disordered minds." Nevertheless, the pope argued that gays

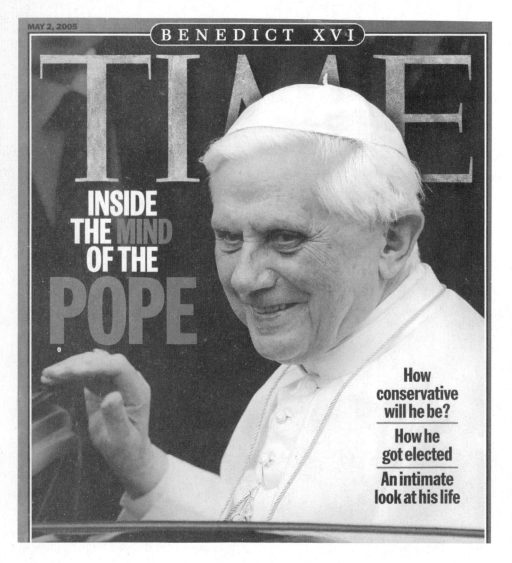

should be treated with "respect, compassion, and delicacy" because homosexuality is a "disorder." Believing that homosexuality might be partially responsible for the many sexual abuse scandals involving priests, the Vatican ordered seminaries in 2005 to bar candidates for the priesthood who "practice homosexuality," have "deeply rooted homosexual tendencies," or support "gay culture." It did not call for the removal of gays who are already priests.

The Church has sexual problems of its own as its clergy are charged in many countries of sexually abusing believers. All American cardinals were called to Rome in 2002 to be lectured on the impermissibility of such behavior. However, when the United States Conference of Catholic Bishops approved of a zero-tolerance policy on sexually abusive priests in October 2002, the Vatican demanded major revisions. In April 2008 Benedict made his first visit to the U.S. as pope and made the first papal visit to the White House in 30 years. The crowd in the Rose Garden sang Happy Birthday to celebrate his 81st anniversary. He celebrated huge masses at Nationals Park stadium in Washington and in St. Patrick's Cathedral in New York. But his trip was dominated by the sexual abuse scandal involving 12,000 children and 5,000 priests and costing the Church $2 billion in settlements. A half-dozen bankrupt dioceses were closed.

In 2001 the pope apologized to China for errors of the colonial past and pleaded for diplomatic relations, broken in 1951, in order to protect Chinese Roman Catholics from continued persecution. This is made difficult because the Vatican maintains diplomatic relations with Taiwan. But in 2006 the Vatican hinted that it is willing to break with Taiwan and recognize Beijing in order to improve the lives of the 10 million practicing Catholics in China. In May 2008 the China Philharmonic Orchestra performed Mozart's Requiem with the Shanghai Opera House Chorus for Pope Benedict XVI in the Paul VI Audience Hall at the Vatican. This was an unprecedented event aimed at signaling a possible thaw in the chilly China-Vatican relationship.

The Church also clashed with Russia's Orthodox Church in 2002 when it created four new dioceses in that country, which has an estimated 1.3 million Catholics. Orthodox leaders charged that Rome seeks to poach converts. On the pope's 100th foreign trip during his papacy in 2003, he reached out to leaders of the Orthodox Church to try to heal the rift that has divided the two faiths since the Great Schism of 1054. In 2004 he agreed to establish a joint committee to help improve relations with the Russian Orthodox

Church. He also called on the Catholic majority in Croatia to seek reconciliation with Orthodox Serbs. In 2004 he returned the bones of two saints to Ecumenical Patriarch Bartholomew I to underscore his determination to reconcile with Orthodox Christianity and forge pan-Christian unity.

The Papacy of Pope Benedict XVI (2005–)

John Paul II passed away a few days after Easter 2005. The able hand of Cardinal Joseph Ratzinger, the guardian of theological orthodoxy during most of John Paul II's reign, organized the pope's memorable funeral in St. Peter's Square. It was attended by 300,000, including three U.S. presidents, the secretary of state, and dozens of other heads of state and government. This was the first time in history any American president had attended a papal funeral. Millions more watched on huge screens all over Rome. Not only did the world's 1.1 billion Catholics (17.3% of the world's population) mourn the loss of their spiritual leader, but also two billion people all over the globe, one-third of the world's population, turned on their televisions to witness the departure of an extraordinary man who had accomplished extraordinary things.

It was also Cardinal Ratzinger who organized the election of a new Pontiff. Centuries of tradition govern the process. Nine days of official mourning (known as "novemdiales") follow the burial. The conclave must be held no sooner than 15 days after the pope's death and no later than 20 days. All cardinals under the age of 80 can vote. Of the 117 electors who qualified, 58 came from Europe (20 from Italy, the largest national contingent), 21 from Latin America, 14 from North America, 11 from Africa, 11 from Asia and one each from Australia and New Zealand.

During the process cardinals are not permitted to use phones, computers, radios, televisions, cameras or recording devices. Phone lines are disconnected. All cardinals take an oath of secrecy and may only confer with each other. The winner must have a two-thirds majority. If after 12 days and 30 votes no candidate has achieved that, the cardinals can change the rules. They can either elect the pope by a simple majority or by holding a runoff vote between the two top candidates in the most recent ballot. After each vote, the ballots are burned with the addition of special chemicals, and the smoke exits from the Vatican palace roof. Black smoke indicates an inconclusive vote. White means the world has a new pope. In 2005, for the first time, the traditional white smoke for a winner was accompanied by the ringing of bells.

Emerging as the winner after only four votes in fewer than 24 hours was the 78-year-old Ratzinger himself, the first German Pope in 482 years. He took the name Benedict XVI. The son of a police officer from rural Bavaria, he, like most young Germans, had joined the Hitler Youth and served briefly in an antiaircraft unit before deserting in 1944. Like his brother, he became a priest, and his sister became a nun. A religious scholar and powerful intellectual, he held professorships at the Universities of Tübingen and Regensburg and is a gifted linguist (ten languages including heavily accented English, French and Italian). After serving as Archbishop of Munich for only four years, Pope John Paul II called him to Rome to head the Congregation for the Doctrine of Faith, the Vatican's ministry for maintaining orthodoxy. He was no doubt elected Pope because of his deep knowledge of the Vatican bureaucracy, leadership qualities, intellectual prowess, and his reputation for shoring up the fundamentals of the faith.

Because of his age, his reign will be shorter than that of his predecessor. In the first months of his papacy, Benedict XVI waived the traditional five-year waiting period and ordered the launching of the process to make his predecessor a saint. A special commission will review John Paul's life and work and look for miracles. One is required for beatification, and a second for canonization.

Benedict confronts enormous challenges, including how to stem the Church's erosion in Europe. This traditional bastion is in decline, even in such predominantly Catholic countries as Italy, Ireland, and Spain, the country that changed more than any other during John Paul II's reign. The latter appealed repeatedly in vain to have a reference to Europe's Christian heritage included in the preamble of the ill-fated EU constitution, which instead referred to the Roman and Greek heritage. In 2007 he apologized to the Muslim world for a speech in which he seemed to equate Islam with violence.

One in six humans on earth were baptized Catholics, but many Europeans and North Americans describe themselves as "cultural Catholics" while blithely ignoring the pope's teaching when it does not suit them. However, in Poland many analysts credit a pastoral letter from native son, Pope John Paul II, for persuading the required number of people (50%) to vote in a June 2003 referendum that approved the country's entry into the EU. His letter, which was read in churches across Poland the weekend before the voting, called EU membership "an act of historical justice."

Its former political influence in Italy was greatly diminished by the collapse of

Vatican City

the Christian Democracy party. Nevertheless, Pope John Paul II gave a historic address to the Italian parliament in November 2002, the first time this had ever happened. Appealing to Italians to meet the "crisis of the birth rate," he received a standing ovation, which was in part a tribute to his physical perseverance. The appearance was a sign that the turbulent relationship between Italy and the Church has become warmer.

Its political influence has not completely vanished in Italy. A reminder was given in June 2005, when a referendum took place to decide whether to abrogate parts of a 2004 fertility law that banned research using stem cells from embryos. The law also imposed stringent requirements on test-tube pregnancies. In order to pass, a majority had to turn out to vote, and a majority had to vote yes. Pope Benedict XVI and the country's bishops and priests told the faithful to boycott the referendum. As a result, only 26% showed up to vote, and 90% of those voted yes. Italians once again showed the power of their Church.

In Spain only 14% of young people described themselves as religious in 2005. The Spanish Socialist government is aggressively pursuing an agenda that contravenes almost every tenet of Catholic doctrine. It legalized gay marriage in July 2005 and allows gay couples to adopt children. It introduced fast-track divorce and relaxed abortion rules. The Archbishop of Madrid said his country had turned into "Sodom and Gomorrah." Benedict XVI himself is on record calling homosexuality "intrinsic moral evil." There will be no doctrinal change under a pope who considers rock music a "vehicle of antireligion" and who opposes women priests in order to "protect true doctrine, to safeguard the communion and unity of the Church and to guide consciences of the faithful." He did, however, order the Church to rethink its ban on condoms. The church is experiencing its greatest growth in Africa and is alert to the impact that AIDS is having on that troubled continent.

FUTURE

The fact that a third of mankind and the world's major political leaders observed John Paul II's funeral in April 2005 demonstrates that the influence and spiri-

tual attraction of the Roman Catholic Church have not disappeared even if they are weaker than they once were. Because of his advanced age, Pope Benedict XVI will probably be a transitional leader until the Church decides how it might respond differently to a rapidly changing world.

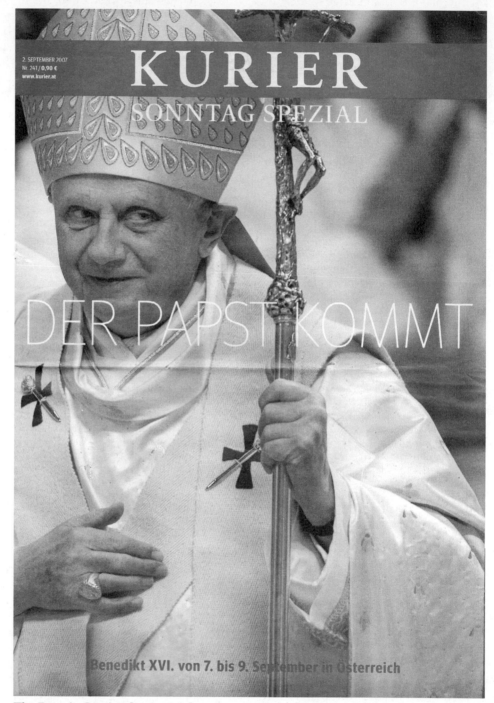

The Pope is Coming [to Austria]

342

The Sovereign Military Order of Malta

(The Roman Catholic *Sovereign Military Hospitaler Order of St. John of Jerusalem, of Rhodes and of Malta*)

Area: The Malta Palace (Palazzo di Malta) and the Villa Malta, about three acres.

Population: International membership in the Order is about 9,600, all of whom retain their own nationality.

Neighboring Countries: Located in Rome, Italy.

Religion: Roman Catholicism.

Chief of State (Head of the Order): The Prince and Grand Master (since 1988), His Most Eminent Highness Frà Andrew Bertie (b. 1929).

Flag of State: A plain white cross on a red field, (of the Grand Master)—The white Maltese Cross on a red field.

Only with a magnifying glass can one see the world's smallest country on a Rome city map. Completely surrounded by a wall and with a territorial size equivalent to half a football field, The Sovereign Military Order of Malta (SMOM) is the only country in the world which has *no* citizens whatsoever and which is small enough to be assigned a street address: 68 Via Condotti, a very elegant street just a stone's throw from Rome's famous Span-

ish Steps. By peeping through the keyhole of the main gate of Villa Malta on the Aventine Hill, a palace which is also part of SMOM, one can gain the kind of view normally available only to astronauts: one can see three sovereign countries, namely the SMOM, Italy and the Vatican.

The Prince and Grand Master is elected by the Council Complete of State and is duly confirmed by the pope. Today this ancient entity maintains diplomatic relations with the Holy See, on which it depends as a religious order, but not as a sovereign, and with 48 nations (but not with the United States). It has delegations to the Council of Europe and UNESCO. It sent a delegate to the UN Millennium Summit in New York, September 2000, who was imaginative in getting himself and his sovereign order noticed. Publication of the official photograph of world leaders was delayed because a man in the photo could not be identified. It turned out that he was Count Carlos Maruulo di Condojanni, Grand Chancellor of the Sovereign Military Order of Malta, who somehow slipped past security into history.

It enjoys the same status of extra–territoriality that the Italian government grants to any embassy; that is, it is considered to be foreign soil. On January 28, 1961, the civil courts of Rome declared the order an "international sovereign society." Issuing its own passports and conducting its affairs without interference, this tiny state is truly an oddity in the contemporary world.

The hospital–infirmary dedicated to St. John the Baptist was founded in Jerusalem about the middle of the 11th century. Originally connected with the Benedictines, but later independent, it was administered by a monastic community dedicated to the care of those Christians who fell ill during their pilgrimages to the Holy Land.

In the same century Pope Urban II urged the formation of a great crusade in order to sweep the Moslems from the cradle of Christianity and to expand the reach of the Roman Catholic Church. In 1096, a growing army, led by French knights and joined by noblemen and simple folk from many nations, progressed on

The Sovereign Military Order of Malta

horseback and foot across Europe and toward the Holy Land. The crusader knights were young, ranging from 16 to 30 years, and they were brimming with enthusiasm, self–confidence, a strong taste for adventure and (for many) visions of riches. They seized Jerusalem in 1099 and surrounding areas in a series of bloody battles. During the first years the hospital's prior installed some of them into the Order of St. John of Jerusalem as defenders. To confirm their intense dedication at the time of their induction they held out their swords, which were blessed under flickering torches.

In 1113 the community of the Hospital of St. John was recognized by the pope as a religious order of the Church, free from all lay interference. This was the germ of the order's sovereignty. In the 1130s, because of the need to protect the sick, the pilgrims and the Christian settlements in the Holy Land, the order acquired the additional military character and became a monastic–chivalric order, in which monks were knights and knights took the monas-

H.M.E.H. The Prince and Grand Master

tic vows. The order's military edge was first felt in 1118 when its knights did more than protect; they openly attacked the Moslems. Stories of their bravery made them living legends, and new recruits continued to join their ranks every year.

In 1187 the overwhelming forces of Saladin, Sultan of Egypt and Syria, drove the knights, who suffered terrible losses, from the Latin Kingdom of Jerusalem. All of them were at least wounded, and only a handful survived, including the Grand Master. Those who remained escaped. The kingdom and the order continued at Acre (Akka). In even greater numbers than before, knights came from all over Europe to join the struggle against the "infidels." There were eight crusades until 1291, but each grew weaker. The crusaders were never permanently able to wrest Jerusalem from Moslem control. The Moslems wiped the kingdom out in 1291, and the order moved to Cyprus. But the Knights of St. John remained dedicated to their task of defending Christianity.

They used Cyprus as a base for the next 120 years, continuing to battle the Moslems on or around the Mediterranean Sea. The island was never considered ideal for their purposes because the coastline was too extensive to defend adequately. In 1310 the knights attacked and captured Rhodes, a beautiful island of meadowlands and forests lying some 25 miles (40 km.) off the southwestern coast of Turkey. Establishing their headquarters there, they continued to expand their navy and constructed a watchtower on the nearby islet of Simi in order to foil any naval attack.

The Malta Palace, 68 Via Condotti

The Sovereign Military Order of Malta

In the following years their control extended over most of the islands off the western coast of Turkey, some little more than outcroppings of jagged rock. Their activity excited admiration throughout Europe because the knights could effectively challenge Turkish domination in the Mediterranean Sea. In recognition of this role, Pope Nicholas V recognized the Grand Master of the order as the Sovereign Prince of Rhodes in 1446.

The Turks overran Asia Minor and were moving into Europe—in 1453 they put an end to the Byzantine Empire and proceeded to launch attacks on Rhodes. Over and over the Turks made massive attacks against the island, but not until 1532 did they succeed in overwhelming the knights and forcing them to leave. During the following eight years the knights were homeless, but in 1530 the Holy Roman Emperor, Charles V, gave the order the island of Malta, on which they built the finest hospital in Europe at that time. Included were the nearby islands, as well as the African mainland fortress–city, Tripoli, a city which the knights soon abandoned.

During the next 268 years they vigilantly patrolled the waters to protect trade routes for Christian merchants. They continued to raid Turkish ships and those of Barbary pirates (see The Republic of Malta).

The Prince Grand Master of the Order, who since 1630 has the rank equal to that of a Cardinal, was the undisputed ruler of Malta and was a sovereign who entered into treaties with other nations and enjoyed the usual rights accorded to a chief of state. Of course, the order's very existence, powers, privileges and immunities remained under the protective umbrella of the Roman Catholic Church, and these were therefore respected throughout Christendom. Splendid architectural monuments, churches, public buildings and fortifications still bear witness to the order's sovereign rule in Malta.

It took periodic interest in acquiring territory in the New World. In 1653 Louis XIV of France gave the order four Caribbean islands—St. Kitts, St. Martin, St. Croix and St. Barthélemy—but it later decided to sell them to the French West India Company.

In 1794 it approached James Monroe, the U.S. Ambassador to France, with an offer of ports, provisions and protection for American sailors in the Mediterranean in return for lands in America. Monroe responded that the order was welcome to purchase land, but that such property could not become a part of another sovereign government and would have to remain under the jurisdiction of the United States. Although the order was not interested in buying under these terms, its personal ties with the United States have remained strong—approximately 1,500 out of 9,600 of the order's knights are presently living in the U.S., and they include such prominent American Catholics as former Treasury Secretary William E. Simon, the late Clare Boothe Luce, William F. Buckley, Jr., and the late Terrence Cardinal Cooke, Archbishop of New York. However, Americans can never ascend to the highest ranks of the order because only persons of long–standing nobility are admitted to high leadership positions.

Napoleon's forces, engaged in a campaign against Egypt, occupied the island of Malta in 1798 and drove out the order. The knights were overwhelmingly French and were reportedly somewhat sympathetic to the French general. But they again found themselves without a home. This was followed by what has been called the Russian *coup d'état* (1798–1803).

Tsar Paul I of Russia was a bitter opponent of the French Revolution and also had hopes of setting up a Russian naval base in the Mediterranean. He had shown himself as a friend of the order. He now had himself proclaimed Grand Master by

Interior courtyard of the Malta Palace

345

The Sovereign Military Order of Malta

Location and grounds of the Villa Malta on the Aventine Hill

dent in 1964. Surviving knights scattered throughout Europe attempted after 1802 to persuade European powers once again to give the order a base. Various islands were considered, but no nation seemed interested in donating even a small one to what they considered to be a fading order of knighthood. The Sovereign Order's headquarters moved to Sicily and then to Ferrara. Finally, in 1834 the 16th century Malta Palace in Rome, which had been the Order's embassy to the Papal State since the early 1600s, became the order's headquarters and remains so to the present time.

Maintaining health institutions throughout the world, from small dispensaries and leper colonies to 10 hospitals, the order has returned to its original mission of caring for the sick. Yet those persons who dismiss The Sovereign Military Order of Malta as being neither sovereign nor military are only half right. It no longer performs a military function, despite the shining swords that the knights still bear on festive occasions. It does perform an admirable humanitarian function in a world that, in many places, is still largely gripped by disease and misery. And it is a sovereign entity by international recognition, even if it only has three acres in Rome to call its very own.

a handful of knights who had gone to live in Russia, instead of the Grand Master Frà Ferdinand von Hompesch, who had abandoned Malta to the French. This proclamation of a married non–Catholic as head of a Catholic religious order was wholly illegal and void; the Holy See never recognized it, which was a necessary condition for legitimacy. Accordingly, Paul I, who was nevertheless accepted by many knights and a number of governments, can only be regarded as a Grand Master *de facto*, never one *de jure*. This was only a brief interlude. Paul was murdered in 1801 and was succeeded by his 24–year–old son, Alexander I. The new Tsar helped the order to return to legitimate rule. In 1803 Frà Giovanni Battista Tommasi was elected Grand Master.

In the meantime, the British had seized the island of Malta from Napoleon in 1801. They specified in the 1802 Treaty of Amiens with France that Malta must be restored to the order. This never happened, though, and Britain continued to rule the island until it became indepen-

Peeping through the keyhole of Villa Malta

The Republic of Malta

Mdina—old capital of Malta

Courtesy: Alexandra Schaerrer

Area: 122 sq. mi. (316 sq. km., one–tenth the size of Rhode Island, twice the size of Washington D.C.).

Population: 407,000 (UN, 2007).

Capital City: Valletta (Pop. 21,000, estimated).

Climate: Mild and sunny Mediterranean.

Neighboring Countries: Italy lies to the north, Libya to the south.

Official Languages: Maltese, English. Italian is also widely spoken.

Other Principal Tongues: Italian is understood.

Ethnic Background: Mixture of Phoenician, Carthaginian, Arab, Sicilian, Norman, Spanish, Italian, British.

Principal Religion: Roman Catholic (98%).

Main Exports: Tourism, machinery, transport equipment, ship repair, clothing, food manufacturing and processing, textiles.

Main Customers: EU: 42.3% of exports and 67.3% of imports, Italy (40%), Germany (15%), France (9%), UK (6%).

Currency: Maltese lira.

Former Colonial Status: British Crown Colony.

Independence Day: September 21, 1964, within the British Commonwealth of Nations; Republic declared on December 13, 1974. Government: Parliamentary democracy.

Chief of State: Eddie Fenech Adami, President (since April 2004).

Head of Government: Lawrence Gonzi, Prime Minister (since March 2004).

National Holiday: Republic Day, December 13.

National Flag: Two large vertical white and red stripes with a gray cross in the upper left–hand corner.

Malta is a small but historically and strategically important group of five islands (two of which are uninhabited) in the central Mediterranean Sea 60 miles (96 km.) south of Sicily and 180 miles (290 km.) north of Libya. After Monaco, it has the greatest population density in Europe and the third-greatest in the world, with 1,196 persons per square kilometer, three times that of the Netherlands. For centuries Malta, with its well–sheltered anchorage, has been squarely in the middle of the many struggles to control the Mediterranean Sea and with that, the traffic between Europe, Africa and the Middle East. Because of its strategic importance and small size, Malta has always been dependent upon exterior powers.

Malta's people and culture today clearly reflect the influence of the many conquerors who have dominated the islands. Ethnically, the Maltese people are predominantly of Carthaginian and Phoenician origin. The latter named the islands "Maleth," meaning "hiding place," from which the country's present name is derived. The Maltese culture is a mixture of Italian and Arabic traditions. Maltese is a Semitic language arising from the mixture of Arabic and Sicilian Italian, with influences from English and French. It is the only Semitic language that is written in Latin script, and it is the only official language in the EU that is Semitic. To the stranger it sounds very much like Arabic. Because of long British rule, many Maltese speak impeccable English. Today Britons constitute only 2.1% of the population, which is dominated by 95.7% Maltese. The official language since 1934, Maltese is the most widely used medium of communication. It is also the language of instruction in the schools, which are patterned on the British educational system, and is used by one television and nine radio networks. Scholars disagree whether the European or the Arabic component predominates in the Maltese character and nature, but they do agree that the Maltese have a distinct culture and identity of their own.

HISTORY

The Early Period

Archaeologists have uncovered evidence of Neolithic cave dwellers from approximately 3800 B.C. on Malta, and it is probable that the islands were a center of Mediterranean civilization before Crete was. Between the 9th and 6th centuries B.C. the Phoenicians, Greeks and Carthaginians established colonies in Malta and the islands' inhabitants came into contact with Semitic cultures along the southern and eastern rim of the Mediterranean. In 218 B.C. the islands fell under Roman control.

Christian Beginnings

According to Biblical legend, a Roman ship carrying St. Paul crashed on offshore rocks in 60 A.D., and Paul saved himself by swimming shore. The Maltese still use the favorite saying when everything seems to go wrong: "Don't forget that even St. Paul was shipwrecked on Malta!" He wasted no time in converting the population, and the majority of Malta's population has been Christian ever since.

Arabs and Normans

When the Roman Empire approached total collapse in the 4th century A.D., Malta fell under the domination of Constantinople. Until the 16th century the islands were ruled successively by Arabs, who came in 870 A.D. and placed their indelible stamp on the Maltese, by Normans, who displaced the Arabs in 1000 A.D. and who improved Maltese political and legal structures, and later by other European nations.

Control by the Knights

In 1520 Malta came under the control of the Order of the Hospital of St. John of Jerusalem (otherwise known as the "Knights Hospitalers," or the "Maltese Knights"), a Roman Catholic religious order. It had been founded in Jerusalem before the Crusades in order to protect Christian pilgrims. Later, it had established its headquarters on the Greek island of Rhodes before being driven out by the Turks. The Holy Roman Emperor of the time, Charles V, granted Malta to the knights, which they turned into a fortress against Islam.

Their military mission was to keep the Turks out of the western Mediterranean and to clear the southern Mediterranean of pirates. Their raids on the immense Ottoman Empire so enraged the Turkish Sultan that he sent a huge army of 40,000 men and a navy of 200 ships against the heavily fortified islands. The four–month Turkish siege was one of the bloodiest in history, and of 9,000 Maltese Knights and soldiers, fewer than 1,000 survived unwounded. But their valor, under Grand Master Jean de La Valette, a shrewd military tactician after whom Malta's present capital city was named, forced the Turks to withdraw. Never again did the Turks attempt to penetrate the western Mediterranean.

The victorious and prosperous knights began to build the capital city of Valleta

The Republic of Malta

on a rocky headland. They built innumerable splendid baroque palaces, churches and public buildings, financed primarily by booty from their naval adventures against the Turks. Many of these structures still survive and testify to the great prosperity of that time. The famed Sacra Infermeria Hospital, whose construction began in 1571, was recently converted to a magnificent and modern Mediterranean conference center in an attempt to make Malta a major trade center.

Napoleon and British Rule

Napoleon Bonaparte seized the islands in 1798. Because of sympathetic French knights, his troops scarcely had to fire a shot. However, realizing that he would be unable to defend the islands against the British Navy, he decided to return them to the knights soon thereafter. Not wishing this to happen, a sizable number of Maltese rebelled and demanded to be placed under British sovereignty. Always attentive to the strategic needs of its empire and navy, and bracing itself for a bitter struggle against Napoleonic France, Britain gladly accepted in 1800. The Treaty of Paris confirmed British sovereignty over Malta in 1814. The Maltese Knights never returned to the islands as rulers, but each June they return from all over the world in full regalia for the Feast of St. John at St. John's Cathedral.

Throughout the 19th century, a British governor ruled Malta, and its economy grew almost entirely dependent upon the proceeds from British military facilities on the islands, a dependence which Malta has never been able to overcome successfully. Immediately following World War I the British granted internal autonomy to the Maltese, but the experiment failed and in 1933 Malta reverted to its status of a Crown Colony. During World War II, this "unsinkable aircraft carrier," as Winston S. Churchill called it, heroically resisted brutal German bombing and refused to surrender even though the islands were frequently cut off from supplies for months at a time. Malta played an extremely significant role in the successful Allied efforts in North Africa, Sicily and southern Europe. In 1947 the islands were again granted self–government, but a British–appointed governor maintained control over foreign affairs, defense and currency.

In 1955 the Maltese Labor Party won a parliamentary majority and made a radical proposal for full integration of Malta into the United Kingdom. This proposal, which now appears highly surprising in view of the party's later stand on independence, received the support of three–fourths of the voters in a referendum in 1956. However, negotiations to work out such integration broke down two years later, and by 1960 the Maltese support for the tie had disappeared. Independence, not integration, became the new goal, and the Nationalist Party, which had won the 1964 parliamentary elections, achieved this the same year.

GOVERNMENT

The constitution of 1964, which had made Malta an independent parliamentary monarchy within the British Commonwealth, was revised in 1974 to create a republican parliamentary democracy. A 65–member unicameral parliament, called the House of Representatives, is elected by universal suffrage of all citizens over the age of 18 on the basis of proportional representation (PR) using the single-transferable-vote system at least every five years. Since 1987 any party that wins a majority of the popular vote is assured a majority of parliamentary seats, despite PR. In deference to the country's Catholic majority and past, all members of parliament take the constitutional oath of loyalty in the traditional manner, by kissing a cross held out to them. The majority party appoints the prime minister and cabinet, who exercise executive power, but who remain responsible to the House of Representatives. An indirectly elected, largely ceremonial president serves as the head of state for a five–year term. In 2004 former Prime Minister Eddie Fenech Adami was elected.

The government of the country is highly centralized in the capital city although Sliema is actually the country's largest city. There is little established local government. The major exception to this is the island of Gozo, which has a locally elected Civic Council which rules that small island in conjunction with a commissioner appointed by the central government in Valletta. Malta has an independent judicial system consisting of lower courts and a Constitutional Court, a Superior Court and a Court of Appeal.

POLITICS

Only two political parties have a significant number of seats in the House of Representatives or play an important role in Maltese politics. The opposition Labour Party (LP) sees itself as a socialist party and depends upon the support of workers and the powerful trade unions. From 1961 until 1971 the LP was embroiled in such a bitter struggle with the Catholic Church that the Church declared any vote or other active support for this party to be sufficient grounds for excommunication. The lifting of this ban in 1971 enabled the party to maintain its position.

For many years the character of the LP was shaped by the personality of its mercurial former leader, Dom Mintoff, who stepped down as prime minister in 1984. His hand–picked successor, Carmelo

Hon. Alfred Sant
Leader, *Labour Party*

Mifsud–Bonnici, succeeded him. The LP favored an independent and neutral Malta playing the role of bridge between Europe and the Arab world and an anti-colonialist foreign policy involving close ties with the "Third World." To strengthen its European credentials, it joined the Council of Europe in 1965.

The LP advocates foreign investment and economic help to industrialize the islands. At the same time, it seeks the redistribution of property and income in order to create a more egalitarian society. In many ways, these last two objectives are in conflict with one another. Under Mintoff's premiership the government took over broadcasting, telecommunications, oil and gas and a full or majority interest in all banks. It also established a national airline and shipping line, and it introduced a minimum wage, a 40–hour workweek and mandatory wage increases to keep pace with inflation.

The LP clashed with the Catholic Church because of Mintoff's decision to nationalize hospitals and schools. He expelled all nuns and doctors who refused to comply with the state takeover of the hospitals. He refused all state assistance to the country's private (mainly Catholic) schools, which educate about a third of all Maltese children. The government's campaign against Catholic schools was stepped up in 1984 when it was announced that private schools could no longer charge tuition. This move was followed by widespread violence, including a raid on Catholic Church headquarters, reportedly led by Mifsud–Bonnici.

Hostility between the Church and the LP had been intensified when the latter introduced a bill to authorize state seizure of about three–fourths of the Church's property in Malta. Not surprisingly, Vatican spokesmen warned that such action would have "predictable repercussions on religious peace." But in 1985 Mifsud–

President Eddie Fenech Adami

Bonnici signed an agreement with the Vatican designed to end the controversy over government control of Catholic schools.

The Church remains influential in Malta, where 98% are Catholic. Divorce and abortion are illegal. A 2005 poll revealed that 55% opposed divorce, while only 38% found it necessary. Opposition to abortion was even more pronounced: 95.7% opposed it in cases where a woman becomes pregnant outside marriage, 85.7% in cases of incest. Even 76% opposed it in cases of rape. When the pope visited the country in 1990, half the entire population gathered in a large square to see him.

Under the leadership since 1992 of Alfred Sant, a pragmatic Harvard PhD in business administration and former diplomat in Brussels, the party shook off its confrontational socialist image. He severed the party's formal links with the trade unions and admits that economic liberalization has benefited Malta. Not all LP militants supported these changes. The fiery Dom Mintoff opposed his party's plan to lease state land to an American consortium to build a new yacht marina. When he voted against his government, it fell and lost the 1998 elections. In the April 2003 and March 2008 elections it lost again, receiving 48.8% of the votes and 34 seats the second time.

The ruling Nationalist Party (NP), led by Prime Minister Lawrence Gonzi, who took over from Eddie Fenech Adami in March 2004, stands much closer to the Catholic Church and to the Maltese middle class. It wishes to safeguard Malta's Catholic Church and European traditions. The NP advocates Malta's following the example of other minute European states, such as Andorra, Monaco and Liechtenstein, in lowering taxes so that foreign wealth and business enterprises are attracted to the islands. This reduces the island's dependence on financial handouts from other countries and brings prosperity to Malta. The NP advocates closer relations with Europe and the U.S.

The NP ruled from 1987 to 1996. The transition of power in 1987 went more smoothly than many observers had feared. Fenech Adami had vowed that his government would work to bring about national reconciliation in a land bitterly polarized in many ways: labor unions based in the dockyards versus the middle class; clans with generations of hostility; villages divided in their loyalty to competing saints; townships torn by rivalry between clubs which parade on holy days and by disagreements on whether to root for Italian or British soccer teams.

The transition from violent confrontational politics succeeded. Party allegiance no longer dominates every issue, and the pervasive tension is gone. In 1998 the NP

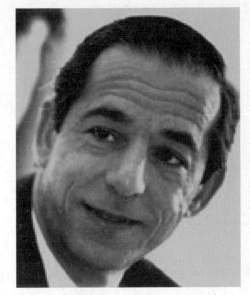

Prime Minister Lawrence Gonzi

regained the reins of power. In the April 2003 parliamentary election that revolved around the question of joining the EU, the pro-membership NP won almost 52% of the votes and carried the day. In March 2008 it dropped 2.5%, but it still came out on top, winning 49.34% of the votes. Although it only captured 31 seats outright, it was awarded four extra seats because it got more of the popular votes than LP. Thus, it formed a majority government with 35 seats. Turnout dropped to 93%, the lowest figure since 1971. Like his predecessor, Gonzi is a devout Roman Catholic and favors pragmatic solutions to stubborn political and economic issues.

A third party, the Democratic Alternative, is politically active, but it is irrelevant in the House of Representatives. It got only 1.31% of the votes in 2008. It describes itself as "green–progressive" and focuses on corruption and social and environmental issues. It publishes a monthly newspaper, *XPRESS*.

Foreign and Defense Policy

Malta had difficulty solving its major long–standing economic and foreign policy problem: how to survive economically without the rental fees paid by Britain for use of Maltese defense facilities. In 1971 the strong–willed Mintoff abrogated the Mutual Defense and Assistance Agreement of 1964; after months of difficult negotiations a new seven–year agreement was reached tripling the rental fees Britain was required to pay. He again demanded an increase in 1973. Britain finally decided it could live without Malta's base facilities and withdrew from the island in 1979, after 179 years of military presence there. Mintoff hailed this as "the day of light, freedom day, the day of the new Malta."

The Republic of Malta

The economic problems caused by the loss of more than $70 million in revenue were not solved by that freedom. No country was inclined to help Mintoff.

A modest amount of development assistance the People's Republic of China had given Malta since 1971 to construct a dry dock to handle tankers was much too small to solve Malta's problems. Therefore, Mintoff turned to that oil–rich state to the south, whose leader had shown himself willing to support practically any state or group whose policies are directed against the industrialized West: Libya. Mintoff announced in 1979, "Europe showed us the cold shoulder, but Libya heartily and spontaneously accepted our suggestions for collaboration." Libya's flamboyant and erratic leader, Col. Moamer al Ghadafi, took a 500–man delegation to the ceremony in Malta marking the British withdrawal, and promised the country unlimited aid.

Ghadafi delivered oil and gasoline to Malta almost without charge, and the Maltese government was able to derive even greater profit from this gift by imposing a stiff local consumption tax on the petroleum. Libya also invested approximately $150 million in the islands, entered a defense pact with Malta and provided helicopters and coastal patrol boats.

Ghadafi proudly proclaimed Malta as the "northern outpost of the Arabic world" and even aspired to introduce pure Arabic as Malta's official language (Arabic is no longer compulsory in secondary schools.). Such pronouncements merely aggravated many Maltese, who from the beginning had misgivings toward this strange marriage of convenience. NP leaders called it an exchange of "one type of colonialism for another."

The marriage was scarcely a year old when a disagreement erupted. Both governments claimed oil rights in the waters between the two states. An angry Mintoff declared Libya "a danger to peace in the Mediterranean" and expelled as "security risks" 50 Libyan military personnel who had been sent to train Maltese helicopter pilots. By 1984 differences with Libya were settled. Both countries agreed to submit their dispute over oil rights in the sea to the International Court of Justice, which rendered a decision satisfactory to both parties. They signed a military cooperation treaty under which Libya would help to train and supply the Maltese forces and help to protect Malta "in case of threats or acts of aggression." In 1981 Malta had signed an agreement with the Soviet Union, which pledged to respect

350

The Republic of Malta

Malta's neutrality in return for the right to store up to 300,000 tons of oil on the islands. Mintoff claimed that Moscow was not committed to defend the island if Maltese territory were violated.

Under Fenech Adami, Malta steered a more pro–Western course. The NP has a tradition of strong sympathies with Italy. Under Labour rule, Malta had already secured assistance from its nearest northern neighbor. Arguing that Maltese neutrality was in Italy's and NATO's interest and threatening to allow the Soviet navy to use the harbor of Valletta, it persuaded Italy to support Malta. The Italian government rather liked the idea of assuming greater responsibility in the Mediterranean area. In 1980 it promised Malta technical assistance and financial support. Until 1994 Italy covered a third of Malta's budget deficit, enabling that shortfall to remain below 4% of GDP.

The islands, which for five years had maintained a consultative arrangement with NATO, received in 1981 military guarantees from Italy, which stationed 47 air force personnel in Malta to operate two helicopters. In exchange, Malta formally declared neutrality and promised not to allow any foreign military bases. In 1987 the Maltese constitution was changed in order to entrench both non-alignment and neutrality and to forbid foreign military bases.

In 1986 the former LP prime minister admitted having tipped off Ghadafi minutes before the American bombing raid on Libya, thereby possibly saving the Libyan leader's life. The NP government did not show such "even–handedness." Malta maintained economic ties with Libya and renegotiated its friendship treaty with it. But Fenech Adami emphasized that he had widened the political distance with Ghadafi and that the military clauses, which had obligated Malta to warn Libya of American air strikes, had been removed. Fenech Adami's government severed air links with Libya and honored the UN embargo imposed after Libya's complicity in the bombing of a Pan Am plane over Lockerbie, Scotland, appeared obvious. Britain's and the United States' diplomatic opening to Libya in 2004 will no doubt provide favorable investment and trade prospects to Maltese businesses.

In 1996 former Prime Minister Sant informed Brussels that he had put Malta's application for EU membership on hold because joining was supposedly not in the tiny country's interest. After the 1998 election, the new NP government renewed the country's EU application. In one of his first acts, Sant formally withdrew Malta from NATO's Partnership for Peace program "because it contradicts our constitutional neutrality." Malta allots about 3.5%

($29 million) of its budget to the maintenance of its small army, navy and air force of 2,140 troops. There are also 47 Italian air force personnel stationed in Malta flying two AB-212 aircraft. However, it could never defend itself alone.

Malta's most pressing foreign policy problem is the influx of unwanted illegal immigrants from Africa. It faces south to a 2,000-mile (3,200 km.) North African coastline, located less than 200 miles (320 km.) away. The passage can be made in open fishing boats, which often capsize. In the four years to June 2006, almost 6,000 migrants had washed ashore, more than 1,822 in the first five months of 2006 alone. In proportion to the resident population, this would be like Germany being inundated by a million migrants or the U.S. by 3.5 million. Many of them were heading for Italy but got blown off course; others use it as a backdoor to the EU after it joined in 2004. Because of the high costs and diplomatic complications, Malta cannot return them to their homelands, and many feel trapped in their dingy barracks where they are confined. Malta pleads for help from the EU, but many of its partners are facing the same problem. The leader of a Maltese anti-immigrant party said: "We have never had minorities, and we don't want minorities."

ECONOMY

Malta is a highly over–crowded mini–state with four–tenths of a million people on only 122 square miles (316 sq. km). Only one-third the size of New York City, it has one vehicle for every two residents, making it Europe's most traffic-congested nation. It has no natural resources except limestone, and its terrain is very unsuited to agriculture. It can supply only about 20% of its food needs, and only 6% of its population can find employment in agriculture. Its major agricultural products are potatoes, cauliflower, grapes, wheat, barley, tomatoes, citrus fruit, cut flowers, hogs, poultry and eggs. Desalination plants provide half of Malta's fresh water.

Its major industry, thanks to its deep-water harbors, is ship repair. This provides 5% of total employment although it has fallen on hard times. In an austerity move, the workforce at the docks was cut by 3,000. In the related area of aircraft maintenance, Lufthansa services its smaller planes at Malta's airport and plans to do the same for its widebody fleet in the future. The government's efforts since independence to diversify the economy have had modest success, and Malta now has some light manufacturing enterprises in the clothing, textile, building and food processing sectors. Foreign investments contributed significantly to this success,

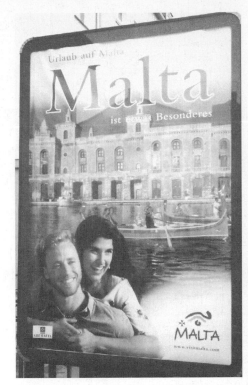

Advertising for tourists in Germany

but they have meant that more than half of Malta's industrial production is in foreign hands. Maltese industry will be lucky if it can continue employing a fourth of the workforce. Not wanting to compete as a low–wage economy, it faces a particular obstacle in that it must import so many raw materials in order to export finished products at a profit.

An Achilles heel was the fact that more than half of its exports are textile products. In the industrialized nations to which it exports, there are increasingly loud demands to erect barriers against textile imports in order to protect their own clothing industries. Diversification has reduced this problem. Malta must still import most consumer and industrial needs, including fuels and raw materials.

A fourth of its GDP is derived from tourism, its biggest revenue earner. The number of foreign tourists who visit Malta is three times as large as the country's population. The government believes that with a million tourists every year (predominantly Britons) the three islands have reached the saturation point. Therefore, it aims to restructure the industry to attract more up-market tourists. This would bring more income from fewer visitors. They arrive at the country's two usable airfields, one major and two minor harbors.

In order to try to overcome Malta's economic stagnation, the former NP government liberalized the economy, which was

351

The Republic of Malta

over–protected and state–dominated. Through "tax holidays," it lured foreign investment from the West. Some other countries and the OECD criticized its status as a tax haven. Therefore, in June 2000 it joined five other small states in agreeing to cooperate with international efforts to curb abusive and criminal tax-avoidance schemes. It largely completed its first priority of improving the infrastructure by overhauling the telecommunications network and building a new power station, desalination plants, and a second airport terminal.

It attracted some higher-skill and technology industries, such as pharmaceuticals, to replace traditional ones, like textiles, which are threatened by low-cost competition from North Africa and Asia. It also has high hopes for its growing financial-services industry, which is attracting most of the incoming investment and which is supported by a small government-owned stock exchange located in a former military chapel. Although it lists only 13 stocks, its equity index jumped by 40% in 2004 and 60% in 2005. There are about 250 hedge funds. The government has sold off a variety of state-owned businesses, including the telecoms provider Maltacom, bought in 2006 by Dubai Tecom.

With one or more cars per family, there is an air of prosperity in the country. Growing wealth has created the same phenomenon in Malta as in other developed European countries: a lowering of the fertility rate to only 1.5 (2.1 are needed to maintain the population level). Life expectancy is 81 for women and 77 for men. The feeling that Malta is already performing rather well was an important reason why many voters did not view EU entry as an urgent necessity.

Since 1971 Malta has had a special trade relationship with the EU, to which it sent 68% of its exports and from which it bought 78% of its imports in 1990, the year in which it applied for full membership. The NP government drafted all its legislation with eventual EU membership in mind. Prime Minister (now President) Fenech Adami had announced, "Malta is a European country. To us, this will be a homecoming." Voters saw it differently in 1996, but they changed their minds in September 1998. Malta's EU application was renewed. In December 1999 the EU invited Malta back to formal talks leading to membership.

The talks went so well that Malta won more concessions than any of the other nine accession countries. Its workers are allowed unrestricted entry into EU countries although it won the right to bar foreign labor for up to seven years. It also secured the right to block nonresidents indefinitely from buying second homes on the islands.

In March 2003 the Nationalist Party government was ready to put the emotional question of membership to the voters. Rallies for and against joining drew thousands of people. Many Maltese feared that Europe would take away the hard-earned independence they had finally won in 1964. As the least populous country in the EU, Malta risked being overshadowed by the large EU nations and might not have a voice that would be listened to. The Labour Party led the charge against EU membership. However, arguing that membership is vital for Malta's economy and international credibility, the government prevailed. In the March 9 referendum, 53.6% supported accession, while 46.4% said no.

Malta's constitution required that the referendum be confirmed by a general election, which took place April 12. Interest was at such a high pitch that plane loads of Maltese returned to vote, benefiting from reduced fares by state-owned Air Malta. In an election whose central issue was the EU, the government won almost 52%. Four days later ex-Prime Minister Adami traveled to Athens to sign the EU accession treaty, with formal membership following on May 1, 2004. The accession of Malta and Cyprus undoubtedly strengthens the EU's Mediterranean dimension. Malta replaces Luxembourg as the smallest country in the EU, and it is also likely to be the most socially conservative, given the fact that abortion and divorce are illegal. In July 2005 parliament unanimously ratified the ill-fated EU constitution. It joined Schengen in 2007.

In the past two decades, Malta has experienced robust annual economic growth. Its public-sector finances are solid, with an overall public debt of 36% of GDP (down from 75% in 2004), lower than any EU country except Luxembourg. In 1993 employment in the service sector overtook private direct production for the first time signaling that Malta has a modern economy. Malta's per capita income, at 11,170 euros ($17,000), exceeds that of Portugal and Greece and is the highest of any of the 10 countries that entered the EU in May 2004. Real growth has remained strong in recent years, and unemployment and inflation have stayed low.

The large government budget debt (6% of GDP in 2004) was brought down to below 3% in order to qualify for the euro, which went into circulation on January 1, 2008. Malta is a good example of how countries are inspired to reform their economies in order to meet EU entry requirements. Many of the Maltese government's austerity measures, such as freezing public employment, would have been unimaginable without the lure of the euro. Three-fourths of its trade is with the EU. As central-bank governor, Michael Bonello, noted: "For a trading nation like ours, it is one headache less." Of course, problems remain. Internal market rigidities weaken competition and deter productive investment. Malta must reform its pension system and deregulate and privatize its economy. These matters remain contentious in the domestic political context.

FUTURE

With a Nationalist prime minister and with economic optimism in the air, Malta looks into a future of prosperous alignment with Europe as a full member of the EU. It adopted the euro in 2008. Prospects for the tiny island nation are good.

Source: BBC

Source: BBC

Maltese celebrating EU referendum victory

Iberian Peninsula

Contemporary Mutual Relations

The Iberian Peninsula is located at the southwest periphery of Europe, separated from the rest of the Continent by the high Pyrenees Mountains. Most of the population is settled around the coastal areas, with certain prominent exceptions, most notably Madrid, where a third of Spain's inland population is concentrated. The land area is distributed very unevenly among the three countries on the peninsula; Spain occupies about 85% of the space, and Portugal occupies most of the rest. Tiny Andorra has a very small chunk of mountainous land in the northeastern corner, and Britain still controls a strategically important toehold on the rock of Gibraltar at the southern tip of Spain.

Spain and Portugal do not have identical characteristics and problems. But they undeniably have very much in common. Perhaps most obviously, if one casts a quick glance at the globe, are their strategically significant locations. They are placed between the continents of Europe and Africa and face the Atlantic and, in the case of Spain, the Mediterranean Sea.

They possess islands in the Atlantic Ocean that are important links between the Western and Eastern Hemispheres: the Canary Islands are Spanish, and the Azores and Madeira are Portuguese. The Spanish also possess the Balearic Islands in the Mediterranean, the largest of which is the tourist Mecca of Majorca. Spain also owns a few islands off the Moroccan coast and the cities of Ceuta and Melilla on the northern coast of Morocco. In 1987 the

Portuguese agreed to relinquish to China their small enclave of Macau on the southern coast of China. It was their highly valuable strategic positions which enabled Spain and Portugal to escape prolonged international isolation and to regain a status of relative respectability after 1945, despite the fact that until the mid–1970s they had authoritarian political systems that were repugnant to most persons in the democratic countries of the world.

These lands were formerly mighty colonial powers that spread their languages and cultures to colonies in Latin America and Africa, which were many times greater in size and population than the mother countries. Their empires have by now almost completely disappeared. The process of decolonization brought the fascist regime to its knees in Portugal in 1974 and was a consequence of the collapse of fascism in Spain in 1975.

Portuguese and Spaniards speak languages that are derived from Latin and that are very similar to each other. Although their words are spelled and pronounced somewhat differently, they understand the gist of what each other is saying. However, the Spaniard, except in Galicia, generally has more trouble understanding Portuguese than *vice versa*. Both countries are also predominantly Roman Catholic, and the Catholic Church has traditionally wielded considerable power and influence in them.

Both countries have similar political backgrounds, traditions, institutions and problems. They had monarchies that col-

lapsed in the first third of the 20th century because of chronic political turmoil and violence. In neither country did experiments with republican and democratic forms of government go well, and in 1926 in Portugal and 1936 in Spain the military seized power. Such seizure was quick and bloodless in Portugal, but painful and bloody in Spain. The carnage that lasted for three years in Spain was portrayed with great force by Picasso's unforgettable painting, *Guernica*, and by Ernest Hemingway's moving novel, *For Whom the Bell Tolls*.

Both countries lived under fascism for several decades. In the mid–1970s they reemerged from fascism, but experienced different transitions. Portugal dived headlong into revolutionary and democratic government and passed through two tense years of political experimentalism and uncertainty until it could gain its balance in the political center. By contrast, Spain experienced, in 1975, a long and carefully planned entry into democracy and a restoration of the monarchy, which has proven to be one of the major bulwarks of democracy.

During the last decade and a half of fascist rule, Spain underwent rapid and extensive industrialization. By contrast, Portugal did not, and it entered its new democratic era as the poorest country in western Europe. Although Spain was one of its poorest countries, its economic head start over Portugal strengthened the inclination of Spaniards to regard the poorer, smaller Portugal in a condescending, patronizing way. In the 21st century, both are experiencing an economic boom.

In 1983 the Spanish prime minister traveled to Portugal for a summit conference designed to bury "historical ghosts." He called for "a new era in our relations." His Portuguese counterpart responded by announcing, "the mistrust and reservations which many Portuguese continue to feel toward Spain are no longer justified. Portugal has survived eight centuries of independence and nation identity, and Spain, a great country, has respected and will continue to respect our independence." Clichés remain, though. Some Portuguese still see Spaniards as explosively talkative, opinionated, aggressive, arrogant, sociable and dressed beyond their means, with a barely concealed contempt for Portugal, while the Portuguese are quieter, more reserved and self–deprecating.

In 1986 they again pledged closer cooperation and agreed on frequent and regular meetings between the heads of their governments. As a symbol of closer ties, they agreed to build a bridge over the Guadiana River frontier. In 1989 they adapted their narrow–gauged railway systems to the one used in the rest of Eu-

Iberian Peninsula

rope so that rail cars will not need to be changed at Iberia's frontier with the rest of Europe. Portugal launched a major effort to streamline and modernize its rail system and highways toward Spain.

The results of their cooperation are clear: Between 1985 and 1989 trade trebled between them, and it doubled again in the 1990s. By 2005, 9.3% of Spain's foreign trade was with Portugal, and it is Portugal's largest supplier and its third biggest market. In 2007 Portugal bought 29% of its imports from Spain, more than from any other country. Portugal sends 13.5% of its exports to its eastern neighbor. Spain trades more with it than with all of Latin America. After the U.S., Spain is the largest investor in Latin America, and it invests more heavily in Portugal than anywhere else in Europe. By 2003 there were over 2,500 Spanish firms in Portugal, compared with only 400 in 1989. Spanish banks control about one-sixth of Portugal's banking. Many multinational corporations deal with Portugal through their headquarters in Madrid. About two–thirds of foreigners visiting Portugal are Spanish. Portugal has about 300 companies operating in Spain. Its income per capita was half that of Spain in 1991. By 2007 its per capita GDP had increased to $17,460, compared with $26,090 in Spain.

The relationship is asymmetrical, partly because of the different size and partly because of their past: Spain began encouraging competition and entrepreneurship during the Franco years, while Portugal did not. Spain was also largely free of the costly colonial wars, disruptive revolution and political upheaval that set Portugal back. Some Portuguese worry about Spain's economic influence on them. In 2003, forty Portuguese economists and business leaders published an open letter entitled "Patriots' Manifesto," warning against the steady move of their country's economic decision-making centers abroad.

Portugal and Spain have long traditions of military intervention in politics. Since the 19th century, soldiers in the peninsula have viewed themselves as the guarantors of their nations' sovereignty and integrity. Although soldiers in both lands symbolically show their loyalty to the state by kissing the respective national flags at ceremonial occasions, their commitment to democracy was not entirely certain, as the attempted *coup d'état* in 1981 by elements within the Spanish military revealed. In the constitution of Spain, the military as an institution is granted explicit political powers. From the 1974 revolution until 1986 the highest political office in Portugal, the presidency, was occupied by high–ranking officers. The potential political activity of the military sets these nations off from the rest of western Euro-

pean nations, where the military is indisputably subordinate to the elected political leadership. Nevertheless, by the 1990s democracy had set deep roots in both countries, and the danger of military intervention had diminished significantly. This adjustment to the western European norm was strengthened by Spain's entry into NATO in 1982 (Portugal was a founding member), as well as by both lands joining the EU in 1986.

The Early Period

Many things that Portugal and Spain have in common stem from 2,000 years of shared history. The most ancient human remains found on the peninsula, and so far in all of Europe, date from 800,000 B.C. They were uncovered at the Atapuerca archaeological site in Burgos in northern Spain. It is likely that the first settlers began arriving on the Iberian Peninsula from 3000 to 2000 B.C. and were followed by waves of Celts, Phoenicians, Greeks and Carthaginians from the rest of Europe and Africa. Most of the settlers were firmly unified under Roman rule by 19 B.C. although individual tribes and cultures in the interior and northern parts of the peninsula continued to exist.

Tensions between the center and the periphery have continued to plague Spain and Portugal to the present day although they are certainly less significant in contemporary Portugal than in Spain. The Romans brought the Latin language to the peninsula, from which both modern Spanish and Portuguese developed. They also brought Roman law and administrative practices. In the 4th century they introduced Christianity to the area. From the important Roman cities in the South and

East of the peninsula came many of the Roman Empire's great leaders, such as Hadrian, Lucan, Marcus Aurelius, Seneca and Trajan.

Visigoth and Moslem Rule

The collapse of Rome in the 5th century A.D. was followed by three centuries of rule in Spain by the Visigoths, who had stormed the peninsula by force. Taking advantage of divisions and quarrels among the Visigoth leaders, Moors from North Africa began crossing the Strait of Gibraltar in 711 A.D. Within a very short time Muslims controlled virtually all the Roman cities in the South and East of the peninsula. Iberian art and commerce bloomed under the new Muslim rule, which was, on the whole, tolerant toward Jews and Christians.

Christians ensconced in strongholds in northwestern Spain hammered away at the Muslim realm in Iberia. It was further weakened by quarrels and intrigues among the Muslim rulers themselves, whose grip on the peninsula began to loosen. The newly emerging kingdom of Castile, which combined with Leon and whose military prowess is symbolized by its hero El Cid, and the kingdom of Aragon, which in 1137 combined with Catalonia, slowly but steadily pushed back the Muslims. Their rule in most of the peninsula had been broken by the mid 13th century, although a small Muslim kingdom hung on in Granada until 1492.

Moslem Decline; Portugal and Spain Separate

While the reconquest of the peninsula from the Muslims was taking place, Portugal began to sever its ties with Leon and

Spain under Roman rule

354

Iberian Peninsula

The Iberian Peninsula about 1150

to establish itself as an independent country. In 1095 Count Henri of the House of Burgundy became the direct ruler over Portugal, and in 1140, after a nine–year rebellion against the king of Leon–Castille, Henri's son, Alfonso Henriques, declared himself to be the king of Portugal. The Burgundians ruled Portugal until 1383, during which time Portugal's borders were expanded from the original Oporto and Coimbra. Lisbon was snatched from the Moslems in 1147. Since the second half of the 13th century, Portugal's boundaries have been the same as today, with the exception of the district of Olivenza, which Spain took in 1801 and continues to hold.

Portuguese Exploration and Conquest

As a country facing the sea, Portuguese sights were always directed outward, and the bulk of the population was attracted to the coast because of this maritime and external commercial orientation. By 1337 their mariners had already landed on the Canary Islands. Overseas exploration was particularly encouraged by Prince Henry the Navigator (1394–1460), a farsighted and imaginative man who established a maritime school to assemble and extend his country's knowledge of the sea. Portuguese mariners explored the African coast, and in 1488 Bartolommeo Dias rounded the Cape of Good Hope and reached East Africa. In 1497 Vasco da Gama set sail for India. He not only reached it, but he returned to describe the land to a receptive and curious Europe. Pedro Alvares Cabral landed in Brazil in 1500.

Such activity stimulated important advances in cartography and astronomy and also helped redirect the attention of Europe outward toward the larger world. It enabled Portugal to build up a massive empire which included Mozambique, Angola and Guinea–Bissau in Africa, Brazil in South America, East Timor, Macau (which the Chinese gave to Portugal as a reward for its fight against pirates), Portuguese India (with its capital of Goa) in South and Southeastern Asia, and the Atlantic islands of the Azores and Madeira. Portuguese naval squadrons were stationed permanently in strongholds in or around the Atlantic and Indian Oceans. The Portuguese also began to send settlers to some of these imperial holdings, especially to the Azores, Madeira and Brazil.

These colonial activities brought advantages to Portugal, as they did to Spain. They provided it with gold and other precious stones, silks and spices, which were treasured in Europe at that time, and needed foodstuffs, especially wheat. They also provided an occupation for those portions of the feudal nobility that could no longer be supported by domestic agricultural production. Settlement in the colonies offered many Portuguese the hope for a better life. Finally, the desire to convert the peoples of the world to Roman Catholicism furnished the enterprise with a spirit of crusade and gave it a religious and spiritual justification.

Spanish Colonial Activities

Portugal's most avid competitor was its only neighbor—Spain. Spanish attention had remained largely focused on Iberia until 1492, which was a very significant date. In that year the Spanish captured Granada, the last Moslem foothold on Spanish soil. The triumphant entry into that city of Ferdinand and Isabella, whose marriage had sealed the unity of Aragon and Castile, signified the end of the seven and one–half century reconquest of the Iberian peninsula. Thus, Spain took shape as a unified kingdom over an ethnically diverse area three and a half centuries after Portugal. The reconquest sparked a flourish of Spanish literature and artistic achievement that lasted at least two centuries. It also allowed Spaniards to concentrate their energy on overseas expansion and exploration.

As every American school child knows, the year 1492 was significant for another event: Christopher Columbus, a native of Genoa (Italy) working for the Spanish, sailed west in search of India, but instead bumped into the island of Santo Domingo in the Caribbean. His discovery opened the eyes of Europeans to an entirely new part of their world and launched an era of Spanish colonialism that spread Hispanic culture and languages to dozens of modern–day countries.

In order to minimize a potentially dangerous rivalry between Spain and Portugal in the wake of Columbus' discovery, the sovereigns of the two countries agreed in the Treaty of Tordesillas (1494) to divide the world in such a way that Spain would receive the Philippines (named after the Spanish king) and most of the Western Hemisphere (including large chunks of the contemporary U.S., such as California, the Southwest and Florida) with Portugal receiving what is now Brazil, and parts of Africa and Asia. Both countries continued generally to observe this agreement, which had the Pope's approval, but to their consternation, other interested powers, especially Britain, France and the Netherlands, did not.

Like Portugal, Spain had several different motives for establishing and maintaining an empire. Dominican and Franciscan friars were always close on the heels of the *conquistadores* in order to convert and educate the native populations. Also, the *conquistadores*, the royal court and the private companies that stood behind them clearly sought wealth, status and power. The Spanish kings insisted that all trade

Iberian Peninsula

with the colonies be conducted through Seville and be reserved for Castile although most of the trade was actually organized by Genoese and southern German merchants.

The Spanish kings also claimed one–fifth of all precious metals imported from the New World. Such metals greatly enriched the Spanish treasury, but they also heated inflation within Spain and created serious economic distortions. This wealth was used to add glitter to the royal and noble courts, to finance massive Spanish imports, and also to finance Spanish armies and navies. These military forces were constantly embroiled abroad maintaining an empire which encompassed the present–day BENELUX countries, Italy and, through the Hapsburg throne, all of the Austrian Empire. Throughout the 17th century Spanish money and troops also supported the Catholic struggle against Protestantism. Since almost none of its wealth was invested in productive facilities within the home country itself, Spain remained poor despite its temporary wealth.

Temporary Unity

The 16th century had been Portugal's "Golden Age," but it was dealt a devastating blow in the aftermath of events in Morocco, where King Sabastião and much of the nobility were slain while trying to protect the kingdom's holdings there. Spain claimed the Portuguese throne on the grounds that the mother of King Philip II of Spain was descended from Portuguese nobility. Thus, in 1580 the two countries were united in a dual monarchy, which was supposed to leave the Portuguese with domestic autonomy. In fact, Spaniards were appointed to Portuguese offices.

Despite initial economic advantages that Portugal gained through a dropping of customs barriers between the two lands, it was compelled to enter and to help finance through heavy taxes a costly and protracted war against England. This not only cost Portugal most of its lucrative markets in the Orient, but the bulk of its fleet as well. Both consequences directly benefited England and the Netherlands. Disillusioned about Spanish rule, and taking advantage of a revolt in Catalonia, the Portuguese also revolted. French support helped the rebellion succeed in 1640, when the House of Bragança was established as the Portuguese ruling family (which it remained until the monarchy fell in 1910). The Portuguese still mark the anniversary of this revolt that ended Spanish rule, and much of their subsequent history can be summarized as a struggle against absorption by its big neighbor. The Spanish did not accept Portuguese independence without a fight, though, and

until 1668 they struggled unsuccessfully to win back the country. As late as the early 20th century, King Alfonso XIII, grandfather of currently reigning King Juan Carlos, was considering the annexation of Portugal.

In order to guarantee that it would never again fall under Spanish domination, Portugal entered an alliance with the sea power, Britain, which always had a sharp strategic eye for coastal countries that could be useful allies. This alliance lasts into the 21st century. The struggle against Spain affirmed and strengthened Portuguese national identity, which still defines itself most clearly in terms of its distinctiveness from the Spanish nation. The loss of many of its colonies and markets in the Orient necessitated a shift of Portugal's colonial attention from the Indian Ocean to Brazil. The revenues from Brazilian sugar, coffee, diamonds, gold and other minerals became extremely important to the Portuguese economy.

Separation

The separation of Portugal from Spain was, for the latter, merely one of a series of foreign political setbacks following the destruction of the Spanish Armada, a mighty fleet sent to subdue England in 1588. Spain squandered its wealth on endless wars on the European Continent, and its European holdings were gradually whittled away. The last blow was the War of the Spanish Succession that erupted after the death in 1700 of Charles II, the last of the Hapsburg rulers in Spain. This conflict ended in the establishment of a Bourbon dynasty in Spain. In practical terms, this meant French domination of Spain's foreign policy. Occasionally Spain seemed about to be ready to rear its proud head once again and to assert primacy in its own affairs. However, any chance of Spain's restoring its former imperial

grandeur and power was undercut by that social and political convulsion which changed Europe irrevocably—the French Revolution and the accompanying French military conquest of most of Europe.

As an ally of England, Portugal intervened much earlier, in 1793, in the war against revolutionary France. In 1807 the French entered Portugal, prompting the royal court to flee to Brazil. French troops also invaded Spain, and in 1808 Napoleon placed his brother, Joseph, on the Spanish throne. Many Spaniards valiantly resisted this foreign invasion, as Goya's powerful paintings portray.

The Grand Army was nevertheless able to conquer most of the peninsula by 1809. Yet its hold on Spain was only temporary. The English Duke of Wellington, supported by Spanish guerrillas, advanced from Portugal and delivered a crushing defeat at Talavera in 1809. By 1811 the French had been driven out by British troops and by Portuguese soldiers who had been placed under the command of an English general, Lord Beresford. In the Portuguese king's absence, Beresford continued to dominate Portuguese politics long after Napoleon's troops had departed. Wellington defeated the French again at Vitoria in June 1813.

Both Spain and Portugal faced the post–Napoleonic era with restored monarchies but with the liberal ideas of the French Revolution in the heads of many of their citizens. These ideas would not permit a quiet return to the authoritarian government of earlier years. Also, these new notions, combined with the long rupture in reliable communication with their American colonies, spelled the end of their empires in the Western Hemisphere. The Spanish and Portuguese had fought heroically for their national independence. Now their American colonies decided to do the same.

Driving the Moors from Spain

356

Kingdom of Spain

Area: 194,897 sq. mi. (504,750 sq. km.), some 640 miles (1,034 km.) from east to west, 530 miles (848 km.) from north to south.

Population: 44.9 million (estimate 2008).

Capital City: Madrid (Pop. 3.2 million, almost 6 million in greater Madrid region).

Climate: Varying from Madrid's 2,000-foot (610 meters) elevation, making the area cold in winter and hot and dry in summer, to the Mediterranean coast that is hot in summer, mild in winter.

Neighboring Countries: France, Andorra (north); Portugal (west); Morocco lies only eight and a half miles across the Strait of Gibraltar.

Languages: Spanish (primarily the Castilian dialect), with Catalan, Basque, Galician, Valencian, regional languages which are once again flourishing and comprise an important part of the tongues spoken every day.

Principal Religion: Roman Catholic.

Chief Commercial Exports: Machinery, iron and steel, fruits and vegetables, footwear, textiles, energy products.

Major Customers: EU25 (72.1% of exports and 60.8% of imports), France (19.2% of exports and 14.2% of imports), Germany (11.4% of exports and 14.6% of imports), UK (8.4% of exports and 5.7% of imports), Italy (8.5% of exports and 8.9% of imports), Portugal (9.3% of exports).

Currency: Euro.

National Holiday: October 12 (1492)—*Dia de la Hispanidad* (Columbus Day). This holiday was called *Dia de la Raza* until it was changed before the Franco era. A second national holiday is December 6 to commemorate the passage of the present constitution by referendum in 1978.

Chief of State: His Majesty King Juan Carlos I (b. 1938). Married Princess Sophia of Greece, 1962. Proclaimed King of Spain, November 22, 1975.

Heir Apparent: His Royal Highness Crown Prince Felipe, Prince of the Asturias (b. 1968). Married Letizia Ortíz, Princess of Asturias, May 22, 2004.

Head of Government: José Luis Rodríguez Zapatero, President of the Government (since April 2004).

National Flag: Three horizontal stripes of red, yellow, and red, with the center yellow stripe twice as wide as the red ones. The Spanish royal crest is set off center on the left of the flag.

For as long as most people could remember, Spain was, by European standards, a poor, thinly populated country on the edge of the Continent and separated from the rest of Europe by more than the high peaks of the Pyrenees Mountains. Its people had produced a language and a high culture which had been spread to

Spain

most countries in the New World, but in politics it appeared excessively passionate, polarized, and generally ungovernable by any other means than authoritarianism. The Spanish kings had never thoroughly integrated this heterogeneous country, and at times it threatened to split apart, with the Basque and Catalan provinces in the northeast leading the way. Unceasing political instability prevailed, punctuated by longer or shorter periods of authoritarian rule. The last such interlude lasted until the end of 1975 and was guided by a diminutive general named Francisco Franco, called *El Caudillo* (the Leader). His fascist regime made Spain an embarrassment to and, for a long time, an outcast in western Europe.

After Franco's death Spain began to move in a different direction. Indeed, he would scarcely recognize the land he claimed to have "saved" in 1939. Wishing both to create a parliamentary democratic order and to avoid a bloody repeat of the turmoil and civil war of the 1930s, the major contenders for political power have displayed a remarkable willingness to cooperate with each other and to moderate their political demands.

Spain's regions have been offered autonomy statutes that reduce Madrid's hold on the country's politics. Communist and Socialist–led trade unions operate freely and act with moderation and responsibility. Many political parties compete for seats in the national parliament, but Spanish voters have overwhelmingly supported the moderate democratic parties in the political center. A king, picked and trained by Franco, has shown unswerving determination to create and to preserve a democratic order and has therefore won the admiration of most of his countrymen. Spain also moved into western Europe by joining NATO and by entering the EU, which enjoys a broad consensus within the country.

It is true that every November the anniversary of Franco's death still brings some Spaniards out into the streets to wear and wave fascist paraphernalia and to hear inflammatory speeches against the new democratic order. There is also a small minority within the army that sometimes vents its dissatisfaction with the new Spain and makes democrats nervous. But democracy in Spain, as well as in Portugal, is working. The Pyrenees are no longer the edge of Europe.

CONTEMPORARY HISTORY

The Post–Napoleonic Period

The liberation of Spain from French occupation and the restoration of the Bourbon dynasty by no means brought the country peace and stability. Spain's isolation from its American colonies during the Napoleonic wars had loosened its grip and had given Latin American leaders a taste of local rule they liked. They therefore revolted. Again, the Spanish treasury was drained by protracted war far from its own territory. After the disastrous Spanish defeat at the battle of Ayacucho in 1825, the vast and mighty Spanish empire had been reduced to the islands of Cuba, Puerto Rico, the Philippines and three Pacific archipelagos—the Carolinas, the Marianas (which included Guam), and Palaos. Spain kept these archipelagos for one year and then sold them to Germany in 1899.

Spanish domestic politics was marred by almost continuous political, social and economic crises. This turmoil began with the king's revocation in 1814 of the admirably liberal Cadiz Constitution, which had been approved in 1812. By 1820 the dim–witted Ferdinand VII had alienated many important groups, especially the liberals and the military, and in the midst of widespread demonstrations and riots throughout the country, the military revolted. In an unsuccessful attempt to salvage his throne, the king allowed the Cadiz Constitution to be proclaimed again, but it was exactly such democratic constitutions which most of the conservative monarchs of Europe could not tolerate. Therefore, in April 1823 French armies again invaded Spain on behalf of most other European powers (with the notable exception of England) and restored Ferdinand VII to absolute power.

The next decade and a half were filled with reaction and unrest, followed by another quarter-century of rule by generals and a scandal–ridden Queen Isabella II, who was finally deposed in 1868 by military officers. When they tried to appoint a Prussian Hohenzollern to the throne, they provided the spark for the war between France and Prussia in 1870, which resulted in German unification. A brief and unsuccessful republican experiment ended again in military intervention and the restoration in 1874 of the monarchy under Alfonso XII, the son of Isabella II. A parliament (*Cortes*), for which only property owners could vote, was also created. In order to achieve some measure of stability, the Conservative and Liberal parties agreed to alternate power. However, this system of *turno político* had broken down by the end of the 19th century.

The Spanish–American War and Ensuing Turbulence

Spain was badly shaken in 1898 by its war against the United States. This conflict was sparked by an explosion of dubious origin on a U. S. vessel, the Maine, which was anchored in Havana harbor.

American soldiers, including those led by Theodore Roosevelt's "Roughriders," entered the battlefield with the cry, "Remember the Maine!" The war left Spain with 200,000 dead in Cuba, a sorely humiliated officer corps, an empty treasury, and a denuded empire. The U. S took Cuba, Puerto Rico, Guam and the Philippines, and Spain retained only a smattering of holdings in West Africa and Morocco.

Widespread domestic dissatisfaction increasingly began to manifest itself again, urban workers began to be attracted to Marxism and syndicalism (radically political trade unionism), and anarchism infected the downtrodden workers in Barcelona and the peasants in southern Spain. Corruption and inefficiency in Madrid, combined with bitter disappointment at losing the 1898 Spanish-American War (called "The Disaster") and many colonies, stimulated separatist sentiments in the Basque and Catalan regions. Political parties took shape. Political violence became commonplace, and Spanish politics was in a state of utter confusion. Between 1902 and 1923 the country averaged one government every 18 months.

Spain managed to remain neutral in World War I, but in 1921 it experienced such a stinging military reversal at the hands of the Moors at Annual in North Africa that public pressure forced the government to conduct an investigation of that institution which had never contented itself with mere military matters—the army. However, before the investigation could be completed, the military's rage at such "impudence" boiled over. The army seized power in 1923 and formed a government under General Miguel Primo de Rivera. Primo de Rivera's government banned all opposition parties, slapped severe controls on the press and the universities and openly expressed great admiration for the kind of fascist political order that Mussolini was establishing in Italy.

The new Spanish leader did launch an extensive public works program and, with the help of the French, ended the war in Morocco in 1926. But without the support of the masses or of the youth or intelligentsia, Primo de Rivera's authoritarian government could not survive the jolt which the worldwide depression gave to Spain and most other European countries at the end of the 1920s. He therefore resigned in January 1930. Demonstrations in favor of a republic and elections in which republican candidates won in all important cities became so worrisome that King Alfonso XIII was forced to flee the country April 13, 1931. The almost immediate proclamation of the Second Republic (the first being in the early 1870s) unleashed such enthusiasm from its supporters that 200 churches were burned to the ground. Of course, such anti-clericalism had been building up throughout the 19th century. This helps explain why the church supported Franco so strongly and why he protected it in turn.

Many Spaniards today look back very carefully to Spain's entry into democracy in 1931 in order to try to insure that earlier mistakes which helped lead to the downfall of the democratic republic would not be repeated. The new constitution of December 1931 legalized all political parties and created a unicameral *Cortes* (parliament) to which the government was responsible. The new government under Manuel Azaña launched a full–scale attack on the old ruling pillars: the church, the army and the wealthy. The Jesuit order was expelled, and fully state schools were established in order to eliminate religious influence over education. Large estates were confiscated, and the beginnings of a land reform were introduced. Railroads and the Bank of Spain were nationalized, the eight–hour workday introduced and the army officer corps reduced by almost half.

It soon became clear that many of the new government's reforms were unrealistic. Both the delay in their implementation and the fear that they might actually be implemented brought peasants, workers, anarchists, fascists and monarchists out into the streets. Spain was bubbling with conspiracies and intrigues. It experienced one government after the other; in the five years of the republic, there were 18 different governments. This came to a head shortly after the beginning of 1936 when a Popular Front on the French model, composed of socialists, communists, anarcho–syndicalists, and Basque and Catalan nationalists, was formed and won an electoral victory. The assassination on July 13, 1936, of the former finance minister under Primo de Rivera, Calvo Sotelo, was the cue for the army to launch a long–planned coup against the Republic.

Civil War

On July 18, 1936, a diminutive general, Francisco Franco, flew to Morocco from the Canary Islands and drew his sword against the republic. Within a few days the revolt spread to garrisons within metropolitan Spain, and within ten days troops were flown in German planes from Morocco to secure strategically important positions. Unlike early military rebellions, which usually succeeded very quickly, this one thrust Spain into a savage three–year civil war that not only destroyed democracy and liberty in Spain, but temporarily moved the country into the center of the world political conflict between the proponents and opponents of fascist dictatorship.

The revolt was successful in certain parts of Spain, but not in such key cities as Madrid. Also, the provinces of Catalonia and Basque strongly supported the Republic because the latter had guaranteed them a large measure of autonomy. Further, Franco did not have the support of the navy, the air force and part of the army.

It is probable that the coup would have collapsed within a few months if Franco had not received crucial military assistance from fascist Germany and Italy. The Italians sent more than a thousand planes, four infantry divisions, tanks, artillery and other military equipment. The German contribution was smaller but highly effective. The Germans sent a tank battalion. The major contribution was the Condor Legion, composed of four fighter–bombers, four fighters, one reconnaissance, and two seaplane squadrons. The German aerial bombing of the city of Guernica on April 26, 1937, outraged world opinion and prompted an indignant Pablo Picasso to paint his famous *Guernica*. Sixty years later Germany agreed to donate almost $2 million to the city in symbolic compensation for the destruction.

Franco and Fascism

The republic called for help, but France and Britain refused to respond to its calls and limited their reactions to verbal protests. It did have on its side some loyal army and naval units, as well as units hastily formed with trade unionists, students, and Catalan and Basque nationalists. In addition, several thousand generally poorly equipped and insufficiently trained international volunteers organized in such units as the Abraham Lincoln and Ernst Thälmann brigades came to fight for the republic. This conflict inspired to action many idealistic young people throughout Europe and the United States, who saw in Spain the only determined struggle against fascism. The Soviet Union also sent limited aid in the form of advisers, technicians, tanks and aircraft. However, the Soviet Union itself was in the grips of a terrifying purge at home, which spilled over to communist units fighting in Spain. In such a state of paralysis, the Soviets withdrew their aid to the Republic a year before the end of the war.

Ultimately the military balance tipped in favor of Franco's fascists. In the spring of 1939 armed resistance in Catalonia was broken, and soon thereafter Franco's forces entered the severely bombed and starving capital of Madrid. The human costs of this brutal civil war were extremely high: approximately a million Spaniards were either killed or forced to emigrate. The war left most Spaniards with an intense fear of another such armed conflict on their own territory.

A victim of the civil war amidst the ruins of her home

Spain

Despite Hitler's pressure and threats, Franco did maintain an official policy of neutrality during World War II, although he openly sympathized with Germany and Italy. He even sent a "Blue Division" of volunteers to fight on Germany's side against the Soviet Union from 1941–43. But Franco was always sensitive to the direction political winds blew, and after disastrous German setbacks on the Eastern front in 1943, he decided to maintain his official policy of neutrality more strictly.

Franco created an authoritarian, fascist regime, supported by the army and, initially, by the Catholic Church. This regime remained fundamentally unchanged until his death in November 1975. He always was skillful in playing different groups against each other, but he did not dare create any democratic institutions. The *Cortes* was restructured so that it could not effectively challenge Franco; in reality it was a cheerleader for the rulers. The news media were subjected to close censorship. Franco abolished all political parties except his own *Movimiento Nacional* (National Movement).

The right–wing Falangist Movement, which had elaborated fascist ideals for Franco in the early days, gradually declined in influence and ultimately became strictly an agency to administer the bureaucracy. The Catholic Church's support of the regime gradually waned as the years went on, but the Catholic lay organization, *Opus Dei*, did grow in influence, especially within the educational and economic spheres. The *Opus Dei* became more open to progressive ideas and was a force behind Spain's rapid industrialization and robust economic growth that began in the 1960s.

Although Franco was the undisputed dictator from the very beginning, in 1947 he officially made himself chief of state for life, with the right to appoint his own successor. He declared Spain to be a monarchy, but not until 1969 did he name Prince Juan Carlos of Bourbon, whom he had educated and groomed for years to prepare him for his new role, to be the new king upon his death.

Isolation and Economic Progress

Because of Franco's open sympathy with Germany and Italy during World War II, the victorious allies initially isolated Spain in the international community and for years refused to allow it to enter the UN. But the Cold War brought many former enemies onto better terms with each other, and Spain was no exception. The emerging hostilities between the Soviet Union and the nations in the Atlantic Alliance greatly enhanced the value of Spain's strategic location. Therefore, in 1953 the U. S. reached an agreement with Franco providing for American financial assistance in return for the right to establish four air and naval bases in Spain. This agreement was of great military significance for the U. S., but Franco's many opponents never regarded it kindly. The former Socialist leader, Felipe González, for instance, admitted that his attitude toward the U. S. had always been negative, in large part because the picture of former President Dwight D. Eisenhower smilingly shaking hands with Franco had remained firmly etched in his memory.

All in all, the fascist movement failed to stimulate much mass enthusiasm in Spain. It rested on widespread apathy fed by most Spaniards' intense desire for order after the Civil War. Franco had created a panoply of corporatist organizations that were designed to mobilize and control the diverse elements of society. But as years passed, dissatisfaction and unrest began to manifest themselves since Spain's fundamental problems had by no means been solved. Labor and student unrest, high inflation, growing opposition with the church, increasing Basque extremism and revolutionary events in neighboring Portugal, beginning in 1974, continually chipped away at the foundations of the fascist state. Yet only one event could wipe away the trappings of fascism and set the process of democracy in motion: the death of Franco, which finally occurred in November 1975.

King Juan Carlos

The most visible sign for a new democratic spirit of reconciliation and national unity quickly became King Juan Carlos de Borbón y Borbón. Even former Communist Party chief, Santiago Carrillo, had to admit, "without Juan Carlos, Spaniards would probably be fighting each other again." Few persons had expected that the monarch would become a major linchpin for democracy in Spain.

Franco had chosen Juan Carlos (the grandson of former King Alfonso XIII) over the head of his father, Don Juan, who lived in Portuguese exile and who had always been an outspoken critic of Franco. From his father, Juan Carlos had learned several very important lessons: to install a democracy in Spain, to shun the everyday dealings of political parties, and never to play the army against the people.

Young Juan Carlos was an uninspiring pupil and rather introverted, especially after accidentally shooting his brother with an air gun at age 16. Remembering a suggestion the Italian fascist leader, Benito Mussolini, had once made to him, Franco brought the nine–year old Juan Carlos back to Spain in 1947 and had him educated under his watchful eye. The boy was sent to the army, navy and air force academies in Zaragoza, Marín and San Javier, respectively. He enjoyed his life at these academies, making contacts within the military that later were to be important to him as king. He had plenty of time for his favorite hobbies of athletics, ham radios and fast motorcycles. He also became a jet pilot, and he still flies himself around Spain for official visits.

When Franco decided in 1964 that the young Prince had had enough education, he entered a very trying phase in his life waiting for a task. He married Sophia, sister of the former Greek King Constantine, a public relations agent in London, who was one of the king's few close friends. Not until 1969 was he officially proclaimed the crown prince after he had sworn allegiance to Franco's basic principles before the parliament and after he had had a serious argument with his own

Prince Juan Carlos as a schoolboy

360

father over his decision to accept the Spanish crown from Franco's own hand. He was therefore distrusted by Don Juan and by many Spanish democrats, who thought that the prince had become *El Caudillo's* stooge.

Many in Franco's coterie also distrusted him because he did not ingratiate himself to them. Their suspicions were fed by the fact that Juan Carlos began establishing contacts with political opponents of the Franco regime, including, through an intermediary, communist leaders in Paris. With Franco on his death bed in late 1975, Juan Carlos gave a revealing glimpse of his sentiments by flying to Spanish Sahara and telling the troops there that they would have to withdraw because Spanish colonialism had come to an end.

He was installed as king after Franco's death, but he proceeded cautiously. In fact, the Spanish experiment of making a step–by–step transition from a dictatorship to a parliamentary democracy, while continuing to observe the existing laws of the land, was unique in European history. He temporarily retained Franco's last prime minister, Carlos Arias Navarro. Through wise appointments, he gained influence over the Council of the Realm, a small body whose only clear function was to insure that the new regime would remain within the bounds of Francoism. By the summer of 1976 he was able to have

Arias eased out of office and to have a man with reformist designs, Adolfo Suárez, appointed in his place. The king gave Suárez unmistakable instructions to proceed as rapidly as possible toward the goal which Juan Carlos shared with most of his countrymen: "to restore sovereignty to the Spanish people."

As king, Juan Carlos set about to demonstrate that the bitter controversies of the past could be ended. When he visited Mexico three years after becoming king, he requested that veteran republicans who had fled from Franco's rule be invited to the Spanish Embassy, where he received them with demonstrative cordiality. Also, in a public speech he called the civil war a fratricidal tragedy; Franco had always referred to it as a "glorious crusade."

He chooses to live in the relatively small Zarzuela Palace outside of Madrid, rather than the stately palace his ancestors had built in the middle of the capital. He prevents anything like a palace clique to congeal around him. Realizing that most Spaniards are not ardent monarchists, he keeps protocol to a minimum and leads a relatively austere private life. But his patience, tact, shrewdness and courage in guiding the nation have won him respect from even those Spaniards who had always considered the very word "monarchist" an insult.

Seeds of Democracy

The National Movement (*Movimiento Nacional*), which Franco had formed out of various political movements, was withering on the vine. The best-known component of the National Movement was the fascist–oriented *Falange*, named after the infantry formations which Alexander the Great had called phalanx. The trappings of fascist salutes, paramilitary youth organizations and the calls to revitalize Spain through order, authority and hierarchy remained, but membership in the National Movement had for most Spaniards become a mere formal prerequisite for a government job. In fact, many of Spain's foremost reformers after Franco's death, including Adolfo Suárez, under whose premiership Spain became a modern parliamentary democracy in the second half of the 1970s, had attained political prominence within the National Movement.

Spain felt its way slowly and nervously out of the authoritarian political order created and maintained by Franco. Many Spaniards looked back uneasily to the 1930s, and they saw certain parallels between that period and the 1970s. At both times political parties were legalized after dictatorships had ended, and the Communist Party supported the young democracy both times. At the beginning of the two democracies the vast majority of Spaniards voted for the moderate parties

The ancient city of Toledo, capital of Spain under Roman rule and home of the illustrious artist El Greco

Spain

of the center. Also, world economic crises set in at the inception of both Spanish democracies. Basque and Catalan nationalists demanded autonomy, and a fraction of their numbers resorted to grisly violence to provoke the military and press for their aims. Thus, in both eras, Spanish democratic leaders had to face a declining economy, a wave of strikes and demands for better wages, and extremist violence, while creating a political order which would later be, in the words of King Juan Carlos, "a just order, equal for all," supported by "public activity as much as private activity, under legal safeguards."

Economic Progress

Despite the parallels between the 1930s and the 1970s, one must notice also the many significant differences between Spanish society in the heyday of Franco's rule and in the 1970s. One difference was the evolution of the church in Spain, traditionally one of the most conservative in the entire Catholic world.

A further development that favored the post–Franco democratic experiment was economic progress. The recession of the 1970s was not nearly as deep as that of the 1930s and did not shake the democratic foundations of the European countries as was the case earlier. Most important, Spain's economic structure has changed drastically since Franco seized power. *El Caudillo* sought to establish complete Spanish self–reliance, which amounted to sealing Spain off economically from the rest of the world. An international outcast after World War II, Spain was not permitted to receive Marshall Plan assistance. This greatly widened the gap between Spain and most of the rest of western Europe. But in 1950 the UN lifted the trade boycott against Spain, and capital and modern production and business ideas began to enter the country.

The result was a doubling of industrial production in the course of the 1950s. This upswing did bring a doubling of prices, which stimulated labor unrest, but it also gave Spanish technocrats the courage to draw up a Stabilization Plan in 1959. This significant plan devalued the peseta to a level that would favor Spanish exports, began to eliminate some unnecessary economic controls, buried the old economic isolation policy (known as autarky) in theory as well as practice, and headed Spain in a dynamic capitalist direction. This new direction was not only good for the living standards of the people, but also for the later stabilizing of democracy. In the last decade of Franco's rule economic growth in Spain was an enviable 7% per year, one of the highest in western Europe.

Rapid economic growth not only increased the size of the middle class and gradually began to level out class differences, but it changed the country's outlook and demography. As Spaniards' economic expectations grew, their eyes turned more toward western Europe, where democracy and prosperity were linked. Their contact with other Europeans was enormously increased by the lightning expansion of the Spanish tourist industry, which soon made Spain the number one tourist country in all of Europe. Although the bulk of Spain's tourists flock to the beaches, seldom venturing into the interior, they brought millions of Spanish into direct contact with western Europeans and their ideas and spending habits.

Many Spaniards themselves began to pull up stakes and seek a better economic life elsewhere. In the 1960s more than three million Spaniards moved from the poorer countryside into the country's major industrial areas, especially Madrid, Catalonia and the Basque country. Well over two million Spaniards left the rural areas for industrialized countries north of the Pyrenees, especially to France, West Germany and Switzerland, sending much–needed foreign currency remittances back to Spain. Entire villages were deserted.

The trend greatly reduced the number of Spaniards engaging in agriculture and left many pockets of rural poverty, especially in the South and in the province of

West of Madrid in the foothills of the bleak Sierra de Guadarrama stands El Escorial, the brooding, magnificent blue-gray slate and stone symbol of the unchangeable spirit of Spain. Combining a royal palace, basilica, monestery and art gallery, it was built by Philip II, heir to the boundless riches of the New World, the most powerful monarch of the 16th century.

Galicia. Such rapid industrial growth also left more polluted air, sea, rivers and tap water in Spain. It transformed quiet, picturesque fishing villages into loud, overcrowded mass tourist places with tasteless and cheaply constructed hotels, an army of souvenir vendors and thieves, and much higher prices. Large parts of the beautiful coastline were scarred with factories, chemical and power plants and blocks of apartments. Also, many of the suburbs around industrial cities shot up almost overnight and were often built without paved streets, or medical, educational and leisure facilities. Some became slums and centers for delinquency and crime. Spain paid a price for its rapid industrialization.

Yet Spain's social base had changed significantly. Workers increasingly began to own their own homes or apartments. They also began to buy cars and take vacations far from home. Although Franco had tried to keep them by and large politically apathetic, more and more Spaniards began under Franco to make public demands on the political system through strikes and demonstrations. Workers began to support the illegal trade union movement that grew out of the 1950s. Workers' Committees (*Comisiones Obreras*) emerged in larger factories to represent workers in negotiations with the management. By the 1970s they had successfully infiltrated the official unions, thereby weakening that prop of the Francoist system. In 1967 workers acquired the right to strike as long as such strikes were peaceful and strictly nonpolitical.

Franco's Legacy

The changes in the Catholic Church, the economy and the social structure had already eaten away at the roots of Francoism long before *El Caudillo* had closed his

General Francisco Franco

eyes for the last time. But the main reason why Spain's second attempt at democracy had a better chance to succeed was that Spaniards had a good memory. They remembered that four decades earlier half of Spain conquered the other after untold suffering and grief and that years of authoritarianism had followed. This time, Spaniards were ready for reconciliation with each other.

The willingness to ignore the things they once fought over has been referred to as a *pacto de olvido*, an agreement to forget. For example, for a while, even after more than a dozen years of Socialist rule, many plazas still bore Franco's name, and almost all monuments and memorials one-sidedly honored Franco's rebels. This is no longer the case, even in his birthplace. In 1977, two years after his death, an amnesty was granted to his collaborators, and unlike in several other European countries, there was no collective declaration of guilt or rejection of the past even though hundreds of thousands of Franco's opponents had been killed, sent to concentration camps, or forced into exile. There were no war crimes trials or purges of the security apparatus.

In 1980 the new democratic regime dared to sponsor the first balanced exhibition of the Civil War. Videotapes, old news films, and tapes of the songs of both sides were played. Documents, flags, weapons, posters and newspapers were shown. Rather than rekindling old passions, the exhibition seemed to strengthen a very powerful sentiment in contemporary Spain—*never again civil war*.

By 2002, nearly 40% of Spaniards either had not been born when Franco ruled or were too young to remember him. They form a new political class of Spaniards not involved in the old regime. Democracy has been firmly established and reinforced by NATO and EU membership, and it now seems less dangerous for the country's cohesion to glance backwards into Spain's past. A flood of books on the Franco era has appeared, as well as a major exhibition (officially opened by the king) on the history of those were forced into exile, and a popular TV series, "*Cuéntame cómo pasó*" ("Tell me how it happened"), based on the day-to-day life of an ordinary Madrid family as Spain began to change in the 1960s. Many communal graves of republican fighters and sympathizers have been located for excavation and transformation into memorials; about 500 mass graves have been found in Andalusia alone. Retrospection is no longer taboo in Spain.

The generation of President of the Government José Luis Rodriguez Zapatero, elected in 2004, was too young to have taken part in the negotiated amnesia fol-

Crown Prince Filipe and family

lowing Franco's death in 1975. One of his Socialist Party's campaign pledges was to change it. In the fall of 2007 his government passed a statute, known as the Law of Historical Memory, formally condemning Franco's rule for the first time. It mandates the removal of all fascist symbols, forbids all political acts at grave sites, dismisses the verdicts of the summary trials staged by Franco's Nationalists during the Civil War, and requires local governments to fund the excavation of mass graves so that those Republican victims who had been denied a decent burial can finally have one. The law not only honors the many war dead, including the hundreds of priests and nuns murdered by Republican supporters, but also the countless victims of persecution by the later Franco regime. This is very personal for Zapatero: his grandfather, a captain in the Republican army, was executed by Franco's forces in 1936. The law was opposed by the opposition Popular Party on the grounds that it is a mistake to revisit the past.

A further reminder of the country's undigested past was given in early 2008, when an attempt to provide words to the national anthem, *La Marcha Real* (The Royal March), failed. The earlier text was dropped after Franco's death and never replaced. This left sports fans with nothing to sing when their anthem was played at contests. Therefore, the Spanish Olympic Committee launched a contest to seek proposals for the lyrics, and it received 7,000 entries. One was chosen, but then it had to be withdrawn a few days later amid criticism that it harked back to the

Spain

The Spanish Royal Family: (l. to r.) Princess Elena, Crown Prince Felipe, Queen Sophia, King Juan Carlos I, and Princess Cristina.

fascist past. It opened with *Viva España* (Long Live Spain), the rallying cry of the Franco dictatorship. Anything smacking of fervent patriotism remains suspect. A further problem is the fact that this is one of Europe's most decentralized countries, with many groups within its borders that consider themselves "nations." One can hardly imagine a stirring anthem that would satisfy both left and right and not offend Basques, Catalans, or Galicians.

GOVERNMENT

Monarch as Head of State

The king works hard and is informed about the minutest details of his country's policies. However, unlike Franco, he does not attend cabinet meetings, and he usually keeps himself aloof from day–to–day political affairs. He preserves his real political authority for critical issues and times. Some Spaniards were critical of his outspoken support of joining NATO's integrated command structure and the EU's single currency. But communist leader Julio Anguita's demand in 1996 that the king resign unleashed a public furor. Polls in the same year revealed that the monarchy was Spain's most highly rated institution.

The king operates under strong constitutional constraints. However, he is able to influence the complexion of the government, and he is the supreme commander of the armed forces. Unlike any other monarch in Europe, he deals directly with

the political and military leaders in his own country. He is without question Europe's most powerful and influential monarch although he probably is the one with the least personal wealth. He performs all the ceremonial duties of a chief–of–state, but because of his guiding role in Spanish politics, he is a far more important conversation partner for foreign leaders than are most European heads of state.

Sometimes he can be very direct. In November 2007 he participated in an Ibero-American summit of 19 Latin American countries plus Spain and Portugal in Santiago, Chile. When Venezuela's mercurial president, Hugo Chávez, kept interrupting the proceedings, repeatedly calling Spain's former ruler José María Aznar a "fascist," the infuriated king turned to Chávez and told him: "Why don't you just shut up?" Juan Carlos later stormed out of the meeting when Nicaragua's president, Daniel Ortega, supported Chávez and attacked Spanish businesses. His comment was a big hit back home. A ring tone featuring his words, *"Por qué no te callas?"*, netted more than $2 million sales in a couple of weeks. Websites, t-shirts and coffee mugs dedicated to the incident were on the market by Christmas.

By the 21st century the monarchy was probably respected more than it was at any time since 1800. Its popularity was strengthened in the aftermath of the March 11, 2004, terrorist bombings in Madrid when Crown Prince Felipe led a

march of millions through the streets of the capital to protest against terrorism and to commemorate the victims of the attacks. This was the first time he had participated in a public rally.

His marriage in May 2004 to the commoner and divorced TV journalist Letizia Ortíz, a beautiful and intelligent woman with a PhD from Mexico, was a welcome diversion and catharsis for a shocked nation. Security concerns were so great that the Schengen treaty permitting free movement across EU borders was suspended for a week, and Madrid's city center was blocked to traffic for almost 24 hours. There is a historical precedent for such caution since his great-grandfather, Alfonso XIII, was almost killed at his wedding in 1906 when a Catalan anarchist threw at the newlyweds a bomb wrapped in a bouquet of flowers.

Felipe and Letizia have two daughters, Leonor (b. 2005) and Sofia (b. 2007), who are next in line for the throne after their father. All political parties are in agreement that the law of male primogeniture should be abolished in order to permit a woman to ascend the throne before her younger brothers. This would not be retroactive and affect Crown Prince Felipe, who has two older sisters. Such a constitutional change requires a referendum, and some fear that it could degenerate into a plebiscite between monarchists and republicans.

The king influences the selection of the president of the government and the cabi-

**President of the Government
José Luis Rodríguez Zapatero**

net, and he formally appoints both. The cabinet is technically not responsible to the *Cortes*. However, according to recent practice, a government is expected to have a majority in the Chamber of Deputies or at least to have the support on key votes of a majority of deputies. The leader and most important political figure is not called "prime minister," as in most European democracies, but "president of the government."

Parliament

A national referendum in December 1976 established a bicameral parliament. In another referendum in December 1978, 87.8% of all voting Spaniards approved of a new constitution, which contained few traces of Francoism.

The upper house of the *Cortes*, the 259-seat Senate, is the less important chamber. Senators are elected in two ways: 208 are chosen by direct election in provincial constituencies in an electoral system that gives each voter four votes. Each provincial constituency selects four senators regardless of population. This is designed to protect the interests of the smaller provinces. There are variations for the Balearic and Canary Islands. The enclaves of Ceuta and Melilla choose two each. The remaining 51 are chosen through proportional representation in the autonomous communities (regions). Each region chooses one senator and an additional one for every million inhabitants. The senators are designated by the parliament of each region in a manner that differs from region to region. This complicated system is one indication of the extent to which Spain had become a federal state. The king is no longer permitted to appoint senators.

The 350 members of the lower house, the Chamber of Deputies, are elected by a modified form of proportional representation by which voters choose from a list established by each party. Independent candidates are forbidden to run for election unless they can combine to form a list. Seats are distributed to the various provinces according to population, with the smallest province receiving at least three seats.

The electoral system is designed to favor the large parties at the expense of the smaller ones. For example, in the 2008 parliamentary elections the two largest parties won almost 84% of the votes and 323 of 350 seats; that percentage is steadily growing. Parties have the power to expel maverick parliamentarians from the party but not to take their seats away. This possibility strengthens members' loyalty toward their parties. One can only marvel at the way the Spanish, who were not permitted to vote in free elections for more than 40 years, could in the early years of the democracy competently sort their way through more than 60 parties and groups, using two different electoral systems at the same time, and produce a similar result in both houses of the *Cortes*. In 2008, ten parties (down from 11) won seats in the lower house out of more than two dozen that presented candidates. Over a third were women, and in the cabinet that followed, women outnumbered men nine to eight. The new defense minister was a woman: Carme Chancón.

Political Parties

In 1977 Spain's major parties signed the Moncloa Pact with each other, named after the small governmental palace in Madrid. By signing this pact, the parties agreed to drop their party dogma for the good of the country. The voters appreciated the major parties' moderation. In the first free elections since 1936, the Spanish showed their preference for the parties that are unmistakably in favor of the democratic order. The more radical parties of the left and right found themselves represented in parliament, but without anything close to a majority.

Political parties entered the post–Franco era with well–founded nervousness. In Spain's past, parties were always plagued by division. Like Greece, Spain was one of the few European countries to experience a civil war in the 20th century. The political parties had been in the thick of that tragic struggle. From 1939 to 1975 they had been unable to operate freely, and most of them had been driven underground or into exile, where their members were often isolated from each other, and where their leaders had great problems in establishing and maintaining unity. They also had difficulty following political developments within Spain.

When Franco died, the parties had to organize themselves very quickly. Fortunately Spain had an intelligent and able king who could stabilize the transition while the democratic parties prepared themselves. Portugal had not been so fortunate and had to experience two years of chaos before the moderate democratic parties could gain their footing.

Socialists

Only two of the major parties existed before 1975. The Spanish Socialist Labor Party (PSOE) which, together with the Catalan Socialist Party and the Basque Socialist Party, is generally referred to as The Socialists. Founded in 1879, it is the oldest Spanish party. Yet it acquired a young image after a thorough change of leadership in the early 1970s.

Its former leader, Felipe González, was an attractive and charismatic man, who was a labor lawyer and who had engaged in anti–Francoist underground activity. He and the other leaders were able to lead the PSOE from a radical leftist Marxist stance during the Franco era to a pragmatic political course that sought to open the party toward the political center. He was a master of compromise, tactics and organization.

A majority within the PSOE decided in 1976 to call itself Marxist, over the urgent protest of González. The latter argued that the party should return to the ethical and undogmatic socialism of the party's founders and consider Marxism merely as "an interesting intellectual exercise, but not the holy writ." He, himself, publicly declared that he is not a Marxist. González resigned in protest, and as a result the popularity of the party plummeted. Therefore a special party congress was called in 1979 to vote by 86% to reinstate him as head of a moderate party executive committee. The PSOE is still a party with a broad political spectrum, but González brought the left wing within the party largely under control. The PSOE calls for a classless, pluralistic, democratic and decentralized Spain with a market economy. Its slogan is: "Socialism is freedom!"

The party is strong in industrial centers, and many large cities have Socialist mayors. It is also strong in the agricultural region of Andalusia. It is the only Socialist party in southern Europe that has strong support from a significant independent trade union, the UGT. It also has a well–developed local base, so it is the only Spanish party with solid roots in the factories, local neighborhoods and national and regional parliaments.

One of the PSOE's major advantages had always been its unity in the face of opposing parties' disunity. But that ended as fighting within González's party

Spain

erupted over the question of what a socialist government should do. One faction, the *renovadores* (renewers), supported González's pragmatic free market policies, aimed at opening up monopolies, curbing the budget deficit, and creating conditions favorable for job creation and business. The *Guerristas*, named after their leader, Alfonso Guerra, regard themselves as orthodox Socialists. The government's economic austerity fueled such strong discontent on the labor front that the unions called several 24–hour general strikes in 1988, 1992, and 1994. The 1988 work stoppage was the first successful general strike in Spain since 1934.

González was sometimes accused of abandoning socialist principles by failing to redistribute wealth. The charge is not entirely fair. During his four terms, education spending rose, as the school–leaving age was raised to 16 and the number of university students doubled. Health services and pension rights were extended to the entire population, and a nation– wide unemployment benefit scheme was created. His victory in 1993 left him the only Socialist ruler in any major western European country and the only leader in any European country to win a fourth term. His moderate, pragmatic party personified Spain's post–Franco modernization.

His government found itself embroiled in a series of scandals that severely dented his credibility. Early elections in 1996 resulted in the defeat of the incumbent by a narrow margin. In opposition, González stepped down as leader in 1997. At the end of his era, Spaniards reflected on the dramatic transformation their country had undergone during his rule: Spain is solidly democratic. Francoism has lost its force even though old Francoists have suffered little persecution. The army no longer intervenes in politics. The country is more decentralized, with more power having passed to the regions. The nature of Spanish socialism has changed to the extent that most now refer to themselves as "social democrats," and the middle class is no longer hostile to Socialists.

Economically, González championed the free market, was often firm with the trade unions, and privatized some state enterprises. He made Spain look modern, and in 1995 the UN ranked Spain ninth in the world for its "quality of life." In foreign affairs, he led Spain into the EU and NATO, and he permitted the U.S. to retain its military bases in the country.

The party got a new leader in 2000: José Luis Rodríguez Zapatero, a 39-year-old lawyer from northern Castile who had won his first *Cortes* seat at age 26. Polls had indicated that his party would lose the 2004 elections, but everything changed

**Ex-President of the Government
José Maria Aznar**

in Spain on March 11, three days before the elections, when terrorist bombs in commuter trains killed 191 persons and injured more than 1,400. The conservative government's initial insistence that the Basque terrorist group, ETA, had committed the bloody act came to be perceived by many voters as deceptive and self-serving. The quickly emerging realization that the perpetrators were Islamic terrorists led some voters to blame the Aznar government's policy of supporting the U.S. war effort in Iraq, which had been very unpopular in Spain, for allegedly bringing their country into the gun sights of fanatic religious killers. Zapatero had pledged to withdraw the 1,300 Spanish troops from Iraq, a promise that three-fourths of Spaniards favored.

A traumatized people, which gathered in the streets by the millions to protest against terrorism, decided in record time to vote against the conservative government, whose leader's authoritarian and divisive style was increasingly resented. Voter turnout increased dramatically from 69% in 2000 to 77% in 2004. In a poll, 86% of respondents expressed the belief that the terrorist attacks had influenced the results, and 20% said they had galvanized them to vote. The Socialists were reelected in March 2008, climbing to 43.64% of the votes (up from 42.6%) and 169 seats (up from 164). Turnout was 75%. They still fell short of an absolute majority and had to turn to regional parties to put them over the top.

In 2008 those regional parties won 25 seats in the *Cortes* (down from 33), and

they lost a quarter of their support. The Basque Nationalists (PNV/EAJ) won 1.2% of the votes and six seats. Navarre Yes (including Basque Solidarity—EA) got .25% and one seat. Convergence and Union (in Catalonia) won 3% and 10 seats, while the Republican Left of Catalonia captured 1.17% and three seats. The center-right Canary Coalition (CC) won .65% and two seats, and the left-wing Galicia Nationalist Bloc (BNG) received .82% and two seats. Finally Union, Progress and Democracy scraped together 1.2% and one seat. Imagine having to sort through these minuscule parties to form a majority.

The Communists

The other party with deep historical roots is the Spanish Communist Party (PCE). Founded in 1920, it was heavily involved in the Spanish Civil War on the Republican side. The Communists worked closely with the Soviet Union's participants in the civil war. This collaboration was too close and gave Spanish Communists a clear look at Marxist–Leninist practices. This fact helps to explain why the exiled party was the first communist party in Europe to reject the Soviet model of communism and the notion of the dictatorship of the proletariat. It condemned the Warsaw Pact invasion of Czechoslovakia in 1968, as well as similar actions against Afghanistan and Poland in 1979 and 1981. In 1977 former party chief Santiago Carrillo published a book, Eurocommunism and the State, in which he repeated his contention that the Soviet model had so discredited itself that it was beyond rescue. The party continues this moderate, independent course.

The party's operations within Spain began again long before the death of Franco. It built up party cells in the factories, neighborhoods, youth groups, hospitals and even in the government ministries. It is still the most disciplined and best organized mass party in Spain, despite factional splits. The working class provides 80% of its voters, who are predominantly male. Its strongest areas are in the industrialized zones of Madrid and Catalonia.

Despite its turn from Stalinism and despite its pragmatic approach and support for the democratic regime, it had little electoral success. In the 1979 national parliamentary elections, it received only about 10% of the votes, and it has declined steadily ever since. Combining forces with other elements of the old Marxist left under the banner, United Left (IU), it and its allies lost a quarter of their voters and managed to garner only 3.8% of the votes in 2008 and two seats (down from five).

It has become almost irrelevant in Spanish politics. While its cells are well entrenched in numerous organizations in the country, it lacks popular support. Its membership had fallen to about 62,000 from its peak of 200,000 in 1978. Although it is supported by the Workers' Commissions, this most powerful trade union federation is losing ground to the Socialist-dominated UGT.

Some Spanish are still aware of the remorseless and cunning tactics that the Communists used during the civil war to gain control over Socialists and leftist Republicans. Their heavy–handedness caused many Spanish to forget their more moderate actions during the Popular Front days before the outbreak of hostilities. Although the PCE now advocates a "peaceful road to socialism," there are several other ultra-left and violent groups in Spain that call themselves "communist." They therefore help keep alive the inclination of many Spaniards to associate communism with unrest and violence.

The hardest nut for the splintered PCE to crack is the presence of an attractive Socialist Party for Spanish voters who want a moderate, democratic leftist-oriented party. In fact, the Communist Party faces a dilemma: it knows that no party in Spain has a chance without a democratic program and policy. But the more the PCE moderates itself and embraces democracy, the more it becomes indistinguishable from the PSOE. Thus, there is little reason to vote for the PCE, which has become politically marginalized.

The Political Right

The existence of two parties on the political left which could together capture about half of the votes presented a serious challenge to the more conservative political forces. The die–hard supporters of the Franco dictatorship had to learn through stinging electoral defeats that Francoism could not survive in Spain without *El Caudillo* himself.

The two dominant parties in Spain today—the PSOE and the People's Party (PP, until 1989 called the Popular Alliance or AP)—support the democratic order; this makes the present political situation far different from the early 1930s. Indeed, the emergence of a basically two–party system strengthens Spanish democracy.

The most conservative of the major parties, the People's Party, was refounded, renamed and revamped in 1989. At first it thought it could win votes by hammering against crime and the alleged Marxist danger and thereby polarizing the society. Young thugs identifying themselves as AP adherents roamed the streets with sticks and bicycle chains attacking persons wearing Socialist badges. The result was a miserable showing in the 1977 elections.

In post–Franco Spain, the word "right" is still a red flag for many voters, who want to see any conservative policies advocated from the center–right. The party decided to move closer to the political center and to draw a clear line between itself and the anti–regime parties on the right. It rejects violence, supports the monarchy, advocates reforms and a "social market economy," and opposes monopolies. It seeks a broad alliance of voters.

Its former leader was Manuel Fraga Iribarne, one of Spain's most colorful politicians. Like almost all earlier leaders of the party, he was a high functionary in the earlier regime. But he became a strong proponent of parliamentary democracy. He was such a skilled and hard–hitting speaker that he even scared some people in his own party. His party became Spain's second largest political force, despite its lingering associations with the Franco era. Fraga left the national scene to become head of Galicia's regional government. This left the party free to construct a more modern alternative to the Socialist government.

The June 2005 regional elections were a cliff-hanger, as the octogenarian Fraga tried to win his fifth consecutive term as premier of Galicia. This is his and Franco's birthplace, as well as that of opposition leader Mariano Rajoy. On election night it was too close to call, and the final count had to wait a week for all émigré votes to be received and counted. In the end, Fraga and his PP fell 10,000 votes short, and the Socialists claimed victory in alliance with Galician nationalists. Fraga's defeat cut the last political tie to the Franco era.

The party was led until 2004 by José María Aznar, who was able to do what other conservative leaders had failed to accomplish: unite former Francoists, Christian Democrats, and free–market liberals. A master of consensus politics, he insists, "I am a centrist." He narrowly escaped an assassination attempt in 1995. The People's Party has the fewest members of any other major party and is well represented only in the upper civil service and the army. Its views are expressed by *La Razón*, a newspaper that few read. Most conservatives read *El Mundo*, which often supports the PP. The monarchist, conservative Madrid daily, *ABC*, is not important.

It is particularly strong in small towns and predominantly rural areas. Its chief problem was that González's pragmatic socialism left little room for a conservative party beyond tax cutting. But it benefited from his difficulties.

In the 2000 parliamentary elections a rightist party, albeit one that now calls itself the "reformist center," won an outright majority of seats in democratic elections for the first time. It captured also for the first time the majority of votes from young Spaniards and from voters in the industrial quarters in Madrid. It performed very well in the Catalonia and the Basque regions.

Approaching the 2004 elections, Aznar honored his promise to serve only two terms as president of the government. He turned over leadership of the party to his hand-picked successor, Mariano Rajoy. But because of the tragic bombings on March 11, 2004, emotional and angry Spanish voters threw out the PP government, despite the economic accomplishments which had made it the favorite for reelection. It vehemently rejects allegations that the Aznar government had deliberately sought to conceal evidence of the Islamist threat and that it had withheld information from voters to deny any link between its unpopular occupation role in Iraq and the Madrid bombings.

Post–Franco Spain has undergone three peaceful transfers of power, from the center to the left, then from the left to the right, and again back to the left in 2004; this demonstrates that democracy has come of age. In another way Aznar's government represented a *Second Transition* (the title of his 1994 book): it brought to power a new generation of leaders in their thirties and forties who were students when Franco died in 1975. The PP's leadership allayed Spanish fears that the old Francoist right would dismantle the welfare state and that fascist intolerance might return to Spain. Aznar had a strong historical motive to operate by consensus. Most of his policies—privatization of industries, full integration with NATO, and fiscal austerity to qualify for the euro—continued the Socialists' program.

Aznar benefited from a booming economy and from his brand of government that purged the authoritarian reputation that once haunted the country's conservatives. His governance did not provoke the trade unions or the students, and street violence was practically unknown on his watch. He gradually withdrew subsidies from ailing industries, privatized nearly every publicly owned enterprise, including the steel industry, which he made competitive, closed the shipyards in Cadiz, lowered top tax rates from 56% to 48% and public spending from 48% of GDP to 40%, reshaped the welfare state, loosened the rigid labor market, and balanced the budget. Under his rule, Spain was the fastest-growing large economy in Europe. His stewardship of the economy was his government's greatest gift. He strengthened the delicate consensus that has maintained stability in Spanish politics since Franco's death. Aznar directed the country's politics into the center.

Aznar challenged nationalists' hold in the regions, and his party did well in elections there. His policy was one of national

Spain

unity. He stressed that the constitution mandates that Spain remain one country. He refused to grant the Basques a referendum on self-determination or to talk to ETA terrorists until they renounce violence. He also enacted a controversial ad hoc criminal law threatening the Basque regional president if he dared conduct a referendum. He reportedly did have conversations with terrorists in the past although he did not emphasize this. Following the defeat of his party in 2004 he accepted a visiting professorship at Georgetown University in Washington D.C.

In the 2008 elections, PP raised its share of the vote from 37.6% to 40.1% and its seats from 148 to 154. Nevertheless, it fell 15 seats behind the Socialists and suffered its second defeat in a row. It remains in the opposition, and it is unclear how long the unpopular Mariano Rajoy can hold on to the party's reins.

The Military and Politics

While Spain's parties are doing much to pull Spain's democratic forces together, there are certain elements which place strains on the Spanish constitutional order: the military, regional separatists and a governmental bureaucracy in need of reform.

After Franco's death the civilians carefully removed the 40,000-man National Police from military control and gave the ministry of the interior coequal power with the military over the 75,000-man Civil Guard. The latter troops, highly efficient, proud and dressed in dull-green uniforms and black patent-leather tricorn hats, have been used since 1844 as an internal security force by the central government and under Franco as an apparatus of repression. No country can ever make an absolutely clean break with its past, and an essential fact of Spain's past is the military's arrogation to itself of special political responsibility. Every officer takes an oath "to preserve the unity of Spain," and Article 8 of the constitution names the military as ultimate arbiter of Spanish sovereignty and constitutional rights.

Most of Spain's officers are politically conservative and highly disciplined. Most will obey whoever is in power. After the inception of democracy many officers openly grumbled about the new kind of politics, which, they say, gave free rein to criminals, terrorists, opponents of a unified Spain, bickering political parties and assertive trade unions. They also resented what they saw as politically motivated military promotions and neglect of the military's needs. By the end of the 1980s only about 9% of the central government's budget was spent on defense.

Soldiers also criticized the civilian government's failure to cope with domestic

Col. Tejero brandishes a pistol on the podium of the Cortés

terrorism. These groups include the Basque separatists (ETA), a leftist–sounding GRAPO (the Spanish initials for "Groups of Antifascist Resistance First of October," which scarcely exists anymore), the rightist Apostolic Alliance and the Warriors of Christ the King. All aim to destroy confidence in the government, polarize society and (except ETA) provoke the armed forces to take over power and establish a dictatorship. Their motives are, of course, different.

The ultra-rightists want a dictatorship for its own sake, and the ultra-leftists want one as a prelude to some kind of Marxist paradise. It cannot be denied that these terrorists know their country's history very well. Domestic violence has time and again destroyed the constitutional order and provoked the establishment of dictatorships to restore order. Fortunately none of these groups, except ETA, poses a serious threat to Spain today. The chief terrorist threat to Spain now comes from radical Islamic groups.

The 1981 Attempted Coup

One event especially showed that the essential political issues of parliamentary supremacy and civilian control over the military had not yet been entirely solved within the first decade after the restoration of democracy. On February 23, 1981, only three weeks after President of the Government Suárez had announced his resignation thereby plunging Spain into a parliamentary crisis, a colonel in the Civil Guard, Antonio Tejero Molina, led 200 guardsmen into the ornate Chamber of Deputies and held the parliament and the

cabinet hostage for 18 hours. It was the most outrageous event in the *Cortes* since 1874, when General Manuel Pavia rode his horse up the steps of the parliament building and dismissed the horrified deputies.

The intruders roughed up Deputy President of the Government Manuel Gutierrez Mellado, a liberal general in the army and unleashed bursts of machine gun fire toward the ceiling, forcing most deputies to take cover under their desks. Since the plotters forgot that the session was being televised, Spaniards outside the *Cortes* were able to witness the shameful spectacle. Tejero had received a slap on the wrist only a year earlier for his part in a harebrained plot to kidnap the cabinet, and he was not acting alone. Other officers were also involved. The regional commander in Valencia put his troops on alert and sent his tanks into the streets, and all but two of the nine regional commanders hesitated to do anything while waiting to see if the coup (called *el golpe* in Spain) would succeed.

It was at this critical juncture that Juan Carlos, who had fortunately canceled a long–planned trip to the U.S. in order to be in Madrid during the political crisis, acted to save Spanish democracy. He ordered the creation of a "governmental commission" composed of ministerial undersecretaries to assume provisional civilian governmental power while the cabinet was in captivity. He skillfully turned one of the highest–ranking plotters, his military tutor in the 1950s and chief military adviser after 1975, General Alfonso Armada Comyn, away from the venture by declaring that the plotters would "have to put two bullets in me before they take over" and then dispatching the general to help suppress the uprising.

The king then turned to his many contacts within the army to assure them that he opposed the coup and would die to defend Spain's democracy. Ironically, one can thank Franco for having sent the king to the military academies and thereby having provided Juan Carlos with so many friends within the armed forces. He persuaded the officers of the elite Brunete armored division on the outskirts of Madrid to keep their tanks in the camp and out of the streets of Madrid. If the capital city had become filled with tanks, it is likely that the coup would have acquired uncontrollable momentum. The King phoned all the captains–general in the nine military districts to coax or pressure them into supporting him.

Finally, at 1:15 A.M. he went on national television, wearing a general's uniform and sitting in front of the royal coat of arms, to announce that "the crown, symbol of the permanence and unity of the nation, cannot tolerate, in any form, actions or attitudes attempting to interrupt the democratic process." This announcement was a tremendous comfort to a people that places great importance on symbols. The next morning Tejero saw that he was alone and gave up.

Spanish democracy had passed an important test. According to opinion polls, only 4% of Spaniards wanted the coup to succeed, while 76% were hostile to it. Most soldiers had supported their civilian rulers. Only hours after the abortive coup, the king met with political leaders and warned: "I invite all to reflect and reconsider postures that might lead to greater unity in Spain and more agreement among the Spanish people."

All democratic forces thereafter had to be more cautious and to strive much harder to adopt policies and wage settlements that rest on a consensus, which would include the military. Reforms were slowed down, and a conscientious effort was made to woo the military. For the first time, the army was given an actual role in a stepped–up campaign against Basque terrorism by being deployed along the French border. The *Cortes* passed a law defining states of alarm, siege and emergency, during which times certain civil rights dealing with press freedom, search and detention could be revoked.

Spain's political leaders were faced with a dilemma as to what to do with the plotters. If they cracked down too hard, they might provoke an unfortunate military response. Spanish history clearly shows that nothing is more dangerous than a humiliated military. However, if the coup leaders were not given stiff sentences, then they might be encouraged to try again. After all, most of the key figures in the coup had been given the mildest suspended sentences for their part in earlier attempts to overthrow the government.

One year after the coup attempt, 32 officers and one civilian were brought to trial before a military tribunal. In the closing statements no defendant showed the slightest regret or guilt for his actions, and instead all stressed their love for Spain, their honor as officers and their wish to save the motherland. Tejero probably best expressed the standpoint of a person who learns nothing and understands even less: "I would like to express my utter contempt for those high–ranking officers who have betrayed their motherland." He and the other major conspirator, General Milan del Bosch, were sentenced to 30 years in jail.

The potential strength of the far right was also demonstrated at the time by the *Fuerza Nueva* ("New Force"), which had wanted to turn back the wheel of history. Although this and other ultraright groups never got many votes, they were visible and audible. The leader was Blas Piñar, a highly skilled demagogue who was at his best in rallies complete with outstretched arms giving the fascist salute, fascist paraphernalia everywhere, and the sounds of Franco's hymn, "Cara al Sol" (Face the Sun) blaring in the background. At one time this group could mobilize 300,000 Spaniards in the streets of Madrid every November to honor their dead idol, and their bullies roamed the streets menacingly. The *Fuerza Nueva* idolized the military, especially those soldiers who seized the *Cortes* in 1981, and it promised to help establish a "free Spain." Few Spaniards cared much for its notion of freedom. It disappeared because it had been ignored by those it had hoped to protect: the Church, conservatives and the military.

Spaniards protest by the millions against terrorism

Spain

González bent over backwards to quiet the soldiers' nerves. Shortly after assuming office, he visited the crack Brunete armored division, which had been deeply implicated in the 1981 plot. He picked up on the initiatives of his predecessor to modernize the army by streamlining and professionalizing it and by giving it better equipment. In 1983 the government moved to tighten control over the military by appointing a single chief of defense responsible to the defense minister. It moved the Brunete armored division to Extremadura on the Portuguese border.

It reduced the number and rank of Spain's most senior officers. In 1985 the defense minister abolished the guarantee that every officer would be promoted at least to the rank of brigadier general before retirement. But he had to concede the right that all would be made colonels, a policy unheard of in any other western army. In 1989 Spain introduced promotions based on merit, and those who cannot perform satisfactorily are retired early. These were important steps toward greater professionalization.

Spain has come a long way since the 1981 plot, but the military's history of intervening in political disputes continues to cast a shadow. In January 2006 the supreme commander of the country's ground forces, General José Mena Aguado, expressed his concern about increasing Catalan autonomy. He cited Article 8 of the Constitution, which establishes that the armed forces are responsible for defending the country's "territorial integrity" and "the constitutional order." "It is our obligation to warn that there could be serious consequences for the armed forces as an institution." He hinted that other soldiers shared his views.

The government's reaction to these impermissible comments was swift and firm. He was placed under house arrest, relieved of his command, and retired early from the army. An army captain who published similar opinions in *Melilla Hoy* was disciplined by his superiors and admitted afterwards that his chances for promotion were doomed.

Terrorism

Spain has known terrorist violence by radical Basque separatists for decades, and that form of violence has not disappeared. But the variety that poses the most danger to Spaniards today is Islamic radicalism, stemming particularly from Morocco, with which Spain has had troubled relations over the years. Al-Qaeda inspiration, but not direction, is apparent. Al-Qaeda has claimed many times that it seeks to reestablish "al-Andalus," the vast area of Spain the Moors ruled for 800 years until 1492.

EL PAIS
DIARIO INDEPENDIENTE DE LA MAÑANA

MIÉRCOLES 14 DE ABRIL DE 2004
Año XXIX. Número 9.813

EDICIÓN E
www.

España y varios países europeos piden a sus ciudadanos que salgan de Irak

Un portavoz de EE UU afirma que hay 40 secuestrados de 12 países

La inseguridad de Irak y la oleada de secuestros de extranjeros en los últimos días —un portavoz de EE UU en Bagdad informó ayer de que hay 40 rehenes de 12 países— ha hecho saltar las alarmas en varias cancillerías acreditadas en la capital iraquí. España, Alemania, Francia, Portugal y la República Checa han pedido a sus ciudadanos que no viajen al país árabe y que salgan todos aquellos cuya presencia no sea imprescindible. "Hay que extremar las precauciones", afirmó ayer el encargado de negocios español, Marcos Vega.

El clérigo Hazem al Arayi, al ser detenido ayer en un hotel de Bagdad. / AP

El diplomático aconsejó ayer a los residentes y periodistas españoles que, mientras dure la actual situación, "lo prudente es que se reduzca el personal al mínimo imprescindible y que quienes tengan que estar en Irak eviten desplazamientos por carretera y restrinjan sus movimientos al máximo". Francia, Alemania y Portugal fueron más lejos y recomendaron a sus ciudadanos salir de Irak.

El Gobierno francés exhortó al centenar de compatriotas que se encuentran en Irak a que abandonasen el país y pidió el aplazamiento de cualquier viaje previsto. "La situación evoluciona como lo temíamos desde el comienzo de la crisis", afirmó ayer el

RELEVO CON DOSSIERES. El presidente del Gobierno en funciones, José María Aznar, y el líder d José Luis Rodríguez Zapatero, cerraron ayer en La Moncloa, durante un desayuno, el traspaso de podere ocasión primó la cordialidad y se alcanzó un compromiso: los ministros entrantes, que previsiblemente ju cargos el domingo, recibirán informes sobre la situación en cada departamento. **Página 17 / Editorial en la**

Zapatero depende de ERC para salir investido en primera votació

Old and new President of the Government

On March 11, 2004 (referred to in Spain as 11-M), Spaniards suffered their most savage attack since the civil war from 1936–1939. About a dozen terrorists left 13 backpacks and gym bags in commuter trains as they pulled into three crowded stations, including the central Atocha station, during the morning rush hour. Each contained about 25 pounds of high explosive. The detonators were wired to cell phones, and when they rang, 10 bombs went off almost simultaneously. The force of the blasts crumpled rail cars like aluminum cans and scattered burned and twisted bodies alongside the train tracks. The ghastly result was 191 dead (47 of whom were foreigners) and over 1,400 injured, many seriously. Suddenly the Spanish had experienced the shock and the terrible confusion Americans had on 9-11. An estimated 11 million Spaniards took to the streets in cities all over Spain to show solidarity with the victims and with each other. In Madrid, 2.5 million shouted: "We were all in that train!"

Three of the bombs had failed to detonate, permitting the police to examine the cell phones and cell phone cards inside the bags and thereby trace the presumed perpetrators of the crime. Arrests were

made quickly, and on April 3 seven of the Islamist terrorists, including the cell leader, suspected of carrying out the rail bombings blew themselves up after police cornered them in a suburban Madrid apartment. The same kind of explosives was found under tracks 40 miles south of Madrid used by the country's high-speed AVE trains a couple of weeks later. Fortunately the bomb had been poorly wired, and it failed to ignite.

The investigations focused on the Moroccan Islamic Combatant Group, which was linked both to al-Qaeda and the 2003 suicide attacks against Spanish interests in Casablanca, Morocco. They revealed that the equipment and explosives used in the bombings had been financed by the sale of hashish and ecstasy. As in the U.S., there is now more cooperation among police and intelligence services, as well as with Spain's allies, to try to deal with this deadly problem.

Spanish authorities are aggressively pursuing suspected terrorists in the courts. In February 2007, a trial for 29 (seven of whom had already blown themselves up, and two had fled) began in connection with the March 11 attacks. This was the largest legal proceeding against

Spain

Spanish Autonomus Communities

terrorism to take place in Europe to date. Most were Moroccans, and all but one (the Spaniard who provided the explosives) were from North Africa or the Middle East. The trials were held in a high security building constructed for that purpose on the outskirts of Madrid.

In November 2007 the court sentenced 21 persons. Seven were acquitted, and only three were found guilty of murder. The rest were convicted of belonging to an Islamist terrorist cell. Most were angry young North Africans who had settled in Spain. They had been inspired by al-Qaeda, but they were not directed by it. The Madrid bombings had changed Spanish politics by opening up a rift between left and right over who ordered the attacks and how to counter terrorism in general. The court concluded that ETA had not been involved, thereby taking some of the wind out of a popular conspiracy theory propagated by the People's Party.

Since the Madrid bombings, police are very aggressive in breaking up suspected Islamist plots. Police arrested 11 men on charges of belonging to a group that recruits people to carry out suicide attacks in Iraq. They arrested five men on suspicion of planning to bomb the country's High Court and Real Madrid's Bernabeu soccer stadium. They disrupted a plot by a cell of Islamic radicals to blow up the headquarters for the country's top antiter-

rorism investigators and judges. They uncovered a Pakistani cell suspected of planning an attack in Barcelona. In January 2008 they apprehended 14 men (12 Pakistanis and two Indians) on suspicion of planning a suicide attack on Barcelona's public transportation system. Laws in place to deal with Basque terror allow the state to imprison terrorist suspects for up to four years without trial.

The picture that emerged was a complicated and mixed one; the Madrid conspiracy was wider and more destructive than previously suspected. Most suspects were Moroccan, but some come from elsewhere, such as the local leader of the cell responsible for March 11. He was Tunisian and was a successful real estate agent before turning radical. A few were native Spaniards, such as the miner who provided the explosives for the March 11 bombings. Some were radicalized Muslims while others are common criminals. Based on a two-year investigation, authorities concluded in 2006 that ETA played no role in the Madrid bombings and that while the terrorist threat is homegrown, a major inspiration was the Iraq and Afghanistan wars even though the al-Qaeda cells were well established in Spain long before the conflicts and took part in the planning of the September 11, 2001, attacks in New York and Washington. In 2004-05 Spain began trying 22 Spain-

based Muslims charged with providing logistical support to the September 11 killers. Authorities have arrested hundreds of Islamic terror suspects since the 2001 attacks in America.

The authorities consider organized crime to be as big a threat as terrorism and are particularly worried about its ability to corrupt local politicians, judges and police officers. They are detaining Mafia bosses of diverse origin, including eastern Europe. Spain is determined to crack down on crime syndicates that have flocked to the Mediterranean coast to launder money through the booming construction and real estate businesses.

Spain faces the problem of how to deal with attacks in the future. The dangers make their dealing with the country's 600,000 Muslims (more than a half million of whom are legal Moroccan residents) more difficult. Even though a 2007 poll revealed that only 16% of them thought that suicide bombing was often or sometimes justified, the question remains: how would they affect Spain's immigrant population of 4.5 million (10% of the population—higher than in France, the UK or Germany—and half of them undocumented) and the growing hostility toward foreigners within its borders? Polls in 2004 indicated that a majority of Spaniards thought there were too many foreigners in the country. How can authorities prevent Islamic militants from operating out of the many tiny, makeshift mosques without violating the country's freedom of religion? How do the dangers affect relations with Europe and the Middle East? Many cities have toned down their traditional festivals that for three centuries celebrated the expulsion of the Muslim rulers by staging provocative mock battles between Christians and Moors and by destroying effigies of Mohammed.

Regionalization and Decentralization

A second element that places a heavy strain on the democratic regime is the attempt to decentralize Spanish government and to grant a satisfactory measure of autonomy to the regions. For reasons related to the Moslem conquest, the prolonged expulsion of them and the vast overextension of imperial power, Spain was never a fully integrated country. This is true of many other European countries. Madrid is in the middle and is therefore a logical site for the capital. It is surrounded like a bull's-eye by the harsh, sparsely-populated, mainly Castilian Meseta. Around this tableland is the more densely populated and highly diverse periphery.

Tension between the center and the periphery has been a constant factor in politics. Even today, a fourth of all citizens speak another language in addition to

371

Spain

Castilian Spanish. There are economic disparities. For example, Catalonia, the Basque area and Madrid produce half of Spain's GDP, while almost half the population in Galicia and a third in Extremadura and Castile still work on the land, compared to only 6% in Catalonia and the Basque region. New industries and tourism have helped narrow the gap between these rich and poor regions.

Most Spaniards note regional idiosyncrasies, and many clichés are current: Cordobans are stoic; Galicians are stubborn and moody; Catalans and Valencians are artistic and entrepreneurial; Andalusians are a bit wild and Moorish; and Castilians are austere and noble. Yet all benefit from being a part of the larger Spanish economy and are held together by such strong common interests that no region would vote for secession.

The regions particularly were suppressed under Franco, who in part justified his military coup and subsequent rule as the preservation of unity. Franco gained the lasting hatred of the Basques after ordering the devastating bombing of Guernica on April 26, 1937. This situation did not change immediately after Franco's death, and in the Basque country there were some regrettable incidents involving the suppression of cultural events. But in modern Spanish history transitions to greater freedom and democracy were always accompanied by demands for more home rule in the regions, and the post–Franco era was no exception. Fortunately the new leaders had pluralist political sentiments and were therefore willing to make many compromises.

Spain introduced, in 1979, the most ambitious plan to decentralize political power since the foundation of the Federal Republic of Germany in 1949. It has already become one of Europe's most decentralized states. Between 1994 and 2000, the central government shed 45,000 employees, and the regions gained 235,000 more. There are 17 autonomous regions, each with its own government and parliament, though with differing degrees of power. They have almost total responsibility for health and education. Basques and Catalans have their own police forces and civil law. The Basque country and Navarra collect their own taxes and pay Madrid for the services they receive. Other regions live on funds and grants from Madrid. Regional governments and local governments dispense three-fourths of all public spending. The regions' share had by 2007 grown to 36% after the central government had devolved responsibility for housing, education and healthcare. About a third of the income tax collected in the regions returns to them. There is still constant controversy between the center and the regions over the funding of public services.

Ultimately Spain is to have a fully federal system, with the central government reserving for itself the exclusive right to conduct foreign, defense, monetary, customs and strategic industrial policy, as well as full responsibility over the national police and criminal law. Health, welfare, local administration, local roads, and education were gradually transferred to the regions, but that transfer varies in degree and was still incomplete as Spain entered the new century. The central government negotiates with each of the 17 regions on the powers that should be granted to each. The *Cortes* vets all charters and usually waters them down. No charter gives a region the right of secession, and references to nations are carefully worded. For instance, Andalusia is a "nationality," not a "nation." The Catalans' charter states that they consider their region a nation, but the rest of Spain does not. The system has to be renegotiated between the regions and Madrid every five years.

Since the death of Franco, regional languages and history has been emphasized. Madrid was forced to back down in 1997 when a committee of experts drew up a list of 100 teaching points to be used in history classes all over Spain. Regional minorities, especially in Catalonia and the Basque area, considered the idea that Spain had a unified history to be reactionary and intolerable. However, the question was not put to rest. Government education officials in Madrid argued in 2000 that Castile should regain its place at the heart of Spanish history and as the source of the country's main language. The central government has the ultimate authority to inspect and supervise schools although the regions have input. Regions establish a large part of the curriculum and approve textbooks before they are published. The result is that children learn widely varying things in different parts of the country. Aznar government also favored a return to the basics.

Relations with the demanding regions are never easy for Madrid. Four regions—Catalonia, the Basque Country, Galicia and Andalusia—have more autonomy than the others. As a price for Catalán support for the Aznar minority government in 1996, the central government agreed to increase the proportion of locally raised income taxes the Catalans may keep from 15% to 30% over five years. This percentage differs in each region, so Spain in effect has 17 different tax systems.

The Zapatero government promised to look favorably on reforms as long as they are supported by the majority of parties represented in the regional parliaments and do not violate the Spanish constitution. Zapatero rejected Catalonia's demand for a new financial agreement with the central government that would end the region's situation where it pays out more money to the rest of Spain than it takes in. The 2006 Catalan autonomy statute does allow Catalonia to keep more of the revenues it raises. He maintains that the wealthy regions must help the poorer ones. That is especially true after Spain lost most of its subsidies from the EU; some of these funds were used to finance development in poor areas.

Basque Separatism

Basque nationalism remains the Achilles heel of Spanish democracy. There are 2.2 million Basques in Spain (just 5% of the country's population) and about 200,000 in France, which declared in 1981 that it would no longer permit its territory to be used as a base for illegal operations in Spain. The relative prosperity of the Basque area had long attracted immigrants from poorer Spanish regions. The result is that half of the residents are not Basque. Only 30% of the people speak Basque.

An ancient people of obscure origins and speaking a language which is unrelated to any language of Europe and which almost no outsiders speak, the Basques have always been sharply aware of their separate identity. This awareness was greatly enhanced by the suppression of things Basque during the Franco era. People were forced to adopt Spanish names, and local administration and police work was placed in the hands of non–Basques who had no comprehension or sympathy with the local language or culture.

Acting more like an army of occupation than a protector of public safety, the Civil Guard antagonized the local population to such an extent that the latter could not help sympathizing with a group of Basque nationalists and student activists that took shape in 1952 under the name of *Euskadi ta Askatasuna* ("Basque Country and Freedom," or ETA). In 1968 ETA began resorting to violence to accomplish its aims. This caused it to split into a militant, hyper–nationalist wing, called *ETA–Militar*, staffed by predominantly young, well–educated Basques from middle- and working-class backgrounds and a more moderate wing that now disavows violence. Since 1968 ETA was directly responsible for 812 deaths by May 2003, when the organization stopped its frenzied killing. In the next four years it killed "only" four persons.

ETA–Militar reportedly received training and material support from Libya, Cuba, Yemen and from Palestinian terrorist organizations. It was closely linked to the only Basque party that opposed regional autonomy in 1980, *Herri Batasuna* ("Popular Unity"), renamed *Euskal Herritarok* (EH) in 1998. Both organizations demand a revision of the Spanish constitution that would be a prelude for an independent *Euskadi*, based on the right of self–determination. Only a third of Basque voters had supported Spain's new constitution in 1978. That document declares Spain's unity to be forever indivisible, and most parties outside of the Basque region consider that wording to preclude any form of referendum on self-determination. However, that is precisely what all Basque nationalists, including the majority that renounces violence, demand. Opponents retort that any tampering with that clause would lead quickly to the dissolution of Spain.

Short of amending the constitution, there is little else Madrid can offer Basques. They already have wide autonomy, a parliament, the power to raise taxes, control over most aspects of education, health, transport, and local police (although anti-terrorism is a federal matter). Nor are Basques the victims of discrimination. In fact, the reverse is more likely correct. They man the police force and otherwise have good jobs. Their language is spreading and is used in the schools.

EH gave signals that it would like to negotiate with the Spanish government in order to escape from the cycle of violence. But until 1998 the government refused publicly to enter into such negotiations. The other radical nationalist coalition in *Euskadi*, the more moderate *Euskadiko Ezkerra* ("Basque Left"), fused with the Basque Communist Party and publicly disavowed violence.

The major political force in *Euskadi* is the more conservative Basque Nationalist Party (PNV), formerly led by Josu Jon Imaz. He spoke of creating a civic society for all Basques, not an ethnic one, condemned ETA and ruled out pacts with Batasuna. By 2008 it had dominated Basque politics for three decades. It is rural, conservative and Catholic. A party calling itself *Eusko Alkartasuna* (EA) broke away from PNV, thereby dividing the moderate Basques. The Basque subsidiary of the Socialist party is the *Partido Socialista de Euskadi* (PSE), which regards itself as progressive, modern, and secular; it appeals mainly to non-nationalists. The PSE is not to be confused with the *Abertzale Sozialistak* (AS), which the Spanish Supreme Court declared in May 2007 to be front group for the outlawed Batasuna. There is a Basque branch of the People's Party. More and more Basques are political moderates. They are no longer so afraid to speak out against ETA.

EL PAIS

DIARIO INDEPENDIENTE DE LA MAÑANA

JUEVES 23 DE MARZO DE 2006
Año XXXI. Número 10.516

EDICIÓN EUROPA
www.elpais.es

LA BANDA AFIRMA QUE "LA SUPERACIÓN DEL CONFLICTO, AQUÍ Y AHORA, ES POSIBLE"

ETA anuncia un "alto el fuego permanente"

Zapatero pide prudencia y serenidad para un proceso "largo y difícil" al que convoca a todos los partidos políticos

ETA declaró ayer un "alto el fuego permanente" que entrará en vigor mañana, según un escueto comunicado en el que la banda concluye: "La superación del conflicto, aquí y ahora, es posible". El presi-

dente, José Luis Rodríguez Zapatero, pidió "responsabilidad, prudencia y serenidad" ante un proceso que se anuncia "largo y difícil", para el que convocó a todos los partidos. "Hasta ahora nos unía el

espanto del horror; confío en que ahora nos una la esperanza", declaró Zapatero, quien hizo en el Congreso una apelación al PP y a su líder, Mariano Rajoy: "Nos han separado muchas cosas, pero sé que

ustedes también desean la paz. Tenemos que recorrer juntos este camino". Rajoy lamentó que el alto el fuego anunciado sea sólo "una pausa" de ETA y no la "disolución" definitiva de la banda.

La banda terrorista, que ha cometido 817 asesinatos en los últimos 36 años, anunció el alto el fuego en un vídeo remitido a la televisión pública vasca. En él, una terrorista encapuchada, escoltada por otros dos miembros de ETA, lee un comunicado en el que explica las intenciones de la banda: "Impulsar un proceso democrático en Euskal Herria para construir un nuevo marco en el que sean reconocidos los derechos que como pueblo nos corresponden (...). La decisión que los ciudadanos vascos adoptemos sobre nuestro futuro deberá ser respetada". En el comunicado no hay ninguna referencia a la violencia callejera ni a la extorsión de los empresarios.

La tregua de ETA llega tras 1.028 días sin muertos en atentado. En los últimos meses, Zapatero ha reiterado su confianza en que se acercaba "el principio del fin" de la banda. En agosto de 2004, cuatro meses después de asumir el poder, el presidente recibió una carta en la que ETA le pedía establecer una comunicación con su Gobierno. Fue el arranque del actual proceso.

Zapatero anunció que se tomará tiempo para analizar si "se dan las condiciones para pedir el aval del Congreso ante un posible diálogo" con ETA. Rajoy le ofreció su apoyo siempre que no se pague un precio político y las fuerzas y cuerpos de Seguridad y los jueces sigan actuando contra los terroristas.   **Páginas 15 a 31**

Rajoy minusvalora la tregua porque es sólo "una pausa" ● El presidente del Gobierno recibió la primera carta de la organización terrorista en agosto de 2004 ● La sociedad vasca acoge la noticia con esperanza y cautela ● París, Londres y Washington hablan de "paso decisivo" para la paz

Tres terroristas de ETA anuncian el "alto el fuego permanente" en un vídeo remitido a la televisión pública vasca. / AP

La UE busca una política energética común pese a sus divisiones internas

Los jefes de Estado y de Gobierno de la UE debaten desde hoy en Bruselas la puesta en marcha de una política europea de energía. Los Veinticinco están divididos sobre las ofertas de compra de firmas del sector y las medidas adoptadas por los Gobiernos para proteger su mercado nacional. INTERNACIONAL. **Páginas 2 y 3**

CAROD descarta que ERC vote 'no' en el referéndum sobre el Estatuto de Cataluña. ESPAÑA. **Página 32**

CUATRO AÑOS de cárcel para el dueño de un bar de Barcelona por exceso de ruido. SOCIEDAD. **Página 35**

ARQUITECTOS DE ÉLITE debaten en Barcelona sobre la construcción del entorno. CULTURA. **Página 40**

The central government has recognized their specific needs by granting Basques the right to raise their own taxes and pay none to the federal treasury, as well as to form an all–Basque police force of 6,000 to replace the Civil Guards and national police. Schools, roads, courts and police are all run by the Basques themselves. There are three types of schooling available: in Spanish, Basque, or a mixture of both languages. Fewer than 15% of the schools teach only in Spanish. The predominance of Basque (*Euskerra*) was shown in 2008 when regional education authorities turned down free copies of Al Gore's film, "An Inconvenient Truth," because it had not been translated into Basque. A 2000 poll determined that almost two-thirds of Basques feel both Basque and Spanish. A groundswell of opinion sees violence as futile and profoundly damaging to the Basque economy. ETA and EH supporters came to realize that their extremism was so unpopular that it undermined their cause.

The autonomy measures cut into public support for the separatist alternative. Also, the antiterrorist campaign by the Spanish police increased French cooperation, and disillusionment among many Basques with the brutality shown by ETA reduced the number of terrorist attacks and paved the way to temporary ceasefires in 1998 and March 2006. Spaniards were greatly relieved that ETA terrorists had not disrupted the Barcelona Olympics in 1992. Prior to the games the Spanish and French authorities had launched a determined campaign against ETA.

In 1992 ETA's top leaders were arrested, but authorities found the organization to be more complex than had previously been imagined. It still remains a mystery. Its fighters were equipped with advanced technology, weapons, lots of money, and a back–up leadership ready to take over in case the top members were arrested, as was the case. ETA traditionally based its command and support structures in southwest France. There its armed units

Spain

were equipped and trained and then sent across the border into Spain to make its bloody strikes. In October 2004 joint Spanish-French operations bagged 21 ETA members, including its political leader Mikel Albizu Iriarte, in southwestern France, and in May 2005 three more were apprehended.

As ETA became more isolated, it attacked higher–profile targets. In 1995 José María Aznar, who was president of the government from 1996 to 2004, barely escaped death when a car bomb went off near his home. ETA also failed in an attempt to assassinate King Juan Carlos in 1995. A year later the mastermind of this abortive plot, Julián Atxurra Egurola, was arrested in France, whose three southwest departments, together with the four northern Spanish regions, the Basque terrorists claim for the independent Basque country they dream of. The house in which Egurola was captured was a true arsenal, containing explosives, timers, grenade launchers, antitank rockets, machine guns, pistols and ammunition.

The 1997 killing of a town councilor, Miguel Ángel Blanco, from the ruling People's Party wiped out any remaining support for *Herri Batasuna* outside the Basque area and caused revulsion across Europe and massive protests throughout Spain. In December the entire 23–member leadership of *Herri Batasuna* was sentenced to seven years in prison for helping ETA guerrillas. Losing support steadily, the ETA declared a temporary ceasefire in 1998 to enable it to regroup.

Aznar stuck to his government's policy of seeking a political solution to the problem, while continuing to rule out the Basque nationalists' long-standing demand for a "right to self-determination"

to be expressed in a referendum. This would require an alteration of the 1978 constitution that declares Spain to be indissoluble.

The government released more than 130 Basque prisoners and transferred dozens more to jails closer to their families in the Basque region. But this was not enough for ETA, which ended its 14-month truce in December 1999. This sparked protest marches and condemnations throughout both the region and Spain involving the mainstream Basque Nationalist Party, the PP and other parties. Aznar concluded that the cease-fire had been a ruse to give ETA guerrillas a breathing space.

The September 11, 2001, terrorist attacks were a shock to Spaniards and created more backing for the president of the government's tough stand against ETA. The government reacted by arresting many al-Qaeda suspects, sharing intelligence with the U.S. and other allies, and cooperating with police authorities in France and elsewhere. The Americans responded by putting 21 ETA names on their "wanted" list. A series of ETA attacks in 2002 persuaded Aznar that it was time to outlaw its political arm, Batasuna, and the *Cortes* approved in June 2002. The Spanish Supreme Court agreed to this in March 2003 under a new law allowing political parties to be banned if they do not condemn terrorism and if they maintain even tenuous links with terrorist groups. Two months later the United States and EU acceded to Spain's request to add Batasuna to their list of terrorist organizations. The moment Batasuna became illegal, the PNV became more radical in its objectives. Batasuna was seriously weakened by the arrests of scores of members and many top leaders and by the squeeze on its financial assets

Catalonian symbol

abroad as a result of increased international cooperation. The arrests and convictions continued in October 2007, when the Batasuna leadership was apprehended at a secret meeting, and in December 2007, when 47 Basques were sentenced for links with ETA.

In 2003 the Spanish government closed down the only newspaper printed in the Basque language, *Euskaldunon Egunkaria*, for allegedly aiding ETA. This did not dissuade the more moderate PNV regional government under Juan José Ibarretxe from guiding through a divided regional assembly in October 2003 a plan for a referendum to determine whether the Basque region should become a "free state associated with Spain." A *Euskobarómetro* poll a month later revealed that 32% of Basques favor the status quo, 31% a federal model of greater autonomy, and only 31% independence. His plan would involve its own foreign policy, separate courts, and representation in the EU. Citizens would have dual Basque-Spanish citizenship, and they would perhaps share the monarchy. It would fall far short of ETA's claims to a greater Basque state that includes the province of Navarre and part of southwest France.

Such a state was rejected by a majority of Basque voters in their April 2005 regional elections. The Socialists jumped from 13 to 18 seats in the 75-seat parliament in Vitoria. Its gains came at the expense of the PNV, which had hoped that a big win would force the Spanish government to accept its demands for an "associated free state" with Spain. The PNV and its allies who advocate independence lost a quarter of their support, sinking from 33 to 29 seats. The Communist Party of the Basque People, which had previously been a marginal group and which maintains close ties to Batasuna, won 12% of the votes and nine seats. The PP fell to third place with 15 seats.

Zapatero announced that while his government would not amend the 1978 constitution to permit secession of any part of Spain, it would be more flexible and offer Basque nationalists an alternative that would not violate the constitution but address Basques' concerns. That alternative

The sign was written in both languages—Spanish and Catalan. The Spanish was crossed out, leaving only the Catalan with the added comment: "In Catalonia, in Catalan," meaning that in Catalonia, it has to be written in Catalan

would not include independence. In May 2005 he got the *Cortes* to accept an explosive motion supporting "dialogue between the competent authority within the state and whoever decides to give up violence." The country was ready for this. The March 2004 train bombings in Madrid had eliminated most residual support for terrorist groups and reduced their political audience. The government had also come as close as is possible to defeating ETA terrorist operatives. With most of their senior commanders in jail, 700 arrests in Spain and France since 2000, and its support at home halved since the 1998 ceasefire, ETA had been greatly weakened and degraded to more an irritant than a serious security threat. This is especially true after the 2004 Madrid bombings, which strengthened public revulsion against terrorism in general.

On March 22, 2006, a woman wearing combat fatigues, a white face mask and a black beret, flanked by two similarly clad guerrillas, made a dramatic announcement in a video: ETA was prepared to shift from violence to "a democratic process in which our rights as people will be recognized." The organization declared a permanent cease-fire with the aim "to drive a democratic process in the Basque country." The Zapatero government responded cautiously but resolutely to ETA. Talks started in the summer of 2006. The opposition PP, which nearly defeated ETA while in government, accused the president of bowing to terrorism.

On December 30, 2006, whatever peace had prevailed was shattered by an ETA bombing at Madrid's Barajas Airport, which flattened a five-story parking garage and killed two Ecuadorians sleeping in their cars. This act made a mockery of Zapatero's optimism about a peace process on which he had staked so much of his political credibility. He called off the peace talks. In March 2007 the opposition PP, which had fiercely resisted every Socialist attempt to solve the Basque problem, organized a mass demonstration of several hundreds of thousands in Madrid to demand tougher government action against separatists. This coincided with the dedication of a towering monument located outside Atocha railroad station to those killed in the March 11, 2004, bombings.

Complaining that the government had not reciprocated, ETA called off its 14-month ceasefire in June 2007. There was a surge of ETA attacks in the months leading up to the March 2008 elections. Just two days before the voting, a former Socialist town councilor in the Basque country was shot to death outside his house in front of the eyes of his wife and daughter. Fearing that it might set a precedent for Basques, the Spanish government refused to recognize Kosovo's independence from Serbia in February 2008.

Catalonia

Viewed from Madrid, Catalonia appears almost as the model of civic responsibility, when compared with its Basque neighbors. It is much larger, with a population of 7.1 million; almost one-sixth of Spaniards live there. Catalans are Spain's richest and culturally most illustrious minority. The architect Antoni Gaudi, cellist Pablo Casals, and painters Joan Miró and Salvador Dalí were all from this region. Its capital, Barcelona, is one of Europe's most stylish and fun metropolises. International business surveys conducted by Cushman & Wakefield consistently rank it first in the world in terms of quality of life. It receives 20 million tourists each year. In the past its literature and language, spoken by about 4 million persons (some Catalans claim 10 million), was suppressed. Under Franco one could be put in jail for singing "El Cant dels Segadors," the Catalan national anthem.

Catalans are a pragmatic and patient people, who are inclined to wait for more promising times, rather than to revolt. As one Castilian observer noted, "the difference between the Basque and Catalan nationalists is that the Basques want to leave Spain, and the Catalans want to run it." Most Catalan nationalists do not want to secede; they want Catalonia accepted as a nation within Spain, with its own language, traditions and history. Most Catalan political parties want autonomy, not independence, with the same taxing power as the Basques now have and with their own court system. In 1992, the Olympic Games were held in Barcelona 500 years after Columbus's discovery of America. They were a source of great pride for Catalans. All events and results were announced first in the Catalan language, and then in Spanish, English and French.

Since 1979 Catalonia has had an autonomy statute similar to that of the Basque country. However, by the time it was able to manage many of its own affairs, an important change had taken place. The region's dynamic industry and commerce had attracted so many immigrants from the poorer Spanish regions that nearly half of the region's population was no longer of Catalan origin. A minority of the newcomers refused to learn the Catalan language or to adjust to the cultural tradi-

Roman bridge in Orense, Galicia

Spain

tions in the area. Some become enthusiastic Catalans. After years of teaching it in schools, almost everybody now speaks Catalan. Catalonia had a struggle to define its own identity within the Spanish nation. But by the end of the last century the Catalan language had revived remarkably. About 95% of the residents can use it. The regional government is strict in enforcing its use. In 2004 it fined the Spanish postal service 30,000 euros (then $37,500) for not having all its labels and stamps in Catalan. The 2006 autonomy statute officially makes Catalan the "preferential" language and states that it is the duty of all residents to learn it.

Barcelona's clout in Madrid was dramatically increased by the fact that both the Socialist and PP governments became dependent on the seats of the two-party alliance, Convergence and Union's (CIU), to have a majority. The skillful former leader, Jordi Pujol, had by 2000 won six regional elections by proclaiming both Catalan nationalism and loyalty to Spain. He knew how to use the CIU's leverage. With the Socialists, he negotiated a measure of fiscal autonomy for the Catalan government to keep 15% of the income tax raised in the region. In 1996 he forced the newly elected Aznar to raise that to 30% within five years. He also stepped up the campaign, supported by all parties, to make Catalan the language used in the schools. When the blockbuster film, "Harry Potter," premiered in 2001, he insisted that it be dubbed in Catalan, not in Castilian Spanish. In 2008 education authorities turn down free copies of Al Gore's film, "An Inconvenient Truth," for the schools because it was not in Catalan. Pujol kept his focus on his central ambition: a loosely federated Spain in which the King of Spain would become the "King of the Spains."

Pujol stepped down in 2003 although his party, the nationalist Convergence and Union (CIU), had come out on top in elections to the 135-seat regional assembly. The Catalan Republican Left (ERC), a leftist pro-independence party, joined the Socialists and Greens to form a governing coalition under the leadership of Pasquall Maragall. But it was shaken in 2004 when ERC leader Josep Lluis Carod-Rovira admitted that he had secretly recently met with ETA leaders.

Maragall pressed ahead with plans for a new statute recognizing the region as a nation. He got a powerful boost after the 2004 Spanish elections when the Zapatero's new Socialist government became dependent on the votes of regional parties, including those in Catalonia, to support his minority government. Zapatero agreed to respect Catalan aspirations and to support the elevation of the Catalan language to official status within the EU. However, Maragall and the ERC were furious when Spain's foreign minister asked the EU in 2004 to make Catalan, Valencian, Basque, and Galician official languages. Catalans consider Valencian to be a mere dialect of Catalan. An ERC spokesman accused the government in Madrid of "ignorance, lack of culture and bad political faith." In the end, only Catalan won EU recognition as an official regional language, along with Irish.

In June 2006 three-quarters (74%) of voters in the region approved the Catalan Statute of Autonomy, which had been approved by the *Cortes* earlier in the year. Many voters greeted the statute with a gaping yawn. In polls before the referendum, 70% admitted they knew nothing about the new charter, half said the result was of little or no concern to them, and few had read it. The low turnout of only 49% cast some doubt on its legitimacy. But the law passed nevertheless. Much of the campaign had revolved around symbolic issues, such as the right to call Catalonia a "nation," which its charter does. Article 2 of the Spanish constitution already recognizes that the country contains different "nationalities."

Catalonia now has more taxing powers and pays less to Spain than it did before although it was not allowed to include a revenue-sharing formula in its new statute. It gained authority over immigration and judicial matters, but its courts cannot override Spain's highest courts. Despite its limitations, the statute could be a model for other regions, including Andalusia, Galicia, Valencia, the Balearic Islands, and the Basque area. However, it was fiercely resisted by the opposition PP and was unpopular elsewhere in Spain. Parts of it might be struck down by the constitutional court.

Ironically, the debate over the statute led to the breakup of the Catalan regional government and prompted early regional elections in November 2006. Although the CIU won the most seats, Catalonia got a new coalition government composed of three left-wing parties, led by the Socialists.

Catalonia is booming economically, and its seven million people generate 20% of Spain's GDP. Pujol's favorite statistics were that Catalonia has 6% of Spain's territory, 13% of its population, 25% of its exports, and 38% of its industrial exports. Barcelona is still Spain's industrial heart. Foreign investment pours in. Catalonia receives $50 million each year in EU grants and since 2006 is authorized to negotiate directly with the EU on matters affecting the region. It has its own seat in such international bodies as UNESCO.

Other Regions

The other Spanish regions are also making their way toward one form of autonomy or the other. About half the inhabitants of País Valencia (the provinces of Valencia, Castellón and Alicante) speak Valencian, which is related to but not the same as Catalan. However, the majority is in favor of autonomy, while remaining consciously within the Catalan cultural community, which also embraces the Balearic Islands, Andorra and Roussillon in France.

Spain's largest region, Andalusia, approved its autonomous statute in 1981, and voters in a 2007 referendum approved a revised charter that calls their people a "nationality." It is one of Spain's poorest regions, with an illiteracy rate estimated at 30%, but accounting for half of Spain's population growth. It needs all the financial assistance it can get from the wealthier regions and the EU.

In order to stimulate the region's economy and build up its infrastructure, its capital, Seville, hosted "Expo 92," 500 years since Columbus set foot on Santo Domingo. Visitors saw the pavilions around the 15th–century Santa María de la Cuevas, where Columbus planned his last voyage to America and where he is buried. His voyages were retraced by reproductions of the Niña and Pinta and two of the Santa María, which sailed to San Salvador and New York, where three of the ships will remain as part of the Metropolitan Museum's permanent collection. The second Santa María proceeded through the Panama Canal and on to Japan, where Columbus had hoped to arrive.

In Galicia, 28.4% of eligible voters went to the polls to approve overwhelmingly its autonomy statute. Aragón, Asturias and other regions are also moving toward limited self–government. In the Canary Islands the separatist Union of the Canary People demands self–determination for the islands and the removal of the Spanish army.

Source: *The Economist*

Bureaucracy Reform

A third major problem facing Spain was to reform the bureaucracy while maintaining a reasonable level of services. Large numbers of state employees had some trouble adjusting to the new democratic environment, where public servants are really expected to serve the public. Many functionaries long regarded their positions as practically their own property, and many old usages have persisted, such as the right of each department to collect fees for the services it performs. Also, financial inspectors expected to receive a percentage of the taxes they collected.

Each department still has a strong sense of self–interest and internal loyalty that often takes priority over serving the public. They are often inefficient and excruciatingly slow, especially when it comes to paying money they owe. They are also greatly overstaffed. This was made worse by such measures as the requirement that the government bureaucracy absorb 35,000 members of Franco's disbanded *sindicatos*, or state–controlled unions. Work had to be created for this vast unproductive group, and there was understandably lots of sitting or standing around in many of the departments.

González moved quickly to create the kind of civil service appropriate to a democratic and modern Spanish state. His government began immediately to enforce the conflict–of–interest law passed by the *Cortes* in 1982. Civil servants, cabinet ministers, members of parliament and top executives of state companies are allowed to have only one job and one salary. Civil servants, who had become accustomed to a 26- to 28–hour work week, are required to be at work at 8 A.M. and to work eight and one–half hours, with a half-hour lunch break. Also, the first Spanish ombudsman was appointed, with the task of looking into complaints of abuses and neglects inflicted on the people by ministers, administrative authorities or public servants.

In 2006 the Zapatero government abolished the mid-afternoon two-hour lunch break for civil servants by limiting lunch to one hour beginning at noon. The aim is to stop the practice of pushing the workday into night and keeping parents away from their families. It is hoped that the private sector will follow suit. Already some large firms, like Coca-Cola and Ibérica, have decreed 45-minute lunch breaks and clock off at 6 PM. But the private sector is slow to change the traditional siesta. Spain still has the longest working hours in Europe.

FOREIGN AND DEFENSE POLICY

Franco's death enabled Spain to modify its course in foreign policy. In February 1976 Spain relinquished Spanish Sahara, with its rich phosphate deposits, to Morocco and Mauritania, with the hope that the inhabitants could determine their own future. Algeria greatly resented this solution, and a bloody struggle occurred over control of this colony. Morocco simply annexed the former colony.

The major change in Spain's foreign policy, however, was that it turned its primary attention toward Europe. Spain was the only country in western Europe that did not belong either to the EU, EFTA or NATO. It had been permitted to join the UN in 1950 and eventually became a member of virtually all world bodies.

Latin America

Spain's entry into western Europe signaled certain other foreign policy changes. Franco established a special relationship with Latin America, where there were many authoritarian regimes similar to his own. Now Spaniards openly condemn most Latin American dictatorships. The King left no doubt when he was awarded a prize in Germany for his work toward European unity that although Spain is rooted in Europe, it is also a part of the Hispanic world. Spain's policy during the Falkland Islands conflict underscored this fact.

The earlier Socialist government showed its special interest in helping to bring about peace talks in Central America, if Spain had been asked to do so. During a visit to Cuba in 1986, Cuban leader, Fidel Castro, referred to González as "dear friend Felipe" and pinned Cuba's highest distinction, the order of José Martí, on his lapel. In the mid-1990s Spain became the leading investor and a key western economic and diplomatic intermediary for Cuba, which,

EL PAIS

DIARIO INDEPENDIENTE DE LA MAÑANA

DOMINGO 25 DE ABRIL DE 2004
Año XXIX. Número 9.824

EDICIÓN EUROPA
www.elpais.es

President Zapatero meets Moroccan King Mohamed VI in Casablanca

Spain

unlike the Philippines, still exerts an emotional pull on Spaniards. Relations cooled after Aznar and the PP came to power. But in 1999 King Juan Carlos became the first Spanish monarch to visit Cuba, joining the leaders of 14 Latin American countries and Portugal for an Ibero-American summit.

The Socialist government that came to power in March 2004 was determined to reinforce Spain's relations with Cuba. Madrid disagrees with the American embargo against Cuba, and in December 2004 it restored diplomatic relations with Cuba, followed a month later by most other major European countries. When Foreign Minister Moratinos visited Havana in 2007 without meeting with dissidents, U.S. Secretary of State Condoleezza Rice criticized him. But Moratinos insists that the Americans "should trust in a faithful, solid ally like Spain."

The Zapatero government tries to play an active role in Latin America. In March 2005 it announced plans to host a summit in Colombia of three South American leaders from Venezuela, Colombia and Brazil to forge closer cooperation against terrorism and drug trafficking. Venezuela's leader, Hugo Chávez, greeted the opportunity to have Spain as a possible ally to offset a tense relationship with the U.S. In April 2005 Spain agreed to sell Venezuela $2.3 billion in military equipment, including a dozen unarmed transport and maritime surveillance aircraft and eight patrol boats to combat smuggling. This is Spain's largest ever defense contract. Washington was not pleased and tried to block it by forbidding Spain to outfit the planes with American surveillance electronics. But Madrid announced it would get the electronics from other NATO allies and go ahead with the deal.

This sale fits Spain's policy of deliberately courting left-wing and populist regimes in Latin America. However, by 2007 it had cooled toward the mercurial Chávez as he became increasingly autocratic. It also became less supportive of Chávez's admirer in Bolivia, Evo Morales, when the latter nationalized the gas sector, in which the Spanish energy giant Repsol had major stakes.

Despite the importance that Spain places on *Hispanidad*, its growing European focus weakens its ties with Latin America. Its historical links with its colonies were severed much earlier than were those of Britain and France. Its trade with Latin America is insignificant. The major partners are Venezuela and Mexico. Spain is the leading foreign investor in Latin America after the U.S., and this is visible in Cuba, where Spanish hotels are everywhere on the island. The Spanish could never really dominate Latin America; the size of its economy is roughly the same as Brazil's and only about twice the size of Mexico's. Since 1991 both Spain and Portugal maintain formal ties with Latin America and the Caribbean through annual summits, bringing together the leaders of 21 countries and 489 million people. This is merely a forum for discussion.

In 1992, Spain had hoped to celebrate in grand style the 500th anniversary of Columbus' voyage. But it found at a meeting in Madrid of 19 presidential guests from Latin America and Portugal that the New World now has mixed feelings about that explorer who sailed under the Spanish flag.

North Africa and Spanish Enclaves

Franco had also established another special relationship with the Arab states. Until 1986 Spain did not recognize Israel, for instance. But since Franco's death the Arab states have shown little gratitude for this long–standing policy. Morocco has refused to help implement self–determination for the almost totally nomadic residents of former Spanish Sahara.

With the backing of Arab states, Morocco periodically revives its claims to Ceuta (where 15,000 out of a total population of 85,000 are Muslims, and which is located only 14 kilometers from the Spanish mainland) and Melilla (where 27,000 Moroccans and 45,000 Spaniards, including 15,000 soldiers, live). These are the remnants of a string of fortresses Spain built in North Africa after Andalusia was reconquered. These bases have lost most of their strategic importance, and the Spanish and Moroccan militaries exercise and interact with each other quite well even though Morocco has never formally recognized Spain's footholds there. There is tension between Arab residents (many of whom are illegal) and Spaniards, who show no signs of wanting to be ruled by Morocco.

In 1997, Spain fenced off the enclaves to prevent illegal immigrants from using them to gain access to Europe. The reason is that Spain's per capita GDP is 12 times higher than that of Morocco. However, these 2.5-meter high barriers were easy to overcome and did not prevent the enclaves from becoming centers for illegal immigration to southern Europe. The razor-wire barriers around Melilla were breached in October 2005 when close to 700 Africans, some of whom having trekked for two years to get there, scaled the fence in a pre-dawn rush. Surprised security officials repelled about half of them, but nine were killed, and 135 immigrants and seven police were injured. The same had happened a week earlier in Ceuta, where five were killed. Newer, higher, and more high-tech walls were built.

In February 2006 Zapatero defied decades of Moroccan warnings and made the first visit by a Spanish leader to the enclaves since 1980. The Moroccan newspaper, *Le Matin*, called it an unnecessary provocation for him to visit "the last vestiges of a colonial occupation." He wanted to reassure the two cities that Spain would defend them and their borders and be tough on immigration. But faced with imminent passage of a Catalan autonomy statute, with more to follow in other regions, he also felt a need to burnish his credentials at home as a staunch defender of the Spanish state and territorial integrity.

Although Morocco was not pleased, it is aware of the steps the Spanish leader has made to improve bilateral cooperation. Spain sent a joint peacekeeping force to Haiti in 2004, combats Islamic terrorist groups that also threaten Morocco, and helps Moroccan officials establish closer ties with the EU. They also have a 1992 agreement obligating Morocco to take back sub-Saharan Africans who try to enter the enclaves by land. That caused an international outcry in 2005 when Morocco rounded up the migrants and abandoned them several hundred kilometers in the desert without food or water.

Although Ceuta is only a 90-minute boat-ride from mainland Spain, it is a dangerous trip. In 2001 alone, about 710 persons drowned in the attempt to reach Europe from North Africa. One Moroccan association in Spain claims that about 4,000 persons perished in this way from 1997 to 2003. Arabs in the enclaves have the same rights as Spanish citizens. Muslim leaders negotiated with local Spanish officials to improve their social and political conditions, but resistance to their demands remains strong within the Spanish majority.

Perhaps in order to press its sovereignty claim over the enclaves, a group of Moroccan gendarmes occupied on July 11, 2002, the tiny, uninhabited island of Perejil (Parsley, but known in Arabic as Leila) located 200 meters off the North African coast and claimed by both Spain and Morocco. Moroccan marines quickly replaced them, and escalation followed rapidly. The Spanish government dispatched five warships, a submarine, and helicopters and other aircraft to the area and put the 7,000 troops of Spain's Foreign Legion, who defend the two enclaves, on alert. On July 17 Spanish commandos recaptured the island without firing a shot, and a Foreign Legion unit moved in to hold it.

Moroccans accused Spain of hypocrisy for demanding that Britain hand over Gibraltar while refusing to talk to them about doing the same for the enclaves. U.S. Secretary of State Colin Powell was asked to mediate the crisis. After he made an estimated three dozen phone calls to both parties, a deal was reached to return the island to its previous demilitarized status. Spanish troops left and both sides agreed not to send troops there again.

Following a post-Franco tradition, newly elected President of the Government Zapatero made his first foreign visit to Morocco in April 2004. Relations have improved markedly since he took office. He also appointed as his foreign minister Miguel Angel Moratinos, a veteran diplomat who had served for seven years as the top Middle East advisor for EU High Representative Javier Solana, himself a former Spanish Socialist foreign minister. To symbolize an improvement of relations in January 2005, King Juan Carlos made his first state visit to Morocco in more than a quarter of a century. Largely because of the proximity and near total dependence on Arab oil, Madrid is still more sensitive to Arab sentiments than are most other western European countries.

Defense Policy and NATO

Spain's strategic location brought it into an indirect relationship with NATO through a series of bilateral defense agreements with the U.S. beginning in 1953. According to the provisions of this agreement, the U.S. would provide military assistance to the Spanish armed forces in return for the right to have air bases in Torrejon and Zaragoza, a naval base in Rota, and scattered communications installations throughout the country. About 10,000 U.S. troops are stationed in Spain. The periodic renegotiation of these agreements has never been pleasant or easy.

In 1982 Spain became the first country to enter NATO since Germany did so in 1956. Although a majority within the *Cortes* approved membership, the PSOE and PCE opposed it, and public opinion polls indicated that more Spaniards were against NATO membership than for it. There is an undercurrent of neutralism in Spain. Nevertheless the earlier government pressed on without a referendum on the issue in order, in the words of the former defense minister, "to bring us back into European and democratic circles and to strengthen the democratic system in Spain."

Thus, not only would Spanish defense be boosted, but its officers would be brought into closer contact with foreign officers who are committed to democracy and civilian rule. Army officers would have to learn foreign languages, travel to other NATO countries and acquire modern military skills. They would have to accept a promotion system based not on mere seniority but on professional competence, as was already the case for young officers in the Spanish air force and navy.

Modernization is also desirable for strictly military reasons. The army is poorly equipped and has very few mobile units that are up to NATO standards. The air force is competent, but it is scarcely large enough to provide for Spain's own air defense needs. Therefore, the government decided to purchase 72 American–made F18A fighter planes. It also acquired an aircraft carrier, called the *Príncipe de Asturias*, equipped with a dozen vertical take–off Sea Harrier jets and leading a task force that will include four new anti–submarine frigates. Still, Spanish studies concluded that Spain has half the necessary capability for defending its own airspace; the U.S. provided the other half from its bases in Zaragoza and Torrejon (now vacated).

The armed forces had by 2004 been reduced to 150,700 active duty forces (95,600 army, 22,900 navy and 22,750 air force), including 3,800 women. It has a total reserve strength of 328,500. Soldiers are no longer required to perform nonmilitary duties, such as serving as chauffeur of officers' wives, doing laundry or making house repairs with the commanders taking payment on the black market. Also, serving better food lifted morale. When possible, recruits serve near their homes, and they are never posted outside of Spain. The Aznar government announced plans in 1996 to phase out conscription in favor of a smaller, better-equipped professional army, and this completed in 1998. It was to be paid for by raising defense spending from 1.5% of GDP in 1997 to over 2%, but this had actually declined to only 1.4% by 2000. Nevertheless, Spain was one of the few EU countries that was increasing its defense spending before the Socialists resumed power in 2004.

NATO also derived important advantages from Spain's entry. It is well–situated for resupply from the U.S. Spain also provides important bases and surveillance posts to protect Mediterranean and Atlantic shipping routes, and it can help deny the exit of enemy ships from the Mediterranean into the Atlantic.

In 1979 the Spanish required the U.S. to withdraw its nuclear weapons from Rota. The African Union has issued a resolution supporting independence for these enclaves, as well as for the Canary Islands. Partly for that reason, the Spanish have declared the latter to be out of bounds for NATO facilities. Spain insists that Spanish officers command all units on Spanish territory. Until January 1, 1999, Spain remained outside NATO's integrated military command structure. It is an active NATO member.

Despite his 1982 electoral rhetoric, González became more pragmatic about his party's opposition to NATO. He brought it to accept the view that Spain's democracy and political stability, as well

SÁBADO 15 DE MARZO DE 2003
Año XXVIII. Número 9.421

DIARIO INDEPENDIENTE DE LA MAÑANA

EDICIÓN EUROPA
www.elpais.es

Bush, Blair y Aznar se reúnen en Azores para sacar adelante el ultimátum a Irak

La Casa Blanca afirma que la cumbre significa el "fin de la vía diplomática"

El presidente estadounidense, George W. Bush; el primer ministro británico, Tony Blair, y el presidente del Gobierno español, José María Aznar, tienen previsto reunirse mañana en las islas portuguesas de Azores, en mitad del Atlántico, para abordar la crisis iraquí. Los tres líderes, invitados por el primer ministro portugués, Jose Manuel Durão Barroso, se verán a medio camino entre EE UU y Europa para discutir la estrategia ante la práctica imposibilidad de conseguir el apoyo del Consejo de Seguridad de Naciones Unidas.

La Casa Blanca calificó la cumbre de "esfuerzo de último minuto" en el proceso diplomático para encontrar una salida pacífica a la crisis iraquí. La asesora de Seguridad de Bush, Condoleezza Rice, lo resumió así: "Ha llegado el momento de la verdad".

Los tres copatrocinadores de la segunda resolución de Naciones Unidas, que da un ultimátum al régimen de Irak para que ofrezca garantías de desarme superiores a las certificadas por los inspectores de la ONU, han comprobado que no tienen votos suficientes

Schröder propone recortes en las ayudas sociales para salir de la crisis

El canciller alemán anunció ayer en la presentación de los presupuestos medidas "dolorosas" y recortes sociales para superar la crisis. INTERNACIONAL. Página 10
Editorial en la página 16

El embajador de España en la ONU, Inocencio Arias, ayer, en la sede de Nueva York. / REUTERS

España subordinó sus decisiones en la ONU a la "aquiescencia" de EE UU

Spain

as its commitment to Europe, would be best served if Spain remained inside of NATO. He considered it the "logical consequence" of Spain's entry into the EU, which took place on January 1, 1986.

Nevertheless, in March 1986, he fulfilled his earlier promise to allow Spaniards to express their opinion in a referendum. This was the first time that a member of either NATO or the Warsaw Pact permitted a popular vote on continued membership. Polls had indicated that a majority was against remaining in NATO. To sweeten the pill, González set terms: Spain would not join the integrated command structure, would not permit the entry or stockpiling of nuclear weapons on its territory, and would negotiate the progressive reduction of the U.S. military presence in Spain.

The results stunned many anxious observers: 52.5% voted in favor of continued membership, while fewer than 40% voted for withdrawal. An earlier opponent, Socialist Foreign Minister Javier Solana, was named NATO secretary–general in 1995. The opposition parties were left shocked and divided, while González's moderate and pragmatic brand of socialism was reinforced. More important, Spain had finally and dramatically ended centuries of isolation. No longer would the French be able to joke that Africa begins at the Pyrenees.

In 1988 González carried through with his promise to reduce American military forces in the country. No reductions were sought at Rota, which plays a key role in supporting the U.S. 6th Fleet. But the 5,000 American servicemen and 72 F16 fighters of the 401st Tactical Air Wing at Torrejon, which is located only 12 miles from Madrid and had become a convenient symbol for anti–U.S. protesters, were ordered to leave by 1991. The bilateral defense agreement in effect since 1953 was renewed in 2001 allowing full use of the naval base in Rota and the nearby Moron Air Base. Torrejon could be used for fuel stops.

Spain's government made a crucial decision during the 1991 Gulf war against Iraq to support its allies actively. Before the fighting began it sent three warships to the Persian Gulf to help enforce the UN embargo against Iraq. When the air war commenced, Spain permitted the Americans to launch B–52 bombing raids escorted by Spanish fighter planes from Moron air base near Seville, a base jointly used by both air forces. It ferried bombs to the U.S. planes and even supplied ordnance from its own stocks when the Americans ran low. At first, this was highly unnerving and unpopular in a country whose last war outside its borders was in 1898, when Cuba was lost to the Americans. However,

public opinion swung around when reports of Iraqi atrocities in Kuwait began arriving.

It was an enormous political risk for González, but it paid off handsomely. He said: "That is what allies are for," and "for the first time in modern history, Spain has stood where it should be." It marked a defining moment in Spain's effort to end its long isolation and shoulder more international responsibility. It buoyed Spanish confidence and helped sweep away memories of neutrality in the First World War and fascist sympathies in the Second.

In 1992–3 Spain again demonstrated its expanded role in international affairs and the increased professionalism of its military by deploying the Spanish Legion to war–torn Bosnia. This elite unit had been formed in 1920 as a colonial force for Africa and gained a fearsome reputation in the Civil War on Franco's side.

Spanish troops participate in the international force sent to Bosnia in 1995 to implement the peace agreement. The contingent in Bosnia (numbering 1,200 in 2004) was the largest Spanish force to be deployed outside the country since the Blue Division fought in Russia on the side of Nazi Germany. In 1996 González led an OSCE investigative team to Serbia, which ordered that the country's communist president recognize opposition victories in local elections. In 1999 Spain sent four F–18 fighter aircraft to join NATO's air war against Yugoslavia that aimed to stop ethnic cleansing in Kosovo, and it permitted American military aircraft to stopover at bases across Spain.

Public opinion was mixed concerning this action, especially after the Spanish ambassador's residence in Belgrade had been mistakenly damaged in a bombing raid. It sent peacekeeping forces to Bosnia and Kosovo. In 2004 it had 1,300 peacekeepers deployed in Kosovo. However, it was unable to bring itself to recognize Kosovo's independence from Serbia in February 2008 out of fear that Basques would see that as a precedent and push even harder for their own independence. It also offered in 2000 to provide 10% of its military personnel to a future EU rapid-reaction force. By 2004 it was already the largest contributor to the NATO Response Force (NRF) with 2,200 troops plus ships, aircraft and helicopters.

Following the September 11, 2001, terrorist attacks against the United States, Spain offered unhesitating support to its ally and sent troops to Afghanistan to participate in the peacekeeping effort after the defeat of the Taliban. In May 2003 Spaniards mourned the death of 62 of their peacekeepers on their way home after a four-month tour in Afghanistan. The 15-year-old Ukrainian Yak-42 plane, char-

tered by a NATO agency, crashed into a mountain in bad weather while trying to land in Turkey. It was the worst accident in Spanish military history.

In 2005 it had 540 troops deployed in Afghanistan but 17 died in a helicopter crash. In January 2005 NATO agreed to expand its mission in the country after Spain committed its troops to western Afghanistan. It moved almost all of its troops out of the relatively secure capital city of Kabul to set up a provincial reconstruction team (PRT) and to help protect four other PRTs operating in the area. At the end of 2004, Spain dispatched military medical teams to the Asian countries devastated by the tsunamis.

Iraq

Spain served on the UN Security Council during the Iraq war in 2003. The Spanish government and president of the government worked hard to strengthen the strategic relationship between Europe and the U.S. He opposed any signs of resurging anti-Americanism: "We don't always have to agree on everything. But I don't see what's to be gained by beating the drums every time there is a divergence." President George W. Bush appreciated this consideration. In his maiden trip to Europe as president in 2001, he made his first stop in Spain, and his description of former President of the Government Aznar was sincere: "José María is a man of principle and a man of courage."

Aznar had a dramatic opportunity to display this in the 2003 crisis in Iraq. While polls indicated that as many as 90% of his countrymen opposed war against Saddam Hussein's regime, he steadfastly supported the U.S. and UK. Although he sent no combat troops to Iraq, he dispatched 200 soldiers to help defend Turkey within the NATO framework, a hospital ship with 900 personnel on board, a frigate, an oiler, and mine-clearing and chemical weapons decontamination units. After the war he sent 1,300 troops to participate in the postwar stabilization force in Iraq although he forbade them to engage in combat missions.

Until they were ordered home by the new Socialist government in April 2004, a Spanish brigade served in a division with Ukrainian forces, led by Poland, and a Spanish officer was the deputy commander. Spain utilized its traditionally close ties with Arab nations to help mediate between the U.S. and the Arab world. Aznar emphasized his conviction that "Europe and the United States have to act together. Any weakening of the Atlantic alliance is directly opposed to Europe's interests." When France and Germany moved to block U.S. policy in Iraq, Aznar enlisted seven other like-minded European lead-

Spain

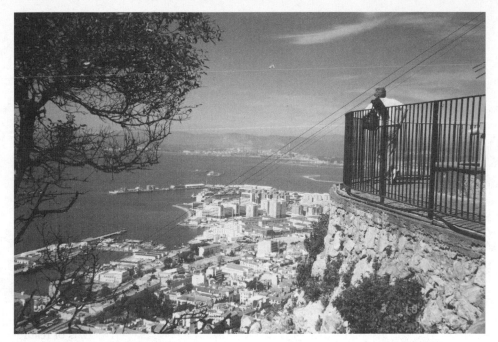

View of the port of Gibraltar   Photo by Eugenia Elseth

for president in 2004. He even offered to go to America and campaign for Kerry, who found this unusual intrusion into the domestic politics of another country embarrassing and unwelcome. President Bush showed his displeasure by refusing to accept a congratulatory call from the Spanish leader after the election.

Within 24 hours of taking office, Zapatero announced the withdrawal of Spain's 1,300 troops from Iraq. He had spoken during the campaign about such a prospect only in the event that the United Nations did not assume a leading role in the transfer of sovereignty to Iraqis. Sensitive to charges of "appeasement," he insisted that the withdrawal had nothing to do with the March 11 terrorist attacks and that Spain would continue its help to rebuild Iraq by honoring its pledges made at the Iraq donor's conference. Spain provided 20 million euros ($30 million) to help finance Iraq's successful elections on January 30, 2005. Taking a swipe at Aznar, he pledged that Spanish troops would never again be sent on foreign missions "behind the backs of its citizens."

Both Spain and the U.S. signaled their desire to normalize their relationship in June 2007, when Secretary of State Rice became the highest American official to visit Spain in three years. Although there were disagreements on how to deal with Cuba, she noted with regard to Iraq that "we had our differences. We have overcome them with Spain." Nevertheless, Zapatero is one of the few European leaders who have never visited the White House.

Gibraltar

The Spanish government also hopes that NATO membership will prepare the way for Spanish sovereignty over Gibraltar, a piece of rock three and a half square miles (6 sq. km.) in size, where a Muslim army under Tarik ibn Zeyad (thus the

ers to sign an open letter praising a strong U.S.-European relationship.

However, Aznar's deeper motives were to put an end to Spain's peripheral position in Europe and within the EU and to move it into the center of continental foreign policy, heretofore dominated by France and Germany. He saw this as a second transition in Spain following the successful transition to parliamentary democracy after Franco's death in 1975. As one of his aides put it, he hoped to make Spain "one of the few and not one of the many." He himself said: "Spain can no longer be just a nice country. It has to assume its responsibilities." The country's newly established economic strength gave the government confidence that Spain could support a more activist foreign policy and form its own alliances.

By siding with the U.S. and the UK, he furthered his twin goals of raising his country's international profile and gaining American support for his government's fight against Basque terrorists. This policy was fraught with domestic political dangers because not all Spaniards were convinced that a prominent international role is good for them. Since the civil war and Franco's military dictatorship, they are distrustful of military displays. Some were also convinced that Aznar had degraded himself to being a yes-man for the American president. There was no doubt that Spain's international stature and visibility had increased during Aznar's rule.

The Socialist victory in the March 2004 elections brought a dramatic change in Spain's foreign policy. The Socialist party

had always denounced the shift away from the large European continental powers, Germany and France, and towards the U.S. and Britain. President of the Government Zapatero reoriented the main focus of Spanish foreign policy from being a global player back toward Europe and the EU. He pledged to "return to the heart of Europe" and restore previously "magnificent" relations with France and Germany. This included accepting those countries' views on the new EU constitutional treaty. In February 2005, Spaniards were the first to hold a referendum to ratify the constitution; 77% voted in favor although only 42% turned out to cast their votes. By contrast, the French rejected it solidly in May. He emphasized that the chief goal is to forge a common EU foreign policy that can deal with the United States as an equal. "It is Europe that must have a great relationship with the United States before any individual country. That will make Europe strong."

He announced a two-track approach toward the United States. On the one hand, he tries to portray Spain as a reliable ally. Foreign Minister Moratinos said that the terror attacks in Madrid on March 11, 2004, proved that Spain "needs the United States more than ever." On the other hand, Zapatero rails against the U.S. policy in Iraq, describing it as a disaster, "neocolonial," and a "huge mistake." He accused both British Prime Minister Tony Blair and President George W. Bush of having gone to war "on the basis of lies." He suggested publicly that American voters should follow the Spaniards' example and change their leadership by supporting John Kerry

Hon. Peter Caruana

381

Spain

Arab name for the rock, *gib al–Tarik*) landed an army from North Africa in 711 to begin the conquest of Spain. England snatched the rock during the War of the Spanish Succession in 1704 and has held it ever since.

The 32,000 Gibraltarians are not of Spanish descent, although they tend to speak more Spanish among themselves than English. Their habits are more English, though. They lunch at noon, not in mid–afternoon, and eat and drink more British fare. They read English newspapers, and their currency is sterling, albeit Gibraltar sterling. They are descendants of various Mediterranean immigrants brought to Gibraltar and include Genoese, Catalans, Jews, Portuguese and Maltese. The Spanish maintain that the population is artificial and the mere remnant of a foreign naval base and is therefore not entitled to self–determination in the decolonization process. The UN has upheld this claim.

Britain, on the other hand, maintains that no change in the status of Gibraltar could be legitimate without the approval of the population. The preamble to Gibraltar's 1969 constitution reads that Britain "will never enter into arrangements under which the people of Gibraltar would pass under the sovereignty of another state against their freely and democratically expressed wishes." Gibraltarians remain ardently pro–British and profoundly suspicious of Spain. They have their own miniature Westminster–style democracy, and the attempted coup in Madrid in 1981 helped confirm their preference, expressed in a 1967 referendum, when 12,138 voted to remain British subjects; only 44 voted against it.

In 1969 Spain sealed the border between the mainland and the rock. In 1980 Britain agreed to negotiate a settlement. When Prince Charles and his bride decided to visit Gibraltar during their honeymoon cruise, Juan Carlos refused to attend the wedding in London. Also, the Falkland Islands conflict in the spring of 1982 caused further delays. Spain was the only western European land not to support the British in the crisis, and many Spanish see parallels between the Argentines' claim to the islands and the Spanish claim to Gibraltar. Nevertheless, both sides continue to profess the desire to settle their differences. During the Falklands war, Spain did prevent a number of Argentines from launching an attack on Gibraltar from Spanish territory.

Spain made a goodwill gesture in 1982 by opening the border to pedestrians. In 1985 it was opened to vehicular traffic. Britain and Spain reached an agreement in 1988 to share Gibraltar's airport although until 2006 Spain maintained re-

strictions on airlines approaching Gibraltar and denied them use of its airspace. Planes had to leave from Britain and perform dangerous approaches onto the Rock. The area is so small that its airstrip cannot accommodate large aircraft; it is also built on an isthmus that Spain does not recognize as British territory.

On a visit to London in 1991 González called Gibraltar an "anachronism" and noted that for the British, discussions with Spain about it are like an annual visit to the dentist, while for Spain it is like a permanent stone in its shoe. In 1997 Spain proposed "shared sovereignty" of the Rock. Although the British rejected it, they noted that the Spanish no longer rule out the idea of Gibraltar's independence, only that "independence will never be granted against Spanish wishes." That is not the same as insisting that the Rock must one day be Spanish.

The concept of "shared sovereignty" was central to the talks that recommenced

in 2002. It will be at the heart of any agreement even though Chief Minister Caruana, who refused an invitation to attend the talks unless he were to be granted a veto, rejects the concept, as did 99% of the rock's population (with 85% voting) in a November 2002 referendum on the single question: "Do you approve of the principle that Britain and Spain should share sovereignty over Gibraltar?" London refused to recognize this polling, which was an effort of the Gibraltar government to thwart British plans for a compromise with Spain. It complicates the British government's effort to settle this lingering sore point with Spain once and for all.

The UK's interest in holding on to the colony has waned, and it would like to be rid of it. Gibraltar no longer has the enormous strategic value it once had. Mines, long–range missiles and nuclear weapons make it far easier to block the strait of Gibraltar than to keep it open. The Rock does contain 30 miles of underground

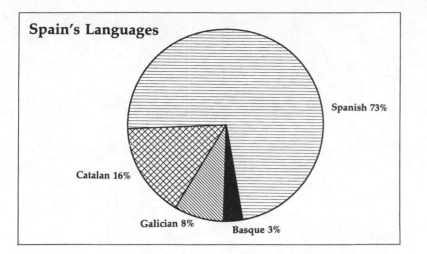

Spain's Languages

Spanish 73%

Catalan 16%

Galician 8%

Basque 3%

tunnels, a hidden strategic command center and berths for atomic submarines, all of which are important for NATO.

In 1991 Britain withdrew the last of its ground forces stationed there. That was an economic blow since spending by British soldiers and their dependents amounted to 18% of Gibraltar's revenues and provided a fourth of the jobs. Tourists replace some of the losses. Their numbers leaped from 600,000 in 1984, the last full year of the Spanish siege, to more than 3 million annually in the 1990s. In 2000 the OECD named Gibraltar as an unfair tax haven.

In 1996 Gibraltarians elected a new chief minister, a young pro–business lawyer, Peter Caruana. His Social Democrats captured 52% of the votes and eight of 15 seats in the House of Assembly. He tries to improve diplomatic relations with Madrid, while maintaining the Rock's colonial relationship with British. The British welcome this approach, after the more abrasive style of his predecessor, Joe Bossano, whose dream was for the Rock to be independent of both Britain and Spain.

Nevertheless, tensions remain. Spanish leaders are always wary of any moves by Gibraltar to represent itself on the international stage, insisting that it operate through the British foreign office. However, in 2000 Spain and the UK agreed to allow banking and insurance firms based in Gibraltar to sell products across the EU and to have identity cards issued in Gibraltar recognized throughout the EU.

After the sovereignty negotiations collapsed with the referendum in 2002, the UK and Spain agreed to set this paramount issue aside and to concentrate on cooperation. A trilateral "forum" was created in 2004 to tackle practical problems, but not to discuss sovereignty.

In September 2006 the three parties reached a deal that resolves many disagreements except sovereignty. The airport will get a new terminal that straddles the border so that passengers can exit directly either into Spain or Gibraltar. They can take direct flights from Spanish cities to the colony. Border controls are relaxed. Spain now recognizes Gibraltar's international dialing code making direct dialing possible.

ECONOMY

At one time, Spain was a country with a layer of wealthy persons stretched thin over a large population that lived in varying degrees of poverty. Its industry was small, highly protected, unaggressive and suffering from a general mental inertia. Its agriculture was unproductive, by comparison with other western European nations north of the Pyrenees. The chronically unstable political conditions in the 19th and 20th centuries always hampered economic development and delayed the industrial revolution. In the 1940s Spain's national income had fallen to the level of 1906–07, and not until 1954 was the 1936 level reached.

All of that has changed now that the country has undergone an almost miraculous economic transformation. The Spanish are now prosperous, and they have the eighth largest economy in the world, the fifth largest in Europe. Their incomes are converging with those of northern Europe. There are plenty of cars on the roads. In 2005 Spain was the third largest automobile manufacturer in the EU (the sixth largest in the world) although manufacturing jobs in that and other sectors will continue to decline as producers shift jobs to the lower-wage new members in the East and Asia. From 2002 to 2005, more than 40 multinational companies closed or sold factories.

Sixty percent of Spanish families own their own homes (compared with slightly over one–half in Britain and France); this gives Spain one of Europe's highest home ownership rates. Spaniards built 58%

more houses in 2003 than they did in 1996, and in 2006 they built more than France, Germany and Italy combined. Housing prices more than doubled between 1995 and 2007. The construction boom drove the economy, accounting for 18% of GDP, twice the share in other European nations. However, the economy became overheated, and in 2007-8 the bubble burst causing a temporary slowdown in economic growth. Nevertheless, Spanish self-confidence is demonstrated by its companies' acquisition spree, first in Latin America and now in Europe.

It cannot be denied that Spain has come a very long way since the 1950s. Its economy grew by 4% per year since 1997, double the EU average. In 2007 it was growing 4.1%, but slowed down to about 1.8% in 2008, its slowest since 1993. Per capita GDP had climbed to 87% of the EU average in 2004, up from 78% in 1975. It has overtaken Italy in terms of per capita wealth. Its prosperity is boosted by a less generous welfare state, moderate trade unions, budget discipline, the willingness to experiment, such as introducing flexible short-term labor contracts, and long-lived stable governments.

Prosperity is distributed geographically unequally. In Catalonia, the Basque country and Madrid, incomes are 25% higher than the national average, and in most of Andalusia, Extremadura, Galicia and Castilla-la-Mancha, incomes are 30% below the national average. In 2008 unemployment stood at 9.3% (lower in the Madrid region), roughly the EU average and dramatically down from 23% in 1996. In 2006 it created nearly 700,000 jobs, about half the total generated in the entire EU.

As in all Mediterranean countries, Spain has a sizable "submerged economy," which accounts for an estimated one–fifth of GDP. Up to one–third of the unemployed has an income from unofficial work. Taking this into account, the real unemployment figure is lower. Joblessness is also unevenly distributed. It is much higher in Andalusia, Extremadura, and the Basque country. For those under age 25, the jobless rate is around 40%, and it was 12.4% for foreigners in 2008. It is a testimony to the resilience of the extended family–based society that the Spanish can bear joblessness. Almost two-thirds (62%) of Spanish women are in the workforce, but their unemployment is almost double that of men.

In an attempt to maintain Spanish firms' economic competitiveness, the Socialist government introduced the concept of "temporary contracts" in 1984, followed by other labor market reforms in 1994 hoping to make it easier for companies to hire and fire. These measures an-

Spain

Goya's epic painting *El 3 de mayo de 1808*, which hangs in the Prado Museum in Madrid, commemorates the resistance to the French invasion which placed Napoleon's brother, Joseph, on the Spanish Throne.

tagonized labor unions and voters, who had grown accustomed since the Franco era to life–time job guarantees. But enough obstacles remain to make Spain's labor market one of the world's most rigid. Employers must pay 20 days salary for each year of employment to workers "fairly" dismissed, and 45 days to those "unfairly" dismissed. The courts almost always rule that dismissal is "unfair."

Not wishing to hire full–time employees who would receive this kind of protection, employers can, since 1984, hire them on "temporary contracts," which provide no job security. Thus, a two–tier labor market has developed: one for older workers with such protection that they have little incentive to be productive or to restrain their pay demands, and younger ones who stagger from one short–term contract to the other without building real careers. By 2008 almost a third (compared with 13% in the U.S. and over 12% in Germany, Italy and France) of all workers (and two-thirds of young people under age 25) had such contracts. On the positive side, these give Spanish companies a competitive edge over their French and German rivals. In 2006 the World Bank

ranked Spain 30th out of 155 countries studied in terms of competitiveness.

Nationwide collective–bargaining agreements are negotiated for each industry. This makes it hard for individual firms to adjust their employment conditions to their own particular economic circumstances. The result is unemployment higher than it should be.

Economy growth has stalled, and it buys more than it sells. Its current accounts deficit reached 10% by 2008, second only to that of the U.S. Nevertheless, foreign capital still comes in. Spain once surpassed the United States as the largest foreign investor in Latin America, but that was reversed in 1999 when Spanish investments there declined rapidly. By 2007 the budget was in the black by 1.7% of GDP, but that melted to zero in 2008 as a result of the economic turndown. The total foreign debt stands at 39.8% of GDP. Public spending fell from 48% of GDP in the mid-1990s to 40.8% a decade later. Government employment has been cut. Perhaps most significantly, the historical phenomenon in Spain of disinterest or lack of prestige accorded to business activity has disappeared.

There are problems. Spain has an aging population with a birth rate among native Spaniards of 1.35; however, immigrants are more than offsetting the shrinking native population. Its inflation fell from 14% in 1981 to 2.4% in 2007, but it rose to 4.5% a year later. Productivity is low. Exports are weak and the trade deficit high. Corporate taxes and wages are significantly higher than those of its competitors making it more difficult to compete. Perhaps the greatest problem is the failure to invest sufficiently in research, development and technology. In 2005 it invested only 1.03% of GDP in research and development, compared with an EU average of 1.9% and 2.6% in the U.S. Its number of active patents is 300 per 100,000, compared with 5,800 in the U.S. It has a weak technology base, and high-tech manufactured exports account for 7% of its total, compared with 32% in the U.S. and 40% in Ireland.

The welfare system looks more like that of the UK rather than of France and Germany. It has caught up with many other western European countries in terms of social welfare benefits. Almost a third of its unemployed receive some form of as-

Spain

Philip II by Sánchez Coello 1531–88

sistance, and the social security system is able to provide free or cheap medical care, although its facilities are often overcrowded. It provides pensions, welfare and other social assistance. From 80% to 85% of its funds are provided by a payroll tax on employees. This tax increases labor costs, though, by about 35%.

Madrid was the biggest net beneficiary of EU funds by far, something that changed after 10 new and poorer members joined the EU in 2004 (and two more in 2007). It received annually about $7.5 billion in EU regional, social and "cohesion" funds, plus $6.75 billion from the EU's Common Agriculture Policy (CAP). The total was more than 90 billion euros ($112.5 billion). After subtracting Spain's $6.4 billion in annual payments into the EU budget, it chalked up a net gain of almost 8 billion euros each year or roughly 1% of GDP.

In recent years EU funds financed from 30% to 50% of infrastructure construction in Spain. In general, that money was used wisely as one sees from its up-to-date infrastructure and general prosperity. Its roads and railroads are modern and well laid out, helping connect poorer regions to more developed ones. Its new interstate highways are first-rate, and most of them run north, connecting the country with Europe. The Spanish government accepted that it would receive fewer subsidies after 2007 although EU guidelines still permitted subsidies to four of the 17 Spanish regions. It phased in the cuts slowly. Starting in 2012 Spain will become a net contributor to the EU budget.

It is no wonder that most Spaniards think that membership in the EU is both beneficial and good. It has brought prosperity, and per capita income has risen. But belonging to the EU was never pri-

marily a matter of money for Spain. It was a symbol of European norms of social progress, democracy and freedom. It is also a context within which Spain's strength and size can count. It was significant that the EU asked former President Felipe González in 2008 to chair a committee that reflects upon the future of the EU and how to prevent the economic and geopolitical decline of Europe.

That inflation is under control is partially due to the largely responsible way in which the major labor unions, the communist–controlled Confederation of Workers' Commissions (CCOO) and the Socialist–dominated General Workers' Union (UGT), which work closely together, responded to the economic challenges facing the country. Only one worker in seven (15%) belongs to a union. Yet Spain has the EU's second worst record for days lost in strikes per 1,000 employees (197.4), after Greece (580).

As in all European countries, the rapid rise in energy prices in the 1970s exacerbated the country's economic problems. Spain is dependent on imported oil for about 60% of its total energy needs. It is only able to produce domestically 2% of the oil it uses. It receives 60% of its natural gas from Algeria via a pipeline through Morocco.

In years of normal rainfall Spain can provide 15% of its power generation through hydroelectricity. However, since 2004 it experienced a series of droughts that are increasingly worrisome for the future. Scientists predict that because of global warming, most of the country will be desert within a half century. Water is already so scarce that during the summer months it must be brought by ship to Barcelona from Marseilles and a desalination plant in Almería.

It has had modest success in relieving its excessive reliance on imported oil by increasing its use of hydro, coal and nuclear power. Local opposition to atomic power has caused Spain's nuclear ambitions to be revised downward. Nevertheless, in 2007 nine nuclear power plants were generating 23% of Spain's electricity.

Its greatest hope lies in renewable sources to provide for its future energy needs. Its natural conditions are favorable for them: it is Europe's second most mountainous country after Switzerland, and it is one of Europe's least populated. Combined with the increasing desertification, Spain has the right climate and geography for wind and solar power. It is already the world's second largest producer of wind energy after Germany and slightly ahead of the U.S. It is also in the front ranks in solar power and biofuels.

Spain has a modern economy, with 30% of the workforce employed in industry

(producing 29.2% of GDP) and 65% in services (turning out 66.8% of GDP). Its industries are, as a rule, much smaller than in most EU countries. It has few multinational corporations. Of the FT–500 top European companies, only 24 are Spanish. Businesses tend not to be as high–tech as in some competitor countries. Half of Spain's biggest companies (including all the auto industry—Europe's third biggest—and nine out of ten top exporters) are owned by foreign companies.

The previous conservative government privatized most of the economy. However, a Spanish Society for Industrial Participation (SEPI, which replaced the earlier state holding company, National Institute of Industry—INI, created during the Franco era) controls companies that still remain under state control. The state monopolies on telephones (through Telefónica), petroleum (though Campsa) and tobacco (through Altadis, earlier named Tabacalera) have ended although the state retains some shares in those specific companies.

Foreign trade accounts for 38% of Spain's economy, and the emphasis is on Europe. Almost three-fourths of total Spanish merchandise exports go to the EU, up from half in 1985, and 60% of its imports are from the EU, compared with 37% in 1985. Thanks in part to incentives for investment, Spain attracted needed foreign investments. Favorite sectors for their foreign investors are in the auto and chemical industries, financial institutions and the hotel business. This is no one-way street. Spanish companies are also investing heavily in Europe and North America. In 2005 its deals outside the country were 69% higher than in the previous year. Such activities make Spanish companies global leaders in some industries.

A major problem that continues to cool the enthusiasm of foreign investors and seriously burdens the economy in certain areas of Spain is the terrorist activity, especially in the Basque country, traditionally one of the most industrialized and economically dynamic regions in Spain. There the ETA forced "revolutionary taxes" on the companies and kidnapped and even killed some leading industrialists and engineers. These tactics prompted other businessmen to leave with their families. The al-Qaeda-related bombings in Madrid on March 11, 2004, gave potential investors pause, but they have had little economic effect. Nevertheless, Spain will not be wholly attractive for business activity and investments until terrorism has been brought under control.

The "primary sector" of agriculture, forestry and fishing employs 5% of the Spanish, produces 4.1% of the GDP, and constitutes less than 20% of its exports. Its horticulture, poultry farming, wine and

Spain

The horror of April 26, 1937, in Guernica . . .

. . . and Picasso's stark depiction—*Guernica*

Guggenheim Bilbao Museum

fruit growing are highly productive, but its meat and cereal production is low. Despite the large size of its territory and agricultural population, Spain is not entirely self–sufficient in food. It remains one of Europe's major wine growers and is the fourth-largest exporter to the U.S., supplying 5% of the American market. However, Spain finds it increasingly difficult to compete with wines from countries like Australia, New Zealand, Chile and South Africa.

It needs to reorganize its agricultural production. But the results of such improvement would be to increase rural unemployment and thus stimulate the flight into the cities and industrialized countries. Among the rural problems which must be solved in order to improve the country's agricultural output are insufficient water supplies, especially in the South, forest and brush fires, soil erosion, the preponderance of small, uneconomical farms in the North and the West and the existence of large underutilized estates in the South.

A Spaniard eats an estimated three times more fish than the average west European. To supply this immense seafood appetite, the country has built up the largest fishing fleet in the EU and the third largest in the world. This caused concern over Spain's entry into the EU, and members fight bitterly over fishing quotas. Spain accounts for a fifth of the EU's catch. In 1988 a French coast guard vessel fired on Basque fishing boats that were exceeding Spain's quota. Canada captured a Spanish vessel over fishing off its coast in 1994 and found on board doctored records and illegal nets designed to catch undersized fish. Despite being caught red–handed, Spanish public opinion was enflamed by this "act of piracy." One of its diplomats proclaimed: "We may not be big in anything else, but in fish we are a superpower."

Two of Spain's major economic assets have been the sun and the sea, and since the 1960s Spain has been one of Europeans' favorite tourist countries. It is close behind France as Europe's leader in terms of tourist earnings and is the world's second favorite destination after France. With 53.5 million overnight foreign tourists in 2004 and 55 million in 2005, tourism is an important source of income and employment. It is Spain's biggest earner of foreign exchange and generates 12% of GDP directly or indirectly. However, Spain is becoming too expensive for the mass tourism market. Also the tourist industry is vulnerable to recession in the rest of Europe and to international terrorism. It had only one million American tourists in 2002. Not only do Americans spend more money on vacation, but they are more likely than Europeans to visit cultural sites in the interior of the country as opposed to sunning themselves on Spain's beaches.

For a long time, Spain relied on its beaches and good weather to attract tourists, but as the euro hardens, prices have risen, and many tourists look elsewhere. This presents challenges to the industry. In order to stimulate both tourism and its economy in general, Spain decided in 1988 to modernize its railroad, which is one of Europe's oldest, slowest and financially troubled. It adapted its narrow-gauge railway system to the one used by the rest of Europe and introduced its first high-speed train (known as AVE) between Madrid and Seville in 1992. Travel time is less than two and one-hours, and its AVE trains are punctual, clean, safe and highly profitable. The project to create a similar AVE line from Madrid to Barcelona had by 2003 gone only as far as the Catalan town of Lerida and was completed in 2008 although its terminal point inside Barcelona is still under discussion. Future links to France will require an eight-kilometer tunnel through the Pyrenees.

CULTURE

Languages

Spain's culture and language have taken root far beyond its own borders. In fact, 400 million speak Spanish as a mother tongue, making it the only real challenger to English as a world language. Spanish is the favorite foreign language in American high schools and universities, and as many as 35 million citizens and residents of the U.S. speak Spanish as a mother tongue. The official language in Spain is the Castilian dialect of Spanish. It differs in some respect from the many different dialects of Spanish spoken in South and Central America, to say nothing of the Basque, Galician and Catalán languages. The most audible difference is that the "s" or soft "c" sound in Castilian Spanish sounds like the English "th" sound.

There are, of course, many languages spoken within Spain itself, and three are especially important. In Galicia one speaks Gallego, which is more similar to Portuguese than are other Spanish languages. In Catalonia, Valencia and the Balearic Islands, variations of a separate language called Catalán are spoken. It is a Romance language closely related to Provençal and Languedoc, spoken in France. It has a rich written literature and has always been a crucially important cultural tool for preserving Catalán national identity. Cataláns want the EU to recognize their tongue as an official language.

Basque, a language with neither Romance nor other Indo–European roots, is spoken mainly in the villages of the Basque country and is seldom heard in the two major Basque cities of Bilbao and San Sabastian. It remains, however, a very important vehicle for Basque identity.

Spain

Literature and Arts

Spain was always a crossroads between the European and Islamic Oriental cultures. Indeed, some of Europe's greatest writers wrote in Spanish. During the "Golden Age" of the 16th and 17th centuries, Cervantes wrote his classic, Don Quixote, a humorous story of chivalry and lofty, idealistic aspirations beyond all human capacity to achieve. Today, the word "Quixotic" is used in English to refer to any naive venture which, because of hopeless odds, is doomed to failure from the very start. In the 20th century, Spain produced several internationally renowned poets, most notably Juan Ramón Jiménez, who won a Nobel Prize in 1956, and Federico García Lorca, who was murdered during the Civil War. Its novelists, such as Manuel Vázquez, José Heirro, Soledad Puertolas, Arturo Perez-Reverte, Antonio Muñoz Molina, Almudena Grandes, Miguel Delibes and Manuel Rives have international reputations. In 1989, Camilo José Cela was awarded the Nobel Prize for Literature. Author of 60 disturbing and powerful books, Cela lived an exciting, risky and iconoclastic life, disdaining authority in all forms. His regular newspaper columns and television appearances also helped make him a legend in Spain.

In art Spain has also distinguished itself. El Greco (words which mean "the Greek" and applied to Kyriakos Theotokopoulos, who lived and worked in Toledo) established his own characteristic style in the 16th century. Diego Rodríguez de Silva Velázquez painted revealing and astonishingly uncomplimentary portraits of the Spanish court during the 17th century, and Francisco José de Goya painted powerful portrayals of revolution and resistance in the 18th and 19th centuries.

In the 20th century, Salvador Dalí, Joan Miró and Pablo Picasso inalterably influenced modern painting. Because of political disagreements, these artists lived a part of their working lives outside of Spain. Dalí's personalized museum in the former theater of his Catalan hometown of Figueres, just south of the French border, is unforgettable.

The most ringing protest against Franco, and of course, against war itself, was Picasso's *Guernica*, which he painted for the Spanish pavilion of the Paris World Fair in 1937 in order to invoke the memory of the German bombing of the Basque city of Guernica. He then lent the painting to the Museum of Modern Art in New York and ordered that it not be returned to Spain until democracy had been restored in his homeland. In 1980, after a

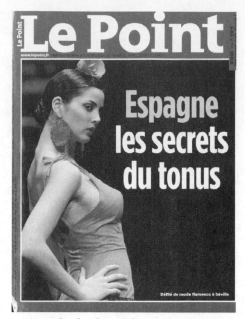

As only the Spanish can dance it—
El Flamenco

long legal wrangle with Picasso's heirs, the painting was finally returned to the magnificent Prado Museum in Madrid. In 1992 it was moved to the new modern art museum, Centro de Arte Reina Sofia. Spanish viewers, who often exclaim in museums, are hushed when face to face with the shrieking victims portrayed in this stark mural. The Thyssen-Bornemisza Museum in Madrid opened in the 1990s to rave reviews.

A major addition to Spanish culture is the Guggenheim Museum in Bilbao, opened in 1997. Costing $171 million to build, this is the anchor project in an effort to preempt Basque violence by emphasizing national pride and culture in a positive way. Basque officials requested that *Guernica*, the work of art most symbolic of the region, be moved or lent to the museum, which is located only 12 miles from the town of Guernica. Citing the painting's deteriorating condition and concerns over its safety in the Basque area, the request was turned down. This decision sparked fierce controversy. Nevertheless, the experiment of stimulating the entire Basque region through this art magnet is a smashing success. In its first 18 months, tourism in the Basque country increased by 28%, most of it attributable to the museum. It has become a symbol of the area's economic and cultural resurgence that could be secured by the permanent end of separatist violence. In an effort to give a similar cultural boost to the south, a museum in Malaga to honor its most famous son, Pablo Picasso, draws large crowds.

Secluded, elegant entrances to several Andalusian homes

Cinema

Over two-thirds of all films shown in Spain are American, and only 16% are Spanish. Spanish directors have created some very good ones. Luis Buñuel, who for decades lived in exile in France, Hollywood and Mexico, was especially acclaimed for his playful and charming films. He aims his subtle but deadly arrows toward the Spanish bourgeoisie, from which he is descended.

In 2000, Spanish director Pedro Almodovar's film, "All About My Mother," won the Academy Award for best foreign-language film, and his 2002 film, "Talk to Her," won the Best Original Screenplay Oscar. He comes from a poor village in La Mancha to the south of Madrid, and his loyalty to his roots, despite past criticism of some aspects of Spain, endeared him to most of his compatriots. Two cabinet ministers accompanied him to Hollywood, and in accepting his statue he dedicated the prize "to Spain and Spaniards." The entire country cheered, and King Juan Carlos and former President of the Government José María Aznar sent him congratulatory telegrams. Others are hard on his heels, such as the female film director and screenwriter Icíar Bollaín ("Take My Eyes"), Julio Medem ("Sex and Lucía") and Alejandro Amenábar ("The Others"). Amenábar's "Mar Adentro" (The Sea Inside) took an Oscar in 2005. Javier Bardem, who acts in both English and Spanish, can almost single-handedly make a film succeed. Spain's film success has also helped Latin America: over half of Spain's co-productions in 2002 involved at least one Latin American country.

The kinds of Spanish films that have won international acclaim are facing domestic competition from another kind of movie which has sprung alive after 1975—pornography. Barcelona has become one of Europe's centers for this art form. Of course, pornography is in the eye of the beholder: one man's treat is another man's horror. But even the most tolerant must be surprised to see a film entitled "Would you like to be my husband's lover?" being shown in a Granada movie house named Isabel la Católica (Isabel the Catholic). Although some argue that such films have driven away family audiences from the cinemas, Spain has developed such a tolerant society that it seems unaffected by this type of license. Prostitution (though not pimping) is legal, and even conservative newspapers publish explicit ads for their services.

Two–thirds of the foreign TV films purchased are from the U.S. Only slightly more than 10% of Spaniards go to the theater, despite heavy state subsidies of theater tickets. Many more follow bull fighting closely: 40% according to polls, although a 2008 survey revealed that 70% of Spaniards disapproved of the sport. Only soccer is more popular. Bull fighting nets over one billion dollars every year. It is an expensive spectacle. A normal event requires six bulls, which cost from $25,000 to $100,000 a head. The price for a matador can run from $25,000 to $120,000 for a single afternoon.

Media

The lifting of censorship in Spain brought a flowering daily and weekly press, even though newspaper readership remains low. Only about 8% of Spaniards buy a newspaper, which is half as many as in France and a fifth as many as in Britain. One in seven young adults claims to read any printed medium at all.

Three of the best papers in Europe now come from Spain: *Cambio*, a weekly modeled on *Time*, the conservative daily, *Vanguardia* (circulation 198,000), and the liberal broadly pro-Socialist daily, *El Pais*, which is unloved by the police, army, and church. *El Pais* is the leading paid daily with a circulation of 434,000 copies; it often supports the Socialist Party, for which it is criticized. As a sign of its political influence, former Socialist President Filipe González banned its reading before cabinet meetings out of fear that members would be swayed by its opinion. A new nationalist daily, *Público*, hit the stands in September 2007. To the left of *El Pais*, it is irreverent and aims to attract young people who had not bought newspapers before. *El Mundo* (312,000) is its livelier conservative rival. *La Razón* (149,000) is another voice on the right. Even the right–wing monarchist daily, *ABC* (279,000), improved its standards and converted to democracy. Most papers are partisan in one-way or the other. As of 2006, the largest general-circulation newspaper, with a total readership of 2.3 million, is the free sheet, *20 Minutos*, which surged past *El Pais*. With another free paper, *Metro*, nipping at its heels, almost half of all newspapers in Spain are distributed free.

It is still an offense to question the honor of the royal family or the legitimacy of the monarchy or the unity of Spain. That began to change somewhat after the Crown Prince's royal wedding, but the press still does not delve in the personal peccadilloes of the royals. The press is also technically forbidden to challenge the honor of the armed forces. But this is changing as one saw when the press roundly condemned criticism by two generals of the new Catalán autonomy law in 2006. Despite these continuing limitations on the freedom of the press, it should not be forgotten that for the first time in Spanish history people can generally speak and write about politics and religion without fear of being jailed.

Television is the real molder of society. Polls indicate that about two–thirds of adults form their political opinions from television, which 87% watch daily. The

Spanish Students at the College of Europe

Spain

state remains a large owner and voice in the media. It appoints the heads of state TV and radio, as well as of the national news agency, EFE. Critics say this limits the objectivity and selection of images and news. Others argue that the private sector provides an adequate balance. The autonomous governments also run regional channels. In 1991 private TV was established. There are two central and seven regional public-sector channels, four private channels, a subscription company called Canal Plus, and the state's two main TVE networks, which also operate TVE Internacional and a rolling news channel, 24 Horas. The private channels, *Antena 3* and Tele-5, have more viewers than TVE-1. Two of the private channels appeared recently: Cuartro in 2005 and La Sexta in 2006.

Catholic Church

The church had been one of Franco's chief supporters, and he repaid the favor by restoring its role in the schools, and by granting it generous state subsidies. He effectively had the power to appoint bishops, a prerogative which Juan Carlos eliminated. On Spanish coins Franco was called "leader of Spain by God's grace."

In the 1960s, though, the church's support for El Caudillo began to change. Many Spanish priests adopted the ethic of social justice. They formed social action groups and spoke out in support of disadvantaged workers and peasants. Priests in the Basque country, Spain's most fervently

Catholic area, sometimes publicly supported the Basque nationalists.

In the 1960s the Catholic lay organization, Opus Dei (Latin for "God's Work"), which began its existence in 1928 as a highly conservative effort to become firmly rooted in the society's elite, changed its thinking. It became an important force for rationalizing the economy. From a force for reaction, Opus Dei became one of Spain's most important forces for industrial innovation. Although it had largely lost its influence on public policy by the end of the 1980s, its Spanish membership had by 2006 settled at 35,000 of the world total of 85,000. Pope John Paul II ordered in 1982 that Opus Dei become a "personal" bishopric, meaning that its members owe spiritual allegiance to its head, not to the local bishop. In 2003 he canonized its founder, José María Escriva de Balaguer, who died only in 1975.

By 1972 most of Spain's bishops were moderate. Franco's displeasure was demonstrated by his government's threat in 1974 to cancel the Concordat (treaty) with the Vatican. Most Spaniards favored maintaining this Concordat with Rome; it provides the state with a voice in appointing bishops, while the Church receives a modest subsidy. The church had changed from a major foundation for the Franco regime to a skeptical semi-opponent. However, in 2000 it decided not to plead forgiveness for siding with Franco after the civil war.

The Church now claims to stay out of party politics, but the Socialist Zapatero government accuses it of meddling in electoral politics. In 2008 the Church urged voters not to support parties that talked with ETA, favored abortion and gay rights, including same-sex marriage, and advocated reducing the importance of religion in the school curriculum.

In the 1980s, the church accepted the Socialist Party's law permitting the sale of contraceptives. But it fought in vain to prevent the full legalization of abortion and divorce, problems that could not be so easily hidden in the medicine cabinet. It is understandable why many Spanish supported the Socialist government's reform to de-penalize abortion in 1985 in cases such as rape or where the mother's life is in danger. The Zapatero government changed the law in order to permit abortions within the first 12 weeks of pregnancy for whatever reason. Illegal abortions have become rare, and 90% of terminations happen within this 12-week period. They can also take place within the first 22 weeks if there is a risk of fetal malformation and at any stage of pregnancy if the mother's mental or physical health is at risk.

The church hierarchy and the conservative opposition expressed outrage and are helpless against Europe's steepest drop in the birth rate, from 19 births per 1,000 Spaniards in 1975 to 11 by 1989. By 2002 the average Spanish woman had become the least reproductive in the EU, with a birth rate of only 1.22 children, down from 2.8 in 1975, but up in 2006 to 1.35. Italy and Greece were close behind with 1.25 and 1.3 respectively. This is well below the 2.1% needed to keep a population steady. The immigrant population helps bring this rate up. Despite the fact that Spaniards have the longest life expectancy in the EU (84.2 years for women and 77.7 for men), the overall population is expected to begin declining around 2010.

It is influenced by the fact that 62% of Spanish women are already in the workforce (compared with 75% in northern Europe), and 70% under age 30 have or are seeking employment. Although Spanish families are still cohesive and close, they continue to become less male–dominated than they once were. The Zapatero government introduced tough penalties against wife battering and discrimination against women at the workplace.

In 2007 a far-reaching new gender-equality act came into force. It mandates equal pay for equal work. It requires companies with more than 250 employees to implement "equality plans" and become more "family friendly." Since office hours still sometimes end at 8 PM or later, many women have to drop out of the workforce

Plaza de Colón, Madrid

when they have children. Female unemployment (11.4% in 2007) is almost double the rate for men. More controversially, the law requires listed companies to balance men and women on corporate boards. In 2007, two-thirds of companies had no women on their boards, and fewer than 6% of directors were female.

Families have become less heterosexual. Spain has a vibrant, flamboyant and politically active gay community. Some form of civil "unions" short of marriage were already in place in most of the 17 autonomous regions by 2004. Gay marriage was favored by two-thirds of Spaniards in 2005. By a vote of 187 to 147, the *Cortes* legalized same-sex marriages in June 2005. This included the rights to adopt children and inherit each other's property. In the first half of 2006 alone, there were 4,500 same-sex marriages that included army officers and politicians of the conservative People's Party.

The changed environment in Spain is reflected by opinion polls, which indicated that fewer than 15% of Spaniards considered marriage to be indissoluble. Yet the roots of social conservatism in Spain were also revealed in the fact that it took six years after Franco's death to pass a liberal divorce law, which permitted civil divorce by mutual consent one year after the couple had been legally separated. The debate exasperated church leaders so much that they told Spanish Catholics that the law does not apply to them.

The Zapatero government wasted no time in enacting an agenda that contravenes almost every tenet of Catholic doctrine, including fast-track divorce, relaxed rules on abortion, and legal stem-cell research. The Archbishop of Madrid, Cardinal Rauco Varela, despaired: "Madrid has turned into Sodom and Gomorrah." Spain has become the main battleground in the new Pope Benedict XVI's attack against the evil of "moral relativism" encroaching all of Europe.

The church's stand on these issues does not persuade many Spaniards, 80% of whom consider themselves to be "culturally Catholic" and are formally members of the church. In his May 2003 visit to Spain, Pope John Paul II pleaded with the people: "Do not break with your Christian roots!" He claimed, "the Christian and Catholic faith constitutes the identity of the Spanish people." His successor, Pope Benedict, made a one-day visit to Spain in July 2006 to carry the message that the family was "founded on indissoluble marriage between a man and a women." Zapatero and his deputy president, Maria Teresa Fernandez de la Vega, paid a 15-minute courtesy visit to the pope, and the king and queen saw him off at Valencia airport.

El Congreso refrenda el regreso de las tropas con el voto en contra del PP

Todos los grupos parlamentarios condenan las torturas a presos en Irak

El Congreso de los Diputados respaldó ayer por 185 votos a favor, 141 en contra y cuatro abstenciones la retirada inmediata de las tropas españolas en Irak ordenada el pasado 18 de abril por el presidente del Gobierno, José Luis Rodríguez Zapatero. El PP fue el único que votó en contra de una proposición no de ley donde se censuraba la gestión que hizo el Gobierno de José María Aznar sobre el conflicto de Irak y se apoyaba la decisión de "hacer regresar las tropas en el menor tiempo y con la mayor seguridad posibles".

El PSOE aventaja en 10 puntos al PP en intención de voto, según el CIS

ESPAÑA. Página 20

12 PALESTINOS mueren en una represalia del Ejército israelí en Gaza
INTERNACIONAL. Página 7

LA FAMILIA GANDHI recupera el poder en India tras un gran vuelco electoral
INTERNACIONAL. Página 8
Editorial en la página 16

UN TRIBUNAL condena a dos etarras y otro les absuelve por falta de pruebas
ESPAÑA. Página 25

El pleno del Congreso aprobó ayer la propuesta que el Partido Popular evitó que se votara hace 15 días en la sesión monográfica que el presidente del Gobierno explicó los motivos de su orden de retirada inmediata de las tropas.

Los grupos parlamentarios favorables al regreso de los militares españoles sumaron ayer una nueva razón a sus argumentos: el escándalo de las torturas de militares estadounidenses a presos iraquíes.

El socialista Diego López Garrido consideró que las torturas denunciadas expresan "la ilegalidad originaria de la guerra, que al final conduce a que quienes ejecutan esa guerra se sientan impunes para cometer actos ilegales".

El PP, que soportó los reproches de todos los grupos parlamentarios por haber apoyado desde el Gobierno la guerra de Irak, también condenó en la sesión parlamentaria "los abyectos y repulsivos comportamientos de

Estreno de Letizia ante la realeza europea

REUTERS

Rumsfeld dice en la prisión d Abu Ghraib q los torturadore serán castigad

El secretario de Defens EE UU, Donald Rumsfeld, i zó ayer una visita sorpresa prisión de Abu Ghraib, sed las torturas que han salido luz en las últimas semanas, centenares de soldados, R feld reconoció el golpe que sufriendo por las denunci prometió que "los culpable rán castigados". Lo ocur aseguró tras soportar las r das de los presos, "no volv pasar jamás". La víspera, R feld declaró ante un subco del Senado que las técnicas cadas en los interrogatorios legales y están aprobadas pc abogados del Pentágono co me a la Convención de Gin Ésta se aplica en Irak y Afg tán, dijo, aunque no en Gu namo. Los congresistas est ayer divididos sobre si debe vulgarse las nuevas prueba torturas. Rumsfeld asegura su difusión violaría la Cor ción de Ginebra. **Páginas**

Entrevista con
Robert MacNama

"¿Era necesar ir a la guerra Mi respuesta es no"

El ex secretario de Defens EE UU Robert McNamar que la Casa Blanca debía l

---

Most Spaniards favor the strict separation between Church and state, which was enshrined in the constitution in 1978. A 2006 poll revealed that while 80% still call themselves Catholics, only 42% say they believe in God. In 1975, 61% had claimed to go to mass regularly; by 2008 that figure had fallen to less than 20% (even less in urban areas); 46% of those saying they are Catholic admit that they "almost never go." In 2004 only 12% of young Spaniards between ages 13 and 24 said they go to mass every week; in 2005 only 14% of young people described themselves as "religious." A year later, 80% of young Spaniards said they distrusted the church, to which they gave a lower approval rating than to NATO and multinational corporations. Even the clergy is shrinking. In 1952 Spain had 77,800 priests and 7,050 seminarians studying for the priesthood; today the figures are 18,500 and 1,800. From 10% to 15% of parishes have no priest at all.

Although Spain is officially a secular state, the government and church are closely intertwined. Since 1979, Spaniards can check a box on their income tax designating about half a percent (.052%) of their taxes to the church. However, the number of taxpayers doing so has steadily declined to under 40%. The government makes up the shortfall of what the church needs with direct subsidies, which account for about 30% of the church's income.

Education

The role of the church in contemporary Spanish society is not a burning political issue. It has largely turned away from active intervention in politics. But it does raise its voice on certain issues, such as religious instruction and parochial schools. The church energetically defends its influence on parochial schools, which about a third of all Spanish schoolchildren attend (twice the figure even of the Franco years) and which have a higher social reputation. These Catholic schools are fully funded by the government. The church is willing to accept some standards and guidelines by the state, such as teacher training and financial accountability. But it wishes to avoid any state control over the content of education in its schools, which it insists must remain religious.

The first Socialist government before 1996 aroused the ire of the church by pass-

Spain

ing legislation guaranteeing the right to free secular education and thereby reducing the church's influence in the schools. The government also announced that for the first time, books and teaching materials would be distributed free of charge to some 200,000 school children attending rural public and private schools. The school–leaving age was lifted to 16. The second Socialist government refused in 2004 to allow a controversial law to go into effect that would have made religious instruction a required part of the curriculum in state schools. Instead the government allows optional religion courses, while integrating religion as a cultural topic in other subjects. All regions permit religious instruction, but it is optional. Spain must seek to improve education. In 2007 it spent only half the OECD average on schools. It also ranked only 29th in the world (behind Morocco and South Africa) as an attractive research and development location.

Drugs and Immigration

Spain has replaced the Netherlands as the most important conduit into Europe for illegal drugs. European addicts receive 40% of their cocaine via Spain. In part this is explained by the more open borders to other EU partners, the congenial Spanish–speaking environment for Latin American drug runners, and the 1983 decriminalization of possession of small quantities of soft or hard drugs for personal use. Drug use by individuals in the privacy of their homes is tolerated. The González government had made the country's drug laws among the most lax in Europe, and the rapid spread of drug abuse brought a reaction. Spain has Europe's highest incidence of drug abuse and AIDS. It is faced with an epidemic: it has an estimated 100,000 heroin addicts, and cocaine use has spread into the middle–class. It is reckoned that 1.5 million smoke marijuana often. Most of Spain's heavy drug users are young. The earlier Socialist government had tried to fight back by increasing maximum prison sentences, fines and indictments for drug traffickers, but critics called these measures too little, too late.

Racial violence was a shock for many Spaniards, despite polls that suggest that they are more tolerant of outsiders than are most other Europeans. By 2008 Spain had about 4.5 million foreigners, or 10% of the total population (higher than in France, the UK or Germany), compared with only 1.6% in 1998. This includes Europe's largest Romanian (mainly Roma—gypsy) community outside of Romania, numbering 530,000 registered residents. Foreigners can bring in their families only one year after receiving a residency per-

mit. A half million Moroccans live legally in Spain. They have more trouble integrating than do other large immigrant groups, such as Latin Americans and Eastern Europeans.

Spain overtook France as the favored European destination for immigrants; in fact only the U.S. accepts more. That is a dramatic change from the 1950s and 1960s when it was a net exporter of people. Spain remains open to many newcomers. They are good for the economy. Without them Spain would suffer severe labor shortages and wage inflation. About two million of them pay into the social security system. This is important for a country trying to maintain its pay-as-you-go pensions while experiencing a declining birth rate. It decided in 2006 to lift restrictions on the movement of labor from the EU's new members. But most troubling, it is the closest thing in the EU to a frontier with Africa, with nautical distances of nine miles (14 km.) at the Strait of Gibraltar and land borders along the enclaves.

Most immigrants arrive by plane and quickly get jobs on building sites or in households. Of those arriving by sea in 2006, the greatest flood was pouring over the shores of the Canary Islands, a 600-mile (1,000 km.) week to ten-day journey on dangerously flimsy boats from countries as far south as Mauritania and Senegal. An estimated 1,000 have perished at sea. As an area that depends on 12 million annual tourists, the islanders feel a mortal economic threat. In 2005 alone, 4,700 illegal immigrants were registered in the Canaries, and that number was topped in the first six months of 2006.

Spanish law gives authorities only 40 days to determine the country of origin and deport an illegal alien. This is often impossible since most migrants get rid of all their passports and identification documents before they set sail. Thus many are

turned over to the Red Cross and are allowed to remain in Spain or migrate elsewhere in Europe. In desperation, Spain asked for EU help. Because of the backlash against out-of-control immigration in Europe, the organization agreed in May 2006 to deploy patrol boats, planes and rapid-reaction aid teams from eight nations to the Canaries. Its European Refugee Fund can be used to pay the cost of sending illegal migrants back home.

Former Foreign Minister Javier Solana (now EU High Representative) said, "Spain is a country where others have always been taken in with great generosity and solidarity." To try to demonstrate this, the conservative government adopted a law in 1996 giving legal foreign residents the right both to vote and to run for office in municipal elections starting in 1999. Another law in 1999 made it possible for 70,000 illegal immigrants to have residence permits and to bring their dependents into Spain. Nearly a quarter-million applied. This was advertised as one of Europe's most liberal immigration policies.

In 2005 the government offered another three-month amnesty, under which 700,000 illegal immigrants were given work and residency permits if they could prove that they had resided in Spain since August 2004 and had a six-month work contract. Ecuadorians made up a fifth of the applicants, followed by Romanians, Moroccans and Colombians. Other EU countries were not happy with this amnesty since legal residents can freely move within the Union.

In 2000 the government created of a department for integrating immigrants. Most immigrants live along the Mediterranean coast and in the main cities. Madrid and Catalonia are the favored destinations, with the former preferred by Latin Americans and the latter by North Africans. Demography experts calculate that Spain will need 12 million immi-

Seaside town of Salobreña on the southern coast   Photo by Eugenia Elseth grants until 2030 in order to prevent the population from shrinking below its 2000 level. In other words, they help lift Spain's low fertility rate. One in seven children is now born to an immigrant mother. A half-million immigrant children attend schools.

The March 11, 2004, terrorist bombings in Madrid focused the spotlight on Spain's deeply ambivalent attitudes toward immigrants. Of the 191 who died in the attack, 47 were foreigners, and all of the suspects arrested were foreigners, most of them Islamic militants from Morocco. Opinion polls reveal that hostility and mistrust toward foreigners are growing fast, as well as the perceptions that immigrants burden the social welfare system, take jobs from Spaniards and drive up the crime rate. Verbal abuse and derogatory graffiti are more noticeable, but there was no violent backlash against the Muslim community. They also worry about the effect of so many foreigners on their Spanish national identity. As the government responds by tightening up legal immigration, the illegal variety soars despite the redoubled efforts to deport illegals and to prevent others from trying to enter the country illegally.

Defenders of immigration as a necessity for the country's demographic health point out that the low-paid newcomers do work that Spaniards do not wish to do, and they actually increase employment. For example, cheap nannies enable more Spanish women to go to work. The tourist and construction industries depend on foreigners. Immigrant workers are net contributors to the welfare system and generate more than twice the tax revenue they consume. Nevertheless, a majority of Spaniards believe there are too many foreigners in the country.

FUTURE

Spain's future continues to be promising despite an economic downturn and burst of its real estate bubble. Its dynamism was praised by a special report in the European edition of *Time* that appeared on March 3, 2004, only eight days before the tragic terrorist bombings in Madrid that killed 191 persons. "Spain rocks," it asserted, calling modern Spaniards "the New Conquistadores" in the arts, business, foreign affairs, food and sports. At the same time, Spaniards have created one of the most tolerant and permissive societies in Europe.

Spain has a democratic constitution and a king who has shown that he is willing to die to defend democracy. Spanish voters avoid extremist parties, trade unions show responsibility and moderation, and politicians cooperate with each other. Time has dampened passions over the civil war, fears of military coups, and emotions over NATO. Its stability and democratic confidence allow it to reexamine its Franco past without tearing the nation apart. Separatist terrorism in the Basque region returned after a "permanent" cease-fire declared by ETA in March 2006 broke down. But after March 11, 2004, the supreme threat facing the country is radical Islamic terrorism, stemming primarily from Morocco. The liberal, parliamentary order has definitely sunk its roots deeply. It has already long outlived the earlier republic, during which 18 governments fell before Franco took full control.

On March 14, three days after the tragic bombings occurred in Madrid, the Socialists, led by José Luis Rodríguez Zapatero, were catapulted into power by the emotional force of a people in shock, grief and anger. Spain recovered quickly from the attacks, which had no noticeable effect on the economy. Zapatero stuck rather closely to his predecessor's successful economic policies. The world's eighth-largest economy is troubled by slower economic growth, falling house prices, and rising unemployment and inflation. The budget surplus also disappeared, and its gaping current-accounts deficit has risen to 10% of GDP.

Upon becoming only the fifth president of the government since Franco's death in 1975 Zapatero immediately honored his campaign promise to withdraw Spanish troops from Iraq despite the friction that caused with the American and British allies. He pledged to fight terrorism "in all its forms." He took steps to increase cooperation among the country's intelligence and security services and to hire 36,000 more policemen over four-year period. His negotiations with ETA failed, and he is unlikely to attempt them again. The long-standing cross-party consensus on how to fight terrorism broke down. Spaniards remain divided on how to deal with ETA and how to think about the March 11 tragedy.

As is the custom for new Spanish leaders, Zapatero made his first foreign trip to Morocco, from where most of the Islamic terrorists had come. The king also made a state visit there in 2005. The following year the president made the first trip by a Spanish leader to the North African enclaves since 1980 to demonstrate his readiness to protect Spanish unity. Spain faces daunting problems of illegal immigration. The president pledged to shift Spain's foreign policy from an Atlanticist orientation to one of close partnership with France and Germany. But he has chosen not to play a visible and major role on the European stage and instead to focus on internal reforms. Secretary of State Rice's visit to Spain in June 2007 signaled a desire on both sides to restore good relations.

Zapatero promised a leadership style of dialogue and consensus rather than the confrontation of his predecessor. This applies to relations with the regions. Although he stresses the importance of the constitution, a codeword in Spanish political rhetoric for national unity, he is much more open to the wishes of Basques and Catalans. This is partly explained by the fact that he needs the votes of regional parties in both houses of the *Cortes* to form his government. He promised to discuss greater Basque and Catalan autonomy, and he supported statutes giving Catalonia and Andalucía more self-rule.

Finally the new president of government announced some important social changes. Calling himself a "radical feminist" and promising to make sexual equality an "emblematic task," he appointed nine women to his cabinet in 2008 (up from eight in 2004) and sponsored a law that requires that between 40% and 60% of the candidates in elections be women. He emphasized that women earn one-fifth less than men for the same work, that Spain has one of the highest female jobless rates in Europe, and that only 10% of business executives are female. By law, governing boards of companies must now have 40% to 50% women. His government introduced fast-track divorce. It also made the abortion laws less strict by allowing women to terminate pregnancy in the first 12 weeks for whatever reason, eliminated required religious instruction in public schools, legalized same-sex marriages granting gay couples the right to adopt children, and launched a reexamination of the civil war.

The Zapatero government was thought to have become vulnerable in the March 2008 national elections. Polls had shown that his popularity had shrunk drastically after the breakdown of the peace process involving ETA. He had invested much political capital in the talks, and their failure was a huge personal blow to him. Nevertheless, his party emerged with a 16-seat advantage over the PP. The good news for him was that the opposition PP was absorbed by internal bickering and plots to replace the party leader, Mariano Rajoy, the most unpopular opposition leader in decades. His future as PP chief is uncertain after leading his party to two electoral defeats in a row. With the economy in trouble, Zapatero's second term is likely to be harder than his first. He rules a country that is possibly more polarized politically than in decades.

Portugal

Area: 35,553 sq. mi. (92,082 sq. km.), not counting the Azores or Madeira; (about the size and general shape of Indiana—380 miles north to south, and 140 miles at its widest point).

Population: 10.36 million (estimated).

Capital City: Lisbon (Pop. 2 million). *Lisboa* in Portuguese, pronounced Leesh–boa.

Climate: Mild and rainy weather in late fall and early winter, but cold and snowy in the mountains. From June to September the days are hot, but the air is rather dry.

Neighboring Countries: Spain (North and East); Morocco lies 140 miles across the ocean to the southeast.

Language: Portuguese

Principal Religion: Roman Catholic.

Chief Commercial Exports: Transport equipment, machinery, clothing and footwear, cork, wood and wood products, wine, canned fish, tomato paste, olive oil.

Major Customers: EU25 (79.4% of exports and 73.5% of imports), principally Spain (13.5% of exports and 29% of imports), France (24.9% of exports and 8.5% of imports), Germany (14% of exports and 13.5% of imports), UK (9.6% of exports and 4.6% of imports), U.S. (4% of exports), Italy (5.2% of imports).

Currency: Euro.

National Holiday: June 10 (Luiz de Camões Day, and Day of the Portuguese Communities).

Chief of State: Aníbal Cavaco Silva, President (since March 2006).

Head of Government: José Sócrates, Prime Minister (since March 2005).

National Flag: From the hoist, green and red vertical fields, the green being somewhat less than half of the flag. The Portuguese coat–of–arms is imposed where the two fields meet.

Portugal entered the 1970s as a conservative, industrially underdeveloped country at the bottom of western Europe's economic barrel. It had an authoritarian political order that suppressed all signs of genuine opposition. It therefore was an embarrassment to its NATO allies, which sought to defend democracy on both sides of the Atlantic. It was embroiled in a multitude of hopeless colonial wars in an attempt to maintain control over an empire more than 20 times the size of the mother country.

Yet by the 1980s Portugal offered an almost entirely different picture. It had undergone a revolution that, though claiming almost no lives, drastically altered many aspects of the country. It is now a thriving democracy in which persons of all persuasions can speak and act openly. Although it is one of western Europe's poorest nations, with the continent's highest infant mortality and illiteracy rates, it was willing to accept the economic challenge of entering the EU. It is a country now entirely stripped of its colonial empire, but it is much healthier and stronger as a result. It is a democratically ruled member of NATO with an army radically reduced in size but with military facilities of great strategic importance for the alliance.

The Portuguese are tolerant, friendly, polite and patient, and they form a relatively cohesive society. Without these qualities, the Portuguese would not have survived so well the radical changes that have occurred in the country since 1974. The population is largely homogeneous. But there are over 100,000 blacks from the former African colonies; 10% of Lisbon's population is black, some of whom have been the targets of racist attacks. There are also about 90,000 gypsies, who have not integrated as well in Portugal as they have in Spain.

Few European countries have such a large portion of its population living abroad as does Portugal. Since the 15th century the Portuguese have emigrated in large numbers, first to Brazil, and then after Brazilian independence, to such destinations as North America, Venezuela, Angola and Mozambique. However, after 1955 the greatest number of Portuguese emigrants, two–thirds of whom left agricultural areas in Portugal, went to industrialized western European countries, especially France and Germany, in order to find employment. From 1960 until 1972 a million and a half Portuguese left the country. Emigration has slowed down considerably due to the dramatic economy and political improvements in Portugal after 1974.

The U.S. is now the single country that accepts the greatest annual number of Portuguese emigrants. Indeed, more than a million Portuguese live there. Most of them are from the Azores. By 1987 the total number of Portuguese living abroad was more than four million—roughly 40% of the country's total population. They send back billions in remittances every year.

Portugal is a rectangular–shaped country, a little larger than the state of Maine, but with 10 times as many inhabitants. It has a long Atlantic coastline, along which most of the country's inhabitants live, and it has only one neighbor: Spain. The country is separated into northern and southern halves by the Tagus River. The North is cooler and more mountainous, with small family farms and three–fourths of the entire population. The South is hotter and drier, with rolling plains and large farms, called *latifundios*.

Astride the line between the two halves is Lisbon, where the Tagus empties into the Atlantic Ocean. The capital city is located on seven hills and still reflects a physical character shaped by its Moorish past. It is the heart of a highly centralized country and has all too often in the past looked down upon the rest of the country and has seemed to be uninterested in the fate and welfare of the regions. With all its

suburbs it counts almost two and a half million inhabitants. It and greater Oporto, which is Portugal's only other major city and has 800,000 residents, have attracted three–fourths of the population that is active in the industrial and service sectors of the economy.

Portugal has three main rivers: the Douro in the north, which empties near Oporto, the Tagus in the middle, and the Guadiana, which forms part of the border with Spain and then empties into the Gulf of Cadiz. All originate in Spain, but almost none is navigable between the two countries. Indeed, the transportation links between Spain and Portugal remain difficult. This is a major reason why both countries have stood for so long with their backs practically toward each other facing different directions.

CONTEMPORARY HISTORY

In 1834 Portugal became a constitutional monarchy in a setting of bitter power struggles and intrigues among rival claimants to the throne and between conservatives, who supported the Catholic Church and the nobility, and liberals, who wished to reduce the power of those groups. Except for a relatively brief respite between 1851 and 1910, the century preceding the military takeover of power in 1926 was an era of restlessness, discontent and civil disturbances. It was peppered by wars and revolts which so shook the land that conservatives and liberals finally agreed to avoid bloodshed by alternating power in a system called *rotativismo*.

This rotation system could not prevent the steady erosion of support for the

monarchy, caused by financial and colonial difficulties and by the rising political ambitions of the middle class, which wanted a greater share in political power. In February 1908 King Carlos I, a man of absolutist inclinations and a lust for personal gratification, and the crown prince, were both assassinated. After a spell of uncontrollable political turbulence, the monarchy fell in October 1910. As usual, the military was heavily involved in this overthrow.

The monarchy was replaced by a parliamentary republic, whose main accomplishments were to separate church and state, to end Catholicism's status as the official state religion, and to terminate religious instruction in state schools and state aid to religious schools. But the republic could not find solutions for the country's economic problems or the political factionalism, extremism, terrorism, anarchy, riots, strikes and attempted *coups d'état*, which continued to be a part of daily political life. The republic was further weakened by Portugal's participation in World War I, which in no way unified the many leading groups behind a common objective.

Not only were many politicians corrupt and incompetent, but the rapid turnover of governments prevented any policy continuity. Portugal had an average of three governments per year until 1926, when the military stepped in again and took political power into its own hands. The military takeover was not followed by a bloody civil war, as in Spain a decade later. The reasons are that the years of political havoc had not thoroughly polarized Portuguese society, as had been the case

Lisbon from the Tagus River

Portugal

in Spain. Also Portugal has, in general, a more homogeneous, less fragmented society than its neighbor, Spain.

Military–Fascist Rule

In order to attack the financial problems, especially inflation, which the years of chaos had exacerbated, the generals, in 1928, named an economics professor from the University of Coimbra, Dr. Antonio Oliveira Salazar, as finance minister. In 1932 he became leader of the only legal party and prime minister, the post that until 1974 remained the heart of political power in Portugal. He established a fascist state, called the *Estado Novo* ("New State"), which he guided until his incapacitation in 1968. In 1933 a constitution was promulgated that had a few trappings of parliamentary government, such as a unicameral National Assembly and a directly elected president.

The corporatist character of the new constitution was embodied in an advisory organ called the Corporative Chamber. This allegedly united all classes by bringing together representatives of diverse economic and professional groups in order to evaluate all legislation. Over the years other organizations were established to encompass workers, employers, craftsmen, landowners, rural laborers, fishermen, women and youth, in order to lock all citizens tightly into a bundle of groups, all directed from the top by Salazar. There was only one legal political party, the *União Nacional* ("National Union"), which never played a central role in Portugal, as did the Nazi or Fascist parties in Germany and Italy.

The Portuguese political system was complicated in theory, but it was rather simple in practice. With the advice of trusted cronies from industry, the military and the church, Salazar made all crucial political decisions. Freedom of press and assembly were curtailed, and all written and electronic communications were censored. Critical professors were dismissed, and strikes were outlawed. As every Portuguese knew, the secret police (PIDE) was ever–present. It is estimated that one in 400 Portuguese were paid informants.

When the Spanish Civil War broke out in 1936, Salazar ordered the creation of a "Portuguese Legion" to fight on Gen. Francisco Franco's side. About 6,000 Portuguese fought against the Spanish Republic. Portugal also tolerated the transport of munitions from France across its territory until mid–1937, when the British, Portugal's closest ally for three centuries, pressured Salazar into closing its borders to such war material. On March 17, 1939, Franco and Salazar signed a nonaggression and friendship pact, which was amended on July 29, 1940, to obligate both

governments to discuss their mutual security interests with one another whenever the "independence or security" of one of the countries is endangered. That pact remains valid.

Portugal, like Spain, did not become linked militarily and diplomatically with Germany and Italy before and during World War II. Portugal even profited from its neutrality; the country became one of Europe's major centers for spies from all belligerent countries. However, Salazar's sympathies were revealed when he ordered a day of national mourning after Hitler had committed suicide.

Portugal's valuable strategic position and long–standing relationship with Britain enabled it to become a founding member of NATO, and in 1955 Portugal was admitted to the UN. However, Portugal remained in an economic, social and political condition of stagnation and immobility, ruled and administered by an aging dictator, and a tight clique of generals, admirals and bureaucrats, who, through a swarm of spies, rendered the population submissive, but increasingly dissatisfied and restless.

In 1968 a law professor, Dr. Marcelo Caetano, assumed leadership over this regime, which was in the process of rapid decay. He had high hopes of reforming and liberalizing the authoritarian system that his predecessor had created, but it had become far too late for such reform.

Portugal had just about reached the exploding point, and all that was needed was a spark. That spark came in 1974 from the same institution that had stepped into the Portuguese political sphere many times before and that had established the half–century dictatorship in the first place in 1926—the military.

Colonial Problems

The last straw was the seemingly endless wars in Portugal's African colonies, which the Portuguese preferred to call Ultramar (overseas territories). The Portuguese settlers had always mingled more easily with nonwhite native populations than did the British, French and Belgian colonizers. One still sees the results of this in Brazil, where blacks and whites seem to live together relatively harmoniously (albeit under a predominantly white elite). Also, nothing resembling an official apartheid ("separateness") policy ever developed in the Portuguese colonies, such as in formerly British and Dutch South Africa.

A certain conviction that Portuguese rule was both good and tolerable for the subject peoples, combined with the economic importance for Portugal and with the fact that there were over a million Portuguese living in the colonies, led Portugal to hang on to its empire long after the other European nations had decided to relinquish theirs. Foreign Minister Franco

Salazar greeting Spain's Franco

War in Angola: troop carrier swerves to avoid a road trap

Nogueira even wrote in 1967 that the Portuguese considered themselves "to be an African nation." The obvious point, however, was that the bulk of the native populations in the colonies did not consider themselves to be *Portuguese*.

In 1961 India simply invaded and annexed the mini–territories of Goa, Damão and Diu. Since 1913 the Portuguese had had to quell occasional native uprisings in Africa. In 1961 these uprisings re-erupted, first in Angola around such groups as the Popular Movement for the Liberation of Angola (MPLA), the Angolan National Liberation Front (FNLA) and the National Union for Total Angolan Independence, (UNITA), then in 1963 in Mozambique (led by the Front for the Liberation of Mozambique) and in Guinea–Bissau. The Portuguese government decided to hold on to the African colonies at all costs, fearing that their loss would spell the doom of the Portuguese state. In fact, it was this decision more than any other that led to the ultimate downfall of the Portuguese fascist regime.

Military Unrest

By 1974 there were 170,000 men in the Portuguese army, 135,000 of whom were stationed in Africa. The lion's share of these troops was four–year conscripts, who increasingly resented their role in quelling native rebellions against a regime that fewer and fewer Portuguese wished to preserve. The need to expand the size of the army to cope with the African wars brought many young men from the lower classes and the universities into the offi-

cers' corps. These groups had earlier been largely excluded from the officers' ranks and were more inclined to sympathize with the rebels' aims. These young officers gradually lost faith in the kinds of arguments that had long been used to justify the protracted colonial struggle. Many became inspired by the revolutionary ideas espoused by their African adversaries. They grew to dislike strongly their more traditional military superiors. These radicalized lower–ranking officers formed the illegal Movement of the Armed Forces (MFA), which became the core of opposition to the regime.

Their convictions and confidence were enormously strengthened by the appearance in February 1974 of a book that must be considered one of the most significant in modern Portuguese history: *Portugal and the Future*. It was written by the monacled General António de Spínola, the former commander in Guinea–Bissau, whose legendary bravery in battle had won him the admiration of the lower ranks. Spínola advocated a political solution to the colonial question and the establishment of a sort of Portuguese commonwealth of nations, similar to that of the British. It is not surprising that Dr. Caetano reportedly could not sleep the night after he had read the book.

The "Carnation Revolution"

Plotters in the MFA went to work on a plan to overthrow the regime. In the night of April 25, 1974, troops numbering about 5,000 occupied Lisbon in a well–planned operation. Since most officers had become

indifferent to the survival of the regime, there was no resistance to the surprise coup. Some nervous PIDE agents, (which the underground press had called "Gestaportuguese") who had fled to their headquarters in panic, had reportedly fired on a small crowd (reports differ, but the total casualties did not exceed four). Except for these, not a shot was fired to defend a fascist regime that had ruled Portugal for about half a century. Rarely in history has such a fundamental political change occurred with so little loss of life.

The plotters formed a "Junta of National Salvation," which abolished the PIDE and announced that the colonies would be granted the right of self–determination and that political exiles would be permitted to return to Portugal. Political enthusiasm burst into life, and public debates, rallies and street demonstrations seized a nation in which such things had been forbidden for 48 years.

For two years Portugal was rocked by a succession of provisional governments and confusing revolutionary turmoil. While this turmoil was fired by much emotion, it occurred in the traditional Portuguese style of little actual bloodshed. The new leaders were in such a hurry to cut their former colonies totally loose that they made little effort to try at least to introduce a stable transfer of power in the colonies to groups that might have been willing to legitimize their rule through democratic elections. The MFA's strong Marxist bias inclined it to hand over power in the colonies to like–minded revolutionaries.

Decolonization and Internal Turmoil

Most of Portugal's land area and its world–wide population were reduced by 65% overnight because of the rapid Portuguese withdrawal from the African territories and Timor in the Far East. This created a particularly great refugee problem for the home country. Between 1974 and 1976 at least half a million refugees poured into Portugal, mainly from Angola. In March 1977 the new Marxist leader ordered the expulsion of all persons holding Portuguese passports, so a new wave of expellees began to pour in. The U.S. helped pay for the airlift of the *retornados* (a term Portuguese dislike today because it implies the returnees were not welcome) and gave Portugal more than $1 billion over five years to help cope with the financial crisis.

The returnees arrived in a chaotic Portugal with few possessions and with currencies that were not accepted in Portugal. Many were convinced that their home government had sold out to revolutionary terrorists and were therefore deeply embittered and inclined toward

Portugal

The military *coup*, April 25, 1974

active, anticommunist and conservative politics. Their bitterness was also stimulated by the facts that there were almost no jobs for them in Portugal and that the government could provide only meager financial assistance. Many only found shelter in shantytowns that cropped up everywhere. In some places, especially in Algarve, the government commandeered luxury hotels for the returnees, a logical and humanitarian action which, however, almost bankrupted the country and deprived one of Portugal's most important industries, tourism, of many needed facilities. Ultimately the returnees were dispersed more evenly throughout the country and slowly began to find work. But the initial problems for the shaken country were immense.

There were moderates within the ruling MFA, such as General Spínola, whom the MFA had appointed immediately as provisional president, who believed that the new leaders had moved too far to the left. As a result of unsuccessful countercoups against the leftist elements within the leadership in September 1974 and again in March 1975, the moderate elements within the government were purged and, in some cases such as Spínola himself, were driven into exile.

Those leaders who remained were highly critical of what they derided as "bourgeois democracy." The avowedly pro–Communist Colonel Vasco Gonçalves advocated the creation of Soviet–style "committees for the defense of the Revolution," and the swaggering admirer of Fidel Castro, General Otelo Saraiva de Carvalho, championed the notion of "people's power" to replace the political parties. These leaders, along with a more pliant presidential replacement for Spínola, General Costa Gomes, allowed the Communists and the far left to assume control of the trade unions, the news media and local governments.

They ordered the soldiers not to intervene when left–wing mobs broke up socialist and conservative political gatherings. They nationalized major industries, insurance companies and banks, and they looked on approvingly as workers seized factories and as peasants took over land in the central and southern provinces. Roughly a fourth of Portugal's forest and croplands were seized and most of them were converted to forms of collectively owned farms. But these new farms, especially in the province of Alentejo, where farming had traditionally been done on large estates called *latifundios*, were so in-

efficient that by the end of the 1970s Alentejo produced about a third to half of the grain and livestock it had supplied before the revolution.

The MFA's revolutionary economic experiments were devastating for the country, and they aroused intense opposition. It almost seemed that Portugal was going to return to the political havoc that had stricken the country before 1926. But the politically naive and inexperienced captains, who suddenly wore colonels' and generals' brass on their shoulders, lost sight of one important factor: the Portuguese voter.

They had announced that they intended to hold power for three years, but they did not prevent the holding of elections in April 1975 for an assembly that would produce a new constitution. They dismissed the elections casually as a mere opinion poll that could not possibly lessen their grip on political power. However, the results stunned them. In the first free election in half a century, 92% of eligible voters turned out to give a massive vote of no-confidence to the heavy–handed, revolutionary–authoritarian rulers. Over 70% of the voters supported the three moderate democratic parties, and only 17% supported the soldiers' only friends, the Communists and their allies.

The officers in power made it clear that they had no intention of honoring the results of the election. Instead they moved to eliminate entirely the freedom of the press. The supporters of the democratic parties thereupon poured into the streets to show their disapproval. Beginning in July 1975 anti–Communist riots erupted in the North in reaction to a Communist bombing campaign there. This massive resistance jolted the majority of military officers out of their state of indifference. When far–left paratroopers supporting General Otelo tried to seize full power for themselves on November 25, 1975, Lt. Col. Ramalho Eanes led a crack commando force to foil the uprising. Eanes, who had heretofore been almost unknown, took the revolution back to its democratic purpose. In the aftermath, all Communists and extreme leftists were purged from the MFA and from all governing bodies, and the Communists' hopes of taking command over a radical revolution were dashed.

A decade later, Otelo was put on trial for his continuing support for leftist revolution. The press dubbed it the "trial of the century," and it lasted 19 months. He was convicted in 1987 of belonging to a terrorist organization, Popular Forces of April 25 (FP–25), which was suspected of being responsible for at least 15 assassinations of businessmen and landowners and for attacks against the U.S. embassy, NATO warships and the residences of German airmen. Forty–seven codefendants were also convicted. In 2001 a Lisbon court acquitted Otelo of terrorism charges.

In the mid–1970s foreign observers were left dizzy by all the fundamental shifts, from right to left and then back to center, where Portugal was to stay. Most Portuguese had wanted a revolution, but they had wanted a moderate democratic revolution, one that would bring them a stable and just political order, protection of individual rights, and ultimately economic prosperity. The last 50 years had brought them enough tyranny and extremist politics. Within a year and a half, the Portuguese revolution had been tamed.

In February 1976 the MFA signed a pact with the political parties that greatly restricted the political role of the military. In April 1976 the assembly that had been elected a year earlier to write a new constitution completed its job. Elections in the same month produced another victory for the moderate democratic parties. Eanes, who had been promoted to the rank of general, was elected president in June 1976, an office he occupied for a decade. One month later he swore in Portugal's first truly democratic government since 1926. Within a few months the radically revolutionary military officers disap-

peared from the political stage. In 1996, Portugal's first contemporary history museum, charting the transition from dictatorship to democracy, was opened in Leiria. It contains official archives of the 1974 armed forces revolt.

GOVERNMENT

The Arrival of Democracy

One of the most astonishing aspects of Portuguese events after April 25, 1974, often called the "carnation revolution" because of its bloodless character, was the speed with which the Marxist flirtation expired and the extent to which the revolution became tamed. Within two years, the swaggering officers who had seized power and set Portugal on the fast track toward a radical socialist state had disappeared almost completely. The rigidly orthodox Portuguese Communist Party (PCP) saw much of its electoral support evaporate.

Within two years the moderate democratic parties could claim the support of more than 80% of the voters. Also, a president was in office who had snatched the revolution from the clutches of the extreme left, even though he had moderate leftist sympaties and saw the revolution

as something more than the mere establishment of a politically democratic system. He had left no doubt whatsoever that he would support democracy with all the vigor that his serious and ramrod frame could muster.

The salvation of democracy in Portugal was aided by other important factors. First, the extremists were effectively challenged by a democratically oriented Portuguese Socialist Party (PS), led by Mario Soares, a product of one of the country's most prominent families and one of the most respected Portuguese political figures. His popularity within Portugal helped him counter the Communist grab for power by presenting a responsible, socialist, democratic alternative to the Stalinist, heavy–handed, Moscow–oriented PCP. Also, his prestige abroad helped bind Portugal's untried democracy to the West. The PS was also aided by the existence of attractive social democratic models in other western European countries, such as Germany.

A second factor was U.S. financial assistance. In addition to helping finance the return of many refugees from Africa to metropolitan Portugal, the U.S. granted $1.5 billion in economic assistance from 1975 to 1980. This was the largest contri-

Former President Eanes

Portugal

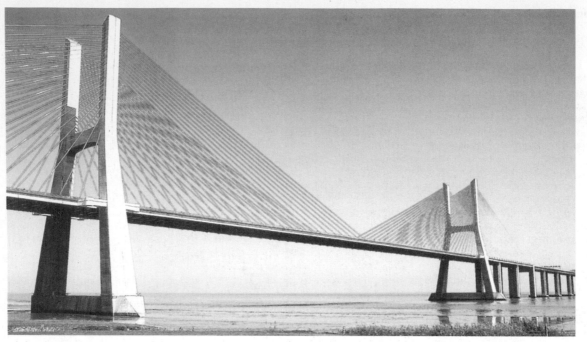

Lisbon: panoramic view of Ponte Vasco da Gama Bridge over the Tagus River

bution any single western country made to the $2.3 billion worth of aid given to Portugal during that period. The U.S. also provided it with long–term, low-interest credit to purchase grain and animal feeds. This example of enlightened self–interest reflected the earlier insights of the Marshall Plan in the rest of Europe after World War II—the best policy against Marxist appeals is economic success. The U.S. held itself aloof from Portugal's domestic battles and thus enabled the democratic forces to expose the blatant Communist attempts to seize power, backed by money from the Soviet Union.

A final factor, and perhaps the most important, was the fact that the Portuguese were tired of 50 years of dictatorship and desperately wanted an effective economy to scrape the country out of the bottom of the western European economic barrel and to set it on the path to stability and prosperity.

In spite of the success in grabbing the revolution out of the eager hands of the extremists, there were significant visible traces of revolutionary enthusiasm left in the constitution and the political and economic system, which could only gradually be erased. One was the far–reaching nationalization of much of the economy; Article 10 of the constitution called for "the collectivization of the main means of production." Second, the constitution of 1976 ruled out the idea of a market economy and placed severe limitations on any nonsocialist government.

Article 1 called for "Portugal's . . . transformation into a society without classes."

Article 2 obligated the nation's leaders to "assure the transition to socialism through the creation of conditions for the democratic exercise of power by the working classes." A third remnant was the appointment of the Revolutionary Council, the governing body of the old Armed Forces Movement, as a kind of watchdog of the revolution. Article 273 of the constitution gave the army the duty to "secure the continuation of the revolution." This body was composed of 14 military officers chosen among themselves, the heads of the three branches of the armed services, and the president of the republic, who was chairman of the Council. It had the power to block or even to veto parliamentary legislation, a power it was not afraid to exercise.

A New Constitution

A fourth remnant is the strong presidency, elected every five years by direct, universal suffrage. A president may be re-elected only once. The president relinquished, in 1981, the post of supreme commander, and he can no longer control promotions within the armed forces. According to the 1982 constitution, the government is responsible only to the parliament, and not to the president. The latter can dismiss a government only after consulting the constitutional committee. But as the country saw in 2004 and 2005, the president indeed retains the power to appoint prime ministers, dissolve parliament and call new elections; former President Jorge Sampaio called this crucial power his "atomic bomb." A president can

veto or delay or block legislation by sending it to the constitutional court or back to parliament. Although the president's formal powers may seem limited, his influence is considerable. The reason is that with so many changes in governments (by 1987 there had been 17 in 13 years) the presidency has been the center of political continuity.

The former president, General António Ramalho Eanes, can undeniably take more credit than anyone else for establishing order and discipline among the country's highly politicized military officers and for purging the leftist extremists within the army. In February 1976 he signed a pact with the leaders of the major political parties that demoted the army to a less direct political role. He ruled as a quiet, shy, serious and very hard–working man from a peasant background. Although he was seldom seen smiling, he was unquestionably the most popular man in Portuguese politics at the time. This is very important in Portugal, where, as in many young democracies, politics is highly personalized. Names tend to be more important than programs.

The winner of the 1986 presidential election was the Socialist, Mario Soares, who jubilantly proclaimed that his election marked "the end of Portugal's transition to a genuine democracy." The event was a watershed in Portuguese politics in that none of the candidates was a military man. It signaled the definite return of the soldiers from politics to the barracks.

Soares relinquished the presidency in 1996 to fellow Socialist, Jorge Sampaio, a lawyer and former Lisbon mayor who defeated ex–Prime Minister Cavaco Silva 53.8% to 46.2%. This was the first time since 1974 that voters chose a president from the same ranks as the ruling party. Sampaio speaks excellent English, having spent part of his boyhood in Baltimore and London. He was comfortably re-elected in January 2001.

He demonstrated how powerful the presidency can be when he decided, in July 2004, that for the sake of stability no new elections would be held when José Manuel Barroso stepped down as prime minister to become president of the European Commission. After the new prime minister, Pedro Santana Lopes, seemed to have lost control after only five months despite commanding a majority in parliament, it was Sampaio who ordered the parliament to be dissolved and new elections held in 2005, again for the sake of long-term stability. This was unprecedented, but it was within the president's authority.

In January 2006, Anibal Cavaco Silva defeated five center-left candidates to win the presidency on the first round of voting, garnering 50.7% of the votes. An economist who studied at Britain's York University, he is a pragmatic Social Democratic politician with long experience as prime minister from 1985–1995. He is the first president since the overthrow of the dictatorship in 1974 who is not of the left. He crushed not only popular poet, Manuel Alegre, who won almost 21%, but also former President Mario Soares, who at age 81 won an embarrassingly low 14%. It was an inglorious end to Soares's noble political career.

Cavaco Silva is of a different party than Socialist Prime Minister José Sócrates and made clear his intention to be more politically active than his predecessors. But one

The National Theater, Lisbon

Lisbon newspaper called them "twin souls" who can easily cohabit. More unites the two leaders than divides them. Both are pragmatists who prefer action over rhetorical grandstanding. They both seek the same things: to salvage the economy, reduce government spending, trim the public sector and improve a school system in which 45% drop out before completing secondary school.

Changes in Government Structure

There are some institutions, policies and trends that have steadily reduced the revolutionary stamp on political life. One is the unicameral parliament, called the Assembly of the Republic, with 230 seats elected for a maximum four–year term by proportional representation in 20 multi-member constituencies. At the head of the majority within the assembly is a relatively strong prime minister. Since 1974 regional governors or parliaments have not been able to block either the prime minister's or the president's powers since Portugal is a highly centralized, unitary state. It has also developed a stable political system. From 1975 to 1985, the average life of a government was only ten months. The average from 1975 to 2005 was two years. Since 1987, all but one government has served out its full four-year term.

For administrative purposes Portugal is divided into 18 districts, each with a governor appointed by the ministry of internal administration upon the approval of the prime minister and his cabinet. A plan to devolve more power to the regions failed in 1998 when an overwhelming 64% of voters in a referendum rejected it; the majority feared that it would destroy na-

tional unity, undermine budgetary discipline, and create another wasteful layer of bureaucracy. A few months earlier only a third of voters turned out to express their opinion on the country's strict abortion laws; since a majority did not vote, the results were invalid. This had been Portugal's first–ever referendum, a device whose introduction a year earlier had been hailed as the completion of a finely balanced constitution.

All institutionalized control by the military over the civilian government was eliminated, and military officers were banned from politics. This does not mean that all military influence in Portuguese politics will vanish. Indeed, military intervention in politics has historical roots too deep in Portugal to disappear completely. But it did mean that a civilian Council of State and Constitutional Council, appointed jointly by the parliament, the government and the president replaced the Revolutionary Council. The adoption of the new constitution in 1982 marked the formal end of the "carnation revolution" and the coming of age of Portugal's parliamentary democracy.

A further move to strengthen the Portuguese incentive to remain on the road of democracy was the decision in 1976 to seek entry into the EC (now EU) and thereby to tighten the links that bind Portugal to the older democracies of western Europe. Perhaps the most important trend that has reduced the revolutionary stamp on public life in Portugal has been the string of electoral victories for the moderate democratic political parties. This is particularly significant for a country in which all earlier attempts at democratic

President Anibal Cavaco Silva

Portugal

rule collapsed partly because of a paralyzing multiparty system.

POLITICAL PARTIES

Social Democratic Party (PSD)

The Social Democratic Party (PSD) changed its name from the People's Democratic Party (PPD), in order to give itself a sharper programmatic definition. It is a moderate, progressive and organizationally decentralized party without a rigid ideological position. It is an avowedly anti–Marxist party which supports basic democratic freedoms and the market economy. It draws its voters mainly from the middle class in small and medium-sized towns, from the independent professions and from mid- and upper–level technical cadres. It is traditionally strongest in the Azores and Madeira archipelagos and in northern and central Portugal.

Under former leader Aníbal Cavaco Silva it became, in 1987, the first party since 1974 to win a majority of either votes or seats. It was also the first time that the parties of the left did not win most of the votes. The 1991 elections demonstrated the steadiness of his free market policies, economic privatization, and encouragement of private initiative and foreign investment. For the first time since the founding of the republic 81 years earlier, a democratically elected party won two consecutive absolute majorities. This was a stunning change for a country whose only previous periods of political stability were under fascist dictatorship.

The PSD was defeated in the 1995 and 1999 parliamentary elections. Its fortunes changed in the March 2002 elections, when it captured 40.1% of the votes and 102 of the 230 seats. José Manuel Barroso, a former foreign minister who had lived seven years in the U.S. and taught at Georgetown University, became prime minister at the head of a coalition government that included the People's Party. In 2004 he stepped down to became EC president after a bitter struggle in Brussels among the major powers within the EU to find a candidate acceptable to everyone. Thanks to his fluent French acquired while working on an MA in political science in Geneva, he was acceptable to the French.

He passed the prime ministry to Lisbon's flamboyant mayor, Pedro Santana Lopes in July 2004. It turns out that Barroso left a mess. Lopes's government proved to be so erratic, blunder-prone and media-obsessed that after only four months in office then President Jorge Sampaio decided that the country had had enough. He called new elections for February 2005. Lopes felt betrayed: "I'm covered in scars from being stabbed in the

back." With a turnout of 65%, the largest in a decade, the PSD was unceremoniously thrown out of power, dropping from 40% to 29% of the votes. However, the current president since March 2006, Aníbal Cavaco Silva, is from the PSD.

The People's Party

The People's Party (PP, formerly called the Democratic and Social Center—CDS or Christian Democrats) is the newest and most conservative of Portugal's four major parties. It has an anti–Marxist, Euroskeptic, Christian and humanistic orientation and a politically moderate leadership. It is the only major party that rejects socialism as a goal. It finds its members and voters chiefly among industrial management, the service industries, independent farmers and the *retornados* from the former colonies. Women also vote disproportionately for it. The party is strongest in the north, where the influence of the Catholic Church has not sunk as rapidly after 1974 as in Lisbon and the south.

It is decentralized and organizationally weaker than the other major parties. It does have the backing of the major industrialists' association, the CIP. It did well in the 2002 elections, winning 8.8% and 14

seats and entered the coalition government with the PSD. The party did very poorly in the 2005 elections and finds itself in the opposition. However, its founder and former leader, Diego Freitas do Amaral, was appointed foreign minister in the Socialist government.

Socialist Party (PS)

Along with some close associates, Mario Soares had founded the Socialist Party (PS) in Münstereifel, Germany, in 1973, with the helping hand of the then ruling Social Democratic Party of Germany. When the Portuguese revolution erupted in 1974, Soares rushed back from his Paris exile, and the PS was thrust into the forefront of the turbulent events without having time to become well organized for its new role. The PS and Soares certainly share much of the credit for channeling the revolution into a democratic direction. But after being the country's most important political party for a few years, its extreme fragmentation and organizational difficulties, along with the widespread unsatisfied economic expectations of the Portuguese, caused it to suffer a string of election failures, which shook the party's confidence.

Young Communists call for action in Faro (Algarve)

The party is organized in a decentralized way. Unlike all other Portuguese parties, its voting strength has traditionally been spread fairly evenly over the entire country and was found primarily in the working and lower middle classes. It is backed by the moderate General Union of Workers, (UGT), which, since 1979, increasingly challenged Communist domination of the organized labor movement. The party program was officially Marxist, but the existence of a rigid and stubborn Communist Party to its left, with which the PS refuses to form any coalition, pushed the party toward the political center. In the minds of most politically active Portuguese, the desire to overcome economic difficulties has replaced earlier aspirations of establishing socialism.

The Socialists ruled Portugal from 1995 to 2002. It got 37.9% of the votes and 95 seats in the March 2002 elections and was the main opposition party. Its fortunes turned around under the leadership of a new dynamic and charismatic leader, José Sócrates. The environment minister in the previous Socialist government from 1995 to 2002, he took over the leadership in September 2004. The son of an architect from a northern Portuguese village, he was 16 years old when the fascist regime crashed down. After studying civil engineering and getting an MBA, he has worked his way up in Socialist politics. Known to be straightforward, courageous, determined and methodical, he also brings a certain youthful flair to the party, representing a younger generation of modernizing, pro-market Socialists. He draws inspiration from Britain's Tony Blair. One fashion designer designated him as the best dressed politician in Portugal.

In the February 2005 elections the Socialists achieved an overwhelming victory, winning an absolute majority in parliament for the first time in the party's history. Not only did it win 121 of the 230 seats, but the left parties together won nearly two-thirds of the seats. Prime Minister Sócrates promised a "technological shock" aimed at copying the economic success of two other small EU countries—Ireland and Finland. "I want to use this victory to modernize the country, to create more economic growth, more innovation, more investment and more opportunities." After four prime ministers in four years, the four uninterrupted years of Socialist rule will provide the stability for sustained economic reforms that most Portuguese regard as essential.

Portuguese Communist Party (PCP)

The final major party is the Portuguese Communist Party (PCP), once led by Alvaro Cunhal, then Carlos Carvalhas and Jerónimo de Sousa. The PCP is still fairly orthodox. During the fascist rule many of its leading functionaries were either in prison or in exile in the Soviet Union. Cunhal himself was in prison eight years and is too bitter and frozen in his thinking to change now. It is Portugal's oldest party and is the only one with roots in the first republic from 1910 to 1926. This is also the country's best-organized party. It was a tight, clandestine group during the fascist period, and when the revolution came in 1974 it was immediately prepared to jump into the political fray and attempt to take all the reins of power in its own hands.

Its major base of power since the summer of 1975, when its patrons within the army lost most of their own power, was the landless farmers in the Alentejo region, where the party helped organize collectivized agricultural enterprises (UCP), and the trade unions, especially the powerful General Confederation of Portuguese Workers (CGTP–*Intersindical*), which organizes almost three–fourths of all trade union leaders. The PCP has also attracted some intellectuals.

Geographically the party's electoral fortresses were the agricultural area of Alentejo and the industrial zone around Lisbon. In the north, it faced almost complete rejection, except in the city of Oporto. The disillusioned, more educated party members defected in droves. Among the party's problems are a general de-radicalization of the working class and the rise of a younger wing within the PCP that advocates less dogmatic policies. In the 2005 elections the PCP and the radical *Bloco de Esquerda* (Bloc of the Left) together captured about 15% of the votes and won representation in parliament.

Foreign and Defense Policies

Because of its small size and limited economic prowess, Portugal is accustomed to playing a low-key role in international affairs. In 2004 José Manuel Barroso departed from this mold and stepped into the international spotlight to become the president of the European Commission. Many regard this as the most important international post ever held by a Portuguese citizen. Being a part of an integrated Europe is a major foundation stone for its foreign policy.

Its defense policy has long been based on its membership in NATO. Its Atlantic location is central to its approach to the world. It was access to this body of water that enabled it to expand its language and culture to far-flung lands. As a traditional ally of Great Britain since 1386, it was a founding member of the Atlantic Alliance in 1949. In fact, its historical partnership with the UK is the longest-standing pact in Europe. Portugal's major contribution to the alliance has never been in the form of combat troops.

During the decade and a half preceding the 1974 revolution, Portugal's army was bogged down in colonial wars, but between September 1974 and November 1975 these millstones were cast off one by one: first Portuguese Guinea (now Guinea–Bissau), then Mozambique, Angola, the Cape Verde Islands, São Tomé and Príncipe.

In 1996 Portugal and its six former colonies, including Brazil, fulfilled a long–held ambition by uniting their 230 million people (of whom 183 million are Brazilians) in the Community of Por-

Portugal

tuguese–Speaking Countries (CPLP). Its task is to protect their common language and promote cooperation. The post of secretary general is rotated alphabetically every two years. The African Union has designated Portuguese as one of the organization's official languages, and China has observer status because of Macao. Portuguese is a global language, spoken on every continent, but it is not an international language, used in business and diplomacy.

Prime Minister Sócrates reaffirmed the country's three-sided foreign policy in 2005: "Portugal's external policy is a strategic triangle that unites our commitment to being at the heart of Europe with our Atlantic ties and our commitment to the Lusophone community." The country was a partner in the attempt to stabilize Iraq after the March 2003 war, but many Portuguese, including the Socialist government's foreign minister, Diogo Freitas do Amaral, were critical of Washington's Iraq policy. Amaral was particularly blunt, calling the war "illegal" and even comparing President George W. Bush to Hitler. His appointment was the most controversial decision the prime minister made because Portugal's relationship with the U.S. is a key element in its foreign policy.

Macau

The only actual colony that remained until the end of the century was Macau, a tiny (six sq. miles) outpost on the southern coast of the People's Republic of China, 40 miles (64 km.) across the Canton River Estuary from Hong Kong. Only about 10,000 of the estimated 427,000 are Portuguese, although 110,000 hold Portuguese passports and can therefore live and work anywhere in the EU if they choose. Few of the Chinese who live there speak Portuguese. In fact, English is used far more than Portuguese. After the 1974 revolution, Lisbon wanted to give up the colony, which is an important trade outlet and source of foreign capital for Beijing. In 1979 officials from both countries met secretly in Paris, where the Portuguese acknowledged Chinese sovereignty over the territory and agreed to administer it until China wanted it back. China assumed full control on December 19, 1999, after 442 years of Portuguese rule.

Although nominally under Portuguese administration, Portuguese officials made no pretense of being in charge. Indeed, all it would have taken for the Chinese to regain control of the colony earlier was a phone call from Beijing. There is little popular agitation for greater democracy, as in Hong Kong. The Chinese promised to respect Macau's Western, capitalist society and economy until at least 2050 and leave it with considerable autonomy in local affairs. The Portuguese were a bit nostalgic. Fernando Lima, a journalist and author of several books on Macau, wrote: "At least Portuguese can look back with some pride. We created a special culture you don't find anywhere else in the world, a melting pot of people of mixed-European, Indian, and Asian descent."

East Timor

Technically speaking, Portugal still had another colony until 2002, namely Portuguese Timor. Neither Portugal nor the UN ever officially recognized the annexation of this half of the Timor Island by Indonesia on July 17, 1976. Almost half of East Timor's population died as a result of Indonesia's invasion and a native independence movement still resists Indonesian authority. The situation recaptured the world's attention in 1991, when Indonesian soldiers and police opened fire on peaceful demonstrators, killing dozens in front of western journalists' cameras. All over Portugal, flags were flown at half-mast, newspapers appeared with black bands, and ceremonies and church vigils were held. Portugal's talks with Indonesia on this issue in 1992 ended with no concrete results.

In 1996 the Nobel Peace Prize was awarded to José Ramos–Horta, a U.S.–educated human rights activist whose leftist Portuguese father had been deported to East Timor, and to Roman Catholic Bishop Carlos Filipe Ximenes Belo, a native of Timor, who had studied in missionary schools in Portugal and Rome. President Jorge Sampaio, whose country had provided refuge for many East Timorese dissidents and had conducted the UN–sponsored negotiations with Indonesia for 12 years, called the award "a wonderful surprise" that reflects the two men's "indefatigable work in the service of human rights and peace in the territory." Portugal was rewarded by being given a two–year seat on the UN Security Council in 1997. Ramos-Horta went on to become president of the new country, but he almost died of an assassination attempt in February 2008.

The situation changed dramatically in 1998 when the Indonesian government of longtime ruler Suharto was overthrown, and the new leaders offered the 800,000

Timorese the opportunity to choose autonomy or independence. In May 1999, following more than 15 years of UN–sponsored negotiations in which the Portuguese were more closely involved than any other nation, Portugal signed an agreement with Indonesia calling for a referendum on August 8. A majority voted for independence, but violence continued. Portugal dispatched 1,000 troops to help reestablish and keep the peace.

The UN decision to make Portuguese the official language of independent East Timor ignited an intense protest and debate about what it means to be East Timorese. Only 10%, most of them older people, speak it. Proponents, like resistance fighter Joao Carrascalo, argue, "we have a strong and long link with Portugal. They were benevolent colonialists. It makes sense for us to speak the language." Opponents, such as youth leader Nino Pereira, disagree: "If that [Portuguese] is what they want to speak, how are we supposed to be involved in the new government? The old people have this nostalgia with Portugal, but they have to realize that we are moving forward. The colonial days are over." In August 2001 voters elected a constituent assembly that produced a constitution. In 2002 East Timor became an independent state.

The Azores

The Azores, nine mountainous and beautiful islands of volcanic origin which are located about 1,000 miles (1,600 km.) west of Lisbon, are a vital stepping-stone for NATO airborne forces moving toward the Mediterranean, Middle East, Persian Gulf or Africa. Former President Eanes was certainly correct in calling them "a pillar of support in the defense of Europe." American Air Force General Larry Wright underscored this: "Whoever controls the Azores controls the Atlantic."

Azores

Of particular importance is the U.S. air base at Lajes on the island of Terceiram, which the U.S. leases from Portugal, renewable every five years. Lajes is a refueling station, and about 250 U.S. aircraft touch down each month. It is also a base for P–3 Orion maritime surveillance planes that patrol 2.5 million square miles in the North Atlantic.

A serious financial dispute arose in 1988 when the U.S. announced that it would provide less aid. The prime minister noted, "expectations are not being met." Many of his countrymen had the impression that Portugal was being taken for granted, now that democracy had been stabilized. Unlike the situation in Spain concerning Torrejon Air Base, where the issue was political, not financial, there is no public resentment over the American military presence at Lajes. In 1988 the Portuguese government announced that it did not want the F16 fighter-bombers that were being evicted from Spain to be redeployed in Portugal. It called for a formal review of the base agreement, and a solution was found in 1989: the U.S. supplied the Portuguese armed forces with 20 F16s, as well as a battery of Hawk ground–to–air missiles, 57 antisubmarine, combat and utility helicopters, air defense radar, and a hydrographic vessel. U.S. financial aid for 1989 was set at $150 million, down from $208 million in 1985. All this assistance enables Portugal to shift its military emphasis in NATO from leasing bases to a more active antisubmarine role in the mid–Atlantic.

In the 1990s the U.S. pulled some of its military assets out of the Azores after Soviet activity in the Atlantic had ended. The U.S., which maintains 1,800 military personnel and 1,900 dependents on the island, also has an underwater terminal on the island of Santa Maria to monitor submarine movements in the Atlantic and a network of underground supply areas throughout the islands whose contents can be airlifted to any transatlantic area within hours. France also operates a missile tracking station on the island of Flores. Because of its need for a rapid deployment capability for the Middle East and elsewhere, the U.S. conducted a major buildup of its military facilities here, aimed at providing a "viable support base" eastward and southward.

When, in 1975, the leftist Portuguese government allowed Cuban planes carrying troops to Angola to use Santa Maria for refueling stops, a pro–American Azores separatist movement sprang up, but it withered again when more moderate leaders came to power in Lisbon. This movement indicated the basic strength of the ties between the 200,000 residents of the Azores and the U.S., where more than

600,000 Azoreans now live, mainly on the east and west coasts. The issue of possible abuse of landing rights reemerged again in 2007 when allegations were made that CIA-operated planes with suspected terrorists refueled on the islands; Prime Minister Sócrates said there was no evidence of that.

A dispute in 1986 over the elevation of the Azorean flag and anthem to equal status with those of the motherland served as a reminder of local pride. They had been waved and played in official ceremonies since 1980. Nevertheless, because of the symbolic importance, President Soares vetoed the islands' revised autonomy statute, which had been approved by the Portuguese parliament. This was the first use of the presidential veto under the 1976 constitution, and it indicated how a flag and anthem question can revive Lisbon's fears of possible Azorean separatism.

The Madeira Archipelago

The Madeira Archipelago is not only the home of a desirable aperitif wine, which rivals sherry for popularity. It guards the southern approaches to Europe and the Strait of Gibraltar and is the southernmost NATO territory. The island of Porto Santo has excellent airport and deep–water port facilities, which at times has been used for military purposes, such as in 1978 when it was used as a refueling stop for aircraft carrying Belgian troops to Zaire. NATO military planners are very interested in Madeira because the Spanish made it clear that their Canary Islands, which lie only 300 miles (480 km.) south of Madeira, would not be considered NATO territory once Spain entered the Atlantic Alliance.

Portugal is wary about allowing Madeira to become a military bastion like the Azores. A major reason is that this could create a conflict with the African Union, in which voices have long been raised that the Madeira archipelago is colonized African territory and should therefore be liberated. After all, Madeira lies only 350 miles (560 km.) west of Morocco. Lisbon is trying to forge closer links with its former African colonies in order to regain some of their lucrative markets and to send them some of their excess work force.

Mozambique and Angola

Both Mozambique and Angola, the two richest of the former colonies, have realized the benefits the more skilled Portuguese could bring to their countries and have asked the Portuguese to return under a new guise. This reconciliation with its former colonies has been made politically easier since Portugal supported the Black African position toward South

Portugal

Stripping cork

Africa. One–seventh of the white South Africans are of Portuguese origin.

In 1991 Portugal mediated the "Estoril Accord," ending Angola's 16–year civil war. The key mediator in the talks was José Manuel Barroso, who went on to become Portuguese prime minister and then president of the European Commission. Portugal also participated, along with American, Russian and Angolan observers, in the political–military commission to supervise the truce and prepare for elections. It sent peacekeeping forces to Mozambique in the early 1990s. Portugal supported peaceful change in part because it wants to avoid the kind of refugee flood it experienced in the 1970s. Emotional ties with Africa are still strong, but economic links have become much weaker. By the 1990s only about 1% of Portugal's foreign trade was with Angola and Mozambique.

Defense

After the 1974 revolution had been tamed, Portugal could afford neither politically nor economically to continue maintaining a large land army. Therefore the size of the armed forces was cut from nearly half a million to about 44,900 politically obedient troops (26,700 army; 10,950 navy; 7,250 air force) in 2004, including 2,300 female volunteers and 9,100 conscripts. Compulsory service dropped to 4 months for all services. It is scheduled to disappear altogether as Portugal shifts to a professional army with modern rapid reaction capability. The military's share in the budget fell from 50% in 1970 to less than 10% by 2000. What Portugal can contribute to NATO is the use of strategically important facilities on the mainland, where NATO has naval and air facilities, and in the Azores and Madeira island groups, which are autonomous parts of Portugal.

In 1991 it supported its allies' war to dislodge the Iraqi aggressors from Kuwait. It sent 900 troops to Bosnia to help NATO implement the 1995 Dayton Peace Accord. In 2004 it still maintained peacekeeping forces in both Bosnia (330) and Kosovo (313). Its diplomatic support for the U.S. is not due exclusively to the fact that the U.S. provides Portugal economic and military aid. The two nations now share democratic values and common interests and therefore have a solid foundation for good relations.

Portugal is trying to improve its relations with the nations of the Middle East. Portugal was the first ally to heed President Carter's call in 1979 for sanctions against Iran when Iranian mobs had seized the U.S. embassy. It also levied sanctions against the Soviet Union when it invaded Afghanistan although President Soares' visit to Moscow in 1987 signaled a normalization of relations with Russia.

Portugal supported the U.S., UK and Spain in the 2003 war in Iraq although it supplied no troops or military aid. It hosted in the Azores a summit meeting of the leaders of these three allies on March 16, 2003. It culminated in a final 24-hour notice to the UN Security Council to act, or a decision to take military action would be made without the UN. After the conflict, it dispatched 120 peacekeepers to Iraq and maintained 20 troops in Afghanistan and 655 in East Timor. It turned to Washington for help in rebuilding its neglected armed forces. At its June 2003 summit, NATO decided to locate a sea-based joint task force in Portugal.

ECONOMY

Under fascist rule, Portugal's economy was relatively isolated and sheltered from the rest of Europe. Its industry was primarily in the hands of rather inefficient family businesses, which were protected from stiff western European competition and which had a comfortable export and import monopoly with their country's African colonies. A third of the Portuguese worked in agriculture. After 1974 much of Portugal's economic situation changed for the better.

The 1974 revolution did, however, create additional economic problems, beyond the temporary scaring away of tourists and their much–needed foreign currencies. Most of the earlier large private industrial and financial groups were broken down, and a wide range of economic activities that were not foreign owned was brought under state control. These included banks, insurance, airlines, railways, electricity, oil, gas, petrochemicals, cement, breweries, tobacco, wood pulp, steel, shipping and ship–building, urban transit, trucking, metallurgy, chemicals, food processing and textiles. Many of these sectors were combined in a huge publicly–owned conglomerate called Quimigal.

In all, 60% of Portugal's industry was nationalized after 1974. These nationalized industries exacerbated Portugal's problems. In 2007 government expenditures still accounted for 42.4% of GDP (down from 47.7% in 2005). Although many firms escaped the sword of nationalization because of their small size, it is not surprising that an immediate result of this policy was that investment capital was scared away. Productivity dropped and, because wages were doubled after 1974, inflation soared. Such nationalizations merely added to the weight of Portugal's already cumbersome bureaucracy. The state–owned companies also sap the lion's share of the government's economic subsidies, but these funds are insufficient to convert them into efficient companies able to compete well in international markets.

The Cavaco Silva government vowed in 1985 to end state domination of the economy, which he blamed for keeping Portuguese living standards so far below the western European average. His reelection in 1987 boosted his program to begin gradually selling off most industries and financial institutions nationalized after

1974. Cavaco Silva noted, "the state should control only companies of particular importance to public service," such as power, water and public–transport utilities. The government's extensive media holdings, including newspapers, are also earmarked for sale, save one television and radio channel. "The era of state paternalism will soon be over."

Progress on this privatization program has been slow. One problem is that there are too few large Portuguese groups with enough money to buy what is up for sale. Not wishing to sell most of these assets to foreigners, rigid, but ineffective, limits on how much foreigners can buy were established. Beginning in 1993 foreigners could buy control in state firms on a case–by–case basis; that included the national airlines, TAP-Air Portugal.

A welcome reform after the 1974 revolution was the lifting of the ban against strikes and independent trade unions. However, in the heady days after the revolution the well–organized Communists seized control of the major labor union, the CGTP–Intersindical. This union drives an extremely hard bargain and became accustomed to getting what it demands. It is highly politicized and is able to threaten the government through potentially crippling strikes.

The decolonization of Portugal's empire forced Portugal to compete with other nations for markets and brought close to a million bitter and penniless *retornados* to the motherland. What was worse, it cut off the country's most important sources of raw materials, especially energy. With no fossil fuel resources of its own, it must import about 80% of its primary energy needs. It can produce only about 20% of the energy it needs, and it brings in all of its oil and 83% of its coal. It generates 58% of its electricity from foreign oil, and it imports substantial amounts of electricity from Spain and France. Its bill for energy imports is about 10% of GDP, compared with only 1% in 1973. It does have the alternative of using its one untapped energy source, namely the 8,000 tons of proven uranium reserves, mostly located in the northern area of Urgerica, to produce nuclear energy.

It manages for several reasons. It has the lowest per capita energy consumption in Western Europe and also the lowest ownership of automobiles per inhabitant although the number of cars doubled between 1985 and 1990, causing congestion in Lisbon. Of increasing importance is the fact that it is among the top three countries in Europe (after Sweden and Austria) in terms of renewable energy sources. Almost one-fifth of its total energy needs and about 41% of its total electricity production are met by alternative sources.

That percentage is growing, as is energy demand in general, and it is hoped that they will constitute 60% of the country's electricity by 2020.

Unlike most other European countries, which have already developed their own hydroelectricity to a maximum, Portugal's is only half used, and it is building 18 hydropower projects. The Guadinana river was dammed to create Western Europe's largest reservoir, and a project is moving along to dam the Sabor River. Recurrent droughts and environmental protests plague hydroelectric plans and make this source less certain. Portugal is already one of the world's top ten producers of wind power. One of the world's largest wind farms is being built in the northwest Alto Minho region. Outside the town of Moura the world's biggest photovoltaic power plant is being constructed to take advantage of the country's abundant sunlight. General Electric's huge solar energy plant contains 52,000 solar panels capable of lighting and heating 8,000 homes. Portugal will start up the world's first commercial wave-driven power plant off the coast of Porto, and planners hope that 20% of electricity needs will one day be met by wave power.

Agriculture and Fishing

Portuguese agriculture is traditionally inefficient, and 13% of all Portuguese are engaged in agriculture (down from 44% in 1960). Farming contributes only 2.8% of Portugal's GDP; if one adds fishing and forestry, the figure would double that. Portugal continues to have proportionately the EU15's largest agricultural sector. The country must still import half of its food and animal feeds. Food makes up one–fifth of the nation's total imports.

Portugal is dependent on the Americans for a large portion of foodstuffs, including 90% of its wheat.

It has the lowest per capita productivity in Western Europe. It is only a about 40% of the EU average and two–thirds that of Spain and Greece. This is due to several factors, including the rocky, hilly soil, the low level of mechanization, the inefficient collective farms in the South, the insufficient size of family farms in the North, and the farmers' general resistance to change. Portuguese farmers' inability to compete successfully within a single European market has left a majority of them living at subsistence levels on incomes a third as big as their Spanish counterparts.

The revolution of 1974 did not create Portugal's agricultural problems. However, the initial leaders' fervor created particular problems in the south, where the land conquered from the Moors in the 13th century was distributed in large tracts to Portuguese nobility. These large land–owners often lived in Lisbon and had their large estates worked by low–paid agricultural laborers. These large estates were ripe for picking in revolutionary times.

The Communists, supported by the ruling leftist military leaders, seized many of the estates and converted them into large collective farms. In other cases, they forced the owners to hire more workers than could be employed profitably. By the 1990s more than half the seized estates had been returned to their original owners, and all owners have received some compensation for their former holdings. Nevertheless, about one–fifth of Portugal's forest and cropland remains collectivized. But these collectively–owned

Wine-growing country around the Douro River Valley

Portugal

Diário de Notícias

ALARGAMENTO

Europa
em festa

A UE passou de 378 para 455 milhões de habitantes e de 3,2 para 3,7 milhões de km2

■■■A partir de hoje a União Europeia está mais ampla, tem mais cidadãos e é politicamente mais estável. Mas também tem novos problemas para resolver. Os dez novos Estados membros, recebidos em festa pela família europeia, são vistos pelo antigo secretário de Estado dos Assuntos Europeus, Vítor Martins, como «nossos potenciais aliados». PÁGINAS 2 a 7

→ **Teresa Villaverde filma visão portuguesa.** Pág. 47

GRANDE REPORTAGEM
→ **Os novos países que vêm do frio**

BERLIM. Cidadãos dos dez novos países fizeram uma largada de balões

OUTROS DESTAQUES

SÁBADO

OPINIÃO

VASCO PULIDO VALENTE

Santana 'Pop Star' PÁGINA 64

MEMÓRIA

Ayrton Senna, 10 anos depois do acidente fatal Pág. 34 a 37

PROMOÇÃO

Amanhã
Não perca este livro, com o DN.

€ 9,90 SENNA

Esta Segunda
Grátis capa dura e 1º fascículo, com o DN.

GRÁTIS

Esta Segunda
Grátis a caixa + livro caderneta, com o DN.

GRÁTIS

MOÇAMBIQUE

14 detidos por posse de órgãos em Nampula

■■■A polícia moçambicana deteve 14 indivíduos, em Nampula, depois de descobrir braços, pernas e corações humanos guardados em panelas de barro. A magia negra parece estar na origem destes casos, com os detidos a confessarem ter retirado os órgãos de parentes já mortos. O Presidente Joaquim Chissano desafiou a sociedade do país a dar um combate sem tréguas ao que classificou como «crime hediondo» de rapto, assassínio e tráfico de órgãos em Moçambique. PÁGINA 23

IRAQUE

PROVAS. CBS mostrou as fotos

Imagens de tortura chocam o mundo

■■■Imagens fotográficas de interrogatórios efectuados a iraquianos na prisão de Abu Gharib, nos arredores de Bagdad, estão a chocar o mundo. Nas fotos vêem-se militares norte-americanos a torturarem e humilharem presos iraquianos, o que já levou à suspensão do general Janis Karpinski, responsável pelos centros de detenção da coligação. As fotografias foram reveladas pela cadeia de televisão norte-americana CBS e retransmitidas pelas estações árabes Al-Jazeera e Al-Arabiya. George W. Bush já condenou o sucedido. PÁGINA 21

DEBATE NO PARLAMENTO

Acusação de Louçã irrita Durão Barroso

■■■Um violento confronto verbal entre o deputado do Bloco de Esquerda Francisco Louçã e Durão Barroso marcou ontem o debate mensal do primeiro-ministro no Parlamento. Louçã questionou o papel da CGD e insinuou favorecimentos públicos ao grupo Carlyle. Durão irritou-se e disse: «ou prova o que diz ou então mente». PÁGINA 9

INDIGNADO. Primeiro-ministro reagiu

COIMBRA

Perseguição policial provoca um morto

■■■Um morto e um ferido grave foi o resultado de uma tentativa de fuga de três reclusos. Os três detidos, de nacionalidade ucraniana, tentaram fugir de um carro celular que os transportava de Leiria para a prisão central de Coimbra. Os guardas que os acompanhavam conseguiram pôr termo à fuga após perseguição. PÁGINA 25

Europe celebrates EU enlargement

---

farms have, on the whole, been poorly managed. They therefore now produce only a third to a half of the grain and livestock that they supplied before the revolution. Because of legal tangles, the government did not move as fast to de-collectivize farming in the South as it had hoped.

Portugal faces a problem of what to do about its inefficient farming and antiquated fishing fleet, which is already unable to withstand competition in its home waters. Also, it has few agricultural products that can compete in the EU. The ones that can are wines, tomato concentrate and cork. The heart of its wine growing is in the Douro River Valley, from which port wine (named for the city of Oporto) comes.

Portugal's fishing fleet is the oldest and least productive in all of western Europe. Many of its vessels have no engines. It has world-class ship repair; its repair yards are among the world's biggest and handle more tonnage than their top four competitors together. In 1969 the Portuguese government granted Spain, which has a fishing fleet that is larger than that of all 15 EU countries combined, unrestricted rights to fish in Portugal's waters. Most leaders in Lisbon now view that decision as a cardinal error and have been trying hard to undo it.

Portugal's chief export is cork, of which it supplies half of the world's supply (most of the rest comes from Spain.) and 68% of the wine corks. The industry creates 3% of the country's GDP, but it is threatened by the rising popularity of synthetic corks and twist-off caps, which are capturing more and more of the world market. It has invested heavily in research to improve cork effectiveness as a stopper. This substance is the bark that is stripped off the cork oak trees every 11 years, a process which leaves the trees a bright red color. Cork production suffered a setback in the mid–1970s, when following the seizure of large estates in Alentejo thousands of cork trees were uprooted to make way for wheat, a crop unsuited for the region. The Communist–inspired wheat drive at least temporarily destroyed cork–growing there.

In order to irrigate more than 272,000 acres in the Alentejo region, the government closed the giant Alqueva dam in 2002 in order to create the largest artificial lake in western Europe. When filled, it will submerge the village of Luz, a million trees and hundreds of Stone Age rock drawings. Environmentalists decry the damage this project does to nature. Droughts and resulting forest fires are a perpetual threat to the country.

Membership in EU

Portugal's political leaders, supported by a large majority of the population, chose a formidable challenge to prepare their country for a more prosperous future—entry into the EU. Before becoming a full member in 1986, it was a member of EFTA. In 1972 Portugal had entered into an agreement with the EU providing free trade of industrial products. Its leaders, as well as those in the EU member countries, hoped that such entry would help solidify the democratic foundations in Portugal, as well as provide a mighty boost for the country's economy. By 2007, 79.4% of its exports went to EU countries (the larg-

Former Prime Minister and current EC President Manuel Durão Barroso

est market being France, followed by Germany and Spain), more than double the proportion a decade earlier. In general, Portugal derives 73.5% of its imports from the EU.

Portugal has developed a modern economy that employs 33% of its workforce in industry (producing 22.3% of GDP) and 55% in services (creating 74.9% of GDP). By 2008 the country had reached a tipping point where it exports more technology than it imports, invests more in science and research than ever before, and earns more from its export of business services than from cheap textiles and footwear. It is clearly evolving from a low-cost manufacturing economy to a knowledge-based one. The introduction of greater incentives through a reform of personal taxation, which some observers described as the most punitive in all of western Europe, stimulated the economy. Corporate taxes have already fallen to 20% from 2006 on. Portuguese industry enjoys other advantages. Its smallness and fragmented nature lend it some flexibility.

However, its poor remain the poorest in Western Europe, and the gap between the rich and poor within the country is widening. More than two million Portuguese (a fifth of the population) live on less than 350 euros ($525) per month, and the sluggish economic growth (an annual average of only .6% from 2001-5 and at 1.9% in 2007 the lowest in Europe) offers little

Fado star

hope. Its basic strength was in the cheapness of labor, the lowest in Western Europe, but that advantage is eroding. Its GDP per capita grew from 55% of the EU average in 1975 to 80% and then back down to just over 70% in 2008. In terms of GDP per head, the Czech Republic, Greece, Malta and Slovenia have all overtaken it. The OECD estimated in 2005 that it will take another 40 years to catch up with the EU average. Its productivity was only 40% of the EU average in 2007, compared with 120% in Ireland and 96% in Spain. Part of the reason is that its research and development, up to only 1% of GDP, is still little over half the EU average of 1.9%, but it is improving. Inflation was 2.5% in 2006, and its rising 8% unemployment rate in 2008 was at a six-year high, double the rate of 2001, and a little above the EU average. Living standards have risen visibly.

Entry into the EU brought needed social and regional funds to Portugal; from 3% to 4% of its GDP was derived from financial transfers from Brussels, a total of $30 billion between 1986 and 2003. Those funds began to decline in 2006, and new ones are going to new members in central Europe. However, these monies have made a real economic difference. One can see this in Portugal's infrastructure. In 1987 it had only 240 kilometers (144 miles) of freeways; by 1998, it had 840 kilometers (504 miles). This is more in terms of distance per inhabitant than in any other EU member state. Critics say these freeways do not link the poorer and richer regions as they should, nor do they tie in well with Spain's road network, leaving Portu-

gal relatively isolated from Europe. Its railway system has not been modernized at the same pace as its roadways.

This country, which was so successful in establishing a democratic political order despite enormous problems and the absence of a democratic tradition, is meeting the economic challenges associated with becoming a full economic partner in Europe. It met the qualifications to enter the European Monetary Union (EMU) and adopted the euro. It enjoys a higher profile in the EU because of the EC presidency of José Manuel Barroso and because of its successful half-year presidency in 2007, which culminated in the signing of semi-constitutional Lisbon Treaty.

In 2001 Portugal became the first country to exceed the 3% limit for a budget deficit and to face a penalty. The prior conservative government was compelled to impose painful budget cuts, freeze civil servants' pay, end special credit terms for first-time home buyers, and raise the sales tax to 19%. It tried to make the overstaffed, underproductive and expensive public-sector workers more efficient. Its wages cost 15% of GDP versus 10.3% EU average. As of 2004 automatic promotion and guaranteed top performance reports were scrapped, and promotion is now based on merit.

These measures sparked widespread strikes among civil servants and created the circumstances for the conservatives' electoral defeat in February 2005. The EU gave the country three years until 2007 to bring it back to 3%. The reduction of the budget deficit, which was down to 2.6% in 2007 (the lowest since Portugal's return

Vasco da Gama, Museum of Ancient Art, Lisbon

Portugal

to democracy), remains a top priority for Sócrates's government. It also reduced total public debt to 63.6% of GDP by 2007.

Among the controversial measures the Socialist government is taking is to raise the minimum retirement age for state employees in stages from age 60 to 65. They make up one-sixth of the work force and under the constitution cannot be fired. People with fewer than two children are expected to contribute more toward their pensions. These steps are crucial if the country is to solve its pension crisis. Retirement benefits are among the world's most generous, with some people receiving more than they did while working. Given a birth rate that has fallen by 35% between 1975 and 2005 (from a 2.6 fertility rate to only 1.5), more than a third of the population will be over age 65 in 2050, compared with 17% in 2005.

The state is hiring only one new state employee for every two who leave. It lowered their sickness pay from 100% to 65% and reduced the maximum personal income tax to 42% (thereby limiting tax evasion). The VAT was raised from 19% to 21% and then dropped back to 20% in 2008. Despite demonstrations and strikes by judges, public prosecutors, doctors, nurses, teachers, police, soldiers and other state workers against radical changes to their pension, health and pay benefits, the

Sócrates government stuck to its guns. Courts were forced to stay open during the summer, except for a one-month holiday. To cut red tape and to stimulate the creating of new businesses, the time needed to set up a new company was lowered to less than an hour, the fastest in the EU.

The magnitude of the challenges was revealed in July 2005 when the finance minister and architect of Sócrates's draconian measures unexpectedly resigned after only four months in office. His replacement, Fernando Teixeira dos Santos, became the country's fourth finance minister in little more than a year. In the October 2005 local elections throughout the country, the ruling Socialists lost in more than two-thirds of the municipalities, and their candidate was crushed in the 2006 presidential election.

Tourism continues to be an important component of the economy, accounting for approximately 11% of its GDP and providing employment for one in 10 workers. However, tourist officials would like to attract visitors year-round to areas beyond the beaches of the Algarve, which now produces about half of Portugal's tourist earnings. One form of tourism that is increasingly popular is "wine tourism," especially in the Douro Valley. Optimists predict that the tourist industry will account for almost 23% of employment by 2018.

Foreign investment is coming in, two-thirds of it from the EU. With 75% of its GDP derived from foreign trade, Portugal is one of the most open countries in Europe. It is therefore natural that it became a part of the world's largest economic market, and it is doing well. Its huge Autoeuropa car plant, owned by Volkswagen, accounts for 12% of exports. The U.S. is one of the country's leading investors, and among the major American firms active in Portugal are Ford, Microsoft, Texas Instruments, Compaq, Johnson and Johnson, Unisys, Citibank, and Chase Manhattan. General Motors sparked strikes in 2006 when it rejected its workers' cost-cuts aimed at keeping its van factory in Portugal open. The U.S. purchases almost 6% of Portugal's exports and provides over a quarter of its non-EU imports. An active American Chamber of Commerce in Portugal promotes this important bilateral trade.

Since the 1990s the state has been selling off its interests in oil, gasoline, natural gas, electricity, banks and telecommunications companies. In 2000 it unloaded an additional 20% of the national power company, Electricidade de Portugal. It sold most of its remaining interest in Portugal Telecom (PT). In 2004 the state sold a stake in Portucel, the state-owned pulp and paper company. It announced the sale of a large part of Galp Energia, the country's dominant oil utility. However, the government maintains close ties with formerly state-owned firms. It keeps "golden shares" that allow it to veto mergers, even when it retains only a minority stake in a company.

The existence of a lively "submerged economy" makes it more difficult to get an exact picture of Portugal's economic condition. This kind of activity is done at home, in the streets, or on the job while the boss is looking the other way. It takes place behind the backs of government statisticians and tax collectors. If the production of goods and services from such an invisible economy were able to be included in the official economic figures, an estimated 10% to 25% would have to be added to the GDP, and real unemployment would be below the official figures.

There were two showcases of the country's economic development in 1998. The world exposition in Lisbon commemorated the 500th anniversary of Vasco da Gama's first voyage to Brazil and drew millions of visitors. Also the dramatic 11–mile Vasco da Gama Bridge spanning the Tagus River opened.

CULTURE

Portugal is a nation whose cultural influence extends far beyond its own bor-

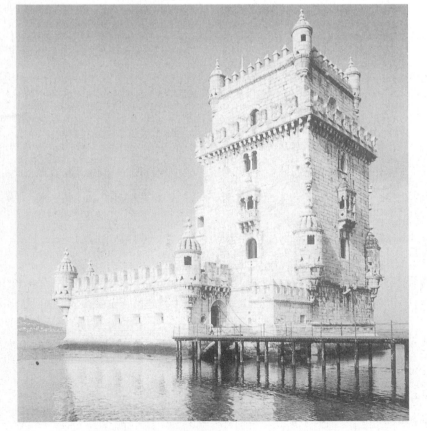

Belem Tower, 16th century, Lisbon

ders. Today nearly 200 million people speak Portuguese. Its outward–looking orientation was beautifully reflected in its greatest literary figure, Luiz de Camões (1524–80), who wrote poetry and dramatic comedies. In 1572 he published perhaps the greatest piece of Portuguese literature, *Os Lusíadas* ("The Lusitanians"), a long epic poem celebrating Portuguese history and heroes. His story is linked with that of Vasco da Gama's voyage to India and is infused with much Greek mythology. In general, Portuguese today are nostalgic about their country's great past, and they have a term for this yearning: *saudade*.

Portuguese culture has also been enriched by experiences or influences from abroad. For instance, the novelist, John Dos Passos, and the undisputed king of march music, John Philip Sousa, were both sons of Portuguese emigrants and received their artistic inspiration in the U.S. No one who has heard fado (meaning "fate") music sung in Portugal can ever forget its deep feeling for love, nostalgia and yearning. Used during the fascist era to promote nationalism (along with Fatima and football), it has become the country's most successful cultural export.

In 1998 a Portuguese writer won the Nobel Prize for literature for the first time. Jose Samarago was born into a home with no books, grew up in poverty, never went to the university, and toiled as a metalworker until the fall of dictator Antonio Salazar enabled him, an active Communist, to publish his first novel in 1974. The best known of his imaginative novels are *Baltasar and Blimunda* and *The Year of the Death of Ricardo Reis*. He expressed his hope on receiving the honor that "Portuguese will become more visi-

ble and more audible." Earlier in the century Egas Moniz had won the Nobel prize for medicine.

Immigrants from Portugal's former colonies have changed the face of Portuguese society and made it much more heterogeneous. Historically the Portuguese were an emigrant people, settling all corners of the globe. By the 21st century, the flow had reversed, and Portugal had become a net importer of labor. In 2005 there were roughly 256,000 legal immigrants in the country, almost half of them from Africa. An increasing number comes from central and eastern Europe. Unlike in some other European countries, this ethnic mixing has not been accompanied by serious racial tension. In 2005 newcomers were issued high-tech identity cards in an effort to fight illegal immigration.

Influence of Brazil

Perhaps the greatest foreign cultural influence comes from Brazil. Soap operas from there fill Portugal's air waves with Brazilian slang, songs, accents and dress. Many imports are aired on Portugal's two state–owned and run channels, RTP 1 and 2, on its two newer private commercial channels, SIC and TV1 and on a multitude of cable and satellite channels.

Chiefly because of its small size and high degree of centralization, there are few different dialects spoken within Portugal, except in Miranda do Douro in the northeast. But of the 230 million persons in the world who speak Portuguese as a

Portugese student

native language, only a little over 10 million live in the mother country; 183 million live in Brazil and speak what writer Eca de Queiroz calls "Portuguese with sugar." At newsstands one finds many Brazilian publications mixed with Portuguese ones: Lisbon alone has five morn-

Robed freshmen students are initiated into the University, Libson

Portugal

ing and four afternoon papers, the most popular being the tabloid *Correio da Manha*. In 1991 the last state–owned daily newspaper, *Diario de Noticias*, established in 1864, was sold into private hands; it is respected as a serious paper and has been given a modernized look. Other dailies are *Publico*, *Correio da Manha* and the *Jornal de Noticias*. There are also hot-selling weeklies, such as *Expresso*, *O Jornal*, *Semanario* and *Independente*. *The Portugal News* is available for English-readers.

It is not surprising that the Portuguese spoken outside, especially in Brazil is changing the language spoken in this small country. Oral expression is being strongly penetrated by Brazilian words and idiomatic phrases. The economic prowess of Brazil has meant that the Portuguese being learned by foreigners abroad is now primarily Brazilian. Most magazines on Portugal's newsstands are from Brazil.

A passionate debate began in 1986 over whether Portugal should simply recognize this fact and negotiate a linguistic agreement with Brazil and other former colonies. Proponents argue that a common structure of the language must be preserved and that the constant evolution of the language should be incorporated in the mother country. Critics decry the "crime against the patrimony of the Portuguese language" and "a disgusting resignation to Brazil's economic interests." It

Students at Coimbra University

cannot be expected that, in the long run, any effort to erect a barrier against the flood of foreign cultural influences could succeed in a country like Portugal that is adapting itself so quickly to the changing world it faces. Millions of Portuguese really want no such barrier anyway. Nevertheless, the government established tough requirements that 40% of all TV shows have to be in Portuguese. Three–fourths must be produced in Portugal.

Education

Postrevolutionary Portugal inherited considerable educational problems. These included a shortage of schools and teachers, a clear and discriminatory separation of the elite lycée (high school) from the trade schools, a poor geographic distribution of educational facilities throughout the country, and especially the concentration of higher education along the coast. By the 1990s there were 12 state universities, 14 polytechnic schools, and a growing number of private universities.

For a couple of years after the *ancien regime* was swept from power, the educational system became the wet clay in the hands of leftist and Marxist teachers and reformers. Many Marxist textbooks replaced the outdated books from the Salazar era, schools were taken over by management committees which excluded most parental influence in the schools, and pupils were examined on their "collective work" and even had a voice in the grades they received.

When the Socialist Party finally gained a firm grip on the reins of government in the second half of 1975, the textbooks were changed again to reflect the more moderate and pluralistic character of the new leadership. Parents were again given some say in the school system, the former strict grading system was reintroduced, and hundreds of leftists were removed from the schools and the ministry of education. With order restored in the schools, the education system was more or less back where it had been in 1974, but the ground had been laid for important changes.

In 1977 a system of preschool instruction was introduced, and the preuniversity schooling was established at 11 years, with the possibility of a twelfth year later. All pupils in Portugal now receive six years of elementary education, which is obligatory, and some secondary schooling. All children must remain in school until age 14, but almost 40% drop out of school before they have finished four years of secondary school. This is more than double the 16% EU average. This means that only a fifth of the population aged 25 to 64 have a secondary education, compared with two-thirds on average elsewhere in the EU. Its percentage of university graduates in the population is 12% (up from only 2% in 1974), half the EU average of 24%. This low level of education has an adverse effect on the economy, including competitiveness and productivity. The government wants to raise the sec-

Portugese journalist

ondary-school completion rate to 65%. The Sócrates government succeeded in introducing the teaching of English in the primary schools.

Those who wish to stay in school have six years of secondary school, which over half finish. After the one–year transition class, qualified students can enter the university for a "short advanced education" of two to three years, or for the "diverse superior courses" of four or five years. The number of students is still low with only one in five going on to higher education, and 12% completing a degree. But the number is six times higher than in 1974.

The educational system remains a matter of concern. Only a third of people age 25–34 had completed 12 years of school, compared with an average of three-fourths in the rest of the OECD. Portugal spends 5.7% of its national income on public schools and universities, a relatively high proportion by OECD standards. It also spends more per student in secondary education than most countries, in part because its teachers' salaries are relatively high, consuming 93% of spending on education, compared with the OECD average of 75%. Its average ratio of one teacher to nine students is one of the highest in the world. But the outcomes are nevertheless among the worst in Europe. Portugal is trying to overcome this at the highest level by entering into research

Three children reportedly visited by the Virgin at Our Lady of Fatima.

partnership agreements with leading U.S. universities, including MIT, Carnegie Mellon, The University of Texas and Harvard Medical School.

All kinds of scholarly and cultural endeavors are generously supported in Portugal by the Gulbenkian Foundation, established and richly funded by a foreign oil magnate who made Portugal his home. Since the foundation is massively involved in supporting a wide range of cultural activities, is private and has carefully steered clear of government control, it was able to support research with critical political implications, which the politicians in power viewed with some distrust. The Luso-American Foundation sponsors scholarships for American students of Portuguese descent and provides funding for hiring American professors at MBA programs at Portuguese universities.

Cultural activity also got a boost in 1986 with a new law (called the "Maecenas Law") that concedes tax breaks to corporations that support cultural initiatives. Up to 60% of any "cultural financing" costs can be written off taxes. Since only about 1% of the national budget is allotted to culture, and public support is very scarce, this new measure is most welcome.

Religion

Portuguese society has experienced some social transformation in the past decade and a half, but religion has not changed as much as in many other western European countries. Divorce was permitted after the revolution. The Catholic Church continued to oppose birth control, but Portuguese of childbearing age are inclined to ignore that opposition.

Despite bitter protests by the Catholic Church, parliament voted in 1984 to permit abortions following rape, or whenever medically advisable. Nevertheless, until 2007 it had the strictest abortion laws of any EU country except Ireland. Legal abortion was rare, and illegal abortions continued. It was estimated in 2002 that as many as 40,000 women a year had them. One 23-year-old female journalist stated, "I would say 60% of the women I know have had abortions. If they're rich, they go to Spain, and if they're not, they go to midwives, often in really bad conditions."

The trial and conviction in 2002 of a female abortionist who performed illegal operations in a clean, modern clinic provoked outrage among pro-choice groups. But in 2004 a judge in Aveiro dropped charges against seven women who had abortions deemed to be illegal. The dramatic lowering of Portugal's infant mortality rate from 85 to only six per 1,000 births reinforced the conviction of supporters that abortions should be con-

ducted in modern hospitals, not in back rooms. In a February 2007 referendum, 59% of voters backed the legalization of abortion within the first ten weeks of pregnancy. Since fewer than 50% of eligible voters (31%) turned out to cast their ballots, the result was not binding on the government. But the Socialist-dominated parliament approved of the reform anyway.

Religious superstitions and symbols remain strong. One sees "Our Lady of …" various things everywhere. A popular pilgrimage site is the shrine of Our Lady of Fatima, where the virgin reportedly appeared to three shepherd children in 1917. Hundreds of thousands of pilgrims attend candlelight masses at the rural shrine twice a year. Portuguese are conscientious church–goers, by European standards. Although only about a third of all Catholics attend regularly, this compares with less than a fifth in Spain and a sixth in France. About two out of three choose to get married in a church, compared with nine out of ten in 1960. The divorce rate has shot up to approximately 14,000 a year, from only a few hundred before the 1974 revolution. A fifth of all babies are born out of wedlock, compared with one in 14 in 1970. Portugal has the second highest rate of teenage pregnancy in Europe after the UK.

Perhaps the greatest social change involves women. Before 1974, a woman had to get her husband's permission to go into higher education, take a job, or get a passport. In 1960, only about a fifth of women of working age had paying jobs. Now the proportion is 63%, at the top end of the EU range. Women account for about half the work force and 60% of university students and graduates, up from a fourth in 1960. As a result of increased education and employment possibilities, fertility rates have plummeted from the highest in Europe to among the lowest. Portuguese are also living longer: 81.2 years for women and 75 years for men.

Reflecting a shifting attitude in Europe, Portugal adopted in 2002 a new approach to the problem of drug addiction by decriminalizing all drug use. Users (now officially called "consumers") are no longer viewed as criminals, but as victims of a drug culture that tough laws cannot control. One worrisome fact, however, is that Portugal has the highest HIV infection rate in all of Europe. Starting in 2008 Portuguese lungs are benefiting from a ban on smoking in all public places.

FUTURE

Since 1974, Portugal has established a democratic political order that is capable of surviving. Its extrication from costly colonial wars not only aided its own econ-

Portugal

omy, but it enabled Portugal to concentrate its military attention on common NATO objectives. With the continued need for the U.S. and its allies to be able to project their military presence into the Mediterranean and Middle Eastern regions, Portugal's Azores and Madeira archipelagos in the Atlantic Ocean will continue to have strategic importance.

Portugal has undergone a dramatic transformation since joining the EU in 1986. The economy experienced an unprecedented boom and has been modernized and liberalized. Despite poverty that still exists, standards of living have been raised, unemployment is low although it is rising to slightly over the EU average, the budget deficit is at an all-time low, and most Portuguese have experienced progress. The economy has passed the tipping point in its transformation from a low-cost manufacturing one to a knowledge-based one, and this process will continue.

One sees manifestations of economic progress in modern construction, huge shopping malls, diverse renewable energy-producing infrastructure and the emergence of a new technocratic class. However, the success is uneven throughout the country. It has launched an international advertising campaign to change its image from a backwater to being "the West Coast of Europe," a play on California. It depicts Portugal as rich in beauty, tradition and environmental technology.

The country's euphoria of joining the eurozone has given way to despondency as the challenges of globalization and EU enlargement have exposed its economic weaknesses. The Socialist government of José Sócrates is dealing with the feeling of uneasiness that Portugal has again fallen behind the rest of Europe. He described the climate as "pessimism, discouragement and disappointment." There is a broad consensus that something must be done.

In 2004 Portugal gained a high profile in the EU when the post of European Commission president went to former Prime Minister José Manuel Barroso. This is the highest international position ever held by a Portuguese. In July 2007 Portugal also assumed the EU's revolving six-month presidency. The EU's two most senior jobs are occupied for a half a year by Portuguese. Prime Minister Sócrates shifted the organization's focus from the East to Africa and Brazil and presided over summits with leaders from these two places. It paved the way to the signing of a new EU super-treaty, appropriately named the Lisbon Treaty, which will change some of the ways the organization operates.

Portugal's democratic constitution has been reformed and strengthened, and Portuguese have rediscovered a sense of national pride. In April 2004 they celebrated the 30th anniversary of the "Carnation Revolution." They can look with satisfaction on the legacies of that revolution: a stable parliamentary democracy, membership and leadership in the EU, and sustained economic growth that has raised living standards.

Snake dance Lisbon style

414

Andorra

The church Sant Cristòfol d'Anyós high in the Andorran Pyrenees dates from the 12th century

Area: 188 sq. mi. (487 sq. km.)

Population: 75,000. More than 80% are foreigners.

Capital City: Andorra la Vella, population with adjoining Encamp, 22,000.

Climate: Cool, dry summer and snowy, mountain winter climate.

Official Language: Catalan; Spanish and French are also widely spoken.

Ethnic Background: Catalan stock; about 15% of residents are native Andorrans, 61% Spanish, 6% French.

Principal Religion: Roman Catholic

Major Industries: Tourism, free port for consumer goods, tobacco products, hydroelectric power, timber.

Major Customers: France, Spain, Germany, Japan.

Currency: Euro.

Year of Independence: 1278.

Government: Since 1993 a self–ruling sovereign state.

Chiefs of State: Figurehead Co–Princes are the President of the French Republic and the Spanish Bishop of Seo de Urgel, who are represented locally by officials called Veguers.

Head of Government: Albert Pintat, Prime Minister (since April 2005).

National Flag: Three vertical bands of blue, yellow, and red with the national coat of arms in the center.

Perched high in the Pyrenees Mountains is the largest of Europe's six microscopic independent states: Andorra. Mountain peaks rising to 9,000 feet (2,743 meters) overlook six deep valleys on the southern slopes of the Pyrenees. Border-

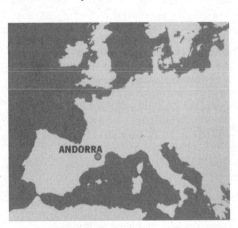

ing on France to the north and on Spain to the south, Andorra, with its ruggedly beautiful landscape, is a geographic blend of glacial valleys, lakes, fresh water springs and Alpine meadows. Abundant rainfall and snow give this tiny land a green, rich look half the year and a white mountain look the other half. In the 58 villages and hamlets in the highlands, with their typically granite, wood and slate houses, live many of the native Andorrans, who now comprise only about 15% of the population.

They have a strong affinity with the region of Catalonia in northern Spain. They speak Catalan, a rich romance language related to Provencal, spoken by approximately six million persons in the region that encompasses French and Spanish Catalonia. In the age of the automobile, Andorra has been ripped from the Middle Ages, and its dizzying economic advance-

ment has attracted thousands of Spaniards and French, who now comprise 61% and 6% of Andorra's residents respectively. These developments have made Andorrans a minority in their own country, but they have also given the land a prosperous, international character.

There is evidence of human settlements in Andorra dating many thousands of years ago, and the first written records date from the third century B.C. It is a local legend that the mountain people in these valleys helped a grateful Charlemagne drive the Moors from the area in 806 A.D. Charlemagne's son, Louis the Pious, granted the six valleys to the Spanish Bishop of Seo de Urgel in 819 A.D. In 1278 the French count of Foix and the bishop recognized each other as co–princes of Andorra. Over the years, the count of Foix's claims passed to the king of Navarre, then to the king of France, and finally to the president of the French Republic. Except for a brief period during the French Revolution, when the French occupied Andorra and declared it a republic, it has retained to the present day its co–allegiance to France and the Bishop of Seo de Urgel.

Until 1993 the co–allegiance was formally acknowledged by a token annual tribute (*questia*) of 960 French francs (about $190) to France and 460 Spanish pesetas (about $15) to Spain in alternating years. Because of this tribute and because the country existed as a result of a feudal grant, Andorra was technically not a state, according either to international law or to its own statutes. It was a fief, a feudal

415

Andorra

carry–over from the Middle Ages with no equivalence in modern Europe.

POLITICAL SYSTEM

In 1990 reformer Josep Maria Beal was elected Sindic, pledging to modernize the country's institutions to enable it to survive in the new Europe. With the support of his successor, Jordi Farras, and other Andorran leaders, such as Oscar Ribas Reig, his pledge was fulfilled. In 1993 the tiny country adopted its first–ever constitution. With three–quarters of the eligible voters participating, 74.2% opted for sovereignty. By choosing self–rule, they acquired the right to have their own judicial system and foreign policy.

Andorrans are now completely free to establish political parties. Traditionally, all Andorran candidates ran as independents. In 1976 Andorra's first political party, the Andorran Democratic Association, was formed. In the April 2005 elections for the 28 seats in the General Council, the Unio Lliberal (Liberals) lost its absolute majority, but won exactly half the seats. The center-left Social Democrats won 12. Competing for the remaining votes were the center–right Agrupament Nacional Democratic, Nova Democracia, and the National Democratic Initiative. Albert Pintat, who had been foreign minister in the previous Liberal government led by Marc Forné Molné, became prime minister.

The right to vote is very restricted. Only the 10,000 Andorrans whose families have had Andorran citizenship for three generations are permitted to vote. This amounts to only 15% of the population. Women citizens were granted suffrage in 1970. Over time the new constitution is bound to affect every preexisting political institution in the country.

The President of France and the Bishop of Seo de Urgel are figurehead Co–Princes of Andorra and until 1993 had full executive, legislative and judicial power. In practice, *Veguers* (their designated representatives) and *Battles* (magistrates) represented them in the country. These feudal offices were combined with more modern elected offices.

Prime Minister Albert Pintat

**His Excellency
The Honorable Nicolas Sarkozy
President of the French Republic**

**His Excellency
The Most Reverend Joan Martí Alanis
Bishop of Seo de Urgel**

The country had no constitution before 1993, but a "Plan of Reform," adopted in 1866. It established the groundwork for a General Council of 28 members (at least four of whom are elected from each of the six Parishes in the six valleys—Andorra, Canillo, Encamp, La Massana, Ordino, and Sant Julià). Each member is elected to a four–year term, and half the members were elected every two years. Before the new constitution was implemented, the General Council had no formal legislative power, but it was the supreme administrative body. It elected for three–year terms a Sindic (manager) and Sub–Sindic to implement its decisions. There was usually tension within the General Council between the four representatives from the capital city, where two–thirds of the country's population lives, and the remaining 20 representatives from the more rural parishes. When the capital's four representatives request funds for facilities needed by the rapidly growing capital city, the remaining members are inclined to demand similar facilities for their parishes. This often created deadlocks on important issues.

The judicial system is now independent. It is based on French secular and Spanish ecclesiastical law. That such a hybrid legal system could function in Andorra is demonstrated by the fact that the entire country maintains only six jail cells, most of which usually are empty. The constitution emboldened the judiciary in 1993 to arrest the director of state security and president of the Olympic committee in a new effort to fight corruption. Earlier, the country's main families had been powerful enough to suppress scandals through their dominance of the French and Spanish courts in Andorra. The tiny mountainous land has sent athletes to the Winter Olympics since 1976.

Andorra has no defense forces, but all able–bodied men between the ages of 16 and 60 are required to arm themselves and be ready to serve without pay or uniforms in the People's Militia, which has not fought in a war for 700 years. This strange, unorganized army regards all its "soldiers" as officers. In practice, France and Spain provide for Andorra's defense, and the Barcelona police and French gendarmerie alternate year by year in assisting the 160–man Andorran police to maintain order within the country.

Andorra is a member of UNESCO, but until 1993 France played the primary role in handling its diplomatic affairs, the Bishop of Seo de Urgel having no official international status. Its 1993 constitution permits Andorra to conduct its own foreign policy. It immediately joined the UN as a full member, entered the Council of Europe in 1994, and tightened

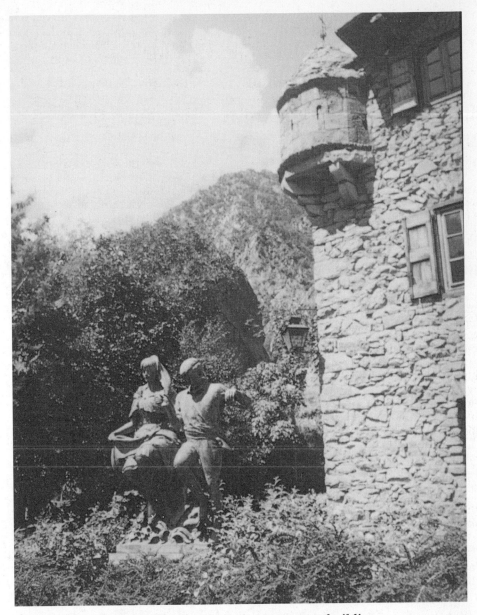

Statue in front of the main government building

Hon. Marc Forné Molné

its ties with the EU. The United States' relations with Andorra have traditionally been conducted through its consulate in Barcelona.

ECONOMY

Since only 4% of the country's land can be cultivated, most of its food must be imported. It owes its livelihood to tourism and to its status as a free port (duty–free marketplace) for manufactured goods from many industrialized nations. This duty–free status makes Andorra one of the most active smuggling centers of Europe, an activity which French and Spanish customs officials have difficulty controlling due to the country's remote and rugged frontier, and due also to the impossibility of checking all the thousands

of automobiles which cross its borders daily. Andorra refuses to make smuggling a penal offense. Therefore, dealing in contraband, by either organized criminals or legal merchants, thrives.

The same has been true of money laundering and the hiding of assets. In 2000 the OECD placed Andorra on a list of "uncooperative tax havens." It reached an agreement with the EU in 2003 to collect taxes for bank account interest and return 75% of it to the country of residence without providing account holders' names. The tiny country wants to get off the OECD's list.

This tiny country absorbs 11 million visitors each year. Two–thirds of them are from Spain, mainly day-trippers. What awaits this throng of visitors is one huge mall with good bargains at gaudy shops,

Andorra

but also long traffic jams, tight parking, exhaust–filled air, shoulder–to–shoulder walking, and almost interminable waiting at the border. Commerce trumps charm. For export, it manufactures cigars and cigarettes, matches, anisette liqueur and sandals. It also produces for sale that customary product of microstates: beautiful postage stamps, although no postage whatsoever is required for mail *within* the country. In January 2002 the euro became the official currency.

Both France and Spain want to limit Andorra's duty–free business. For example, cigarettes are 60% cheaper than in neighboring France. Many Andorrans fear that the attractiveness of a shopping trip to their country will decline in the future. Andorra's favorable trade agreements with Spain and France give it legal trade outlets to the entire EU. In 1990, for the first time in 700 years, Andorra signed an international treaty, approving a trade agreement with the EU. It makes Andorra a member of the EU customs union. It permits industrial goods to flow freely to and from the EU and obligates Andorra to apply the EU's external tariffs on such goods to third countries. Full EU membership must wait. Spain insists that Andorra introduce adequate labor and social security laws for the 20,000 Spaniards who work in Andorra, mainly in tourism, before the tiny country is considered for EU membership. Andorra's 1993 constitution permits the establishment of labor unions, hitherto banned.

It has a hydroelectric plant at Escaldes, which provides electricity for Andorra and exports a modest amount of power to the northern part of Barcelona province and to southern France. Residents of Andorra pay no personal income taxes.

The 1993 constitution grants freedom of religion although Roman Catholicism remains the established church. Andorra's school system is a cumbersome combination of French secular schools and Spanish parochial schools, financed and staffed by France and Spain, and terminating educational possibilities within Andorra at age 14. Because there is no university, young Andorrans go to France or Spain for higher education. Only half of them return, in part because the exorbitant property prices, which have spiraled to Parisian levels, keep them away.

Andorra has two daily newspapers, *Diari d'Andorra* and *El Periodic*, and one monthly, *Andorra Magazine*. Radio service is provided by *Radio Nacional d'Andorra*, which operates *Radio Andorra* and *Andorra Musica*. Andorrans can receive many Spanish and French television stations, as well as its own TVA, operated by *Radio i Televiso d'Andorra*. There are no railroad or airport facilities, but good roads tie the country to Spain and, except in the winter months, to France.

FUTURE

Andorra has undergone great social, economic, and political changes, from a traditional pastoral and farming fiefdom and economy to a sovereign ministate thriving on commerce and tourism. This process, which has led to a quadrupling of Andorra's population in a quarter of a century, brings both promise and problems to the future Andorra. Population density has become and will remain very high. There has been too little snow in recent years, which damages overnight tourism, and economic problems in neighboring Spain have taken some of the shine off the principality's economy. Tourism can no longer be counted on to provide prosperity for years to come, and it is uncertain anyway whether it will destroy Andorra's traditions and mountain tranquility. Nevertheless, Western Europe's newest sovereign state, with a new constitution and its first general elections in 1993, Andorra can face the future with relative confidence.

Web Sites and Bibliography of Key English-Language Books

WEB SITES

Useful Web Sites on the UN, EU, OECD, NATO and other:

www.un.org (Web site for United Nations. Many links.)

www.unsystem.or (Official UN website)

http://europa.eu.int (EU server site)

http://ue.eu.int (The Council of European Union site)

http://europa.eu.int/comm (European Commission site)

http://www.euobserver.com (EU news)

http://www.euractiv.com (European news)

www.EU-Values.org (Site maintained by students and staff of the College of Europe, Bruges)

http://www.europarl.eu.int (European Parliament)

http://european-convention.EU.int/ (Site for EU constitutional convention)

www.euractiv.com (Diverse news on EU and Europe)

www.aktion-euro.de (Site for the euro currency)

www.europeanaccess.co.uk (Links to various subjects)

www.eurunion.org (EU delegation of the European Commission to the U.S.)

http://www.europeanvalues.nl/ (site for European values)

Knoweurope.net (search engine for all documents published by EU institutions— by subscription)

www.oecd.org/daf/cmis/fdi/statist.htm (OECD site)

www.osce.org (Site of OSCE)

www.nato.int/structur/nids/nids.htm (NATO documentation, NATO Review)

www.nato.org and www.NATO.int (Web sites for NATO. Many links.)

www.wto.org (World Trade Organization site)

www.worldbank.org/html/Welcome.html (World Bank news, publications with links to other financial institutions)

www.ceip.org (Carnegie Endowment for International Peace, using a fully integrated Web-database system)

www.cia.gov/index.html (Central Intelligence Agency)

www.odci.gov/cia (Includes useful CIA publications, such as The World Factbook and maps)

www.state.gov/www/ind.html (U.S. Department of State, including country reports)

lcweb2.loc.gov/frd/cs/cshome.html (Library of Congress with coverage of over 100 countries)

www.xe.com/ucc/ (Site with most up-to-date foreign currency values)

http://www.linktoyourroots.hamburg.de (an internet database to help Americans trace their European roots)

Newspapers, Journals and Television with good coverage on European affairs:

www.chicagotribune.com (Named best overall US newspaper online service for newspapers with circulation over 100,000.)

www.csmonitor.com (Respected U.S. newspaper, *Christian Science Monitor*. Named best overall US newspaper online service for newspapers with circulation under 100,000.)

www.economist.com (British weekly news magazine)

www.nytimes.com (Respected U.S. newspaper, *The New York Times*)

www.washingtonpost.com

www.IHT.com (*International Herald Tribune*, published and distributed in Europe)

www.Europeanvoice.com (Weekly newspaper with EU and European news)

www.timeeurope.com (European edition of *Time*)

www.FT.com (authoritative British newspaper, *Financial Times*)

www.foreignaffairs.org (One of best-known international affairs journal)

www.cnn.com (Latest news with external links)

www.news.BBC.co.uk (British Broadcasting Corporation site)

www.c-span.org (Includes C-SPAN International)

www.libertaddigital.es (Spain's first online newspaper)

Country Web Sites:

www.embassy.org (This website contains links to all embassies in Washington)

www.britain-info.org (British press reports with links)

www.fco.gov.UK (British Foreign and Commonwealth Office site)

www.pm.gov.uk (Prime minister site)

www.number-10.gov.uk (Prime minister site)

www.parliament.gov.uk (Parliament site)

www.mod.uk (British Ministry of Defense site)

http://www.european-defence.co.uk (UK defense)

www.margaretthatcher.org (Margaret Thatcher's site)

www.irlgov.ie/frmain.htm (Irish government cite)

www.info-france-usa.org (French culture and government)

www.French-news.com (an English-language newspaper)

www.NBT.nl (Netherlands, with links to many subjects)

www.parlement.nl (Dutch parliamentary site)

http://www.minaz.nl/english/index.html (Dutch Ministry of General Affairs)

www.kabinetderkoningin.nl/en/home.html (Dutch Queen's Office)

www.expatica.com (Dutch news)

http:\\www.koninklijkhuis.nl/English/content.jsp?objectid=13817 (Dutch royal family)

www.Belgium.fgov.be (Cite of Belgian government)

www.vlaanderen.be (Flemish Community in Belgium)

www.cfwb.be (French Community in Belgium)

www.wallonie.org (Walloon Region in Belgium)

www.europeonline.com/bel/index_gb.htm (Belgian cite)

www.restena.lu/luxembourg/(various topics with links)

www.admin.ch (Swiss cite)

www.firstlink.li (Liechtenstein site)

www.news.li (news of Liechtenstein)

www.tourismus.li (Liechtenstein tourism)

www.greekembassy.org/pressoffice (Greek embassy press office)

http://www.governo.it/ (Italian government)

http://www.esteri.it/eng/index.htm (Italian Ministry of Foreign Affairs)

www.mi.cnr.it/WOI/ (Italian history and cities)

http://cca.imediata.pt (American Chamber of Commerce in Portugal)

www.vatican.va/ (Vatican site)

http://searchmalta.com (Malta)

http://www.magnet .mt (Malta's government website)

www.timesofmalta.com

www.independent.com.mt (Maltese newspaper in English)

http://inthenet.sm/rsm/intro.htm (San Marino)

www.greekembassy.org (Greek embassy)

www.mfa.gr (Greek Foreign Ministry)

http://greece.flash.gr (Greek news)

www.casareal.es/esp/familia/index.html (Spanish royal family)

GENERAL

Anderson, Stephanie B. *Crafting EU Security Policy: In the Pursuit of a European Identity*. Boulder, CO: Lynne Rienner, 2008.

Barzini, Luigi. *The Europeans*. New York: Simon Schuster, 1983.

Bauman, Zugmunt. *Europe. An Unfinished Adventure*. Malden, MA: Polity Press, 2004.

Bell, David S. *Western European Communists and the Collapse of Communism*. Oxford: Berg, 1993.

Biscop, Sven. *The European Security Strategy*. Abington, UK: Ashgate, 2005.

_____ and Johan Lembke, eds. *EU Enlargement and the Transatlantic Alliance:*

Bibliography

A Security Relationship in Flux. Boulder, CO: Lynne Rienner, 2007.

Black, Cyril E., et al. *Rebirth. A History of Europe Since World War II*. Boulder, CO: Westview, 1992.

Brimmer, Esther, ed. *The EU's Search for a Strategic Role*. Washington: Brookings, 2004.

Calleo, David P. *Rethinking Europe's Future*. Princeton: Princeton University Press, 2001.

Craig, Gordon A. *Europe Since 1815*. 3rd ed. New York: Holt, Rinehart Winston, 1971.

Curtis, Michael. *Western European Government and Politics*. New York: Longman, 1997.

De Grazia, Victoria. *America's Advance Through Twentieth-Century Europe*. Cambridge, MA: Harvard University Press, 2005.

Dinan, Desmond. *Europe Recast: A History of European Union*. Boulder, CO: Lynne Rienner, 2004.

———, ed. *Encyclopedia of the European Union*. Updated ed. Boulder, CO: Lynne Rienner, 2000.

———. *Ever Closer Union: An Introduction to European Integration*. 3d ed. Boulder, CO: Lynne Rienner, 2005.

Dragnich, Alex N., Rasmussen, Jorgen S, and Moses, Joel C. *Major European Governments*. 9th ed. Chicago: The Dorsey Press, 1994.

Dunkerley, David et al. *Changing Europe. Identities, Nations and Citizens*. New York: Routledge, 2002.

Dyson, Kenneth, and Featherstone, Kevin. *The Road to Maastricht. Negotiating Economic and Monetary Union*. New York: Oxford University, 2000.

Duroselle, Jean–Baptiste. *Europe: A History of its Peoples*. New York: Viking, 1990.

Eichengreen, Barry. *The European Economy Since 1945*. Princeton University Press, 2007.

Gaddis, John Lewis. *The Cold War: A New History*. New York: Penguin, 2006.

Gallagher, Michael, et al. *Representative Government in Western Europe*. 3d ed. New York: McGraw Hill, 2001.

Gärtner, Heinz et al. *Europe's New Security Challenges*. Boulder, CO: Lynne Rienner, 2001.

George, Stephen and Ian Bache. *Politics in the European Union*. New York: Oxford, 2001.

Gillingham, John. *European Integration, 1950–2003*. Cambridge: Cambridge University, 2003.

Giustino, David de. *A Reader in European Integration. A selection of key documents*. New York: Longman, 1996.

Goodby, James, et al. *A Strategy for Stable Peace. Toward a Euroatlantic Security Community*. Washington: Association for Diplomatic Studies and Training, 2002.

Gordon, Philip H. and Shapiro, Jeremy. *Allies at War. America, Europe, and the Crisis over Iraq*. NY: McGraw-Hill, 2004.

Green, David Michael. *The Europeans: Political Identity in an Emerging Polity*. Boulder, CO: Lynne Rienner, 2007.

Hamilton, Daniel S., ed. *Transatlantic Transformations. Equipping NATO for the 21st Century*. Washington: Brookings, 2004.

———, ed. *Conflict and Cooperation in Transatlantic Relations*. Washington: Brookings, 2004.

——— and Quinlan, Joseph P. *Partners in Prosperity. The Changing Geography of the Transatlantic Economy*. Washington: Brookings, 2004.

Hancock, M. Donald, et al. *Politics in Europe*. 4d ed. Washington: CQ Press, 2007.

Hitchcock, William I. *The Struggle for Europe: The Turbulent History of a Divided Continent 1945 to the Present*. NY: Anchor Books, 2004.

Hix, Simon. *The Political System of the European Union*. 2d. ed. New York: Palgrave Macmillan, 2005.

Hoffman, Stanley. *The Atlantic Alliance under Stress*. New York: Cambridge University, 2005.

Hogwood, Patricia and Roberts, Geoffrey K. *European politics today*. 2d ed. Manchester: Manchester University Press, 2003.

Horowitz, Joseph. *Artists in Exile: How Refugees from Twentieth-Century War and Revolution Transformed the American Performing Arts*. New York: Harper Collins, 2008.

Hosli, Madeleine O. *The Euro: A Concise Introduction to Europe's Single Currency*. Boulder, CO: Lynne Rienner, 2005.

Hunter, Robert E. *The European Security and Defense Policy. NATO's Companion—or Competitor?* Santa Monica, CA: Rand, 2002.

Jones, Robert A. *The Politics and Economics of the European Union*. Williston, VT: Edger Elgar, 1996.

Judt, Tony. *Postwar: A History of Europe Since 1945*. New York: Penguin, 2005.

Kaelble, Hartmut, ed. *The European Way. The Societies of Europe in the 19th and 20th Centuries*. New York: Berghahn, 2004.

Kagan, Robert. *Of Paradise and Power. America and Europe in the New World Order*. NY: Alfred A. Knopf, 2003.

Kaplan, Lawrence S. *NATO Divided, NATO United. The Evolution of an Alliance*. Westport, CT: Praeger, 2004.

Kesselman, Mark, et al. *European Politics in Transition*, 4th ed. New York: Houghton Mifflin, 2002.

Klausen, Jytte. *The Islamic Challenge: Politics and Religion in Western Europe*. New York: Oxford University, 2005.

Kramer, Jane. *Europeans*. New York: Penguin, 1992.

Kupchan, Charles A. *The End of the American Era. U.S. Foreign Policy and the Geopolitics of the Twenty-First Century*. NY: Knopf, 2003.

Lane, Jan–Erik and Ersson, Svante O. *European Politics*. 4th ed. Beverly Hills: Sage, 1998.

Laqueur, Walter. *Europe in Our Time. A History, 1945–1992*. New York: Penguin, 1993.

Leach, Rodney. *Europe. A Concise Encyclopedia of the European Union*. 4th ed. London: Profile Books, 2004.

Mahncke, Dieter and Thompson, Wayne C. and Rees, Wyn. *Redefining Transatlantic Relations: The Challenge of Change*. Manchester, UK: Manchester University Press, 2004.

Mair, Peter, ed. *The Western Europe Party System*. Oxford: Oxford University Press, 1990.

Mak, Geert. *In Europe: Travels through the Twentieth Century*. New York: Pantheon, 2007.

Marks, Gary, and Steenbergen, Marco R., eds. *European Integration and Political Conflict*. Cambridge, Cambridge University, 2003.

McCormick, John. *Understanding the European Union. A Concise Introduction*, 2d ed. NY: Palgrave, 2002.

———. *The European Union. Politics and Policies*. 3d ed. Boulder, CO: Westview, 2004.

Merkl, Peter H. *The Rift Between America and Old Europe. The Distracted Eagle*. New York: Routledge, 2005.

Miller, Steven L., ed. *European Unification: A Conceptual Guide for Educators*. Bloomington, IN: ERIC Clearing House for Social Studies, 1995.

Nelsen, Brent F. and Stubb, Alexander, eds. *The European Union: Readings of the Theory and Practice of European Integration*. Boulder, CO: Lynne Rienner, 2003.

Nugent, Neill. *The Government and Politics of the European Union*. 6th ed. NY: Palgrave, 2006.

———, ed. *European Union Enlargement*. New York: Palgrave Macmillan, 2004.

Occhipinti, John D. *The Politics of EU Police Cooperation: Toward a European FBI*. Boulder, CO: Lynne Rienner, 2003.

Patten, Chris. *Cousins and Strangers. America, Britain, and Europe in a New Century*. NY: Times Books/Henry Hold, 2006.

Pells, Richard. *Not Like Us. How Europeans Have Loved, Hated and Transformed American Culture Since World War II*. New York: Basic Books, 1997.

Pinder, John. *European Community. The Building of a Union*. 3d ed. Oxford: Oxford University Press, 1998.

_____, *The European Union. A Very Short Introduction*. Oxford: Oxford University Press, 2001.

Perry, Marvin. *An Intellectual History of Modern Europe.* Boston: Houghton Mifflin, 1993.

Peterson, John and Michael Shackleton. *The Institutions of the European Union.* New York: Oxford University Press, 2002.

Peterson, John and Pollack, Mark A. *Europe, America, Bush: Transatlantic Relations in the Twenty-first Century.* New York: Routledge, 2003.

Pond, Elizabeth. *The Rebirth of Europe,* 2d ed. Washington D.C.: Brookings, 2002.

———. *Friendly Fire. The Near-Death of the Transatlantic Alliance.* Washington D.C.: Brookings, 2003.

Roberts, Geoffrey and Hogwood, Patricia. *European Politics Today.* New York: St. Martin's, 1997.

Salmon, Trevor C. and Alistair Shepherd. *Toward a European Army: A Military Power in the Making?* Boulder, CO: Lynne Rienner, 2003.

Schain, Martin. *The Marshall Plan: Fifty Years After.* NY: Palgrave, 2001.

Schimmelfennig, Frank. *The EU, NATO and the Integration of Europe. Rules and Rhetoric.* Cambridge: Cambridge University Press, 2003.

Serfaty, Simon. *The Vital Partnership. Power and Order. America and Europe Beyond Iraq.* Lanham, MD: Rowman & Littlefield, 2005.

Shawcross, William. *Allies: The U.S., Britain, Europe, and the War in Iraq.* NY: Public Affairs, 2004.

Sloan, Stanley R. *NATO, The European Union, and the Atlantic Community. The Transatlantic Bargain Reconsidered.* Lanham, MD: Rowman & Littlefield, 2003.

Slomp, Hans. *European Politics into the Twenty-First Century. Integration and Division.* Westport, CT: Greenwood, 2000.

Smith, Michael E. *Europe's Foreign and Security Policy. The Institutionalization.* Cambridge: Cambridge University Press, 2004.

Steiner, Jürg. *European Democracies. 2d ed.* NY: Longman, 1991.

Telò, Mario. *Europe: A Civilian Power? European Union, Global Governance, World Order.* London: Palgrave MacMillan, 2006.

Torbiörn, Kjell M. *Destination Europe. The political and economic growth of a continent.* Manchester: Manchester University Press, 2003.

Tsoukalis, Loukas. *The New European Economy.* 3d ed. New York: Oxford University Press, 1996.

Urwin, Derek W. *Western Europe since 1945. A Political History.* 5th ed. New York: Longman, 1997.

———. *The Community of Europe. A History of European Integration since 1945.* 2d. ed. New York: Longman, 1994.

———. *Dictionary of European History and Politics Since 1945.* New York: Longman, 1996.

Warmenhoven, Henri J. *Western Europe.* Guilford, CT: Dushkin, annually updated.

Weidenfeld, Werner, et al. *From Alliance to Coalitions. The Future of Transatlantic Relations.* Washington D.C.: Brookings, 2004.

Wood, Steve and Wolfgang Quaisser. *The New European Union: Confronting the Challenges of Integration.* Boulder, CO: Lynne Rienner, 2007.

Young, John W. *Cold War Europe. 1945–1989.* New York: Routledge, 1991.

Youngs, Richard. *Europe and the Middle East: In the Shadow of September 11.* Boulder, CO: Lynne Rienner, 2006.

Zeff, Eleanor E. and Ellen B. Pirro, eds. *The European Union and the Member States.* 2d ed. Boulder, CO: Lynne Rienner, 2006.

Great Britain

Adolino, Jessica R. *Ethnic Minorities, Electoral Politics, and Political Integration in Britain.* Herndon, VA: Cassell, 1998.

Ascherson, Neal. *Stone Voices: The Search for Scotland.* NY: Hill and Wang, 2003.

Baylis, John. *Anglo–American Relations Since the Second World War.* New York: St. Martin's, 1997.

Blair, Tony. *New Britain. My Vision of a Young Country.* Boulder, CO: Westview, 2004.

Bartle, John and Anthony King, eds. *Britain at the Polls 2005.* Washington: CQ Press, 2005.

Bartlett, C.J. *The Special Relationship. A Political History of Anglo–American Relations since 1945.* New York: Longman, 1992.

Birch, Anthony H. *The British System of Government.* 8th ed. New York: Routledge, 1990.

Blair, Cherie. *Speaking for Myself: The Autobiography.* Boston: Little Brown, 2008.

Bower, Tom. *Gordon Brown.* New York: HarperCollins, 2004.

Brendon, Piers. *The Decline and Fall of the British Empire: 1781-1997.* London: Jonathon Cape, 2008.

Briggs, Asa. *A Social History of England.* London: Weidenfeld Nicolson, 1983.

Budge, Ian et al. *New British Politics.* 3d ed. NY: Pearson Longman, 2004.

Butler, David and Sloman, Anne, eds. *British Political Facts, 1900–1979.* 5th ed. New York: St. Martin's Press, 1980.

Campbell, Alastair. *The Blair Years.* New York: Alfred A. Knopf, 2007.

Cashmore, E. Ellis. *United Kingdom? Class, Race, and Gender since the War.* Winchester: Unwin Hyman, 1989.

Childs, David. *Britain since 1945. A Political History.* 6th ed. New York: Routledge, 2006.

Colley, Linda. *Britons. Forging the Nation, 1707–1837.* New Haven, CT: Yale University Press, 1992.

Copus, Colin. *Party politics and local government.* Manchester: Manchester University Press, 2004.

Croft, Stuart. *British Security Policy. The Thatcher Years and the End of the Cold War.* New York: Routledge, 1992.

Crossman, R. H. S. *Introduction to Bagehot's English Constitution.* London: Fontana, 1963.

Davies, John. *A History of Wales.* New York: Penguin, 2000.

Davis, Charlotte. *Welsh Nationalism in the Twentieth Century.* Westport, CT: Praeger, 1989.

Devine, T.M. *The Scottish Nation. 1700–2000.* New York: Penguin, 2000.

Edgell, Stephen and Duke, Vic. *A Measure of Thatcherism. A Sociology of Britain in the 1980s.* New York: Routledge, 1991.

Evans, Eric J. *Thatcher and Thatcherism,* 2d ed. NY: Routledge, 2002.

Forman, F.N. *Constitutional Change in the United Kingdom.* NY: Routledge, 2002.

Forster, Anthony. *Euroscepticism in British Politics.* NY: Routledge, 2002.

Freedman, Lawrence. *Britain and the Falklands War.* Cambridge, MA: Basil Blackwell, 1988.

Garner, Robert and Richard Kelly. *British Political Parties Today.* 2d ed. Manchester: Manchester University Press, 1998.

Gilbert, Martin. *Churchill and America.* New York: Free Press, 2006.

Goring, Rosemary. *Scotland: The Autobiography—2,000 Years of Scottish History by Those Who Saw it Happen.* London: Viking, 2007.

Hardie, Frank. *The Political Influence of the British Monarchy, 1868–1952.* London: Batsford, 1970.

Harvie, Christopher. *Scotland and Nationalism. Scottish Society and Politics 1707–Present.* 4th ed. New York: Routledge, 2004.

Hattersley, Roy. *Borrowed Time: The Story of Britain Between the Wars.* Boston: Little, Brown, 2007.

Havighurst, Alfred F. *Britain in Transition: the Twentieth Century.* Chicago: University of Chicago Press, 1979.

Hennessy, Peter. *The Prime Minister. The Office and its Holders Since 1945.* London: Penguin, 2000.

Holliday, Ian, ed. *Fundamentals in British Politics.* New York: St. Martin's, 1999.

Hurd, Douglas. *Robert Peel: A Biography.* London: Weidenfeld & Nicolson, 2007.

Irwin, John. *Modern Britain. An Introduction.* 3d ed. New York: Routledge, 1994.

Bibliography

James, Simon. *British Cabinet Government.* New York: Routledge, 1992.

Jenkins, Simon. *Thatcher & Sons: A Revolution in Three Acts.* London: Penguin/Allen Lane, 2006.

Jones, Bill and Kavanagh, Dennis. *British Politics.* 7th ed. Manchester: Manchester University Press, 2003.

———— et al. *Politics UK.* 5th ed. NY: Pearson Longman, 2004.

Jones, R. Brinley, ed. *The Anatomy of Wales.* Peterson–super–Hy: Gwerin, 1972.

Kavanagh, Dennis. *Thatcherism and British Politics. The End of Consensus?* 2d ed. Oxford: Oxford University Press, 1990.

King, Anthony, et al. *New Labour Triumphs: Britain at the Polls.* Chatham, NJ: Chatham House, 1998.

Kirk, Russell. *America's British Culture.* New Brunswick, NJ: Transaction, 1992.

Krieger, Joel. Reagan, *Thatcher, and the Politics of Decline.* New York: Oxford University Press, 1986.

Laybourn, Keith and Collette, Christine F. *Modern Britain Since 1979. A Reader.* NY: Palgrave, 2003.

Lynch, Peter. SNP. The History of the Scottish National Party. Welsh Academic Press, 2002.

Magnusson, Magnus. *Scotland. The Story of a Nation.* Camp Hill, PA: History Book Club, 2004.

Major, John. *John Major: The Autobiography.* London: HarperCollins, 1999.

Marr, Andrew. *A History of Modern Britain.* London: Macmillan, 2007.

Marwick, Arthur. *Culture in Britain Since 1945.* Cambridge, MA: Basil Blackwell, 1991.

Massie, Allan. *The Thistle and the Rose: Six Centuries of Love and Hate Between the Scots and the English.* London: John Murray, 2005.

McCormick, John. *Contemporary Britain.* NY: Palgrave, 2003.

McCrone, David. *Understanding Scotland. The Sociology of a Nation.* NY: Routledge, 2001.

McNaughton, Neil. *Understanding British and European Political Issues.* Manchester: Manchester University Press, 2003.

Mead, Walter Russell. *God and Gold: Britain, America and the Making of the Modern World.* New York: Knopf, 2007.

Meyer, Christopher. *DC Confidential. The Controversial Memoirs of Britain's Ambassador to the U.S. at the Time of 9/11 and the Iraq War.* London: Weidenfeld & Nicolson, 2005.

Mitchell, James. *Governing Scotland. The Invention of Administrative Devolution.* NY: Palgrave, 2003.

Mitchinson, John, and Merullo, Annabil. *British Greats.* London: Cassell, 2000.

Morgan, Kenneth O. *Labour People.* Oxford: Oxford University Press, 1987.

————. ed. *The Oxford History of Britain.* Rev. ed. New York: Oxford University, 1999.

Murkens, Jo Eric, et al. *Scottish Independence. A Practical Guide.* Edinburgh: Edinburgh University Press, 2002.

Naughtie, James. *The Best President We Never Had. The Political Tragedy of Tony Blair.* New York: PublicAffairs, 2004.

Norton, Bruce F. *Politics in Britain.* Washington: CQ Press, 2007.

Norton, Philip. *The British Polity.* 3d ed. New York: Longman, 1994.

Paterson, Alan. *The Law Lords.* London: Macmillan, 1982.

Paxman, Jeremy. *The English. A Portrait of the People.* London: Penguin, 1999.

Pearce, Malcolm and Stewart, Geoff. British *Political History 1867–1990.* New York: Routledge, 1992.

Pilkington, Colin. *Representative Democracy in Britain today.* Manchester: Manchester University Press, 1997.

————. *Britain in the European Union today.* Manchester: Manchester University Press, 2001.

————. *Devolution in Britain today.* Manchester: Manchester University Press, 2003.

Prescott, John. *Prezza—My Story: Pulling No Punches.* London: Headline Review, 2008.

Rasmussen, Jorgen S. *British Politics.* Belmont, CA: Wadsworth, 1993.

Reitan, Earl A. Tory Radicalism. *Margaret Thatcher, John Major, and the Transformation of Modern Britain.* Lanham, MD: Rowman & Littlefield, 1997.

Rentoul, John. *Tony Blair: Prime Minister.* Boston: Little, Brown, 2001.

Riddell, Peter. *The Thatcher Decade. How Britain has Changed During the 1980s.* Cambridge, MA: Basil Blackwell, 1989.

————. *The Odd Couple. Tony Blair's Love Affair with George W. Bush and America.* Politico's Publishing, 2003.

Robbins, Keith. *Nineteenth–Century Britain. England, Scotland and Wales: The Making of a Nation.* Oxford: Oxford University Press, 1988.

Rose, Richard. *Politics in England.* 5th ed. New York: Harper Collins, 1989.

Royle, Edward. *Modern Britain. A Social History, 1750–1997.* 2d ed. New York: Oxford University, 1997.

Russell, Andrew et al. *Neither Left nor right? The electoral politics of the Liberal Democrats.* Manchester: Manchester University Press, 2004.

Sampson, Anthony. *Who Runs this Place? The Anatomy of Britain in the 21st Century.* London: John Murray, 2004.

Särlvik, Bo and Crewe, Ivor. *Decade of Dealignment: The Conservative Victory of 1979 and Electoral Trends in the 1970s.* Cambridge: Cambridge University Press, 1983.

Seitz, Raymond. *Over Here.* London: Phoenix, 1998.

Seldon, Anthony, ed. *Conservative Century. The Conservative Party Since 1900.* Oxford: Oxford University, 1994.

Shaw, Eric. *The Labour Party Since 1979. Crisis and Transformation.* New York: Routledge, 1994.

Shell, Donald and Beamish, David, eds. *The House of Lords at Work.* Oxford: Oxford University, 1993.

Sked, Alan and Chris Cook. *Post-War Britain: A Political History.* 2d ed. New York: Penguin, 1990.

Skidelsky, Robert, ed. *Thatcherism.* Cambridge, MA: Basil Blackwell, 1990.

Smith, Julie and Mariana Tsatsas. *The New bilateralism. The UK's Relations within the EU.* Washington, D.C.: Brookings, 2002.

Smith, Martin J. and Spear, Joanna. *The Changing Labour Party.* New York: Routledge, 1992.

Smith, Michael. *The Spying Game. The Secret History of British Espionage.* Politico's Publishing, 2003.

Solomos, John. *Race and Racism in Britain.* NY: Palgrave, 2003.

Stephens, Philip. *Tony Blair. The Making of a World Leader.* London: Viking, 2004.

Thatcher, Margaret. *The Path to Power and Downing Street Years.* 2 vols. New York: HarperCollins, 1993, 1995.

————. *Statecraft: Strategies for a Changing World.* New York: HarperCollins, 2002.

Thompson, Juliet S. and Wayne C. *Margaret Thatcher. Prime Minister Indomitable.* Boulder, CO: Westview, 1994.

Trevelyan, G. M. *History of England.* London: Longmans, 1963.

Wapshott, Nicholas. *Ronald Reagan and Margaret Thatcher: A Political Marriage.* New York: Sentinel, 2007.

Williams, Glyn and Ramsden, John. *Ruling Britannia. A Political History of Britain 1688–1988.* New York: Longman, 1990.

Young, Hugo. *The Iron Lady. A Biography of Margaret Thatcher.* New York: Farrar Straus and Giroux, 1989.

Young, John W. *Britain and the World in the Twentieth Century.* New York: Oxford University, 1997.

Northern Ireland

Adams, Gerry. *Hope and History. Making Peace in Ireland.* London: Brandon, 2004.

Arthur, Paul. *Government and Politics of Northern Ireland.* Second Edition. New York: Longman, 1984.

————. and Jeffery, Keith. *Northern Ireland Since 1968.* Cambridge, MA: Basil Blackwell, 1988.

Aughey, Arthur. *The Politics of Northern Ireland.* Abington, UK: Routledge, 2005.

Barton, Brian and Patrick J. Roche. *The Northern Ireland Question*. Brookfield, VT: Ashgate, 1999.

Boyle, Keven and Tom Hadden. *Northern Ireland: The Choice*. New York: Praeger, 1998.

Bruce, Steve. *God Save Ulster! The Religion and Politics of Paisleyism*. Oxford: Oxford University Press, 1989.

———. *The Edge of the Union. The Ulster Loyalist Political Vision*. Oxford: Oxford University, 1994.

Coogan, Tim Pat. *The IRA*. Rev. ed. London: HarperCollins, 2000.

Dixon, Paul. *The Northern Ireland Peace Process. Choreography and Theatrical Politics*. New York: Routledge, 2006.

Elliott, Marianne. *The Catholics of Ulster. A History*. NY: Basic Books, 2002.

———. *The Long Road to Peace in Northern Ireland*. Liverpool: Liverpool University Press, 2002.

Farren, Sean, and Mulvihill, Robert F. *Paths to a Settlement in Northern Ireland*. New York: Oxford University, 2000.

Feeney, Brian. *Sinn Fein. A Hundred Turbulent Years*. Madison: University of Wisconsin Press, nd.

Gaffikin, Frank and Morrissey, Mike. *Northern Ireland. The Thatcher Years*. Atlantic Highlands, NJ: Humanities Press, 1990.

Geraghty, Tony. *The Irish War. The Hidden Conflict between the IRA and British Intelligence*. Baltimore: Johns Hopkins University, 2000.

Godson, Dean. *Himself Alone. David Trimble and the Ordeal of Unionism*. New York: HarperCollins, 2004.

Hull, R. H. *Irish Triangle*. Princeton: Princeton University Press, n.d.

Irvine, Maurice. *Northern Ireland. Faith and Faction*. New York: Routledge, 1991.

Maillot, Agnes. *New Sinn Fein. Irish Republicanism in the Twenty-First Century*. New York: Routledge, 2006.

Maloney, Ed. *A Secret History of the IRA*. New York: Norton, 2002.

McDonald, Henry and Jim Cusack. *UDA: Inside the Heart of Loyalist Terror*. Dublin: Penguin Ireland, 2004.

Mitchell, Paul and Rick Wilford, eds. *Politics in Northern Ireland*. Boulder, CO: Westview, 1998.

Murray, Gerard and Jonathan Tonge. *Sinn Fein and the SDLP. From Alienation to Participation*. London: Hurst, 2005.

O'Kane, Eamonn. *Anglo-Irish Relations and the Northern Ireland Conflict*. New York: Routledge, 2006.

Ruane, Joseph and Todd, Jennifer. *The Dynamics of Conflict in Northern Ireland*. New York: Cambridge University Press, 2003.

Tonge, Jonathan. *Northern Ireland*. London: Polity, 2005.

Whyte, John and Fitzgerald, Garret. *Interpreting Northern Ireland*. Oxford: Oxford University Press, 1991.

Wichert, Sabine. *Northern Ireland since 1945*. New York: Longman, 1991.

Republic of Ireland

Ardagh, John. *Ireland and the Irish. Portrait of a Changing Society*. New York: Penguin, 1998.

Boyce, D. George. *Nationalism in Ireland*. 2d ed. New York: Routledge, 1991.

Chubb, Basil. *The Government and Politics of Ireland*. 3d ed. New York: Longman, 1992.

Coakley, John and Michael Gallagher, eds. *Politics in the Republic of Ireland*. 4th ed. Abington, UK: Routledge, 2004.

Collins, Neil and McCann, Frank. *Irish Politics Today*. 3d. ed. New York: St. Martin's, 1997.

Coulter, Colin and Coleman, Steve, eds. *The end of Irish history? Critical approaches to the Celtic Tiger*. Manchester: Manchester University Press, 2003.

Curtis, Edmund. A *History of Ireland*. London: Methuen, 1961.

Fitzgerald, Garret. *All in a Life*. London: Macmillan, 1991.

———. *Reflections on the Irish State*. Dublin: Irish Academic Press, 2002.

Foster, Roy F., ed. *The Oxford History of Ireland*. Oxford: Oxford University Press, 1992.

———. *Luck and the Irish: A Brief History of Change 1970-2000*. Oxford: Oxford University Press, 2007.

Fulton, John. *The Tragedy of Belief. Division, Politics, and Religion in Ireland*. Oxford: Oxford University Press, 1991.

Gallagher, Michael et al, eds. *How Ireland Voted 2002*. NY: Palgrave, 2003.

Johnson, Nuala C. *Ireland, the Great War and The Geography of Remembrance*. Cambridge, Cambridge University, 2003.

Lalor, Brian, ed. *The Encyclopedia of Ireland*. New Haven: Yale University, 2003.

Macardle, Dorothy. *The Irish Republic*. Dublin: Irish Press, 1951.

Mallie, Eamonn and David McKittrick. *Endgame in Ireland*. Hodder & Stoughton, 2001.

McCaffrey, Lawrence J. *Ireland from Colony to Nation–State*. Englewood Cliffs, NJ: Prentice–Hall, 1977.

Munck, Ronnie. *The Irish Economy*. Boulder, CO: Westview Press, 1993.

Patterson, Henry. *Ireland Since 1939: The Persistence of Conflict*. Dublin: Penguin, 2006.

Roy, James Charles. *The Fields of Athenry. A Journey through Ireland*. Boulder, CO: Westview, 2003.

———. *The Back of Beyond. A Search for the Soul of Ireland*. Boulder, CO: Westview, 2004.

Savage, Robert J., Jr., ed. *Ireland in the New Century*. Four Courts Press, 2003.

Tanner, Marcus. *Ireland's Holy Wars: The Struggle for a Nation's Soul, 1500–2000*. New Haven: Yale University Press, 2001.

Townshend, Charles. *Political Violence in Ireland*. Oxford: Oxford University Press, 1985.

———. *Ireland. The 20th Century*. New York: Oxford University, 1999.

Uris, Leon. *Trinity*. New York: Doubleday, 1975.

France

Adams, William James. *Restructuring the French Economy: Government and the Rise of Market Competition Since World War II*. Washington, D.C.: Brookings, 1989.

Alexander, Martin S. *French History Since Napoleon*. New York: Oxford University, 1999.

Ardagh, John. *France in the New Century. Portrait of a Changing Society*. rev. ed. New York: Penguin, 2000.

Bell, David S. *French politics today*. Manchester, Manchester University Press, 2002.

———. *The French Socialist Party*. Oxford: Oxford University Press, 1988.

———. and Criddle, Byron. *The French Communist Party in the Fifth Republic*. Oxford: Oxford University, 1994.

Bernstein, Richard. *Fragile Glory. A Portrait of France and the French*. New York: Alfred A. Knopf, 1990.

Braudel, Fernand. *The Identity of France: History and Environment*. New York: Harper and Collins, 1989.

Brenner, Michael and Guillaume Parmentier. *Reconcilable Differences. U.S.-French Relations in the New Era*. Washington D.C.: Brookings, 2002.

Bridgford, Jeff. *The Politics of French Trade Unionism*. New York: St. Martin's, 1992.

Brogan, D. W. *France Under the Republic (1870–1939)*. New York: Harper and Row, 1940.

Brogan, Hugh. *Alexis de Tocqueville: Prophet of Democracy in the Age of Revolution—A Biography*. New Haven: Yale University, 2006.

Chapman, Herrick and Frader, Laura. *Race in France. Interdisciplinary Perspectives on the Politics of Difference*. New York: Berghahn, 2004.

Cogan, Charles. *French Negotiating Behavior. Dealing with La Grande Nation*. Herndon, VA: United States Institute of Peace Press, 2003.

Cole, Alistair. *François Mitterrand. A Study in Political Leadership*. New York: Routledge, 1994.

Cross, Maire and Sheila Perry. *Population and Social Policy in France*. Herndon, VA: Cassell, 1997.

Davies, Peter. *The Extreme Right in France, 1789 to the Present. From De Maistre to Le Pen*. NY: Routledge, 2002.

Bibliography

De Gaulle, Charles. *The War Memoirs of Charles de Gaulle*. 3 vols. New York: Simon Schuster, 1960.

———. *Memoirs of Hope and Endeavor*. New York: Simon Schuster, 1970.

Doyle, William. *The Oxford History of the French Revolution*. Oxford: Oxford University Press, 1990.

Ehrmann, Henry and Schain, Martin A. *Politics in France*. 5th ed. New York: Harper Collins, 1992.

Esdaile, Charles. *Napoleon's Wars: An International History, 1803-1815*. London, Allen Lane, 2007.

Evans, Jocelyn, ed. *The French party system*. Manchester: Manchester University Press, 2003.

Friend, Julius W. *The Long Presidency: France in the Mitterrand Years, 1981–1995*. Boulder, CO: Westview, 1999.

———. *Unequal Partners. French-German Relations, 1989–2000*. Washington: CSIS Press, 2001.

Fysh, Peter and Wolfreys, Jim. *The Politics of Racism in France*. NY: Palgrave, 2003.

Gaffney, John. *The French Left and the Fifth Republic: The Discourses of Communism and Socialism in Contemporary France*. New York: St. Martin's, 1989.

Gildea, Robert. *France Since 1945*. Oxford: Oxford University Press, 1996.

Godin, Emmanuel and Chafer, Tony, eds. *The French Exception*. New York: Berghahn, 2005.

Gopnik, Adam. *Paris to the Moon*. New York: Random House, 2000.

Gordon, Philip H. *A Certain Idea of France. French Security Policy and the Gaullist Legacy*. Princeton: Princeton University Press, 1993.

——— and Sophie Meunier. *The French Challenge. Adapting to Globalization*. Washington D.C.: Brookings, 2001.

Hanley, David. *Party, Society, Government. Republican Democracy in France*. New York: Berghahn, 2001.

Hauss, Charles. *Politics in France*. Washington: CQ Press, 2007.

Hazareesingh, Sudhir. *Political Traditions in Modern France*. Oxford: Oxford University, 1994.

Higonnet, Patrice. *Paris: Capital of the World*. NY: Belknap, 2002.

Hirschfeld, Gerhard. *Collaboration in France. Politics and Culture during the Nazi Occupation, 1940–1944*. Oxford: Berg, 1989.

Hoffmann, Stanley and Ross, George, eds. *Continuity and Change in Mitterrand's France*. New York: Oxford University Press, 1987.

Hollifield, James F. and Ross, George, eds. *Searching for the New France*. New York: Routledge, 1992.

Holman, Valerie, ed. *France at War in the Twentieth Century. Propaganda, Myth and Metaphor*. New York: Berghahn, 2000.

Horne, Alistair. *Seven Ages of Paris: Portrait of a City*. NY: Alfred A. Knopf, 2002.

Jackson, Julian. *France: The Dark Years, 1940–1944*. Oxford: Oxford University Press, 2001.

Jones, Colin. *The Great Nation: France from Louis XV to Napoleon, 1715–99*. NY: Allen Lane/The Penguin Press, 2002.

Kedward, Rod. *La Vie en Bleu: France and the French since 1900*. New York: Overlook Press, 2006.

Keiger, John. *France and the World in the Twentieth Century*. New York: Oxford University, 2000.

Larkin, Maurice. *France Since the Popular Front. Government and People, 1936–1986*. Oxford: Oxford University Press, 1988.

Lewis–Beck, ed. *How France Votes*. Chatham, NJ: Chatham House, 1999.

May, Catherine. *The Black and the Red*. (Biography of Mitterrand). NY: Harcourt Brace Jovanovich, 1987.

McMillan, James F. *Twentieth Century France. Politics and Society in France, 1898–1991*. New York: Routledge, 1992.

Northcutt, Wayne. *Mitterrand. A Political Biography*. New York: Holmes and Meier, 1992.

Perry, Sheila. *Voices of France. Social, Political and Cultural Identity*. Herndon, VA: Cassell, 1997.

Roger, Philippe. *The American Enemy: The History of French Anti-Americanism*. Chicago: University of Chicago Press, 2005.

Sarkozy, Nicolas. *Testimony: France in the Twenty-First Century*. New York: Pantheon Books, 2007.

Schoenbrun, David. *Soldiers of the Night: The Story of the French Resistance*. New York: New American Library, 1981.

Smith, Leonard V. and Audoin-Rouzeau, Stéphane. *France and the Great War, 1914-1918*. Cambridge, Cambridge University, 2003.

Stevens, Anne. *The Government and Politics of France*. 3d ed. New York: Palgrave, 2003.

Tilly, Charles. *The Contentious French: Four Centuries of Popular Struggle*. Cambridge: Harvard University Press, 1986.

Tocqueville, Alexis de. *The Old Regime and the French Revolution*. New York: Doubleday Anchor, 1955.

Tombs, Robert and Isabelle. *That Sweet Enemy: The French and the British from the Sun King to the Present*. London: William Heinemann, 2006.

Védrine, Hubert with Dominique Moisi. *France in an Age of Globalization*. Washington: Brookings Institution, 2001.

Wahl, Nicholas, ed. *DeGaulle and the United States, 1930–1970*. Oxford: Berg, 1992.

Wall, Irwin M. *France, The United States, and the Algerian War*. Ithaca, NY: Cornell University Press, 2001.

Wawro, Geoffrey. *The Franco-Prussian War. The German Conquest of France in 1870-1871*. Cambridge, Cambridge University, 2003.

Williams, Charles. *Pétain*. New York: Palgrave Macmillan, 2005.

Wright, Vincent. *The Government and Politics of France*. 4th ed. New York: Routledge, 1994.

Zeldin, Theodore. *The French*. New York: Pantheon Books, 1982.

The BENELUX Countries

General

Eych, F. Gunther. *The Benelux Countries: An Historical Survey*. Princeton: Van Nostrand, 1959.

Kossman, E. H. *The Low Countries, 1780–1940*. Oxford: Oxford Univ. Press, 1978.

Stein, George J. *Benelux Security Cooperation*. Boulder, CO: Westview, 1990.

The Netherlands

Ali, Ayaan Hirsi. *Infidel-My Life: The Story of My Enlightenment*. NY: Free Press, 2007.

Anderweg, Rudi B. and Galen A. Irwin. *Governance and Politics of the Netherlands*. New York: Palgrave Macmillan, 2002.

Bakvis, Herman. *Catholic Power in the Netherlands*. Toronto: McGill–Queen's Univ. Press, 1981.

Buruma, Ian. *Murder in Amsterdam: The Death of Theo van Gogh and the Limits of Tolerance*. New York: Penguin, 2006.

Cox, Robert H. *The Development of the Dutch Welfare State*. Pittsburgh: University of Pittsburgh Press, 1993.

Daalder, Hans and Irwin, Galen A. *Politics in the Netherlands. How much change?* Portland, OR: Frank Cass, 1989.

Gladdish, Ken. *Governing from the Center. Politics and Policy–Making in the Netherlands*. DeKalb, IL: Northern Illinois University Press, 1992.

Israel, Jonathan I. *Dutch Primacy in World Trade, 1585–1740*. Oxford: Oxford University Press, 1990.

Lijphart, Arend. *The Politics of Accommodation: Pluralism and Democracy in the Netherlands*. Berkeley: University of California Press, 1968.

Mak, Geert. *Amsterdam*. Cambridge, MA: Harvard University Press, 2000.

Belgium

Belgium: A State of Mind. (ISBN: 9020244649). Lannoo, 2001.

Boudart, Marina, et al. *Modern Belgium*. Palo Alto, CA: SPOSS, 1990.

Cowie, Donald. *Belgium: The Land and the People*. Cranbury, NJ: A. S. Barnes, 1977.

Fox, Renée. *In the Belgian Chateau. The Spirit and Culture of a European Society in an Age of Change*. Chicago: Ivan R. Dee, nd.

Hochschild, Adam. *King Leopold's Ghost. A Story of Greed, Terror, and Heroism in Colonial Africa.* New York: Houghton Mifflin. A Mariner Book, 1998.

Hooghe, Liesbet. *A Leap in the Dark. Nationalist Conflict and Federal Reform in Belgium.* Ithaca, NY: Cornell University Press, 1993.

Fitzmaurice, J. *Politics of Belgium. Crisis and Compromise in a Plural Society.* New York: St. Martin's Press, 1983.

Lijphart, Arend, ed. *Conflict and Coexistence in Belgium.* Berkeley: University of California Press, 1980.

Meeus, Adrien de. *History of the Belgians.* New York: Praeger, 1962.

Strikwerda, Carl. *A House Divided. Catholics, Socialists, and Flemish Nationalists in Nineteenth Century Belgium.* Lanham, MD: Rowman and Littlefield, 1998.

Luxembourg

Barteau, Harry C. *Historical Dictionary of Luxembourg.* Metuchen, NJ: Scarecrow Press, 1996.

Majerus, Pierre. *The Institutions of the Grand Duchy of Luxembourg.* Luxembourg: Ministry of State Press and Information Service, 1976.

Margue, Paul. *A Short History of Luxembourg.* Luxembourg: Ministry of State Press and Information Service, 1976.

Switzerland

Bernath, Magdalena, et al. *Swiss Foreign Policy. Foundations and Possibilities.* NY: Routledge, 2004.

Bonjour, E., et al. *A Short History of Switzerland.* Oxford: Clarendon, 1972.

Bradfield, B. *The Making of Switzerland: From Ice Age to Common Market.* Zurich: Schweizer Spiegel Verlag, 1964.

Church, Clive H. *Switzerland and the European Union.* New York: Routledge, 2006.

Craig, Gordon A. *The Triumph of Liberalism: Zurich in the Golden Age, 1830–1869.* New York: Collier, 1990.

Gabriel, Jürg Martin and Fischer, Thomas. *Swiss Foreign Policy, 1945–2002.* NY: Palgrave, 2003.

Gstöhl, Sieglinde. *Reluctant Europeans: Norway, Sweden, and Switzerland in the Process of Integration.* Boulder, CO: Lynn Rienner, 2002.

Hilowitz, Janet Eve. *Switzerland in Perspective.* Westport, CT: Greenwood, 1990.

Kieser, Rolf and Spillman, Kurt R., eds. *The New Switzerland. Problems and Policies.* Palo Alto, CA: SPROSS, 1996.

Linder, Wolf. *Swiss Democracy.* New York: St. Martin's, 1994.

Luck, Murray J. *History of Switzerland: The First Hundred Thousand Years From Before the Beginning to the Days of the Present.* Palo Alto, CA: SPROSS, 1985.

McPhee, John. *La Place de la Concorde Suisse.* New York: Farrar/Straus/Giroux, 1983.

Milivojevic, Marko, and Mauerer, Pierre. *Swiss Neutrality and Security. Armed Forces, National Defence and Foreign Policy.* New York: St. Martin's, 1991.

Remak, Joachim. *A Very Civil War. The Swiss Sonderbund War of 1847.* Boulder, CO: Westview, 1993.

Sorell, Walter. *The Swiss.* New York: Bobbs–Merrill, 1972.

Steinberg, J. *Why Switzerland.* 2d ed. Cambridge; Cambridge University Press, 1996.

Steiner, Jürg. *Amicable Agreement Versus Majority Rule: Conflict Resolution in Switzerland.* Chapel Hill: University of North Carolina Press, 1974.

———. *Conscience in Politics.* Levittown, PA: Garland, 1996.

Liechtenstein

Kranz, Walter, ed. *The Principality of Liechtenstein: A Documentary Handbook.* Schaan: Lingg, 1973.

Raton, Pierre. *Liechtenstein: History and Institutions of the Principality.* Vaduz: Liechtenstein Verlag, 1970.

Schlapp, Manfred. *This is Liechtenstein.* Stuttgart: Seewald, n.d.

Mediterranean Europe

General

Aliboni, Roberto, ed. *Southern European Security in the 1990s.* New York: St. Martin's, 1992.

Chilcote, Ronald H., et al. *Transitions from Dictatorship to Democracy: Comparative Studies of Spain, Portugal and Greece.* Bristol, PA: Crane Russak, 1990.

Kurth, James, and Petras, James. *Mediterranean Paradoxes. The Politics and Social Structure of Southern Europe.* Oxford: Berg, 1992.

Liebert, Ulrike and Cotta, Maurizio, eds. *Parliament and Democratic Consolidation in Southern Europe. Italy, Spain, Portugal, Greece and Turkey in Comparison.* New York: Columbia University Press, 1990.

Greece

Bahcheci, Tozun. *Greek Turkish Relations Since 1955.* Boulder: Westview Press, 1989.

Bryant, Ralph C. et al. *Greece's Economic Performance and Prospects.* Washington D.C.: Brookings 2002.

Clark, Bruce. *Twice a Stranger: The Mass Expulsions that Forged Modern Greece and Turkey.* Cambridge, MA: Harvard University Press, 2006.

Clogg, R., *Greece in the 1980's.* London: Macmillan, 1983.

———. ed. *The Struggle for Greek Independence.* London: Macmillan, 1973.

———. and Yannopoulos, G. *Greece Under Military Rule.* New York: Basic Books, 1972.

———. *A Concise History of Greece.* 2d. ed. Cambridge: Cambridge University Press, 2002.

Constas, Dimitri, ed. *The Greek–Turkish Conflict in the 1990s. Domestic and External Influences.* New York: St. Martin's, 1991.

Couloumbis, J. A. et al. *Foreign Interference in Greek Politics: An Historical Perspective.* New York: Pella, 1976.

Couloumbis, Theodore A., et al, eds. *Greece in the twentieth century.* London: Frank Cass, 2003.

Featherstone, Kevin, ed. *Political Change in Greece: Before and After the Colonels.* Kent: Croom Helm, 1988.

Featherstone, Kevin, ed. *The Challenge of Modernization: Politics and Policy in Greece.* Special issue of *West European Politics,* Vol. 28, Nr. 2, March 2005.

Fox, Robin Lane. *The Classical World. An Epic History from Homer to Hadrian.* Basic, 2006.

Hadjiyannis, Stylianos. *Social Conflict and Change in Modern Greece.* Bristol, PA: Crane Russak, 1991.

Kazakos, Panos and Ioakimidis, P.C., eds. *Greece and EC Membership Evaluated.* New York: St. Martin's, 1995.

Koliopoulos, J.S. and Thanos M. Veremis. *Greece: the Modern Sequel. From 1821 to the Present.* London: Hurst, 2002.

Kourvetaris, Yorgos A. and Dobratz, Betty A. *A Profile of Modern Greece. In Search of Identity.* Oxford: Oxford University Press, 1988.

Mazower, Mark. *Inside Hitler's Greece. The Experience of Occupation, 1941–44.* New Haven: Yale University Press, 2001.

Nachmani, Amikam. *International Intervention in the Greek Civil War.* Westport, CT: Praeger, 1990.

Pagoulatos, George. *Greece's New Political Economy.* NY: Palgrave, 2003.

Peltifer, James. *The Greeks. The Land and People Since the War.* 2d ed. New York: Penguin, 2000.

Spourdalakis, Michalis. *The Rise of the Greek Socialist Party.* New York: Routledge, 1988.

Stavrakis, Peter J. *Moscow and Greek Communism, 1944–1949.* Ithaca, NY: Cornell University Press, 1992.

Stearns, Monteagle. *Entangled Allies. U.S. Policy Toward Greece, Turkey, and Cyprus.* New York: Council on Foreign Relations Press, 1992.

Tzannatos, Zafiris. *Socialism in Greece.* Brookfield, VT: Gower, 1986.

Winnifrith, Tom and M. P., eds. *Greece—Old and New.* New York: St. Martin's Press, 1982.

Woodhouse, C. M. *Modern Greece: A Short History.* New York: Faber and Faber, 1977.

———. *Karamanlis: The Restorer of Greek Democracy.* New York: Oxford Univ. Press, 1982.

Bibliography

Cyprus

Calotychos, Vangelis, ed. *Cyprus and Its People: Nation, Identity, and the Experience in an Unimaginable Community, 1955–1997.* Boulder, CO: Westview Press, 1998.

Diez, Thomas, ed. *The European Union and the Cyprus conflict.* Manchester: Manchester University Press, 2002.

Dodd, Clement H. *The Cyprus Imbroglio.* Concord, MA: Paul & Company Publishers Consortium, 1998.

Hart, Parker T. *Two NATO Allies at the Threshold of War. Cyprus, a Firsthand Account of Crisis Management, 1965–1968.* Durham, NC: Duke University Press, 1990.

Holland, Robert. *Britain and the Revolt in Cyprus, 1954–1959.* New York: Oxford University Press, 1998.

Joseph, Joseph S. *Cyprus: Ethnic Conflict and International Politics: from Independence to the Threshold of the European Union.* New York: Saint Martin's Press, 1997.

Kitromilides, Paschalis M. *Cyprus.* Santa Barbara, CA: ABC-CLIO, rev. ed 1995.

O'Malley, Brendan. *Cyprus Conspiracy.* New York: I.B. Tauris, 2000.

Pace, Roderick. *The European Union's Mediterranean Enlargement. Cyprus and Malta.* New York: Routledge, 2006.

Panteli, Stavros. *Historical Dictionary of Cyprus.* Lanham, MD: Scarecrow Press, 1995.

Salem, Norma, ed. *Cyprus. A Regional Conflict and its Resolution.* New York: St. Martin's, 1992.

Solstein, Eric, ed. *Cyprus: a Country Study.* Washington, DC: U.S. GPO, 4th ed. 1993.

Italy

Atkinson, Rick. *The Day of Battle: The War in Sicily and Italy, 1943-1944.* New York: Henry Holt, 2007.

Barkan, Joanne. *Visions of Emancipation: The Italian Workers' Movement Since 1945.* New York: Praeger, 1984.

Barzini, Luigi. *The Italians.* New York: Atheneum, 1977.

Bosworth, R.J.B. *Mussolini's Italy. Life Under the Dictatorship, 1915-1945.* New York: Penguin, 2005.

Bull, Martin and Martin Rhodes, eds. *Crisis and Transition in Italian Politics.* Portland, OR: Frank Cass, 1997.

———— and Martin Rhodes, eds. *Italy: A Contested Polity.* Special Issue of *West European Politics,* Vol. 30, Nr. 4, September 2007.

Burnett, Stanton H. and Luca Mantovani. *The Italian Guillotine: Operation Clean Hands and the Overthrow of Italy's First Republic.* Washington D.C.: CSIS, 1998

Catanzaro, Raimondo, ed. *The Red Brigades and Left–Wing Terrorism in Italy.* New York: St. Martin's, 1991.

Caesar, Michael, and Hainsworth, Peter, eds. *Writers and Society in Contemporary Italy.* 2d rev. ed. Oxford: Berg, 1993.

D'Alimonte, Roberto and David Nelken, eds. *Italian Politics. The Center–Left in Power.* Boulder, CO: Westview, 1997.

DiScala, Spencer M. *Italy. From Revolution to Republic. 1700 to the Present.* Boulder, CO: Westview, 2004.

Duggan, Christopher and Wagstaff, Christopher, eds. *Italy in the Cold War. Politics, Culture and Society 1948–1958.* Oxford: Berg, 1993.

Farneti, Paolo. *The Italian Party System.* London: Frances Pinter, 1985.

Furlong, Paul. *Modern Italy. Representation and Reform.* New York: Routledge, 1994.

Giammanco, Rosanna Mulazzi. *The Catholic–Communist Dialogue in Italy: 1944 to the Present.* Westport, CT: Praeger, 1989.

Gilbert, Mark. *The Italian Revolution. The End of Politics, Italian Style?* Boulder, CO: Westview, 1995.

Ginsborg, Paul. *A History of Contemporary Italy. Society and Politics 1943–1988.* New York: Palgrave Macmillan, 2003.

————. *Italy and its Disontents: 1980–2001.* New York: Penguin, 2002.

Gold, Thomas. *The Lega Nord and Contemporary Politics in Italy.* NY: Palgrave, 2003.

Hearder, Harry. *Italy: A Short History.* Cambridge: Cambridge University Press, 1990.

Hibbert, Christopher. *Rome: The Biography of a City.* New York: Viking, n.d.

Hine, David. *Governing Italy. The Politics of Bargained Pluralism.* Oxford: Oxford University Press, 1993.

Jones, Tobias. *The Dark Heart of Italy: Travels Through Space and Time Across Italy.* (A critique of Silvio Berlusconi's government). North Point Press, 2004.

Kertzer, David I. *Comrades and Christians. Religion and Political Struggle in Communist Italy.* Prospect Heights, IL: Waveland, 1992.

Kogan, Norman H. *Political History of Postwar Italy: From the Old to the New Center Left.* New York: Praeger, 1981.

Levy, Carl, ed. *Italian Regionalism. History, Identity and Politics.* New York: Berg, 1996.

Locke, Richard M. *Remaking the Italian Economy.* Ithaca, NY: Cornell University Press, 1997.

Leonardi, Robert and Wertman, Douglas A. *Italian Christian Democracy.* New York: St. Martin's, 1989.

McCarthy, Patrick. *The Crisis of the Italian State.* New York: St. Martin's, 1997.

Morgan, Philip. *The Fall of Mussolini.* Oxford: Oxford University Press, 2007.

Moss, David. *The Politics of Left–Wing Violence in Italy, 1969–85.* New York: St. Martin's, 1990.

Mountjoy, Alan B. *The Mezzogiorno.* New York: Oxford University Press, 1973.

Newell, James, ed. *The Italian General Election of 2001. Berlusconi's Victory.* NY: Palgrave, 2003.

Parker, Simon and Paolo Natale. *Contemporary Italian Politics.* New York: Routledge, 2006.

Partridge, Hillary. *Italian Politics Today.* New York: St. Martin's, 1998.

Pinter Publishers, *Italian Politics, A Review.* New York: Columbia University Press, annual updated editions.

Pridham, Geoffrey. *Political Parties and Coalitional Behavior in Italy.* New York: Routledge, 1988.

Procacci, Giuliano. *History of the Italian People.* Hammondsworth, UK: Penguin Books, 1973.

Putnam, Robert D. *Making Democracy Work. Civic Traditions in Modern Italy.* Princeton: Princeton University Press, 1993.

Riall, Lucy. *Garibaldi: Invention of a Hero.* New Haven: Yale University, 2007.

Richards, Charles. *The New Italians.* New York: Penguin, 1995.

Saviano, Roberto. *Gomorrah: A Personal Journey into the Violent International Empire of Naples' Organized Crime System.* New York: Farrar, Straus and Giroux, 2007.

Sciascia, Leonardo. *The Moro Affair.* Granta Books, 2002.

Trevelyan, J. O. *A Short History of the Italian People.* London: Allen and Unwin, 1956.

Weinberg, Leonard. *The Transformation of Italian Communism.* New Brunswick, NJ: Transaction, 1995.

San Marino

Bent, James T. *A Freak of Freedom or the Republic of San Marino.* Port Washington, NY: Kennikat, 1970.

Rossi, Giuseppe. *San Marino.* San Marino: Governmental Tourist Body Sport and Spectacle, n.d.

————. *A Short History of the Republic of San Marino.* San Marino: Poligrafico Artioli–Modena, n.d.

San Marino. Milan: Ediz. Garami (Garanzini Milano), 1977.

Vatican City

Bernstein, Carl and Marco Politi. *His Holiness. John Paul II and the Hidden History of our Time.* New York: Bandam Doubleday Dell, 1996.

Flamini, Roland. *Pope, Premier, President.* New York: Macmillan, 1980.

Kreutz, Andres. *Vatican Policy on the Palestinian–Israeli Conflict: The Struggle for the Holy Land.* Westport, CT: Greenwood, 1990.

La Bello, Nina. *Vatican Empire.* Frieside: SS, 1970.

Nichols, Peter. *The Pope's Divisions.* New York: Holt, Rinehart and Winston, 1981.

Partner, Peter. *The Lands of St. Peter: The Papal State in the Middle Ages and the*

Early Renaissance. London: Methuen, 1972.

Walsh, Michael J. *Vatican City State.* Santa Barbara: ABC–Clio, 1983.

Malta

Berg, Warren G. *Historical Dictionary of Malta.* Metuchen, NJ: Scarecrow Press, 1995.

Blouet, Brian. *The Story of Malta.* Rev. ed. London: Faber Faber, 1972.

Holland, James. *Fortress Malta. An Island under Siege 1940–1943.* London: Phoenix, 2003.

Pace, Roderick. *The European Union's Mediterranean Enlargement. Cyprus and Malta.* New York: Routledge, 2006.

Sire, H. J. A. *The Knights of Malta.* New Haven, CT: Yale University Press, 1996.

Iberian Peninsula

General

Manuel, Paul C. and Sebastian Royo. *Spain and Portugal in the European Union. The First Fifteen Years.* New York: Routledge, 2004.

Mar–Molinero, Clare and Angel Smith. *Nationalism and the Nation in the Iberian Peninsula. Competing and Conflicting Identities.* New York: Berg, 1996.

Michener, James. *Iberia.* New York: Random House, 1968.

Payne, Stanley G. *A History of Spain and Portugal.* 2 vols. Madison: University of Wisconsin Press, 1973.

Tovias, Alfred. *Foreign Economic Relations of the European Community: The Impact of Spain and Portugal.* Boulder, CO: Lynne Rienner, 1990.

Wiarda, Howard J. *Politics in Iberia. The Political Systems of Spain and Portugal.* New York: HarperCollins, 1993.

———. *Iberia and Latin America. New Democracies, New Policies.* Lanham, MD: Rowman & Littlefield, 1996.

Spain

Alba, Victor. *The Transition in Spain: From Franco to Democracy.* New Brunswick, NJ: Transaction Books, 1978.

———. *The Communist Party in Spain.* New Brunswick, NJ: Transaction Books, 1983.

Archer, E.G. *Gibraltar, Identity and Empire.* New York: Routledge, 2005.

Balfour, Sabastian. *The Politics of Contemporary Spain.* New York: Routledge, 2005.

Beevor, Antony. *The Battle for Spain: The Spanish Civil War 1936-1939.* New York: Penguin, 2006.

Bertrand, Louis, and Petrie, Sir Charles. *The History of Spain. From the Musulmans to Franco.* New York: Collier Books, 1971.

Carr, Raymond, and Fusi, Juan Pablo. *Spain: Dictatorship to Democracy.* 2nd ed. Winchester, MA: Allen and Unwin, 1981.

———. *Spain: 1808–1975.* 2nd ed. New York: Oxford Univ. Press, 1982.

Castro, Americo. *The Spaniards: An Introduction to Their History.* Berkeley: University of California Press, 1985.

Chislett, W. *Spain and the United States: the quest for mutual rediscovery.* Madrid: Real Instituto Elcano de estudios internacionales y estratégicos, 2005.

———. *Spain: Going Places.* Madrid: Telefónica, 2008.

Collins, Roger. *The Basques.* London: Blackwell, 1987.

Conversi, Daniele. *Nationalist Mobilization in Catalonia and the Basque Country.* Reno: University of Nevada, 1995.

Eaton, Samuel D. *The Forces of Freedom in Spain, 1974–1979.* Palo Alto: Hoover, 1981.

Fusi, J. *Franco: A Biography.* New York: Harper and Row, n.d.

Gil, Federico G. and Tulchin, Joseph S., eds. *Spain's Entry Into NATO.* Boulder, CO: Lynne Rienner, 1988.

Gillespie, Richard. *The Spanish Socialist Party. A History of Factionalism.* Oxford: Oxford University Press, 1989.

——— and Richard Youngs, eds. *Spain. The European and International Challenges.* Portland, OR: Frank Cass, 2003.

Gilmour, David. The *Transformation of Spain.* Topsfield, MA: Quartet, 1986.

———. *Cities of Spain.* Chicago: Ivan R. Dee, nd.

Gold, Peter. *Gibraltar. British or Spanish?* New York: Routledge, 2005.

Graham, Helen. *The Spanish Republic at War 1936-1939.* Cambridge: Cambridge University, 2003.

Grugel, Jean and Tim Rees. *Franco's Spain.* New York: St. Martin's, 1997.

Gunther, Richard, ed. *Politics, Society, and Democracy. The Case of Spain.* Boulder, CO: Westview, 1993.

———. et al. *Spain After Franco: The Making of a Competitive Party System.* Berkeley: University of California Press, 1988.

———, et al. *Democracy in Modern Spain.* New Haven, CT: Yale University, 2004.

Holguin, Sandie. *Creating Spaniards. Culture and National Identity in Republican Spain.* Madison: University of Wisconsin Press, nd.

Hooper, John. *The New Spaniards.* Rev. ed. New York: Penguin, 1995.

Jackson, Gabriel. *The Spanish Republic and the Civil War, 1931–1939.* Princeton: Princeton University Press, 1965.

Kamen, Henry. *The Disinherited: The Exiles who Created Spanish Culture.* London: Allen Lane, 2007.

Kenwood, Alun, ed. *The Spanish Civil War. A Cultural and Historical Reader.* Oxford: Berg, 1992.

Kurlansky, Mark. *The Basque History of the World.* New York: Penguin 1999.

Magone, José M. *Contemporary Spanish Politics.* New York: Routledge, 2002.

Maravall, José. *The Transition to Democracy in Spain.* New York: St. Martin's Press, 1983.

Maxwell, Kenneth, ed. *Spanish Foreign and Defense Policy.* Boulder, CO: Westview, 1991.

———. and Steven Spiegel. *The New Spain. From Isolation to Influence.* New York: Council on Foreign Relations, 1994.

McRoberts, Kenneth. *Catalonia.* New York: Oxford University, 2000.

Newton, Michael T. *Institutions of Modern Spain: a Political and Economic Guide.* New York: Cambridge University, 1997.

Parry, J.H. *The Spanish Seaborne Empire.* Berkeley: University of California Press, 1990.

Payne, Stanley G. *The Spanish Civil War, the Soviet Union, and Communism.* New Haven: Yale University, 2004.

———. *The Phoenix: Franco Regime 1936-1975.* Paperback, 2000.

———. *Fascism in Spain, 1923-1977.* Madison: University of Wisconsin, 1999.

———. *Basque Nationalism.* Reno: University of Nevada Press, 1975.

Pilar, Ortuño Anaya. *European Socialists and Spain. The Transition to Democracy, 1959–77.* New York: Palgrave, 2002.

Preston, Paul, ed. *Spain in Crisis: The Evolution and Decline of the Franco Regime.* London: Harvester Press, 1976.

———. *The Triumph of Democracy in Spain.* Methuen, 1986.

———. *The Politics of Revenge. Fascism and the Military in 20th Century Spain.* New York: Harper Collins, 1990.

Rodosh, Ronald, et al, eds. *Spain Betrayed. The Soviet Union in the Spanish Civil War.* New Haven: Yale University Press, 2001.

Salmon, Keith. *The Modern Spanish Economy. Transformation and Integration into Europe.* New York: Columbia University Press, 1991.

Shubert, Adrian. *A Social History of Modern Spain.* New York: Harper Collins, 1990.

Sullivan, J.L. *ETA and Basque Nationalism. The Fight for Euskadi 1890–1986.* Kent: Croom Helm, 1988.

Tortella, Gabriel. *The Development of Modern Spain. An Economic History of the Nineteenth and Twentieth Centuries.* Cambridge, MA: Harvard University Press, 2000.

Tremlett, Giles. *Ghosts of Spain: Travels Through a Country's Hidden Past.* Faber and Faber, 2007.

Bibliography

Vilar, Pierre. *Spain. A Brief History.* 2nd ed. New York: Pergamon, 1980.

Williams, Mark. *The Story of Spain*, 3d ed. Fuengirola, Spain: Santana Books, 2000.

Woolard, Kathryn A. *Double Talk. Bilingualism and the Politics of Ethnicity in Catalonia.* Palo Alto, CA: Stanford University Press, 1989.

Portugal

Birmingham, David. *A Concise History of Portugal.* Cambridge: Cambridge University Press, 2003.

Bruce, N. *Portugal, The Last Empire.* New York: Wiley, 1975.

Bruneau, Thomas C. *Politics and Nationhood. Post–Revolutionary Portugal.* New York: Praeger, 1984.

———. *Political Parties and Democracy in Portugal.* Boulder, CO: Westview, 1997.

———. and Macleod, Alex. *Politics in Contemporary Portugal: Parties and the Consolidation of Democracy.* Boulder, CO: Lynne Rienner, 1986.

dos Passos, John. *The Portugal Story: Three Centuries of Exploration and Discovery.* New York: Doubleday, 1969.

Figueiredo, Antonio de. *Portugal: 50 Years of Dictatorship.* London: Penguin, 1975.

Graham, Lawrence. *The Portuguese Military and the State.* Boulder, CO: Westview Press, 1993.

———. and Makler, Henry, eds. *Contemporary Portugal: The Revolution and its Antecedents.* Austin: Univ. of Texas Press, 1979.

Hamilton, Kimberly A. *Lusophone Africa, Portugal, and the United States.* Boulder, CO: Westview Press, 1992.

Harsgor, Michael. *Portugal in Revolution. The Washington Papers*, Vol. III, No. 32. Beverly Hills: Sage, 1976.

Harvey, Robert. *Portugal: Birth of Democracy.* New York: St. Martin's Press, 1978.

Janitschek, Hans. *Mario Soares. Portrait of a Hero.* New York: St. Martins, 1986.

Livermore, H. V. *Portugal: A Short History.* Princeton: Scholar's Bookshelf, n.d.

MacDonald, Scott B. *European Destiny, Atlantic Transformations. Portuguese Foreign Policy under the Second Republic, 1974–1992.* New Brunswick, NJ: Transaction, 1993.

Magone, José M. *European Portugal: the Difficult Road to Sustainable Democracy.* New York: St. Martin's, 1997.

Marques, Antonio H. *History of Portugal.* 2 vols. New York: Columbia University Press, 1972.

Maxwell, Kenneth. *The Making of Portuguese Democracy.* New York: Cambridge University Press, 1995.

Nataf, Daniel. *Democratization and Social Settlement. The Politics of Change in Contemporary Portugal.* Albany, NY: SUNY, 1995.

Opello, Walter C., Jr. *Portugal. From Monarchy to Pluralist Democracy.* Boulder, CO: Westview Press, 1991.

Pinto, António Costa, ed. *Introducing Modern Portugal.* Palo Alto, CA: SPOSS, 1998.

———. *Salazar's Dictatorship and European Fascism.* New York: Columbia University Press, 1996.

Porch, Douglas. *The Portuguese Armed Forces and the Revolution.* Palo Alto, CA: Hoover Institution, 1991.

Raby, D.L. *Fascism and Resistance in Portugal: Communists, Liberals and Military Dissidents in the Opposition to Salazar, 1941–1974.* New York: St. Martin's, 1988.

Schneidman, Witney W. *Engaging Africa. Washington and the Fall of Portugal's Colonial Empire.* Lanham, MD: University Press of America, 2004.

Silva Lopes, José de, ed. *Portugal and EC Membership Evaluated.* New York: St. Martin's, 1994.

Wheeler, Douglas L. *Historical Dictionary of Portugal.* Metuchen, NJ: Scarecrow Press, 1993.

Andorra

Cameron, Peter. *Andorra.* New York: Ferrar Straus Giroux, 1997.

Carter, Youngman. *On to Andorra.* New York: Norton, 1964.

Deane, Shirley. *The Road to Andorra.* New York: Morrow, 1961.

Morgan, Bryan. *Andorra, the Country in Between.* Nottingham, U.K.: Palmer, 1964.

EU institutions in Brussels

Courtesy: Central audiovisual Library, European Commision